CPA

Comprehensive Exam Review

Accounting & Reporting:

Taxation, Managerial, Governmental & Not-for-Profit Organizations

Nathan M. Bisk, J.D., C.P.A.

ACKNOWLEDGEMENTS

We wish to thank the **American Institute of Certified Public Accountants** and other organizations for permission to reprint or adapt the following copyright © materials:

1. Uniform CPA Examination Questions and Unofficial Answers, Copyright © American Institute of Certified Public Accountants, Inc., Harborside Financial Center, 201 Plaza Three, Jersey City, NJ 07311-3881.

2. Accounting Research Bulletins, APB Opinions, Audit and Accounting Guides, Auditing Procedure Studies, Risk Alerts, Statements of Position, and Code of Professional Conduct, Copyright © American Institute of Certified Public Accountants, Inc., Harborside Financial Center, 201 Plaza Three, Jersey City, NJ 07311-3881.

3. FASB Statements, Interpretations, Technical Bulletins, and Statements of Financial Accounting Concepts, Copyright © Financial Accounting Standards Board, 401 Merrit 7, P.O. Box 5116, Norwalk, CT 06856.

4. GASB Statements, Interpretations, and Technical Bulletins, Copyright © Governmental Accounting Standards Board, 401 Merritt 7, P.O. Box 5116, Norwalk CT 06856-5116.

5. Statements on Auditing Standards, Statements on Standards for Consulting Services, Statements on Responsibilities in Personal Financial Planning Practice, Statements on Standards for Accounting and Review Services, Statements on Quality Control Standards, Statements on Standards for Attestation Engagements, and Statements on Responsibilities in Tax Practice, Copyright © American Institute of Certified Public Accountants, Inc., Harborside Financial Center, 201 Plaza Three, Jersey City, NJ 07311-3881.

6. ISB Standards, Copyright © Independence Standards Board, 6th Floor, 1211 Avenue of the Americas, New York, NY 10036-8775

PREFACE

Our texts provide comprehensive, complete coverage of <u>all</u> the topics tested on all <u>four</u> sections of the CPA Examination, including **Business Law & Professional Responsibilities, Financial Accounting & Reporting, Accounting & Reporting,** and **Auditing**. Used effectively, our materials will enable you to achieve maximum preparedness for the Uniform CPA Examination. Here is a brief summary of the **features** and **benefits** that our texts will provide for you:

1. **Information on the Closed Exam...**Beginning with the May 1996 Exam, the Uniform CPA Examination is non-disclosed. See Appendix B for a full discussion of this issue. This edition contains up-to-date coverage, including complete coverage of all exam changes. This edition also includes all the latest pronouncements of the AICPA and FASB, the current tax rates, governmental and nonprofit accounting, and other topics that are tested on the CPA exam. Our coverage is based on the most recent **AICPA Content Specification Outlines for the Uniform CPA Exam.**

2. **Separate and Complete Volumes...**Each volume includes text, multiple choice and other objective questions with solutions, plus essays and problems where appropriate for that section of the CPA exam. There is no need to refer to any other volume.

3. **More than 2,600 Pages of Text...**Including a selection of more than 3,200 recent CPA Examination questions, problems, and essays with Unofficial Answers. Solving these questions and problems under test conditions with immediate verification of results instills confidence and reinforces our **SOLUTIONS APPROACH**™ to solving exam questions.

4. **Complete Coverage...**No extra materials required. We discuss and explain all important AICPA, FASB, GASB, and ISB pronouncements, including all significant ARBs, APBs, SASs, SSARs, SFACs, and FASB materials. We also cite and identify all authoritative sources including the dates of all AICPA Questions and Unofficial Answers covered in our materials.

5. **Detailed Summaries...**We set forth the significant testable concepts in each CPA exam topic. These highly readable summaries are written in complete sentences using an outline format to facilitate rapid and complete comprehension. The summaries isolate and emphasize topics historically tested by the CPA examiners.

6. **Emphasis on "How to Answer Questions" and "How to Take the Exam"...**We teach you to solve problem, essay, and objective questions using our unique and famous **SOLUTIONS APPROACH**™.

7. **Discussion and Development of...**AICPA grading procedures, grader orientation strategies, examination confidence, and examination success.

8. **Unique Objective Question Coverage and Unofficial Answers Updated...**We explain *why* the multiple choice alternatives are either right or wrong. Plus, we clearly indicate the changes that need to be made in the Unofficial Answers to correctly reflect current business and tax laws and AICPA, FASB, GASB, and other authoritative pronouncements.

9. **Writing Skills...**Financial Accounting & Reporting, Auditing, and Business Law & Professional Responsibilities contain a section to help you brush up on your writing skills for the CPA exam.

10. **Indexes...**We have included a comprehensively compiled index for easy topic reference in all four sections.

11. **Trend Analysis of Recent Exams...**We include short summaries of all essays and problems given on the most recent exams, to assist you in accurately pinpointing topics tested most frequently.

12. **Diagnostic Exam to Test Your Present Level of Knowledge...**And we include a **Practice Exam** to test your exam preparedness under actual exam conditions. These testing materials are designed to help you single out for concentrated study the exam topic areas in which you are dangerously deficient.

Our materials are designed for the candidate who has previously studied accounting. Therefore, the rate at which a candidate studies and learns (not merely reads) our material will depend on a candidate's background and aptitude. Candidates who have been out of school for a period of years might need more time to study than recent graduates. The point to remember is that <u>all</u> the material you will need to know to pass the exam is here. All you need to do is apply yourself and learn this material at a rate that is appropriate to your situation. **As a final thought,** keep in mind that test confidence gained through disciplined preparation equals success.

OUR EDITORIAL BOARD INCLUDES THE NATION'S LEADING CPAs, ATTORNEYS AND EDUCATORS!

The Only CPA Review Texts Developed By Full-Time Experts.

YOU WILL LEARN FROM OUR OUTSTANDING EXPERTS... WITHOUT LEAVING YOUR HOME OR OFFICE.

Consulting Editor

MORTIMER M. CAPLIN, LL.B., J.S.D., LL.D., is a senior partner with the Washington D.C. law firm of Caplin and Drysdale. He served as Commissioner of the Internal Revenue Service and as a member of the President's Task Force on Taxation. He received the Alexander Hamilton Award (the highest award conferred by the Secretary of the Treasury) for outstanding and unusual leadership during service as a U.S. Commissioner of Internal Revenue. For more than 25 years, Mr. Caplin has been in private practice with his present law firm, and has served as adjunct professor for the University of Virginia Law School. He is a nationally acclaimed author of numerous articles on tax and corporate matters.

Consulting Editor

RICHARD M. FELDHEIM, M.B.A., J.D., LL.M., C.P.A. (NY), is a New York CPA as well as an attorney in New York and Arizona. He holds a Masters in Tax Law from New York University Law School. Mr. Feldheim is a member of the New York State Society of CPAs, AICPA, New York State Bar Association, Association of the Bar of the City of New York, Arizona Bar, and American Bar Association. His background includes practice as both a CPA with Price Waterhouse & Co. and as a Senior Partner with the Arizona law firm of Wentworth & Lundin. He has lectured for the AICPA, the Practicing Law Institute, Seton Hall University, and the University of Arizona.

Consulting Editor

WILLIAM J. MEURER, C.P.A. (FL), is former Managing Partner for both the overall operations in Central Florida and the Florida Audit and Business Advisory Services sector of Arthur Andersen LLP. During his 35-year career with the firm, Mr. Meurer developed expertise in several industries, including high technology, financial services, real estate, retailing/distribution, manufacturing, hospitality, professional services, and cable television. A graduate of Regis University, he is a member of both the American Institute of CPAs and the Florida Society of CPAs.

Consulting Editor

THOMAS A. RATCLIFFE, Ph.D., C.P.A. (TX), is Dean of the Sorrell College of Business Administration and Eminent Scholar in Accounting and Finance at Troy State University. He teaches financial accounting courses as well as CPE courses for accountants in public accounting and industry. Dr. Ratcliffe also writes the monthly audio program, *Bisk Audio Accounting and Auditing Report*, published by Bisk Education, Inc.

Consulting Editor

C. WILLIAM THOMAS, M.B.A., Ph.D., C.P.A. (TX), currently serves as J.E. Bush Professor and former Chair of the Department of Accounting and Business Law at Baylor University. He is a member of the AICPA, the Texas Society of CPAs, the Central Texas Chapter of CPAs, and the American Accounting Association, where he is past Chair for the Southwestern Regional Audit Section. Professor Thomas is a nationally known author and has extensive experience in Auditing CPA Review. In addition, he has received recognition for special audit education and curriculum projects he developed for Coopers & Lybrand. His background includes public accounting experience with KPMG Peat Marwick.

CHANGE ALERT

GASB No. 34, *Basic Financial Statements–and Management's Discussion and Analysis–for State and Local Governments,* was issued by the GASB in June 1999, overhauling the governmental reporting model. GASB 34 may be implemented immediately, and is required to be implemented for financial statements for periods beginning after June 15, 2001, at the earliest. The outgoing reporting model is unlikely to be heavily tested after **November 2001,** although it remains eligible to be tested. The transition period, with optional early implementation, makes **both** reporting models eligible to be tested through the **May 2003** exam, and for infrastructure assets, through May 2006. With the issuance of GASB 34, all of the guidance in GASB 11 is superseded. (GASB 11 was never implemented.)

Coverage of GASB No. 35, Basic Financial Statements–and Management's Discussion and Analysis–for Public Colleges and Universities, GASB No. 37, Basic Financial Statements—and Management's Discussion and Analysis—for State and Local Governments: Omnibus—an amendment of GASB Statements No. 21 and No. 34, and GASB No. 38, Certain Financial Statement Note Disclosures is incorporated in this text to the depth likely to be tested on the CPA exam. GASB 35 may be implemented immediately, and component units must implement it as GASB 34 is implemented for the primary government. GASB 35 has the same staggered implementation dates as GASB 34 for non-component units. GASB 37 and GASB 38 are applied when GASB 34 is applied. (Chapters 21 and 22)

GASB No. 39, *Determining Whether Certain Organizations Are Component Units,* was issued by the GASB in May, 2002. The material in GASB No. 39 is unlikely to be tested heavily. GASB No. 39 is effective for periods beginning after June 15, 2003, with early application encouraged. (Chapter 21)

The Job Creation & Worker Assistance Act of 2002 (JCWAA '02) includes business economic stimulus provisions, some general retroactively effective tax breaks, and some relief provisions only for lower-Manhattan entities affected by terrorist acts on September 11, 2001. JCWAA '02 became effective on March 9, 2002, and thus, is eligible to be tested on the November 2002 and later CPA exams. The Bisk Education editors believe details on the provisions applicable only to lower-Manhattan are beyond the scope of the exam.

The Economic Growth and Tax Relief Reconciliation Act of 2001 (EGTRRA '01) changes are pervasive, but not as sweeping as the popular press might have you believe, particularly for the tax years 2002 and 2003. For instance, the changes do not impact the relationship between standard and itemized deductions. In this volume, no effective date is designated for provisions that are not changed. Note that this is the majority of the content. (Chapters 27 through 30)

ACCOUNTING & REPORTING

VOLUME II of IV

TABLE OF CONTENTS

---

* These percentages refer to the proportionate value that the exam allocates to this topic. We recommend that candidates remain cognizant of the depth of coverage of a topic and their proficiency with it when studying for the exam. Make informed decisions about your study plan by reading the information in the **Getting Started** and **Practical Advice** sections of this volume.

QUICK TEXT REFERENCE

The editors strongly recommend that candidates read the entire **Getting Started** and **Practical Advice** sections of this volume, unless they have already read these sections in the *Financial Accounting & Reporting* volume. The references on this page are only intended for conveniently relocating selected parts of the volume. Add items to this list that you find yourself revisiting frequently.

FOREWORD: GETTING STARTED

STEP ONE: READ PART ONE OF THE PRACTICAL ADVICE SECTION

Part One of the **Practical Advice** section (Appendix B) is designed to familiarize you with the CPA examination. Included in **Practical Advice** are general comments about the exam, a schedule of exam dates, addresses and numbers of state boards of accountancy, and attributes required for exam success.

STEP TWO: TAKE THE DIAGNOSTIC EXAMS

The diagnostic exam in this foreword is designed to help you determine your strong and weak areas. This in turn will help you design your personalized training plan so that you spend more time in your weak areas and do not waste precious study time in areas where you are already strong. You can take the exams using either the books or CPA Review Software for Windows™. Don't mark answers in the book; then you can use the diagnostic as a "second" final exam, if you want. The books provide you with a worksheet that makes self-diagnosis fast and easy. CPA Review Software for Windows will automatically score your exams for you and give you a personalized analysis of your strong and weak areas.

NOTE: If you took a previous CPA exam and passed some but not all the sections, also analyze these exam sections to help you determine where you need to concentrate your efforts this time.

NOTE: If you purchase a package that includes software, you will also want to go through all of the software tutorials prior to beginning intensive study. They are each only a few minutes long, but they are loaded with valuable information. There is simply no better way to prepare yourself to study.

STEP THREE: DEVELOP A PERSONALIZED TRAINING PLAN

Based on the results from your diagnostic exams, develop your personalized training plan. If you are taking the exam for the first time, and you are the "average" CPA candidate, we recommend that you train for 20 weeks at a minimum of 20 hours per week. This level of intensity should increase during the final four weeks of your training and peak at a minimum of 40 hours the final week before the exam. Designed to complete your study program, our Intensive Video Series is a concentrated and effective "cram course" that targets the information you must know to pass. The videos will refresh your memory on subjects you covered weeks earlier and clarify topics you haven't yet fully grasped.

If you took the exam previously and did not condition (you still have to take all four sections), and you are the "average" CPA candidate, we recommend that you train for 12 weeks at a minimum of 20 hours per week. Again, this level of intensity should increase during the final four weeks of your training and peak during the final week before the exam. If you have conditioned (you have to take three or less sections), you can adjust these guidelines accordingly.

You may wonder what we mean by an "average" candidate. We are referring to a candidate who is just finishing or has just finished her/his academic training, attended a school that has a solid accounting curriculum, and received above average grades in accounting and business law courses. (An "average" candidate's native language is English.) Remember, "average" is a benchmark. Many candidates are not "average," so adjust your training plan accordingly.

	MON	TUES	WED	THURS	FRI	SAT	SUN
1:00 AM							
2:00 AM							
3:00 AM							
4:00 AM							
5:00 AM							
6:00 AM							
7:00 AM							
8:00 AM							
9:00 AM							
10:00 AM							
11:00 AM							
12:00 PM							
1:00 PM							
2:00 PM							
3:00 PM							
4:00 PM							
5:00 PM							
6:00 PM							
7:00 PM							
8:00 PM							
9:00 PM							
10:00 PM							
11:00 PM							
12:00 AM							

How to Find 20 Hours a Week to Study

The typical CPA candidate is a very busy individual. He or she goes to school and/or works full or part time. Some candidates have additional responsibilities such as a spouse, children, a house to take care of—the list can go on and on. Consequently, your first reaction may be, "I don't have 20 hours a week to devote to training for the CPA exam." Using the chart on the previous page, we will show you how to "find" the time that you need to develop your training schedule.

1. Keeping in mind what you would consider to be a typical week, first mark out in black the time that you know you won't be able to study. For example, mark an "X" in each block which represents time that you normally sleep, have a class, work, or have some other type of commitment. Be realistic.

2. Next, in a different color, put a "C" in each block that represents commute time, an "M" in each block that represents when you normally eat, and an "E" in each block that represents when you exercise.

3. Now pick one hour each day to relax and give your mind a break. Write "BREAK" in one block for each day. Do not skip this step. By taking a break, you will study more efficiently and effectively.

4. In a third color, write "STUDY" in the remaining blocks. Count the "STUDY" blocks. Are there 20? If not, count your "C", "M", and "E" blocks; if needed, these blocks of time can be used to gain additional study time by using Bisk Education CPA Review audio tapes and videotapes. For example, our audios are ideal for candidates on the go, you can listen to them whenever you're in the car or exercising and gain valuable study time each week.

5. If you still do not have 20 "STUDY" blocks, and you scored 70% or more on your diagnostic exams, you may still be able to pass the exam even with your limited study time. If, however, you scored less than 70% on your diagnostic exams, you have 2 options: (1) re-prioritize and make a block that has an "X" in it available study time; or (2) concentrate on conditioning (passing some but not all of the sections) instead of on passing the entire exam. Before you choose to condition, check with your state board about the details. A drastic solution is to skip the managerial portion of the ARE section of the exam if you are extremely pressed. Ordinarily, we do not recommend this strategy.

How to Allocate Your 20 Weeks

Develop your overall training plan. We outline a recommended training plan based on 20 hours per week and 20 weeks of study. The time allocated to each topic was based on the length of the chapter, the difficulty of the material, and how heavily the topic is tested on the exam (refer to the exam specifications and our frequency analysis found in the **Practical Advice** section of your book). Keep in mind that this plan is for the "average" CPA candidate. You should customize this plan based on the results of your diagnostic exams and level of knowledge in each area tested. **Warning:** When studying, be careful not to fall into the trap of spending too much time on an area that rarely is tested on the exam. **NOTE:** For each week listed below there are corresponding Hot•Spot videos and audio tapes for more in-depth study. Call 1-888-CPA-BISK.

Recommended Training Plan (all 4 sections)*

		Hours
Week 1:	READ **GETTING STARTED** AND **PRACTICAL ADVICE** SECTIONS	1
	TAKE DIAGNOSTIC EXAMS	10
	GET ORGANIZED	2
	READ **ACCOUNTING FOR 5%** SECTION	1
	CHAPTER 1—OVERVIEW OF FINANCIAL ACCOUNTING & REPORTING	2
	CHAPTER 2—CASH, SHORT-TERM INVESTMENTS, & RECEIVABLES	4

* Candidates should make modifications to suit their individual circumstances. For instance, this training plan repeats Chapter 21. Candidates may not need to return to Chapter 21, particularly those who took a governmental accounting course.

		Hours
WEEK 11:	OVERALL REVIEW OF FINANCIAL ACCOUNTING & REPORTING	6
	CHAPTER 22—GOVERNMENTAL FUNDS & ACCOUNT GROUPS	7
	CHAPTER 42—ACCOUNTANT'S PROFESSIONAL RESPONSIBILITIES	3
	CHAPTER 43—ACCOUNTANT'S LEGAL RESPONSIBILITIES	4
WEEK 12:	WEEKLY REVIEW OF WEEKS 1 - 11	4
	CHAPTER 21—GOVERNMENTAL OVERVIEW	3
	CHAPTER 23—NONPROFIT ACCOUNTING	7
	CHAPTER 44—CONTRACTS	6
WEEK 13:	WEEKLY REVIEW OF WEEKS 1 - 12	4
	CHAPTER 24—DECISION MAKING	4
	CHAPTER 25—COST ACCOUNTING	4
	CHAPTER 44—CONTRACTS	2
	CHAPTER 45—SALES	6
WEEK 14:	WEEKLY REVIEW OF WEEKS 1 - 13	3
	CHAPTER 27—DECISION MAKING	1
	CHAPTER 26—PLANNING & CONTROL	5
	CHAPTER 28—FEDERAL TAXATION: PROPERTY	5
	CHAPTER 46—NEGOTIABLE INSTRUMENTS	3
	CHAPTER 47—SECURED TRANSACTIONS & DOCUMENTS OF TITLE	3
WEEK 15:	WEEKLY REVIEW OF WEEKS 1 - 14	3
	CHAPTER 27—FEDERAL TAXATION: INDIVIDUALS	10
	CHAPTER 48—BANKRUPTCY	4
	CHAPTER 49—DEBTORS, CREDITORS & GUARANTORS	3
WEEK 16:	WEEKLY REVIEW OF WEEKS 1 - 15	3+
	CHAPTER 29—FEDERAL TAXATION: CORPORATIONS	10
	CHAPTER 50—AGENCY	3
	CHAPTER 51—PARTNERSHIPS	4
WEEK 17:	WEEKLY REVIEW OF WEEKS 1 - 16	4+
	CHAPTER 30—FEDERAL TAXATION: PARTNERSHIPS & OTHER TOPICS	10
	CHAPTER 52—CORPORATIONS	3
	CHAPTER 53—ESTATES & TRUSTS	3
WEEK 18:	WEEKLY REVIEW OF WEEKS 1 - 17	2+
	CHAPTER 54—EMPLOYMENT & ENVIRONMENTAL REGULATION	2
	CHAPTER 55—FEDERAL SECURITIES REGULATION	4
	CHAPTER 56—REAL & PERSONAL PROPERTY	4
	CHAPTER 57—FIRE & CASUALTY INSURANCE	1
	OVERALL REVIEW OF ACCOUNTING & REPORTING	4
	OVERALL REVIEW OF BUSINESS LAW & PROFESSIONAL RESPONS.	3
WEEK 19:	REVIEW AREAS IN WHICH YOU STILL FEEL WEAK	20+
WEEK 20:	TAKE FINAL EXAMS UNDER EXAM CONDITIONS	10
	DO FINAL REVIEWS	10+

YOUR PERSONALIZED TRAINING PLAN:

WEEK	TASK	DIAGNOSTIC SCORE	EST. HOURS	DATE COMPLETE	CHAPTER SCORE	FINAL SCORE
1						
2						
3						
4						
5						
6						
7						
8						
9						

WEEK	TASK	DIAGNOSTIC SCORE	EST. HOURS	DATE COMPLETE	CHAPTER SCORE	FINAL SCORE
10						
11						
12						
13						
14						
15						
16						
17						

WEEK	TASK	DIAGNOSTIC SCORE	EST. HOURS	DATE COMPLETE	CHAPTER SCORE	FINAL SCORE
18						
19						
20						

STEP FOUR: READ THE REST OF THE PRACTICAL ADVICE SECTION

Part Two of the **Practical Advice** section of the book will familiarize you with how the CPA examination is graded and tell you how you can earn extra points on the exam simply by knowing what the grader is going to seek. In addition, in Part Three we explain our Solutions Approach™, an approach that will help you maximize your grade. In Part Four, we discuss examination strategies. In Part Five, we provide information on the AICPA exam content specifications and point distribution.

STEP FIVE: INTEGRATE YOUR REVIEW MATERIALS

In this step, we demonstrate how to integrate the Bisk Education CPA Review products to optimize the effectiveness of your training plan. Find and read the section that corresponds to the package that you purchased. (To facilitate easy reference to your package guidance, you may want to strike through the sections corresponding to other packages.)

VIDEOTAPES

The videotapes are designed to supplement all of the study packages. Note how we recommend using the audiotapes in the following review plans. These recommendations also apply to the videotape programs. FYI: The videotapes have similar content as the online video lectures, but they are not exactly the same. Each of the Hot•Spot™ videotapes concentrates on a few topics. Use them to help you study the areas that are most troubling for you. Each of the Intensive videotapes are designed for a final, intensive review, after a candidate has already done considerable work. If time permits, use the Intensive tapes at both the very beginning (for an overview) and set them aside until the final review in week 19. They contain concise, informative lectures, as well as CPA exam tips, tricks, and techniques that will help you to learn the material needed to pass the exam.

ONLINE PACKAGE: BOOKS, VIDEO LECTURES, AND CPA SOFTWARE FOR WINDOWS

This is our most comprehensive review package. This combination provides the personal advice, discipline, and camaraderie of a classroom setting with the convenience of self-study. It is intended for those candidates who want to make sure that they pass the exam the **first** time. By using this package, you are eligible to qualify for Bisk Education's money-back guarantee. Contact a customer representative for details on the components of this package. Contact your online faculty advisor if you have questions about integrating your materials after viewing the web site guidance. The editors strongly recommend that candidates working full-time take a maximum of 2 sections per six-week session.)

BOOKS, AUDIOTAPES, AND CPA REVIEW SOFTWARE FOR WINDOWS

This is our most comprehensive self-study review package. This combination is designed expressly for the serious CPA candidate. It is intended for those candidates who want to make sure that they pass the exam the **first** time (or *this* time, if you have already taken the exam). In addition, by using this package, you are eligible to qualify for Bisk Education's money-back guarantee.

How to Use This Package:

1. First take the diagnostic exams using CPA Review Software for Windows™. CPA Review Software for Windows™ automatically scores your exams and tells you what your strong and weak areas are. Then view the short tutorial to learn how to use the software features to their fullest.

In chapters where you are strong (i.e., you scored 65% or better on the diagnostic exam):

2. Answer the objective questions using CPA Review Software for Windows™.

3. Read the subsections of the chapter that correspond to your weak areas.

4. Listen to the audiotape for topics covered in this chapter to reinforce your weak areas and review your strong areas.

5. Now, using CPA Review Software for Windows™, answer the objective questions that you previously answered incorrectly. If you answer 70% or more of the questions correctly, you are ready to move to the next chapter. If you answer less than 70% of the questions correctly, handle this chapter as if you scored less than 65% on the diagnostic exam.

6. Answer the related essay questions.

In chapters where you are weak (i.e., you scored less than 65% on the diagnostic exam):

2. Read the chapter in the book.

3. Listen to the audiotape lectures on topics covered in the chapter.

4. Re-read the subsections of the chapter that correspond to your weak subtopics.

5. Using CPA Review Software for Windows™, answer the objective questions for this chapter. If you answer 70% or more of the questions correctly, you are ready to move on to the next chapter. If you get less than 70% of the questions correct, review the subtopics where you are weak. Then answer the questions that you previously answered incorrectly. If you still do not get at least 70% correct, check the exam specification and frequency charts in the Practical Advice section to find out how heavily the area is tested. If this is an area that is heavily tested, continue reviewing the material and answering multiple choice questions until you can answer at least 70% correctly. Allocate more time than you originally budgeted, if necessary. If this is not a heavily tested area, move on, but make a note to come back to this area later as time allows.

6. Answer the related essay questions.

BOOKS AND CPA REVIEW SOFTWARE FOR WINDOWS™

This combination allows you to use the books to review the material and CPA Review Software for Windows™ to practice exam questions. You can also use the books to practice exam questions when you do not have access to a computer. In addition, by using this package, you are eligible to qualify for Bisk Education's money-back guarantee.

How to Use This Package:

1. Take the diagnostic exams using CPA Review Software for Windows™. CPA Review Software for Windows automatically scores your exams and tells you what your strong and weak areas are. Then view the short tutorial to learn how to use the software features to their fullest.

In chapters where you are strong (i.e., you scored 65% or better on the diagnostic exam):

2. Answer the objective questions using CPA Review Software for Windows™.

3. Read the subsections of the chapter that correspond to your weak areas.

4. Now using CPA Review Software for Windows™, answer the objective questions that you previously answered incorrectly. If you answer 70% or more of the questions correctly, you are ready to move on to the next chapter. If you answer less than 70% of the questions correctly, handle this chapter as if you scored less than 65% on the diagnostic exam.

5. Answer the related essay questions.

In chapters where you are weak (i.e., you scored less than 65% on the diagnostic exam):

2. Read the chapter in the book.

3. Using CPA Review Software for Windows™, answer the objective questions for this chapter. If you answer 70% or more of the questions correctly, you are ready to move on to the next chapter. If you get less than 70% of the questions correct, review the subtopics where you are weak. Then answer the questions that you previously answered incorrectly. If you still do not get at least 70% correct, check the exam specification and frequency charts in the Practical Advice section to find out how heavily the area is tested. If this is an area that is heavily tested, continue reviewing the material and answering multiple choice questions until you can answer at least 70% correctly. Allocate more time than you originally budgeted, if necessary. If this is not a heavily tested area, move on, but make a note to come back to this area later as time allows.

4. Answer the related essay questions.

BOOKS AND AUDIOTAPES

This combination is designed for the candidate who does not have access to a computer to study, who spends time commuting or doing other activities that could take valuable time away from studying, and for those who like to reinforce what they read by listening to a lecture on tape.

How to Use This Package:

1. Take the diagnostic exams found in your book. Using the worksheets provided, score your exams to determine your strong and weak areas.

In chapters where you are strong (i.e., you scored 65% or better on the diagnostic exam):

2. Do the objective questions for that chapter. Using the worksheet provided, analyze your strong and weak areas.

3. Read the subsections of the chapter that correspond to your weak subtopics.

4. At this point, listen to the audiotape on topics covered in this chapter to reinforce weak areas and review strong areas.

5. Answer the objective questions that you previously answered incorrectly. If you answer 70% or more of the questions correctly, you are ready to move on to the next chapter. If you answer less than 70% of the questions correctly, handle this chapter as if you scored 65% or less on the diagnostic exam.

6. Answer at least one essay question (if there are any) and review any other essay questions and solutions.

In chapters where you are weak (i.e., you scored less than 65% on the diagnostic exam):

2. First read the chapter in the book.

3. Now listen to the audiotape lectures covering topics in this chapter.

4. Re-read the subsections of the chapter that correspond to your weak subtopics.

5. Do the objective questions and score yourself using the worksheet provided. If you answer 70% or more of the questions correctly, you are ready to move on to the next chapter. If you answer less than 70% of the questions correctly, review the subtopics that are still giving you trouble. Then answer the questions that you have previously answered incorrectly. If you still do not get at least 70% of the questions correct, check the exam specification and frequency charts in the Practical Advice section to find out how heavily this area is tested. If this is an area that is heavily tested, continue reviewing the material and answering questions until you can answer at least 70% of them correctly. Allocate more time than you originally budgeted for if necessary. If this area is not heavily tested, move on, but make a note to come back to this topic later as time allows.

6. Answer at least one essay question (if there are any) and review any other essay questions and solutions.

STEP SIX: USE THESE HELPFUL HINTS AS YOU STUDY

♦   SPEND YOUR WEEKLY REVIEW TIME EFFECTIVELY. DURING EACH WEEKLY REVIEW:

Answer the objective questions that you previously answered incorrectly or merely guessed correctly.

Read through your notes.

Pick one essay question or problem to work. (Do not wait until the end of your 20 weeks to attempt the essay questions.) Read the other essay and problem questions and solutions.

Go through your flashcards.

♦ DO NOT MARK THE OBJECTIVE QUESTION ANSWERS IN THE BOOK.

Do not circle the answer to objective questions in the book. You should work every multiple-choice question at least twice and you do not want to influence your later answers by knowing how you previously answered the question.

♦ MARK THE OBJECTIVE QUESTIONS THAT YOU ANSWER INCORRECTLY OR MERELY GUESS CORRECTLY.

This way you know to answer this question again at a later time.

♦ MAKE NOTES AS YOU STUDY

Make notes and/or highlight when you read the chapters in the book. When possible, make notes when you listen to the tapes. You will find these very useful for weekly reviews and your final review.

♦ MAKE FLASHCARDS

Make flashcards for topics that are heavily tested on the exam or that are giving you trouble. By making your own flashcards, you learn during their creation and you can tailor them to your individual learning style and problem areas. You will find these very useful for weekly reviews and your final review. Replace flashcards of information you know with new material as you progress through your study plan. Keep these handy and review them when you are waiting in line or on hold. This will turn nonproductive time into valuable study time. Review your complete set during the last two weeks before the exam.

♦ EFFECTIVELY USE THE VIDEOTAPES

Watch the videotapes in an environment without distractions. Be prepared to take notes and answer questions just as if you were attending a live class. Frequently, the instructors will have you stop the tape to work a question on your own. This means a 2-hour tape may take 2½ hours or more to view.

♦ EFFECTIVELY USE THE AUDIO TUTOR

Use Audio Tutor to turn nonproductive time into valuable study time. For example, play the tapes or CDs when you are commuting, exercising, getting ready for school or work, doing laundry, etc. Audio Tutor will help you to memorize and retain key concepts. It will also reinforce what you have read in the books. Get in the habit of listening to the tapes or CDs whenever you have a chance. The more times that you listen to each lecture, the more familiar you will become with the material and the easier it will be for you to recall it during the exam.

STEP SEVEN: IMPLEMENT YOUR TRAINING PLAN

This is it! You are primed and ready. You have decided which training tools will work best for you and you know how to use them. As you implement your personalized training plan, keep yourself focused. Your goal is to obtain a grade of 75 or better on each section and, thus, pass the CPA exam. Therefore, you should concentrate on learning new material and reviewing old material only to the extent that it helps you reach this goal. Also, keep in mind that now is not the time to hone your procrastination skills. Utilize the personalized training plan that you developed in step three so that you do not fall behind schedule. Adjust it when necessary if you need more time in one chapter or less time in another. Refer to the AICPA content specification and the frequency analysis to make sure that the adjustment is warranted. Above all else, remember that passing the exam is an **attainable** goal. Good luck!

DIAGNOSTIC EXAMINATION

PROBLEM 1 MULTIPLE CHOICE QUESTIONS (120 to 150 minutes)

1. Which of the following statements is correct regarding comparability of governmental financial reports?
a. Comparability is **not** relevant in governmental financial reporting.
b. Similarly designated governments perform the same functions.
c. Selection of different alternatives in accounting procedures or practices account for the differences between financial reports.
d. Differences between financial reports should be due to substantive differences in underlying transactions or the governmental structure.

(4979)

2. The basic financial statements of a state government that has adopted GASB Statement No. 34, Basic Financial Statements—and Management's Discussion and Analysis—for State and Local Governments
a. Are comprised of the government-wide financial statements and related notes.
b. Are comprised of the primary government funds' financial statements and related notes.
c. Contain more detailed information regarding the state government's finances than is contained in the comprehensive annual financial report.
d. Do not include management's discussion and analysis (MD&A). (6879)

3. Which of the following is required by GASB No. 34, Basic Financial Statements—and Management's Discussion and Analysis—for State and Local Governments?

I. Governmental activities information using the economic resources measurement focus in the government-wide financial statements.
II. Governmental fund information included in the statement of cash flows.

a. I only
b. II only
c. Both I and II
d. Neither I nor II

(6816)

4. Where does GASB Statement No. 34, Basic Financial Statements—and Management's Discussion and Analysis—for State and Local Governments, require management's discussion and analysis (MD&A) to be presented?
a. Before the financial statements
b. Before the notes to the financial statements, but after the financial statements
c. In the notes to the financial statements
d. After the notes to the financial statements, before other required supplementary information

(6873)

5. Hill City's water utility fund held the following investments in U.S. Treasury securities at June 30, 20X4:

Investment	Date purchased	Maturity date	Carrying amount
3-month T-bill	5/31/X4	7/31/X4	$ 30,000
3-year T-note	6/15/X4	8/31/X4	50,000
5-year T-note	10/1/X0	9/30/X5	100,000

In the fund's balance sheet, what amount of these investments should be reported as cash and cash equivalents at June 30, 20X4?
a. $0
b. $ 30,000
c. $ 80,000
d. $180,000

(4448)

6. Proceeds of General Obligation Bonds is an account of a governmental unit that would be included in the
a. Debt service fund.
b. Internal service fund.
c. Capital projects fund.
d. Enterprise fund.

(2163)

ITEMS 7 AND 8 are based on the following:

Ridge Township's governing body adopted its general fund budget, comprised of estimated revenues of $100,000 and appropriations of $80,000. Ridge formally integrates its budget into the accounting records.

7. To record the appropriations of $80,000, Ridge should
a. Credit appropriations control.
b. Debit appropriations control.
c. Credit estimated expenditures control.
d. Debit estimated expenditures control.

(4430)

8. To record the $20,000 budgeted excess of estimated revenues over appropriations, Ridge should
a. Credit estimated excess revenues control.
b. Debit estimated excess revenues control.
c. Credit budgetary fund balance.
d. Debit budgetary fund balance. (4431)

9. Lake County received the following proceeds that are legally restricted to expenditure for specified purposes:

Levies on affected property owners to install sidewalks	$500,000
Gasoline taxes to finance road repairs	900,000

What amount should be accounted for in Lake's special revenue funds?
a. $1,400,000
b. $ 900,000
c. $ 500,000
d. $0 (2659)

10. Arlen City's fiduciary funds contained the following cash balances at December 31, 20X1:

Under the Forfeiture Act—cash confiscated from illegal activities; principal can be used only for law enforcement activities	$300,000
Sales taxes collected by Arlen to be distributed to other governmental units	500,000

What amount of cash should Arlen report in its permanent funds at December 31, 20X1?
a. $0
b. $300,000
c. $500,000
d. $800,000 (4443)

11. The following are Boa City's long-term assets:

Fixed assets used in enterprise fund activities	$1,000,000
Infrastructure assets	9,000,000
All other general fixed assets	1,800,000

What aggregate amount should Boa report in the governmental activities column of the government-wide financial statements?
a. $ 9,000,000
b. $10,000,000
c. $10,800,000
d. $11,800,000 (2665)

12. The following fund types used by Bluff City had total assets as follows:

Special revenue funds	$ 50,000
Agency funds	75,000
Trust funds	100,000

Total fiduciary fund assets amounted to
a. $100,000.
b. $150,000.
c. $175,000.
d. $225,000. (1388)

13. Kew City received a $15,000,000 federal grant to finance the construction of a center for rehabilitation of drug addicts. The proceeds of this grant should be accounted for in the
a. Special revenue funds.
b. General fund.
c. Capital projects funds.
d. Trust funds. (1351)

14. Japes City issued $1,000,000 general obligation bonds at 101 to build a new city hall. As part of the bond issue, the city also paid a $500 underwriter fee and $2,000 in debt issue costs. What amount should Japes City report as other financing sources?
a. $1,010,000
b. $1,008,000
c. $1,007,500
d. $1,000,000 (6994)

15. Dale City is accumulating financial resources that are legally restricted to payments of general long-term debt principal and interest maturing in future years. At December 31, $5,000,000 has been accumulated for principal payments and $300,000 has been accumulated for interest payments. These restricted funds should be accounted for in the

	Debt service fund	General fund
a.	$0	$5,300,000
b.	$ 300,000	$5,000,000
c.	$5,000,000	$ 300,000
d.	$5,300,000	$0

(2668)

16. Which of the following classifications is required for reporting of expenses by all not-for-profit organizations?
a. Natural classification in the statement of activities or notes to the financial statements.
b. Functional classification in the statement of activities or notes to the financial statements.
c. Functional classification in the statement of activities and natural classification in a matrix format in a separate statement.
d. Functional classification in the statement of activities and natural classification in the notes to the financial statements. (6545)

17. Famous, a nongovernmental not-for-profit art museum, has elected not to capitalize its permanent collections. In 20X0, a bronze statue was stolen. The statue was not recovered and insurance proceeds of $35,000 were paid to Famous in 20X1. This transaction would be reported in

I. The statement of activities as permanently restricted revenues.
II. The statement of cash flows as cash flows from investing activities.

a. I only.
b. II only.
c. Both I and II.
d. Neither I nor II. (6812)

18. Dee City's community hospital, which uses enterprise fund reporting, normally includes proceeds from sale of cafeteria meals in
a. Patient service revenues.
b. Other revenues.
c. Ancillary service revenues.
d. Deductions from dietary service expenses. (Similar to 4665, 2566)

19. Buff Co. is considering replacing an old machine with a new machine. Which of the following items is economically relevant to Buff's decision? (Ignore income tax considerations.)

	Carrying amount of old machine	Disposal value of new machine
a.	Yes	No
b.	No	Yes
c.	No	No
d.	Yes	Yes	(2749)

20. In an income statement prepared using the variable costing method, fixed factory overhead would
a. Not be used.
b. Be treated the same as variable factory overhead.
c. Be used in the computation of operating income but **not** in the computation of the contribution margin.
d. Be used in the computation of the contribution margin. (2199)

21. Carr Co. had an unfavorable materials usage variance of $900. What amounts of this variance should be charged to each department?

	Purchasing	Warehousing	Manufacturing
a.	$0	$0	$900
b.	$0	$900	$0
c.	$300	$300	$300
d.	$900	$0	$0

(Similar to 2676)

22. Baby Frames, Inc., evaluates manufacturing overhead in its factory by using variance analysis. The following information applies to the month of May:

	Actual	Budgeted
Number of frames manufactured	19,000	20,000
Variable overhead costs	$4,100	$2 per direct labor hour
Fixed overhead costs	$22,000	$20,000
Direct labor hours	2,100 hours	0.1 hour per frame

What is the fixed overhead spending variance?
a. $1,000 favorable
b. $1,000 unfavorable
c. $2,000 favorable
d. $2,000 unfavorable (6998)

23. The following is a summarized income statement of Carr Co.'s profit center No. 43 for March:

Contribution margin		$70,000
Period expenses:		
Manager's salary	$20,000	
Facility depreciation	8,000	
Corporate expense allocation	5,000	33,000
Profit center income		$37,000

Which of the following amounts would most likely be subject to the control of the profit center's manager?
a. $70,000
b. $50,000
c. $37,000
d. $33,000 (2683)

24. Polo Co. requires higher rates of return for projects with a life span greater than five years. Projects extending beyond five years must earn a higher specified rate of return. Which of the following capital budgeting techniques can readily accommodate this requirement?

	Internal rate of return	Net present value
a.	Yes	No
b.	No	Yes
c.	No	No
d.	Yes	Yes

(2248)

25. Sam Gow's wife died in 1998. Sam did not remarry, and he continued to maintain a home for himself and his dependent infant child during 1999 and 2000, providing full support for himself and his child during these years. For 1998, Sam properly filed a joint return. For 2000, Sam's filing status is

a. Single.
b. Head of household.
c. Qualifying widower with dependent child.
d. Married filing joint return. (1581)

26. Jim and Kay Ross contributed to the support of their two children, Dale and Kim, and Jim's widowed parent, Grant. Dale, a 19-year-old full-time college student, earned $4,500 as a baby-sitter. Kim, a 23-year-old bank teller, earned $12,000. Grant received $5,000 in dividend income and $4,000 in nontaxable social security benefits. Grant, Dale, and Kim are U.S. citizens and were over one-half supported by Jim and Kay. How many exemptions can Jim and Kay claim on their joint income tax return?

a. Two
b. Three
c. Four
d. Five (4619)

27. Harold sustained a serious injury in the course of his employment. As a result of this injury, Harold received the following payments during the same year:

Workers' compensation	$1,200
Reimbursement from his employer's accident and health plan for medical expenses paid by Harold and not deducted by him	600
Damages for personal injuries	4,000

The amount to be included in Harold's gross income should be

a. $6,100.
b. $4,000.
c. $ 600.
d. $0. (1601)

28. James received the following interest income:

On Veterans Administration insurance dividends left on deposit with the VA	$20
On state income tax refund	30

What amount should James include for interest income in his return?

a. $50
b. $30
c. $20
d. $0 (Similar to 1575)

29. With regard to the passive loss rules involving rental real estate activities, which one of the following statements is correct?

a. The term "passive activity" includes any rental activity without regard as to whether or not the taxpayer materially participates in the activity.
b. Passive rental activity losses may be deducted only against passive income, but passive rental activity credits may be used against tax attributable to nonpassive activities.
c. Gross investment income from interest and dividends **not** derived in the ordinary course of a trade or business is treated as passive activity income that can be offset by passive rental activity losses when the "active participation" requirement is **not** met.
d. The passive activity rules do **not** apply to taxpayers whose adjusted gross income is $300,000 or less. (4596)

30. Paul and Lois Kim, both age 50, are married and will file a joint return. Their adjusted gross income was $80,000, including Paul's $75,000 salary. Lois had no income of her own. Neither spouse was covered by an employer-sponsored pension plan. What amount could the Kims contribute to IRAs to take advantage of their maximum allowable IRA deduction in their tax return?

a. $0
b. $2,000
c. $2,250
d. $4,000

(Similar to 1589)

31. During 20X1, Scott charged $4,000 on his credit card for his dependent son's medical expenses. Payment to the credit card company had not been made by the time Scott filed his income tax return in 20X1. However, in 20X1, Scott paid a physician $2,800 for the medical expenses of his wife, who died in 20X0. Disregarding the adjusted gross income percentage threshold, what amount could Scott claim in his 20X1 income tax return for medical expenses?

a. $0
b. $2,800
c. $4,000
d. $6,800

(1557)

32. Taylor, an unmarried taxpayer, had $90,000 in adjusted gross income for the year. Taylor donated land to a church and made no other contributions. Taylor purchased the land ten years ago as an investment for $14,000. The land's fair market value was $25,000 on the day of the donation. What is the maximum amount of charitable contribution that Taylor may deduct as an itemized deduction for the land donation for the current year?

a. $25,000
b. $14,000
c. $11,000
d. $0

(6911)

33. An employee who has had social security tax withheld in an amount greater than the maximum for a particular year, may claim

a. Such excess as either a credit or an itemized deduction, at the election of the employee, if that excess resulted from correct withholding by two or more employers.
b. Reimbursement of such excess from his employers, if that excess resulted from correct withholding by two or more employers.
c. The excess as a credit against income tax, if that excess resulted from correct withholding by two or more employers.
d. The excess as a credit against income tax, if that excess was withheld by one employer. (1559)

34. Kent qualified for the earned income credit. This credit could result in a

a. Refund even if Kent had no tax withheld from wages.
b. Refund only if Kent had tax withheld from wages.
c. Subtraction from adjusted gross income to arrive at taxable income.
d. Carryback or carryforward for any unused portion. (2470)

35. Fred Berk bought a plot of land with a cash payment of $40,000 and a purchase money mortgage of $50,000. In addition, Berk paid $200 for a title insurance policy. Berk's basis in this land is

a. $40,000.
b. $40,200.
c. $90,000.
d. $90,200.

(1613)

36. Under the modified accelerated cost recovery system (MACRS) of depreciation for property placed in service after 1986,

a. Used tangible depreciable property is excluded from the computation.
b. Salvage value is ignored for purposes of computing the MACRS deduction.
c. No type of straight-line depreciation is allowable.
d. The recovery period for depreciable realty must be at least 27.5 years. (5423)

37. A 2001 capital loss incurred by a married couple filing a joint return

a. Is **not** an allowable loss.
b. Will be allowed to the extent of capital gains, plus up to $3,000 of ordinary income.
c. May be carried forward up to a maximum of five years.
d. Will be allowed only to the extent of capital gains. (1619)

38. The following information pertains to the acquisition of a six-wheel truck by Richards, a self-employed contractor:

Cost of original truck traded in	$20,000
Book value of original truck at trade-in date	6,000
List price of new truck	25,000
Trade-in allowance for old truck	9,000
Business use of both trucks	100%

The basis of the new truck is
a. $28,000.
b. $25,000.
c. $22,000.
d. $16,000.   (Similar to 6638)

39. Barr Corp. had the following income:

Income from operations	$700,000
Dividends from unrelated taxable domestic corporation of which Barr owns 30%	4,000

Barr had no portfolio indebtedness. In Barr's taxable income, what amount should be included for the dividends received?
a. $ 600
b. $ 800
c. $3,200
d. $3,400   (1671)

40. Which of the following costs are amortizable organizational expenditures?
a. Professional fees to issue the corporate stock
b. Printing costs to issue the corporate stock
c. Legal fees for drafting the corporate charter
d. Commissions paid by the corporation to an underwriter   (5015)

41. Maple Corp.'s book income, before federal income tax, was $100,000. Included in this $100,000 were the following:

Provision for state income tax	$1,000
Interest earned on U.S. Treasury Bonds	6,000
Interest expense on bank loan to purchase U.S. Treasury Bonds	2,000

Maple's taxable income was
a. $ 96,000.
b. $ 97,000.
c. $100,000.
d. $101,000.   (1658)

42. The following information pertains to Rim Corp.:

Accumulated earnings and profits at January 1	$30,000
Earnings and profits for the year	40,000
Cash distributions to individual stockholders for the year	90,000

What is the total amount of distributions taxable as dividend income to Rim's stockholders for the year?
a. $0
b. $40,000
c. $70,000
d. $90,000   (5763)

43. The accumulated earnings tax
a. Applies only to closely held corporations.
b. Should be self-assessed by filing a separate schedule along with the regular tax return.
c. Can be imposed on S corporations that do not regularly distribute their earnings.
d. Cannot be imposed on a corporation that has undistributed earnings and profits of less than $150,000.   (Similar to 5762)

44. When a consolidated return is filed by an affiliated group of includible corporations connected from inception through the requisite stock ownership with a common parent,
a. Each of the subsidiaries is entitled to an accumulated earnings tax credit.
b. Operating losses of one member of the group offset operating profits of other members of the group.
c. The parent's basis in the stock of its subsidiaries is unaffected by the earnings and profits of its subsidiaries.
d. Intercompany dividends are excludable to the extent of 80%.   (1645)

45. Ati Corp. has two common stockholders. Ati derives all of its income from investments in stocks and securities, and it regularly distributes 51% of its taxable income as dividends to its stockholders. Ati is a
a. Corporation subject to tax only on income **not** distributed to stockholders.
b. Corporation subject to the accumulated earnings tax.
c. Personal holding company.
d. Regulated investment company.   (4157)

46. Pursuant to a plan of corporate reorganization adopted in July 2000, Gow exchanged 500 shares of Lad Corp. common stock that he had bought in January 2000 at a cost of $5,000 for 100 shares of Rook Corp. common stock having a fair market value of $6,000. Gow's recognized gain on this exchange was
a. $1,000 long-term capital gain.
b. $1,000 short-term capital gain.
c. $1,000 ordinary income.
d. $0. (1637)

47. Krol Corp. distributed marketable securities in redemption of its stock in a complete liquidation. On the date of distribution, these securities had a basis of $100,000 and a fair market value of $150,000. What gain does Krol have as a result of the distribution?
a. $0
b. $50,000 capital gain
c. $50,000 Section 1231 gain
d. $50,000 ordinary gain (1652)

48. Which one of the following will render a corporation ineligible for S corporation status?
a. One of the stockholders is a decedent's estate
b. One of the stockholders is a bankruptcy estate
c. The corporation has 100 stockholders
d. The corporation has both voting and nonvoting common stock issued and outstanding (1651)

49. Dale's distributive share of income from the calendar-year partnership of Dale & Eck was $50,000 in 2000. On December 15, 2000, Dale, who is a cash-basis taxpayer, received a $27,000 distribution of the partnership's 2000 income, with the $23,000 balance paid to Dale in May 2001. In addition, Dale received a $10,000 interest-free loan from the partnership in 2000. This $10,000 is to be offset against Dale's share of 2001 partnership income. What total amount of partnership income is taxable to Dale in 2000?
a. $27,000
b. $37,000
c. $50,000
d. $60,000 (1714)

50. Hall and Haig are equal partners in the firm of Azure Associates. On January 1, each partner's adjusted basis in Azure was $40,000. During the year, Azure borrowed $60,000, for which Hall and Haig are personally liable. Azure sustained an operating loss of $10,000 for the year ended December 31. The basis of each partner's interest in Azure at December 31, was
a. $35,000.
b. $40,000.
c. $65,000.
d. $70,000. (4483)

51. Hart's adjusted basis in Best Partnership was $9,000 at the time he received the following non-liquidating distributions of partnership property:

Cash	$ 5,000
Land—Adjusted basis	7,000
Land—Fair market value	10,000

What was the amount of Hart's basis in the land?
a. $0
b. $ 4,000
c. $ 7,000
d. $10,000 (5775)

52. The basis to a partner of property distributed "in kind" in complete liquidation of the partner's interest is the
a. Adjusted basis of the partner's interest increased by any cash distributed to the partner in the same transaction.
b. Adjusted basis of the partner's interest reduced by any cash distributed to the partner in the same transaction.
c. Fair market value of the property.
d. Adjusted basis of the property to the partnership. (2502)

53. A guaranteed payment by a partnership to a partner for services rendered, may include an agreement to pay

I. A salary of $5,000 monthly without regard to partnership income.
II. A 25% interest in partnership profits.

a. I only
b. II only
c. Both I and II
d. Neither I nor II (5447)

54. For income tax purposes, the estate's initial taxable period for a decedent who died on October 24

a. May be either a calendar year, or a fiscal year beginning on the date of the decedent's death.

b. Must be a fiscal year beginning on the date of the decedent's death.

c. May be either a calendar year, or a fiscal year beginning on October 1 of the year of the decedent's death.

d. Must be a calendar year beginning on January 1 of the year of the decedent's death. (6914)

55. On January 3, the partners' percentage interest in the capital, profits, and losses of Able Partnership were:

Dean	25%
Poe	30%
Ritt	45%

On February 4, of the same year, Poe sold her entire interest to an unrelated party. Dean sold his 25% interest in Able to another unrelated party on December 20, of the same year. No other transactions took place in this year. For tax purposes, which of the following statements is correct with respect to Able?

a. Able terminated as of February 4.

b. Able terminated as of December 20.

c. Able terminated as of December 31.

d. Able did **not** terminate. (5777)

56. Following are the fair market values of Wald's assets at the date of death:

Personal effects and jewelry	$150,000
Land bought by Wald with Wald's funds five years prior to death and held with Wald's sister as joint tenants with right of survivorship	800,000

The executor of Wald's estate did not elect the alternate valuation date. The amount includible as Wald's gross estate in the federal estate tax return is

a. $150,000.

b. $550,000.

c. $800,000.

d. $950,000. (1707)

57. Jan, an unmarried individual, gave the following outright gifts in 2002:

Donee	Amount	Use by donee
Jones	$15,000	Downpayment on house
Craig	12,000	College tuition
Kande	5,000	Vacation trip

Jan's 2002 exclusions for gift tax purposes total

a. $28,000.

b. $27,000.

c. $22,000.

d. $11,000. (1705)

58. An executor of a decedent's estate that has only U.S. citizens as beneficiaries is required to file a fiduciary income tax return, if the estate's gross income for the year is at least

a. $ 400.

b. $ 500.

c. $ 600.

d. $1,000. (1697)

59. Hope is a tax-exempt religious organization. Which of the following activities is(are) consistent with Hope's tax-exempt status?

I. Conducting weekend retreats for business organizations.

II. Providing traditional burial services that maintain the religious beliefs of its members.

a. I only.

b. II only.

c. Both I and II.

d. Neither I nor II. (6803)

60. Which of the following acts constitute(s) grounds for a tax preparer penalty?

I. Without the taxpayer's consent, the tax preparer disclosed taxpayer income tax return information under an order from a state court.

II. At the taxpayer's suggestion, the tax preparer deducted the expenses of the taxpayer's personal domestic help as a business expense on the taxpayer's individual tax return.

a. I only.

b. II only.

c. Both I and II.

d. Neither I nor II. (6915)

OTHER OBJECTIVE FORMAT QUESTIONS

PROBLEM 2 (45 to 55 minutes)

ITEMS 61 THROUGH 70 represent various transactions pertaining to a municipality that uses encumbrance accounting.

FOR 61 THROUGH 70, (the municipality's transactions) select the appropriate recording of the transaction (A through L). A method of recording the transactions may be selected once, more than once, or not at all.

ITEMS 71 THROUGH 80 represent the funds and accounts used by the municipality.

FOR 71 THROUGH 80, (the municipality's funds and accounts) select the appropriate method of accounting and reporting (M through V). An accounting and reporting method may be selected once, more than once, or not at all.

Transactions

61. General obligation bonds were issued at par.

62. Approved purchase orders were issued for supplies.

63. The above-mentioned supplies were received and the related invoices were approved.

64. General fund salaries and wages were incurred.

65. The internal service fund had interfund billings.

66. Revenues were earned from a previously awarded grant.

67. Property taxes were collected in advance.

68. Appropriations were recorded on adoption of the budget.

69. Short-term financing was received from a bank, secured by the city's taxing power.

70. There was an excess of estimated inflows over estimated outflows.

Funds and Accounts

71. Enterprise fund fixed assets.

72. Capital projects fund.

73. Internal service fund fixed assets.

74. Private-purpose trust fund cash.

75. Enterprise fund cash.

76. General fund.

77. Agency fund cash.

78. Pension trust fund cash.

79. Special revenue fund.

80. Debt service fund.

Recording of Transactions

A. Credit appropriations control.

B. Credit budgetary fund balance—unreserved.

C. Credit expenditures control.

D. Credit deferred revenues.

E. Credit interfund revenues.

F. Credit tax anticipation notes payable.

G. Credit other financing sources.

H. Credit other financing uses.

I. Debit appropriations control.

J. Debit deferred revenues.

K. Debit encumbrances control.

L. Debit expenditures control.

Accounting and Reporting by Funds

M. Accounted for in a fiduciary fund.

N. Accounted for in a proprietary fund.

O. Accounted for in a quasi-endowment fund.

P. Accounted for in a self-balancing account group.

Q. Accounted for in a special assessment fund.

R. Accounts for major construction activities.

S. Accounts for property tax revenues.

T. Accounts for payment of interest and principal on tax supported debt.

U. Accounts for revenues from earmarked sources to finance designated activities.

V. Reporting is optional. (3395-3413)

PROBLEM 3 (25 to 30 minutes)

Frank and Dale Cumack are married and filing a joint 2002 income tax return. During 2002, Frank, 65, was retired from government service and Dale, 55, was employed as a university instructor. In 2002, the Cumacks contributed all of the support to Dale's father, Jacques, an unmarried French citizen and French resident who had no gross income.

REQUIRED:

FOR ITEMS 81 THROUGH 90, select the correct amount of income, loss, or adjustment to income that should be recognized on page 1 of the Cumack's 2002 Form 1040—Individual Income Tax Return to arrive at the adjusted gross income for each separate transaction. A response may be selected once, more than once, or not at all. Any information contained in an item is unique to that item and is not to be incorporated in your calculations when answering other items.

Amounts			
A.	$0	H.	$ 9,000
B.	$1,000	I.	$ 10,000
C.	$2,000	J.	$ 25,000
D.	$2,500	K.	$ 30,000
E.	$3,000	L.	$125,000
F.	$4,000	M.	$150,000
G.	$5,000		

81. Dale received a $30,000 cash gift from her aunt.

82. Dale contributed $3,000 to her Individual Retirement Account (IRA) on January 15, 2003. In 2002, she earned $60,000 as a university instructor. During 2002, the Cumacks were not active participants in an employer's qualified pension or annuity plan.

83. The Cumacks received a $1,000 federal income tax refund.

84. During 2002, Frank, a 50% partner in Diske General Partnership, received a $4,000 guaranteed payment from Diske for services that he rendered to the partnership that year.

85. Frank received $10,000 as beneficiary of his deceased brother's life insurance policy.

86. Dale's employer pays 100% of the cost of all employees' group term life insurance under a qualified plan. Policy cost is $5 per $1,000 of coverage. Dale's group term life insurance coverage equals $450,000.

87. Frank won $5,000 at a casino and had $2,000 in gambling losses.

88. The Cumacks received $1,000 interest income associated with a refund of their prior years' federal income tax.

89. The Cumacks sold their first and only residence for $200,000. They purchased their home five years ago for $50,000 and have lived there since then. There were no other capital gains, losses, or capital loss carryovers. The Cumacks do not intend to buy another residence.

90. Zeno Corp. declared a stock dividend and Dale received one additional share of Zeno common stock for three shares of Zeno common stock that she held. The stock that Dale received had a fair market value of $9,000. There were no provisions to receive cash instead of stock. (6552-6571)

PROBLEM 4 (10 to 15 minutes)

Reliant Corp., an accrual-basis calendar year C corporation, filed its 20X8 federal income tax return on March 16, 20X9.

FOR ITEMS 91 THROUGH 93, indicate if the items are (F) fully taxable, (P) partially taxable, or (N) nontaxable for regular tax purposes on Reliant's current federal income tax return. All transactions occurred during the current year.

91. Reliant received dividend income from a mutual fund that solely invests in municipal bonds.

92. Reliant, the lessor, benefited from the capital improvements made to its property by the lessee in 20X8. The lease agreement is for one year ending December 31, 20X8, and provides for a reduction in rental payments by the lessee in exchange for the improvements.

93. Reliant collected the proceeds on the term life insurance policy on the life of a debtor who was not a shareholder. The policy was assigned to Reliant as collateral security for the debt. The proceeds exceeded the amount of the debt.

FOR ITEMS 94 THROUGH 98, indicate if the following (I) increase, (D) decrease, or (N) have no effect on Reliant's 20X8 alternative minimum taxable income (AMTI) prior to the adjusted current earnings adjustment (ACE).

94. Reliant used the 70% dividends-received deduction for regular tax purposes.

95. Reliant received interest from a state's general obligation bonds.

96. Reliant used MACRS depreciation on seven-year personal property placed into service January 3, 20X8, for regular tax purposes. No expense or depreciation election was made.

97. Depreciation on nonresidential real property placed into service on January 3, 20X4, was under the general MACRS depreciation system for regular tax purposes.

98. Reliant had only cash charitable contributions for 20X8.

For Items 99 through 105, indicate if the statement is true (T) or false (F) regarding Reliant's compliance with tax procedures, tax credits and the alternative minimum tax.

99. Reliant's exemption for alternative minimum tax is reduced by 20% of the excess of the alternative minimum taxable income over $150,000.

100. The statute of limitations on Reliant's fraudulent 20X1 federal income tax return expires six years after the filing date of the return.

101. The statute of limitations on Reliant's 20X2 federal income tax return, which omitted 30% of gross receipts, expires 2 years after the filing date of the return.

102. The targeted job tax credit may be combined with other business credits to form part of Reliant's general business credit.

103. Reliant incurred qualifying expenditures to remove existing access barriers at the place of employment in 20X8. As a small business, Reliant qualifies for the disabled access credit.

104. Reliant's tax preparer, a CPA firm, may use the 20X8 corporate tax return information to prepare corporate officers' tax returns without the consent of the corporation.

105. Reliant must file an amended return for 20X8 within 1 year of the filing date. (5503-5536)

Problem 5 (5 to 10 minutes)

During 20X0, Adams, a general contractor, Brinks, an architect, and Carson, an interior decorator, formed the Dex Home Improvement General Partnership by contributing the assets below:

	Asset	Adjusted basis	Fair market value	% of share in capital, profits & losses
Adams	Cash	$40,000	$40,000	50%
Brinks	Land	$12,000	$21,000	20%
Carson	Inventory	$24,000	$24,000	30%

The land was a capital asset to Brinks, subject to a $5,000 mortgage, which was assumed by the partnership.

For Items 106 and 107, determine the initial basis of the partner's interest in Dex.

106. Brinks

107. Carson

During 20X0, the Dex Partnership breaks even but decides to make distributions to each partner.

For Items 108 through 113, determine whether the statement is true (T) or false (F).

108. A nonliquidating cash distribution may reduce the recipient partner's basis in his or her partnership interest below zero.

109. A nonliquidating distribution of unappreciated inventory reduces the recipient partner's basis in his or her partnership interest.

110. In a liquidating distribution of property other than money, where the partnership's basis of the distributed property exceeds the basis of the partner's interest, the partner's basis in the distributed property is limited to his or her predistribution basis in the partnership interest.

111. Gain is recognized by the partner who receives a nonliquidating distribution of property, where the adjusted basis of the property exceeds his or her basis in the partnership interest before the distribution.

112. In a nonliquidating distribution of inventory, where the partnership has no unrealized receivables or appreciated inventory, the basis of inventory that is distributed to a partner cannot exceed the inventory's adjusted basis to the partnership.

113. The partnership's nonliquidating distribution of encumbered property to a partner who assumes the mortgage, does not affect the other partners' bases in their partnership interests. (5037-5044)

ANSWERS TO MULTIPLE CHOICE QUESTIONS

1. d	6. c	11. c	16. b	21. b	26. b	31. d	36. b	41. c	46. d	51. b	56. d
2. d	7. a	12. c	17. b	22. d	27. d	32. a	37. b	42. c	47. b	52. b	57. b
3. a	8. c	13. c	18. b	23. a	28. b	33. c	38. c	43. d	48. c	53. a	58. b
4. a	9. b	14. a	19. b	24. d	29. a	34. a	39. b	44. b	49. c	54. a	59. b
5. c	10. b	15. d	20. c	25. c	30. d	35. d	40. c	45. c	50. c	55. c	60. b

PERFORMANCE BY TOPICS

Diagnostic exam questions corresponding to each chapter of the Accounting & Reporting text are listed below. To assess your preparedness for the CPA exam, record the number and percentage of questions you correctly answered in each topic area. The point distribution of the multiple choice questions (not counting the other objective format question) approximates that of the exam. See page F-25 for explanations to these questions and questions 36, 41, 49, and 50.

Chapter 21: Governmental Overview

Question #	Correct √
1	(7)
2	(20)
3	(21)
4	(24)
5	(40)
# Questions	5

Correct _____
% Correct _____

Chapter 22: Governmental Funds & Transactions

Question #	Correct √
6	(3)
7	[8]
8	[8]
9	(20)
10	(30)
11	(32)
12	(50)
13	[62]
14	(63)
15	(26)
# Questions	10

Correct _____
% Correct _____

Chapter 23: Nonprofit Accounting

Question #	Correct √
16	(5)
17	(19)
18	[26]
# Questions	3

Correct _____
% Correct _____

Chapter 24: Decision Making

Question #	Correct √
19	(16)
20	(65)
# Questions	2

Correct _____
% Correct _____

Chapter 25: Cost Accounting

Question #	Correct √
21	[31]
22	(60)
# Questions	2

Correct _____
% Correct _____

Chapter 26: Planning & Control

Question #	Correct √
23	(9)
24	(22)
# Questions	2

Correct _____
% Correct _____

Chapter 27: Federal Taxation—Individuals

Question #	Correct √
25	(3)
26	(9)
27	(26)
28	(33)
29	(88)
30	[90]
31	(56)
32	(99)
33	(105)
34	[70]
# Questions	10

Correct _____
% Correct _____

Chapter 28: Federal Taxation—Property

Question #	Correct √
35	(1)
36	
37	[29]
38	[20]
# Questions	4

Correct _____
% Correct _____

Chapter 29: Federal Taxation—Corporations

Question #	Correct √
39	[26]
40	(22)
41	
42	(49)
43	[56]
44	[69]
45	[103]
46	(63)
47	(77)
48	(78)
# Questions	10

Correct _____
% Correct _____

Chapter 30: Federal Taxation—Partnerships & Other Topics

Question #	Correct √
49	
50	
51	(18)
52	(80)
53	(24)
54	(36)
55	(37)
56	(52)
57	(92)
58	(37)
59	(67)
60	(74)
# Questions	12

Correct _____
% Correct _____

OTHER OBJECTIVE FORMAT QUESTION SOLUTIONS

SOLUTION 2 GOVERNMENTAL ACCOUNTING (Problem 22-6 in Chapter 22, Items 1 - 20)

61.	G	65.	E	69.	F	73.	N	77.	M
62.	K	66.	J	70.	B	74.	M	78.	M
63.	L	67.	D	71.	N	75.	N	79.	U
64.	L	68.	A	72.	E	76.	S	80.	T

SOLUTION 3 FEDERAL TAX—INDIVIDUALS (Problem 27-4 in Chapter 27, Items 10 - 19)

81.	A	83.	A	85.	A	87.	G	89.	A
82.	E	84.	F	86.	C	88.	B	90.	A

SOLUTION 4 FEDERAL TAX—CORPORATIONS (Problem 29-3 in Chapter 29, Items 14 - 28)

91.	N	94.	N	97.	I	100.	F	103.	T
92.	F	95.	N	98.	N	101.	F	104.	T
93.	P	96.	I	99.	F	102.	T	105.	F

SOLUTION 5 FEDERAL TAXATION—PARTNERSHIPS (Problem 30-3 in Chapter 30, Items 1 - 8)

106.	$ 8,000	108.	F	110.	T	112.	T
107.	$25,000	109.	T	111.	F	113.	F

EXPLANATIONS OF MULTIPLE CHOICE ANSWERS

The editors strongly recommend that candidates **not** spend much time on the answers to specific questions that they answered incorrectly on the diagnostic exam, particularly at the beginning of their review. Instead, study the related chapter. The numbers in parenthesis in the performance by topic chart (on the page with the answers to the multiple choice questions) refer to an **explanation** of a question in the related chapters. **The question in the chapter is not necessarily the same question as in the diagnostic exam.** Other explanations are provided here.

36. MACRS is a system similar to the double-declining balance used in financial accounting, except salvage value is ignored and the method coverts to straight line towards the end of the asset life. Used tangible property is eligible for cost recovery. Most realty has a recovery period of at least 27.5 years, but there are exceptions, such as land improvements (15 years).

41. In this case, the taxable income equals book income before FIT. Interest earned on federal debt is not an exclusion from (federal) taxable income. State income tax is an allowable deduction from (federal) taxable income.

49. Generally, a partner is taxed on the income of the partnership, regardless of distributions.

50. Incurring debt increases a partner's basis. A loss reduces a partner's basis. [$40,000 + 0.50 x ($60,000 – $10,000) = $65,000]

THE NATURE OF THE CPA EXAM

See the **Practical Advice** section of this volume for detailed information about the types of questions and point value of various topics. The typical format of the ARE section in the most recent exams was 4 OOAF questions, with a total of about 60 items (40% of the point value) and 60 to 75 multiple choice questions (60% of the point value). These are answered by marking a machine-readable (bubble) sheet with a pencil. There are no essay questions or problems on this section of the exam.

What will the actual exam be like? The questions throughout this book are either former exam questions or based on former exam questions. General predictions of future exams can be made based on previously disclosed exams. Specific predictions about which topics will be stressed or the type of question used to test a specific topic are mere speculation and rather useless. (The examiners try not to make the exam predictable. Candidates must know roughly the same information regardless of the type of questions.) Don't waste time with mere speculation; instead, study and be prepared!

Using Videos to Study

Actively watch video classes, taking notes and answering questions as if it were a live class. If the lecturer recommends you to work an example as the video plays, write the numbers in the viewer guide, rather than merely following along. If the lecturer instructs you to stop the tape to answer questions, stop the tape. If the lecturer advises you to take notes, personalize your copy of the viewer guide. The lecturers provide these instructions with the insight gained from years of CPA review experience.

Each of the Hot•Spot™ videotapes concentrates on a few topics. Use them to help you study the areas that are most troubling for you. If you are strong in a topic, watching the video and answering the questions may be sufficient review. If your strength is moderate in a topic, you should probably read the related text before watching the video. If you are weak in a topic, one successful strategy is to watch the video (including following all of the lecturer's instructions), read the book, and then watch the video again.

Each of the Intensive videotapes are designed for a final, intensive review, after a candidate has already done considerable work. If time permits, use the Intensive tapes at both the very beginning (for an overview) and set them aside until the final review in week 19. They contain concise, informative lectures, as well as CPA exam tips, tricks, and techniques that will help you to learn the material needed to pass the exam.

FYI: The Hot•Spot™ and Intensive videotapes have similar content as the audio tutor and online video lectures, but they are not exactly the same.

CHANGE ALERT

GASB No. 34, *Basic Financial Statements–and Management's Discussion and Analysis–for State and Local Governments,* was issued by the GASB in June 1999, overhauling the governmental reporting model. GASB 34 may be implemented immediately, and is required to be implemented for financial statements for periods beginning after June 15, 2001, at the earliest. The outgoing reporting model is unlikely to be heavily tested after **November 2001,** although it remains eligible to be tested. The transition period, with optional early implementation, makes **both** reporting models eligible to be tested through the **May 2003** exam, and for infrastructure assets, through May 2006. With the issuance of GASB 34, all of the guidance in GASB 11 is superseded. (GASB 11 was never implemented.)

The new reporting model is discussed throughout the **text** of Chapters 21 and 22, except as noted. The examiners historically have clearly labeled **questions** pertaining to any new pronouncement during the implementation period. To be consistent with the exam, this book does the same. Be observant while writing the exam; the examiners may make one general statement regarding this issue applicable to all governmental questions, instead of mentioning GASB 34 in each question.

Coverage of GASB No. 35, Basic Financial Statements–and Management's Discussion and Analysis–for Public Colleges and Universities, GASB No. 37, Basic Financial Statements—and Management's Discussion and Analysis—for State and Local Governments: Omnibus—an amendment of GASB Statements No. 21 and No. 34, and GASB No. 38, Certain Financial Statement Note Disclosures is incorporated in this text to the depth likely to be tested on the CPA exam. GASB 35 may be implemented immediately, and component units must implement it as GASB 34 is implemented for the primary government. GASB 35 has the same staggered implementation dates as GASB 34 for non-component units. GASB 37 and GASB 38 are applied when GASB 34 is applied.

GASB No. 39, *Determining Whether Certain Organizations Are Component Units,* was issued by the GASB in May, 2002. The material in GASB No. 39 is unlikely to be tested heavily. GASB No. 39 is effective for periods beginning after June 15, 2003, with early application encouraged.

CHAPTER 21

GOVERNMENTAL OVERVIEW

EXAM COVERAGE: The governmental and nonprofit accounting portion of the ARE section of the CPA exam is designated by the examiners to be 30 percent of the section's point value. Historically, exam coverage of the topics in this chapter is 4 to 9 percent of the ARE section. Bear in mind that (1) the division of governmental topics into two chapters is somewhat arbitrary, and (2) a thorough grasp of the concepts of the first section of Chapter 21, *Governmental Accounting Environment*, is necessary to understand Chapter 22. Candidates with less than a semester course in fund accounting may need to repeat Chapters 21 and 22. A thorough understanding of the other topics in both governmental chapters should be gained before candidates pursue mastery of the appendix topics.

Material covered in Chapter 21 and Chapter 22 combined has repeatedly covered 23 to 27 percent of the ARE section of the exam. More information about the point value of various topics is included in the **Practical Advice** section of this volume.

CHAPTER 21

GOVERNMENTAL OVERVIEW

I. GOVERNMENTAL ACCOUNTING ENVIRONMENT

A. NATURE OF GOVERNMENTAL ENTITIES

1. **SERVICE** Governmental entities are established by the citizenry through the constitutional and charter process. The primary objective of governmental entities is to render services to those citizens.

2. **LACK OF PROFIT MOTIVE** In most cases, governmental entities do not seek to profit from the activities in which they engage. This general absence of profit motive is the primary distinguishing characteristic of governmental entities as compared to commercial enterprises.

3. **DEPENDENCE ON LEGISLATIVE AUTHORITIES** Governmental entities generally receive their authority to act directly from legislative authorities, which ultimately oversee and circumscribe governmental operations. Although the operation of commercial sector enterprises is also overseen to some extent by public authorities, this type of oversight is regulatory rather than proprietary in nature.

4. **RESPONSIBILITY TO CITIZENS** In financial reporting matters, governmental entities have the responsibility of demonstrating good stewardship over financial resources provided and entrusted to them by the citizenry. In contrast, commercial sector enterprises have a similar stewardship duty to their debt and equity owners.

5. **TAXES AS SOURCE OF REVENUE** The principal source of revenue for governmental entities is taxes levied on the citizenry. Commercial sector enterprises have no comparable source of revenue.

6. **RESTRICTIONS AND CONTROLS** In the absence of a profit motive, a net income bottom line, or other performance indicators, governments are subjected to a variety of restrictions and controls. The most important are overall restrictions on the use of resources (which leads to fund accounting) and exercise of expenditure control through the annual budget (which leads to budgetary accounting).

B. FINANCIAL REPORTING
Financial reporting takes into consideration the influence of the governmental environment on reporting both governmental- and business-type activities, and the information needs of users. NCGA and GASB pronouncements primarily address annual financial statements.

1. **ACCOUNTABILITY AND INTERPERIOD EQUITY** Governmental accountability requires governments to justify the raising of public resources and to disclose the purposes for which they are used. Accountability means that governments must ultimately answer to the citizenry through financial reporting, part of a government's duty in a democratic society. Accountability is the primary objective. Interperiod equity refers to the concept of paying for current-year services so as not to shift the burden to future-year taxpayers. Interperiod equity is an integral part of accountability. The primary objectives of financial reporting are to

   a. Provide assistance in fulfilling government's duty to be publicly accountable and enable users to assess that accountability.

b. Assist users in assessing the operating results of the governmental entity for the year, the level of services that can be provided by the governmental entity, and its ability to meet its obligations as they become due.

2. USERS OF FINANCIAL REPORTS

a. **CITIZENS** This group includes taxpayers, voters, service recipients, the media, advocate groups, and public finance researchers.

b. **LEGISLATIVE AND OVERSIGHT BODIES** This group includes members of state legislatures, county commissions, city councils, boards of trustees, school boards, and executive branch officials with oversight responsibilities.

c. **INVESTORS AND CREDITORS** This group includes individual and institutional investors and creditors, municipal security underwriters, bond rating agencies, bond insurers, and financial institutions.

d. **INTERNAL USERS** Internal users are not considered primary users, although they have many uses for external financial reports.

3. CHARACTERISTICS OF FINANCIAL REPORTING INFORMATION

a. **UNDERSTANDABILITY** To be publicly accountable, financial reports must be understood by those who may not have detailed knowledge of accounting principles.

b. **RELIABILITY** Information in financial reports should be comprehensive, verifiable, free from bias, and representative of what it purports.

c. **RELEVANCE** Information must be reliable and bear a close logical relationship with the purpose for which it is needed.

d. **TIMELINESS** Financial reports should be issued soon after the reported events to facilitate timely decisions.

e. **CONSISTENCY** Financial reports should be consistent over time in regard to accounting principles, reporting and valuation methods, basis of accounting, and determination of the reporting entity. Changes occurring in these areas should be disclosed.

f. **COMPARABILITY** Differences among financial reports should be due to substantive differences in the underlying transactions or structure rather than due to different alternatives in accounting practices or procedures.

g. **LIMITATIONS OF FINANCIAL REPORTING** Users must understand limitations of the information to properly assess needs. Limitations are similar to those in commercial accounting.

4. GOVERNMENTAL-TYPE ACTIVITIES

a. **ACCOUNTABILITY** The need for public accountability in financial reporting arises because of characteristics unique to governmental environments.

(1) Resources are provided by essentially involuntary means, i.e., taxes. Accordingly, difficulties arise when attempting to measure optimal quantity or quality, because consumers cannot choose what or how much to purchase as is the case in the commercial arena.

(2) There is no direct relationship between taxes collected and services rendered except in some instances when fees are charged for specific services. The only relationship that does exist in the governmental sector is a timing relationship, i.e., resources provided and services rendered occurring during the fiscal year.

    (3) Governments have monopolies on some services provided to the public. It is difficult to measure efficiency without the element of competition.

    (4) Because there is no single overall performance measure, the users of governmental financial reports must assess accountability by means of a variety of measures that evaluate performance.

b.   **ANNUAL BUDGET** The annual budget is a plan for the coordination of revenues and expenditures. Legislative approval authorizes expenditures within the limits of the appropriations and any applicable laws. When developing the financial reporting objectives of the budget, the budget is an expression of

    (1) **PUBLIC POLICY** The budget is a result of not only the legislative process but also of the direct or indirect participation of the citizenry.

    (2) **FINANCIAL INTENT** A financial plan sets forth the proposed expenditures for the year and the means for financing them. The balanced-budget concept is important to many who expect governments not to exceed their means.

    (3) **CONTROL** A government should demonstrate that it is accountable from both the authorization and the limitation perspectives, because (a) budgetary allowances and authorizations are the direct result of competition for resources and (b) budget limitations cannot be legally exceeded.

    (4) **PERFORMANCE EVALUATION** The budget may be a means of evaluating performance by comparing actual results to the legally adopted budget.

c.   **USES OF FINANCIAL REPORTS**

    (1) Assessing financial condition and the results of operations

    (2) Determining compliance with finance-related laws and regulations

    (3) Evaluating efficiency and effectiveness

d.   **CAPITAL ASSETS** Commitments to build and maintain infrastructure do not provide a direct return to governments.

5.   **BUSINESS-TYPE ACTIVITIES** Governmental activities resemble private-sector business activities when they provide the same services and/or are self-sufficient, operating as separate, legally constituted organizations.

a.   **EXCHANGE RELATIONSHIP** There is often a direct relationship between charges and services rendered; for example, bus fares and tolls. Users of financial reports are able to measure costs and revenues and the differences between them. Further, users may determine the full cost of operating the activity and the financial implications of subsidies or grants. This information is useful for public policy decision-making.

b.   **ANNUAL BUDGET** The use of the budget and fund accounting is less common in business-type activities. The budget is often merely an internal management process. Similarly, fund accounting is not as common because the business-type activity often represents a single function only.

c.   **USES OF FINANCIAL REPORTS** The primary difference in use for business-type activities is the emphasis on financial condition and results of operations, as opposed to the comparison of actual results with budgeted amounts. Uses include assessing reasonableness of user charges and assessing the potential need to subsidize activities with general governmental revenues.

    d.   **CAPITAL ASSETS** Unlike many governmental-type activities, capital assets of business-type activities have a direct relationship to the entity's revenue-raising capabilities.

6.   **NONPROFIT ORGANIZATIONS** Some nonprofit organizations have strong ties to governments, making it difficult to determine which guidance applies. Along with public corporations and bodies corporate and politic, the following are governments:

    a.   Entities that have one or more of the following traits:

        (1)   Popular election of officers or approval (or appointment) of a controlling majority of the entity's governing board members by state or local government's officials

        (2)   The possibility of unilateral dissolution by a government with the reversion of the entity's net assets to a government

        (3)   The ability to enact and enforce a tax levy

    b.   Entities that have the power to directly issue debt (as opposed to through a state or local authority) that pays interest exempt from federal taxation. Entities having only this trait may refute the presumption that the entity is a government if they provide compelling, relevant evidence.

7.   **GOVERNMENTAL REPORTING ENTITY** The governmental reporting entity often coincides with the legal unit (entity) as defined in law or by charter. However, some governments also control other governmental units, quasi-governmental units, or nonprofit corporations (that are in substance its departments or agencies) and must report them in their financial statements.

C.   DEFINITIONS

Most governmental fund accounting systems use both budgetary accounts and regular accounts. Budgetary accounts are nominal accounts used to record approved budgetary estimates of revenues and expenditures (appropriations). Regular accounts are used to record the actual revenues, expenditures, and other transactions affecting the fund. Although terminology varies, the following accounts are usually employed in governmental funds:

1.   **ESTIMATED REVENUES** Forecasts of asset inflows of estimated sources of fund working capital (except from other financing sources). The *Estimated Revenues Control* account is debited to record the revenue budget (and is closed at the end of the period with a credit).

2.   **APPROPRIATIONS** Forecasts of (and authorizations of) asset outflows of estimated uses of fund working capital (except for other financing uses). The *Appropriations Control* account is credited to record the budgeted expenditures (and is closed at the end of the period with a debit).

3.   **REVENUES** Additions to fund assets or decreases in fund liabilities (except from other financing sources) that increase the residual equity of the fund—inflows (sources) of fund working capital. Governmental fund revenues differ from the commercial concept of revenues in that they often are levied (e.g., taxes) rather than earned per se, and the related financial resources must be available working capital for revenue to be recognized. (Revenue recognition criteria for the various funds are discussed in D., below.)

4.   **OTHER FINANCING SOURCES** Nonrevenue increases in fund net assets and residual equity (e.g., from certain interfund transfers and bond issue proceeds).

5. **EXPENDITURES** Increases in fund liabilities or decreases in fund assets (except for other financing uses) that decrease the residual equity of the fund—outflows (uses) of fund working capital. Expenditures differ from expenses (as defined in commercial accounting) because expenditures include—in addition to current operating expenditures that benefit the current period—capital outlays for general fixed assets and repayment of general long-term debt principal.

6. **OTHER FINANCING USES** Nonrevenue decreases in fund net assets and residual equity—e.g., for interfund transfers.

7. **FUND BALANCE** The fund residual equity account that balances the asset and liability accounts of a governmental fund (and trust funds), thus recording the amount available for expenditures. (The *Fund Balance* account is similar to the owners' equity account of a commercial enterprise only in this balancing feature; however, it does not purport to show any ownership in a fund's assets.)

8. **FUND BALANCE RESERVES** When some of the assets of a governmental fund are not working capital available for expenditure—e.g., assets of one fund have been loaned to another fund for several years—a fund balance reserve is established (e.g., *Fund Balance Reserved for Interfund Advances* or simply *Reserve for Interfund Advances*) and the *Fund Balance* account should be retitled *Unreserved Fund Balance* (but may be called simply *Fund Balance*) and reduced accordingly.

D. **FUNDS**

1. **GOVERNMENTAL FUNDS** Governmental funds are used to finance general government activities such as police and fire protection, courts, inspection, and general administration. Most of their financial resources are subsequently budgeted (appropriated) for specific general government uses (expenditures) by the legislative body. Governmental funds are essentially working capital funds, and their operations are measured in terms of sources and uses of working capital, that is, changes in working capital. Capital assets and long-term general obligation debt are excluded from all governmental fund statements. The accounting equation of most governmental funds is as follows:

Current Assets – Current Liabilities = Fund Balance

a. General fund

b. Special revenue fund

c. Capital projects fund

d. Debt service fund

e. Permanent fund

2. **PROPRIETARY FUNDS** Proprietary funds are used to finance a government's self-supporting business-type activities (for example, utilities). The accounting equation of proprietary funds is identical to that of a business corporation—it includes accounts for **all** related assets and liabilities, not just for current assets and current liabilities, as well as for contributed capital and retained earnings. Proprietary fund operations are measured in terms of revenues earned, expenses incurred, and net income or loss.

a. Enterprise funds (for example, utilities)

b. Internal service funds (for example, central repair shop)

3. **FIDUCIARY FUNDS** Fiduciary funds account for resources (and related liabilities) held by governments in a trustee capacity (trust funds) or as an agent for others (agency funds).

a. Pension trust funds

b. Investment trust funds

c. Private-purpose trust funds

d. Agency funds are purely custodial (assets equal liabilities).

FUNDS: TYPE AND GOVERNMENT-WIDE STATEMENT COLUMN

	Fund	Type	Activities Column
P	**P**ension trust fund	Fiduciary	not in GWS
I	**I**nvestment trust fund	Fiduciary	not in GWS
P	**P**rivate-		
P	**P**urpose trust fund	Fiduciary	not in GWS
A	**A**gency trust fund	Fiduciary	not in GWS
C	**C**apital projects fund	Governmental	Governmental
G	**G**eneral fund	Governmental	Governmental
R	Special **R**evenue fund	Governmental	Governmental
I	**I**nternal service	Proprietary	Governmental (typically)
P	**P**ermanent fund	Governmental	Governmental
E	**E**nterprise	Proprietary	Business-type
S	Debt **S**ervice fund	Governmental	Governmental

NOTE: All PIPPA funds are fiduciary and do not appear in the government-wide financial statements. Amounts from any C GRIPES funds appear in the government-wide statements (GWS). The vowels in C GRIPES indicate the proprietary funds; the consonants indicate the governmental funds.

E. FUND ACCOUNTING

A specific governmental unit is not accounted for through a single accounting entity. Instead, the accounts of a government are divided into several funds. A fund is a fiscal and accounting entity with a self-balancing set of accounts recording cash and other financial resources, together with all related liabilities and residual equities and balances, and changes therein, that are segregated for the purpose of carrying on specific activities or attaining certain objectives in accordance with special regulations, restrictions, or limitations. A government should have only one general fund. It may have one, none, or several of the other types of funds, depending on its activities. Governments should use the minimum number of funds consistent with their laws (and contracts) and sound financial management. Comparisons among the types of funds and account groups are common questions on the exam.

1. **BUDGETS** Annual budgets of estimated revenues and estimated expenditures are prepared for most governmental-type funds. The approved budgets of such funds are recorded in budgetary accounts in the accounting system to provide control over governmental fund revenues and expenditures. Proprietary and fiduciary funds—and most capital projects funds—are not dependent on annual budgets and legislative appropriations of resources, and thus budgets are not usually incorporated into their accounts. The balances of budget accounts are generally the **opposite** of the companion accounts. For instance, the *Revenues* account ordinarily has a credit balance, but *Estimated Revenues* is opened with a debit balance.

2. **ENCUMBRANCE SYSTEM** The encumbrance system is used in governmental funds (General, special revenue, and capital projects funds) to prevent over-expenditure and to demonstrate compliance with legal requirements. When a purchase order is issued or a contract is approved, the estimated amount of the planned expenditure is encumbered (committed) by

debiting *Encumbrances* and crediting *Reserve for Encumbrances*. When the related invoice is received, the encumbrance entry is reversed and the actual expenditure is recorded.

a. The unencumbered balance of the *Appropriations* account is the amount of uncommitted appropriations funds available for expenditures.

$$\text{Unencumbered Appropriations} = \text{Appropriations} - \left(\text{Outstanding Encumbrances} + \text{Year-to-date Expenditures} \right)$$

b. **PRIOR PERIOD ENCUMBRANCES** If funds are encumbered but not yet expended at the end of the period, the usual accounting treatment is to close the encumbrances account (i.e., credit *Encumbrances*, debit *Fund Balance*). This reduces the *Unreserved Fund Balance* account and causes the *Reserve for Encumbrances* account—which merely offsets the *Encumbrances* account during the year—to be a true fund balance reserve. The *Reserve for Encumbrances* account thus is not a liability, but a reservation of *Fund Balance* similar to the appropriated retained earnings of a business enterprise. At the beginning of the subsequent period, the encumbrances closing entry is reversed, returning the *Encumbrances* and *Reserve for Encumbrances* accounts to their usual offsetting relationship.

3. **BASIS OF ACCOUNTING** The basis of accounting used depends on the nature of the fund and the financial statement being presented.

EXHIBIT 1 ♦ BASIS OF ACCOUNTING

	ACCRUAL	**MODIFIED ACCRUAL**
REVENUES	Accrued as earned	Accrued when available and measurable
EXPENSES	Fixed assets are capitalized	Fixed assets are expenditures

a. The modified accrual basis is used in the governmental-type fund statements (general, special revenue, capital projects, and debt service funds), where revenues and **expenditures** are recorded.

b. The accrual basis is used in the government-wide statements for all amounts. The accrual basis is used in proprietary fund statements, where revenues and **expenses** are recorded and net income (loss) is reported. The accrual basis is also used in fiduciary fund statements, except for the recognition of certain liabilities of defined benefit pension plans (GASB 25) and certain postemployment healthcare plans (GASB 26).

II. NEW REPORTING MODEL

A. OVERVIEW

While legal restrictions generally mandate the continuation of fund segregation in accounting systems, many users want to see the government-wide information to assess the overall financial position of the government. Users are interested in both the short-term and the long-term view. The outgoing model provides incomplete information about the long-term perspective of the government's financial position and operations, particularly with regard to governmental funds.

1. **OBJECTIVE** The objective for GASB 34, *Basic Financial Statements–and Management's Discussion and Analysis–for State and Local Governments*, is "to establish a basic financial reporting model that will result in greater accountability by state and local governments by providing more useful information to a wider range of users than the existing model."

a. Operational accountability is important to assess the government's ability to provide services. GASB 34 states that operational accountability "includes the periodic economic cost of the services provided. It also informs users about whether the government is raising sufficient revenues each period to cover that cost, or whether the government is deferring costs to the future or using up accumulated resources to provide current-period services." The government-wide statements (GWS) are designed to provide an economic long-term view of the government that cannot be seen with the presentation of a collection of funds.

b. The outgoing reporting model includes a liftable section termed the *general purpose financial statements*. GASB 34 shifts to the concept of *basic financial statements*, incorporating government-wide statements. The GASB hopes that the new formats will simplify the external reports and create a user-friendly environment. [The GASB encourages governments to issue a CAFR (discussed in Section V).]

2. **UNIVERSITIES** GASB 34 originally excluded public colleges and universities from its scope. GASB 35 includes these institutions and permits those issuing separate financial statements to use the new reporting model guidance for special purpose governments.

3. **EFFECTIVE DATES** Early application is encouraged. The staggered implementation schedule is based on governments' revenues, with implementation required no later than fiscal years beginning after the implementation date for that size government. (There is additional time to implement the requirements for *retroactive* reporting of infrastructure assets.) Institutions that are component units implement the new reporting model at the same time as the primary government.

EXHIBIT 2 ♦ EFFECTIVE DATES FOR GASB 34 AND 35

Phase	Revenue Range (in millions)	General Implementation Date	Retroactive Infrastructure Implementation Date
1	> $100	June 15, 2001	June 15, 2005
2	> $10 and < $100	June 15, 2002	June 15, 2006
3	< $10	June 15, 2003	optional

4. **BASIS OF ACCOUNTING** All amounts in the government-wide statements, including from the governmental funds, are determined using the economic resources measurement focus and accrual basis of accounting. Governmental funds presented in the fund financial statements use current financial resources and modified accrual basis. Proprietary and fiduciary funds use the economic resources focus and accrual basis in the fund statements, with limited exceptions for some fiduciary funds.

5. **BASIC FINANCIAL STATEMENTS** Basic financial statements (BFS) include both the government-wide statements and the fund statements, as well as the notes.

6. **GOVERNMENT-WIDE STATEMENTS** Government-wide statements (GWS) aggregate information for all governmental and business-type activities. GASB 34 requires economic resources measurement focus and accrual basis of accounting for all amounts in the GWS. There are four required columns in the GWS, one each for: governmental activities, business-type activities, the primary government (sum of the previous two), and component units. Note that funds do not explicitly appear in GWS; the amounts in governmental fund, proprietary fund, and component unit statements match or are reconciled to GWS amounts.

7. **FUND STATEMENTS** Fund statements appear between the GWS and the notes. Fund types are retained by GASB 34, but reporting in the fund financial statements shifts to major fund reporting. Users indicated that specific fund information for significant funds is more important than the traditional fund type reporting. The combining statements report funds by type for the fiduciary funds and the combination of nonmajor funds.

a. A reconciliation to government-wide statements appears on the face of the governmental fund financial statements, in a separate schedule, or in the notes.

b. Cash flows statements appear only in the fund statements for proprietary funds. (The governmental funds pose significant problems for developing meaningful information for a government-wide cash flow statement.)

c. Optional combining fund statements (for nonmajor funds) may be presented after the notes to the financial statements.

8. **TERMINOLOGY**

   a. **FIDUCIARY FUNDS** The fiduciary fund category includes only those funds used to report assets held in a trustee or agency capacity for others and that cannot be used to support the government's own programs. *Private-purpose trust funds* and *permanent funds* distinguish between resources held in a fiduciary capacity and those available to the government. Private purpose trusts are fiduciary funds; permanent funds are governmental funds, not fiduciary funds.

   b. **PROPRIETARY FUNDS** Enterprise and internal service funds are *proprietary funds*. If the sponsoring government is the predominant "customer" for the activity, the activities are reported in an internal service fund. Otherwise, an enterprise fund is used. GASB 34 establishes criteria that *require* the use of an enterprise fund in certain circumstances. Internal service fund activities are generally classified as governmental activities in the GWS.

   c. **CAPITAL ASSETS** The concept of *fixed assets* generally refers to land, building, and equipment, as well as improvements to those assets. GASB 34 uses the term *capital assets* to include easements, infrastructure, and all other tangible or intangible assets that are used in operations and that have initial useful lives extending beyond a single reporting period.

   d. **SPECIAL & EXTRAORDINARY ITEMS** Special and extraordinary items are nonoperating sources or uses. They are displayed separately on the statement of activities after the calculation of excess revenues. Special items are transactions or other events *within* the control of management that are *both* abnormally large in size and *either* unusual in nature *or* infrequent in occurrence. An event is presumed to be *within* management's control if management normally can influence the occurrence of that event. Extraordinary items are transactions or other events that are *both* unusual in nature *and* infrequent in occurrence.

   e. **ELIMINATIONS & RECLASSIFICATIONS** Combined statements in the outgoing model do not reflect *eliminations* and *reclassifications* of interfund activities. GASB 34 includes provisions for these adjustments in the aggregated data presented in the government-wide statements. Eliminations deduct the duplication resulting from interfund transfers and internal service fund transactions. Interfund receivables and payables are eliminated, except for residual balances between governmental and business-type activities. Internal events that are essentially allocations of overhead expenses are also eliminated from the statement of activities. Interfund services provided and used between functional categories, such as sales of utilities, are not be eliminated.

   f. **RECIPROCAL INTERFUND ACTIVITY** The internal counterpart to exchange and exchange-like transactions, including loans or interfund services provided and used.

   g. **NONRECIPROCAL INTERFUND ACTIVITY** Includes internal nonexchange transactions such as transfers or reimbursements.

B. **MANAGEMENT'S DISCUSSION & ANALYSIS (MD&A)**

MD&A is required supplementary information (RSI) in the general purpose external financial report. Although MD&A is classified as RSI, it is presented before the financial statements. The GASB encourages entities not to duplicate information in the MD&A and the more subjective letter of transmittal. GASB 37 limits MD&A to eight categories.

- **LETTER OF TRANSMITTAL** Governments that participate in the Government Finance Officers Association (GFOA) Certificate of Achievement for Excellence in Financial Reporting include a *letter of transmittal* in the CAFR. The GASB does not require a transmittal letter or provide specific guidance for its contents, although the GASB recommends including a transmittal letter. The GFOA has revised some components of the transmittal letter to reflect the GASB requirement for an MD&A.

1. **DISCUSSION** Brief discussion of the basic financial statements, including the relationship among them and the significant differences in the perspective that they provide.

2. **COMPARISON** Condensed financial information derived from government-wide statements comparing the current and prior year.

3. **ANALYSIS OF OVERALL FINANCIAL POSITION & RESULTS OF OPERATIONS** This should include reasons for significant changes from the prior year, including important economic factors.

4. **ANALYSIS OF BALANCES AND TRANSACTIONS OF INDIVIDUAL FUNDS**

5. **ANALYSIS OF SIGNIFICANT BUDGET CHANGES** Analysis of differences between original and final budget amounts as well as final budget amounts and actual results for the general fund.

6. **CAPITAL ASSET & LONG-TERM LIABILITY ACTIVITY DESCRIPTION**

7. **INFRASTRUCTURE DISCUSSION** (Only by governments using the modified approach.)

8. **CURRENTLY KNOWN FACTS, DECISIONS, OR CONDITIONS** that are expected to have significant effect on the government's financial condition

C. **GOVERNMENT-WIDE FINANCIAL STATEMENTS**

The only required government-wide statements (GWS) are the Statement of Net Assets and the Statement of Activities. The entity reports net assets, not fund balances or fund equity.

1. **FIDUCIARY ACTIVITIES** Fiduciary activities are not included in the GWS because the assets and liabilities cannot be used to support the government's own programs. (There are two required statements to report fiduciary activities in the fund statements.)

2. **PRIMARY GOVERNMENT** Sum of governmental and business-type activities.

3. **GOVERNMENTAL ACTIVITIES** This classification includes the amounts from the governmental funds (restated on the accrual basis of accounting) plus, typically, the amounts from the internal service funds. An exception applies if the internal service fund provides services primarily to enterprise funds; such a fund is included in business-type activities in the GWS.

4. **BUSINESS-TYPE ACTIVITIES** This classification includes the amounts from the enterprise funds and exceptional internal service funds.

5. **CAPITAL ASSETS & LONG-TERM LIABILITIES** Reporting capital assets and long-term liabilities is required in the GWS. Amounts are presented within the appropriate governmental activities, business-type activities, and component unit classification. Depreciation is not required if governments meet certain criteria for providing alternative information about the condition and financial impact of infrastructure assets and adopt the modified approach for reporting infrastructure. (There is additional time to implement these requirements for *retroactive*

reporting. *Prospective* reporting of infrastructure assets begins at the same time as the general reporting model standards are implemented.)

EXHIBIT 3 ◆ GOVERNMENT-WIDE STATEMENT OF NET ASSETS

Sample City
Statement of Net Assets
December 31, 20X1

	Primary Government			Component Units
	Governmental Activities	Business-Type Activities	Total	
ASSETS				
Cash and cash equivalents	$ 13,597,899	$ 10,279,143	$ 23,877,042	$ 303,935
Investments	27,365,221	—	27,365,221	7,428,952
Receivables (net)	12,833,132	3,609,615	16,442,747	4,042,290
Internal balances [1]	175,000	(175,000)	—	—
Inventories	322,149	126,674	448,823	83,697
Capital assets, net (Note 1)	170,022,760	151,388,751	321,411,511	37,744,786
Total assets	224,316,161	165,229,183	389,545,344	49,603,660
LIABILITIES				
Accounts payable	6,783,310	751,430	7,534,740	1,803,332
Deferred revenue	1,435,599	—	1,435,599	38,911
Noncurrent liabilities (Note 2):				
Due within one year	9,236,000	4,426,286	13,662,286	1,426,639
Due in more than one year	83,302,378	74,482,273	157,784,651	27,106,151
Total liabilities	100,757,287	79,659,989	180,417,276	30,375,033
NET ASSETS				
Invested in capital assets, net of related debt	103,711,386	73,088,574	176,799,960	15,906,392
Restricted for:				
Capital projects[2]	11,705,864	—	11,705,864	492,445
Debt service	3,020,708	1,451,996	4,472,704	—
Community development projects	4,811,043	—	4,811,043	—
Other purposes	3,214,302	—	3,214,302	—
Unrestricted (deficit)	(2,904,429)	11,028,624	8,124,195	2,829,790
Total net assets	$123,558,874	$ 85,569,194	$209,128,068	$19,228,627

6. **NOTES TO THE FINANCIAL STATEMENTS** The notes are considered part of the basic financial statements. GASB 38 highlights the following required disclosures: descriptions of activities within major funds, internal service fund types, and fiduciary fund types; the time period defining "available" for revenue recognition; follow-up on significant finance-related legal or contractual violations; debt service requirements through debt maturity; separate identification of lease obligations, debt principal, and interest for five years subsequent to the financial statement date and in five year increments thereafter; schedule of short-term debt changes and purposes; details on interfund balances and transfers; terms of interest rate changes for variable rate debt; interest requirements using the year-end effective rate for variable rate debt; details about major components of receivables and payables, if obscured by aggregation; identification of long-term receivable balances. Note disclosure requirements tend not to be heavily tested.

7. **STATEMENT OF ACTIVITIES** Fund statements present the traditional revenue and expenditure format, but the net revenue (expense) format is required for the government-wide statement of activities. The net program cost format provides information about the cost of primary functions of the government and outlines how much each of those programs depends on general revenues of the government. This format also introduces the concept of matching

program revenues and costs and allows governments to distributes administrative costs with indirect cost allocations.

EXHIBIT 4 ♦ GOVERNMENT-WIDE OPERATING STATEMENT

Sample City
Statement of Activities
For the Year Ended December 31, 20X1

Functions/Programs	Expenses	Program Revenues			Net (Expense) Revenue and Changes in Net Assets Primary Government			
		Charges for Services	Operating Grants and Contributions	Capital Grants and Contributions	Governmental Activities	Business-type Activities	Total	Component Units
Primary government:								
Governmental activities:								
General government	$ 9,571,410	$ 3,146,915	$ 843,617	$ —	$ (5,580,878)	$ —	$ (5,580,878)	$ —
Public safety	34,844,749	1,198,855	1,307,693	62,300	(32,275,901)	—	(32,275,901)	—
Public works	10,128,538	850,000	—	2,252,615	(7,025,923)	—	(7,025,923)	—
Engineering services	1,299,645	704,793	—	—	(594,852)	—	(594,852)	—
Health and sanitation	6,738,672	5,612,267	575,000	—	(551,405)	—	(551,405)	—
Cemetery	735,866	212,496	—	—	(523,370)	—	(523,370)	—
Culture and recreation	11,532,350	3,995,199	2,450,000	—	(5,087,151)	—	(5,087,151)	—
Community development	2,994,389	—	—	2,580,000	(414,389)		(414,389)	—
Education (payment to school district)	21,893,273	—	—	—	(21,893,273)	—	(21,893,273)	—
Interest on long-term debt	6,068,121	—	—	—	(6,068,121)	—	(6,068,121)	—
Total governmental activities	105,807,013	15,720,525	5,176,310	4,894,915	(80,015,263)	—	(80,015,263)	—
Business-type activities:								
Water	3,595,733	4,159,350	—	1,159,909	—	1,723,526	1,723,526	—
Sewer	4,912,853	7,170,533	—	486,010	—	2,743,690	2,743,690	—
Parking facilities	2,796,283	1,344,087	—	—	—	(1,452,196)	(1,452,196)	—
Total business-type activities	11,304,869	12,673,970	—	1,645,919	—	3,015,020	3,015,020	—
Total primary government	$117,111,882	$28,394,495	$ 5,175,310	$6,540,834	(80,015,263)	3,015,020	(77,000,243)	—
Component units:								
Landfill	$ 3,382,157	$ 3,857,858	$ —	$ 11,397	—	—	—	—
Public school system	31,186,498	705,765	3,937,083	—	—	—	—	487,098
Total component units	$ 34,568,655	$ 4,563,623	$ 3,937,083	$ 11,397	—	—	—	(26,543,650)
								(26,056,552)

	Governmental Activities	Business-type Activities	Total	Component Units
General revenues:				
Taxes:				
Property taxes, levied for general purposes	51,693,573	—	51,693,573	—
Property taxes, levied for debt service	4,726,244	—	4,726,244	—
Franchise taxes	4,055,505	—	4,055,505	—
Public service taxes	8,969,887	—	8,969,887	—
Payment from Sample City	—	—	—	21,893,273
Grants and contributions not restricted to specific programs	1,457,820	—	1,457,820	6,461,708
Investment earnings	1,958,144	601,349	2,559,493	881,763
Miscellaneous	884,907	104,925	989,832	22,464
Special item—Gain on sale of park land	2,653,488	—	2,653,488	—
Transfers	501,409	(501,409)	—	—
Total general revenues, special items, and transfers	76,900,977	204,865	77,105,842	29,259,208
Change in net assets	(3,114,286)	3,219,885	105,599	3,202,656
Net assets—beginning	126,673,160	82,349,309	209,022,469	16,025,971
Net assets—ending	$123,558,874	$85,569,194	$209,128,068	$ 19,228,627

D. FUND FINANCIAL STATEMENTS

GASB 34 shifts to a fund reporting format that presents major fund financial statements to highlight the importance of individual funds and the relationship to the government-wide financial statements. Basic fund financial statements will present a separate column for the General Fund, a separate column for each major fund and a single column to aggregate all nonmajor funds. Governmental and proprietary fund statements are segregated since the bases of accounting are different. (Fund information is reconciled in a summary format to the government-wide statements.)

EXHIBIT 5 ◆ GOVERNMENTAL FUNDS BALANCE SHEET

Sample City
Balance Sheet
Governmental Funds
December 31, 20X1

	General	HUD Programs	Community Redevelopment	Route 7 Construction	Other Governmental Funds	Total Governmental Funds
ASSETS						
Cash and cash equivalents	$ 3,418,485	$1,236,523	—	$ —	$ 5,606,792	$ 10,261,800
Investments	—	—	$13,262,695	10,467,037	3,485,252	27,214,984
Receivables, net	3,644,561	2,953,438	33,340	11,000	10,221	6,972,560
Due from other funds	1,370,757	—	—	—	—	1,370,757
Receivables from other governments	—	119,059	—	—	1,596,038	1,715,097
Liens receivable	791,926	3,195,745	—	—	—	3,987,671
Inventories	182,821	—	—	—	—	182,821
Total assets	$9,408,550	$7,504,765	$13,616,035	$10,478,037	$10,689,303	$ 51,705,690
LIABILITIES AND FUND BALANCES						
Liabilities:						
Accounts payable	$3,408,680	$ 129,975	$ 190,548	$ 1,104,632	$ 1,074,831	$ 5,908,666
Due to other funds	—	25,369	—	—	—	25,369
Payable to other governments	94,074	—	—	—	—	94,074
Deferred revenue	4,250,430	6,273,045	250,000	11,000	—	10,784,475
Total liabilities (Note 2)	7,753,184	6,428,389	440,548	1,115,632	1,074,831	16,812,584
Fund balances:						
Reserved for:						
Inventories	182,821	—	—	—	—	182,821
Liens receivable	791,926	—	—	—	—	791,926
Encumbrances	40,292	41,034	119,314	5,792,586	1,814,122	7,807,349
Debt service	—	—	—	—	3,832,062	3,832,062
Other purposes	—	—	—	—	1,405,300	1,405,300
Unreserved, reported in: [1]						
General fund	640,327	—	—	—	—	640,327
Special revenue funds	—	1,035,342	—	—	1,330,718	2,366,060
Capital projects funds	—	—	13,056,173	3,569,818	1,241,270	17,867,261
Total fund balances	1,655,366	1,076,376	13,175,487	9,362,405	9,623,472	34,893,106
Total liabilities and fund balances	$9,408,550	$7,504,765	$13,616,035	$10,478,037	$10,698,303	

Amounts reported for governmental activities in the statement of net assets (Exhibit 3) are different because (see Note 4, also): [2]

Capital assets used in governmental activities are not financial resources and therefore are not reported in the funds.	161,082,708
Other long-term assets are not available to pay for current-period expenditures and therefore are deferred in the funds.	9,348,876
Internal service funds are used by management to charge the costs of certain activities, such as insurance and telecommunications, to individual funds. The assets and liabilities of the internal service funds are included in governmental activities in the statement of net assets (Exhibit 3).	2,994,691
Long-term liabilities, including bonds payable, are not due and payable in the current period and therefore are not reported in the funds (see Note 4a).	(84,760,507)
Net assets of governmental activities	$123,558,874

EXHIBIT 6 ♦ GOVERNMENTAL FUNDS OPERATING STATEMENT

Sample City
Statement of Revenues, Expenditures, and Changes in Fund Balances
Governmental Funds
For the Year Ended December 31, 20X1

	General	HUD Programs	Community Redevelopment	Route 7 Construction	Other Governmental Funds	Total Governmental Funds
REVENUES						
Property taxes	$51,173,436	$ —	$ —	$ —	$ 4,680,192	$ 55,853,628
Franchise taxes	4,055,505	—	—	—	—	4,055,505
Public service taxes	8,969,887	—	—	—	—	8,969,887
Fees and fines	606,946	—	—	—	—	606,946
Licenses and permits	2,287,794	—	—	—	—	2,287,794
Intergovernmental	6,119,938	2,578,191	—	—	2,830,916	11,529,045
Charges for services	11,374,460	—	—	—	30,708	11,405,168
Investment earnings	552,325	87,106	549,489	270,161	364,330	1,823,411
Miscellaneous	881,874	66,176	—	2,939	94	951,083
Total revenues	86,022,165	2,731,473	549,489	273,100	7,906,240	97,482,467
EXPENDITURES						
Current						
General government	8,630,835		417,814	16,700	121,052	9,186,401
Public safety	33,729,623	—	—	—	—	33,729,623
Public works	497,775	—	—	—	3,721,542	8,697,317
Engineering services	1,299,645	—	—	—	—	1,299,645
Health and sanitation	6,070,032	—	—	—	—	6,070,032
Cemetery	706,305	—	—	—	—	706,305
Culture and recreation	11,411,685	—	—	—	—	11,411,685
Community development	—	2,954,389	—	—	—	2,954,389
Education—payment to school district	21,893,273					21,893,273
Debt service:						
Principal	—	—	—	—	3,450,000	3,450,000
Interest and other charges	—	—	—	—	5,215,151	5,215,151
Capital outlay	—	—	2,246,671	11,281,769	3,190,209	16,718,649
Total expenditures	88,717,173	2,954,389	2,664,485	11,298,469	15,697,954	121,332,470
Excess (deficiency) of revenues over expenditures	(2,695,008)	(222,916)	(2,114,996)	(11,025,369)	(7,791,714)	(23,850,003)
OTHER FINANCING SOURCES (USES)						
Proceeds of refunding bonds	—	—	—	—	38,045,000	38,045,000
Proceeds of long-term capital-related debt	—	—	17,529,560	—	1,300,000	18,829,560
Payment to bond refunding escrow agent	—	—	—	—	(37,284,144)	(37,284,144)
Transfers in	129,323	—	—	—	5,551,187	5,680,510
Transfers out	(2,163,759)	(348,046)	(2,273,187)	—	(219,076)	(5,004,068)
Total other financing sources and uses	(2,034,436)	(348,046)	15,256,373	—	7,392,967	20,266,858
SPECIAL ITEM						
Proceeds from sale of park land	3,476,488					3,476,488
Net change in fund balances (see C-3) [1]	(1,252,956)	(570,962)	13,141,377	(11,025,369)	(398,747)	(106,657)
Fund balances—beginning	2,908,322	1,647,338	34,110	20,387,774	10,022,219	34,999,763
Fund balances—ending	$ 1,655,366	$1,076,376	$13,175,487	$ 9,362,405	$ 9,623,472	$ 34,893,106

1. **LONG-TERM DEBT & CAPITAL ASSETS** These balances are not included in the governmental fund statements.

2. **RECONCILIATION** The link between government-wide and fund statements requires a reconciliation to convert the governmental funds to the economic resources measurement and accrual basis of accounting. Adjustments usually include moving transactions for general capital assets and general long-term liabilities from the operating statements to the balance sheet. Other reconciling items may include adjustments to deferred revenues or internal service fund net assets. If the entity presents summary information on the face of the financial statements, detailed schedules in the notes may be necessary.

EXHIBIT 7 ♦ PROPRIETARY FUNDS BALANCE SHEET

Sample City
Balance Sheet
Proprietary Funds
December 31, 20X1

	Business-type Activities—Enterprise Funds			Governmental Activities—Internal Service Funds (Note 4)
	Water and Sewer	Parking Facilities	Totals [2]	
ASSETS [1]				
Current assets:				
Cash and cash equivalents	$ 8,416,653	$ 369,168	$ 8,785,821	$ 3,336,099
Investments	—	—	—	150,237
Receivables, net	3,564,586	3,535	3,568,121	157,804
Due from other governments	41,494	—	41,494	—
Inventories	126,674	—	126,674	139,328
Total current assets	12,149,407	372,703	12,522,110	3,783,468
Noncurrent assets:				
Restricted cash and cash equivalents	—	1,493,322	1,493,322	—
Capital assets:				
Land	813,513	3,021,637	3,835,150	—
Distribution and collection systems	39,504,183	—	39,504,183	—
Buildings and equipment	106,135,666	23,029,166	129,164,832	14,721,786
Less accumulated depreciation	(15,328,911)	(5,786,503)	(21,115,414)	(5,781,734)
Total noncurrent assets	131,124,451	21,757,622	152,882,073	8,940,052
Total assets	143,273,858	22,130,325	165,404,183	12,723,520
LIABILITIES				
Current liabilities:				
Accounts payable	447,427	304,003	751,430	780,570
Due to other funds	175,000	—	175,000	1,170,388
Compensated absences	112,850	8,827	121,677	237,690
Claims and judgments	—	—	—	1,687,975
Bonds, notes, and loans payable	3,944,609	360,000	4,304,609	249,306
Total current liabilities	4,679,886	672,830	5,353,716	4,125,929
Noncurrent liabilities:				
Compensated absences	451,399	35,306	486,705	—
Claims and judgments	—	—	—	5,602,900
Bonds, notes and loans payable	54,451,549	19,544,019	73,995,568	—
Total noncurrent liabilities	54,902,948	19,579,325	74,482,273	5,602,900
Total liabilities	59,582,834	20,252,155	79,834,989	9,728,829
NET ASSETS				
Invested in capital assets, net of related debt	72,728,293	360,281	73,088,574	8,690,746
Restricted for debt service	—	1,451,996	1,451,996	—
Unrestricted	10,962,731	65,893	11,028,624	(5,696,055)
Total net assets	83,691,024	1,878,170	85,569,194	$ 2,994,691
Total liabilities and net assets	$143,273,858	$22,130,325	$165,404,183	$12,723,520

[1] This statement illustrates the "balance sheet" format; the "net assets" format also is permitted. Classification of assets and liabilities is required in either case.

[2] Even though internal service funds (ISF) are classified as proprietary funds, the nature of the activity accounted for in them is generally governmental. By reporting ISFs separately from the proprietary funds that account for business-type activities, the information in the "Totals" column on this statement flows directly to the "Business-type Activities" column on the statement of net assets, and the need for a reconciliation on this statement is avoided.

EXHIBIT 8 ♦ PROPRIETARY FUNDS OPERATING STATEMENT

Sample City
Statement of Revenues, Expenses, and Changes in Fund Net Assets
Proprietary Funds
For the Year Ended December 31, 20X1

	Business-type Activities—Enterprise Funds			Governmental Activities—Internal Service Funds (Note 5)
	Water and Sewer	Parking Facilities	Totals [1]	
Operating revenues:				
Charges for services	$11,329,883	$ 1,340,261	$12,670,144	$15,256,164
Miscellaneous	—	3,826	3,826	1,066,761
Total operating revenues	11,329,883	1,344,087	12,673,970	16,322,925
Operating expenses:				
Personal services	3,400,559	762,348	4,162,907	4,157,156
Contractual services	344,422	96,032	440,454	584,396
Utilities	754,107	100,726	854,833	214,812
Repairs and maintenance	747,315	64,617	811,932	1,960,490
Other supplies and expenses	498,213	17,119	515,332	234,445
Insurance claims and expenses	—	—	—	800,286
Depreciation	1,163,140	542,049	1,705,189	1,707,872
Total operating expenses	6,907,756	1,582,891	8,490,647	16,863,457
Operating income (loss)	4,422,127	(238,804)	4,183,323	(540,532)
Nonoperating revenues (expenses):				
Interest and investment revenue	454,793	146,556	601,349	134,733
Miscellaneous revenue	—	104,925	104,925	20,855
Interest expense	(1,600,830)	(1,166,546)	(2,767,376)	(41,616)
Miscellaneous expense	—	(46,846)	(46,846)	(176,003)
Total nonoperating revenue (expenses)	(1,146,037)	(961,911)	(2,107,948)	(62,031)
Income (loss) before contributions and transfers	3,276,090	(1,200,715)	2,075,375	(602,563)
Capital contributions	1,645,919	—	1,645,919	18,788
Transfers out	(290,000)	(211,409)	(501,409)	(175,033)
Change in net assets	4,632,009	(1,412,124)	3,219,885	(758,808)
Total net assets—beginning	79,059,015	3,290,294	82,349,309	3,753,499
Total net assets—ending	$83,691,024	$1,878,170	$85,569,194	$ 2,994,691

[1] Even though internal service funds are classified as proprietary funds, the nature of the activity accounted for in them is generally *governmental*. By reporting internal service funds separately from the proprietary funds that account for business-type activities, the information in the "Totals" column on this statement flows directly to the "Business-type Activities" column on the statement of net assets, and the need for a reconciliation on this statement is avoided.

3. **MAJOR FUNDS** Major funds are reported (in both the governmental and the proprietary fund statements) to provide users with detailed fund information on significant activities of the government. The general fund is always major. There are two other criteria for determining major funds. (GASB 37 clarifies that major fund reporting requirements apply if the same element exceeds both the 10 and 5 percent criteria.) In addition to funds that meet the major-fund criteria, any other funds that the government's officials believe are particularly important to financial statement users are reported as major funds. Total assets, liabilities, revenues, or expenditures/expenses of major individual funds are both:

a. At least 10% of the corresponding total for the relevant fund category (governmental or proprietary).

b. At least 5% of the corresponding total for all governmental and proprietary funds combined.

EXHIBIT 9 ♦ PROPRIETARY FUNDS CASH FLOWS STATEMENT

Sample City
Statement of Cash Flows
Proprietary Funds
For the Year Ended December 31, 20X1

	Business-type Activities—Enterprise Funds			Governmental Activities—Internal Service Funds (Note 5)
	Water and Sewer	Parking Facilities	Totals	
CASH FLOWS FROM OPERATING ACTIVITIES				
Receipts from customers	$11,400,200	$ 1,345,292	$12,745,492	$15,356,343
Payments to suppliers	(2,725,349)	(365,137)	(3,090,486)	(2,812,238)
Payments to employees	(3,360,055)	(750,828	(4,110,883)	(4,209,688)
Internal activity—payments to other funds	(1,296,768)	—	(1,296,768)	—
Claims paid	—	—	—	(8,482,451)
Other receipts (payments)	(2,325,483)	—	(2,325,483)	1,061,118
Net cash provided by operating activities	1,692,545	229,327	1,921,872	883,084
CASH FLOWS FROM NONCAPITAL FINANCING ACTIVITIES				
Operating subsidies and transfers to other funds	(290,000)	(211,409)	(501,409)	(175,033)
CASH FLOWS FROM CAPITAL AND RELATED FINANCING ACTIVITIES				
Proceeds from capital debt	4,041,322	8,660,779	12,702,100	—
Capital contributions	1,645,919	—	1,645,919	—
Purchases of capital assets	(4,194,035)	(144,716)	(4,338,751)	(400,086)
Principal paid on capital debt	(2,178,491)	(8,895,000)	(11,073,491)	(954,137)
Interest paid on capital debt	(1,479,708)	(1,166,546)	(2,646,254)	(41,616)
Other receipts (payments)	—	19,174	19,174	131,416
			(3,691,303)	
Net cash (used) by capital and related financing activities	(2,164,993)	(1,526,303)		(1,264,423)
CASH FLOWS FROM INVESTING ACTIVITIES				
Proceeds from sales and maturities of investments	—	—	—	15,684
Interest and dividends	454,793	143,747	598,540	129,550
Net cash provided by investing activities	454,793	143,747	598,540	145,234
Net (decrease) in cash and cash equivalents	(307,655)	(1,364,645)	(1,672,300)	(411,138)
Balances—beginning of the year	8,724,308	3,227,135	11,951,443	3,747,237
Balances—end of the year	$ 8,416,653	$1,862,490	$10,279,143	$ 3,336,099
Reconciliation of operating income (loss) to net cash provided (used) by operating activities				
Operating income (loss)	$ 4,422,127	$ (238,804)	$ 4,183,323	$ (540,532)
Adjustments to reconcile operating income to net cash provided (used) by operating activities:				
Depreciation expense	1,163,140	542,049	1,705,189	1,707,872
Change in assets and liabilities:				
Receivables, net	653,264	1,205	654,469	31,941
Inventories	2,829	—	2,829	39,790
Accounts and other payables	(297,446)	(86,643)	(384,089)	475,212
Accrued expenses	(4,251,369)	11,520	(4,239,849)	(831,199)
Net cash provided by operating activities	$ 1,692,545	$ 229,327	$ 1,921,872	$ 883,084

Note: Required information about noncash investing, capital, and financing activities is not illustrated.

EXHIBIT 10 ♦ FIDUCIARY FUNDS BALANCE SHEET

Sample City
Statement of Fiduciary Net Assets
Fiduciary Funds
December 31, 20X1

	Employee Retirement Plan	Private-Purpose Trusts	Agency Funds
ASSETS			
Cash and cash equivalents	$ 1,973	$ 1,250	$ 44,889
Receivables:			
Interest and dividends	508,475	760	—
Other receivables	6,826	—	183,161
Total receivables	515,301	760	183,161
Investments, at fair value:			
U.S. government obligations	13,056,037	80,000	
Municipal bonds	6,528,019	—	—
Corporate bonds	16,320,047	—	—
Corporate stocks	26,112,075	—	—
Other investments	3,264,009	—	—
Total investments	65,280,187	80,000	—
Total assets	65,797,461	82,010	$228,050
LIABILITIES			
Accounts payable	—	1,234	$ —
Refunds payable and others	1,358	—	228,050
Total liabilities	1,358	1,234	$228,050
NET ASSETS			
Held in trust for pension benefits and other purposes	$65,796,103	$80,776	

Statements of individual pension plans and external investment pools are required to be presented in the notes to the financial statements if separate GAAP statements for those individual plans or pools are not available.

EXHIBIT 11 ♦ FIDUCIARY FUNDS OPERATING STATEMENT

Sample City
Statement of Changes in Fiduciary Net Assets
Fiduciary Funds
For the Year Ended December 31, 20X1

	Employee Retirement Plan	Private-Purpose Trusts
ADDITIONS		
Contributions:		
Employer	$ 2,721,341	—
Plan members	1,421,233	—
Total contributions	4,142,574	—
Investment earnings:		
Net (decrease) in fair value of investments	(272,522)	—
Interest	2,460,871	4,560
Dividends	1,445,273	—
Total investment earnings	3,633,622	4,560
Less investment expense	216,428	—
Net investment earnings	3,417,194	4,560
Total additions	7,559,768	4,560
DEDUCTIONS		
Benefits	2,453,047	3,800
Refunds of contributions	464,691	—
Administrative expenses	87,532	678
Total deductions	3,005,270	4,478
Change in net assets	4,554,498	82
Net assets—beginning of the year	61,241,605	$80,694
Net assets—end of the year	$65,796,103	$80,776

EXHIBIT 12 ♦ COMPONENT UNITS BALANCE SHEET

Sample City
Statement of Net Assets
Component Units
For the Year Ended December 31, 20X1

	Sample City School District	Sample City Landfill	Total
ASSETS			
Cash and cash equivalents	$ 303,485	$ 450	$ 303,935
Investments	3,658,520	1,770,432	5,428,952
Receivables, net	3,717,026	325,264	4,042,290
Inventories	83,697	—	83,697
Restricted assets—landfill closure	—	2,000,000	2,000,000
Capital assets, net (Note 1)	34,759,986	2,984,800	37,744,786
Total assets	42,522,714	7,080,946	49,603,660
LIABILITIES			
Accounts payable	1,469,066	334,266	1,803,332
Deposits and deferred revenue	38,911	—	38,911
Long-term liabilities (Note 2):			
Due within one year	1,426,639	—	1,426,639
Due in more than one year	22,437,349	4,668,802	27,106,151
Total liabilities	25,371,965	5,003,068	30,375,033
NET ASSETS			
Invested in capital assets, net of related debt	12,921,592	2,984,800	15,906,392
Restricted for capital projects	492,445	—	492,445
Unrestricted	3,736,712	(906,922)	2,829,790
Total net assets	$17,150,749	$2,077,878	$19,228,627

Nonmajor component units are aggregated into a single column. Combining statements of nonmajor components have the same status as combining statements for nonmajor funds (supplementary information).

EXHIBIT 13 ♦ COMPONENT UNITS OPERATING STATEMENT

Sample City
Statement of Activities
Component Units
For the Year Ended December 31, 20X1

		Program Revenues			Net (Expense) Revenue and Changes in Net Assets		
	Expenses	Charges for Services	Operating Grants and Contributions	Capital Grants and Contributions	School District	Landfill	Totals
Sample City School District							
Instructional	$16,924,321	$ 147,739	$2,825,109	$ —	$(13,951,473)	$ —	$(13,951,473)
Support services	7,972,559	300	751,711	$ —	(7,220,548)	—	(7,220,548)
Operation of non-instructional services	1,523,340	557,726	359,092	—	(606,522)	—	(606,522)
Facilities acquisition and construction services	48,136	—	1,171	—	(46,965)	—	(46,965)
Interest on long-term debt	546,382	—	—	—	(546,382)	—	(546,382)
Unallocated depreciation (Note F)	4,171,760	—	—	—	(4,171,760)	—	(4,171,760)
Total—Sample City School District	31,186,498	705,765	3,937,083	—	(26,543,650)	—	—
Sample City Landfill							
Landfill operations	3,382,157	3,857,858	—	11,397	—	487,098	487,098
Total component units	$34,568,655	$4,563,623	$3,937,083	$11,397			(26,056,552)
General revenues:							
Payment from Sample City					21,893,273	—	21,893,273
Grants, entitlements, and contributions not restricted to specific programs					6,461,708	—	6,461,708
Investment earnings					674,036	207,727	881,763
Miscellaneous					19,950	2,514	22,464
Total general revenues					29,048,967	210,241	29,259,208
Change in net assets					2,505,317	697,339	3,202,656
Net assets—beginning					14,645,432	1,380,539	16,025,971
Net assets—ending					$ 17,150,749	$2,077,878	$ 19,228,627

4. **PRESENTATION** The fund financial statements for major funds are presented before the notes to the financial statements. Combining statements for nonmajor funds are not required, but may be presented after the notes as supplementary information.

5. **FIDUCIARY FUNDS** Major fund reporting is not used in the fiduciary fund category. Fiduciary statements include separate columns for each fiduciary fund type used by the governmental entity. Financial statements for individual pension plans and investment trusts are presented in the notes to the financial statements of the primary government if separate, audited financial reports are not issued. The *statement of fiduciary net assets* and *statement of changes in fiduciary net assets* are included in the fund statements to report fiduciary activities. GASB 25 and 26 provide guidance for reporting pension trust funds. GASB 31 provides guidance for investment trust funds.

6. **REPORTING** Minimum reporting requirements for fund financial information in the basic financial statements include:

   - Governmental Funds: (1) a Fund Balance Sheet and (2) a Statement of Revenues, Expenditures, and Changes in Fund Balances.
   - Proprietary Funds: (1) a Statement of Fund Net Assets or Fund Balance Sheet; (2) a Statement of Revenues, Expenses, and Changes in Fund Equity or Fund Net Assets; and (3) a Statement of Cash Flows.
   - Fiduciary Funds: (1) a Statement of Fiduciary Net Assets and (2) a Statement of Changes in Fiduciary Net Assets.

E. STATEMENT OF CASH FLOWS

The major differences between the GASB 9 statement and the SFAS 95 statement (see the FAR volume) are that four categories are used for classifying cash flows instead of three and the operating category is more narrowly focused. This statement classifies cash receipts and payments of all proprietary funds as resulting from operating activities, noncapital financing, capital and related financing, or investing activities.

1. **OPERATING ACTIVITIES** Cash inflows, receipts, and payments that do not result from transactions defined as capital and related financing, noncapital financing, or investing activities.

   a. **CASH INFLOWS** Include receipts from cash

      (1) Sales of goods or services, including receipts from collection of accounts receivable and both short- and long-term notes receivable from customers arising from those sales.

      (2) Quasi-external operating transactions with other funds.

      (3) Grants for specific activities that are considered to be operating activities of the grantor government. (A grant arrangement of this type is essentially the same as a contract for services.)

      (4) Other funds for reimbursement of operating transactions.

      (5) Loan programs that are made and collected as part of a governmental program such as student loans or low-income housing mortgages. Investment type loans would not be included in this category.

   b. **CASH OUTFLOWS** Include cash payments

      (1) To acquire materials for providing services and manufacturing goods for resale, including principal payments on accounts payable and both short- and long-term notes payable to suppliers for those materials or goods.

(2) To other suppliers for other goods or services, including employees.

(3) For grants to other governments or organizations for specific activities that are considered to be operating activities of the grantor government.

(4) For taxes, duties, fines, and other fees or penalties.

(5) For quasi-external operating transactions with other funds, including payments in lieu of taxes.

2. **NONCAPITAL FINANCING ACTIVITIES** Include borrowing for purposes other than to acquire, construct, or improve capital assets, as well as repaying borrowed amounts, including interest. This category includes proceeds from all borrowings (such as revenue anticipation notes) not clearly attributable to capital assets, regardless of the form of the borrowing. Also included are certain other interfund and intergovernmental receipts and payments.

    a. **CASH INFLOWS**

        (1) Proceeds from issuing bonds, notes, and other short- or long-term borrowing not clearly attributable to capital assets.

        (2) Receipts from grants or subsidies except those specifically restricted for capital purposes and those for specific activities that are considered to be operating activities of the grantor government.

        (3) Receipts from other funds except those amounts that are clearly attributable to capital assets, quasi-external operating transactions, and reimbursement for operating transactions.

        (4) Receipts from property and other taxes collected for the governmental enterprise and not specifically restricted for capital purposes.

    b. **CASH OUTFLOWS**

        (1) Repayments of amounts borrowed for purposes other than acquiring, constructing, or improving capital assets.

        (2) Interest payments to lenders and other creditors on amounts borrowed or credit extended for purposes other than capital assets.

        (3) Payments as grants or subsidies to other governments or organizations, except those for specific activities that are considered to be operating activities of the grantor government.

        (4) Payments to other funds, except for quasi-external operating transactions.

3. **CAPITAL AND RELATED FINANCING ACTIVITIES** Include acquiring and disposing of capital assets used in providing services or producing goods; borrowing money for acquiring, constructing, or improving capital assets and repaying the amounts borrowed, including interest; and paying for capital assets obtained from vendors on credit.

    a. **CASH INFLOWS** Inflows from

        (1) Issuing or refunding bonds, mortgages, notes, and other short- or long-term borrowing clearly attributable to capital assets.

        (2) Capital grants awarded to the governmental enterprise.

      (3)   Contributions made by other funds, governments, and organizations or individuals for the specific purpose of defraying the cost of capital assets.

      (4)   Sales of capital assets; also, proceeds from insurance on capital assets that are stolen or destroyed.

      (5)   Special assessments or property and other taxes levied specifically to finance capital assets.

    b.   **CASH OUTFLOWS**

      (1)   Payments to acquire, construct, or improve capital assets.

      (2)   Repayments or refundings of amounts borrowed specifically to acquire, construct, or improve capital assets.

      (3)   Other principal payments to vendors who have extended credit directly to acquire, construct or improve capital assets.

      (4)   Payments to creditors for interest directly related to capital assets.

4.   **INVESTING ACTIVITIES** Investing activities include making and collecting loans (except program loans) and acquiring and disposing of debt or equity instruments.

    a.   **CASH INFLOWS** Include: (1) receipts from collections of loans (except program loans) made by the governmental enterprise and sales of other entities' debt instruments (other than cash equivalents) that were purchased by the governmental enterprise; (2) interest and dividends received as returns on loans (except program loans), debt instruments of other entities, equity securities, and cash management or investment pools; and (3) withdrawals from investment pools that the governmental enterprise is not using as demand accounts.

    b.   **CASH OUTFLOWS** Disbursements for: (1) Loans (except program loans) made by the governmental enterprise and payments to acquire debt instruments of other entities (other than cash equivalents); and (2) deposits into investment pools that the governmental enterprise is not using as demand accounts.

F.   **OTHER REQUIRED SUPPLEMENTARY INFORMATION (RSI)**
Required supplementary information is outside the scope of the auditor's opinion. Except for MD&A, RSI is presented after the financial statements.

1.   **BUDGETARY COMPARISON SCHEDULE (BCS)** is presented for the general fund and for each major special revenue fund that has a legally adopted annual budget, on the **budgetary** basis of accounting. The BCS presents both the original and final budget as well as actual inflows, outflows, and balances. It uses the same format, terminology, and classifications as either the budget document or a statement of revenues, expenditures, and changes in fund balances. The BCS is accompanied by a reconciliation (in either a separate schedule or RSI notes) of budgetary information to GAAP information. This reconciliation provides the link from the budgetary comparisons to the GAAP statements in the BFS.

2.   **INFRASTRUCTURE SCHEDULES** (Only for assets reported using the modified approach.) These schedules include (1) information on the assessed condition (assessed at least every 3 years) for at least the 3 most recent assessments (i.e., this information could be from 9 years); and (2) the estimated annual amount to maintain the condition level established and disclosed by the government compared with amounts actually expensed for the past 5 reporting periods. The schedules are accompanied by (1) disclosures on the basis for the condition measurement and the measurement scale; (2) the condition level at which the government intends to preserve assets reported using the modified approach; and (3) factors that could effect trends in these schedules.

III. RECOGNITION OF SPECIFIC REVENUES AND LIABILITIES

A. NONEXCHANGE TRANSACTIONS

GASB 24 provides guidance for food stamps and on-behalf payments for fringe benefits and salaries. All other grants fall within the scope of GASB 33, *Nonexchange Transactions*, as amended by GASB 36. One of the basic principles of GASB 33 is symmetry between expense or expenditure recognition by a provider government and revenue recognition by the recipient government. Recipient governments do not apply the criteria for derived tax revenues or imposed nonexchange revenues on transactions involving provider governments.

1. **APPLICABILITY**

   a. Under the accrual basis of accounting, recipients of resources from nonexchange transactions report assets when the applicable recognition criterion is met or when resources are received, whichever occurs first. Revenues are recognized when the applicable revenue recognition criterion is met. Resources received in advance are recognized as deferred revenues (liabilities). Similar recognition criteria apply to providers.

   b. Under the modified accrual basis of accounting, revenues are not recognized unless resources are available.

2. **DERIVED TAX REVENUES** Derived tax revenues are assessments imposed by governments on exchange transactions and generally include sales taxes, income taxes, motor fuel taxes, and similar taxes on earnings or consumption. Assets are recognized when the underlying exchange transaction occurs. Revenues generally are recognized at the same time.

3. **IMPOSED NONEXCHANGE TRANSACTIONS** Imposed nonexchange revenues represent assessments imposed on non-governmental entities and include property taxes and fines or forfeitures. Assets are recognized when the government has an enforceable legal claim to the resources. Revenues are recognized in the period when use of the resources is required or first permitted, or at the same time as the assets when there is no time requirement. (Time requirements for imposed nonexchange revenue transactions affect the timing of revenue recognition, but not asset recognition. Receivables and deferred revenues are recognized as soon as the government has an enforceable legal claim to the provider's resources.)

4. **GOVERNMENT-MANDATED NONEXCHANGE TRANSACTIONS** Government-mandated nonexchange transactions occur when a government at one level provides resources to a government at another level and requires that government to use the resources for a specific purpose. Intergovernmental grants fall into this category. Recipients recognize assets and revenues when all eligibility requirements have been met. Providers recognize liabilities and expenses using the same criteria. Eligibility requirements include time requirements. Purpose restrictions result in restricted assets until resources are used for the specified purpose. [Noncompliance with time criteria cancels the transaction. Neither the provider nor the recipient recognizes liabilities (or assets) or expenses (or revenues) until all eligibility requirements have been met.]

5. **VOLUNTARY NONEXCHANGE TRANSACTIONS** Voluntary nonexchange transactions result from legislative or contractual agreements, but do not involve an exchange of equal value. Certain grants, entitlements, and donations are classified as voluntary nonexchange transactions. Both parties may or may not be governmental entities. Specific recognition criteria are the same as those for government-mandated nonexchange transactions.

6. **CONTINUING APPROPRIATIONS** If distributions from a provider government are authorized by continuing appropriations (involving no further legislative action), the recipient governments can use any reasonable estimate to accrue revenues.

B. CERTAIN GRANTS & OTHER FINANCIAL ASSISTANCE

GASB 24 requires that cash-conduit arrangements be included in the agency funds. Examples are pass-through grants, food stamps, and on-behalf payments for fringe benefits and salaries. If the recipient government monitors secondary recipients, determines eligibility, or has the ability to exercise discretion for allocating funds, the grant is **not** a cash conduit and should be reported in governmental, proprietary, or trust funds, as appropriate.

1. **STATE GOVERNMENTS** Required to recognize revenues and expenditures when benefits, such as food stamps, are distributed to individual recipients by the entity or its agents.

2. **STATE AND LOCAL GOVERNMENTS** The guidance for on-behalf payments for fringe benefits and salaries affects both state and local governments. If the employer is not legally liable for these benefits, the employer recognizes revenues and expenditures in equal amounts based on payments of the grantor. If the employer is legally liable for these payments, the expenditures are recognized based on the legal provisions associated with the salaries and the accounting standards that apply. Revenues are recognized based on third-party payments or amounts that meet criteria for receivables at year-end. There are required disclosure provisions for both the employer and payor government that are beyond the scope of this discussion.

C. CAPITAL LEASE OBLIGATIONS

The criteria used to determine whether a lease is capital or operating is the same for governments and businesses.

1. **CAPITAL LEASES** If a lease meets any one of the following criteria, it is a capital lease.

    a. Ownership of the property transfers to the lessee by the end of the lease term.

    b. The lease contains an option to purchase the leased property at a bargain price.

    c. The lease term is equal to or greater than 75 percent of the estimated economic life of the leased property.

    d. The present value of the minimum lease payments equals or exceeds 90 percent of the fair value of the leased property at the inception of the lease.

2. **OPERATING LEASES** If none of the criteria for a capital lease is met, the lessee classifies the lease as an operating lease. Payments for assets used by governmental funds are recorded by the using fund as expenditures. Payments for assets used by proprietary funds are recorded by the using fund as expenses.

3. **GOVERNMENTAL FUNDS**

    a. **GOVERNMENTAL-TYPE FUND** The governmental fund records an expenditure and an Other Financing Source, just as if the general fixed asset had been constructed or acquired from debt issue proceeds. The amount to be recorded is the lesser of (1) the present value of the minimum lease payments or (2) the fair value of the leased property.

    b. **DEBT SERVICE FUND** Commonly, governmental units use the Debt Service Fund (DSF) to record capital lease payments because the annual payments are installments of general long-term debt. Although part of each payment is interest at a constant rate on the unpaid balance of the lease obligation, and part is payment on the principal, the *Expenditures* account is debited in the DSF for the full amount of the lease payment. Only the detail records in the DSF show how much of the expenditure was for interest and how much was for principal.

EXHIBIT 14 ♦ LEASED GENERAL FIXED ASSET*

1.	Lease Inception		
	a. Governmental Fund		
	Expenditures	XX	
	Other Financing Sources—Capital Leases		XX
2.	Lease Repayment		
	a. Debt Service Fund		
	Expenditures (principal and interest)	XX	
	Cash		XX

*These entries may be more clear to candidates who are familiar with the material in Chapter 22.

4. **PROPRIETARY FUNDS** Assets acquired under capital leases are depreciated by the proprietary fund. Capital leases are generally recorded as an asset and liability at the lesser of (a) the present value of the minimum lease payments or (b) the fair value of the leased property. Lease payments for capital leases are comprised of interest expense and principal reduction.

EXHIBIT 15 ♦ LEASED PROPRIETARY FIXED ASSET (IN THE RELATED PROPRIETARY FUND)

1.	Lease Inception		
	Equipment	XX	
	Capital Leases Payable		XX
2.	Lease Repayment		
	Expenses—Interest	XX	
	Capital Leases Payable	XX	
	Cash		XX

D. **MUNICIPAL SOLID WASTE LANDFILLS**
Municipal solid waste landfills (MSWLFs) are required by the Environmental Protection Agency (EPA) to follow certain closure functions and postclosure monitoring and maintenance procedures in order to operate. Any state or local government that is required by federal, state, or local laws or regulations to incur MSWLF closure and postclosure care costs is subject to GASB 18.

1. **ESTIMATED TOTAL CURRENT COST** The estimated total current costs of closure and postclosure care should include those costs that result in disbursements near the date that the MSWLF stops accepting solid waste and during the postclosure period: equipment expected to be installed and facilities expected to be built; final cover (capping) costs; and monitoring and maintenance costs. These costs are based on laws or regulations enacted or approved as of the balance sheet date, regardless of their effective date. The estimated current cost is reevaluated annually to adjust for the effects of inflation, deflation, or other changes in estimated costs.

2. **MEASUREMENT AND RECOGNITION** The type of fund or account group employed by the MSWLF determines the recognition method. Estimated total current costs should be based on MSWLF use, not the passage of time. The current year closure and post-closure cost recognition is the difference between the total costs to be recognized to date and the total costs recognized in prior periods. The total costs to be recognized to date are the total estimated costs times the cumulative used percentage of total capacity. (Costs and liabilities are recognized as the MSWLF accepts solid waste.)

a. **PROPRIETARY FUND** Capital assets should be fully depreciated by the date the MSWLF stops accepting solid waste or, in the case of a single cell, the date that cell is closed.

b. **GOVERNMENTAL-TYPE FUND** The MSWLF recognizes expenditures using the modified accrual basis of accounting, with liability reported as with other general long-term debt. Expenditures are disclosed in the notes to the financial statements or appear as a parenthetical display on the statement of operations.

c. **GOVERNMENTAL COLLEGES AND UNIVERSITIES THAT USE THE AICPA COLLEGE GUIDE MODEL** Expenditures and liabilities should be calculated similarly to other governmental-type funds and be reported in an unrestricted current fund.

3. **DISCLOSURE** The disclosure requirements include the nature of closure and postclosure care estimates, the reported liability at the balance sheet date, the estimated total closure and postclosure care cost remaining to be recognized, the percentage of MSWLF capacity used to date, and the estimated remaining MSWLF life in years. Disclosure of how closure and postclosure care financial assurance requirements are being met is also required.

E. **ESCHEAT PROPERTY**
Escheat property is property that reverts to a governmental entity in the absence of legal claimants or heirs. GASB 21 requires escheat property to be reported in either a trust fund (for the new reporting model, GASB 37 specifies a private-purpose trust fund) or the fund to which the property ultimately escheats.

1. **REPORTING REVENUE** Revenue from escheat property should be reduced and a fund liability reported to the probable extent that the property will be reclaimed and paid to claimants. These payments reduce the liability. The total liability represents an estimate of the amount expected to be reclaimed and paid to claimants.

2. **INTERFUND TRANSFERS** When a trust fund is the initial reporting vehicle, amounts that are transferred to the ultimate fund should be reported as an operating transfer. The difference resulting from the transfer when the remaining assets of the trust are less than the liabilities should be reported as an "advance to" in the trust fund and an "advance from" in the ultimate fund. When the assets exceed the liabilities in the trust fund, the difference is reported as fund balance.

IV. APPENDIX: LIMITED SCOPE TOPICS

A. **GOVERNMENTAL COLLEGES AND UNIVERSITIES**
GASB 19 provides guidance on reporting for all **governmental** colleges and universities.

1. **PELL GRANTS** Pell grants are scholarships granted to students requesting financial assistance who meet the federal government criteria for aid. Pell grants must be reported in a restricted current fund.

2. **RISK-TAKING ACTIVITIES** If a single fund is used to account for risk financing activities, it must be reported as an unrestricted current fund.

B. **POSTEMPLOYMENT BENEFITS**

1. **DEFINED BENEFIT PENSION PLANS AND DEFINED CONTRIBUTION PLANS** GASB 25 establishes standards for defined benefit pension plans and defined contribution plans. It does not address healthcare benefits, any plans not providing postretirement income, or the measurement of employer costs.

a. **DEFINED CONTRIBUTION PLANS** Disclosures must include a brief plan description, a summary of significant accounting policies (including the fair value of plan assets), and information about contributions and investment concentrations.

b. **DEFINED BENEFIT PENSION PLANS** Plans may elect to report one or more years of the required information in an additional financial statement or in the notes to the financial statements. A plan and its participating employer(s) must use the same methods and assumptions for financial reporting.

(1) A statement of plan net assets provides information about the fair value and composition of plan assets, liabilities, and net assets.

(2) A statement of changes in plan net assets provides information about the year-to-year changes in plan net assets, for a minimum of six years.

(3) Notes to the financial statements include a short plan description; a summary of significant accounting policies; and information about contributions, legally required reserves, and investment concentrations.

(4) Required supplementary information includes two schedules of historical trend information for a minimum of six years. Disclosures related to these schedules include the actuarial methods and significant assumptions used for financial reporting. The **schedule of funding progress** reports the actuarial value of assets, the actuarial accrued liability, and the relationship between the two over time. The **schedule of employer contributions** provides information about the employer's annual required contributions (ARC) and the percentage of the ARC recognized by the plan as contributed.

2. **POSTEMPLOYMENT HEALTHCARE PLANS** GASB 26 establishes reporting standards for post-employment healthcare plans administered by defined benefit pension plans. Similar to the pension plan standards, plans that administer postemployment healthcare plans **must** present (1) a statement of plan net assets, (2) a statement of changes in plan net assets, and (3) notes to the financial statements. Plans may **elect** to provide historical trend information about the funded status of the plan and the employer's required contributions, either as supplementary information or in additional statements or notes, if they follow certain requirements.

3. **PENSIONS** GASB 27 establishes standards for the measurement, recognition, and display of pension expenditures/expense and related liabilities, assets, disclosures, and required supplementary information. Pension trust funds included in the employer's financial statements are **not** subject to GASB 27. (They are subject to GASB 25.)

a. **ANNUAL COSTS** For single-employer or agent multiple-employer plans, annual pension costs are equal to the employer's annual required contributions (ARC).

b. **MULTIPLE PLANS** When an employer has more than one plan, all recognition requirements should be applied separately for each plan.

c. **MULTIPLE FUNDS** If the contributions are made from more than one fund, the ARC should be allocated on a pro-rata share to the various funds. In addition, the interest and the adjustment to reverse the actuarial amortization should also be allocated on the fund's proportionate share of the beginning balance of the NPO.

d. **MULTIPLE-EMPLOYER PLANS** Employers participating in multiple-employer plans share costs regardless of individual employer member demographics. The actuary usually calculates a single contribution requirement for all participants. Employers recognize pension expenditures equal to this contractual requirement. The plan description in the employer financial statements should include a reference to any separate issuance of pension plan reports.

e. **DISCLOSURES** Requirements are similar to pension plans' requirements. Single or agent employers have additional requirements to outline the annual pension cost, contributions, and NPOs for the current year and two previous years.

f. **TRANSFER OF OBLIGATION** If an insurance company unconditionally undertakes a legal obligation to pay employees' pension benefits, the employer recognizes pension expense equal to the insurance premiums. The notes disclose information about this transfer and describe the benefits provided in the event of the company's default.

g. **DEFINED CONTRIBUTION PLANS** The annual expense or expenditure is based on the amounts required by the plan. Benefits are based on accumulated contributions. Differences between required and actual contributions are accumulated as assets or liabilities, and future contributions do not reflect amortization of previous deficiencies. Note disclosures include identification of the plan, description of the plan provisions, contribution requirements, and actual member and employer contributions.

4. **DEFERRED COMPENSATION PLANS** Under GASB 32, as amended by GASB 34, an IRC §457 deferred compensation plan that meets the criteria in NCGA Statement No. 1 for inclusion in the fiduciary funds of a government is reported as a pension trust fund in the financial statements. The government must determine whether it has fiduciary accountability for IRC §457 plans and whether it holds the assets in a trustee capacity. NCGA guidance generally does not require the use of fiduciary funds when the assets are administered by a third party. The likely result of GASB 32 is that many government employers that formerly reported IRC §457 plan assets on their balance sheet will no longer do so.

C. **SECURITIES LENDING TRANSACTIONS**

Governments lend securities from their investment portfolios to enhance income opportunities. The securities are lent to brokers or financial institutions that need to cover "short" positions until they can purchase the specific securities. GASB 28 establishes standards for income recognition, reporting, and disclosures for securities lending transactions.

1. **BALANCE SHEET** The underlying securities loaned are reported as assets. Cash or securities received as collateral, and the obligation to return these assets is also reported on the balance sheet, unless the lender cannot pledge or sell the collateral. Transactions that are secured by letters of credit or securities that cannot be pledged or sold should not be reported as assets and the liabilities to return this collateral are not included in liabilities of the lending government.

2. **INCOME STATEMENT** Costs of lending transactions (including borrower rebates, interest costs, or agent fees) are reported as expenditures or expenses, **not** netted against income.

3. **DISCLOSURES** The notes include general information about the securities, collateral, terms and conditions of the agreements. Notes also describe the source of legal or contractual authorization for the use of securities lending transactions, any violations of legal restrictions, whether maturities of investments match the maturities of loans, and the credit risk associated with these transactions.

D. **PUBLIC ENTITY RISK POOLS**

GASB 30, *Risk Financing Omnibus*, revises the method that public entity risk pools use for calculating a premium deficiency and expands disclosure requirements for reinsurance, gross, ceded, and net premium and claims costs in the 10 year historical tables.

1. **PUBLIC ENTITY RISK POOLS** Capitalization contributions to public entity risk pools with transfer (or pooling) of risk are reported as deposits if it is probable that the contributions will be returned to the entity upon the dissolution of the pool or an approved withdrawal from the pool. Otherwise, they are reported as prepaid insurance. Contributions made without transfer or pooling of risk are reported as a deposit or a reduction of claims liabilities.

2. **ENTITIES OTHER THAN POOLS** These entities must include specific incremental claim adjustment expenses, salvage, and subrogation in the determination of the liability for unpaid claims. Disclosures must reflect whether liabilities related to claims include these claim adjustment expenses.

E. **INVESTMENTS**

Recent failures (e.g., Orange County) in the governmental sector related to investment performance raised public awareness of investments. GASB 31 requires revenue recognition for changes in the investments' fair value. Internal and external investment pools are required to report, as assets, the equity position of each fund and component unit of the reporting entity that sponsors the pools.

1. **APPLICABILITY** GASB 31 establishes standards for all investments held by external investment pools (EIPs). For most other governmental entities, it establishes fair value standards for investments in participating interest-earning investment contracts, external investment pools, open-end mutual funds, debt securities, and equity securities with readily determinable fair values. GASB 31 does **not** apply to securities that are accounted for under the equity method.

2. **VALUATION** Fluctuations due to market changes are presented in the financial statements. Non-participating contracts may be valued using a cost-based measure. Participating interest-earning investment contracts include investments whose value is affected by market (interest rate) changes. They participate chiefly because they are negotiable, transferable, or their redemption value considers market rates. GASB 31 states that fair value is, "the amount at which a financial instrument could be exchanged in a current transaction between willing parties, other than in a forced or liquidation sale." Broader than *market value* (associated only with the price for an actively traded security), *fair value* includes active, inactive, primary, and secondary assessments based on negotiations between sellers and buyers.

    a. Entities other than EIPs may use amortized cost for money market investments with a remaining maturity of one year or less at the time of purchase.

    b. EIPs may report short-term debt investments with a remaining maturity of up to 90 days at the financial statement date at amortized cost, provided that the fair value of those investments is not significantly affected by market factors.

    c. Investments in open-end mutual funds and EIPs are valued using the fund's current share price. If the investments are in external pools that are not SEC registered, fair value is determined by the fair value per share of the pool's underlying portfolio.

    d. EIPs that are 2a7-like pools are permitted to report their investments at amortized cost. (This standard parallels an SEC rule that allows money market mutual funds to use amortized cost to report net assets. The pool must operate in a manner consistent with this SEC rule.)

3. **REPORTING** The changes in the fair value of investments is included in revenues, captioned *net increase (decrease) in the fair value of investments*. Separate classification for realized and unrealized gains and losses is optional. EIPs can separately display realized gains and losses in their separate reports. Assets are reported in the funds and component units that hold the equity interests. Accounting for the allocations of income based on legal and contractual provisions can be based on those restrictions. For allocations based on management policies, the fund that holds the investment should report the income and record an operating transfer for the amounts transferred to other funds. Notes to the financial statements include:

    a. The methods and significant assumptions used to estimate the fair value of investments, when that fair value is based on other than quoted market prices.

    b. The policy for determining which investments, if any, are reported at amortized costs.

c. Allocations, if any, of income from investments associated with one fund that is assigned to another fund.

d. If realized gains and losses are disclosed separately, the notes should also disclose that

(1) The calculation of realized gains and losses is independent of a calculation of the net change in the fair value of investments.

(2) Realized gains and losses on investments that had been held in more than one fiscal year and sold in the current year were included as a change in the fair value of investments reported in the prior year(s) and the current year.

4. EXTERNAL INVESTMENT POOLS EIPs are organized to consolidate investment holdings for multiple governmental units and improve performance with the resulting larger holdings. As such, EIPs are likely to be more sensitive to investment performance fluctuations.

a. An investment trust fund reports the transactions and balances of the EIPs. The investment trust fund reports the external portion of each pool in the financial statements of the sponsoring government, using the accrual basis of accounting. The external portion of the EIP represents the equity interests of legally separate entities that are not part of the sponsoring government. Financial statements for the investment trust fund should include a statement of net assets and a statement of changes in net assets. The difference between EIP assets and liabilities should be captioned *net assets held in trust for pool participants*.

b. Disclosures in the financial statements of an EIP include: (1) a brief description of any regulatory oversight; (2) the frequency and purpose of determining the fair value of investments; (3) the method used to determine participants shares sold and redeemed and whether that method differs from the method used to report investments; (4) whether the pool sponsor has provided or obtained any legally binding guarantees during the period to support the value of shares; (5) the extent of involuntary participation in the pool, if any; (6) summary of the fair value, the carrying amount (if different from fair value), the number of shares or the principal amount, ranges of interest rates, and maturity dates of each major investment classification; and (7) the accounting policy for defining each of the income components, if the investment income is separated into interest, dividend, and other income versus the net increase or decrease in fair value of investments.

c. Disclosures for the sponsoring government are expanded if the pool does not issue separate financial statements. These additional disclosures include

(1) Disclosures required by GASB 31 for separate pool financial statements.

(2) Disclosures required by GASB 3 and GASB 28 should be presented separately for the external portion of each pool.

(3) Condensed statements of net assets and changes in net assets, for each pool. Pools with internal and external investors should present net assets in total and distinguish between internal and external portions of assets held in trust for pool participants.

F. INVENTORY ACCOUNTING METHODS

Three different means of accounting for inventories are commonly used. Only the consumption method is used in government-wide statements, as the purchases method is not full accrual.

EXHIBIT 16 ♦ COMPARISON OF INVENTORY ACCOUNTING METHODS

	PURCHASES METHOD	**CONSUMPTION METHOD**	**CONSUMPTION METHOD**
	Periodic System	*Periodic System*	*Perpetual System*
Reserve for Supply Inventory	Required	Optional	Optional
Interim Purchase	Expenditures　　　100　　Vouchers Payable　　　100	Expenditures　　　100　　Vouchers Payable　　　100	Supply Inventory　　100　　Vouchers Payable　　　100
Interim Issue/Use	No entry	No entry	Expenditures　　　80　　Supply Inventory　　　80
Year-end (inventory increase)	Supply Inventory　　20　　OFS-Inventory Increase　20　Unreserved FB　　20　　Reserve for Supplies Inv.　20	Supply Inventory　　20　　Expenditures　　　20	No entry—unless there is an overage (decrease expenditures and increase inventory)
Year-end (inventory decrease)	OFS-Inventory Increase　15　　Supply Inventory　　15　Reserve for Supplies Inv.　15　　Unreserved FB　　15	Expenditures　　　15　　Supply Inventory　　15	No entry—unless there is a shortage (increase expenditures and decrease inventory)

G.　SERVICE EFFORTS & ACCOMPLISHMENTS (SEA)
Financial reporting under both the old and new governmental reporting models is limited in scope. Currently, reporting SEA information is optional, but is under discussion.

1.　SAMPLE MEASURES Proposed measures for elementary and secondary education include the following indicators. The number of student days indicates a general measure of workload. The number of students promoted or graduated indicates the degree to which educational requirements are fulfilled. The absenteeism and dropout rates indicate the degree of student participation and interest. The percentage of graduates employed or in college indicates the suitability of preparation for these pursuits.

2.　DIFFICULTIES Implementation of mandatory SEA reporting is hindered by several challenges. Few performance indicators are readily or accurately measurable. By selecting readily measured indicators, there may be poor association of reported performance measures with goals. Actions that do not improve substantive value, but result in favorable measurements, manipulate SEA performance numbers. Because several indicators may be necessary for a well-rounded measurement of a single activity, there is a risk of information overload. Finally, apparently similar programs may have considerable substantive differences, compounding the difficulties of comparison among entities, or even different divisions of the same entity.

H.　COMPONENT UNIT DETERMINATION
GASB 39, Determining Whether Certain Organizations Are Component Units—an Amendment of GASB Statement No. 14, provides additional guidance to determine whether certain entities for which a primary government is not accountable financially must be reported as component units based on the nature and significance of their relationship with the primary government. Generally, it requires reporting, as a component unit, an entity that raises and holds economic resources for the direct benefit of a government.

1.　CRITERIA Legally separate, tax-exempt entities that meet **all** three criteria must be presented discretely as component units.

a.　DIRECT BENEFIT Economic resources received or held by the separate entity are totally—or nearly totally—for the direct benefit of the primary government, its component units, or its constituents.

    b. **MAJORITY** The primary government, or its component units, is entitled to—or has the ability to otherwise access—a majority of the economic resources received or held by the separate entity.

    c. **SIGNIFICANCE** The economic resources received or held by an individual entity that the specific primary government, or its component units, is entitled to, or has the ability to otherwise access, are significant to that primary government.

  2. **PROFESSIONAL JUDGMENT** GASB 14 continues to require the application of professional judgment in determining whether the relationship between a primary government and other organizations for which the primary government is not financially accountable and that do not meet these criteria is such that exclusion of the organization would render the financial statements of the reporting entity misleading or incomplete.

V. APPENDIX: OUTGOING REPORTING MODEL

A. FUNDS AND ACCOUNT GROUPS

The focus of the outgoing reporting model is on individual funds and fund types. The governmental funds and account groups, taken together, account for the general government.

  1. **GOVERNMENTAL FUNDS** Fixed assets and long-term general obligation debt are excluded from all governmental fund balance sheets. All governmental funds use the modified accrual basis of accounting. The **four** governmental fund types are the general, special revenue, capital projects, and debt service funds.

  2. **ACCOUNT GROUPS** The two account groups are memorandum list and offset accounts that provide a record of general government fixed assets and long-term debt, as these are not recorded in the governmental funds. Account groups don't have any operating accounts. (The new reporting model does not use account groups to report capital assets or long-term debt of governmental funds.) Both account groups use the modified accrual basis of accounting. Depreciating fixed assets and reporting infrastructure are both optional and uncommon. If optional accumulated depreciation is reported, the corresponding debit (in the GFAAG) reduces the related *Investment in General Fixed Asset* account, not an expenditure or expense account.

    a. **GENERAL FIXED ASSETS ACCOUNT GROUP (GFAAG)**

    b. **GENERAL LONG-TERM DEBT ACCOUNT GROUP (GLTDAG)**

  3. **PROPRIETARY FUNDS** Proprietary funds are little changed from the outgoing reporting model to the new reporting model. All proprietary funds use the accrual basis of accounting. They record their fixed assets and depreciation expense. The two proprietary fund types are enterprise and internal service funds.

  4. **FIDUCIARY FUNDS** Fiduciary funds account for resources (and related liabilities) held by government entities in a trustee capacity (trust funds) or as an agent for others (agency funds). Unlike in the new reporting model, two fiduciary funds are accounted for using the modified accrual basis of accounting.

    a. Nonexpendable trust funds are accounted for like proprietary funds. For an entity using the outgoing reporting model, a nonexpendable trust fund may be used for escheat property.

    b. Expendable trust funds are accounted for like governmental funds (**modified** accrual).

    c. Investment trust funds are accounted for like proprietary funds.

    d. Pension trust funds are accounted for like proprietary funds.

    e.   Agency funds are purely custodial (assets equal liabilities) and use the **modified** accrual basis of accounting.

FUNDS & ACCOUNT GROUPS: TYPE AND BASIS OF ACCOUNTING

P	**P**ension Trust	Fiduciary	Accrual
I	**I**nvestment Trust	Proprietary	Accrual
P	**P**rivate-		
P	**P**urpose Fund	New: Not used in outgoing model	
A	**A**gency Trust Fund	Fiduciary	Modified Accrual
C	**C**apital Projects Fund	Governmental	Modified Accrual
G	**G**eneral Fund	Governmental	Modified Accrual
R	Special **R**evenue Fund	Governmental	Modified Accrual
I	**I**nternal Service	Proprietary	Accrual
P	**P**ermanent Fund	New: Not used in outgoing model	
E	**E**nterprise	Proprietary	Accrual
S	Debt **S**ervice Fund	Governmental	Modified Accrual
D	Long-Term **D**ebt Account Group		for gov't-type funds only
A	General Fixed **A**ssets Account Group		for gov't-type funds only
N	**N**onexpendable Trust	Fiduciary	Accrual
E	**E**xpendable Trust Fund	Fiduciary	Modified Accrual

NOTE: Two funds and the two account groups (DANE) are eliminated from the financial statements by GASB 34.

B.   **ACCOUNTING**

The accounts of a government are divided into several funds and nonfund account groups. A government should have only one general fund, GFAAG, and GLTDAG. It may have one, none, or several of the other types of funds, depending on its activities.

    1.   **BUDGETS** The budget system is unchanged from the outgoing reporting model to the new reporting model. The outgoing reporting model includes budget information in the general purpose financial statements.

    2.   **ENCUMBRANCE SYSTEM** The encumbrance system is unchanged from the outgoing reporting model to the new reporting model.

    3.   **BASIS OF ACCOUNTING** The basis of accounting used depends on the fund.

FUNDS THAT USE ACCRUAL BASIS

P	**P**ension Trust	Fiduciary
I	**I**nternal Service	Proprietary
I	**I**nvestment Trust	Fiduciary
N	**N**onexpendable Trust	Fiduciary
E	**E**nterprise	Proprietary

---

    a.   The modified accrual basis is used in the governmental-type funds (general, special revenue, capital projects, and debt service funds), where revenues and expenditures are recorded—and in some fiduciary funds (expendable trust and agency funds).

    b.   The accrual basis is used in proprietary (enterprise and internal service) funds, where revenues and expenses are recorded and net income (loss) is reported. The accrual basis is also used in nonexpendable trust, investment trust, and pension trust funds.

4. **CAPITAL LEASE IN A GOVERNMENTAL-TYPE FUND: ACCOUNT GROUP TRANSACTIONS** An asset acquired through a capital lease is recorded in the **GFAAG** at the inception of the lease at the lesser of (1) the present value of the minimum lease payments or (2) the fair value of the leased property. The portion of the lease payment considered to be a payment of principal is also recorded in the GLTDAG. The liability incurred under the capital lease is recorded in the **GLTDAG** at the inception of the lease at the present value of the minimum lease payments.

EXHIBIT 17 ♦ LEASED GENERAL FIXED ASSET: ACCOUNT GROUP TRANSACTIONS*

1. Lease Inception		
a. General Fixed Assets Account Group		
Equipment	XX	
Investment in General Fixed Assets—Capital Leases		XX
b. General Long-Term Debt Account Group		
Amount to Be Provided for Lease Payments	XX	
Amount Available in DSF for Lease Payments	XX	
Capital Leases Payable		XX
2. Lease Repayment (GLTDAG)		
Capital Leases Payable (principal only)	XX	
Amount Available in DSF for Lease Payments		XX
Amount to Be Provided for Payment of		
Capital Lease Principal		XX

*These entries are made in addition to the capital lease entries previously covered, not instead of them. These entries may be more clear to candidates who are familiar with the material in Chapter 22.

C. FINANCIAL STATEMENT OVERVIEW

Governments prepare financial statements for both individual funds and account groups and by fund type and account group for the government in its entirety.

1. **STATEMENT HEADINGS AND FORMATS** All individual fund and combining statements that support and are aggregated to prepare each of the five general purpose financial statements (GPFS) should be in the **same** format. (There are several alternative formats.)

EXHIBIT 18 ♦ STATEMENT HEADINGS

COMBINED STATEMENTS	COMBINING STATEMENTS	INDIVIDUAL STATEMENTS
Name of Government	Name of Government	Name of Government
	Combining	Name of Fund
Combined [Name of Statement]	[Name of Statement and of Fund Type]	[Name of Statement]
Date or Period Ended	Date or Period Ended	Date or Period Ended

2. **COMBINING AND INDIVIDUAL FUND STATEMENTS** The combining and individual fund statements are presented **only** in the comprehensive annual financial report (CAFR).

D. COMPREHENSIVE ANNUAL FINANCIAL REPORT

A Comprehensive Annual Financial Report (CAFR) is prepared following a pyramid reporting concept: GPFS are built from combining statements, which are built from individual statements.

1. **COMBINED GENERAL PURPOSE FINANCIAL STATEMENTS (GPFS)** Present the data for each fund and account group type in a columnar format—the data in each column being the total data for all funds (or account groups) of that type. These may include (optionally) a memorandum-only total column. Five combined GPFS are required in the CAFR, and, with the notes to the financial statements, may be published separately. Note that two statements

are operating statements for the governmental and similar fiduciary fund types: one on the GAAP basis and the other on the budgetary basis.

    a. **COMBINED STATEMENT OF REVENUES, EXPENDITURES, AND CHANGES IN FUND BALANCES** Governmental (and similar fiduciary) fund types [GAAP basis]. (non-PIINE funds)

    b. **COMBINED STATEMENT OF REVENUES, EXPENDITURES, AND CHANGES IN FUND BALANCES: BUDGET AND ACTUAL** General and special revenues fund types (and similar governmental [and fiduciary] fund types) for which annual budgets have been legally adopted [Budgetary basis]. (non-PIINE funds with budgets)

    c. **COMBINED STATEMENT OF REVENUES, EXPENSES, AND CHANGES IN RETAINED EARNINGS/ FUND EQUITY** Proprietary (and similar fiduciary) fund types. (PIINE funds)

    d. **COMBINED BALANCE SHEET** All fund types and account groups [GAAP basis]. The balance sheet includes data on all of the funds and account groups.

    e. **COMBINED STATEMENT OF CASH FLOWS** Proprietary (and similar fiduciary) fund types. (PIINE funds)

  2. **NOTES TO THE GPFS**

  3. **COMBINING STATEMENTS** Statements in which separate columns present the data for each fund of a fund type (e.g., present the data for each of five separate special revenue funds and the fund type total) that appears in the related combined statement. Combining statements are more detailed than and thus support combined statements. Combining statements are essentially a series of individual fund statements presented in adjacent columns with a total column. A total column is required, because the fund type data represented by the totals is GAAP data presented in the **combined** statements.

  4. **INDIVIDUAL FUND STATEMENTS** Statements in which data for one fund or account group are presented in more detail than in the combined and/or combining statements. They are required only when such additional detail is considered necessary for fair disclosure in the CAFR at the individual fund materiality level.

E. **GENERAL PURPOSE FINANCIAL STATEMENTS**

  1. **COMBINED BALANCE SHEET** All fund types and account groups are included.

EXHIBIT 19 ♦ COMBINED BALANCE SHEET

	Governmental Fund Types		Account Groups		Prop Fund Types	Fiduciary Fund Types	[Optional] Memorandum
	Gen. fund	Spec. rev. funds	GFA	GLTD	Enterprise funds	Agency funds	only totals
Assets [list]	XX	XX	XX	XX	XX	XX	XX
Liab. [list]	XX	XX	XX	XX	XX	XX	XX
Fund Equity	XX	XX	XX	XX	XX	XX	XX
	XX	XX	XX	XX	XX	XX	XX

The memorandum only total, if included, may be simply the sum of the data in the columns or it may be net of interfund and similar eliminations. (This applies to all combined statements.)

2. **COMBINED STATEMENT OF REVENUES, EXPENDITURES, AND CHANGES IN FUND BALANCES** All governmental (and similar fiduciary) fund types are prepared on the modified accrual (GAAP) basis. This statement reconciles beginning and ending total fund balances. Alternatively, it may reconcile beginning and ending unreserved fund balances—in which case, a *Changes in Reserves* section would be added immediately above or below the *Fund Balance's* beginning amount. (Note that transfers in/out or to/from are **not** netted. Transfers are reported after revenues and expenditures, as they affect operating results.)

EXHIBIT 20 ♦ COMBINED STATEMENT OF REVENUES, EXPENDITURES, AND CHANGES IN FUND BALANCES

(Heading)	Gen. funds	Spec rev. funds	Debt serv. funds	Cap. proj. funds	Expendable trust funds	[Optional] Memorandum only totals
	Governmental Fund Types				Fiduciary Fund Types	
Revenues [list by source category]	XX	XX	XX	XX	XX	XX
Expenditures [list by proj. or type]	XX	XX	XX	XX	XX	XX
Excess of Revenues Over (Under) Expenditures	XX	XX	XX	XX	XX	XX
Other Financing Sources (Uses) [list, e.g., operating transfers, bond issue proceeds]	XX	XX	XX	XX	XX	XX
Excess of Revenues and Other Financing Sources Over (Under) Expenditures and Other Financing Uses	XX	XX	XX	XX	XX	XX
Fund Balances, Beginning	XX	XX	XX	XX	XX	XX
Residual Equity Transfers In (Out)	XX	XX	XX	XX	XX	XX
Fund Balances, Ending	XX	XX	XX	XX	XX	XX

3. **COMBINED STATEMENT OF REVENUES, EXPENDITURES, AND CHANGES IN FUND BALANCES: BUDGET AND ACTUAL** Presents budgetary comparison data for the annually (legally) budgeted governmental fund types and similar fiduciary fund types. Accordingly, it is presented on the budgetary basis, which may not be modified accrual as required by GAAP. (The budgetary basis is the basis of preparation for the budget.) Any differences between the GAAP basis and the budgetary basis must be explained in the notes to the GPFS. This statement is prepared on the total fund balance approach—since changes in reserves are not budgeted and have no budgetary significance.

EXHIBIT 21 ♦ COMBINED STATEMENT OF REVENUES, EXPENDITURES, AND CHANGES IN FUND BALANCES: BUDGET AND ACTUAL

	(Heading)								
	Governmental Fund Types						Fiduciary Fund Types		
	General fund			Special rev. funds			Expendable trust fund		
	Act.	Budg.	Var.	Act.	Budg.	Var.	Act.	Budg.	Var.
Revenues [listed by source category]	X	Y	X-Y	X	Y	X-Y	X	Y	X-Y
Expenditures [listed by program or type]	X	Y	X-Y	X	Y	X-Y	X	Y	X-Y
Excess (Deficit) of Revenues Over (Under) Expenditures	X	Y	X-Y	X	Y	X-Y	X	Y	X-Y
Other Financing Sources (Uses) [listed]	X	Y	X-Y	X	Y	X-Y	X	Y	X-Y
Excess (Deficit) of Revenues & Other Financing Sources Over (Under) Expenditures & Other Uses	X	Y	X-Y	X	Y	X-Y	X	Y	X-Y
Fund Balances, Beginning	X	X	--	X	X	--	X	X	--
Residual Equity Transfers In (Out)	X	Y	X-Y	X	Y	X-Y	X	Y	X-Y
Fund Balances, Ending	X	Y	X-Y	X	Y	X-Y	X	Y	X-Y

4. **COMBINED STATEMENT OF CASH FLOWS** All proprietary, investment trust, and nonexpendable trust funds.

EXHIBIT 22 ♦ COMBINED STATEMENT OF CASH FLOWS

	(Heading)		
	Proprietary Fund Types		
	Enterprise funds	Internal service funds	Nonexpend. trust funds
Cash flows from operating activities	XX	XX	XX
Cash flows from noncapital financing transactions	XX	XX	XX
Cash flows from capital and related financing activities	XX	XX	XX
Cash flows from investing activities	XX	XX	XX
Net increase (decrease) in cash	XX	XX	XX
Cash at beginning of year	XX	XX	XX
Cash at end of year	XX	XX	XX

5. **COMBINED STATEMENT OF REVENUES, EXPENSES, AND CHANGES IN RETAINED EARNINGS/FUND EQUITY** All proprietary (and similar fiduciary) fund types must follow a prescribed format similar to a business enterprise statement of income and retained earnings. As its title indicates, it may reconcile either beginning and ending retained earnings or total fund equity including contributed capital.

EXHIBIT 23 ♦ COMBINED STATEMENT OF REVENUES, EXPENSES, AND CHANGES IN RETAINED EARNINGS/FUND EQUITY

| | Proprietary Fund Types | | Fiduciary Fund Types | | [Optional] |
| | (Heading) | | | | |
	Enterpr. funds	Internal service funds	Nonexpen. trust funds	Pension trust funds	Memorandum only total
Operating Revenues [list]	XX	XX	XX	XX	XX
Operating Expenses [list]	XX	XX	XX	XX	XX
Operating Income (loss)	XX	XX	XX	XX	XX
Nonoperating Revenues and Expenses [list]	XX	XX	XX	XX	XX
Income before Operating Transfers	XX	XX	XX	XX	XX
Operating Transfers In (Out) [list]	XX	XX	XX	XX	XX
Net Income (Loss)	XX	XX	XX	XX	XX
Retained Earnings/Fund Equity, Beginning	XX	XX	XX	XX	XX
Residual Equity Transfers In (Out) [list]*	XX	XX	XX	XX	XX
Retained Earnings/Fund Equity, Ending	XX	XX	XX	XX	XX

* Would **not** appear in a statement reconciling beginning and ending Retained Earnings.

F.   TRANSITION TO NEW REPORTING MODEL

Account groups, expendable trust funds, and nonexpendable trust funds are not used by the GASB 34 reporting model.

OUTGOING REPORTING MODEL	**NEW REPORTING MODEL**
Nonexpendable trust funds	Permanent funds
	Private-purpose trust funds
Expendable trust funds	Special revenue funds

1.   Nonexpendable trust funds report resources with nonexpendable principal. Under the new reporting model, they become either **permanent funds** or **private-purpose trust funds**. Permanent funds account for resources that are legally restricted to the extent that income, but not principal, may be used for the benefit of the reporting government or its citizenry. (The permanent fund is the only governmental-type fund with a principal preservation implication.) Private-purpose trust funds account for trust arrangements under which principal and income benefit individuals, private organizations, or other governments (as opposed to the reporting government or its citizenry).

2.   Expendable trust funds formerly reported resources with expendable principal. They become either **special revenue funds** or **private-purpose trust funds**. If the government may use the resources to support its programs (in other words, to benefit itself or its citizenry), these resources may be accounted for in special revenue funds.

3.   Account groups do not appear in financial statements prepared using the new reporting model; as a practical matter, entities may first account for assets and long-term debt within the account groups and then adjust the financial statements according to GASB No. 34.

4.   New reporting model statements present the financial information of each major fund in a separate column. Non-major funds are aggregated and displayed in a single column. All fund statements using the modified accrual basis of accounting include a reconciliation to the accrual basis. All the "C GRIPES" funds, except for the proprietary funds (the vowels in "C GRIPES"), are shown on the modified accrual basis of accounting. General capital assets and general long-term liabilities usually are not reported in these statements.

5. In the new reporting model, the proprietary and fiduciary [PIPPA] funds are shown on the accrual basis of accounting, except for certain liabilities of defined benefit pension plans and certain post-employment healthcare plans, in accordance with GASB 25 and 26. Be alert! The internal service fund is still a proprietary fund. In the fund statements, internal service funds use accrual accounting (like enterprise funds), not modified accrual (like governmental-type funds). This is despite the fact, that, in the GWS, the internal service funds generally appear in the governmental activity column.

6. In the new reporting model, fund financial statements for major funds are presented before the notes to the financial statements. (They are part of the basic financial statements.) Combining statements for non-major funds are not required, but may be presented as supplementary information.

CHAPTER 21—GOVERNMENTAL OVERVIEW

PROBLEM 21-1 MULTIPLE CHOICE QUESTIONS (110 to 138 minutes)

1. The primary authoritative body for determining the measurement focus and basis of accounting standards for governmental fund operating statements is the
a. Governmental Accounting Standards Board (GASB).
b. Financial Accounting Standards Board (FASB).
c. Government Accounting and Auditing Committee of the AICPA (GAAC).
d. National Council on Governmental Accounting (NCGA).　(5/91, Theory, #51, amended, 2095)

2. Which of the following lead(s) to the use of fund accounting by a governmental organization?

	Financial control	Legal restrictions
a.	Yes	Yes
b.	Yes	No
c.	No	No
d.	No	Yes

(R/00, AR, #1, 6906)

3. The measurement focus of governmental-type funds is on the determination of

	Flow of financial resources	Financial position
a.	Yes	No
b.	No	Yes
c.	No	No
d.	Yes	Yes

(5/96, AR, #4, 6201)

4. Interperiod equity is an objective of financial reporting for governmental entities. According to the Governmental Accounting Standards Board, is interperiod equity fundamental to public administration and is it a component of accountability?

	Fundamental to public administration	Component of accountability
a.	Yes	No
b.	No	No
c.	No	Yes
d.	Yes	Yes

(11/92, Theory, #51, 3484)

5. What is the basic criterion used to determine the reporting entity for a governmental unit?
a. Special financing arrangement
b. Geographic boundaries
c. Scope of public services
d. Financial accountability　(11/95, AR, #62, 5805)

6. Governmental financial reporting should provide information to assist users in which situation(s)?

I. Making social and political decisions.
II. Assessing whether current-year citizens received services but shifted part of the payment burden to future-year citizens.

a. I only
b. II only
c. Both I and II
d. Neither I nor II　(5/95, AR, #52, 5470)

7. Which of the following statements is correct regarding comparability of governmental financial reports?
a. Comparability is **not** relevant in governmental financial reporting.
b. Similarly designated governments perform the same functions.
c. Selection of different alternatives in accounting procedures or practices account for the differences between financial reports.
d. Differences between financial reports should be due to substantive differences in underlying transactions or the governmental structure.
(11/94, AR, #2, 4979)

8. Which event(s) is(are) supportive of interperiod equity as a financial reporting objective of a governmental unit?

I. A balanced budget is adopted.
II. Residual equity transfers out equals residual equity transfers in.

a. I only
b. II only
c. Both I and II
d. Neither I nor II　(11/95, AR, #59, 5802)

9. Which of the following statements is correct concerning disclosure of reverse repurchase and fixed coupon reverse repurchase agreements?
a. Related assets and liabilities should be netted.
b. Related interest cost and interest earned should be netted.
c. Credit risk related to the agreements need **not** be disclosed.
d. Underlying securities owned should be reported as "Investments."　(11/94, AR, #6, 4983)

10. Property taxes levied in fiscal year 20X0 to finance the general fund budget of fiscal year 20X1 should be reported as general fund revenues in fiscal year 20X1

a. Regardless of the fiscal year in which collected.
b. For the amount collected before the end of fiscal year 20X1 or shortly thereafter.
c. For the amount collected before the end of fiscal year 20X1 only.
d. For the amount collected in fiscal year 20X0 only.   (5/92, Theory, #58, amended, 2751)

11. In which situation(s) should property taxes due to a governmental unit be recorded as deferred revenue?

  I. Property taxes receivable are recognized in advance of the year for which they are levied.
 II. Property taxes receivable are collected in advance of the year in which they are levied.

a. I only
b. Both I and II
c. II only
d. Neither I nor II   (11/94, AR, #17, 4994)

12. Which of the following fund types used by a government most likely would have a Fund Balance Reserved for Inventory of Supplies?

a. General
b. Internal service
c. Nonexpendable trust
d. Capital projects   (11/90, Theory, #52, 2105)

13. The following information pertains to property taxes levied by Oak City for the calendar year 20X1:

Collections during 20X1	$500,000
Expected collections during the first 60 days of 20X2	100,000
Expected collections during the balance of 20X2	60,000
Expected collections during January 20X3	30,000
Estimated to be uncollectible	10,000
Total levy	$700,000

What amount should Oak report for 20X1 net property tax revenues?

a. $700,000
b. $690,000
c. $600,000
d. $500,000   (11/93, PII, #10, amended, 4439)

14. The modified accrual basis of accounting should be used for which of the following funds?

a. Capital projects fund
b. Enterprise fund
c. Pension trust fund
d. Proprietary fund   (5/93, PII, #22, 4130)

15. Under the modified accrual basis of accounting for a governmental unit, revenues should be recognized in the accounting period in which they

a. Are collected.
b. Are earned and become measurable.
c. Become available and measurable.
d. Become available and earned.   (Editors, 2128)

16. Expenditures of a governmental unit for insurance extending over more than one accounting period

a. Must be accounted for as expenditures of the period of acquisition.
b. Must be accounted for as expenditures of the periods subsequent to acquisition.
c. Must be allocated between or among accounting periods.
d. May be allocated between or among accounting periods or may be accounted for as expenditures of the period of acquisition.
          (11/94, AR, #15, 4992)

17. Allen Town has adopted GASB Statement No. 34, *Basic Financial Statements—and Management's Discussion and Analysis—for State and Local Governments*. For which of the following funds does Allen use the modified accrual basis of accounting in the fund financial statements?

a. Capital projects fund
b. Enterprise fund
c. Investment trust fund
d. Pension trust fund   (Editors, 6884)

18. Lys City reports a compensated absences liability in its combined balance sheet. The salary rate used to calculate the liability should normally be the rate in effect

a. When the unpaid compensated absences were earned.
b. When the compensated absences were earned or are to be paid, or at the balance sheet date, whichever results in the lowest amount.
c. At the balance sheet date.
d. When the compensated absences are to be paid.   (11/95, AR, #70, amended, 5813)

19. According to GASB Statement No. 34, *Basic Financial Statements—and Management's Discussion and Analysis—for State and Local Governments*, what is the paramount objective of governmental financial reporting?
a. Accountability
b. Consistency
c. Understandability
d. Usefulness (Editors, 6871)

20. The basic financial statements of a state government that has adopted GASB Statement No. 34, *Basic Financial Statements—and Management's Discussion and Analysis—for State and Local Governments*
a. Are comprised of the government-wide financial statements and related notes.
b. Are comprised of the primary government funds' financial statements and related notes.
c. Contain more detailed information regarding the state government's finances than is contained in the comprehensive annual financial report.
d. Do not include management's discussion and analysis (MD&A). (Editors, 6879)

21. Which of the following is required by GASB No. 34, *Basic Financial Statements—and Management's Discussion and Analysis—for State and Local Governments*?

I. Governmental activities information using the economic resources measurement focus in the government-wide financial statements.
II. Governmental fund information included in the statement of cash flows.

a. I only
b. II only
c. Both I and II
d. Neither I nor II (Editors, 6816)

22. River City has adopted GASB Statement No. 34, *Basic Financial Statements—and Management's Discussion and Analysis—for State and Local Governments*. River has a defined contribution pension plan. How should River report the pension plan in its financial statements?
a. Within the component units column of its government-wide financial statements
b. Within the fiduciary column of its government-wide financial statements
c. Within its fund financial statements
d. Within the governmental activities column of its government-wide financial statements
(Editors, 6876)

23. Arbor City has adopted GASB Statement No. 34, *Basic Financial Statements—and Management's Discussion and Analysis—for State and Local Governments*. What basis of accounting does Arbor use to present the general fund in the financial statements?

I. Modified accrual basis in all financial statements.
II. Accrual basis in the government-wide statement of activities and statement of net assets.
III. Modified accrual basis in the fund financial statements with a reconciliation to the accrual basis.

a. I only
b. II only
c. III only
d. Both II and III (Editors, 6877)

24. Where does GASB Statement No. 34, *Basic Financial Statements—and Management's Discussion and Analysis—for State and Local Governments*, require management's discussion and analysis (MD&A) to be presented?
a. Before the financial statements
b. Before the notes to the financial statements, but after the financial statements
c. In the notes to the financial statements
d. After the notes to the financial statements, before other required supplementary information
(Editors, 6873)

25. GASB Statement No. 34, *Basic Financial Statements—and Management's Discussion and Analysis—for State and Local Governments*, requires governments to include which of the following in management's discussion and analysis (MD&A)?
a. Analysis of significant budget variances
b. Comparisons of current year to prior year, based on government-wide information
c. Currently known facts, decisions, or conditions that are expected to have a significant effect on financial position or results of operations
d. All of the above (Editors, 6894)

26. Which total columns does GASB Statement No. 34, *Basic Financial Statements—and Management's Discussion and Analysis—for State and Local Governments*, require governments to include in the government-wide financial statements?

	Primary government	Entity as a whole
a.	Yes	Yes
b.	Yes	No
c.	No	Yes
d.	No	No

(Editors, 6874)

27. Dale Town has adopted GASB Statement No. 34, *Basic Financial Statements—and Management's Discussion and Analysis—for State and Local Governments*. Dale's public school system is administered by a separately elected board of education. The board of education is not organized as a separate legal entity and does not have the power to levy taxes or issue bonds. Dale's town council approves the school system's budget. Where should Dale report the public school system in its government-wide information?
a. Within the component units column
b. Within the governmental activities column
c. In the notes to the financial statements
d. In the required supplementary information

(Editors, 6875)

28. Chase City uses an internal service fund for its central motor pool. The assets and liabilities account balances for this fund that are not eliminated normally should be reported in the government-wide statement of net assets as
a. Governmental activities
b. Business-type activities
c. Fiduciary activities
d. Note disclosures only

(R/01, AR, #3, 6988)

29. Kellick City has adopted GASB Statement No. 34, *Basic Financial Statements—and Management's Discussion and Analysis—for State and Local Governments*. It is inappropriate to record depreciation expense in the government-wide financial statements related to the assets in which of Kellick's funds?
a. Agency fund
b. Enterprise fund
c. General fund
d. Special revenue fund

(Editors, 6881)

30. Zebra Town has adopted GASB Statement No. 34, *Basic Financial Statements—and Management's Discussion and Analysis—for State and Local Governments*. Which of the following funds will Zebra rarely report within in the same activity column as the general fund in the government-wide financial statements?
a. Debt service fund
b. Enterprise fund
c. Internal service fund
d. Permanent fund

(Editors, 6885)

31. Berry Township has adopted GASB Statement No. 34, *Basic Financial Statements—and Management's Discussion and Analysis—for State and Local Governments*. Berry's eligible infrastructure assets are exempt from depreciation if the modified approach is used. Which of the following are requirements of the modified approach?

I. The entity performs condition assessments of eligible assets and summarizes the results using a measurement scale.
II. The entity annually estimates the amount to preserve the eligible assets at an established and disclosed condition level.
III. The entity assesses asset conditions in comparison to condition levels established by the National Association of Public Works Engineers or a comparable organization.

a. I
b. I and II
c. I and III
d. I, II, and III

(Editors, 6888)

32. GASB Statement No. 34, *Basic Financial Statements—and Management's Discussion and Analysis—for State and Local Governments*, does **not** require depreciation of which of the following assets purchased after June 30, 1980?

I. Land and land improvements
II. Historical treasures and works of art that meet the conditions of an inexhaustible collection
III. Infrastructure assets that are part of a network or subsystem of a network, when the modified approach is used

a. I only
b. I and II only
c. I and III only
d. I, II, and III

(Editors, 6889)

33. Farmer Township has adopted all provisions of GASB Statement No. 34, *Basic Financial Statements—and Management's Discussion and Analysis—for State and Local Governments*. In which financial statements does Farmer present its general-use capital assets?

	Fund	*Government-wide*
a.	Yes	Yes
b.	Yes	No
c.	No	Yes
d.	No	No

(Editors, 6890)

34. Does GASB Statement No. 34, *Basic Financial Statements—and Management's Discussion and Analysis—for State and Local Governments*, allow estimates of general infrastructure assets historical cost based on current replacement cost for assets existing upon adoption of the Statement and does it allow the use of composite methods to calculate depreciation expense?

	Estimates	Composite depreciation
a.	Yes	Yes
b.	Yes	No
c.	No	Yes
d.	No	No	(Editors, 6891)

35. Where does GASB Statement No. 34, *Basic Financial Statements—and Management's Discussion and Analysis—for State and Local Governments*, require fund financial statements for major funds to be presented?
a. Before the notes to the financial statements
b. In the notes to the financial statements
c. After the notes to the financial statements, before other required supplementary information
d. After the notes to the financial statements and required supplementary information (RSI)
(Editors, 6872)

36. Financial statements for which fund type generally report net assets?
a. Capital projects
b. Expendable pension trust
c. Special revenue
d. Enterprise (11/95, AR, #69, amended, 5812)

37. Zephyr City has adopted GASB Statement No. 34, *Basic Financial Statements—and Management's Discussion and Analysis—for State and Local Governments*. Which activities and basis of accounting must appear in Zephyr's statement(s) of cash flows?

I. Business-type activities in the fund financial statements
II. Government-type activities in the fund financial statements
III. Business-type and government-type activities in the government-wide financial statements

a. I only
b. II only
c. III only
d. I and III only (Editors, 6878)

38. Baker Town has adopted GASB Statement No. 34, *Basic Financial Statements—and Management's Discussion and Analysis—for State and Local Governments*. Baker accounts for construction of assets for general use in a single capital projects fund. Which event(s) should Baker include in a statement of cash flows?

I. Cash inflow from issuing bonds to finance city hall construction.
II. Cash outflow from a city utility representing payments in lieu of property taxes.

a. I only
b. II only
c. Both I and II
d. Neither I nor II (Editors, 6880)

39. Dogwood City's water enterprise fund received interest of $10,000 on long-term investments. How should this amount be reported on the Statement of Cash Flows?
a. Operating activities
b. Non-capital financing activities
c. Capital and related financing activities
d. Investing activities (R/01, AR, #5, 6990)

40. Hill City's water utility fund held the following investments in U.S. Treasury securities at June 30, 20X4:

Investment	Date purchased	Maturity date	Carrying amount
3-month T-bill	5/31/X4	7/31/X4	$ 30,000
3-year T-note	6/15/X4	8/31/X4	50,000
5-year T-note	10/1/X0	9/30/X5	100,000

In the fund's balance sheet, what amount of these investments should be reported as cash and cash equivalents at June 30, 20X4?
a. $0
b. $ 30,000
c. $ 80,000
d. $180,000 (11/93, PII, #19, amended, 4448)

41. Vale City has adopted GASB Statement No. 34, *Basic Financial Statements—and Management's Discussion and Analysis—for State and Local Governments*. Vale legally adopts a cash-basis budget. What basis should be used in Vale's budgetary comparison schedule?
a. Accrual
b. Cash
c. Modified accrual
d. Cash or modified accrual (Editors, 6893)

42. GASB Statement No. 34, *Basic Financial Statements—and Management's Discussion and Analysis—for State and Local Governments*, requires presentation of a budgetary comparison schedule in required supplementary information. Which of the following must this schedule include?

I. Actual inflows, outflows, and balances, stated on the basis in the government's budget, with a reconciliation between the budgetary and GAAP information
II. Original budget
III. A separate column to report the variances between the final budget and actual amounts

a. I only
b. I and II only
c. I and III only
d. I, II, and III   (Editors, 6895)

43. When a capital lease of a governmental unit represents the acquisition of a general fixed asset, the acquisition should be reflected as
a. An expenditure but **not** as an other financing source.
b. An other financing source but **not** as an expenditure.
c. Both an expenditure and an other financing source.
d. Neither an expenditure nor an other financing source.   (11/94, AR, #10, 4987)

44. Cy City's Municipal Solid Waste Landfill Enterprise Fund was established when a new landfill was opened May 3, 2000. The landfill is expected to close December 31, 2019. Cy's 2000 expenses would include a portion of which of the year 2020 expected disbursements?

I. Cost of a final cover to be applied to the landfill
II. Cost of equipment to be installed to monitor methane gas buildup

a. I only
b. II only
c. Both I and II
d. Neither I nor II   (5/95, AR, #55, amended, 5473)

45. Polk County's solid waste landfill operation is accounted for in a governmental fund. Polk used available cash to purchase equipment that is included in the estimated current cost of closure and post-closure care of this operation. How would this purchase affect the long-term asset and the long-term liability amounts in Polk's general fund?

	Asset amount	Liability amount
a.	Increase	Decrease
b.	Increase	No effect
c.	No effect	Decrease
d.	No effect	No effect

(11/95, AR, #68, amended, 5811)

46. Which of the following statements meet the measurement and recognition criteria for landfill closure and postclosure costs?
a. Landfills should only be accounted for in the general fund.
b. Total landfill liabilities should be recognized in the general long-term debt account group.
c. Expense recognition should begin when waste is accepted and should continue through the post-closure period.
d. Equipment and facilities included in estimated total current cost of closure and postclosure care should not be reported as capital assets.
(R/99, AR, #19, 6808)

47. River City has a defined contribution pension plan. How should River report the pension plan in its financial statements?
a. Amortize any transition asset over the estimated number of years of current employees' service.
b. Disclose in the notes to the financial statements the amount of the pension benefit obligation and the net assets available for benefits.
c. Identify in the notes to financial statements the types of employees covered and the employer's and employees' obligations to contribute to the fund.
d. Accrue a liability for benefits earned but **not** paid to fund participants.   (11/92, Theory, #58, 3491)

48. Which of the following characteristics of service efforts and accomplishments is the most difficult to report for a governmental entity?
a. Comparability
b. Timeliness
c. Consistency
d. Relevance   (R/99, AR, #20, 6809)

49. Which of the following funds of a governmental unit uses the same basis of accounting as the special revenue fund?
a. Enterprise funds
b. Internal service funds
c. Nonexpendable trust funds
d. Expendable trust funds   (5/95, AR, #56, 5474)

50. Which of the following funds of a governmental unit uses the same basis of accounting as the enterprise fund?
a. Nonexpendable trust funds
b. Expendable trust funds
c. Debt service funds
d. Capital projects funds   (Editors, 2123)

51. The general purpose financial statements of a governmental entity should include

	Combining financial statements	Combined financial statements	Notes to financial statements
a.	Yes	Yes	Yes
b.	No	Yes	Yes
c.	Yes	No	Yes
d.	Yes	Yes	No

(R/99, AR, #18, 6807)

52. Vale City legally adopts a cash-basis budget. What basis should be used in Vale's combined statement of revenues, expenditures, and changes in fund balances—budget and actual?
a. Cash
b. Modified accrual
c. Accrual
d. Modified cash   (11/95, AR, #61, 5804)

53. What funds are **not** used by the reporting model introduced by GASB Statement No. 34, *Basic Financial Statements—and Management's Discussion and Analysis—for State and Local Governments*?
a. Agency funds
b. Expendable trust funds
c. Investment trust funds
d. Pension trust funds   (Editors, 6882)

54. Upon implementation of GASB Statement No. 34, *Basic Financial Statements—and Management's Discussion and Analysis—for State and Local Governments*, resources formerly accounted for in a nonexpendable trust fund will most likely be accounted for in a
a. Permanent fund.
b. Private-purpose trust fund.
c. Special revenue fund.
d. Either a permanent fund or a private-purpose trust fund.   (Editors, 6883)

55. Flax City has adopted GASB Statement No. 34, *Basic Financial Statements—and Management's Discussion and Analysis—for State and Local Governments*. Flax previously had reported a 20-year building rental agreement in the general fixed asset account group. Where should the lease liability be reported in Flax's financial statements?
a. General fund in the fund financial statements
b. General long-term debt account group in the fund financial statements
c. The governmental activities column of the government-wide financial statements
d. The governmental activities column of the government-wide and the general fund in the fund financial statements   (Editors, 6892)

PROBLEM 21-2 ADDITIONAL MULTIPLE CHOICE QUESTIONS (38 to 48 minutes)

56. Which of the following fund types of a governmental unit has(have) income determination as a measurement focus?

	General funds	Capital project funds
a.	Yes	Yes
b.	Yes	No
c.	No	No
d.	No	Yes

(11/95, AR, #57, amended, 5800)

57. Fund accounting is used by governmental units with resources that must be
a. Composed of cash or cash equivalents.
b. Incorporated into combined or combining financial statements.
c. Segregated for the purpose of carrying on specific activities or attaining certain objectives.
d. Segregated physically according to various objectives.   (11/95, AR, #60, 5803)

58. Property taxes and fines represent which of the following classes of nonexchange transactions for governmental units?
a. Derived tax revenues
b. Imposed nonexchange revenues
c. Government-mandated nonexchange transactions
d. Voluntary nonexchange transactions
(R/01, AR, #4, 6989)

59. South City School District has a separate elected governing body that administers the public school system. The district's budget is subject to the approval of the city council. The district's financial activity should be reported in the City's financial statements by
a. Blending only.
b. Discrete presentation.
c. Inclusion as a footnote only.
d. Either blending or inclusion as a footnote.
(11/97, AR, #13, 6541)

60. Marta City's school district is a legally separate entity but two of its seven board members are also city council members and the district is financially dependent on the city. The school district should be reported as a
a. Blended unit.
b. Discrete presentation.
c. Note disclosure.
d. Primary government. (11/97, AR, #14, 6542)

61. For which of the following governmental entities that use proprietary fund accounting should a statement of cash flows be presented?

	Public benefit corporations	Governmental utilities
a.	No	No
b.	No	Yes
c.	Yes	Yes
d.	Yes	No

(5/94, AR, #52, 4657)

62. GASB Statement No. 34, *Basic Financial Statements—and Management's Discussion and Analysis—for State and Local Governments*, requires large governments (annual revenues in the range above $100 million) to

I. Report all fixed assets (land, buildings, and equipment).
II. In fiscal periods beginning after June 15, 2001, report all major general infrastructure asset acquisitions.
III. In fiscal periods beginning after June 15, 2005, retroactively report all major general infrastructure assets acquired in fiscal years

ending after June 30, 1980, and before adoption of GASB Statement No. 34.

a. I only
b. I and II only
c. I and III only
d. I, II, and III   (Editors, 6886)

63. GASB Statement No. 34, *Basic Financial Statements—and Management's Discussion and Analysis—for State and Local Governments*, requires small governments (revenues of less than $10 million) to
a. Report and depreciate all buildings, and equipment, except for infrastructure assets.
b. Report and depreciate all buildings, and equipment, and report all major general infrastructure assets.
c. Report and depreciate all buildings, equipment, and major general infrastructure assets.
d. Report and depreciate all buildings and equipment as well as all major general infrastructure assets acquired in fiscal periods beginning after June 15, 2003.   (Editors, 6887)

64. With regard to the statement of cash flows for a governmental unit's enterprise fund, items generally presented as cash equivalents are?

	2-month treasury bills	3-month certificates of deposit
a.	No	No
b.	No	Yes
c.	Yes	Yes
d.	Yes	No

(11/93, Theory, #58, 4563)

65. The statement of activities of the government-wide financial statements is designed primarily to provide information to assess which of the following?
a. Operational accountability.
b. Financial accountability.
c. Fiscal accountability.
d. Functional accountability. (R/01, AR, #8, 6993)

66. On what accounting basis does GASB recommend that governmental fund budgets be prepared?
a. Cash
b. Modified cash
c. Accrual
d. Modified accrual   (11/94, AR, #4, 4981)

67. It is inappropriate to record depreciation expense in a(n)
a. Enterprise fund.
b. Internal service fund.
c. Nonexpendable trust fund.
d. Capital projects fund.   (11/94, AR, #8, 4985)

68. In which of the following fund types of a city government are revenues and expenditures recognized on the same basis of accounting as the general fund?
a. Nonexpendable trust
b. Internal service
c. Enterprise
d. Debt service   (11/91, Theory, #54, 2561)

69. Which of the following statements about the statistical section of the Comprehensive Annual Financial Report (CAFR) of a governmental unit is true?
a. Statistical tables may **not** cover more than two fiscal years.
b. Statistical tables may **not** include nonaccounting information.
c. The statistical section is **not** part of the basic financial statements.
d. The statistical section is an integral part of the basic financial statements. (R/01, AR, #7, 6992)

70. Valley Town's public school system is administered by a separately elected board of education. The board of education is not organized as a separate legal entity and does not have the power to levy taxes or issue bonds. Valley's city council approves the school system's budget. How should Valley report the public school system's annual financial results?

	Discrete presentation	Blended
a.	Yes	Yes
b.	Yes	No
c.	No	Yes
d.	No	No

(11/98, AR, #21, 6687)

71. Clover City's comprehensive annual financial report contains both combining and combined financial statements. Total columns are
a. Required for both combining and combined financial statements.
b. Optional, but commonly shown, for combining financial statements and required for combined financial statements.
c. Required for combining financial statements and optional, but commonly shown, for combined financial statements.
d. Optional, but commonly shown, for both combining and combined financial statements.
      (11/91, Theory, #58, 2565)

72. Which event(s) should be included in a statement of cash flows for a governmental entity?
I. Cash inflow from issuing bonds to finance city hall construction.
II. Cash outflow from a city utility representing payments in lieu of property taxes.

a. I only
b. II only
c. Both I and II
d. Neither I nor II   (11/95, AR, #63, 5806)

73. Flac City recorded a 20-year building rental agreement as a capital lease. The building lease asset was reported in the general fixed asset account group. Where should the lease liability be reported in Flac's combined balance sheet?
a. General long-term debt account group
b. Debt service fund
c. General fund
d. A lease liability should **not** be reported
      (11/93, Theory, #59, 4564)

74. Frome City signed a 20-year office property lease for its general staff. Frome could terminate the lease at any time after giving one year's notice, but termination is considered a remote possibility. The lease meets the criteria for a capital lease. What is the effect of the lease on the asset amount in Frome's general fixed assets account group and the liability amount in Frome's general long-term debt account group?

	Asset amount	Liability amount
a.	Increase	Increase
b.	Increase	No effect
c.	No effect	Increase
d.	No effect	No effect

(11/95, AR, #67, 5810)

OTHER OBJECTIVE FORMAT QUESTIONS

PROBLEM 21-3 (10 to 15 minutes)

Although it has adopted GASB Statement 34, Central Town uses a general fixed asset account group and a general long-term debit group to track capital assets and long-term debt. Central makes the same entries in these account groups as it did before adopting GASB Statement 34. The following information relates to actual results from Central's general fund for the year ended December 31, 20X1:

	Revenues
Property tax collections:	
Current year taxes collected	$630,000
Prior year taxes due 12/1/X0, collected 2/1/X1 as expected	50,000
Current year taxes due 12/1/X1, collection expected by 2/15/X2	70,000
Other cash receipts	190,000

	Expenditures
General government expenditures:	
Salaries and wages	$160,000
Other	100,000
Public safety and welfare expenditures:	
Salaries and wages	350,000
Other	150,000
Capital outlay	140,000
Transfer to debt service fund	30,000

- *Other cash receipts* includes a county grant of $100,000 for a specified purpose, of which $80,000 was expended; $50,000 in fines; and $40,000 in fees.

- *General government expenditures—other* includes employer contributions to the pension plan and $20,000 in annual capital lease payments for computers over three years; the fair value and present value at lease inception is $50,000.

- *Capital outlay* is for police vehicles.

- *Debt service* represents annual interest payments due December 15th of each year on $500,000 face value, 6%, 20-year term bonds.

Capital projects fund:

Central's council approved $750,000 for construction of a fire station, to be financed by $600,000 in general obligation bonds and a $150,000 state grant. Construction began during 20X1, but the fire station was not completed until April 20X2. The unreserved fund balance at January 1, 20X1, was $110,000.

During 20X1, the following transactions were recorded:

State grant	$150,000
Bond proceeds	610,000
Expenditures	500,000
Unpaid invoices at year end	30,000
Outstanding encumbrances at year end, which do not lapse and are to be honored the following year	25,000

REQUIRED:

FOR ITEMS 1 THROUGH 9, determine the 20X1 year-end amount to be recognized in the particular fund or account group.

		Amounts			
A.	$0	G.	$150,000	M.	$500,000
B.	$ 35,000	H.	$170,000	N.	$525,000
C.	$ 50,000	I.	$190,000	O.	$630,000
D.	$ 55,000	J.	$315,000	P.	$700,000
E.	$ 60,000	K.	$345,000	Q.	$710,000
F.	$140,000	L.	$370,000	R.	$760,000

1. What amount was recorded for property tax revenues in the general fund?

2. What amount was recorded for other revenues in the general fund?

3. What amount was recorded for capital leases of computers in the general fixed assets account group?

4. What amount was recorded as capital outlay for police vehicles in the general fixed assets account group?

5. What amount was recorded for debt service interest payment in the general long-term debt account group?

6. What was the total amount recorded for functional expenditures in the general fund?

7. What amount was recorded for revenues in the capital projects fund?

8. What amount was recorded as construction-in-progress in the general fixed assets account group?

9. What amount was reported as the unreserved fund balance at year-end in the capital projects fund?

REQUIRED:

FOR ITEMS 10 AND 11, select the required reporting disclosure for Central's defined-benefit pension plan.

Reporting Disclosures

A. Notes to the financial statements
B. Required supplementary information after the notes to the financial statements
C. No required disclosure

10. Schedule of employer contributions

11. Classes of employees covered, such as general employees and public safety employees
(11/98, AR, #4, amended, 6698-6708)

PROBLEM 21-4 (15 to 20 minutes)

Rock County adopted GASB Statement No. 34, but still uses its account groups as before adoption. Rock acquired equipment through a noncancelable lease-purchase agreement dated December 31, 20X1. This agreement requires no down payment and the following minimum lease payments:

December 31	Principal	Interest	Total
20X2	$50,000	$15,000	$65,000
20X3	50,000	10,000	60,000
20X4	50,000	5,000	55,000

FOR ITEMS 1 THROUGH 3, select the best answer from the following list:

A. Other Financing Uses Control
B. Other Financing Sources Control
C. Equipment
D. Expenditures Control—Capital Leases
E. Expenses Control—Capital Leases
F. Fund Balance From Capital Lease Transactions
G. Other Financing Sources Control—Capital Leases
H. Investment in General Fixed Assets—Capital Leases
I. Memorandum Entry Only

1. What account should be debited for $150,000 in the general fund at inception of the lease if the equipment is a general fixed asset and Rock does **not** use a capital projects fund?
(5/90, PII, #1, amended, 1364)

2. What account should be credited for $150,000 in the general fixed assets account group at inception of the lease if the equipment is a general fixed asset?
(5/90, PII, #2, amended, 1365)

3. If the equipment is used in enterprise fund operations and the lease payments are to be financed with enterprise fund revenues, what account should be debited for $150,000 in the enterprise fund at inception of the lease?
(5/90, PII, #5, amended, 1368)

4. What journal entry is required in the general long-term debt account group at inception of the lease if the lease payments are to be financed with general government resources?

	Debit	Credit
A.	Expenditures Control	Other Financing Sources Control
B.	Other Financing Uses Control	Expenditures Control
C.	Amount to be Provided for Lease Payments	Capital Lease Payable
D.	Capital Lease Payable	Amount to Be Provided for Lease Payments

(R/99, AR #21, amended, 6810)

FOR ITEMS 5 AND 6, select the best answer from the following list:

A.	Expenditures Control	$65,000
B.	Expenses Control	$65,000
C.	Amount to Be Provided for Lease Payments	$50,000
	Expenditures Control	15,000
D.	Expenditures Control	$50,000
	Amount to Be Provided for Lease Payments	15,000
E.	Capital Lease Payable	$50,000
	Expenses Control	15,000

5. If the lease payments are required to be made from a debt service fund, what account or accounts should be debited in the debt service fund for the first lease payment of $65,000?
(5/90, PII, #4, amended, 1367)

6. If the equipment is used in internal service fund operations and the lease payments are financed with internal service fund revenues, what account or accounts should be debited in the internal service fund for the first lease payment of $65,000?
(5/90, PII, #6, amended, 1369)

SOLUTION 21-1 MULTIPLE CHOICE ANSWERS

GOVERNMENTAL ENVIRONMENT

1. (a) The GASB sets accounting and financial reporting standards for state and local governments. The FASB sets standards for financial reports published by business and nonprofit enterprises.

2. (a) In the absence of a profit motive, a net income bottom line, or other uniform object performance indicators, governments use fund accounting to demonstrate compliance with restrictions and controls.

3. (d) GASB §1300.102 states, "The governmental fund measurement focus is on determination of financial position and changes in financial position..., rather than on net income determination." GASB §C60.108 states, "In governmental funds, the primary emphasis is on the flow of financial resources...."

4. (d) The GASB believes that interperiod equity is a significant component of accountability and is fundamental to public administration. It therefore needs to be considered when establishing financial reporting objectives. In short, financial reporting should help users assess whether current-year revenues are sufficient to pay for services provided that year and whether future taxpayers will be required to assume burdens for services previously provided (Cod. 100.161).

FINANCIAL REPORTING

5. (d) GASB Codification §2100.108 focuses on the ability of a governmental unit to exercise oversight responsibility over an entity when considering that entity's inclusion in a governmental unit. Oversight responsibility includes "financial interdependency, selection of governing authority, designation of management, ability to significantly influence operations, [and] *accountability for fiscal matters.*"

6. (c) GASB §100.132 states that governmental financial reporting is used in making social and political decisions. Section 100.161 states that because interperiod equity is important, financial reporting should help users assess whether current-year revenues are sufficient to provide current services or whether future taxpayers are assuming the burden of previously provided services.

7. (d) According to GASB No. 1, financial reports should be comparable, which implies that differences between financial reports should be due to substance (actual events) rather than form (accounting policies).

8. (a) Interperiod equity is the idea of using the revenues from one period to pay for the expenditures of that same period and that period only. A balanced budget is a plan for this occurrence. Residual equity transfers are between funds, not between periods.

9. (d) The underlying securities owned with regard to reverse repurchase and fixed coupon reverse repurchase agreements should be reported as "Investments." Related assets and liabilities and interest cost and interest earned should not be netted. Credit risk related to such agreements must be disclosed.

DEFINITIONS

10. (b) Governmental funds use the modified accrual basis of accounting, under which, revenues are recognized when they become measurable and available for use. "Available for use" means that the revenues will be collected within the current period or collected early enough in the next period to be used to pay for expenditures incurred in the current period. The property taxes collected before the end of fiscal year 20X1 or shortly thereafter should be reported as revenues in fiscal year 20X1.

11. (b) Revenues are susceptible to accrual at the time they become measurable and available for use under NCGA Statement 1 modified accrual basis guidelines. Significant amounts received prior to the normal time of collection (i.e. early payment of property taxes) are recorded as *Deferred Revenues* (GASB §1600.116).

12. (a) The *Fund Balance Reserved for Inventory of Supplies* account is an equity balance indicating the presence of fund assets that are not available for expenditure. The account would most likely appear in the general fund because the general fund would be more likely to have a significant amount of supplies on hand at the end of the year and it reports a fund balance. Internal service and nonexpendable trust funds report retained earnings rather than fund balance. Capital projects funds report a fund balance, but it is not likely that they would have significant amounts of supplies on hand at year-end. FYI: Nonexpendable trust funds are used under the pre-GASB 34 reporting model.

13. (c) Governmental funds use the modified accrual basis of accounting, under which revenues

susceptible to accrual (e.g., property taxes) are recognized when they become measurable and available for use. "Available for use" means that the revenues will be collected within the current period or collected early enough in the next period (i.e., within 60 days or so) to be used to pay for expenditures incurred in the current period. For 20X1, Oak should report property tax revenues of $600,000, the sum of the property taxes levied and collected in 20X1 and the expected property tax collections during the first 60 days of 20X2.

FUNDS & FUND ACCOUNTING

14. (a) The modified accrual basis of accounting for a governmental unit recognizes revenues in the period in which they become available and measurable. The modified accrual basis is the appropriate basis of accounting for governmental-type funds. Proprietary and fiduciary funds use the accrual basis of accounting. The accrual basis of accounting recognizes revenues in the period in which they become earned and measurable.

15. (c) The modified accrual basis of accounting for governments recognizes revenues in the period they become measurable and available to cover approved expenditures of the period.

16. (d) Expenditures are recorded when fund liabilities are incurred or assets are expended, except in regard to inventory items, interest on general long-term debt, and prepaids such as insurance. This is due to the emphasis on the flow of financial resources in governmental accounting.

17. (a) The modified accrual basis of accounting for a governmental unit recognizes revenues in the accounting period in which they become available and measurable. The modified accrual basis is the appropriate basis of accounting for governmental-type funds (i.e., general, special revenue, capital projects, debt service, and permanent funds). Proprietary and fiduciary funds use the accrual basis of accounting in all financial statements in the GASB 34 reporting model. The accrual basis of accounting recognizes revenues in the period in which they become earned and measurable.

18. (c) GASB Codification §C60.107 states, "Liabilities for compensated absences should be inventoried at the end of each accounting period and adjusted to current salary costs."

FINANCIAL STATEMENT OVERVIEW

19. (a) The objective of GASB 34 is "to enhance the understandability and usefulness of the general purpose external financial reports of state

and local governments..."; however, GASB 34 reiterates Concepts Statement 1, stating, "accountability is the paramount objective of governmental financial reporting—the objective from which all other financial reporting objectives flow." (¶1, 2)

20. (d) The basic financial statements (BFS) consist of both government-wide and fund financial statements along with the accompanying notes (GASB 34, ¶6). Although it is presented before the BFS, MD&A is classified as required supplementary information, not BFS. The MD&A is a component of the *minimum* reporting requirements for state and local governments. A CAFR includes the BFS.

21. (a) Only business-type activities appear in the statement of cash flows. (The governmental funds pose problems for developing meaningful information for a government-wide statement.) All funds use the economic resources measurement focus and accrual basis of accounting in the government-wide statements.

22. (c) GASB 34 (¶6) states, "The government-wide statements should display information about the reporting government as a whole, except for its fiduciary activities." A pension plan is a fiduciary activity, and thus a pension trust fund is reported in the fund financial statements, but not the government-wide statements. GASB 34 (¶6) states, "These statements display information about major funds individually and non-major funds in the aggregate for governmental and enterprise funds. Fiduciary statements should include financial information for fiduciary funds and similar component units. Each of the three fund categories should be reported using the measurement focus and basis of accounting required for that category."

23. (d) GASB 34 requires that government-wide statements aggregate information for all governmental and business-type activities on the accrual basis of accounting (¶16). A reconciliation to the government-wide statement must appear on the face of the governmental-type fund financial statements or in a separate schedule (¶77).

MD&A

24. (a) GASB 34 (¶8) states, "The basic financial statements should be preceded by MD&A, which is required supplementary information. MD&A should provide an objective and easily readable analysis of the government's financial activities based on currently known facts...."

25. (d) In the MD&A, GASB 34 requires comparisons of current to prior year results, based on government-wide information; a brief discussion of

the basic financial statements, an analysis of the government's overall financial position and results of operations to assist users in assessing whether financial position has improved or deteriorated as a result of annual operations; an analysis of balances and transactions of individual funds; significant variances between original and final budget amounts, and between final budget and actual results; a description of significant capital asset and long-term debt activity; and currently known facts, decisions, or conditions that are expected to have a significant effect on financial position or results of operations. Governments that use the modified approach to report infrastructure assets must also discuss significant changes in the assessed condition of infrastructure assets from previous assessments; how the current condition compares with the established condition level; and any significant differences from the estimated annual amount to maintain or preserve infrastructure assets compared with the actual spending during the current period. (¶9, 11)

GWS

26. (b) GASB 34 (¶14) states, "The focus of the government-side financial statements should be on the primary government...A total column should be presented for the primary government. A total column for the government as a whole may be presented, but is not required."

27. (b) GASB 34 (¶6) states, "The government-wide statements should display information about the reporting government as a whole, except for its fiduciary activities. The statements should include separate columns for the governmental and business type activities of the primary government as well as for its component units." GASB 34 (footnote 4) states, "The term *primary government* includes...blended component units, as defined in Statement 14." GASB 14 states, "The reporting entity's financial statements should present the... primary government (including its blended component units, which are, in substance, part of the primary government) and provide an overview of the discretely presented component units....A primary government is also a special-purpose government (for example, a school district...) that meets all of the following criteria: a. It has a separately elected governing body. b. It is legally separate. c. It is fiscally independent...A special-purpose government is fiscally independent if it has the authority to do all three of the following: a. determine its budget..., b. levy taxes...without approval..., c. issue bonded debt without approval by another government." This school district is a unit that is blended, not discretely presented. Thus, it is not reported in the component

unit column, but rather the governmental activities column.

28. (a) Although internal service funds are proprietary funds, they appear in the government-wide statements as governmental activities in the new reporting model.

29. (a) GASB 34 (¶73) states, "Agency funds should be used to report resources held by the reporting government in a purely custodial capacity (assets equal liabilities). Agency funds typically involve only the receipt, temporary investment, and remittance of fiduciary resources to individuals, private organizations, or other governments." Agency funds generally have neither capital assets nor expenses. Also see explanation 33.

30. (b) The governmental-type funds and internal service funds usually appear in the government activities column in the government-wide financial statements. Enterprise funds generally appear in the business-type activities column in the government-wide financial statements (¶15). Note that GASB 34 (¶62) states, "Internal service fund assets and liability balances that are not eliminated in the statement of net assets should normally be reported in the governmental activities column. Although internal service funds are reported as proprietary funds, the activities accounted for in them ...are usually more governmental than business-type in nature. If enterprise funds are the predominant...participants in an internal service fund, however, the governmental should report that internal service funds' residual assets and liabilities within the business-type activities column in the statement of net assets." Also see explanation 17.

CAPITAL ASSETS

31. (b) Infrastructure assets that are part of a network or a sub-system of a network (eligible infrastructure assets) are not required to be depreciated, if the government: documents that eligible infrastructure assets are preserved approximately at (or above) a condition level established and disclosed by the government; has an up-to-date inventory of eligible infrastructure assets; consistently performs condition assessments of eligible assets at least triannually and summarizes the results using a measurement scale; and annually estimates the amount to preserve the eligible assets at a condition level established and disclosed by the government. (GASB 34, ¶23, 24)

32. (d) Unless held as a collection, works of art, historical treasures, and similar assets should be capitalized at historical cost or fair value at date of

donation. GASB 34 merely encourages capitalization of these assets when held as collections. Collections are held for public exhibition, education, or research in furtherance of public service rather than financial gain; protected, kept unencumbered, cared for, and preserved; and are subject to policies that require sales proceeds be used to acquire collection items. An exhaustible capitalized collection must be depreciated over its estimated useful life. Also see explanations 31, 62, and 63. (¶27, 29)

33. (c) GASB 34 (¶80) states, "General capital assets...are not specifically related to activities reported in proprietary or fiduciary funds. [They]... are associated with, and generally arise from, governmental activities....They should **not** be reported as assets in governmental funds, but should be reported in the governmental activities column in the government-wide statement of net assets." (added emphasis)

34. (a) GASB 34 (¶155) states that governments may use any approach that complies with the intent of GASB 34 (when actual historical cost data is not available) to **estimate the costs of existing** general infrastructure assets. Reporting of non-major networks is encouraged but not required (¶156). GASB 34 (¶158) states, "A government may estimate the historical cost of general infrastructure assets by calculating the current replacement cost of a similar asset and deflating this cost through the use of price-level indexes to the acquisition year (or estimated acquisition year if the actual year is unknown)....Accumulated depreciation would be calculated based on the deflated amount, except for general infrastructure assets reported according to the modified approach." GASB 34 (¶160) states, "Other information may provide sufficient support for establishing initial capitalization...include[ing] bond documents used to obtain financing for construction or acquisition of infrastructure assets, expenditures reported in capital project funds or capital outlays in governmental funds, and engineering documents." GASB 34 (¶161) states, "Governments may use any established depreciation method. Depreciation may be based on the estimated useful life of a class of assets, a network of assets, a subsystem of a network, or individual assets. For estimated useful lives, governments can use (a) general guidelines obtained from professional or industry organizations, (b) information for comparable assets of other governments, or (c) internal information. In determining estimated useful life, a government also should consider an asset's present condition and how long it is expected to meet service demands." GASB 34 (¶163) states, "Governments also may use **composite methods** to calculate depreciation expense. Composite methods refer to depreciating

a grouping of similar assets (for example, all the interstate highways in a state) or dissimilar assets of the same class (for example, all the roads and bridges of a state) using the same depreciation rate."

FUND STATEMENTS

35. (a) The major fund financial statements are presented before the notes to the financial statements, as part of the basic financial statements, not RSI (¶1, 2). GASB 34 (¶8) states, "The basic financial statements should be preceded by MD&A, which is required supplementary information." GASB 34 (¶6) states, "The basic financial statements should include... (1) the government-wide statements [that] ...display information about the reporting government as a whole, except for its fiduciary activities... (2) Fund financial statements for the primary government's governmental, proprietary, and fiduciary funds should be presented after the government-wide statements... (3) Notes to the financial statements. Except for MD&A, required supplementary information, including the required budgetary comparison information, should be presented immediately following the notes to the financial statements."

36. (d) Enterprise funds generally report net assets. Capital projects and special revenue funds are governmental-type funds, and thus report a fund balance. Expendable trust funds (under the outgoing reporting model) use fund balance accounts also.

37. (a) Governmental-type funds pose problems for developing a meaningful government-wide cash flows statement. Only funds for business-type activities are required in the statement of cash flows (GASB 34, ¶16, 78, 91, 105).

38. (b) A cash flows statement includes receipts and payments resulting only from the proprietary funds' activities (GASB 34, ¶78, 105, 106). Baker accounts for city hall construction in its capital projects fund, a governmental-type fund. The payments in lieu of property taxes are from an operating activity of an enterprise fund.

STATEMENT OF CASH FLOWS

39. (d) For the statement of cash flows, investing activity cash inflows include interest and dividends received as returns on loans (except program loans), debt of other entities, equity securities, and cash management or investment pools.

40. (c) For purposes of preparing a statement of cash flows, cash equivalents are short-term, highly liquid investments that are both (1) readily convertible into known amounts of cash and (2) so near their maturity that they present insignificant risk

of changes in value because of changes in interest rates. Generally, only investments with original maturities to the reporting entity of three months or less qualify as cash equivalents. Both a 3-month bill and a 3-year note purchased three months from maturity qualify as cash equivalents. However, a note purchased three years ago does not become a cash equivalent when its remaining maturity is three months. Therefore, the amount of the investments that Hill should report as cash and cash equivalents at 6/30/X4 is the sum of the 3-month bill and the 3-year note purchased less than three months from maturity. The note with an original maturity to Hill of five years (i.e., 10/1/X0 to 9/30/X5) will never be reported as a cash equivalent by Hill.

OTHER RSI

41. (b) GASB 34 (¶130, 131) states "Budgetary comparison schedules should be presented as RSI for the general fund and for each major special revenue fund that has a legally adopted annual budget....The budgetary comparison schedule should present both (a) the original and (b) the final...as well as (c) actual inflows, outflows, and balances, **stated on the government's budgetary basis**....Governments may present the budgetary comparison schedule using the same format, terminology, and classifications as the budget document, or using the format, terminology, and classifications in a statement of revenues, expenditures, and changes in fund balances. Regardless of the format used, the schedule should be accompanied by information (either in a separate schedule or in notes to RSI) that reconciles budgetary information to GAAP information...." This reconciliation provides the link from the budgetary comparisons to the GAAP operating statements in the basic financial statements.

42. (b) The budgetary comparison schedule includes the original and final budgets as well as actual inflows, outflows, and balances, stated on the government's budgetary basis of accounting, with a reconciliation between the budgetary and GAAP information (GASB 34, ¶130). The schedule may have the same format as the budget documents or the statement of revenues, expenditures, and changes in fund balances (¶131). A column reporting the variances between the final budget and actual amounts is encouraged, but not required (¶131).

CAPITAL LEASES

43. (c) The acquisition of a general fixed asset is an expenditure, with the asset recorded in the GFAAG. A capital lease is an other financing source, recorded in the GLTDAG.

MSWLF

44. (c) GASB No. 18 establishes accounting standards for MSWLF costs. A portion of the estimated total current costs must be recognized as an expense and as a liability in each period during which the MSWLF accepts solid waste. The estimated total current costs of MSWLF closure and postclosure care should include those costs which result in disbursements near, or after, the date that the MSWLF stops accepting solid waste and during the postclosure period, including the cost of a final cover and monitoring equipment.

45. (d) A MSWLF accounted for in a governmental-type fund should recognize expenditures and fund liabilities on the modified accrual basis of accounting, with the long-term capital assets and liabilities reported in the government-wide financial statements, but not the governmental funds. GASB No. 18, ¶11, states, "Equipment, facilities, services, and final cover included in the estimated total current cost of closure and postclosure care should be reported as a reduction of the reported liability for closure and postclosure care when they are acquired." If the entity uses a GLTDAG, the following entry would be made in the GLTDAG:

DR:	MSWLF Payable	XX
CR:	Amount to Be Provided for	
	Payment of MSWLF Obligation	XX

46. (d) Proprietary funds may account for landfills. Liabilities are recognized in a proprietary fund when a proprietary fund accounts for the landfill. Expense recognition should be finished when the post-closure period begins. Capital assets should be fully depreciated by the date the MSWLF stops accepting solid waste.

LIMITED SCOPE TOPICS

47. (c) Governmental employers identify in the notes to the financial statements the types of employees covered under the defined contribution pension plan and the employer's and employees' obligations to contribute to the fund (GASB Cod. P20.137).

48. (d) Comparability, consistency, and timeliness in SEA reporting are readily accomplished for a single governmental entity. Ensuring that reported performance yardsticks measure goals and desired effects is more complex.

OUTGOING REPORTING MODEL FUNDS

49. (d) The special revenue fund is a governmental-type fund. Expendable trust fund accounting

and reporting parallels that of governmental-type funds (modified accrual basis of accounting). Non-expendable trust funds and pension trust funds are similar to proprietary funds (internal service and enterprise funds) and are accounted for on the accrual basis.

50. (a) **P**ension trust, **I**nternal service, **N**on-expendable trust, and **E**nterprise funds use the accrual basis of accounting under the outgoing model. Governmental-type funds and expendable trust funds all use the modified accrual basis of accounting.

OUTGOING REPORTING MODEL STATEMENTS

51. (b) There are five financial statements plus notes in the general purpose financial statements (GPFS). Combining statements are more detailed than combined statements and are required for a comprehensive annual financial report (CAFR), but not for GPFS presented separately.

52. (a) GASB Codification §2400.104 states that the Statement of Revenues, Expenditures, and Changes in Fund Balances—Budget and Actual should be prepared on the same basis as the budget is adopted. The reconciliation with GAAP-based operating data is disclosed in the notes.

GASB 34 TRANSITION

53. (b) The GASB 34 reporting model uses the following funds: governmental-type funds (general

funds, special revenue funds, capital project funds, debt service funds, and permanent funds); proprietary funds (enterprise and internal service funds); and fiduciary funds (pension trust funds, investment trust funds, private-purpose trust funds, and agency funds). Expendable and nonexpendable trust funds are not used by the new reporting model.

54. (d) Nonexpendable trust funds formerly reported resources with nonexpendable principal. Permanent funds report resources that are legally restated to the extent that income, but not principal, may be used for the benefit of the reporting government or its citizenry (GASB 34, ¶64). (The permanent fund is the only governmental-type fund with a principal preservation implication.) Private-purpose trust funds account for trust arrangements under which principal and income benefit individuals, private organizations, or other governments (¶63). Resources formerly in a nonexpendable trust fund have a principal preservation attribute that is inappropriate for inclusion in a special revenue fund. Special revenue funds most likely are appropriate for resources formerly in expendable trust funds. Also see explanation 53.

55. (c) The long-term debt incurred by a government under a capital lease should be reported in the governmental activities column of the government-wide statements, but not in any of the fund statements. The GASB 34 reporting model specifies the use of neither the general long-term debt account group nor the general fixed asset account group.

SOLUTION 21-2 ADDITIONAL MULTIPLE CHOICE ANSWERS

GOVERNMENTAL ENVIRONMENT

56. (c) The general and capital project funds are governmental-type funds. All governmental-type funds have the fund flow measurement focus. GASB Codification §1300.102 places the measurement focus of both these funds on "determination of financial position and changes in financial position, rather than on net income determination."

57. (c) Fund accounting is used when there are legal separations between sources and uses of funds. Fund accounting may be used to account for assets aside from cash and cash equivalents. Combined or combining financial statements may be used with or without fund accounting. The resources may be physically in the same account or location.

58. (b) Imposed nonexchange revenues are assessments on non-governmental entities, and include property taxes and fines or forfeitures.

FINANCIAL STATEMENTS

59. (b) According to GASB No. 14, component units should be presented discretely unless either (a) the components unit's governing body is substantively the same as the governing body of the primary government, or (b) the component unit provides services almost entirely to the primary government, or almost exclusively benefits the primary government although it does not provide services directly to it.

60. (b) According to GASB No. 14, component units should be presented discretely unless either (a) the components unit's governing body is substantively the same as the governing body of the primary government, or (b) the component unit provides services almost entirely to the primary government, or almost exclusively benefits the primary government although it does not provide services directly to it.

61. (c) A statement of cash flows is required for *all* proprietary funds, including public benefit corporations and governmental utilities.

62. (d) GASB 34 requires all governments to report all current fixed assets and new capital assets. Capital assets include assets formerly listed in the general fixed asset account group (land, buildings, and equipment) and infrastructure assets. The retroactive infrastructure asset reporting requirements are required for the largest two categories of governments and optional for small governments (annual revenues under $10 million). GASB 34 (¶149) states, "If determining the actual historical cost of general infrastructure assets is not practical because of inadequate records, governments should report the estimated historical cost for major general infrastructure assets that were acquired or significantly reconstructed, or that received significant improvements, in fiscal years ending after June 30, 1980." Capital assets should be depreciated over their estimated useful lives unless they are either inexhaustible or are eligible infrastructure assets reported using the modified approach (¶21); however, the modified approach (condition assessment) is not one of the answer options.

63. (d) GASB 34 requires all governments to report all new capital assets at historical cost (¶18). Capital assets include assets formerly listed in the general fixed asset account group (land, buildings, equipment) and infrastructure assets (¶19). Capital assets should be depreciated over their estimated useful lives unless they are either inexhaustible or are eligible infrastructure assets reported using the modified approach (¶21). The retroactive infrastructure reporting requirements are optional for small governments (¶148). Also see explanation 17.

64. (c) For purposes of preparing a statement of cash flows, cash equivalents are short-term, highly liquid investments that are both (1) readily convertible into known amounts of cash and (2) so near their maturity that they present insignificant risk of changes in value because of changes in interest rates. Generally, only investments with original maturities to the entity holding the investment of three months or less qualify under as cash equivalents. Examples of items that the GASB considers to be cash equivalents are Treasury bills, commercial paper, certificates of deposit, money market funds, and cash management pools. Therefore, both the 2-month Treasury bill and the 3-month certificate of deposit should be presented as a cash equivalent by the governmental unit.

65. (a) The government-wide statements, which include the statement of activities, are designed to provide operational accountability by showing an economic long-term view of a government's ability to provide services. Operational accountability includes the periodic economic cost of the services provided.

OUTGOING REPORTING MODEL

66. (d) The appropriate method of accounting for governmental fund budgets is the modified accrual basis, recommended by GASB.

67. (d) Capital projects funds are designed only for construction in progress and have a limited life encompassing the construction period. Depreciation is not recorded during construction.

68. (d) Both the general fund and the debt service fund use the modified accrual basis of accounting. The modified accrual basis is the appropriate basis of accounting for governmental funds, expendable trust funds, and agency funds. **P**ension trust funds, **I**nternal service funds, **N**onexpendable trust funds, and **E**nterprise funds all use the accrual basis of accounting.

69. (c) The basic financial statements include both the government-wide statements and the fund statements, as well as the notes, but not the statistical section.

70. (c) GASB 14 states, "The reporting entity's financial statements should present the...primary government (including its blended component units, which are, in substance, part of the primary government) and provide an overview of the discretely presented component units....A primary government is also a special-purpose government (for example, a school district...) that meets all of the following criteria: a. It has a separately elected governing body. b. It is legally separate. c. It is fiscally independent...A special-purpose government is fiscally independent if it has the authority to do all three of the following: a. Determine its budget..., b. Levy taxes...without approval..., c. Issue bonded debt without approval by another government."

71. (c) Where a governmental unit has more than one fund of a given type (e.g., five Special Revenue Funds), combining statements for all funds of that type should be presented in columnar format. The total columns of these combining statements should agree with the amounts reported in the combined statements. Thus, total columns are required for combining statements. The combined statements present the data for all funds and account groups in a columnar format—the data in each column being the total data for all funds (or account groups) of that type as reported in the total columns of the combining

statements. Although commonly shown, the reporting of a "memorandum only" total column is optional in combined financial statements.

72. (b) The Statement of Cash Flows for a governmental entity only includes receipts and payments resulting from the activities of proprietary and non-expendable trust funds. City hall construction would not be handled in these funds. The payments in lieu of property taxes made by a city utility is from an operating activity of an enterprise fund.

73. (a) The debt incurred by a governmental unit under a capital lease should be recorded in the General Long-Term Debt Account Group (GLTDAG) at the inception of the lease at the present value of the minimum lease payments. The following entry would be made to record the lease in the GLTDAG:

DR: Amount to Be Provided for
          Capital Lease   XX
CR: Capital Lease Payable   XX

Debt service funds account for the accumulation of resources for, and the payment of, general long-term debt principal and interest. Debt service funds do not account for any long-term debt themselves; rather they maintain resources that are then used to meet "general government" obligations as they become due. The unmatured general obligation debt is not recorded as a liability of the general fund but in the GLTDAG. The only long-term debt included in the general fund is that which has matured and is payable from the current resources of the general fund. The lease liability should be reported in the GLTDAG.

74. (a) The following entry would be made in the GFAAG:

DR: Equipment   XX
CR: Investment in General
          Fixed Assets—Capital Leases   XX

The following entry would be made in the GLTDAG:

DR: Amount to Be Provided for
          Payment of Capital Lease   XX
CR: Capital Lease Payable   XX

PERFORMANCE BY SUBTOPICS

Each category below parallels a subtopic covered in Chapter 21. Record the number and percentage of questions you correctly answered in each subtopic area.

Governmental Environment

Question	# Correct √
1	
2	
3	
4	
# Questions	4
# Correct	
% Correct	

Financial Reporting

Question	# Correct √
5	
6	
7	
8	
9	
# Questions	5
# Correct	
% Correct	

Definitions

Question	# Correct √
10	
11	
12	
13	
# Questions	4
# Correct	
% Correct	

Funds & Fund Accounting

Question	# Correct √
14	
15	
16	
17	
18	
# Questions	5
# Correct	
% Correct	

Financial Statement Overview

Question	# Correct √
19	
20	
21	
22	
23	
# Questions	5
# Correct	
% Correct	

MD&A

Question	# Correct √
24	
25	
# Questions	2
# Correct	
% Correct	

GWS

Question	# Correct √
26	
27	
28	
29	
30	
# Questions	5
# Correct	
% Correct	

Capital Assets

Question	# Correct √
31	
32	
33	
34	
# Questions	4
# Correct	
% Correct	

Fund Statements

Question	# Correct √
35	
36	
37	
38	
# Questions	4
# Correct	
% Correct	

Statement of Cash Flows

Question	# Correct √
39	
40	
# Questions	2
# Correct	
% Correct	

Other RSI

Question	# Correct √
41	
42	
# Questions	2
# Correct	
% Correct	

Capital Leases

Question	# Correct √
43	
# Questions	1
# Correct	
% Correct	

MSWLF

Question	# Correct √
44	
45	
46	
# Questions	3
# Correct	
% Correct	

Limited Scope Topics		Outgoing Reporting Model Funds		Outgoing Reporting Model Statements		GASB 34 Transition	
Question	# Correct √	Question	# Correct √	Question	# Correct √	Question	# Correct √
47		49		51		53	
48		50		52		54	
# Questions	2	# Questions	2	# Questions	2	55	
						# Questions	3
# Correct		# Correct		# Correct		# Correct	
% Correct		% Correct		% Correct		% Correct	

OTHER OBJECTIVE FORMAT QUESTION SOLUTIONS

SOLUTION 21-3 REVENUES, ASSETS & PENSIONS

1. **P** The current year property tax revenues include those collections of taxes due during the current year that are expect to be collected within about 60 days of year end, as well as the current year taxes actually collected. The prior year taxes collected in the current year as expected were already included in the prior year revenues and are not recorded as revenues again. ($630,0000 + $70,000 = $700,000)

2. **H** Whereas unrestricted grants are recognized immediately as revenue, if available, restricted grants must be expended for the specific purposes to be considered earned. ($50,000 + $40,000 + $80,000 = $170,000)

3. **C** The liability incurred under a capital lease is recorded in the GLTDAG at the present value of the minimum lease payments.

4. **A** The GFAAG doesn't record capital outlay. The GFAAG is only a list of the general fixed assets.

5. **A** Interest payments are not recorded in the GLTDAG. The GLTDAG is only a list of (the principal of) unmatured general long-term debt.

6. **R** $160,000 + $100,000 + $350,000 + $150,000 = $760,000

7. **G** The $150,000 state grant is the capital project fund's only revenue. Bond issue proceeds are an other financing source.

8. **M** The recorded expenditures of $500,000 are transferred to the GFAAG at the close of the year. The outstanding encumbrances represent work yet to be done. The $30,000 of unpaid invoices is included in recorded expenditures; the credit merely was made to vouchers payable, not cash.

9. **K** $110,000 + $150,000 + $610,000 – $500,000 – $25,000 = $345,000

10. **B** GASB 25 requires RSI to include two schedules of historical trend information for defined-benefit pension plans for a minimum of six years: the schedules of funding progress and of employer contributions.

11. **A** GASB 25 requires notes to the financial statements to include a plan description, which includes the type of plan; the number and type of employees covered by the plan, including their plan status; a description of plan provisions; and the authority under which benefits are provided or may be amended.

SOLUTION 21-4 CAPITAL LEASE OBLIGATIONS

1. **D** The noncancelable lease-purchase agreement should be recorded in the general fund as an expenditure and an "other financing source" at the lesser of (1) the present value of the minimum lease payments (i.e., $150,000) or (2) the fair value of the leased property (not given in this problem). The following entry would be made to record the lease in the general fund:

Expenditures Control—Capital Leases   150,000
   Other Financing
     Sources—Capital Leases   150,000

2. **H** General fixed assets acquired by a governmental unit under a lease-purchase agreement should be recorded in the general fixed assets account group (GFAAG) at the inception of the lease at the lesser of (1) the present value of the minimum lease payments or (2) the fair value of the leased property. The following entry would be made to record the lease in the GFAAG:

Equipment   150,000
   Investment in General
     Fixed Assets—Capital Leases   150,000

3. **C** Because the enterprise fund is a proprietary fund, it records assets acquired and liabilities incurred in the same manner as commercial business enterprises. Thus, fixed assets used in fund operations are recorded in the accounts of the

enterprise fund. The following entry would be made in the enterprise fund to record the asset acquired and the liability incurred under the lease-purchase agreement at the inception of the lease:

Equipment	150,000	
Capital Lease Payable		150,000

4. C The debt incurred by a governmental unit under a lease-purchase agreement is recorded in the general long-term debt account group (GLTDAG) at the inception of the lease at the present value of the minimum lease payments. Account groups do not have expenditures or other financing uses or sources. The GLTDAG accounting equation is *Amount Available in DSF for GLTD Principal Retirement* plus *Amount to be Provided in Future Years for GLTD Principal Retirement* equals *GLTD Payable*. The following entry would be made to record the lease in the GLTDAG:

Amount to Be Provided for Lease Payments	150,000	
Capital Lease Payable		150,000

5. A Commonly, governmental units use a debt service fund to record capital lease payments because the annual payments are merely installments of general government long-term debt. Part of each payment is interest at a constant rate on the unpaid balance of the lease obligation, and part is payment on the principal. The following entry would be made in the debt service fund to record the first lease payment:

Expenditures Control	65,000	
Cash		65,000

Although the lease payment consists of a payment of interest and a $50,000 payment on principal, expenditures control is debited for the full amount of the lease payment. Only the detail records in the debt service fund would show how much of the expenditure was for interest and how much was for principal.

6. E Because the internal service fund is a proprietary fund, it records assets, liabilities, revenues, and expenses in the same manner as commercial business enterprises. The lease-purchase agreement meets the criteria of a capital lease under SFAS 13, *Accounting for Leases*; therefore, the lease payment is comprised of (1) interest expense and (2) a reduction of the principal. The following entry would be made in the internal service fund to record the lease payment:

Capital Lease Payable	50,000	
Expenses Control—Interest Expense	15,000	
Cash		65,000

VIDEOTAPE CROSS REFERENCE

The videotapes are designed to supplement all of our study packages. They contain concise, informative lectures, as well as CPA exam tips, tricks, and techniques to help you learn the material needed to pass the exam. The **HotSpots**™ videotapes concentrate on particular topics. Use them to study the areas that are most troubling for you. Each one of the **Intensive** video programs covers one of the four exam sections. The **Intensive** videotapes are designed for final, intensive review, after you already have done considerable work. Alternatively, the **Intensive** videotapes may be used as both a preview and a final review. Please see the information in the **Getting Started** section of this volume for a discussion on integrating videos into your study plan. This information is accurate as we go to press, but it is subject to change without notice.

Video Title	Text Chapters	Approx. Time
HotSpots™ Cash, Receivables & Marketable Securities	2	2:30
HotSpots™ Inventory, Fixed Assets & Intangible Assets	3, 4, 5	2:45
HotSpots™ Bonds & Other Liabilities	6, 7	4:00
HotSpots™ Leases & Pensions	8, 9	2:50
HotSpots™ Owners' Equity & Miscellaneous Topics	10, 15 - 18	2:20
HotSpots™ Revenue Recognition & Income Statement Presentation	11, 12	3:00
HotSpots™ FASB 109: Accounting for Income Taxes	13	2:00
HotSpots™ FASB 95: Statement of Cash Flows	14	2:00
HotSpots™ Consolidations	19, 20	5:00
HotSpots™ Governmental & Nonprofit Accounting	21 - 23	5:15
HotSpots™ Cost & Managerial Accounting	24 - 26	3:20
HotSpots™ Gross Income, Tax Liabilities & Credits	27, 29	2:45
HotSpots™ Individual Taxation	27	3:00
HotSpots™ Property Taxation	28	2:30
HotSpots™ Corporate Taxation	29	3:20
HotSpots™ Partnerships & Other Tax Topics	30	3:05
HotSpots™ Audit Standards & Planning	31, 32	2:45
HotSpots™ Internal Control	33, 34	2:10
HotSpots™ Audit Evidence	35, 36	2:25
HotSpots™ EDP Auditing & Statistical Sampling	37, 38	2:50
HotSpots™ Standard Audit Reports	39	2:50
HotSpots™ Other Reports, Reviews & Compilations	40, 41	1:50
HotSpots™ Contracts	44	2:35
HotSpots™ Sales	45	2:00
HotSpots™ Commercial Paper & Documents of Title	46	2:00
HotSpots™ Secured Transactions	47	1:10
HotSpots™ Bankruptcy & Suretyship	48, 49	1:30
HotSpots™ Business Organizations	50 - 53	2:15
HotSpots™ Government Regulation of Business	54, 55	1:20
HotSpots™ Real Property, Personal Property & Insurance	56, 57	1:45
HotSpots™ Professional & Legal Responsibilities	42, 43	1:30

Intensive Video Review	FARE	ARE	AUD	BLPR	Total
Text Chapters	1 - 20	21 - 30	31 - 41	42 - 57	
Approximate Time	6:00	6:00	3:30	3:30	19:00

CHAPTER 22

GOVERNMENTAL FUNDS & TRANSACTIONS

EXAM COVERAGE: The governmental and nonprofit accounting portion of the ARE section of the CPA exam is designated by the examiners to be 30 percent of the section's point value. Exam coverage of the topics in this chapter is 15 to 20 percent of the ARE section. Historically material covered in Chapter 21 and Chapter 22 combined has repeatedly covered 23 to 27 percent of the ARE section of the exam. More information about the point value of various topics is included in the **Practical Advice** section of this volume.

CHAPTER 22

GOVERNMENTAL FUNDS & TRANSACTIONS

I. GOVERNMENTAL-TYPE FUNDS

A. OVERVIEW

The governmental funds and nonfund account groups are used to account for the general government activities of a state or local government. The fund flow accounting for governmental funds is one of the **truly unique aspects** of state and municipal accounting and its **most heavily tested** aspect on CPA exams. There are three types of journal entries: those to record (and close) the budget, those to record (and close) encumbrances, and those to record (and close) actual activity.

1. **BUDGET** Budgetary accounting is used by governmental-type funds.

   a. **ESTABLISH** The following entry is typical of the general fund's entry to record the budget at the beginning of the year.

Estimated Revenues Control	700	
Estimated Other Financing Sources	200	
Budgetary Fund Balance (DR or CR)		75
Estimated Other Financing Uses		300
Appropriations		525

   b. **CLOSE** The following entry is typical of the general fund's entry to close the budget at the end of the year. (Note the same dollar amounts are used as the recording entry.)

Estimated Other Financing Uses	300	
Appropriations	525	
Budgetary Fund Balance (CR or DR)	75	
Estimated Revenues Control		700
Estimated Other Financing Sources		200

   c. **TRANSFERS** Note that GASB §1700 states, "The appropriations constitute maximum expenditure authorization during the fiscal year." Thus estimated transfers (other financing sources and uses) are merely a specific kind of appropriation. Transfers (either budgeted or actual) are not netted.

2. **ENCUMBRANCES** Encumbrance accounting records obligations to spend (purchase orders) to prevent overspending of appropriations. Encumbrances are not liabilities.

   a. An encumbrance entry is made when an item is ordered in the amount of the estimated cost. Many amounts are controlled by another means and are frequently not encumbered. For example, salaries and wages are set by contract and controlled by established payroll procedures and are not encumbered.

   b. The reverse entry is made for the same dollar amount when the invoice arrives.

   c. Outstanding encumbrances at year end are carried forward as a reserve of fund balance with a corresponding deduction of unreserved fund balance.

   d. The spending of a prior year's outstanding encumbrances is a use of reserved fund balance, not a current year expenditure.

3. **ACTUAL ACTIVITY** The emphasis on reporting activity is on cash flow, as opposed to profit and loss. The matching principle of accrual accounting is not applicable. NCGA Statement 1 offers the following **modified** accrual basis guidelines:

a. **REVENUES** Revenues are recorded as received in cash except for revenues susceptible to accrual and revenues of a material amount that have not been received at the normal time of receipt. Revenues are considered susceptible to accrual at the time they become **measurable** and **available** for use.

(1) **BILLED** Available means collected or collectible within the current period or early enough in the next period (e.g., within 60 days or so) to be used to pay for expenditures incurred in the current period (for example, property taxes). If revenue-related assets (e.g., taxes receivable) are **not** available, a *Deferred Revenue* account should be credited initially; when the assets become available, the *Deferred Revenue* account is debited and *Revenue* is credited.

(2) **RECEIVED** GASB No. 22, *Accounting for Taxpayer-Assessed Tax Revenues in Governmental Funds*, guides revenue recognition. All governmental entities that report using governmental funds should recognize revenues from taxpayer-assessed taxes in the accounting period in which they become susceptible to accrual. In other words, these revenues are recognized when they become both **measurable** and **available** to finance expenditures of the fiscal period.

(a) Personalty and realty property taxes.

(b) Taxpayer-assessed sales and income taxes.

(c) Sales taxes **collected** and held by one government agency for another at year-end should be accrued if they are remitted in time to be used as a resource for payment of obligations incurred during the preceding year. Remitted in time means collected during the year or within about 60 days after year-end.

(3) **RESTRICTED** Whereas *unrestricted* grants should be recognized immediately as revenue of governmental funds, if available, *restricted* grants should not be recognized as revenue until they are earned. A restricted grant must be expended for the specific purposes to be considered earned. Deferred grant revenue is recorded initially, and the grant revenue is recognized only when qualifying expenditures are incurred.

(4) **EXCEPTION** Significant amounts received before the normal collection time (i.e., early property tax payments) are recorded as deferred revenues.

b. **EXPENDITURES** Expenditures (not expenses) are recorded when fund liabilities are incurred or assets are expended, except

(1) Inventory items may be recorded as expenditures either (a) at the time of purchase or (b) at the time the items are used.

(2) Expenditures normally are **not** allocated between years by the recording of prepaids (e.g., a two-year insurance policy). Prepaid **expenses** may be recorded as expenditures or may be allocated to periods (in funds using accrual accounting).

(3) Interest on **general** long-term debt, usually accounted for in debt service funds, normally are recorded as an expenditure on its due date rather than being accrued prior to its due date.

   c.   **OTHER FINANCING SOURCES/USES** Transfers in/out or to/from are not netted. Transfers are reported after revenues and expenditures, as they affect operating results.

   d.   **ASSETS** Assets are treated as (capital outlay) expenditures and are not capitalized within the fund. Capital assets are not carried in governmental-type funds, but are listed in the general fixed asset account group (GFAAG). Fixed assets are rarely expected to contribute to revenues. Depreciation expense is **not** recorded in the governmental-type funds. Under the outgoing reporting model, infrastructure assets need not be listed in the GFAAG.

   e.   **DEBT** Long-term debts are not carried in governmental-type funds, but are listed in the general long-term debt account group (GLTDAG). Money is repaid through the debt service fund.

B.   **GENERAL FUND**
This primary governmental fund is used to account for most routine operations of the governmental entity. All general government resources that are not required to be accounted for in another fund are accounted for in the general fund. General fund revenues primarily consist of taxes (property, sales, income, and excise), licenses, fines, and interest. General fund expenditures are budgeted (and appropriated for) by the legislative body.

1.   **PURPOSE** The general fund finances other funds through capital contributions and operating subsidies. An example is found in the section of the chapter on interfund transactions.

2.   **OPERATION** The general fund [C GRIPES] uses modified accrual accounting. Budgetary, encumbrance, and actual activity entries usually appear in the general fund.

EXHIBIT 1 ♦ SAMPLE GENERAL FUND ENTRIES

1. To record the budget:

Estimated Revenues Control	1,000	
Estimated Other Financing Sources	100	
Appropriations Control		625
Appropriations: Estimated Other Financing Uses		425
Budgetary Fund Balance [difference—the **planned** change in		
fund balance during year. May be Dr. or Cr.]		50

NOTE: Estimated operating transfers are recorded separately as *Estimated Other Financing Sources (Uses)*; they are not included with *Estimated Revenues* or *Appropriations*.

NOTE: Some governments use the *Fund Balance* account for both actual and budgetary amounts. Their budgetary entry causes the *Fund Balance* account to be carried during the year at its planned end-of-year balance. Then, the year-end closing entries adjust the *Fund Balance* account from its planned year-end balance to its actual year-end balance. This combination of actual and budget amounts is theoretically less sound than the approach illustrated here.

2. To record actual revenues:

Cash or Receivables	600	
Allowance for Uncollectible Receivables		30
Revenues Control		570

NOTE: Governmental fund revenues are recorded net of estimated bad debts. That is, estimated uncollectible accounts are recorded as direct reductions from revenues rather than as expenditures. If all the revenues are collected in cash, there would not be a credit to the allowance account.

(continued on next page)

3. To record an encumbrance, in the form of a purchase order issued or contract commitment, for two shipments (one for $120, and one for $10 close to year end):

Encumbrances Control [expected cost]	130	
Reserve for Encumbrances		130

NOTE: Alternatively, the credited account may be titled *Budgetary Fund Balance Reserved for Encumbrances*.

4. To record expenditures (for slightly more than the purchase order total) upon receipt of an invoice for the first shipment:

Reserve for Encumbrances [reverse entry 3.]	120	
Encumbrances Control		120
Expenditures Control [actual cost]	125	
Vouchers Payable		125

5. To record unencumbered expenditures incurred:

Expenditures Control - Salaries	490	
Vouchers Payable		490

6. To record increase in supplies inventory on hand at year-end (supplies purchased were previously recorded as expenditures):

Supplies Inventory	20	
Fund Balance Reserved for Supplies Inventory [indicates that a portion of fund balance is not available]		20

NOTE: This customary entry compounds these two more proper entries:

a.
Supplies Inventory	20	
Fund Balance		20

b.
Fund Balance	20	
Fund Balance Reserved for Supplies Inventory		20

The entry(ies) would be reversed had the supplies inventory decreased. The increase (decrease) in supplies inventory is reported as an *Other Financing Source (Use)* in the governmental fund operating statement.

7. To record receipt of a grant from the state government and a bond issue:

Cash (or Receivable)	350	
Grant Revenues		100
Other Financing Sources: Bond Proceeds		250

8. To record payment of a grant to the school district:

Other Financing Uses	245	
Cash (or Payable)		245

(continued on next page)

9. To record closing entries at year-end:

Appropriations Control [budgeted]	625	
Appropriations: Estimated Other Financing Uses [budgeted]	425	
Budgetary Fund Balance [difference—debit or credit]	50	
Estimated Revenues Control [budgeted]		1,000
Estimated Other Financing Sources [budgeted]		100
Revenues Control [actual]	670	
Other Financing Sources [actual]	250	
Expenditures Control [actual]		615
Other Financing Uses [actual]		245
Fund Balance [difference—debit or credit]		60
Fund Balance	10	
Encumbrances Control [amount outstanding at year-end]		10

The third closing entry reduces the (*Unreserved*) *Fund Balance* account by the amount of the encumbrances outstanding and causes the *Reserve for Encumbrances* account—which is offset by the *Encumbrances* account during the year-to become a true fund balance reserve account at year-end. Alternatively, a compound closing entry may be made. The amount is the $10 shipment that has not been received ($130 – $120 = $10).

NOTE: Since closing the budgetary accounts (i.e., *Estimated Revenues, Appropriations, Estimated Other Financing Sources*, and *Estimated Other Financing Uses*) simply reverses the entry to record the budget, their closing has no effect on fund balance. It is the closing of the activity accounts (i.e., *Revenues, Other Financing Sources, Expenditures, Encumbrances*, and *Other Financing Uses*) that increases or decreases the fund balance.

10. To record encumbrance reversing entry—beginning of next year:

Encumbrances Control	10	
Fund Balance		10

NOTE: This entry reverses the encumbrance closing entry, restoring the *Encumbrances* and *Reserve for Encumbrances* accounts to their usual off-setting relationship.

NOTE: None of the exhibits in this chapter are related to the other exhibits.

C. SPECIAL REVENUE FUNDS

Used to account for revenues that are externally restricted or designated by the legislative body for specific general government purposes other than capital projects.

EXHIBIT 2 ♦ SAMPLE SPECIAL REVENUE FUND ENTRIES

1. To record endowment earnings that are restricted for library purposes:

Cash (or Due From Permanent Fund)	45	
Other Financing Sources: Library Permanent Fund		45

2. To record expenditures for library purposes:

Expenditures—Library Books	40	
Cash or Payable		40

3. To close the accounts at year-end:

Other Financing Sources: Library Permanent Fund	45	
Expenditures—Library Books		40
Fund Balance		5

1. **USE** The deciding factor for use of this fund as opposed to an enterprise fund is intent. If the intent is to recover less than 50 percent of expenses from user fees, then the activity is handled in a special revenue fund. The deciding factor for use of this fund as opposed to a private-purpose trust fund are the beneficiaries. If the beneficiaries are citizens or the reporting entity, then the activity is handled in a special revenue fund. If the beneficiaries are individuals, private organizations, or other governments, then the activity is handled in a private-purpose trust fund.

EXHIBIT 3 ♦ EXAMPLES OF SPECIAL REVENUES AND CORRESPONDING USES

Source	Use
Hotel bed tax	Operate tourist center
Gasoline tax	Maintain streets
Parking fines	Operate traffic court
Library fines	Operate library
Donations	Purchase library books
Endowment income	Maintain public cemetery
State Juvenile Rehabilitation Grant	Operate youth programs

2. **OPERATION** The special revenue fund uses modified accrual accounting. Budgetary, encumbrance, and actual activity entries usually appear in special revenue funds. Accounting practices for special revenue funds [C GRIPES] parallel those for the general fund, so the only sample entries presented are related to a permanent fund endowment.

D. CAPITAL PROJECTS FUND

Used to account for the acquisition and use of financial resources to construct or otherwise acquire major long-lived general government capital facilities. Does not include assets used by trusts or proprietary funds. Most capital project(s) fund [C GRIPES] entries are similar to those illustrated earlier for the general fund.

1. **USE** Each capital project fund has a life limited to the construction period of the project. Alternatively, several overlapping capital projects may be accounted for in one capital projects fund, which exists as long as any one project is under construction. The acquisition of mobile property (for example, a car) need not be accounted for in a capital projects fund unless required by law or contractual agreement.

2. **OPERATION** Capital project(s) funds use modified accrual accounting. Encumbrance and actual activity entries usually appear in the capital projects fund. Budget entries are optional, and are usually used when accounting for more than one project in the same fund. Budget and encumbrance entries are similar to those in the general fund.

3. **FINANCIAL RESOURCES** Typically are provided by bond issue proceeds, other funds, and interest earnings.

   a. Interfund transfers are classified as operating transfers (other financing sources) or residual equity transfers, as appropriate.

   b. Bond issue proceeds are classified as other financing sources. Premiums and discounts are recorded as other financing sources and uses, respectively. Debt issue costs paid out of proceeds are reported as expenditures. A net premium is usually transferred to the debt service fund.

4. **INTERIM FINANCING** Often needed during the early stages of the capital projects to pay for expenditures incurred before the bond issue proceeds or other resources are received.

a. The interim financing may be obtained from funds of other governmental units, bond anticipation notes (BANS), or borrowings from local banks.

b. Interim borrowing, if short-term, is a current liability of the capital projects fund and is credited to *Notes Payable or Due To (Fund)*.

c. Certain BANs are an exception to the above rule if (1) all legal steps have been taken to refinance the bond anticipation notes and (2) the intent is supported by an ability to consummate refinancing the short-term note on a long-term basis in accordance with the criteria set forth in SFAS 6, *Classification of Short-Term Obligations Expected to Be Refinanced*.

EXHIBIT 4 ♦ SAMPLE CAPITAL PROJECT FUND ENTRIES

1. To record deferred revenues and other financing received and accrued:

Due From Federal Grantor Agency	200	
Cash	300	
Deferred Grant Revenues		
[unearned until expended for project]		225
Bond Issue Proceeds		
[a nonrevenue other financing source]		275

2. To recognize grant revenue earned through expenditures having been incurred (recorded previously) for specified purposes:

Deferred Grant Revenues [amount earned through project expenditures]	225	
Grant Revenues		225

NOTE: Other capital projects fund entries are illustrated later in Interfund Transactions and Interfund-Account Group Transactions (see Section V).

E. DEBT SERVICE FUNDS

Used to account for the accumulation of resources for the periodic payment of interest on and principal of general obligation long-term debt. Only general obligation long-term debt recorded in the general long-term debt account group (GLTDAG) should be serviced through debt service funds [C GRIPE**S**]. The debt service fund uses modified accrual accounting. Budgetary, encumbrance, and actual activity entries usually appear in the debt service fund.

EXHIBIT 5 ♦ SAMPLE DEBT SERVICE FUND ENTRIES

1. Debt service fund budgetary accounts **may** be used to record the estimated revenues (e.g., from taxes), estimated other financing sources (e.g., from interfund transfer from the general fund for retirement of debt principal and for payment of matured interest), and estimated income (e.g., from investments). To record the budget:

Estimated Other Financing Sources [e.g., from interfund transfers]	350	
Required Additions [estimated tax revenues]	250	
Required Earnings [estimated investment income]	150	
Appropriations [for debt service payments		700
Budgetary Fund Balance [planned change—debit or credit]		50

2. To record actual tax revenues and other financing sources (for example, loans):

Cash or Receivables	550	
Allowance for Uncollectible Taxes		10
Tax Revenues		240
Operating Transfer From General Fund		300

(continued on next page)

3. Debt service payments are recorded by debiting liability accounts (and crediting cash). To record expenditures for debt principal retirement (at maturity date) and interest (at due date):

Expenditures	700	
Bonds Payable (or Matured Bonds Payable)		50
Interest Payable (or Matured Interest Payable)		650

4. **Maturing** bond or other long-term debt principal and related interest and fiscal agent charges are recorded as debt service fund expenditures and liabilities when **due**. At that time the debt principal is removed from the general long-term debt account group. To record payment of matured debt and interest due:

Bonds Payable	70	
Interest Payable	650	
Cash		700

NOTE: Payment of matured debt and interest due is generally effected by transferring the required amount of cash to a bank or other fiscal agent, who then pays the creditors.

5. Any matured debt principal and interest that is **unpaid** at year-end (e.g., because bond interest coupons have not been presented to the fiscal agent for payment) should be recorded, as should the cash with fiscal agent, in the year-end adjusting entry process.

To record unpaid liabilities and cash with fiscal agent at year-end:

Cash With Fiscal Agent	50	
Unredeemed Bonds Payable		30
Unredeemed Interest Coupons Payable		20

6. To record closing entries:

Appropriations	700	
Required Additions		250
Required Earnings		150
Estimated Other Financing Sources		350
Budgetary Fund Balance [difference—debit or credit]	50	
Tax Revenues	240	
Investment Revenues (entry to record revenue not shown)	210	
Operating Transfer From General Fund	300	
Expenditures		700
Fund Balance [difference—debit or credit]		50

F. PERMANENT FUNDS

Used to account for nonexpendable resources that may be used for the government's programs, in other words, to benefit the reporting entity or its citizens. The permanent funds [C GRIPES] use modified accrual accounting. Budgetary and encumbrance entries usually aren't made in permanent funds. Accounting practices for permanent funds parallel those for the general fund, so few sample entries are presented.

EXHIBIT 6 ♦ SAMPLE PERMANENT FUND ENTRIES

1. To record receipt of a gift of an investment portfolio to establish an endowment; the principal (corpus) including capital gains and losses, must be maintained intact, but the other earnings are to be transferred to a special revenue fund (SRF) to support the operations of the city library:

Cash	100	
Investments	1,000	
Contribution Revenues		1,100

NOTE: Donations are recorded as revenue at fair value, regardless of their cost to the donor, reported at fair value at statement dates, and closed to *Fund balance—Principal* at year-end.

2. To close revenue and expense accounts to determine earnings to transfer to the SRF:

Revenues—Investments	100	
Expenses—Commissions		30
Expenses—Administration		10
Expenses—Other		5
Fund Balance—Earnings		55

NOTE: Revenue and expense accounts, but not investment gains, are closed to *Fund balance—Earnings* to determine the earnings as defined by the donor. (The entries recording revenues, expenses, and gains are not illustrated.)

3. To record transfer of earnings, as defined, to an special revenue fund:

Other Financing Uses: Transfer to Library SRF	55	
Cash (or Due to Library SRF)		55

NOTE: A transfer does not necessarily indicate that cash has been disbursed, but may be accrued—and should be accrued if its necessity is indicated in a CPA exam question. Accounting for interfund transfers is discussed further in a later part of this chapter.

4. To close the remaining accounts:

Fund Balance—Earnings	55	
Other Financing Uses: Transfer to Library SRF		55
Gain on Sale of Investments	20	
Contribution Revenues	1,100	
Fund Balance—Principal		1,120

NOTE: The gains on sale of investments are closed to principal because the donor's restrictions specified that earnings are to be computed without regard to gains or losses on sale of investments.

II. ACCOUNT GROUPS

A. OVERVIEW

The account groups are remnants from the outgoing reporting model. They are not required by GASB 34 and are eliminated as a line item or column heading anywhere in the new reporting model financial statements. Although account groups are not required by the new reporting model, governments will most likely use them to track these amounts. General fixed assets (GFA) and general long-term debt (GLTD) must be reported in the GWS in the governmental activity column. They are not reported in fund financial statements, except as summary reconciling items (in the reconciliation from the fund financial statements to the government-wide statements).

1. **ACCOUNTING FOR GENERAL FIXED ASSETS AND GENERAL LONG-TERM DEBT** GASB 34 addresses reporting, not accounting. Therefore, GASB 34 doesn't specify how to account for GFA and GLTD.

2. **OUTGOING REPORTING MODEL** The reporting for specific fund (proprietary and fiduciary funds) fixed assets and long-term debt remains essentially unchanged. Prior to GASB 34 implementation, accounting standards require a general fixed asset account group (GFAAG) and a general long-term debt account group (GLTDAG). These account groups are illustrated in this chapter. Governments will most likely continue to use the systems that they have in place to account for GFA and GLTD. For most governments, these systems involve account groups.

   a. **GENERAL FIXED ASSETS** Neither depreciation expense for GFA nor infrastructure reporting are required (and rarely are recorded).

   b. **GENERAL LONG-TERM DEBT** Debt related to a specific fund must also appear in the GLTDAG if the general government has an obligation in the event of default by the proprietary or fiduciary fund. This can result in the same debt appearing twice in the government's financial statements.

3. **NOTE DISCLOSURES** Disclosures include major classes of capital assets (land, buildings, etc.) and long-term liabilities (bonds, capital leases, compensated absences, etc.) plus the assignment between governmental and business-type activities and allocations to each of the functions in the statement of activities.

   a. **GENERAL FIXED ASSETS** Capital asset disclosures include: beginning and ending balances, acquisitions, disposals, and current depreciation expense allocated to each of the functions in the statement of activities.

   b. **GENERAL LONG-TERM DEBT** The portions of each item that are due within one year of the statement date and which governmental funds typically have liquidated other long-term liabilities (compensated absences, pension liabilities, etc.) in prior years.

ACCOUNT GROUPS (NOT FUNDS)

D Long-Term **D**ebt Account Group
A General **A**ssets Account Group } for governmental-type funds only

---

B. **GENERAL FIXED ASSET ACCOUNT GROUP (GFAAG)**
   A **nonfund** account group used to record the general government funds' **capital** assets, including an equity interest in a joint venture and infrastructure. Fixed assets that relate to a specific (proprietary or fiduciary) fund are recorded in the related fund rather than in the GFAAG. The GFAAG is not a fund because it does not record expendable assets or related liabilities, but only general capital asset accountability. The GFAAG does **not** have operating accounts, and no GFAAG operating statement is prepared. Under the outgoing reporting model, this is named the general **fixed** asset account group (as it excludes infrastructure assets). Under the new reporting model, it might be renamed the general **capital** asset account group to reflect its broader scope.

   1. **ACCOUNTING EQUATION** GFAAG accounting procedures follow a simple self-balancing or list and offset approach. The GFAAG accounting equation is simply the following:

      General Capital Assets = *Investment in General Assets*
      (By Asset Type)   *(By Financing Source)*

2. **ACQUISITION OF ASSETS** General assets are recorded in appropriately titled asset accounts and the accounting equation is balanced by a credit balance in the *Investment in General Assets* account or a series of such accounts indicating how the fixed assets were financed.

    a. Typical asset accounts are *Land, Building, Other Improvements, Machinery and Equipment, Construction in Process*, and *Infrastructure*.

    b. Typical financing source accounts are *Investment in General Fixed Assets—Federal Grants, Investment in General Fixed Assets—General Revenues,* and *Investment in General Fixed Assets—Bond Issues*.

EXHIBIT 7 ♦ SAMPLE GFAAG ENTRIES

---

1. To record general assets (e.g., police cars or fire trucks) acquired by the general fund or special revenue funds:

Machinery and Equipment (for police cars or fire trucks)	100	
Investment in General Fixed Assets—General Revenues		100

NOTE: The acquisition of capital assets is recorded by the acquiring governmental fund as an expenditure. Prior to adoption of GASB No. 34, reporting of infrastructure (e.g., roads, bridges, streets, sidewalks, etc.) and similar assets that are immovable and of value only to the governmental unit is **optional**.

2. To record construction in process at the end of the first year of a two-year capital project:

Construction in Process	770	
Investment in General Fixed Assets—Bond Issues		550
Investment in General Fixed Assets—Federal Grants		220

NOTE: The credits to the source of financing accounts in capitalizing construction in process are based on the **estimated** percentage of the final cost of the project to be financed by each financing source.

3. To record completion of the two-year capital project

Land	140	
Building	730	
Other Improvements	20	
Construction in Process		770
Investment in General Fixed Assets—Bond Issues		90
Investment in General Fixed Assets—Federal Grants		30

NOTE: This entry (a) records the total costs of the completed general assets, (b) removes the *Construction in Process* account balance, and (c) adjusts the financing sources accounts to indicate the actual amount of the total project cost financed by each source.

4. To record disposal of general assets by their removal from the GFAAG:

Investment in General Fixed Assets—Bond Issues	400	
Investment in General Fixed Assets—General Revenues	50	
Land		120
Buildings		330

NOTE: Any sale proceeds are recorded as revenues in the appropriate **governmental** fund—usually the general fund—and gain (loss) on general fixed asset disposal is **not** recognized in the governmental funds.

---

3. **VALUATION OF ASSETS**

    a. Purchased assets are recorded at cost.

b. Assets acquired through capital leases are recorded at the lesser of the present value of the minimum lease payments (at inception) or the fair value of the property (at inception).

c. Construction is recorded at total cost. GASB 37 eliminates the requirement to capitalize construction-period interest for general governmental assets.

d. Forfeitures are recorded at the cost to perfect title.

e. Donated fixed assets (acquired by gift) are recorded at their fair value when received.

4. **DISPOSAL OF ASSETS** When general fixed assets are disposed of, they are simply removed (reversed) from the GFAAG accounts. Any sale proceeds are recorded as revenues in the appropriate **governmental** fund, usually the general fund. No gain or loss is recognized in the fund.

5. **ACCUMULATED DEPRECIATION** When an *Accumulated Depreciation* account is credited, an *Investment in General Fixed Assets* account is debited. Depreciation **expense** is not recorded by governmental-type funds, as the cost of the asset was an **expenditure** at the time of purchase. Depreciation **expense** is not recorded by the account group, as it has no operating accounts. Typically, for depreciation expense, only a worksheet entry is made to reconcile to amounts in the GWS.

a. Adopting the modified approach for infrastructure is fraught with political pitfalls, making it unlikely to be widespread in practice. GASB 37 clarifies that adopting the modified approach for infrastructure assets that previously were depreciated is a change in accounting estimate, and hence, is accounted for prospectively.

b. Governments are encouraged, but not required, to depreciate collections. The definition and treatment of collections are similar to that of collections of non-governmental non-profit organizations.

C. **GENERAL LONG-TERM DEBT ACCOUNT GROUP (GLTDAG)**
A **nonfund** account group used to record the **unmatured** principal of the general government long-term debt. GLTD of a government can be defined as all of its unmatured long-term debt except that of proprietary or fiduciary funds. The GLTDAG is not a fund because it does not record expendable assets or related current liabilities, but only general long-term debt accountability.

1. **ACCOUNTING EQUATION** GLTDAG accounting procedures follow a simple self-balancing or list and offset approach. Thus, the GLTDAG **accounting equation** is simply

Assets		
Amount **Available** in Debt Service Funds for GLTD Principal Retirement	+ Amount to be **Provided** in Future Years of GLTD Principal Retirement	= Liabilities GLTD Payable

a. The general long-term debts are recorded in appropriately titled liability accounts, e.g., *Bonds Payable, Long-term Notes Payable*, and *Capital Leases Payable*.

b. The accounting equation is balanced by debit balance accounts indicating (1) the amounts accumulated in the debt service funds that may be used to retire GLTD principal, and (2), the amount of money that must be raised in future years to pay off GLTD principal (the difference between the total GLTD and the amount available to retire the GLTD).

2. **ELIGIBILITY FOR DEBT IN THE GLTDAG**

   a. **UNMATURED** Matured general government long-term debt is removed from the GLTDAG and recorded as a debt service fund expenditure and liability, as noted in Exhibit 8.

   b. **SPECIFIC FUND DEBT** Specific fund long-term debt that relates to and will only be repaid from a specific fund is recorded in that fund **rather** than in the GLTDAG. All proprietary and fiduciary fund debt is specific fund debt, which is recorded in the related specific proprietary or fiduciary fund, rather than in the GLTDAG. None of the governmental funds has specific fund long-term debt. (Under the outgoing reporting model, specific fund long-term debt and special assessment debt is included in GLTDAG if the general government is obligated. This could result in one debt being reported twice.)

   c. **SHORT-TERM DEBT IN THE GLTDAG** A government unit might issue bond anticipation notes (BANs) to provide funds to defray costs expected to be incurred before the related bonds are issued. Such notes are accounted for in the GLTDAG, even if due within one year, if (1) they are to be repaid with the proceeds of the bond issue, (2) all legal steps have been taken to refinance the notes, and (3) the intent is supported by an ability to refinance the short-term notes on a long-term basis.

3. **MATURITY** When the GLTD **matures**, it is removed from the GLTDAG and is recorded as an expenditure and current liability of the governmental fund from which it is to be repaid, usually a debt service fund. Thus, the GLTDAG does **not** have operating accounts, and **no** GLTDAG operating statement is prepared.

EXHIBIT 8 ♦ SAMPLE GLTDAG ENTRIES

1. To record general long-term debt incurred:

Amount to Be Provided for Payment of Bonds	300	
Amount to Be Provided for Payment of Long-Term Notes	200	
Amount to Be Provided for Payment of Capital Lease Principal	100	
Bonds Payable		300
Long-Term Notes Payable		200
Capital Lease Payable [principal]		100

2. To record amount of the debt service fund (DSF) fund balance (or change therein) available for GLTD principal retirement, in this case for bond principal retirement:

Amount Available in DSF for Bond Retirement	300	
Amount to Be Provided for Payment of Bonds		300

   NOTE: While in practice the amount available and amount to be provided adjusting entry usually is made at year-end, CPA exam candidates should make this type of adjusting entry whenever an exam question indicates that amounts have been provided in a DSF for GLTD **principal** payment.

3. To record the removal (reversal) of matured general long-term debt principal from the GLTDAG, including the principal portion of capital lease payments due:

Bonds Payable	300	
Long-Term Notes Payable	200	
Capital Lease Payable [principal]	100	
Amount Available in DSF for Bond Retirement		300
Amount to Be Provided for Payment of Long-Term Notes		200
Amount to Be Provided for Payment of Capital Lease Principal		100

   (continued on next page)

> **NOTE**: This entry presumes that the bonds will be repaid through a DSF in which resources have already been provided, while the long-term notes and capital lease will be paid through the general fund or perhaps a special revenue fund. The key point here is that when a GLTD **matures**, the liability account and the related amount available and amount to be provided accounts are removed from the GLTDAG accounts by **reversal**.

III. PROPRIETARY FUNDS

A. OVERVIEW

While the governmental funds and the nonfund account groups account for the general government activities of a state or local government, its business type activities are accounted for in **proprietary** funds essentially as if they were private sector profit-seeking business enterprises. The proprietary fund accounting equation is the familiar business accounting equation.

$$\underset{\text{Assets}}{\text{Cur.}} + \underset{\text{Assets}}{\text{Fixed}} + \underset{\text{Assets}}{\text{Other}} = \underset{\text{Liab.}}{\text{Cur.}} + \underset{\text{Debt}}{\text{Long-Term}} + \underset{\text{Assets}}{\text{Net}}$$

1. BUSINESS-TYPE ACCOUNTING Revenues and **expenses** (not expenditures) are measured using the accrual basis of accounting, as in business accounting. Fixed assets and long-term debt are recorded in the fund as well as the associated depreciation and interest charges. Contributed capital is no longer separated from retained earnings in the balance sheet; both are labeled *Net Assets*.

2. NOT-FOR-PROFIT ACCOUNTING AND FINANCIAL REPORTING GASB 29 allows the use of either the Nonprofit (or AICPA) model or the Governmental model for accounting and reporting by state or local governmental units that have previously applied the principles of SOP 78-10 or *Audits of Voluntary Health and Welfare Organizations*. However, proprietary funds that implement FASB pronouncements released after November 31, 1989, should only apply those pronouncements that are intended for business (as opposed to nonprofit) organizations.

3. REFUNDINGS OF DEBT REPORTED BY PROPRIETARY ACTIVITIES GASB 23 provides standards of accounting and reporting for current refundings and advance refundings resulting in defeasance of debt reported by proprietary activities (proprietary funds and other governmental entities that use proprietary fund accounting). GASB 23 requires that the difference between the reacquisition price and the net carrying amount of the old debt be deferred and amortized as a component of interest expense over the remaining life of the old debt or the life of the new debt, whichever is shorter. The deferred amount is reported on the balance sheet as an addition to or a deduction from the new debt liability. Additionally, current refundings reported by proprietary activities are subject to the disclosure requirements of GASB 7, *Advance Refundings Resulting in Defeasance of Debt*.

    a. CURRENT REFUNDINGS Involve the issuance of new debt, the proceeds of which are to be used immediately.

    b. ADVANCE REFUNDINGS Involve the issuance of new debt that is placed in escrow to be used at a later date to pay principal and interest on the old debt.

B. INTERNAL SERVICE FUNDS

Internal service funds [C GRIPES] are used to account for *in-house* business enterprise activities; that is, to account for the financing of goods or services provided by **one** government department or agency to **other** departments or agencies of the government (and perhaps also to other governments) on a **cost reimbursement** basis. Common examples of internal service funds (ISF) are those used to account for government motor pools, central repair shops and garages, data processing departments, and photocopy and printing shops.

1. **ZERO PROFIT** ISFs are supposed to break even annually and/or over a period of years. That is, the charges to other departments—that are accounted for as ISF revenues—are intended to **recoup** ISF **expenses**. ISF thus are, in essence, cost accounting and cost distribution (to other funds) accounting entities. They are accounted for in essentially the same manner as enterprise funds.

2. **ESTABLISHMENT** The initial capital to finance an ISF may come from the general fund, the issuance of general obligation bonds, transfers from other funds, or advances from other governments. Permanent capital contributions (i.e., residual equity transfers) must be distinguished from loans and advances that are to be repaid.

3. **DIFFERENCES BETWEEN ENTERPRISE FUND AND INTERNAL SERVICE FUND ACCOUNTING**

   a. Only the fixed assets that are expected to be replaced through the ISF are recorded therein and depreciated. Thus, the printing equipment for a central printing shop located in the basement of a county courthouse would be recorded in (and depreciated in) the print shop ISF. The courthouse remains in the GFAAG, a portion of the courthouse cost would **not** be recorded in the ISF.

   b. An account such as *Billings to Departments* serves as the ISF sales account rather than the usual *Revenues* account.

C. **ENTERPRISE FUNDS**
   Enterprise funds [C GRIPES] **must** be used to account for a government's business-type operations that are financed and operated like private businesses—where the government's **intent** is that **all** costs (expenses, including depreciation) of providing goods or services to the general public on a continuing basis are to be financed or recovered primarily through user charges. Most government-owned public utilities (e.g., electricity, gas, water, and sewage systems) must be accounted for in enterprise funds under these mandatory criteria.

   1. **OPTIONAL USE** NCGA Statement 1 also **permits** governments to account for virtually any type of self-contained business-type activity in enterprise funds if it prefers to do business-type accounting rather than general government accounting. City bus or other mass transit systems are examples of government activities that are often accounted for through enterprise funds under the NCGA's permissive criteria.

   2. **SUBFUNDS** If capital, debt service, trust, or agency funds related to an enterprise activity are required (e.g., by bond indentures, other contractual agreements, grant provisions, or laws), they are accounted for as enterprise fund subfunds rather than as separate funds.

      a. Assets and liabilities of such subfunds are accounted for by using separate asset and liability accounts (e.g., *Cash—Construction, Contracts Payable—Construction, Investments—Debt Service, Accrued Interest Payable—Debt Service,* and *Cash—Customer Deposits*) and need not balance, though all except agency subfunds may be balanced by net assets reserve accounts such as *Reserve for Construction* or *Reserve for Debt Service.*

      b. Revenues and expenses related to the subfunds are recorded as enterprise revenues and expenses, **not** in separate subfund revenue and expense accounts.

      c. Customers' security deposits that cannot be spent for normal operating purposes should be classified in the balance sheet of the enterprise funds as both a restricted asset and a liability.

EXHIBIT 9 ♦ SAMPLE ENTERPRISE FUND ENTRIES

1. To record operating revenues:

Cash or Receivables	850	
Revenues—Sale of Electricity		725
Revenues—Sale of Appliances		50
Revenues—Other		75

2. To record federal grants for operating and capital purposes:

Cash or Receivables	100	
Cash—Construction	350	
Revenues—Federal Grants [operating grant]		100
Contributed Capital—Federal Grants [capital grant]		350

NOTE: If grants must be expended to be considered earned, they are initially credited to deferred revenues and deferred contributed capital accounts, then credited to revenue and contributed capital accounts when earned by being expended. Also, this entry (and entry 4) assumes that a capital projects subfund is required by federal grant and/or bond indenture provisions.

3. To record operating expenses:

Expenses—Cost of Electricity Purchased	400	
Expenses—Depreciation	100	
Expenses—Salaries and Wages	100	
Expenses—Other	50	
Accumulated Depreciation		100
Cash		500
Payables		50

4. To record issuance of enterprise revenue bonds to finance new electricity distribution lines and acquiring transmission equipment under capital lease:

Cash—Construction	450	
Bonds Payable		450
Transmission Equipment	200	
Capital Leases Payable		200

5. To record use of revenue bond issue proceeds to build new electricity distribution lines:

Transmission Lines	750	
Cash—Construction (or Payables—Construction)		750

6. To record payment of bond and capital lease principal and interest:

Bonds Payable	15	
Expenses—Interest [on bonds]	35	
Cash—Debt Service		50
Capital Leases Payable	10	
Expenses—Interest [on capital lease]	20	
Cash		30

NOTE: This entry assumes that a debt service subfund is used for bond debt service but that the capital lease is serviced from enterprise fund operating cash.

(continued on next page)

7. To close the accounts at year-end:

Revenues—Sale of Electricity	725	
Revenues—Sale of Appliances	50	
Revenues—Federal Grants [operating grant]	100	
Revenues—Other	75	
Expenses—Cost of Electricity Purchased		400
Expenses—Depreciation		100
Expenses—Salaries and Wages		100
Expenses—Interest ($20 + $35)		55
Expenses—Other		50
Net Assets [debit or credit]		245

NOTE: The revenue and expense accounts may be closed initially to a *Revenue and Expense Summary* account, which is then closed to *Net Assets*.

IV. FIDUCIARY FUNDS

A. OVERVIEW

Fiduciary funds are used to account for a government's fiduciary or stewardship responsibilities as an agent (agency funds) or trustee (trust funds) for other governments, funds, organizations, and/or individuals.

1. **NEW REPORTING MODEL** All fiduciary funds [PIPPA] are accounted for on the accrual basis, in essentially the same manner as proprietary funds.

2. **OUTGOING REPORTING MODEL** Under the outgoing reporting model, both agency funds and expendable trust funds are accounted for on the **modified** accrual basis in essentially the same manner as governmental funds. Nonexpendable trust funds and pension trust funds are accounted for on the accrual basis, in essentially the same manner as proprietary funds. There are no private-purpose trust funds in the outgoing model.

3. **TRANSITION** Both expendable and nonexpendable trust funds are eliminated by the new reporting model. Former expendable trust funds that benefit the reporting entity or its citizens become special revenue funds [C GRIPES]. Former nonexpendable trust funds that benefit the reporting entity or its citizens become permanent funds [C GRIPES]. Both expendable and nonexpendable trust funds that benefit other governments, funds, organizations, and/or individuals become private-purpose trust funds [PIPPA].

B. PENSION TRUST FUNDS

Used to account for a government's fiduciary responsibilities and activities in managing pension or retirement trust funds for its retired, active, and former employees and their beneficiaries.

1. **USE** Pension trust funds are needed only by governments that manage their own pension plans rather than participate in statewide plans or contract with an insurance or pension management company to manage the plans. (While relatively few businesses manage their own pension plans, many governments do so.)

2. **BASIS OF ACCOUNTING** Pension trust funds [PIPPA] are accounted for in essentially the same manner as proprietary funds. Accordingly, all contributions to and earnings of the plan are accounted for as revenues; and all benefit payments, refunds of contributions, and pension plan administrative costs are accounted for as **expenses**. Depreciation expense is recorded on depreciable fixed assets used in administering the pension plan. A unique series of fund balance reserve accounts is employed to account for the equities of the several types of plan participants.

C. INVESTMENT TRUST FUNDS

Used to account for a government's fiduciary responsibilities and activities in managing an investment plan. [PIPPA] Further details are in Chapter 21 in the Limited Scope Topics Appendix.

D. PRIVATE-PURPOSE TRUST FUNDS

Private-purpose trust funds [PIPPA] are used to account for fiduciary responsibilities and activities in managing all other trust arrangements that benefit individuals, private organizations, or other governments.

E. AGENCY FUNDS

Used to account for the custodial activities of a government serving as an agent for other governments, private organizations, or individuals. Agency funds [PIPPA] are purely custodial (assets equal liabilities). The government has no equity in agency funds. Further, agency funds do not have operating accounts (for instance, *Revenues*). No operating statement is prepared for agency funds.

1. ACCOUNTING EQUATION

Current Assets = Current Liabilities

2. COMMON TYPES

The most common type of agency fund is the tax agency fund—used when one government collects property (or other) taxes for several governments, usually including the collecting government. Also, some governments use a payroll withholding agency fund to accumulate the payroll taxes, insurance premiums, etc., withheld in its several funds, then remit them to the proper governments, insurance companies, etc.

EXHIBIT 10 ♦ SAMPLE PROPERTY TAX AGENCY FUND ENTRIES

1. To record property taxes, levied by other governments (in this instance, the city and school district) and for other county funds, which are to be collected through the county's property tax agency fund:

Taxes Receivable—Other Funds and Units	2,000	
Due to City		250
Due to School District		250
Due to General Fund [of county]		1,500

NOTE: The county general fund will be paid the county's share of the property taxes collected plus any collection fees charged the city and school district.

The property tax levies will be recorded also in the county general fund and in the appropriate city and school district governmental funds in the manner illustrated earlier. An allowance for uncollectible taxes is not recorded in the agency fund since the county is responsible for collecting all taxes possible and returning the uncollected tax receivables to the city and school districts (and the county general fund) for further collection effort.

County's General Fund:

Taxes Receivable—Current	1,500	
Allowance for Uncollectible Taxes		75
Revenues—Property Taxes		1,425

2. To record tax collections:

Cash	1,975	
Taxes Receivable—Other Funds and Units		1,975

(continued on next page)

3. To record payment of tax collections to other units and to the county general fund:

Due to City [collections less any fee] ($245 – $5)	240
Due to School District [collections less any fee] ($245 – $5)	240
Due to General Fund [collections **plus** any fees] ($1,485 + $5 + $5)	1,495
Cash	1,975

NOTE: Entries in the general funds would be the following:

County's General Fund:

Cash	1,495	
Taxes Receivable—Current		1,485
Revenues—Property Tax Collection Fees		10

City's and School District's General Funds:

Cash	240	
Expenditures—Property Tax Collection Fees	5	
Taxes Receivable—Current		245

V. INTERFUND AND INTERFUND-ACCOUNT GROUP TRANSACTIONS AND RELATIONSHIPS

A. OVERVIEW

The preceding discussions and illustrations focus primarily on accounting for each of the several different types of funds and account groups. Interfund and interfund account group transactions and relationships are important aspects of governmental accounting. This part of the chapter focuses on interfund transactions (where one transaction affects two or more funds) and interfund-account group transactions (where one transaction affects one or more funds and one or both account groups). These discussions and illustrations also review and expand upon the material covered earlier in this chapter.

B. INTERFUND TRANSACTIONS

Interfund transactions simultaneously affect two or more funds of the government. Transfers are **nonreciprocal** shifts of resources among funds and are **not** intended to be repaid. GASB 34 details three types of interfund transactions in the new reporting model. (NCGA Statement 1 previously provided specific guidance on accounting for four types of interfund transactions.)

1. **QUASI-EXTERNAL TRANSACTIONS** These are transactions that would result in recognizing revenues and expenditures or expenses, as appropriate, if they were with organizations apart from the government. These transactions should also result in recognition of revenues and expenditures or expenses, as appropriate, when they occur between or among funds of the government. Examples include routine employer contributions to pension trust funds, enterprise and internal service fund billings to government departments, and enterprise fund payments in lieu of taxes to the general fund or other governmental funds.

EXHIBIT 11 ♦ SAMPLE QUASI-EXTERNAL TRANSACTIONS ENTRIES

1. To record billings to departments financed by the general fund for services rendered through enterprise and internal service fund departments:

a.	*General Fund:*		
	Expenditures—Services	115	
	Due to Enterprise Fund		35
	Due to Internal Service Fund		80
b.	*Enterprise Fund:*		
	Due From General Fund	35	
	Revenues—Services		35

(continued on next page)

```
c.   Internal Service Fund:
     Due From General Fund                          80
       Billings for Services                               80
```

NOTE: Note that an account such as *Billings for Services* is used in internal service fund accounting instead of *Revenues*.

2.   To record employer contributions from the general and enterprise funds to the pension trust fund:

```
a.   General Fund:
     Expenditures—Pension Contribution              300
       Due to Pension Trust Fund (or Cash)                 300
b.   Enterprise Fund:
     Expenses—Pension Contribution                  100
       Due to Pension Trust Fund (or Cash)                 100
c.   Pension Trust Fund:
     Due From General Fund (or Cash)                300
     Due From Enterprise Fund (or Cash)             100
       Revenues—Employer Contributions                     400
```

NOTE: The cash account would be used if an actual cash transfer had occurred.

2.   **REIMBURSEMENTS** These are transactions that reimburse one fund for expenditures or expenses initially recorded there but properly attributable to another fund. Reimbursements are recorded as expenditures or expenses, as appropriate, in the reimbursing fund and as reductions of the recorded expenditures or expenses (**not** as revenues) in the fund that is reimbursed.

3.   **TRANSFERS** The difference between operating transfers and residual equity transfers (RETs) of the outgoing reporting model is not always easy to distinguish and practice varies widely. GASB 34 eliminated the **requirement** to distinguish between operating transfers and RETs. (The following illustrations distinguish between the two, as candidates may encounter this terminology.) GASB 34, ¶420 notes that all transfers must be reported as *Other Financing Sources* or *Other Financing Uses*. [See the sample financial statements. Note that transfers don't include quasi-external transactions and reimbursements.]

EXHIBIT 12 ♦ SAMPLE TRANSFER ENTRIES

1.   To record transfers made from the general fund to establish a new internal service fund:

```
a.   General Fund:
     OFU: Residual Equity Transfer to Internal Service Fund   500
       Cash                                                         500
b.   Internal Service Fund:
     Cash                                                     500
       OFS: Residual Equity Transfer From General Fund             500
```

NOTE: This is a residual equity transfer. In internal service funds, the RET account(s) will be closed to a *Contribution From Municipality* (or similar contributed capital) account. The general fund RET accounts will be closed to *Fund Balance*.

(continued on next page)

2. To record routine transfers from the general fund to a debt service fund:

   a. *General Fund:*
OFU: Operating Transfer to Debt Service Fund	350	
Cash		350

   b. *Debt Service Fund:*
Cash	350	
OFS: Operating Transfer From General Fund		350

   NOTE: All interfund transfers that are not RETs are operating transfers.

4. **FINANCIAL STATEMENT PRESENTATION** These three types of transactions all appear in the operating statements of the affected funds. Quasi-external transactions and reimbursements are buried in expenditures, expenses, and revenues account detail. Transfers (RETs and operating) appear in the *Other Financing Sources (Uses)* section.

5. **INTERFUND LOANS** Amounts that are expected to be repaid appear in the balance sheets of affected funds. They have no impact on operating statements. Both short-term and noncurrent loans are indicated using *Receivable* and *Payable* accounts, appropriately classified in the balance sheets. Governments are encouraged, but not required, to present assets and liabilities in order of their relative liquidity. Liabilities whose average maturities are greater than one years should be reported in two components (a short-term component and a noncurrent component).

EXHIBIT 13 ♦ OTHER SAMPLE INTERFUND ENTRIES

1. To record reimbursement of the general fund for previously recorded operating expenditures that are properly attributable to special revenue and enterprise funds:

   a. *General Fund:*
Cash	125	
Expenditures—Operating		125

   b. *Special Revenue Fund:*
Expenditures—Operating	40	
Cash		40

   c. *Enterprise Fund:*
Expenses—Operating	85	
Cash		85

   NOTE: If cash was not involved, appropriate *Due From* and *Due to* accounts would be debited and credited rather than *Cash*.

2. To record four payments from an enterprise fund to the general fund—(1) a routine payment to subsidize general fund operations, (2) a payment in lieu of taxes, (3) a payment to reimburse the general fund for enterprise fund wages erroneously recorded in the general fund, and (4) a payment reducing the municipality's contributed capital investment in the enterprise fund:

   a. *Enterprise Fund:*
Operating Transfer to General Fund	50	
Expenses—Payments in Lieu of Taxes	130	
Expenses—Wages	40	
Residual Equity Transfer to General Fund	350	
Cash		570

   (continued on next page)

b. *General Fund:*

Cash	570	
Operating Transfer From Enterprise Fund		50
Revenues—Payments in Lieu of Taxes		130
Expenditures—Wages		40
Residual Equity Transfer From Enterprise Fund		350

NOTE: These entries demonstrate and review accounting for quasi-external transactions, reimbursements, residual equity transfers, and operating transfers.

3. To record a short-term loan from the general fund to a special revenue fund:

   a. *General Fund:*

Due From Special Revenue Fund	100	
Cash		100

   b. *Special Revenue Fund:*

Cash	100	
Due to General Fund		100

NOTE: In the outgoing reporting model, the *Due to* and *Due From* accounts indicate a short-term interfund loan that is expected to be repaid during the current year or early the next year. The new reporting model uses an account title including the word *payable,* although governments may still use the old account titles internally. The new reporting model shows the short-term and noncurrent payables separately.

4. To record a long-term loan from the general fund to an enterprise fund:

   a. *General Fund:*

Advance to Enterprise Fund	200	
Cash		200
Fund Balance (or Unreserved Fund Balance)	200	
Reserve for Advance to Enterprise Fund		200

   b. *Enterprise Fund:*

Cash	200	
Advance From General Fund		200

NOTE: (a) The terms *advance to* and *advance from* denote accounts for noncurrent or long-term interfund loans; and (b) since the amount loaned to the enterprise fund on a long-term basis does not now represent current assets available to finance general fund expenditures, an appropriate fund balance reserve must be established in the general fund. (The general fund reserve will be reduced when the advance becomes an available current asset—in full or in installments.)

5. To record closing of selected operating transfer and RET accounts in governmental (e.g., the general) and proprietary (e.g., enterprise and internal service) funds:

   a. *General Fund:*

Operating Transfer From Enterprise Fund	XX	
Residual Equity Transfer From Enterprise Fund	XX	
Operating Transfer to Enterprise Fund		XX
Residual Equity Transfer to Internal Service Fund		XX
Fund Balance [difference—debit or credit]		XX

   b. *Enterprise Fund:*

Operating Transfer From General Fund	XX	
Retained Earnings [difference—debit or credit]	XX	
Operating Transfer to General Fund		XX

(continued on next page)

		XX	
Contributions From Municipality (or Contributed Capital)		XX	
Residual Equity Transfer to General Fund			XX

c. *Internal Service Fund:*

Residual Equity Transfer From General Fund	XX	
Contributions From Municipality (or Contributed Capital)		XX

NOTE: All transfers are closed to *Fund Balance* accounts of **governmental** funds. In **proprietary** funds: (a) operating transfers are closed to *Retained Earnings*, since they affect reported operating results, while (b) residual equity transfers are considered capital (**not** operating) transactions, and thus, are closed to the *Contributions From Municipality* (or similar contributed capital) account.

C. INTERFUND-ACCOUNT GROUP TRANSACTIONS

Interfund-account group transactions simultaneously affect one or more funds and one or more nonfund account groups. Since the account groups record general fixed assets and general long-term debt, interfund-account group transactions arise in general government capital outlay and long-term debt transactions.

EXHIBIT 14 ♦ SAMPLE INTERFUND-ACCOUNT GROUP ENTRIES

1. To record a general obligation bond issued for **capital outlay** purposes at a premium:

   a. *Capital Projects Fund:*

Cash	505	
Bond Issue Proceeds		505

   b. *General Long-Term Debt Account Group:*

Amount to Be Provided for Payment of Bonds	505	
Bonds Payable		505

   NOTE: (a) The bond issue proceeds are recorded in the capital projects fund at the amount received, even if more or less than par, and (b) no bond issue premium or discount is recorded in capital projects funds. The same practice is followed in recording proceeds of refunding bond issues in debt service funds and in any other governmental fund in which bond issue proceeds are recorded—e.g., in the general fund should bonds be issued to finance a general fund deficit.

2. To record transfer of the bond issue premium to a debt service fund to be used to retire bond principal:

   a. *Capital Projects Fund:*

Operating Transfer to Debt Service Fund	5	
Cash		5

   b. *Debt Service Fund:*

Cash	5	
Operating Transfer From Capital Projects Fund		5

   c. *General Long-Term Debt Account Group:*

Amount Available in Debt Service Fund for Bond Retirement	5	
Amount to Be Provided for Payment of Bonds		5

   NOTE: Had the transfer to the debt service fund been for **interest payments**, entry c. would **not** have been made.

(continued on next page)

3. To record the maturity of long-term debt for bonds serviced through the debt service fund:

   a. *Debt Service Fund:*

Expenditures—Bond Principal	300	
Expenditures—Interest on Bonds	15	
Matured Bonds Payable (or Cash)		300
Matured Interest Payable (or Cash)		15

   b. *General Long-Term Debt Account Group:*

Bonds Payable	300	
Amount Available in Debt Service Fund for Bond Retirement		300

4. To record capital outlay expenditures made from (a) the general fund (equipment) and (b) a capital projects fund (land and buildings) financed by bond issues and federal grants:

   a. *General Fund:*

Expenditures—Capital Outlay	150	
Cash or Payable		150

   b. *Capital Projects Fund:*

Expenditures—Capital Outlay	700	
Cash or Payable		700

   c. *General Fixed Assets Account Group:*

Equipment	150	
Land	175	
Buildings	525	
Investment in General Fixed Assets—Revenues		150
Investment in General Fixed Assets—Bond Issues		500
Investment in General Fixed Assets—Federal Grants		200

5. To record the sale of general capital assets (land)—originally financed from a capital projects fund (bonds) that has been terminated—and deposit of the sale proceeds in the debt service fund bank account for bond retirement:

   a. *Debt Service Fund:*

Cash	120	
Revenues—Sale of General Fixed Assets		120

   b. *General Fixed Assets Account Group:*

Investment in General Fixed Assets—Bond Issues	120	
Land		120

   c. *General Long-Term Debt Account Group:*

Amount Available in Debt Service Fund for Bond Retirement	120	
Amount to Be Provided for Payment of Bonds		120

   NOTE: If bonds or other debt that financed the general fixed assets sold are still outstanding, the sale proceeds usually are recorded in a debt service fund. Otherwise, they usually are recorded in the general fund.

(continued on next page)

6. To record the transfer of equipment previously used in enterprise fund activities to the city street department, which is financed from the general fund:

    a. *Enterprise Fund:*

Accumulated Depreciation—Equipment	195	
Loss (or gain) on Disposal of Equipment	35	
Contribution From Municipality (fair value of asset)	25	
Equipment		255

    b. *General Fixed Assets Account Group:*

Equipment	25	
Investment in General Fixed Assets—Fund Contributions		25

    NOTE: (a) **No** transfer is reported since the transaction involves a (nonfund) account group, and (b) the transaction is recorded at the **fair value** of the equipment at transfer.

VI. APPENDIX: OUTGOING REPORTING MODEL

A. OVERVIEW

The preceding discussions and illustrations focus primarily on accounting under the new reporting model. There are some differences in accounting under the outgoing model. Many of these differences are mentioned within this chapter. While there is some emphasis of points already discussed, the purpose of this section is to discuss the remaining differences, not to be a stand-alone discussion of the outgoing model.

1. **ELIMINATED FUNDS** Both expendable and nonexpendable trust funds were eliminated by the new reporting model. These are both fiduciary funds under the outgoing model.

2. **ACCOUNT GROUPS ELIMINATED** Both account groups were eliminated from the financial statements by the new reporting model. Although not required to do so, many governments still use account groups to account for capital assets and long-term obligations.

B. NONEXPENDABLE TRUST FUND

Used only under the outgoing reporting model to account for a government's fiduciary responsibilities and activities in managing trusts when either (1) the trust is nonexpendable as to principal but its earnings are expendable or (2) the trust is purely nonexpendable.

EXHIBIT 15 ♦ SAMPLE NONEXPENDABLE TRUST FUND ENTRIES

1. To record receipt of a gift of an apartment complex and cash to establish an endowment fund; the principal (corpus) must be maintained intact, but the earnings—computed without regard to building depreciation expense—are to be transferred to an expendable trust fund to support the operations of the city library:

Cash	100	
Land	115	
Buildings	600	
Equipment	120	
Mortgage Payable		365
Fund Balance—Principal		570

    NOTE: Any liabilities against properties given in trust are assumed by the trust. Properties received are recorded at fair value, regardless of their cost to the donor.

(continued on next page)

2. To close revenue and expense accounts to determine the trust earnings to be transferred to the expendable trust fund:

Revenues—Rentals	130	
Expenses—Maintenance		25
Expenses—Utilities		20
Expenses—Administrative		15
Expenses—Other		10
Expenses—Depreciation of Equipment		5
Fund Balance—Earnings		55

NOTE: All revenue and expense accounts **except** *Building Depreciation Expense*, which is charged against principal rather than earnings in this case, are closed *to Fund Balance—Earnings* to determine the trust earnings as defined in this trust agreement.

3. To record transfer of trust earnings, as defined, to an expendable trust fund:

Operating Transfer to Library Expendable Trust Fund	55	
Cash (or Due to Expendable Trust Fund)		55

NOTE: A transfer does not necessarily indicate that cash has been disbursed, but may be accrued—and should be accrued if its necessity is indicated in a CPA exam question.

4. To close the operating transfer and building depreciation expense accounts:

Fund Balance—Earnings	55	
Operating Transfer to Library Expendable Trust Fund		55
Fund Balance—Principal	15	
Expenses—Depreciation of Buildings		15

NOTE: The building depreciation expense was closed to *Fund Balance—Principal* here because the trust agreement specified that trust earnings were to be computed without regard to building depreciation expense. Otherwise, it would have been closed to determine trust earnings.

1. **EXPENDABLE EARNINGS** An endowment gift of securities or an apartment complex in trust—where the principal must be maintained intact but the earnings may be expended for library purposes—is an example of a trust that is nonexpendable as to principal but expendable as to earnings.

2. **NONEXPENDABLE EARNINGS** Both the trust principal (corpus) and its earnings must be maintained intact and accumulated, and neither may be expended. When both the principal and the earnings are to be maintained intact—for example, a county loan fund where the earnings could be loaned to government employees and the interest earned used to make other loans—the trust fund would be purely nonexpendable.

3. **BASIS OF ACCOUNTING** Nonexpendable trust funds are accounted for on the accrual basis to determine revenues earned, expenses incurred, and net income (loss). However, a **unique** income determination feature of endowment and similar gifts in trust—where the earnings are expendable for specified purposes—is that the trust grantor can specify which revenues and expenses enter the determination of the trust earnings that are expendable. For example, a common endowment provision is that trust earnings **before** depreciation are expendable and shall be transferred to an Expendable trust fund. In such cases depreciation expense **is** recorded, but is closed to the trust **principal** *Fund Balance* account at year-end.

C. **EXPENDABLE TRUST FUND**
Used only under the outgoing reporting model to account for a government's fiduciary responsibilities and activities in managing trusts whose net assets **may** be expended for specified purposes.

Expendable trust funds are similar to governmental-type funds; they use modified accrual accounting.

1. **EXAMPLES** A Library expendable trust fund to account for the expenditure of the earnings of the Endowment nonexpendable trust (in B., above) for library purposes is a typical city or county expendable trust fund. Some federal grants also require the state or local government to establish an expendable trust fund.

2. **BASIS OF ACCOUNTING** Expendable trust fund accounting and reporting is on the modified accrual basis and parallels that for the governmental-type funds. Thus, expendable trust fund accounting warrants only a brief illustration here.

EXHIBIT 16 ♦ SAMPLE LIBRARY EXPENDABLE TRUST FUND ENTRIES

1. To record earnings of the nonexpendable trust fund that are restricted for library purposes:

Cash (or Due From Endowment Nonexpendable Trust Fund)	55	
Operating Transfer From Endowment Nonexpendable Trust Fund		55

2. To record expenditures and interfund transfer for library purposes:

Expenditures—Library Books	40	
Operating Transfer to Library Special Revenue Fund	5	
Cash or Payable		40
Due to Library Special Revenue Fund		5

NOTE: This entry assumes that some library expenditures are made directly from the Library expendable trust fund, but some of its resources are transferred to a Library special revenue fund to subsidize library expenditures made there. Alternatively, all expenditures might be made directly from the Library expendable trust fund or all available resources might be transferred to other funds through which library expenditures are financed.

3. To close the accounts at year-end:

Operating Transfer From Endowment Nonexpendable Trust Fund	55	
Expenditures—Library Books		40
Operating Transfer to Library Special Revenue Fund		5
Fund Balance		10

D. **ACCOUNT GROUPS**
The account groups appear in the balance sheet, but not in any operating statement.

1. **GENERAL FIXED ASSETS** Infrastructure is not required to be reported, and rarely appears. Depreciation is rarely accumulated on general fixed assets.

2. **GENERAL LONG-TERM DEBT** All the long-term liabilities of the governmental funds appear in the GLTDAG. If the general government is obligated in any manner for the debt of a proprietary or fiduciary fund, this debt appears in both the specific fund and the account group, resulting in it appearing twice in the financial statements.

E. **TRANSFERS**
The outgoing reporting model distinguishes between operating transfers and retained equity transfers as well as short-term and noncurrent interfund receivables and payables.

1. **RESIDUAL EQUITY TRANSFERS** These are nonrecurring, nonroutine, or unusual transfers of equity between funds. Under the outgoing reporting model, they should be (a) recorded in distinctive *Residual Equity Transfers From (To) [Name of Fund]* or *Residual Equity Transfers In (Out)* accounts, and (b) reported **after** the results of operations in the fund's operating statement. Examples include the transfer of initial capital from the general fund to establish an enterprise or internal service fund, return of all or part of that initial capital to the general fund upon abolishing or reducing the scope of activities of an enterprise or internal service fund, and transfers of residual balances of terminated funds to the general fund or to a debt service fund. Note that residual equity transfers (RETs) are involved in either establishing or closing a proprietary fund, but only in closing a governmental-type fund.

2. **OPERATING TRANSFERS** This term encompasses all interfund transactions **except** quasi-external transactions, reimbursements, and residual equity transfers. Under the outgoing reporting model, operating transfers should be (a) recorded in distinctive *Operating Transfers From (To)* [Name of Fund] or *Operating Transfers In (Out)* accounts, and (b) reported **after** revenues and expenditures or expenses, but **before** determining the results of operations in the fund's operating statement. Examples include routine transfers from the general fund to debt service funds, transfers of earnings from nonexpendable trust funds to expendable trust funds, transfers from the general fund to capital project fund or special revenue funds to an enterprise or internal service fund, and transfers of bond issue premiums from capital project funds to debt service funds.

3. **INTERFUND LOANS** Short-term loans are indicated using *Due from (to)* accounts. Long-term loans are indicated using *Advance From (to)* accounts. The fund making the loan reserves part of its fund balance to show that the resources are unavailable for other purposes.

_____

Time Management

Approximately 10% of the multiple choice questions in every section of every exam given after November 1995 are questions that are being pretested. These questions are **not** included in candidates' final grades; they are presented only so that the Board of Examiners may evaluate them for effectiveness and possible ambiguity.

The Scholastic Achievement Test and the Graduate Record Exam both employ similar but not identical strategies. Those tests include an extra section, which is being pretested, and test-takers do not know which section is the one that will not be graded. On the Uniform CPA Examination, however, the extra questions are mixed in among the graded questions.

This makes time management particularly crucial. Candidates who are deciding how much time to spend on a difficult multiple choice question must keep in mind that there is a 10% chance that the answer to the question will not affect them either way. Also, candidates should not allow a question that seems particularly difficult or confusing to shake their confidence or affect their attitude towards the rest of the test; it may not even count.

This experimental 10% will work against candidates who are not sure whether or not they have answered enough questions to earn 75%. Candidates should try for a safety margin, so that they will have accumulated enough correct answers to pass, even though some of their correctly answered questions will not be scored.

———————————

CHAPTER 22—GOVERNMENTAL FUNDS & TRANSACTIONS

PROBLEM 22-1 MULTIPLE CHOICE QUESTIONS (120 to 150 minutes)

1. Fish Road property owners in Sea County are responsible for special assessment debt that arose from a storm sewer project. If the property owners default, Sea has no obligation regarding debt service, although it does bill property owners for assessments and uses the monies it collects to pay debt holders. What fund type should Sea use to account for these collection and servicing activities?
a. Agency
b. Debt service
c. Expendable trust funds
d. Capital projects   (11/95, AR, #64, 5807)

2. Receipts from a special tax levy to retire and pay interest on general obligation bonds should be recorded in which fund?
a. General
b. Capital projects
c. Debt service
d. Special revenue   (11/97, AR, #12, 6540)

3. Proceeds of General Obligation Bonds is an account of a governmental unit that would be included in the
a. Debt service fund.
b. Internal service fund.
c. Capital projects fund.
d. Enterprise fund.   (Editors, 2163)

4. The portion of special assessment debt maturing in 5 years, to be repaid from general resources of the government, should be reported in the
a. General fund column.
b. Governmental activities column.
c. Agency fund column.
d. Capital projects fund column.
          (11/94, AR, #13, amended, 4990)

5. Cal City maintains several major fund types. The following were among Cal's cash:

Unrestricted state grant	$1,000,000
Interest on bank accounts held for employees' pension plan	200,000

What amount of these cash receipts should be accounted for in Cal's general fund?
a. $1,200,000
b. $1,000,000
c. $ 200,000
d. $0   (11/93, PII, #8, amended, 4437)

6. The town of Hill operates municipal electric and water utilities. In which of the following funds should the operations of the utilities be accounted for?
a. Enterprise fund
b. Internal service fund
c. Agency fund
d. Special revenue fund   (5/93, PII, #28, 4135)

7. For the 20X1 budgetary year, Maple City's general fund expects the following inflows of resources:

Property taxes, licenses, and fines	$9,000,000
Proceeds of debt issue	5,000,000
Interfund transfers for debt service	1,000,000

In the budgetary entry, what amount should Maple record for estimated revenues?
a. $ 9,000,000
b. $10,000,000
c. $14,000,000
d. $15,000,000   (11/93, PI, #3, amended, 4432)

8. The budget of a governmental unit, for which the appropriations exceed the estimated revenues, was adopted and recorded in the general ledger at the beginning of the year. During the year, expenditures and encumbrances were less than appropriations; whereas revenues equaled estimated revenues. The budgetary fund balance account is
a. Credited at the beginning of the year and debited at the end of the year.
b. Credited at the beginning of the year and **not** changed at the end of the year.
c. Debited at the beginning of the year and credited at the end of the year.
d. Debited at the beginning of the year and **not** changed at the end of the year.
          (5/91, Theory, #52, 2096)

9. The revenues control account of a governmental unit is increased when
a. The encumbrances account is decreased.
b. Appropriations are recorded.
c. Property taxes are recorded.
d. The budget is recorded.   (11/95, AR, #65, 5808)

10. Which of the following journal entries should a city use to record $250,000 for fire department salaries incurred during May?

		Debit	Credit
a.	Salaries expense	$250,000	
	Appropriations		$250,000
b.	Salaries expense	$250,000	
	Encumbrances		$250,000
c.	Encumbrances	$250,000	
	Salaries payable		$250,000
d.	Expenditures—salaries	$250,000	
	Salaries payable		$250,000

(11/96, AR, #12, amended, 6305)

11. On December 31, 20X1, Hill City paid a contractor $5,000,000 for the total cost of a new municipal annex built during the year on city-owned land. Financing was provided by a $3,000,000 general obligation bond issue sold at face amount on December 31, 20X1, with the remaining $2,000,000 transferred from the general fund. What account and amount should be reported in Hill's 20X1 financial statements for the general fund?
a. Other financing uses control, $2,000,000
b. Other financing sources control, $3,000,000
c. Expenditures control, $5,000,000
d. Other financing sources control, $5,000,000

(Editors, 9200)

12. The following information pertains to Spruce City's 20X1 liability for claims and judgments:

Current liability at January 1	$100,000
Claims paid during the year	800,000
Current liability at December 31	140,000
Noncurrent liability at December 31	200,000

What amount should Spruce report for 20X1 claims and judgments expenditures?
a. $1,040,000
b. $ 940,000
c. $ 840,000
d. $ 800,000   (11/93, PII, #7, amended, 4436)

13. The following information pertains to Pine City's general fund for 20X1:

Appropriations	$6,500,000
Expenditures	5,000,000
Other financing sources	1,500,000
Other financing uses	2,000,000
Revenues	8,000,000

After Pine's general fund accounts were closed at the end of 20X1, the fund balance increased by
a. $3,000,000.
b. $2,500,000.
c. $1,500,000.
d. $1,000,000.   (11/90, PII, #46, amended, 1350)

14. In 20X1, New City issued purchase orders and contracts of $850,000 that were chargeable against 20X1 budgeted appropriations of $1,000,000. The journal entry to record the issuance of the purchase orders and contracts should include a
a. Credit to vouchers payable of $1,000,000.
b. Credit to reserve for encumbrances of $850,000.
c. Debit to expenditures of $1,000,000.
d. Debit to appropriations of $850,000.

(11/94, AR, #18, amended, 4995)

15. The following information pertains to Park Township's general fund at December 31, 20X1:

Total assets, including $200,000 of cash	$1,000,000
Total liabilities	600,000
Reserved for encumbrances	100,000

Appropriations do not lapse at year-end. At December 31, 20X1, what amount should Park report as unreserved fund balance in its general fund balance sheet?
a. $200,000
b. $300,000
c. $400,000
d. $500,000   (11/93, PII, #20, amended, 4449)

16. During its fiscal year ended June 30, 20X1, Cliff City issued purchase orders totaling $5,000,000, which were properly charged to encumbrances at that time. Cliff received goods and related invoices at the encumbered amounts totaling $4,500,000 before year end. The remaining goods of $500,000 were not received until after year end. Cliff paid $4,200,000 of the invoices received during the year. What amount of Cliff's encumbrances were outstanding at June 30, 20X1?
a. $0
b. $300,000
c. $500,000
d. $800,000   (11/93, PII, #4, amended, 4433)

17. A budgetary fund balance reserved for encumbrances in excess of a balance of encumbrances indicates
a. An excess of vouchers payable over encumbrances.
b. An excess of purchase orders over invoices received.
c. An excess of appropriations over encumbrances.
d. A recording error. (11/93, Theory, #52, 4557)

18. Elm City issued a purchase order for supplies with an estimated cost of $5,000. When the supplies were received, the accompanying invoice indicated an actual price of $4,950. What amount should Elm debit (credit) to the reserve for encumbrances after the supplies and invoice were received?
a. $(50)
b. $ 50
c. $4,950
d. $5,000 (11/93, PII, #5, 4434)

19 When a purchase order is released, a commitment is made by a governmental unit to buy a computer to be manufactured to specifications for use in property tax administration. This commitment should be recorded in the general fund as a (an)
a. Appropriation.
b. Encumbrance.
c. Expenditure.
d. Fixed asset. (R/00, AR, #3, 6908)

20. Lake County received the following proceeds that are legally restricted to expenditure for specified purposes:

Levies on affected property owners to
  install sidewalks $500,000
Gasoline taxes to finance road repairs   900,000

What amount should be accounted for in Lake's special revenue funds?
a. $1,400,000
b. $ 900,000
c. $ 500,000
d. $0 (5/92, PII, #27, 2659)

21. The following information pertains to certain monies held by Blair County at December 31, 20X1, that are legally restricted to expenditures for specified purposes:

Proceeds of short-term notes to be used
  for advances to permanent trust funds $ 8,000
Proceeds of long-term debt to be used for
  a major capital project   90,000

What amount of these restricted monies should Blair account for in special revenue funds?
a. $0
b. $ 8,000
c. $90,000
d. $98,000 (11/93, PII, #18, amended, 4447)

22. Financing for the renovation of Fir City's municipal park, begun and completed during 20X1, came from the following sources:

Grant from state government $400,000
Proceeds from general obligation
  bond issue   500,000
Transfer from Fir's general fund   100,000

In its 20X1 capital projects fund operating statement, Fir should report these amounts as

	Revenues	Other financing sources
a.	$1,000,000	$0
b.	$ 900,000	$ 100,000
c.	$ 400,000	$ 600,000
d.	$0	$1,000,000

(11/93, PII, #11, amended, 4440)

23. In 20X1, Mentor Town received $4,000,000 of bond proceeds to be used for capital projects. Of this amount, $1,000,000 was expended in 20X1. Expenditures for the $3,000,000 balance were expected to be incurred in 20X2. These bonds proceeds should be recorded in capital projects funds for
a. $4,000,000 in 20X1.
b. $4,000,000 in 20X2.
c. $1,000,000 in 20X1 and $3,000,000 in 20X2.
d. $1,000,000 in 20X1 and in the general fund for $3,000,000 in 20X2. (Editors, 9201)

24. Grove Township issued $50,000 of bond anticipation notes at face amount in 20X1 and placed the proceeds into its capital projects fund. All legal steps were taken to refinance the notes, but Grove was unable to consummate refinancing. In the capital projects fund, what account should be credited to record the $50,000 proceeds?
a. Other Financing Sources Control
b. Revenues Control
c. Deferred Revenues
d. Bond Anticipation Notes Payable
(5/90, PII, #10, amended, 1373)

25. Wood City, which is legally obligated to maintain a debt service fund, issued the following general obligation bonds on July 1, 20X1:

Term debt	10 years
Face amount	$1,000,000
Issue price	101
Stated interest rate	6%

Interest is payable January 1 and July 1. What amount of bond premium should be amortized in Wood's debt service fund for the year ended December 31, 20X1?
a. $1,000
b. $ 500
c. $ 250
d. $0   (11/93, PII, #6, amended, 4435)

26. Dale City is accumulating financial resources that are legally restricted to payments of general long-term debt principal and interest maturing in future years. At December 31, 20X1, $5,000,000 has been accumulated for principal payments and $300,000 has been accumulated for interest payments. These restricted funds should be accounted for in the

	Debt service fund	General fund
a.	$0	$5,300,000
b.	$ 300,000	$5,000,000
c.	$5,000,000	$ 300,000
d.	$5,300,000	$0

(5/92, PII, #36, amended, 2668)

27. The debt service fund of a governmental unit is used to account for the accumulation of resources for, and the payment of, principal and interest in connection with a

	Private-purpose trust fund	Proprietary funds
a.	No	No
b.	No	Yes
c.	Yes	Yes
d.	Yes	No

(11/94, AR, #12, 4989)

28. Tott City's serial bonds are serviced through a debt service fund with cash provided by the general fund. In a debt service fund's statements, how are cash receipts and cash payments reported?

	Cash receipts	Cash payments
a.	Revenues	Expenditures
b.	Revenues	Operating transfers
c.	Operating transfers	Expenditures
d.	Operating transfers	Operating transfers

(5/91, Theory, #54, 2098)

29. Cedar City issued $1,000,000, 6% revenue bonds at par on April 1, to build a new water line for the water enterprise fund. Interest is payable every six months. What amount of interest expense should be reported for the year ended December 31?
a. $0
b. $30,000
c. $45,000
d. $60,000   (R/01, AR, #6, 6991)

30. Arlen City's fiduciary funds contained the following cash balances at December 31, 20X1:

Under the Forfeiture Act—cash confiscated from illegal activities; principal can be used only for law enforcement activities	$300,000
Sales taxes collected by Arlen to be distributed to other governmental units	500,000

What amount of cash should Arlen report in its permanent funds at December 31, 20X1?
a. $0
b. $300,000
c. $500,000
d. $800,000   (11/93, PII, #14, amended, 4443)

31. Palm City acquired, through forfeiture as a result of nonpayment of property taxes, a parcel of land that the city intends to use as a parking lot for general governmental purposes. The total amount of taxes, liens, and other costs incurred by Palm incidental to acquiring ownership and perfecting title was $20,000. The land's fair market value at the forfeiture date was $60,000. What amount should be reported in the governmental activities column of the government-wide financial statements for this land?
a. $0
b. $20,000
c. $60,000
d. $80,000   (11/93, PII, #15, amended, 4444)

32. The following are Boa City's long-term assets:

Fixed assets used in enterprise fund activities	$1,000,000
Infrastructure assets	9,000,000
All other general fixed assets	1,800,000

What aggregate amount should Boa report in the governmental activities column of the government-wide financial statements?
a. $ 9,000,000
b. $10,000,000
c. $10,800,000
d. $11,800,000   (5/92, PII, #33, amended, 2665)

33. Dodd Village adopted GASB Statement No. 34, but still uses account groups to track long-term assets and liabilities. Dodd received a gift of a new fire engine from a local civic group. The fair value of this fire engine was $400,000. The entry to be made in the general fixed assets account group for this gift is

		Debit	Credit
a.	Memorandum Entry Only	--	--
b.	General Fund Assets	$400,000	
	Private Gifts		$400,000
c.	Investment in General		
	Fixed Assets	$400,000	
	Gift Revenue		$400,000
d.	Machinery and Equipment	$400,000	
	Investment in General		
	Fixed Assets From		
	Private Gifts		$400,000

(11/93, PII, #16, amended, 4445)

34. Carille City adopted GASB Statement No. 34, but still uses account groups to track long-term assets and liabilities. Carille sold old equipment for less than its carrying amount. The sale reduces the investment in general fixed assets' balance by the
a. Difference between the cost of the equipment and the sales price.
b. Difference between the carrying amount of the equipment and the sales price.
c. Selling price of the equipment.
d. Carrying amount of the equipment.
(5/91, Theory, #56, amended, 2100)

35. Finch City adopted GASB Statement No. 34, but still uses account groups to track long-term assets and liabilities. On March 2, 20X1, Finch City issued 10-year general obligation bonds at face amount, with interest payable March 1 and September 1. The proceeds were to be used to finance the construction of a civic center over the period April 1, 20X1 to March 31, 20X2. During the fiscal year ended June 30, 20X1, no resources had been provided to the debt service fund for the payment of principal and interest. On June 30, 20X1, Finch's governmental funds balance sheet and government-wide statement of net assets should report the construction in progress for the civic center in the

	Capital projects fund	General fixed assets account group
a.	Yes	Yes
b.	Yes	No
c.	No	Yes
d.	No	No

(11/90, Theory, #57, amended, 2110)

36. Kingwood Town paid $22,000 cash for a flatbed trailer to be used in the general operations of the town. The expected useful life of the trailer is 6 years with an estimated $7,000 salvage value. Which of the following amounts would be reported?
a. $15,000 increase in equipment in the general fund.
b. $15,000 increase in the governmental activities column for fixed assets.
c. $22,000 increase in the governmental activities column for fixed assets.
d. $22,000 increase in equipment in the general fund. (R/99, AR, #16, amended, 6805)

37. Tuston City adopted GASB Statement No. 34, but still uses account groups to track long-term assets and liabilities. Tuston Township issued the following bonds during the year ended June 30:

Bonds issued for the garbage collection enterprise fund that will service the debt	$700,000
Revenue bonds to be repaid from admission fees collected by the township zoo enterprise fund	500,000

What amount of these bonds should be accounted for in Tuston's general long-term debt account group?
a. $1,200,000
b. $ 700,000
c. $ 500,000
d. $0 (11/95, AR, #66, amended 5809)

38. Oak County incurred the following expenditures in issuing long-term bonds:

Issue cost	$400,000
Debt insurance	90,000

When Oak establishes the accounting for operating debt service, what amount should be deferred and amortized over the life of the bonds?
a. $0
b. $ 90,000
c. $400,000
d. $490,000 (5/92, PII, #28, amended, 2660)

39. The following obligations were among those reported by Fern Village at December 31:

Vendor financing with a term of 10
months when incurred, in connection
with a capital asset acquisition that is
not part of a long-term financing plan $ 150,000
Long-term bonds for financing of
capital asset acquisition 3,000,000
Bond anticipation notes due in six
months, issued as part of a long-term
financing plan for capital purposes 400,000

What aggregate amount should Fern report as general long-term capital debt at December 31?
a. $3,000,000
b. $3,150,000
c. $3,400,000
d. $3,550,000 (5/92, PII, #34, amended, 2666)

40. Silver City adopted GASB Statement No. 34, but continues to use account groups to track long-term assets and liabilities. Silver City's debt service fund received funds for the future repayment of bond principal. As a consequence, Silver City has
a. An increase in the amount available in debt service funds and an increase in the fund balance.
b. An increase in the amount available in debt service funds and an increase in the amount to be provided for bonds.
c. An increase in the amount available in debt service funds and a decrease in the amount to be provided for bonds.
d. No changes in any amount until the bond principal is actually paid.
(11/91, Theory, #56, amended, 2563)

41. The orientation of accounting and reporting for all proprietary funds of governmental units is
a. Income determination.
b. Project.
c. Flow of funds.
d. Program. (11/94, AR, #3, 4980)

42. The following equity balances are among those maintained by Cole City:

Enterprise funds $1,000,000
Internal service funds 400,000

Cole's proprietary equity balances amount to
a. $1,400,000.
b. $1,000,000.
c. $ 400,000.
d. $0. (11/93, PII, #12, 4441)

43. Shared revenues received by an enterprise fund of a local government for operating purposes should be recorded as
a. Operating revenues.
b. Nonoperating revenues.
c. Other financing sources.
d. Interfund transfers. (5/94, AR, #56, 4661)

44. An enterprise fund would be used when the governing body requires that

I. Accounting for the financing of an agency's services to other government departments be on a cost-reimbursement basis.
II. User charges cover the costs of general public services.
III. Net income information be provided for an activity.

a. I only
b. I and II
c. I and III
d. II and III (11/91, Theory, #55, 2562)

45. A state government had the following activities:

I. State-operated lottery $10,000,000
II. State-operated hospital 3,000,000

Which of the above activities should be accounted for in an enterprise fund?
a. Neither I nor II
b. I only
c. II only
d. Both I and II (11/94, AR, #22, 4999)

46. How would customers' security deposits which can **not** be spent for normal operating purposes be classified in the balance sheet of the enterprise fund of a governmental unit?

	Restricted asset	Liability	Fund equity
a.	No	Yes	No
b.	Yes	Yes	No
c.	Yes	Yes	Yes
d.	Yes	No	Yes

(Editors, 2155)

47. Fixed assets of an enterprise fund should be accounted for in the
a. Enterprise fund, but **no** depreciation on the fixed assets should be recorded.
b. Enterprise fund, and depreciation on the fixed assets should be recorded.
c. General fixed asset account group, and depreciation on the fixed assets should be recorded.
d. General fixed asset account group, but **no** depreciation on the fixed assets should be recorded.
(Editors, 2132)

48. Which of the following does **not** affect an internal service fund's net income?
a. Depreciation expense on its fixed assets
b. Operating transfer sources
c. Residual equity transfers
d. Temporary transfers
(11/93, Theory, #55, amended, 4560)

49. The billings for transportation services provided to other governmental units are recorded by the internal service fund as
a. Transportation appropriations.
b. Operating revenues.
c. Interfund exchanges.
d. Intergovernmental transfers.
(11/95, AR, #73, 5816)

50. The following fund types used by Ridge City had total assets at December 31, 20X1, as follows:

Special revenue funds	$100,000
Agency funds	200,000
Pension funds	400,000

Total fiduciary fund assets amounted to
a. $300,000.
b. $400,000.
c. $600,000.
d. $700,000.
(Editors, 1388)

51. Both Curry City and the state have a general sales tax on all merchandise. Curry City's tax rate is 2 percent and the state's rate is 4 percent. Merchants are required by law to remit all sales tax collected each month to the state by the 15th of the following month. By law, the state has 45 days to process the collections and to make disbursements to the various jurisdictions for which it acts as an agent. Sales tax collected by merchants in Curry total $450,000 in May and $600,000 in June. Both merchants and the state make remittances in accordance with statutes. What amount of sales tax revenue for May and June is included in the June 30 year-end financial statements of the state and Curry?

	State	Curry
a.	$1,050,000	$0
b.	$1,050,000	$350,000
c.	$ 700,000	$350,000
d.	$ 300,000	$150,000

(R/00, AR, #2, 6907)

ITEMS 52 AND 53 are based on the following:

Elm City contributes to and administers a single-employer defined benefit pension plan on behalf of its covered employees. The plan is accounted for in a pension trust fund. Actuarially determined employer contribution requirements and contributions actually made for the past three years, along with the percentage of annual covered payroll, were as follows:

	Contribution made		Actuarial requirement	
	Amount	Percent	Amount	Percent
20X3	$11,000	26	$11,000	26
20X2	5,000	12	10,000	24
20X1	None	None	8,000	20

52. What account should be credited in the pension trust fund to record the 20X3 employer contribution of $11,000?
a. Revenues Control
b. Other Financing Sources Control
c. Due From Special Revenue Fund
d. Pension Benefit Obligation
(5/90, PII, #7, amended, 1370)

53. To record the 20X3 pension contribution of $11,000, what debit is required in the governmental-type fund used in connection with employer pension contributions?
a. Other Financing Uses Control
b. Expenditures Control
c. Expenses Control
d. Due to Pension Trust Fund
(5/90, PII, #8, amended, 1371)

54. Maple City's public employee retirement system (PERS) reported the following account balances at June 30, 20X1:

Reserve for employer's contributions	$5,000,000
Actuarial deficiency in reserve for	
employer's contributions	300,000
Reserve for employees' contributions	9,000,000

Maple's PERS fund balance at June 30, 20X1, should be
a. $ 5,000,000.
b. $ 5,300,000.
c. $14,000,000.
d. $14,300,000. (5/92, PII, #22, amended, 2654)

55. The following information pertains to Grove City's interfund receivables and payables at December 31, 20X1:

Due to special revenue fund from
  general fund $10,000
Due to agency fund from special
  revenue fund 4,000

In Grove's special revenue fund balance sheet at December 31, 20X1, how should these interfund amounts be reported?
a. As an asset of $6,000
b. As a liability of $6,000
c. As an asset of $4,000 and a liability of $10,000
d. As an asset of $10,000 and a liability of $4,000
(11/93, PII, #9, amended, 4438)

56. On December 31, 20X1, Walk Township paid a contractor $3,000,000 for the total cost of a new police building built in 20X1. Financing was by means of a $2,000,000 general obligation bond issue sold at face amount on December 31, 20X1, with the remaining $1,000,000 transferred from the general fund. What amount should Walk record as revenues in the capital projects fund in connection with the bond issue proceeds and the transfer?
a. $0
b. $1,000,000
c. $2,000,000
d. $3,000,000 (Editors, 1381)

57. In preparing combined financial statements for a governmental entity, interfund receivables and payables should be

a. Reported as reservations of fund balance.
b. Reported as additions to or reductions from the unrestricted fund balance.
c. Reported as amounts due to and due from other funds.
d. Eliminated. (5/95, AR, #53, 5471)

58. For which of the following funds do operating transfers affect the results of operations?

	Governmental funds	Proprietary funds
a.	No	No
b.	No	Yes
c.	Yes	Yes
d.	Yes	No

(11/94, AR, #11, 4988)

59. Gem City's internal service fund received a residual equity transfer of $50,000 cash from the general fund. This $50,000 transfer should be reported in Gem's internal service fund as a credit to
a. Revenues.
b. Other Financing Sources.
c. Accounts Payable.
d. Contributed Capital. (5/92, PII, #31, 2663)

60. Which of the following transactions is an expenditure of a governmental unit's general fund?
a. Contribution of enterprise fund capital by the general fund
b. Transfer from the general fund to a capital projects fund
c. Operating subsidy transfer from the general fund to an enterprise fund
d. Routine employer contributions from the general fund to a pension trust fund
(11/94, AR, #19, 4996)

PROBLEM 22-2 ADDITIONAL MULTIPLE CHOICE QUESTIONS (80 to 100 minutes)

61. Central County received proceeds from various towns and cities for capital projects financed by Central's long-term debt. A special tax was assessed by each local government, and a portion of the tax was restricted to repay the long-term debt of Central's capital projects. Central should account for the restricted portion of the special tax in which of the following funds?
a. Internal service fund
b. Enterprise fund
c. Capital projects fund
d. Debt service fund (5/93, PII, #34, 4141)

62. Kew City received a $15,000,000 federal grant to finance the construction of a center for rehabilitation of drug addicts. The proceeds of this grant should be accounted for in the
a. Special revenue funds.
b. General fund.
c. Capital projects funds.
d. Trust funds. (11/90, PII, #47, 1351)

63. Japes City issued $1,000,000 general obligation bonds at 101 to build a new city hall. As part of the bond issue, the city also paid a $500 underwriter fee and $2,000 in debt issue costs. What amount should Japes City report as other financing sources?
a. $1,010,000
b. $1,008,000
c. $1,007,500
d. $1,000,000   (R/01, AR, #9, 6994)

ITEMS 64 AND 65 are based on the following:

On March 2, 20X1, Finch City issued 10-year general obligation bonds at face amount, with interest payable March 1 and September 1. The proceeds were to be used to finance the construction of a civic center over the period April 1, 20X1 to March 31, 20X2. During the fiscal year ended June 30, 20X1, no resources had been provided to the debt service fund for the payment of principal and interest.

64. Proceeds from the general obligation bonds may be recorded in the
a. General fund.
b. Capital projects fund.
c. General long-term debt account group.
d. Debt service fund.
          (11/90, Theory, #55, amended, 2108)

65. The liability for the general obligation bonds may be recorded in the
a. General fund.
b. Capital projects fund.
c. General long-term debt account group.
d. Debt service fund.
          (11/90, Theory, #56, amended, 2109)

66. The following proceeds received by Arbor City are legally restricted to expenditure for specified purposes:

Expendable donation mandated
   by a benefactor to provide meals
   for the needy $100,000
Sales taxes to finance the maintenance of
   tourist facilities in the shopping district   300,000

What amount should be accounted for in Arbor's special revenue funds?
a. $0
b. $100,000
c. $300,000
d. $400,000   (Editors, 1384)

67. Which of the following accounts of a governmental unit is credited when taxpayers are billed for property taxes?
a. Appropriations
b. Taxes Receivable—Current
c. Estimated Revenues
d. Revenues   (11/93, Theory, #53, 4558)

68. Which of the following accounts of a governmental unit is credited when supplies previously ordered are received?
a. Expenditures Control
b. Encumbrances Control
c. Fund Balance Reserved for Encumbrances
d. Appropriations Control   (Editors, 2157)

69. The estimated revenues control account of a governmental unit is debited when
a. Actual revenues are recorded.
b. Actual revenues are collected.
c. The budget is recorded.
d. The budget is closed at the end of the year.
          (11/95, AR, #72, 5815)

70. The budgetary fund balance reserved for encumbrances account of a governmental-type fund is increased when
a. The budget is recorded.
b. Appropriations are recorded.
c. Supplies previously ordered are received.
d. A purchase order is approved.
          (11/92, Theory, #53, 3486)

71. When Rolan County adopted its budget for the year ending June 30, 20X1, $20,000,000 was recorded for estimated revenues control. Actual revenues for fiscal year 20X1 amounted to $17,000,000. In closing the budgetary accounts at June 30, 20X1,
a. Revenues Control should be debited for $3,000,000.
b. Estimated Revenues control should be debited for $3,000,000.
c. Revenues Control should be credited for $20,000,000.
d. Estimated Revenues control should be credited for $20,000,000.
          (11/90, PII, #57, amended, 1360)

72. Which account should Spring Township credit when it issues a purchase order for supplies?
a. Appropriations control
b. Vouchers payable
c. Encumbrance control
d. Reserve for encumbrances
          (11/95, AR, #71, 5814)

73. The encumbrance account of a governmental unit is debited when
a. The budget is recorded.
b. A purchase order is approved.
c. Goods are received.
d. A voucher payable is recorded.

(11/93, Theory, #51, 4556)

74. A county's balances in the general fund included the following:

Appropriations	$745,000
Encumbrances	37,250
Expenditures	298,000
Vouchers payable	55,875

What is the remaining amount available for use by the county?
a. $353,875
b. $391,125
c. $409,750
d. $447,000

(R/99, AR, #17, 6806)

ITEMS 75 THROUGH 77 are based on the following:

Park City uses encumbrance accounting and formally integrates its budget into the general fund's accounting records. For the year ending July 31, 20X1, the following budget was adopted:

Estimated revenues	$30,000,000
Appropriations	27,000,000
Estimated transfer to debt service fund	900,000

75. When Park's budget is adopted and recorded, Park's budgetary fund balance would be a
a. $3,000,000 credit balance.
b. $3,000,000 debit balance.
c. $2,100,000 credit balance.
d. $2,100,000 debit balance.

(5/92, PII, #23, amended, 2655)

76. Park should record budgeted appropriations by a
a. Credit to appropriations control, $27,000,000.
b. Debit to estimated expenditures, $27,000,000.
c. Credit to appropriations control, $27,900,000.
d. Debit to estimated expenditures, $27,900,000.

(5/92, PII, #24, amended, 2656)

77. Park incurred salaries and wages of $800,000 for the month of April 20X1. What account should Park debit to record this $800,000?
a. Encumbrances control
b. Salaries and wages expense control
c. Expenditures control
d. Operating funds control

(5/92, PII, #25, amended, 2657)

78. When a snowplow purchased by a governmental unit is received, it should be recorded in the general fund as a(an)
a. Encumbrance.
b. Expenditure.
c. Fixed Asset.
d. Appropriation.

(11/94, AR, #9, 4986)

ITEMS 79 THROUGH 84 are based on the following:

Cliff Township's fiscal year ends on July 31. Cliff uses encumbrance accounting. On October 2, 20X1, an approved $5,000 purchase order was issued for supplies. Cliff received these supplies on November 2, 20X1, and the $5,000 invoice was approved for payment by the general fund.

During the year ended July 31, 20X2, Cliff received a state grant of $150,000 to finance the purchase of a senior citizens recreation bus, and an additional $15,000 grant to be used for bus operations during the year ended July 31, 20X2. Only $125,000 of the capital grant was used during the year ended July 31, 20X2 for the bus purchase, but the entire operating grant of $15,000 was disbursed during the year.

Cliff's governing body adopted its general fund budget for the year ending July 31, 20X3, comprising estimated revenues of $50,000,000 and appropriations of $40,000,000. Cliff formally integrates its budget into the accounting records.

79. The senior citizens recreation bus program is accounted for as part of Cliff's general fund. What amount should Cliff report as grant revenues for the year ended July 31, 20X1, in connection with the state grants?
a. $165,000
b. $150,000
c. $140,000
d. $125,000

(Editors, 9245)

80. What accounts should Cliff debit and credit on October 2, 20X1, to record the approved $5,000 purchase order?

	Debit	Credit
a.	Encumbrances Control	Appropriations Control
b.	Appropriations Control	Encumbrances Control
c.	Encumbrances Control	Budgetary Fund Balance—
	Reserved for	
	Encumbrances	
d.	Budgetary Fund Balance—	Encumbrances Control
	Reserved for	
	Encumbrances	(Editors, 9246)

81. What accounts should Cliff debit and credit on November 2, 20X1, upon receipt of the supplies and approval of the $5,000 invoice?

	Debit	Credit
a.	Budgetary Fund Balance— Reserved for Encumbrances	Encumbrances Control
	Expenditures Control	Vouchers Payable
b.	Encumbrances Control	Budgetary Fund Balance— Reserved for Encumbrances
	Appropriations Control	Vouchers Payable
c.	Appropriations Control	Encumbrances Control
	Supplies Inventory	Vouchers Payable
d.	Encumbrances Control	Appropriations Control
	Expenditures Control	Vouchers Payable

(Editors, 9247)

82. To record the $40,000,000 of budgeted appropriations, Cliff should
a. Debit estimated expenditures control.
b. Credit estimated expenditures control.
c. Debit appropriations control.
d. Credit appropriations control. (Editors, 9248)

83. The $10,000,000 budgeted excess of revenues over appropriations should be
a. Debited to budgetary fund balance—unreserved.
b. Credited to budgetary fund balance—unreserved.
c. Debited to estimated excess revenues control.
d. Credited to estimated excess revenues control.
(Editors, 9249)

84. When Cliff records budgeted revenues, estimated revenues control should be
a. Debited for $10,000,000.
b. Credited for $10,000,000.
c. Debited for $50,000,000.
d. Credited for $50,000,000. (Editors, 9250)

85. Which of the following amounts are included in a general fund's encumbrance account?

I. Outstanding vouchers payable amounts
II. Outstanding purchase order amounts
III. Excess of the amount of a purchase order over the actual expenditure for that order

a. I only
b. I and III
c. II only
d. II and III (5/91, Theory, #53, 2097)

86. The debt service fund of a governmental unit is used to account for the accumulation of resources to pay, and the payment of, general long-term debt

	Principal	Interest
a.	Yes	Yes
b.	No	Yes
c.	No	No
d.	Yes	No

(Editors, 2145)

87. In connection with Alma Township's long-term debt, the following cash accumulations are available to cover payment of principal and interest on

Bonds for financing of water treatment
plant construction $2,000,000
General long-term obligations 700,000

The amount of these cash accumulations that should be accounted for in Alma's debt service funds is
a. $0.
b. $ 700,000.
c. $2,000,000.
d. $2,700,000. (Editors, 1385)

ITEMS 88 AND 89 are based on the following events relating to the City of Arrow's debt service funds that occurred during the year ended December 31, 20X1:

All principal and interest due in 20X1 were paid on time.

Debt principal matured $3,000,000
Unmatured (accrued) interest on
outstanding debt at Jan. 1, 20X1 45,000
Interest on matured debt 700,000
Unmatured (accrued) interest on
outstanding debt at Dec. 31, 20X1 93,000
Interest revenue from investments 800,000
Cash transferred from general fund
for retirement of debt principal 2,000,000
Cash transferred from general fund
for payment of matured interest 600,000

88. What is the total amount of expenditures that Arrow's debt service funds should record for 20X1?
a. $ 700,000
b. $ 745,000
c. $3,700,000
d. $3,745,000 (Editors, 1413)

89. How much revenue should Arrow's debt service funds record for 20X1?
a. $ 800,000
b. $2,600,000
c. $2,800,000
d. $3,400,000 (Editors, 1414)

90. Fixed assets donated to a governmental unit should be recorded
a. At the donor's carrying amount.
b. At estimated fair value when received.
c. At the lower of the donor's carrying amount or estimated fair value when received.
d. As a memorandum entry only.
(11/95, AR, #58, 5801)

91. A major exception to the general rule of expenditure accrual for governmental units relates to unmatured

	Principal of general long-term debt	Interest on general long-term debt
a.	Yes	Yes
b.	Yes	No
c.	No	Yes
d.	No	No

(11/94, AR, #14, 4991)

92. Which of the following funds of a governmental unit may use the general long-term debt account group to account for unmatured general long-term liabilities?
a. Internal service
b. Capital projects
c. Investment trust
d. Enterprise
(Editors, 9202)

93. Which of the following bases of accounting should a government use for its proprietary funds in measuring financial position and operating results?

	Modified accrual basis	Accrual basis
a.	No	Yes
b.	No	No
c.	Yes	Yes
d.	Yes	No

(11/90, Theory, #51, 2104)

94. The following information for the year ended June 30, 20X1, pertains to a proprietary fund established by Glen Village in connection with Glen's public parking facilities:

Receipts from users of parking facilities	$600,000
Expenditures	
Parking meters	410,000
Salaries and other cash expenses	96,000
Depreciation of parking meters	94,000

For the year ended June 30, 20X1, this proprietary fund should report net income of
a. $0.
b. $ 94,000.
c. $ 96,000.
d. $410,000.
(Editors, 9203)

95. Through an internal service fund, New County operates a centralized data processing center to provide services to New's other governmental units. In 20X1, this internal service fund billed New's parks and recreation fund $150,000 for data processing services. What account should New's internal service fund credit to record this $150,000 billing to the parks and recreation fund?
a. Data Processing Department Expenses
b. Intergovernmental Transfers
c. Interfund Exchanges
d. Operating Revenues Control
(11/93, PII, #13, amended, 4442)

96. Seaside County collects property taxes levied within its boundaries and receives a 1% fee for administering these collections on behalf of the municipalities located in the county. In 20X1, Seaside collected $1,000,000 for its municipalities and remitted $990,000 to them after deducting fees of $10,000. In the initial recording of the 1% fee, Seaside's agency fund should credit
a. Fund Balance—Agency Fund, $10,000.
b. Fees Earned—Agency Fund, $10,000.
c. Due to Seaside County General Fund, $10,000.
d. Revenues Control, $10,000. (Editors, 1396)

97. A city's electric utility, which is operated as an enterprise fund, rendered billings for electricity supplied to the general fund. Which of the following accounts should be debited by the general fund?
a. Appropriations
b. Expenditures
c. Due to Electric Utility Enterprise Fund
d. Other Financing Uses—Operating Transfers Out
(11/94, AR, #16, 4993)

98. Operating transfers received by a governmental-type fund should be reported in the Statement of Revenues, Expenditures, and Changes in Fund Balance as a(an)
a. Addition to contributed capital.
b. Addition to retained earnings.
c. Other financing source.
d. Reimbursement. (11/94, AR, #20, 4997)

ITEMS 99 AND 100 are based on the following:

Smallville has not yet adopted GASB Statement No. 34.

99. The recording of accumulated depreciation in Smallville's general fixed assets account group is
a. Never allowed.
b. Dependent on materiality.
c. Optional.
d. Mandatory. (11/93, Theory, #57, amended, 4562)

100. Which of the following accounts would be included in the fund equity section of Smallville's combined balance sheet for the general fixed asset account group?

	Investment in general fixed assets	Fund balance reserved for encumbrances
a.	Yes	Yes
b.	Yes	No
c.	No	Yes
d.	No	No
		(Editors, 2151)

OTHER OBJECTIVE FORMAT QUESTIONS

PROBLEM 22-3 (20 to 25 minutes)

Jey City adopted GASB Statement No. 34. Jey requires its landfill to recover its cost through user fees. The following events affected the financial statements of Jey City during 20X1:

Budgetary activities:

- Total general fund estimated revenues $8,000,000

- Total general fund budgeted expenditures   7,500,000

- Planned construction of a courthouse improvement expected to cost $1,500,000, and to be financed in the following manner: $250,000 from the general fund, $450,000 from state entitlements, and $800,000 from the proceeds of 20-year, 8% bonds dated and expected to be issued at par on June 30, 20X1. Interest on the bonds is payable annually on July 1, together with one-twentieth of the bond principal from general fund revenues of the payment period.

- A budgeted general fund payment of $180,000 to subsidize operations of a solid waste landfill enterprise fund.

Actual results included the following:

- Jey recorded property tax revenues of $5,000,000 and a related allowance for uncollectibles—current of $60,000. On December 31, 20X1, the remaining $56,000 balance of the allowance for uncollectibles—current was closed, and an adjusted allowance for uncollectibles—delinquent was recorded equal to the property tax receivables balance of $38,000.

- A police car with an original cost of $25,000 was sold for $7,000.

- Office equipment to be used by the city fire department was acquired through a capital lease. The lease required 10 equal annual payments of $10,000 beginning with the July 1, 20X1, acquisition date. Using a 6% discount rate, the 10 payments had a present value of $78,000 at the acquisition date.

- The courthouse was improved and financed as budgeted except for a $27,000 cost overrun that was paid for by the general fund. Jey plans to transfer cash to the debt service fund during 20X2 to service the interest and principal payments called for in the bonds.

- Information related to the solid waste landfill at December 31, 20X1.

Capacity	1,000,000 cubic yards
Usage prior to 20X1	500,000 cubic yards
Usage in 20X1	40,000 cubic yards
Estimated total life	20 years
Closure costs incurred to date	$ 300,000
Estimated future costs of closure and postclosure care	1,700,000
Expense for closure and postclosure care recognized prior to 20X1	973,000

FOR ITEMS 1 THROUGH 10, determine the amounts based solely on the above information.

1. What was the net effect of the budgetary activities on the general fund balance at January 1, 20X1?

2. What was the total amount of operating transfers out included in the general fund's budgetary accounts at January 1, 20X1?

3. What amount of interest payable related to the 20-year bonds should be reported by the general fund at December 31, 20X1?

4. What lease payment amount should be included in 20X1 general fund expenditures?

5. What amount was collected from 20X1 property taxes in 20X1?

6. What was the total amount of the capital project fund's 20X1 revenues?

7. What amount should be reported as long-term liabilities in the government-wide statement of net assets in the governmental activities column at December 31, 20X1?

8. What net increase in capital assets should be reported in the government-wide statement of net assets in the governmental activities column at December 31, 20X1?

9. What 20X1 closure and postclosure care expenses should be reported in the solid waste landfill enterprise fund?

10. What should be the December 31, 20X1, closure and post closure care liability reported in the solid waste landfill enterprise fund?

FOR ITEMS 11 AND 12, indicate the measurement focus of the Jey fund mentioned.

A. Subsidy restrictions
B. Bond restrictions
C. Expenditures
D. Financial resources
E. Capital maintenance/intergenerational equity

11. Capital project fund

12. Solid waste landfill enterprise fund
        (11/96, AR, #3, amended, 6317-6328)

PROBLEM 22-4 (10 to 15 minutes)

Duration City adopted GASB Statement No. 34, but continues to use account groups to track long-term assets and liabilities.

FOR ITEMS 1 THROUGH 10, select the **best** answer from the following list:

A. General long-term debt account group
B. General fixed assets account group
C. General fund
D. Capital projects fund
E. Debt service fund
F. Permanent fund
G. Special revenue fund
H. Private-purpose trust fund
I. Pension trust fund
J. Investment trust fund
K. Agency fund
L. Internal service fund

1. If Duration's general fund has an equity interest in a joint venture, this equity interest is recorded in which fund or account group?   (Editors, 4982)

2. Duration's fixed assets, other than those accounted for in proprietary or fiduciary funds, may be accounted for in which fund or account group?   (Editors, 4984)

3. Duration's unmatured general obligation bonds payable may be accounted for in the liability section of which fund or account group?
        (Editors, 2133)

4. Duration's municipal motor pool maintains all city-owned vehicles and charges the various departments for the cost of rendering those services. In which fund or account group does Duration account for the cost of such maintenance?   (Editors, 4139)

5. Which of Duration's funds or account groups may account for general long-term debt?
        (Editors, 2169)

6. Deferred compensation plans, for other than proprietary fund employees, adopted under IRC §457 should be reported in which fund?
        (Editors, 5000)

7. In which of the following funds or account groups should the debt service transactions of a special assessment issue for which the government is **not** obligated in any manner be reported?
        (Editors, 5001)

8. Taxes collected and held by Duration City for a separate school district would be accounted for in which fund or account group?   (Editors, 4662)

9. Stone Corp. donated investments to Duration and stipulated that the income from the investments be used to acquire art for the city's museum. Which fund or accounting group should be used to account for the investments?
        (Editors, 4145)

10. Which type of fund may have either nonexpendable or expendable resources?   (Editors, 5002)

PROBLEM 22-5 (8 to 15 minutes)

Dane City adopted GASB Statement No. 34. The following information relates to Dane City during its fiscal year ended December 31, 20X1:

- On October 31, 20X1, to finance the construction of a city hall annex, Dane issued 8% 10-year general obligation bonds at their face value of $600,000. Construction expenditures during the period equaled $364,000.

- Dane reported $109,000 from hotel room taxes, restricted for tourist promotion, in a special revenue fund. The fund paid $81,000 for general promotions and $22,000 for a motor vehicle.

- 20X1 general fund revenues of $104,500 were transferred to a debt service fund and used to repay $100,000 of 9% 15-year term bonds, and to pay $4,500 of interest. The bonds were used to acquire a citizens' center.

- At December 31, 20X1, as a consequence of past services, city firefighters had accumulated entitlements to compensated absences valued at $86,000. General fund resources available at December 31, 20X1, are expected to be used to settle $17,000 of this amount, and $69,000 is expected to be paid out of future general fund resources.

- At December 31, 20X1, Dane was responsible for $83,000 of outstanding general fund encumbrances, including the $8,000 for supplies indicated below.

- Dane uses the purchases method to account for supplies. The following information relates to supplies:

Inventory—1/1/X1	$ 39,000
12/31/X1	42,000
Encumbrances outstanding—1/1/X1	6,000
12/31/X1	8,000
Purchase orders during 20X1	190,000
Amounts credited to vouchers	
payable during 20X1	$181,000

FOR ITEMS 1 THROUGH 10, determine the amounts based solely on the above information.

1. What is the amount of 20X1 general fund operating transfers out?

2. How much should be reported as 20X1 general fund liabilities from entitlements for compensated absences?

3. What is the 20X1 reserved amount of the general fund balance?

4. What is the 20X1 capital projects fund balance?

5. What is the 20X1 fund balance on the special revenue fund for tourist promotion?

6. What is the amount of 20X1 debt service fund expenditures?

7. What amount should be included in the general fund for capital assets acquired in 20X1?

8. What amount stemming from 20X1 transactions and events decreased the long-term liabilities reported in the government activities column of the government-wide statements?

9. Using the purchases method, what is the amount of 20X1 supplies expenditures?

10. What was the total amount of 20X1 supplies encumbrances?
    (11/95, AR, #117-126, amended, 5860-5869)

PROBLEM 22-6 (45 to 55 minutes)

ITEMS 1 THROUGH 10 are listed in the left-hand column and represent various transactions pertaining to a municipality that uses encumbrance accounting.

ITEMS 11 THROUGH 20 represent the funds and accounts used by the municipality.

FOR 1 THROUGH 10, (the municipality's transactions) select the appropriate recording of the transaction (A through L). A method of recording the transactions may be selected once, more than once, or not at all.

FOR 11 THROUGH 20, (the municipality's funds and accounts) select the appropriate method of accounting and reporting (M through V). An accounting and reporting method may be selected once, more than once, or not at all.

Transactions

1. General obligation bonds were issued at par.

2. Approved purchase orders were issued for supplies.

3. The above-mentioned supplies were received and the related invoices were approved.

4. General fund salaries and wages were incurred.

5. The internal service fund had interfund billings.

6. Revenues were earned from a previously awarded grant.

7. Property taxes were collected in advance.

8. Appropriations were recorded on adoption of the budget.

9. Short-term financing was received from a bank, secured by the city's taxing power.

10. There was an excess of estimated inflows over estimated outflows.

Recording of Transactions

A. Credit appropriations control.

B. Credit budgetary fund balance—unreserved.

C. Credit expenditures control.

D. Credit deferred revenues.

E. Credit interfund revenues.

F. Credit tax anticipation notes payable.

G. Credit other financing sources.

H. Credit other financing uses.

I. Debit appropriations control.

J. Debit deferred revenues.

K. Debit encumbrances control.

L. Debit expenditures control.

Funds and Accounts

11. Enterprise fund fixed assets.

12. Capital projects fund.

13. Internal service fund fixed assets.

14. Private-purpose trust fund cash.

15. Enterprise fund cash.

16. General fund.

17. Agency fund cash.

18. Pension trust fund cash.

19. Special revenue fund.

20. Debt service fund.

Accounting and Reporting by Funds

M. Accounted for in a fiduciary fund.

N. Accounted for in a proprietary fund.

O. Accounted for in a quasi-endowment fund.

P. Accounted for in a self-balancing account group.

Q. Accounted for in a special assessment fund.

R. Accounts for major construction activities.

S. Accounts for property tax revenues.

T. Accounts for payment of interest and principal on tax supported debt.

U. Accounts for revenues from earmarked sources to finance designated activities.

V. Reporting is optional.
   [11/92, PII, #4 (61-80), amended, 3395-3413]

PROBLEM 22-7 (5 to 10 minutes)

Dease City has adopted GASB Statement No. 34.

ITEMS 1 THROUGH 5 represent transactions by governmental-type funds and account groups based on the following selected information taken from Dease City's 20X1 financial records:

General fund

Beginning fund balance	$ 700,000
Estimated revenues	10,000,000
Actual revenues	10,500,000
Appropriations	9,000,000
Expenditures	8,200,000
Ending encumbrances	500,000
Ending vouchers payable	300,000
Operating transfers in	100,000
20X1 property tax levy	9,500,000
20X1 property taxes estimated to be uncollectible when property tax levy for 20X1 recorded	100,000
20X1 property taxes delinquent at end of 20X1	150,000

Capital projects fund

Operating transfers in	100,000
Construction of new library wing started and completed in 20X1	
• Proceeds from bonds issued at 100	2,000,000
• Expenditures	2,100,000

FOR ITEMS 1 THROUGH 5, determine the amounts solely on the above information.

1. What was the net amount credited to the budgetary fund balance when the budget was approved?

2. What was the amount of property taxes collected on the property tax levy for 20X1?

3. What amount for the new library wing was included in the capital projects fund balance at the end of 20X1?

4. What amount for the new library wing was reported in the government-wide statement of net assets in the governmental activities column at the end of 20X1?

5. What amount for the new library wing bonds was reported in the government-wide statement of net assets in the governmental activities column at the end of 20X1?

(5/97, AR, #2, amended, 6355-6359)

PROBLEM 22-8 (25 to 35 minutes)

Bel City, whose first fiscal year ended December 31, 20X1, has adopted GASB Statement No. 34. Bel has only the long-term debt specified in the information and only the funds necessitated by the information.

1. General fund:

- The following selected information is taken from Bel's 20X1 general fund financial records:

	Budget	Actual
Property taxes	$5,000,000	$4,700,000
Other revenues	1,000,000	1,050,000
Total revenues	$6,000,000	$5,750,000
Total expenditures	$5,600,000	$5,700,000

Property taxes receivable—delinquent	$ 420,000
Less: Allowance for estimated uncollectible taxes—delinquent	50,000
	$ 370,000

- There were no amendments to the budget as originally adopted.
- No property taxes receivable have been written off, and the allowance for uncollectibles balance is unchanged from the initial entry at the time of the original tax levy.
- There were no encumbrances outstanding at December 31, 20X1.

2. Capital project fund:

- Finances for Bel's new civic center were provided by a combination of general fund transfers, a state grant, and an issue of general obligation bonds. Any bond premium on issuance is to be used for the repayment of the bonds at their $1,200,000 par value. At December 31, 20X1, the capital project fund for the civic center had the following closing entries:

Revenues	$ 800,000	
Other financing sources— bond proceeds	1,230,000	
Other financing sources— operating transfers in	500,000	
Expenditures		$1,080,000
Other financing uses— operating transfers out		30,000
Unreserved fund balance		1,420,000

- Also, at December 31, 20X1, capital project fund entries reflected Bel's intention to honor the $1,300,000 purchase orders and commitments outstanding for the center.
- During 20X1, total capital project fund encumbrances exceeded the corresponding expenditures by $42,000. All expenditures were previously encumbered.
- During 20X2, the capital project fund received no revenues and no other financing sources. The civic center building was completed in early 20X2 and the capital project fund was closed by a transfer of $27,000 to the general fund.

3. Water utility enterprise fund:

- Bel issued $4,000,000 revenue bonds at par. These bonds, together with a $700,000 transfer from the general fund, were used to acquire a water utility. Water utility revenues are to be the sole source of funds to retire these bonds beginning in year 20X9.

FOR 1 THROUGH 16, indicate if the answer to each item is yes (Y) or no (N).

ITEMS 1 THROUGH 8 relate to Bel's general fund.

1. Did recording budgetary accounts at the beginning of 20X1 increase the fund balance by $50,000?

2. Should the budgetary accounts for 20X1 include an entry for the expected transfer of funds from the general fund to the capital projects fund?

3. Should the $700,000 payment from the general fund, which was used to help to establish the water utility fund, be reported as an "other financing use—operating transfers out"?

4. Did the general fund receive the $30,000 bond premium from the capital projects fund?

5. Should a payment from the general fund for water received for normal civic center operations be reported as an "other financing use—operating transfers out"?

6. Does the net property taxes receivable of $370,000 include amounts expected to be collected after March 15, 20X2?

7. Would closing budgetary accounts cause the fund balance to increase by $400,000?

8. Would the interaction between budgetary and actual amounts cause the fund balance to decrease by $350,000?

ITEMS 9 THROUGH 16 relate to Bel's financial statements.

9. In the government-wide statement of net assets, is there a total elimination of interfund transactions?

10. In the government-wide statement of activities, are general revenues separated from program revenues?

11. In the government-wide statement of net assets, is the internal service fund reported as a governmental activity?

12. In the primary government's financial statements, is the general fund a nonmajor fund?

13. In the government-wide statements of net assets, are fiduciary funds reported as business-type activities?

In which fund should Bel report capital and related financing activities in its statement of cash flows?

14. Debt service fund.

15. Capital project fund.

16. Water utility enterprise fund.

FOR 17 THROUGH 22, determine the amount.

ITEMS 17 AND 18 relate to Bel's general fund.

17. What was the amount recorded in the opening entry for appropriations?

18. What was the total amount debited to property taxes receivable?

ITEMS 19 THROUGH 22 relate to Bel's funds other than the general fund.

19. What was the completed cost of the civic center?

20. How much was the state capital grant for the civic center?

21. In the capital project fund, what was the amount of the total encumbrances recorded during 20X1?

22. In the capital project fund, what was the unreserved fund balance reported at December 31, 20X1?
    [5/95, AR, #2 (#61-84), amended, 5479-5502]

PROBLEM 22-9 (20 to 30 minutes)

Shar City has adopted GASB Statement No. 34. The following selected information is taken from Shar City's general fund operating statement for the year ended December 31, 20X2:

Revenues	
Property taxes—20X2	$825,000
Expenditures	
Current services	
Public safety	428,000
Capital outlay (police vehicles)	100,000
Debt service	74,000

Expenditures—20X2	$1,349,000
Expenditures—20X1	56,000
Expenditures	$1,405,000
Excess of revenues over expenditures	$ 153,000
Other financing uses	(125,000)
Excess of revenues over expenditures and other financing uses	$ 28,000
Decrease in reserve for encumbrances during 20X2	15,000
Residual equity transfers out	(190,000)
Decrease in unreserved fund balance during 20X2	$ (147,000)
Unreserved fund balance January 1, 20X2	304,000
Unreserved fund balance December 31, 20X2	$ 157,000

The following selected information is taken from Shar's December 31, 20X2, general fund balance sheet:

Property taxes receivable—
delinquent—20X2 $ 34,000
Less: Allowance for estimated
uncollectible taxes—delinquent 20,000
Vouchers payable $ 89,000
Fund balance—
reserved for encumbrances—20X2 $ 43,000
reserved for supplies inventory 38,000
unreserved 157,000

Additional Information:

- Debt service was for bonds used to finance a library building and included interest of $22,000.

- $8,000 of 20X2 property taxes receivable were written-off; otherwise, the allowance for uncollectible taxes balance is unchanged from the initial entry at the time of the original tax levy at the beginning of the year.

- Shar reported supplies inventory of $21,000 at December 31, 20X1.

REQUIRED:

FOR ITEMS 1 THROUGH 3, indicate the type of classification used by Shar.
  A. Character
  B. Function
  C. Object

1. Expenditures—current services
2. Expenditures—capital outlay
3. Expenditures—health

FOR ITEMS 4 THROUGH 6, select the best answer.

4. What recording method did Shar use for its general fund supplies inventory?
  A. Consumption
  B. Purchase
  C. Perpetual inventory

5. How should fund equity be reported in Shar's electric utility enterprise fund?
  A. An amount described as fund balance
  B. An amount described as net assets
  C. Separately for amount due to general fund and retained income

6. Shar's electric utility enterprise fund borrowed $1,000,000 subject to Shar's general guarantee.

Where should the liability be reported in the government-wide statement of net assets?
  A. The business-type activities column
  B. The general long-term debt account group
  C. Both the business-type activities column and the general long-term debt account group

FOR ITEMS 7 THROUGH 13, indicate the part of Shar's general fund statement of activities affected by the transaction.

  A. Revenues
  B. Expenditures
  C. Other financing sources
  D. Other financing uses
  E. Statement of activities is **not** affected

7. An unrestricted state grant is received.

8. The general fund paid pension fund contributions that were recoverable from an internal service fund.

9. The general fund paid $60,000 for electricity supplied by Shar's electric utility enterprise fund.

10. General fund resources were used to subsidize Shar's swimming pool enterprise fund.

11. $90,000 of general fund resources were loaned to an internal service fund.

12. A motor pool internal service fund was established by a transfer of $80,000 from the general fund. This amount will not be repaid unless the motor pool is disbanded.

13. General fund resources were used to pay amounts due on an operating lease.

FOR ITEMS 14 THROUGH 19, calculate the numeric amount.

14. What was the reserved fund balance of the 20X1 general fund?

15. What amount was collected from 20X2 tax assessments?

16. What amount is Shar's liability to general fund vendors and contractors at December 31, 20X2?

17. What amount should be included in the government-wide statement of net assets in the governmental activities column for capital assets acquired in 20X2 through the general fund?

18. What amount arising from 20X2 transactions decreased long-term liabilities reported in the government-wide statement of net assets in the governmental activities column?

19. What amount of total actual expenditures should Shar report in its 20X2 general fund statement of activities?

(5/96, AR, #17-35, amended, 6214-6232)

SOLUTION 22-1 MULTIPLE CHOICE ANSWERS

DETERMINING FUND OR GROUP

1. (a) The agency fund is used to account for the custodial activities of the governmental unit. The debt service fund is used to account for the repayment of the general long-term debt. The capital projects fund accounts for the project itself, not the repayment of debt.

2. (c) The debt service fund is used to account for the accumulation of resources for the periodic payment of interest and principal of general obligation long-term debt. Special revenue funds are used when other governmental-type funds are not more appropriate.

3. (c) Capital projects funds are used to account for the acquisition and use of financial resources to construct or otherwise acquire long-lived "general government" real property and equipment. Project resources, which include proceeds of general obligation bonds, are recorded as received or accrued.

4. (b) General government fixed assets and long-term debt, are *not* recorded in the governmental funds, but are shown in the governmental activities column of the government-wide financial statements. General long-term debt to be repaid from general resources of the government should not be reported in any fund.

5. (b) The $1,000,000 unrestricted grant received from the state should be accounted for as revenue in Cal City's general fund. The $200,000 of interest received on bank accounts held for employees' pension plans should be accounted for in Cal City's pension trust fund.

6. (a) Enterprise funds are used to account for a government's "business-type" operations that are financed and operated like private businesses (i.e., where the government's intent is that all costs, including depreciation, of providing goods or services to the general public on a continuing basis are to be financed or recovered primarily through user charges). Most government-owned public utilities must be accounted for in the enterprise funds under these criteria. Internal service funds account for the financing of goods or services provided by one department or agency to other departments or agencies of a governmental unit, or to other governmental units, on a cost-reimbursement basis. Agency funds account for resources held by a government as an agent for individuals or other governmental units. Special revenue funds account for general government resources that are restricted by law or contract for specific purposes.

GENERAL FUND: BUDGETS

7. (a) The general fund records the expected $9,000,000 of inflows of resources for property taxes, licenses, and fines as estimated revenues in the entry to record the adoption of the budget. In this same entry, the expected inflows of resources from the proceeds of the debt issue and the interfund transfers for debt service are recorded as other financing sources.

8. (c) The *fund balance* account of the governmental unit is *debited* at the beginning of the year because appropriations *exceed* estimated revenues, shown in Entry (1). During the year, revenues *equaled* estimated revenues; therefore, the *fund balance* account is *not affected* by the revenue closing entry, as in Entry (2). During the year, expenditures and encumbrances were *less than* appropriations; therefore, the *fund balance* account is *credited* for the closing entry for the appropriations, expenditures, and encumbrances, as in Entry (3).

(1)	Estimated Revenues Control	XX	
	Fund Balance (to balance)	XX	
	Appropriations Control		XX
(2)	Revenues Control	XX	
	Estimated Revenues Control		XX
(3)	Appropriations Control	XX	
	Expenditures Control		XX
	Encumbrances Control		XX
	Fund Balance (to balance)		XX

GENERAL FUND: ACTUAL

9. (c) When property taxes are recorded, *Property Taxes—Receivable* is debited and *Revenues* is credited. When the budget is recorded, the *Appropriations* account is credited and the *Estimated Revenues* account is debited. The *Encumbrance*

account is decreased when an invoice for an encumbered item is received.

10. (d) Fire department salaries are *expenditures* of the general government, not *expenses* of a propriety fund. While goods and services committed for by purchase order or contract are encumbered in governmental funds to avoid overspending appropriations, some expenditures are controlled by other means and need not be encumbered. Salaries are set by contract and controlled by established payroll procedures and are not encumbered.

11. (a) The $2,000,000 from the general fund was only "transferred" to the capital projects fund. The *Other Financing Uses Control* account should be used to report the interfund transfer in the financial statements for the general fund. The issuance of the $3,000,000 general obligation bond issue for capital outlay purposes is not recorded in the general fund and, thus, is not reported in its financial statements. (The issuance of the bond is recorded in the capital projects fund and optionally, in the general long-term debt account group.)

12. (c) In governmental funds, the primary emphasis is on the flow of financial resources. Accordingly, the amount of claims and judgments recorded as expenditures (and liabilities) in governmental funds is the amount accrued during the year that would normally be liquidated with expendable available financial resources. Optionally, noncurrent claims and judgment liabilities are recorded initially in the GLTDAG. They only become governmental fund expenditures in the year in which they mature or become current liabilities.

Claims paid during the year	$800,000
Increase in current liability for claims and judgments during the year ($140,000 – $100,000)	40,000
Annual claims and judgment expenditures	$840,000

13. (b) *Appropriations* is a budgetary account which will be closed. However, since closing the budgetary accounts (which are not all given) simply reverses the entry to record the budget, their closing has no effect on fund balance. The closing entry for the activity accounts given would increase the fund balance, as follows:

Revenues	8,000,000	
Other Financing Sources	1,500,000	
Expenditures		5,000,000
Other Financing Uses		2,000,000
Fund Balance (difference)		2,500,000

GENERAL FUND: ENCUMBRANCES

14. (b) To record purchase orders issued or contract commitments, the *Encumbrances* account is debited and *Reserve for Encumbrances* is credited.

15. (b) Because Park's appropriations do not lapse at year-end, the *Fund Balance Reserved for Encumbrances* account is converted from an offsetting memorandum account in the general ledger to a true reservation of *Fund Balance* at year-end. The amount that Park should report as *Unreserved Fund Balance* in its general fund balance sheet is computed as follows:

Total assets	$1,000,000
Less: Total liabilities	600,000
Total fund balance	400,000
Less: Fund balance reserved for encumbrances	100,000
Unreserved fund balance, December 31	$ 300,000

16. (c) The amount of Cliff's encumbrances that were outstanding at June 30 is $500,000 (i.e., $5,000,000 – $4,500,000). When the purchase orders were issued, the following entry was made:

Encumbrances Control (estimated cost)	5,000,000	
Reserve for Encumbrances		5,000,000

Upon receipt of the goods and related invoices, the following entries were made:

Reserve for Encumbrances	4,500,000	
Encumbrances Control		4,500,000
(reverse original entry)		
Expenditures (actual cost)	4,200,000	
Vouchers Payable		4,200,000

17. (d) The *Encumbrance* and *Budgetary Fund Balance Reserved for Encumbrances* (BFBRFE) accounts increase by equal amounts when a $200 purchase order is approved:

Encumbrances (estimated cost)	200	
Reserve for Encumbrances		200

The *Encumbrance* and BFBRFE accounts decrease by equal amounts when the receipt of the related goods for $203 and the vouchers payable are recorded:

Fund Balance Reserved for Encumbrances	200	
Encumbrances (estimated cost)		200
Expenditures (actual cost)	203	
Vouchers Payable		203

The *Encumbrance* and BFBRFE accounts will have identical balances unless a recording error was made.

18. (d) When the purchase order for the supplies was issued, the following entry was made:

Encumbrances Control (estimated cost)   5,000
     Reserve for Encumbrances   5,000

Upon receipt of the supplies and invoice, the following entries were made:

Reserve for Encumbrances
    (reverse original entry)   5,000
     Encumbrances Control   5,000
Expenditures (actual cost)   4,950
     Vouchers Payable   4,950

19. (b) Commitments made by a government are encumbrances. Appropriations are amounts budgeted to be spent. Expenditures are amounts that have been spent. A fixed assets account is not debited until the property is placed in service.

SPECIAL REVENUES FUND

20. (b) The $900,000 of gasoline taxes collected to finance road repairs should be accounted for in a Special Revenue Fund. Special Revenue Funds are used to account for revenues that have been legally restricted as to expenditure. The NCGA provides several examples of revenues which would fall under the heading: (1) a state gasoline tax collected in order to maintain streets, (2) proceeds from parking meters which finance the local traffic court, and (3) state juvenile rehabilitation grants used to operate and maintain juvenile rehabilitation centers. In each of these cases, a service is being provided, but the funding comes from a specific revenue source rather than from property taxes or any other general revenues.

21. (a) Special revenue funds are used to account for financial resources that are restricted by law or by contractual agreement to specific purposes *other than for permanent funds or major capital projects.* Thus, neither the $8,000 of proceeds of the short-term notes to be used for advances to permanent fund nor the $90,000 of proceeds on long-term debt to be used for a major capital project should be accounted for in a special revenue fund.

CAPITAL PROJECTS FUND

22. (c) The capital projects fund reports unrestricted grants received from other governmental units as revenue. Therefore, the $400,000 grant from the state is reported as revenue in Fir's capital projects fund's operating statement. The capital projects fund reports long-term debt proceeds and operating transfers from other funds as other financing sources. Therefore, the $500,000 proceeds from the general obligation bond issue and the $100,000 transfer from Fir's general fund are reported as other financing sources of $600,000 in the capital project fund's operating statement.

23. (a) Debt proceeds should be recognized by a capital projects fund at the time the debt is incurred, rather than the time the debt is authorized or when the proceeds are expended. Debt proceeds should be reported in the capital projects fund as *Other Financing Sources* rather than as *Revenues.* The entry in the capital projects fund to record the issuance of the bonds is as follows:

Cash   4,000,000
    Other Financing Sources—
      Bond Proceeds   4,000,000

24. (d) A governmental unit would issue bond anticipation notes to provide funds to defray costs expected to be incurred before the related bonds are issued. Such notes are treated as long-term debt, even if due within one year, if (1) they are to be repaid with the proceeds of the bond issue, (2) all legal steps have been taken to refinance the notes, and (3) the intent is supported by an ability to refinance the short-term notes on a long-term basis. Since all of these criteria are not met for the bond anticipation notes in question, they are reported as a liability of the capital projects fund.

DEBT SERVICE FUND

25. (d) Governmental-type funds do not defer and amortize a bond premium or discount over the life of the bonds. Bond issue proceeds are recorded in the appropriate governmental fund at the amount received, net of any bond premium or discount.

26. (d) See the explanation to question #86.

27. (a) Only general obligation long-term debt should be serviced through debt service funds. Fiduciary and proprietary fund debt are rarely general government obligations.

28. (c) The debt service fund of a governmental unit is used to account for accumulation of resources for, and the payment of, general long-term debt principal and interest. The debt service fund reports cash receipts from the general fund as operating transfers. Cash payments for long-term debt principal and related interest are reported as expenditures in the fund.

29. (c) Since this is an enterprise fund, accrual applies. Interest expense for the year includes the $30,000 ($1,000,000 x 6% x 1/2 year) paid on October 1st and the $15,000 ($1,000,000 x 6% x 1/4 year) accrued expense from October 1st through December 31.

PERMANENT FUND

30. (a) The cash, which can be used only for law enforcement activities, should be accounted for in special revenue fund because the Act does not require the preservation of fund principal and the principal may be used for Arlen's benefit. An agency fund is established to account for assets received by a government in its capacity as an agent for individuals, businesses, or other governments. Therefore, the sales taxes collected by Arlen to be distributed to other governments are accounted for in an agency fund.

GFAAG

31. (b) General fixed assets acquired by foreclosure are recorded at the lower of (1) the amount due for taxes, special assessments, penalties and interest, plus foreclosure costs or (2) appraised fair market value. Therefore, since the $20,000 Palm incurred for taxes, liens, and other costs incidental to acquiring ownership and perfecting title is less than the land's $60,000 fair market value at the forfeiture date, the land is reported in the government-wide statements and may be capitalized in the GFAAG at $20,000.

32. (c) The government-wide financial statements report all general capital assets (fixed assets plus infrastructure) in the governmental activity column. Usually internal service fund fixed assets also appear in this column. Enterprise fund fixed assets appear in a different column. Fiduciary funds do not appear in the GWS.

33. (d) Because no fund assets are relinquished in acquiring donated property, transactions of this type are recorded in the General Fixed Assets Account Group (GFAAG) but not in any governmental fund. The donated property is recorded at its estimated fair value to the government at the time of donation. Account groups don't have revenues or expenditures. The GFAAG accounting equation is:

$$\begin{array}{ccc} \text{General} & & \text{Investment in} \\ \text{Fixed Assets} & = & \text{General Fixed Assets} \\ \text{(By asset type)} & & \text{(By financing source)} \end{array}$$

34. (d) The General Fixed Assets Account Group (GFAAG) may be used to account for capital assets of governmental funds. The proceeds from the sale of the machine are not recorded in the GFAAG; they are recorded as revenues in the recipient governmental fund. The accounting equation for the GFAAG is as follows:

$$\begin{array}{ccc} & & \text{Investment in} \\ \text{General Fixed Assets} & = & \text{General Fixed Assets} \\ \text{(By asset type)} & & \text{(By financing source)} \end{array}$$

The following entry is made in the GFAAG to record a machine acquired by a governmental fund:

Machinery and Equipment   XX
    Investment in General Fixed
     Assets—Financing Source   XX

The machine's carrying amount in the GFAAG is its original cost plus the cost of any additions and betterments less any accumulated depreciation.

35. (d) General government fixed assets may be accounted for in the General Fixed Assets Account Group (GFAAG), regardless of which fund finances them. The cost of construction work undertaken but incomplete at a balance sheet date is accounted for in the GFAAG in the *Construction Work In Process* account. When the project is completed, these costs are transferred to the appropriate fixed asset account in the GFAAG. However, the GFAAG itself doesn't appear in government-wide or fund financial statements.

36. (c) Purchased assets are reported at cost. Long-term capital assets are not recorded in any governmental fund.

GLTDAG

37. (d) Enterprise funds carry their own debt. Both of these funds are enterprise funds. The general long-term debt account group may carry long-term obligations of the general government.

38. (a) Neither the bond issue costs nor the debt insurance are deferred and amortized over the life of the bonds. The bond issue proceeds are recorded at the amount received net of any issue and insurance costs incurred.

39. (c) Fern should report $3,400,000 as long-term capital debt. This amount is comprised of (1) long-term bonds for financing of capital asset acquisition and (2) bond anticipation notes (BANs) due in six months that were issued as part of a long-term financing plan for capital purposes. Although the BANs are due in six months, the intent is to refinance the BANs on a long-term basis. The vendor

financing is not reported as long-term capital debt because it is not part of a long-term financing plan.

40. (c) The GLTDAG may account for the unmatured general obligation debt of a government. The GLTDAG accounting equation is as follows:

Assets		Liabilities
Amount Available in Debt Service Funds +	*Amount to Be Provided for Retirement of General Long-Term Debt* =	*General Long-Term Debt Payable*

When general obligation debt is incurred, the principal of the debt owed is credited to an appropriate liability account; the corresponding debit is to *Amount To Be Provided for Retirement of General Long-Term Debt*. As amounts are made available to the debt service fund for payment of **principal**, the GLTDAG records an increase in the *Amount Available in Debt Service Funds* and a corresponding decrease in the *Amount to be Provided for Retirement of General Long-Term Debt*.

PROPRIETARY FUNDS

41. (a) Proprietary funds are accounted for essentially as if they were private sector, profit-seeking business enterprises. Therefore, the orientation of these funds is income determination.

42. (a) The proprietary funds consist of the enterprise and internal service funds. Therefore, Cole's proprietary equity balances amount to $1,400,000 (i.e., $1,000,000 + $400,000).

ENTERPRISE FUND

43. (b) Grants, entitlements, and shared revenues received by proprietary funds should be reported as nonoperating revenues unless they are externally restricted to capital acquisitions.

44. (d) Enterprise funds should be used to account for operations (1) that are financed in a manner to private business enterprises—where the intent of the governing body is that the costs, including depreciation, of providing goods or services to the general public on a continuing basis be financed or recovered primarily through user charges or (2) where the governing body has decided that periodic determination of revenues earned, expenses incurred, and/or net income is appropriate for capital maintenance, public policy, management control, accountability, or other purposes. Internal service funds are used to account for the financing of goods or services provided by one department or agency to other departments or

agencies of a government, or to other governments, on a cost reimbursement basis.

45. (d) Where the government's intent is that all costs of providing goods or services to the general public are to be financed or recovered primarily through user charges, an enterprise fund must be used. The assumption that the lottery is not intended to be subsidized by the state is easily reached, since this is not an ordinary purpose of government. Those who are able to pay will likely be charged by the hospital, without contrary information stated in the question. The state likely has a separate program to pay for qualified indigents' healthcare, with reimbursement available to any qualified provider. In this case, the state hospital would be similar to a private facility in regard to reimbursement from state and federal indigents' healthcare programs. Thus, the hospital's costs are to be recovered *primarily* through user charges. Alternatively, the hospital may be heavily subsidized by the state, in which case it should *not* be accounted for in an enterprise fund.

46. (b) The customers' security deposits cannot be spent for normal operating purposes. In the balance sheet of the enterprise fund, the cash received is classified as a restricted asset and a liability is created for the customer deposits payable.

47. (b) The enterprise fund is a self-supporting fund which provides goods and/or services to the general public. Revenues and expenses are recorded in the same manner as in commercial business enterprises. Fixed assets are recorded in the fund as well as the associated depreciation charges.

INTERNAL SERVICE FUND

48. (d) An internal service fund's net income is not affected by temporary transfers. Internal service funds report residual equity transfers in and out as other financing sources and other financing uses, respectively. An internal service fund's net income is affected by operating revenues and expenses, nonoperating revenues and expenses, and operating and residual equity transfers.

49. (b) Internal service funds are accounted for in a similar manner to enterprise funds. A *Revenues* or *Billings To Others* account is used for services provided to other departments or other governments. Appropriations accounts are budgetary accounts. Interfund exchanges would be between departments in the same government unit. Intergovernmental transfers are used when the same entity is doing the accounting for both governments.

50. (c) Fiduciary funds are used to account for assets held by a governmental unit acting as a trustee or agent for individuals, organizations, other governmental units, or other funds of the same government. Four distinct types of fiduciary funds exist: (1) pension trust funds, (2) investment trust funds, (3) private-purpose trust funds, and (4) agency funds. Ridge City's total fiduciary fund assets amounted to $600,000 ($200,000 of agency fund assets and $400,000 of pension trust fund assets). The special revenue fund is a governmental, not a fiduciary, fund.

FIDUCIARY FUNDS

51. (c) Under the modified basis of accounting, governments accrue sales tax revenue when it is measurable and available for use. "Available for use" means that the revenues will be collected within the current period or early enough in the next period (i.e., within 60 days or so) to be used to pay for expenditures incurred in the current period. All of these revenues will be collected within 60 days. Curry City's portion of the total is not reported as revenues in the state's financial statements. Curry's portion is reported in the state's books in an agency fund (which does not have operating accounts) in an account such as *Due to City*.

52. (a) All pension trust fund contributions and earnings are accounted for as fund revenues. The pension trust fund makes the following entry to record employer contributions:

Cash	11,000	
Revenues Control—Employer		
Contribution		11,000

53. (b) *Governmental-type funds* record contributions to the pension trust fund as *expenditures*. A governmental-type fund would make the following entry to record its contribution:

Expenditures Cntrl—Pension Contribution	11,000	
Cash		11,000

It is important to note that *proprietary-type funds* (i.e., enterprise and internal service funds) record contributions to the pension trust fund as *expenses*. The following entry would be recorded in a proprietary-type fund to reflect its contribution to the pension trust fund:

Expenses Control—Pension Contribution	XX	
Cash		XX

54. (d) The PERS should be accounted for in a pension trust fund. Under the traditional approach of accounting for pension trust funds under NCGA Statement 1, the $14,300,000 Fund Balance of the pension trust fund can be determined by adding the Reserve for Employee Contributions (i.e., $9,000,000), the Reserve for Employer Contributions (i.e., $5,000,000), and the Actuarial Deficiency in Reserve for Employer's Contributions (i.e., $300,000).

INTERFUND TRANSACTIONS

55. (d) The interfund receivables and payables of a governmental fund should not be netted. Therefore, the special revenue fund should report an asset of $10,000 for the amount *due from* the general fund and a liability of $4,000 for the amount *due to* the agency fund.

56. (a) Capital projects fund inflows from intergovernmental grants and from interest on investments are considered *revenue*. On the other hand, capital projects fund inflows from bond or other long-term general obligation debt issues and transfers from other funds should be reported as *other financing sources*. Therefore, Walk should report a total of $3,000,000 ($2,000,000 from the bond issue + $1,000,000 from the general fund) in the *Other Financing Sources Control* account, not in revenue.

57. (c) GASB Section 2200.903 illustrates interfund receivables and payables reported as amounts due to and due from other funds. They are not reported as reservations of fund balance or additions to or reductions from the unrestricted fund balance. Section 2200.108 allows the option of eliminating the interfund assets and liabilities, but requires that such eliminations be apparent from the headings, or be disclosed in the notes to the financial statements.

58. (c) Operating transfers should be reported in *Other Financing Sources Uses* or *Other Financing* accounts and reported after revenues and expenditures or expenses, but before determining the results of operations in the operating statements.

59. (b) Residual equity transfers are as *Other Financing Sources* or *Other Financing Uses*.

60. (d) NCGA Statement 1 provides specific guidance on accounting for four types of interfund transactions. This is a quasi-external transaction, or one that would result in recognizing revenues and expenditures or expenses, as appropriate, as if it was with an organization apart from the government. The transactions in the other answers would not occur with an independent organization.

SOLUTION 22-2 ADDITIONAL MULTIPLE CHOICE ANSWERS

DETERMINING FUND

61. (d)   Since it is a governmental fund, long-term debt of the capital projects fund is not reported in the fund, although it may be accounted for in the General Long-Term Debt Account Group. Debt service funds account for the accumulation of resources for, and the payment of, general long-term debt principal and interest. Therefore, the portion of the special tax that is restricted to repay the long-term debt of the capital projects fund should be accounted for in a debt service fund.

62. (c)   Capital project funds are used to account for financial resources that are to be used to construct or otherwise acquire major long-lived "general government" capital facilities—such as buildings and infrastructure. Since the federal grant is restricted to construction of a center for rehabilitation of drug addicts, it should be accounted for in the capital project funds.

63. (a)   GASB 34 requires long-term debt issued ($1,000,000) to be reported as an other financing source. Premiums ($10,000) and discounts are reported as other financing sources and uses, respectively. Debt issue costs paid out of proceeds are reported as expenditures. Therefore, the city should report the entire $1,010,000 as an other financing source, not net of expenditures.

64. (b)   Capital project funds are used to account for the acquisition and use of financial resources to construct or otherwise acquire long-lived general government fixed assets. Project resources, which include *proceeds* of general obligation bonds, are recorded in the capital project funds as received or accrued. The General Long-Term Debt Account Group may be used to account for the *liability* for the general obligation bonds. Debt service funds account for the accumulation of resources for, and the payment of, general long-term debt principal and interest. Thus, a debt service fund would not account for the general obligation bond itself; rather it would maintain **resources** that are then used to meet the general obligation bonds as they become due.

65. (c)   The General Long-Term Debt Account Group may be used to account for the unmatured general obligation debt of a government. None of the governmental funds carry unmature specific long-term fund debt. Debt service funds account for the accumulation of resources for, and the payment of, general long-term debt principal and interest. Debt service funds do not account for any unmature long-term debt themselves; rather they maintain resources that are then used to meet general obligations as they become due.

66. (c)   Special revenue funds are used to account for revenues that have been legally restricted as to expenditure. The NCGA provides several examples of revenues which would fall under this heading: (1) a state gasoline tax collected in order to maintain streets, (2) proceeds from parking meters which finance the local traffic court, and (3) state juvenile rehabilitation grants used to operate and maintain juvenile rehabilitation centers. In each of these cases, a service is being provided, but the funding comes from a specific source rather than from general revenues. The sales taxes collected to finance the maintenance of tourist facilities in the shopping district should be accounted for in a special revenue fund. The donation mandated to provide meals for the needy should be accounted for in a private-purpose trust fund. Special revenue funds are used to account for resources held in trust by a government for a specific purpose where both the principal and any earnings may be expended for government programs. Private-purpose trust funds are resources to be expended for the benefit of individuals, organizations, or other governments.

GENERAL FUND

67. (d)   Taxes Receivable—Current is *debited* when taxpayers are billed for property taxes. *Appropriations* and *Estimated Revenues* accounts are affected when the budget is recorded. The following entry is made to record the assessment of property taxes:

Taxes Receivable—Current	XX	
Allowance for Uncollectible Taxes—Current		XX
Revenues—Property Taxes		XX

68. (b)   When $100 of supplies are ordered, the following entry is made:

Encumbrances Control (expected cost)	100	
Reserve for Encumbrances		100

Upon receipt of the supplies and an invoice for $105, the following entries are made:

Reserve for Encumbrances (reverse prior entry)	100	
Encumbrances Control		100
Expenditures (actual cost)	105	
Vouchers Payable		105

69. (c) The *Estimated Revenues* account is a budgetary account. Budgetary accounts are generally opened with balances opposite of the corresponding actual account.

70. (d) The *Budgetary Fund Balance Reserved for Encumbrances* is increased when a purchase order is approved. The *Budgetary Fund Balance Reserved for Encumbrances* is not affected when the budget (along with the related appropriations) is recorded. Upon the receipt of the item previously ordered, *Budgetary Fund Balance Reserved for Encumbrances* is decreased. The following entry is made when a purchase order is approved:

Encumbrances	XX
Budgetary FB Reserved for Encumbrances	XX

71. (d) The *Estimated Revenues Control* account of a governmental fund type is a budgetary account (i.e., it is not used to record actual revenues). Its balance is eliminated when the budgetary accounts are closed. The entry to close the *Estimated Revenues Control* and *Revenues Control* accounts to *Fund Balance* is as follows:

Revenues Control	17,000,000	
Fund Balance (difference)	3,000,000	
Estimated Revenues Control		20,000,000

72. (d) The *Appropriations* account is credited when the budget is recorded. The entry when a $100 purchase order is issued is as follows:

DR:	Encumbrances	100
CR:	Reserve for Encumbrances	100

When a corresponding invoice is received for $105, the following two entries are made:

DR:	Reserve for Encumbrances	100
CR:	Encumbrances	100

DR:	Expenditures	105
CR:	Vouchers Payable	105

73. (b) The following entry is made when a purchase order for $50 is approved:

Encumbrances (estimated cost)	50	
Reserve for Encumbrances		50

The following entries would be made to record the receipt of the related goods for $55 and the vouchers payable:

Fund Balance Reserved for Encumbrances	50	
Encumbrances (estimated cost)		50
Expenditures (actual cost)	55	
Vouchers Payable		55

The *Encumbrances* account is not affected when the budget is recorded. The following entry would be made to record the budget:

Estimated Revenues	XX	
Estimated Other Financing Sources	XX	
Appropriations		XX
Estimated Other Financing Uses		XX
Fund Balance (difference—debit or credit)		XX

74. (c) Appropriations are budgeted expenditures. Encumbrances are commitments for purchases that are not yet received. Expenditures are paid or accrued for purchases already received. $745,000 - $37,250 - $298,000 = $409,750

75. (c) Although authorized transfers to other fund entities may be viewed as appropriation expenditures from the point of view of the general fund entity, for purposes of financial reporting they are distinguished from expenditures. Control over authorized transfers to other fund entities is achieved by recording them as estimated other financing uses at the beginning of the period for which they are authorized (budgeted), rather than by including them in the budget entry for appropriations. The journal entry to record the adoption of the budget is as follows:

Estimated Revenues Control	30,000,000	
Appropriations Control		27,000,000
Estimated Other Financing Uses		900,000
Fund Balance (to balance)		2,100,000

76. (a) See the explanation to question #75.

77. (c) While goods and services committed for by purchase order or contract are encumbered in governmental funds to avoid overspending appropriations, some expenditures are controlled by other means and need not be encumbered. Salaries and wages are set by contract and controlled by established payroll procedures and are *not* encumbered. Salaries and wages should be recorded as follows:

Expenditures Control	800,000	
Vouchers Payable		800,000

78. (b) Governmental fund types include the general fund and use the modified accrual basis of accounting. This basis of accounting follows the "flow of financial resources" concept, and the term "expenditure" means decreases in (uses of) fund financial resources. (GASB 1800.114) The acquisition of a general fund fixed asset is a use of financial resources or an expenditure. The asset has been received and not just ordered. The fixed asset may be recorded in the general fixed asset account group. Appropriations relate to a budgetary account

that is only changed upon budget modification or closure.

79. (c) Grant revenues are recognized as being earned when expended. Prior to expenditure, they should be reported as deferred revenue. During the current fiscal year, Cliff spent $125,000 of the capital grant and $15,000 of the operating grant. Therefore, $140,000 should be reported as grant revenues for the period. The $25,000 not yet expended is reported as deferred revenue at the end of the period.

80. (c) When the purchase order was approved, the following journal entry was made:

Encumbrances Control	5,000	
Budgetary Fund Balance—		
Reserved for Encumbrances		5,000

81. (a) When the supplies are received, the encumbering entry is reversed, and the actual amounts are recorded.

Budgetary Fund Balance—		
Reserved for Encumbrances	5,000	
Encumbrances Control		5,000
Expenditures Control	5,000	
Vouchers Payable		5,000

82. (d) The journal entry to record the adoption of the budget is as follows:

Estimated Revenues Control	50,000,000	
Appropriations Control		40,000,000
Budgetary Fund Balance—Unreserved		10,000,000

83. (b) See the explanation to item #82.

84. (c) See the explanation to item #82.

85. (c) The encumbrance system is used by governmental funds to prevent overexpenditure and to demonstrate compliance with legal requirements. When a purchase order is issued, the estimated amount of the planned expenditure is **encumbered** by debiting *Encumbrances* and crediting *Fund Balance Reserved for Encumbrances*. When the related invoice is received, the encumbrance entry is reversed and the actual expenditure is recorded. Thus, the balance of the *Encumbrance* account will equal the outstanding purchase order amounts until the books are closed at year-end.

DEBT SERVICE FUND

86. (a) Debt service funds are used to account for the accumulation of resources for, and the payment of, general long-term debt principal and interest.

87. (b) Debt service funds are used to account for the accumulation of resources for, and the payment of, general long-term debt principal and interest. Therefore, the cash accumulation of $700,000 pertaining to general long-term obligations should be accounted for in Alma's debt service fund. The proprietary funds (enterprise and internal service funds) record their own assets, liabilities, revenues, and expenses. Therefore, the cash accumulation related to the bonds issued to finance the construction of the water treatment plant should be accounted for in an enterprise fund—not in Alma's debt service fund.

88. (c) **Mature** long-term debt principal and related interest are recorded as debt service fund expenditures when *due*. Debt service funds are used to account for resources for repayment of all general long-term debt and payment of related interest.

89. (a) Debt service fund budgetary accounts may be used to record estimated revenues from taxes or other financing sources, or estimated investment earnings. Actual amounts are then recorded as revenues. The operating transfer from the general fund is recorded as an other financing source, not revenue.

ACCOUNT GROUPS

90. (b) GASB Codification §1400.113 states that fixed assets donated to a governmental unit are recorded at fair value when received.

91. (a) GASB §1600.122 begins…"A major exception to the general rule of expenditure accrual relates to unmatured principal and interest on general long-term debt…" This question relates to the criterion related to the expenditure recognition on debt known as the "when due" criterion. Entities that budget cash outflows for debt when they legally become due include budget appropriations for debt in the year in which the cash outflow occurs. Because the financial flow of funds to make payment has not been budgeted for, interest and principal payments are not subject to accrual.

92. (b) A capital projects fund is used to account for resources used to acquire or build long-lived property (e.g., a city library). Neither the asset itself (e.g., the building) nor the long-term liability is recorded in the capital projects fund. The asset may be recorded in the General Fixed Assets Account Group and the bond issued to finance construction may be recorded in the GLTDAG. All proprietary and fiduciary fund debt is "specific fund" debt, which is recorded in the related specific fund, rather than in the GLTDAG. The account groups don't appear in

any financial statements; amounts from account groups appear in the government-wide financial statements.

PROPRIETARY FUNDS

93. (a) The appropriate basis of accounting for proprietary and fiduciary funds is the accrual basis, under which revenues are recognized in the accounting period in which they are earned and become measurable.

94. (d) Proprietary funds account for their fixed assets in the same manner as commercial enterprises; therefore, the expenditure for the parking meters should be recorded in the fund's fixed asset accounts. Enterprise funds and internal service funds are the two types of proprietary funds. The fund in question is an enterprise fund because it is a self-supporting fund which provides goods and/or services to the general public.

Receipts from users of parking facilities		$600,000
Less: Salaries and other cash expenses	$96,000	
Depreciation of parking meters	94,000	(190,000)
Net income		$410,000

95. (d) Billings for services provided to other governmental units are recorded by the internal service fund as operating revenues.

FIDUCIARY FUNDS

96. (c) Agency funds do not have revenues or a fund balance. Seaside County's tax agency fund should record all levies as follows:

Taxes Receivable for Other Units	XX	
Due to Other Funds and Units		XX

The fund should record the taxes collected for the county's municipalities during the period as follows:

Cash	1,000,000	
Taxes Receivable for Other Units		1,000,000

Upon the collection of the taxes, the fund should make the following entry to record the fund's liability for the distribution of the collections:

Due to Other Funds and Units	1,000,000	
Due to Municipalities		990,000
Due to General Fund		10,000

INTERFUND TRANSACTIONS

97. (b) NCGA Statement 1 provides specific guidance on accounting for interfund transactions. This is a quasi-external transaction, or one that would result in recognizing revenues and expenditures or expenses, as appropriate, as if it was with an organization apart from the government. The general fund expenditures account is debited when the general fund liabilities increase.

98. (c) Operating transfers should be recorded in distinctive Operating Transfers From (To) [Name of Fund] or Operating Transfers In (Out) accounts and reported after revenues and expenditures or expenses, but before determining the results of operations in the fund's operating statement.

OUTGOING REPORTING MODEL

99. (c) Although depreciation expense is not recorded in the General Fixed Assets Account Group (GFAAG), accumulated depreciation may be recorded in the government's balance sheet.

100. (b) The General Fixed Assets account is included in the asset section of the combined balance sheet of a government. The Investment in General Fixed Assets account is included in the fund equity section of the combined balance sheet. The Fund Balance Reserved for Encumbrances is not applicable to the GFAAG. The accounting equation for the General Fixed Asset Account Group (GFAAG) is as follows:

$$\text{General Fixed Assets (By asset type)} = \text{Investment in General Fixed Assets (By financing source)}$$

PERFORMANCE BY SUBTOPICS

Each category below parallels a subtopic covered in Chapter 22. Record the number and percentage of questions you correctly answered in each subtopic area.

Determining Fund or Group

Question #	Correct √
1	
2	
3	
4	
5	
6	

\# Questions   6

\# Correct _____
% Correct _____

General Fund: Budgets

Question #	Correct √
7	
8	

\# Questions   2

\# Correct _____
% Correct _____

General Fund: Actual

Question #	Correct √
9	
10	
11	
12	
13	

\# Questions   5

\# Correct _____
% Correct _____

General Fund: Encumbrances

Question #	Correct √
14	
15	
16	
17	
18	
19	

\# Questions   6

\# Correct _____
% Correct _____

Special Revenues Fund

Question #	Correct √
20	
21	

\# Questions   2

\# Correct _____
% Correct _____

Capital Projects Fund

Question #	Correct √
22	
23	
24	

\# Questions   3

\# Correct _____
% Correct _____

Debt Service Fund

Question #	Correct √
25	
26	
27	
28	
29	

\# Questions   5

\# Correct _____
% Correct _____

Permanent Fund

Question #	Correct √
30	

\# Questions   1

\# Correct _____
% Correct _____

GFAAG

Question #	Correct √
31	
32	
33	
34	
35	
36	

\# Questions   6

\# Correct _____
% Correct _____

GLTDAG

Question #	Correct √
37	
38	
39	
40	

\# Questions   4

\# Correct _____
% Correct _____

Proprietary Funds

Question #	Correct √
41	
42	

\# Questions   2

\# Correct _____
% Correct _____

Enterprise Fund

Question #	Correct √
43	
44	
45	
46	
47	

\# Questions   5

\# Correct _____
% Correct _____

Internal Service Fund

Question #	Correct √
48	
49	
50	

\# Questions   3

\# Correct _____
% Correct _____

Fiduciary Funds

Question #	Correct √
51	
52	
53	
54	

\# Questions   4

\# Correct _____
% Correct _____

Interfund Transactions

Question #	Correct √
55	
56	
57	
58	
59	
60	

\# Questions   6

\# Correct _____
% Correct _____

OTHER OBJECTIVE FORMAT QUESTION SOLUTIONS

SOLUTION 22-3 BUDGETS, ASSETS & LIABILITIES

1. $70,000

The general fund budgetary entry is as follows:

DR:	Estimated Revenues	8,000,000	
CR:	Budgetary Fund Balance		70,000
CR:	Appropriations		7,500,000
CR:	Est. Other Financing Uses (capital proj.)		250,000
CR:	Est. Other Financing Uses (enter. fund)		180,000

2. $430,000

($250,000 + $180,000 = $430,000) Also see the explanation to #1.

3. -0-

Interest is recorded when due.

4. $10,000

The full $10,000 lease payment amount should be included in general fund expenditures. In total, $78,000 would be debited in the general fund. The other $68,000 would be credited to Other Financing Sources—Capital Leases in the general fund.

5. $5,018,000

Because the December 31 balance of $56,000 was closed and a delinquent receivables account was established for only $38,000, $18,000 must have been collected. (The $4,000 difference between $60,000 and $56,000 was written off during the year.) The estimate for uncollectible taxes was not increased, so apparently the full $5,000,000 of the original entry was collected. ($5,000,000 + $56,000 – $38,000 = $5,018,000) The original entry to record property taxes is:

DR:	Property tax receivable	5,060,000	
CR:	Allowance for estimated		
	uncollectible taxes		60,000
CR:	Property tax revenue		5,000,000

6. $450,000

The state entitlements are revenues. The general fund money and debt proceeds are Other Financing Source, not revenue.

7. $868,000

The amount of the principal on the bonds ($800,000) plus the net present value of $68,000 for the capital lease (not counting the $10,000 payment already made) are included.

8. $1,580,000

The courthouse improvements ($1,527,000), police car retirement ($25,000), and office equipment acquisition ($78,000) all had an impact on the capital assets amount. The $7,000 paid for the car would not affect the capital assets.

9. $107,000

Usage to date (in cubic yards)	540,000
Divided by: Total capacity	1,000,000
Equals: Capacity used to date (percentage)	54%
Times: Est. closure & post-closure costs	$2,000,000
Total to be recognized to date	$1,080,000
Total previously recognized	973,000
Current year recognition	$ 107,000

10. $780,000

Total to be recognized to date	$1,080,000
Total incurred to date	300,000
Closure & post-closure liability	$ 780,000

11. D The primary focus of a capital project is not exceeding available resources.

12. E The primary focus of an MSWLF fund is concerned with not allowing a shortfall of resources for future closure and post-closure costs.

SOLUTION 22-4 DETERMINING FUND OR GROUP

1. B The general fixed assets account group may be used to record the general government fixed assets. The proprietary and fiduciary funds each account for only those fixed assets that relate to that particular fund.

2. B See the explanation to #1. The capital projects fund is used only for projects under construction. The general long-term debt account group is for debt only. The general fund has no fixed assets accounts.

3. A The general long-term debt account group (GLTDAG) may be used to account for the unmatured general obligation debt of a governmental unit. The accounting equation for the GLTDAG is as follows:

Assets		Liabilities
Amount Available in Debt Service Funds	+ Amount to Be Provided for Retirement of General Long-Term Debt	= General Long-Term Debt Payable

The general fund and capital projects funds do not have specific fund debt. Debt service funds account for the accumulation of resources for, and the payment of, general long-term debt principal and interest. Debt service funds do not account for any long-term debt themselves; rather they maintain resources that are then used to meet "general government" obligations as they become due.

4. L   The municipal motor pool which maintains all city-owned vehicles and charges the various departments for the cost of rendering those services should be accounted for in an internal service fund. Internal service funds account for departments or agencies of a governmental unit that provide goods or services to other departments or agencies on a cost-reimbursement basis. The general fund accounts for financial resources that are not required to be accounted for in another fund. Special revenue funds account for general government resources that are restricted by law or contract for specific purposes.

5. L   Internal service funds (ISF) are proprietary funds, and as such record their own assets, liabilities, revenues, and expenses. This is in order to ensure that the fees ISFs charge are sufficient to cover the costs of providing services.

6. I   As amended by GASB 34, GASB 32 requires an IRC §457 deferred compensation plan to be displayed in a *pension trust* fund.

7. K   GASB Section S40.119 specifies, "The debt service transaction of a special assessment issue for which the government is not obligated in any manner should be reported in an *agency* fund rather than a debt service fund, to reflect the fact that the government's duties are limited to acting as an agent for the assessed property owners and the bondholders."

8. K   An agency fund is used to account for the custodial activities of a government serving as an agent for other governments, funds, organizations, or individuals. Taxes, for example, are occasionally collected by one governmental unit on behalf of another. Until that money is physically transferred to the proper authority, it is recorded in an agency fund. Special revenue funds are used to account for revenues that have been legally restricted as to expenditure (e.g., a state gasoline tax collected in order to maintain streets). Internal service funds are used to account for any department or agency that provides services within the government on a cost-reimbursement basis. A trust fund accounts for assets received and held by a governmental unit acting in the capacity of trustee or custodian. The aim in trust fund accounting is to ensure that the money or other resources are handled in accordance with the terms of the trust agreement and/or applicable trust laws.

9. F   Duration should establish a Permanent Fund to account for the donated investments because the donor intended the principal to be held intact and only the income from the investments be expended. Assets held by the government as a trustee or custodian that may be used to benefit the government are accounted for in the permanent or special revenue funds depending on their expendability. Duration should establish a special revenue fund to account for the investment income since the investment income earned is to be used to finance Duration's activities. GASB 34 eliminates expendable and nonexpendable trust funds

10. H   Private-purpose trust funds may hold both expendable and nonexpendable resources.

SOLUTION 22-5 GOVERNMENTAL-TYPE FUNDS

1. $104,500

The general fund operating transfers out (other financing uses) are composed of the $104,500 for bond principal and interest payment.

2. $17,000

Compensated absences are valued at the salary and wage rates in effect as of the balance sheet date. The liabilities in the general fund are the amounts expected to be settled with resources available at the balance sheet date. The remainder of $69,000 would appear in the government-wide statement of net assets as long-term liability but is not booked in the general fund.

3. $125,000

The reserved amount is the $83,000 for total encumbrances outstanding at December 31 and the $42,000 in ending supplies inventory. The reserve for supplies inventory indicates that a portion of fund balance is not available.

4. $236,000

The capital projects fund fund balance is $600,000 – $364,000 = $236,000.

5. $6,000

The special revenue fund fund balance is $109,000 – $81,000 – $22,000 = $6,000.

6. $104,500

The debt service fund expenditures for 20X1 are the $100,000 of principal repaid and the $4,500 of interest paid.

7. $0

The cost of capital assets acquired in 20X1 is $22,000 from the special revenue fund's purchase of a motor vehicle plus $364,000 from the capital projects fund. This appears in the government-wide financial statements in the governmental activities column, but is not booked in the general fund.

8. $100,000

The $100,000 repayment of debt decreased the reported long-term liabilities.

9. $181,000

Under the encumbrances method, the amount of 20X1 supplies expenditures is the $181,000 credited to the *Vouchers Payable* account during 20X1 less the $6,000 credited to *Vouchers Payable* account and debited to the *Fund Balance Reserved for Encumbrances* account for the encumbrances outstanding as of 1/1/X1. Under the purchases method, the fund balance is not reserved for prior year encumbrances, and thus the amount for 20X1 expenditures is the full $181,000.

10. $190,000

The $190,000 of purchase orders issued during 20X1 is the total amount of 20X1 supplies encumbrances.

SOLUTION 22-6 TRANSACTIONS & FUNDS

1. G   Proceeds of general obligation bonds should not be recorded as a credit to fund liabilities or revenues. Instead they should be recorded as a credit to other financing sources.

Cash	XX	
Other Financing Sources—Bond Proceeds		XX

2. K   When a purchase order is approved, the following journal entry is made:

Encumbrances Control	XX	
Budgetary Fund Balance—Reserved for Encumbrances		XX

3. L   When the supplies are received, the original encumbering entry is reversed, and the actual amounts are entered into the accounts as follows:

Budgetary Fund Balance—Reserved for Encumbrances	XX	
Encumbrances Control		XX
Expenditures Control	XX	
Vouchers Payable		XX

4. L   The general fund salaries and wages incurred should be recorded as follows:

Expenditures Control	XX	
Vouchers Payable		XX

5. E   The billings of the internal service fund is a "quasi-external" transaction. The internal service fund: (1) debits to receivable for the amount due, and (2) credits interfund revenues.

6. J   Where revenues are not properly recognized at the time the grant is awarded, Entry (1) is appropriate. When the conditions of the previously awarded grant are met, the deferred revenue is recognized as revenue, as in Entry (2).

Due From Grantor	XX	
Deferred Revenues		XX
Deferred Revenues	XX	
Revenues		XX

7. D   A deferred revenue account is credited if property taxes are collected prior to the year they apply.

8. A   The appropriations control account is credited when the following entry is made to record the budget:

Estimated Revenues Control	XX	
Appropriations Control		XX
Budgetary Fund Balance—Unreserved (to balance)		XX

9. F   Local banks customarily meet the working capital needs of a governmental unit by accepting a "tax anticipation note" from the unit. The journal entry to record the short-term financing received from the bank that is secured by the city's taxing power is as follows:

Cash   XX

    Tax Anticipation Notes Payable   XX

10. **B**   If there is an excess of estimated inflows over estimated outflows at the adoption of the budget, the Budgetary Fund Balance—Unreserved account is increased (i.e., credited). This can be seen from the following journal entry to record the adoption of the budget in question:

Estimated Revenues Control   XX

Estimated Other Financing Sources   XX

    Appropriations Control   XX

    Estimated Other Financing Uses   XX

    Budgetary Fund Balance—

       Unreserved (to balance)   XX

11. **N**   The enterprise fund is a proprietary fund. Therefore, it records its own assets and liabilities, including fixed assets and long-term debt.

12. **R**   Capital projects funds are used to account for financial resources that are to be used to construct or otherwise acquire major long-lived "general government" capital facilities—such as buildings, highways, storm sewer systems, and bridges.

13. **N**   The internal service fund is a proprietary fund. (See the explanation to #11.)

14. **M**   The private-purpose trust fund is a fiduciary fund. (Also see the explanation to #17.)

15. **N**   The enterprise fund is a proprietary fund. Proprietary funds are used to account for a government's continuing business-type activities that are similar to private business enterprises.

16. **S**   Property taxes usually are a major revenue source of local governments. Unless the property taxes are restricted for specific purposes or required to be accounted for in another fund, they are accounted for in the general fund.

17. **M**   The agency fund is a fiduciary fund. Fiduciary funds are used to account for assets held by a government in a trustee or agency capacity.

18. **M**   The pension fund is a fiduciary fund. (Also see the explanation to #17)

19. **U**   Special revenue funds account for proceeds of specific revenue sources that are restricted by law or contract for specified purposes.

20. **T**   Debt service funds account for the accumulation of resources for, and the payment of, general long-term debt principal and interest.

SOLUTION 22-7 TRANSACTIONS & FUNDS

1. $1,000,000

The budgetary entry is as follows:

DR: Estimated Revenues   10,000,000

CR: Appropriations   9,000,000

CR: Budgetary Fund Balance   1,000,000

2. $9,350,000

There were no write-offs of current year property taxes. Therefore, the amount collected is the amount of the current year property tax levy ($9,500,000) less the current-year property taxes delinquent at the end of the year ($150,000).

3. -0-

$100,000 + $2,000,000 − $2,100,000 = -0- All the current year expenditures are transferred out of the capital projects fund upon completion of the project.

4. $2,100,000

The full cost of the library wing is reported.

5. $2,000,000

The full amount of the bond debt is reported.

SOLUTION 22-8 COMPREHENSIVE ILLUSTRATION

1. **N**   The following entry would be made to record the budget in the General Fund, based on budgeted amounts:

Estimated Revenues   5,000,000

Estimated Other Financing Sources   1,000,000

    Appropriations   4,400,000 [2]

    Estimated Other Financing Uses   1,200,000 [1]

    Budgetary Fund Balance   400,000

Explanation of Amounts:

[1]   Capital Projects Fund ($500,000) operating transfer plus Water Utility Fund ($700,000) residual equity transfer.

[2]   Total budgeted expenditures minus Other financing uses ($5,600,000 − $1,200,000 = $4,400,000).

2. **Y**   Although authorized transfers to other fund entities may be viewed as appropriation expenditures from the point of view of the General Fund entity, for purposes of financial reporting they are distinguished from expenditures. Control over authorized transfers to other fund entities is achieved by recording them as estimated other financing uses at the beginning of the period for which they are authorized (budgeted), rather than by including them in the budget entry for appropriations.

3.　N　　This nonrecurring transfer of equity between funds is recorded in a distinctive Residual Equity Transfers to Water Utility Enterprise Fund account and is reported after the results of operations in the general fund's operating statement. GASB Section 1800.106 distinguishes between two major types of interfund transfers (residual equity and operating) and provides the specific example of the contribution of enterprise fund capital by the general fund as a residual equity transfer.

4.　N　　Bond proceeds are classified as other financing sources and are recorded at the net amount received, including premiums and deducting discounts and issuance costs. A net premium is usually transferred to the Debt Service fund, which is used to account for the accumulation of resources for payment of general long-term debt principal and interest (GASB Section 1500.109).

5.　N　　Quasi-external transactions are transactions that would result in recognizing revenues and expenditures or expenses, as appropriate, if they were with organizations apart from the government.

6.　N　　GASB Section P70.103 states, "The revenue produced from any property tax assessment should be recognized in the fiscal period for which it was levied, provided the available criteria are met. Available means then due, or past due and receivable within the current period, and collected within the current period or expected to be collected soon enough thereafter to be used to pay liabilities of the current period. Such time thereafter shall not exceed 60 days." Since the fiscal year ends December 31, and March 1 is 60 days later, the net delinquent property taxes receivable should be expected to be collected before March 15.

7.　N　　The entry to close budgetary accounts is the exact opposite of the one to record the budget. Thus, there is a credit of $400,000 to the *budgetary* fund balance. (Also see the explanation to #1.)

8.　N　　The net budgetary effects are zero and the actual amount is a credit of $50,000, so the net impact on the year-end general fund balance is $50,000.

9.　N　　Interfund transactions are partially eliminated in the government-wide statement of net assets.

10.　Y　　General and program revenues are separated in the government-wide statement (GWS) of activities.

11.　Y　　The ISF typically is reported in the GWS in the governmental activities column.

12.　N　　The general fund is always a major fund.

13.　N　　Fiduciary funds do not appear in the government-wide statements.

14.　N　　Only proprietary funds report in the statement of cash flows. Governmental-type funds do not report a statement of cash flows.

15.　N　　See the explanation to question #14.

16.　Y　　Proprietary funds report in the statement of cash flows. Enterprise funds are proprietary funds.

17.　$5,600,000

Per GASB Section 1700.105, "The appropriations constitute maximum expenditure authorizations during the fiscal year."

18.　$4,750,000

The total amount debited to property taxes receivable is the actual amount of property taxes. The entry to record property taxes is:

Property taxes receivable	4,750,000	
Allowance for estimated		
uncollectible taxes		50,000
Property tax revenue		4,700,000

19.　$2,473,000

The total cost of the project is calculated as follows:

20X1 revenues	$　800,000
20X1 bond proceeds	1,230,000
Less: Transfer to debt service fund	(30,000)
20X1 operating transfers in	500,000
Less: Transfer to general fund at close	(27,000)
Total cost of project	$2,473,000

20.　$800,000

Grants from another government for a capital project are recorded as deferred revenues in the capital project fund until expended for the project and are then transferred to a revenue account for the remainder of the construction period. Since the state grant is the only grant involved in the project, the amount of the state grant must be the balance in the revenues account at the end of the project life.

21. $2,422,000

The total expenditures in 20X1 were $1,080,000, and the related encumbrances were greater by $42,000. To calculate the total encumbrances, add to this sum the unpaid encumbrances of $1,300,000. [($1,080,000 + $42,000) + $1,300,000 = $2,422,000]

22. $120,000

The fund balance is affected by the opening and closing budget entries and the (actual) closing entries. The illustrated closing entry has a $1,420,000 credit entry to unreserved fund balance. Since there is no opening balance and the budget entries are equal in amount and opposite in direction, the combined closing entry amounts are also the ending balance. (**NOTE:** $1,420,000 − $1,300,000 = $120,000) The illustrated closing entry omits the following entry.

Fund Balance	1,300,000	
Encumbrances Control		1,300,000

Solution 22-9 Comprehensive Illustration

1. **A** GASB Section 1800.119 states, "Expenditures should be further classified by *character*, that is, on the basis of the fiscal period they are presumed to benefit. The major character classifications of expenditures are 'Current Expenditures,' which benefit the current fiscal period..." GASB 1800.118 explains the *activity* classification as facilitating evaluation of the economy and efficiency of operations by providing information for figuring costs per unity of activity.

2. **A** GASB Section 1800.119 states, "Expenditures should be further classified by *character*, that is, on the basis of the fiscal period they are presumed to benefit. The major character classifications of expenditures are 'Current Expenditures,' which benefit the current fiscal period; 'Capital Outlays,' which are presumed to benefit both the present and future fiscal periods; and 'Debt Service,' which presumably benefits prior fiscal periods as well as current and future periods. 'Intergovernmental,' a fourth character classification, is appropriate where one governmental unit transfers resources to another.... Character classification may be accomplished by grouping the object classification..., which are subdivisions of the character classifications." GASB 1800.120 defines the classification *object classes* as the types of items purchased or services obtained (sales and wages).

3. **B** GASB Section 1900.115 explains that the *function* or *program* classification provides information on the overall purposes of expenditures.

4. **B** GASB Section 1600.122 states, "Other alternative expenditure recognition methods in governmental fund accounting, usually of a relatively minor nature, include: inventory items (for example, materials and supplies) may be considered expenditures either when purchased (purchases method) or when used (consumption method), but significant amounts of inventory should be reported in the balance sheet...." GASB Section 2200.903.b (a nonauthoritative discussion) states, "Under the *consumption* method (1) inventory acquisitions are recorded in inventory accounts initially and charged as expenditures when used, and (2) an equity reserve for inventories need not be established unless minimum amounts of inventory must be maintained and, thus, are not available for use (expenditure). Under the *purchases* method (1) inventories are recorded as expenditures on acquisition, and (2) significant inventories on hand at year-end are reflected in the *Assets* section of the balance sheet and are fully reserved in the equity section." These sections make no mention of perpetual inventory beyond what is mentioned for the consumption method. As no mention of minimum inventories is included in the given information, we must assume there is no such requirement. Because the reserve for inventory exists, Shar City must be using the purchase method.

5. **B** Proprietary funds account use the term net assets. Fund balances are appropriate in governmental-type funds. A debt is liability, not equity.

6. **A** Proprietary fund debt is reported in the business-type activity column. The account groups may be used to account for long-term debt and capital assets, but they do not appear in the financial statements.

7. **A** Unrestricted grants are reported as revenues.

8. **E** The general fund has a receivable due from the internal service fund (ISF).

9. **B** The purchase of goods or services by a governmental-type fund from a proprietary fund are handled like purchases from other vendors.

10. **D** Operating transfers to internal service or enterprise funds are other financing uses.

11. **E** Loans to an internal service fund would be recorded in the general fund as follows:

DR:	Receivable from Internal Service Fund	90,000
CR:	Cash	90,000

DR: Fund Balance (or Unreserved Fund Bal.)   90,000
CR: Reserve for Advance to Int. Serv. Fund   90,000

12.   D   A transfer to establish a proprietary fund is a residual equity transfer, which is reported as an other financing use.

13.   B   General fund payments on operating leases are expenditures.

14. $79,000

The fund balance reserve for encumbrances for 20X2 year-end is $43,000. The decrease in reserve for encumbrances is $15,000. Working back to 20X1 year-end, the 20X1 year-end fund balance reserve for encumbrances was $43,000 + $15,000 = $58,000. The reserve for supplies inventory at 20X1 year-end was $21,000.   ($58,000 + $21,000 = $79,000)

15. $811,000

As $8,000 was written-off, $845,000 remained to be collected. Of this, $34,000 was uncollected at year-end, meaning $811,000 was collected during the year. The initial property tax entry was as follows:

DR: Property Taxes Receivable $853,000
CR: Allow. Property Taxes Uncollectible   28,000
CR: Property Tax Revenues   825,000

16. $89,000

Vouchers payable is $89,000. Encumbrances are not liabilities until the goods or services are provided.   Then they are removed from the encumbrances account and recorded in the payable account.

17. $100,000

The only capital outlay for governmental activities was the purchase of the police vehicles.

18. $52,000

The total debt service expenditure was $74,000. This amount included interest of $22,000; the rest reduced debt principal.   ($74,000 − $22,000 = $52,000)

19. $1,392,000

Total actual expenditures for 20X2 are the $1,349,000 made in 20X2 and the $43,000 that will be made in 20X3 for 20X2 encumbrances.

Accounting & Reporting Coverage
by Bisk Education Chapter

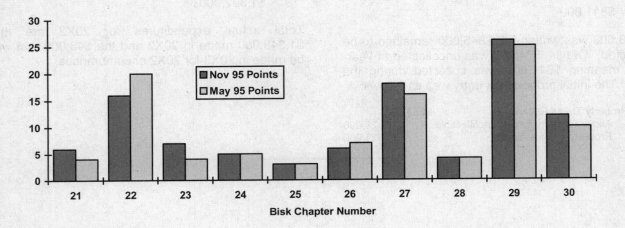

While reviewing this graph, please be aware that the content specification slightly decreased individual and corporate taxation coverage and increased partnership and other topics coverage since the November 1995 exam (the last fully disclosed exam). Also, realize that the split between Chapters 21 and 22 is somewhat artificial.

More information is in the **Practical Advice** appendix.

CHAPTER 23

NONPROFIT ACCOUNTING

EXAM COVERAGE: Historically, exam coverage of the topics in Chapter 23 is 3 to 7 percent of the ARE section. It is also heavily concentrated on the first section, *Standard Nonprofit Accounting*, and, to a lesser degree, the second section, *Unique Accounting Features*.

CHAPTER 23

NONPROFIT ACCOUNTING

I. STANDARD NONPROFIT ACCOUNTING

A. CONCEPTS

The fundamental presumption used by the FASB in developing financial reporting standards for (non-governmental) nonprofit organizations (NPO) is that the financial reporting practices of non-profit entities should be the same as those for commercial entities.

1. **STANDARDS** Statement on Auditing Standards No. 69, *The Meaning of "Present Fairly in Conformity With Generally Accepted Accounting Principles" in the Independent Auditor's Report*, establishes a parallel hierarchy where non-governmental nonprofit entities are subject to the FASB rather than the GASB standards. In SFAS 117, the FASB requires non-profit entities to provide financial statements on an entity-wide basis similar to the concept of consolidated statements for business entities.

2. **FUND ACCOUNTING** Disaggregated financial statements, common with fund accounting, are insufficient, by themselves, to meet the requirements of SFAS 117. Use of fund accounting for nonprofit organizations is allowed but not required by SFAS 117. This relegates fund statements to a supplementary role for external reporting purposes. Although fund account-ing is redundant with the adoption of SFAS 117, fund accounting remains an option, and many entities may be slow to eliminate it. [Expect the majority of (nongovernmental) nonprofit accounting CPA exam points to be in areas other than fund accounting.] NPOs generally do not use budgetary and encumbrance accounting.

B. DEFINITIONS

1. **BOARD-RESTRICTED** The governing board of an entity may earmark assets for specific purposes as long as these do not conflict with donor conditions. These assets may be des-ignated board-restricted in the financial statements, but they remain in the unrestricted category.

2. **ENDOWMENT FUND** A fund of assets to provide support for the activities of a not-for-profit organization. Endowment funds are typically composed of donor-restricted gifts to provide a permanent source of support. However, use of the fund assets may also be temporarily restricted or unrestricted.

3. **FUNCTIONAL CLASSIFICATION** A manner of arranging costs by the activities for which the costs are attributable. Program services and supporting activities are the two main classifications.

4. **OBJECT CLASSIFICATION** A manner of arranging costs by the item or service obtained. For example, utilities and salaries.

5. **PERMANENT RESTRICTION** A donor-imposed restriction. The principal of a permanent endowment may not be exhausted.

6. **PROGRAM SERVICES** Activities that further the mission of the organization. For example, a university's program services might include instruction and research.

7. **SUPPORTING ACTIVITIES** Activities that are secondary to the mission of the organization. These include administration activities, general activities, fund-raising activities, and member development activities.

8. **TEMPORARY RESTRICTION** A donor-imposed restriction that will lapse upon occurrence of conditions specified by the donor. The principal of a temporary endowment or donation may be used after the conditions of the restriction are fulfilled. The allowable use of the income of a temporarily restricted asset may also be restricted by the terms of the donation.

9. **UNRESTRICTED ASSETS** The assets from donations unrestricted by the donors, and assets formerly temporarily restricted by the donors that have since become unrestricted. Unrestricted assets may include board-restricted assets.

C. FINANCIAL STATEMENTS

SFAS 117 requires that nonprofit organizations present at least three statements. The statements exhibited in this section are similar to those used by a commercial entity. Some entities may choose to also disclose the fund statements. Several formats are acceptable for nonprofit entities. However, in order to meet the requirements of SFAS 117, *aggregated* statements must be used.

1. **STATEMENT OF FINANCIAL POSITION** Entities report assets, liabilities, and net assets in this statement. Entities are required to classify net assets based upon the existence or absence of donor-imposed restrictions. Thus, net assets are classified into at least three categories: permanently restricted, temporarily restricted, and unrestricted. Assets are arranged by relative liquidity. Assets restricted to a particular use assume the liquidity of that use. For instance, cash and marketable securities restricted for the purchase of property, plant, and equipment (PPE) are presented below inventories.

EXHIBIT 1 ♦ STATEMENT OF FINANCIAL POSITION

Name of Nonprofit Entity
Statement of Financial Position
December 31, 20X0

Assets:		Liabilities:	
		Accounts Payable	$ 1,285
Cash	$ 38	Grants Payable	438
Contributions Receivable	1,512	Annuity Obligation	842
Accounts Receivable	1,065	Bonds Payable	2,750
Marketable Securities	700	Total Liabilities	$ 5,315
Inventory	300	Net Assets	
Prepaid Expenses	5	Unrestricted	$ 57,614
Assets Restricted to Investment: PPE	2,605	Temporarily Restricted	12,171
Property, Plant, and Equipment	30,850	Permanently Restricted	71,010
Long-term Investments	109,035	Total Net Assets	140,795
Total Assets	$146,110	Total Liabilities and Net Assets	$146,110

2. **STATEMENT OF ACTIVITIES** This statement is similar to a for-profit entity's income statement. The change in the net assets is reported in the Statement of Activities. The revenues, expenses, gains, and losses are classified into the same three groups as in the statement of financial position (unrestricted, temporarily restricted, and permanently restricted).

a. **SUBTOTALS** Subtotals are required for income from **C**ontinuing operations, income from **D**iscontinued operations, **E**xtraordinary items, and the of e**F**fect Accounting changes (CDEF).

b. **SEQUENCE** The Statement of Activities is presented in the following sequence:

Revenues and Other Additions
Expenditures and Other Deductions
Transfers Among Funds
Net Increase (Decrease) in Net Assets
Net Assets—Beginning of Year
Net Assets—End of Year

c. **CHANGE** Entities display the change in each of the three classes of net assets.

EXHIBIT 2 ♦ STATEMENT OF ACTIVITIES

Name of Nonprofit Entity
Statement of Activities
Year Ending December 31, 20X1

	Total	Unrestricted	Temporarily Restricted	Permanently Restricted
Revenues and Gains:				
Contributions	$ 8,515	$ 4,320	$ 4,055	$ 140
Services Fees	2,700	2,700		
Investment Income	4,575	3,225	1,290	60
Net Unrealized and Realized Gains on				
Long-term Investments	7,900	4,114	1,476	2,310
Other	75	75		
Net Assets Released From Restrictions:				
Expiration of Time Requirements		5,995	(5,995)	
Fulfilled Conditions of Equipment Acquisition		750	(750)	
Fulfilled Conditions of Program Services		625	(625)	
Total Revenues, Gains, and Other Support	$ 23,765	$21,804	$ (549)	$ 2,510
Expenses and Losses:				
Program Expenses	$ 13,700	$13,700		
Administration Expenses	1,210	1,210		
Fund-raising Expenses	1,075	1,075		
Loss on Sale of Equipment	40	40		
Actuarial Loss on Annuity Obligations	15		15	
Total Expenses and Losses	$ 16,040	$16,025	$ 15	
Change in Net Assets (or change in equity)	$ 7,725	$ 5,779	$ (564)	$ 2,510
Net Assets at December 31, 20X0	133,070	51,835	12,735	68,500
Net Assets at December 31, 20X1	$140,795	$57,614	$12,171	$71,010

3. **ALTERNATIVE TWO-PART FORMAT** The statement of activities may be divided into two parts, as illustrated in Exhibits 3 and 4.

a. **STATEMENT OF ACTIVITIES: STATEMENT OF UNRESTRICTED REVENUES, EXPENSES, AND OTHER CHANGES IN UNRESTRICTED NET ASSETS** This alternative format divides the statement into two parts. The statements exhibited in this section are what an entity using optional fund accounting might present. The first part of the Statement of Activities is based on the operation of the General Funds. It may also be named Statement of Operations. Increases and decreases in donor-restricted funds are considered in the other part.

b. **STATEMENT OF ACTIVITIES: STATEMENT OF CHANGES IN NET ASSETS** This part summarizes the first part and reports the changes in restricted assets.

4. **STATEMENT OF FUNCTIONAL EXPENSES** The Statement of Functional Expenses is required only for Voluntary Health and Welfare Organizations (VHWO). This details the expenses on the Statement of Activities by functional and object (or natural) classification, as opposed to only the functional classification in the Statement of Activities. This statement is illustrated in Exhibit 12.

5. **STATEMENT OF CASH FLOWS** This statement reports the change in cash and cash equivalents similar to commercial enterprises. SFAS 117 amends SFAS 95, *Statement of Cash Flows*, to extend the provisions of SFAS 95 to nonprofit organizations. Furthermore, SFAS 117 expands the description of cash flows from financing activities to include certain donor-restricted cash that must be used for long-term purposes.

EXHIBIT 3 ♦ HEALTH CARE ENTITY STATEMENT OF ACTIVITIES: PART I

Name of Nonprofit Entity
Statement of Unrestricted Revenue, Expenses,
and Other Changes in Unrestricted Net Assets
Year Ending December 31, 20X1

Unrestricted Revenues and Gains:		
Contributions	$ 4,320	
Service Fees	2,700	
Investment Income	3,225	
Net Unrealized and Realized Gains on Long-term		
Investments	4,114	
Investment Income	75	
Net Assets Released From Restrictions:		
Expiration of Time Requirements	5,995	
Fulfilled Conditions of Equipment Acquisition	750	
Fulfilled Conditions of Program Services	625	
Total Unrestricted Revenues, Gains, and Other Support		$ 21,804
Expenses and Losses:		
Program Expenses	$ 13,700	
Administration Expenses	1,210	
Fund-raising Expenses	1,075	
Loss on Sale of Equipment	40	
Total Expenses and Losses		$ 16,025
Change in Unrestricted Net Assets		$ 5,779

EXHIBIT 4 ♦ STATEMENT OF ACTIVITIES: PART 2

Name of Nonprofit Entity
Statement of Changes in Net Assets
Year Ending December 31, 20X1

Unrestricted Net Assets		
Total Unrestricted Revenues and Gains	$ 14,434	
Net Assets Released From Restrictions	7,370	
Total Expenses and Losses	(16,025)	
Change in Unrestricted Net Assets		$ 5,779
Temporarily Restricted Net Assets		
Contributions	$ 4,055	
Investment Income	1,290	
Net Unrealized and Realized Gains on Long-term		
Investments	1,476	
Actuarial Loss on Annuity Obligations	(15)	
Net Assets Released From Restrictions	(7,370)	
Change in Temporarily Restricted Net Assets		$ (564)
Permanently Restricted Net Assets (Endowment Funds)		
Contributions	$ 140	
Long-Term Investment Income	60	
Net Unrealized and Realized Gains on Long-term		
Investments	2,310	
Change in Permanently Restricted Net Assets		$ 2,510
Change in Net Assets		$ 7,725
Net Assets at December 31, 20X0		133,070
Net Assets at December 31, 20X1		$140,795

EXHIBIT 5 ♦ STATEMENT OF CASH FLOWS

Name of Nonprofit Entity
Statement of Cash Flows
Year Ending December 31, 20X3

Cash Flows From Operating Activities:	
Cash Received From Service Recipients	$ 5,220
Cash Received From Contributors	8,030
Collections on Pledges	2,616
Interest and Dividends Received	8,570
Miscellaneous Receipts	150
Cash Paid to Vendors and Employees	(23,808)
Cash Paid for Interest	(382)
Cash Paid for Grants	(424)
Net Cash Used by Operating Activities	$ (28)
Cash Flows From Investing Activities:	
Cash Paid for Purchase of Investments	$(74,900)
Cash Received from Sale of Investments	76,100
Cash Paid for Property, Plant, and Equipment	(1,500)
Cash Received from Sale of Property, Plant, and Equipment	250
Net Cash Used by Investing Activities	$ (50)
Cash Flows From Financing Activities:	
Proceeds from Contributions Restricted for:	
Investment in Endowment	$ 200
Investment in Term Endowment	70
Investment in Property, Plant, and Equipment	1,210
Investment Income Restricted for Reinvestment	200
Interest and Dividends Restricted for Reinvestment	300
Less: Payment of Annuity Obligations	(146)
Less: Payment of Notes Payable	(1,140)
Less: Payment on Bonds Payable	(1,000)
Net Cash Used by Financing Activities	$ (306)
Net Increase in Cash and Cash Equivalents	$ (384)
Cash and Cash Equivalents at December 31, 20X2	460
Cash and Cash Equivalents at December 31, 20X3	$ 76
Reconciliation of Change in Net Assets to Net Cash Used by Operating Activities	
Change in Net Assets	$ 15,450
Reconciling Adjustments:	
Plus: Depreciation	$ 3,200
Plus: Loss on Sale of Equipment	80
Plus: Actuarial Loss on Annuity Obligations	30
Less: Increase in Accounts and Interest Receivable	(460)
Less: Increase in Contributions Receivable	(324)
Plus: Decrease in Inventories and Prepaid Expenses	390
Less: Decrease in Refundable Advance	(650)
Less: Decrease in Grants Payable	(424)
Plus: Increase in Accounts Payable	1,520
Less: Contributions Restricted for Long-Term Investment	(2,740)
Less: Investment Income Restricted for Long-Term Investment	(300)
Less: Net Unrealized and Realized Gains on Long-Term Investment	(15,800)
Net Cash Used by Operating Activities	$ (28)
Supplemental Data for Noncash Investing and Financing Activities:	
Gifts of Property, Plant, and Equipment	$ 140
Gifts of Paid-up Life Insurance, Cash Surrender Value	80

6. **DISCLOSURES** SFAS 136 requires an NPO that discloses in its financial statements a ratio of fundraising expenses to amounts raised, to also disclose how it computes that ratio.

D. **CONTRIBUTIONS**

SFAS 116 governs contributions received and made for nonprofit entities. Contributions are unconditional donations, or gifts, of assets, including both property (either for general operating purposes or restricted for a specific purpose) and services (under certain limited circumstances).

EXHIBIT 6 ♦ SAMPLE DONATION ENTRIES

1. To record gifts, bequests, and donations received:

Cash (or other assets)	XX	
Nonoperating Gains—(Unrestricted) Contributions		XX
Liabilities (if any are assumed)		XX
(Restricted) Revenue		XX

NOTE: Unrestricted gifts, bequests, and donations are recorded as nonoperating gains, generally. If restricted, they are recorded as permanently or temporarily restricted revenue in the appropriate donor-restricted fund.

2. To record donations (to a hospital) of pharmacy supplies and professional services:

Inventory of Pharmacy Supplies	XX	
Operating Expenses (functional expense accounts)	XX	
Contributions—Donated Pharmacy Supplies		XX
Contributions—Donated Professional Services		XX

NOTE: Report the contributions as operating gains or revenue or nonoperating gains depending on whether the donation constitutes the entity's major or central operations or are peripheral and incidental to the entity's operations.

1. **ASSETS** Donated assets are recorded as revenue at **fair value** as of the date of the gift.

a. Donated assets other than property and equipment—If **unrestricted**, report as operating gains or revenue or nonoperating gains depending on whether the donations constitute the entity's ongoing major or central operations or are peripheral and incidental to the entity's operations. If **restricted**, report as restricted gain or revenue.

b. Donations of property and equipment, or of assets to acquire property and equipment, may be initially reported as restricted gain or revenue. A transfer to the unrestricted net assets is reported when the donated property or equipment is placed in service, or when the donated assets are used to acquire property and equipment. If the entity recognizes an implicit restriction in the donation (to be used for the life of the asset, for instance), then the transfer is to the restricted net assets.

c. A nonprofit organization has the option of not recognizing the contributions of artwork, antiques, and similar items if the donated property is added to a collection that meets three criteria: (1) held for research or exhibition for public service as opposed to monetary gain; (2) are preserved and kept unencumbered; and (3) proceeds from sales of collection components must be used to acquire other artwork or antiques for collections. Contributed collection assets are recognized as revenues if collections are capitalized and not recognized as revenues if collections are not capitalized.

2. **SERVICES** Report the fair value of donated services (e.g., doctors, nurses) as both an expense and a revenue if (1) the services would otherwise be purchased; (2) the value of the services is measurable; and (3) the entity controls the employment and duties of the service donors (i.e., there is the equivalent of an employer-employee or hired contractor relationship).

    a.   Contributions of services are recognized as revenues only if (1) nonfinancial assets are created or enhanced, and (2) special skills are required that would otherwise be purchased. The debit depends on the form of the benefit received.

    b.   Participation of volunteers in philanthropic activities generally does not meet the foregoing criteria because there is no effective employer-employee relationship.

3.   **CLASSIFICATION** Contributions are classified as gains when they are peripheral or incidental to the activities of the entity. However, they are classified as revenue in those circumstances in which these sources are deemed to be ongoing major or central activities by which the provider attempts to fulfill its basic function. For example, donor's contributions are revenues if fund-raising is an ongoing major activity by which the provider attempts to fulfill its basic function. The same donations, however, would be a gain to a provider that does not actively seek contributions and receives them only occasionally.

4.   **PLEDGES** Pledges are reported in the period in which they are made, net of an allowance for uncollectible amounts. Pledges are also called promises to give. Conditional pledges are not recorded until they become unconditional.

    a.   Unrestricted pledges are reported in the statement of revenue and expenses. If part of the pledge is to be applied during some future period, that part is reported as restricted revenue. A pledge to give in the future has an **implied** restriction for future use.

    b.   Restricted pledges are reported as restricted revenues.

5.   **INTERMEDIARY TRANSACTIONS** When a nonprofit organization (NPO) receives assets in a nonexchange transaction from a resource provider, with the proviso that the assets be redistributed to another specific organization (or ultimate recipient) chosen by the resource provider, the NPO intermediary is functioning as an agent. However, if the NPO has some discretion as the timing, manner, and recipient of the assets, the NPO intermediary may then be either an agent for the resource provider or a donee. The degree of discretion exercised by the NPO intermediary determines the classification of the event as a donation or as an agency transaction.

EXHIBIT 7 ♦ SOME GUIDELINES FOR SEPARATING DONATIONS FROM AGENCY TRANSACTIONS

Attribute	Donation Status	Agency Status
NPO's assertions when requesting donations.	Requests assets to provide for own activities.	Requests assets to provide for others or is not much involved in requesting assets.
Composition of assets	Changes while NPO holds assets (Land received, cash redistributed).	Assets redistributed in same composition. (Land received, land redistributed).
Legal title to assets.	NPO holds legal title.	NPO doesn't hold legal title.
Intent of transfer.	NPO commonly has programs that the assets are intended to support.	NPO doesn't commonly have programs that the assets are intended to support.
Donor awareness.	Providers unaware of ultimate recipient.	Providers are aware of ultimate recipient.
Type of NPO operation.	NPO has programs.	NPO exists to collect and redistribute assets.

E.   CONTRIBUTIONS FOR OTHERS (SFAS 136)
SFAS 136, *Transfers of Assets to a Not-for-Profit Organization or Charitable Trust That Raises or Holds Contributions for Others*, applies to contributions for others and also to transactions that are not contributions because the transfers are revocable, repayable, or reciprocal.

1.   DEFINITIONS

a.   RECIPIENT A not-for profit entity or charitable trust that accepts assets from donors and agrees to use those assets on behalf of, or transfer those assets to, another entity specified by the donor. This transfer of assets includes the assets, the return on investment of those assets, or both.

b.   FINANCIALLY INTERRELATED ORGANIZATIONS (ENTITIES) One entity has the ability to influence the operating and financial decisions of the other and one entity has an ongoing economic interest in the net assets of the other.

2.   RECIPIENT A recipient that accepts assets from a donor on behalf of a specified beneficiary recognizes the fair value of those assets as a liability concurrent with the recognition of the assets. If the donor explicitly gives the recipient variance power or if the recipient and the specified beneficiary are financially interrelated entities, the recipient instead recognizes the transaction as a contribution. Four circumstances exist in which a transfer of assets by a donor is recognized by the recipient as a liability and by the donor as an asset.

a.   DONOR MAY REDIRECT The transfer is subject to the donor's unilateral right to redirect the use of the assets to another beneficiary.

b.   DONOR MAY REVOKE The transfer is accompanied by the donor's conditional promise to give or is otherwise revocable or repayable.

c.   DONOR CONTROLS The donor controls the recipient and specifies an unaffiliated beneficiary.

d.   DONOR BENEFITS The donor specifies itself or its affiliate as the beneficiary and the transfer is not an equity transaction.

3.   BENEFICIARY A specified beneficiary recognizes rights to assets held by a recipient as an asset (either an interest in the net assets of the recipient, a beneficial interest, or a receivable) unless the donor has explicitly granted variance power to the recipient.

a.   NET ASSET INTEREST If the beneficiary and the recipient are financially interrelated entities, the beneficiary recognizes an interest in the net assets of the recipient, adjusting that interest for its share of the change in the recipient's net assets.

b.   BENEFICIARY INTEREST If the beneficiary has an unconditional right to specified cash flows from a charitable trust or other identifiable pool of assets, the beneficiary is required to recognize that beneficial interest, at fair value as of the transaction date and reporting dates.

c.   NONRECOGNITION If the recipient is explicitly granted variance power, the specified beneficiary doesn't recognize an asset.

d.   RECEIVABLE In all other circumstances, a beneficiary recognizes its rights as a receivable.

4.   EQUITY TRANSACTION If the transfer is an equity transaction and the donor specifies itself as beneficiary, the donor records an interest in the net assets of the recipient. If the donor specifies an affiliate as beneficiary, the donor records an equity transaction as a separate line item in its statement of activities, and the beneficiary records an interest in the net assets of the recipient entity. The recipient entity records an equity transaction as a separate line item in its statement of activities.

5. **DISCLOSURES** If a NPO transfers assets to a recipient and specifies itself or an affiliate as beneficiary or if it includes a ratio of fundraising expenses to amount raised in its financial statements, the NPO must make the following disclosures for each period that it presents a statement of financial position: recipient identity; whether variance power was granted to the recipient and the terms of any variance power; the distribution conditions; and the classification (as a beneficial interest or an interest in the net assets of the recipient, etc.) and aggregate amount recognized in the statement of financial position for these transfers.

F. INVESTMENTS

SFAS 124, *Accounting For Certain Investments Held by Not-for-Profit Organizations*, applies to all investments of all NPOs in debt securities and to investments in equity securities that have a readily determinable market value for all nonprofit organizations. Investments in equity securities accounted for under the equity method, or that are consolidated, are not within the scope of SFAS 124.

1. **APPLICABILITY** Fair value of equity securities is deemed to be readily determinable if any of the following conditions are met:

   a. Sales prices or bid-and-ask quotations are available on an exchange which is registered with the SEC or where over-the-counter quotations are reported by NASDAQ or the National Quotation Bureau.

   b. For securities traded in a foreign market, the market must be of breadth and scope to make it comparable to a U.S. market which meets the condition just mentioned.

   c. For mutual funds, the fair value per share or unit is determined and published, and represents the basis for current transactions.

2. **VALUATION** SFAS 124 requires that all applicable investments be measured at fair value. Gains and losses on the investments are included in the statement of activities as increases and decreases, respectively, in unrestricted net assets unless the use of the securities is temporarily or permanently restricted in accordance with the definitions found in SFAS 117.

3. **INVESTMENT INCOME** Any dividends, interest, or other investment income are to be included in the statement of activities as earned. Such amounts would be reported as adjustments to unrestricted net assets unless some restriction exists.

4. **DISCLOSURES**

   a. Composition of the investment return including investment income, net realized gains or losses on investments reported at other than fair value, and net gains or losses on investments reported at fair value.

   b. A reconciliation of investment return to amounts reported in the statement of activities, if investment return is separated into operating and nonoperating amounts, together with a description of the policy used to determine the amount that is included in the measure of operations and a discussion of circumstances leading to a change in the policy.

   c. Aggregate carrying amount of the investment by major types.

   d. Basis for determining the carrying amount for investments, other than those to which SFAS 124 applies.

e. Methods and significant assumptions used to estimate the fair values of investments other than financial instruments, if those other investments are reported at fair value.

f. Aggregate amount of the deficiencies for all donor-restricted endowment funds for which the fair value of the assets at the reporting date is less than the level required by donor stipulations or law.

g. The nature and carrying amount of each individual investment group which represents a significant concentration of market risk.

G. DEPRECIATION

SFAS 93, *Recognition of Depreciation by Not-for-Profit Organizations*, requires all nonprofit organizations to recognize depreciation in general purpose external financial statements. SFAS 93 does not cover matters of financial statement display, recognition of assets, or measurement, such as the amount of depreciation to be recognized for a particular period.

1. REQUIRED DISCLOSURES

a. Depreciation expense for the period

b. Depreciable asset balances, by nature or function of asset

c. Total accumulated depreciation, or accumulated depreciation for the major classes of assets

d. The depreciation method or methods used for each major class of assets

2. EXCEPTION
Depreciation should not be recognized on individual pieces of artwork or antiquities. Artwork or antiquities shall be deemed to have those characteristics only if verifiable evidence exists that

a. The asset has cultural, aesthetic, or historical value that is worth preserving perpetually.

b. The holder has the technological and financial ability to protect and preserve, essentially undiminished, the service potential of the asset and is doing so.

H. RELATED ORGANIZATIONS

Reporting of Related Entities by Not-For-Profit Organizations (SOP 94-3) unifies guidance involving reporting related organizations.

1. REQUIRED CONDITIONS
A foundation, auxiliary, or guild is considered to be related to a nonprofit entity if one of the following conditions is met:

a. The nonprofit entity **controls** the separate organization through contracts or other legal documents that provide the entity with the authority to direct the separate organization's activities, management, and policies.

b. The nonprofit entity is considered to be the **sole beneficiary** of the organization because one of the three following circumstances exists:

(1) The organization has solicited funds in the name of the nonprofit entity and substantially all of the funds were intended by the contributor to be transferred to or used by the nonprofit entity.

(2) The nonprofit entity has transferred some of the resources to the organization, and substantially all of the organization's resources are held for the benefit of the entity.

(3) The entity has assigned certain of its functions (e.g., the operation of a dormitory) to the organization, which is operating primarily for the benefit of the entity.

c. The nonprofit entity, upon liquidation of the group, is **liable** for any deficit or due the net assets of the group.

2. DISCLOSURE If the nonprofit entity both **controls** the separate organization and is considered to be its **sole beneficiary**, and if the financial statements of the entity and the related organization are not consolidated or combined in accordance with ARB 51, *Consolidated Financial Statements*, then the entity should disclose summarized financial information about the related organization (e.g., total assets, total liabilities, results of operations, and changes in net assets) and describe the nature of the relationship in a note to the nonprofit entity's financial statements.

II. UNIQUE ACCOUNTING FEATURES

A. HEALTH CARE ENTITIES

All revenues (restricted and unrestricted) and expenses are recognized on the accrual basis. The basis and timing of the recognition of expenses for health care entities are generally the same as for other business organizations. Thus, **depreciation** and amortization is reported in conformity with commercial GAAP, as is the provision for **bad debts**.

1. UNRESTRICTED REVENUES AND EXPENSES Mostly classified as **operating** because they arise from activities associated with the provision of health care services. Unrestricted revenues are further classified as *patient service revenue* or *other revenue*.

a. The major classifications of **functional expenses** include nursing and other professional, general, fiscal, and administrative services; bad debts; depreciation; and interest.

b. **Other revenues** include tuition from educational programs, cafeteria revenues, parking fees, fees for copies of medical records, gift shop revenues, and other activities somewhat related to the provision of patient service revenues.

2. PATIENT SERVICE REVENUE Patient service revenue (revenue from health care services) is recorded gross, at the provider's regularly established rates, regardless of collectibility. **Charity** care is **not** included in patient service revenues because these services were provided free of charge and, thus, were never expected to result in cash flows.

a. **DEDUCTIONS FROM PATIENT SERVICE REVENUES** Provisions for *contractual adjustments* (i.e., the difference between established rates and third-party payor payments) and *other adjustments* are recorded on the accrual basis and deducted from gross patient service revenue to determine *net patient service revenue*.

b. **BAD DEBTS** The *provision for bad debts* is reported as an expense in accordance with GAAP. It is not acceptable to deduct an allowance for uncollectible accounts from gross patient service revenues in determining net patient service revenue.

3. OTHER REVENUE Normally includes revenue from services other than health care provided to patients, as well as sales and services to nonpatients. Depending on the relation to the health care entity's operations, other revenue may include:

a. Revenue from educational programs, including tuition from schools, such as nursing.

b. Revenue from research and other gifts and grants, either unrestricted or for a specific purpose.

c. Revenue such as gifts, grants, or endowment income restricted to finance charity care.

d. Revenue from miscellaneous sources, such as (1) proceeds from sale of cafeteria meals and guest trays to employees, medical staff, and visitors; (2) proceeds from sales at gifts shops, snack bars, newsstands, parking lots, and vending machines; and (3) fees charged for copies of medical records.

4. GAINS AND LOSSES Are generally classified as nonoperating because they generally result from transactions that are peripheral or incidental to the provision of health care services. However, a gain or loss closely related with the provision of health care services may be classified as operating. Therefore, depending on the relation of the transactions to the health care entity's ongoing or major operations, gains (losses) normally include:

a. Contributions

b. Returns on investments (i.e., interest, dividends, rents, and gains and losses resulting from increases and decreases in the value of investments). Investment income essential to the provision of health care services is reported as revenue (e.g., a provider with a large endowment that provides funds that are necessary for the provider to operate).

c. Amounts from Endowment Funds that are available for general operating purposes, which include interest and dividends on Endowment Fund investments. Realized gains or losses on the sale of investments of Endowment Funds are recorded as restricted revenue or gains in the Endowment Fund principal unless such amounts are legally available for other use or are chargeable against other funds.

d. Miscellaneous gains (losses) such as a gain or loss on the sale of the entity's properties.

5. RECEIVABLES Receivables for health care services do not include charges related to charity care. They are reported net of valuation allowances for uncollectibles and contractual and other adjustments.

EXHIBIT 8 ♦ SAMPLE HEALTH CARE ENTITY JOURNAL ENTRIES

1. To record gross charges to patients at established rates:

   Accounts Receivable   XX
      Patient Service Revenues   XX

   NOTE: Charity care is not included in gross patient service revenues because the services are provided free of charge.

2. To record deductions from gross patient service revenues:

   Contractual and Other Adjustments   XX
      Accounts Receivable   XX

   NOTE: Contractual and other adjustments are recognized as deductions from patient service revenues rather than as operating expenses.

   (continued on next page)

3. To record hospital operating expenses and other revenues (that is, operating revenues other than patient service revenues):

Operating Expenses (functional expense accounts)	XX	
Depreciation Expense	XX	
Cash or Payable		XX
Inventory		XX
Accumulated Depreciation		XX
Cash or Receivables	XX	
Other Revenues		XX

6. OTHER HEALTH CARE ENTITIES

a. COMMERCIAL Financial statements of investor-owned health care entities are similar to those of other investor-owned entities.

b. GOVERNMENTAL The financial activities of a health care entity operated by a governmental unit should be accounted for as an enterprise fund when incorporated into the basic financial statements or CAFR of the governmental unit.

B. COLLEGES & UNIVERSITIES

Also see annuity and life income funds (in Section IV).

1. REVENUE Where standard established tuition and fee charges are waived, whether partially or entirely, the full amounts of the standard tuition and fees are recognized as revenues and the amounts waived are recorded as expenditures. The amount of *tuition remissions* allowed to faculty members' families and *scholarships* are also recorded as both a revenue and an expenditure. The amount of *class cancellation refunds*, however, are not classified as either a revenue or an expenditure.

2. TYPICAL OPERATING ACCOUNTS Revenues, expenditures, and transfers typically are recorded in accounts such as the following, which are adapted from NACUBO's *College and University Business Administration* (CUBA) chart of accounts:

- Tuition and Fees
- Appropriations [by source, e.g., state, local]
- Grants and Contracts [by source, e.g., federal]
- Private Gifts, Grants, and Contracts
- Endowment Income
- Sales and Service of Educational Activities [e.g., testing services]
- Auxiliary Enterprises [e.g., residence halls, food service, athletic programs, hospitals]

- Educational and General [subclassified—e.g., Instruction, Research, Public Services, Academic Support, Student Services, Institutional Support, Operation and Maintenance of Plant, Scholarships and Fellowships]
- Mandatory Transfers
- Nonmandatory Transfers
- Auxiliary Enterprises [e.g., as contra to the revenue account]
- Other

NOTE: Past CPA exam problems have required knowledge of the eight functional subclassifications within Educational and General.

3. STATEMENT OF ACTIVITIES The university Statement of Activities is usually presented in a columnar format with one column for each fund group or major subdivision. (Exhibit 9)

EXHIBIT 9 ♦ UNIVERSITY STATEMENT OF ACTIVITIES COLUMN HEADINGS

Current Fund		Trust Funds				Plant Funds		
			Endowment &	Annuity & life			Renewals &	Investment
Unrestricted	Restricted	Loan funds	similar funds	income funds	Unexpended		replacements	in plant

NOTE: These fund groups may be viewed in three categories: (1) current funds, (2) trust funds, and (3) plant funds—though the university accounting literature does not use the trust funds label as such. Agency funds are not included in this statement because agency funds are purely custodial—assets equal liabilities—and, thus, do not have net assets.

4. **GOVERNMENTAL COLLEGES & UNIVERSITIES** Governmental colleges and universities usually do not record depreciation expense (prior to adoption of GASB No. 34).

EXHIBIT 10 ♦ UNIVERSITY STATEMENT OF CHANGES IN UNRESTRICTED NET ASSETS

(Heading)

	Current Funds			
	Unrestricted	Temporarily restricted	Permanently restricted	Total
Revenues:				
Educational and General [listed by major source]	XX			XX
State Appropriations	XX			XX
Federal Grants and Contracts		XX	XX	XX
Private Gifts, Grants, and Contracts	XX	XX	XX	XX
Endowment Income	XX	XX	XX	XX
Expired Term Endowment	XX	XX		XX
Interest Income	XX			XX
Auxiliary Enterprises	XX	XX	XX	XX
Total Revenues	XX	XX	XX	XX
Net Assets Released From Restrictions:				
Expiration of Time Requirements	XX	XX		
Fulfilled Conditions of Equipment Acquisition	XXX	XXX		
Fulfilled Conditions of Program Services	XX	XX		
Total Net Assets Released From Restrictions	XXX	XXX		
Expenditures and Mandatory Transfers:				
Educational and General Expenditures [listed by type]	XX		XX	XX
Total Educational and General Expenditures	XX		XX	XX
Mandatory Transfers for:				
Debt Service Principal and Interest	XX			XX
Loan Fund Equity	XX		XX	XX
Plant Expansion, Renewal, and Replacement	XX			XX
Total Mandatory Transfers	XX		XX	XX
Auxiliary Enterprises:				
Expenditures	XX		XX	XX
Mandatory Transfers	XX		XX	XX
Total Auxiliary Enterprises	XX		XX	XX
Total Expenditures and Mandatory Transfers	XX		XX	XX
Other Transfers and Additions (Deductions):				
Excess of Restricted Receipts and Accruals over Amounts Reported as Revenues			XX	XX
Nonmandatory Transfers to Plant Funds	XX		—	—
Increase (Decrease) in Net Assets	XX	XX	XX	XX

C. **VOLUNTARY HEALTH & WELFARE ORGANIZATIONS (VHWO)**
Voluntary health and welfare organizations (VHWOs) offer free or low cost services to the general public or to certain segments of society, and are supported primarily by public contributions. Examples include the United Way, the American Heart Association, Girl Scouts, Boy Scouts, the YMCA, and the YWCA. **Four** statements are required for VHWOs: the same statements required for all NPOs, plus a fourth, the Statement of Functional Expenses.

1. **STATEMENT OF FUNCTIONAL EXPENSES** The "extra" primary VHWO statement is in substance a schedule detailing expenses. SFAS 117 prescribes that the information in this statement be disclosed for VHWO's. One format of this statement is illustrated in Exhibit 12.

2. **STATEMENT OF FINANCIAL POSITION**

3. **STATEMENT OF CASH FLOWS**

4. **STATEMENT OF ACTIVITIES (OR SUPPORT, REVENUE, AND EXPENSES AND CHANGES IN NET ASSETS)** Many features of typical VHWO accounting and reporting are apparent in the primary VHWO operating statement, which may be presented in the format shown in Exhibit 11. Note that there is a distinct difference between support and revenue.

EXHIBIT 11 ♦ VHWO STATEMENT OF ACTIVITIES

	Current Funds Unrestricted	Current Funds Restricted	Land, Building, and Equipment Fund	Endowment Fund	Total
PUBLIC SUPPORT AND REVENUE					
Public Support:					
Operating Contributions (net)	XX	XX			XX
Capital Contributions (net)			XX	XX	XX
Legacies and Bequests		XX	XX	XX	XX
Special Events (net of related costs)	XX	XX	XX		XX
United Way [or similar federated or nonfederated support organizations]	XX				XX
Total Public Support	XX	XX	XX	XX	XX
Revenue:					
Membership Dues	XX				XX
Investment Income	XX	XX	XX	XX	XX
Investment Gains	XX	XX	XX	XX	XX
Client Service Fees	XX				XX
Total Revenue	XX	XX	XX	XX	XX
EXPENSES					
Program Services:					
Research	XX	XX	XX		XX
Education	XX	XX	XX		XX
Community Services	XX		XX		XX
Total Program Services	XX	XX	XX		XX
Supporting Services:					
Management and General	XX		XX		XX
Fund Raising	XX		XX		XX
Total Supporting Services	XX	XX	XX		XX
OTHER CHANGES IN NET ASSETS					
Fixed Asset Acquisitions From Unrestricted Funds	(XX)		XX		
Transfer of Realized Endowment Appreciation	XX			(XX)	
Returned to Grantor or Donor		(XX)			(XX)
Net Assets, Beginning	XX	XX	XX	XX	XX
Net Assets, Ending	XX	XX	XX	XX	XX

EXHIBIT 12 ♦ VHWO STATEMENT OF FUNCTIONAL EXPENSES

	Program Services				Support Services			
(Heading)	Research	Education	Community Services	Total	Management and General	Fund Raising	Total	Grand Total
Salaries	XX	XX	XX	XX	XX	XX	XX	XX
Employee Benefits	XX	XX	XX	XX	XX	XX	XX	XX
Payroll Taxes	XX	XX	XX	XX	XX	XX	XX	XX
Total	XX	XX	XX	XX	XX	XX	XX	XX
Professional Fees and Contractual Services	XX	XX	XX	XX	XX	XX	XX	XX
Supplies	XX	XX	XX	XX	XX	XX	XX	XX
Telephone	XX	XX	XX	XX	XX	XX	XX	XX
Miscellaneous	XX	XX	XX	XX	XX	XX	XX	XX
Total	XX	XX	XX	XX	XX	XX	XX	XX
Total Expenses Before Depreciation	XX	XX	XX	XX	XX	XX	XX	XX
Depreciation	XX	XX	XX	XX	XX	XX	XX	XX
Total Expenses	XX	XX	XX	XX	XX	XX	XX	XX

D. OTHER NONPROFIT ORGANIZATIONS (ONPO)

Other nonprofit organizations include all nonbusiness organizations **except** (1) those covered by AICPA audit guides, and (2) entities that operate essentially as commercial businesses for the direct economic benefit of stockholders or members (for example, mutual insurance companies or farm cooperatives). Examples of the types of organizations classified as ONPOs are in Exhibit 13. ONPOs are required to present the standard three basic financial statements. The ONPO funds are similar to those of VHWOs.

EXHIBIT 13 ♦ TYPES OF ORGANIZATIONS CLASSIFIED AS ONPO

Civic organizations	Social and country clubs	Performing arts organizations
Labor unions	Cemetery organizations	Private and community foundations
Political parties	Professional organizations	Private elementary and secondary schools
Trade associations	Fraternal organizations	Public broadcasting stations
Libraries	Religious organizations	Research and scientific organizations
Museums	Other cultural institutions	Zoological and botanical societies

III. APPENDIX: HEALTH CARE ENTITY FUND ACCOUNTING

A. CONCEPTS

All (optional) fund formats are insufficient on their own, without the aggregate information required by SFAS 117. Nonprofit health care entities may use fund accounting to account for resources received from donors and grantors and to satisfy their fiduciary responsibilities. The fund accounting model and procedures used are closer to business accounting than to governmental fund accounting. For example, the entity's revenues, expenses, gains, and losses are accounted for and reported in a manner similar to businesses.

1. Except for the aggregate amount reported for revenues and gains in excess of expenses and losses, all other changes in the net assets of the General Fund reported in the Statement of Operations are not reported in the Statement of Revenues and Expenses of General Funds. For example, transfers to the General Fund from the Plant Replacement and Expansion Fund are treated as restricted revenues.

2. Note that investment income restricted for a specific operating purpose by donors and grantors is reported as restricted revenues in the appropriate donor-restricted fund. Unrestricted income of the donor-restricted funds is reported in the Statement of Revenues and Expenses of General Funds.

B. FUND TYPES
To facilitate reporting on the use of assets available for (the governing board's) use versus assets held under external restrictions, health care entities use two categories of funds—the General Funds and donor-restricted funds—each consisting of a self-balancing group of accounts composed of assets, liabilities, and net assets. All **unrestricted** resources and obligations are accounted for in the General Funds. Donor-restricted funds are used to account for financial resources that are *externally restricted* for specified operating or research, capital outlay, or endowment purposes. The fund structure of a health care entity is readily apparent in the format of its Statement of Financial Position, which is presented in Exhibit 14 in the pancake format with each fund reported separately.

EXHIBIT 14 ♦ HEALTH CARE ENTITY STATEMENT OF FINANCIAL POSITION, FUND ACCOUNTING

```
                              (Heading)
                            GENERAL FUNDS

Current assets: (e.g., cash, receivables,        Current liabilities: (same as business
   due from Specific-Purpose Funds)      XX         entities)                             XX
Assets whose use is limited              XX      Long-term debt: (same as business
Property and equipment, net of                      entities)                            XX
   accumulated depreciation:             XX      Contingencies: (same as business
Other assets (e.g., investment in affiliated company) XX  entities)                       XX
                                         XX      Net assets: Unrestricted                 XX

                         DONOR-RESTRICTED FUNDS

                        Specific-Purpose Funds

Cash                                     XX      Due to General Funds                     XX
Investments                              XX      Net Assets: Temp. Restricted             XX
Due from Endowment Funds                 XX      Net Assets: Perm. Restricted             XX
                                         XX                                               XX

                  Plant Replacement and Expansion Funds

Cash                                     XX      Accounts payable                         XX
Investments                              XX      Contracts payable                        XX
Due from Endowment Funds                 XX      Net Assets (Temp. or Perm. Restricted)   XX
                                         XX                                               XX

                           Endowment Funds

Cash                                     XX      Due to Specific-Purpose Funds            XX
Investments                              XX      Due to Plant Replacement and
Pledges receivable, net                  XX      Expansion Funds                          XX
Property and Equipment, net              XX      Mortgage Assets (related)                XX
                                                 Net Assets (Temp. or Perm. Restricted)   XX
                                         XX                                               XX
```

1. **GENERAL FUNDS** Account for all assets and liabilities that are not required to be accounted for in a donor-restricted fund, including assets whose use is limited, Agency Funds, and property and equipment related to the general operations of the entity. Assets and liabilities of General Funds are classified as current or noncurrent in conformity with GAAP.

   a. Assets whose use is limited include assets set aside by the governing board for identified purposes. The board retains control over the board-restricted assets and may, at its discretion, subsequently use them for other purposes.

b. Agency funds are included in General Funds as both an asset and a liability. Transactions involving receipt and disbursement of agency funds are not included in the results of operations.

c. Property and equipment used for general operations, and the related liabilities, are reported in General Funds. Property and equipment whose use is restricted (e.g., real estate investments of Endowment Funds) are reported in the appropriate donor-restricted fund.

2. **DONOR-RESTRICTED FUNDS** Account for resources whose use is restricted by donors or grantors and essentially act as holding funds until the resources are used. Donor-restricted funds may be temporarily or permanently restricted and include resources for specific operating purposes, additions to property and equipment, and endowments. Increases and decreases in the donor-restricted fund types are recorded as additions to and deductions from the appropriate fund net assets and are reported in the Statement of Activities (after original recognition as revenue).

> **Hospital Funds**
> **U** Unrestricted general
> **P** Plant replacement
> **S** Specific purpose
> **E** Endowment
> **T** Term Endowment

a. Specific-Purpose Funds account for resources restricted by donors and grantors for specific operating purposes (e.g., research or education). They are recorded as restricted revenue (or gains) when received. Their expenditure (1) decreases the net assets of the Specific-Purpose Fund and (2) are generally recorded as expenses and net assets released from restrictions in the General Funds.

b. Plant Replacement and Expansion Funds account for resources restricted by donors and grantors for capital outlay purposes. They are recorded as restricted revenues (or gains) when received. Their expenditure (1) decreases the net assets of the Plant Replacement and Expansion Fund, and (2) increases property and equipment and the net assets of the General Funds. Neither the plant assets acquired nor any long-term debt issued for capital outlay purposes is accounted for in the Plant Replacement and Expansion Funds.

c. Endowment Funds include resources whose principal may not be expended (i.e., an Endowment Fund is generally a permanently restricted fund).

(1) The receipt of gifts and bequests restricted for endowments are reported as permanently restricted revenues of the Endowment Fund.

(2) Realized gains or losses on the sale of investments of Endowment Funds are reported as restricted revenues of the Endowment Fund unless such amounts are legally available for other use.

(3) Investment income of Endowment Funds is accounted for in accordance with the donor's instructions. If unrestricted, the income is generally reported as a (unrestricted) nonoperating gain in the General Funds. Investment income is reported as a temporarily or permanently restricted revenue (a) in the Specific Purpose Fund if restricted for a specified operating purposes (e.g., research or education), or (b) in the Plant Replacement and Expansion Fund if restricted for capital outlay purposes.

d. Term Endowment Funds account for resources whose principal may be expended after the donor-imposed restrictions are satisfied (e.g., for 15 years or until after the donor's death). Term endowments are accounted for as discussed above during the endowment term. When the term of the endowment ends, the assets are transferred to other funds, as specified by the donor. The transfer increases the net assets of the specific purpose fund or plant replacement and expansion fund, as appropriate, if restricted for specified operating or capital outlay purposes. If the assets are available for general operating purposes, the transfer is generally recorded as an increase in the unrestricted net assets in the general funds.

IV. APPENDIX: UNIVERSITY FUND ACCOUNTING

A. CONCEPTS
University (and college) fund accounting is both similar and different from that for governments and hospitals. Universities have only a few fund groups, as do hospitals, but divide these into major fund group subdivisions that resemble the municipal funds.

University Funds

Current Funds [Unrestricted Current Funds, Restricted Current Funds]

Plant Funds

Agency Funds

Loan Funds

Annuity Fund

Life Income Fund

Endowment Fund [Endowment Funds (pure), Term Endowment Funds, Quasi-Endowment Funds]

---

1. **TRANSFERS** Universities account for interfund quasi-external transactions, reimbursements, and transfers similarly to governments.

2. **NUMBER OF FUND GROUPS** Like hospitals, universities **may** use only one fund of each group for accounting purposes. Alternatively, they may use a separate fund for each major sub-division or may use many separate funds as do municipalities.

B. RESTRICTED VS. UNRESTRICTED CURRENT FUNDS
Unrestricted Current Funds are used to account for all university financial resources (and related current liabilities) that are expendable for any legal and reasonable institutional purposes and that have **not** been (1) externally restricted by donors or grantors for specified purposes, or (2) designated by the governing board and, thus, accounted for as Net Assets—Unrestricted in another fund. Financial resources (and related current liabilities) that are externally restricted for current operating purposes of the university are accounted for in the *Restricted Current Funds*.

C. CURRENT FUND UNIQUE ACCOUNTING CONVENTIONS
Current Funds are accounted for on the accrual basis of accounting.

1. **UNRESTRICTED CURRENT FUNDS**

    a. Where the **full amount** of specific fees or other revenue sources is legally or contractually restricted for *debt service* or *capital outlay* purposes, the fees are recorded as restricted revenues of the appropriate plant funds rather than as current fund revenues.

    b. Where only **part** of specific fees or other revenue sources is legally or contractually restricted for *debt service* or *capital outlay* purposes, (1) the full amount is reported as unrestricted current fund revenue, and (2) the restricted amount is recorded as a mandatory transfer to the appropriate plant funds.

    c. Where the governing board has **designated** unrestricted resources for purposes usually financed in other funds, the revenues are reported in the unrestricted current fund, as is a *nonmandatory* transfer to the other fund(s). Likewise, returns of such sums are recorded as transfers to the unrestricted current fund rather than as revenues.

d. Residual balances of endowment and similar funds and annuity and life income funds that become unrestricted at the end of their term are recorded in distinctively titled *Net Assets Released From Restrictions* (NARFR) accounts in the unrestricted current fund.

e. Inventory may be accounted for on the consumption or use method whereby (a) inventory purchases are charged to *Expenses*, but (b) the change in inventories during the year is recorded as an adjustment to the *Expenses* account at year-end. (No inventory reserve is needed unless there is a base stock of inventories that is not available for use.)

2. **RESTRICTED CURRENT FUNDS**

a. Financial resources restricted for operating purposes are recorded as assets and restricted revenues—in the restricted current funds.

b. Restricted current fund expenditures are recorded in expenditures accounts of that fund—**not** of the unrestricted current funds.

D. **CURRENT FUND BUDGETARY ACCOUNTS**
Universities may use budgetary accounts—particularly in the current funds—in a manner like that illustrated for a municipal general fund.

1. **ENCUMBRANCE ACCOUNTING** Generally used in budgeted university funds, parallel to that for municipal general and special revenue funds.

2. **BUDGETS** The university budgetary account entry usually varies somewhat from that for a municipal general fund. This entry follows a budgetary fund balance approach in that the *Unallocated (or Unassigned) Budget Balance* account is a balancing or offsetting account. The budgetary entry is reversed in the year-end closing entries.

E. **TRUST & AGENCY FUNDS**
Accounting for university loan funds, endowment and similar funds, and agency funds parallels that for municipalities and/or hospitals.

F. **ANNUITY & LIFE INCOME FUNDS**
Annuity and life income funds are used to account for assets (and related liabilities) given to the university on the condition that the university either (1) make annuity payments of a fixed amount periodically to a named recipient(s) for a fixed or determinable period of time (annuity fund), or (2) pay the income earned by the fund to a named recipient(s) for a fixed or determinable period of time, often the donor's and/or the recipient's lifetime (life income fund).

1. **FUNDAMENTAL DISTINCTION** The annuity fund guarantees the recipient(s) a fixed dollar payment periodically during its term, while the life income fund involves no guarantees except that whatever income is earned will be paid to the recipient(s) during its term.

a. **INITIAL RECORDING** No payable to the beneficiary is recorded at the inception of the Life Income Fund because there is no obligation to make fixed payments to the beneficiary. (The beneficiary is entitled only to receive the **income** from the fund's assets, if any.)

b. **CLOSING ENTRIES** Revenues are **not** credited for the income generated by the life income fund's assets, since the income is payable to the beneficiary. Therefore, life income fund income is credited to an *Income Payable to Beneficiary* account.

2. **CLOSING** At the end of their terms, the fund balances of both annuity funds and life income funds become expendable for unrestricted and/or specified restricted purposes and are transferred to the unrestricted current fund or to the appropriate restricted fund.

G. **PLANT FUNDS**

The plant funds group is used to account for financial resources restricted and/or designated for university capital outlay and debt service, its fixed assets, and its long-term debt. All fixed assets and long-term debt that are not related to the university's trust funds are recorded in the plant funds. This is reasonable since most universities cannot incur long-term debt except for fixed asset acquisitions. The four plant fund subdivisions are closely related, and their accounting procedures are relatively simple.

U	**Unexpended** Plant Fund
R	Fund for **Renewals** and **Replacements**
R	Fund for **Retirement** of Indebtedness
I	**Investment** in Plant

1. **UNEXPENDED PLANT FUNDS** Used to account for financial resources restricted or designated for acquisition of **new** fixed assets, the current and long-term liabilities related to such unexpended financial resources, and the net amount available for expenditure for new fixed assets. The new fixed assets acquired consist of both new fixed assets and existing fixed assets newly acquired for university purposes—as opposed to renovating existing university fixed assets. The new fixed assets are capitalized in the *Investment in Plant* accounts.

2. **PLANT FUNDS FOR RENEWALS AND REPLACEMENTS** Identical to unexpended plant funds except the financial resources are used to renovate or perhaps replace existing university fixed assets. Long-term debt is not often incurred for such purposes and most renovations, in particular, are not capitalized in the *Investment in Plant* accounts—though major betterment and replacements are capitalized in the *Investment in Plant* accounts.

NOTE: Both unexpended plant funds and plant funds for renewals and replacements are similar to municipal capital projects funds, except that long-term debt may be accounted for temporarily in these plant fund subdivisions. Because of their similarity, it is acceptable to account for both of these plant fund subdivisions in one plant fund subdivision, provided that separate *Net Assets* accounts distinguish the net assets of the two subfunds.

3. **PLANT FUNDS FOR RETIREMENT OF INDEBTEDNESS** Used to account for restricted and designated financial resources to be used for university debt service, related current liabilities for long-term debt principal and interest payable, and the net amount available for future debt service expenditures. The accounting procedures for plant funds for retirement of indebtedness parallel those for municipal debt service funds.

4. **INVESTMENT IN PLANT** An account group in a governmental accounting sense, which is used to record the university's general fixed assets, general long-term debt, and the difference between its fixed assets and long-term debt, referred to as net investment in plant. Thus, the investment in plant fund functions like a combination of the pre-GASB 34 municipal general fixed assets and general long-term debt account groups. Nongovernmental colleges and universities *must* report accumulated depreciation on these assets and the periodic depreciation provision *must* be reported in the Statement of Activities. Colleges and universities that are part of a government have the option of not reporting these amounts (prior to adoption of GASB No. 34) and, historically, have not done so.

H.   STATEMENT OF FINANCIAL POSITION
The university fund group and major fund subdivisions structure is readily apparent in the format of the university Statement of Financial Position (balance sheet), when presented in the fund pancake format. (See Exhibit 15.)

1.   **UNRESTRICTED AND RESTRICTED CURRENT FUNDS** Similar to municipal general and special revenue funds, respectively, and the restricted current fund is like a hospital specific purpose fund.

2.   **TRUST FUNDS** The loan fund, endowment funds, and annuity and life income funds are all trust funds. The loan fund is like one of the municipal nonexpendable trust funds. The annuity and life income funds are special types of trust funds.

3.   **AGENCY FUND** Similar to the simpler municipal agency funds.

4.   **PLANT FUNDS** Like a combination of municipal (a) capital projects funds—the unexpended funds and fund for renewals and replacements; (b) debt service funds—the funds for retirement of indebtedness; and (c) general fixed assets and general long-term debt account groups—the investment in plant fund. The distinction between the unexpended funds and the fund for renewals and replacements is that (a) the unexpended funds are used to account for resources (and related debt) to be expended for new construction (capitalized in the *Investment in Plant* accounts), while (b) the fund for renewals and replacements are used to account for financial resources to be expended for renovation of existing fixed assets (which are **not** usually capitalized in *Investment in Plant* accounts).

EXHIBIT 15 ♦ UNIVERSITY STATEMENT OF FINANCIAL POSITION, FUND ACCOUNTING

(Heading)			
Assets		Liabilities and Net Assets	
CURRENT FUNDS			
Unrestricted		Unrestricted	
Current Assets [list]	XX	Current Liabilities [list]	XX
		Net Assets: Unrestricted	XX
	XX		XX
Restricted		Restricted	
Current Assets [list]	XX	Current Liabilities [list]	XX
		Net Assets: Temporarily Restricted	XX
		Net Assets: Permanently Restricted	XX
Total Current Funds	XX	Total Current Funds	XX
LOAN FUNDS			
Current Assets [list]	XX	Net Assets:	
Loan Notes Receivable	XX	Unrestricted	XX
Long-Term Investments	XX	Temporarily Restricted	XX
Total Loan Funds	XX	Permanently Restricted	XX
		Total Loan Funds	XX
ENDOWMENT AND SIMILAR FUNDS			
Current Assets [list]	XX	Current Liabilities [list]	XX
Long-Term Investments [list]	XX	Long-Term Liabilities [list]	XX
Fixed Assets [list, net of			XX
accumulated depreciation]	XX	Net Assets:	
		Perm. Restricted: Endowment	XX
		Temp. Restricted: Term Endowment	XX
		Unrestricted: Quasi-Endowment	XX
Total Endowment and Similar Funds	XX	Total Endowment and Similar Funds	XX
(continued on next page)			

ANNUITY AND LIFE INCOME FUNDS			
Current Assets [list]	XX	Annuities Payable	XX
Long-Term Investments	XX	Life Income Earnings Payable	XX
		Net Assets: Permanently Restricted	
		Annuity Funds	XX
		Life Income Funds	XX
Total Annuity and Life Income Funds	XX	Total Annuity and Life Income Funds	XX

PLANT FUNDS			
Unexpended		Unexpended	
Current Assets [list]	XX	Current Liabilities [list]	XX
Long-Term Investments	XX	Notes Payable	XX
Construction in Process	XX		XX
		Net Assets:	
		Unrestricted	XX
		Temporarily Restricted	XX
		Permanently Restricted	XX
Total Unexpended Plant Funds	XX	Total Unexpended Plant Funds	XX
For Renewals and Replacements		For Renewals and Replacements	
Current Assets [list]	XX	Current Liabilities [list]	XX
Long-Term Investments	XX	Net Assets:	
		Unrestricted	XX
		Temporarily Restricted	XX
		Permanently Restricted	XX
Total for Renewals and Replacements	XX	Total for Renewals and Replacements	XX
For Retirement of Indebtedness		For Retirement of Indebtedness	
Current Assets [list]	XX	Net Assets:	
Long-Term Investments	XX	Restricted (Temp. or Perm)	XX
Sinking Fund—Bank Trustee	XX	Unrestricted	XX
Total for Retirement of Indebtedness	XX	Total for Retirement of Indebtedness	XX
Investment in Plant		Investment in Plant	
Fixed Assets [list]	XX	Long-Term Debt [list]	XX
		Net Investment in Plant	XX
Total Investment in Plant	XX	Total Investment in Plant	XX

V. APPENDIX: VHWO FUND ACCOUNTING

A. CONCEPTS

The VHWO fund structure is similar to that used by universities; furthermore, VHWOs use only one fund of each fund type. Note that fund accounting is **not** required. Whereas hospital accounting records all revenues and expenses in a single unrestricted fund, VHWOs record revenues and expenses in **each** fund—summarizing them in the total column of a columnar Statement of Activities.

B. FUND TYPES

1. **LAND, BUILDING, AND EQUIPMENT (OR PLANT) FUND** Used to account for (a) unexpended restricted resources to be used to acquire VHWO fixed assets, (b) the VHWO's general fixed assets, (c) long-term debt related to the VHWO's fixed assets, and (d) the net investment in VHWO general fixed assets. (This fund is identical to the university plant fund—although VHWOs may record debt service in the current unrestricted fund rather than in the plant fund.)

   a. VHWO general fixed assets and related general long-term debt are recorded in the land, buildings, and equipment (or plant) fund, while those related to endowments are recorded in the endowment fund.

   b. If fixed assets are donated to a VHWO to be sold and the proceeds used for operating purposes, the fixed assets are recorded in the current unrestricted fund or current restricted fund pending their sale, depending on whether the use of the sale proceeds is unrestricted or restricted.)

c. Net Assets of the land, buildings, and equipment (or plant) fund are classified as between (1) expended and (2) unexpended, as well as between unrestricted and temporarily and permanently restricted.

2. **CUSTODIAN FUND** Used to account for resources held by the VHWO in an agency capacity for other organizations or individuals. (This fund is identical to the university agency fund and to simple municipal agency funds.)

3. **RESTRICTED CURRENT FUND** Used to account for available financial resources (and related current liabilities) that are expendable only for operating purposes specified by the donor or grantor. (This fund is identical to the university restricted current fund.)

4. **UNRESTRICTED CURRENT FUND** Used to account for all unrestricted resources (and related current liabilities) except those invested in fixed assets, which are accounted for in the land, buildings, and equipment (or plant) fund. (This fund is identical to the university unrestricted current fund.)

5. **ENDOWMENT FUND** Used to account for the principal (corpus) of gifts or bequests accepted with donor stipulations that (a) the principal is to be maintained intact—in perpetuity or for a fixed or determinable term of time, and (b) the earnings may be expended for unrestricted purposes and/or specified restricted purposes. (The VHWO endowment fund is identical to those of hospitals and universities and is like some municipal nonexpendable trust funds.)

6. **LOAN AND ANNUITY FUND** Used to account for resources restricted to making loans and/or annuity payments to specified recipients for a specified term—after which the VHWO is the remainderman beneficiary of the net assets, which may be unrestricted or restricted to use. (This fund is similar to the university annuity and life income fund.)

A·CRUEL

Asset—Land, Building, and Equipment (or Plant) Fund

Custodian Fund

Restricted Current Fund

Unrestricted Current Fund

Endowment Fund

Loan and Annuity Fund

ARE HOT•SPOT™ VIDEO DESCRIPTIONS
(Partial list; subject to change without notice.)

CPA 2040 Governmental & Nonprofit Accounting
Following previous exam emphasis, this program concentrates on accounting for governments. Funds, their uses, and their presentation are examined. Encumbrance, budget, and modified accrual accounting are clarified. This program also covers accounting for healthcare organizations, colleges & universities, and voluntary health & welfare organizations. Robert Monette explains two extensive examples, 40 multiple choice questions, and two other objective format problems as well as discussing problem-solving techniques and introducing proven mnemonics. Approximately 5 hours.

CPA 2290 Cost & Managerial Accounting
Robert Monette thoroughly discusses managerial topics such as break-even analysis, profitability analysis, and capital budgeting with examples worked throughout the lecture. An in-depth examination of direct vs. absorption costing is provided, as well as coverage of incremental analysis, budgeting, the time value of money, economic order quantity, and various graphing techniques. Recurring exam topics are highlighted in the lecture and over 40 multiple choice questions. Approximately 3 hours and 20 minutes.

In order to ensure current materials, Bisk Education leases (rather than sells) videos to candidates for one year. At lease completion (after your exam), contact your customer service representative regarding the return of videos. If needed, extensions on leases are available—but with material this effective, it's a rare occurrence.

Call a customer representative toll-free at 1 (800) 874-7877 for more details about videos.

CHAPTER 23—NONPROFIT ACCOUNTING

PROBLEM 23-1 MULTIPLE CHOICE QUESTIONS (60 to 75 minutes)

1. Cancer Educators, a not-for-profit organization, incurred costs of $10,000 when it combined program functions with fund raising functions. Which of the following cost allocations might Cancer report in its statement of activities?

	Program services	Fund raising	General
a.	$0	$0	$10,000
b.	$0	$6,000	$ 4,000
c.	$ 6,000	$4,000	$0
d.	$10,000	$0	$0

(11/94, AR, #26, 5003)

2. Functional expenses recorded in the general ledger of ABC, a nongovernmental not-for-profit organization, are as follows:

Soliciting prospective members	$45,000
Printing membership benefits brochures	30,000
Soliciting membership dues	25,000
Maintaining donor list	10,000

What amount should ABC report as fund raising expenses?
a. $ 10,000
b. $ 35,000
c. $ 70,000
d. $110,000   (R/99, AR, #2, 6811)

3. In hospital accounting, restricted funds are
a. **Not** available unless the board of directors removes the restrictions.
b. Restricted as to use only for board-designated purposes.
c. **Not** available for current operating use; however, the income generated by the funds is available for current operating use.
d. Restricted as to use by the donor, grantor, or other source of the resources.

(5/93, PII, #29, 4136)

4. The expenditure element "salaries and wages" is an example of which type of classification?
a. Object
b. Program
c. Function
d. Activity   (5/95, AR, #54, 5472)

5. Which of the following classifications is required for reporting of expenses by all not-for-profit organizations?
a. Natural classification in the statement of activities or notes to the financial statements.
b. Functional classification in the statement of activities or notes to the financial statements.
c. Functional classification in the statement of activities and natural classification in a matrix format in a separate statement.
d. Functional classification in the statement of activities and natural classification in the notes to the financial statements. (11/97, AR, #17, 6545)

6. The Jackson Foundation, a not-for-profit organization, received contributions during the year as follows:

- Unrestricted cash contributions of $500,000.
- Cash contributions of $200,000 to be restricted to acquisition of property.

Jackson's statement of cash flows should include which of the following amounts?

	Operating activities	Investing activities	Financing activities
a.	$700,000	$0	$0
b.	$500,000	$200,000	$0
c.	$500,000	$0	$200,000
d.	$0	$500,000	$200,000

(11/97, AR, #18, 6546)

7. In 20X1, Gamma, a not-for-profit organization, deposited at a bank $1,000,000 given to it by a donor to purchase endowment securities. The securities were purchased January 2, 20X2. At December 31, 20X1, the bank recorded $2,000 interest on the deposit. In accordance with the bequest, this $2,000 was used to finance ongoing program expenses in March 20X2. At December 31, 20X1, what amount of the bank balance should be included as current assets in Gamma's classified balance sheet?
a. $0
b. $ 2,000
c. $1,000,000
d. $1,002,000   (11/96, AR, #11, amended, 6304)

8. In a statement of activities of the People's Environmental Protection Association, a voluntary community organization, depreciation expense should
a. Not be included.
b. Be included as an element of support.
c. Be included as an element of other changes in net assets.
d. Be included as an element of expense.

(11/94, AR, #29, amended, 5006)

9. On January 2, 20X1, the Baker Fund, a non-governmental not-for-profit corporation, received a $125,000 contribution restricted to youth activity programs. During 20X1, youth activities generated revenues of $89,000 and had program expenses of $95,000. What amount should Baker report as net assets released from restrictions for the current year?
a. $0
b. $ 6,000
c. $ 95,000
d. $125,000

(R/00, AR, #5, amended, 6910)

10. On December 30, Leigh Museum, a not-for-profit organization, received a $7,000,000 donation of Day Co. shares with donor stipulated requirements as follows:

- Shares valued at $5,000,000 are to be sold with the proceeds used to erect a public viewing building.
- Shares valued at $2,000,000 are to be retained with the dividends used to support current operations.

As a consequence of the receipt of the Day shares, how much should Leigh report as temporarily restricted net assets on its statement of financial position?
a. $0
b. $2,000,000
c. $5,000,000
d. $7,000,000

(5/95, AR, #57, amended, 5475)

11. In its fiscal year ended June 30, 20X0, Barr College, a private nonprofit institution, received $100,000 designated by the donor for scholarships for superior students. On July 26, 20X0, Barr selected the students and awarded the scholarships. How should the July 26 transaction be reported in Barr's statement of activities for the year ended June 30, 20X1?
a. As both an increase and a decrease of $100,000 in unrestricted net assets
b. As a decrease only in unrestricted net assets
c. By footnote disclosure only
d. Not reported

(5/96, AR, #5, amended, 6202)

12. A labor union had the following receipts:

Per capita dues	$680,000
Initiation fees	90,000
Sales of organizational supplies	60,000
Nonexpendable gift restricted by donor for loan purposes for 10 years	30,000
Nonexpendable gift restricted by donor for loan purposes in perpetuity	25,000

The union's constitution provides that 10% of the per capita dues are designated for the Strike Insurance Fund to be distributed for strike relief at the discretion of the union's executive board. In the statement of activity, what amount should be reported as permanently restricted revenues?
a. $123,000
b. $ 93,000
c. $ 55,000
d. $ 25,000

(Editors, 1361)

13. Child Care Centers, Inc., a not-for-profit organization, receives revenue from various sources during the year to support its day-care centers. The following cash amounts were received during the year:

- $2,000 restricted by the donor to be used for meals for the children.
- $1,500 received for subscriptions to a monthly child-care magazine with a fair market value to subscribers of $1,000.
- $10,000 to be used only upon completion of a new playroom that was 75% complete at December 31.

What amount should Child Care Centers record as contribution revenue in its Statement of Activities?
a. $ 2,000
b. $ 2,500
c. $10,000
d. $11,000

(11/97, AR, #15, amended, 6543)

14. A not-for-profit organization receives $150 from a donor. The donor receives two tickets to a theater show and an acknowledgment in the theater program. The tickets have a fair market value of $100. What amount is recorded as contribution revenue?
a. $0
b. $ 50
c. $100
d. $150

(11/97, AR, #16, 6544)

15. The Pel Museum, a nonprofit organization, received a contribution of historical artifacts. It need **not** recognize the contribution if the artifacts are to be sold and the proceeds used to
a. Support general museum activities.
b. Acquire other items for collections.
c. Repair existing collections.
d. Purchase buildings to house collections.
(5/95, AR #59, amended, 5477)

16. Land valued at $400,000 and subject to a $150,000 mortgage was donated to Beaty Hospital without restriction as to use. Which of the following entries should Beaty make to record this donation?

a. Land   400,000
   Mortgage Payable   150,000
   Permanently Restricted Revenues   250,000
b. Land   400,000
   Net Assets   150,000
   Contributions   250,000
c. Land   400,000
   Net Assets   150,000
   Temporarily Restricted Revenues   250,000
d. Land   400,000
   Mortgage Payable   150,000
   Unrestricted Revenues   250,000
(Editors, 4133)

17. In 20X1, Jones Foundation received the following support:

- A cash contribution of $875,000 to be used at the board of directors' discretion

- A promise to contribute $500,000 in 20X2 from a supporter who has made similar contributions in prior periods

- Contributed legal services with a value of $100,000, which Jones would have otherwise purchased

At what amounts would Jones classify and record these transactions as revenue?

	Unrestricted	Temporarily restricted
a.	$1,375,000	$0
b.	$ 875,000	$500,000
c.	$ 975,000	$0
d.	$ 975,000	$500,000

(R/00, AR, #4, amended, 6909)

18. Allan Rowe established a $100,000 endowment, the income from which is to be paid to Elm Hospital for general operating purposes. The present value of the income is estimated at $95,000. Elm does not control the endowment's principal. Rowe appointed West National Bank as trustee. What journal entry is required by Elm to record the establishment of the endowment?

		Debit	Credit
a.	Beneficiary Interest in Trust	$ 95,000	
	Nonexpendable Endowment:		
	Net Assets		$ 95,000
b.	Beneficiary Investment in Trust	$ 95,000	
	Permanently Restricted		
	Revenues: Contributions		$ 95,000
c.	Beneficiary Interest in Trust	$100,000	
	Permanently Restricted		
	Revenues: Contributions		$100,000
d.	Memorandum entry only	--	--

(Editors, 1420)

19. Famous, a nongovernmental not-for-profit art museum, has elected not to capitalize its permanent collections. In 20X0, a bronze statue was stolen. The statue was not recovered and insurance proceeds of $35,000 were paid to Famous in 20X1. This transaction would be reported in

I. The statement of activities as permanently restricted revenues.
II. The statement of cash flows as cash flows from investing activities.

a. I only.
b. II only.
c. Both I and II.
d. Neither I nor II. (R/99, AR, #23, amended, 6812)

20. The League, a not-for-profit organization, received the following pledges:

Unrestricted $200,000
Restricted for capital additions   150,000

All pledges are legally enforceable; however, the League's experience indicates that 10% of all pledges prove to be uncollectible. What amount should the League report as pledges receivable, net of any required allowance account?
a. $135,000
b. $180,000
c. $315,000
d. $350,000   (5/93, PII, #35, 4142)

ITEMS 21 THROUGH 23 are based on the following:

Metro General is a municipally owned and operated hospital and a component unit of Metro City. The hospital received $7,000 in unrestricted gifts and $4,000 in unrestricted bequests. The hospital has $1,200,000 in fixed assets.

The hospital has transferred certain resources to a hospital guild. Substantially all of the guild's resources are held for the benefit of the hospital. The hospital controls the guild through contracts that provide it with the authority to direct the guild's activities, management, and policies. The hospital has also assigned certain of its functions to a hospital auxiliary, which operates primarily for the benefit of the hospital. The hospital does **not** have control over the auxiliary. The financial statements of the guild and the auxiliary are **not** consolidated with the hospital's financial statements. The guild and the auxiliary have total assets of $20,000 and $30,000, respectively.

Before the hospital's financial statements were combined with those of the city, the city's statements included data on one special revenue fund and one enterprise fund. The city's statements showed $500,000 in enterprise fund fixed assets and $6,000,000 in general fixed assets.

21. What account or accounts should generally be credited for the $7,000 of unrestricted gifts and the $4,000 of unrestricted bequests?
a. Other revenue $11,000
b. Nonoperating gains $11,000
c. Other revenue $ 7,000
   Nonoperating gains $ 4,000
d. Nonoperating gains $ 7,000
   Other revenue $ 4,000 (Editors, 1430)

22. In the hospital's notes to financial statements, total assets of hospital-related organizations required to be disclosed amount to
a. $0.
b. $20,000.
c. $30,000.
d. $50,000. (Editors, 1432)

23. The hospital's fixed assets are reported in the city's government-wide statement of net assets as
a. Special revenue fund fixed assets of $1,200,000 in a separate discrete presentation hospital column.
b. Part of $7,200,000 general fixed assets in the governmental activities column.
c. Part of $1,700,000 enterprise fund type fixed assets in the business-type activities column.
d. Part of $7,200,000 fixed assets in the general fixed assets account group column.
(Editors, 1433)

24. Midtown Church received a donation of marketable equity securities from a church member. The securities had appreciated in value after they were purchased by the donor, and they continued to appreciate through the end of Midtown's fiscal year. At what amount should Midtown report its investment in marketable equity securities in its year-end balance sheet?

a. Donor's cost
b. Market value at the date of receipt
c. Market value at the balance sheet date
d. Market value at either the date of receipt or the balance-sheet date (5/93, PII, #38, 4144)

25. Under Abbey Hospital's established rate structure, the hospital would have earned patient service revenue of $6,000,000 for the year. However, Abbey did not expect to collect this amount because of charity care of $1,000,000 and discounts of $500,000 to third-party payors. How much should Abbey record as patient service revenue for the year?
a. $6,000,000
b. $5,500,000
c. $5,000,000
d. $4,500,000 (Editors, 1422)

26. Valley's community hospital normally includes proceeds from sale of cafeteria meals in
a. Deductions from dietary service expenses.
b. Ancillary service revenues.
c. Patient service revenues.
d. Other revenues. (5/94, AR, #60, 4665)

27. For the summer session, Unity University assessed its students $3,000,000 for tuition and fees. However, the net amount realized was only $2,900,000 because of the following reductions:

Tuition remissions granted to faculty
   members' families $30,000
Class cancellation refunds   70,000

How much unrestricted current funds revenues from tuition and fees should Unity report for the period?
a. $2,900,000
b. $2,930,000
c. $2,970,000
d. $3,000,000 (Editors, 1406)

28. The following expenditures were among those incurred by Hope University during the year:

Administrative data processing $100,000
Fellowships   200,000
Operation and maintenance of
   physical plant   400,000

The amount to be included in the functional classification "Institutional Support" expenditures account is
a $100,000.
b. $300,000.
c. $500,000.
d. $700,000. (Editors, 1408)

29. A not-for-profit hospital issued long-term tax exempt bonds for the hospital's benefit. The hospital is responsible for the liability. Which fund may the hospital use to account for this liability?
a. Enterprise
b. Specific purpose
c. General
d. General long-term debt account group

(5/94, AR, #58, 4663)

30. Which of the following accounts would appear in the plant fund of a not-for-profit private college?

	Fuel inventory for power plant	Equipment
a.	Yes	Yes
b.	No	Yes
c.	No	No
d.	Yes	No

(5/93, Theory, #57, 9209)

PROBLEM 23-2 ADDITIONAL MULTIPLE CHOICE QUESTIONS (64 to 80 minutes)

31. The Board of Trustees of Rose Foundation designated $200,000 for college scholarships. The foundation received a bequest of $400,000 from an estate of a benefactor who specified that the bequest was to be used for hiring teachers to tutor handicapped students. What amount should be accounted for as restricted resources?
a. $0
b. $200,000
c. $400,000
d. $600,000

(Editors, 1391)

32. At the end of the year Cram University had $15,000,000 of unrestricted assets (including $300,000 restricted by the donors for use the next year for any board-designated purpose) and $9,000,000 of liabilities. What are Cram's unrestricted net assets?
a. $ 5,700,000
b. $ 6,000,000
c. $ 6,300,000
d. $15,000,000

(Editors, 4134)

33. Hunt Community Development Agency (HCDA), a financially independent authority, provides loans to commercial businesses operating in Hunt County. This year, HCDA made loans totaling $500,000. How should HCDA classify the disbursements of loans on the cash flow statement?
a. Operating activities.
b. Noncapital financing activities.
c. Capital and related financing activities.
d. Investing activities. (R/01, AR, #2, 6987)

34. A labor union had the following expenses:

Labor negotiations	500,000
Fund-raising	100,000
Membership development	50,000
Administrative and general	200,000

In the statement of activity, what amount should be reported under the classification of program services?
a. $850,000
b. $600,000
c. $550,000
d. $500,000

(Editors, 1362)

35. The following funds were among those held by State College at December 31:

Principal specified by the donor as nonexpendable	$500,000
Principal expendable after the year 2010	300,000
Principal designated from current funds	100,000

What amount should State College classify as regular endowment funds?
a. $100,000
b. $300,000
c. $500,000
d. $900,000

(5/92, PII, #35, amended, 2667)

36. What describes a private nonprofit university's internally designated asset, the income from which will be used for a specified purpose?
a. Endowment
b. Term endowment
c. Quasi-endowment
d. Restricted

(Editors, 9204)

37. FASB Statement No. 117, *Financial Statements of Not-for-Profit Organizations*, focuses on
a. Basic information for the organization as a whole.
b. Standardization of funds nomenclature.
c. Inherent differences of not-for-profit organizations that impact reporting presentations.
d. Distinctions between current fund and non-current fund presentations.

(11/94, AR, #30, 5007)

38. Pharm, a nongovernmental not-for-profit organization, is preparing its year-end financial statements. Which of the following statements is required?
a. Statement of changes in financial position.
b. Statement of cash flows.
c. Statement of changes in fund balance.
d. Statement of revenue, expenses and changes in fund balance. (R/01, AR, #10, 6995)

39. The Jones family lost its home in a fire. On December 25, 20X1, a philanthropist sent money to the Amer Benevolent Society, a nonprofit organization, to purchase furniture for the Jones family. During January 20X2, Amer purchased this furniture for the Jones family. How should Amer report the receipt of the money in its 20X1 financial statements?
a. As an unrestricted contribution
b. As a temporarily restricted contribution
c. As a permanently restricted contribution
d. As a liability (5/95, AR, #58, amended, 5476)

40. Lori Hospital received a pure endowment grant. The pure endowment grant
a. May be expended by the governing board only to the extent of the principal since the income from this fund must be accumulated.
b. Should generally be reported as a nonoperating gain when the full amount of principal is expended.
c. Should be recorded as a memorandum entry only.
d. Should be recorded as donor-restricted revenue upon receipt. (Editors, 1428)

41. A large not-for-profit organization's statement of activities should report the net change for net assets that are

	Unrestricted	Permanently restricted
a.	Yes	Yes
b.	Yes	No
c.	No	No
d.	No	Yes

(11/95, AR, #74, 5817)

42. Which basis of accounting should a voluntary health and welfare organization use?
a. Accrual basis for some resources and modified accrual basis for resources
b. Modified accrual basis
c. Accrual basis
d. Cash basis (Editors, 9205)

43. In a statement of activities of a voluntary health and welfare organization, contributions to the building fund should
a. Be included as an element of support.
b. Be included as an element of revenue.
c. Be included as an element of other changes in net assets.
d. Not be included. (Editors, 9210)

44. In 20X1, Citizens' Health, a voluntary health and welfare organization, received a bequest of a $200,000 certificate of deposit maturing in 20X2. The testator's only stipulations were that this certificate be held until maturity and that the interest revenue be used to finance salaries for a preschool program. Interest revenue for 20X2 was $16,000. When the certificate matured and was redeemed, the board of trustees adopted a formal resolution designating $40,000 of the proceeds for the future purchase of equipment for the preschool program. What amount should Citizen report in its 20X2 year-end current funds balance sheet as net assets designated for the preschool program?
a. $0
b. $16,000
c. $40,000
d. $56,000 (5/93, PII, #21, amended, 4129)

45. Super Seniors is a not-for-profit organization that provides services to senior citizens. Super employs a full-time staff of 10 people at an annual cost of $150,000. In addition, two volunteers work as part-time secretaries replacing last years' full-time secretary who earned $10,000. Services performed by other volunteers for special events had an estimated value of $15,000. These volunteers were employees of local businesses and they received small-value items for their participation. What amount should Super report for salary and wage expenses related to the above items?
a. $150,000
b. $160,000
c. $165,000
d. $175,000 (5/93, PII, #30, 4137)

46. Stanton College, a not-for-profit organization, received a building with no donor stipulations as to its use. Stanton does not have an accounting policy implying a time restriction on donated assets. What type of net assets should be increased when the building was received?

I. Unrestricted.
II. Temporarily restricted.
III. Permanently restricted.

a. I only.
b. II only.
c. III only.
d. II or III. (R/01, AR, #1, 6986)

47. Lema Fund, a voluntary welfare organization funded by contributions from the general public, received unrestricted pledges of $200,000 during 20X1. It was estimated that 10% of these pledges would be uncollectible. By the end of 20X1, $130,000 of the pledges had been collected. It was expected that $50,000 more would be collected in 20X2 and that the balance of $20,000 would be written off as uncollectible. What amount should Lema include under public support in 20X1 for net contributions?
a. $200,000
b. $180,000
c. $150,000
d. $130,000 (5/90, PII, #13, amended, 4601)

48. A voluntary health and welfare organization received a cash donation in 20X1 from a donor specifying that the amount donated be used in 20X3. The cash donation should be accounted for as
a. Revenue in 20X1.
b. Revenue in 20X1, 20X2, and 20X3, and as a deferred credit in the balance sheet at the end of 20X1 and 20X2.
c. Revenue in 20X3, and **no** deferred credit in the balance sheet at the end of 20X1 and 20X2.
d. Revenue in 20X3, and as a deferred credit in the balance sheet at the end of 20X1 and 20X2. (Editors, 4602)

49. In May 20X1, Ross donated $200,000 cash to a church with the stipulation that the revenue generated from this gift be paid to Ross during Ross' lifetime. The conditions of this donation are that, after Ross dies, the principal may be used by the church for any purpose voted on by the church elders. The church received interest of $16,000 on the $200,000 for the year ended June 30, 20X1, and the interest was remitted to Ross. In the church's June 30, 20X1 annual financial statements
a. $200,000 should be reported as revenue.
b. $184,000 should be reported as revenue.
c. $16,000 should be reported under support and revenue.
d. The gift and its terms should be disclosed only in notes to the financial statements. (Editors, 4599)

50. Which of the following normally would be included in other operating revenues of a hospital?

	Revenues from educational programs	Unrestricted gifts
a.	No	No
b.	No	Yes
c.	Yes	No
d.	Yes	Yes

(11/94, AR, #28, 5005)

51. Which of the following normally would be included in Other Revenue of a hospital?

	Revenue from grants, specified by the donor for research	Revenue from a gift shop
a.	No	No
b.	No	Yes
c.	Yes	No
d.	Yes	Yes

(Editors, 2171)

52. Which of the following should normally be considered ongoing or central transactions for a not-for-profit hospital?

I. Room and board fees from patients
II. Recovery room fees

a. Neither I nor II
b. Both I and II
c. II only
d. I only (11/95, AR, #75, 5818)

53. For the fall semester, Ames University assessed its students $3,000,000 for tuition and fees. The net amount realized was only $2,500,000 because scholarships of $400,000 were granted to students, and tuition remissions of $100,000 were allowed to faculty members' children attending Ames. What amount should Ames report for the period as unrestricted current fund gross revenues from tuition and fees?
a. $2,500,000
b. $2,600,000
c. $2,900,000
d. $3,000,000 (5/93, PII, #33, amended, 4140)

54. Unrestricted earnings on specific purpose fund investments that are part of a hospital's central operations are reported as
a. Specific purpose fund restricted revenues.
b. Specific purpose fund unrestricted revenues.
c. General fund deferred revenues.
d. General fund unrestricted revenues.

(5/92, Theory, #60, amended, 2753)

55. Calvin College makes a discretionary transfer of $100,000 to its library fund. This transfer should be recorded by a debit to
a. Unrestricted current fund net assets.
b. Restricted current fund net assets.
c. General fund expenditures.
d. Library fund expenditures.

(5/92, PII, #37, amended, 2669)

56. Maple Church has cash available for investments in several different accounting funds. Maple's policy is to maximize its financial resources. How may Maple pool its investments?
a. Maple may **not** pool its investments.
b. Maple may pool all investments, but must equitably allocate realized and unrealized gains and losses among participating funds.
c. Maple may pool only unrestricted investments, but must equitably allocate realized and unrealized gains and losses among participating funds.
d. Maple may pool only restricted investments, but must equitably allocate realized and unrealized gains and losses among participating funds.

(5/93, PII, #40, 4146)

57. Community College had the following encumbrances at December 31:

Outstanding purchase orders	$12,000
Commitments for services not received	50,000

What amount of these encumbrances should be reported as liabilities in Community's balance sheet at December 31?
a. $62,000
b. $50,000
c. $12,000
d. $0

(5/92, PII, #38, amended, 2670)

ITEMS 58 AND 59 are based on the following:

Burr Foundation is a voluntary welfare organization funded by contributions from the general public. Burr sold a computer for $36,000. Its cost was $42,000 and its book value was $30,000. Burr made the correct entry to record the gain on sale.

58. In addition to the entry recording the gain on sale of the computer, the other accounts that Burr should debit and credit in connection with this sale are

	Debit	Credit
a.	Current Unrestricted Funds	NetAssets—Undesignated
b.	Excess Revenues Control	Sale of Equipment
c.	Net Assets—Unexpended	Net Assets—Expended
d.	Net Assets—Expended	Net Assets—Unexpended

(Editors, 9211)

59. The amount that should be debited and credited for the additional entry in connection with the sale of the computer is
a. $ 6,000.
b. $30,000.
c. $36,000.
d. $42,000.

(Editors, 9212)

60. The current funds group of a not-for-profit private university includes which of the following?

	Loan funds	Plant funds
a.	No	No
b.	No	Yes
c.	Yes	Yes
d.	Yes	No

(Editors, 2149)

61. A college's plant funds group includes which of the following subgroups?

I. Renewals and replacement funds
II. Retirement of indebtedness funds
III. Restricted current funds

a. I and II
b. I and III
c. II and III
d. I only

(5/91, Theory, #58, 2102)

62. In 20X1, Smith University's board of trustees established a $100,000 fund to be retained and invested for scholarship grants. The fund earned $6,000 which had not been disbursed at December 31. What amount should Smith report in a quasi-endowment fund's net assets at December 31, 20X1?
a. $0
b. $ 6,000
c. $100,000
d. $106,000

(11/93, PII, #17, amended, 4446)

OTHER OBJECTIVE FORMAT QUESTIONS

PROBLEM 23-3 (15 to 25 minutes)

Community Service, Inc. is a nongovernmental not-for-profit voluntary health and welfare calendar-year organization that began operations on January 1, 20X1. It performs voluntary services and derives its revenue primarily from voluntary contributions from the general public. Community implies a time restriction on all promises to contribute cash in future periods. However, no such policy exists with respect to gifts of long-lived assets.

ITEMS 1 THROUGH 4 are based on the following selected transactions that occurred during Community's 20X2 calendar year:

- Unrestricted written promises to
  contribute cash—20X1 and 20X2
  — 20X1 promises (collected in 20X2) $22,000
  — 20X2 promises (collected in 20X2)   95,000
  — 20X2 promises (uncollected)   28,000

- Written promises to contribute cash
  restricted to use for community college
  scholarships—20X1 and 20X2
  — 20X1 promises (collected and
    expended in 20X2)   10,000
  — 20X2 promises (collected and
    expended in 20X2)   20,000
  — 20X2 promises (uncollected)   12,000

- Written promise to contribute $25,000
  if matching funds are raised for the
  capital campaign during 20X2
  — Cash received in 20X2 from con-
    tributor as a good faith advance   25,000
  — Matching funds received in 20X2   0

- Cash received in 20X1 with donor's only
  stipulation that a bus be purchased
  — Expenditure of full amount
    of donation July 1, 20X2   37,000

REQUIRED:

ITEMS 1 THROUGH 4 represent the 20X2 amounts that Community reported for selected financial statement elements in its December 31, 20X2, statement of financial position and 20X2 statement of activities. For each item, indicate whether the amount was overstated, understated, or correctly stated.

List	
O.	Overstated.
U.	Understated.
C.	Correctly stated.

1. Community reported $28,000 as contributions receivable.

2. Community reported $37,000 as net assets released from restrictions (satisfaction of use restrictions).

3. Community reported $22,000 as net assets released from restrictions (due to the lapse of time restrictions).

4. Community reported $97,000 as contributions—temporarily restricted.

ITEMS 5 THROUGH 11 are based on the following selected transactions that occurred during Community's 20X2 calendar year:

- Debt security endowment received in
  20X2; income to be used for
  community service
  — Face value $90,000
  — Fair value at time of receipt   88,000
  — Fair value at December 31, 20X2   87,000
  — Interest earned in 20X2   9,000

- 10 concerned citizens volunteered   2,000
  to serve meals to the homeless
  (400 hrs. free; fair market value of
  services $5 per hr.)

- Short-term investment in equity
  securities in 20X2
  — Cost   10,000
  — Fair value December 31, 20X2   12,000
  — Dividend income   1,000

- Music festival to raise funds for a local
  hospital
  — Admission fees   5,000
  — Sales of food and drinks   14,000
  — Expenses   4,000

- Reading material donated to Community
  and distributed to the children in 20X2
  — Fair market value   8,000

- Federal youth training fee
  for service grant
  — Cash received during 20X2   30,000
  — Instructor salaries paid   26,000

- Other cash operating expenses
  — Business manager salary   60,000
  — General bookkeeper salary   40,000
  — Director of community activities
      salary   50,000
  — Space rental (75% for community
      activities, 25% for office activities)   20,000
  — Printing and mailing costs for
      pledge cards   2,000

- Interest payment on short-term bank
  loan in 20X2   1,000

- Principal payment on short-term bank
  loan in 20X2   20,000

REQUIRED:

FOR ITEMS 5 THROUGH 11, determine the amounts for the following financial statement elements in the 20X2 statement of activities. Select your answer from the following list of amounts. An amount may be selected once, more than once, or not at all.

Amounts					
A.	$0	F.	$ 9,000	K.	$87,000
B.	$2,000	G.	$14,000	L.	$88,000
C.	$3,000	H.	$16,000	M.	$90,000
D.	$5,000	I.	$26,000	N.	$94,000
E.	$8,000	J.	$50,000	O.	$99,000

5. Contributions—permanently restricted

6. Revenues—fees

7. Investment income—debt securities

8. Program expenses

9. General fund-raising expenses (excludes special events)

10. Income on long-term investments— unrestricted

11. Contributed voluntary services

ITEMS 12 THROUGH 19 are based on the fact pattern and financial information found in **both Part A and Part B**.

REQUIRED:

ITEMS 12 THROUGH 19 represent Community's transactions reportable in the statement of cash flows. For each of the items listed, select the classification that best describes the item. A classification may be selected once, more than once, or not at all.

Classifications	
O.	Cash flows from operating activities.
I.	Cash flows from investing activities.
F.	Cash flows from financing activities.

12. Unrestricted 20X1 promises collected

13. Cash received from a contributor as a good faith advance on a promise to contribute matching funds

14. Purchase of bus

15. Principal payment on short-term bank loan

16. Purchase of equity securities

17. Dividend income earned on equity securities

18. Interest payment on short-term bank loan

19. Interest earned on endowment
     (5/98, AR, #3, amended, 6656-6674)

PROBLEM 23-4 (5 to 10 minutes)

Alpha Hospital, a large not-for-profit organization, has adopted an accounting policy that does not imply a time restriction on gifts of long-lived assets.

FOR ITEMS 1 THROUGH 6, indicate the manner in which the transaction affects Alpha's financial statements. Select the **best** answer for each item.

A. Increase in unrestricted revenues, gains, and other support
B. Decrease in an expense
C. Increase in temporarily restricted net assets
D. Increase in permanently restricted net assets
E. No required reportable event

1. Alpha's board designates $1,000,000 to purchase investments whose income will be used for capital improvements.

2. Income from investments in item 1, which was not previously accrued, is received.

3. A benefactor provided funds for building expansion.

4. The funds in item 3 are used to purchase a building in the fiscal period following the period the funds were received.

5. An accounting firm prepared Alpha's annual financial statements without charge to Alpha.

6. Alpha received investments subject to the donor's requirements that investment income be used to pay for outpatient services.
(11/95, AR, #111-116, amended, 5854-5859)

SOLUTION 23-1 MULTIPLE CHOICE ANSWERS

DEFINITIONS

1. (c) AICPA SOP 87-2, *Accounting for Joint Costs of Informational Materials and Activities of NFP Organizations that Include a Fund-Raising Appeal*, allows that all joint costs of informational materials or activities should be reported as fundraising expense, unless it can be demonstrated that a program or management and general function has been conducted in conjunction with the appeal for funds. In this question, it appears that a program function and a fundraising appeal are joint costs. There is the alternative of no cost allocation and classifying all costs as fundraising costs, but this is not one of the options. Answers (a) and (b) are not appropriate; no general service is mentioned as having been accomplished. Since no general services are mentioned, no allocation would be appropriate to this function. Only answer (c), which allows for joint allocation, might be appropriate. One must assume that the 60/40 allocation is appropriate under the circumstances—although no information is given to verify this assumption.

2. (a) Maintaining a donor list is a fund raising activity. Soliciting prospective members, printing membership benefit brochures, and soliciting dues are member development activities.

3. (d) In hospital accounting, restricted funds account for financial resources that are externally restricted by donors and grantors for specified operating or research, capital outlay, or endowment purposes. The board of directors of a hospital cannot remove restrictions on the use of financial resources imposed by donors and grantors. While unrestricted resources may be appropriated or designated by the governing board of a hospital for special uses, the board nevertheless has the authority to rescind such actions. Therefore, board-designated assets of a hospital are accounted for in the General Fund. The income generated by a restricted fund may or may not be available for current operating use, depending upon the restrictions imposed upon such income by the donor or grantor.

4. (a) GASB Section 1800.120 defines the classification *object classes* as the types of items purchased or services obtained (salaries and wages). Section 1800.116 explains that the *function* or *program* classification provides information on the overall purposes of expenditures. Section 1800.118 explains the *activity* classification as facilitating evaluation of the economy and efficiency of operations by providing information for figuring costs per unit of activity.

FINANCIAL STATEMENTS

5. (b) SFAS 117, para. 26 states, "...a statement of activities or notes to financial statements shall provide information about expenses reported by their functional classification such as major classes of program services and supporting activities. [VHWO]...shall report that information as well as information about expenses by their natural classification...in a separate financial statement. Other [NPO]...are encouraged, but not required, to provide information about expenses by their natural classification."

6. (c) SFAS 117 expands the description of cash flows from financing activities in SFAS 95 to include donor-restricted cash that must be used for long-term purposes. Unrestricted cash from contributors is included in operating activities. Investing activities includes the sale and purchase of investments and PP&E.

7. (b) Assets restricted to a particular use assume the liquidity of that use. Endowment funds are typically long-term assets. (Endowment implies a permanent restriction.)

8. (d) SFAS 93 requires all (nongovernmental) nonprofit organizations to recognize depreciation in external financial statements.

9. (c) The $125,000 contribution is not restricted to the shortfall between youth activity program revenue and expenses; thus, the entire amount of program expenses satisfies the restriction on $95,000 of the contribution. (The youth activity program revenues are not restricted.)

10. (c) SFAS 117 requires that net assets be allocated among three classifications for nonprofits: unrestricted, temporarily restricted, and permanently restricted. The $2,000,000 is permanently restricted because only the income may be used to support current operations. The $5,000,000 for the public viewing building is temporarily restricted because the terms of the donation will be met when the building is built.

11. (a) When the terms of a gift are met, the assets and net assets are reclassified, increasing unrestricted net assets. With the concurrent use of the assets, unrestricted net assets decreases.

12. (d) Only donor restrictions create restricted revenue. Permanently restricted revenue is restricted in perpetuity. Restrictions that lapse are temporary.

CONTRIBUTIONS

13. (b) By recording the full $1,500 as a contribution, the entity would overstate the amount of contributions. Only that portion exceeding the fair market value of a benefit received by the contributor should be included in contribution revenue. A donor-imposed restriction limits the use of contributed assets to a use more specific than broad limits resulting from the nature of the organization, etc. A donor-imposed restriction on a contributed assets considered revenue if it is an unconditional transfer or promise to transfer. In contrast, a donor-imposed condition specifies a future and uncertain event whose occurrence or failure to occur gives the promisor a right of return of transferred assets, or release a promisor form its obligation to transfer promised assets. [$2,000 + $1,500 – $1,000]

14. (b) By recording the full $150 as a contribution, the entity would overstate the amount of contributions. Only that portion exceeding the fair market value of a benefit to the contributor is included in contribution revenue.

15. (b) SFAS 116 has an exemption to the rule of recognizing donations of collections of historical artifacts if they are held as a collection or are sold and the proceeds used to acquire other items for collections.

16. (d) The land was donated to the hospital without restriction as to use; therefore, the hospital records the donation with a debit to Land, a credit to Mortgage Payable, and a credit to Unrestricted Revenues for the excess of the fair value of the land over the mortgage assumed by the hospital.

17. (d) Contributions that may be used at the board of directors' discretion are unrestricted. Pledges are recognized in the period they are made, net of any appropriate allowance for uncollectible amounts. There is an implicit time restriction on the $500,000 donation, because it will not be made until the next year. The fair value of donated services is recognized as both a revenue and expense if the services (1) would otherwise be purchased, (2) the value of the services is measurable, and (3) there is the equivalent of an employer-employee or hired contractor relationship.

18. (b) The establishment of an endowment requires a nonprofit organization (NPO) to recognize restricted contribution revenue. The NPO includes an asset in its balance sheet. When a beneficiary has an unconditional right to specific cash flows from a trust, the beneficiary interest is measured and subsequently remeasured at fair value, using a valuation technique such as the present value of estimated expected future cash flows. (SFAS 136, ¶15).

19. (b) Contributed collection assets are recognized as revenues if collections are capitalized. Revenues are not recognized if collections are not capitalized. Cash flows from operating activities are generally the cash effect of events that enter into the determination of income. Cash flows from financing activities include paying or incurring debt principal, paying dividends, or issuing or acquiring stock.

20. (c) Since the League is an ONPO and all of its pledges are legally enforceable, the League should report $315,000 [i.e., ($200,000 + $150,000) x (100% – 10%)] as pledges receivable, net of the allowance for uncollectible pledges.

21. (b) The revenues of a hospital are generally separated into three broad classifications: (1) patient service revenue, (2) other revenue, and (3) nonoperating gains. Patient service revenues are charges assessed for services provided to patients. This revenue would include fees for intensive care, surgery, nursing services, laboratory work, etc. Other revenues include amounts transferred from donor-restricted funds; tuition from nursing students; and cafeteria, gift shop, and parking lot revenues.

Nonoperating gains generally include *gifts, bequests*, and investment income.

RELATED ORGANIZATIONS

22. (b) Metro General should disclose the assets of the guild (i.e., $20,000) in the notes to the financial statements because it controls the guild through contracts or other legal documents that provide Metro General with the authority to direct the guild's activities, management, and policies; and Metro General is considered to be the sole beneficiary of the guild (i.e., Metro General has transferred certain resources to the guild, and substantially all of the guild's resources are held for the benefit of Metro General). Although Metro General is considered to be the sole beneficiary of the auxiliary (i.e., Metro General has assigned certain of its functions to the hospital auxiliary, which operates primarily for the benefit of Metro General), Metro General does *not* have control over the auxiliary.

23. (c) The hospital's fixed assets should be reported as part of the enterprise fund fixed assets in the business-type activities column (i.e., $1,200,000 + $500,000 = $1,700,000). There are only four columns in the government-wide statement of net assets: governmental activities, business-type activities, primary government total (sum of previous two), and component units. (See Chapter 21.) Alternatively, the hospital could be a discretely presented component unit, but as that option isn't included in the answer choices, we must assume that a blended presentation is appropriate.

INVESTMENT SECURITIES

24. (c) Investments of nonprofit organizations are recorded initially at cost, except that donated securities are recorded at their fair market value at date of receipt. Thereafter, marketable equity and debit securities are accounted for in accordance with SFAS 124 (fair market value at balance sheet date).

UNIQUE HEALTHCARE FEATURES

25. (c) Abbey's patient service is determined by subtracting the charity care from the patient service revenue that would have been recorded at Abbey's established rate for all healthcare services provided (i.e., $6,000,000 − $1,000,000 = $5,000,000). Charity care is not included in patient service revenues because these services were provided free of charge and, thus, were never expected to result in cash flows. On the other hand, the discounts to third party payors are reported as *deductions* from patient service revenues to determine *net* patient service revenue. Note that the

amount that would be reported as *net* patient service revenue is $4,500,000 (i.e., $5,000,000 − $500,000).

26. (d) Other Revenue of a healthcare entity is the usual day-to-day revenue that is not derived from patient care and services, and generally includes (1) proceeds from the sale of cafeteria meals, (2) revenue from educational programs, and (3) revenues from miscellaneous sources, such as revenue from gift shops and parking lots. The proceeds from the sale of cafeteria meals do not offset dietary service expenses. Under the old AICPA *Hospital Audit Guide*, Ancillary Service Revenue represented a subcategory of Patient Service Revenue consisting of professional services such as lab fees, radiology fees, etc. Patient service revenues consist of revenue from routine services (e.g., room, board, general nursing and home health), other nursing services (e.g., operating room, recovery room, and delivery room), and professional services (e.g., physicians' care, laboratories, radiology, and pharmacy).

UNIQUE UNIVERSITY FEATURES

27. (b) Tuition and fees are recorded at standard established rates, with amounts waived (such as scholarships or tuition remissions) recorded as expenditures. Actual refunds of tuition or fees should be recorded as a reduction of revenues. Therefore, Unity should include $2,930,000 ($3,000,000 − $70,000) in the unrestricted current funds as revenues from tuition and fees.

28. (a) There are separate functional classifications for expenditures pertaining to "Institutional Support," "Scholarships and Fellowships," and "Operation and Maintenance of Plant." Therefore, the only expenditure in question that should be included in the functional classification "Institutional Support" expenditures account is the one for administrative data processing.

FUND ACCOUNTING

29. (c) Healthcare entities have only two categories of funds: (1) the general funds and (2) the donor-restricted funds. The general fund is used to account for all assets and liabilities that are not required to be accounted for in a donor-restricted fund. Since the bonds in question were issued for the hospital's benefit and are unrelated to any donor-restricted assets, they should be accounted for in the general fund. Both enterprise funds and the general long-term debt account group are utilized by state and local governments rather than by nonprofit healthcare entities. Specific-purpose funds are a type of donor-restricted funds that are used to

account for resources restricted by donors and grantors for specific operating purposes.

30. (b) The asset accounts in the Investment in Plant subgroup of the Plant Funds group of a college contain the carrying amounts of the

institution's fixed assets. Therefore, the equipment would be reported in the Investment in Plant subgroup of the Plant Funds group of the college. The fuel inventory for the college's power plant should be reported in the Unrestricted Current Funds under Inventory of Materials and Supplies.

SOLUTION 23-2 ADDITIONAL MULTIPLE CHOICE ANSWERS

DEFINITIONS

31. (c) The bequest of $400,000 received by the foundation from the estate of the benefactor who specified that the bequest was to be used for hiring teachers to tutor handicapped students is restricted. Restricted resources are financial resources that are *externally restricted* for specified purposes. On the other hand, the *board-designated* resources of $200,000 are unrestricted. Restrictions imposed by the Board of Trustees may be removed by the Board; they therefore do not impose restrictions as to when or how the resources may be used and should not be presented in the foundation's financial statements as restrictions.

32. (b) If the Board may change the designation, the assets are not restricted.

Unrestricted assets (including the $300,000)	$15,000,000
Liabilities	9,000,000
Unrestricted net assets	$ 6,000,000

33. (a) Hunt Community Development Agency provides loans as its operating activity, not as financing or investing activities.

34. (d) Expenses of nonprofit organizations are reported in two categories: program services and support services. Program services are related directly to the primary missions of the nonprofit organization. A labor union would report the cost of labor negotiations under the classification of program services. Support services do not relate to the primary missions of the nonprofit organization and include such costs as management and general administration, membership development, and fund-raising.

35. (c) The $500,000 donated for which a donor or external agency has specified that the principal remains intact in perpetuity should be accounted for in an Endowment Fund. The $300,000 of principal expendable after the year 2010 should be accounted for in a Term Endowment Fund because the principal may be expended after a specified period of time. The $100,000 of principal designated from Current Funds should be accounted for in a

Quasi-Endowment Fund because the amount was set aside by the governing board of the institution to function as endowments.

36. (c) Assets with *internal* restrictions (i.e., designation by the governing board) are quasi-endowments. Endowment, term-endowment, and restricted current signify resources with *donor* restrictions.

FINANCIAL STATEMENTS

37. (a) SFAS 117 focuses on basic information for the organization as a whole. Standardization of fund nomenclature is a secondary consideration. As this statement establishes standards for financial reporting applicable to all nonprofit organizations, it focuses on the similarities between different organizations or types of organizations. Distinctions between current and noncurrent presentations are also secondary.

38. (b) SFAS 117 requires nonprofit organizations to present, at a minimum, a statement of financial position, a statement of activities, and a statement of cash flows.

39. (b) SFAS 116 requires that nonprofits' donations be recognized in income in the period of receipt and that donations be allocated among three classifications: unrestricted, temporarily restricted, and permanently restricted. This is a temporary restriction because, upon meeting the conditions of the donor, the donation may be disbursed.

40. (d) SFAS 116 requires that donations be recognized in the period of receipt, not in the period of expenditure for the donor's specified purpose. The principal of a pure endowment may *not* be expended. The receipt of the pure endowment grant is recorded as permanently restricted revenues upon receipt.

41. (a) SFAS 117 requires the statement of activities to report the net change for all three types of net assets: unrestricted, temporarily restricted, and permanently restricted.

42. (c) Nongovernmental nonprofit organizations, including voluntary health and welfare organizations (VHWOs), use the accrual basis of accounting for all external reporting purposes.

43. (a) The contributions to the building fund are included as support in the statement of activities of a voluntary health and welfare organization.

CONTRIBUTIONS

44. (c) The voluntary health and welfare organization (VHWO) used an endowment fund to account for the certificate of deposit because the testator stipulated that the certificate be held until maturity and that the interest revenue be restricted for a special purpose (i.e., to be used to finance salaries for a preschool program). In 2000, the restrictions on the endowment fund principal lapsed (i.e., the certificate of deposit matured). Since the testator did not place any restrictions on the principal of the certificate, that amount was transferred to the current unrestricted fund. The board of trustees then adopted a formal resolution designating $40,000 of the proceeds of the certificate of deposit for the future purchase of equipment for the preschool program. Therefore, $40,000 should be reported in the current funds balance sheet as net assets designated by the governing board for the preschool program. The interest revenue is restricted per testator specifications for a special purpose. Therefore, it cannot be reported in the current funds balance sheet as net assets designated by the governing board for the preschool program.

45. (b) Other nonprofit organizations (ONPOs) should report donated services as revenue and expense if the following conditions are met: (1) the services are a normal part of the program or supporting services and would otherwise be performed by salaried personnel, (2) the organization exercises control over the employment and duties of the donors of the services, (3) the ONPO has a clearly measurable basis for the amount, (4) the services are significant, and (5) the services of the ONPO are not primarily for the benefit of its members. Since all of the above conditions are met for the part-time secretaries, Super Seniors should report salary and wages expense of $160,000, comprised of the $150,000 annual cost of its full-time staff and the $10,000 estimated value of the donated secretarial services.

46. (a) Only a donor may impose temporary or permanent restrictions on assets. Otherwise, donated assets are unrestricted.

47. (b) SFAS 116 prescribes the accounting for contributions received and made. Pledges are reported in the period in which they are made, net of an allowance for uncollectible accounts.

48. (a) Contributions received in advance of the year the donor intends them to be used—even if usable then for unrestricted purposes—are initially recorded in a "restricted support" account. They should be accounted for as support in the year the unconditional promise to give is made. The term "deferred" is no longer applied to donations.

49. (a) The principal of life income gifts (where a specified person is to receive the income from the assets for life or another determinable period of time) should be reported as restricted support in the balance sheet of a nonprofit organization, until the terms of the life income gift have been met.

UNIQUE FEATURES

50. (c) Operating revenues include "Net Patient Revenue" and "Other Revenues." Other revenues of a hospital are defined as amounts generated from *activities that are major and central to ongoing operations other than patient services*. This classification includes activities from gift shops, cafeterias, education programs, snack bars, newsstands, parking lots, etc. However, unrestricted gifts are not included and are classified as "Nonoperating Gains," a separate and distinct section of the operating statement.

51. (d) Other Revenue of a healthcare entity is the usual day-to-day revenue that is not derived from patient care and services, and generally includes (1) revenue from grants for such specific purposes as research and education; (2) revenue from educational programs; and (3) revenues from miscellaneous sources, such as revenue from gift shops and parking lots. Additional sources of Other Revenue include rentals of hospital plant, sales of supplies to physicians, and fees charged for copies of documents.

52. (b) Room and board for patients and recovery room activities are both central to a hospital's services.

53. (d) Tuition and fees are recorded as revenue at standard established rates, with amounts waived (such as scholarships or tuition remissions) recorded as expenditures. Therefore, Ames University should report $3,000,000 as unrestricted current fund revenues from tuition and fees.

FUND ACCOUNTING

54. (d) Unrestricted earnings on specific purpose fund investments that are part of a hospital's

central operations are reported as general fund unrestricted revenues. If, on the other hand, the investment earnings were restricted by donors or grantors for a specified operating purpose (e.g., research or education), they would be reported as restricted revenues in the specific purpose fund. Deferred revenue is no longer used in nongovernmental nonprofit accounting.

55. (a)   The question implies that the library fund is separate from the current fund. Therefore, a discretionary transfer could only be made from the unrestricted portion of the current fund. Consequently, the transfer should be recorded by a debit to the unrestricted current fund net assets.

56. (b)   The church is an other nonprofit organization (ONPO). ONPOs may establish investment pools. Such pools should be accounted for on a market value basis to ensure equitable allocations of realized and unrealized gains and losses among participating funds. An ONPO may pool both unrestricted and restricted investments.

57. (d)   Outstanding encumbrances cannot be reported as liabilities. Any encumbrance outstanding should be reported as part of the equity section of the balance sheet.

58. (d)   Voluntary health and welfare organizations record fixed asset and depreciation transactions in the Land, Building, and Equipment Fund. Two entries should be recorded in this fund in connection with the sale of the equipment. The following entry should be made to record the sale:

Cash	36,000	
Accumulated Depreciation—		
Equipment ($42,000 – $30,000)	12,000	
Equipment		42,000
Gain on Sale of Equipment		6,000

In addition, the following entry should be made to reduce the Net Assets—Expended account and increase the Net Assets—Unexpended account for the net book value of the equipment sold:

Net Assets—Expended	30,000	
Net Assets—Unexpended		30,000

The Net Assets—Expended account represents the net book value of fixed assets not represented by indebtedness. It is debited to reduce it for the net book value of the equipment sold. The Net Assets—Unexpended account represents the assets available for future expenditure for plant. It is credited for the same amount in this entry. The logic of this credit is explained below. The Net Assets—Unexpended account (the assets available for future expenditure for plant) must increase by the $36,000 cash received from the sale. To accomplish this, the account is credited for (1) the $30,000 book value of the equipment sold per the preceding entry, and (2) the $6,000 gain on the sale when the gain is closed out to this account at year-end.

59. (b)   See the explanation to #58.

60. (a)   The fund groups generally used by colleges and universities are (1) current funds, (2) loan funds, (3) endowment and similar funds, (4) annuity and life income funds, (5) plant funds, and (6) agency funds. Loan funds and plant funds are not included in the current funds group as they are separately disclosed.

61. (a)   The plant funds group for colleges and universities includes four subgroups: (1) unexpended plant funds, (2) funds for renewals and replacements, (3) funds for retirement of indebtedness, and (4) investment in plant. A college's plant funds group does not include a subgroup for restricted current funds.

62. (d)   Quasi-Endowment Funds are used by colleges and universities to account for amounts set aside by the governing board to function as endowments. Smith University should report as quasi-endowment fund net assets at December 31, the sum of the $100,000 set aside by the governing board to be invested for scholarship grants and the $6,000 of fund earnings which had not been disbursed at December 31.

PERFORMANCE BY SUBTOPICS

Each category below parallels a subtopic covered in Chapter 23. Record the number and percentage of questions you correctly answered in each subtopic area.

Definitions

Question #	Correct √
1	
2	
3	
4	
# Questions	4

Correct _____
% Correct _____

Financial Statements

Question #	Correct √
5	
6	
7	
8	
9	
10	
11	
12	
# Questions	8

Correct _____
% Correct _____

Contributions

Question #	Correct √
13	
14	
15	
16	
17	
18	
19	
20	
21	
# Questions	9

Correct _____
% Correct _____

Related Organizations

Question #	Correct √
22	
23	
# Questions	2

Correct _____
% Correct _____

Investment Securities

Question #	Correct √
24	
# Questions	1

Correct _____
% Correct _____

Unique Healthcare Features

Question #	Correct √
25	
26	
# Questions	2

Correct _____
% Correct _____

Unique University Features

Question #	Correct √
27	
28	
# Questions	2

Correct _____
% Correct _____

Fund Accounting

Question #	Correct √
29	
30	
# Questions	2

Correct _____
% Correct _____

OTHER OBJECTIVE FORMAT QUESTION SOLUTIONS

SOLUTION 23-3 FINANCIAL STATEMENTS

1. U   Contributions receivable should be at least $40,000, to include the unrestricted $28,000 and the restricted $12,000 of 20X2 promised contributions that are uncollected.

2. U   The 20X1 promises to contribute cash in 20X2 and the bus purchase cash are both assets released from restrictions.

3. C   The 20X1 promises to contribute cash of $22,000 are restricted by time only.

4. O   Temporarily restricted cash is composed of uncollected 20X2 promises to give in future years. At most this is ($28,000 + $12,000) $40,000. The $25,000 matching funds advance is a liability, as the conditions of the potential contributor are apparently not met.

5. L   Permanently restricted contributions for the year are the debt security endowment, at its fair value at time of receipt.

6. D   The only revenues that Community had during the year are the admission fees to the music festival.

7. E   Investment income includes interest earned plus the change in fair value from time of receipt to the balance sheet date. ($9,000 – $1,000)

8. O   Program expenses are those connected with the NPO's mission. These include reading materials distributed to children, instructor salaries, the director of community activities' salary, and a portion of the space rental.

9. B   The printing and mailing costs for pledge cards are the only general fund-raising expenses.

10. A   There is no unrestricted income from long-term investments.

11. A   There are no contributed voluntary services that qualify to be included on the statement of activities (i.e., that result from an employer-employee type of relationship).

12. O   Cash flows from operating activities include most contributions; certain donor-restricted cash that must be used for long-term purposes is included in financing activities.

13. O   Cash flows from operating activities include most contributions; certain donor-restricted cash that must be used for long-term purposes is included in financing activities.

14. I   Transactions involving investments as well as property, plant, and equipment generally are classified as investing activities.

15. F   Principal repayments are cash flows used by financing activities.

16. I   Cash paid for, and received from, transactions involving investments and property, plant, and equipment generally is classified as investing.

17. O   Interest and dividends received are cash flows from operating activities.

18. O   Interest payments are cash flows used by operating activities.

19. O   Interest and dividends received are cash flows from operating activities.

SOLUTION 23-4 CONTRIBUTIONS

1. E   Board designated assets are unrestricted. Only donor restrictions "restrict" assets for external reporting purposes.

2. A   Income from board-designated assets is unrestricted revenue.

3. C   The donation is restricted only until the donor's conditions are met.

4. A   As Alpha does not have an accounting policy that implies a time restriction on gifts of long-lived assets, the building expansion funds are unrestricted when the building is built.

5. A   The measurable fair value of donated services that would otherwise be purchased are recorded as both revenue and expense if (1) non-financial assets are created or enhanced, (2) the performance of the services is controlled by the NPO, and (3) special skills are required. All of these conditions are met. As the terms of the inherent restriction (to purchase accounting services) is met within the period of donation, this is an unrestricted donation.

6. D   The donation is subject to the donor's restriction, a requirement that cannot be fulfilled with the passage of time or the accomplishment of a specific objective.

CHAPTER 24

DECISION MAKING

EXAM COVERAGE: The managerial accounting portion of the ARE section of the CPA exam is designated by the examiners to be 10 percent of the section's point value. Historically exam coverage of the topics in this chapter hovers at 3 to 6 percent of the ARE section. Candidates should plan their use of study time accordingly. More information about the point value of various topics is included in the **Practical Advice** section of this volume.

CHAPTER 24

DECISION MAKING

I. MANAGERIAL ACCOUNTING OVERVIEW

A. COST DEFINITIONS

EXHIBIT 1 ♦ COST COMPONENTS IN THE MANUFACTURING FIRM

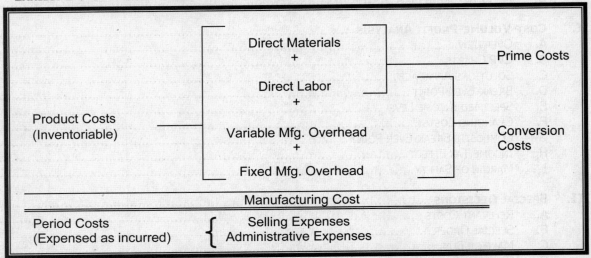

1. **CONVERSION COST** Conversion cost is the sum of the direct labor and manufacturing overhead. It represents the manufacturing costs to convert raw materials to finished products.

2. **MANUFACTURING COST ELEMENTS** Manufacturing cost is the sum of all three elements of production. These are collectively equivalent to the cost of purchases in a merchandising enterprise.

   a. Direct materials are the materials that become an integral part of the finished product and are easily traceable to the finished product. Examples include desk tops and legs used in making steel desks.

   b. Direct labor represents the labor that acts directly on the product and physically transforms or manipulates the product. Direct labor costs are easily traceable to the product. Examples include the labor costs of workers who assemble desk tops or operate melting equipment. Direct labor does not include wages paid to a maintenance worker or a supervisor in a factory.

   c. Manufacturing overhead costs consist of all production costs other than direct material and direct labor costs. In other words, manufacturing overhead costs are those production costs that cannot be easily traced to a specific product. Other terms that are synonymous with manufacturing overhead are factory overhead and indirect factory costs. Examples include indirect labor, indirect materials, repairs and maintenance on factory machinery, factory utilities, factory equipment depreciation, etc.

   • The overtime premium paid to all factory workers (direct labor as well as indirect labor) is usually considered to be a part of manufacturing overhead. The overtime premium is considered to be attributable to the heavy overall volume of work; thus, its cost should be borne by all units produced.

3. **PERIOD COSTS** Period costs are costs that are not incurred in the production of physical units and are not inventoried. Period costs are charged to expense in the period in which incurred. All selling and administrative costs are period costs.

4. **PRIME COST** Prime cost is the sum of the direct materials and direct labor costs.

5. **PRODUCT COSTS** Product costs are costs that are inventoriable (i.e., that are directly **or** indirectly related to physical units). These costs become an expense when the goods to which the costs attach are sold. All **manufacturing** cost elements, including depreciation on factory equipment and other manufacturing overhead, are product costs.

B. COST CLASSIFICATION
Different methods of classification satisfy different needs of various information users. (Also see quality control programs.)

1. **BEHAVIOR** Costs are classified as fixed or variable according to their response to changes in levels of activity.

2. **CONTROLLABILITY** Costs are also categorized according to whether they can be influenced by managers of a particular segment of the entity within a specified period of time. (Also see responsibility accounting.)

3. **FUNCTION** Under this arrangement, costs are classified according to the function they perform within the business, for example, as manufacturing, selling, or administrative costs.

4. **OBJECT OF EXPENDITURE** This involves classifying costs according to the goods or services they purchase, for example, as wages, rent, or advertising.

5. **TRACEABILITY** Costs are classified according to whether or not they can be traced to, and directly identified with, a finished unit of production. The distinction may be described as that between direct and indirect manufacturing costs.

C. COST BEHAVIOR
Definitions of fixed and variable costs refer to **total** cost behavior, not **unit** cost behavior.

1. **FIXED COSTS** Fixed costs are those costs that tend to remain constant in total within a given period of time and over a wide range of activity. This range of activity is referred to as the relevant range.

    a. **COMMITTED COSTS** Represent fixed costs that arise from having property, plant, and equipment, and a functioning organization. These costs remain even when the production volume is zero. Committed costs include depreciation of buildings and long-term lease payments.

    b. **DISCRETIONARY COSTS** Represent annual budget appropriations. These fixed costs are often unrelated to volume and include, for example, advertising costs and research and development costs.

EXHIBIT 2 ♦ BEHAVIOR OF FIXED COSTS

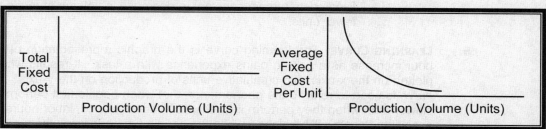

2. **VARIABLE COSTS** Variable costs are those costs that tend to remain constant per unit but that vary in total in direct proportion to changes in the level of activity.

EXHIBIT 3 ♦ BEHAVIOR OF VARIABLE COSTS

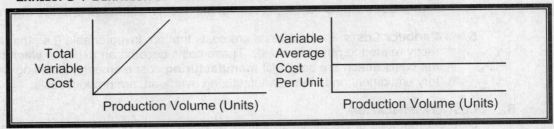

3. **MIXED (SEMIVARIABLE) COSTS** Are comprised of both variable and fixed cost elements. Due to their variable cost element, mixed costs change in total with a change in volume, but not in direct proportion because of their fixed cost element. Due to their fixed cost element, average mixed cost per unit **decreases** (increases) with an **increase** (decrease) in volume. Mixed costs include electricity, maintenance, etc. Mixed costs are typically split into fixed and variable elements for purposes of cost-volume-profit analysis and budgeting.

   a. In practice, arbitrary assumptions are often made about the cost behavior patterns of mixed costs. For example, the cost of electric power may be classified entirely as a variable cost, even though it has both fixed and variable elements.

   b. The fixed and variable elements of mixed costs can be determined through mathematical models such as regression analysis, scatter diagrams, and the high-low estimation method.

4. **STEP-VARIABLE COSTS** Costs that are relatively fixed over a small range of output, but are variable over a large range of output. For example, supervision costs may be fixed over a given production volume. However, additional shifts or work crews may be added to increase production. This will require additional supervisors and thus the added cost will go up in a lump sum or "stair step" pattern.

5. **COMPARISON**

   a. **TOTAL COSTS** Total fixed cost does not change with a change in volume (within the relevant range). **Total** variable cost has a **direct** relationship with volume. The total variable cost increases or decreases in direct proportion to the change in volume.

   b. **AVERAGE COSTS** Average fixed cost per unit has an **inverse** relationship with volume. Average variable cost per unit does not change with volume; it remains constant.

      (1) The average fixed cost per unit decreases as volume increases. Because total fixed costs remain constant, an increase in volume spreads the fixed costs over more units.

      (2) The average fixed cost per unit increases as volume decreases. Because total fixed costs remain constant, a decrease in volume spreads the fixed costs over fewer units.

6. **LEARNING CURVE** The learning curve is the graphic representation of how units per labor hour increase as a person gains experience with a task. It results when time per unit are plotted on the x-axis with cumulative units of production on the y-axis. The phrase *learning curve* is used to refer to the phenomenon that when people first perform a task, they will be slower than when they perform it for the 100th time. Hence, labor hours will be greater (and associated costs will be higher) when the people are performing the work for the first time.

7. **EXPERIENCE CURVE** The experience curve is the graphic representation of time (and costs) for a broad category of tasks decreasing as a group gains experience with a set of tasks. This phrase can refer to several situations. For example, it may refer to the reduced time for a group to train a new member or to reduced time (and costs) for a number of cost areas (perhaps including distribution and customer service) to add their part to the value chain.

EXHIBIT 4 ♦ COST BEHAVIOR PATTERNS

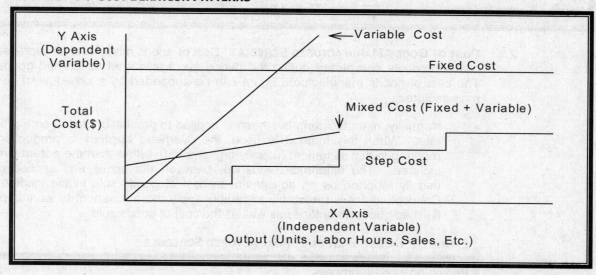

D. **MANUFACTURING FIRM STATEMENTS**

1. **COMPARISON WITH MERCHANDISING FIRMS** The income statement of a manufacturing firm is similar to that of a merchandising firm except that the cost of goods sold section will include a "cost of goods manufactured" schedule. Essentially, the difference between the two cost of goods sold sections is that in a manufacturing firm, cost of goods manufactured replaces purchases.

EXHIBIT 5 ♦ COMPARISON OF INCOME STATEMENTS: MANUFACTURING VS. MERCHANDISING FIRM

Manufacturing Co.			Merchandising Co.		
Sales		$ 500,000	Sales		$ 500,000
Cost of goods sold:			Cost of goods sold:		
Finished goods, Jan. 1, 2000	$125,000		Merchandise inventory, Jan. 1, 2000	$125,000	
Cost of goods mfd. (see schedule)	300,000		Purchases, net	300,000	
Cost of goods available for sale	425,000		Cost of goods available for sale	425,000	
Finished goods, Dec. 31, 2000	120,000		Merchandise inventory, Dec. 31. 2000	120,000	
Cost of goods sold		(305,000)	Cost of goods sold		(305,000)
Gross margin		195,000	Gross margin		195,000
Selling & administrative expense		(160,000)	Selling & administrative expense		(160,000)
Net income		$ 35,000	Net Income		$ 35,000

EXHIBIT 6 ♦ ACCOUNT ACTIVITY FOR A TYPICAL MANUFACTURING COMPANY

Raw Material Inventory	Work-in-Process Inventory	Finished Goods Inventory
Beginning Balance	Beginning Balance	Beginning Balance
Plus: Purchases	Plus: Raw Material, Labor, OH Used	Plus: Goods Finished (From WIP)
Equals: Available for Use	Equals: Available to Finish	Equals: Available for Sale
Less: Raw Material Used (To WIP)	Less: Goods Finished (To FG)	Less: Cost of Goods Sold
Equals: Ending Balance	Equals: Ending Balance	Equals: Ending Balance

2. **COST OF GOODS MANUFACTURED SCHEDULE** Cost of goods manufactured represents the cost of the products **completed** during the period and transferred to finished goods inventory. The cost of goods manufactured figure can be supported by a schedule of cost of goods manufactured.

- Normally, manufacturing overhead is applied to production based on a predetermined rate. When this method is used, the overhead **applied** to production would be reported in this statement (usually one amount), rather than the **actual** overhead cost incurred. The difference (variance) between the actual and applied overhead is usually reported as an adjustment to cost of goods sold in the income statement. Conceptually, it is preferable to ratably apply the adjustment to work-in-process and finished goods inventories as well as the cost of goods sold.

EXHIBIT 7 ♦ COST OF GOODS MANUFACTURED SCHEDULE

Beginning work-in-process			$ 55,000
Beginning inventory		$ 32,000	
Add purchases		116,000	
Materials available for use		148,000	
Less: Ending inventory		(28,000)	
Direct materials used		$120,000	
Direct labor		60,000	
Indirect material	$ 25,000		
Indirect labor	30,000		
Miscellaneous	35,000		
Manufacturing overhead		90,000	
Add: Total current manufacturing costs incurred			270,000
Total manufacturing costs to account for			325,000
Less: Ending work-in-process			(25,000)
Cost of goods manufactured			$300,000

EXHIBIT 8 ♦ COST OF GOODS MANUFACTURED SCHEDULE (ALTERNATIVE FORMAT)

Direct materials used (same as similar section in Exhibit 7)	$120,000
Direct labor (same as in Exhibit 7)	60,000
Manufacturing overhead (same as in Exhibit 7)	90,000
Total manufacturing cost incurred	270,000
Add: Beginning work-in-process	55,000
Total manufacturing cost to account for	325,000
Less: Ending work-in-process	(25,000)
Cost of goods manufactured	$300,000

II. COST-VOLUME-PROFIT ANALYSIS

A. OVERVIEW

Break-even and cost-volume-profit (CVP) analyses are concerned with the effect upon operating income (or net income) of various decisions regarding sales and costs. CVP analysis is management's study of the relationships among cost, volume, and profit. This study is used in planning, controlling, and evaluating the incremental impact of business decisions. The general assumptions are:

1. The behavior of costs and revenues has been reliably determined and is linear over the relevant range.

2. Costs are classified as fixed or variable.

3. Variable costs change at a linear rate.

4. Fixed costs remain unchanged over relevant range.

5. Selling prices do not change as sales volume changes.

6. For multi-products, the sales mix remains constant.

7. Productive efficiency does not change.

8. Inventory levels remain constant, i.e., production equals sales.

9. Volume is the only relevant factor affecting costs.

10. There is a relevant range for which all of the other underlying assumptions and concepts are valid.

B. CVP CHARTS

1. **COST-VOLUME-PROFIT CHART** The cost-volume-profit (CVP) chart (Exhibit 9) shows the profit or loss potential for the range of volume within the relevant range. At any given level of output, the predicted profit or loss is the vertical difference between the sales line and the total cost line. The **break-even point** is at the intersection of sales and total costs. The **contribution margin** at any level of output is the vertical difference between the sales line and the variable costs line. Note that the total costs and variable costs lines are parallel, with the difference between them equal to fixed costs.

   • All the relationships graphed on the CVP chart are valid only within a band of activity called the **relevant range**. Outside the relevant range, the same relationships are unlikely to hold true. For example, some fixed costs may increase at high levels of output.

EXHIBIT 9 ◆ COST-VOLUME-PROFIT (CVP) CHART

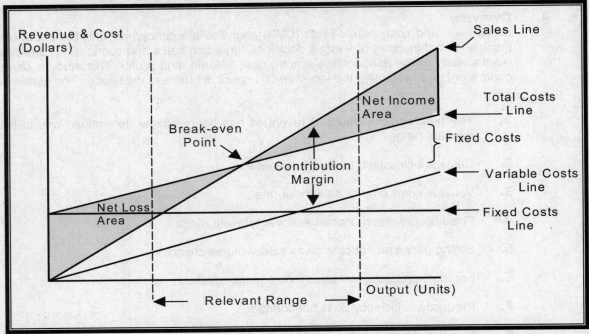

2. **PROFIT-VOLUME CHART** The profit-volume chart is a simpler version of the CVP chart which is useful if management is primarily interested in the effect of changes in volume on net income.

EXHIBIT 10 ◆ PROFIT-VOLUME (P/V) CHART

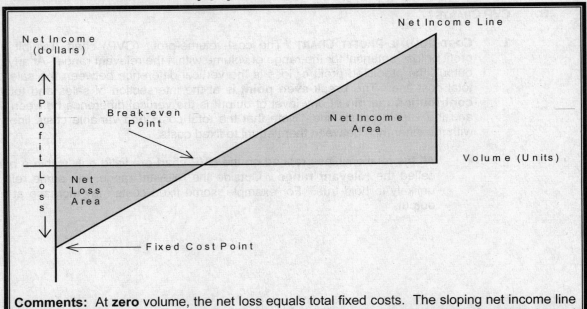

Comments: At **zero** volume, the net loss equals total fixed costs. The sloping net income line moves upward from the fixed costs point at the rate of the **unit contribution margin** and intersects the volume axis at the **break-even** point. Each unit sold beyond the break-even point increases net income by the amount of the unit contribution margin.

C. SOLUTIONS APPROACH

1. **DEFINE THE PROBLEM** Determine the objectives of the problem or problem situation. These generally include the following:

   a. Break-even point in units or dollars.

   b. Desired sales (units or dollars) to obtain a specified profit level.

   c. Desired sales in units or dollars to obtain the break-even point or a specified profit level, given that changes will occur in the selling price, fixed cost, and/or variable cost.

   d. Amount of profit or loss that will result at a specified volume level based on the current or anticipated selling price and cost/volume relationships.

   e. Selling price to be charged based on anticipated changes in cost, volume, and/or profit level.

2. **SELECT A COMPUTATIONAL METHOD**

   a. The Income Equation Method

   Sales = Variable expenses + Fixed expenses + Net income

   or

   Net income = Sales – Variable expenses – Fixed expenses

   b. The Contribution Margin Method

   (1) Contribution margin = Sales – Variable costs

   (2) Unit contribution margin = Unit sales price – Unit variable costs

   (3) Contribution margin ratio = $\dfrac{\text{Unit contribution margin}}{\text{Unit sales price}}$

   or

   Contribution margin ratio = $\dfrac{\text{Total contribution margin}}{\text{Total sales}}$

   (4) Variable cost ratio = $\dfrac{\text{Variable cost}}{\text{Sales}}$

   (5) Break-even point in units = $\dfrac{\text{Fixed expenses}}{\text{Unit contribution margin}}$

   (6) Break-even point in dollars = $\dfrac{\text{Fixed expenses}}{\text{Contribution margin ratio}}$

   (7) Dollar sales to achieve a desired profit = $\dfrac{\text{Fixed costs \& desired net income*}}{\text{Unit contribution margin}}$

   (8) Unit sales to achieve a desired profit = $\dfrac{\text{Fixed costs \& desired net income*}}{\text{Contribution margin ratio}}$

   * A predicted operating loss would be subtracted from fixed costs in the numerator.

3. **CLASSIFY COSTS** Mixed (semi-variable) costs must be split into fixed and variable elements.

4. **SOLVE FOR UNKNOWNS** Insert all the given information into the appropriate computational formats and solve for the unknowns.

D.   BREAK-EVEN POINT

The point where sales less fixed and variable costs result in zero profit. Thus, the break-even point is **defined** as the point where net income equals zero. The terms break-even point analysis and cost-volume-profit analysis are sometimes used interchangeably.

EXAMPLE 1 ♦ BREAK-EVEN POINT

Bob's Deli specializes in Bob's Bagel Delight. Production and sales data are provided below.

	Per unit	%
Selling price	$ .90	100.00
Variable cost	.60	(66.67)
Contribution margin	$ .30	33.33
Total fixed cost	$ 300	

REQUIRED: Solve for the break-even point in dollars and in units using the two methods given in this chapter.

SOLUTION:

Income equation method:

a.   Sales in dollars (S) = Variable costs + Fixed costs + Net income

$$S = .6667 S + \$300 + 0$$

$$S = \$300/.3333 = \underline{\$900}$$

b.   Sales in units (Su)

$$\$0.90\ Su = \$0.60\ Su + \$300 + 0$$

$$\$0.30\ Su = \$300$$

$$Su = \$300/\$0.30 = \underline{1,000}\ \text{units}$$

Contribution margin method:

a.   Sales in dollars $= \dfrac{\text{Fixed costs + Net income}}{\text{Contribution margin ratio}}$

$$= \frac{\$300 + 0}{0.3333} = \$900$$

b.   Sales in units $= \dfrac{\text{Fixed costs + Net income}}{\text{Unit contribution margin}}$

$$= \frac{\$300 + 0}{\$0.30} = 1,000\ \text{units}$$

PROOF:

Sales (1,000 x $.90)	$900
Variable costs (1,000 x $.60)	(600)
Contribution margin	300
Fixed costs	(300)
Net income	$ 0

E. **SPECIFIED INCOME LEVEL**

EXAMPLE 2 ♦ SALES TO OBTAIN A SPECIFIED NET INCOME LEVEL

Use the same facts from Example 1 plus a desired income level of $100.

REQUIRED: Determine the target sales, using the contribution margin method.

SOLUTION:

In units	*In sales dollars*
$\dfrac{\text{Fixed cost + Desired net income}}{\text{Unit contribution margin}}$	$\dfrac{\text{Fixed cost + Desired net income}}{\text{Contribution margin ratio}}$
$= \dfrac{\$300 + \$100}{\$0.30}$	$= \dfrac{\$300 + \$100}{.3333}$
$= \underline{1,333}$ units	$= \underline{\$1,200}$

F. **CHANGING COSTS**

1. **SALES** Desired sales in units or dollars given that the selling price, fixed cost, and/or variable cost will change.

EXAMPLE 3 ♦ CHANGING COSTS GIVEN IN PERCENTAGES

Use the facts from Example 1 with the following changes:

Selling price decreased	11.11%
Variable costs decreased	33.33%
Fixed costs increased	33.33%
Desired profit (based on sales)	10%

REQUIRED: Determine the target sales in units (Su) and in dollars (S), using the contribution margin method.

SOLUTION:

	Per unit	%
Selling price, $.90 (1 − .1111)	$ .80	100%
Variable cost, $.60 (1 − .3333)	(.40)	(50%)
Revised contribution margin	$ .40	50%

In units	*In dollars*
$\dfrac{FC(1 + \% \text{ incr.}) + NI \text{ as } \% \text{ of sales}}{\text{Unit contribution margin}}$	$\dfrac{FC(1 + \% \text{ incr.}) + NI \text{ as } \% \text{ of sales}}{\text{Contribution margin ratio}}$
$Su = \dfrac{\$300(1.3333) + .10\,(\$.80Su)}{\$0.40}$	$S = \dfrac{\$300(1.3333) + .10\,S}{.50}$
$Su = \dfrac{\$400 + \$.08Su}{\$.40}$	$.50S = \$400 + .10S$
$\$.40\,Su = \$400 + \$.08Su$	$.40S = \$400$
$Su = \dfrac{\$400}{\$.32}$	$S = \dfrac{\$400}{.4}$
$Su = \underline{1,250} \text{ Units}$	$S = \underline{\$1,000}$

2. **SELLING PRICE** Required selling price based on change in cost, volume, and/or profit level.

EXAMPLE 4 ♦ CHANGING COSTS

Use the facts in Example 1, except that variable cost increased $0.10. The present contribution margin ratio is to be maintained.

REQUIRED: Determine new unit sale price.

SOLUTION:

Present	Per Unit	%
Selling price	$ 0.90	100.00
Variable cost	(0.60)	(66.67)
Contribution margin	$ 0.30	33.33

$$\text{Contribution margin ratio (CMR)} = \frac{\text{Unit contribution margin (CM)}}{\text{Unit selling price (SP)}}$$

$$SP = \frac{CM}{CMR}$$

$$SP = \frac{SP - \text{Revised variable costs (VC)}}{CMR}$$

$$SP = \frac{SP - (\$0.60 + \$0.10)}{0.3333}$$

$$.3333\ SP = SP - \$.70$$
$$.6667\ SP = \$.70$$
$$SP = \underline{\$1.05}$$

NOTE: The break-even point in dollars does not change since the contribution margin ratio remains the same. However, the break-even point in units does change as a result of the revised contribution margin per unit.

Revised data	Per unit	%
Selling price (per above)	$ 1.05	100.00
Variable cost ($.60 + $.10)	(0.70)	(66.67)
Contribution margin	$ 0.35	33.33

Break-even point
In units $300 / $0.35 = 857 units (rounded)   In dollars $300 / .333 = $900

G. COMPOSITE BREAK-EVEN POINT

1.   When a company sells more than one product, a break-even point can be determined for each product based on the expected sales mix and the composite or combined contribution margin.

EXAMPLE 5 ♦ MIXED SALES

	Product		
	A	B	C
Selling price	$ 1.00	$ 2.00	$ 3.00
Variable cost	(0.50)	(1.50)	(2.00)
Contribution margin	$ 0.50	$ 0.50	$ 1.00
Sales mix ratio	1/8	3/8	4/8
Total fixed costs	$60,000		

REQUIRED: Compute the break-even point in units and dollars for Products A, B, and C.

SOLUTION:

Composite contribution margin

	A	B	C	Composite contribution margin
Contribution margin	$ .50	$ .50	$1.00	
Sales mix ratio	x 1	x 3	x 4	
Weighted CM	$ .50	$ 1.50	$4.00	$6.00

Total break-even point

$$\frac{\text{Fixed costs}}{\text{Composite contribution margin}} = \text{Composite units*}$$

$$\frac{\$60,000}{\$6.00} = \underline{10,000} \text{ composite units}$$

* A composite unit is the "package" made up of 1 unit of A, 3 units of B, and 4 units of C.

Break-even point for each product

	A	B	C
Composite units	10,000	10,000	10,000
Sales mix ratio	x 1	x 3	x 4
Break-even, units	10,000	30,000	40,000
Selling price	x $1.00	x $2.00	x $3.00
Break-even, dollars	$10,000	$60,000	$120,000

PROOF:

A (10,000 x $.50)	$ 5,000
B (30,000 x $.50)	15,000
C (40,000 x $1.00)	40,000
Contribution margin	$60,000
Fixed costs	(60,000)
Net income	$ 0

2. The composite contribution margin can be determined from the separate multi-product contribution rates and the forecasted sales mix in dollars, by use of the following formula:

$$\text{Composite Contribution Margin} = \sum \left[\text{Sales mix ratio in dollars, product}_i \times \text{Contribution margin ratio}_i \right]$$

EXAMPLE 6 ♦ MIXED SALES

Product	X	Y	Z
$ Sales mix ratio	1/19	6/19	12/19
CMR	50%	25%	33.33%
Total fixed costs	$60,000		

REQUIRED: Compute break-even point in dollars. [Since we are not given the selling price per unit, we can't determine break-even sales in number of units.]

SOLUTION:

Composite CMR $= \Sigma$ ($ Sales mix ratio, product$_i$ x CMR$_i$)

$= 1/19(50\%) + 6/19(25\%) + 12/19(33.33\%)$

$= .02632 + .07895 + .21053 = .31580$

Composite sales break-even $= \dfrac{\text{Fixed cost}}{\text{Composite CMR}}$

$= \dfrac{\$60,000}{.31580}$

$= \underline{\$190,000}$ (rounded)

H. INCOME TAX EFFECT

Most cost-volume-profit CPA Exam problems ignore income taxes. A modified formula is required to include the impact of income taxes.

$$\frac{Fixed\ cost + \dfrac{Net\ income}{1 - Tax\ rate}}{Contribution\ margin}$$

EXAMPLE 7 ♦ INCOME TAX CONSIDERATIONS

Fixed costs = $300; Desired net income = $100; Tax rate = 40%; Unit contribution margin = $0.30; Contribution margin rate = 33.33%

REQUIRED: Compute the sales for net income after tax of $100.

SOLUTION:

In units	In dollars
$\dfrac{\$300 + \dfrac{\$100}{\$1 - .40}}{\$.30}$	$\dfrac{\$300 + \dfrac{\$100}{\$1 - .40}}{.3333\%}$
$= \dfrac{\$300 + \$166.67}{\$.30}$	$= \dfrac{\$300 + \$166.67}{\$.30}$
$= \mathbf{1{,}556}$ units	$= \mathbf{\$1{,}400}$

I. MARGIN OF SAFETY

The margin of safety (M/S) can be defined as the excess of budgeted (or actual) sales over the break-even volume of sales. It states the amount by which sales can drop before losses begin to be incurred in an organization.

1. **DOLLARS** The formula for the calculation of the margin of safety in dollars is

Total sales – Break-even sales = Margin of safety (M/S)

2. **PERCENTAGE** The M/S can also be expressed in percentage form. This percentage is obtained by dividing the M/S in dollar terms by total sales.

$$\frac{M/S \ in \ dollars}{Total \ sales} = M/S \ percentage$$

III. SPECIAL DECISIONS

A. RELEVANT COSTS

Relevant costs are expected future costs that will differ among alternatives. The concept of cost relevance is important in the decision-making process, especially in decisions that are nonroutine. Differential cost analysis is the study of relevant costs that are associated with a decision among possible courses of action so that the most appropriate alternative may be selected.

1. **AVOIDABLE COSTS** Costs that will not be incurred if an activity is suspended.

2. **DIFFERENTIAL (INCREMENTAL) COSTS** The difference in cost between two alternatives.

3. **MARGINAL COSTS** The addition to total cost of producing or selling one more unit of output.

4. **OUT-OF-POCKET COSTS** Immediate or near future cash outlays.

5. **OPPORTUNITY COSTS** The foregone benefits (revenues minus costs) from alternatives not selected. Opportunity costs do not require an actual current or future cash outlay. Although relevant, opportunity costs are generally not incorporated in the accounting system nor included in differential cost analyses, as they are difficult to measure objectively. However, the use of opportunity cost is a practical means of reducing the alternatives under consideration.

6. **IRRELEVANT COSTS** Historical costs are always **irrelevant per se,** although they may be helpful in predicting relevant costs. In order to be relevant for decision making, an item must meet both of the following criteria.

    a. It is an expected **future** cost or revenue.

    b. Its amount will **differ** among alternatives.

7.   **SUNK COSTS** Historical costs incurred as a result of past decisions; they are not relevant in current decision making.

EXAMPLE 8 ♦ OPPORTUNITY COSTS

	Alternatives considered		Alternatives not considered	
	#1	#2	#3	#4
Relevant revenues	$1,000	$ 2,000	$ 3,000	$300
Relevant cost	(500)	(1,750)	(2,800)	0
Differential income	$ 500	$ 250	$ 200	$300

REQUIRED: Prepare an opportunity cost analysis.

SOLUTION:

	Alternatives		Differential
	#1	#2	
Relevant revenues	$1,000	$ 2,000	$(1,000)
Relevant costs	(500)	(1,750)	1,250
Opportunity costs—contribution foregone from next best alternative	(300)	(300)	0
Net advantage	$ 200	$ (50)	$ 250

NOTE: Notice that the net differential amount between alternative #1 and #2 is still $250. Note also that if all the results of the alternatives formally considered were negative, such a result would indicate that the best **excluded** alternative was in fact optimal.

EXAMPLE 9 ♦ RELEVANT COSTS

The Sky Company is planning to expand its production capacity. Its plans consist of purchasing a new machine for $100,000 and selling the old machine for $10,000. The new machine has a 5-year life. The old machine has a 5-year remaining life and a carrying amount of $50,000. The new machine will reduce labor costs from $40,000 per year to $20,000 per year. Assume that there are no other related machine costs and that the disposal value at the end of each machine's estimated life is zero.

REQUIRED: What are the relevant and differential costs? Ignore present value and income taxes.

SOLUTION:

	Relevant costs		Differential
	Keep	Replace	
Labor costs			
($40,000 x 5)	$200,000		
($20,000 x 5)		$100,000	$ 100,000
Disposal value of old		(10,000)	10,000
Cost of new machine		100,000	(100,000)
Total relevant costs	$200,000	$190,000	$ 10,000

COMMENT: The $50,000 carrying amount of the old machine is a sunk cost and is not relevant to the decision.

B.   **SPECIAL ORDER**
This type of problem usually involves an order at a price lower than the regular selling price, and there are often some cost differences as well. Generally, the requirement is to determine whether the special order should be accepted or rejected, and its effect on pretax income. Only incremental

variable costs are relevant, unless additional fixed costs must be incurred because of the special order. If available capacity is not fully utilized, a differential cost analysis may indicate the advisability of accepting a special order at a price lower than the existing unit cost (which includes allocated **fixed** overhead). If the variable cost is covered, any additional revenue can contribute to the recovery of fixed costs.

- When only differential manufacturing costs are taken into account for special order pricing, it is essential to assume that acceptance of the order will not affect regular sales.

EXAMPLE 10 ♦ SPECIAL ORDER

The Bike Company has enough idle capacity available to accept a special order of 10,000 bicycles at a unit price of $80. There are no additional selling expenses or fixed manufacturing costs associated with the special order. Acceptance of the special order will not affect regular sales. Estimated income for the year <u>without</u> the special order is as follows:

	Per Unit		Total
Sales	$100		$100,000,000
Manufacturing costs			
Variable	$40		$40,000,000
Fixed	20	60	20,000,000	60,000,000
Gross margin		40		40,000,000
Selling expenses			
Variable	$20		$20,000,000
Fixed	10	30	10,000,000	30,000,000
Operating income		$ 10		$ 10,000,000

REQUIRED: Determine the net effect on operating income of the acceptance of the special order.

SOLUTION:

	Differential
Incremental revenues 10,000 x $80	$800,000
Incremental costs 10,000 x $40	400,000
Increase in operating income	$400,000

or

Per unit change approach

Relevant selling price	$ 80
Relevant variable mfg. costs	40
Unit contribution margin	$ 40
	x 10,000 units
Increase in operating income	$400,000

Contribution margin statement approach

	Without special order	With special order	Special order difference
Sales	$100,000,000	$100,800,000	$800,000
Variable costs			
Manufacturing	40,000,000	40,400,000	400,000
Selling & Adm.	20,000,000	20,000,000	0
	60,000,000	60,400,000	400,000
Contribution margin	40,000,000	40,400,000	400,000
Fixed costs			
Manufacturing	20,000,000	20,000,000	0
Selling & Adm.	10,000,000	10,000,000	0
Operating income	$ 10,000,000	$ 10,400,000	$400,000

C.   **MAKE OR BUY**
The relevant cost of manufacturing a given product is compared to the cost of purchasing it from an outside supplier. For differential analysis purposes, the relevant cost of production includes variable costs and "fixed" costs that would be **eliminated** if the product were purchased. Any opportunity cost of using production facilities for some other purpose (e.g., manufacturing of a different product, leasing or selling facilities, etc.) is subtracted from the cost of **purchasing** the product from the outside supplier or added to the cost of production.

EXAMPLE 11 ♦ MAKE OR BUY

The Sun Lamp Company needs 20,000 units of Part 109 used in its production cycle. If Sun Lamp Company buys the required parts rather than producing them, it will eliminate $1 of fixed overhead per unit. The remaining fixed overhead will continue even if the part is purchased from outsiders. The cost to buy the part is $22. The following information is available:

Direct material	$ 4
Direct labor	8
Variable overhead	8
Fixed overhead applied	4
Cost to make the part	$24

REQUIRED: Should Sun Lamp manufacture Part 109, or should it buy it from the outside supplier? Determine the relevant unit cost, relevant total costs, and differential costs.

SOLUTION:

Relevant Unit Costs	Make	Buy
Direct material	$ 4	
Direct labor	8	
Variable overhead	8	
Fixed overhead which can be eliminated ($4 – $3)	1	
Total	$21	$22

The relevant costs to make Part 109 are $420,000 (20,000 x $21). The relevant costs to buy the part are $440,000 (20,000 x $22). It is to Sun Lamp's advantage ($20,000) to continue to manufacture Part 109.

EXAMPLE 12 ♦ MAKE OR BUY

The same situation as Example 11, except that the facilities presently used to manufacture Part 109 could be used to manufacture Part 007 for product ABC and generate an operating profit of $30,000. The incremental costs to manufacture Part 109 (i.e., $420,000) must now be compared to the cost of purchasing the part less the operating profit generated in the manufacture of Product ABC (i.e., $440,000 – $30,000). Therefore, it would now be $10,000 ($420,000 – $410,000) cheaper to buy the part.

D.   **SCRAP OR REWORK**
The relevant cost is the added cost of reworking the inventory, compared to the differential revenue from the sale of the refinished goods (i.e., the difference between the scrap value of the inventory and the value of the refinished goods).

EXAMPLE 13 ♦ SCRAP OR REWORK

The Hippy Company has 1,000 obsolete lava lamps that are carried in inventory at a cost of $20,000. If these parts are reworked for $10,000 they could be sold for $15,000. If they are scrapped, they could be sold for $1,000.

REQUIRED: Should these lamps be reworked or scrapped? Determine the relevant and differential costs, sunk costs, and opportunity cost.

SOLUTION: The rework alternative is more attractive since it yields a greater excess of relevant revenues over relevant costs. The $10,000 rework costs are incremental costs; therefore, they are relevant costs. The $20,000 inventory cost represents a sunk cost. It is not relevant to the decision to scrap or rework. The opportunity cost is the $1,000 of revenue foregone from not selling the obsolete inventory as scrap.

	Alternatives		
	Scrap	Rework	Differential
Relevant revenues	$1,000	$ 15,000	$ 14,000
Relevant costs	0	(10,000)	(10,000)
	$1,000	$ 5,000	$ 4,000

E.   SELL OR PROCESS FURTHER

This is another application of relevant cost and revenue analysis. The additional revenues obtainable from further processing the product are compared to the additional costs that would be incurred. If the additional revenues derived exceed the additional costs, the product should be processed further. The joint costs allocated to the product is **irrelevant** to the decision whether to subject the product to further processing.

EXAMPLE 14 ♦ SELL OR PROCESS FURTHER

The White Company uses a joint process to produce products A, B, and C. Each product may be sold at its split-off point or processed further. Additional processing costs are entirely variable. Joint production costs were $100,000 and are allocated using the relative-sales-value at split-off approach. The following information is available:

Products	Sales value at split-off	Additional processing costs	Final sales value
A	$ 50,000	$20,000	$100,000
B	100,000	20,000	120,000
C	20,000	30,000	40,000
	$170,000	$70,000	$260,000

REQUIRED: Should the products be sold at the split-off point or should they be further processed? Determine the net differential income.

SOLUTION: The joint production costs are not relevant (i.e., do not differ between alternatives) and therefore do not affect the decision to process further or sell now. The optimum course of action is to sell product C at the split-off point, further process product A, and either sell at split-off or further process product B, depending on qualitative factors

	A	B	C
Final sales value	$100,000	$ 120,000	$ 40,000
Sales value at split-off	(50,000)	(100,000)	(20,000)
Incremental revenues	50,000	20,000	20,000
Incremental costs	(20,000)	(20,000)	(30,000)
Differential	$ 30,000	$ 0	$(10,000)

F.   ELIMINATE PRODUCT LINE OR DIVISION

In addition to the differential items relating to the line or division, the effect on sales of related lines or divisions may be relevant. Furthermore, a line may be unprofitable but still contribute to the recovery of total fixed costs. The contribution margin of the line must be compared to its relevant fixed costs (i.e., the fixed costs that would be eliminated if the line were discontinued). If the contribution margin of the line exceeds the fixed costs that would be eliminated, the line should **not** be discontinued. The fixed costs that cannot be eliminated are **irrelevant** to the decision because they will continue regardless of the decision.

EXAMPLE 15 ♦ ELIMINATING A PRODUCT LINE

Management is considering eliminating product line B.

	Products			
	A	B	C	Total
Revenue	$1,000	$ 2,000	$ 3,000	$ 6,000
Variable costs	(500)	(1,500)	(1,000)	(3,000)
Contribution margin	500	500	2,000	3,000
Fixed costs				
Avoidable	200	100	1,000	1,300
Unavoidable	100	500	200	800
	(300)	(600)	(1,200)	(2,100)
Net income	$ 200	$ (100)	$ 800	$ 900

REQUIRED: Determine if product line B should be eliminated, based on the given information.

SOLUTION: Product line B should not be eliminated because net income will decrease $400. The $500 of unavoidable fixed costs allocated to product line B are irrelevant because they will continue regardless of the decision.

	Alternative #1 Keep Product Line B	Alternative #2 Eliminate Product Line B	Difference
Revenues	$ 6,000	$ 4,000	$ 2,000
Variable costs	(3,000)	(1,500)	(1,500)
Contribution margin	3,000	2,500	500
Fixed costs			
Avoidable	1,300	1,200	100
Unavoidable	800	800	0
	(2,100)	(2,000)	(100)
Net income	$ 900	$ 500	$ 400

G.   PRODUCT PRICING

Product pricing involves the integration of various disciplines such as economics, statistics, industrial engineering, marketing, and accounting. The objective of product pricing is to maximize profits and thus, shareholders' wealth. Often, costs are the starting point for a pricing decision. Two common approaches to product pricing are the contribution margin approach and cost-plus pricing.

1.   **CONTRIBUTION MARGIN APPROACH** Under this approach, product pricing is based upon all relevant variable costs plus any additional fixed costs necessary for the increased production level.

2.   **COST-PLUS PRICING** This method takes the product's cost and adds a predetermined markup to compute the targeted selling price. A predetermined markup that is expressed as a percentage of the product's selling price (e.g., a gross margin of 20% is desired) must be converted to a percentage markup on cost by the following formula:

$$\text{Percentage markup on cost} = \frac{\text{Percentage markup on selling price}}{100\% - \text{Percentage markup on selling price}}$$

EXAMPLE 16 ♦ COST-PLUS PRICING

> Pallex Co. wants to sell a product at a gross margin of 20%. The cost of the product is $4.00.
>
> **REQUIRED:** Determine the selling price of the product.
>
> **SOLUTION:**
>
> Percentage markup on cost $= \dfrac{\text{Percentage markup on selling price}}{100\% - \text{Percentage markup on selling price}}$
>
> $\qquad\qquad\qquad\qquad\qquad = \dfrac{20\%}{100\% - 20\%}$
>
> $\qquad\qquad\qquad\qquad\qquad = 25\%$
>
> Selling price $\quad = $ Cost of product + Gross margin
>
> $\qquad\qquad\qquad = \$4.00 + 25\% \,(\$4.00)$
>
> $\qquad\qquad\qquad = \underline{\$5.00}$

IV. DIRECT (VARIABLE) COSTING

A. OVERVIEW

Direct costing (variable costing) is an inventory costing method whereby direct materials, direct labor, and variable manufacturing overhead are considered to be product costs (inventoriable costs), while fixed manufacturing overhead is considered to be a period cost (cost expensed in the period incurred).

1. COMPONENTS OF INVENTORY Under direct costing, only variable manufacturing costs are included in inventory. No **fixed** manufacturing costs are included in inventory.

2. FORMAT OF INCOME STATEMENT Under direct costing, the income statement subtracts all variable expenses from sales to arrive at contribution margin. All fixed expenses are subtracted from contribution margin to arrive at operating income. (There is no gross margin.)

3. REPORTING Direct costing is used for internal reporting purposes only. Its uses include inventory valuation, income measurement, relevant cost analysis, cost-volume-profit analysis, and other short-run, decision-making situations. Direct costing is not acceptable for external financial reporting (i.e., GAAP) and federal income tax reporting. Companies that use direct costing for internal reporting must convert to absorption costing (GAAP) for external financial reporting.

B. ACCOUNTING FOR FIXED MANUFACTURING OVERHEAD

No selling or administrative costs are ever part of product costs under either method.

1. DIRECT COSTING The costs to be inventoried include only the variable manufacturing costs. Fixed manufacturing overhead is expensed as incurred as a period cost, along with all selling and administrative costs.

2. ABSORPTION COSTING The costs to be inventoried include **all** manufacturing costs, both variable and fixed.

EXHIBIT 11 ♦ COMPARISON OF INVENTORIED COSTS

	Direct Costing	Absorption Costing
Direct materials	$XX	$XX
Direct labor	XX	XX
Variable manufacturing overhead	XX	XX
Fixed manufacturing overhead	--	XX
Variable selling and administrative costs	--	--
Fixed selling and administrative costs	--	--
Total product cost	$XX	$XX

C.   EFFECTS ON NET INCOME
Under direct costing, income tends to move with sales, whereas under absorption costing, income may be influenced by production levels. Thus, net income can be influenced by inventory changes under absorption costing, but not under direct costing.

1.   **PRODUCTION EXCEEDS SALES** When production exceeds sales (that is, when work-in-process and finished goods inventories are increasing), absorption costing shows a **higher** profit than does direct costing. The reason is that in absorption costing, a greater portion of the fixed manufacturing cost of the period is charged to inventory and thereby deferred to future periods. The total fixed cost charged against revenue of the period, therefore, is less than the amount of fixed cost incurred during the period.

2.   **SALES EXCEED PRODUCTION** When sales exceed production (that is, when work-in-process and finished goods inventories are decreasing), absorption costing shows a lower profit than does direct costing. Under absorption costing, fixed costs previously deferred in inventory are charged against revenue in the period in which the goods are sold. Total fixed costs charged against revenue, therefore, exceed the amount of fixed cost incurred during the period.

3.   **PRODUCTION EQUALS SALES** When sales and production are in balance, net income will be the same under direct and absorption costing (assuming that fixed manufacturing costs per unit do not change). Since there is no change in inventories, the fixed manufacturing overhead cost incurred during the period will be charged to expense under both methods. Thus, net income will be the same using either costing method.

4.   **RECONCILIATION BETWEEN NET INCOME UNDER ABSORPTION COSTING AND DIRECT COSTING**
If the fixed manufacturing overhead per unit cost does not change between periods, the difference between the reported net income under the two costing methods can be reconciled as follows:

$$\text{Difference in net income} = \text{Change in inventory level} \times \text{Fixed manufacturing overhead per unit}$$

EXHIBIT 12 ♦ DIRECT AND ABSORPTION COSTING

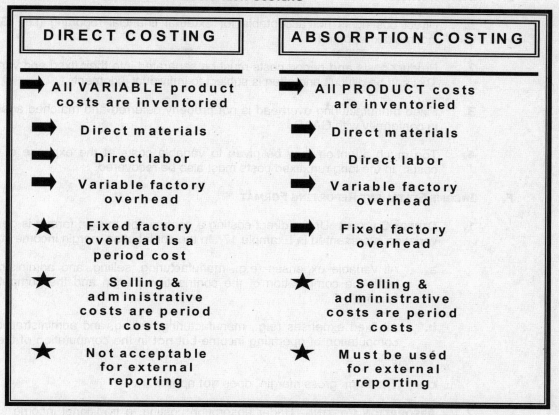

DIRECT COSTING	ABSORPTION COSTING
➡ All VARIABLE product costs are inventoried	➡ All PRODUCT costs are inventoried
➡ Direct materials	➡ Direct materials
➡ Direct labor	➡ Direct labor
➡ Variable factory overhead	➡ Variable factory overhead
★ Fixed factory overhead is a period cost	➡ Fixed factory overhead
★ Selling & administrative costs are period costs	★ Selling & administrative costs are period costs
★ Not acceptable for external reporting	★ Must be used for external reporting

D. ADVANTAGES

1. All fixed costs (i.e., manufacturing, selling, and administrative) are expensed in the period incurred. This highlights the effect of fixed costs on net income.

2. Fixed manufacturing overhead is not accounted for as an inventoriable cost. This simplifies record keeping and provides a more visible basis for controlling the total fixed manufacturing overhead costs.

3. Net income is not influenced by production and inventory changes. Net income tends to vary with sales.

4. The income statement reporting format (i.e., the contribution margin format) is extremely useful for management purposes, e.g., cost-volume-profit relationships, contribution margin data, etc.

   a. When absorption costing is used, break-even analysis assumes: (1) sales volume equals production volume (i.e., inventory levels remain constant), (2) unit variable costs are unchanged over the relevant range, and (3) a given sales mix is maintained for all volume changes.

   b. If direct costing is used, no fixed manufacturing costs are applied to inventory, and hence it does not matter if sales volume equals production volume. All fixed costs are expensed when incurred.

E.   DISADVANTAGES

1.   Direct costing is not acceptable for external financial reporting (i.e., GAAP) and federal income tax reporting.

2.   Product costs **and** period costs must be separated into their fixed and variable components. This can be difficult and often is subject to individual judgment.

3.   Fixed manufacturing overhead is not properly deferred and matched against sales revenue in conformity with GAAP.

4.   Too much attention may be given to variable costs at the expense of disregarding fixed costs. In the long run, fixed costs must also be recovered.

F.   INCOME STATEMENT REPORTING FORMAT

1.   **DIRECT COSTING** Under direct costing a contribution margin format is generally used. One variation is presented in Example 17. In the contribution margin income statement:

   a.   All variable expenses (e.g., manufacturing, selling, and administrative) are used in **both** the computation of the contribution margin and the computation of operating income.

   b.   All fixed expenses (e.g., manufacturing, selling, and administrative) are used in the computation of operating income but **not** in the computation of the contribution margin.

   c.   The term "gross margin" does **not** appear.

2.   **ABSORPTION COSTING** Under absorption costing, a traditional income statement format is used. One variation is presented in Example 17.

EXAMPLE 17 ♦ DIRECT COSTING VS. FULL ABSORPTION COSTING INCOME STATEMENTS

The records of the Nickerson Company reveal the following information:

	20X1	20X2
Beginning inventory balance, in units	0	3,500
Production	10,000	9,000
Available for sale	10,000	12,500
Less units sold	(6,500)	(11,500)
Ending inventory balance, in units	3,500	1,000
Sales ($2/unit)	$13,000	$ 23,000
Variable manufacturing cost ($0.75/unit)	7,500	6,750
Fixed manufacturing cost	5,000	5,400
Selling and administrative expenses	4,500	7,500

REQUIRED: Prepare Nickerson's partial income statements for 20X1 and 20X2 using both direct costing and absorption costing. Selling and administrative expenses are 50% fixed and 50% variable. Assume a FIFO inventory flow. Ignore income taxes.

SOLUTION:

20X1 Absorption Costing Statement

Sales (6,500 x $2)		$ 13,000
Var. mfg. costs		
(6,500 x $0.75)	$4,875	
Fixed mfg. Costs		
(6,500 x $0.50)	3,250	
CGS		(8,125)
Gross margin		$ 4,875
S&A expense		(4,500)
Operating income		$ 375

Difference in operating income: $375 – ($1,375) = $1,750

Change in inventory level	3,500
Fixed manufacturing OH per unit	$ 0.50
Reconciliation of 20X1 operating income:	$1,750

20X1 Direct Costing Statement

Sales		$ 13,000
Var. mfg. costs		
(6,500 x $0.75)	$4,875	
Var. S&A ($4,500 x 0.50)	2,250	
Less: Variable costs		(7,125)
Contribution margin		$ 5,875
Less: Fixed mfg. costs	$5,000	
Fixed S&A	2,250	(7,250)
Operating loss		$ (1,375)

20X2 Absorption Costing Statement

Sales (11,500 x $2)		$ 23,000
Var. mfg. Costs		
(11,500 x $0.75)	$8,625	
Fixed mfg. Costs		
(3,500 x $0.50)	1,750	
(8,000 x $0.60)	4,800	
CGS		(15,175)
Gross margin		$ 7,825
S&A expense		(7,500)
Operating income		$ 325

Difference in operating income: $325 – $1,475 = $1,150

3,500 units x $5,000/10,000 =	$1,750
8,000 units x $5,400/9,000 =	4,800
Fixed costs expensed under absorption costing:	$6,550
Fixed costs expensed under direct costing:	5,400
Reconciliation of 20X2 operating income:	$1,150

20X2 Direct Costing Statement

Sales		$ 23,000
Var. mfg. costs		
(11,500 x $0.75)	$8,625	
Var. S&A		
($7,500 x 0.50)	3,750	
Less: Variable costs:		(12,375)
Contribution margin		$ 10,625
Less: Fixed mfg. costs		(5,400)
Fixed S&A		(3,750)
Operating income		$ 1,475

Using Audio Tutor to Study

Actively listen to the audio tapes, taking notes if convenient. In the Audio Tutor product, the lecturers supplement the content in this material with the insight gained from years of CPA review experience.

If you are strong in a topic, your audio review and question drill may be sufficient. If your strength is moderate in a topic, you might find that reading the related text before listening to the audio tapes is helpful. If you are weak in a topic, one successful strategy is to listen to the audio tapes, read the book, and then listen to the audio tapes again.

FYI: The Audio Tutor tapes have similar content as the Hot*Spot, Intensive, and online video lectures, but they are not exactly the same. Audio Tutor and this book have topics arranged in essentially the same chapters, although material might be organized differently within the chapters.

Call a customer service representative for more details about Audio Tutor.

CHAPTER 24—DECISION MAKING

PROBLEM 24-1 MULTIPLE CHOICE QUESTIONS (60 to 75 minutes)

1. Gram Co. develops computer programs to meet customers' special requirements. How should Gram categorize payments to employees who develop these programs?

	Direct costs	Value-adding costs
a.	Yes	Yes
b.	Yes	No
c.	No	No
d.	No	Yes

(11/95, AR, #45, 5788)

2. The following information pertains to the August manufacturing activities of Griss Co.:

Beginning work-in-process	$12,000
Ending work-in-process	10,000
Cost of goods manufactured	97,000
Direct materials issued to production	20,000

Factory overhead is assigned at 150 percent of direct labor. What was the August direct labor?
a. $30,000
b. $30,800
c. $31,600
d. $50,000

(11/98, AR, #22, 6688)

3. When production levels are expected to increase within a relevant range, and a flexible budget is used, what effect would be anticipated with respect to each of the following costs?

	Fixed costs per unit	Variable costs per unit
a.	Decrease	Decrease
b.	No change	No change
c.	No change	Decrease
d.	Decrease	No change

(11/93, Theory, #46, 4551)

4. Day Mail Order Co. applied the high-low method of cost estimation to customer order data for the first 4 months of the year.

Month	Orders	Cost
January	1,200	$ 3,120
February	1,300	3,185
March	1,800	4,320
April	1,700	3,895
	6,000	$14,520

What is the estimated variable order filling cost component per order?
a. $2.00
b. $2.42
c. $2.48
d. $2.50

(5/95, AR, #36, amended, 5454)

5. Sender Inc. estimates parcel mailing costs using data shown on the chart below.

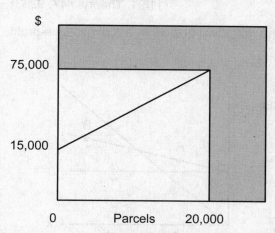

What is Sender's estimated cost for mailing 12,000 parcels?
a. $36,000
b. $45,000
c. $51,000
d. $60,000

(11/95, AR, #39, 9235)

6. In the budgeted profit-volume chart below, EG represents a two-product company's profit path. EH and HG represent the profit paths of products #1 and #2, respectively.

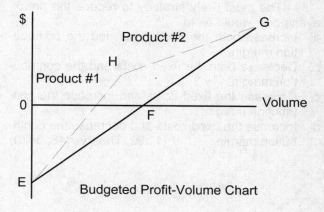

Budgeted Profit-Volume Chart

Sales prices and cost behavior were as budgeted, actual total sales equaled budgeted sales, and there were no inventories. Actual profit was greater than budgeted profit. Which product had actual sales in excess of budget, and what margin does OE divided by OF represent?

	Product with excess sales	OE/OF
a.	#1	Contribution margin
b.	#1	Gross margin
c.	#2	Contribution margin
d.	#2	Gross margin

(11/91, Theory, #47, 9233)

7. The diagram below is a cost-volume-profit chart.

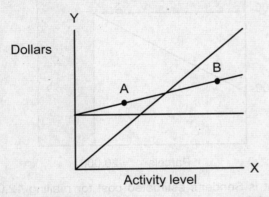

At point A compared to point B, as a percentage of sales revenues

	Variable costs are	Fixed costs are
a.	Greater	Greater
b.	Greater	The same
c.	The same	The same
d.	The same	Greater

(5/90, Theory, #46, 9234)

8. The most likely strategy to reduce the break-even point, would be to
a. Increase both the fixed costs and the contribution margin.
b. Decrease both the fixed costs and the contribution margin.
c. Decrease the fixed costs and increase the contribution margin.
d. Increase the fixed costs and decrease the contribution margin. (11/92, Theory, #46, 3479)

9. Cuff Caterers quotes a price of $60 per person for a dinner party. This price includes the 6% sales tax and the 15% service charge. Sales tax is computed on the food plus the service charge. The service charge is computed on the food only. At what amount does Cuff price the food?
a. $56.40
b. $51.00
c. $49.22
d. $47.40 (5/95, AR, #50, 5468)

ITEMS 10 AND 11 are based on the following:

Slick Co. sells radios for $30 each. Fixed expenses total $15,000. Variable expenses are $20 per unit.

10. How many radios must Slick sell to earn an operating income of $35,000?
a. 5,000
b. 3,500
c. 2,500
d. 1,500 (Editors, 1450)

11. What total dollar amount must Slick sell to break even?
a $20,000
b. $37,500
c. $45,000
d $60,000 (Editors, 1451)

12. Product Cott has sales of $200,000, a contribution margin of 20%, and a margin of safety of $80,000. What is Cott's fixed cost?
a. $16,000
b. $24,000
c. $80,000
d. $96,000 (11/95, AR, #43, 5786)

13. At annual sales of $900,000, the Ebo product has the following unit sales price and costs:

Sales price	$20
Prime cost	6
Manufacturing overhead	
Variable	1
Fixed	7
Selling & admin. costs	
Variable	1
Fixed	3
	18
Profit	$ 2

What is Ebo's breakeven point in units?
a. 25,000
b. 31,500
c. 37,500
d. 45,000 (R/00, AR, #16, 6921)

14. Based on potential sales of 500 units per year, a new product has estimated traceable costs of $990,000. What is the target price to obtain a 15% profit margin on sales?
a. $2,329
b. $2,277
c. $1,980
d. $1,935   (11/95, AR, #55, 5798)

15. For 20X1, Abel Co. incurred direct costs of $500,000 based on a particular course of action during the year. If a different course of action had been taken, direct costs would have been $400,000. In addition, Abel's 20X1 fixed costs were $90,000. The incremental cost was
a. $ 10,000.
b. $ 90,000.
c. $100,000.
d. $190,000.   (5/92, PII, #56, amended, 2688)

16. Buff Co. is considering replacing an old machine with a new machine. Which of the following items is economically relevant to Buff's decision? (Ignore income tax considerations.)

	Carrying amount of old machine	Disposal value of new machine
a.	Yes	No
b.	No	Yes
c.	No	No
d.	Yes	Yes

(5/92, Theory, #56, 2749)

17. Clay Co. has considerable excess manufacturing capacity. A special job order's cost sheet includes the following applied manufacturing overhead costs:

Fixed costs	$21,000
Variable costs	33,000

The fixed costs include a normal $3,700 allocation for in-house design costs, although no in-house design will be done. Instead the job will require the use of external designers costing $7,750. What is the total amount to be included in the calculation to determine the minimum acceptable price for the job?
a. $36,700
b. $40,750
c. $54,000
d. $58,050   (5/94, AR, #49, 4654)

18. When only differential manufacturing costs are taken into account for special order pricing, an essential assumption is that
a. Manufacturing fixed and variable costs are linear.
b. Selling and administrative fixed and variable costs are linear.
c. Acceptance of the order will **not** affect regular sales.
d. Acceptance of the order will **not** cause unit selling and administrative variable costs to increase.
(11/90, Theory, #49, 2183)

ITEMS 19 AND 20 are based on the following:

Golden, Inc., has been manufacturing 5,000 units of Part 10541 which is used in the manufacture of one of its products. At this level of production, the cost per unit of manufacturing Part 10541 is as follows:

Direct materials	$ 2
Direct labor	8
Variable overhead	4
Fixed overhead applied	6
Total	$20

Brown Company has offered to sell Golden 5,000 units of Part 10541 for $19 a unit. Golden has determined that it could use the facilities presently used to manufacture Part 10541 to manufacture Product RAC and generate an operating profit of $4,000. Golden has also determined that two-thirds of the fixed overhead applied will continue even if Part 10541 is purchased from Brown.

19. In deciding whether to make or buy the part, the total relevant costs to make the part are
a. $70,000.
b. $80,000.
c. $90,000.
d. $95,000.   (Editors, 9236)

20. Should Golden accept Brown's offer, and why?
a. No, because it would be $11,000 cheaper to make the part
b. No, because it would be $15,000 cheaper to make the part
c. Yes, because it would be $5,000 cheaper to buy the part
d. Yes, because it would be $9,000 cheaper to buy the part   (Editors, 9237)

21. Gandy Company has 5,000 obsolete desk lamps that are carried in inventory at a manufacturing cost of $50,000. If the lamps are reworked for $20,000, they could be sold for $35,000. Alternatively, the lamps could be sold for $8,000 to a jobber located in a distant city. What alternative is more desirable and what are the total relevant costs for that alternative?
a. Neither, since there is an overall loss under either alternative
b. Rework and $20,000
c. Rework and $70,000
d. Scrap and $50,000   (Editors, 9238)

22. One hundred pounds of raw material W is processed into 60 pounds of X and 40 pounds of Y. Joint costs are $135. X is sold for $2.50 per pound and Y can be sold for $3.00 per pound or processed further into 30 pounds of Z (10 pounds are lost in the second process) at an additional cost of $60. Each pound of Z can then be sold for $6. What is the effect on profits of processing product Y further into product Z?
a. $60 increase.
b. $30 increase.
c. No change.
d. $60 decrease.   (R/00, AR, #19, 6924)

23. Big Corporation currently operates two divisions that had operating results for the calendar year 20X1, as follows:

	West Division	East Division
Sales	$ 900,000	$ 300,000
Variable costs	(510,000)	(230,000)
Contribution margin	390,000	70,000
Fixed costs for the division	(110,000)	(50,000)
Margin over direct costs	280,000	20,000
Allocated corporate costs	(135,000)	(45,000)
Operating income (loss)	$ 145,000	$ (25,000)

Since the East Division also sustained an operating loss during 20X0, Big's president is considering the elimination of this division. The East Division fixed costs could be avoided if the division was eliminated. If the East Division had been eliminated on January 1, 20X1, Big Corporation's 20X1 operating income would have been
a. $20,000 lower.
b. $25,000 higher.
c. $45,000 lower.
d. $70,000 higher.   (Editors, 1453)

24. Brent Co. has intracompany service transfers from Division Core, a cost center, to Division Pro, a profit center. Under stable economic conditions, which of the following transfer prices is likely to be most conducive to evaluating whether both divisions have met their responsibilities?
a. Actual cost
b. Standard variable cost
c. Actual cost plus mark-up
d. Negotiated price   (5/94, AR, #44, 4649)

25. Vince Inc. has developed and patented a new laser disc reading device that will be marketed internationally. Which of the following factors should Vince consider in pricing the device?

I. Quality of the new device
II. Life of the new device
III. Customers' relative preference for quality compared to price

a. I and II only
b. I and III only
c. II and III only
d. I, II, and III   (11/93, Theory, #50, 4555)

26. Using the variable costing method, which of the following costs are assigned to inventory?

	Variable selling and administrative costs	Variable factory overhead costs
a.	Yes	Yes
b.	Yes	No
c.	No	No
d.	No	Yes
		(5/95, AR, #40, 5458)

27. Jago Co. has 2 products that use the same manufacturing facilities and cannot be subcontracted. Each product has sufficient orders to utilize the entire manufacturing capacity. For short-run profit maximization, Jago should manufacture the product with the
a. Lower total manufacturing costs for the manufacturing capacity.
b. Lower total variable manufacturing costs for the manufacturing capacity.
c. Greater gross profit per hour of manufacturing capacity.
d. Greater contribution margin per hour of manufacturing capacity.   (5/95, AR, #49, 5467)

28. In calculating the break-even point for a multiproduct company, which of the following assumptions are commonly made when variable costing is used?

I. Sales volume equals production volume.
II. Variable costs are constant per unit.
III. A given sales mix is maintained for all volume changes.

a. I and II
b. I and III
c. II and III
d. I, II, and III   (5/92, Theory, #52, 9253)

29. In an income statement prepared as an internal report using the variable costing method, variable selling and administrative expenses would
a. Not be used.
b. Be used in the computation of operating income but **not** in the computation of the contribution margin.
c. Be treated the same as fixed selling and administrative expenses.
d. Be used in the computation of the contribution margin.   (Editors, 2207)

30. In its first year of operations, Magna Manufacturers had the following costs when it produced 100,000 and sold 80,000 units of its only product:

Manufacturing costs:
Fixed	$180,000
Variable	160,000

Selling & admin. costs:
Fixed	90,000
Variable	40,000

How much lower would Magna's net income be if it used variable costing instead of full absorption costing?
a. $36,000
b. $54,000
c. $68,000
d. $94,000   (R/01, AR, #19, 7004)

PROBLEM 24-2 ADDITIONAL MULTIPLE CHOICE QUESTIONS (70 to 88 minutes)

31. A direct labor overtime premium should be charged to a specific job when the overtime is caused by the
a. Increased overall level of activity.
b. Customer's requirement for early completion of job.
c. Management's failure to include the job in the production schedule.
d. Management's requirement that the job be completed before the annual factory vacation closure.   (11/91, Theory, #43, 2551)

32. Fab Co. manufactures textiles. Among Fab's June manufacturing costs were the following salaries and wages:

Loom operators	$120,000
Factory foremen	45,000
Machine mechanics	30,000

What was the amount of Fab's June direct labor?
a. $195,000
b. $165,000
c. $150,000
d. $120,000   (5/92, PII, #42, amended, 2674)

33. Following are Mill Co.'s production costs for October:

Direct materials	$100,000
Direct labor	90,000
Factory overhead	4,000

What amount of costs should be traced to specific products in the production process?
a. $194,000
b. $190,000
c. $100,000
d. $ 90,000   (11/92, PII, #30, 3364)

ITEMS 34 THROUGH 36 are based on the following information pertaining to Harp Company's manufacturing operations:

Inventories	May 1	May 31
Direct materials	$18,000	$15,000
Work-in-process	9,000	6,000
Finished goods	27,000	36,000

Direct materials purchased in May	$42,000
Direct labor payroll in May	30,000
Direct labor rate per hour in May	7.50
Factory overhead rate per direct labor hour in May	10.00

34. For the month of May, prime cost was
a. $45,000.
b. $60,000.
c. $72,000.
d. $75,000.   (Editors, 1459)

35. For the month of May, conversion cost was
a. $45,000.
b. $70,000.
c. $72,000.
d. $85,000.   (Editors, 1460)

36. Cost of goods manufactured in May was
a. $109,000.
b. $112,000.
c. $115,000.
d. $118,000.   (Editors, 1461)

37. In job cost systems, manufacturing overhead is

	An indirect cost of jobs	A necessary element in production
a.	No	Yes
b.	No	No
c.	Yes	Yes
d.	Yes	No

(11/91, Theory, #41, amended, 2549)

38. Given that demand exceeds capacity, that there is no spoilage or waste, and that there is full utilization of a constant number of assembly hours, the number of components needed for an assembly operation with an 80 percent learning curve should

I. Increase for successive periods.
II. Decrease per unit of output.

a. I only.
b. II only.
c. Both I and II.
d. Neither I nor II.   (R/01, AR, #17, 7002)

39. Mat Co. estimated its material handling costs at two activity levels as follows:

Kilos handled	Cost
80,000	$160,000
60,000	132,000

What is the estimated cost for handling 75,000 kilos?
a. $150,000
b. $153,000
c. $157,500
d. $165,000   (5/94, AR, #36, amended, 4641)

40. In the profit-volume chart below, EF and GH represent the profit-volume graphs of a single-product company for 20X1 and 20X2, respectively.

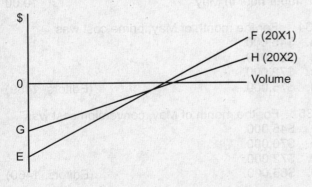

If 20X1 and 20X2 unit sales prices are identical, how did total fixed costs and unit variable costs of 20X2 change compared to 20X1?

	20X2 Total fixed costs	20X2 Unit variable costs
a.	Decreased	Increased
b.	Decreased	Decreased
c.	Increased	Increased
d.	Increased	Decreased

(5/91, Theory, #49, amended, 9232)

41. Briar Co. signed a government construction contract providing for a formula price of actual cost plus 10%. In addition, Briar was to receive one-half of any savings resulting from the formula price being less than the target price of $2,200,000. Briar's actual costs incurred were $1,920,000. How much should Briar receive from the contract?
a. $2,060,000
b. $2,112,000
c. $2,156,000
d. $2,200,000   (5/94, AR, #48, 4653)

42. Del Co. has fixed costs of $100,000 and break-even sales of $800,000. What is its projected profit at $1,200,000 sales?
a. $ 50,000
b. $150,000
c. $200,000
d. $400,000   (5/95, AR, #39, 5457)

43. The contribution margin ratio always increases when the
a. Variable costs as a percentage of net sales increase.
b. Variable costs as a percentage of net sales decrease.
c. Break-even point decreases.
d. Break-even point increases.   (Editors, 2223)

44. The following information pertains to Casa Co.'s cost-volume-profit relationships:

Break-even point in units sold	1,000
Variable costs per unit	$ 500
Total fixed costs	$300,000

How much will be contributed to profit before income taxes by the 1,001st unit sold?
a. $1,300
b. $1,000
c. $ 300
d. $0   (Editors, 1444)

45. At the break-even point, the contribution margin equals total
a. Variable costs.
b. Sales revenues.
c. Selling and administrative costs.
d. Fixed costs.   (11/93, Theory, #48, 4553)

46. The following information is taken from Wampler Co.'s contribution income statement:

Sales	$200,000
Contribution margin	120,000
Fixed costs	90,000
Income taxes	12,000

What was Wampler's margin of safety?
a. $ 50,000
b. $150,000
c. $168,000
d. $182,000   (5/98, AR, #8, amended, 6645)

47. The following information pertains to Syl Co.:

Sales	$800,000
Variable costs	160,000
Fixed costs	40,000

What is Syl's break-even point in sales dollars?
a. $200,000
b. $160,000
c. $ 50,000
d. $ 40,000   (11/92, PII, #36, 3370)

48. Break-even analysis assumes that over the relevant range
a. Unit revenues are nonlinear.
b. Unit variable costs are unchanged.
c. Total costs are unchanged.
d. Total fixed costs are nonlinear.
        (11/95, AR, #44, 5787)

49. Lake Company increased its direct labor wage rates. All other budgeted costs and revenues were unchanged. How did this increase affect Lake's budgeted break-even point and budgeted margin of safety?

	Budgeted break-even point	Budgeted margin of safety
a.	Increase	Increase
b.	Increase	Decrease
c.	Decrease	Decrease
d.	Decrease	Increase

        (5/92, Theory, #54, amended, 2747)

50. The following information pertains to Clove Company:

Budgeted sales	$1,000,000
Break-even sales	700,000
Budgeted contribution margin	600,000
Cashflow break-even	200,000

Clove's margin of safety is
a. $300,000.
b. $400,000.
c. $500,000.
d. $800,000.   (5/92, PII, #50, amended, 2682)

51. At December 31, Caine Co. had a machine with an original cost of $104,000, accumulated depreciation of $70,000, and an estimated salvage value of zero. On December 31, Caine was considering the purchase of a new machine having a five-year life, costing $130,000, and having an estimated salvage value of $30,000 at the end of five years. In its decision concerning the possible purchase of the new machine, how much should Caine consider as sunk cost at December 31?
a. $130,000
b. $100,000
c. $ 34,000
d. $ 4,000   (Editors, 1448)

52. The manufacturing capacity of Gorb Company's facilities is 30,000 units of product a year. A summary of operating results for the calendar year 20X1 is as follows:

Sales (18,000 units @ $50)	$ 900,000
Variable manufacturing and selling costs	(495,000)
Contribution margin	405,000
Fixed costs	(247,500)
Operating income	$ 157,500

A foreign distributor has offered to buy 15,000 units at $45 per unit during 20X2. Assume that all of Gorb's costs would be at the same levels and rates in 20X2 as in 20X1. If Gorb accepted this offer and rejected some business from regular customers so as not to exceed capacity, what would be the total operating income for 20X2?
a. $195,000
b. $352,500
c. $420,000
d. $427,500   (Editors, 1449)

53. Dale Company manufactures products Dee and Eff from a joint process. Product Dee has been allocated $5,000 of total joint costs of $40,000 for the 1,000 units produced. Dee can be sold at the split-off point for $6 per unit, or it can be processed further with additional costs of $2,000 and sold for $10 per unit. If Dee is processed further and sold, the result would be
a. A break-even situation.
b. An additional gain of $2,000 from further processing.
c. An overall loss of $2,000.
d. An additional gain of $4,000 from further processing. (Editors, 9239)

54. Rice Co. plans to discontinue a department with a $24,000 contribution to overhead, and allocated overhead of $48,000, of which $21,000 cannot be eliminated. What would be the effect of this discontinuance on Rice's pretax profit?
a. Increase of $24,000
b. Decrease of $24,000
c. Increase of $3,000
d. Decrease of $3,000 (Editors, 9240)

ITEMS 55 AND 56 are based on the following:

Sand Company has a calendar fiscal year and produces a single product that sells for $20 per unit. Sand uses an actual (historical) cost system. In the first year of operations, 100,000 units were produced and 80,000 units were sold. There was no work-in-process inventory at December 31. Manufacturing costs and selling and administrative expenses were as follows:

	Fixed costs	Variable costs
Raw materials	--	$4.00 per unit produced
Direct labor	--	2.50 per unit produced
Factory overhead	$240,000	1.50 per unit produced
Selling and administrative	140,000	2.00 per unit sold

55. What is Sand's operating income under the variable (direct) costing method?
a. $228,000
b. $420,000
c. $468,000
d. $660,000 (Editors, 1478)

56. What is Sand's finished goods inventory at December 31, under the absorption costing method?
a. $160,000
b. $208,000
c. $220,000
d. $248,000 (Editors, 1479)

57. A manufacturing company prepares income statements using both absorption and variable costing methods. At the end of a period actual sales revenues, total gross profit, and total contribution margin approximated budgeted figures, whereas net income was substantially greater than the budgeted amount. There were no beginning or ending inventories. The most likely explanation of the net income increase is that, compared to budget, actual
a. Manufacturing fixed costs had increased.
b. Selling and administrative fixed expenses had decreased.
c. Sales prices and variable costs had increased proportionately.
d. Sales prices had declined proportionately less than variable costs. (5/93, Theory, #45, 4232)

ITEMS 58 AND 59 are based on the following information concerning the operations of Gordon Company for its initial calendar year. There were no work-in-process inventories at year-end.

Units produced	10,000
Units sold	9,000
Direct materials used	$20,000
Direct labor incurred	$10,000
Fixed factory overhead	$12,500
Variable factory overhead	$ 6,000
Fixed selling and administrative expenses	$15,000
Variable selling and administrative expenses	$ 2,250
Finished goods inventory, January 1	None

58. What is Gordon's finished goods inventory cost at December 31, under the variable (direct) costing method?
a. $3,600
b. $3,825
c. $4,000
d. $4,850 (Editors, 1480)

59. Which costing method, absorption or variable costing, would show a higher annual operating income and by what amount?

	Costing method	Amount
a.	Absorption costing	$1,250
b.	Variable costing	$1,250
c.	Absorption costing	$2,750
d.	Variable costing	$2,750

(Editors, 1481)

60. Cay Co.'s fixed manufacturing overhead costs totaled $100,000, and variable selling costs totaled $80,000. Under direct costing, how should these costs be classified?

	Period costs	Product costs
a.	$0	$180,000
b.	$ 80,000	$100,000
c.	$100,000	$ 80,000
d.	$180,000	$0

(11/92, PII, #33, amended, 3367)

61. Lynn Manufacturing Co. prepares income statements using both standard absorption and standard variable costing methods. For 20X2, unit standard costs were unchanged from 20X1. In 20X2, the only beginning and ending inventories were finished goods of 5,000 units. How would Lynn's ratios using absorption costing compare with those using variable costing?

	Current Ratio	Return on Stockholders' Equity
a.	Same	Same
b.	Same	Smaller
c.	Greater	Same
d.	Greater	Smaller

(11/95, AR, #56, amended, 5799)

62. Dowell Co. manufactures a wooden item. Which of the following is included with the inventoriable cost under absorption costing and excluded from the inventoriable cost under variable costing?
a. Cost of electricity used to operate production machinery
b. Straight-line depreciation on factory equipment
c. Cost of scrap pieces of lumber
d. Wages of assembly line personnel

(11/98, AR, #23, 6689)

63. During May, Kern Co. produced and sold 10,000 units of a product. Manufacturing and selling costs incurred during May were as follows:

Direct materials and direct labor	$200,000
Variable manufacturing overhead	45,000
Fixed manufacturing overhead	10,000
Variable selling costs	5,000

The product's unit cost under direct (variable) costing was
a. $24.50.
b. $25.00.
c. $25.50.
d. $26.00.

(Editors, 1475)

64. Operating income using direct costing as compared to absorption costing would be higher
a. When the quantity of beginning inventory is less than the quantity of ending inventory.
b. When the quantity of beginning inventory is more than the quantity of ending inventory.
c. When the quantity of beginning inventory equals the quantity of ending inventory.
d. Under no circumstances. (Editors, 9252)

65. In an income statement prepared using the variable costing method, fixed factory overhead would
a. Not be used.
b. Be treated the same as variable factory overhead.
c. Be used in the computation of operating income but not in the computation of the contribution margin.
d. Be used in the computation of the contribution margin. (Editors, 2199)

OTHER OBJECTIVE FORMAT QUESTIONS

PROBLEM 24-3 (40 to 50 minutes)

Asta, Inc., is a medical laboratory that performs tests for physicians. Asta anticipates performing between 5,000 and 12,000 tests during the month of April.

Compared to industry averages, at the low range of activity Asta has a lower sales price per test, higher fixed costs, and the same break-even point in number of tests performed. At the high range of activity, Asta's sales price per test and fixed costs are the same as industry averages, and Asta's variable costs are lower. At the low range of activity (0 to 4,999 tests performed) fixed costs are $160,000. At the high range of activity (5,000 to 14,999 tests performed) fixed costs are $200,000.

Sales price per test	$60
Variable costs per test	20

ITEMS 1 THROUGH 8 represent costs incurred by Asta. Two responses are required for each item: determine how the cost should be categorized from the given list and indicate if the cost is fixed (F) or variable (V).

Categories
A. Direct materials cost
B. Direct labor cost
C. Overhead cost for testing
D. General and administrative cost

1. Office manager's salary
2. Cost of electricity to run laboratory equipment

3. Hourly wages of part-time technicians who perform tests
4. Cost of lubricant used on laboratory equipment
5. Cost of distilled water used in tests
6. Accelerated depreciation on laboratory equipment
7. Straight-line depreciation on laboratory building
8. Cost of expensive binders in which test results are given to physicians

FOR ITEMS 9 THROUGH 12, calculate the amount.

9. Contribution margin per test
10. Break-even point in number of tests at low activity range
11. Break-even point in number of tests at high activity range
12. Number of units sold to achieve a gross profit of $160,000

ITEMS 13 THROUGH 15 refer to Asta's costs in comparison to industry averages. For each item, indicate if Asta's costs are greater than (G), lesser than (L), or the same as (S) the industry average.

13. Variable costs at low activity range
14. Contribution margin at high activity range
15. Break-even point at high activity range
            (11/93, PII, #4, amended, 4490-4501)

PROBLEM 24-4 (5 to 10 minutes)

The following information pertains to a product for a 10-week budget period:

- Manufacturing and sales of 70,000 units are expected to occur evenly over the period.
- Materials are paid for in the week following use.
- There are no beginning inventories.

Sales price	$11 per unit
Materials	$3 per unit
Manufacturing conversion costs—Fixed	$210,000
Variable	$2 per unit
Selling and administrative costs—Fixed	$45,000
Variable	$1 per unit
Beginning accounts payable for materials	$40,000

Determine the correct amount using the accompanying information. Any information contained in an item is unique to that item and is **not** to be incorporated in your calculations when answering other items.

1. What amount should be budgeted for cash payments to material suppliers during the period?
2. Using variable costing, what is the budgeted income for the period?
3. Using absorption costing, what is the budgeted income for the period?
4. Actual results are as budgeted, except that 60,000 of the 70,000 units produced were sold Using absorption costing, what is the difference between the reported income and the budgeted net income?
5. If a special order for 4,000 units would cause a loss of 1,000 regular sales, what minimum amount of revenue must be generated from the special order so that net income is not reduced? (All cost relationships are unchanged.)
            (11/96, AR, #4, 6329-6333)

SOLUTION 24-1 MULTIPLE CHOICE ANSWERS

COST CLASSIFICATION

1. (a) Direct costs can be traced easily to a cost object. Value-adding costs are costs for which a customer would be willing to pay. The payments to the employees who develop computer programs can be traced easily to the cost of the computer programs. Costs incurred for employees who work directly on a product desired by a customer are value-adding costs. Therefore, the payments are both direct and value-adding costs.

2. (a) With beginning WIP of $12,000, direct materials added of $20,000, and cost of goods manufactured of $97,000, the only way to have an ending WIP balance of $10,000 is to add $75,000 of direct labor (DL) and factory overhead (FOH) combined. FOH is assigned at 1½ the rate of DL, so 1.5 DL + 1.0 DL = $75,000 and so 2.5 DL = $75,000 and thus DL = $75,000 / 2.5 = $30,000.

3. (d) Since total fixed costs remain constant within the relevant range of activity, an increase in the level of production decreases the fixed costs per unit because the same total fixed costs are allocated over more units. Variable costs do not change on a per unit basis with changes in the level of activity within the relevant range.

COST ESTIMATION

4.   (a)   The high month is March with 1,800 orders at a cost of $4,320. The low month is January with 1,200 orders at a cost of $3,120. The estimated variable order filling cost can be obtained by dividing the change in cost by the change in orders, because only variable costs change in total with a change in the order volume.

$$\frac{\$4,320 - \$3,120}{1,800 - 1,200} = \frac{\$1,200}{600} = \$2/\text{order}$$

CVP CHARTS

5.   (c)   The variable cost per parcel is determined using the high-low method by dividing the change in total costs by the change in number of parcels: ($75,000 – $15,000) / (20,000 parcels – 0 parcels) = $60,000 / 20,000 parcels = $3/parcel. The fixed costs are the amount of total cost when no parcels are mailed. The total variable costs are $36,000 ($3/parcel x 12,000 parcels). The estimated total cost for mailing parcels is equal to the fixed costs plus the total variable costs, or $15,000 + $36,000 = $51,000.

6.   (a)   Total actual sales equaled budgeted sales and sales prices and cost behavior were as budgeted. Thus, the increase in profit cannot be due to additional sales, and neither the contribution margin per unit of either of the products nor total fixed costs changed. The only plausible explanation of the increase in profit is that the sales mix of the two products changed. Total sales must have consisted of a greater percentage of the high contribution margin product and a lower percentage of the low contribution margin product. Since profit line EH for Product 1 has a steeper slope than profit line HG for Product 2, Product 1 has a higher contribution margin. Thus, actual sales of Product 1 must have exceeded budgeted sales while actual sales of Product 2 must have been less than budgeted sales. Point E, the point at which the profit line intersects the vertical axis, represents total fixed costs. Point F, the point at which the profit line intersects the horizontal axis, represents the break-even level of sales because there is no profit or loss at this level of activity. At the break-even point, contribution margin equals total fixed costs. Therefore, Line OE represents total contribution margin at the break-even point. Line OF represents the sales volume at the break-even point. Thus, Line OE (total contribution margin at the break-even point) divided by Line OF (sales volume at the break-even point) represents the average contribution margin percentage.

7.   (d)   Cost-volume-profit (CVP) analysis assumes that both the selling price and variable cost per unit do not change with volume changes; therefore, variable costs are the same percentage of sales revenues at points A and B. CVP analysis also assumes that fixed costs remain unchanged over the relevant range. Therefore, fixed costs are a greater percentage of revenues at point A than point B because revenues are lower at point A.

COMPUTATIONAL METHODS

8.   (c)   The break-even point is computed by dividing fixed costs by the contribution margin. Since fixed costs is the numerator of the formula, a decrease in fixed costs would *decrease* the break-even point. Since contribution margin is the denominator of the formula, an increase in this amount would also *decrease* the break-even point.

9.   (c)   Let F = sales price of the food only.

Let   C   =   Service charge = 0.15F
      T   =   Sales tax   = 0.06 (F + 0.15F)
                             = 0.06 (1.15F) = .069F

$60   =   F + C + T
$60   =   F + 0.15F + 0.069F = 1.219F
F   = $60 / 1.219 = $49.22

10.   (a)   Let X = number of radios sold.

X – Variable expenses – Fixed expenses = Operating income
$30X – $20X – $15,000 = $35,000
$10X = $50,000
X = 5,000 radios sold

11.   (c)   Let X = dollar amount of sales.

X – Variable expenses – Fixed expenses = Operating income
X – ($20/$30)X – $15,000 = $0
1/3 X = $15,000
X = $45,000

BREAK-EVEN ANALYSIS

12.   (b)   Margin of safety (MOS) equals actual sales less break-even (BE) sales; thus, actual sales less MOS equals BE point sales. At BE point, sales are $120,000 ($200,000 – $80,000) and total contribution margin (CM) equals $24,000 ($120,000 x 20%). At BE point, CM equals fixed cost.

13.   (c)   Dividing the annual sales by the sales price provides the annual budgeted units [$900,000 / $20/unit = 45,000 units] used for determining fixed costs. Thus, annual fixed costs are ($7 + $3) x 45,000 units = $450,000. The breakeven point is that point at which there is zero profit. Sales minus variable and fixed costs equals profit. If X is the

number of units at the breakeven point, ($20/unit − $8/unit) * X − $450,000 = 0; or X = $450,000 / 12 = 37,500 units. Candidates also may use trial and error with the responses to determine the answer.

14. (a) Let P = the target price per unit necessary to realize a 15% profit margin on sales.

500P	− $990,000	=	0.15(500)P
500P	− $990,000	=	75P
	425P	=	$990,000
	P	=	$2,329.41 or approx. $2,329

RELEVANT COSTS

15. (c) Incremental cost is the difference in total cost between the two alternatives. The total amount of fixed costs does not differ between the two alternatives.

16. (b) The carrying amount of the old machine is irrelevant because it is a sunk (historical) cost. The disposal value of the new machine is relevant because it is an expected future cash inflow that differs between alternatives.

SPECIAL ORDER

17. (b) The fixed costs are not relevant to the decision as they remain constant in total whether or not Clay Co. accepts the special order. The relevant costs are the variable costs and the additional cost of using the external designers.

Variable costs	$33,000
Plus: Cost of using external designers	7,750
Minimum acceptable price	$40,750

18. (c) When only differential manufacturing costs are taken into account for special order pricing, it is essential to assume that acceptance of the order will not affect regular sales. It is not necessary to assume that costs are linear or that they will not change.

MAKE OR BUY DECISIONS

19. (b) The fixed overhead that would continue ($6 x 2/3) even if Part 10541 is purchased is irrelevant to the decision to make or buy.

Direct materials	$ 2
Direct labor	8
Variable overhead	4
Fixed overhead eliminated ($6 x 1/3)	2
Incremental (total relevant) unit cost	$ 16
Times: Units to be manufactured	x 5,000
Incremental cost to manufacture 5,000 units	$80,000

20. (a) The incremental costs to manufacture Part 10541 must be compared to the net cost of purchasing the part. It is $11,000 (i.e., $91,000 − $80,000) cheaper to manufacture the part.

Incremental manufacturing cost (Question #19)	$80,000
Purchase price of 5,000 units (5,000 x $19)	95,000
Less: Operating profit generated in the manufacture of Product RAC	(4,000)
Net cost of purchasing Part 10541	$91,000

SCRAP OR REWORK

21. (b) The $27,000 ($35,000 − $8,000) of incremental revenues exceed the $20,000 incremental rework costs.

SELL OR PROCESS FURTHER

22. (c) Product Y can be sold for a revenues of $120 ($3 / lb. x 40 lb.) or used to create 30 lbs. of Z that can be sold for revenues of $180 ($6 / lb. x 30 lb.) less additional costs of $60 = $120. There is no increase or decrease to profits from processing product Y into Z. The cost of raw material W assigned to Y is irrelevant.

ELIMINATE LINE OR DIVISION

23. (a) All amounts relative to East Division through "Margin over direct costs" would be eliminated if the division were eliminated. Therefore, the $20,000 margin would be lost, and income would be reduced by that amount. Note that the $45,000 allocated corporate costs would *not* be eliminated.

PRODUCT PRICING

24. (b) If actual cost or actual cost plus a markup is used, the selling division can pass on inefficiencies to the buying division. Negotiated price may not result in the most efficient transfer pricing, due to inequities in negotiating power. Standard variable cost should be used since the selling division is a cost center and has no incentive to make a profit on the transfer. Furthermore, with standard variable costing, inefficiencies will not be passed on to the buying division, which is concerned with profits.

25. (d) In pricing the new device, the quality and life of the new device should be considered, along with customers' relative preference for quality compared to price.

DIRECT VS. ABSORPTION COSTING

26. (d) Under the variable costing method only variable production costs are treated as inventoriable or product costs. Fixed overhead cost is treated as a period cost. Variable factory overhead costs are assigned to inventory. However, under variable costing, as well as under absorption costing, selling and administrative costs (whether

variable or fixed) are period costs, not product costs assigned to inventory.

27. (d) When there are products competing for a scarce resource, the company should produce and sell the product that has the greater contribution margin per unit of the scarce resource. In this case, manufacturing capacity is the scarce resource. Therefore, Jago Co. should manufacture the product with the greater contribution margin per hour of manufacturing capacity. This will result in a greater total contribution margin and thus a greater short-run profit.

28. (c) Using absorption costing, break-even analysis assumes: (I) sales volume equals production volume (i.e., inventory levels remain constant), (II) unit variable costs are unchanged over the relevant range and (III) a given sales mix is maintained for all volume changes. Using direct costing, no fixed manufacturing costs are applied to inventory because all fixed costs are expensed when incurred. Hence, it does not matter if sales volume equals production volume.

29. (d) Variable sales and administration expenses are used in both the computation of the contribution margin and the computation of operating income. The format of an income statement prepared using variable costing is as follows:

Sales		$XXX
Less variable expenses:		
Production	$XXX	
Selling and administrative	XXX	XXX
Contribution margin		XXX
Less fixed expenses:		
Production	XXX	
Selling and administrative	XXX	XXX
Operating income		$XXX

30. (a) The only difference between variable (or direct) and full absorption costing income is the treatment of fixed manufacturing costs. Variable costing expenses the full $180,000. Full absorption costing includes a share of the fixed manufacturing costs in inventory for the 20,000 finished but unsold units. (20,000 units x $180,000 / 100,000 units = $36,000)

SOLUTION 24-2 ADDITIONAL MULTIPLE CHOICE ANSWERS

COST CLASSIFICATION

31. (b) A direct labor overtime premium is generally considered to be attributable to the heavy overall volume of work, and its cost is thus regarded as part of manufacturing overhead, which is borne by all units produced. Sometimes the direct labor overtime premium is not random. For example, a special or rush job may clearly be the sole source of the overtime. In such instances, the premium is regarded as a direct cost of the products made for that job.

32. (d) Direct labor includes all labor that is physically traceable to the finished goods in an economically feasible manner. The labor of a factory machine operator (e.g., a loom operator) and an assembler are common examples of direct labor. Since wages paid to factory foremen and machine mechanics are not physically traceable to the finished goods in an economically feasible manner, they would be included in manufacturing overhead.

33. (b) Direct materials are those materials that are traceable to and an integral part of the finished good. Direct labor is factory labor that is traceable to specific products. Factory overhead is the sum of all indirect product costs (i.e., all product costs except direct materials and direct labor).

Therefore, the costs that are traced to specific products in the production process is the sum of the direct materials and direct labor costs.

34. (d) Prime cost is the sum of direct materials cost and direct labor cost.

Beginning inventory	$18,000
Add: Purchases	42,000
Direct materials available for use	60,000
Less: Ending inventory	(15,000)
Direct materials used in production	$45,000
Direct labor cost (given)	30,000
Prime cost incurred	$75,000

35. (b) Conversion cost is the sum of direct labor cost and manufacturing overhead cost.

Direct labor cost (given)		$30,000
Direct labor cost	$30,000	
Direct labor rate per hour	÷ $7.50	
Direct labor hours incurred	4,000	
Factory overhead rate per direct labor hour	x $10.00	
Manufacturing overhead cost applied		40,000
Conversion cost incurred		$70,000

36. (d)

Beginning work-in-process		$ 9,000
Direct materials cost	$45,000	
Direct labor cost	30,000	
Overhead cost applied	40,000	
Manufacturing costs added		115,000
Manufacturing costs to account for		$124,000
Ending work-in-process		(6,000)
Cost of goods manufactured		$118,000

37. (c) Direct materials, direct labor, and manufacturing overhead are the three major elements in the cost of a manufactured product. Manufacturing overhead consists of all manufacturing costs other than direct materials and direct labor.

38. (a) This learning curve pertains to the assembly operation. As workers learn to assemble components faster, they will assemble more components per period in successive time periods. Learning how to assemble components faster has no effect on the number of components needed to produce a unit of output.

COST ESTIMATION

39. (b) The variable cost (VC) per kilo handled can be estimated by dividing the change in cost by the change in kilos handled. Thus, the estimated VC per kilo handled is $1.40 ($28,000 / 20,000 kilos handled). The total VC can be obtained by multiplying the VC per kilo handled times the number of kilos handled. The total cost less the total VC equals the fixed cost. The VC cost for the 75,000 kilos handled can be estimated by multiplying the 75,000 kilos handled by the $1.40 VC per kilo handled. Adding the total VC and the fixed cost gives the total estimated cost for handling 75,000 kilos.

Change in cost: $160,000 – $132,000 = $28,000
Change in kilos handled: 80,000 – 60,000 = 20,000

Total cost	$ 160,000	$132,000
Less: Total variable cost		
80,000 K x $1.40/K	(112,000)	
60,000 K x $1.40/K		(84,000)
Fixed cost	$ 48,000	$ 48,000

Total variable cost (75,000 K x $1.40/K)	$105,000
Fixed cost	48,000
Total estimated cost for 75,000 K	$153,000

CVP CHARTS

40. (a) Lines EF and GH depict profit lines for 20X1 and 20X2, respectively. Points E and G, the points at which the profit lines intersect the vertical axis, represent the total fixed costs for 20X1 and 20X2, respectively, because there are no variable costs at zero volume. Since Line OG (20X2) is less than Line OE (20X1), total fixed costs decreased in

20X2. The profit lines slope upward from the fixed cost points at the rate of the unit contribution margin. Since the 20X2 profit line (GH) has a less steep slope than the 20X1 profit line (EF), the unit contribution margin decreased in 20X2, meaning that variable costs increased in 20X2.

COMPUTATIONAL METHODS

41. (c)

Actual costs incurred		$1,920,000
Plus: Markup (10%)		192,000
Formula price		$2,112,000
Target price	$ 2,200,000	
Less: Formula price	(2,112,000)	
Savings	$ 88,000	
Additional revenues	x 50%	44,000
Amount Briar should receive		$2,156,000

42. (a) The contribution margin equals fixed costs at the break-even point. Thus, the contribution margin is also $100,000 at the break-even point. The contribution margin ratio is the contribution margin divided by sales. The contribution margin ratio computes to 12.5% ($100,000 ÷ $800,000). Multiplying the sales in dollars by the contribution margin ratio gives the contribution margin in dollars. Because fixed costs remain constant in total when volume changes, the fixed costs can be subtracted from the contribution margin to determine the profit.

Sales		$1,200,000
Times: Contribution margin ratio		x 12.5%
Contribution margin		$ 150,000
Less: Fixed costs		(100,000)
Profit		$ 50,000

43. (b) Questions of this type are usually best answered by setting forth the equation for the required variable (i.e., contribution margin ratio in this case) and then analyzing the effect of changes in the other variables. Based on the equation below, you can easily see that a decrease in variable costs would increase the contribution margin ratio.

$$\frac{\text{Contribution}}{\text{margin ratio}} = \frac{\text{Sales} - \text{Variable costs}}{\text{Sales}}$$

44. (c) For each unit sold above the break-even point, the company will obtain net income equal to the CM / U. Therefore, the 1,001[st] unit sold will contribute $300 to profits before income taxes.

$$\frac{\text{Break-even}}{\text{(units)}} = \frac{\text{Fixed costs}}{\text{Contribution margin per unit}}$$

$$1,000 \text{ units} = \frac{\$300,000}{\text{CM / unit}}$$

CM / unit = $300,000 / 1,000 units = $300 per unit

BREAK-EVEN ANALYSIS

45. (d) Contribution margin less fixed costs equals operating income. At the break-even point, operating income is zero. At the break-even point, the contribution margin equals fixed costs.

46. (a) The margin of safety is actual sales less break-even (BE) sales ($200,000 – $150,000 = $50,000). BE sales are sales equal to the sum of variable and fixed costs. The variable manufacturing costs at actual sales (actual sales less the actual contribution margin, or $200,000 – $120,000 = $80,000) are ($80,000 / $200,000 =) 40% of sales. Income taxes generally are not included in calculating the margin of safety. Let SB = break-even sales and F = fixed costs, then .4SB = variable costs (at break-even sales), and

$$SB = 0.4SB + F$$
$$0.6SB = F = \$90,000$$
$$SB = \$90,000 / 0.6 = \$150,000$$

47. (c) To compute the break-even point in sales dollars, the contribution margin percentage must first be computed. The contribution margin percentage is 80% [i.e., ($800,000 sales – $160,000 variable costs) ÷ $800,000 sales)].

$$\text{Break-even point in dollars} = \frac{\text{Fixed costs}}{\text{Contribution margin percentage}}$$

$$= \$40,000 / 80\% = \mathbf{\$50,000}$$

48. (b) Break-even analysis assumes that costs behave in a linear relationship within the relevant range. Break-even analysis assumes that fixed costs remain constant in total and that variable costs are fixed or unchanged on a per-unit basis.

49. (b) The increase in the direct labor wage rates increased the variable cost per unit, thereby decreasing the contribution margin ratio because the selling price per unit is unchanged. With unchanged budgeted fixed costs and a decreased contribution margin ratio, the budgeted break-even point increases. The margin of safety is the excess of budgeted revenues over the level of revenues at the break-even point. Since budgeted revenues were unchanged and the budgeted break-even point increased, the budgeted margin of safety decreased.

50. (a) The margin of safety is the excess of budgeted revenues over the level of revenues at the break-even point (i.e., $1,000,000 – $700,000).

SPECIAL DECISIONS

51. (c) Sunk costs are costs incurred as a result of past decisions and *not* relevant to future decisions. The carrying amount of the machine ($104,000 – $70,000) is a sunk cost with no bearing on the decision to keep or replace the machine.

52. (b) Variable costs per unit are $27.50 ($495,000 / 18,000 units)

	Regular sales (15,000 units)	Special order (15,000 units)	Total (30,000 units)
Sales	$ 750,000	$ 675,000	$1,425,000
Variable costs	(412,500)	(412,500)	(825,000)
Contribution margin	$ 337,500	$ 262,500	$ 600,000
Fixed costs			(247,500)
Operating income			$ 352,500

53. (b) The $5,000 of joint costs allocated to the product is *irrelevant* to the decision whether to subject the product to further processing.

Incremental revenues [1,000 x ($10 – $6)]	$ 4,000
Additional costs	(2,000)
Additional gain from further processing	$ 2,000

54. (c) The department contributes $24,000 to overhead. Allocated overhead amounts to $48,000, of which $21,000 cannot be eliminated; thus, $27,000 of overhead can be eliminated by discontinuing the department. This will *increase* Rice's pretax profit by $3,000 (i.e., $27,000 – $24,000).

DIRECT VS. ABSORPTION COSTING

55. (b) Under variable (direct) costing, direct materials, direct labor, and variable manufacturing overhead are product costs, i.e., they are not expensed until the produced item is sold. Fixed manufacturing overhead and all selling and administrative costs are expensed in the period incurred. Sand's operating income under variable costing can be computed as follows:

Sales (80,000 units @ $20 per unit)		$1,600,000
Less: Var. mfg. costs [80,000 x		
($4.00 + $2.50 + $1.50)]	$(640,000)	
Var. S & A (80,000 x $2/unit)	(160,000)	(800,000)
Contribution margin		$ 800,000
Less: Fixed manufacturing costs		(240,000)
Fixed selling and administrative		(140,000)
Operating income		$ 420,000

56. (b) Under absorption costing, all manufacturing costs are product costs (and thus inventoriable). The variable manufacturing costs that attach to each produced unit total $8 ($4.00 raw materials + $2.50 direct labor + $1.50 variable overhead). The fixed manufacturing cost that attaches to each produced unit equals $2.40 ($240,000 fixed overhead / 100,000 units). With each unit having

$10.40 of costs (variable + fixed) attaching to it, the ending inventory (100,000 units produced – 80,000 units sold) would be carried on the books at $208,000 (20,000 units x $10.40 per unit).

57.	(b)	The following income statement formats show that operating income is measured under both absorption costing and variable costing.

Absorption Costing Method		
Sales		$XX
Less: Cost of goods sold		XX
Gross margin		XX
Selling	$XX	
Administrative	XX	
Less operating expenses:		XX
Operating income		$XX

Variable Costing Method		
Sales		$XX
Variable production	$XX	
Variable selling	XX	
Variable administrative	XX	
Less variable costs:		XX
Contribution margin		XX
Fixed production	XX	
Fixed selling	XX	
Fixed administrative	XX	
Less fixed costs:		XX
Operating income		$XX

With respect to the income statement prepared using the variable costing method, the manufacturing company's sales revenues and total contribution margin approximated budgeted figures; therefore, the company's total variable expenses also approximated budgeted figures. Thus, it is unlikely that the higher net income figure was due to a decrease in variable manufacturing or variable selling and administrative expenses. With respect to the income statement prepared using the absorption costing method, sales revenues and gross profit approximated budgeted figures; therefore, the company's total manufacturing expenses also approximated budgeted figures. Thus, it is also unlikely that the higher net income figure was due to a decrease in fixed manufacturing expenses. Since it is unlikely that the higher net income figure was due to a decrease in either variable manufacturing expenses, variable selling and administrative expenses, or fixed manufacturing expenses, the most likely explanation of the higher net income figure is that fixed selling and administrative expenses had decreased.

58.	(a)	Using direct costing, only variable production costs are inventoriable. Fixed factory overhead is expensed when incurred as a period cost.

Direct materials	$20,000
Direct labor	10,000
Variable factory overhead	6,000
Total variable production costs	$36,000
Portion allocated to ending inventory (1,000 ÷ 10,000)	x .10
Cost of ending inventory	$ 3,600

59.	(a)	Under variable costing, the entire fixed factory overhead is charged to expense as a period cost. Under absorption costing, fixed factory overhead is a product cost (i.e., an inventoriable cost) and is expensed only to the extent included in cost of goods sold. The portion of fixed overhead allocated to goods not sold during the period becomes part of the ending inventory for the period.

FOH expensed, variable costing	$ 12,500
FOH expensed, absorption costing (9/10 x $12,500)	(11,250)
Excess expense recognized under variable costing	$ 1,250

60.	(d)	Under direct costing, both the fixed manufacturing overhead costs and the variable selling costs are classified as period costs. Under direct costing, only variable manufacturing costs (i.e., direct materials, direct labor, and variable manufacturing overhead) are inventoried as product costs. Fixed manufacturing overhead and *all* selling and administrative costs are considered to be period costs, and are therefore expensed when incurred.

61.	(d)	When there is no change in standard costs and inventories, the absorption costing method and variable costing will give the same net income. However, the cost of inventory will be greater under absorption costing because inventory includes fixed overhead cost under absorption costing but not under variable costing. Inventory is a current asset. Costing methods have no effect on other current assets or on the amount of current liabilities. The current ratio is the ratio between current assets and current liabilities. Because inventory is greater under absorption costing, the current ratio will also be greater under absorption costing. Because inventory is greater under absorption costing, stockholders' equity will also be greater under absorption costing. Return on stockholders' equity is net income divided by stockholders' equity. Since the income is the same under both methods, the return on stockholders' equity will be smaller under absorption because of the greater denominator.

62.	(b)	Under direct (variable) costing only variable manufacturing costs are inventoried. Fixed manufacturing costs are expensed in the period incurred. Absorption costing includes all manufacturing costs in inventory.

63.	(a)	Under direct costing, only variable product costs (i.e., direct materials, direct labor, and variable manufacturing overhead) are inventoried. The fixed manufacturing overhead and variable selling costs are considered to be period costs (rather than product costs) and are expensed when incurred.

Direct materials and direct labor	$200,000
Variable manufacturing overhead	45,000
Total variable product costs	$245,000
Units produced during period	÷ 10,000
Unit cost under direct costing	$ 24.50

64. (b) When sales exceed production (i.e., the quantity of beginning inventory is more than ending inventory), the operating income reported using direct costing will generally be higher than operating income reported using absorption costing. When more inventory is sold than is produced, inventories are drawn down, and the amount of fixed manufacturing overhead cost released to expense using absorption costing is greater than the amount that was incurred during the period.

65. (c) Fixed factory overhead is used in the computation of operating income but *not* in the computation of the contribution margin. The format of an income statement using the variable costing method is as follows.

Sales		$XXX
Less variable expenses:		
Manufacturing	$XXX	
Selling and administrative	XXX	XXX
Contribution margin		XXX
Less fixed expenses:		
Manufacturing	XXX	
Selling and administrative	XXX	XXX
Operating income		$XXX

PERFORMANCE BY SUBTOPICS

Each category below parallels a subtopic covered in Chapter 24. Record the number and percentage of questions you correctly answered in each subtopic area.

Cost Classification

Question #	Correct √
1	
2	
3	
# Questions	3

Correct _____
% Correct _____

Cost Estimation

Question #	Correct √
4	
# Questions	1

Correct _____
% Correct _____

CVP Charts

Question #	Correct √
5	
6	
7	
# Questions	3

Correct _____
% Correct _____

Computational Methods

Question #	Correct √
8	
9	
10	
11	
# Questions	4

Correct _____
% Correct _____

Break-Even Analysis

Question #	Correct √
12	
13	
14	
# Questions	3

Correct _____
% Correct _____

Relevant Costs

Question #	Correct √
15	
16	
# Questions	2

Correct _____
% Correct _____

Special Order

Question #	Correct √
17	
18	
# Questions	2

Correct _____
% Correct _____

Make or Buy Decisions

Question #	Correct √
19	
20	
# Questions	2

Correct _____
% Correct _____

Scrap or Rework

Question #	Correct √
21	
# Questions	1

Correct _____
% Correct _____

Sell or Process Further

Question #	Correct √
22	
# Questions	1

Correct _____
% Correct _____

Eliminate Line or Division

Question #	Correct √
23	
# Questions	1

Correct _____
% Correct _____

Product Pricing

Question #	Correct √
24	
25	
# Questions	2

Correct _____
% Correct _____

Direct vs. Absorption Costing

Question #	Correct √
26	
27	
28	
29	
30	
# Questions	5

Correct _____
% Correct _____

OTHER OBJECTIVE FORMAT QUESTION SOLUTIONS

SOLUTION 24-3 TYPES OF COSTS

1. D, F The office manager's salary is a general and administrative cost. The office manager's salary will not be affected by the number of tests performed.

2. C, V Overhead cost for testing is the sum of all indirect costs of testing (i.e., all testing costs except direct materials and direct labor). Therefore, the cost of electricity to run laboratory equipment is an overhead cost for testing. The electricity to run laboratory equipment changes in total with a change in the number of tests; therefore, it is variable.

3. B, V Direct labor cost includes all labor that is physically traceable to the laboratory tests in an economically feasible manner. Therefore, the hourly wages of part-time technicians who perform tests is a direct labor cost. The wages will change in total with a change in the number of tests performed; therefore, it is variable.

4. C, V Overhead cost for testing is the sum of all indirect costs of testing. The cost of lubricant used on laboratory equipment is an overhead cost for testing. The cost of lubricant used on laboratory equipment changes in total with a change in the number of tests; therefore, it is variable.

5. A, V The water is physically traceable to the tests; therefore, it is a direct material cost. The water used in tests changes in total with a change in the number of tests; therefore, it is variable.

6. C, F Overhead cost is the sum of all indirect costs. Therefore, depreciation is an overhead cost. The amount of depreciation will not be affected by the number of tests; therefore, it is fixed.

7. C, F See the explanation to item #6.

8. A, V Direct material cost includes all materials that are traceable to the tests in an economically feasible manner. Therefore, the cost of the expensive binders is a direct material cost. The cost of the binders will change in total with a change in the number of tests; therefore, it is variable.

9. $40

Sales price per test	$ 60
Variable costs per test	(20)
Contribution margin per test	$ 40

10. 4,000

$$\text{Break-even point in units at low range of activity} = \frac{\text{Fixed costs for low range of activity}}{\text{Contribution margin per test}}$$

$$= \$160,000 \, / \, (\$60 - \$20)$$

$$= 4,000 \text{ tests}$$

The break-even point of 4,000 tests is within the low range of activity of 0 to 4,999 tests.

11. 5,000

$$\text{Break-even point in units at high range of activity} = \frac{\text{Fixed costs for high range of activity}}{\text{Contribution margin per test}}$$

$$= \$200,000 \, / \, (\$60 - \$20)$$

$$= 5,000 \text{ tests}$$

The break-even point of 5,000 tests is within the high range of activity of 5,000 to 14,999 tests.

12. 9,000

It must first be determined if Asta can achieve a gross profit of $160,000 at the low range of activity.

$$\text{Unit sales} = \frac{\text{Fixed costs at low range of activity + Desired profit}}{\text{Contribution margin per unit}}$$

$$= (\$160,000 + \$160,000) \, / \, (\$60 - \$20)$$

$$= 8,000 \text{ units}$$

Since 8,000 units exceeds the low range of 0 to 4,999 tests, Asta cannot achieve the desired gross profit at the low range of activity. Next, it must be determined if Asta can achieve the desired gross profit at the high range of activity. The required 9,000 unit sales is within the high range of activity of 5,000 to 14,999 tests.

$$\text{Unit sales} = \frac{\text{Fixed costs at high range of activity + Desired profit}}{\text{Contribution margin per unit}}$$

$$= (\$200,000 + \$160,000) \, / \, (\$60 - \$20)$$

$$= 9,000 \text{ units}$$

13. L At the low range of activity, Asta has the same break-even point in number of tests performed as the industry average, despite having higher fixed costs than the industry average. Therefore, Asta's contribution margin per test must be greater than the industry average at the low range of activity. Since Asta has a lower sales price

per test and a higher contribution margin per test than the industry average at the low range of activity, Asta's variable cost per test must be *lower* than the industry average at the low range of activity.

14. **G** At the high range of activity, Asta has the same sales price per test and lower variable costs per test as compared to the industry average. Therefore, Asta's contribution margin per test is greater than the industry average at the high range of activity. Asta's fixed costs are the same as industry averages at the high range of activity; therefore, since Asta's contribution margin per test is greater than the industry average at the high range of activity, Asta's break-even point in units is lower than the industry average at the high range of activity.

15. **L** At the high range of activity, Asta has the same sales price per test as the industry average and lower variable costs per test. Therefore, Asta's contribution margin per test is greater than the industry average at the high range. Asta's fixed costs are the same as industry averages at the high range of activity; therefore, since Asta's contribution margin per test is greater than the industry average at the high range of activity, Asta's break-even point in number of tests performed is lower than the industry average at the high range of activity.

SOLUTION 24-4 DIRECT COSTING & BUDGETING

1. $229,000

Beginning accounts payable	$ 40,000
9 payments ($3 x 7,000 units per week)	189,000
Total payments during the 10 weeks	$229,000

2. $95,000

As all units are produced and sold in the same period, direct and absorption costing produces the same income in this circumstance.

Sales per unit	$ 11
Variable costs per unit ($3 + $2 + $1)	6
Contribution margin per unit	$ 5
Times: Units	70,000
Contribution margin	$350,000
Fixed expenses ($210,000 + $45,000)	255,000
Budgeted income	$ 95,000

3. $95,000

Also see the explanation to #2.

Sales ($11 x 70)	$770
CGS: Variable ($5 x 70)	350
CGS: Fixed ($210 / 70 x 70)	210
Gross Income	$210
S&A [($1 x 70) + $45]	115
Budgeted Income (in 1,000s)	$ 95

4. $20,000

$95,000 − $75,000 = $20,000
Also see the explanation to #3.

Sales ($11 x 60)	$660
CGS: Variable ($5 x 60)	300
CGS: Fixed ($210 / 70 x 60)	180
Gross Income	$180
S&A [($1 x 60) + $45]	105
Actual Income (in 1,000s)	$ 75

5. $29,000

This question is answered by developing an income statement with the known values and "backing in" the unknown values. The fixed amounts will not change regardless of the amount of production or sales, if all production is sold. If the special order must generate net income of $5,000 (to keep total net income the same), then it must generate $9,000 of gross income and $29,000 of sales.

	Total	Regular	Special
Units	73	69	4
Sales (Regular $11/unit)	?	$759	?
CGS: Variable ($5/unit)	365	345	20
CGS: Fixed	210	210	-NA-
Gross Income	?	$204	?
S&A: Variable ($1/unit)	73	69	4
S&A: Fixed	45	45	-NA-
Actual Income	$ 95	$ 90	$ 5

Alternatively, 1,000 units lost of regular sales results in $5,000 lost contribution margin. The revenue from the special order must replace this lost margin, as well as covering variable costs of $6/unit. 4,000 units x $6/unit + $5,000 = $29,000

Post-Exam Diagnostics

The AICPA Board of Examiners' Advisory Grading Service provides state boards of accountancy with individual diagnostic reports for all candidates along with the candidates' grades. The diagnostic reports show the candidate's level of proficiency on each examination section. The boards of accountancy **may** mail the diagnostic reports to candidates along with their grades: candidates should contact the state board in their jurisdiction to find out its policy on this.

Remember that candidates are required to sign a statement of confidentiality in which they promise not to reveal questions or answers. Due to the nondisclosure requirements, Bisk Education's editors are no longer able to address questions about specific examination questions, although we continue to supply help with similar study problems and questions in our texts.

Grades are mailed approximately **90 days** after the examination.

See the **Practical Advice** appendix for more information.

_____

CHAPTER 25

COST ACCOUNTING

Some abbreviations used in this chapter:

EU	=	equivalent units	WIP	=	work-in-process
FIFO	=	first in, first out	WA	=	weighted average
AP	=	actual price per unit	AQ	=	actual quantity per unit
SP	=	standard price per unit	SQ	=	standard quantity per unit

EXAM COVERAGE: The managerial accounting portion of the ARE section of the CPA exam is designated by the examiners to be 10 percent of the section's point value. Historically, exam coverage of the topics in this chapter hovers at 1 to 4 percent of the ARE section. (Familiarity with, rather than knowledge of, overhead variance analysis is recommended for the CPA exam.) Candidates should plan their use of study time accordingly. More information about the point value of various topics is in the **Practical Advice** section of this volume.

CHAPTER 25

COST ACCOUNTING

I. JOB ORDER COSTING

A. OVERVIEW
Job order costing is the accumulation of costs by specific jobs (i.e., physical units, distinct batches, or job lots). This costing method is appropriate when direct costs can be identified with specific units, or groups of units, of production. Job order costing is widely used in industries such as construction, aircraft manufacturing, printing, auto repair, and professional services. (Service organizations frequently use job order costing.)

B. PROCEDURES
Direct materials and direct labor are traced to a particular job. Costs not directly traceable (i.e., manufacturing overhead) are applied to individual jobs using a predetermined overhead application rate.

1. **RATE** The overhead rate is a predetermined yearly rate using a base that is common to all units produced, such as direct labor hours, machine hours, or direct labor cost.

$$\text{Overhead application rate} = \frac{\text{Estimated Factory Overhead}}{\text{Estimated Direct Labor Hours}}$$

2. **ACCOUNT** The *Factory Overhead Control* account is debited as actual factory overhead costs are incurred. The *Factory Overhead Applied* account is credited as factory overhead is applied to inventory costs at the predetermined rate.

3. **CLOSING** As a practical matter, the difference between overhead applied and actual overhead incurred is often closed to **cost of goods sold** (CGS) at the end of the period. Theoretically, the difference should be closed to WIP, finished goods, and CGS.

II. PROCESS COSTING

A. OVERVIEW
Process costing is a cost accumulation method that aggregates production costs by departments or by production phases. Unit cost is determined by dividing the total costs charged to a cost center by the output of that cost center. Process costing is appropriate for enterprises that produce a continuous mass of like units through a series of production steps called operations or processes. Process costing is generally used in the manufacturing of homogeneous products (such as chemicals, petroleum, textiles, paints, and food processing).

1. **COST OF PRODUCTION REPORT** Summarizes the total cost charged to a department and the distribution of that total cost between the ending work-in-process inventory and the units completed and transferred to the next department or finished goods inventory.

2. **EQUIVALENT UNITS** The expression of the physical units of output in terms of doses or units. For example, 600 units that are one-third complete and 400 units that are one-half complete are both 200 equivalent units. Equivalent units are frequently figured on separate inventory components (material, labor, etc.) as product may be complete with respect to material, but only partially complete in regard to conversion costs.

3. **STAGE OF COMPLETION** The degree, point, or phase in the manufacturing process at which a product currently stands; used in determining the equivalent units of production in beginning and ending work-in-process (WIP) inventory.

4. **TRANSFERRED-IN COST** The material, labor, and overhead cost transferred-in from a prior department. By definition, transferred-in costs are always at the 100% stage of completion.

5. **SOLUTIONS APPROACH TO PROCESS COSTING**

a. Compute the physical flow of units. (Beginning WIP inventory + Units started = Units transferred out + Ending WIP inventory)

b. Compute equivalent units of production separately for beginning WIP, materials, and conversion costs.

c. Determine the total costs, classified by major categories.

d. Calculate the equivalent unit cost, depending on the cost flow assumption used.

e. Allocate total costs between ending work-in-process and finished (i.e., transferred out) goods.

B. **COST FLOW ASSUMPTIONS**

Only two flow assumptions are generally used—FIFO and weighted average. Under weighted average, the costs in the **beginning** inventory are averaged with the **current** period's costs to determine one average unit cost for all units passing through the department in a given period. Under FIFO, costs in the beginning inventory are **not** mingled with the current period costs, but are transferred out as a separate batch of goods at a different unit cost than units started and completed during the period.

EXAMPLE 1 ♦ COST OF PRODUCTION REPORT, FIFO

Beginning WIP inventory is 200 units (at 40% completion). Beginning WIP inventory material costs are $200. Beginning WIP inventory conversion costs are $400.

All material for a product is added at the beginning of the production process. Conversion takes place continuously throughout the process. During the period 500 units were started. Material costs for the period are $600. Conversion costs for the period are $5,527.50.

Ending WIP inventory is 100 units (at 30% completion).

REQUIRED: Prepare a cost of production report, using a FIFO cost flow assumption.

SOLUTION:

1. *Step One:* Calculate the physical flow in units.

	Physical Flow		Physical Flow
Beginning WIP (40% complete)	200	Units completed	600
Units started	500	Ending WIP (30% complete)	100
Units to account for	700	Units accounted for	700

2. *Step Two:* Compute the equivalent units of production.

	Equivalent Units			
	Materials		Conversion cost	
Units completed	(600 x 100%)	600	(600 x 100%)	600
Ending WIP (30% complete)	(100 x 100%)	100	(100 x 30%)	30
WA EU	(200 x 100%)	700	(200 x 40%)	630
Beginning WIP (40% complete)		(200)		(80)
FIFO EU		500		550

NOTE: Material is added at the beginning of the process and thus is 100% complete. Conversion costs are incurred evenly throughout the process and thus are 40% and 30% complete.

(continued on next page)

3. *Step Three:* Determine total costs.

	Beginning WIP	Current costs	Total costs
Materials	$200.00	$ 600.00	$ 800.00
Conversion costs	400.00	5,527.50	5,927.50
Total costs to account for	$600.00	$6,127.50	$6,727.50

4. *Step Four:* Calculate equivalent unit cost.

	Current costs	FIFO EU Divisor	Equivalent unit cost
Materials	$ 600.00	500	$ 1.20
Conversion costs	5,527.50	550	10.05
Total current costs	$6,127.50		$11.25

5. *Step Five:* Allocate total costs between work-in-process and finished goods.

		Total Costs
Total costs (from Step 3)		$6,727.50
Ending WIP material costs (100 units x 100% x $1.20/unit)	$120.00	
Ending WIP conversion costs (100 units x 30% x $10.05/unit)	301.50	
Less: Ending WIP		421.50
Cost of finished goods		$6,306.00*

* Proof:
FG = Beginning WIP cost + Cost to complete beginning WIP + Units started and completed
   = $600 + (200 x [1 – 0.4] x $10.05) + (400 x $11.25) = $6,306

6. *Step Six:* Cost of Production Report (complete solution)

	Physical Flow
Beginning WIP (40% complete)	200
Units started	500
Units to account for	700

		Equivalent Units	
		Materials	Conversion cost
Units completed	600	600	600
Ending WIP (30% complete)	100	100	30
Units accounted for	700		
Weighted average EU		700	630
Beginning WIP (40% complete at beginning of period)		(200)	(80)
FIFO EU		500	550

	Allocation of Costs to Product				
	Total costs	Beginning WIP	Current costs	EU Divisor	Current unit cost
Materials	$ 800.00	$200.00	$ 600.00	500	$ 1.20
Conversion costs	5,927.50	400.00	5,527.50	550	10.05
Total costs to account for	$6,727.50	$600.00	$6,127.50		$11.25
Total costs accounted for	$6,727.50				
Ending WIP	421.50				
Goods completed	$6,306.00				

EXAMPLE 2 ♦ COST OF PRODUCTION REPORT, WEIGHTED AVERAGE

REQUIRED: Prepare a cost of production report under the same conditions as for the FIFO example, using a weighted average cost flow assumption.

SOLUTION:

1. *Step One:* Calculate the physical flow in units. (This is the same as the FIFO example.)

2. *Step Two:* Compute the equivalent units of production. (Note the FIFO example similarities.)

	Equivalent Units			
	Materials		Conversion cost	
Units completed	(600 x 100%)	600	(600 x 100%)	600
Ending WIP (30% complete)	(100 x 100%)	100	(100 x 30%)	30
WA EU		700		630

3. *Step Three:* Determine total costs. (This is the same as the FIFO example.)

4. *Step Four:* Calculate equivalent unit costs.

	Total costs	WA EU Divisor	Equivalent unit cost
Materials	$ 800.00	700	$ 1.14
Conversion costs	5,927.50	630	9.41
Total current costs	$6,727.50		$10.55

5. *Step Five:* Allocate total costs between work-in-process and finished goods.

Total costs		$6,727.50
Ending WIP material costs (100 units x 100% x $1.14/unit)	$114.00	
Ending WIP conversion costs (100 units x 30% x $9.41/unit)	282.30	
Less: Ending WIP		396.30
Cost of finished goods		$6,331.20

6. *Step Six:* Cost of Production Report (The physical flow is the same as for FIFO.)

	Physical	Equivalent Units	
	Units	Materials	Conversion cost
Units completed	600	600	600
Ending WIP (30% complete)	100	100	30
Units accounted for	700	700	630

	Allocation of Costs to Product				
	Current costs	Beginning WIP	Total costs	EU Divisor	Current unit cost
Materials	$ 600.00	$200.00	$ 800.00	700	$ 1.14
Conversion costs	5,527.50	400.00	5,927.50	630	9.41
Total costs to account for	$6,127.50	$600.00	$6,727.50		$10.55
Goods completed			$6,331.20		
Ending WIP			396.30		
Total costs accounted for			$6,727.50		

C. USING STANDARD COSTS WITH PROCESS COSTING

The use of standard costs for inventory valuation simplifies process cost computations. Standard costing eliminates the need to compute the cost per equivalent unit (i.e., Step 4.) because the standard cost **is** the cost per equivalent unit. Standard costs eliminate the complications of WA or FIFO inventory methods, thus simplifying Step 5.

III. SPOILAGE

A. OVERVIEW
Spoilage is production that does not result in good finished units.

1. **NORMAL SPOILAGE** Normal spoilage is inherent in the manufacturing process and is uncontrollable in the short run. Management establishes a normal spoilage rate, which is the rate of spoilage that is acceptable under a given combination of production factors. Normal spoilage is a cost of goods produced and, thus, is inventoried as a product cost.

2. **ABNORMAL SPOILAGE** Abnormal spoilage is spoilage beyond the normal spoilage rate. It is considered controllable because it is a result of inefficiency. Abnormal spoilage is not a cost of good production, but rather is a **loss** for the period.

3. **SPOILED GOODS** Units that do not meet quality or dimensional standards and are junked or sold for salvage (disposal) value.

4. **DEFECTIVE UNITS** Units that do not meet quality or dimensional standards and are sold at a reduced price or reworked and sold at the regular or a reduced price.

5. **SCRAP** Material residue of the manufacturing process that has measurable but minor recovery value. Scrap may be sold or reused. Examples: Wood or metal shavings in woodworking operations and foundries, bolt-ends of fabric in clothing manufacturing. Generally, the sales value of scrap is regarded as a decrease to factory overhead control. In some job-order situations, the sales value of scrap is credited to the particular job that yielded the scrap.

6. **WASTE** Material that is lost in the manufacturing process by evaporation, shrinkage, etc., or material residue that has no measurable recovery value. Disposal of waste may entail additional cost, as in the cost of antipollution devices to clean gaseous wastes. The cost of waste from shrinkage, evaporation, etc., usually is not traced and is not recognized in the accounts. In a standard cost system, an allowance for waste may be included in the determination of standard product cost. Shrinkage in excess of standard is thus revealed as a material usage or quantity variance.

7. **REWORK** The cost of reworking defective units is generally charged to manufacturing overhead. The predetermined overhead rate should include a provision for costs of rework.

B. PROCESS COST SYSTEM
Both normal spoilage and abnormal spoilage are incorporated into process costing procedure. Additionally, a normal spoilage rate is included in the predetermined overhead application rate.

1. In computing the physical flow in units, the count of spoiled units must take into consideration the stage of production at which the spoilage occurred. Generally, spoilage is deemed to occur at the time of inspection; therefore, the cost of spoiled units is generally allocated to the manufacturing process from this point forward. If spoiled units are discovered at the end of the process, the entire cost of spoilage should be charged to the completed units.

2. Abnormal spoilage is included in the equivalent unit calculation to the extent of the completion stage where abnormal spoilage occurs.

C. JOB ORDER COST SYSTEM

1. **ABNORMAL SPOILAGE** Abnormal spoilage is recognized as a loss when discovered. WIP is credited for the total amount of spoilage, an asset account is debited for the disposal value, and a loss on abnormal spoilage account is debited for the difference.

2. **NORMAL SPOILAGE ALTERNATIVES** The predetermined overhead application rate may or may not include a provision for normal spoilage.

   a. **INCLUDED** When spoilage occurs, WIP is credited for the total amount of spoilage, an asset account is debited for the disposal value, and manufacturing overhead is debited for the difference.

   b. **NOT INCLUDED** This method is used when spoilage is viewed as directly attributable to the nature of particular jobs. When spoilage occurs, WIP (of a specific job) is credited and an asset account is debited for the disposal value of the spoiled units. Thus, the remaining good units in the specific job bear the cost of net normal spoilage.

IV. JOINT-PRODUCT AND BY-PRODUCT COSTING

A. DEFINITIONS
Deciding if a product is a joint-product or a by-product is sometimes a matter of judgment. (CPA exam questions usually give a clear indication of the nature of the product.)

1. **BY-PRODUCTS** By-products are products that (1) have minor sales value as compared with the sales value of the main products and (2) are not identifiable as separate products until their split-off point.

2. **JOINT-PRODUCT COSTS** Exist where two or more products are produced from processing the same raw material by a single process. Moreover, the various products are not separately identifiable until a certain stage of production known as the **split-off point**. The cost of the input factors incurred prior to split-off must be allocated to the joint products.

3. **NET REALIZABLE VALUE** Sales value less estimated cost to complete and sell.

4. **SEPARABLE COST** Additional processing cost after the split-off point.

5. **SPLIT-OFF POINT** Represents the stage of production where the various products become identifiable as separate individual products. These products can be further processed or sold at the split-off point.

B. NEED FOR ALLOCATION
None of the individual products can be produced without the others.

1. **REPORTING** Allocation of joint costs, however arbitrary, becomes necessary if inventories are carried forward from period to period. In other words, cost allocation is essential for inventory valuation and determining cost of goods sold.

2. **DECISIONS** Joint product cost allocation should **not** be used in deciding whether to further process or sell the products at the split-off point. Joint costs are **irrelevant** for decision-making purposes.

C. RELATIVE MARKET (SALES) VALUE METHOD OF ALLOCATING JOINT COSTS

1. **SPLIT-OFF POINT** This method allocates joint costs to products based on their relative sales value at the split-off point. It is considered to be the best allocation method because it allocates the joint cost in proportion to the products' ability to absorb these costs.

2. **NET REALIZABLE VALUE** Frequently, joint products have no sales value at the split-off point (i.e., separable costs must be incurred before the products become salable). Joint costs are then allocated on the basis of each product's net realizable value. Net realizable value is defined as the difference between sales value and estimated costs to complete and sell. Varying degrees of additional processing often result in increasingly higher sales value. For the purpose of allocating joint costs, net realizable value should be computed on the basis of the **first** sales value obtained as a result of additional processing.

EXAMPLE 3 ♦ JOINT PRODUCTS

The ABC Company produces two products, Y and Z, from the same raw material. Joint product costs are $900. The process yields 200 units of Y and 400 units of Z. Products Y and Z have no sales value at split-off. Additional processing yields the following results:

Product	Separable Costs	Sales Value
Y	$100	$1,300
Z	200	2,000

REQUIRED: Allocate joint costs on the basis of net realizable value (NRV).

SOLUTION:

Product	Sales value	Separable cost	NRV	Ratio	Allocated joint costs	Total Cost
Y	$1,300	$100	$1,200	12/30	$360	$ 460
Z	2,000	200	1,800	18/30	540	740
	$3,300	$300	$3,000		$900	$1,200

D. BY-PRODUCT METHODS

Generally, the relative sales value of the by-product(s) should be used to reduce the cost of the main product(s).

1. The net revenue from by-product(s) sold reduces the cost of the main product(s) **sold**; or

2. The net realizable value of by-product(s) produced is deducted from the cost of the main product(s) **produced**. This approach is conceptually superior because it allocates the benefits derived from the by-product(s) between cost of goods sold and ending inventory.

V. ALLOCATION OF SERVICE DEPARTMENT COSTS

A. PURPOSE

All manufacturing costs, whether originating in production **or** service departments, must be assigned to the goods produced for proper inventory valuation and cost of goods sold determination. Costs allocated to service departments, as well as costs directly traceable to these departments, must be allocated to production departments. This is necessary for product costing and financial reporting. Ideally, costs incurred by service departments should be allocated on the basis of a **cause and effect** relationship. However, such direct relationships are often not present. This calls for allocation of costs on some other basis, as illustrated by Exhibit 1.

EXHIBIT 1 ♦ SAMPLE COST ALLOCATION BASES

Service Department	Bases of Allocation to Other Departments
Factory cafeteria	Number of employees
Factory maintenance	Square footage
Factory storeroom	Material requisitions
General factory administration	Direct labor hours
Power department	Kilowatt hours used

B. DIRECT METHOD

The direct method allocates the costs of each service department directly to producing departments. No consideration is given to services performed by one service department for another service department.

C. STEP METHOD

The step method involves allocation of service department costs to both service and production departments.

1. Costs of the most widely used service department (or the department with the greatest total cost) are first allocated to all other departments. The costs of the next most widely used service department are then allocated. These costs will include those previously allocated from the first department. These "steps" continue until all service costs are allocated.

2. Once a department's costs have been allocated, no further allocations are made to it from other departments. (**Reciprocal** services among departments are **not** considered.)

EXAMPLE 4 ♦ SERVICE COST ALLOCATION

	Production Departments		Service Departments	
	A	B	General plant	Maintenance
Overhead—Production depts.	$40,000	$50,000		
Total costs—Service depts.			$20,000	$10,000
Square footage occupied	50,000	30,000	5,000	4,000
Direct labor hours	60,000	40,000	15,000	20,000

Allocation bases: General plant services are allocated on the basis of direct labor hours. Maintenance services are allocated on the basis of square footage occupied.

REQUIRED:

A. Allocate each service department's cost to the production departments using the (1) direct and (2) step methods.

B. Compute the overhead rate based on direct labor hours for the production departments using the (1) direct and (2) step methods.

SOLUTION A: Schedules of Cost Allocation

(1) Direct Method	Dept. A	Dept. B	General plant	Maintenance
Total cost			$ 20,000	$ 10,000
Production overhead	$40,000	$50,000		
Reallocation:				
General plant:			(20,000)	
(60,000 / 100,000*) x $20,000	12,000			
(40,000 / 100,000) x $20,000		8,000		
Maintenance:				(10,000)
(50,000 / 80,000*) x $10,000	6,250			
(30,000 / 80,000) x $10,000		3,750		
Production department overhead after allocation	$58,250	$61,750	$ 0	$ 0

(2) Step Method	Dept. A	Dept. B	General plant	Maintenance
Total cost			$ 20,000	$ 10,000
Production overhead	$40,000	$50,000		
Reallocation:				
General plant:			(20,000)	
(60,000 / 120,000*) x $20,000	10,000			
(40,000 / 120,000) x $20,000		6,667		
(20,000 / 120,000) x $20,000				3,333
Maintenance:				(13,333)
(50,000 / 80,000*) x $13,333	8,333			
(30,000 / 80,000) x $13,333		5,000		
Production department overhead after allocation	$58,333	$61,667	$ 0	$ 0

(continued on next page)

SOLUTION B: Overhead Rates

		Dept. A		Dept. B
(1)	Direct Method	($58,250 / 60,000) = $0.9708		($61,750 / 40,000) = $1.5438
(2)	Step Method	($58,333 / 60,000) = $0.9722		($61,667 / 40,000) = $1.5417

* The denominator must equal the sum of the allocation bases used in order for the service departments' total costs to be allocated.

VI. ACTIVITY-BASED COSTING

A. OVERVIEW

Activity-based costing (ABC) in many cases is an improvement over traditional methods of allocating overhead to product costs on a volume-related basis. In the past, when production was more labor intensive, nonvolume-related costs were a much smaller portion of total product costs compared to the high technology environments in which companies operate today, thus volume plays a smaller role in driving overhead costs. ABC follows the idea that products consume activities. ABC's purpose is to assign costs to activities performed in an organization and then assign them to products according to each product's use of the activities.

1. **ACTIVITIES** Procedures or processes that cause work. Materiality and the cost/benefit of relevant information determines the need for dividing the organization into smaller and smaller pieces. In a large company, an example of an activity as it relates to accounts payable might be matching invoices, purchase orders, and receiving reports. Another activity could be batching vouchers for data entry. For a small company, an activity could incorporate the whole accounts payable function.

   - Activities may be identified as batch-level activities and product-level activities. A batch-level activity would be the manufacture of breaker panels for which customers have specified the number and size of holes to be cut in ordered boards. The setup activity for this order benefits the entire batch, as opposed to performing the activity for each product unit.

2. **COST DRIVERS** May be thought of as the root cause of a cost or the factor used to measure how a cost is incurred and how best to charge the cost to activities or products. Cost drivers are used to reflect the consumption of costs by activities and products. An example for an accounts payable department may be the number of invoices processed.

3. **OCCUPANCY GROUP** The occupancy group is the most appropriate cost driver for distributing fixed costs based on the physical location of activities or assets. An example would be the distribution of property taxes, building depreciation, and security guard service charges based upon square footage occupied by each activity.

4. **COST CENTERS** The lowest level of detail for which costs are accumulated and distributed, and can consist of a single activity or group of activities.

5. **PRODUCT DIVERSITY** Occurs when products consume activities and inputs in different proportions. Thus, there is a difference in the size, complexity, material components, and other characteristics and demands made on a firm's resources by product lines.

6. **VOLUME DIVERSITY** Occurs when there is a difference in the number of units manufactured by product lines.

7. **MATERIAL DIVERSITY** Occurs when products having materials that take longer to process consume a disproportionate share of the unit-level inputs.

B.   APPLICATION

Activity-based costing is appropriate for selling, administrative, and general business functions as well as manufacturing and revenue-producing service processes. ABC assigns costs of activities to products using both volume- and nonvolume-based cost drivers. Thus, if some product-related activity is unrelated to the number of units manufactured, using only volume-based allocations would distort the product's cost. As an example, for determining overhead allocation, cost accountants should instead apply the factors that cause activities to occur.   This establishes the requirements placed on an activity by a product. Once costs are assigned to activities performed in an organization, the costs can be allocated to products (or services) based on each product's use of the activities. General steps in establishing an ABC system are:

1.   Identify relevant activities.

2.   Organize activities by cost centers.

3.   Identify major elements of indirect costs.

4.   Identify cost drivers, assign costs to activities, assign activities to products.

5.   Establish a cost flow chart.

6.   Establish appropriate cost conversion tools.

7.   Gather data information for the ABC system.

8.   Establish the cost flow model to develop costing rates.

EXHIBIT 2 ♦ ACTIVITY-BASED COSTING

This exhibit illustrates how an inappropriate cost system can lead an organization to make pricing decisions that reward the company with contracts for which the company has actually underpriced itself, and at the same time, making itself noncompetitive by overpricing bids that could have created a profit at a lower price.

A homeowner obtained quotes from two remodeling companies for renovations on her home. The two remodeling companies are identical except for their method of costing and pricing their services. The Overhaul Remodeling Company uses the standard industry practice of charging 50 percent of the material's sales price for its installation, whereas the ABC Remodeling Company uses the activity-based costing method for determining costs incurred and the prices to charge for various installation activities. Both companies submitted bids of $2,430 for the following materials and services:

- Provide and install two 3' x 9' French doors
- Provide and install one 48" x 72" bay window
- Provide and install three rolls Grade A wallpaper
- Paint and trim out new window and door

Material Portion of Bid:		Overhaul	ABC
2-3' x 9' French doors	@$400/ea.	$ 800	$ 800
1-48" x 72" bay window	@$300	300	300
3-Rolls of wallpaper	@$40/ea.	120	120
Paint and trim	@$20/ft.	400	400
Total Material Bid		$1,620	$1,620

Installation/Application Portion of Bid:	Overhaul (@50%)	ABC	ABC charge per unit
Installation of French doors	$400	$500	(@$100/hr.)
Installation of bay window	150	200	(@$100/hr.)
Application of wallpaper	60	30	(@$10/roll)
Application of paint & trim	200	80	(@$4/ft.)
Total Installation Bid	$810	$810	

The actual costs of providing the materials and services, using activity-based costing, are as follows:

	Materials		Installation/Application		Total
2-3' x 9' French doors	@$380/ea.	$ 760	@$90/hr.	$450	$1,210
1-48" x 72" bay window	@$275	275	@$90/hr.	180	455
3-Rolls wallpaper	@$20/ea.	60	@$5/roll	15	75
Paint and trim	@$10/ft.	200	@$3/ft.	60	200
Total Actual Cost		$1,295		$705	$2,000

The Overhaul Company is actually losing money by pricing the installation of the French doors and bay windows using the old method. This is because the installation of these items is labor intensive (since more employees are required for these procedures) and also because special tools are needed, adding the cost of maintenance, depreciation, and so forth, that are all part of the cost of using this equipment. Overhaul is making up for the loss in performing the finishing work. If the homeowner contracts with Overhaul to install the French doors and bay windows and with the ABC Company for the finishing work, the Overhaul Company would lose money due to an inappropriate bid.

VII. STANDARD COST ACCOUNTING

A. PURPOSE

Comparison of standard (or estimated) to actual costs aids management in identifying problems and is a basis for judging performance. Standard costing is used to value inventory, plan and control costs, measure performance, prepare budgets, and motivate employees. Standard costing can be used in a wide variety of organizations; it is not limited to manufacturing activities. Standard costing can be used with process or job-order costing.

1. **VARIANCES** Variances are the differences between standard and actual costs. A variance is favorable if actual costs are less than standard costs, and unfavorable if actual costs exceed standard costs. Analysis of variances reveals the causes of deviations between actual and standard costs. This feedback aids in setting goals, estimating future costs, and evaluating performance.

2. **MANAGEMENT BY EXCEPTION** Reports of activities and performance show actual and budgeted amounts, and variances. Attention is focused on deviations from the budget, rather than on those parts of the operation that adhere to the budget.

B.   DEVELOPMENT OF STANDARD COSTS
Standard costs are predetermined, or target, unit costs that should be attained under efficient conditions. A standard cost system records activities at both standard and actual costs. Physical standards are determined by analyses of the kinds and amounts of material, labor, and factory overhead needed to produce one unit. The entire production cycle is divided into various operations, and inputs are estimated for each operation. Physical standards are multiplied by appropriate price factors to determine standard costs. Standards can be set at different levels, depending on management's objectives.

1. **BASIC COST STANDARDS** Standards that are unchanged year after year. Useful in tracing trends in price effects and efficiency, except when products change frequently.

2. **PERFECTION (IDEAL) COST STANDARDS** Absolute minimum costs attainable under perfect operating conditions (i.e., "factory heaven"). No allowance is made for factors beyond management's control. They may depress employee morale since they frequently result in unfavorable variances.

3. **CURRENTLY ATTAINABLE COST STANDARDS** Standards that can be attained under efficient operating conditions. Widely used because they serve a variety of purposes. Useful for employee motivation, product costing, and budgeting.

C.   OVERHEAD COSTS
Variances in overhead costs represent differences between budgeted (predetermined) and actual overhead.

1. **VARIABLE OVERHEAD** Application of **variable** overhead requires that the **incremental** overhead costs of production be determined. A standard variable overhead rate is obtained and applied to production on the basis of some common denominator, such as direct labor cost, direct labor hours, or machine hours. Note that, by definition, the total amount of **variable** overhead incurred and applied varies **directly** with the level of production.

2. **FIXED OVERHEAD** Since the total amount of **fixed** overhead remains **constant** over the relevant range of activity, the amount of fixed overhead per unit varies **inversely** with the level of production. Therefore, in order to obtain a standard fixed overhead rate it is necessary to select a predetermined (budgeted) level of activity. This activity should be measured on the basis of standard inputs allowed, such as direct labor cost, direct labor hours, or machine hours. If the fixed overhead rate was determined on the basis of actual outputs (i.e., finished units), it would be influenced by how **efficiently** those units were produced.

$$\frac{\text{Fixed overhead}}{\text{standard rate}} = \frac{\text{Budgeted fixed manufacturing overhead}}{\text{Predetermined level of activity (measured in standard inputs)}}$$

D.   ISOLATING VARIANCES
Accounting depends upon when variances are isolated in the flow of elements through the accounts. A common method is to isolate material price variances at the time of purchase and to isolate all other variances in the work-in-process account. (This method makes the formulas for variances, discussed later, relatively easy to remember.)

1. Accumulate direct materials at actual quantity times standard prices. The difference between actual and standard price is charged or credited to the direct material price variance account.

2. Accumulate actual cost of direct labor and manufacturing overhead.

3. Transfer direct material, direct labor, and overhead to the work-in-process account at standard quantity times standard price. The differences between actual and standard direct material and labor prices are isolated in material quantity, labor rate, and labor efficiency variances. Thus, work-in-process includes no inefficiencies.

4. The cost of completed units is transferred to finished goods at standard quantities times standard prices. No variances are recognized at this time.

E. DISPOSITION OF VARIANCES
At the end of the period, the variances must be **disposed** of to arrive at the proper net income. The commonly used alternatives for disposing of these variances are

1. **EXPENSE OR INCOME ITEM** Close out the variance to the income summary account and present the net variance as an income or expense item in the income statement.

2. **COST OF GOODS SOLD** Close out the variance to cost of goods sold and present the net variance as an adjustment to cost of goods sold in the income statement.

3. **ALL INVENTORIES** Close out the variances by allocating them between inventories and cost of goods sold. This is the most conceptually sound and most commonly used approach.

   a. Inventories may be carried at standard costs for external reporting purposes only if the standards are frequently adjusted so as to approximate the costs that would be inventories under one of the cost flow assumptions recognized by GAAP.

   b. Each specific variance is allocated in proportion to the related standard cost included in each account. For example, the material price variance would be allocated based on the ratio of total material price variance to the total material cost included in the raw materials, work-in-process, and finished goods inventories and cost of goods sold. All other variances should be allocated to work-in-process and finished goods inventories, and cost of goods sold.

F. VARIANCES IN PRIME COSTS
Efficiency variances are generally more controllable by management than price variances, and are thus of more interest to most enterprises.

1. **PRICE VARIANCES** Price variances are differences between **actual unit prices** and **standard unit prices**, multiplied by **actual inputs**. A positive result (i.e., a positive V_p) indicates an **increase** in costs (i.e., an unfavorable variance), while a negative V_p indicates a cost **reduction** (i.e., a favorable variance). Price variances reflect changes between the expected price and actual price of direct materials and labor.

$$V_p = (AP - SP) \times AQ$$

   a. Unfavorable direct **material** price variances may be related to unwise purchasing decisions. However, price variances are often caused by price fluctuations that cannot be controlled by management. Therefore, in many enterprises, the price variance is isolated solely to separate it from efficiency variances.

   b. Material price variances may be isolated at the time of purchase to remove the influence of price changes from efficiency reports, or to control purchasing activities.

   c.   Unfavorable **labor** price variances may be the result of unavoidable increases in labor rates or the use of overqualified persons for a job, resulting in payment of higher rates than standard.

  2. **EFFICIENCY VARIANCES** Efficiency variances are differences between the quantity of inputs (materials or labor) that should have been used and inputs that were actually used, based on the **standard unit price**.

$$V_e = (AQ - SQ) \times SP$$

   a.   Unfavorable material efficiency variances indicate excessive usage of materials.

   b.   Unfavorable labor efficiency variances indicate that inefficient labor methods resulted in more hours worked than would be budgeted for the level of production achieved.

  3. **DISTINGUISHING THE VARIANCE FORMULAS OF PRIME COSTS** Remembering these two formulas is easy, if one assumes isolation of the material price variances at the time of purchase (a common practice). At the time of purchase, the standard quantity is not known, so it cannot be used in the price variance formula. Then keep in mind that the efficiency variance formula must account for all of the remaining variance from standard cost.

G. **VARIANCES IN VARIABLE OVERHEAD COSTS**

  1. **EFFICIENCY VARIANCE** The variable overhead efficiency variance reflects the differences in actual and budgeted variable overhead costs that are incurred because of the inefficient use of resources such as direct labor or machine hours.

$$VOHV_e = (AQ - SQ) \times SP$$

  2. **SPENDING VARIANCE** The variable overhead spending variance reflects the differences in actual and budgeted variable costs that result from price changes in indirect materials and labor, poor budget estimates, and insufficient control of costs of specific overhead items.

$$VOHV_s = (AP - SP) \times AQ$$

H. **VARIANCES IN FIXED OVERHEAD COSTS**

  1. **TOTAL FIXED OVERHEAD VARIANCE (FOHV)** Total FOHV (i.e., **under-** or **overapplied** overhead) is the difference between **actual** fixed overhead incurred and FOH applied to production (generally on the basis of standard direct labor hours, machine hours, etc., allowed for good production output). Total FOHV combines the FOH **volume** variance and the FOH **budget** (spending) variance.

$$\text{Total } FOHV = FOH \text{ \textit{incurred}} - FOH \text{ \textit{applied}}$$

$$= FOH \text{ incurred} - \left[\begin{array}{c} FOH \text{ standard} \\ rate \end{array} \times \begin{array}{c} Standard \text{ inputs allowed} \\ (DLH, \text{ mach. hours, etc.}) \end{array} \right]$$

  2. **VOLUME VARIANCE** Fixed overhead volume (denominator) variance results when the actual activity level (direct labor, machine hours, etc.) differs from the budgeted quantity used in determining the fixed overhead application rate. In developing a predetermined fixed overhead rate, the denominator represents the expected activity level. The denominator variance arises when the activity level for a period does not coincide with the predetermined activity level. A volume variance is a measure of the cost of failure to operate at the budgeted activity level, and may be caused by failure to meet sales goals or idleness due to poor scheduling, machine breakdowns, etc.

FOH volume
(denominator) = (Budgeted FOH – FOH applied)
variance

$$= \left[\begin{array}{c} \text{FOH standard} \\ \text{rate} \end{array} \times \begin{array}{c} \text{Budgeted standard} \\ \text{inputs*} \end{array} \right] - \left[\begin{array}{c} \text{FOH standard} \\ \text{rate} \end{array} \times \begin{array}{c} \text{Standard inputs} \\ \text{allowed} \end{array} \right]$$

$$= \left[\begin{array}{c} \text{Budgeted} \\ \text{Standard inputs*} \end{array} - \begin{array}{c} \text{Standard inputs} \\ \text{allowed} \end{array} \right] \times \left[\begin{array}{c} \text{FOH standard rate} \end{array} \right]$$

_____

* Budgeted standard inputs based on some level of activity, e.g., normal or maximum capacity.

3. **BUDGET (SPENDING) VARIANCE** Fixed overhead budget (spending) variance is the difference between actual fixed overhead incurred and fixed overhead budgeted. *This difference is not affected by the level of production.* Fixed overhead, by definition, does not change in total with the level of activity within the relevant range. The budget variance is caused solely by events such as unexpected changes in prices, unforeseen repairs, etc.

$$\begin{array}{lll} \textit{FOH budget} \\ \textit{variance} & = & \textit{Actual FOH} - \textit{Budgeted FOH} \end{array}$$

$$= \quad \textit{Actual FOH} - \left[\begin{array}{c} \textit{FOH} \\ \textit{Standard rate} \end{array} \times \begin{array}{c} \textit{Budgeted production} \\ \textit{(DL, machine hours, etc.)} \end{array} \right]$$

4. **EFFICIENCY VARIANCE** There are no FOH efficiency variances because fixed overhead does not change regardless of whether productive resources are used **efficiently** or not (e.g., real estate taxes are not affected by whether production is being carried on efficiently or not).

EXHIBIT 3 ♦ POSSIBLE FIXED OVERHEAD VARIANCES

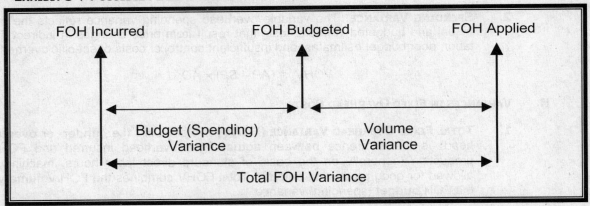

I. VARIANCE ANALYSIS

Variances between standard and actual costs may be analyzed to discover price or efficiency differences in prime costs (labor and direct material), spending or efficiency differences in variable overhead costs, and budget or volume differences in fixed overhead costs. Variance analysis is subject to the same cost-benefit tests as other phases of an information system.

1. **PURPOSE** Variances that are material in amount may indicate that further investigation is warranted to pinpoint their exact cause. For example, a material efficiency variance may be caused by faulty workmanship or an improper mix of materials. Consistently high variances (favorable **or** unfavorable) may be indicative of faulty standards. Standards should be examined and revised if appropriate.

2. **METHODS** Variance analysis generally consists of a two-way prime cost variance analysis and a two-, three-, or four-way overhead variance analysis, depending on the significance of the variance amounts compared to the cost of analysis. Note that the three-way analysis is a refinement on the two-way analysis and the four-way analysis is a refinement on the three-way analysis.

a. **Two-way** direct material and direct labor variance analysis involves the computation of **price** and **efficiency** variances for each of those cost elements.

b. **Two-way** overhead variance analysis

    (1) Volume variance   =   Fixed overhead (OH) volume variance

    (2) Budget variance   =   { Variable OH efficiency variance +
Variable OH spending variance +
Fixed OH budget variance

c. **Three-way** overhead variance analysis

    (1) Volume variance   =   Fixed OH volume variance

    (2) Efficiency variance   =   Variable OH efficiency variance

    (3) Spending variance   =   { Variable OH spending variance +
Fixed OH budget variance

d. **Four-way** overhead variance analysis

    (1) Fixed OH volume variance

    (2) Variable OH efficiency variance

    (3) Variable OH spending variance

    (4) Fixed OH budget variance

EXAMPLE 5 ♦ VARIANCE ANALYSIS

	Standard		Standard cost for one
	Quantity	Price	completed unit
Material	3 lbs.	$2.00	$ 6.00
Labor	2 hrs.	$4.00	8.00
Overhead:			
Variable	2 hrs.	$1.00	2.00
Fixed	2 hrs.	$2.00	4.00
			$20.00

Budgeted Activity: 50 Standard direct labor hours

Actual Data:	Units produced	20
	Material = 100 pounds at a total cost of	$225
	Labor—30 hours at $4.10	$123
	Overhead	
	Variable	$ 45
	Fixed	$115

REQUIRED: Compute the following variances:

a.   Material price
b.   Material quantity
c.   Labor rate
d.   Labor quantity
e.   Total net overhead

SOLUTION:

a.   *Material price variance (AP – SP)AQ*

Price difference   ($2.25 – $2.00) times Actual quantity or:
$.25 x 100 = $25 Unfavorable

b.   *Material quantity variance (AQ – SQ)SP*

Quantity difference (100 – 60) times Standard price or:
40 x $2 = $80 Unfavorable
NOTE: AP = $225 / 100 = $2.25, SQ = 20 units x 3 lbs. = 60

c.   *Labor rate variance (AP – SP)AQ*

Rate difference   ($4.10 – $4.00) times Actual quantity or:
$.10 x 30 = $3.00 Unfavorable

d.   *Labor efficiency variance (AQ – SQ)SP*

Quantity difference (30 – 40) times Standard rate or:
(10) x $ 4 = $(40) Favorable
NOTE: SQ = 20 units x 2 hrs./unit = 40 hrs.

e.   *Total net overhead variance*

Actual overhead ($45 + $115)	$ 160	
Less: Overhead appl. (SQ x SP = 40 x $3)	(120)	
Underapplied overhead	$ 40	Unfavorable

EXHIBIT 4 ♦ RELATIONSHIPS OF 1-, 2-, AND 3-WAY ANALYSES

	(1) Actual factory overhead incurred	(2) Flexible budget based on actual inputs ($1 x 30 un.)	(3) Flexible budget based on actual outputs (2hrs. x $1 x 20 un.)	(4) Factory overhead applied (2hrs. x $1 x 20 un.)
V	$ 45	$ 30	$ 40	$ 40
				(2hrs. x $2 x 20 un.)
F	115	$100	$100	80
Combined	$160	$130	$140	$120

3-Way Analysis

	Spending Var. (1) – (2)	Efficiency Var. (2) – (3)	Volume Var. (3) – (4)
V	$15 U	$10 F	
F	15 U	N/A	$20 U
Combined	$30 U	$10 F	$20 U

2-Way Analysis

	Controllable (budget) Var. (1) – (3)		Volume Var. (3) – (4)
V	$ 5 U		N/A
F	15 U		$20 U
Combined	$20 U		$20 U

1-Way Analysis

Net Overhead Variance (Underapplied)

	(1) – (4)
V	$ 5 U
F	35 U
Combined	$40 U

Frequency of Tested Areas

Heavily Tested

Ch. 21   Governmental Overview
Ch. 22   Governmental Funds & Transactions
Ch. 27   Federal Taxation: Individuals
Ch. 29   Federal Taxation: Corporations
Ch. 30   Federal Taxation: Partnerships & Other Topics

Moderately Tested

Ch. 23   Nonprofit Accounting
Ch. 28   Federal Taxation: Property

Lightly Tested

Ch. 24   Decision Making
Ch. 25   Cost Accounting
Ch. 26   Planning & Control

More information is in the **Practical Advice** appendix.

CHAPTER 25—COST ACCOUNTING

PROBLEM 25-1 MULTIPLE CHOICE QUESTIONS (60 to 75 minutes)

1. Under Pick Co.'s job order costing system, manufacturing overhead is applied to work in process using a predetermined annual overhead rate. During January, Pick's transactions included the following:

Direct materials issued to production	$ 90,000
Indirect materials issued to production	8,000
Manufacturing overhead incurred	125,000
Manufacturing overhead applied	113,000
Direct labor costs	107,000

Pick had neither beginning nor ending work-in-process inventory. What was the cost of jobs completed in January?
a. $302,000
b. $310,000
c. $322,000
d. $330,000   (5/94, AR, #42, amended, 4647)

2. In a traditional job order cost system, the issue of indirect materials to a production department increases
a. Stores control.
b. Work-in-process control.
c. Factory overhead control.
d. Factory overhead applied.

(5/93, Theory, #41, 4228)

3. The following information pertains to Lap Co.'s Palo Division for the month of April:

	Number of units	Cost of materials
Beginning work-in-process	15,000	$ 5,500
Started in April	40,000	18,000
Units completed	42,500	
Ending work-in-process	12,500	

All materials are added at the beginning of the process. Using the weighted-average method, the cost per equivalent unit for materials is
a. $0.59.
b. $0.55.
c. $0.45.
d. $0.43.   (5/94, AR, #40, 4645)

4. In computing the current period's manufacturing cost per equivalent unit, the FIFO method of process costing considers current period costs

a. Only.
b. Plus cost of beginning work-in-process inventory.
c. Less cost of beginning work-in-process inventory.
d. Plus cost of ending work-in-process inventory.

(11/92, Theory #47, 3480)

5. In process 2, material G is added when a batch is 60% complete. Ending work-in-process units, which are 50% complete, would be included in the computation of equivalent units for

	Conversion costs	Material G
a.	Yes	No
b.	No	Yes
c.	No	No
d.	Yes	Yes

(5/90, Theory, #42, 2185)

6. A process costing system was used for a department that began operations in January. Approximately the same number of physical units, at the same degree of completion, were in work in process at the end of both January and February. Monthly conversion costs are allocated between ending work-in-process and units completed. Compared to the FIFO method, would the weighted-average method use the same or a greater number of equivalent units to calculate the monthly allocations?

	Equivalent units for weighted-average compared to FIFO	
	January	February
a.	Same	Same
b.	Greater number	Greater number
c.	Greater number	Same
d.	Same	Greater number

(5/91, Theory, #42, amended, 2175)

7. In its April production, Hern Corp., which does not use a standard cost system, incurred total production costs of $900,000, of which Hern attributed $60,000 to normal spoilage and $30,000 to abnormal spoilage. Hern should account for this spoilage as
a. Period cost of $90,000.
b. Inventoriable cost of $90,000.
c. Period cost of $60,000 and inventoriable cost of $30,000.
d. Inventoriable cost of $60,000 and period cost of $30,000.   (5/95, AR, #41, amended, 5459)

8. During March, Hamilton Company incurred the following costs on Job 10 for the manufacture of 200 motors:

Direct materials	$ 330
Direct labor	400
Factory overhead (150% of direct labor)	600
Original cost accumulation:	$1,330
Direct materials	$ 50
Direct labor	80
Direct costs of reworked 10 units:	$ 130

The rework costs were attributable to exacting specifications of Job 10 and the full rework costs were charged to this specific job. The cost per finished unit of Job 10 was
a. $7.90
b. $7.30
c. $7.00
d. $6.65   (Editors, 1501)

9. The Forming Department is the first of a two-stage production process. Spoilage is identified when the units have completed the Forming process. Costs of spoiled units are assigned to units completed and transferred to the second department in the period spoilage is identified. The following information concerns Forming's conversion costs in May:

	Units	Conversion costs
Beginning work-in-process (50% complete)	2,000	$10,000
Units started during May	8,000	75,500
Spoilage—normal	500	
Units completed & transferred	7,000	
Ending work-in-process (80% complete)	2,500	

Using the weighted average method, what was Forming's conversion cost transferred to the second production department?
a. $59,850
b. $64,125
c. $67,500
d. $71,250   (11/95, AR, #46, amended, 5789)

10. For purposes of allocating joint costs to joint products, the sales price at point of sale, reduced by cost to complete after split-off, is assumed to be equal to the
a. Joint costs.
b. Total costs.
c. Net sales value at split-off.
d. Sales price less a normal profit margin at point of sale.   (11/95, AR, #48, 5791)

11. A processing department produces joint products Ajac and Bjac, each of which incurs separable production costs after split-off. Information concerning a batch produced at a $60,000 joint cost before split-off follows:

Product	Separable costs	Sales value
Ajac	$ 8,000	$ 80,000
Bjac	22,000	40,000
Total	$30,000	$120,000

What is the joint cost assigned to Ajac if costs are assigned using the relative net realizable value?
a. $16,000
b. $40,000
c. $48,000
d. $52,000   (R/00, AR, #17, 6922)

12. Kode Co. manufactures a major product that gives rise to a by-product called May. May's only separable cost is a $1 selling cost when a unit is sold for $4. Kode accounts for May's sales by deducting the $3 net amount from the cost of goods sold of the major product. There are no inventories. If Kode were to change its method of accounting for May from a by-product to a joint product, what would be the effect on Kode's overall gross margin?
a. No effect
b. Gross margin increases by $1 for each unit of May sold
c. Gross margin increases by $3 for each unit of May sold
d. Gross margin increases by $4 for each unit of May sold   (5/95, AR, #43, 5461)

13. Parat College allocates support department costs to its individual schools using the step method. Information for May is as follows:

	Support departments	
	Maintenance	Power
Costs incurred	$99,000	$54,000
Services percentages provided to:		
Maintenance	—	10%
Power	20%	—
School of Education	30%	20%
School of Technology	50%	70%
	100%	100%

What is the amount of May support department costs allocated to the School of Education?
a. $40,500
b. $42,120
c. $46,100
d. $49,125   (11/95, AR, #49, amended, 5792)

14. A basic assumption of activity-based costing (ABC) is that
a. All manufacturing costs vary directly with units of production.
b. Products or services require the performance of activities, and activities consume resources.
c. Only costs that respond to unit-level drivers are product costs.
d. Only variable costs are included in activity cost pools. (R/00, AR, #13, 6918)

15. What is the normal effect on the numbers of cost pools and allocation bases when an activity-based cost (ABC) system replaces a traditional cost system?

	Cost pools	Allocation bases
a.	No effect	No effect
b.	Increase	No effect
c.	No effect	Increase
d.	Increase	Increase

(5/94, AR, #41, 4646)

16. Which of the following is true about activity-based costing?
a. It should not be used with process or job costing.
b. It can be used only with process costing.
c. It can be used only with job costing.
d. It can be used with either process or job costing. (R/01, AR, #11, 6996)

17. Book Co. uses the activity-based costing approach for cost allocation and product costing purposes. Printing, cutting, and binding functions make up the manufacturing process. Machinery and equipment are arranged in operating cells that produce a complete product starting with raw materials. Which of the following are characteristic of Book's activity-based costing approach?

I. Cost drivers are used as a basis for cost allocation.
II. Costs are accumulated by department or function for purposes of product costing.
III. Activities that do not add value to the product are identified and reduced to the extent possible.

a. I only.
b. I and II.
c. I and III.
d. II and III. (5/92, Theory, #55, 2748)

18. In an activity-based costing system, cost reduction is accomplished by identifying and eliminating

	All cost drivers	Nonvalue-adding activities
a.	No	No
b.	Yes	Yes
c.	No	Yes
d.	Yes	No

(11/93, Theory, #45, 4550)

19. In an activity-based costing system, what should be used to assign a department's manufacturing overhead costs to products produced in varying lot sizes?
a. A single cause and effect relationship
b. Multiple cause and effect relationships
c. Relative net sales values of the products
d. A product's ability to bear cost allocations (5/95, AR, #44, 5462)

20. Companies in what type of industry may use a standard cost system for cost control?

	Mass production industry	Service industry
a.	Yes	Yes
b.	Yes	No
c.	No	No
d.	No	Yes

(5/95, AR, #42, 5460)

21. In connection with a standard cost system being developed by Flint Co., the following information is being considered with regard to standard hours allowed for output of one unit of product:

Average historical performance for the past three years	1.85
Production level to satisfy average consumer demand over a seasonal time span	1.60
Engineering estimates based on attainable performance	1.50
Engineering estimates based on ideal performance	1.25

To measure controllable production inefficiencies, what is the best basis for Flint to use in establishing standard hours allowed?
a. 1.25
b. 1.50
c. 1.60
d. 1.85 (11/92, PII, #31, amended, 3365)

ITEMS 22 AND 23 are based on the following information pertaining to 1,200,000 papers that were processed by DEP Company:

Total cost	$1,050,000
Labor cost	$ 950,000
Labor hours	190,000

The following processing standards have been set for DEP Co.'s clerical workers:

Number of hours per 1,000 papers processed	150
Normal number of papers processed per year	1,600,000
Wage rate per 1,000 papers	$ 750
Standard variable cost of processing 1,600,000 papers	$1,280,000
Fixed costs per year	$ 200,000

22. DEP Company's expected total cost to process 1,200,000 papers, assuming standard performance, is
a. $1,480,000.
b. $1,280,000.
c. $1,160,000.
d. $1,100,000. (Editors, 1509)

23. DEP's labor rate variance is
a. $50,000 unfavorable.
b. $40,000 favorable.
c. $10,000 unfavorable.
d. $0. (Editors, 1510)

24. Nile Co. uses a predetermined factory over-head application rate based on direct labor cost. Nile's budgeted factory overhead was $300,000, based on a budgeted volume of 25,000 direct labor hours, at a standard direct labor rate of $6.00 per hour. Actual factory overhead amounted to $310,000, with actual direct labor cost of $162,500. Overapplied factory overhead was
a. $10,000.
b. $12,500.
c. $15,000.
d. $25,000. (Editors, 1512)

ITEMS 25 AND 26 are based on the following:

Hart Company uses job order costing. Factory over-head is applied to production at a determined rate of 150% of direct-labor cost. Any over- or under-applied factory overhead is closed to the cost of goods sold account at the end of each month.

- Job 1001 was the only job in process at the end of April, with accumulated costs as follows:

Direct materials	$4,000
Direct labor	2,000
Applied factory overhead	3,000
	$9,000

- Jobs 1002, 1003, and 1004 were started during May.
- Direct materials requisitions for May totaled $26,000.
- Direct-labor cost of $20,000 was incurred for May.
- Actual factory overhead was $32,000 for May.
- The only job still in process at the end of May was Job 1004, with costs of $2,800 for direct materials and $1,800 for direct labor.

25. The cost of goods manufactured for May was
a. $77,700.
b. $78,000.
c. $79,700.
d. $85,000. (Editors, 9290)

26. Over- or underapplied factory overhead should be closed to the cost of goods sold account at the end of May, in the amount of
a. $ 700 overapplied.
b. $1,000 overapplied.
c. $1,700 underapplied.
d. $2,000 underapplied. (Editors, 9291)

ITEMS 27 AND 28 are based on the following inventory balances and manufacturing cost data for the month of January for Summit Company. Under Summit's cost system, any over- or under-applied overhead is closed to the cost of goods sold account at the end of the calendar year.

Inventories:	Beginning	Ending
Direct materials	$15,000	$20,000
Work-in-process	7,500	10,000
Finished goods	32,500	25,000

	Month of January
Cost of goods manufactured	$257,500
Factory overhead applied	75,000
Direct materials used	95,000
Actual factory overhead	72,000

27. What was the total amount of direct-material purchases during January?
a. $ 90,000
b. $ 95,000
c. $ 97,500
d. $100,000 (Editors, 9220)

28. How much direct-labor cost was incurred during January?
a. $85,000
b. $87,500
c. $90,000
d. $93,000   (Editors, 9221)

29. The following information pertains to Roe Co.'s June manufacturing operations:

Standard direct labor hours per unit	2
Actual direct labor hours	10,500
Number of units produced	5,000
Standard variable overhead per standard direct labor hour	$ 3
Actual variable overhead	$28,000

Roe's June unfavorable variable overhead efficiency variance was
a. $0.
b. $1,500.
c. $2,000.
d. $3,500.   (11/92, PII, #25, amended, 3359)

30. Mason Company uses a job-order cost system and applies manufacturing overhead to jobs using a predetermined overhead rate based on direct-labor dollars. The rate for the current year is 200 percent of direct-labor dollars. This rate was calculated last December and will be used throughout the current year. Mason had one job, No. 150, in process on August 1 with raw materials costs of $2,000 and direct-labor costs of $3,000. During August, raw materials and direct labor added to jobs were as follows:

	No. 150	No. 151	No. 152
Raw materials	—	$4,000	$1,000
Direct labor	$1,500	5,000	2,500

Actual manufacturing overhead for the month of August was $20,000. During the month, Mason completed Job Nos. 150 and 151. For August, manufacturing overhead was
a. Overapplied by $4,000.
b. Underapplied by $7,000.
c. Underapplied by $2,000.
d. Underapplied by $1,000.   (R/00, AR, #12, 6917)

PROBLEM 25-2 ADDITIONAL MULTIPLE CHOICE QUESTIONS (96 to 120 minutes)

31. Birk Co. uses a job order cost system. The following debits (credit) appeared in Birk's work-in-process account for the month of April:

April	Description	Amount
1	Balance	$ 4,000
30	Direct materials	24,000
30	Direct labor	16,000
30	Factory overhead	12,800
30	To finished goods	(48,000)

Birk applies overhead to production at a predetermined rate of 80% of direct labor cost. Job No. 5, the only job still in process at the end of April, has been charged with direct labor of $2,000. What was the amount of direct materials charged to Job No. 5?
a. $ 3,000
b. $ 5,200
c. $ 8,800
d. $24,000   (5/92, PII, #44, amended, 2676)

32. A job order cost system uses a predetermined factory overhead rate based on expected volume and expected fixed cost. At the end of the year, underapplied overhead might be explained by which of the following situations?

	Actual volume	Actual fixed costs
a.	Greater than expected	Greater than expected
b.	Greater than expected	Less than expected
c.	Less than expected	Greater than expected
d.	Less than expected	Less than expected

(11/90, Theory, #42, 2181)

33. In a job order cost system, the use of direct materials previously purchased usually is recorded as an increase in
a. Work-in-process control.
b. Factory overhead applied.
c. Factory overhead control.
d. Stores control.   (Editors, 2205)

34. In a process cost system, the application of factory overhead usually would be recorded as an increase in
a. Finished goods inventory control.
b. Factory overhead control.
c. Cost of goods sold.
d. Work-in-process inventory control.
(5/92, Theory, #51, 2744)

35. In developing a predetermined factory overhead application rate for use in a process costing system, which of the following could be used in the numerator and denominator?

	Numerator	Denominator
a.	Actual factory overhead	Actual machine hours
b.	Actual factory overhead	Estimated machine hours
c.	Estimated factory overhead	Actual machine hours
d.	Estimated factory overhead	Estimated machine hours

(5/91, Theory, #46, 2179)

36. In the computation of manufacturing cost per equivalent unit, the weighted-average method of process costing considers
a. Current cost less cost of beginning work-in-process inventory.
b. Current costs plus cost of ending work-in-process inventory.
c. Current costs plus cost of beginning work-in-process inventory.
d. Current costs only. (Editors, 2224)

37. Yarn Co.'s inventories in process were at the following stages of completion at the end of April:

No. of units	Percent complete
200	90
100	80
400	10

Equivalent units of production amounted to
a. 300.
b. 360.
c. 660.
d. 700. (Editors, 2677)

38. Bing Company had no beginning work-in-process inventory, and the ending work-in-process inventory is 50% complete as to conversion costs. The number of equivalent units as to conversion costs would be
a. The same as the units completed.
b. The same as the units placed in process.
c. Less than the units placed in process.
d. Less than the units completed. (Editors, 2229)

39. Kerner Manufacturing uses a process cost system to manufacture laptop computers. The following information summarizes operations relating to laptop computer model #KJK20 during the quarter ending March 31:

	Units	Direct Materials
Work-in-process inventory, January 1	100	$ 70,000
Started during the quarter	500	
Completed during the quarter	400	
Work-in-process inventory, March 31	200	
Costs added during the quarter		$750,000

Beginning work-in-process inventory was 50% complete for direct materials. Ending work-in-process inventory was 75% complete for direct materials. What were the equivalent units of production with regard to materials for the quarter?
a. 450
b. 500
c. 550
d. 600 (R/01, AR, #12, 6997)

40. Mart Co. adds materials at the beginning of the process in Department M. The following information pertains to units in Department M's work-in-process during April:

Work-in-process, April 1 (60% complete as to conversion cost)	1,500
Started in April	12,500
Completed	10,000
Work-in-process, April 30 (75% complete as to conversion cost)	4,000

Under the weighted-average method, the equivalent units for conversion cost are
a. 13,000.
b. 12,500.
c. 12,000.
d. 10,900. (Editors, 1487)

41. Kerner Manufacturing uses a process cost system to manufacture laptop computers. The following information summarizes operations relating to laptop computer model #KJK20 during the quarter ending March 31:

	Units	Direct Materials
Work-in-process inventory, January 1	100	$ 50,000
Started during the quarter	500	
Completed during the quarter	400	
Work-in-process inventory, March 31	200	
Costs added during the quarter		$720,000

Beginning work-in-process inventory was 50% complete for direct materials. Ending work-in-process inventory was 75% complete for direct materials. What is the total value of material costs in ending work-in-process inventory using the FIFO unit cost, inventory valuation method?
a. $183,000
b. $194,000
c. $210,000
d. $216,000 (R/01, AR, #15, 7000)

42. A department adds material at the beginning of a process and identifies defective units when the process is 40% complete. At the beginning of the period, there was no work in process. At the end of the period, the number of work-in-process units equaled the number of units transferred to finished goods. If all units in ending work-in-process were 66-2/3% complete, then ending work-in-process should be allocated
a. 50% of all normal defective unit costs.
b. 40% of all normal defective unit costs.
c. 50% of the material costs and 40% of the conversion costs of all normal defective unit costs.
d. None of the normal defective unit costs.
(5/91, Theory, #41, 2174)

43. During June, Delta Co. experienced scrap, normal spoilage, and abnormal spoilage in its manufacturing process. The cost of units produced includes
a. Scrap, but **not** spoilage.
b. Normal spoilage, but **neither** scrap **nor** abnormal spoilage.
c. Scrap and normal spoilage, but **not** abnormal spoilage.
d. Scrap, normal spoilage, and abnormal spoilage.
(11/91, Theory, #44, 2552)

44. Simpson Company manufactures electric drills to the exacting specifications of various customers. During April, Job 43 for the production of 1,100 drills was completed at the following costs per unit:

Direct materials	$ 5
Direct labor	4
Applied factory overhead	6
	$15

Final inspection of Job 43 disclosed 50 defective units and 100 spoiled units. The defective drills were reworked at a total cost of $250, and the spoiled drills were sold to a jobber for $750. What would be the unit cost of the good units produced on Job 43?

a. $16.50
b. $16.00
c. $15.00
d. $14.50 (Editors, 9213)

45. The sale of scrap from a manufacturing process usually would be recorded as a(an)
a. Decrease in factory overhead control.
b. Decrease in finished goods control.
c. Increase in factory overhead control.
d. Increase in finished goods control.
(Editors, 2204)

46. The diagram below represents the production and sales relationships of joint products P and Q. Joint costs are incurred until split-off, then separable costs are incurred in refining each product. Market values of P and Q at split-off are used to allocate joint costs.

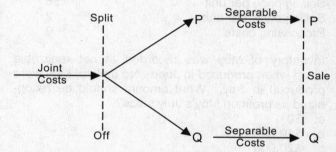

If the market value of P at split-off increases and all other costs and selling prices remain unchanged, then the gross margin of

	P	Q
a.	Increases	Decreases
b.	Increases	Increases
c.	Decreases	Decreases
d.	Decreases	Increases

(5/90, Theory, #44, 9215)

47. Actual sales values at the split-off point for joint products Y and Z are not known. For purposes of allocating joint costs to products Y and Z, the relative sales value at split-off method is used. An increase in the costs beyond split-off occurs for product Z, while those of product Y remain constant. If the selling prices of finished products Y and Z remain constant, the percentage of the total joint costs allocated to product Y and product Z would
a. Decrease for product Y and increase for product Z.
b. Decrease for product Y and product Z.
c. Increase for product Y and product Z.
d. Increase for product Y and decrease for product Z. (Editors, 2189)

48. Rome Co. produces two joint products, BEC and CAL. Joint production costs for June were $30,000. During June, further processing costs beyond the split-off point, needed to convert the products into saleable form, were $25,000 and $35,000 for 800 units of BEC and 400 units of CAL, respectively. BEC sells for $100 per unit, and CAL sells for $200 per unit. Rome uses the net realizable value method for allocating joint product costs. For June, the joint costs allocated to product BEC were
a. $20,000.
b. $16,500.
c. $13,500.
d. $10,000.   (Editors, 1489)

49. The following information pertains to a by-product called Moy:

Sales in July	5,000 units
Selling price per unit	$6
Selling costs per unit	2
Processing costs	0

Inventory of Moy was recorded at net realizable value when produced in June. No units of Moy were produced in July. What amount should be recognized as profit on Moy's July sales?
a. $0
b. $10,000
c. $20,000
d. $30,000   (5/92, PII, #47, amended, 2679)

50. Mig Co. produces gasoline and a gasoline by-product. The following information is available pertaining to sales and production of the first year of operations:

Total production costs to split-off point	$120,000
Gasoline sales	270,000
By-product sales	30,000
Gasoline inventory, ending	15,000
Additional by-product costs:	
Marketing	10,000
Production	15,000

Mig accounts for the by-product at the time of production. What are Mig's cost of sales for gasoline and the by-product for the first year of operations?

	Gasoline	By-product
a.	$105,000	$25,000
b.	$115,000	$0
c.	$108,000	$37,000
d.	$100,000	$0

(11/92, PII, #32, amended, 3366)

51. In accounting for by-products, the value of the by-product may be recognized at the time of

	Production	Sale
a.	Yes	Yes
b.	No	Yes
c.	No	No
d.	Yes	No

(Editors, 2206)

52. Alley Co. produces main products Kul and Ju. The process also yields by-product Bef. Net realizable value of by-product Bef is subtracted from joint production cost of Kul and Ju. The following information pertains to production in July at a joint cost of $54,000:

Product	Units produced	Market value	Additional cost after split-off
Kul	1,000	$40,000	$0
Ju	2,500	60,000	0
Bef	500	9,000	5,000

If Alley uses the net realizable value method for allocating joint cost, how much of the joint cost should be allocated to product Kul?
a. $13,500
b. $14,286
c. $20,000
d. $33,333   (Editors, 9216)

53. When a manager is concerned with monitoring total cost, total revenue, and net profit conditioned upon the level of productivity, an accountant would normally recommend

	Flexible budgeting	Standard costing
a.	Yes	Yes
b.	Yes	No
c.	No	Yes
d.	No	No

(11/90, Theory, #45, 2182)

54. Fount Company uses a standard cost system. For April, total overhead is budgeted at $80,000 based on the normal capacity of 10,000 direct-labor hours. At standard, each unit of finished product requires two direct-labor hours. The following data are available for April production activity:

Equivalent units of product	4,750
Direct-labor hours worked	9,250
Actual total overhead incurred	$79,500

What amount should Fount credit to the applied factory overhead account for April?
a. $76,000
b. $78,000
c. $79,500
d. $80,000 (Editors, 1520)

55. A standard cost system may be used in
a. Neither process costing nor job order costing.
b. Process costing but **not** job order costing.
c. Either job order costing or process costing.
d. Job order costing but **not** process costing.
(11/91, Theory, #42, 2550)

56. Which of the following standard costing variances would be **least** controllable by a production supervisor?
a. Overhead volume
b. Overhead efficiency
c. Labor efficiency
d. Material usage (5/93, Theory, #43, 4230)

57. Rigley Company has underapplied overhead of $55,000 for the calendar year. Before disposition of the underapplied overhead, selected year-end balances from Rigley's accounting records are:

Sales $1,200,000
Cost of goods sold 900,000
Direct materials inventory 150,000
Work-in-process inventory 200,000
Finished goods inventory 100,000

Under Rigley's cost accounting system, over or underapplied overhead is allocated to appropriate inventories and cost of goods sold based on year-end balances. In its annual income statement, Rigley should report costs of goods sold as
a. $858,750.
b. $863,333.
c. $936,667.
d. $941,250. (Editors, 1519)

58. The following were among Gage Co.'s April costs:

Normal spoilage $ 5,000
Freight out 10,000
Excess of actual manufacturing costs
over standard costs 20,000
Standard manufacturing costs $100,000
Actual prime manufacturing costs 80,000

Gage's April actual manufacturing overhead was
a. $ 40,000.
b. $ 45,000.
c. $ 55,000.
d. $120,000. (5/92, PII, #43, amended, 2675)

59. Which of the following variances would be useful in calling attention to a possible short-term problem in the control of overhead costs?

	Spending variance	Volume variance
a.	Yes	Yes
b.	No	Yes
c.	Yes	No
d.	No	No

(Editors, 2188)

60. Baby Frames, Inc., evaluates manufacturing overhead in its factory by using variance analysis. The following information applies to the month of May:

	Actual	Budgeted
Number of frames manufactured	19,000	20,000
Variable overhead costs	$4,100	$2 per direct labor hour
Fixed overhead costs	$22,000	$20,000
Direct labor hours	2,100 hours	0.1 hour per frame

What is the fixed overhead spending variance?
a. $1,000 favorable
b. $1,000 unfavorable
c. $2,000 favorable
d. $2,000 unfavorable (R/01, AR, #13, 6998)

61. Kemper Company follows a practice of isolating variances at the earliest point in time. When is the appropriate time to isolate and recognize a direct material price variance?
a. When a purchase order is originated
b. When material is purchased
c. When material is used in production
d. When material is issued (Editors, 2234)

62. The following direct labor information pertains to the manufacture of product Glu:

Time required to make
one unit 2 direct labor hours
Number of direct workers 50
Number of productive hours
per week, per worker 40
Weekly wages per worker $500
Workers' benefits treated as
direct labor costs 20% of wages

What is the standard direct labor cost per unit of product Glu?
a. $30
b. $24
c. $15
d. $12 (5/92, PII, #46, 2678)

63. The standard direct material cost to produce a unit of Lem is 4 meters of material at $2.50 per meter. During May, 4,200 meters of material costing $10,080 were purchased and used to produce 1,000 units of Lem. What was the material price variance for May?
a. $400 favorable
b. $420 favorable
c. $ 80 unfavorable
d. $480 unfavorable
(11/95, AR, #47, amended, 5790)

64. Yola Co. manufactures one product with a standard direct labor cost of four hours at $12.00 per hour. During June, 1,000 units were produced using 4,100 hours at $12.20 per hour. The unfavorable direct labor efficiency variance was
a. $1,220.
b. $1,200.
c. $ 820.
d. $ 400.
(11/92, PII, #21, 3355)

65. For April, Stork Co.'s records disclosed the following data relating to direct labor:

Actual cost	$10,000
Rate variance	1,000 favorable
Efficiency variance	1,500 unfavorable
Standard cost	$ 9,500

For April, actual direct labor hours totaled 1,000. Stork's standard direct labor rate per hour was
a. $11.00.
b. $10.00.
c. $ 9.50.
d. $ 9.00.
(Editors, 1515)

66. Tyro Co. uses a standard cost system. The following information pertains to direct labor for product B for the month of May:

Actual rate paid	$ 8.40 per hour
Standard rate	$ 8.00 per hour
Standard hours allowed for actual production	2,000 hours
Labor efficiency variance	$ 800 unfavorable

What were the actual hours worked?
a. 1,900
b. 1,905
c. 2,095
d. 2,100
(Editors, 1511)

67. When using the two-variance method for analyzing factory overhead, the difference between the budget allowance based on standard hours allowed and the factory overhead applied to production is the

a. Controllable variance.
b. Net overhead variance.
c. Volume variance.
d. Efficiency variance.
(Editors, 2225)

68. Columbia Company uses a standard cost system and prepared the following budget at normal capacity for the month of June:

Direct-labor hours	12,000
Variable factory overhead	$24,000
Fixed factory overhead	$54,000
Total factory overhead per direct-labor hour	$ 6.50
Actual June direct labor hours worked	11,000
Actual June total factory overhead	$73,500
Standard direct labor hours allowed for capacity attained in June	10,500

Using the two-way analysis of overhead variances, what is the budget (controllable) variance for June?
a. $1,500 favorable
b. $2,500 favorable
c. $4,500 favorable
d. $5,250 unfavorable
(Editors, 1523)

69. Under the two-variance method for analyzing overhead, which of the following variances consists of both variable and fixed overhead elements?

	Controllable (budget) variance	Volume variance
a.	No	No
b.	Yes	No
c.	Yes	Yes
d.	No	Yes

(Editors, 9217)

70. Information on Wright Company's overhead costs for the June production activity is as follows:

Budgeted fixed overhead	$ 37,500
Standard fixed overhead rate per direct-labor hour	$ 3
Standard variable overhead rate per direct-labor hour	$ 6
Standard direct-labor hours allowed for actual production	12,000
Actual total overhead incurred	$110,000

Wright has a standard absorption and flexible budgeting system, and uses the two-variance method (two-way analysis) for overhead variances. The volume (denominator) variance for June is
a. $1,500 unfavorable.
b. $1,500 favorable.
c. $2,000 unfavorable.
d. $2,000 favorable.
(Editors, 9223)

71. Under the two-variance method for analyzing factory overhead, which of the following is used in the computation of the controllable (budget) variance?

	Budget allowance based on actual hours	Budget allowance based on standard hours
a.	No	No
b.	Yes	No
c.	Yes	Yes
d.	No	Yes

(Editors, 2202)

72. Under the three-variance method for analyzing factory overhead, which of the following is used in the computation of the spending variance?

	Actual factory overhead	Budget allowance based on actual hours
a.	Yes	No
b.	No	No
c.	No	Yes
d.	Yes	Yes

(Editors, 2212)

ITEMS 73 AND 74 are based on the following information available from Rust Company:

Actual factory overhead	$30,000
Fixed overhead, actual	$14,400
Fixed overhead, budgeted	$14,000
Actual hours	7,000
Standard hours	7,600
Variable overhead rate per direct-labor hour	$ 2.50

Rust uses a three-way analysis of overhead variances.

73. What is the spending variance?
a. $1,500 favorable
b. $1,500 unfavorable
c. $1,900 favorable
d. $3,000 unfavorable   (Editors, 9218)

74. What is the efficiency variance?
a. $1,500 favorable
b. $1,500 unfavorable
c. $1,900 favorable
d. $3,000 unfavorable   (Editors, 9219)

75. A department's three-variance overhead standard costing system reported unfavorable spending and volume variances. The activity level selected for allocating overhead to the product was based on 80% of practical capacity. If 100% of practical capacity had been selected instead, how would the reported unfavorable spending and volume variances be affected?

	Spending variance	Volume variance
a.	Increased	Unchanged
b.	Increased	Increased
c.	Unchanged	Increased
d.	Unchanged	Unchanged

(5/91, Theory, #43, amended, 2176)

ITEMS 76 THROUGH 78 are based on the following information pertaining to Rand Company:

Units actually produced	76,000
Actual direct labor hours worked	160,000
Actual variable overhead incurred	$500,000
Actual fixed overhead incurred	384,000

Based on monthly normal volume of 100,000 units (200,000 direct labor hours), Rand's standard cost system contains the following overhead costs:

Variable	$6 per unit
Fixed	4 per unit

76. The fixed overhead budget variance was
a. $ 8,000 unfavorable.
b. $ 8,000 favorable.
c. $16,000 unfavorable.
d. $16,000 favorable.   (Editors, 9226)

77. The unfavorable variable overhead spending variance was
a. $12,000.
b. $20,000.
c. $24,000.
d. $44,000.   (Editors, 1513)

78. The fixed overhead volume variance was
a. $96,000 unfavorable.
b. $96,000 favorable.
c. $80,000 unfavorable.
d. $80,000 favorable.   (Editors, 1514)

OTHER OBJECTIVE FORMAT QUESTIONS

PROBLEM 25-3 (6 to 9 minutes)

ITEMS 1 AND 2 are based on the accompanying diagram, with the line OW representing the standard labor cost at any output volume expressed in direct labor hours. Point S indicates the actual output at standard cost, and Point A indicates the actual hours and actual costs required to produce S.

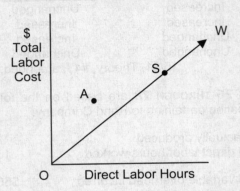

REQUIRED: FOR ITEMS 1 AND 2, indicate if each variance is favorable (F) or unfavorable (U).

1. Rate variance
2. Efficiency variance

ITEMS 3 THROUGH 5 are based on the accompanying diagram, depicting a factory overhead flexible budget line DB and standard overhead application line OA. Activity is expressed in machine hours with Point V indicating the standard hours required for the actual output in September. Point S indicates the actual machine hours (inputs) and actual costs in September.

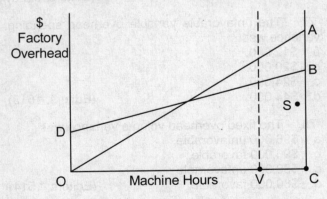

REQUIRED: FOR ITEMS 3 AND 4, indicate if each variance is favorable (F) or unfavorable (U).

3. Volume (capacity) variance
4. Efficiency variance
5. The budgeted total variable overhead cost for C machine hours is

A. AB.
B. BC.
C. AC minus DO.
D. BC minus DO.
   (11/90, Theory, #41-#44, amended, 9221-9225)

PROBLEM 25-4 (15 to 25 minutes)

Bilco, Inc. produces bricks and uses a standard costing system. On the accompanying diagram, the line OP represents Bilco's standard material cost at any output volume expressed in direct material pounds to be used. Bilco had identical outputs in each of the first three months of 1997, with a standard cost of V in each month. Points Ja, Fe, and Ma represent the actual pounds used and actual costs incurred in January, February, and March, respectively.

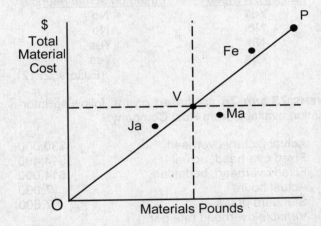

REQUIRED: FOR ITEMS 1 THROUGH 5, determine whether each variance is favorable (F) or unfavorable (U).

1. January material price variance.
2. January material usage variance.
3. February material price variance.
4. February material usage variance.
5. March material net variance.
   [5/92, Theory, #2 (61-65), amended]

PROBLEM 25-5 (7 to 12 minutes)

The accompanying diagram depicts a manufacturing total cost flexible budget line KI and standard cost line OI. Line OJ is parallel to line KI, and revenues are represented by line OH.

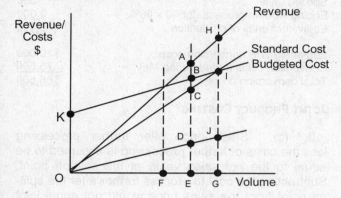

REQUIRED: FOR ITEMS 1 THROUGH 5, identify the line on the graph that represents each item.

1. The budgeted fixed cost at volume OE.
2. The budgeted variable cost at volume OE.
3. The standard gross profit at volume OE.
4. The budgeted gross profit at volume OE, assuming **no** change between beginning and ending inventories.
5. The normal capacity, assuming standard costs are based on normal capacity.

[11/92, Theory, #2 (69-73)]

SOLUTION 25-1 MULTIPLE CHOICE ANSWERS

JOB ORDER COSTING

1. **(b)**   Indirect materials are a part of manufacturing overhead. Therefore, they are included in the manufacturing overhead cost and should not be added again. Doing so would result in double counting the cost of indirect materials. The jobs completed during January should be charged with the manufacturing overhead applied, not the manufacturing overhead incurred. Some overhead costs are not incurred uniformly during the year. Applying overhead to production using a predetermined annual overhead rate helps to prevent some jobs from being overcosted and others from being undercosted.

Direct materials issued to production	$ 90,000
Direct labor costs	107,000
Manufacturing overhead applied	113,000
Total manufacturing costs	$310,000
Add: Beginning WIP	0
Total costs in WIP	$310,000
Less: Ending WIP	0
Cost of jobs completed during January	$310,000

2. **(c)**   In a job order cost system, the issue of indirect materials to a production department is recorded as an increase to the Factory Overhead Control account, as follows:

Factory Overhead Control	XX	
Stores Control		XX

PROCESS COSTING

3. **(d)**   The weighted-average method of process costing assumes that all units in the beginning inventory were completed during the current period. The equivalent units (EU) of production are the completed units plus the units in the ending work-in-process (WIP) inventory times the percentage of completion. In this case, all materials are added at the beginning of the process. Thus, the units in the ending inventory are 100% complete as to materials. To determine unit costs under the weighted-average method, the cost of beginning WIP is added to costs incurred during the period. The total cost is then divided by the EU of production. The result is the cost per EU: $23,500 / 55,000 = $0.43/unit.

Units completed	42,500
Units in ending WIP (12,500 x 100%)	12,500
Equivalent units of production	55,000

Cost of materials in beginning WIP	$ 5,500
Cost of materials added during period	18,000
Total cost of materials	$23,500

4. **(a)**   The first-in, first-out (FIFO) method of process costing separates the costs of the beginning work-in-process inventory from the costs of current production. Current-period costs are divided by current-period equivalent units (EU) to determine the current period's manufacturing cost per EU.

5. **(a)**   In the process, material G is added when a batch is 60% complete. Since the ending work-in-process (WIP) units are only 50% complete, they have not reached the stage of production where

material G is added. Therefore, we do not assume that there are any equivalent units (EU) of material G in the ending WIP units. On the other hand, conversion costs (i.e., direct labor and manufacturing overhead) are assumed to be incurred evenly throughout the process. Therefore, the ending WIP units are assumed to be 50% complete as to conversion costs. It is important to note that the answer to this question is not dependent on whether the weighted-average method or the FIFO method of process costing is used. Both of these methods use the EU in the ending WIP units to compute the EU of production of the period.

6. (d)   Under the FIFO method of process costing, the costs of the beginning work-in-process (WIP) are separated from the cost of current production. Therefore, in the computation of equivalent units (EU) for the period under FIFO, the EU in beginning WIP are subtracted. In the weighted-average method, all costs (including that of beginning WIP) are lumped together and a single cost of EU of production is computed. Thus, for any period for which there is a beginning WIP, EU for the weighted-average method will exceed the EU for the FIFO method by the number of EU in beginning WIP. Since there was no WIP at January 1, both methods yield the same results in January. However, since there was WIP at February 1, the number of EU is greater for the weighted-average method in February.

SPOILAGE

7. (d)   Normal spoilage is considered as a necessary cost of production. Therefore, the $60,000 normal spoilage cost is treated as a product or inventoriable cost. The $30,000 in abnormal spoilage cost is treated as a period cost because this cost is not usually incurred in making the product.

8. (a)   The unit cost of Job 10 = $1,580/200 = $7.90.

	Original cost accumulation	Rework costs	Total costs
Direct materials	$ 330	$ 50	$ 390
Direct labor	400	80	480
Factory overhead (150% of DL)	600	120	720
Total	$1,330	$250	$1,580

9. (c)   The weighted average method treats partially completed units in the beginning work-in-process inventory as if they were started and completed in the current period. Normal spoilage is treated as a normal cost of production, and the cost of spoilage is transferred to the second production department. The equivalent units (EUs) of production

for purposes of determining the costs to be transferred also include the spoiled units. The conversion cost per EU is $9.00 ($85,500 / 9,500). $9.00 x 7,500 = $67,500.

Units completed and transferred	7,000
Spoiled units	500
Ending work-in-process (2,500 x 80%)	2,000
Equivalent units of production	9,500

Beginning WIP conversion costs	$10,000
Conversion costs added during May	75,500
Total conversion costs	$85,500

JOINT PRODUCT COSTING

10. (c)   Sales price after further processing less the costs of further processing is assumed to be equal to the net sales value at the split-off point. Subtracting the cost to process further after the split-off point from the sales price would not equal joint costs or total costs because subtracting further processing costs from sales price would not equal costs. Such a difference would not equal the sales price less a normal profit margin.

11. (c)   As Ajac has 80% of net realizable value [($80,000 − $8,000) / ($120,000 − $30,000) = 80%], it is assigned 80% of joint cost. [$60,000 x 80% = $48,000]

BY-PRODUCTS

12. (b)   There would be no effect on Kode Co.'s overall profit, but there will be an effect on the company's gross margin. The gross margin will be $1 higher for each unit of May sold if May is accounted for as a joint product rather than as a by-product. The reason is that selling expenses are not subtracted in arriving at overall gross margin. This problem is best illustrated with an example. Assume that the major product sells for $100 and costs $60 to make. If May is accounted for as a by-product, the overall gross margin is $43.

Sales		$100
Cost of major product	$60	
Less: Sale of May ($4 − $1)	(3)	
Cost of goods sold		57
Overall gross margin		$ 43

If May is accounted for as a joint product, the overall gross margin is $44, although the overall profit is $43. Therefore, the overall gross margin will be $1 higher for each unit of May sold if May is accounted for as a joint product rather than as a by-product.

| | | | Sales ($100 + $4) | | $104 |
Sales ($100 + $4) $104
Less: Cost of goods sold .... (60)
Overall gross margin .... $ 44
Less: Selling expense .... (1)
Overall profit .... $ 43

SERVICE COSTS

13. (c)   Under the step method, costs are allocated from the service departments to other service departments and to the operating departments. In this case, the maintenance department costs must be allocated first because if the power department costs are allocated first, the answer doesn't appear in the options. Once costs are allocated from a service department, costs are not allocated back to that department. Neither can costs be allocated from a service department to the same service department based on a measure of service that such service department receives. Any percentage of use by the same service department or by a service department that has already had its costs allocated are ignored and new ratios must be computed using the relative usage of the remaining departments. The power department costs are allocated 2/9 to the School of Education and 7/9 to the School of Technology.

	Maintenance	Power	School of Education	School of Technology
Costs	$ 99,000	$ 54,000		
Allocation of Maintenance Costs:				
2/10 x $99,000	(19,800)	19,800		
3/10 x $99,000	(29,700)		$29,700	
5/10 x $99,000	(49,500)			$ 49,500
Total Power Costs		$ 73,800		
Allocation of Power Costs:				
2/9 x $73,800		(16,400)	16,400	
7/9 x $73,800		(57,400)		57,400
Totals	$ 0	$ 0	$46,100	$106,900

ACTIVITY-BASED COSTING

14. (b)   ABC assumes that creating production requires activities that consume resources. ABC allows for more complex relationships to be included in costing than traditional methods. An ABC system may use unit-, batch-, and plant-level drivers and both variable and fixed costs.

15. (d)   In such a system, costs are assigned to cost centers or cost pools and then to products using a volume basis. The most commonly used bases for allocating overhead are direct labor hours, direct labor cost, and machine hours. In an ABC system, costs are first charged to activities and then to products using cost drivers. Activities may be combined into homogeneous cost pools if the products consume the activities in the same proportion.

Cost drivers should have a causal relationship to the incurrence of cost. Thus, in an ABC system there are usually more cost pools and more allocation bases (cost drivers). An ABC system is more complex, but it should be more accurate than a traditional cost system.

16. (d)   Activity-based costing is a method for allocating overhead to products. It may be applied to either job or process costing.

17. (c)   Activity-based accounting systems have activities as the fundamental cost objects (they do not accumulate costs by department or function for purposes of product costing). Activity-based accounting systems use cost drivers as a basis for cost allocation (a cost driver is any factor whose effects cause an increase in the total cost of a related cost object). Under an activity-based accounting system, activities that do not add to the value of the product are identified and reduced to the extent possible.

18. (c)   ABC systems have activities as the fundamental cost objects; they do not accumulate costs by department, or function for purposes of product costing. ABC systems identify cost drivers as a basis for cost allocation. No attempt is made to eliminate the cost drivers. A cost driver is any factor whose effects cause an increase in the total cost of a related cost object. Under an ABC system, activities that do not add to the value of the product are identified and eliminated to the extent possible.

19. (b)   In an ABC system, costs are first assigned to activities based upon the costs those activities consume. Next, the costs are assigned to cost objects such as products based upon the activities those cost objects consume. For example, some costs are batch level costs, such as the cost to set up a machine. Other costs are related to volume. There may be various kinds of batch level costs related to different activities. ABC uses a multiple cause and effect relationship in an attempt to arrive at the most accurate cost possible.

STANDARD COST CONCEPTS

20. (a)   Standard costing is appropriate for mass production industries, as well as for service industries. Standard costing may be used in various types of companies in which repetitive tasks are performed in making and selling a product or in delivering a service.

21. (b)   Engineering standards based on attainable performance is the best basis to use in establishing standard hours allowed because they

reflect the costs that should be incurred under efficient operating conditions. Standards based on attainable performance are less stringent than those based on ideal performance because of allowance for normal spoilage, ordinary machine breakdowns, and lost time. However, standards based on attainable performance are usually set strict enough so that the achievement of standard performance is a satisfying accomplishment for the workers. The average historical performance for the past three years may contain many inefficiencies, which should not be permitted to influence future performance measurement. In addition, the past may not be reflective of current economic conditions, technology, and supply and demand characteristics. Engineering estimates based on ideal performance do not allow for imperfections or inefficiencies of any type. Standards based on ideal performance are rarely, if ever, attained. The production level to satisfy average consumer demand over a seasonal time span also should not be used.

22. (c) The expected total cost to process the papers is comprised of the expected variable and fixed costs of processing, given standard performance.

Standard variable cost of processing 1,600,000 papers	$1,280,000
Divide by: 1,600,000 papers	÷1,600,000
Standard variable cost of processing one paper	$ 0.80
Papers processed during period	x 1,200,000
Expected variable cost of processing 1,200,000 papers	$ 960,000
Expected fixed cost of processing (given)	200,000
Expected total cost to process papers produced	$1,160,000

VARIANCES

23. (d) Since there is no difference between the standard and actual labor rate, there is no labor rate variance. To determine the labor rate variance it is necessary to determine the standard rate and actual rate per labor hour.

Standard labor cost to process 1,000 papers	$ 750
Standard labor hours to process 1,000 papers	÷ 150
Standard rate per labor hour	$ 5.00

Labor cost incurred to process 1,200,000 papers	$950,000
Labor hours incurred to process 1,200,000 papers	÷190,000
Actual rate per labor hour	$ 5.00

24. (c) The predetermined factory overhead application rate is based on direct labor cost. Budgeted factory overhead was $300,000 and budgeted direct labor cost was $150,000 (25,000 DLH x $6.00) resulting in a predetermined factory overhead application rate of 200% ($300,000 ÷ $150,000) of direct labor cost.

Factory overhead applied ($162,500 x 200%)	$ 325,000
Factory overhead incurred	310,000
Overapplied factory overhead	$ 15,000

DISPOSITION OF VARIANCES

25. (a) Cost of goods manufactured for May is determined by first adding the costs in beginning WIP, direct costs incurred during May, and OH applied; this is then reduced by ending WIP. Note that any over- or underapplied OH is closed to cost of goods sold; it is not reflected in cost of goods manufactured or ending WIP.

Beginning WIP	$ 9,000	
Direct materials	26,000	
Direct labor	20,000	
Applied OH ($20,000 x 150%)	30,000	
Total manufacturing costs applied		$ 85,000
Direct materials	$ 2,800	
Direct labor	1,800	
Applied OH ($1,800 x 150%)	2,700	
Less ending WIP		(7,300)
Cost of goods manufactured		$ 77,700

26. (d) Hart does not allocate over- or underapplied OH to inventories and cost of goods sold. Thus, the entire $2,000 is charged to CGS.

Factory overhead incurred	$ 32,000
Factory overhead applied ($20,000 x 150%)	(30,000)
Underapplied overhead	$ 2,000

PRIME COST VARIANCES

27. (d) To compute the amount of direct materials purchased in January, it is necessary to analyze the changes in the direct materials inventory.

Beg. inventory + Purchases = Materials used + End inventory

$$\$15,000 + X = \$95,000 + \$20,000$$
$$X = \$100,000$$

28. (c) In computing the amount of direct-labor cost, it is necessary to isolate the costs that were applied during January. The cost-of-goods manufactured of $257,500 includes the $7,500 of cost in beginning WIP. Beginning WIP must be subtracted because it involves costs applied in a prior period. In the same respect, the $10,000 of costs of the ending WIP must be added in because such costs were applied in January. Now that the total costs applied in January are isolated, the amounts applied for direct materials used and factory overhead are subtracted, yielding $90,000 direct-labor costs ($260,000 – $75,000 – $95,000). It should be noted that the amount of actual factory overhead is *not* subtracted because any over- or underapplied overhead is closed to cost of goods sold at the *end* of the year.

VARIANCES IN OH COSTS

29. (b)   In the four-way analysis of factory over-head, the variable overhead efficiency variance is computed by multiplying the difference between the actual direct labor hours incurred and the standard direct labor hours (DLH) allowed for the units produced by the variable overhead rate (DLH).

Actual direct labor hours	10,500
Standard DLH allowed for quantity	
produced (5,000 x 2)	10,000
Excess of actual DLH over standard DLH	500
Times: Variable overhead rate per standard DLH	x $3
Variable overhead efficiency variance (unfavorable)	$ 1,500

30. (c)   In August, $9,000 ($1,500 + $5,000 + $2,500) of direct labor was added to jobs, so $18,000 ($9,000 x 2) of manufacturing overhead was applied, or $2,000 less than actual manufacturing overhead of $20,000.

SOLUTION 25-2 ADDITIONAL MULTIPLE CHOICE ANSWERS

JOB ORDER COSTING

31. (b)

Beginning work-in-process		$ 4,000
Direct materials	$24,000	
Direct labor	16,000	
Factory overhead applied	12,800	
Manufacturing costs added during month		52,800
Manufacturing costs to account for		56,800
Less: Transfer to finished goods		48,000
Ending work-in-process—Job No. 5		8,800
Less: Direct labor (given)		(2,000)
Factory overhead applied		
($2,000 x 80%)		(1,600)
Direct materials charged to Job No. 5		$ 5,200

32. (c)   The predetermined factory overhead rate is determined by dividing the estimated factory overhead cost by the estimated level of activity. Underapplied overhead could result if the actual level of activity was less than the estimated level of activity used to determine the overhead rate. Under-applied overhead could also result if actual fixed costs were greater than the estimated fixed costs used to determine the overhead rate.

33. (a)   In a job order cost system, use of direct materials previously purchased usually is recorded as an increase in the *WIP Control* account.

Work-in-Process Control—Job "X"	XX	
Stores Control		XX

PROCESS COSTING

34. (d)   In either a process or job order cost system, the application of factory overhead is usually recorded as an increase in the *Work-in-Process Control* account.

Work-in-Process Control—Job "X"	XX	
Factory Overhead Applied		XX

Finished Goods Inventory Control is increased when goods are completed. *Factory Overhead Control* is increased when factory overhead costs are incurred. Cost of goods sold is increased when finished goods are sold.

35. (d)   The predetermined factory overhead application rate is computed by dividing the estimated factory overhead costs by the estimated level of activity, usually measured in direct labor hours, direct labor cost, or machine hours.

36. (c)   The weighted-average method of process costing intermingles the costs in beginning work-in-process (WIP) inventory with the costs incurred in the current period. These costs are then allocated to all the equivalent units of production, including the equivalent units in beginning inventory. By contrast, the first-in, first-out (FIFO) method of process costing treats the beginning WIP as a separate batch.

37. (a)   Equivalent units (EU) of production are used in process costing to express a given number of partially completed units in terms of a smaller number of fully completed units. The EU of production for the inventories in question is 300 [i.e., (200 x 90%) + (100 x 80%) + (400 x 10%)].

38. (c)   Assuming no beginning work-in-process (WIP), the number of equivalent units (EU) as to conversion costs will be the sum of the number of units finished during the period, plus the product of multiplying the number of units in ending WIP by the percentage of completion of those units. Thus, the number of EU of conversion costs will be greater than the number of units finished, but less than the number of units initially placed in production.

39. (b)   Assume the WIP beginning inventory, 100 units 50% complete, are among the 400 units completed during the quarter. That would use 50 units of direct materials. Of the 500 units started during the quarter, 300 were completed, using 300 units of direct materials. Finally, 200 of the

500 units started were only 75% completed, using (75% x 200 units) 150 units of direct materials. Production units used during the quarter would be 50 to complete the original 100, plus 300 started & completed during the quarter, plus the 150 used to process 200 units to 75% completion, or 500 total units. Notice that the dollar figures given in the question are irrelevant to the solution.

40. (a) Under the weighted-average method, the equivalent units (EU) for conversion cost are determined by adding the EU of conversion cost embodied in the units completed and ending WIP.

	Physical Units	Percentage complete as to conversion cost		Equivalent units of conversion cost
Completed	10,000 x	100%	=	10,000
Ending work-in-process	4,000 x	75%	=	3,000
				13,000

41. (d) FIFO assumes the WIP beginning inventory, 100 units 50% complete, are among the 400 units completed during the quarter. That would use 50 equivalent finished units (EFU's) of direct materials. Of the 500 units started during the quarter, 300 EFU's were completed, using 300 units of direct materials. Finally, 200 of the 500 units started were only 75% completed, using (75% x 200 units) 150 EFU's of direct materials. Production units used during the quarter are 50 EFU's to complete the original 100, plus 300 started & completed, plus 150 EFU's used to process 200 units 75%, or 500 EFU's. Divide the direct material costs added during the quarter, $720,000, by the 500 EFU's of direct materials used during the quarter, to get direct material cost per unit, $1,440. 150 EFU's x $1,440 per EFU equals $216,000.

SPOILAGE

42. (a) Because defective units are identified when production is 40% complete, and all of the completed units and all of the work-in-process (WIP) units are past that point, all units should receive the same amount of spoilage cost. Because, at the end of the period, the number of WIP units equaled the number of completed units, the ending WIP should be allocated 50% of the defective unit costs.

43. (c) The cost of units produced usually includes scrap and normal spoilage, but *not* abnormal spoilage. *Scrap* is the residue from manufacturing operations that has measurable but relatively minor recovery value. The sales value of scrap is *usually* recorded as a decrease to the *Factory Overhead Control* account (although it is important to note that an alternative in a job order

cost situation would be to trace sales of scrap to the job that yielded the scrap and decrease the *Work-in-Process Control* account). The cost of the units produced should include *normal spoilage* because it is an inherent result of the particular process; it was expected to occur under efficient operating conditions. On the other hand, *abnormal spoilage* is not inventoried because it is not an inherent result of the selected production process; it was not expected to be incurred under efficient operating conditions.

44. (b) The original production of 1,100 drills cost $16,500 (1,100 drills x $15 per drill). The reworking of the defective drills increased the cost total to $16,750. The $750 received from the sale of the 100 defective units should be subtracted from the total cost incurred in producing the 1,100 drills. Therefore, the total cost for producing *1,000* good drills equals $16,000 ($16,500 + $250 − $750).

45. (a) Scrap is the residue from manufacturing operations that has measurable but relatively minor recovery value. The sales value of scrap is usually recorded as a decrease to the *Factory Overhead Control* account. An alternative method in a job-cost situation would be to trace sales of scrap to the jobs that yielded the scrap and decrease the *Work-in-Process Control* account.

JOINT PRODUCT COSTING

46. (d) The market values of joint products P and Q at split-off are used to allocate their joint costs. If the market value of P at split-off increases, while the market value of Q at split-off remains unchanged, the relative market value at split-off increases for P and decreases for Q. Thus, more of the joint product costs would be allocated to P and less would be allocated to Q. Since the separable costs and the final selling prices of P and Q remain constant, the gross margin of P would decrease due to its increased allocation of joint costs, and the gross margin of Q would increase due to its decreased allocation of joint costs.

47. (d) When the actual sales values at the split-off point for joint products are not known, joint costs are allocated on the basis of each product's net realizable value. Net realizable value is the excess of the product's sales value less costs beyond the split-off point. Since the selling prices of products Y and Z remain constant, and the costs beyond the split-off point increase for product Z, its net realizable value decreases. Less joint costs will be allocated to product Z and more will be allocated to product Y.

48. **(b)** The joint costs (in 1,000's) are allocated as follows.

	Total Sales value	Costs beyond split-off	NRV at split-off	%	Joint costs to allocate	Joint costs allocated
BEC	$ 80	$25	$ 55	55%	$30	$16.5
CAL	80	35	45	45	$30	13.5
	$160	$60	$100	100%		$30.0

BY-PRODUCTS

49. **(a)** Net realizable value (NRV) is the estimated selling price of an inventory item less the estimated costs that will be incurred in preparing the item for sale and selling it. Since the inventory in question was recorded at net realizable value when produced, no profit will be recognized on its sale.

Selling price per unit		$6.00
Less: Selling costs per unit	$2.00	
Carrying amount per unit ($6.00 – $2.00)	4.00	6.00
Profit recognized on each unit at time of sale		$ 0

50. **(d)** Mig accounts for the by-product at the time of production, whereby the net realizable value (i.e., sales value less additional costs) of the by-product is deducted from the total cost of production of the main product. This method directly matches the cost-reduction power of the by-product to the production costs of the main product. No cost of sales is reported for the gasoline by-product because its NRV is deducted from the total cost of production of the gasoline.

Total production costs to split-off point (i.e., the joint product costs)	$120,000
Less: Net realizable value of by-product [$30,000 – ($15,000 + $10,000)]	5,000
Net production costs of gasoline	115,000
Less: Gasoline inventory, ending	15,000
Cost of sales for gasoline	$100,000

51. **(a)** There are two general approaches to accounting for the value of by-products. First of all, the value of by-products may be recognized at the time of production. Under this approach, the net realizable value of the by-products produced is deducted from the cost of the major products produced. Alternatively, the value of the by-products may be recognized at the time of sale. Under this approach, the net revenue from the by-products sold is deducted from the cost of the major products sold.

52. **(c)** Subtracting the net realizable value (NRV) of Bef (i.e., $9,000 – $5,000) from the joint cost of $54,000 leaves $50,000 to be allocated to products Kul and Ju. Kul's portion of this cost is computed as follows:

Sales value	– Additional cost	= NRV	
$40,000	– $0	= $40,000	
NRV ratio	x Joint cost	= Allocated portion	
40/(40+60)	x $50,000	= $20,000	

STANDARD COST CONCEPTS

53. **(a)** Whenever levels of production change, cost variances should be calculated based on a flexible budget. Standard costing allows control over variances from actual costs to standard flexible budget cost at the appropriate level of production.

54. **(a)** Fount should apply factory overhead based on the equivalent units of production, the standard direct-labor hours per unit, and the standard amount of overhead per direct-labor hour (overhead rate).

$$\frac{\text{Overhead}}{\text{rate}} = \frac{\text{Total overhead budgeted}}{\text{Normal capacity}} = \frac{\$80,000}{10,000} = \frac{\$8 / \text{direct}}{\text{labor hour}}$$

Equivalent units of product	4,750
Standard direct-labor hours per unit	x 2
Standard direct-labor hours	9,500
Overhead rate	x $8
Applied factory overhead	$76,000

55. **(c)** A standard cost system is one whereby costs are charged to work-in-process on the basis of predetermined standard rates. Standard costs may be applied to a single unit as in job order costing or to many units as in process costing.

56. **(a)** The overhead volume variance is a measure of the utilization of available plant facilities; it does not measure the efficient use of inputs used in production. The volume variance is considered to be beyond the immediate control of a production supervisor because it is an activity-related variance that is explainable only by activity and is controllable only by activity—which is often geared to anticipated sales. Efficiency variances (e.g., overhead efficiency, labor efficiency, and material usage) measure the difference between the quantity of inputs that should have been used at the actual output level achieved and the quantity of inputs that were actually used. Efficiency variances are considered to be controllable by a production supervisor.

57. (d) The under (over) applied overhead should be prorated to the balances of work-in-process, finished goods, and cost of goods sold.

	Dec. 31 unadjusted balance	%	% x under-applied overhead	Dec. 31 adjusted balance
Cost of goods sold	$ 900,000	75	$41,250	$ 941,250
Finished goods	100,000	8 1/3	4,583	104,583
Work-in-process	200,000	16 2/3	9,167	209,167
	$1,200,000	100	$55,000	$1,255,000

58. (a)

Standard manufacturing costs	$100,000
Add: Excess of actual manufacturing costs over standard costs	20,000
Actual manufacturing (conversion) costs	$120,000
Actual prime manufacturing costs	80,000
Actual manufacturing overhead costs, April	$ 40,000

59. (c) The relationships in the three-variance method for analyzing factory overhead are identified below:

Actual Factory overhead incurred	Budget allowance based on actual hours	Budget allowance based on standard hours	Factory overhead applied
	Spending variance	Efficiency variance	Volume variance

The spending variance is affected by (1) price increases over what was shown in the flexible budget and (2) waste or excessive usage of overhead materials. Since the spending variance represents the difference between the actual factory overhead incurred and the budget allowance based on actual hours, waste will automatically show up as part of this variance, along with any excessive prices paid for overhead items. Generally the price element in this variance will be small, so the variance permits a focusing of attention on that thing over which the supervisor probably has the greatest control—the usage of overhead in production. On the other hand, the volume variance is a measure of utilization of available plant facilities; it does not measure over- or underspending. Most companies consider the volume variance to be beyond immediate control because it is an activity-related variance that is explainable only by activity and is controllable only by activity—which is often geared to anticipated sales.

60. (d) An unfavorable variance exists when actual cost exceeds standard cost. Since Baby Frames actually overspent the fixed overhead budget by $2,000, the spending variance is $2,000 unfavorable.

PRIME COST VARIANCES

61. (b) If the company follows a practice of isolating variances at the earliest point in time, a direct material price variance will be isolated at purchase time. This is the earliest time at which the company knows that the actual price differs from its standard price.

62. (a)

Weekly wages per worker	$ 500
Number of productive hours per week per worker	÷ 40
Hourly wage per worker	12.50
Add: Workers' benefits treated as direct labor cost ($12.50 x 20%)	2.50
Direct labor cost per productive hour	15.00
Times: Direct labor hours required to produce one unit	x 2
Standard direct labor cost per unit	$30.00

63. (b) The material price variance (MPV) is equal to the difference between the actual price and the standard price times the actual quantity purchased: MPV = (AP – SP) AQ. The actual price is $2.40 ($10,080 / 4,200). MPV = ($2.40 – $2.50) x 4,200 = ($420). The cost variance is considered favorable because the actual cost is less than the standard cost.

64. (b)

Actual direct labor hours	4,100
Standard direct labor hours (1,000 x 4 DLH)	4,000
Excess of actual over standard direct labor hours	100
Times: Standard direct labor rate	x $12
Direct labor efficiency variance—Unfavorable	$1,200

65. (a)

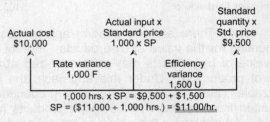

Actual cost $10,000	Actual input x Standard price 1,000 x SP	Standard quantity x Std. price $9,500
	Rate variance 1,000 F	Efficiency variance 1,500 U

1,000 hrs. x SP = $9,500 + $1,500
SP = ($11,000 ÷ 1,000 hrs.) = $11.00/hr.

66. (d) The labor efficiency variance is $800 unfavorable and the standard rate per direct labor hour is $8.00; thus, 100 ($800 ÷ $8) direct labor hours were incurred above the 2,000 standard hours allowed for actual production. Actual hours worked were 2,100 hours (2,000 + 100).

2-VARIANCE OH METHOD

67. (c)   The difference between the budget allowance based on standard hours allowed and the factory overhead applied to production is the volume variance. (Also see the diagram in the explanation to question #71.)

68. (a)   The budget (controllable) variance is the difference between the actual overhead incurred and the budgeted overhead based on the standard costs for the attained capacity. The actual overhead incurred was $73,500. The budgeted overhead was $75,000 [$54,000 for fixed overhead and $21,000 ($2 budgeted variable overhead per direct-labor hour x 10,500 standard direct-labor hours allowed for attained capacity) for variable overhead]. Thus, the actual overhead incurred was $1,500 less than the budgeted overhead for the capacity attained.

69. (b)   This diagram identifies the relationships in the two-variance method for analyzing factory overhead.

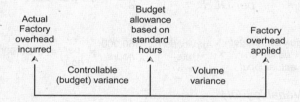

The controllable (budget) variance consists of both variable and fixed overhead elements. The amount of the variable overhead element included in the actual factory overhead incurred (i.e., the actual variable overhead incurred) and that included in the flexible budget based on standard hours allowed (i.e., the variable overhead rate multiplied by the standard hours allowed) differ. The amount of the fixed overhead element included in the actual factory overhead incurred (i.e., the actual fixed overhead incurred) and that included in the flexible budget based on standard hours allowed (i.e., the original estimate of budgeted fixed overhead for the period) also differ. On the other hand, the volume variance consists only of a fixed overhead element. The amount of the variable overhead element included in the flexible budget based on standard hours allowed is the same as that included in the amount of factory overhead applied (i.e., the variable overhead rate multiplied by the standard hours allowed). On the other hand, the amount of the fixed overhead element included in the flexible budget based on standard hours allowed (i.e., the original estimate of budgeted fixed overhead for the period) differs from the amount of the fixed factory overhead included in the amount of factory overhead applied (i.e., the fixed overhead rate multiplied by the standard hours allowed).

70. (a)   The volume (denominator) variance in either the two-, three-, or four-way analysis of overhead can be computed as the difference between the budgeted fixed overhead and the fixed overhead applied to production.

Budgeted fixed overhead		$37,500
Standard DLHs allowed for actual production	12,000	
Standard fixed overhead rate per DLH	x $3.00	
Fixed overhead applied to production:		36,000
Volume (denominator) variance (unfavorable)		$ 1,500

The volume variance is unfavorable because the company operated at an activity level (12,000 DLHs) below that planned for the period [12,500 DLH (i.e., $37,500 / $3.00)].

71. (d)   The budget allowance based on standard hours is used in the computation of the controllable (budget) variance. The budget allowance based on actual hours is not used in the two-variance method of analyzing factory overhead. The following diagram identifies relationships in the two-variance method of analyzing factory overhead.

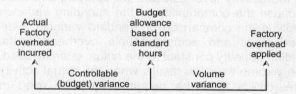

3-VARIANCE OH METHOD

72. (d)   Actual factory overhead and the budget allowance based on actual hours are used to determine the spending variance under the three-variance method for analyzing factory overhead. The relationships in the three-variance method for analyzing factory overhead are identified below:

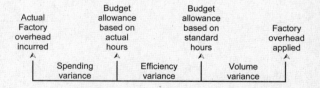

73. (a)   Under the three-way analysis of overhead, the spending variance is computed as the difference between the amount of actual factory overhead incurred and the amount of factory overhead budgeted for the actual hours incurred. The spending variance is favorable because less factory overhead was incurred than that budgeted for the actual direct labor hours incurred.

Actual factory overhead (given)		$30,000
Actual DLH incurred	7,000	
Times: Variable overhead rate per DLH	x $2.50	
Budgeted variable overhead for actual DLH	$17,500	
Budgeted fixed overhead (given)	14,000	
Budgeted factory overhead for actual hours		31,500
Spending variance (favorable)		$ 1,500

74. (a) Under the three-way analysis of overhead, the efficiency variance is computed as the difference between the amount of budgeted factory overhead for the actual hours incurred and the amount of budgeted factory overhead for the standard hours allowed. The efficiency variance is favorable because less factory overhead is budgeted at the actual hours incurred than that for the standard hours allowed.

Budgeted factory overhead for actual DLH incurred		
(see explanation for previous question)		$31,500
Standard DLH	7,600	
Times: Variable overhead rate per DLH	x $2.50	
Budgeted variable overhead for		
standard DLH	$19,000	
Budgeted fixed overhead (given)	14,000	
Budgeted factory overhead for		
standard hours allowed		33,000
Efficiency variance (favorable)		$ 1,500

75. (c) The spending variance is **not** affected by the activity level selected for applying overhead because the computation of the spending variance involves the comparison of standard variable overhead costs and actual variable overhead costs, holding quantity constant at the actual quantity used. The volume variance results when the actual activity level differs from the budgeted quantity used in determining the fixed overhead application rate. If the application rate had been based on 100% capacity rather than 80%, a lower application rate would have resulted. Because the volume variance was unfavorable at an 80% level of application, standard production must have been lower than 80% of capacity. The lower application rate based on 100% would have made the underapplication of fixed costs even greater.

76. (d) The fixed overhead budget variance in the four-way analysis of overhead is computed as the difference between the budgeted fixed overhead and the actual fixed overhead incurred. The fixed overhead budget variance is favorable because less fixed overhead was incurred than was budgeted.

Budgeted fixed overhead (100,000 units x $4/unit)	$ 400,000
Actual fixed overhead incurred (given)	(384,000)
Fixed overhead budget variance (favorable)	$ 16,000

77. (b)

$$\begin{array}{ccc} \text{Variable FOH} & & \text{Flexible budget} \\ \text{spending} = \text{Actual} - \text{based on} \\ \text{variance} & \text{VFOH} & \text{actual inputs} \\ & & \text{x application} \\ & & \text{rate} \end{array}$$

$$\begin{array}{c} \text{Standard direct} \\ \text{labor hours} = \dfrac{200,000 \text{ hrs.}}{100,000 \text{ units}} = 2 \text{ hrs./unit} \\ \text{per unit} \end{array}$$

$$\begin{array}{c} \text{Application rate} \\ \text{per DLH} = \dfrac{\$6}{2} = \$3 \text{ per DLH} \end{array}$$

$$\begin{array}{c} \text{Flexible budget} \\ \text{based on} \times \begin{array}{c}\text{Application}\\\text{rate}\end{array} = \begin{array}{c}160,000\\\text{hours}\end{array} \times \begin{array}{c}\$3\\\text{per}\\\text{hour}\end{array} = \$480,000 \\ \text{actual input} \end{array}$$

$$\begin{array}{c} \text{Variable FOH} \\ \text{spending} = \$500,000 - \$480,000 = \mathbf{\$20,000} \\ \text{variance} \end{array}$$

78. (a)

FOH Volume Variance	=	FOH budgeted – Applied FOH
	=	(100,000 x $4) – (76,000 x $4)
	=	$400,000 – $304,000
	=	$96,000 Unfavorable

PERFORMANCE BY SUBTOPICS

Each category below parallels a subtopic covered in Chapter 25. Record the number and percentage of questions you correctly answered in each subtopic area.

Job Order Costing

Question #	Correct √
1	
2	
# Questions	2

Correct _____
% Correct _____

Process Costing

Question #	Correct √
3	
4	
5	
6	
# Questions	4

Correct _____
% Correct _____

Spoilage

Question #	Correct √
7	
8	
9	
# Questions	3

Correct _____
% Correct _____

Joint Product Costing

Question #	Correct √
10	
11	
# Questions	2

Correct _____
% Correct _____

By-Products

Question #	Correct √
12	
# Questions	1

Correct _____
% Correct _____

Service Costs

Question #	Correct √
13	
# Questions	1

Correct _____
% Correct _____

Activity-Based Costing

Question #	Correct √
14	
15	
16	
17	
18	
19	
# Questions	6

Correct _____
% Correct _____

Standard Cost Concepts

Question #	Correct √
20	
21	
22	
# Questions	3

Correct _____
% Correct _____

Variances

Question #	Correct √
23	
24	
# Questions	2

Correct _____
% Correct _____

Disposition of Variances

Question #	Correct √
25	
26	
# Questions	2

Correct _____
% Correct _____

Prime Cost Variances

Question #	Correct √
27	
28	
# Questions	2

Correct _____
% Correct _____

Variances in OH Costs

Question #	Correct √
29	
30	
# Questions	2

Correct _____
% Correct _____

OTHER OBJECTIVE FORMAT QUESTION SOLUTIONS

SOLUTION 25-3 VARIANCES & GRAPHS

1. **U** The direct labor rate variance is unfavorable because the direct labor cost incurred for the actual direct labor hours incurred was more than the amount that would have been incurred if the actual direct labor hours had been incurred at the standard direct labor hour rate. This can be determined by noting where lines drawn from the following points intersect the direct labor cost axis: (1) Point A and (2) the point where a line drawn from Point A intersects line OW (a point we will now refer to as Point Z). Actual direct labor cost incurred is determined where the line drawn from Point A intersects the direct labor cost axis. The standard direct labor cost allowed for the actual hours incurred is determined where the line drawn from Point Z intersects the direct labor hours axis (i.e., the point at which the line drawn from Point A intersects line OW represents the actual direct labor hours incurred at the standard direct labor hour rate; since line OW represents the standard labor cost at any output volume, all points on line OW are a function of the standard direct labor hour rate). Since the line drawn from Point A intersects the direct labor cost axis further away from the origin than the line drawn from Point Z, the direct labor cost incurred for the actual direct labor hours incurred was more than the amount that would have been incurred if the actual direct labor hours had been incurred at the standard direct labor hour rate.

2. **F** The direct labor efficiency variance is favorable because the actual direct labor hours incurred were less than the direct labor hours allowed for the output achieved. This can be easily determined by noting where lines drawn from Points A and S intersect the direct labor hour axis. Actual direct labor hours incurred is determined where the line drawn from Point A intersects the direct labor hours axis. Standard direct labor hours allowed for the output achieved is determined where the line drawn from Point S intersects the direct labor hours axis. Since the line drawn from Point A intersects the direct labor hours axis closer to the origin than the line drawn from Point S, the actual direct labor hours incurred were less than the direct labor hours allowed for the output achieved.

3. **F** At volume V, overhead cost applied (shown on Line OA) exceeds budgeted overhead costs (shown on Line DB). Therefore, more overhead was applied than was budgeted and the volume variance is favorable.

4. **U** Actual machine hours (Point S) exceed standard hours allowed for good production (Point V); therefore, the efficiency variance is unfavorable.

5. **D** Line DB depicts the factory overhead flexible budget line. At zero volume, Point O, no variable costs are budgeted. Thus, Line DO represents budgeted fixed costs. Fixed costs are budgeted to remain constant in total within the relevant range, regardless of changes in volume. Therefore, budgeted variable costs at Point C are equal to total budgeted costs at Point C (Line BC) less budgeted fixed costs at Point C (Line DO).

SOLUTION 25-4 DIRECT MATERIAL VARIANCES

1. **U** The January material price variance is unfavorable because the actual cost incurred for the actual materials pounds used is greater than the amount that would have been incurred if the actual materials pounds used had been purchased at their standard price. This can be determined by noting where horizontal lines drawn from the following points intersect the total material cost axis: (1) Point Ja and (2) the point where a vertical line drawn from Point Ja intersects line OP (a point we will now refer to as Z). Actual total material cost is determined where the horizontal line drawn from Point Ja intersects the total material cost axis. Standard total material cost for the actual materials pounds used is determined where the horizontal line drawn from Point Z intersects the total material cost axis (i.e., the point at which the vertical line drawn from Point Ja intersects line OP represents actual materials pounds used at standard price; since line OP represents standard material cost at any output volume, all points on line OP are a function of the standard price of the material). Since the horizontal line drawn from Point Ja intersects the total material cost axis further away from the origin than the horizontal line drawn from Point Z, actual material cost is more than the amount that would have been incurred if the actual materials pounds used had been acquired at their standard price. Hence, the January material price variance is unfavorable.

2. **F** The January material usage variance is favorable because actual materials pounds used is less than standard materials pounds allowed for the output volume achieved. This can be easily seen by noting where vertical lines drawn from Points Ja and V intersect the materials pounds axis. Actual materials pounds is determined where the vertical line from Point Ja intersects the materials pounds axis. Standard materials pounds allowed for the output volume

achieved is determined where the vertical line drawn from Point V intersects the materials pounds axis. Since the vertical line drawn from Point Ja intersects the materials pounds axis closer to the origin than the vertical line drawn from Point V, actual materials pounds used is less than standard materials pounds allowed for the output volume achieved. Hence, the January material usage variance is favorable.

3. U   The February material price variance is unfavorable because the actual cost incurred for the actual materials pounds used is greater than the amount that would have been incurred if the actual materials pounds used had been purchased at their standard price. This can be determined by noting where horizontal lines drawn from the following points intersect the total material cost axis: (1) Point Fe and (2) the point where a vertical line drawn from Point Fe intersects line OP (a point we will now refer to as S). Actual total material cost is determined where the horizontal line drawn from Point Fe intersects the total material cost axis. Standard total material cost for the actual materials pounds used is determined where the horizontal line drawn from Point S intersects the total material cost axis (i.e., the point at which the vertical line drawn from Point Fe intersects line OP represents actual materials pounds used at standard price; since line OP represents standard material cost at any output volume, all points on line OP are a function of the standard price of the material). Since the horizontal line drawn from Point Fe intersects the total material cost axis further away from the origin than the horizontal line drawn from Point S, actual material cost is more than the amount that would have been incurred if the actual materials pounds used had been acquired at their standard price. Hence, the February material price variance is unfavorable.

4. U   The February material usage variance is unfavorable because actual materials pounds used is greater than standard materials pounds allowed for the output volume achieved. This can be easily seen by noting where vertical lines drawn from Points Fe and V intersect the materials pounds axis. Actual materials pounds is determined where the vertical line from Point Fe intersects the materials pounds axis. Standard materials pounds allowed for the output volume achieved is determined where the vertical line drawn from Point V intersects the

materials pounds axis. Since the vertical line drawn from Point Fe intersects the materials pounds axis further away from the origin than the vertical line drawn from Point V, actual materials pounds used is greater than standard materials pounds allowed for the output volume achieved. Hence, the February material usage variance is unfavorable.

5. F   The March material net variance is favorable because Point Ma (actual material cost incurred in March) is below the horizontal line drawn through Point V which represents the standard cost for the output volume achieved in March.

SOLUTION 25-5 BUDGETS & STANDARD COSTS

1. BD   Budgeted variable cost is the line which begins at the origin that is below and parallel to the budgeted cost line. Budgeted cost is comprised of budgeted variable cost and budgeted fixed cost. At volume OE, budgeted cost is represented by the line BE and budgeted variable cost is represented by line DE. Thus, budgeted fixed cost at volume OE is represented by line BD.

2. DE   Budgeted variable cost is the line which begins at the origin that is below and parallel to the budgeted cost line. At volume OE, budgeted variable cost is represented by line DE.

3. AC   Standard gross profit is the difference between revenue and standard cost. At volume OE, revenue is represented by line AE and standard cost is represented by line CE. Thus, standard gross profit at volume OE is represented by line AC.

4. AB   Budgeted gross profit is the difference between revenue and budgeted cost. At volume OE, revenue is represented by line AE and budgeted cost is represented by line BE. Thus, budgeted gross profit at volume OE is represented by line AB.

5. OG   Normal capacity is the point at which standard costs equal budgeted costs since standard costs are determined by dividing budgeted costs by normal volume. These cost are equal at point I. Therefore, normal capacity is represented by line OG.

Wondering how to allocate
your study time?

In your excitement to answer multiple choice questions, don't forget that the examiners ask questions in other formats!

The first pass through a chapter:

1.   Strive to answer **all** the multiple choice questions in the first problem.

2.   Choose one or more of the other objective format questions to answer.

When you review the chapter later:

1.   Answer **at least** those multiple choice questions that you did not understand the first time. (If you had a lucky guess, did you really understand?)

2.   Select a new other objective format question to answer.

When you review the chapter for the final time (for some chapters, the second time may **be** the final time):

1.   Only review the notes you would review just before the exam. For a whole exam sec-tion, this should take less than five minutes. Answer the questions "cold turkey" (without reviewing the text materials just before answering questions).

2.   Answer **at least** those multiple choice questions that you did not understand the first time.

3.   Select a new other objective format question to answer.

Remember, with the techniques and information in your material,

A passing score is well within reach!

_____

CHAPTER 26

PLANNING & CONTROL

EXAM COVERAGE: The managerial accounting portion of the ARE section of the CPA exam is designated by the examiners to be 10 percent of the section's point value. Historically, exam coverage of the topics in this chapter hovers at 1 to 4 percent of the ARE section. Candidates should plan their use of study time accordingly. More information about the point value of various topics is included in the **Practical Advice** section of this volume.

CHAPTER 26

PLANNING & CONTROL

I. BUDGETS

A. OVERVIEW
A budget is a quantitative expression of the objectives and goals of an enterprise. Budgeting compels management planning, provides definite expectations that are a objective framework for judging subsequent performance, and promotes communication and coordination among the various segments of the enterprise. Budgets may be used for planning, evaluating performance, implementing plans, communicating plans, motivating personnel, and authorizing actions.

B. MASTER BUDGET
A master budget represents a comprehensive plan for the overall activities of the enterprise. A master budget generally summarizes the forecasts contained in the operating budget, the capital expenditures budget, and the financial budget. Formulating a master budget involves preparing the operating income budget and using that information to develop a financial budget and a capital expenditure budget.

1. **OPERATING BUDGET** An operating budget forecasts income, predicts sales volume, as well as estimates cost of goods sold and operating expenses.

   a. Prepare a sales forecast, generally based on estimates by the sales staff, statistical analyses, and group executive judgment.

   b. Prepare a schedule of desired ending inventory levels.

   c. Prepare a production budget based on the sales forecast. Units to produce = Desired ending finished goods inventory + Budgeted sales (units) − Beginning finished goods inventory

   d. Prepare a schedule of inventory costs based on production level.

      (1) Prepare a schedule of direct material usage and purchases. Usage will depend on the level of production as budgeted. Purchases will depend on the desired ending material inventory plus usage less beginning material inventory.

      (2) Prepare a schedule of direct labor costs based on estimated production, labor rates, and labor methods.

      (3) Prepare a schedule of manufacturing overhead costs. This schedule consists of two parts: variable overhead and fixed overhead. Variable overhead is determined by the production budget and the per-unit budgeted costs. Fixed overhead remains stable over a wide production range.

   e. Prepare a cost of goods sold budget, using the information already gathered.

   f. Prepare a budget of selling, administrative, and other expenses, often determined by group executive judgment and statistical analyses.

   g. Prepare a budgeted income statement, based on the information gathered thus far.

2. **FINANCIAL BUDGET** A financial budget forecasts the flow of cash and other funds in the business and charts the expected balance sheet for the end of the planning period.

a. Prepare a cash budget, predicting the effects on cash position of the level of operation forecast in step g., above. Note that noncash expenses such as depreciation and amortization are not included. Future dividend payments may or may not be included in the cash budget. Prepare a budgeted statement of cash flows using the information gathered for other budgets.

(1) Beginning cash + Cash collections = Total cash available before financing activity

(2) Cash disbursements = Purchases of materials + Salaries and wages + Other cash outlays + Purchases of fixed assets + Investments

(3) Financing requirements include repayments of obligations, interest expense, and other investments that may be planned.

(4) Ending cash balance = Beginning cash balance + Cash collections − Cash disbursements

b. Prepare a budgeted balance sheet, using the information gathered for other budgets. For example, accounts receivable equals budgeted sales, plus beginning accounts receivable balance, less estimated cash receipts.

3. **CAPITAL EXPENDITURES BUDGET** A capital expenditures budget summarizes expenditures for individual capital projects. The time period of this budget depends on the entity's planning horizon. Capital expenditures that are budgeted include replacement, acquisition, or construction of plants and major equipment. Prepare a capital expenditures budget taking into account the facilities, equipment, etc., required to achieve the budgeted level of production, long-range expansion plans, and the cash available for capital expenditures (from the cash budget).

C. **FLEXIBLE BUDGET**
A flexible budget does not confine itself to only one level of activity but rather is geared toward a range of activity. A flexible budget may be prepared for production, selling, or administrative activities.

1. **USE OF A VARIABLE BUDGET** A static budget is not adjusted or altered, regardless of changes in volume during the period. In the planning phase, the flexible budget can be geared toward all levels of activity within the relevant range. In the controlling phase, the flexible budget can be tailored for the level of activity achieved. That is, a manager can look at what activity level was attained during a period and then turn to the flexible budget to determine what costs should have been at that level.

2. **EFFECTS ON COSTS** When using a flexible budget, it is important to know the effect that changes in production levels within the relevant range have on variable, fixed, and total costs.

a. Variable costs are costs that remain constant per unit but that vary in total in direct proportion to changes in the level of production. Thus, with an increase in production levels within the relevant range, total variable costs increase; with a decrease in production levels within the relevant range, total variable costs decrease.

b. Fixed costs are costs that tend to remain constant in total, regardless of changes in production levels within the relevant range. However, fixed costs per unit have an inverse relationship with changes in production levels. Fixed costs per unit decrease with an increase in production levels because total fixed costs are spread over more units. Fixed costs per unit increase with a decrease in production levels because total fixed costs are spread over fewer units.

    c.   Total costs vary with changes in the level of production due to the change in total variable costs. Thus, with an increase in production levels within the relevant range, total costs increase; with a decrease in production levels within the relevant range, total costs decrease.

D.   RESPONSIBILITY ACCOUNTING

Responsibility accounting systems recognize various decision centers (or responsibility centers) throughout an organization and trace costs (and revenues, assets, and liabilities, where pertinent) to the individual managers who are primarily responsible for the costs in question. Generally, the manager in question is not held responsible for her/his own salary or other factors beyond control. Controllable costs for responsibility accounting purposes are those costs that are directly influenced by a given manager within a given period of time.

    1.   **COST CENTER** The manager is responsible only for **controllable costs**. The manager has no control over sales or over the generating of revenue. Cost centers are evaluated by means of performance reports, in terms of meeting cost standards that have been set.

    2.   **REVENUE CENTER** The manager is responsible only for **controllable revenues**. For instance, a sales manager has no control over manufacturing costs.

    3.   **PROFIT CENTER** The manager is responsible for both controllable **revenues and costs.** Profit centers are evaluated by means of contribution income statements, in terms of meeting revenue and cost objectives.

    4.   **INVESTMENT CENTER** The manager is responsible for controllable revenues, costs, and **investment funds**. Investment centers are also evaluated by means of contribution income statements, but normally in terms of the rate of return they are able to generate on invested funds.

II. QUALITY CONTROL PROGRAMS

A.   CATEGORIES OF COST

Quality control programs commonly recognize four, or occasionally five, categories of costs. Quality control programs are also applicable when the "product" is a service.

    1.   **PREVENTION COSTS** The costs of avoiding producing products not conforming to specifications.

    2.   **APPRAISAL COSTS** The costs of discovering which individual units don't conform to the specifications.

    3.   **INTERIOR FAILURE COSTS** The costs incurred when a non-conforming product is discovered before shipment to the customer; for example, rework of a partially complete product.

    4.   **EXTERIOR FAILURE COSTS** The costs incurred when a non-conforming product is discovered after shipment to the customer; for example, rework of returned product and reshipping charges.

    5.   **OPPORTUNITY COSTS** These include the estimated "costs" of lost sales or dissatisfied customers. An example of an opportunity cost is lost margin on products that could have been produced when a full capacity plant was instead reworking defective parts. These indistinct costs are less frequently included in quality program reports, as they are rarely readily available or verifiable.

B.   COST MANAGEMENT SYSTEMS

    1.   Traditional methods usually base production on forecast sales. Standard cost systems are often used to measure variances that result in operations improvement. However, using variances without discretion may lead to dysfunctional behavior. (For example, an extreme emphasis on the materials price variance may encourage the purchaser to obtain the lowest price without regard for quality or warehousing costs.)

2. Process value analysis (or value chain analysis) attempts to reduce all nonvalue added costs, keeping costs low and flexibility to customer requirements at a maximum. This system is also referred to as a just-in-time (JIT) system.

    a. Companies applying PVA techniques often negotiate long-term contracts with a limited number of vendors that specify acceptable prices and quality, eliminating the need to compute a material price variance. By only working with suppliers who deliver quality raw materials on a timely basis, less raw material inventory is required as a safety stock.

    b. By eliminating nonvalue-adding work (for example, materials handling) and costs (for example, warehousing costs), throughput time is minimized, enabling customer demand to stimulate production (inventory is produced after a sale is made), so excess and obsolete finished goods inventory is reduced. This is referred to as a "pull" system (each department's work is initiated by demand from the department ahead of it), as opposed to a "push" system (work is pushed from beginning to end, based on forecasts of customer demand).

    c. By concentrating on quality, rework and reshipping costs are minimized and customer satisfaction is maximized.

C. **INVENTORY TRACKING SYSTEMS**

1. **SEQUENTIAL COSTING** Sequential (or synchronous) tracking methods attempt to time entries with physical production events. This can be expensive, especially when material and time tickets are linked to individual products or operations.

2. **BACKFLUSH COSTING** Backflush costing systems eliminate the need to record work-in-process inventory by delaying recording production changes until finished goods (or sometimes even sales) occur. At this point, standard costs are used to allocate manufacturing costs to finished goods. Other names for this system include delayed costing or endpoint costing. Although backflush costing can be used with any production system, it frequently appears with a just-in-time (JIT) inventory system. Entities using backflush costing usually (a) want a simple accounting system, (b) have a standard cost for each product, and (c) achieve about the same end results with backflush costing as with sequential tracking.

III. TIME VALUE OF MONEY

A. **FUTURE VALUE OF AN AMOUNT**
Due to the time value of money, a dollar a year from now is worth less than a dollar today. The future value of a lump-sum amount (and other time values) may be determined by using factors from pre-calculated tables. The CPA exam usually provides an assortment of time value factors, rather than complete tables, and requires candidates to determine the correct factor to use in a given situation. The formula (used to develop the factors) is itself not tested on the CPA exam. Selection, manipulation, and use of the correct factor is tested. (See Appendix C for present value and future value tables as well as additional examples.)

EXAMPLE 1 ♦ FUTURE VALUE OF AN AMOUNT (LUMP-SUM)

> Sam deposits $1,000 in a CD at the bank for two years at 5%. The future value interest factor for 2 years at 5% (FVIF 2, 5%) is 1.1025.
>
> **REQUIRED:** What will be the total of the CD at maturity?
>
> **SOLUTION:** FV = PV x FVIF (2, 5%) = $1,000 x 1.1025 = $1,102.50
>
> **PROOF:** Value at end of first year = principal + interest = $1,000 + $1,000 x .05 = $1,050.00
> Value at end of second year = principal + interest = $1,050 + $1,050 x .05 = $1,102.50

B.   PRESENT VALUE OF A FUTURE AMOUNT
This looks at the future value of money from a slightly different perspective. Note that present value factors may be derived from future value factors by simple algebraic manipulation. Manipulation of the figures from a present value table will provide future values and vice versa. A similar manipulation is also possible with annuity factors.

EXAMPLE 2 ♦ PRESENT VALUE OF AN AMOUNT

> Patricia wants to deposit enough money in a CD at the bank at 5% to have $5,000 in 2 years. The future value interest factor for 2 years at 5% (FVIF 2, 5%) is 1.1025. The present value interest factor for 2 years at 5% (PVIF 2, 5%) is 1 / 1.1025 = 0.907029.
>
> **REQUIRED:** What amount will Patricia need to deposit now?
>
> **SOLUTION:** PV = FV x PVIF (2, 5%) = $5,000 x 0.907029 = $4,535 (rounded)
>
> **PROOF:** Value at end of first year = principal + interest = $4,535 + $4,535 x .05 = $4,761.75
> Value at end of second year = principal + interest = $4,762 + $4,762 x .05 = $5,000.10

C.   ANNUITIES
An annuity is a series of payments of a fixed amount for a specified number of years. With an **ordinary** annuity (an annuity in **arrears**) the payment occurs at the **end** of the year. With an annuity **due** (an annuity in **advance**) the payment is made at the **beginning** of the year.

1.   **ORDINARY ANNUITIES** The present and future value factors for ordinary annuities are applied in a manner similar to the factors for lump-sum payments.

2.   **ANNUITIES DUE** The factors used for ordinary annuities can be used for annuities in advance, with a slight modification.

   a.   **FUTURE VALUE OF AN ANNUITY DUE** Value of annuity in advance of amount A at the end of n periods = Value of ordinary annuity for (n + 1) periods – A.

   b.   **PRESENT VALUE OF AN ANNUITY DUE** Present value of annuity in advance of amount A for n periods = Present value of ordinary annuity for (n – 1) periods + A.

D.   COMPOUNDING PERIODS OTHER THAN A YEAR
For compounding periods other than a year, the interest rate and the number of periods to get a factor are modified appropriately. In the case of quarterly compounding, the present value factor for 4 times the number of periods and one-quarter of the interest rate is used. In the case of monthly compounding, the present value factor for 12 times the number of periods and one-twelfth of the interest rate is used.

EXAMPLE 3 ♦ PRESENT VALUE OF AN ANNUITY AND A SINGLE SUM COMBINED

Rick won $160,000 in a state lottery. He will receive an immediate payment of $30,000, three annual payments of $30,000 (at the end of each year), and a payment of $40,000 at the end of the fourth year. Rick only has the following time value factors.

Ordinary annuities: PVIFA (3 years, 8%) = 2.577097   PVIFA (4 years, 8%) = 3.312127
Annuities due: PVIFAA (4 years, 8%) = 3.577097   PVIFAA (5 years, 8%) = 4.312127

REQUIRED: Determine the present value of Rick's payments, discounted at a rate of 8%, using only: (A) the ordinary annuity factors, and (B) the annuity due factors.

SOLUTION A: Add together the value of the immediate payment, the present value of an annuity of $30,000 for three years, and the present value of one $40,000 payment at the end of four years. (The present value of the immediate payment is its face value.)

   PV   = $30,000 + $30,000 x PVIFA (3, 8%) + $40,000 x [PVIFA (4, 8%) – PVIFA (3, 8%)]
        = $30,000 + $30,000 x 2.577097 + $40,000 x (3.312127 - 2.577097)
        = $30,000 + $30,000 x 2.577097 + $40,000 x 0.735030
        = $30,000 + $77,313 + $29,401 = <u>$136,714</u>

SOLUTION B: Add together the present value of an annuity due of $30,000 for five years and the present value of one $10,000 payment at the beginning of the fifth year. (The end of the fourth year is the same as the beginning of the fifth year.)

   PV   = $30,000 x PVIFAA (5, 8%) + $10,000 x [PVIFAA (5, 8%) – PVIFAA (4, 8%)]
        = $30,000 x 4.312127 + $10,000 x 0.735030 = $129,364 + $7,350 = <u>$136,714</u>

NOTE: PVIF (4 years, 8%) = 0.735030. This is shown in Appendix C, Table 2, *Present Value of $1*. This is calculated here from the difference between the annuity factors of different lengths of time. (See Solution A.)

IV. CAPITAL BUDGETING

A. OVERVIEW

Capital budgeting pertains to the allocation of capital among alternative investment opportunities. An important aspect of the capital budgeting process is the application of various investment criteria to proposed projects in order to determine which one would be the most profitable for the firm to implement. Another important concept in this context is that of the firm's cost of capital. Before considering investment criteria and the cost of capital, depreciation and the tax shield are discussed.

B. DEPRECIATION AND THE TAX SHIELD

Incremental earnings from a project have a related incremental tax liability. Since depreciation is deductible as a regular business expense, it reduces taxable incremental earnings, and therefore reduces incremental tax liability. Thus, depreciation "shields" part of the cash inflow from taxation when income taxes are a factor.

EXAMPLE 4 ♦ DEPRECIATION

A company buys a new machine for $10,000 that increases its annual earnings by $5,000. The tax rate is 30% and the machine has a 10-year life and no salvage value. Using straight-line depreciation, the annual depreciation provision would be $1,000. The yearly incremental tax liability would be $1,200 [($5,000 – $1,000) x .30]. Depreciation reduces the tax liability by $300 ($1,000 x .30).

1. **EXCLUDED** When income tax considerations are ignored, depreciation expense is excluded from the calculations for the (a) net present value, (b) internal rate of return, and (c) payback methods. These methods focus on cash flow, and depreciation expense is not a cash flow, but an allocation of past cost. Deduction of depreciation would constitute a double counting of a cost, because the initial cost of the project has already been considered as a lump-sum cash outflow.

2. **INCLUDED** Even when income taxes are ignored, depreciation expense is included when calculating the accounting rate of return.

C. INVESTMENT EVALUATION METHODS

1. **ACCOUNTING RATE OF RETURN ON AVERAGE INVESTMENT** This is the average annual net income from the project divided by the average investment in the project. The numerator is the average annual increase in **net income**, not **cash flow**, so depreciation and incremental income taxes are subtracted. The denominator also takes account of depreciation in the carrying amount of the asset.

   a. An advantage of the accounting rate of return method is that it is easily understood because its terms and computation are based upon financial accounting income, and since it is based upon the average annual financial accounting income the project generates, revenue over the entire life of the project is used.

   b. Disadvantages of the method are that it is based upon financial accounting income that uses the accrual basis (capital budgeting decisions should generally rely on estimates of cash flows) and it ignores the time value of money.

2. **PAYBACK PERIOD** This is the length of time required to recover the initial cash outflow from the incremental cash benefits after tax. Thus, if we have an investment of $10,000 that yields $4,500 each year after tax, it would take us 2.22 years (i.e., $10,000 ÷ $4,500) to recover the original investment from the cumulative net cash inflows. (We assume here that the $4,500 cash inflow during any given year is spread uniformly over the year.) Depreciation expense is excluded from the calculation when income taxes are ignored.

   a. Advantages of the payback method are (1) it is based upon cash flows, (2) it serves as a rough screening device to determine the time it will take to recoup the original investment, and (3) it is simple to understand and easy to compute.

   b. Disadvantages of the method are (1) the time value of money is ignored, (2) not all of the cash flow over the life of the project is used—all cash flow beyond the payback period for the investment is ignored, and (3) it does not measure profitability.

3. **INTERNAL RATE OF RETURN** This is the rate of interest that would make the present value of the future cash flows from the project equal to the cost of the initial investment. Projects with a rate less than a minimum rate (or hurdle rate) set by the company are eliminated from consideration.

   a. Advantages of the internal rate of return method are (1) all of the cash flow over the life of the project is used, including the estimated residual sales value of the project, (2) the time value of money is explicitly recognized, and (3) the project's rate of return is estimated.

   b. Disadvantages of the internal rate of return method are (1) cash flows are assumed to be reinvested at the rate earned by the project, and (2) it is more difficult to use than other less sophisticated capital budgeting techniques.

4. **NET PRESENT VALUE** Net present value (NPV) is the present value of the future cash inflows from the project **minus** the cost of the initial investment. Unlike the internal rate of return

method where the rate of interest is an unknown to be determined, a certain rate at which to compute the present value of the cash inflows is given. This rate is called the cost of capital, a concept that will be explained later in this section. A project that will earn exactly the desired rate of return will have a NPV of zero. A positive net present value identifies projects that will earn in excess of the minimum rate of return.

a.   Advantages of the net present value method are (1) all of the cash flow over the life of the project is used, including the estimated residual sales value of the project, (2) the time value of money is explicitly recognized, and (3) cash flows are assumed to be reinvested at the enterprise's cost of capital.

b.   Disadvantages of the method are (1) it does not estimate the project's rate of return but merely tests the rate against a minimum rate (i.e., the enterprise's cost of capital), (2) it is more difficult to use than other less sophisticated capital budgeting techniques, and (3) it is difficult to apply to strategic investments that do not generate identifiable cash flows. However, such investments can be more critical to an entity's success than more tangible investments.

c.   It is important to note that both the net present value and the internal rate of return methods (1) can be used regardless of whether cash flows from period to period are uniform or uneven, (2) do not use depreciation expense when income tax considerations are ignored, and (3) can both easily accommodate a requirement that projects with longer lives must earn a higher specified rate of return. For instance, projects with less than a five-year life must earn a return of 10%, while those with a life of five years or more must earn a return of 12%.

5.   **PROFITABILITY INDEX** Because projects can differ greatly in size, it would not be meaningful to compare the NPVs of different projects directly. Instead, a **profitability index** is used.

$$\text{Profitability index} \quad = \quad \frac{\text{Present value of cash flow}}{\text{Initial investment}}$$

EXAMPLE 5 ♦ PROFITABILITY INDEX

A machine, purchased for $10,000, yields cash inflows of $5,000, $4,000, and $4,000. The cost of capital is 10%.

REQUIRED: Determine the profitability index.

SOLUTION:

Year	Cash flow	PV factor at 10%	PV of cash flow
1	$5,000	.909	$ 4,545
2	4,000	.826	3,304
3	4,000	.751	3,004
		Total	$10,853

Net present value = $10,853 – $10,000 = $853

$$\text{Profitability index} = \frac{\$10,853}{\$10,000} = \underline{1.0853}$$

D.   COST OF CAPITAL

The firm's cost of capital is a weighted average of the costs of debt and equity funds. Equity funds here include both capital stock and retained earnings. These costs are expressed in terms of a percentage per annum. An entity's **cost of capital** is equal to the weighted average of the cost of debt, preferred and common stock, and retained earnings, with their market values as weights. (The tax rate adjustment is made to the cost of debt because interest payments are deductible for income tax purposes.)

1. Cost of debt = $\dfrac{\text{Interest payments x (1 – tax rate)}}{\text{Average market value of debt (e.g., bonds)}}$

2. *Cost of preferred stock* = Preferred dividends / Average market value of preferred stock.

3. Cost of common stock = $\dfrac{\text{Dividends on common stock}}{\text{Average market value of common stock}}$ + $\begin{array}{l}\text{Expected growth} \\ \text{rate in dividends}\end{array}$

4. *Cost of retained earnings* = $(1 - t_s)$ x Cost of common stock, where t_s is the marginal tax rate per dollar for the firm's stockholders.

EXAMPLE 6 ◆ CALCULATION OF THE COST OF CAPITAL

REQUIRED: Given the following facts, determine a firm's cost of capital.

Total interest payments	$10,000	Total market values of	
Common dividends	14,560	Bonds	$200,000
Annual common dividend growth	3%	Common stock	150,000
Preferred dividends	6,000	Preferred stock	100,000
Company tax rate	40%	Retained earnings	50,000
Stockholders' marginal tax rate	30%	Total	$500,000

SOLUTION: Firm's cost of capital = .4(3%) + .3(12.7%) + .2(6%) + .1(8.9%) = 7.1%

	Cost			Weight	
Debt	$10,000 (1 – .4) / $200,000	=	3%	$200,000 / $500,000	= .4
Preferred stock	$6,000 / $100,000	=	6%	$100,000 / $500,000	= .2
Common stock	$14,560 / $150,000 + 3%	= 12.7%		$150,000 / $500,000	= .3
Retained earnings	(1 – .3) x 12.7%	=	8.9%	$ 50,000 / $500,000	= .1

E. RETURN ON INVESTMENT

The return on investment measures the relationship of profit to invested capital for a unit of account-ability. The return on investment is **increased** when operating income increases or when average invested capital decreases. Return on investment **decreases** when operating income decreases or when average invested capital increases. Operating income increases when costs decrease, and decreases when costs increase.

$$\begin{array}{ll}\text{Return on} \\ \text{investment}\end{array} = \begin{array}{ll}\text{Percentage of} \\ \text{profit to sales}\end{array} \text{x} \begin{array}{ll}\text{Capital-employed} \\ \text{turnover rate}\end{array}$$

$$= \dfrac{\text{Operating income}}{\text{Sales}} \text{ x } \dfrac{\text{Sales}}{\text{Average invested capital}}$$

$$= \dfrac{\text{Operating income}}{\text{Average invested capital}}$$

F. RESIDUAL INCOME

The objective of maximizing residual income assumes that as long as the accounting unit earns a rate of return in excess of the imputed interest charge for invested capital, the unit should expand. Residual income is a unit's operating income less an imputed interest charge on its average invested capital.

$$\text{Residual income} = \text{Operating income} - \left[\begin{array}{l}\text{Imputed} \\ \text{Interest rate} \\ \text{(cost of capital)}\end{array} \text{ x } \begin{array}{l}\text{Average} \\ \text{Invested} \\ \text{capital}\end{array}\right]$$

V. ECONOMIC ORDER QUANTITY (EOQ)

A. BASIC FORMULA

The economic order quantity is the purchase order size that minimizes the total of inventory order cost and inventory carrying costs. It is important to note: (1) this formula can be used by a manufacturer to determine the optimum size for a production run by replacing "order cost" with the "set-up costs" necessary for a production run, (2) the formula assumes that periodic demand for the good is known, (3) inventory cost flow assumptions, such as LIFO and FIFO, do not affect the computation, and (4) neither the actual cost per inventory unit, the cost of carrying safety stock, nor the cost of a stockout are used in the formula.

$$\text{Economic order quantity} = \sqrt{\frac{2 \text{ x Order cost x Annual demand}}{\text{inventory carrying cost per unit}}}$$

EXAMPLE 7 ♦ ECONOMIC ORDER QUANTITY

Pierce plans to manufacture 10,000 blades for its electric lawn mower division. The blades will be used evenly throughout the year. The setup cost every time a production run is made is $80, and the cost to carry a blade in inventory for the year is $.40. Pierce's objective is to produce the blades at the lowest cost possible.

REQUIRED: Determine the number of production runs Pierce should make.

SOLUTION:

$$\text{Optimal production run} = \sqrt{\frac{2 \text{ x } 80 \text{ x } 10,000}{.40}} = \mathbf{2,000} \text{ units}$$

Annual demand	10,000
Divided by: Optimal production run	÷ 2,000
Number of production runs	5

B. LEAD TIME AND REORDER POINT

Lead time is the time lag between placing an order and the receipt of the goods. If safety stock is ignored, the reorder point is computed as the anticipated demand during the lead time. If safety stock is considered, the reorder point is computed as the anticipated demand during the lead time plus the level of safety stock.

C. SAFETY STOCK

If the demand during the lead time is not known with certainty, it may be important to keep extra inventory (known as safety stock) on hand so as to avoid the possibility of a stockout in case the lead time demand was higher than average. Its level is determined by balancing the cost of a stockout (i.e., lost business and customer goodwill) against the cost of carrying extra inventory.

EXAMPLE 8 ♦ ECONOMIC ORDER QUANTITY, SAFETY STOCK

Eagle Company's material A will be required evenly throughout the year.

Annual usage in units	7,200	Normal lead time in working days	20
Working days per year	240	Maximum lead time in working days	45

REQUIRED: Determine reorder point and the level of safety stock.

(continued on next page)

SOLUTION:

Average usage of units per work day (7,200 / 240)	30
Times: Maximum lead time in working days	45
Maximum demand during lead time = Reorder point with safety stock	1,350
Maximum demand during lead time	1,350
Less: Expected demand during lead time [(7,200 ÷ 240) × 20]	600
Safety stock	**750**

VI. PROBABILITY AND EXPECTED VALUE

A. THEORY

Probability theory helps formulate quantitative models to deal with situations involving uncertainty. Such situations are formally described by means of random variables. A **random variable** can take several values, each with a specified probability. The set of values that a random variable can take, together with the associated probabilities, constitutes a **probability distribution**. The probabilities are non-negative numbers, each being less than or equal to one. Since the variable must take one of the values, the probabilities add up to one. Probability analysis is an extension of sensitivity analysis.

EXAMPLE 9 ♦ PROBABILITY

The Wing Manufacturing Corporation has manufactured a chemical compound, product X, for the past 20 months. Demand for product X has been irregular and at present there is no consistent sales trend. During this period, there have been five months with 8,000 units sold, twelve months with 9,000 units sold, and three months with 10,000 units sold.

REQUIRED: Compute the probability of sales of product X of 8,000, 9,000, or 10,000 units in any month.

SOLUTION:

Units sales per month	Number of months	Probability
8,000	5	5/20 = 25%
9,000	12	12/20 = 60%
10,000	3	3/20 = 15%
	20	100%

B. STANDARD DEVIATION

The conventional measure of the dispersion of a probability distribution for a single variable is the standard deviation. The standard deviation is the square root of the mean of the squared differences between the observed values and the expected value.

C. JOINT PROBABILITY

Two events A and B may be either **independent** or **dependent**.

1. If they are **independent**, the probability that either one of them will occur does not depend on the probability of the other event occurring. The **joint probability**, P(AB), which is the probability that both A and B occur, is equal to P(A) x P(B).

2. If two events are dependent, the probability that A occurs, given that B has occurred, is different from P(A). This is called the conditional probability of A given B, denoted by P(A/B). P(AB) = P(A/B) x P(B) = P(B/A) x P(A).

D.   EXPECTED VALUE

The information provided by a probability distribution can be summarized by means of the expected value of the random variable. This is a weighted average of all the values the variable can take, with the respective probabilities as weights. To compute the expected value, the various values are multiplied by their probabilities and then added together. The expected value concept furnishes business managers with a decision-making tool when dealing with situations characterized by uncertainty. Suppose the decision maker has to choose from among several courses of action. There are several possible outcomes, with known probabilities. The decision maker would compute the monetary value (gain or loss) that would result from each action/outcome combination. For each action, the **expected monetary value** would next be calculated. The action whose expected monetary value is the highest (the highest gain or the least loss) would be selected as the optimum course of action.

EXAMPLE 10 ♦ EXPECTED MONETARY VALUE

Lex Co. is considering introducing a new product, Vee. The following probability distribution indicates the relative likelihood of monthly sales volume levels and related income (loss) for Vee.

Monthly sales volume	Probability	Income (loss)
6,000	.10	$ (70,000)
12,000	.20	10,000
18,000	.40	60,000
24,000	.20	100,000
30,000	.10	140,000

REQUIRED: Determine the expected value of the added monthly income if Lex markets Vee.

SOLUTION:

Monthly sales volume	Probability	x	Income (loss)	=	Expected value
6,000	.10		$ (70,000)		$ (7,000)
12,000	.20		10,000		2,000
18,000	.40		60,000		24,000
24,000	.20		100,000		20,000
30,000	.10		140,000		14,000

Expected value of added monthly income .... $ 53,000

VII. REGRESSION & CORRELATION

A.   REGRESSION ANALYSIS

Regression analysis tries to estimate the relationship between a *dependent* variable and one or more *independent* variables from a set of actual observations on these variables. Regression analysis produces a measure of *probable* error, but does not establish a cause and effect relationship. *Simple* regression analysis measures the change in one dependent variable associated with the change in one independent variable. *Multiple* regression analysis measures the change in *one* dependent variable associated with the change in *more than one* independent variable.

EXHIBIT 1 ♦ REGRESSION EQUATION

$$y = A + Bx$$

y	=	dependent variable (e.g., total overhead cost)
A	=	the y intercept (e.g., fixed overhead cost)
B	=	the slope of the line (e.g., the variable overhead cost per direct labor hour)
x	=	independent variable (e.g., direct labor hours)
Bx	=	total variable overhead cost

B. COEFFICIENT OF CORRELATION

The coefficient of correlation (R) measures the degree of linearity in the relationship between two variables—one dependent and one independent variable. It can vary only between +1 and –1. These two values (perfect correlation) imply a perfect linear relationship between the two variables. The data points in a scatter diagram would lie on a straight line in such a case. The two variables move in the same direction when the correlation coefficient is positive and in opposite directions if it is negative. If the data points in a scatter diagram appear as random points, the coefficient of correlation between the two variables is zero.

EXHIBIT 2 ♦ SCATTER DIAGRAMS DEPICTING DIFFERENT DEGREES OF CORRELATION

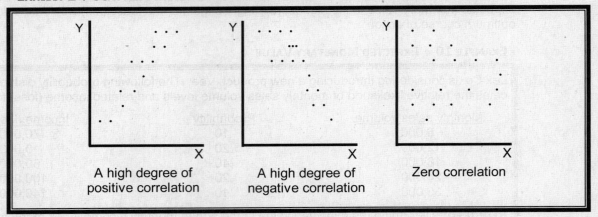

| A high degree of positive correlation | A high degree of negative correlation | Zero correlation |

C. COEFFICIENT OF DETERMINATION

The coefficient of determination, which is the square of the coefficient of correlation (R^2), lies between 0 and 1. As the coefficient of determination approaches +1, we are given a higher level of assurance that the independent variable accounts for most of the variability in the dependent variable.

EXAMPLE 11 ♦ COEFFICIENT OF DETERMINATION

Box Co. has developed the following regression equation to analyze the behavior of its maintenance costs (Y) as a function of machine hours (X):

Y = $12,000 + $10.50X

Box used 30 monthly observations to develop the foregoing equation. The related coefficient of determination (R^2) was .90.

REQUIRED: Determine the related point estimate of total maintenance cost if 1,000 machine hours are worked in one month.

SOLUTION: Total maintenance costs = $12,000 + $10.50 (1,000) = $22,500

The .90 coefficient of determination does **not** affect the above computation. However, since it approaches +1, we are given a high level of assurance that the independent variable, machine hours, accounts for most of the variability in the dependent variable, total maintenance cost.

CHAPTER 26—PLANNING & CONTROL

PROBLEM 26-1 MULTIPLE CHOICE QUESTIONS (80 to 100 minutes)

1. Mien Co. is budgeting sales of 53,000 units of product Nous for April. The manufacture of one unit of Nous requires 4 kilos of chemical Loire. During April, Mien plans to reduce the inventory of Loire by 50,000 kilos and increase the finished goods inventory of Nous by 6,000 units. There is no Nous work-in-process inventory. How many kilos of Loire is Mien budgeting to purchase in April?
a. 138,000
b. 162,000
c. 186,000
d. 238,000   (11/95, AR, #40, amended, 5783)

2. The basic difference between a master budget and a flexible budget is that a master budget is
a. Only used before and during the budget period and a flexible budget is only used after the budget period.
b. For an entire production facility and a flexible budget is applicable to single departments only.
c. Based on one specific level of production and a flexible budget can be prepared for any production level within a relevant range.
d. Based on a fixed standard and a flexible budget allows management latitude in meeting goals.
(11/95, AR, #41, 5784)

3. Lean Company is preparing its cash budget for November. The following information pertains to Lean's past collection experience from its credit sales:

Current month's sales	12%
Prior month's sales	75%
Sales two months prior to current month	6%
Sales three months prior to current month	4%
Cash discounts (2/30, net 90)	2%
Doubtful accounts	1%

Credit sales:

November—estimated	$100,000
October	90,000
September	80,000
August	95,000

How much is the estimated credit to accounts receivable as a result of collections expected during November?
a. $85,100
b. $87,100
c. $88,100
d. $90,000   (Editors, 1471)

4. A flexible budget is appropriate for a

	Marketing budget	Direct material usage budget
a.	No	No
b.	No	Yes
c.	Yes	Yes
d.	Yes	No

(5/94, AR, #37, 4642)

5. When a flexible budget is used, an increase in production levels within the relevant range would
a. Not change variable costs per unit.
b. Not change fixed costs per unit.
c. Not change total variable costs.
d. Change total fixed costs.   (Editors, 2746)

6. Cook Co.'s total costs of operating five sales offices last year were $500,000, of which $70,000 represented fixed costs. Cook has determined that total costs are significantly influenced by the number of sales offices operated. Last year's costs and number of sales offices can be used as the bases for predicting annual costs. What would be the budgeted costs for the coming year if Cook were to operate seven sales offices?
a. $700,000
b. $672,000
c. $614,000
d. $586,000   (11/92, PII, #34, 3368)

7. Wages earned by machine operators in producing the firm's product should be categorized as

	Direct labor	Controllable by the machine operators' foreman
a.	Yes	Yes
b.	Yes	No
c.	No	Yes
d.	No	No

(11/90, Theory, #41, 2180)

8. Controllable revenue would be included in a performance report for a

	Profit center	Cost center
a.	No	No
b.	No	Yes
c.	Yes	No
d.	Yes	Yes

(11/93, Theory, #49, 4554)

9. The following is a summarized income statement of Carr Co.'s profit center No. 43 for December:

Contribution margin		$70,000
Period expenses:		
Manager's salary	$20,000	
Facility depreciation	8,000	
Corporate expense allocation	5,000	33,000
Profit center income		$37,000

Which of the following amounts would most likely be subject to the control of the profit center's manager?
a. $70,000
b. $50,000
c. $37,000
d. $33,000   (5/92, PII, #51, amended, 2683)

10. Key Co. changed from a traditional manufacturing operation with a job order costing system to a just-in-time operations with a back-flush costing system. What is(are) the expected effect(s) of these changes on Key's inspection costs and recording detail of costs tracked to jobs in process?

	Inspection costs	Detail of costs tracked to jobs
a.	Decrease	Decrease
b.	Decrease	Increase
c.	Increase	Decrease
d.	Increase	Increase

(11/95, AR, #51, 5794)

11. Rework costs should be regarded as a cost of quality in a manufacturing company's quality control program when they are

I.   Caused by the customer.
II. Caused by internal failure.

a. I only.
b. II only.
c. Both I and II.
d. Neither I nor II.   (R/01, AR, #18, 7003)

12. Which measures would be useful in evaluating the performance of a manufacturing system?

I.   Throughput time
II. Total setup time for machines/Total production time
III. Number of rework units/Total number of units completed

a. I and II only
b. II and III only
c. I and III only
d. I, II, and III   (5/95, AR, #46, 5464)

13. Which changes in costs are most conducive to switching from a traditional inventory ordering system to a just-in-time ordering system?

	Cost per purchase order	Inventory unit carrying costs
a.	Increasing	Increasing
b.	Decreasing	Increasing
c.	Decreasing	Decreasing
d.	Increasing	Decreasing

(5/95, AR, #47, 5465)

14. Which of the following is **not** a typical characteristic of a just-in-time (JIT) production environment?
a. Lot sizes equal to one
b. Insignificant setup times and costs
c. Push-through system
d. Balanced and level workloads
          (R/99, AR, #24, 6813)

15. Pole Co. is investing in a machine with a 3-year life. The machine is expected to reduce annual cash operating costs by $30,000 in each of the first 2 years and by $20,000 in year 3. Present values of an annuity of $1 at 14% are:

Period		
	1	0.88
	2	1.65
	3	2.32

Using a 14% cost of capital, what is the present value of these future savings?
a. $59,600
b. $60,800
c. $62,900
d. $69,500   (5/95, AR, #38, 5456)

16. On March 15, 20X1, Ashe Corp. adopted a plan to accumulate $1,000,000 by September 1, 20X5. Ashe plans to make four equal annual deposits to a fund that will earn interest at 10% compounded annually. Ashe made the first deposit on September 1, 20X1. Future value and future amount factors are as follows:

Future value of 1 at 10% for 4 periods	1.46
Future amount of ordinary annuity of 1 at 10% for 4 periods	4.64
Future amount of annuity in advance of 1 at 10% for 4 periods	5.11

Ashe should make four annual deposits (rounded) of
a. $250,000.
b. $215,500.
c. $195,700.
d. $146,000.   (11/91, PI, #9, amended, 2397)

17. Major Corp. is considering the purchase of a new machine for $5,000 that will have an estimated useful life of five years and no salvage value. The machine will increase Major's after-tax cash flow by $2,000 annually for five years. Major uses the straight-line method of depreciation and has an incremental borrowing rate of 10%. The present value factors for 10% are as follows:

Ordinary annuity with five payments   3.79
Annuity due for five payments   4.17

Using the payback method, how many years will it take to pay back Major's initial investment in the machine?
a. 2.50
b. 5.00
c. 7.58
d. 8.34   (11/92, PII, #38, 3372)

18. Neu Co. is considering the purchase of an investment that has a positive net present value based on Neu's 12% hurdle rate. The internal rate of return would be
a.   0%.
b.   12%.
c.   > 12%.
d.   < 12%.   (11/92, PII, #37, 3371)

19. Which of the following characteristics represent an advantage of the internal rate of return technique over the accounting rate of return technique in evaluating a project?

   I.   Recognition of the project's salvage value
  II.   Emphasis on cash flows
III.   Recognition of the time value of money

a. I only
b. I and II
c. II and III
d. I, II, and III   (11/92, Theory, #49, 3482)

20. A project's net present value, ignoring income tax considerations, is normally affected by the
a. Proceeds from the sale of the asset to be replaced.
b. Carrying amount of the asset to be replaced by the project.
c. Amount of annual depreciation on the asset to be replaced.
d. Amount of annual depreciation on fixed assets used directly on the project.
           (5/93, Theory, #47, 4234)

21. Oak Company bought a machine which they will depreciate on the straight-line basis over an estimated useful life of seven years. The machine has no salvage value. They expect the machine to generate after-tax net cash inflows from operations of $110,000 in each of the seven years. Oak's minimum rate of return is 12%. Information on present value factors is as follows:

- Present value of $1 at 12% at the
  end of seven periods   0.0452
- Present value of an ordinary annuity
  of $1 at 12% for seven periods   4.564

Assuming a positive net present value of $12,000, what was the cost of the machine?
a. $480,000
b. $490,040
c. $502,040
d. $514,040   (R/00, AR, #18, 6923)

22. Polo Co. requires higher rates of return for projects with a life span greater than five years. Projects extending beyond five years must earn a higher specified rate of return. Which of the following capital budgeting techniques can readily accommodate this requirement?

	Internal rate of return	Net present value
a.	Yes	No
b.	No	Yes
c.	No	No
d.	Yes	Yes

           (5/90, Theory, #48, 2248)

23. The following selected data pertain to the Darwin Division of Beagle Co. for 20X1:

Sales	$400,000
Operating income	40,000
Capital turnover	4
Imputed interest rate	10%

What was Darwin's 20X1 residual income?
a. $0
b. $ 4,000
c. $10,000
d. $30,000   (11/95, AR, #50, amended, 5793)

24. Residual income of an investment center is the center's
a. Income plus the imputed interest on its invested capital.
b. Income less the imputed interest on its invested capital.
c. Contribution margin plus the imputed interest on its invested capital.
d. Contribution margin less the imputed interest on its invested capital.   (11/92, Theory, #48, 3481)

25. Select Co. had the following financial statement relationships:

Asset turnover   5
Profit margin on sales   0.02

What was Select's percentage return on assets?
a. 0.1%
b. 0.4%
c. 2.5%
d. 10.0%   (5/95, AR, #45, amended, 5463)

26. The following information pertains to Bala Co. for the year ended December 31, 20X1:

Sales	$600,000
Net income	100,000
Capital investment	400,000

Which of the following equations should be used to compute Bala's return on investment?
a. $(4 \div 6) \times (6 \div 1) = ROI$
b. $(6 \div 4) \times (1 \div 6) = ROI$
c. $(4 \div 6) \times (1 \div 6) = ROI$
d. $(6 \div 4) \times (6 \div 1) = ROI$
     (5/92, PII, #53, amended, 2685)

27. The following information pertains to Quest Co.'s Gold Division:

Sales	$311,000
Variable cost	250,000
Traceable fixed costs	50,000
Average invested capital	40,000
Imputed interest rate	10%

Quest's return on investment was
a. 10.00%.
b. 13.33%.
c. 27.50%.
d. 30.00%.   (5/94, AR, #43, amended, 4648)

28. In Belk Co.'s "just-in-time" production system, costs per setup were reduced from $28 to $2. In the process of reducing inventory levels, Belk found that there were fixed facility and administrative costs that previously had not been included in the carrying cost calculation. The result was an increase from $8 to $32 per unit per year. What were the effects of these changes on Belk's economic lot size and relevant costs?

	Lot size	Relevant costs
a.	Decrease	Increase
b.	Increase	Decrease
c.	Increase	Increase
d.	Decrease	Decrease

     (11/92, PII, #26, 3360)

29. In computing the reorder point for an item of inventory, which of the following is used?

I. Cost
II. Usage per day
III. Lead Time

a. I and II
b. II and III
c. I and III
d. I, II, and III   (R/00, AR, #14, 6919)

30. As a consequence of finding a more dependable supplier, Dee Co. reduced its safety stock of raw materials by 80%. What is the effect of this safety stock reduction on Dee's economic order quantity?
a. 80% decrease
b. 64% decrease
c. 20% increase
d. No effect   (5/94, AR, #46, 4651)

31. The following information pertains to material X which is used by Harbor Co.:

Annual usage in units	40,000
Working days per year	250
Safety stock in units	800
Normal lead time in working days	30

Units of material X will be required evenly throughout the year. The order point is
a. 1,600.
b. 3,200.
c. 4,800.
d. 5,600.   (Editors, 1548)

32. Probability (risk) analysis is
a. Used only for situations involving five or fewer possible outcomes.
b. Used only for situations in which the summation of probability weights is greater than one.
c. An extension of sensitivity analysis.
d. Incompatible with sensitivity analysis.
     (5/94, AR, #47, 4652)

33. Which tool would most likely be used to determine the best course of action under conditions of uncertainty?
a. Cost-volume-profit analysis
b. Expected value (EV)
c. Program evaluation and review technique (PERT)
d. Scattergraph method   (R/99, AR, #25, 6814)

34. Under frost-free conditions, Cal Cultivators expects its strawberry crop to have a $60,000 market value. An unprotected crop subject to frost has an expected market value of $40,000. If Cal protects the strawberries against frost, then the market value of the crop is still expected to be $60,000 under frost-free conditions and $90,000 if there is a frost. What must be the probability of a frost for Cal to be indifferent to spending $10,000 for frost protection?
a. .167
b. .200
c. .250
d. .333   (11/95, AR, #53, 5796)

35. In probability analysis, the square root of the mean of the squared differences between the observed values and the expected value is the
a. EOQ.
b. Objective function.
c. Optimum corner point.
d. Standard deviation.   (Editors, 2266)

36. Which of the following may be used to estimate how inventory warehouse costs are affected by both the number of shipments and the weight of materials handled?
a. Economic order quantity analysis
b. Probability analysis
c. Correlation analysis
d. Multiple regression analysis
(11/90, Theory, #50, 2246)

37. Using regression analysis, Fairfield Co. graphed the following relationship of its cheapest product line's sales with its customers' income levels:

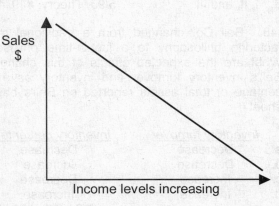

If there is a strong statistical relationship between the sales and customers' income levels, which of the following numbers best represents the correlation coefficient for this relationship?

a. −9.00
b. −0.93
c. +0.93
d. +9.00   (5/93, Theory, #50, 4237)

38. To determine the best cost driver of warranty costs relating to glass breakage during shipments, Wymer Co. used simple linear regression analysis to study the relationship between warranty costs and each of the following variables: type of packaging, quantity shipped, type of carrier, and distance shipped. The analysis yielded the following statistics:

Independent Variable	Coefficient of Determination	Standard Error of Regression
Type of packaging	0.60	1,524
Quantity shipped	0.48	1,875
Type of carrier	0.45	2,149
Distance shipped	0.20	4,876

Based on these analyses, the best driver of warranty costs for glass breakage is
a. Type of packaging.
b. Quantity shipped.
c. Type of carrier.
d. Distance shipped.   (11/97, AR, #19, 6547)

39. Sago Co. uses regression analysis to develop a model for predicting overhead costs. Two different cost drivers (machine hours and direct materials weight) are under consideration as the independent variable. Relevant data were run on a computer using one of the standard regression programs, with the following results:

	Machine hours	Direct materials weight
Y intercept coefficient	2,500	4,600
B coefficient	5.0	2.6
R^2	0.70	0.50

Which regression equation should be used?
a. Y = 2,500 + 5.0x
b. Y = 2,500 + 3.5x
c. Y = 4,600 + 2.6x
d. Y = 4,600 + 1.3x   (11/92, PII, #22, 3356)

40. Multiple regression differs from simple regression in that it
a. Provides an estimated constant term.
b. Has more dependent variables.
c. Allows the computation of the coefficient of determination.
d. Has more independent variables.
(R/00, AR, #11, 6916)

PROBLEM 26-2 ADDITIONAL MULTIPLE CHOICE QUESTIONS (64 to 80 minutes)

41. Rolling Wheels purchases bicycle components in the month prior to assembling them into bicycles. Assembly is scheduled one month prior to budgeted sales. Rolling pays 75% of component costs in the month of purchase and 25% of the costs in the following month. Component costs included in budgeted cost of sales are:

April	May	June	July	August
$5,000	$6,000	$7,000	$8,000	$8,000

What is Rolling's budgeted cash payments for components in May?
a. $5,750
b. $6,750
c. $7,750
d. $8,000   (R/01, AR, #20, 7005)

42. The flexible budget for a production department may include

	Direct labor	Factory overhead
a.	Yes	No
b.	No	No
c.	No	Yes
d.	Yes	Yes

(Editors, 2219)

43. When production levels are expected to decline within a relevant range, and a flexible budget is used, what effect would be anticipated with respect to each of the following?

	Variable costs per unit	Fixed costs per unit
a.	No change	No change
b.	Increase	No change
c.	No change	Increase
d.	Increase	Increase

(11/91, Theory, #46, 2554)

44. Lanta Restaurant compares monthly operating results with a static budget. When actual sales are less than budget, would Lanta usually report favorable variances on variable food costs and fixed supervisory salaries?

	Variable food costs	Fixed supervisory salaries
a.	Yes	Yes
b.	Yes	No
c.	No	Yes
d.	No	No

(5/91, Theory, #44, 2177)

45. Controllable revenues would be included in the performance reports of which of the following types of responsibility centers?

	Cost centers	Investment centers
a.	Yes	No
b.	Yes	Yes
c.	No	No
d.	No	Yes

(5/91, Theory, #47, 9254)

46. The benefits of a just-in-time system for raw materials usually include
a. Elimination of nonvalue adding operations.
b. Increase in the number of suppliers, thereby ensuring competitive bidding.
c. Maximization of the standard delivery quantity, thereby lessening the paperwork for each delivery.
d. Decrease in the number of deliveries required to maintain production.   (5/93, Theory, #44, 4231)

47. Nonfinancial performance measures are important to engineering and operations managers in assessing the quality levels of their products. Which of the following indicators can be used to measure product quality?

I.   Returns and no allowances
II. Number and types of customer complaints
III. Production cycle time

a. I and II only
b. I and III only
c. II and III only
d. I, II, and III   (5/93, Theory, #49, 4236)

48. Bell Co. changed from a traditional manufacturing philosophy to a just-in-time philosophy. What are the expected effects of this change on Bell's inventory turnover and inventory as a percentage of total assets reported on Bell's balance sheet?

	Inventory turnover	Inventory percentage
a.	Decrease	Decrease
b.	Decrease	Increase
c.	Increase	Decrease
d.	Increase	Increase

(5/94, AR, #50, 4655)

49. For the next 2 years, a lease is estimated to have an operating net cash inflow of $7,500 per annum, before adjusting for $5,000 per annum tax basis lease amortization, and a 40% tax rate. The present value of an ordinary annuity of $1 per year at 10% for 2 years is $1.74. What is the lease's after-tax present value using a 10% discount factor?
a. $ 2,610
b. $ 4,350
c. $ 9,570
d. $11,310   (11/95, AR, #42, 5785)

50. Lin Co. is buying machinery it expects will increase average annual operating income by $40,000. The initial increase in the required investment is $60,000, and the average increase in required investment is $30,000. To compute the accrual accounting rate of return, what amount should be used as the numerator in the ratio?
a. $20,000
b. $30,000
c. $40,000
d. $60,000   (11/92, PII, #39, 3373)

51. The capital budgeting technique known as accounting rate of return uses

	Revenue over life of project	Depreciation expense	Time value of money
a.	No	Yes	No
b.	No	No	Yes
c.	Yes	No	Yes
d.	Yes	Yes	No
			(Editors, 2247)

52. Which of the following is a strength of the payback method?
a. It considers cash flows for all years of the project.
b. It distinguishes the sources of cash inflows.
c. It considers the time value of money.
d. It is easy to understand.   (R/01, AR, #14, 6999)

53. Para Co. is reviewing the following data relating to an energy saving investment proposal:

Cost	$50,000
Residual value at the end of 5 years	10,000
Present value of an annuity of 1 at 12% for 5 years	3.60
Present value of 1 due in 5 years at 12%	0.57

What would be the annual savings needed to make the investment realize a 12% yield?
a. $ 8,189
b. $11,111
c. $12,306
d. $13,889   (5/94, AR, #38, 4643)

54. How are the following used in the calculation of the internal rate of return of a proposed project? Ignore income tax considerations.

	Residual sales value of project	Depreciation expense
a.	Exclude	Include
b.	Include	Include
c.	Exclude	Exclude
d.	Include	Exclude
	(11/91, Theory, #49, 2556)	

55. Mudd Co. is planning to buy a coin-operated machine costing $20,000. For tax purposes, this machine will be depreciated over a five-year period using the straight-line method and no salvage value. Mudd estimates that this machine will yield an annual cash inflow, net of depreciation and income taxes, of $6,000. At the following discount rates, the net present values of the investment in this machine are:

Discount rate	Net present value
12%	+ $1,629
14%	+ 599
16%	– 354
18%	– 1,237

Mudd's expected internal rate of return on its investment in this machine is
a. 3.3%.
b. 10.0%.
c. 12.0%.
d. 15.3%.   (Editors, 1540)

56. Which of the following capital budgeting techniques implicitly assumes that the cash flows are reinvested at the company's minimum required rate of return?

	Net present value	Internal rate of return
a.	Yes	Yes
b.	Yes	No
c.	No	Yes
d.	No	No
	(11/90, Theory, #47, 2244)	

57.   A proposed project has an expected economic life of eight years. In the calculation of the net present value of the proposed project, salvage value would be
a.   Excluded from the calculation of the net present value.
b.   Included as a cash inflow at the future amount of the estimated salvage value.
c.   Included as a cash inflow at the estimated salvage value.
d.   Included as a cash inflow at the present value of the estimated salvage value.   (Editors, 2258)

58.   The discount rate (hurdle rate of return) must be determined in advance for the
a.   Payback period method.
b.   Time adjusted rate of return method.
c.   Net present value method.
d.   Internal rate of return method.
                         (5/91, Theory, #48, 2241)

59.   To determine the inventory reorder point, calculations normally include the
a.   Ordering cost.
b.   Carrying cost.
c.   Average daily usage.
d.   Economic order quantity.   (R/01, AR, #16, 7001)

60.   The invested capital-employed turnover rate would include
a.   Invested capital in the numerator.
b.   Invested capital in the denominator.
c.   Net income in the numerator.
d.   Sales in the denominator.   (Editors, 2260)

61.   Division A is considering a project that will earn a rate of return which is greater than the imputed interest charge for invested capital, but less than the division's historical return on invested capital. Division B is considering a project that will earn a rate of return which is greater than the division's historical return on invested capital, but less than the imputed interest charge for invested capital. If the objective is to maximize residual income, should these divisions accept or reject their projects?

	Project A	Project B
a.	Accept	Accept
b.	Reject	Accept
c.	Reject	Reject
d.	Accept	Reject

                         (11/90, Theory, #48, 2245)

62.   Kim Co.'s profit center Zee had 20X1 operating income of $200,000 before a $50,000 imputed interest charge for using Kim's assets. Kim's aggregate net income from all of its profit centers was $2,000,000. During 20X1, Kim declared and paid dividends of $30,000 and $70,000 on its preferred and common stock, respectively. Zee's 20X1 residual income was
a. $140,000.
b. $143,000.
c. $147,000.
d. $150,000.   (11/92, PII, #28, amended, 3362)

63.   Following is information relating to Kew Co.'s Vale Division for 20X1:

Sales	$500,000
Variable costs	300,000
Traceable fixed costs	50,000
Average invested capital	100,000
Imputed interest rate	6%

Vale's residual income was
a. $144,000.
b. $150,000.
c. $156,000.
d. $200,000.   (5/92, PII, #52, amended, 2684)

64.   To assist in an investment decision, Gift Co. selected the most likely sales volume from several possible outcomes. Which of the following attributes would selected sales volume reflect?
a.   The midpoint of the range
b.   The median
c.   The greatest probability
d.   The expected value   (11/92, Theory, #50, 3483)

65.   During 20X1 Deet Corp. experienced the following power outages:

Number of outages per month	Number of months
0	3
1	2
2	4
3	3
	12

Each power outage results in out-of-pocket costs of $400. For $500 per month, Deet can lease an auxiliary generator to provide power during outages. If Deet leases an auxiliary generator in 20X2, the estimated savings (or additional expenditures) for 20X2 would be
a.   ($3,600).
b.   ($1,200).
c. $1,600.
d. $1,900.   (11/95, AR, #54, amended, 5797)

66. Kane Corp. estimates that it would incur a $100,000 cost to prepare a bid proposal. Kane estimates also that there would be an 80% chance of being awarded the contract if the bid is low enough to result in a net profit of $250,000. What is the expected value of the payoff?
a. $0
b. $150,000
c. $180,000
d. $220,000 (5/92, PII, #55, 2687)

67. A vendor offered Wyatt Co. $25,000 compensation for losses resulting from faulty raw materials. Alternately, a lawyer offered to represent Wyatt in a lawsuit against the vendor for a $12,000 retainer and 50% of any award over $35,000. Possible court awards with their associated probabilities are:

Award	Probability
$75,000	0.6
0	0.4

Compared to accepting the vendor's offer, the expected value for Wyatt to litigate the matter to verdict provides a
a. $ 4,000 loss.
b. $18,200 gain.
c. $21,000 gain.
d. $38,000 gain. (R/00, AR, #20, 6925)

68. In statistical analysis, a weighted average using probabilities as weights is the
a. Objective function.
b. Coefficient of variation.
c. Expected value.
d. Standard deviation. (5/90, Theory, #50, 2250)

69. Much Co. has developed a regression equation to analyze the behavior of its maintenance costs (Q) as a function of machine hours (Z). The following equation was developed by using 30 monthly observations with a related coefficient of determination of .90: $Q = \$5,000 + \$6.50Z$.

If 1,000 machine hours are worked in one month, the related point estimate of total maintenance costs would be
a. $11,500.
b. $11,000.
c. $ 6,500.
d $ 5,850. (Editors, 1531)

70. Multiple regression analysis
a. Produces measures of probable error.
b. Establishes a cause and effect relationship.
c. Involves the use of independent variables only.
d. Is **not** a sampling technique. (Editors, 2268)

71. Box Co. uses regression analysis to estimate the functional relationship between an independent variable (cost driver) and overhead cost. Assume that the following equation is being used:

$$y = A + Bx$$

What is the symbol for the independent variable?
a. y
b. x
c. Bx
d. A (5/92, PII, #54, 2686)

OTHER OBJECTIVE FORMAT QUESTIONS

PROBLEM 26-3 (10-15 minutes)

ITEMS 1 THROUGH 4 are based on the following:

Tam Co. is negotiating for the purchase of equipment that would cost $100,000, with the expectation that $20,000 per year could be saved in after-tax cash costs if the equipment were acquired. The equipment's estimated useful life is 10 years, with no residual value, and would be depreciated by the straight-line method. Tam's predetermined minimum desired rate of return is 12%. Present value of an annuity of 1 at 12% for 10 periods is 5.65. Present value of 1 due in 10 periods at 12% is .322.

1. Rounded to the nearest $10, what is the net present value? (5/92, PII, #57, 2689)

2. Rounded to the nearest tenth of a year what is the payback period? (5/92, PII, #58, 2690)

3. What is the accrual accounting rate of return based on initial investment? (5/92, PII, #59, 2691)

4. In estimating the internal rate of return, the factors in the table of present values of an annuity should be taken from the columns closest to what amount? (5/92, PII, #60, 2692)

ITEMS 5 THROUGH 7 are based on the following:

Helm invested $400,000 in a five-year project at the beginning of 20X1. Helm estimates that the annual cash savings from this project will amount to $130,000. The $400,000 of assets will be depreciated over their five-year life on the straight-line basis. On investments of this type, Helm's desired rate of return is 12%. Information on present value factors is as follows:

	At 12%	At 14%	At 16%
Present value of 1 for 5 periods	0.57	0.52	0.48
Present value of an annuity of 1 for 5 periods	3.60	3.40	3.30

5.   What is the net present value of the project?
(Editors, 1535)

6.   Helm's internal rate of return on this project is
A.   Less than 12%.
B.   Less than 14%, but more than 12%.
C.   Less than 16%, but more than 14%.
D.   More than 16%.   (Editors, 1536)

7.   For the project's first year, what would be Helm's accounting rate of return, based on the project's average book value for 20X1?   (Editors, 1537)

PROBLEM 26-4 (10 to 15 minutes)

A company has two mutually exclusive projects, A and B, which have the same initial investment requirements and lives. Project B has a decrease in estimated cash inflows each year, and project A has an increase in estimated net cash inflows each year. Project A has a greater total net cash inflow. Diagram I below depicts the net cash inflows of each project by year. Diagram II depicts the net present value (NPV) of each project assuming various discount rates.

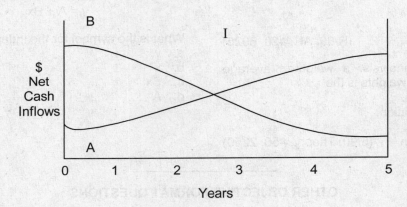

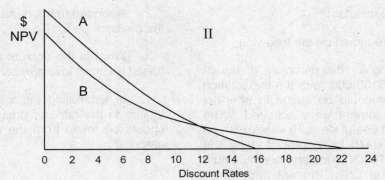

FOR ITEMS 1 THROUGH 4, select your answer from the following list:

A. Project A
B. Project B
C. Both projects equal

1. Which project would be likely to have the shorter payback period?

2. Which project would have the greater average accounting rate of return?

3. Which project would have the greater internal rate of return?

4. Assume, due to innovation, the projects were to terminate at the end of year 4 with cash flows remaining as projected for the first 4 years and no cash flows in year 5. Which project would have the greater internal rate of return?

[11/93, Theory, #2, (#66-69)]

PROBLEM 26-5 (20 to 30 minutes)

EDITOR'S NOTE: Candidates may want to review all the managerial chapters before answering this problem.

Isle, Inc., commenced operations on January 2, 20X1. Isle's three products (Aran, Bute, Cilly) are produced in different plants located in the same community. Apart from initial build-ups in raw materials and finished goods inventories, production schedules are based on sales forecasts. The following selected information is taken from Isle's internal 20X1 contribution income statement, based on standard costs:

Isle, Inc.
20X1 CONTRIBUTION INCOME STATEMENT

| | Products | | | |
	Aran	Bute	Cilly	Total
Sales (Aran 80,000 units)	$1,200,000	$800,000	$500,000	$2,500,000
Standard Costs:				
Direct Materials	180,000			
Direct Labor (Aran 20,000 hours)	240,000			
Variable Manufacturing Overhead	80,000			
Total Variable Manufacturing Costs	500,000	(Detail omitted)		
Less: Finished Goods Inventory December 31	100,000			
Variable Cost of Goods Sold	400,000			
Variable Selling and Administrative Costs	120,000			
Total Variable Costs	520,000			
Standard Contribution Margin	680,000	176,000	144,000	1,000,000
Fixed Manufacturing Overhead Costs	440,000	(Detail omitted)		
Fixed Selling and Administrative Costs	140,000			
Total Fixed Costs	580,000			
Standard Operating Income	100,000	35,000	25,000	160,000
Variances—Favorable (F)/Unfavorable (U):				
Direct Materials—Price	2,000(F)			
Usage	16,000(U)			
Direct Labor— Rate	12,000(U)	(Detail omitted)		
Efficiency	24,000(U)			
Manufacturing Overhead—Total	43,000(U)			
Selling and Administrative—Total	7,000(U)			
Operating Income, Net of Variances	$ 0	$ 41,000	$ 36,000	$ 77,000

(continued on next page)

Additional Information:

Manufacturing Capacity Utilization	75%	80%	70%
Average Investment	$1,000,000	$800,000	$400,000

- Demand for Aran is somewhat seasonal and moderately difficult to project more than 3 years
- Demand for Bute is constant and easy to project more than 3 years
- Demand for Cilly is very seasonal and very difficult to project more than 3 years
- Isle also prepared standard absorption costing statements using full capacity (based on machine hours) to allocate overhead costs.
- Fixed costs are incurred evenly throughout the year.
- There is no ending work-in-process.
- Material price variances are reported when raw materials are taken from inventory.

FOR ITEMS 1 THROUGH 13, determine whether the answer is yes (Y) or no (N).

1. Does Isle practice a just-in-time philosophy?

2. Should Isle include standard indirect material costs in standard fixed overhead costs?

3. Should Isle categorize the operation of production equipment as a value-adding activity?

4. If Isle's three products were produced in a single plant, would activity-based costing provide more useful total production cost information for Aran, Bute, and Cilly than traditional standard costing?

5. Is the regression analysis technique helpful in determining the variable cost component of Isle's manufacturing overhead costs?

6. In Isle's internal performance reports, should normal spoilage costs be reported in fixed manufacturing overhead costs?

7. The computation of Bute's normal spoilage assumes 10 units in 1,000 contain defective materials, and, independently, 15 units in 1,000 contain defective workmanship. Is the probability that is used in computing Bute's normal spoilage less than .025?

8. Isle has contracted to sell units of Aran to a customer in a segregated market during the off-season. Ignore variances and the costs of developing and administering the contract, and assume that standard cost patterns are unchanged except that variable selling and administrative costs are one-half the standard rate. Isle will sell Aran at a price which recoups the variable cost of goods sold at the standard rate, plus variable selling and administrative costs at one-half of the standard rate. Will Isle break even on the contract?

9. Were the actual 20X1 direct labor hours used in manufacturing Aran less than the standard hours?

10. Would Aran's 20X1 operating income reported using absorption cost be lower than the amount reported using variable costing?

11. Was the total amount paid for direct materials put into process for the manufacture of Aran more than the standard cost allowed for the work done?

ITEMS 12 AND 13 are based on the following:

Isle is considering investing $60,000 in a 10-year property lease that will reduce Aran's annual selling and administration costs by $12,000. Isle's cost of capital is 12%. The present value factor for a 10-year annuity at 12% is 5.65.

12. Is there a positive net present value for the lease investment?

13. Is the internal rate of return for the lease investment lower than the cost of capital?

FOR ITEMS 14 THROUGH 17, select the best answer from the following responses:

A. Aran
B. Bute
C. Cilly

14. For which product is evaluation of investments by the payback method likely to be more appropriate?

15. For which product is the economic order quantity formula likely to be most useful when purchasing raw materials to be used in manufacturing?

16. Ignore 20X1 reported variances and assume that Isle used expected demand to allocate manufacturing overhead costs. Which product would be most likely to have a substantial percentage of

underapplied or overapplied fixed manufacturing overhead costs on quarterly statements?

17. Which product had the greatest actual return on investment?

18. If Isle sells $10,000 more of Bute and $10,000 less of Cilly, what is the effect on Isle's standard dollar breakeven point (A) increase, (B) decrease, or (C) no effect?

19. What is Aran's budgeted standard per unit cost for variable selling and administrative costs on sales of 75,000 units?

20. What is Aran's budgeted standard fixed selling and administrative costs on sales of 75,000 units?

21. What is Isle's standard breakeven point in sales dollars for the actual sales mix achieved?

22. What amount of Aran's direct material and direct labor variances might be regarded, wholly or partially, as direct labor employees' responsibility?

23. Isle uses the graph shown to estimate Aran's total standard manufacturing costs. What amount does Y represent?
(11/94, AR, #100-122, amended, 6164-6184)

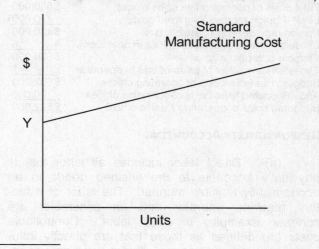

SOLUTION 26-1 MULTIPLE CHOICE ANSWERS

BUDGETS

1. (c)

Budgeted Sales of Nous, in units	53,000
Add: Increase in Finished Goods Inventory	
of Nous	6,000
Units of Nous to Produce	59,000
Times: Kilos of Loire per Unit of Nous	x 4
Kilos of Loire Needed	236,000
Less: Decrease in Inventory of Loire	(50,000)
Kilos of Loire to Purchase	186,000

2. (c)   A master budget is based on the anticipated activity level for the period the budget covers. A flexible budget shows costs by behavior. A flexible budget shows total fixed costs and variable costs on a per unit basis. Thus, a flexible budget can be prepared for any activity level within the relevant range.

3. (c)   The question asks for the computation of the estimated *credit* to *Accounts Receivable*—not the estimated amount of cash received—as a result of November collections. Therefore, cash discounts are disregarded. The doubtful accounts adjustment of 1% can also be discarded because it would be a credit to *Allowance for Doubtful Accounts*, not to *Accounts Receivable*.

Collections from Nov. sales 12% x	$100,000	$ 12,000
Collections from Oct. sales 75% x	90,000	67,500
Collections from Sept. sales 6% x	80,000	4,800
Collections from Aug. sales 4% x	95,000	3,800
		$ 88,100

4. (c)   A flexible budget is one that shows budgeted costs for different activity levels. A flexible budget is appropriate for a direct materials usage budget because the quantity of direct materials used will vary with the level of production. Therefore, the cost of direct materials used will also vary with the level of production.

A flexible budget is also appropriate for a marketing budget because some marketing costs are variable. The variable marketing costs would vary with sales rather than production. Other marketing costs may be semi-variable or fixed. The semi-variable costs must be broken down into their variable and fixed elements. The variable costs are added to the variable cost element of the semi-variable costs and the resulting total variable costs are estimated for various levels of activity. The fixed and the fixed element of the semi-variable costs are also shown. Finally, the total budgeted marketing costs for various levels of activity are shown.

5. (a)   Variable costs do not change on a per unit basis with changes in the level of activity. Total variable costs increase in direct proportion to an

increase in the level of activity. Fixed costs decrease on a per unit basis with an increase in the level of activity. Total fixed costs remain constant regardless of changes in the level of activity within the relevant range.

6. (b)

Total costs of operating five sales offices	$ 500,000
Less: Portion representing fixed costs	(70,000)
Portion representing variable costs	$ 430,000
Divide by: Number of sales offices in operation	÷ 5
Variable cost per sales office	$ 86,000
Times: New number of sales offices in operation	x 7
Budgeted variable costs of operating offices	$ 602,000
Add: Budgeted fixed costs of operating offices	70,000
Budgeted costs of operating 7 sales offices	$ 672,000

RESPONSIBILITY ACCOUNTING

7. (a)   Direct labor includes all labor that is physically traceable to the finished goods in an economically feasible manner. The labor of a factory machine operator and an assembler are common examples of direct labor. Controllable costs are defined as those that are directly influenced by a given manager within a given time span. Therefore, the wages earned by machine operators is considered to be a controllable cost of the machine operators' foreman because the foreman controls these costs by scheduling who operates the machines, how they work, and by controlling when they work (i.e., overtime).

8. (c)   The manager of a profit center is responsible for controllable revenues and controllable costs. The manager of a cost center is only responsible for controllable costs. Thus, controllable revenues would be included in a performance report for a profit center but would not be included in such a report for a cost center.

9. (a)   The manager of a profit center is responsible for both controllable revenues and controllable costs. Controllable costs are defined as those that are directly influenced by a given manager within a given time span and, thus, would include the center's variable costs. Therefore, the manager of a profit center would most likely be responsible for the center's contribution margin (i.e., the center's revenues less the center's variable costs). On the other hand, the manager of a profit center should not be held responsible for costs that cannot be directly influenced by the manager within a given time frame (i.e., uncontrollable costs). The manager of a profit center would normally not be held responsible for her/his salary, facility depreciation, or the corporate expense allocation.

QUALITY CONTROL PROGRAMS

10. (a)   When a company changes from a job order cost system to a just-in-time (JIT) system with backflush costing, inspection costs should decrease. A JIT system places a high emphasis on quality. The company would buy from fewer vendors and these vendors would have been approved as to the quality of their materials. Also, the line workers take on more responsibility for quality. Quality should improve because of a greater emphasis on prevention. Inspection costs would go down as quality improves. The amount of detail tracked to jobs should also decrease under a backflush costing system. There are different levels of backflush costing systems. At the extreme, all production costs are charged to cost of goods sold. Any inventories at the end of a period are backflushed to the inventory accounts by reducing cost of goods sold. Under these systems, little detail is tracked to individual jobs.

11. (b)   Rework costs caused by internal failure are within the control of the manufacturer and therefore should be considered costs of quality. Rework costs caused by the customer, not by product failure, are beyond the manufacturer's control, and are not costs of quality.

12. (d)   All three measures should be useful in evaluating the performance of a manufacturing system. Total throughput time is a measure of how long the system takes to manufacture a product from start to finish. (Some companies may begin counting throughput time when a customer places an order and may end the counting of throughput time when the product is delivered to the customer.) Setup time is time devoted to a non-value-added activity. By measuring setup time as a percentage of total production time, the company obtains a ratio of time devoted to this non-value-added activity to the total time the product spends in production. Quality is important in the manufacturing environment. The cost of rework is an internal failure cost of quality. By dividing the number of reworked units by the total number of units completed, the company can better assess its quality control procedures in an attempt to minimize total quality costs.

13. (b)   In a just-in-time (JIT) system there are frequent orders and the company maintains little, if any, inventory. If the cost of placing a purchase order is decreasing, this is conducive to a JIT system because the company will be placing more orders in a JIT system than in a traditional inventory ordering system. If the unit carrying cost is increasing, this will be conducive to switching to a JIT system.

14. (c) By eliminating non-value-adding work and costs, JIT techniques seek to minimize through-put time, enabling customer demand to stimulate production, so excess and obsolete finished goods inventory is minimal. This is referred to as a "pull" system, rather than a "push" system.

TIME VALUE OF MONEY

15. (c) The present value for a single sum in 3 years is the difference between the present value of an annuity for 3 years and the present value of an annuity for 2 years. (2.32 – 1.65 = 0.67)

Reduction in costs for the first 2 years ($30,000 x 1.65)	$ 49,500
Reduction in costs for Year 3 ($20,000 x 0.67)	13,400
Present value of future cost savings	$ 62,900

16. (c) To determine the amount of the periodic payments required to accumulate to a given sum, with the first payment to be made *immediately*, the factor for the future amount of an *annuity in advance* is used. The factor for the future amount of an annuity in advance of 1 at 10% for 4 periods is given as 5.11.

Annual deposit amount	x	Applicable factor for future amount of annuity in advance	=	Future annuity in advance

Annual deposit x 5.11 = $1,000,000
Annual deposit   = $1,000,000 / 5.11 = $195,700

INVESTMENT EVALUATION

17. (a) The payback period is the period of time it takes for the cumulative sum of annual net cash inflows from a project to equal the initial cash outlay. Since the net cash inflows from the project in question are a constant amount, the payback period is = $5,000 / $2,000 = 2.5.

$$Payback\ period = \frac{Initial\ cash\ outlay}{Annual\ net\ cash\ inflows}$$

18. (c) The internal rate of return (IRR) is the discount rate which would make the net present value of the project equal to zero. Since the investment has a positive net present value at a discount rate of 12%, the IRR of the investment is greater than 12%.

19. (c) The capital budgeting technique, known as internal rate of return (IRR), determines the rate of interest (or discount) that would make the present value of the future cash flows from the project equal to the cost of the initial investment. Therefore, this method uses all of the cash flows over the entire life of the project and the time value of the money. On the other hand, the accounting rate of return (ARR) method of capital budgeting does not recognize the time value of money because it does not focus on cash flows. Rather, it focuses on accounting net income. The ARR is computed by dividing the expected increase in future average annual accounting net income by the initial (or average) increase in the required investment. Both capital budgeting techniques recognize the project's salvage value. The IRR method recognizes the project's salvage value as a future cash inflow. The ARR method subtracts the incremental expenses of the project, including depreciation, from the estimated revenues over the life of the project to determine the expected increase in future average annual accounting income. The ARR method recognizes the project's salvage value in determining the depreciable base of the project.

20. (a) Under the net present value method of capital budgeting, the present value of all cash inflows associated with an investment project are compared to the present value of all cash outflows. Ignoring income taxes, a project's net present value is increased by the amount of proceeds received from the sale of the asset to be replaced. The carrying amount of the asset to be replaced, the amount of annual depreciation on the asset to be replaced, and the amount of annual depreciation on fixed assets used directly on the project do not affect the net present value of the project because they do not represent inflows or outflows of cash.

21. (b) The net present value (NPV) of $12,000 is the present value of the ordinary annuity of $110,000 less the unknown cash outflow (X).

$110,000 x 4.564 – X = $12,000
X = $502,040 – $12,000 = $490,040

22. (d) The internal rate of return and net present value capital budgeting techniques can both easily accommodate Polo's requirement that projects extending beyond five years must earn a higher specified rate of return. Polo can compare the rate of return of projects with a life of five years or less to one specified rate of return (e.g., 10%) and compare the rate of return of projects with a life of greater than five years to a higher specified rate of return (e.g., 12%). Only projects meeting or exceeding the applicable specified rate of return should be accepted.

RESIDUAL INCOME

23. (d) Residual income is equal to operating income less imputed interest (the product of a required rate of return and operating assets). The operating assets are equal to the sales divided by

the capital turnover ratio. Thus, the operating assets are $100,000 ($400,000 / 4).

Operating Income	$ 40,000
Less: Imputed Interest (10% x $100,000)	(10,000)
Residual Income	$ 30,000

24. (b) Residual income is the income of an investment center less an imputed interest charge on the invested capital used by the center.

$$\text{Residual Income} = \text{Operating income} - \left(\begin{array}{c} \text{Imputed} \\ \text{interest} \\ \text{rate} \end{array} \times \begin{array}{c} \text{Average} \\ \text{invested} \\ \text{capital} \end{array} \right)$$

PERCENTAGE RETURN ON ASSETS

25. (d) Return on Assets = Profit Margin on Sales (0.02) x Asset Turnover (5) = 0.10 = 10.0%

RETURN ON INVESTMENT

26. (b) The following equation should be used to determine Bala's return on investment:

$$\begin{array}{rcl} \text{Return on Investment} &=& \text{Profit Margin on sales} \times \text{Capital -employed turnover rate} \\ \\ &=& \dfrac{\text{Net income}}{\text{Sales}} \times \dfrac{\text{Sales}}{\text{Capital Investment}} \\ \\ &=& \dfrac{\$100,000}{\$600,000} \times \dfrac{\$600,000}{\$400,000} \end{array}$$

27. (c) A division's return on investment (ROI) is its segment margin divided by the average invested capital. There is no deduction for imputed interest on invested capital. The ROI is compared to the target ROI to evaluate the performance of the division manager. Imputed interest on capital invested is also used in the calculation of residual income. $11,000 / $40,000 = 0.275 = 27.50%

Sales	$ 311,000
Less: Variable Costs	(250,000)
Contribution Margin	$ 61,000
Less: Traceable Fixed Costs	(50,000)
Segment Margin	$ 11,000

ECONOMIC ORDER QUANTITY

28. (d) The economic lot size formula is:

$$\text{Economic lot size} = \sqrt{\dfrac{2 \times \text{Setup costs} \times \text{Annual demand}}{\text{Inventory carrying cost per unit}}}$$

Since setup costs are in the numerator of the formula, a decrease in setup costs will *decrease* the economic lot size. Since inventory carrying cost per unit is the denominator of the formula, an increase in this amount will also *decrease* the economic lot size. Since both the decrease in setup costs and the increase in the inventory carrying amount decrease the economic lot size, the economic lot size *decreases*. Relevant costs can be defined as expected future costs that differ in amount between alternative courses of action. Since the costs per setup are a variable cost and they were reduced, relevant costs *decrease*. Since the increase in inventory carrying cost is due to *fixed costs* that have been incurred, but not included in the carrying cost calculation, their inclusion does not increase relevant costs.

29. (b) The EOQ formula doesn't include the cost of inventory. It is as follows:

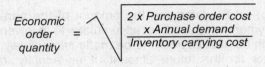

$$\text{Economic order quantity} = \sqrt{\dfrac{2 \times \text{Purchase order cost} \times \text{Annual demand}}{\text{Inventory carrying cost}}}$$

30. (d) The economic order quantity (EOQ) minimizes the sum of carrying costs and ordering costs. The EOQ is the square root of the following: two times the annual demand in units times the order cost for one order with the resulting product divided by the annual cost to carry one unit. Safety stock is important in determining when to place an order. However, changing the safety stock has no effect on the EOQ.

31. (d)

Annual usage, in units	40,000
Working days per year	÷ 250
Daily usage, in units	160
Normal lead time, working days	× 30
Units required for lead time	4,800
Safety stock, in units	800
Order point, in units	5,600

PROBABILITY & EXPECTED VALUE

32. (c) Probability (risk) analysis is an extension of sensitivity analysis. Sensitivity analysis involves determining how sensitive the result is to a change in one or more variables. Probability analysis involves weighting scenarios by the probability of their occurrence. Both are used to assess the risk that the predicted outcome may not occur. They are used for such activities as operational budgeting, capital budgeting, and linear programming.

33. (b) The expected value of a random variable summarizes probability distribution information. Cost-volume-profit analysis examines the operating income effect of sale and cost decisions. PERT is a

project control technique. A scattergraph is used to consider correlation.

34. (b) The difference in the value of the crop between protecting and not protecting it if frost occurs is $50,000 ($90,000 – $40,000). Dividing the $10,000 cost to protect the crop by this $50,000 difference equals 0.20. Thus, 0.20 is the probability of frost occurring at which Cal would be indifferent between the two courses of action. $50,000 x 0.20 = $10,000

35. (d) By definition, the standard deviation in probability analysis is the square root of the mean of the squared differences between the observed values and the expected value. It is the conventional measure of the dispersion of a probability distribution.

REGRESSION & CORRELATION

36. (d) Multiple regression analysis could be used to estimate the relationship between the dependent variable (e.g., inventory warehouse costs) and the two independent variables (e.g., number of shipments, weight of materials handled), based on a set of actual observations in these variables. Correlation analysis could not be used in this fact situation because there are three variables. Correlation analysis relates only two variables (i.e., one independent variable and the dependent variable). Economic order quantity analysis and probability analysis are not used to relate behavior of variables.

37. (b) The coefficient of correlation measures the degree of linearity in the relationship between two variables. It can range only between +1 and –1. The two variables move in the same direction when the correlation coefficient is positive and in opposite directions if it is negative. Since the dollar amount of Fairfield's sales (i.e., the dependent variable) decreases as customer income levels (i.e., the independent variable) increase, the correlation coefficient is negative. Therefore, only answer (b), –0.93

satisfies these requirements. Answers (a) and (d) cannot be correct because the correlation coefficient must range between +1 and –1. Answer (c) is incorrect because the correlation coefficient for the relationship in question is negative (i.e., the dollar amount of Fairfield's sales decreases as customer income levels increase).

38. (a) As the coefficient of determination approaches positive 1, users are given a higher level of assurance that the independent variable accounts for most of the variability in the dependent variable.

39. (a) The coefficient of determination (R^2), which is the square of the coefficient of correlation, lies between 0 and 1. As the coefficient of determination approaches 1, we are given a higher level of assurance that the independent variable accounts for most of the variability in the dependent variable.

Since the regression equation using machine hours has a higher coefficient of determination than the regression equation using direct materials weight (i.e., 0.70 > 0.50), the regression equation using machine hours should be used.

$$y = A + Bx$$
$$y = 2,500 + 5.0x$$

In this equation:

y	=	dependent variable (i.e., total overhead costs)
A	=	the y intercept (i.e., fixed overhead costs)
B	=	the slope of the line (i.e., the variable overhead cost per machine hour)
x	=	the independent variable (i.e., machine hours)
Bx	=	total variable overhead cost

40. (d) Multiple regression uses several independent variable to predict one dependent variable. Both simple and multiple regression have an estimated constant term, have one dependent variable, and allow the computation of the coefficient of determination.

SOLUTION 26-2 ADDITIONAL MULTIPLE CHOICE ANSWERS

BUDGETS

41. (c) In May, Rolling Wheels purchases components for bicycles it would assemble in June for sales in July. It pays in May for 75% of these components' costs. July's budgeted component costs are $8,000, so Rolling Wheels will pay ($8,000 x 75%) $6,000 in May for these components. It will also pay in May for the remaining 25% for components purchased in April for June sales

($7,000 x 25%), or $1,750. Total payments in May for components ($6,000 + $1,750) equal $7,750.

42. (d) The flexible budget for a production department is based upon different levels of activity and takes into account the department's cost of direct materials, *direct labor*, and *factory overhead* at such different levels of activity. It allows a comparison for measuring the actual costs incurred against

the costs that were budgeted for the particular activity level achieved.

43. (c) Variable costs do not change on a per unit basis with changes in the level of activity within the relevant range. Since total fixed costs remain constant in total within the relevant range of activity, a decline in the level of production increases the fixed cost per unit because the same total fixed cost is allocated over fewer units.

44. (b) A static budget is of limited usefulness because it is based upon only one level of volume. When actual sales are less than that level, total variable costs should be lower simply because of lower volume (the variable cost per unit does not change). Total fixed costs, however, should not change with a change in volume. Thus, total fixed costs should be the same at the level of volume assumed in the static budget and that actually achieved.

RESPONSIBILITY ACCOUNTING

45. (d) The manager of a cost center is only responsible for controllable costs. Thus, controllable revenues would not be included in the performance report of a cost center. The manager of an investment center is responsible for controllable revenues, controllable costs, and investment funds. Thus, controllable revenues would be included in the performance report of an investment center.

QUALITY CONTROL PROGRAMS

46. (a) The benefits of a just-in-time (JIT) system usually include elimination of nonvalue added operations—that is, operations that do not affect how customers perceive a product. Eliminating non-value added operations saves the manufacturer money and does no harm to customer relations. Holding inventory is a nonvalue added activity. Hence, under a JIT system, inventory is regarded as an evil, and rigid limits are therefore imposed on all inventories, from raw materials through all stages of production. A JIT system would not seek the maximization of the standard delivery quantity of raw materials or a decrease in the number of deliveries of raw materials required to maintain production because the objective is to minimize inventory levels. Use of a JIT system does not necessarily increase the number of suppliers and ensure competitive bidding.

47. (a) Both (I) returns and allowances and (II) number and types of customer complaints are indicators which can be used to measure product

quality. The production cycle time cannot be used to directly measure product quality.

48. (c) The just-in-time philosophy emphasizes the reduction of waste and maintaining low inventories. Shipments should arrive frequently and just in time to go into production. Inventory turnover is determined by dividing cost of goods sold by the average inventory. Assuming that cost of goods sold remains constant, the inventory turnover will increase because average inventory will decrease. Inventory as a percentage of total assets will decrease because the average inventory will decrease. Although the total assets will also decrease by the reduction in the average inventory, the percentage will still decrease.

TIME VALUE OF MONEY

49. (d) The amortization deduction does not require the use of cash. However, the amortization deduction does reduce taxable income. The tax liability reduces cash flow. Thus, the first step is to determine the tax. Next, the tax liability is subtracted from the cash flow before taxes to determine the after-tax cash flow. This amount is then multiplied by the present value of an annuity factor to determine the after-tax present value of the lease.

Cash Flow Before Amortization and Taxes	$ 7,500
Less: Amortization Deduction	(5,000)
Taxable Income	$ 2,500
Tax Rate	40%
Tax Liability	$ 1,000

Cash Flow Before Amortization and Taxes	$ 7,500
Less: Tax Liability	(1,000)
Net Cash Flow After Taxes	$ 6,500
Times: PV Factor of a 10% Annuity for 2 Years	1.74
After Tax Present Value of Lease	$11,310

INVESTMENT EVALUATION

50. (c) The accrual accounting rate of return (ARR) for a project is computed by dividing the average annual income the project generates by the initial (or average) increase in required investment. Thus, the numerator of the ratio is the increase in average annual operating income of $40,000. (To compute the accrual ARR on the initial investment, the denominator is the $60,000 initial increase in the required investment. The $30,000 average increase in the required investment would be used as the denominator to compute the rate of return on the average investment.)

51. (d) Unlike the net present value, internal rate of return, and payback methods of capital budgeting, the accounting rate of return (ARR) method does not focus on cash flows. Rather, it focuses on

accounting net income. The ARR is computed by dividing the expected increase in future average annual accounting net income by the initial (or average) increase in required investment. The expected increase in future average accounting net income is determined by subtracting the incremental expenses of the project, including depreciation, from the estimated revenues over the life of the project and dividing this amount by the estimated useful life of the project. The time value of money is *not* considered in computing the ARR.

52. (d) Payback method advantages include its: basis on cash flows, rough determination of the time to recoup the original investment, and simplicity & ease of use.

53. (c) The annual savings needed to realize a 12% yield can be obtained by dividing the $44,300 by the 3.60 present value of an annuity at 12% for 5 years. Thus, the annual savings needed are $12,306 ($44,300 / 3.60), rounded to the nearest dollar.

Cost	$50,000
Less: PV of Residual Value ($10,000 x 0.57)	(5,700)
Present Value of Annual Savings Needed	$44,300

54. (d) The internal rate of return (IRR) capital budgeting method determines the rate of interest which would make the present value of the future cash flows equal to the cost of the initial investment. These cash flows include the net cash generated by the operation of the project plus the cash obtained from its ultimate disposal. Depreciation is a noncash expense, representing merely the allocation of the depreciable base of a plant asset over its estimated useful life. When income taxes are ignored, the IRR method excludes depreciation expense from its computation because no cash flow is involved.

55. (d) The internal rate of return (IRR) of an investment is the discount rate that would yield a net present value (NPV) of $0. The table of net present values included in this problem indicates that a 14% discount rate yields a positive NPV, whereas a 16% rate yields a negative NPV. Therefore, IRR is between 14% and 16%; only answer (d), 15.3%, satisfies this requirement.

56. (b) The net present value method uses a predetermined discount or "hurdle" rate to discount all positive and negative cash flows to their present value. The discounted cash flows are then netted; if the resulting amount is positive, the investment has a rate of return greater than the required rate, and vice versa. The internal rate of return (IRR) method uses the expected cash inflows and outflows (and

their timing) to determine the IRR implicit in the investment.

57. (d) The net present value of the project is determined by discounting the cash flows generated by the project at the cost of capital. These cash flows include the net cash generated by the operation of the project plus the cash obtained from its ultimate disposal.

58. (c) The net present value method of investment analysis uses a predetermined discount or "hurdle" rate to discount all positive and negative cash flows to their present value. The discounted cash flows are then netted; if the resulting amount is positive, the investment has a rate of return greater than the required rate, and vice versa. The payback period method ignores return rates—it simply divides the initial investment by the periodic cash inflow to determine the number of periods required to recover the investment. Answers (b) and (d) are incorrect because these two methods (which are actually the same) use the expected cash inflows and outflows (and their timing) to determine the internal rate of return implicit in the investment.

ECONOMIC ORDER QUANTITY

59. (c) The inventory reorder point is figured as anticipated demand during lead time, the time lag between ordering and receiving goods. The reorder point can be calculated by multiplying average daily usage by lead time in days.

RESIDUAL INCOME

60. (b) The capital-employed turnover rate is determined as follows:

$$\frac{\text{Capital-employed}}{\text{turnover rate}} = \frac{\text{Sales}}{\text{Invested capital}}$$

61. (d) Residual income is the income of an investment center less an imputed interest charge on the invested capital used by the center, and is determined as follows:

$$\frac{\text{Residual}}{\text{Income}} = \frac{\text{Operating}}{\text{income}} - \left(\begin{array}{c} \text{Imputed} \\ \text{interest} \\ \text{rate} \end{array} \times \begin{array}{c} \text{Average} \\ \text{invested} \\ \text{capital} \end{array} \right)$$

To maximize residual income, projects earning more than the imputed interest charge would be accepted, while projects earning less than that charge would be rejected. Division A's project should be accepted because it will earn a rate of return greater than the imputed interest rate on invested capital. Division B's project should not be accepted because it will earn a rate of return less than the imputed interest rate on invested capital.

62. (d)   Zee's residual income is $150,000 (i.e., $200,000 – $50,000). The residual income of a profit center is computed by subtracting an imputed interest charge for invested capital from the operating income of the center.

63. (a)   Residual income is the operating income of an investment center less an imputed interest charge on the invested capital used by the center. To compute Kew's residual income, it is first necessary to determine Kew's operating income. Kew's residual income can then be determined.

Sales		$ 500,000
Less: Variable costs	$300,000	
Traceable fixed costs	50,000	(350,000)
Operating income		$ 150,000

$$\frac{\text{Residual}}{\text{income}} = \frac{\text{Operating}}{\text{income}} - \frac{\text{Imputed interest on}}{\text{average invested capital}}$$

$$= \$150,000 - (\$100,000 \times 6\%) = \underline{\$144,000}$$

PROBABILITY & EXPECTED VALUE

64. (c)   The "most likely sales volume" is the sales volume with the greatest probability. The midpoint of the range and the median are statistics derived by combining the estimates of likely sales volume. The expected value of a random variable is a weighted average of all the values the variable can take, with the respective probabilities as weights.

65. (c)

Months with zero outages	0	x	3	=	0
Months with one outage	1	x	2	=	2
Months with two outages	2	x	4	=	8
Months with three outages	3	x	3	=	9
Total Number of Expected Outages					19
Out-of-pocket Costs per Outage					$ 400
Expected Out-of-pocket Costs					$ 7,600
Less: Cost of Auxiliary Generator ($500 x 12)					(6,000)
Estimated Net Savings by Leasing the Generator					$ 1,600

66. (c)   The expected value of the payoff is computed adding the products of each level of income (loss) multiplied by its probability.

Probability	x	Income(loss)	=	Expected value
0.20		$(100,000)		$ (20,000)
0.80		$ 250,000		200,000
1.00				$180,000

67. (a)   The expected value is a weighted average of all the values the variable can take, with the respective probabilities as weights. The value of winning the case is $43,000 = $75,000 – [$12,000 +

1/2 x ($75,000 – $35,000)]. The expected value of accepting the offer is $4,000 greater than the expected value of litigation ($25,800 – $4,800 = $21,000).

Outcome	Probability	Value of Outcome	Weighted Average
Win	0.6	$43,000	$25,800
Lose	0.4	$0 - $12,000	(4,800)

68. (c)   The information provided by a probability distribution can be summarized by means of the expected value of the random variable. This is a weighted average of all the values the variable can take, with the respective probabilities as weights. To compute the expected value, the various values are multiplied by their probabilities and then added together.

REGRESSION & CORRELATION

69. (a)   The estimated total maintenance cost incurred at 1,000 machine hours is determined as follows:

Total cost = $5,000 + $6.50 (machine hours)

= $5,000 + $6.50 (1,000) = $11,500

The .90 coefficient of determination does not affect the above computation. However, since it approaches +1, we are given a high level of assurance that the independent variable, machine hours, accounts for most of the variability in the dependent variable, total maintenance cost.

70. (a)   Regression analysis (multiple or simple) produces measures of the probable error associated with both the uncertainty associated with the location of the regression line (standard error of the estimate) and the uncertainty associated with the variance of the predicted dependent variable. Regression analysis only identifies the association between variables without establishing a cause and effect relationship. Multiple regression almost always involves a sample of observations. Multiple regression analysis involves the use of more than one independent variable in estimating the value of the dependent variable.

71. (b)   The equation being used is that for a straight line: y = A + Bx. In this equation:

y = dependent variable (i.e., total overhead cost)
A = the y intercept (i.e., fixed overhead cost)
B = the slope of the line (i.e., the variable overhead cost per cost driver)
x = independent variable (i.e., the cost driver)
Bx = total variable overhead cost

PERFORMANCE BY SUBTOPICS

Each category below parallels a subtopic covered in Chapter 26. Record the number and percentage of questions you correctly answered in each subtopic area.

Budgets

Question #	Correct √
1	
2	
3	
4	
5	
6	
# Questions	6

\# Correct _____
% Correct _____

Responsibility Accounting

Question #	Correct √
7	
8	
9	
# Questions	3

\# Correct _____
% Correct _____

Quality Control Programs

Question #	Correct √
10	
11	
12	
13	
14	
# Questions	5

\# Correct _____
% Correct _____

Time Value of Money

Question #	Correct √
15	
16	
# Questions	2

\# Correct _____
% Correct _____

Investment Evaluation

Question #	Correct √
17	
18	
19	
20	
21	
22	
# Questions	6

\# Correct _____
% Correct _____

Residual Income

Question #	Correct √
23	
24	
# Questions	2

\# Correct _____
% Correct _____

Percentage Return on Assets

Question #	Correct √
25	
# Questions	1

\# Correct _____
% Correct _____

Return on Investment

Question #	Correct √
26	
27	
# Questions	2

\# Correct _____
% Correct _____

Economic Order Quantity

Question #	Correct √
28	
29	
30	
31	
# Questions	4

\# Correct _____
% Correct _____

Probability & Expected Value

Question #	Correct √
32	
33	
34	
35	
# Questions	4

\# Correct _____
% Correct _____

Regression & Correlation

Question #	Correct √
36	
37	
38	
39	
40	
# Questions	5

\# Correct _____
% Correct _____

OTHER OBJECTIVE FORMAT QUESTION SOLUTIONS

SOLUTION 26-3 INVESTMENT EVALUATION METHODS

1. $13,000

Under the net present value method, the present value of all cash inflows associated with an investment project are compared with the present value of all cash outflows. The difference between the present value of these cash flows is the net present value of the project and determines whether or not the project is an acceptable investment.

Annual cash inflows	$ 20,000
Times: Present value annuity factor	x 5.65
Present value of cash inflows	$ 113,000
Less: Initial investment	(100,000)
Net present value of project	$ 13,000

2. 5.0 years

The payback period is the period of time it takes for the cumulative sum of annual net cash inflows from a project to equal the initial cost outlay. When the annual net cash inflows from the project are a constant amount, the payback period for the project is determined as follows:

$$\text{Payback period} = \frac{\text{Initial cash outlay}}{\text{Annual net cash inflows}} = \frac{\$100,000}{\$20,000} = 5.0 \text{ years}$$

3. 10%

The accrual accounting rate of return on initial investment is computed by dividing the average annual accounting income the machine generates by the cost of the machine. The average annual accounting income generated by the machine is the expected annual after-tax cash savings in operating expenses less annual depreciation expense [i.e., $20,000 – ($100,000 ÷ 10) = $10,000].

$$\text{Accounting rate of return on initial investment} = \frac{\text{Average annual accounting income}}{\text{Initial investment cost}}$$

$$= \frac{\$10,000}{\$100,000}$$

4. 5.00

The internal rate of return is the interest rate which would make the present value of the future expected cash flows equal to the initial investment. Since the annual net cash inflows from the project are a constant amount, the internal rate of return of the proposed investment is calculated as follows:

$$\frac{\text{Annual}}{\text{Cash flows}} \times \frac{\text{Present}}{\text{value factor}} = \frac{\text{Cost of}}{\text{initial investment}}$$

$20,000 x Present value factor = $100,000

Present value factor = $100,000 / $20,000

Present value factor = 5.00

5. $68,000

The net present value of the project is the amount of the excess of the present value of the cash flows over the cost of the project. As the entity is a tax-exempt organization, the effect of income taxes is irrelevant.

Annual cash flow	$ 130,000
Present value annuity factor	x 3.6
Present value of cash flows	$ 468,000
Less: Cost of project	(400,000)
Net present value of project	$ 68,000

6. D   To determine the internal rate of return on this project, the net present value of the project is computed at 12%, 14%, and 16%. Since the machine has a positive net present value at a discount rate of 14%, the internal rate of return exceeds 14%. Since the machine has a positive net present value at a discount rate of 16%, the internal rate of return exceeds 16%.

	14%	16%
Annual cash flow	$ 130,000	$ 130,000
PV annuity factor	x 3.4	x 3.3
PV of cash flows	$ 442,000	$ 429,000
Less: Cost of project	(400,000)	(400,000)
Net present value	$ 42,000	$ 29,500

7. 13.9%

To determine the accounting rate of return (ARR), based on the project's average book value for 20X1, annual depreciation expense and the average book value for 20X1 must be computed. Depreciation expense on the straight-line basis is $80,000 [($400,000 – $0) / 5 years]. The book value of the machine at the end of 20X1 is $320,000 ($400,000 – $80,000). The machine's average book value for 20X1 is $360,000 [($400,000 + $320,000)/ 2]. The ARR, based on the project's average book value for 20X1, is computed as follows:

$$\text{Accounting rate of return on average book value} = \frac{\text{Average annual accounting income}}{\text{Initial investment cost}}$$

$$= \frac{\$130,000 - \$80,000}{\$360,000} = 13.9\%$$

SOLUTION 26-4 INVESTMENT EVALUATION METHODS

1. **B** The payback period is the period of time it takes for the cumulative sum of annual net cash inflows from a project to equal the initial cash outlay. When cash inflows are not uniform, the payback period computation takes a cumulative form. That is, each year's net cash inflows are accumulated until the initial cash outlay is recovered. The question states that Projects A and B have the same initial cash outlay and lives. Per a review of Diagram I, most of the net cash inflows of Project B occur in the first three years of the project's life, and most of the net cash inflows of Project A occur in the last three years of that project's life. Therefore, Project B would be more likely to have the shorter payback period.

2. **A** The average annual accounting income generated by a project is the numerator of the average accounting rate of return (ARR) method of capital budgeting. This amount is computed by subtracting average annual depreciation expense from the average annual net cash inflows generated by the project. Projects A and B have the same initial investment requirements and lives. Therefore, annual average depreciation expense is the same for both projects. Project A has a greater total net cash inflow. Therefore, Project A has greater average annual net cash inflows and thus a greater average ARR.

3. **B** The internal rate of return (IRR) is the discount rate which would make the present value of the project equal to zero. Per a review of Diagram II, projects A and B have a zero present value at discount rates of 16% and 22%, respectively. Hence, projects A and B have internal rates of return of 16% and 22%, respectively. The 22% IRR of project B exceeds the 16% IRR of project A.

4. **B** The internal rate of return (IRR) is the discount rate which would make the present value of a project equal to zero. Per a review of Diagram II, based on 5-year lives, projects A and B have a zero present value at discount rates of 16% and 22%, respectively. Hence, based on 5-year lives, projects A and B have internal rates of return of 16% and 22%, respectively. The 22% internal rate of return of project B based on a 5-year life exceeds the 16% internal rate of return of project A based on a 5-year life. If both projects were to terminate at the end of year 4 with cash flows remaining as projected for the first 4 years and no cash flows in year 5, per a review of Diagram I, the present value of net cash inflows lost by project B is less than that lost by project A. Therefore, although the IRR of both projects would decrease if the projects were to

terminate at the end of year 4, the IRR of project B would still exceed that of project A.

SOLUTION 26-5 INVENTORY

1. **N** Isle does not practice a just-in-time (JIT) philosophy. Having no work-in-process inventories is characteristic of a JIT system. However, other facts lead to the conclusion that Isle does not practice a JIT philosophy. For one thing, production schedules are based upon sales forecasts. In a JIT system, customer demand is what stimulates production. There is a substantial finished goods inventory for the Aran product. In addition, Isle uses a standard cost system to measure variances that lead to attempts to improve operations. Using variances under a standard cost system can lead to dysfunctional behavior. For example, a materials price variance encourages the purchaser to obtain the lowest price with less attention paid to quality. High quality is a key aspect of a JIT system. Also, in a JIT system, the company often negotiates long-term contracts with vendors that specify acceptable prices and quality, eliminating the need for a materials price variance to be computed.

2. **N** Indirect materials costs are costs that are variable, not fixed. These costs vary with production. Thus, they should not be included in standard fixed overhead costs.

3. **Y** A value-adding activity is one that a customer is willing to pay for. Customers are willing to pay for the reasonable cost of operating the equipment necessary to produce a product. Examples of non-value-adding activities include material moves, inspections, and rework.

4. **Y** If Isle's three products were produced in a single plant, activity-based costing (ABC) would provide more accurate, and thus more useful, production cost information than would traditional standard costing. Traditional standard costing uses a volume-based measure to allocate overhead costs to production. If some of the overhead costs are not related to volume, high volume products are over costed and low volume products are undercosted. ABC overcomes this systematic bias by tracing the cost of the activities necessary to produce each product to each product.

5. **Y** When overhead costs are mixed or semivariable, there are a number of ways to separate the costs into their fixed and variable components. One such way is the high-low method. However, this method is deficient in that it takes only the high cost point and the low cost point and their corresponding activity levels into account. Another

method is the scattergraph method in which the analyst uses judgment to draw a line of best fit through the points representing total costs. Regression analysis is superior to both of these methods, taking all points into account and plotting a line of best fit through the points. This regression line minimizes the sum of the squared deviations between the points and the regression line. The point where the line intercepts the Y axis represents the fixed cost element. The slope of the line represents the variable costs per unit of activity.

6. N   Normal spoilage would be expected to increase or decrease as production increases or decreases. Thus, normal spoilage represents a variable cost, not a fixed cost.

7. Y   Because the estimate of the number of units containing defective materials and the number of units containing defective workmanship were made independently, the probability used to determine normal spoilage is less than 0.025. The reason is that some of the units that contain defective workmanship are likely to contain defective materials also. Although the probability estimates were made independently, the two types of defects are not independent events. Indeed, a unit with defective materials would be more likely to have defective workmanship also. The probability estimate would be 0.025 less the probability that a unit has defective materials and defective workmanship.

8. Y   Isle will break even on the contract using variable costing. The fixed costs do not change in total. The sales price exactly offsets the variable costs that would be incurred. Under absorption costing, Isle would show a loss on the contract because fixed manufacturing overhead costs would be allocated to the products sold under the contract.

9. N   The direct labor hours used in producing Aran were greater than the standard hours allowed because the direct labor efficiency variance is unfavorable. The direct labor efficiency variance is the standard labor rate times the difference between the actual hours and the standard hours: SR (AH − SH). If this variance is positive, it is unfavorable because the actual hours were greater than the standard hours. If this variance is negative, the negative sign is dropped and the variance is called favorable because the actual hours were less than the standard hours. Since the direct labor variance was unfavorable for the production of Aran, the direct labor hours used were greater than the standard hours.

10. N   Because Isle began operations in 20X1, there was no beginning inventory of Aran. The ending variable cost of finished goods inventory of Aran is reported to be $100,000. Thus, inventory increased. Absorption costing would result in a greater net income because under absorption costing, some of the fixed manufacturing overhead costs would be deferred as a part of the ending finished goods inventory. Thus, costs charged against income would be less and the net income would be higher. Under variable costing, all fixed manufacturing overhead costs are charged as an expense of the period. If inventory were to decrease during a period, then variable costing would yield a greater net income than would absorption costing.

11. Y   The total amount paid for the direct materials put into process was more than the standard cost allowed for the work done because the total materials variance was unfavorable. The total materials variance was $14,000 unfavorable. It consists of the combination of the $16,000 unfavorable usage variance and the $2,000 favorable price variance. Although the price paid for the materials was favorable, Isle used far more than the standard quantity of materials allowed for the work done. Thus, the total amount paid is more than the standard cost allowed for the work done.

12. Y   The present value of the cash inflows is $67,800 (5.65 x $12,000). Subtracting the $60,000 investment from this amount gives a positive net present value of $7,800 ($67,800 − $60,000).

13. N   The internal rate of return (IRR) on the lease is greater than the cost of capital. The IRR is the rate of return that, when used in the discount rate in the net present value computations, yields a net present value of exactly zero. Because the net present value of this investment is positive, the IRR is greater than the cost of capital. The internal rate of return on this investment is approximately 15.1%.

14. B or C (The Editors prefer answer C.) Of the three products, the payback method is likely to be more appropriate for evaluating investments in Cilly. The payback method is not a discounted cash flow method. The payback method is often used as a crude measure of risk. The payback period is computed by dividing the cost of the investment by the cash flows per year, assuming the cash flows are constant. If the cash flows are not constant, the cash flows for each year are subtracted from the investment. The payback period is the point in time from the time the investment was made to the point where the cost of the investment is recovered in full. Investments in Cilly are more risky because demand

is difficult to project for more than 3 years. Thus, the payback method would be important because the company would want to recover any investment in Cilly as soon as possible.

15. B   Of the three products that Isle produces, the economic order quantity would be most useful when purchasing raw materials for Bute. The reason is that the demand for Bute is constant and easy to project. Estimating demand is important because the economic order quantity is determined by taking the square root of the following formula:

$$\sqrt{\frac{2 \times \text{the order cost for each order} \times \text{the annual demand in units}}{\text{cost to carry one unit of inventory for one year}}}$$

16. C   Cilly would be more likely to have a substantial percentage of under- or overapplied fixed manufacturing overhead costs on quarterly statements because demand for Cilly is very seasonal, yet fixed costs are incurred evenly throughout the year.

17. C   The actual return on investment is determined by dividing the operating income, net of variances, by the average investment. The return on investment for each of the three products is computed as follows:

Aran: $0 / $1,000,000   =   0.000%
Bute: $41,000 / $800,000   =   5.125%
Cilly: $36,000 / $400,000   =   9.000%

18. A   Bute's standard contribution margin ratio is 22% ($176,000/$800,000). Cilly's standard contribution margin ratio is 28.8% ($144,000/ $500,000). Thus, by selling $10,000 more of Bute and $10,000 less of Cilly, Isle would lower its standard weighted average contribution margin ratio. The breakeven point in sales dollars is fixed costs divided by the weighted average contribution margin ratio. Therefore, by lowering its standard weighted average contribution margin ratio, Isle would increase its standard dollar break-even point.

19. $1.50

Aran's standard variable selling and administrative costs per unit can be computed by dividing the standard variable selling and administrative costs by the 80,000 units sold. Thus, the variable selling and administrative costs per unit are $1.50 ($120,000 / 80,000 units). Because variable costs are fixed per unit, Aran's budgeted standard per unit cost for variable selling and administrative costs at a sales level of 75,000 units is the same $1.50.

20. $140,000

Fixed costs are fixed in total and vary on a per unit basis. If Aran's standard fixed selling and administrative costs are $140,000 at a sales level of 80,000 units, such fixed costs should remain at $140,000 at a sales level of 75,000 units.

21. $2,100,000

Isle's standard break-even point in sales dollars can be determined by dividing the standard total fixed costs by the standard weighted average contribution margin ratio. Isle's standard total fixed costs can be determined by subtracting the standard operating income from the standard contribution margin. Thus, Isle's standard total fixed costs are $840,000 ($1,000,000 – $160,000). Isle's standard weighted average contribution margin ratio can be determined by dividing the standard contribution margin by the standard sales revenue. Thus, Isle's standard weighted average contribution margin ratio is 40% or 0.4 ($1,000,000 / $2,500,000). Therefore, the standard break-even point in sales dollars is $2,100,000 ($840,000 / 0.4).

22. $40,000

The direct materials usage variance and the direct labor efficiency variance might be partially or wholly the responsibility of the direct labor employees. Thus, the total amount of the variances that might be regarded partially or wholly as the responsibility of the direct labor employees is $40,000 ($16,000 + $24,000). The direct materials price variance would be the responsibility of the purchasing manager. The direct labor rate variance is the responsibility of management.

23. $440,000

The Y represents the total standard manufacturing cost that would be incurred at a production level of zero units. If no units were produced, the only manufacturing costs that would be incurred would be the fixed manufacturing costs.

WHICH YEAR WILL BE TESTED?

"Candidates are responsible for knowing accounting and auditing pronouncements, including the pronouncements in the governmental and not-for-profit organizations area, six months after a pronouncement's *effective* date, unless early application is permitted. When early application is permitted, candidates are responsible for knowing the new pronouncement six months after the *issuance* date. In this case, candidates are responsible for knowing both the old and new pronouncements until the old pronouncement is superseded. For the federal taxation area, candidates are responsible for knowing the Internal Revenue Code and federal tax regulations in effect six months before the examination date."

The above excerpt from the AICPA's *Information for Uniform CPA Examination Candidates* indicates that the November 2002 exam (for instance) will have questions asking about situations in the 2002 tax year, except as changed by tax laws passed after April. However, note that questions asked in November 2000 (for instance) had 1999 dates in them. The examiners have repeatedly asked questions on the November exam for the previous calendar year, but there is no assurance that they will continue to do so. The editors recommend that candidates study the laws applicable to both years. If candidates feel they must limit their studies to one tax year, the editors suggest that it be the previous calendar year.

The examiners tend to focus on fundamentals, rather than changes from one year to the next. The amounts of inflation-adjusted figures, in particular, usually are given in questions; candidates must demonstrate that they understand when and how to apply these figures.

2002 and 2001 TAX ACTS

The Job Creation & Worker Assistance Act of 2002 (JCWAA '02) includes business economic stimulus provisions, some general retroactively effective tax breaks, and some relief provisions only for lower-Manhattan entities affected by terrorist acts on September 11, 2001. JCWAA '02 became effective on March 9, 2002, and thus, is eligible to be tested on the November 2002 and later CPA exams. The Bisk Education editors believe details on the provisions applicable only to lower-Manhattan are beyond the scope of the exam.

The Economic Growth and Tax Relief Reconciliation Act of 2001 (EGTRRA '01) changes are pervasive, but not as sweeping as the popular press might have you believe, particularly for the tax years 2001 through 2003. For instance, the changes do not impact the relationship between standard and itemized deductions. In this volume, no effective date is designated for provisions that are not changed. Note that this is the majority of the content.

Bisk Education CPA review materials are designed to help you pass the current exam. Provisions that are not yet effective are not tested; thus you unnecessarily would add time to your review by studying them. We do not discourage your interest in these provisions, but we caution you not to delude yourself that this study is exam preparation. Generally, provisions that are not effective until 2004 or later are not in this edition—which already is more than you are likely to need. Some future changes to current provisions are discussed when the additional space to do so is not significant. Future editions and updating supplements will provide information about provisions as they become eligible for testing. Study those provisions that are applicable to your exam.

CHAPTER 27

FEDERAL TAXATION: INDIVIDUALS

CHAPTER 27

FEDERAL TAXATION: INDIVIDUALS

I. INTRODUCTION

A. EXAM COVERAGE

About 20% of the Accounting and Reporting section of the CPA exam will be devoted to federal income taxation of individuals. This includes the taxation of property. To concisely and effectively present property taxation topics (eligible to be tested under the any of the four taxation divisions of the ARE exam section), they are discussed in a separate chapter. Keep in mind that per AICPA guidelines, candidates are responsible for knowledge of the Internal Revenue Code (IRC) and the Federal Tax Regulations in effect six months before the exam. Questions on the **May 2003** exam will cover the law in effect for 2002. The editors expect that questions on the **November 2003** exam will cover the law in effect for 2002. Questions on the **May 2004** exam will cover the law in effect for 2003. (As we go to press, many 2003 amounts are unknown. Updating Supplements, if needed, are available with applicable changes in mid-September.)

B. FLOW OF FORM 1040

To help you understand how an individual's tax liability is determined, presented below is a summary of the flow of the Individual Income Tax Return, Form 1040.

STEP ONE: DETERMINE GROSS INCOME

1. Wages, salaries, tips
2. Interest (Schedule B)
3. Dividends (Schedule B)
4. Taxable refunds of state and local taxes
5. Alimony received
6. Business income (Schedule C)
7. Capital gain or (loss) (Schedule D)
8. Other gains or (losses) (Form 4797)
9. IRA distributions, pensions, and annuities
10. Rents, royalties, partnerships, estates, trusts, etc. (Schedule E)
11. Unemployment compensation
12. Social Security benefits
13. Other income

STEP TWO: LESS ADJUSTMENTS FOR GROSS INCOME (ABOVE-THE-LINE DEDUCTIONS)

1. IRA
2. Medical savings account
3. Moving expenses
4. One-half of self-employment tax
5. Self-employed health insurance
6. Keogh or SEP
7. Penalty for early withdrawal of savings
8. Alimony paid
9. Educational loan interest paid

STEP THREE: EQUALS ADJUSTED GROSS INCOME (AGI)

STEP FOUR: LESS THE GREATER OF THE STANDARD DEDUCTION OR ITEMIZED DEDUCTIONS (SCHEDULE A)

1. Medical and dental expenses
2. Taxes paid
3. Interest paid
4. Charitable contributions
5. Casualty and theft losses
6. Miscellaneous expenses (including unreimbursed employee expenses)

STEP FIVE: LESS EXEMPTIONS

STEP SIX: EQUALS TAXABLE INCOME

STEP SEVEN: DETERMINE TENTATIVE TAX LIABILITY

STEP EIGHT: LESS CREDITS

1. Child and dependent care
2. Credit for the elderly or the disabled
3. Foreign tax credit
4. Other credits (education, child, adoption, etc.)

STEP NINE: PLUS ADDITIONAL TAXES

1. Self-employment tax
2. Alternative minimum tax
3. Recapture taxes
4. Social security tax on tip income
5. Tax on qualified retirement plans

STEP TEN: LESS PAYMENTS

1. Federal income tax withheld
2. Estimated tax payments
3. Overpayment applied to current year liability
4. Earned income credit
5. Amount paid with extension (Form 4868)
6. Excess FICA
7. Other payments

STEP ELEVEN: EQUALS AMOUNT OVERPAID OR BALANCE DUE

C.   **FILING STATUS**
The tax rate applicable to a taxpayer's taxable income depends on her/his filing status. The amount of a taxpayer's standard deduction is also influenced by filing status.

1.   **SINGLE (S)** Taxpayers who are not married or heads of households. Legally separated spouses who are living apart are also considered single, unless they qualify as head of household.

2.   **MARRIED FILING JOINTLY (MFJ)** This status is available to taxpayers who meet all of the following conditions:

   a.   Married and not legally separated at the end of the tax year. If the taxpayer's spouse died during the tax year, the surviving spouse may file a joint return for that year unless s/he remarries before the end of the year. If a marriage is annulled, the annulment is retroactive and thus, both individuals must file amended returns as single taxpayers.

b. Neither spouse was a nonresident alien at any time during the year. If one spouse was a nonresident alien, the couple can elect to file jointly by agreeing to be taxed on combined worldwide income.

c. Both spouses' tax years begin on the same date. (They may have separate accounting methods, i.e., cash basis vs. accrual basis.)

d. Both spouses sign the return.

3. **MARRIED FILING SEPARATELY (MFS)** Married individuals may elect to file separate returns. In a separate property state, each spouse must report her/his own income, deductions, exemptions, and credits. In a community property state, each spouse is allocated 50% of the income, deductions, exemptions, and credits.

4. **SURVIVING SPOUSE (SS)** (Also called Qualifying Widow[er]). If the surviving spouse maintains a household that is the principal place of residence for the entire year of a child who qualifies as her/his dependent, s/he may use the joint return rates for two years after the death of her/his spouse.

5. **HEAD OF HOUSEHOLD (HH)** To qualify, both of the following must be met: (1) the taxpayer must not be married or a surviving spouse at the end of the year, and (2) the taxpayer must maintain as her/his home a household that is the principal place of residence for more than 50% of the year for her/his child, grandchild, stepchild, adopted child, parent, grandparent, uncle, aunt, nephew, niece, or certain step-relatives and in-laws.

D. EXEMPTIONS

Each taxpayer may be entitled to an exemption for her/him, her/his spouse, and for each dependent. For 2002, each exemption is $3,000.

1. **PERSONAL EXEMPTION** Each taxpayer is entitled to an exemption for her/him unless s/he is claimed as a dependent on another taxpayer's return.

- If a husband and wife file a joint return, neither one may be claimed as a dependent on another taxpayer's return unless they are filing a return only to obtain a refund.

2. **SPOUSAL EXEMPTION** The spousal exemption is **not** a dependency exemption. It is a personal exemption based on the marital relationship. Therefore, it is **not** subject to the support test for a dependency exemption.

a. If the taxpayer's spouse dies during the year, the taxpayer may still claim the spousal exemption for that year if s/he has not remarried.

b. If the taxpayers are divorced or legally separated at the end of the year, neither one may claim the other as an exemption.

c. A married spouse filing separately may take only one personal exemption unless the other spouse is the filing spouse's dependent and has no gross income for the tax year.

3. **DEPENDENCY EXEMPTIONS** A taxpayer is allowed an exemption for each dependent. In order for the taxpayer to claim another person as a dependent, five tests must be satisfied.

a. **GROSS INCOME** The person's (taxable) gross income must be less than the personal exemption amount for that tax year. However, this gross income test does **not** apply to children of the taxpayer who are either (1) under 19 years old or (2) a full-time student for at least five calendar months of the year and under 24 years old at the close of the tax year.

    b.   **SUPPORT** Taxpayer furnishes over one-half of dependent's support for the calendar year in question.

        (1)   Amounts contributed by the dependent for her/his own support are included in determining this test. This includes tax-exempt items such as social security benefits received by the dependent, but only if used for her/his support.

        (2)   Scholarships and life insurance proceeds payable to the dependent are not included as support for this test.

        (3)   In the case of children of divorced or separated parents, the **custodial parent** gets the exemptions. However, the custodial parent can waive the exemption without jeopardizing other tax provisions that are contingent upon the dependency exemption (e.g., head-of-household status, earned income credits, or child care credits).

    c.   **RELATIONSHIP OR HOUSEHOLD** Dependent is a lineal descendant (child or grandchild), ancestor (parent or grandparent), or sibling of the taxpayer by whole or half blood, including father-, mother-, sisters-, and brothers-in-law. Also included in the dependency relationship are unrelated individuals who live in the taxpayer's home for the entire taxable year. A person can be a member of the taxpayer's household and not live with her/him. For example, a person may live in a nursing home for the entire year and still be a member of the taxpayer's household.

    d.   **RETURN STATUS** Dependent must not have filed a joint return. However, spouses may be dependents of a third person and still file a joint return if neither spouse is required to file a return, and the joint return was filed solely for a refund, not for the payment of taxes.

    e.   **CITIZENSHIP OR RESIDENCE** Dependent must be a citizen or resident of the U.S., or a citizen of Mexico or Canada.

4.   **MULTIPLE SUPPORT AGREEMENT** A multiple support agreement is used when more than one taxpayer contributes to the support of an individual but no one person contributes more than 50% of the support. A taxpayer who would otherwise qualify for the exemption may claim it if the others agree, as long as s/he contributes more than 10% of the individual's support. The agreement must be signed by all of the contributors and attached to the return of the taxpayer claiming the exemption.

5.   **PHASE-OUT OF PERSONAL AND DEPENDENCY EXEMPTIONS** The exemption amounts are phased out by 2% for each $2,500 or portion thereof by which the taxpayer's adjusted gross income (AGI) exceeds the threshold amounts. (Contrast this with the itemized deduction 3% phase-out rule, discussed later in this chapter.)

EXHIBIT 1 ♦ 2002 PHASE-OUT THRESHOLD AMOUNTS SCHEDULE

Joint Returns	$206,000
Head of Household	171,650
Single Individual	137,300
Married Filing Separately	103,000

E.   **FILING REQUIREMENTS**

1.   **GENERAL** Generally, an individual must file a tax return if her/his income is greater than the sum of her/his personal exemption plus her/his standard deduction. The following individuals are also required to file:

a. An individual who has net earnings from self-employment of $400 or more;

b. An individual who can be claimed as a dependent on another taxpayer's return and has unearned income of $1 or more and gross income of $650 or more;

c. Individuals who receive advance payments of the earned income credit; or

d. Married individuals who file separately must file if their income is greater than their personal exemption.

2. **DUE DATE** An individual's tax return is due on or before the 15th day of the fourth month following the close of the year. For a calendar year taxpayer, the return is due on or before April 15th of the following year. If the due date of the return falls on a weekend or a legal holiday, the return is due the next business day.

3. **EXTENSION** An automatic four month extension will be granted for a taxpayer who is unable to file her/his return by the due date. An additional two month extension is available if the taxpayer can show cause for needing the extra time. The extensions extend only the time to file, not the time to pay the tax. Therefore, to avoid penalty, the taxpayer must pay all taxes due by the 15th day of the fourth month following the close of the year.

4. **ASSESSMENT** Generally, all taxes must be assessed within three years after the later of the due date or the filing date. If the taxpayer omitted more than 25% when reporting her/his gross income, this three-year period is extended to six years. In the case of fraud, there is no statute of limitations. A taxpayer must file to claim a refund by the later of three years from the time the return was filed, or two years after the payment of tax. A return that is filed before the due date is treated as if it were filed on the due date. Individuals have the same deadlines when amending returns (Form 1040X).

F. **TAX PROCEDURES**
The IRS has the burden of proof in any court proceeding with respect to a factual issue regarding a taxpayer's tax liability, if the taxpayer introduces credible evidence and satisfies four conditions. These conditions are (1) the taxpayer must substantiate items, (2) the taxpayer must maintain adequate records, (3) the taxpayer must comply with reasonable requests for interviews and information, and (4) taxpayers must have a net worth of less than $7 million. The net worth condition is inapplicable to individuals.

II. GROSS INCOME

A. **DEFINITION**
Gross income includes all income from whatever source derived **unless** there is a specific exclusion provided by law. Gross income includes money, property, or services. Property and services received are included in gross income at their fair market values.

EXAMPLE 1 ♦ GROSS INCOME

> Sally, a real estate agent, closes a big deal and her boss compensates her by giving her a new BMW. The fair market value of that BMW is gross income to Sally, and it is a deductible trade or business expense for the employer.

B. **REALIZATION & RECOGNITION**
Income is taxable when it is both realized and recognized by the taxpayer.

1. **CONSTRUCTIVE RECEIPT** A cash basis taxpayer is taxed on income once it is **constructively** received even though it may not be **actually** received. Constructive receipt occurs when the income is credited to the taxpayer or made available to her/him without any restrictions or substantial limitations.

2. **INCOME IN RESPECT OF A DECEDENT (IRD)** This income is included in the decedent's final income tax return or the heir's return. Common examples are accrued salary (earned before death) and tax-deferred pension plans paid to heirs or beneficiaries

C. **SPECIFIC EXCLUSIONS FROM GROSS INCOME**
Income items that are not included in gross income and are not subject to income tax. Do not confuse an exclusion with a deduction. Generally, exclusions are not required to be shown on the tax return while deductions must be shown.

1. **LIFE INSURANCE** Generally, life insurance proceeds (the face amount of the policy) paid by reason of death of the insured are excluded from gross income.

   a. **INSTALLMENT OPTIONS** If the beneficiary elects to receive the benefits in installments, the **interest portion** is includible in income.

   b. **DIVIDENDS** Dividends received that are considered a return of premiums paid are **not** included in income.

2. **ANNUITIES** Annuities are excluded from gross income to the extent that they are a return of capital. The excludable portion of an annuity payment is determined by multiplying the total payment by the exclusion ratio. The remainder is included in the income of the recipient. The exclusion ratio equals the net cost of the annuity divided by the expected return. Once the total amount of the investment has been recovered, all remaining payments are included in income. Additionally, if the recipient dies before completely recovering her/his investment, the unrecovered portion may be deducted on her/his final tax return.

3. **GIFTS, BEQUESTS, AND INHERITANCES** Gifts, bequests, and inheritances are excluded from income. However, the income from this property is not excluded.

4. **CERTAIN PRIZES AND AWARDS** Prizes and awards generally are included in gross income **unless** the prize or award is received for religious, charitable, scientific, educational, artistic, literary, or civic achievement, **and** the following conditions are met:

   a. The recipient is selected without any action on her/his part to enter the contest or proceeding;

   b. The recipient is not required to render substantial future services as a condition for receiving the prize or award; and

   c. The prize or award is transferred by the payor to a governmental unit or to a charitable organization pursuant to the recipient's request.

5. **SCHOLARSHIPS AND FELLOWSHIPS** Gross income does not include amounts received as a qualified scholarship by an individual who is a candidate for a degree at an approved educational institution.

   a. A qualified scholarship is any amount that is used to pay for tuition, fees, books, supplies, and equipment. Amounts used for other purposes are included in gross income.

   b. Amounts that represent payment for teaching, research, or other services are not excludable from gross income.

6. **GAIN ON SALE OF PRINCIPAL RESIDENCE** A taxpayer may exclude the gain from gross income. (Examples and additional details are in Chapter 28.)

7. **AMOUNTS RECEIVED FOR PERSONAL INJURY** Are not included in gross income. This rule applies to workers' compensation payments, damages received (except for punitive damages), accident and health insurance claims (except those attributable to employer

contributions that were not income to the employee), and disability benefits. EGTRRA '01 declares Holocaust restitution payments received starting in 2001 to be excluded from income as well as not taken into account for any calculation that picks up otherwise excludable gross income, such as Social Security benefits.

8. **INTEREST ON TAX-EXEMPT GOVERNMENT OBLIGATIONS** Gross income does not include interest on bonds issued by a state or any of its political subdivisions, the District of Columbia, and U.S. possessions.

   - This exclusion does not apply to arbitrage bonds, hedge bonds, private activity bonds that are not qualified, or to pre-August 16, 1986, industrial development bonds.

9. **SOCIAL SECURITY BENEFITS** Social security benefits and other types of welfare payments are generally excluded from gross income. A taxpayer may have to include up to 85% of the amount of benefits received during any year that the taxpayer's provisional income exceeds a base amount.

   a. Modified adjusted gross income, for this purpose, equals adjusted gross income computed without regard to the foreign earned income exclusion, the exclusion for income earned in U.S. possessions and Puerto Rico, or social security benefits, and increased by any tax-exempt interest income.

   b. The first base amount is equal to $32,000 for married individuals filing jointly, $0 for married individuals filing separately, and $25,000 for all other individuals.

      - In years when provisional income exceeds the first base amount, in such a year, the taxpayer must include in income, the lesser of one-half of the benefits, or one-half of the amount, if any, by which the sum of the taxpayer's modified adjusted gross income, tax-exempt income, and one-half of the benefits exceed the base amount.

   c. The second base amount is equal to $44,000 for married individuals filing jointly, $0 for married individuals filing separately, and $34,000 for all other individuals.

      - In years when the provisional income exceeds a second base amount, gross income includes the lesser of (a) 85% of the social security benefit, or (b) the sum of 85% of the excess of provisional income over the new threshold and the smaller of the amount that would otherwise be included under IRC §86(a)(1) or $4,500 for single taxpayers or $6,000 for married taxpayers filing jointly.

EXHIBIT 2 ♦ TAXABLE SOCIAL SECURITY BENEFITS SCHEDULE

Percentage of Benefits Taxed	Provisional Income Amounts		
	MFJ	Single	MFS
0%	$1 to $31,999	$1 to $24,999	none
50%	$32,000 to $43,999	$25,000 to $33,999	none
85%	$44,000 and above	$34,000 and above	$1 and above

EXAMPLE 2 ♦ SOCIAL SECURITY BENEFITS

FYI: Example 2B is likely more in-depth than will be tested on the CPA exam.

A. Doug and Barbara are both 66 years old. Together they receive $8,100 of social security benefits for the calendar year. They have an adjusted gross income of $28,000 from employment, net rents, royalties, interest, and dividends. Additionally, they receive $4,200 of tax-exempt income from municipal bonds. They file jointly.

(continued on next page)

B.   Steve and Nancy are both 66 years old. Together they receive $8,100 of social security benefits for the calendar year. They have an adjusted gross income of $46,000 from employment, net rents, royalties, interest, and dividends. Additionally, they receive $4,200 of tax-exempt income from municipal bonds. They file jointly.

	Example 2A.	Example 2B.
Adjusted Gross Income (AGI)	$28,000	$ 46,000
Tax exempt income	4,200	4,200
Modified AGI	32,200	50,200
50% of social security benefits ($8,100 × 50%)	4,050	4,050
Provisional income	$36,250	$ 54,250
Provisional income	$36,250	
Less: First base amount (MFJ)	(32,000)	
Excess	4,250	
Over first base amount—multiply by 50%	× .50	
Amount to compare to 50% of benefits	$ 2,125	
Amount to include in AGI (lesser of two)	$ 2,125	
Provisional income		$ 54,250
Less: Second base amount (MFJ)		(44,000)
Excess		10,250
Over second base—multiply by 85%		× .85
85% of excess over second base amount		$ 8,712
Lesser of 50% of benefits or $6,000 (MFJ)		4,050
Amount to compare to 85% of benefits (lesser of two)		$ 12,762
Benefits		8,100
Over second base—use 85% of benefits		× .85
Amount to include in AGI (lesser of two)		$ 6,885

10. **PROPERTY SETTLEMENTS** Property transfers from an individual to a spouse or a former spouse incidental to a divorce are nontaxable transactions. A transfer is incident to a divorce if it occurs within one year after the marriage ends or is related to the ending of the marriage.

11. **CHILD SUPPORT** Payments made that are specifically designated as child support by the terms of the divorce instrument are not included as income by the recipient and are non-deductible by the payor. Additionally, any reductions in alimony that are related to a **contingency** involving the child will cause the amount of the reduction to be treated as child support for tax purposes. Furthermore, if the divorce decree specifies that a fixed amount of the payment is for child support, and the payor pays less than the total amount of the pay-ment, then the payment is treated as child support to the extent of this designated amount.

EXAMPLE 3 ♦ CHILD SUPPORT

Harold pays Winnona $400 in alimony per month under the terms of a divorce decree. The terms of the decree also provide that the amount is to be reduced to $300 in the event that David, the child of Harold and Winnona, marries, reaches age 21, or dies. Winnona must include $300 (while she is receiving the entire $400) in her gross income, and Harold is entitled to a $300 deduction. The remaining $100 is deemed child support and it is not deductible by Harold or considered as gross income to Winnona (or to David). Alimony payments received by a taxpayer are includible in the gross income of the recipient and deductible by the payor.

EXAMPLE 4 ♦ CHILD SUPPORT

Per the terms of a divorce agreement, Howard is required to pay $200 a month for the full year to his former wife Wilma, $100 of which is for the support of their minor children. If Howard only pays Wilma $200 a month for 9 months ($1,800), $1,200 is considered to be child support. The remaining $600 is treated as alimony.

12. **EMPLOYEE BENEFITS** Certain fringe benefits are excluded from an employee's income.

   a. **GROUP TERM LIFE INSURANCE** Premiums paid by the employer for up to $50,000 worth of insurance coverage is excluded.

   b. **ACCIDENT AND HEALTH PLANS** Premiums paid by an employer are excluded if they compensate the employee for the following:

      (1) Loss of earnings due to personal injuries and illness (the benefits are includible unless the employer contributions are included in the employee's income, in which case the benefits would be excluded).

      (2) Reimbursement of medical care expenses for employee, spouse, or dependents (the employee cannot take an itemized deduction for these expenses).

      (3) Permanent injury or loss of bodily function.

   c. **MEALS OR LODGING** Meals or lodging furnished for the convenience of the employer on the employer's premises are excluded.

   d. **FRINGE BENEFITS** Fringe benefits are excluded from gross income if

      (1) No additional cost service (e.g., free stand-by flights to airline employees)

      (2) Qualified employee discounts (i.e., employee discounts on employer goods or services)

      (3) Working condition fringe benefit (e.g., use of company car for employer business)

      (4) *De minimis* (minimal) fringe (e.g., use of employer copy machine for personal business)

   e. **DEPENDENT CARE SERVICES** Employer-provided dependent care services are excluded if they are pursuant to a written, nondiscriminatory plan. The amount excludable is limited to $5,000 per year ($2,500 for married individuals filing separate tax returns).

   f. **EDUCATIONAL ASSISTANCE PROGRAMS** Payments of up to $5,250 per year for tuition, fees, books, etc., may be excluded. Assistance for undergraduate courses is excludable. EGTRRA '01 makes assistance for graduate-level courses starting in 2002, or later, excludable.

   g. **WORKERS' COMPENSATION** Workers' compensation is excluded if received for an occupational sickness or injury and paid under a workers' compensation act or statute.

   h. **QUALIFIED ADOPTION EXPENSES** The limitations, restrictions, and phase-out amounts for the credit are equally applicable to the exclusion of expenses paid by employers.

i. **PARKING FRINGE BENEFIT** A taxpayer may exclude employer-provided parking from taxable compensation, even if a cash option is offered. If the taxpayer elects to take the cash, it is taxable compensation.

j. **QUALIFIED RETIREMENT PLANNING SERVICES** Starting in 2002, EGTRRA '01 excludes qualified retirement planning services from taxable compensation.

k. **RETIREMENT PLANS** A taxpayer excludes retirement benefits (both defined benefit and defined contribution plans) from income in the year of service. (Benefits are taxable when paid.) Employees may defer up to the lesser of 25% of annual compensation or $35,000 for all annual additions (everything except earnings and gains) to all plans of the same employer. (Employers often match or partially match employee contributions.) Starting in 2002, EGTRRA '01 increases the limit to $40,000.

   (1) **CASH OR DEFERRED ARRANGEMENTS (CODA)** Under a 401(k), 403(b), or SEP plan in 2002, employees may defer up to the lesser of 15% of annual compensation or $11,000 under any combination of deferred arrangement plans for all employers. Employer matches are not part of this annual limit. EGTRRA '01 increases this limit to $12,000 for 2003. Starting in 2003, EGTRRA '01 allows employees to make contributions to a separate account through the employer plan that are deemed IRAs or Roth IRAs (discussed later in this chapter) and not considered deferred compensation.

   (2) **SIMPLE 401(k) OR IRA** All funds in SIMPLE plans are fully vested. Under a SIMPLE 401(k) plan in 2002, employees may defer up to the lesser of $7,000 of elective contributions or 15% of annual compensation. Employers may match up to $7,000 or 3% of annual compensation. EGTRRA '01 increases this limit to $8,000 for 2003.

   (3) **SECTION 457 PLAN DEFERRALS** Tax-exempt organizations and state and local governments may offer §457 deferred compensation plans to employees. Under a §457 plan in 2002, employees generally may defer up to the lesser of $11,000 of elective contributions or one-third of annual compensation. A special catch-up rule allows participants to increase the annual limit for the three years before retirement by the lesser of $15,000 or the sum of the otherwise applicable limit and the amount by which a previous year's limit exceeded that year's deferrals. EGTRRA '01 increases this limit to $12,000 for 2003.

   (4) **CATCH-UP CONTRIBUTIONS** Starting in 2002, EGTRRA '01 increases the limit of contributions for individuals age 50 or older before the end of the plan year. Participants in 401(k), 403(b), or 457 plans may defer up to an additional $1,000 for 2002 and $2,000 for 2003. Participants in SIMPLE plans may defer up to an additional $500 for 2002 and $1,000 for 2003. No catch-up contributions are allowed in the last three years before retirement for participants in 457 plans.

   (5) **ROLLOVER PROVISIONS** Starting in 2002, EGTRRA '01 allows 401(k), 403(b), or 457 plan participants or their surviving spouses to rollover funds among these plans as well as IRAs. There are no provisions for tax-free rollover of after-tax amounts from an IRA.

13. **SAVINGS BONDS** The interest income from qualified U.S. savings bonds, such as series EE, redeemed to finance qualified higher education costs for the taxpayer, her/his spouse, or dependents is excluded. Qualified higher education costs include tuition and fees. To qualify, the taxpayer must be the sole owner of the bonds or a joint owner with her/his spouse. This exclusion is subject to a phase-out range above which no exclusion is allowed. For

2002, the phase-out ranges begin at $86,400 for married individuals filing a joint tax return, and $57,600 for single individuals and heads of households.

14. **SURVIVOR ANNUITY** The survivor annuity of a public safety officer killed on duty is tax-exempt to the deceased officer's spouse, ex-spouse, or child.

15. **ADOPTION ASSISTANCE** Amounts received by an adoptive parent under an adoption assistance agreement with a state pursuant to the Adoption Assistance and Child Welfare Act of 1980 are not taxable income.

D. INCLUSIONS IN GROSS INCOME

Gross income includes all items from whatever source derived except those items specifically excluded. This section discusses some of the more common income items included in gross income.

1. **COMPENSATION** Including wages, salaries, fees, bonuses, commissions, tips, death benefits, and fringe benefits that do not qualify for statutory exclusions. If compensation is received in the form of property, the amount included in gross income is the fair market value of the property received.

   a. **JURY DUTY PAY** If an employee surrenders jury duty pay to her/his employer in exchange for receiving her/his salary during the time of jury service, then the payment for jury duty is deductible for AGI.

   b. **REIMBURSED EMPLOYEE BUSINESS EXPENSES** Employee business expenses that are reimbursed are deductible **for** AGI if the employer includes these reimbursements in the employee's gross income. Reimbursed employee expenses that are **not** included in the employee's gross income are not deductible **from** AGI. Any excess reimbursement by the employer must be included in gross income by the employee. Unreimbursed employee business expenses are only deductible from AGI as miscellaneous itemized deductions subject to the 2% floor and a 50% limitation on meal and entertainment expenses. Also, no deduction is allowed for any type of club dues.

EXAMPLE 5 ♦ REIMBURSED TRAVEL EXPENSES

ABC Co. fully reimburses its employees for travel expenses, including transportation and accommodations and, in addition, provides a $20 daily allowance for meals and entertainment. In a recent 10-day trip, Joe, an ABC Co. employee, incurred the following expenses:

Airfare	$ 400
Hotel rooms	550
Rental car	150
Meals and entertainment	350
Total cost incurred	$1,450

ABC reimbursed Joe for $1,300 (the cost of the airfare, hotel, and car rental as detailed by Joe plus the maximum $20-per-day meal and entertainment allowance for 10 days). On his return, Joe will neither include in income nor deduct the $1,300 in reimbursed expenses subject to a detailed accounting. Of the remaining $150, Joe may deduct $75 (50%), but only as a miscellaneous deduction subject to a 2% of AGI floor.

2. **INTEREST** Unless specifically exempt from tax, interest is taxable gross income. Examples of taxable interest include amounts received for certificates of deposit, corporate and U.S. government bonds, and imputed interest from below-market-rate and interest-free loans.

3. **DIVIDENDS** A distribution of money, securities, or other property by the corporation to its shareholders out of accumulated or current earnings and profits. Dividends are taxed to the shareholder as ordinary income.

4. **REFUNDS** If a taxpayer obtains a refund for which s/he received a prior tax **benefit** (i.e., deduction) then this refund is included in gross income. A typical example would be a refund of state or local taxes paid by the taxpayer.

5. **ALIMONY** Alimony received is included in gross income.

   a. **QUALIFIED PAYMENTS** To qualify as alimony, the payment must be (1) made pursuant to a divorce or separate maintenance agreement, (2) consist of **cash** payments, (3) not be made to someone who lives in the same household at the time of the payment, (4) must not continue after the death of the payee-spouse (i.e., to the payee's estate), and (5) must not be designated as anything other than alimony (i.e., child support).

   b. **RECAPTURE RULES** A three-year recapture rule applies to excess alimony payments to prevent property settlement payments from qualifying as alimony. Excess alimony is defined as the sum of the excess payments made in both the first and second post-separation year. It must be recaptured in the third post-separation year. The excess payments in the first year equal the amount that exceeds the average of the second year payments (minus any excess payments) and third year payments by more than $15,000. Similarly, the excess payments in the third year equal the amount that exceeds the average payments in the third year by more than $15,000. The recapture rules do not apply if the payments were terminated due to the death or remarriage of the payee-spouse.

EXAMPLE 6 ♦ RECAPTURE OF ALIMONY

Henry and June were divorced in 20X0. Per the terms of the divorce agreement, Henry paid June $50,000 in 20X0, $30,000 in 20X1, and $10,000 in 20X2. How much does Henry need to recapture in 20X2?

SOLUTION:

1) Amount to recapture from 20X1 equals the amount paid in 20X1 ($30,000), that is in excess of the sum of the amount paid in 20X2 ($10,000) plus $15,000.

Amount to recapture = $30,000 − ($10,000 + $15,000)
= $30,000 − $25,000 = $ 5,000

2) Amount to recapture from 20X2 equals the amount paid in 20X0 ($50,000) that exceeds the sum of the average amount paid in 20X1 ($30,000) less any recapture from 20X1 ($5,000) and the average amount paid in 20X2 ($10,000) plus $15,000.

Amount to recapture $= \$50,000 - \left[\dfrac{(\$30,000 - \$5,000 + \$10,000)}{2} + \$15,000 \right]$

$= \$50,000 - \$32,500 = \$17,500$

3) Total amount to recapture = $5,000 + $17,500 = $22,500

6. **NET SELF-EMPLOYMENT INCOME** The gross income from an individual's trade or business less allowable deductions equals net self-employment income. These net earnings are included in the taxpayer's gross income and are subject to the self-employment tax.

a. Director's fees are self-employment income to the recipient.

b. Some otherwise allowable deductions are not allowed because of the taxpayer's method of accounting. For example, a cash basis taxpayer is not allowed a bad debt expense from uncollectible account receivables because these receivables were not previously included in income.

7. CAPITAL GAINS & LOSSES A capital gain or loss occurs when a capital asset is sold or exchanged. Capital assets include all assets *except* the following: (a) inventory or other property held primarily for the sale to customers in the ordinary course of the taxpayer's trade or business, (b) a trade note or account receivable, (c) depreciable business property or real property used in the taxpayer's trade or business, and (d) a copyright; a literary, musical, or artistic composition; a letter, memorandum, or similar property held by the creator or one whose basis in the property is determined from the creator. (Capital gains and losses are covered more thoroughly in Chapter 28.)

a. DEDUCTIBILITY OF CAPITAL LOSSES Individuals may deduct capital losses to the extent of capital gains plus $3,000 per year. Any losses that are not deductible in the current year may be carried forward indefinitely. Personal gains (gains resulting from the disposal of assets acquired for personal use) are taxable, but personal losses are not deductible.

b. TAXATION OF CAPITAL GAINS Schedule D is used to ensure that the amount of income taxes paid on net capital gains does not exceed one of several capital gain rates that are lower than regular tax rates.

8. UNEMPLOYMENT COMPENSATION Unemployment compensation is fully taxable.

9. GAMBLING WINNINGS Winnings from gambling are taxable. Gambling losses are deductible to the extent of gambling winnings, but only as itemized deductions.

10. DISTRIBUTIVE SHARE OF PARTNERSHIP OR S CORPORATION INCOME

11. NET RENTS & ROYALTIES Rental and royalty payments, including nonrefundable deposits, premiums, and lease breaking payments, are taxable in the period received, regardless of the taxpayer's basis of accounting. (Rent and royalty income and expenses are reported on Schedule E.) Unlike gambling losses, related expenses not exceeding the income are frequently deducted directly from it.

- **RENTAL OF VACATION HOME** The deductibility of vacation home rental expenses depends on the allocation between the rental and personal use of the property.

  (1) If the property is rented for **less than 15** days, no expenses are deductible except for those ordinarily deductible **from** AGI (mortgage interest, real estate taxes, and casualty loss expenses), and no rental income is includable in gross income.

  (2) If the property is rented for 15 or more days and is **not** used for personal purposes for (a) more than 14 days or (b) more than 10% of the number of days it was rented at a fair market value price, whichever is greater, then the property is treated as a rental and the expenses are deductible subject to the passive activity loss rules.

  (3) If the property is rented for 15 or more days but use exceeds the personal use test, then rental expenses are limited to the amount that gross income exceeds the deductions otherwise allowable such as mortgage interest and taxes.

12. INCOME FROM THE DISCHARGE OF INDEBTEDNESS Income from the discharge of indebtedness is taxable **unless** the debt is discharged in a bankruptcy proceeding, the discharge is a gift, or a student loan is discharged because the individual fulfilled a service obligation.

13. PASSIVE ACTIVITY LOSSES A passive activity is a trade or business activity in which the taxpayer does not materially participate. In addition, all rental activities are deemed to be passive activities (except some real estate professionals). Generally, passive activity losses may be used only to offset passive activity income. In other words, they may not be deducted against ordinary (earned) or portfolio (interest, dividends, etc.) income. Any passive activity losses that cannot be used in the current year are suspended and carried forward indefinitely until there is sufficient income from passive activities to absorb them. Any losses that remain suspended when the activity is sold in a taxable transaction may be deducted against both ordinary and portfolio income.

    a. RENTAL ACTIVITY EXCEPTION Up to $25,000 of losses from rental activities may be deducted against ordinary and portfolio income if the taxpayer actively participates in the activity. The individual must own at least a 10% interest in the activity to be considered an active participant for purposes of this exception. This exception is phased out for taxpayers whose AGI exceeds $100,000. The deduction is reduced by 50% of the AGI over the phase-out amount. Therefore, the deduction is zero when AGI reaches $150,000.

    b. REAL ESTATE PROFESSIONAL EXCEPTION Real estate professionals are able to offset nonpassive income with their rental real estate losses. A taxpayer is considered a *real estate professional* if more than half of the personal services performed by the taxpayer during the year are performed in real property businesses in which the taxpayer materially participates and the taxpayer also performs more than 750 hours of service during the tax year in the same real property business.

III. ADJUSTED GROSS INCOME (AGI)

A. ADJUSTMENT OVERVIEW
Gross income minus deductions **for** AGI equals adjusted gross income (AGI). Many limitations on below-the-line, or itemized, deductions are based on a taxpayer's AGI. In addition, other phase-outs that reduce specified tax benefits are based on AGI. Adjustments are certain deductions taken from gross income to arrive at AGI. Therefore, these deductions are considered to be **above-the-line** deductions and AGI is "the line." Any one adjustment may be claimed without regard for the others.

B. INDIVIDUAL RETIREMENT ACCOUNT (IRA)
Taxpayers may contribute money to an IRA to defer income tax on IRA earnings. Individuals who are ineligible to deduct IRA contributions may still have the opportunity to defer income tax on IRA earnings.

1. CONTRIBUTIONS For 2002 through 2004, any employee (not a self-employed individual) may contribute the lesser of the individual's earned income or $3,000 to an IRA annually. Annual contributions can be split between IRAs of all types (except education IRAs). A taxpayer with a nonworking spouse may also set up a spousal IRA, with a combined contribution limit of the lesser of double the individual limit or earned income for the year. (The total contribution may be allocated in any way between the two IRAs as long as no more than the individual limit is allocated to either one.) If both spouses work, each may contribute the lesser of total earned income or the individual limit to an IRA. Alimony payments received are treated as earned income for purposes of determining how much an individual is allowed to contribute to an IRA.

2. DEDUCTIONS Contributions may be deductible for AGI depending on AGI before deductions for IRA contributions and participation in an employer-sponsored retirement plan. The term *active participant* generally includes individuals who are eligible to participate in an employer-sponsored plan, even if no amounts are currently being credited to the employee's account.

a. **NOT AN ACTIVE PARTICIPANT** If the taxpayer (and her/his spouse if filing jointly) is not an active participant, contributions are deductible to the extent of the aforementioned limits.

b. **ACTIVE PARTICIPANTS** Individuals who are active participants in a retirement plan are still able to deduct their contributions if their AGI (before deducting IRA contributions) is less than the phase-out amount. If they are in the phase-out range, they may deduct at least $200 of their contributions.

EXHIBIT 3 ◆ 2002 ACTIVE PARTICIPANT IRA DEDUCTIBILITY SCHEDULE

Filing Status	AGI Before IRA Deduction
MFJ	$54,000 to $64,000
S or HH	$34,000 to $44,000
MFS	$0 to $10,000

c. **SPOUSE OF AN ACTIVE PARTICIPANT** Spouses of active participants are able to deduct a $3,000 contribution if their AGI (before deducting IRA contributions) is less than a spousal phase-out range of $150,000 to $160,000.

EXAMPLE 7 ◆ INDIVIDUAL RETIREMENT ACCOUNTS

Thomas earned $80,000 at Tall Corporation in 2002, where he is an active participant in the pension plan. Isabelle earned $1,500 from a part-time job at Fresh Florist where there is no pension plan. Thomas is 45 years old.

REQUIRED: What is the maximum amount that may be contributed to Thomas' and Isabelle's individual retirement accounts and deducted from gross income?

SOLUTION: As Thomas is an active participant in his employer's plan and Thomas and Isabelle have AGI greater than the phase-out range, none of his contribution is deductible. However, $3,000 may be contributed to an IRA for each person: $3,000 for Thomas based on his earned income and $3,000 for Isabelle under the non-working spouse provisions. As the AGI is less than $150,000, Isabelle's $3,000 contribution is fully deductible.

3. **PENALTY** Early withdrawals (before age 59½) are subject to a 10% penalty tax, in addition to regular income tax, unless the withdrawal is due to participant death, participant disability, or other specific conditions, including:

a. **MEDICAL EXPENSES** Medical expenses in excess of 7.5% of AGI.

b. **MEDICAL INSURANCE** Medical insurance by individuals who have received 12 consecutive weeks of unemployment compensation under federal or state law. Self-employed individuals are also eligible if they would otherwise be eligible to collect unemployment compensation.

c. **EDUCATION** College tuition, fees, books, supplies, and equipment (plus room and board, if the student attends school on at least a half-time basis) for the taxpayer, the taxpayer's spouse, or the taxpayer's or taxpayer's spouse's child or grandchild.

d. **FIRST HOME** Up to $10,000 of withdrawals used within 120 days to acquire a first home, as the principal residence for the taxpayer, the taxpayer's spouse or any child, grandchild, or ancestor of the taxpayer or the taxpayer's spouse. The taxpayer (and spouse, if married) must be a first time homebuyer. A first time homebuyer is one who has not had an ownership interest in a principal residence during the two-year period ending on the acquisition date of the home.

4. **ROTH IRA** All Roth IRA contributions are nondeductible. Earnings of a Roth IRA are tax deferred and all qualified distributions are exempt from income tax. There is no age limit for contributions.

    a. The maximum Roth IRA contribution is phased out for taxpayers whose AGI exceeds a threshold (single: $95,000–$110,000; married: $150,000–$160,000). Roth spousal IRAs may be established under the same rules as a traditional spousal IRA.

    b. Qualified distributions are made at least five years after the first year an original contribution is made **and** the distribution is made on account of the participant reaching age 59½, participant death, participant disability, or qualified first-time homebuyer expenses. The holding period begins with the related tax year, not the actual date of the contribution. Unqualified distributions are subject to a 10% excise tax in addition to the regular income tax.

    c. A taxpayer with AGI of less than $100,000 (computed without regard to any amount that must be included in income as a result of the rollover) may roll over a traditional IRA (deductible or nondeductible) into a Roth IRA. The five-year holding period begins at the date of conversion.

C. ARCHER MEDICAL SAVINGS ACCOUNT (MSA)

Archer Medical Savings Accounts (MSAs) are trust accounts (similar to IRAs) that may be established by a limited number of taxpayers. There is a trial period for MSAs through 2003. The details concerning MSAs are more complex than discussed here. We expect exam coverage to be minimal because this is a trial program with a limited number of eligible participants.

1. A self-employed individual or an employee of a small employer is eligible to establish an MSA. An individual must be covered under a high deductible medical plan before s/he can establish an MSA, but may not be covered under another medical plan except: Medicare supplemental insurance; insurance for a specific disease; insurance that provides a fixed payment for hospitalization; or insurance under which the coverage relates primarily to worker's compensation, tort liability, or property liability (i.e., auto insurance).

2. Within limits, amounts contributed to an MSA are deductible by an eligible individual and excludable from the employee's income if the contribution is made by the employer. Contributions are limited to 65% of the deductible of the taxpayer's high-deductible plan for single coverage and 75% for family coverage. Earnings of MSAs are nontaxable. Distributions from MSAs are not taxable, if made for medical expenses of an eligible individual. If not made for eligible medical expenses, a 15% excise tax is imposed, unless the payment is made after age 65 or on account of death or disability.

D. MOVING EXPENSES

An employee or a self-employed individual may deduct moving expenses paid or incurred in connection with the commencement of work at a new principal place of employment.

1. **DISTANCE RULE** The new place of work must be at least 50 miles farther from the old residence than the old place of work was from the old residence.

2. **TIME RULES** The time rules are waived if the taxpayer dies, becomes disabled, is transferred by the employer, or is laid off by the employer for other than willful misconduct.

    a. **EMPLOYEE** The individual must be employed at the new place of employment for at least 39 weeks out of the 12 months following the move.

    b.   **SELF-EMPLOYED**   If the individual is self-employed, s/he must be self-employed 78 weeks during the 24 months following the move. In addition, at least 39 of those weeks must fall in the 12-month period that immediately follows the individual's arrival at the new place of work.

3.   **ALLOWABLE EXPENSES**   Allowable expenses include (1) the cost of moving goods and (2) costs of travel including lodging (but not meals) to the new residence. Actual automobile expenses or $0.10/mile may be deducted.

4.   **DISALLOWED EXPENSES**   Disallowed expenses include (1) costs of house-hunting trips; (2) temporary living expenses; (3) expenses incurred in selling the old residence, buying the new residence, or settling an unexpired lease; and (4) meal expenses.

5.   **REIMBURSEMENTS EXCLUDED**   Reimbursements received from an employer for moving expenses are excluded from the employee's income. However, the same expense cannot be reimbursed (and thus excluded from income) **and** deducted from income.

E.   **SELF-EMPLOYMENT TAX**
A self-employed individual can deduct ½ of the self-employment tax paid for the year.

F.   **SELF-EMPLOYED HEALTH INSURANCE**
A self-employed individual may deduct 70% for 2002 (100% thereafter) of medical insurance for the taxpayer, the taxpayer's spouse, and dependents. This deduction cannot be greater than the net self-employment earnings (self-employment earnings less 1/2 of the self-employment earnings tax). This deduction is **not** allowed for any individual who is eligible to participate in any subsidized health plan of an employer of the individual or the individual's spouse.

G.   **KEOGH PLAN**
Generally, a self-employed individual subject to the self-employment tax may set up a Keogh plan. The maximum contribution is limited to the lesser of

    1. $30,000, or

    2.   25% of net self-employment earnings after the Keogh deduction (or 20% of gross earnings).

H.   **PENALTIES FOR PREMATURE WITHDRAWALS OF TIME DEPOSITS**
All the interest is included in gross income and then the penalty amount is subtracted for AGI.

I.   **ALIMONY PAID**
Amounts paid pursuant to a divorce or separate maintenance agreement are deductible for AGI by the payer.

J.   **EDUCATIONAL LOAN INTEREST**
Interest on qualified educational loans is deductible, subject to modified adjusted gross income (MAGI) thresholds. The maximum interest deduction is $2,500. Starting in 2002, EGTRRA '01 changes the income phase-out ranges to $100,000 to $130,000 for MFJ and $50,000 to $65,000 for single and HH filers

    1.   **MAGI**   AGI increased by the following exclusions: foreign earned income, social security income, adoption assistance, and U.S. Savings Bonds used for education; as well as increased by the following adjustments: IRA contributions, passive losses, and educational loan interest.

    2.   **REQUIREMENTS**   Married couples must file a joint return in order to claim the deduction. No deduction is allowed under this provision if a deduction is allowed under another provision (for instance, a home equity interest deduction). A dependent may not claim a deduction for educational loan interest.

3. **QUALIFIED EDUCATION LOAN** A loan incurred to pay qualified educational expenses (tuition, fees, books, room, and board reduced by scholarships, U.S. Savings Bond provisions, or state qualified tuition programs) for at least half-time attendance for the taxpayer, the taxpayer's spouse, or an individual who was the taxpayer's dependent when the debt was incurred.

4. **AGI IMPACT** This adjustment does not impact the calculation of AGI for purposes of determining exclusions from income for social security, U.S. Savings Bond interest used to pay for education, adoption expenses, IRA contributions, and passive activity loss limitations.

K. **HIGHER EDUCATION EXPENSES**
Starting in 2002, EGTRRA '01 allows deduction of qualified higher education expenses paid by the taxpayer during a tax year. The definition of *qualified higher education expense* is the same as for the HOPE credit (discussed later in this chapter).

1. **DEDUCTION** In 2002 and 2003, a taxpayer with AGI not exceeding $65,000 (double for MFJ) may claim a maximum deduction of $3,000 annually. Taxpayers exceeding the AGI limit get no deduction.

2. **INTERACTION** This deduction may not be claimed if (a) a HOPE or Lifetime Learning credit is claimed in the same year for the same student; (b) expenses are paid by distributions from and education IRA (discussed in Chapter 30); or (c) expenses are paid by the amount of interest excludable with respect to education savings bonds; or (d) the expenses are paid by a distribution from a qualified tuition plan that is excluded from income (discussed in Chapter 30). However, a taxpayer may claim a deduction for the amount of a distribution from a qualified tuition plan that is not attributable to earnings.

L. **EDUCATOR'S PAID EXPENSES**
JCWAA '02 allows, in 2002 and 2003, some teachers to get a deduction for amounts paid for classroom materials for up to $250 per year for books, non-athletic supplies, and other equipment or supplementary materials used by the teacher in the classroom. The deduction is available for K-12 teachers who work in a school for at least 900 hours during a school year, instructors, counselors, and principals.

IV. **DEDUCTIONS FROM AGI**

A. **STANDARD DEDUCTION**
The standard deduction depends on the taxpayer's filing status. Either the standard deduction or itemized deductions are used on any one return, **not** both.

1. **INCREASED AMOUNT** Taxpayers who are 65 years old (or older) or blind are entitled to an increased standard deduction. The standard deduction for a married person (filing jointly or separately) or for a surviving spouse is increased $900 for 2002. For an unmarried individual, (filing as single or head of household) the standard deduction is increased $1,150 for 2002. The standard deduction increase is doubled if the taxpayer is **both** blind and 65 or older.

2. **ANOTHER'S DEPENDENT** For 2002, taxpayers claimed as another taxpayer's dependent have a standard deduction that is the lesser of the standard deduction for single taxpayers or the greater of $750 or the dependent taxpayer's earned income plus $250.

EXHIBIT 4 ♦ 2002 STANDARD DEDUCTION SCHEDULE

Married filing joint (MFJ) and surviving spouses	$7,850
Single	4,700
Heads of household (HH)	6,900
Married filing separate (MFS)	3,925
MFS, Spouse itemizes	-0-

B. OVERVIEW OF ITEMIZED DEDUCTIONS

Itemized deductions are taken only if together they are greater than the taxpayer's allowable standard deduction. There are six classes of itemized deductions, which are subject to phase-out when the taxpayer's AGI exceeds certain thresholds. An individual whose AGI in 2002 exceeds $137,300 ($68,650 for MFS) is required to reduce the amount of allowable itemized deductions by 3% of the excess over the threshold amount. This limitation (called the 3% phase-out rule) is applied **after** taking other limitations into account.

1. **EXCEPTION** No reduction is required for medical expenses, investment interest, casualty and theft losses, or gambling losses.

2. **CAP** The reduction cannot exceed 80% of the individual's allowable deductions that are subject to the 3% rule. (All deductions except those in 1. above.)

C. MEDICAL EXPENSES

Taxpayers are allowed a deduction for expenses paid during the taxable year for medical care for themselves, their spouses, dependents, and those who would otherwise qualify as dependents except that they did not pass the income test.

1. **LIMITATION** Medical expenses are deductible only to the extent that they **exceed** 7.5% of AGI.

2. **CASH BASIS ONLY** The deduction is allowable only for medical expenses **actually paid** during the taxable year regardless of when the expense was incurred or the taxpayer's method of accounting. The deduction is the amount actually paid, less any insurance reimbursement. If the taxpayer is reimbursed in a later year for medical expenses deducted in an earlier year, the reimbursement is includible in gross income to the extent that the prior-year medical expense deduction decreased the income subject to taxes. Medical expenses charged on a credit card are considered paid when **charged**, not when paid to the credit card company.

3. **QUALIFIED EXPENSES** Medical care expenses include amounts paid for (a) the diagnosis, cure, mitigation, treatment, or prevention of disease, (b) the purpose of affecting any structure or function of the body, or for **transportation** primarily for and essential to medical care, (c) prescription drugs and insulin, (d) premiums for medical care **insurance**, and (e) lodging (not exceeding $50 per night, per individual) incurred while away from home in seeking medical care provided by a physician in a hospital or a facility related to, or the equivalent of, a hospital (e.g., the Mayo Clinic). The deduction for lodging expenses also encompasses the amounts incurred for those persons accompanying the patient. School **tuition** is deductible when the primary reason for enrollment is the availability of medical care.

4. **HOME ALTERATIONS** A medical expense deduction is also allowed for the cost of making a home more amenable to the needs of the handicapped. These medically related costs include (a) building entrance ramps, (b) widening of interior and exterior doors and hallways, (c) installing railings or support bars in bathrooms, (d) modifying kitchen cabinetry and equipment to make them accessible to the handicapped, and (e) relocating electrical fixtures and outlets. Only those costs in excess of an increase in the value of the residence are deductible.

5. **NONQUALIFIED EXPENSES** Expenses paid for cosmetic surgery **not** necessary to treat a deformity, a congenital abnormality, a personal injury trauma, or a disfiguring disease are **not** deductible.

D. TAXES

A deduction is allowed for the following taxes: (1) state, local, and foreign real property taxes paid by the owner, (2) state and local personal property taxes paid by the owner, and (3) state, local, and foreign income taxes. A deduction is not allowed for the following taxes: (1) federal income taxes, (2) federal excess profits taxes, (3) federal, state, and local inheritance, legacy, and gift taxes, (4) social security taxes, (5) taxes on real property that are apportioned to another taxpayer due to the sale of the property, and (6) special assessments paid for local benefits such as sidewalks, streets, and sewer systems, except if the assessment is made for maintenance or repair purposes.

1. **CASH-METHOD TAXPAYERS** Taxes are generally deductible in the year they are paid. Buyers and sellers of real estate allocate the tax liability and deduction based on the proportion of which each party was in possession during the real property taxable year. The party in possession on the due date actually pays the entire tax liability.

2. **ACCRUAL-METHOD TAXPAYERS** Taxes generally are deductible only in the year in which they accrue.

3. **OBSERVATIONS** (1) Tax surcharges paid by a tenant as additional rent on a rented residence are **not** deductible as real property tax payments. (2) Refunds of state, local, and foreign income taxes are includible in the year of receipt **if** the taxpayer itemized the deduction for the taxes paid in the prior year **and** received a tax benefit from the prior-year deduction. Conversely, refunds may be excluded in whole or part to the extent that they **exceed** the portion of the refund that provided a tax benefit in the prior year of deduction.

EXAMPLE 8 ♦ LOCAL TAX REFUND

During 2002, Basil (a single cash-basis taxpayer) had $2,600 withheld from his wages for state income taxes and paid local property taxes of $2,000. Basil elected to itemize. In 2003, he received a refund of $350 on his 2002 state income taxes.

ANALYSIS: Basil's total itemized deductions were $4,600 on the 2002 return. The refund of state income taxes would usually be included as taxable income on the 2002 federal tax return. Because Basil could have elected the 2002 standard deduction of $4,500, instead of the revised itemized deductions of $4,250 ($4,600 − $350), only $50 ($4,600 − $4,550) of the refund is recognized as taxable income in 2003.

E. INTEREST

Interest expense is deductible for mortgages for home acquisition, home equity indebtedness, and investment interest expense. Personal or consumer interest is no longer deductible.

1. **ACQUISITION INDEBTEDNESS** Interest on up to $1,000,000 of debt incurred to buy, construct, or substantially improve a first or second home is deductible as qualified residence interest.

2. **HOME EQUITY INDEBTEDNESS** Debt that is secured by the taxpayer's first or second home but is not acquisition indebtedness. Interest on up to $100,000 of debt is deductible as home equity interest expense. The proceeds from a home equity loan do not have to be used for home improvements—if they are, the debt is acquisition indebtedness.

EXAMPLE 9 ♦ INTEREST

> Mr. and Mrs. McKee purchased a home for $80,000 ten years ago, paying 20% down and financing the balance. The outstanding balance on their home mortgage is $55,000. The house has been currently appraised at $250,000. In the current year, the McKees borrowed $125,000 against a second mortgage on the house to buy a boat.
>
> **ANALYSIS:** The $55,000 balance on the first mortgage is acquisition indebtedness. The $125,000 is home equity indebtedness and is limited to the lesser of the current appraised value of the residence minus any acquisition indebtedness ($250,000 − $55,000 = $195,000). However, only interest on up to $100,000 of home equity debt is tax deductible. Thus, the $125,000 qualifies as home equity indebtedness, but only interest expense on $100,000 of this $125,000 debt is deductible.

3. **INVESTMENT INTEREST** Interest paid or accrued on indebtedness incurred to purchase or carry property held for investment is deductible to the extent of net investment income. Any excess may be carried over indefinitely. Investment interest does **not** include interest earned from or paid on a loan to secure an interest in a passive activity.

   a. Net investment income is the excess of investment income over investment expenses.

   b. Investment income includes the following:

      (1) Gross income from interest, dividends, rents, and royalties

      (2) Portfolio income generated by a passive activity

      (3) Gain from sale or other disposition of investment property (subject to restrictions in paragraph c)

   c. Net capital gain is excluded from investment income for purposes of computing the investment income limitation unless the taxpayer makes a special election. A taxpayer may elect to include an unlimited amount of the net capital gain in investment income, if the taxpayer also reduces the amount of net capital gain eligible for the maximum capital gains rate by the same amount. This prevents a high income taxpayer from deducting investment interest against the top rate of 39.6%, while simultaneously taking advantage of the lower rates on long-term capital gains.

   d. Investment expenses are generally those ordinary and necessary expenses directly connected with the production of investment income. Investment expenses are a tier 2 miscellaneous deduction (subject to the 2% of AGI floor limitation). Expenses incurred for the production of tax-exempt interest income are not deductible.

F. **CHARITABLE CONTRIBUTIONS**
Actually paid to a qualified donee during the year are deductible subject to a percentage of AGI limitation. The contribution may be in cash or property. If the contribution is made using a credit card, it is considered paid when the charge is made regardless of when the charge is actually paid. Political contributions are **not** deductible.

1. **QUALIFIED DONEES** Include (1) federal, state, or local governments, **if** the gift is made exclusively for public purposes and (2) domestic organizations and foundations operated exclusively for religious, charitable, scientific, literary, or educational purposes.

2. **CONTRIBUTION BASE** The taxpayer's adjusted gross income computed without regard to any net operating loss carryback. Contributions made that exceed these limits may be carried forward for **five** years.

a. The deduction cannot exceed **50%** of the taxpayer's contribution base for donations to (1) churches, (2) educational organizations, (3) hospitals, (4) governmental units, (5) private operating foundations, (6) certain organizations holding property for state and local colleges and universities, and (7) an organization organized and operated for religious, charitable, educational, scientific, or literary purposes. A contribution cannot exceed 30% of the taxpayer's contribution base to a qualifying organization that is not a 50% organization, such as a war veterans organization or a fraternal order.

b. If the individual makes a contribution of appreciated long-term capital gain property, the amount of the contribution is equal to the fair market value of the property contributed, but if the contribution is to a 50% charity, the 50% limitation is reduced to 30% unless the taxpayer elects to use her/his basis in the property as the amount contributed. If the contribution is made to a 30% charity, the 30% limitation is reduced to 20% and there is no special election available.

3. **PREMIUM** If the taxpayer receives something of value for the contribution, the allowable deduction is reduced by this amount. For example, if a taxpayer makes a charitable contribution by purchasing a ticket to a dinner that costs $100 and the actual cost of the dinner is $40, only $60 is allowed as a charitable deduction.

EXAMPLE 10 ♦ CHARITABLE CONTRIBUTIONS

Mr. and Mrs. Maladroit had adjusted gross income of $100,000 and made the following cash contributions. For the contribution to the operatic society, the Maladroits received four free tickets valued at $300.

Recipient	Amount
Carlsbad Community Hospital	$25,000
Committee to Re-elect Commissioner Huff	1,000
Carlsbad Operatic Society	20,000
Fraternal Order of Swamp Rats	6,000

ANALYSIS: The political contribution is not a charitable contribution and is not deductible. The other contributions are deductible, subject to limitations.

Hospital	$25,000		
Operatic society ($20,000 – $300)	19,700		
Public charity donations			$44,700
Plus the lesser of:			
(1) 30% x $100,000		$30,000 or	
(2) 50% x $100,000	$50,000		
Reduced by public charity donations	44,700		
Private charity donations		5,300	5,300
Current year contribution deduction			$50,000
Carry-forward contributions ($6,000 – $5,300)			$ 700

EXAMPLE 11 ♦ CHARITABLE CONTRIBUTIONS

> Mr. and Mrs. Fellow had adjusted gross income of $50,000 and cash contributions of $1,000 to the Carlsbad Community Hospital and $18,000 to the Fraternal Order of Swamp Rats.
>
> **ANALYSIS:** The contributions are deductible, subject to limitations.
>
> | | | | |
> |---|---|---|---|
> | Public charity donations (hospital) | | | $ 1,000 |
> | Plus the lesser of: | | | |
> | (1) 30% x $50,000 | | $15,000 or | |
> | (2) 50% x $50,000 | $25,000 | | |
> | Reduced by public charity donations | 1,000 | | |
> | Qualified private charity donations | | 24,000 | 15,000 |
> | Current year contribution deduction | | | $16,000 |
> | Carry-forward contributions ($19,000 – $16,000) | | | $ 3,000 |

4. **VALUATION** Appreciated property that would realize long-term capital gain if sold instead of donated is valued at fair market value. Other property is valued at the lesser of basis or fair market value.

5. **STUDENTS** Amounts paid to maintain a domestic or foreign student in one's home are deductible if (1) the student is not a relative or dependent of the taxpayer, (2) the student is in the 12th grade or lower, (3) there is a written agreement with a qualified charitable organization, and (4) no reimbursement is received. The deduction is limited to $50 per month.

6. **EXPENSES** A taxpayer may deduct unreimbursed out-of-pocket expenses incurred as a result of donating services to a qualified charitable organization including actual automobile expenses or 14¢ per mile in 2002. However, there is **no** deduction for the value of the services contributed.

7. **DOCUMENTATION** No deductions are allowed for any charitable contributions of $250 or more unless the taxpayer has written substantiation from the donee organization.

G. **CASUALTY & THEFT LOSSES**
    Casualty and theft losses attributable to property **not** connected with a trade or business or with a transaction entered into for profit (i.e., personal casualties and thefts) are allowable as a deduction to the extent such losses exceed gains from other personal casualties and thefts and to the extent that the total excess losses exceed 10% of the taxpayer's adjusted gross income. In addition, there is a $100 floor per casualty. Furthermore, if the casualty is covered by insurance, the loss is deductible only if the taxpayer files a timely insurance claim. The loss must be reduced by any amount recovered through insurance.

    1. A casualty loss must be due to some sudden, unexpected, or unusual cause. The gradual erosion of a private beach is not a casualty loss. However, the loss of a beach due to a hurricane, tornado, etc., is a casualty loss.

    2. A loss arising from theft is deductible in the year in which the taxpayer discovers the loss.

    3. A casualty loss is allowed as a deduction only for the taxable year in which the loss occurred. A loss sustained in a federal declared disaster area may be deducted in the preceding year by filing an amended tax return for that year.

EXAMPLE 12 ♦ CASUALTY AND THEFT LOSSES

Scott had adjusted gross income of $15,000 and incurred the following gains and losses:

- A $1,200 stereo component system was stolen from his house. The system, which originally cost him $2,000, was not insured.

- A flood washed away and totally destroyed his 1985 Mercedes, which he purchased for $5,000. The insurance proceeds for the car amounted to $6,000.

- In another burglary, $4,500 worth of collector's plates were stolen. The plates cost $4,000 and were uninsured.

ANALYSIS: The theft of the stereo results in a $1,100 theft loss [i.e., $1,200 (lesser of basis or decrease in FMV) – $100]. The theft of the plates resulted in a loss of $3,900 ($4,000 – $100). Thus, Scott's total tax losses amounted to $5,000. The loss of the car in the flood yielded a gain of $1,000 [i.e., $6,000 (proceeds) – $5,000 (basis)]. The $1,000 gain is offset by $1,000 of the losses. The excess $4,000 loss is deductible as an itemized deduction to the extent it exceeds 10% of Scott's AGI. 10% of $15,000 equals $1,500. Scott may deduct $2,500 ($4,000 – $1,500) in losses if he itemizes.

H. MISCELLANEOUS DEDUCTIONS

There are two broad types of miscellaneous deductions, **first-tier** and **second-tier** deductions. Second-tier deductions are allowable only to the extent that in the aggregate, they exceed 2% of AGI. First-tier deductions are not subject to this 2% floor.

1. EXAMPLES OF FIRST-TIER DEDUCTIONS

    a. Impairment-related work expenses for handicapped employees

    b. Estate tax related to income in respect of a decedent

    c. Deductions allowable in connection with personal property used in a short sale

    d. Certain deductions related to computation of tax where the taxpayer restores a substantial amount held under a claim of right

    e. Unrecovered investment in an annuity when payments cease

    f. Amortization of premium on bonds purchased before October 23, 1986.

    g. Deductions relating to certain cooperative housing corporations

    h. Gambling losses to the extent of gambling winnings

    i. Deductions for educator paid expenses above $250 that would otherwise qualify for deduction before AGI under JCWAA '02.

2. EXAMPLES OF SECOND-TIER DEDUCTIONS

    a. Home office expenses

    b. Continuing educational expenses

    c. Employee expenses such as uniforms, safety equipment, small tools, supplies, dues to professional organizations, union dues, subscriptions to professional journals, expense of looking for a job in the taxpayer's present occupation, unreimbursed travel, transportation, and 50% of business entertainment expenses

d. Expenses of producing income including certain legal and accounting fees, safe deposit box rental (to the extent used to protect income-producing property), custodial fees, investment counsel fees, etc.

e. Tax return preparation fees

f. Appraisals to determine casualty losses

g. Legal fees to procure alimony

V. INCOME TAX COMPUTATION

A. TAX RATES

Income tax is levied on an individual's taxable income.

EXHIBIT 5 ♦ 2002 TAX RATE SCHEDULE

Rate	MFJ*	HH	Single	MFS
10%	0-$12,000	0-$10,000	0-$6,000	0-$6,000
15%	$12,001-$46,700	$10,001-$37,450	$6,001-$27,950	$6,001-$23,350
27%	$46,701-$112,850	$37,451-$96,700	$27,951-$67,700	$23,351-$56,425
30%	$112,851-$171,950	$96,701-$156,600	$67,701-$141,250	$56,426-$85,975
35%	$171,951-$307,050	$156,601-$307,050	$141,251-$307,050	$85,976-$153,525
38.6%	Over $307,050	Over $307,050	Over $307,050	Over $153,525

* Also surviving spouse.

1. The 38.6% rate is actually created by imposing a 10% surtax (i.e., 10% times the 35% top rate = 3.6% surtax added to the 35% rate).

2. The maximum tax rates on **capital gains** for individuals are 27% or lower. Therefore, if a taxpayer has net capital gains, s/he probably will need to use Schedule D to correctly compute her/his income tax liability.

B. SELF-EMPLOYMENT TAX
The combined self-employment tax rate is 15.3% of which 2.9% is the Medicare portion. The maximum earnings from self-employment subject to the full tax in 2002 is $84,900, with no maximum for the 2.9% Medicare tax.

C. SOCIAL SECURITY (FICA)
Is imposed on both employers and employees. The employees' share is 7.65% of which 1.45% is for Medicare. The maximum wages in 2002 subject to the full 7.65% tax is $84,900, with no maximum for the 1.45% Medicare tax. If an individual works for more than one employer, the FICA withheld may exceed the maximum amount required. If this happens, the individual is allowed to take a credit on her/his income tax return to offset the amount of income tax liability due.

D. TAX ON CHILDREN'S UNEARNED INCOME
The net **unearned** income of children who have not reached age **14** by the end of the tax year is taxed at the parent's top rate instead of at the child's rate. The amount taxed at the parent's rate in 2002 is the child's unearned income less the sum of $750 and either (1) $750 or (2) itemized deductions related to the production of the unearned income that are over 2% of the child's AGI.

E. ALTERNATIVE MINIMUM TAX (AMT)
The purpose of the alternative minimum tax (AMT) is to ensure that all taxpayers who have realized gains or income during the year pay at least a minimum amount of tax. The AMT only applies if a taxpayer's AMT liability is greater than her/his regular tax liability. AMT paid in a taxable year may

be carried over as a credit to subsequent taxable years. The credit is allowed to reduce future regular tax liability but not future alternative minimum tax liability. It may be carried forward indefinitely. The following is a simplified version of the calculation of AMT liability.

1. **REGULAR TAXABLE INCOME**

2. **PLUS (ADD BACK) NOL DEDUCTION**

3. **PLUS OR MINUS AMT ADJUSTMENTS** These are: (a) standard deduction, (b) medical expenses must be computed using a 10% floor instead of 7.5%, (c) miscellaneous itemized deductions from Schedule A subject to the 2% threshold, (d) taxes from Schedule A, (e) refund of taxes (always a subtraction), (f) home mortgage interest not due to acquisition, (g) investment interest expense, (h) depreciation on tangible property placed in service after 1986, (i) circulation and research and experimental expenditures paid or incurred after 1986, (j) mining exploration and development costs paid or incurred after 1986, (k) long-term contracts entered into after February 28, 1986, (l) pollution control facilities placed in service after 1986, (m) installment sales of certain property, (n) adjusted gain or loss, (o) incentive stock options, (p) certain loss limitations, (q) tax shelter farm activities, (r) passive activity loss, and (s) beneficiaries of estates and trusts.

4. **JCWAA '02 SUSPENSION** There is no need for an AMT adjustment for property qualifying under the JCWAA '02 for bonus depreciation (see Chapter 28). JCWAA '02 also has a broader application than the Section 179 election in that it applies, for example, to estates, trusts, and non-corporate lessors, which the Section 179 election would not. The way the eligible for bonus depreciation. The way the law currently is written, Congress essentially said that if property is eligible for bonus depreciation—whether taken or not—there are no necessary depreciation adjustments for AMT for that property.

5. **PLUS TAX PREFERENCES** These are: (a) private activity bonds tax-exempt interest, (b) percentage depletion, (c) pre-1987 real property accelerated depreciation, (d) pre-1987 leased personal property accelerated depreciation, and (e) intangible drilling costs.

6. **EQUALS ALTERNATIVE MINIMUM TAXABLE INCOME (AMTI)**

   ### EXAMPLE 13 ♦ ALTERNATIVE MINIMUM TAXABLE INCOME

   > Anne and Mike Temple are married, file jointly, have no dependents, and have regular taxable income before personal exemptions of $171,000. Tax-exempt municipal bond interest of $2,000 and private activity bond (issued in March 1992) interest of $900 are not included in this figure. Included in the calculation of their regular taxable income are the following itemized deductions:
   >
   > | | |
   > |---|---:|
   > | Property taxes on primary residence | $3,000 |
   > | State and local income taxes | 6,500 |
   > | Interest on acquisition indebtedness for the primary residence | 7,000 |
   > | Interest on a home equity loan used to buy a personal-use boat in 2002 (secured by the primary residence) | 4,600 |
   >
   > **REQUIRED:** What is the Temple's alternative minimum taxable income?
   >
   > **SOLUTION:**
   >
   > | | | |
   > |---|---:|---:|
   > | Regular taxable income | | $171,000 |
   > | Adjustments: | | |
   > | Plus: Taxes ($3,000 + $6,500) | 9,500 | |
   > | Plus: Home equity loan interest | 4,600 | |
   > | Plus: Preferences—Private activity bond interest | 900 | |
   > | Alternative minimum taxable income | | $186,000 |

7. **LESS EXEMPTION** The exemption is reduced by 25% of the amount by which AMTI exceeds a phase-out amount.

EXHIBIT 6 ♦ AMT EXEMPTION & PHASE-OUT SCHEDULE (2001 THROUGH 2004)

Filing status	Exemption	Phase-out
Married, filing jointly	$49,000	$150,000 - $330,000
Single or Head of household	$35,750	$112,500 - $247,500
Married, filing separately	$24,500	$ 75,000 - $165,000

8. **MULTIPLIED BY THE AMT RATE** A 26% rate applies to the first $175,000 of a taxpayer's AMTI over the exemption amount. A 28% rate is applied to AMTI in excess of $175,000 over the exemption amount ($87,500 for MFS).

9. **LESS SELECT CREDITS** The foreign tax credit, retirement savings credit, and the refundable child tax credit are the only tax credits allowed when computing the AMT liability.

10. **EQUALS ALTERNATIVE MINIMUM TAX**

EXAMPLE 14 ♦ ALTERNATIVE MINIMUM TAX

Anne and Mike Temple are married, file jointly, and have alternative minimum taxable income of $186,000 (See Example 13).

REQUIRED: a. What is the Temple's AMT exemption?
b. What is the Temple's alternative minimum tax?

SOLUTION:

a.	Base exemption		$ 49,000
	AMT income	$ 186,000	
	Less: Threshold	(150,000)	
	Excess	$ 36,000	
	Times: Percentage	25%	
	Less: Reduction		(9,000)
	AMT exemption		$ 40,000
b.	AMT income		$186,000
	AMT exemption		(40,000)
	Nonexempt AMT income		146,000
	Times: Percentage		26%
	Alternative minimum tax		$ 37,960

VI. TAX PAYMENTS

A. TAX CREDITS
Tax credits directly reduce taxes payable on a dollar-for-dollar basis.

1. **CHILD CARE CREDIT** A credit of between 20% and 30% of eligible expenses is available in 2002 up to a maximum of $2,400 for one qualifying dependent and $4,800 for two or more (in 2003, up to $3,000 and $6,000, respectively). This credit is available to individuals who maintain a household for one or more dependents under the age of 13 for whom an exemption can be claimed or for a spouse or dependent of the taxpayer who is unable to care for her/him. In 2003, the upper percentage increases to 35%.

a. The full 30% is available if the taxpayer's AGI is $10,000 or less. The credit is reduced 1% for each $2,000 or portion thereof of AGI in excess of $10,000. However, the credit is not reduced below 20%.

b. The credit is limited to the taxpayer's earned income (or the spouse's earned income, if less).

c. To qualify for the credit, generally, at least one spouse must be working. However, if a non-working spouse is physically or mentally incapable of self care, or is a full-time student, then that spouse is treated as being gainfully employed. The spouse is deemed to earn $200 per month if there is one, and $400 a month if there are two or more, qualifying dependent(s).

d. Married taxpayers must file a joint return to claim the credit. For divorced or separated parents, the credit is available to the parent who had custody for the majority of the year.

e. Payments to a relative qualify for the credit unless the taxpayer claims a dependency exemption for the relative, or if the relative is the taxpayer's child and is less than 19 years old.

2. **CREDIT FOR ELDERLY & PERMANENTLY DISABLED** A credit of 15% of eligible income is available to individuals who are either 65 or older, or permanently disabled.

a. The initial amount of the credit depends on the taxpayer's filing status.

b. These initial amounts are reduced by annuities, pensions, social security, or disability income that is excluded from gross income and further reduced by 50% of AGI in excess of a ceiling that depends on filing status.

EXHIBIT 7 ♦ SCHEDULE FOR CREDIT FOR THE ELDERLY OR PERMANENTLY DISABLED

Filing Status	Initial Amount	Ceiling
Single	$5,000	$ 7,500
Married filing jointly, one spouse qualifies	5,000	10,000
Married filing jointly, both spouses qualify	7,500	10,000
Married filing separately	3,750	5,000

3. **FOREIGN TAX CREDIT** A taxpayer may take either a deduction or a tax credit for amounts paid or accrued for foreign income taxes. A separate limitation is calculated for certain categories of income, such as passive income. The credit limitation is

$$\text{Tentative U.S. tax (before credit)} \times \frac{\text{Taxable income from foreign sources}}{\text{Total taxable income}}$$

4. **CHILD CREDIT** A credit of $600 may be claimed against income taxes due for each qualifying child under the age of 17 at the end of the year. Qualifying children are children, descendants, stepchildren, and foster children who meet the dependency criteria. The names and social security numbers of qualifying children must be included on the tax return. The phase-out ranges start at $110,000 of modified AGI for MFJ, $55,000 for MFS, and $75,000 for singles. For each $1,000, or portion of $1,000, of modified AGI above the thresholds, the credit reduction is $50.

a. The child credit is refundable to the extent of 10% of the taxpayer's earned income in excess of $10,000. This amount is indexed for inflation, beginning in 2002.

b. Taxpayers with three or more qualifying children may be able to claim a refund with an *additional* credit, for the amount of the employee's share of withheld FICA taxes that exceed the earned income credit, if that amount is greater than the refundable credit based on the taxpayer's earned income in excess of $10,000. The editors do not expect this calculation to be tested on the CPA exam, and thus, details are not presented here.

    c.   The refundable portion of the child credits is excluded from the definition of income and may not be considered as resources for purposes of determining eligibility or the amount or nature of benefits or assistance under a federal program or any state or local program financed with federal funds.

5.   **EARNED INCOME CREDIT** The earned income credit (EIC) is a **refundable** credit. This means that if the credit is greater than the individual's tax liability, the individual will receive a refund. To qualify, the individual must have earned income, must be eligible to work in the U.S., and, if married, must file a joint return. Any income earned under a *Workfare* program, to the extent subsidized under a state program, will not constitute earned income for this credit.

    a.   A qualifying child shares the taxpayer's principal place of abode for over one-half of the year and is either (1) less than 19 years old, (2) less than 24 years old and a full-time student, or (3) permanently disabled. The qualifying child must also meet one of the following relationship tests: (1) a son, daughter, stepchild, or her/his descendant; (2) a sibling, step-sibling, or her/his descendant if cared for as the taxpayer's own child; or (3) a foster child who lived with the taxpayer.

    b.   A reduced credit is available to low-income workers over the age of 22 who do not have any qualifying children, and who cannot be claimed as a dependent on another return.

    c.   The credit is reduced if the individual has earned income (or greater AGI) in excess of a threshold or investment income greater than $2,550 in 2002. Nontaxable employee compensation is not included in earned income for EIC purposes. For MFJ taxpayers, the beginning and ending of the phase-out is increased by $1,000, for 2002 and 2003, and by $2,000 for 2004 through 2006.

    d.   Taxpayers making fraudulent EIC claims (later determined to be ineligible) are barred from claiming the credit for the next 10 years. For taxpayers making claims with reckless or intentional disregard for the tax law, the disallowance period is two years.

EXHIBIT 8 ♦ 2002 EARNED INCOME CREDIT AMOUNTS

Qualifying Children	Credit Rate	Computed on Earned Income of:	Maximum Credit	Start of Phase-out	Complete Phase-out
0	7.65%	$ 4,910	$ 376	$ 6,150	$11,060
1	34%	7,370	2,506	13,520	29,201
2	40%	10,350	4,140	13,520	33,178

6.   **GENERAL BUSINESS CREDIT** The general business credit is comprised of the investment tax credit that includes the rehabilitation, energy, and reforestation credits, the targeted jobs credit, the alcohol fuel credit, the research credit, the low-income housing credit, the enhanced oil recovery credit, the disabled access credit, and the renewable electricity production credit. The welfare-to-work credit is in effect for employers with qualified employees (long-term family assistance recipients) who begin work after December 31, 1997.

    a.   The general business credit may not exceed net income tax less the greater of the tentative minimum tax or 25% of net regular tax liability greater than $25,000.

    b.   Any portion of the credit that cannot be used in the current tax year may be carried back 1 year and forward 20 years.

c. Starting in 2002, EGTRRA '01 adds a small business pension plan startup costs credit to the general business credit. It is 50% of the first $1,000 of qualified costs for the first three years. This credit cannot be carried back before the effective date.

7. ADOPTION EXPENSES CREDIT A $10,000 credit is permitted for qualified adoption expenses (adoption, attorney, and court fees). No credit is allowed for reimbursed expenses. Fees from the adoption of a step-child are ineligible for this credit.

a. The credit is claimed in the year that the adoption becomes final, or that payment occurs, whichever is later. Married couples must file a joint return to claim this credit.

b. The phase-out range is $150,000 to $190,000 of modified AGI. Phased-out credits can be carried forward for 5 years.

c. A special needs child is a U.S. citizen or resident who a state determines cannot or should not be returned to her/his parents' residence and who is unlikely to be adopted without assistance. A special needs child's adoption has no requirement for qualified adoption expenses. No credit with respect to a special needs child's adoption is allowed if the adoption is not finalized.

d. For expenses paid or incurred before 2001, the prior limits ($5,000 for most adoptions or $6,000 for a special needs child with a phase-out range at $75,000 to $115,000 of modified AGI) apply.

8. EDUCATION CREDITS Many of the education provisions have phase-out ranges based on different definitions of modified AGI (MAGI). Different provisions also consider different types of expenses; some consider only tuition and fees, while others also consider books or room and board. For the following two credits, any expenses for tuition and fees must be reduced by excludable scholarships and other excludable assistance (but not gifts, bequests, or loans) before the credit is calculated. A dependent may not claim a credit; however, any qualifying expenses paid by the dependent student may be attributed to the parent and may be used in calculating the credit claimed on the parent's return. A tax credit may not be claimed for any amount that any other provision of the tax law provides for a deduction. The credits are phased-out at MAGI of $82,000 to $102,000 for MFJ, and $41,000 to $51,000 for a single filer or HH. MAGI is AGI plus any income earned outside the U.S. and not subject to U.S. tax.

a. **HOPE EDUCATION TAX CREDIT** A taxpayer may claim a nonrefundable credit for tuition and fees for the first two years of post-secondary education in a degree program for her/him, a spouse, or a dependent. This credit is limited to $1,500 per year per student. The student must be at least a half-time student. The credit is 100% of the first $1,000 and 50% of the second $1,000 of qualifying expenses.

b. **LIFETIME LEARNING TAX CREDIT** A taxpayer may claim a nonrefundable 20% credit for tuition and fees of up to $5,000 for the same people who qualify for the Hope credit. This credit is limited to $1,000 per year per taxpayer (not per student). The student need **not** be at least a half-time student. There is **no** limit to the number of years that the credit may be claimed and it may be used for graduate courses.

c. **CREDIT INTERACTION** The Hope and Lifetime Learning credits are **not** available for the same student in the same year. These credits may be claimed in the same year that amounts are distributed from a qualified state tuition program, but **not** in the same year that the taxpayer receives a *nontaxable* distribution from an education IRA.

9. RETIREMENT SAVINGS CREDIT Starting in 2002, eligible individuals are able to claim from 10% to 50% of a annual retirement savings contribution maximum of $2,000 as a credit. Eligible individuals are age 18 or older, other than full-time students or those claimed as a dependent on another person's tax return. Eligible taxpayers have joint returns with AGI of

$50,000 or less, HH returns with AGI of $37,500 or less, and single returns with AGI of $25,000 or less. Eligible retirement savings are IRAs as well as 401(k) and similar plans.

10. **EMPLOYER-PROVIDED CHILD CARE FACILITIES CREDIT** From 2002 to 2006, employers are eligible for a credit equal to 25% of qualified expenses for employee child care and 10% of qualified expenses for child care resource and referral services. The maximum total credit is $150,000 per tax year.

    A. **QUALIFIED EXPENSES** Include costs (1) to acquire, construct, rehabilitate, or expand property to be used as the taxpayer's qualified child care facility; (2) to operate the qualified child care facility; or (3) under a contract with a qualified child care facility to provide child care service to the taxpayer's employees.

    B. **QUALIFIED CHILD CARE FACILITY** The principal use of the facility must be for child care (unless it is the taxpayer's principal residence) and the facility must meet applicable state and local laws and regulations. The facility also must (1) have open enrollment to the taxpayer's employees; (2) not discriminate in favor of highly compensated employees; (3) have, as minimum, 30% of enrolled children who are dependents of the taxpayer's employees, if the facility is the principal trade or business of the taxpayer.

    C. **DEDUCTIONS** Amounts otherwise allowable as deductions must be reduced by the amount of credits. Credit claimed for costs of acquiring, constructing, rehabilitating, or expanding a facility reduces the employer's basis in the facility. If the facility is sold within 10 years of placing the facility in service, recapture rules apply.

B. **ESTIMATED PAYMENTS**
If an individual does not pay enough taxes during the year through withholding, s/he must make quarterly estimated tax payments in order to avoid a penalty for underpayment of tax.

1. **REQUIRED PAYMENTS** There is no penalty if the underpayment is $1,000 or less. To avoid a penalty, an individual must pay, through withholding and estimated payments, the lesser of either

    a. 90% of the current year's tax, or

    b. A safe harbor percentage of the prior year's tax. The safe harbor percentage for an individual with AGI of $150,000 or less is 100%. Any individual with a return with an AGI of more than $150,000 ($75,000 for a married individual filing a separate return) must have paid 105% of the preceding year's tax liability for 2001, 112% for 2002, and 110% thereafter. (The roller coaster swing of percentages is due to the phase-in of TRA '97.)

2. **DUE DATES** These quarterly payments are due on the 15th day of the 4th, 6th, and 9th month of the year, and the 15th day of the 1st month of the following year. For a calendar year taxpayer, this would mean April 15, June 15, September 15, and January 15 of the following year. If any of these dates fall on a weekend or a legal holiday, the payment is due the next business day.

CHAPTER 27—FEDERAL TAXATION: INDIVIDUALS

PROBLEM 27-1 MULTIPLE CHOICE QUESTIONS (160 to 200 minutes)

1. While Emma and John were married, John died on July 1, 2000. With regard to John's and Emma's filing status for 2000, Emma should file
a. As a single individual, and a separate return should be filed for John as unmarried head of household.
b. As a qualifying widow, and a separate return should be filed for John as married head of household.
c. As a qualifying widow, and a separate return should be filed for John as a single deceased individual.
d. A joint return, including John, as married taxpayers.　(Editors, 9258)

2. For head of household filing status, which of the following costs are considered in determining whether the taxpayer has contributed more than one half the cost of maintaining the household?

	Food consumed in the home	Value of services rendered in the home by the taxpayer
a.	Yes	Yes
b.	No	No
c.	Yes	No
d.	No	Yes

(11/92, PII, #10, 3344)

3. Sam Gow's wife died in 20X1. Sam did not remarry, and he continued to maintain a home for himself and his dependent infant child during 20X2 and 20X3, providing full support for himself and his child during these years. For 20X1, Sam properly filed a joint return. For 20X3, Sam's filing status is
a. Single.
b. Head of household.
c. Qualifying widower with dependent child.
d. Married filing joint return.　(Editors, 1581)

4. Which of the following is(are) among the requirements to enable a taxpayer to be classified as a "qualifying widow(er)"?

I. A dependent has lived with the taxpayer for six months.
II. The taxpayer has maintained the cost of the principal residence for six months.

a. I only
b. II only
c. Both I and II
d. Neither I nor II　(5/95, AR, #13, 5431)

5. A husband and wife can file a joint return even if
a. The spouses have different tax years, provided that both spouses are alive at the end of the year.
b. The spouses have different accounting methods.
c. Either spouse was a nonresident alien at any time during the tax year, provided that at least one spouse makes the proper election.
d. They were divorced before the end of the tax year.　(5/91, PII, #33, 1560)

6. Joe and Barb are married, but Barb refuses to sign a joint return. On Joe's separate return, an exemption may be claimed for Barb if
a. Barb was a full-time student for the entire school year.
b. Barb attaches a written statement to Joe's income tax return, agreeing to be claimed as an exemption by Joe.
c. Barb was under the age of 19.
d. Barb had **no** gross income and is **not** claimed as another person's dependent.
　(11/93, PII, #30, amended, 4465)

7. Smith, a divorced person, provided over one half the support for his widowed mother, Ruth, and his son, Clay, both of whom are U.S. citizens. Ruth did not live with Smith. She received $9,000 in social security benefits. Clay, a full-time graduate student, and his wife lived with Smith. Clay had no income but filed a joint return for the year, owing an additional $500 in taxes on his wife's income. How many exemptions was Smith entitled to claim on his tax return?
a. 4
b. 3
c. 2
d. 1　(5/95, AR, #14, amended, 5432)

8. Al and Mary Lew are married and filed a joint 2001 income tax return in which they validly claimed the $2,900 personal exemption for their dependent 17-year-old daughter, Doris. Since Doris earned $6,400 from a part-time job at the college she attended full-time, Doris was also required to file an income tax return. What amount was Doris entitled to claim as a personal exemption in her individual income tax return?
a. $0
b. $1,450
c. $2,900
d. $3,600　(11/90, PII, #24, amended, 4597)

9. Jim and Kay Ross contributed to the support of their two children, Dale and Kim, and Jim's widowed parent, Grant. Dale, a 19-year-old full-time college student, earned $4,500 as a baby-sitter. Kim, a 23-year-old bank teller, earned $12,000. Grant received $5,000 in dividend income and $4,000 in nontaxable social security benefits. Grant, Dale, and Kim are U.S. citizens and were over one-half supported by Jim and Kay. How many exemptions can Jim and Kay claim on their joint income tax return?

a. Two
b. Three
c. Four
d. Five   (5/94, AR, #14, amended, 4619)

10. In 20X0, Alan Cox provided more than half the support for his following relatives, none of whom qualified as a member of Alan's household:

    Cousin
    Nephew
    Foster parent

None of these relatives had any income, nor did any of these relatives file an individual or a joint return. All of these relatives are U.S. citizens. Which of these relatives could be claimed as a dependent on Alan's 20X0 return?

a. No one
b. Nephew
c. Cousin
d. Foster parent   (Editors, 9259)

11. Sarah Hance, who is single and lives alone in Idaho, has no income of her own and is supported in full by the following persons:

	Amount of support	Percent of total
Alan (an unrelated friend)	$ 7,200	48
Barbara (Sarah's sister)	6,450	43
Chris (Sarah's son)	1,350	9
	$15,000	100

Under a multiple support agreement, Sarah's dependency exemption can be claimed by

a. No one.
b. Alan.
c. Barbara.
d. Chris.   (Editors, 9260)

12. On April 15, 20X1, a married couple filed their joint 20X0 calendar-year return showing gross income of $120,000. Their return had been prepared by a professional tax preparer who mistakenly omitted $45,000 of income, which the preparer in good faith considered to be nontaxable. No information with regard to this omitted income was disclosed on the return or attached statements. By what date must the Internal Revenue Service assert a notice of deficiency before the statute of limitations expires?

a. April 15, 20X7
b. December 31, 20X6
c. April 15, 20X4
d. December 31, 20X3   (11/92, PII, #6, amended, 3340)

13. A taxpayer filed his income tax return after the due date but neglected to file an extension form. The return indicated a tax liability of $50,000 and taxes withheld of $45,000. On what amount would the penalties for late filing and late payment be computed?

a. $0
b. $ 5,000
c. $45,000
d. $50,000   (R/01, AR, #25, 7010)

14. A claim for refund of erroneously paid income taxes, filed by an individual before the statute of limitations expires, must be submitted on Form

a. 1139.
b. 1045.
c. 1040X.
d. 843.   (5/95, AR, #20, 5438)

15. A calendar-year taxpayer files an individual tax return for 20X1 on March 20, 20X2. The taxpayer neither committed fraud nor omitted amounts in excess of 25% of gross income on the tax return. What is the latest date that the Internal Revenue Service can assess tax and assert a notice of deficiency?

a. March 20, 20X5
b. March 20, 20X4
c. April 15, 20X5
d. April 15, 20X4   (5/94, AR, #18, amended, 4623)

16. If an individual paid income tax in 20X1 but did **not** file a 20X1 return because his income was insufficient to require the filing of a return, the deadline for filing a refund claim is

a. Two years from the date the tax was paid.
b. Two years from the date a return would have been due.
c. Three years from the date the tax was paid.
d. Three years from the date a return would have been due.   (11/90, PII, #22, amended, 1562)

17. A cash basis taxpayer should report gross income
a. Only for the year in which income is actually received in cash.
b. Only for the year in which income is actually received whether in cash or in property.
c. For the year in which income is either actually or constructively received in cash only.
d. For the year in which income is either actually or constructively received, whether in cash or in property. (5/95, AR, #15, 5433)

18. Perle, a dentist, billed Wood $600 for dental services. Wood paid Perle $200 cash and built a bookcase for Perle's office in full settlement of the bill. Wood sells comparable bookcases for $350. What amount should Perle include in taxable income as a result of this transaction?
a. $0
b. $200
c. $550
d. $600 (11/93, PII, #21, 4450)

19. Unless the Internal Revenue Service consents to a change of method, the accrual method of tax reporting is mandatory for a sole proprietor when there are

	Accounts receivable for services rendered	Year-end merchandise inventories
a.	Yes	Yes
b.	Yes	No
c.	No	No
d.	No	Yes

(11/92, PII, #13, 3347)

20. In 20X1, Emily Judd received the following dividends from:

Grainte Life Insurance Co., on Emily's life insurance policy (total dividends received have not yet exceeded accumulated premiums paid)	$100
National Bank, on bank's common stock	300
Roe Mfg. Corp., a Delaware corporation, on preferred stock	500

What amount of dividend income should Emily report in her 20X1 income tax return?
a. $900
b. $800
c. $500
d. $300 (Editors, 1598)

21. With regard to the inclusion of social security benefits in gross income, which of the following statements is correct?
a. The social security benefits in excess of modified adjusted gross income are included in gross income.
b. The social security benefits in excess of 85% the modified adjusted gross income are included in gross income.
c. 85% of the social security benefits is the maximum amount of benefits to be included in gross income.
d. The social security benefits in excess of the modified adjusted gross income over $34,000 are included in gross income. (5/94, AR, #4, amended, 4609)

22. In a tax year where the taxpayer pays qualified education expenses, interest income on the redemption of qualified U.S. Series EE Bonds may be excluded from gross income. The exclusion is subject to a modified gross income limitation and a limit of aggregate bond proceeds in excess of qualified higher education expenses. Which of the following is (are) true?

I. The exclusion applies for education expenses incurred by the taxpayer, the taxpayer's spouse, or any person whom the taxpayer may claim as a dependent for the year.
II. "Otherwise qualified higher education expenses" must be reduced by qualified scholarships not includible in gross income.

a. I only
b. II only
c. Both I and II
d. Neither I nor II (5/94, AR, #2, 4607)

23. Klein, a master's degree candidate at Briar University, was awarded a $12,000 scholarship from Briar in 1996. The scholarship was used to pay Klein's 1996 university tuition and fees. Also in 1996, Klein received $5,000 for teaching two courses at a nearby college. What amount is includible in Klein's 1996 gross income?
a. $0
b. $ 5,000
c. $12,000
d. $17,000 (11/97, AR, #1, 6529)

24. Jean accepted and received a $20,000 award for outstanding civic achievement. Jean was selected without any action on her part, and no future services are expected of her as a condition of receiving the award. What amount should Jean include in adjusted gross income in connection with this award?
a. $0
b. $ 5,000
c. $10,000
d. $20,000 (Editors, 1578)

25. Darr, an employee of Sorce C corporation, is not a shareholder. Which of the following would be included in a taxpayer's gross income?
a. Employer-provided medical insurance coverage under a health plan.
b. A $10,000 gift from the taxpayer's grandparents.
c. The fair market value of land that the taxpayer inherited from an uncle.
d. The dividend income on shares of stock that the taxpayer received for services rendered.
(R/01, AR, #30, 7015)

26. Harold sustained a serious injury in the course of his employment. As a result of this injury, Harold received the following payments during the current year:

Workers' compensation	$ 6,500
Reimbursement from his employer's insurance plan for medical expenses paid by Harold and not deducted by him	4,000
Damages for personal injuries	16,000

The amount to be included in Harold's gross income for the current year should be
a. $26,500.
b. $16,000.
c. $ 4,000.
d. $0. (Editors, 1601)

27. Walt's employer pays 100% of the cost of all employees' group-term life insurance under a qualified plan. Under this plan, the maximum amount of tax-free coverage that may be provided for Walt by his employer is
a. $100,000.
b. $ 50,000.
c. $ 10,000.
d. $ 5,000. (Editors, 1593)

28. Ash had the following cash receipts:

Wages	$13,000
Interest income from U.S. Treasury bonds	350
Workers' compensation following a job-related injury	8,500

What is the total amount that must be included in gross income on Ash's income tax return?
a. $13,000
b. $13,350
c. $21,500
d. $21,850 (R/99, AR, #1, amended, 6790)

29. Which of the following conditions must be present in a post-1984 divorce agreement for a payment to qualify as deductible alimony?

I. Payments must be in cash.
II. The payments must end at the recipient's death.

a. I only.
b. II only.
c. Both I and II.
d. Neither I nor II. (R/01, AR, #27, 7012)

30. John and Mary were divorced in 20X0. The divorce decree provides that John pay alimony of $10,000 per year, to be reduced by 20% on their child's 18th birthday. During 20X4, John paid $7,000 directly to Mary and $3,000 to Spring College for Mary's tuition. What amount of these payments should be reported as income in Mary's 20X4 income tax return?
a. $ 5,600
b. $ 8,000
c. $ 8,600
d. $10,000 (11/93, PII, #24, amended, 4453)

31. Mock operates a retail business selling illegal narcotic substances. Which of the following item(s) may Mock deduct in calculating business income?

I. Cost of merchandise.
II. Business expenses other than the cost of merchandise.

a. I only
b. II only
c. Both I and II
d. Neither I nor II (R/01, AR, #24, 7009)

32. Billings, a retired corporate executive, earned consulting fees of $9,000 and director's fees of $4,000 in the current year. Billings' gross income from self-employment in the current year was
a. $0.
b. $ 4,000.
c. $ 9,000.
d. $13,000. (Editors, 1573)

33. Kent received the following interest income:

On Veterans Administration insurance
   dividends left on deposit with the VA $20
On U.S. Treasury certificates   30
On state income tax refund   40

What amount should Kent include for interest income in his tax return?
a. $90
b. $70
c. $50
d. $20   (Editors, 1575)

34. Lewis is single, with no dependents. Lewis received wages of $11,000 and state unemployment compensation benefits of $2,000. He had no other source of income. The amount of state unemployment compensation benefits that should be included in Lewis' adjusted gross income is
a. $2,000.
b. $1,000.
c. $ 500.
d. $0.   (Editors, 1582)

35. Jane won $6,000 in a state lottery. Also in the current year, Jane spent $300 for the purchase of lottery tickets. Jane elected the standard deduction on her current year income tax return. The amount of lottery winnings that should be included in Jane's current year taxable income is
a. $0.
b. $2,000.
c. $5,700.
d. $6,000.   (Editors, 1583)

36. Baum, an unmarried optometrist and sole proprietor of Optics, buys and maintains a supply of eyeglasses and frames to sell in the ordinary course of business. In 20X1, Optics had $350,000 in gross business receipts and its year-end inventory was not subject to the uniform capitalization rules. Baum's 20X1 adjusted gross income was $90,000 and Baum qualified to itemize deductions. During 20X1, Baum recorded the following information:

Business expenses:
Optics cost of goods sold $35,000
Optics rent expense $28,000
Liability insurance premium on Optics $ 5,250

Other expenditures:
Baum's self-employment tax $29,750
Baum's self-employment health insurance $ 8,750
Estimated payments of 20X1 federal
   income taxes $13,500

What amount should Baum report as 20X1 net earnings from self-employment?
a. $243,250
b. $252,000
c. $273,000
d. $281,750   (R/99, AR, #2, amended, 6791)

37. On December 1, 20X1, Krest, a self-employed cash basis taxpayer, borrowed $200,000 to use in her business. The loan was to be repaid on November 30, 20X2. Krest paid the entire interest amount of $24,000 on December 1, 20X1. What amount of interest was deductible on Krest's 20X1 income tax return?
a. $0
b. $ 2,000
c. $22,000
d. $24,000   (5/98, AR, #3, amended, 6640)

38. Jason Heron, CPA, reports on the cash basis. In April 20X1, Heron billed a client $3,500 for the following professional services:

Personal estate planning $2,000
Personal tax return preparation   1,000
Compilation of business financial
   statements   500

No part of the $3,500 was ever paid. In April 20X2, the client declared bankruptcy, and the $3,500 obligation became totally uncollectible. What loss can Heron deduct on his 20X2 tax return for this bad debt?
a. $0
b. $ 500
c. $1,500
d. $3,500   (Editors, 1603)

39. Don Wolf became a general partner in Gata Associates on January 1, 20X1, with a 5% interest in Gata's profits, losses, and capital. Gata is a distributor of auto parts. Wolf does not materially participate in the partnership business. For 20X1, Gata had an operating loss of $100,000. In addition, Gata earned interest of $20,000 on a temporary investment. Gata has kept the principal temporarily invested while awaiting delivery of equipment that is presently on order. The principal will be used to pay for this equipment. Wolf's passive loss for 20X1 is
a. $0.
b. $4,000.
c. $5,000.
d. $6,000.   (11/90, PII, #27, amended, 1566)

40. Easel Co. elected to reimburse employees for business expenses under a nonaccountable plan. Easel does not require employees to provide proof of expenses and allows employees to keep any amount not spent. Under the plan, Mel, an Easel employee for a full year, gets $400 per month for business automobile expenses. At the end of the year Mel informs Easel that the only business expense incurred was for business mileage of 12,000 at a rate of 30 cents per mile, the IRS standard mileage rate at the time. Mel encloses a check for $1,200 to refund the overpayment to Easel. What amount should be reported in Mel's gross income for the year?

a. $0
b. $1,200
c. $3,600
d. $4,800   (R/99, AR, #3, amended, 6792)

41. Destry, a single taxpayer, reported the following on his U.S. Individual Income Tax Return Form 1040:

Income:

Wages	$ 5,000
Interest on savings account	1,000
Net rental income	4,000

Deductions:

Personal exemption	$ 2,700
Standard deduction	4,200
Net business loss	16,000
Net short-term capital loss	2,000

What is Destry's net operating loss that is available for carryback or carryforward?

a. $ 7,000
b. $ 9,000
c. $15,100
d. $16,000   (R/99, AR, #7, 6796)

42. Adams owns a second residence that is used for both personal and rental purposes. During 2001, Jackson used the second residence for 50 days and rented the residence for 200 days. Which of the following statements is correct?

a. Depreciation may not be deducted on the property under any circumstances.
b. A rental loss may be deducted if rental-related expenses exceed rental income.
c. Utilities and maintenance on the property must be divided between personal and rental use.
d. All mortgage interest and taxes on the property will be deducted to determine the property's net income or loss.   (R/01, AR, #22, 7007)

43. Nare, an accrual-basis taxpayer, owns a building which was rented to Mott under a ten-year lease expiring August 31, 2008. On January 2, Mott paid $30,000 as consideration for canceling the lease. On November 1, Nare leased the building to Pine under a five-year lease. Pine paid Nare $10,000 rent for the two months of November and December, and an additional $5,000 for the last month's rent. What amount of rental income should Nare report in its current year income tax return?

a. $10,000
b. $15,000
c. $40,000
d. $45,000   (11/93, PII, #23, amended, 4452)

44. Dale received $1,000 in the current year for jury duty. In exchange for regular compensation from her employer during the period of jury service, Dale was required to remit the entire $1,000 to her employer. In Dale's income tax return, the $1,000 jury duty fee should be

a. Claimed in full as an itemized deduction.
b. Claimed as an itemized deduction to the extent exceeding 2% of adjusted gross income.
c. Deducted from gross income in arriving at adjusted gross income.
d. Included in taxable income without a corresponding offset against other income.
            (5/91, PII, #26, amended, 1552)

45. The self-employment tax is
a. Fully deductible as an itemized deduction.
b. Fully deductible in determining net income from self-employment.
c. One-half deductible from gross income in arriving at adjusted gross income.
d. Not deductible.   (5/94, AR, #6, 4611)

46. Which allowable deduction can be claimed in arriving at an individual's adjusted gross income?
a. Alimony payment.
b. Charitable contribution.
c. Personal casualty loss.
d. Unreimbursed business expense of an outside salesperson.   (11/93, PII, #27, 4456)

47. Grey, a calendar year taxpayer, was employed and resided in New York. On February 2, Grey was permanently transferred to Florida by his employer. Grey worked full-time for the entire year. Grey incurred and paid the following unreimbursed expenses in relocating:

Lodging and travel expenses while moving $1,000
Pre-move househunting costs   1,200
Costs of moving household furnishings
  and personal effects   1,800

What amount was deductible as moving expense on Grey's tax return?
a. $4,000
b. $2,800
c. $1,800
d. $1,000   (5/95, AR, #6, amended, 5424)

48. For calendar year 20X1, Ralph earned $1,000 interest at Ridge Savings Bank on a certificate of deposit scheduled to mature in 20X3. In January 20X2, before filing his 20X1 income tax return, Ralph incurred a forfeiture penalty of $500 for premature withdrawal of the funds. Ralph should treat this $500 forfeiture penalty as a
a. Reduction of interest earned in 20X1, so that only $500 of such interest is taxable on Ralph's 20X1 return.
b. Deduction from 20X2 adjusted gross income, deductible only if Ralph itemizes his deductions for 20X2.
c. Penalty **not** deductible for tax purposes.
d. Deduction from gross income in arriving at 20X2 adjusted gross income.   (Editors, 1595)

49. Mike and Julia Crane are married, and filed a joint return for 2002. Mike earned a salary of $80,000 in 2002 from his job at Troy Corp., where Mike is covered by his employer's pension plan. In addition, Mike and Julia earned interest of $3,000 on their joint savings account. Julia is not employed, and the couple had no other income. On January 15, 2003, Mike contributed $3,000 to a traditional IRA for himself, and $3,000 to an IRA for his spouse. The allowable IRA deduction in the Cranes' 2002 joint return is
a. $0.
b. $2,000.
c. $3,000.
d. $6,000.   (Editors, 1580)

50. Val and Pat White filed a joint return. Val earned $35,000 in wages and was covered by his employer's qualified pension plan. Pat was unemployed and received $5,000 in alimony payments for the first 4 months of the year before remarrying. The couple had no other income. Each contributed $3,000 to an IRA account. The allowable IRA deduction on their joint 2002 tax return is
a. $6,000.
b. $3,000.
c. $2,000.
d. $0.   (5/94, AR, #7, amended, 4612)

51. Davis, a sole proprietor with no employees, has a Keogh profit-sharing plan to which he may contribute 15% of his annual earned income. For this purpose, "earned income" is defined as net self-employment earnings reduced by the
a. Deductible Keogh contribution.
b. Self-employment tax.
c. Self-employment tax and one-half of the deductible Keogh contribution.
d. Deductible Keogh contribution and one-half of the self-employment tax.   (11/93, PII, #28, 4457)

52. Which of the following requirements must be met in order for a single individual to qualify for the additional standard deduction amount?

	Must be age 65 or older or blind	Must support dependent child or aged parent
a.	Yes	Yes
b.	No	No
c.	Yes	No
d.	No	Yes

    (11/91, PII, #21, amended, 2469)

53. Poole, 45 years old and unmarried, is in the 15% tax bracket. He has 2002 adjusted gross income of $22,000. The following information applies to Poole:

Medical expenses $7,000
Standard deduction   4,700
Personal exemption   3,000

Poole wishes to minimize his income tax. What is Poole's 2002 total income tax?
a. $3,300.00
b. $2,145.00
c. $2,047.50
d. $1,800.00   (11/93, PII, #38, amended, 4467)

54. Tom and Sally White, married and filing joint income tax returns, derive their entire income from the operation of their retail stationery shop. Their adjusted gross income was $100,000. The Whites itemized their deductions on Schedule A. The following unreimbursed cash expenditures were among those made by the Whites during the current year:

Repair and maintenance of motorized
   wheelchair for physically
   handicapped dependent child $ 600
Tuition, meals, and lodging at special
   school for physically handicapped
   dependent child in an institution
   primarily for the availability of medical
   care, with meals and lodging furnished
   as necessary incidents to that care   8,000

Without regard to the adjusted gross income percentage threshold, what amount may the Whites claim as qualifying medical expenses?
a. $8,600
b. $8,000
c. $ 600
d. $0   (5/95, AR, #12, amended, 5430)

55. Carroll, an unmarried taxpayer with an adjusted gross income of $100,000, incurred and paid the following unreimbursed medical expenses for the year:

Doctor bills resulting from a serious fall $ 5,000
Cosmetic surgery that was necessary
   to correct a congenital deformity   15,000

Carroll had no medical insurance. For regular income tax purposes, what was Carroll's maximum allowable medical expense deduction, after the applicable threshold limitation, for the year?
a. $0
b. $12,500
c. $15,000
d. $20,000   (R/01, AR, #21, 7006)

56. During 20X1, Scott charged $4,000 on his credit card for his dependent son's medical expenses. Payment to the credit card company had not been made by the time Scott filed his income tax return in 20X2. However, in 20X1, Scott paid a physician $2,800 for medical expenses of his wife, who died in 20X0. Disregarding the adjusted gross income percentage threshold, what amount could Scott claim in his 20X1 income tax return for medical expenses?
a. $0
b. $2,800
c. $4,000
d. $6,800   (5/91, PII, #31, amended, 1557)

57. In 20X1, Wells paid the following expenses:

Premiums on an insurance policy
   against loss of earnings due to
   sickness or accident $3,000
Physical therapy after spinal surgery   2,000
Premium on an insurance policy that
   covers reimbursement for the cost of
   prescription drugs   500

In 20X1, Wells recovered $1,500 of the $2,000 that she paid for physical therapy through insurance reimbursement from a group medical policy paid for by her employer. Disregarding the adjusted gross income percentage threshold, what amount could be claimed on Wells' 20X1 income tax return for medical expenses?
a. $4,000
b. $3,500
c. $1,000
d. $ 500   (5/94, AR, #13, amended, 4618)

58. Matthews was a cash basis taxpayer whose records showed the following:

20X1 state and local income taxes withheld $1,500
20X1 state estimated income taxes paid
   December 30, 20X1   400
20X1 federal income taxes withheld   2,500
20X1 state and local income taxes paid
   April 17, 20X2   300

What total amount was Matthews entitled to claim for taxes on her 20X1 Schedule A of Form 1040?
a. $4,700
b. $2,200
c. $1,900
d. $1,500   (5/95, AR, #8, amended, 5426)

59. In 20X1, Farb, a cash basis individual taxpayer, received an $8,000 invoice for personal property taxes. Believing the amount to be overstated by $5,000, Farb paid the invoiced amount under protest and immediately started legal action to recover the overstatement. In November, 20X2, the matter was resolved in Farb's favor, and he received a $5,000 refund. Farb itemizes his deductions on his tax returns. Which of the following statements is correct regarding the deductibility of the property taxes?

a. Farb should deduct $8,000 in his 20X1 income tax return and should report the $5,000 refund as income in his 20X2 income tax return.
b. Farb should **not** deduct any amount in his 20X1 income tax return and should deduct $3,000 in his 20X2 income tax return.
c. Farb should deduct $3,000 in his 20X1 income tax return.
d. Farb should **not** deduct any amount in his 20X1 income tax return when originally filed, and should file an amended 20X1 income tax return in 20X2.   (11/93, PII, #33, amended, 4462)

60.   Jackson owns two residences. The second residence, which has never been used for rental purposes, is the only residence that is subject to a mortgage. The following expenses were incurred for the second residence:

Mortgage interest	$5,000
Utilities	1,200
Insurance	6,000

For regular income tax purposes, what is the maximum amount allowable as a deduction for Jackson's second residence?
a. $6,200 in determining adjusted gross income.
b. $11,000 in determining adjusted gross income.
c. $5,000 as an itemized deduction.
d. $12,200 as an itemized deduction.
                   (5/98, AR, #2, amended, 6639)

61.   The 2002 deduction by an individual taxpayer for interest on investment indebtedness is
a. Limited to the investment interest paid in 2002.
b. Limited to the taxpayer's 2002 interest income.
c. Limited to the taxpayer's 2002 net investment income.
d. Not limited.   (5/94, AR, #8, amended, 4613)

62.   The Browns borrowed $20,000, secured by their home, to pay their son's college tuition. At the time of the loan, the fair market value of their home was $400,000, and it was unencumbered by other debt. The interest on the loan qualifies as
a. Deductible personal interest.
b. Deductible qualified residence interest.
c. Nondeductible interest.
d. Investment interest expense.
                   (5/94, AR, #10, 4615)

63.   On January 2, 20X1, the Philips paid $50,000 cash and obtained a $200,000 mortgage to purchase a home. In 20X3, they borrowed $15,000 secured by their home, and used the cash to add a new room to their residence. That same year they took out a $5,000 auto loan. The following information pertains to interest paid in 20X7:

Mortgage interest	$17,000
Interest on room construction loan	1,500
Auto loan interest	500

For 20X7, how much interest is deductible, prior to any itemized deduction limitations?
a. $17,000
b. $17,500
c. $18,500
d. $19,000   (5/94, AR, #11, amended, 4616)

64.   Moore, a single taxpayer, had $50,000 in adjusted gross income for the current year. During the current year, she contributed $18,000 to her church. She had a $10,000 charitable contribution carryover from her prior year church contribution. What was the maximum amount of properly substantiated charitable contributions that Moore could claim as an itemized deduction for the current year?
a. $10,000
b. $18,000
c. $25,000
d. $28,000   (5/95, AR, #7, amended, 5425)

65.   Deet, an unmarried taxpayer, qualified to itemize 20X1 deductions. Deet's 20X1 adjusted gross income was $40,000 and he made a $1,500 substantiated cash donation directly to a needy family. Deet also donated art, valued at $11,000, to a local art museum. Deet had purchased the art work two years earlier for $2,000. What was the maximum amount of the charitable contribution allowable as an itemized deduction on Deet's 20X1 income tax return?
a. $15,000
b. $11,000
c. $ 3,500
d. $ 2,000   (11/97, AR, #4, amended, 6532)

66.   In 1996, Wood's residence had an adjusted basis of $150,000 and it was destroyed by a tornado. An appraiser valued the decline in market value at $175,000. Later that same year, Wood received $130,000 from his insurance company for the property loss and did not elect to deduct the casualty loss in an earlier year. Wood's 1996 adjusted gross income was $60,000 and he did not have any casualty gains. What total amount can Wood deduct as a 1996 itemized deduction for the casualty loss, after the application of the threshold limitations?
a. $39,000
b. $38,900
c. $19,900
d. $13,900   (11/97, AR, #3, 6531)

67. An individual's losses on transactions entered into for personal purposes are deductible only if
a. The losses qualify as casualty or theft losses.
b. The losses can be characterized as hobby losses.
c. The losses do not exceed $3,000 ($6,000 on a joint return).
d. No part of the transactions was entered into for profit. (5/91, PII, #29, 1555)

68. Which items are subject to the phase out of the amount of certain itemized deductions that may be claimed by high-income individuals?
a. Charitable contributions
b. Medical costs
c. Nonbusiness casualty losses
d. Investment interest deductions
(5/95, AR, #11, 5429)

69. Which of the following is **not** a miscellaneous itemized deduction?
a. An individual's tax return preparation fee
b. Education expense to meet minimum entry level education requirements at an individual's place of employment
c. Custodial fees for a brokerage account
d. An individual's subscription to professional journals (5/94, AR, #9, amended, 4614)

70. Baker, a sole proprietor CPA, has several clients that do business in Spain. While on a four-week vacation in Spain, Baker took a five-day seminar on Spanish business practices that cost $700. Baker's round-trip airfare to Spain was $600. While in Spain, Baker spent an average of $100 per day on accommodations, local travel, and other incidental expenses, for total expenses of $2,800. What amount of educational expense can Baker deduct on Form 1040 Schedule C, "Profit or Loss From Business?"
a. $ 700
b. $1,200
c. $1,800
d. $4,100 (R/99, AR, #6, 6795)

71. Don Mills, a single taxpayer, had $70,000 in taxable income before personal exemptions. Mills had no tax preferences. His itemized deductions were as follows:

State and local income taxes	$5,000
Home mortgage interest on loan to acquire residence	6,000
Miscellaneous deductions that exceed 2% of adjusted gross income	2,000

What amount did Mills report as alternative minimum taxable income before the AMT exemption?
a. $72,000
b. $75,000
c. $77,000
d. $83,000 (5/95, AR, #17, amended, 5435)

72. Alternative minimum tax preferences include

	Tax exempt interest from private activity bonds issued during 1994	Charitable contributions of appreciated capital gain property
a.	Yes	Yes
b.	Yes	No
c.	No	Yes
d.	No	No
		(5/95, AR, #18, 5436)

73. The credit for prior year alternative minimum tax liability may be carried
a. Forward for a maximum of 5 years.
b. Back to the 3 preceding years or carried forward for a maximum of 5 years.
c. Back to the 3 preceding years.
d. Forward indefinitely. (5/94, AR, #16, 4621)

74. To qualify for the child care credit on a joint return, at least one spouse must

	Have an adjusted gross income of $10,000 or less	Be gainfully employed when related expenses are incurred
a.	Yes	Yes
b.	No	No
c.	Yes	No
d.	No	Yes
		(11/92, PII, #11, 3345)

75. Which of the following credits can result in a refund even if the individual had **no** income tax liability?
a. Credit for prior year minimum tax
b. Elderly and permanently and totally disabled credit
c. Earned income credit
d. Child and dependent care credit
(5/94, AR, #17, 4622)

76. Which of the following credits is a combination of several tax credits to provide uniform rules for the current and carryback-carryover years?
a. General business credit
b. Foreign tax credit
c. Minimum tax credit
d. Enhanced oil recovery credit
(11/94, AR, #49, 5025)

77. Sunex Co., an accrual-basis, calendar-year domestic C corporation, is taxed on its worldwide income. In the current year, Sunex's U.S. tax liability on its domestic and foreign source income is $60,000 and no prior-year foreign income taxes have been carried forward. Which factor(s) may affect the amount of Sunex's foreign tax credit available in its current-year corporate income tax return?

	Income source	The foreign tax rate
a.	Yes	Yes
b.	Yes	No
c.	No	Yes
d.	No	No

(R/99, AR, #11, 6800)

78. An accuracy-related penalty applies to the portion of tax underpayment attributable to

I. Negligence or a disregard of the tax rules or regulations.
II. Any substantial understatement of income tax.

a. I only
b. II only
c. Both I and II
d. Neither I nor II   (5/95, AR, #16, 5434)

79. Chris Baker's adjusted gross income on her 2001 tax return was $160,000. The amount covered a 12-month period. For the 2002 tax year, Baker may avoid the penalty for the underpayment of estimated tax if the timely estimated tax payments equal the required annual amount of

I. 90% of the tax on the return for the current year, paid in four equal installments.
II. 100% of prior year's tax liability, paid in four equal installments.

a. I only
b. II only
c. Both I and II
d. Neither I nor II   (5/95, AR, #19, amended, 5437)

80. Krete, an unmarried taxpayer with income exclusively from wages, filed her initial income tax return for the 20X0 calendar year. By December 31, 20X0, Krete's employer had withheld $16,000 in federal income taxes and Krete had made no estimated tax payments. On Monday, April 17, 20X1, Krete timely filed an extension request to file her individual tax return and paid $300 of additional taxes. Krete's 20X0 income tax liability was $16,500 when she timely filed her return on April 30, 20X1, and paid the remaining income tax liability balance. What amount would be subject to the penalty for the underpayment of estimated taxes?

a. $0
b. $ 200
c. $ 500
d. $16,500   (5/98, AR, #4, 6641)

PROBLEM 27-2 ADDITIONAL MULTIPLE CHOICE QUESTIONS (48 to 60 minutes)

81. Clark bought Series EE U.S. Savings Bonds after 1989. Redemption proceeds will be used for payment of college tuition for Clark's dependent child. One of the conditions that must be met for tax exemption of accumulated interest on these bonds is that the
a. Purchaser of the bonds must be the sole owner of the bonds (or joint owner with his or her spouse).
b. Bonds must be bought by a parent (or both parents) and put in the name of the dependent child.
c. Bonds must be bought by the owner of the bonds before the owner reaches the age of 24.
d. Bonds must be transferred to the college for redemption by the college rather than by the owner of the bonds.   (5/91, PII, #28, 1554)

82. Which payment(s) is (are) included in a recipient's gross income?

I. Payment to a graduate assistant for a part-time teaching assignment at a university. Teaching is not a requirement toward obtaining the degree.
II. A grant to a Ph.D. candidate for his participation in a university-sponsored research project for the benefit of the university.

a. I only
b. II only
c. Both I and II
d. Neither I nor II   (5/95, AR, #1, 5419)

83.   Ed and Ann Ross were divorced in January of the current year. In accordance with the divorce decree, Ed transferred the title in their home to Ann. The home, which had a fair market value of $150,000, was subject to a $50,000 mortgage that had 20 more years to run. Monthly mortgage payments amounted to $1,000. Under the terms of settlement, Ed is obligated to make the mortgage payments on the home for the full remaining 20-year term of the indebtedness, regardless of how long Ann lives. Ed made 12 mortgage payments the current year. What amount is taxable as alimony in Ann's current year return?
a. $0
b. $ 12,000
c. $100,000
d. $112,000   (11/90, PII, #25, amended, 1565)

84.   Charles and Marcia are married cash-basis taxpayers. They had interest income as follows:

- $500 interest on federal income tax refund.
- $600 interest on state income tax refund.
- $800 interest on federal government obligations.
- $1,000 interest on state government obligations.

What amount of interest income is taxable on Charles and Marcia's joint income tax return?
a. $ 500
b. $1,100
c. $1,900
d. $2,900   (11/93, PII, #22, amended, 4451)

85.   Rich is a cash basis self-employed air-conditioning repairman with gross business receipts of $20,000. Rich's cash disbursements were as follows:

Air conditioning parts	$2,500
Yellow Pages listing	2,000
Estimated federal income taxes on self-employment income	1,000
Business long-distance telephone calls	400
Charitable contributions	200

What amount should Rich report as net self-employment income?
a. $15,100
b. $14,900
c. $14,100
d. $13,900   (5/94, AR, #5, amended, 4610)

86.   Lee, an attorney, uses the cash receipts and disbursements method of reporting. In December of the current year, a client gave Lee 500 shares of a listed corporation's stock in full satisfaction of a $10,000 legal fee the client owed to Lee. This stock had a fair market value of $8,000 on the date it was given to Lee. The client's basis for this stock was $6,000. Lee sold the stock for cash in January. In Lee's current year income tax return, what amount of income should be reported in connection with the receipt of the stock?
a. $10,000
b. $ 8,000
c. $ 6,000
d. $0   (5/91, PII, #24, amended, 1550)

87.   If an individual taxpayer's passive losses and credits relating to rental real estate activities cannot be used in the current year, then they may be carried
a. Forward up to a maximum period of 15 years, but they cannot be carried back.
b. Forward indefinitely or until the property is disposed of in a taxable transaction.
c. Back three years or forward up to 15 years, at the taxpayer's election.
d. Back three years, but they cannot be carried forward.   (Editors, 1576)

88.   With regard to the passive loss rules involving rental real estate activities, which one of the following statements is correct?
a. The term "passive activity" includes any rental activity without regard as to whether or not the taxpayer materially participates in the activity.
b. Passive rental activity losses may be deducted only against passive income, but passive rental activity credits may be used against tax attributable to nonpassive activities.
c. Gross investment income from interest and dividends **not** derived in the ordinary course of a trade or business is treated as passive activity income that can be offset by passive rental activity losses when the "active participation" requirement is **not** met.
d. The passive activity rules do **not** apply to taxpayers whose adjusted gross income is $300,000 or less.   (Editors, 4596)

89.   Jim owns a two-family house which has two identical apartments. Jim lives in one apartment and rents out the other. In 20X1, the rental apartment was fully occupied and Jim received $7,200 in rent. During 20X1, Jim paid the following:

Real estate taxes	$6,400
Painting of rental apartment	$ 800
Annual fire insurance premium	$ 600

In 20X1, depreciation for the entire house was determined to be $5,000. What amount should Jim include in his adjusted gross income for 20X1?

a. $2,900
b. $ 800
c. $ 400
d. $ 100   (Editors, 1594)

90.   Paul and Sally Lee, both age 50, are married and filed a joint return for 2002. Their adjusted gross income was $180,000, including Paul's $89,000 salary and Sally's $90,000 investment income. Neither spouse was covered by an employer-sponsored pension plan. What amount could the Lee's contribute to IRAs for 2002 to take advantage of their maximum allowable IRA deduction in their 2002 return?
a. $0
b. $2,000
c. $3,000
d. $6,000   (Editors, 1589)

91.   Matilda, who is divorced, received taxable alimony of $25,000 in 2002. In addition, she received $900 earnings from a part-time job. Her employer did *not* provide a retirement plan for part-time employees. What was the maximum IRA contribution that Matilda could have made for 2002, which she could have deducted on her 2002 individual tax return, assuming that everything was done on a timely basis?
a. $ 250
b. $ 900
c. $2,000
d. $3,000   (Editors, 1602)

92.   Bell, a cash basis calendar year taxpayer, died on June 1, 20X1. Prior to her death, Bell incurred $2,000 in medical expenses. The executor of the estate paid the medical expenses, which were a claim against the estate, on July 1, 20X1. If the executor files the appropriate waiver, the medical expenses are deductible on
a.   The estate tax return.
b.   Bell's final income tax return.
c.   The estate income tax return.
d.   The executor's income tax return.
            (11/94, AR, #56, amended, 5032)

93.   Which one of the following expenditures qualifies as a deductible medical expense for tax purposes?
a.   Vitamins for general health **not** prescribed by a physician
b.   Health club dues
c.   Transportation to physician's office for required medical care
d.   Mandatory employment taxes for basic coverage under Medicare A   (11/90, PII, #33, 1569)

94.   Ruth and Mark Cline are married and will file a joint income tax return. Among their expenditures during the current year were the following discretionary costs that they incurred for the sole purpose of improving their physical appearance and self-esteem:

Face lift for Ruth, performed by a
    licensed surgeon $5,000
Hair transplant for Mark, performed
    by a licensed surgeon   3,600

Disregarding the adjusted gross income percentage threshold, what total amount of the aforementioned doctors' bills may be claimed by the Clines in their return as qualifying medical expenses?
a. $0
b. $3,600
c. $5,000
d. $8,600   (5/91, PII, #30, amended, 1556)

95.   In 20X1, Smith paid $6,000 to the tax collector of Wek City for realty taxes on a two-family house owned by Smith's mother. Of this amount, $2,800 covered back taxes for 20X0, and $3,200 covered 20X1 taxes. Smith resides on the second floor of the house, and his mother resides on the first floor. In Smith's itemized deductions on his 20X1 return, what amount was Smith entitled to claim for realty taxes?
a. $6,000
b. $3,200
c. $3,000
d. $0   (11/90, PII, #32, amended, 1568)

96.   William did not itemize his deductions on his 20X0 and 20X1 federal income tax returns. However, William plans to itemize his deductions for 20X2. The following information relating to his state income taxes is available:

Taxes withheld in 20X2 $2,000
Refund received in 20X2 of 20X1 tax   300
Assessment paid in 20X2 of 20X0 tax   200

What amount should William utilize as state and local income taxes in calculating itemized deductions for his 20X2 federal income tax return?
a. $1,700
b. $1,900
c. $2,000
d. $2,200   (Editors, 9261)

97. For regular tax purposes, with regard to the itemized deduction for qualified residence interest, home equity indebtedness incurred
a. Includes acquisition indebtedness secured by a qualified residence.
b. May exceed the fair market value of the residence.
c. Must exceed the taxpayer's net equity in the residence.
d. Is limited to $100,000 on a joint income tax return. (5/91, PII, #27, amended, 1553)

98. Which expense, both incurred and paid in the current year, can be claimed as an itemized deduction subject to the two-percent-of-adjusted-gross-income floor?
a. Self-employed health insurance
b. One-half of the self-employment tax
c. Employee's unreimbursed moving expense
d. Employee's unreimbursed business car expense (5/95, AR, #9, amended, 5427)

99. Taylor, an unmarried taxpayer, had $90,000 in adjusted gross income for the year. Taylor donated land to a church and made no other contributions. Taylor purchased the land ten years ago as an investment for $14,000. The land's fair market value was $25,000 on the day of the donation. What is the maximum amount of charitable contribution that Taylor may deduct as an itemized deduction for the land donation for the current year?
a. $25,000
b. $14,000
c. $11,000
d. $0 (R/00, AR, #6, amended, 6911)

100. Stein, an unmarried taxpayer, had adjusted gross income of $80,000 for the year, and qualified to itemize deductions. Stein had no charitable contribution carryovers and only made one contribution during the year. Stein donated stock, purchased seven years earlier for $17,000, to a tax-exempt educational organization. The stock was valued at $25,000 when it was contributed. What is the amount of charitable contributions deductible on Stein's current year income tax income tax return?
a. $17,000
b. $21,000
c. $24,000
d. $25,000 (R/99, AR, #8, 6797)

101. Spencer, who itemizes deductions, had adjusted gross income of $60,000 in 20X1. The following additional information is available:

Cash contribution to church	$4,000
Purchase of art object at church bazaar (with a fair market value of $800 on the date of purchase)	1,200
Donation of used clothing to Salvation Army (fair value evidenced by receipt received)	600

What is the maximum amount Spencer can claim as a deduction for charitable contributions in 20X1?
a. $5,400
b. $5,200
c. $5,000
d. $4,400 (11/93, PII, #31, amended, 4460)

102. Dole's adjusted gross income exceeds $500,000. After the application of any other limitation, itemized deductions are reduced by
a. The *lesser* of 3% of the excess of adjusted gross income over the applicable amount or 80% of *certain* itemized deductions.
b. The *lesser* of 3% of the excess of adjusted gross income over the applicable amount or 80% of *all* itemized deductions.
c. The *greater* of 3% of the excess of adjusted gross income over the applicable amount or 80% of *certain* itemized deductions.
d. The *greater* of 3% of the excess of adjusted gross income over the applicable amount or 80% of *all* itemized deductions. (5/94, AR, #12, amended, 4617)

103. Which one of the following types of itemized deductions is included in the category of unreimbursed expenses deductible only if the aggregate of such expenses exceeds 2% of the taxpayer's adjusted gross income?
a. Interest expense
b. Medical expenses
c. Employee moving
d. Tax return preparation fees (5/91, PII, #32, 9231)

104. Mr. and Mrs. Sloan paid the following expenses on December 15, 2002, when they adopted a child:

Child's medical expenses	$4,000
Legal expenses	8,500
Agency fee	2,000

What amount of the above expenses may the Sloans claim as an adoption credit on their 2002 joint income tax return?
a. $14,500
b. $12,500
c. $10,500
d. $10,000 (Editors, 4463)

105. An employee who has had social security tax withheld in an amount greater than the maximum for a particular year, may claim

a. Such excess as either a credit or an itemized deduction, at the election of the employee, if that excess resulted from correct withholding by two or more employers.

b. Reimbursement of such excess from his employers, if that excess resulted from correct withholding by two or more employers.

c. The excess as a credit against income tax, if that excess resulted from correct withholding by two or more employers.

d. The excess as a credit against income tax, if that excess was withheld by one employer.

(5/91, PII, #34, 1559)

OTHER OBJECTIVE FORMAT QUESTIONS

PROBLEM 27-3 (40 to 50 minutes)

Green is self-employed as a human resources consultant and reports on the cash basis for income tax purposes. Listed below are Green's business and nonbusiness transactions, as well as possible tax treatments. For each of Green's transactions (**Items 1 through 25**), select the appropriate tax treatment. A tax treatment may be selected once, more than once, or not at all.

TRANSACTIONS

1. Retainer fees received from clients.

2. Oil royalties received.

3. Interest income on general obligation state and local government bonds.

4. Interest on refund of federal taxes.

5. Death benefits from term life insurance policy on parent.

6. Interest income on U.S. Treasury bonds.

7. Share of ordinary income from an investment in a limited partnership reported in Form 1065, Schedule K-1.

8. Taxable income from rental of a townhouse owned by Green.

9. Prize won as a contestant on a TV quiz show.

10. Payment received for jury service.

11. Dividends received from mutual funds that invest in tax-free government obligations.

12. Qualifying medical expenses not reimbursed by insurance.

13. Personal life insurance premiums paid by Green.

14. Expenses for business-related meals where clients were present.

15. Depreciation on personal computer used for business.

16. Business lodging expenses, while out of town.

17. Subscriptions to professional journals used for business.

18. Self-employment taxes paid.

19. Qualifying contributions to a simplified employee pension plan.

20. Election to expense business equipment purchased in the current year.

21. Qualifying alimony payments made by Green.

22. Subscriptions for investment-related publications.

23. Interest expense on a home-equity line of credit for an amount borrowed to finance Green's business.

24. Interest expense on a loan for an auto used 75% for business.

25. Loss on sale of residence.

TAX TREATMENTS

A. Taxable as other income on Form 1040.

B. Reported in Schedule B—Interest and Dividend Income.

C. Reported in Schedule C as trade or business income.

D. Reported in Schedule E—Supplemental Income and Loss.

E. Not taxable.

F. Fully deductible on Form 1040 to arrive at adjusted gross income.

G. Fifty percent deductible on Form 1040 to arrive at adjusted gross income.

H. Reported in Schedule A—Itemized Deductions (deductibility subject to threshold of 7.5% of adjusted gross income).

I. Reported in Schedule A—Itemized Deductions (deductibility subject to threshold of 2% of adjusted gross income).

J. Reported in Form 4562—Depreciation and Amortization and deductible in Schedule A—Itemized Deductions (deductibility subject to threshold of 2% of adjusted gross income).

K. Reported in Form 4562—Depreciation and Amortization, and deductible in Schedule C—Profit or Loss from Business.

L. Fully deductible in Schedule C—Profit or Loss from Business.

M. Partially deductible in Schedule C—Profit or Loss from Business.

N. Reported in Form 2119—Sale of Your Home, and deductible in Schedule D—Capital Gains and Losses.

O. Not deductible.
[5/93, PII, #4(61-85), amended, 4166-4188]

PROBLEM 27-4 (25 to 30 minutes)

Select the **best** answer for each item.

a. The Internal Revenue Service is auditing Oate's 20X1 Form 1040—Individual Income Tax Return. Oate, an unmarried custodial parent, had one dependent three-year-old child and worked in a CPA firm. For 20X1, Oate, who had adjusted gross income of $40,000, qualified to itemize deductions and was subject to federal income tax liability.

REQUIRED:

FOR ITEMS 1 THROUGH 9, select from the accompanying list of tax treatments the appropriate tax treatment. A tax treatment may be selected once, more than once, or not at all.

Tax Treatments
A. Not deductible on Form 1040.
B. Deductible in full on Schedule A—Itemized Deductions.
C. Deductible in Schedule A—Itemized Deductions subject to a limitation of 50% of adjusted gross income.
D. Deductible in Schedule A—Itemized Deductions as miscellaneous deduction subject to a threshold of 2% of adjusted gross income.
E. Deductible in Schedule A—Itemized Deductions as miscellaneous deduction **not** subject to a threshold of 2% of adjusted gross income.
F. Deductible on Schedule E—Supplemental Income and Loss.
G. A credit is allowable.

1. Oate paid $900 toward continuing education courses and was not reimbursed by her employer.

2. Oate had a $30,000 cash charitable contribution carryover from her 20X0 cash donation to the American Red Cross. Oate made no additional charitable contributions during 20X1.

3. Oate had investment interest expense that did not exceed her net investment income.

4. Oate's lottery ticket losses were $450. She had no gambling winnings.

5. Oate paid $2,500 in real property taxes on her vacation home, which she used exclusively for personal use.

6. Oate paid a $500 premium for a homeowner's insurance policy on her principal residence.

7. Oate paid $1,500 to an unrelated baby-sitter to care for her child while she worked.

8. Oate paid $4,000 interest on the $60,000 acquisition mortgage of her principal residence. The mortgage is secured by Oate's home.

9. Oate paid $3,600 real property taxes on residential rental property in which she actively participates. There was no personal use of the rental property.

b. Frank and Dale Cumack are married and filing a joint 2002 income tax return. During 2002, Frank, 65, was retired from government service and Dale, 55, was employed as a university instructor. In 2002, the Cumacks contributed all of the support to Dale's father, Jacques, an unmarried French citizen and French resident who had no gross income.

REQUIRED:

FOR ITEMS 10 THROUGH 19, select the correct amount of income, loss, or adjustment to income that should be recognized on page 1 of the Cumack's 2002 Form 1040—Individual Income Tax Return to arrive at the adjusted gross income for each separate transaction. A response may be selected once, more than once, or not at all. Any information contained in an item is unique to that item and is not to be incorporated in your calculations when answering other items.

Amounts			
A.	$0	H.	$ 9,000
B.	$1,000	I.	$ 10,000
C.	$2,000	J.	$ 25,000
D.	$2,500	K.	$ 30,000
E.	$3,000	L.	$125,000
F.	$4,000	M.	$150,000
G.	$5,000		

10. Dale received a $30,000 cash gift from her aunt.

11. Dale contributed $3,000 to her Individual Retirement Account (IRA) on January 15, 2003. In 2002, she earned $60,000 as a university instructor. During 2002, the Cumacks were not active participants in an employer's qualified pension or annuity plan.

12. The Cumacks received a $1,000 federal income tax refund.

13. During 2002, Frank, a 50% partner in Diske General Partnership, received a $4,000 guaranteed payment from Diske for services that he rendered to the partnership that year.

14. Frank received $10,000 as beneficiary of his deceased brother's life insurance policy.

15. Dale's employer pays 100% of the cost of all employees' group term life insurance under a qualified plan. Policy cost is $5 per $1,000 of coverage. Dale's group term life insurance coverage equals $450,000.

16. Frank won $5,000 at a casino and had $2,000 in gambling losses.

17. The Cumacks received $1,000 interest income associated with a refund of their prior years' federal income tax.

18. The Cumacks sold their first and only residence for $200,000. They purchased their home five years ago for $50,000 and have lived there since then. There were no other capital gains, losses, or capital loss carryovers. The Cumacks do not intend to buy another residence.

19. Zeno Corp. declared a stock dividend and Dale received one additional share of Zeno common stock for three shares of Zeno common stock that she held. The stock that Dale received had a fair market value of $9,000. There were no provisions to receive cash instead of stock.

REQUIRED:

FOR ITEM 20, determine whether the Cumacks overstated (O), understated (U), or correctly determined (C) the number of both personal and dependency exemptions.

20. The Cumacks claimed 3 exemptions on their 2002 joint income tax return.
    (11/97, AR #2, amended, 6552-6571)

PROBLEM 27-5 (25 to 40 minutes)

Mrs. Vick, a 40-year-old cash basis taxpayer, earned $45,000 as a teacher and $5,000 as a part-time real estate agent in 20X1. Mr. Vick, who died on July 1, 20X1, had been permanently disabled on his job and collected state disability benefits until his death. For all of 20X1 and 20X2, the Vick's residence was the principal home of both their 11-year-old daughter, Joan, and Mrs. Vick's unmarried cousin, Fran Phillips, who had no income in either year. During 20X1, Joan received $200 a month in survivor social security benefits that began on August 1, and will continue at least until her 18th birthday. In 20X1 and 20X2, Mrs. Vick provided over one-half the support for Joan and Fran, both of whom were U.S. citizens. Mrs. Vick did not remarry. Mr. and Mrs. Vick received the following in 20X1:

Earned income	$50,000
State disability benefits	1,500
Interest on:	
Refund from amended tax return	50
Savings account and certificates of deposit	350
Municipal bonds	100
Gift	3,000
Pension benefits	900
Jury duty pay	200
Gambling winnings	450
Life insurance proceeds	5,000

- Mrs. Vick received the $3,000 cash gift from her uncle.
- Mrs. Vick received the pension distributions from a qualified pension plan, paid for exclusively by her husband's employer.
- Mrs. Vick had $100 in gambling losses.
- Mrs. Vick was the beneficiary of the life insurance policy on her husband's life. She received a lump-sum distribution. The Vicks had paid $500 in premiums.
- Mrs. Vick received Mr. Vick's accrued vacation pay of $500 in 20X2.

FOR ITEMS 1 AND 2, determine and select from the choices below, BOTH the filing status and the number of exemptions for each items.

Filing Status

S Single
M Married filing joint
H Head of household
Q Qualifying widow with dependent child

1. Determine the filing status and the number of exemptions that Mrs. Vick can claim on the 20X1 federal income tax return, to get the most favorable tax results.

2. Determine the filing status and the number of exemptions that Mrs. Vick can claim on the 20X2 federal income tax return to get the most favorable tax results, if she solely maintains the costs of her home.

FOR ITEMS 3 THROUGH 9, determine the amount, if any, that is taxable and should be included in Adjusted Gross Income (AGI) on the 20X1 federal income tax return filed by Mrs. Vick.

3. State disability benefits
4. Interest income
5. Pension benefits
6. Gift
7. Life insurance proceeds

8. Jury duty pay
9. Gambling winnings

During 20X1, the following payments were made or losses were incurred. FOR ITEMS 10 THROUGH 23, select the appropriate tax treatment. A tax treatment may be selected once, more than once, or not at all.

Tax Treatment

A. Not deductible.

B. Deductible in Schedule A—Itemized Deductions, subject to threshold of 7.5% of adjusted gross income.

C. Deductible in Schedule A—Itemized Deductions, subject to threshold of 2% of adjusted gross income.

D. Deductible on page 1 of Form 1040 to arrive at adjusted gross income.

E. Deductible in full in Schedule A—Itemized Deductions.

F. Deductible in Schedule A—Itemized Deductions, subject to threshold of 50% of adjusted gross income.

Payments and Losses

10. Premiums on Mr. Vick's personal life insurance policy.

11. Penalty on Mrs. Vick's early withdrawal of funds from a certificate of deposit.

12. Mrs. Vick's substantiated cash donation to the American Red Cross.

13. Payment of estimated state income taxes.

14. Payment of real estate taxes on the Vick home.

15. Loss on the sale of the family car.

16. Cost in excess of the increase in value of residence, for the installation of a stairlift in January, related directly to the medical care of Mr. Vick.

17. The Vicks' health insurance premiums for hospitalization coverage through Mrs. Vick's employer.

18. CPA fees to prepare the tax return for the previous year.

19. Amortization over the life of the loan of points paid to refinance the mortgage at a lower rate on the Vick home.

20. One-half the self-employment tax paid by Mrs. Vick.

21. Mrs. Vick's $100 in gambling losses.

22. Mrs. Vick's union dues.

23. 20X0 federal income tax paid with the Vick's tax return on April 15, 20X1.

FOR ITEMS 24 THROUGH 31, determine whether the statement is true (T) or false (F) regarding the Vicks' 20X1 income tax return.

24. The funeral expenses paid by Mr. Vick's estate is a 20X1 itemized deduction.

25. Any federal estate tax on the income in respect of decedent, to be distributed to Mrs. Vick, may be taken as a miscellaneous itemized deduction not subject to the 2% of adjusted gross income floor.

26. A casualty loss deduction on property used in Mrs. Vick's part-time real estate business is reported as an itemized deduction.

27. The Vicks' income tax liability will be reduced by the credit for the elderly or disabled.

28. The CPA preparer is required to furnish a completed copy of the income tax return to Mrs. Vick.

29. Since Mr. Vick died during the year, the income limitation for the earned income credit does not apply.

30. Mr. Vick's accrued vacation pay, at the time of his death, is to be distributed to Mrs. Vick in 20X2. This income should be included in the 20X1 Federal income tax return.

31. The Vicks paid alternative minimum tax in 20X0. The amount of alternative minimum tax that is attributable to "deferral adjustments and preferences" can be used to offset the alternative minimum tax in following years.

(11/94, AR, #78-99, amended, 5045-5073)

PROBLEM 27-6 (25 to 40 minutes)

Tom and Joan Moore, both CPAs, filed a joint 20X2 federal income tax return showing $70,000 in taxable income. Tom's daughter Laura, age 17, resided with Tom's former spouse. Laura had no income of her own and was not Tom's dependent. The Moores' total medical expenses were less than 7.5% of adjusted gross income.

FOR ITEMS 1 THROUGH 10 determine the amount of income or loss, if any, that should be included on page one of the Moores' Form 1040.

1. The Moores had no capital loss carryovers from prior years. The Moores had the following stock transactions which resulted in a net capital loss:

	Date acquired	Date sold	Sales price	Cost
Revco	2-1-X1	3-17-X2	$15,000	$25,000
Abbco	2-18-X2	4-1-X2	8,000	4,000

2. In 20X0, Joan received an acre of land as an inter vivos gift from her grandfather. At the time of the gift, the land had a fair market value of $50,000. The grandfather's adjusted basis was $60,000. Joan sold the land in 20X2 to an unrelated third party for $56,000.

3. The Moores received a $500 security deposit on their rental property in 20X2. They are required to return the amount to the tenant.

4. Tom's wages were $53,000. In addition, Tom's employer provided group-term life insurance on Tom's life in excess of $50,000. The value of such excess coverage was $2,000.

5. The Moores received a $2,500 federal tax refund and a $1,250 state tax refund for 20X1 overpayments. In 20X1, the Moores were not subject to the alternative minimum tax and were not entitled to any credit against income tax. The Moores' 20X1 adjusted gross income was $80,000 and itemized deductions were $1,450 in excess of the standard deduction. The state tax deduction for 20X1 was $2,000.

6. Joan received $1,300 in unemployment compensation benefits. Her employer made a $100 contribution to the unemployment insurance fund on her behalf.

7. The Moores received $8,400 in gross receipts from their rental property. The expenses for the residential rental property were:

Bank mortgage interest	$1,200
Real estate taxes	700
Insurance	500
MACRS depreciation	3,500

8. The Moores received a stock dividend from Ace Corp. They had the option to receive either cash or Ace stock with a fair market value of $900 as of the date of distribution. The par value of the stock was $500.

9. Joan received $3,500 as beneficiary of the death benefit provided by her brother's employer. Joan's brother did not have a non-forfeitable right to receive the money while living.

10. Tom received $10,000, consisting of $5,000 each of principal and interest, when he redeemed a Series EE savings bond in 20X2. The bond was issued in his name in 1990 and the proceeds were used to pay for Laura's college tuition. Tom had not elected to report the yearly increases in the value of the bond.

FOR ITEM 11, determine the amount of the adjustment, if any, to arrive at adjusted gross income.

11. As required by a 1990 divorce agreement, Tom paid an annual amount of $8,000 in alimony and $10,000 in child support during 20X2.

FOR ITEMS 12 TO 23, select the appropriate tax treatment. A tax treatment may be selected once, more than once, or not at all. During 20X2, the following events took place.

12. On March 23, Tom sold 50 shares of Zip stock at a $1,200 loss. He repurchased 50 shares of Zip on April 15.

13. Payment of a personal property tax based on the value of the Moores' car.

14. Used clothes were donated to church organizations.

15. Premiums were paid covering insurance against Tom's loss of earnings.

16. Tom paid for subscriptions to accounting journals.

17. Interest was paid on a $10,000 home-equity line of credit secured by the Moores' residence. The fair market value of the home exceeded the mortgage by $50,000. Tom used the proceeds to purchase a sailboat.

18. Amounts were paid in excess of insurance reimbursement for prescription drugs.

19. Funeral expenses were paid by the Moores for Joan's brother.

20. Theft loss was incurred on Joan's jewelry in excess of insurance reimbursement. There were no personal casualty gains.

21. Loss on the sale of the family's sailboat.

22. Interest was paid on the $300,000 acquisition mortgage on the Moores' home. The mortgage is secured by their home.

23. Joan performed free accounting services for the Red Cross. The estimated value of the services was $500.

	List of Sources
A.	Not deductible on Form 1040
B.	Deductible in full in Schedule A—Itemized Deductions.
C.	Deductible in Schedule A—Itemized Deductions, subject to a threshold of 7.5% of adjusted gross income.
D.	Deductible in Schedule A—Itemized Deductions, subject to a limitation of 50% of adjusted gross income.
E.	Deductible in Schedule A—Itemized Deductions, subject to a $100 floor and a threshold of 10% of adjusted gross income.
F.	Deductible in Schedule A—Itemized Deductions, subject to a threshold of 2% of adjusted gross income.

FOR ITEMS 24 TO 29, indicate if the statement is true (T) or false (F) regarding the Moores' tax return.

24. The Moores were subject to the phaseout of half their personal exemptions for regular tax because their adjusted gross income was $75,000.

25. The Moores' unreimbursed medical expenses for AMT had to exceed 10% of adjusted gross income.

26. The Moores' personal exemption amount for regular tax was not permitted for determining AMT.

27. The Moores paid $1,200 in additional taxes when they filed their return on April 14, 20X3. Their 20X2 federal tax withholdings equaled 100% of 20X1 tax liability. Therefore, they were not subject to the underpayment of tax penalty.

28. The Moores, both being under age 50, were subject to an early withdrawal penalty on their IRA withdrawals used for medical expenses.

29. The Moores were allowed an earned income credit against their tax liability equal to a percentage of their wages.
[11/95, AR, #3 (82-104), amended, 5825-5853]

SOLUTION 27-1 MULTIPLE CHOICE ANSWERS

FILING STATUS

1. (d) A joint return may be filed when one or both spouses died during the tax year. A joint return may not be filed with the deceased spouse if the surviving spouse remarries before the end of the year in which the deceased spouse died.

2. (c) The cost of maintaining the household must be an actual cash expenditure. Therefore, the cost of food is included, but the value of the services rendered is not included for purposes of determining whether the taxpayer has contributed more than one-half of the cost of maintaining the household.

3. (c) Because Sam did not remarry, he was able to file a joint return in the year his wife died, and maintained a home during the year for his dependent child, he meets the definition of a qualifying widower under §2(a). This status allows Sam to use the married filing joint tax rates for two years after the year of death.

4. (d) Section 2(a)(1) defines a surviving spouse as a taxpayer whose spouse died during either of the two preceding tax years and who maintains as his or her home a household which is the principal place of abode for the taxable year of a dependent son, stepson, daughter, or stepdaughter. A taxpayer is deemed to maintain the household if over half the cost of maintaining the household is furnished by the taxpayer. Not all dependents will qualify the taxpayer as a qualifying widow(er). The dependent must be a child or stepchild. In addition, except for allowable temporary absences, the child or stepchild must live with the taxpayer for the entire taxable year, not just for six months. In this case, if the cost of maintaining the household is the same for each month, the taxpayer would have provided exactly half the cost of maintaining the household. Section 2(a)(1) requires that the taxpayer provide over half the cost of maintaining the household. Therefore, neither statement is a requirement for the taxpayer to qualify as a qualifying widow(er).

5. (b) The same accounting method does not have to be used by both husband and wife. For example, if the husband regularly uses the accrual method, and the wife the cash basis, each one computes his or her own income according to the appropriate accounting method, and the amounts so determined are aggregated for the purposes of the joint return. In order to file a joint return, the taxable years of both spouses must begin and end on the same day. As indicated in §6013(g), one spouse may be a nonresident alien, but *both* must make the election which subjects their worldwide income to U.S. taxation. Only married couples may file joint returns, and marital status is determined as of the last day of the taxable year.

6. (d) Section 151(b) provides that a taxpayer may claim an exemption for a spouse if no joint return is filed and the spouse has no gross income and is not a dependent of another taxpayer.

EXEMPTIONS

7. (c) Smith is entitled to claim an exemption deduction for himself under §151. Section 151(c)(1) allows an exemption deduction for each dependent. Smith is entitled to an exemption for his widowed mother, Ruth. Although §151(c)(1) states that the dependent must have gross income that is less than the personal exemption amount, Ruth's social security benefits are excluded from her gross income under §86 because of her income level. Ruth meets the tests for a dependent of §152(a) because she is his mother and Smith provided over half of her support. There is no requirement that a relative live with the taxpayer to qualify as a dependent. Section 151(c)(2) disallows a dependency exemption for a married person who would otherwise qualify as a dependent if such person files a joint return. There is an exception if neither spouse is required to file a return, there would be no gross tax liability if the couple filed separate returns, and the joint return is filed solely to receive a refund.

8. (a) No personal exemption is allowed on the return of an individual who is claimed as a dependent on another taxpayer's return.

9. (b) Jim and Kay may each claim an exemption for themselves under §151(a). Dale fails the gross income test of §151(c)(1)(A) because his gross income is greater than the personal exemption amount. However, he meets the exception under §151(c)(1)(B) because he is a full-time student under the age of 24. No exemption is allowed on Jim and Kay's joint return for Kim. Kim fails the gross income test of §151(c)(1)(A) and does not meet an exception to it provided by §151(c)(1)(B). She is not a full-time student and she is not under age 19. Neither is an exemption allowed for Grant because he fails the gross income test of §151(c)(1)(A). There is no exception from the gross income test for the taxpayer's parent. Thus, Jim and Kay may claim three exemptions on their joint return.

10. (b) In order to qualify as a dependent, an individual must pass five tests. The first four, gross income, support, joint return, and citizenship or residence tests are passed by all of the relatives. However, the fifth test an individual must pass is the relationship test or the member of household test. Since none of the relatives qualified as a member of Alan's household, only the ones which pass the relationship test may be claimed as a dependent. Per §152, the following pass the relationship test: child or dependent of child; stepchild; brother or sister (including half-blood); stepbrother or stepsister; father, mother, or ancestor of either; stepfather or stepmother; nephew or niece; uncle or aunt; and brother-, sister-, father-, mother-, son-, or daughter-in-law.

11. (c) Alan fails the relationship or member of household test. Chris provides less than 10% of Sarah's support. Barbara passes both the relationship and the 10% test. In order for her to claim the exemption, Alan would have to sign the multiple support agreement.

FILING REQUIREMENTS

12. (a) The general rule is that all income taxes must be assessed within three years after the later of the due date or the filing date of the original return. However, if income is understated by more than 25% of the amount stated on the return, then there is a 6-year statute of limitations period. The Burgs omitted $45,000 which is equal to 37.5% of the gross income stated on their return. Therefore, the statute of limitations expires on April 15, 20X7.

13. (b) The tax liability at the due date is the tax on the return less tax payments withheld ($50,000 – $45,000), $5,000. This is the unpaid tax liability on which the penalties for late filing & late payment would be computed.

14. (c) Form 1040X is an amended income tax return for individuals. Form 1139 is a claim for tentative refund of a corporation's income taxes for, among other things, a carryback of net operating losses. Form 1045 is a tentative claim for refund for an individual's income taxes for, among other things, a carryback of net operating losses. Form 843 is a claim for refund that is used for other types of taxes.

15. (c) Section 6072(a) requires that the individual who uses a calendar year file his federal income tax return by April 15 of the following year unless the taxpayer receives an extension under §6081(a). Section 6501(a) provides that in general no assessment of additional taxes may be made after 3 years from the time the tax return was filed. However, §6501(b)(1) provides that a return that is filed early will be deemed to have been filed on its due date. Thus, the return filed on March 20, 20X2, is deemed to have been filed on April 15, 20X2, for purposes of §6501. Section 6501(a) then gives the IRS until April 15, 20X5, to assess additional taxes and assert a notice of deficiency.

16. (a) In a case where the taxpayer had income tax withheld, but did not file a return due to insufficient income, a claim for refund must be filed within *two years* from the date the income tax was *paid* [§6511(a)].

REALIZATION & RECOGNITION

17. (d) Section 451(a) provides that any amount of income is to be included in the taxpayer's gross income for the taxable year in which such amount is received by the taxpayer, unless the taxpayer's method of accounting requires the amount to be included in gross income for a different year. Regulation §1.451-2(a) provides that income, although actually received, is constructively received by a taxpayer when the income is made available to him or her and is not subject to any substantial restrictions or limitations. Section 61(a) states that gross income includes all income from whatever source unless the item of income is excluded from gross income by other sections of the Internal Revenue Code or other applicable law. Regulation §1.61-1(a) states that income may be realized in any form including cash, services, or property.

18. (c) Perle must include $550 in taxable income. The $200 cash is included and the $350

fair market value of the bookcase must also be included [§61(a)(2)]. Regulation §1.61-2(d)(1) states "...if services are paid for in property, the fair market value of the property taken in payment must be included in income as compensation." Therefore, Perle must include the fair market value of what he received, not what he billed.

19. (d)   Generally, if a taxpayer carries merchandise inventories, the accrual method of accounting must be used. However, if a taxpayer has accounts receivable for services rendered, the taxpayer is not precluded from using the cash method.

EXCLUSIONS FROM GROSS INCOME

20. (b)   The term "dividend" means any distribution of property made by a corporation to its shareholders out of accumulated or current earnings and profits [§316(b)(1)]. This definition does *not* apply to the term "dividend" as used in reference to dividends of insurance companies paid to policyholders as such [§316(b)(1)].

21. (c)   Section 86(a) provides that the amount of social security benefits included in gross income is the lesser of one-half of the social security benefits or one-half of the excess described in §86(b)(1). Section 86(b) provides that this amount is the amount by which the sum of modified adjusted gross income plus one-half of the social security benefits exceeds a base amount. The base amount depends upon filing status as described in §86(c). This is altered for taxpayers whose modified adjusted gross income plus one-half of the social security benefits is equal to $44,000 for married taxpayers filing jointly or $34,000 for all other taxpayers. In these situations, up to 85% of social security benefits are taxable. Thus, 85% of social security benefits received is the maximum amount that is includible in gross income.

22. (c)   Section 135 states that qualified higher education expenses include tuition and fees for the enrollment or attendance of the taxpayer, the taxpayer's spouse, or any dependent of the taxpayer at an eligible institution. Section 135 states that the higher education expenses are to be reduced by any qualified scholarship that is excluded from gross income under §117. Thus, both statements are true.

23. (b)   Section 117(a) excludes from gross income amounts received as qualified scholarships by individuals who are degree candidates at a qualified educational organization. Section 117(b) defines qualified scholarships as payments for tuition, fees, books, supplies, and equipment related to

the courses of instruction. The payments received for teaching are compensation for services. [**NOTE**: This question is unchanged from the Nov. 1997 exam. The examiners asked about tax year 1996, even though they specify that candidates should know the law in effect six months before the exam. In this case, the law is the same in 2001 and 2002 as in 1996.]

24. (d)   In order for a prize or award to be excludable from income, the recipients must (1) be selected without any action on their part; (2) not be required, as a condition of receipt, to render substantial future services; and (3) assign the award to a charitable or governmental organization. As the third condition is not met, the full $20,000 is includible in AGI.

25. (d)   Dividends are included in gross income and taxed as ordinary income to shareholders. Employer-provided health coverage, gifts, and inheritances are generally excluded from a taxpayer's gross income.

26. (d)   Section 104 provides for the exclusion from gross income of certain types of compensation received for injury or sickness. The types of compensation which are excluded include amounts received under workers' compensation acts as compensation for personal injury or sickness, and the amount of any damages received on account of personal injuries or sickness. Furthermore, §105(b) generally states "gross income does not include... (amounts that are received by an employee through accident or health insurance plans that are attributable to employer contributions which were not includible in the gross income of the employee)...if such amounts are paid, directly or indirectly, to the taxpayer to reimburse the taxpayer for expenses incurred by him for...medical care..." and for which no deduction was taken under §213. Therefore, none of the amounts received by Harold are includible in his gross income.

27. (b)   Section 79(a) provides that up to $50,000 of group-term life insurance provided by an employer is excludable from gross income for an employee. Any amounts expended by the employer for additional life insurance coverage will be included in the employee's gross income.

INCLUSIONS IN GROSS INCOME

28. (b)   All income is taxable unless specifically exempt. Compensation for injuries is exempt. U.S. Treasury bond interest and wage income are not exempt.

29. (c) To qualify as alimony, payments must be: made pursuant to a divorce or separate maintenance agreement, made in cash, not made to someone in the same household, stopped upon the death of the payee-spouse, and not designated as anything other than alimony.

30. (b) Section 71(a) states that gross income includes alimony and that alimony is any payment made in cash and required by the divorce decree. It also states that alimony does not include payments made to support minor children. Furthermore, if any amount specified in the divorce decree will be reduced on the happening of a contingency relating to a child such as attaining a specified age or at a time which can clearly be associated with such a contingency, then an amount equal to such reduction will be considered as payments made to support minor children. Thus, the $10,000 alimony must be reduced by the 20% by which it will be reduced on their child's 18th birthday, and the alimony is considered to be $8,000. Child support payments received are not included in the gross income of the recipient. Section 71 (b)(1)(A) states that payments made in cash to third parties on behalf of the payee spouse under the terms of the divorce or separation instrument can be alimony. The fact that $3,000 of the $10,000 payment is paid to Spring College on behalf of Mary does not disqualify the $3,000 payment as alimony. Total alimony payments = $3,000 tuition payment + $5,000 cash.

31. (a) Mock may deduct the cost of merchandise, but may not deduct other amounts paid or incurred as business expenses of her/his illegal drug sales.

32. (d) Self-employment income, under Reg. §1.1402(b)-1 includes both earnings as a self-employed consultant and as a director of a corporation.

33. (b) All interest income, unless specifically excluded by law, is includible in taxable income, regardless of the source. Interest is exempt on certain bonds of state governments, but this does not include interest earned on state income tax refunds. There is no provision for excluding interest income from most federal debt. Interest earned on dividends left on deposit with the V.A. is not included in taxable income (Rev. Rul. 91-14, 1991-1, C.B. 18).

34. (a) Recipients of state unemployment compensation benefits must include the entire amount of benefits received in gross income regardless of the level of adjusted gross income.

35. (d) Jane must include the entire state lottery winnings in gross income. If Jane is a non-professional gambler (that is, one who does not continuously and regularly engage in the trade or business of gambling to make a profit), she may take her gambling losses as an itemized deduction on Schedule A. As Jane decided to take the standard deduction, she cannot itemize the $300 of gambling losses.

36 (d) Net earnings (reported on Schedule C) include the gross business receipts less cost of goods sold, rent expense, and business liability insurance. Self-employment tax and health employment insurance premiums are adjustments to gross income, and are not involved in the calculation of net earnings.

37. (b) Interest expense is deductible in the period that it accrues, regardless of the taxpayer's basis of accounting.

38. (a) Section 166 provides a deduction for debts that become partially or wholly worthless. However, the amount of the deduction is limited to the taxpayer's adjusted basis in the debt as provided in §1011. Since the debt arose from services provided and Heron is cash basis taxpayer, his basis in the debt is zero and no part of it is deductible.

39. (c) A passive loss is any loss from activities involving the conduct of a trade or business in which the taxpayer does not materially participate. With respect to this partner, any loss generated from operations will be considered a passive loss since he is not a material participant. Passive loss is calculated as 5% (partnership percentage) x $100,000 = $5,000. This passive loss may generally be used only to offset income from passive activities.

40. (d) All income is taxable unless specifically exempt. There is no exemption for employee expense reimbursements under a non-accountable plan.

41. (a) The net business loss may only offset business income. Wages and rental income are considered business income. Interest income is deemed non-business income. $5,000 + $4,000 – $16,000 = $7,000

42. (c) The deductibility of a vacation home's expenses depends on the allocation of personal and rental use of the property. Depreciation may be allowed, but losses are not.

43. (d) Cancellation payments are rent to the landlord in the year received so Nare must include

the $30,000 received in cancellation of Mott's lease. Although Nare is an accrual basis taxpayer he must include $5,000 for the last month's rent when received rather than when earned under the claim of right doctrine. Nare also must include the $10,000 for November and December. Thus, Nare must include a total of $45,000 as rental income for the current year.

DEDUCTIONS FOR AGI

44. (c) Employees who remit jury duty pay to employers in exchange for their regular compensation during the jury service period may deduct the jury duty pay from gross income in arriving at AGI.

45. (c) Section 164 provides that one-half of the self-employment tax imposed for the year is deductible and provides that this deduction is to be attributed to a trade or business activity that does not consist of the performance of services as an employee. Section 62(a)(1) states that business expenses are deductible from gross income in arriving at AGI if the trade or business does not consist of the performance of services as an employee.

46. (a) Alimony paid is deductible in arriving at AGI under §62(a)(10). The other items are deductible **from** AGI as itemized deductions.

47. (b) Section 217 allows an adjustment for moving expenses, but imposes tests that must be met before any deduction for moving expenses is allowed. The taxpayer's new place of work must be more than 50 miles further from the former residence than was the former place of work. The taxpayer must be employed full time for 39 weeks of the 12-month period following the move. The move from New York to Florida meets the 50-mile test. The taxpayer was employed from February 2 to December 31, meeting the time test. Section 217(b)(1) defines moving expenses as the reasonable expenses of moving household goods and the expense of traveling, including lodging, to the new residence. Grey may not deduct the pre-move househunting costs. ($1,000 + $1,800).

48. (d) The forfeited interest penalty for premature withdrawal of time deposits is a deduction from gross income in arriving at AGI [§62(a)(9)].

49. (c) Generally, under §219, an employee and his or her non-working spouse may each contribute (and deduct) up to $3,000 of earnings to an IRA. If one spouse is covered by an employer pension plan, and their AGI is greater than $54,000 in 2002, the participating spouse's deduction is disallowed. Mike is covered by his employer's plan

and the AGI of Mike and Julia is $83,000, so Mike's contribution is not deductible. Because their AGI is less than $150,000, Julia's contribution is fully deductible. Contributions to an IRA may be made up to April 15 of the year after the taxable year. Thus, a contribution may be made in January of the next year.

50. (a) Compensation for purposes of a qualified retirement contribution includes alimony. Under §219(b), an individual may take a deduction for a qualified retirement contribution up to the lesser of $3,000 or the individual's compensation. Val and Pat would each be entitled to deduct $3,000. The amount deductible is disallowed when an employee is covered by an employer pension plan in 2002, when AGI before the IRA deduction is greater than $64,000. The phase-out of deductibility starts at $54,000 for 2002. The AGI for this purpose is $40,000 ($35,000 + $5,000), or below the limit. Thus, there is no reduction in the deduction for their contributions to their IRAs

51. (d) Section 401(c)(2)(A) defines earned income as the net earnings from self-employment after certain deductions allowed by §404. Section 404(a)(8) allows a deduction for the Keogh contribution and 50% of the self-employment tax.

DEDUCTIONS FROM AGI

52. (c) A taxpayer 65 years old (or older) or blind is entitled to a larger standard deduction amount. The support of a dependent is **not** an eligibility requirement for the increased standard deduction amount.

53. (c) Poole's deductible medical expenses must be reduced by a 7.5% of AGI floor. Thus, Poole's deductible medical expenses are $5,350 ($7,000 – $1,650). The deductible medical expenses exceed the standard deduction amount, so Poole itemizes.

AGI		$ 22,000.00
Less: Itemized deductions		
[$7,000 – ($22,000 X 0.075)]		(5,350.00)
Less: Personal exemption		(3,000.00)
Taxable income		$ 13,650.00
Tax rate		15%
Income tax		$ 2,047.50

54. (a) Section 213(a) authorizes a deduction for medical care expenses incurred on behalf of a dependent to the extent such expenses exceed 7.5% of AGI. Regulation §1.213-1(e)(1)(iii) provides that expenditures for the maintenance or operation of a capital asset are deductible medical expenses if such expenditures have medical care as their

primary purpose. Regulation §1.213-1(e)(1)(v)(a) provides that the cost of medical care includes the cost of special schooling for handicapped individuals. The individual's condition must be such that the resources of the school for alleviating the handicap are a principal reason that the person is enrolled in the special school. This regulation further provides that the cost of meals and lodging is deductible as a medical expense if the meals and lodging are necessary incidents to the medical care. Thus, the tuition, meals, and lodging at the special school qualify. The total amount that may be deducted as a medical expense before the 7.5% AGI floor is $8,600 ($600 + $8,000).

55. (b) Cosmetic surgery expenses are only deductible for deformity, congenital abnormality, personal injury trauma, or disfiguring disease. The medical expenses in this question are deductible to the extent they exceed 7.5% of Carroll's AGI (7.5% x $100,000). Total deductible medical expenses of $20,000, less $7,500, equal $12,500.

56. (d) The use of bank credit cards is deemed to be payment for purposes of timing the deductibility of charitable and medical expenses. Therefore, the $4,000 Scott charged on his credit card for his dependent son's medical expenses can be claimed by Scott as a medical expense in the year charged. Scott can also claim the $2,800 of medical expenses Scott paid in 20X1 on his 20X1 tax return because medical expenses are deductible in the year paid and the medical expenses were for his spouse at the time the expenses were incurred.

57. (c) Section 213 allows a deduction for medical care that is not compensated for by insurance or otherwise. Wells must reduce the $2,000 cost of physical therapy by the $1,500 insurance reimbursement. The remaining $500 is deductible. Wells may also deduct the $500 for an insurance policy that covers the cost of prescription drugs. Wells may not deduct the cost of the insurance policy that covers loss of earnings due to sickness or accident. Section 213 provides that the cost of insurance for medical care including transportation is deductible. Thus, Wells is entitled to a deduction for medical care before the 7.5% AGI floor of $1,000.

58. (c) Section 164 (a)(3) allows a deduction for state and local income taxes that are paid or accrued during the year. Section 275(a)(1) disallows any deduction for federal income taxes. Because Matthews is on the cash basis of accounting, she may deduct state and local income taxes in the year paid. The $1,500 in state and local income tax withheld is deemed paid when withheld by the employer. Matthews is also allowed to deduct the

$400 state estimated income taxes paid on December 30. To deduct this $400 payment, Matthews must have a good faith belief that this payment represents payment for taxes due and owing over and above the $1,500 withheld. The fact that Matthews owes an additional $300 in state and local income taxes for 20X1 is indicative of such a good faith belief. Because the additional $300 in state and local income taxes for tax year 20X1 were not paid until 20X2, Matthews may not deduct this $300 in 20X1. Taxes are deductible on Schedule A as an itemized deduction from adjusted gross income ($1,500 + $400 = $1,900).

59. (a) Section 461(f) provides that a deduction will be allowed in the year that money or other property is transferred to provide for satisfaction of an asserted liability that the taxpayer is contesting. Section 1.461-2(a)(3) provides that refunds of any portion of a contested liability for which a deduction has been allowed are included in gross income under the tax benefit rule of §111 and the regulations thereunder. Thus, Farb should deduct $8,000 in 20X1 under §164(a) and recognize $5,000 gross income in 20X2.

60. (c) Home mortgage interest is deductible as an itemized deduction. Personal utility and insurance expenses are not deductible.

61. (c) Section 163(d)(1) limits the deduction of an individual's investment interest to the individual's net investment income for the taxable year.

62. (b) Section 163 allows a deduction for all interest paid or accrued within the taxable year on indebtedness. However, §163 denies deductions for personal interest expense. Section 163 excludes any qualified residence interest from the term personal interest. Section 163 includes interest on home equity indebtedness with respect to any qualified residence as qualified residence interest. Section 163 defines home equity indebtedness as any indebtedness other than acquisition indebtedness secured by a qualified residence to the extent that the fair market value of such residence does not exceed the acquisition indebtedness. However, §163 limits the amount of home equity indebtedness to $100,000. Section 163 defines a qualified residence as the taxpayer's principal residence and one other residence that the taxpayer uses as a residence. Thus, the Browns meet the definition and limitations of §163 and are entitled to deduct the interest on this loan as qualified residence interest.

63. (c) Section 163 allows a deduction for all interest paid or accrued within the taxable year on indebtedness. However, the interest on the auto

loan is not deductible because no deduction is allowed for personal interest. An auto loan is not mentioned in the exceptions to personal interest listed in §163. However, §163 excludes any qualified residence interest from the term personal interest and includes interest on acquisition indebtedness as qualified residence interest. Section 163 states that acquisition indebtedness includes any indebtedness incurred in acquiring, constructing, or substantially improving any qualified residence of the taxpayer, and is secured by such residence. Section 163 limits the aggregate amount of acquisition indebtedness to $1,000,000. Section 163 defines a qualified residence as the taxpayer's principal residence and one other residence that the taxpayer uses as a residence. The mortgage interest and the interest on the room construction loan meet the definition and are within the limit to qualify as interest on acquisition indebtedness. Thus, the mortgage interest and the interest on the room construction loan are qualified residence interest.

64. (c) Section 170(a)(1) authorizes a deduction for charitable contributions that are paid during the taxable year. Section 170(f)(8) requires that contributions of $250 or more be substantiated by a contemporaneous receipt from the charitable organization. Moore's contributions are properly substantiated. Section 170(b)(1) limits an individual's deduction for charitable contributions to 50% of the taxpayer's contribution base and defines contribution base as AGI computed without regard to the deduction for net operating loss carrybacks. Section 170(d)(1)(A) provides that the charitable contributions in excess of 50% of the contribution base are to be carried over for 5 years, with contributions made for the current year deducted first. Moore deducts the $18,000 of charitable contributions made in the current year. Moore also deducts $7,000 of the charitable contribution carryover from the prior year for a total deduction of $25,000, which equals 50% of Moore's AGI for the current year. Moore has a charitable contribution carryover of $3,000 ($10,000 − $7,000) from the prior year to future years.

65. (b) Amounts actually paid to a qualified donee during the year are deductible subject to a percentage of AGI limitation. Qualified donees include domestic organizations and foundations operated exclusively for religious, charitable, scientific, literary, or educational purposes, but not individuals. The deduction of a charitable contribution of appreciated property depends on the status of the property. Capital gain property is an asset that would have realized a *long-term* capital gain if the taxpayer had sold the asset instead of donating it to charity on the date of the contribution.

66. (d) Section 165(a) allows a deduction for any loss that is not compensated for by insurance or from any other source. Although §165(c) places limitations on the deductibility of losses by individuals, §165(c)(3) allows deductions for an individual's casualty losses. Section 165(h)(1) reduces the casualty loss by $100 for each casualty. Section 165(h)(2)(A) then places a limit on the deductibility of casualty losses. If casualty losses exceed casualty gains, the excess is subject to a 10% of AGI floor. Section 165(b) limits the amount of the loss before insurance reimbursement to the adjusted basis of the property. Regulation §1.165-7(b)(1) provides that the amount of the casualty loss before insurance reimbursement for personal use property is the lesser of the property's adjusted basis or the decline in the fair market value (FMV) of the property because of the casualty. In this case, the decline in the property's FMV equals the property's adjusted basis. [**NOTE**: This question is unchanged from the Nov. 1997 exam. The examiners asked about tax year 1996, even though they specify that candidates should know the law in effect six months before the exam. In this case, the law is the same in 2002 and 2003 as in 1996.]

Adjusted basis or decline in FMV, the lesser	$ 150,000
Less: Insurance reimbursement	(130,000)
Casualty loss before the floors	$ 20,000
Less: $100 floor	(100)
Casualty loss before the 10% AGI floor	$ 19,900
10% AGI floor ($60,000 x 10%)	(6,000)
Deductible casualty loss	$ 13,900

67. (a) An individual may deduct a loss under §165(c) in the following circumstances: (1) the loss is incurred in a trade of business, (2) the loss is incurred in a transaction entered into for profit, or (3) the loss is caused by casualty or by theft. Thus, an individual's losses on transactions entered into for personal purposes are deductible only if the losses qualify as casualty or theft losses.

68. (a) Section 68(a) places an overall limitation on itemized deductions for taxpayers whose adjusted gross income exceed amounts stated in §68(b). However, §68(c)(1) states that the deduction allowed for medical expenses under §213 is not included in the term itemized deductions solely for purposes of the overall limitation on itemized deductions imposed by §68(a). Likewise, §68(c)(2) provides that the deduction for investment interest allowed by §163 is not subject to the overall limitation. Also, §68(c)(3) provides that the deduction for

casualty losses of individuals allowed under §165 is not subject to the overall limitation.

69. (b) Regulation §1.162-5(b)(2)(i) states that an individual's educational expenses that are required to meet the minimum educational requirements for qualification in his employment are not deductible. Thus, the education expense to meet the minimum entry level education requirements at an individual's place of employment is not deductible as any type of deduction. Section 67(b) defines miscellaneous itemized deductions as itemized deductions other than those listed therein. Tax return preparation fees, subscriptions to professional journals, and custodial fees for a brokerage account are not listed in §67(b). Thus, they are itemized deductions. The tax return preparation fees and the custodial fees for a brokerage account would be deductible under §212. The subscriptions to professional journals would be deductible under §162(a) as an itemized deduction if incurred by an employee under §62(a)(1).

70. (b) The cost of the seminar and daily living expenses are a direct result of education that maintains or improves skills connected to the current business. The primary purpose of the trip is not education-related (as evidenced by the percentage of time for the seminar), so the airfare is not an education expense.

AMT

71. (c) Section 56(b)(1)(A)(i) disallows any deduction for an individual's miscellaneous itemized deductions in computing alternative minimum taxable (AMT) income. Section 56(b)(1)(A)(ii) disallows any deduction for taxes described in §164(a). Section 164(a)(3) includes state and local income taxes. Hence, state and local income taxes are not deductible in arriving at AMT income. Section 56(b)(1)(C)(i) disallows the deduction for qualified residence interest in arriving at AMT income. Instead §56(e) allows a deduction for qualified housing interest which includes interest on acquisition indebtedness but not other home equity loans, unless the taxpayer used the loan proceeds to improve the residence. Thus, the home mortgage interest on a loan to acquire a residence is deductible in arriving at AMT income and accordingly does not have to be added back to taxable income. Section 55(b)(2) defines AMT income as the taxable income of the taxpayer, determined with regard to the adjustments required by §§56 and 58 and increased by the preferences described in §57. Taxable income, as defined in §63(a), is gross income minus deductions. Section 56(b)(1)(E) disallows the standard deduction and deduction for

personal exemptions in arriving at AMT income. Don Mills' AMT income before the AMT exemption is determined as follows:

Taxable income before personal exemption	$70,000
Add back: Miscellaneous itemized deductions	2,000
State and local income taxes	5,000
AMT income before the AMT exemption	$77,000

72. (b) Section 57(a)(5)(A) treats interest on specified private activity bonds as a tax preference for purposes of the alternative minimum tax. Section 57(a)(5)(C) defines these bonds as any private activity bonds issued after August 7, 1986, the interest on which is excluded from gross income under §103. Charitable contributions of capital gain property are not included in the list of tax preferences in §57.

73. (d) Section 53(a) allows a credit against the alternative minimum tax (AMT). Section 53(b) provides that the AMT credit for the taxable year is the excess, if any, of the adjusted minimum tax imposed for all prior taxable years after 1986 over the amount allowable as a credit for such prior taxable years. Thus, the AMT credit may be carried forward indefinitely.

TAX CREDITS

74. (d) The child care credit is available in full if the taxpayer's AGI is $10,000 or less. A reduced credit is still available if the taxpayer's AGI is greater than $10,000. Generally, *both* spouses must work in order to qualify for the credit. However, if one spouse does not work but is a full-time student, or is physically or mentally incapable of taking care of him or herself, the credit is still available.

75. (c) Section 26 limits the amount of any credits allowed in Subpart A of Part IV of Subchapter A of Chapter 1 to the excess of the taxpayer's regular tax liability over the tentative minimum tax. The child and dependent care credit is allowed by §21 (in Subpart A). The credit for the elderly and totally disabled is allowed by §22 (in Subpart A). Section 53(c) limits the amount of the credit for prior year minimum tax to the excess of the regular tax liability reduced by certain other credits over the tentative minimum tax for the year. The earned income credit (EIC) is allowed by §32 which is in Subpart C "Refundable Credits" of Part IV of Subchapter A of Chapter 1. Thus, the EIC is refundable and the other credits listed are not refundable.

76. (a) Section 38(b) provides that the general business credit is the sum of 11 credits listed therein. The enhanced oil recovery credit is one of the 11 credits so listed. Section 38(a) allows the general

business credit against the tax, including carrybacks and carryforwards of such credit. The foreign tax credit and the minimum tax credit are single credits.

77. (a) A taxpayer may take either a deduction or a tax credit for amounts paid for foreign income taxes. A separate calculation is involved for certain categories of income, such as passive income.

ESTIMATED TAX PAYMENTS

78. (c) Section 6662(a) imposes a 20% accuracy-related penalty for underpayment of tax for reasons specified in §6662. Section 6662(b) states that the penalty will apply to underpayment of tax for negligence or disregard of rules and regulations and for any substantial underpayment of income tax.

79. (a) Section 6654 allows an individual to avoid the penalty for underpayment of estimated tax by paying in 90% of the tax shown on the return in timely installments. In general, §6654 provides that an individual may avoid the penalty for underpayment of estimated tax by paying 100% of the tax shown on the return for the preceding tax year. However, if an individual's AGI exceeds $150,000, the individual may avoid the penalty for underpayment of estimated tax in 2002, by paying 112%, rather than 100%, of the tax shown on the return for the prior year. (This percentage is 110% thereafter.)

80. (a) The extension of the time to file does not include an extension of the time to pay. The full amount of liability is due on April 15. Taxpayers are permitted an underpayment of *estimated* taxes up to $1,000 without a penalty if taxes are paid on time.

SOLUTION 27-2 ADDITIONAL MULTIPLE CHOICE ANSWERS

EXCLUSIONS FROM GROSS INCOME

81. (a) Section 3105 indicates that Series EE savings bonds, bought after 1989, can be redeemed tax free if the proceeds of the bonds are used to pay tuition and fees for higher education for the taxpayer, his or her spouse or dependents. To qualify, the taxpayer must be the sole owner or, a joint owner with his or her spouse. There is no requirement that says a purchaser must be a parent. The bonds must be issued to an individual who is at least 24 years of age. There is no requirement that the bonds be transferred to, and redeemed by, the college.

82. (c) Section 117(a) excludes from gross income amounts received as qualified scholarships by individuals who are degree candidates at a qualified educational organization. Section 117(b) defines qualified scholarships as payments for tuition, fees, books, supplies, and equipment related to the courses of instruction. However, §117(c) states that the exclusion provided by §117(a) shall not apply to payments received for teaching, research, and other services as a condition for receiving the scholarship. In substance, these payments are compensation for services, rather than bona fide scholarships.

INCLUSIONS IN GROSS INCOME

83. (a) A transfer of property other than cash to a former spouse under a decree of divorce is not a taxable event. Cash payments are not taxable if under the decree the payor spouse is liable for payment after the death of the payee spouse.

Therefore, none of the transferred property or payments is taxable on Ann's return.

84. (c) The $1,000 interest on state government obligations is excluded from gross income under §103(a). The remaining items are included in gross income under §61(a)(4). Thus, the amount included in gross income is $1,900 ($500 + $600 + $800).

85. (a) Under §1402(a) net self-employment income includes the gross income from a trade or business less trade or business expenses allowable under §162. Estimated tax payments are treated as a prepayment of income taxes rather than as a deductible business expense. Charitable contributions are deductible as an itemized deduction on Schedule A rather than as a business expense on Schedule C. The other expenses are deductible as business expenses. The net self-employment income is determined as follows:

Gross business receipts	$20,000
Less: Air conditioning parts	$ (2,500)
Yellow Pages listing	(2,000)
Business long-distance telephone calls	(400)
Total business expenses	(4,900)
Net self-employment income	$15,100

86. (b) A taxpayer who receives property in exchange for his or her services must, under §83, report the fair market value of the property or services as income in the year the property is received, free of any restrictions. If services are rendered at a stipulated price, that price, in absence of contrary evidence, is presumed to be the fair market value of

the property. As Lee accepted property with a known fair market value of $8,000 in full payment of his legal services, he must report this amount as income on his tax return. There is contrary evidence ($8,000 known fair market value) that overrules the stipulated original price of $10,000. In other words, Lee's services must really be worth $8,000 as he accepted this amount in full satisfaction of his services. The client's basis in the property before the exchange will be used in computing gain on the client's return, not Lee's return. The cash method of accounting recognizes property, as well as cash, in the year it is received.

87. (b) If passive losses and credits cannot be used in the current year, they are carried forward indefinitely or until the property is disposed of under §469(b).

88. (a) Code §469(c)(2) defines a passive activity to include *any* rental activity. However, a taxpayer is allowed to deduct a certain amount of a rental property's losses if he materially participates in the rental activity. Interest and dividends are *never* treated as passive activity income. Passive activity credits *are* subject to the same rules as passive activity losses (i.e., the credits have to be used against tax that is attributable to passive activity income). The passive activity rules apply to *everyone*. (Code §469(c)(2) provides an exception for qualified real estate professionals.)

89. (c)

Rental payments received		$ 7,200
Real estate taxes paid ($6,400 / 2)	$3,200	
Payment for painting of rental apartment	800	
Fire insurance premium paid ($600 / 2)	300	
Depreciation ($5,000 / 2)	2,500	
Deductible expenses		(6,800)
Net rental income		$ 400

DEDUCTIONS FOR AGI

90. (d) Since neither Paul nor Sally was covered by an employer-sponsored pension plan, the Lees could take a total IRA deduction of $6,000, regardless of who had earned the income.

91. (d) Section 219 provides a qualifying individual with a deduction up to the lesser of $3,000, or an amount equal to the compensation includible in the individual's gross income for the taxable year. This deduction is not affected by Matilda's status as a divorcee, and she is thus entitled to a maximum deduction of $3,000. For purposes of determining an individual's maximum contribution to an IRA, alimony payments are considered "compensation."

92. (b) The $2,000 in unpaid medical expenses could be deducted from the gross estate in arriving at the taxable estate on the estate tax return as a claim against the estate under §2053. The executor may elect, under §642(g), to deduct certain expenses on the estate's income tax return, rather than taking them as a deduction on the estate tax return. However, Regulation §1.642(g)-2 states that medical expenses of the decedent that are paid by the estate of the decedent are not among those expenses. Section 213 and Regulation §1.213-1 provides that for purposes of §213, medical expenses paid by a decedent's estate within one year of the date of the decedent's death shall be treated as paid by the decedent at the time the medical services were rendered. Section 213 and Regulation §1.213-1 requires that the executor of the decedent's estate file a waiver of the right to claim the medical expenses as a deduction from the gross estate under §2053. The medical expenses may be deducted on Bell's final income tax return as an itemized deduction subject to the 7.5% AGI floor.

DEDUCTIONS FROM AGI

93. (c) Transportation expenses incurred for medical care are deductible as a medical expense subject to 7.5% of AGI. This includes transportation to and from a point of treatment, as well as for a parent accompanying a child who is receiving medical care. A person giving assistance to someone traveling to receive medical care is also allowed this deduction. The other answers are specifically included in the Code as being nondeductible medical expenses.

94. (a) The Revenue Reconciliation Act of 1991 denies a deduction for unnecessary cosmetic surgery. Any cosmetic surgery will be considered unnecessary unless the surgery or procedure is necessary to ameliorate (1) a deformity arising from, or directly related to, a congenital abnormality, (2) a personal injury resulting from accident or trauma, or (3) a disfiguring disease. In general, cosmetic surgery includes any procedure which is directed at improving the patient's appearance and does not meaningfully promote the proper function of the body or prevent or treat illness or disease. Both procedures mentioned in the problem are discretionary cosmetic surgery, so nothing may be deducted.

95. (d) To be deductible, real estate taxes must be paid by the person on whom the tax is imposed. Smith is not eligible to deduct the real estate taxes since he does not own the house. Had Smith owned the house, all the real estate taxes paid during that year would have been deductible

because cash basis taxpayers deduct real estate taxes when paid and not in the year assessed.

96. (d)   Section 164(a) states that a deduction will be allowed for the taxable year within which state income taxes are paid or accrued. The refund of tax is not included in income, nor does the refund reduce the current deduction for taxes, because William never claimed a deduction for the payment of the 20X1 tax (§111).

97. (d)   Home equity indebtedness is limited to $100,000 on a joint income tax return ($50,000 if MFS). Home equity indebtedness does *not* include acquisition indebtedness (i.e., indebtedness incurred in acquiring, constructing, or substantially improving a qualified residence of the taxpayer). Home equity indebtedness may **not** exceed the taxpayer's net equity in the qualified residence.

98. (d)   An employee's unreimbursed business car expenses are deductible as an itemized deduction from AGI. Section 67(a) states that miscellaneous itemized deductions are allowed only to the extent they exceed 2% of AGI. Section 67(b) states that miscellaneous itemized deductions are those itemized deductions not listed in §67(b). Unreimbursed employee business expenses are not listed in §67(b). Moving expenses allowed by §217 are deductible in arriving at AGI under §62(a)(15). One half of the self-employment tax is deductible in arriving at AGI under §62(a)(1). The self-employed health insurance deduction allowed by §162(1) is deductible in arriving at AGI under §62(a)(1).

99. (a)   Generally, the fair market value of appreciated property donated to a qualified charity may be deducted if it doesn't exceed 50% of the donor's AGI. $25,000 < 50% x $90,000

100. (c)   Generally, in-kind charitable contributions are limited to 30% of a taxpayer's adjusted gross income. $80,000 x 30% = $24,000

101. (c)   Spencer can deduct the cash contribution under §170. The used clothing is likewise deductible. Spencer can also deduct $400 for the purchase of the art object which is the difference between what he paid and the fair market value of the art object ($1,200 − $800 = $400).

102. (a)   Section 68(a) provides that the amount of itemized deductions otherwise allowable shall be reduced by the lesser of 3% of the excess of AGI over the applicable amount or 80% of the itemized deductions otherwise allowable. However, §68(c) states that certain itemized deductions are excluded from the definition of itemized deductions for purposes of §68. Thus, the itemized deductions are reduced by the lesser of 3% of the excess of AGI over the applicable amount or 80% of certain itemized deductions.

103. (d)   Tax return preparation fees are a second tier miscellaneous deduction. Interest expense is specifically exempted from the 2% of AGI floor. Medical expenses are subject to a 7.5% of AGI floor. Employee moving expenses are fully deductible *for* AGI.

TAX CREDITS

104. (d)   Generally, up to a $10,000 adoption credit is available to the extent of adoption expenses ($8,500 + $2,000 = $10,500). Section 213(a) authorizes an itemized deduction, not a credit, for a dependent's medical expenses.

105. (c)   Any employee who has worked for two or more employers in any one taxable year and has been subjected to excessive FICA withholding may correct the over withholding by taking the excess amount as a credit against his or her income tax on Form 1040.

PERFORMANCE BY SUBTOPICS

Each category below parallels a subtopic covered in Chapter 27. Record the number and percentage of questions you correctly answered in each subtopic area.

Filing Status

Question #	Correct √
1	
2	
3	
4	
5	
6	
# Questions	6

Correct _____
% Correct _____

Exemptions

Question #	Correct √
7	
8	
9	
10	
11	
# Questions	5

Correct _____
% Correct _____

Filing Requirements

Question #	Correct √
12	
13	
14	
15	
16	
# Questions	5

Correct _____
% Correct _____

Realization & Recognition

Question #	Correct √
17	
18	
19	
# Questions	3

Correct _____
% Correct _____

Exclusions From Gross Income

Question #	Correct √
20	
21	
22	
23	
24	
25	
26	
27	
# Questions	8

Correct _____
% Correct _____

Inclusions in Gross Income

Question #	Correct √
28	
29	
30	
31	
32	
33	
34	
35	
36	
37	
38	
39	
40	
41	
42	
43	
# Questions	16

Correct _____
% Correct _____

Deductions for AGI

Question #	Correct √
44	
45	
46	
47	
48	
49	
50	
51	
# Questions	8

Correct _____
% Correct _____

Deductions From AGI

Question #	Correct √
52	
53	
54	
55	
56	
57	
58	
59	
60	
61	
62	
63	
64	
65	
66	
67	
68	
69	
70	
# Questions	19

Correct _____
% Correct _____

AMT

Question #	Correct √
71	
72	
73	
# Questions	3

Correct _____
% Correct _____

Tax Credits

Question #	Correct √
74	
75	
76	
77	
# Questions	4

Correct _____
% Correct _____

Estimated Tax Payments

Question #	Correct √
78	
79	
80	
# Questions	3

Correct _____
% Correct _____

OTHER OBJECTIVE FORMAT SOLUTIONS

SOLUTION 27-3 TAX TREATMENT OF INDIVIDUAL ITEMS

1. C   Schedule C is used to report trade or business income and expenses. Retainer fees from clients are an example of trade or business income.

2. D   Schedule E is used to report income or loss from rental real estate, royalties, partnerships, S corporations, estates, and trusts.

3. E   Interest income on general obligation state and local government bonds is not taxable.

4. B   The interest income from a refund of federal taxes is an example of interest income which is taxable on Schedule B.

5. E   Death benefits from a life insurance policy are not taxable income.

6. B   Interest on U.S. Treasury bonds is taxable income and is reported on Schedule B.

7. D   Schedule E is used to report income or loss from rental real estate, royalties, partnerships, S corporations, estates, and trusts. Income from a limited partnership is an example of Schedule E partnership income.

8. D   Schedule E is used to report income or loss from rental real estate, royalties, partnerships, S corporations, estates, and trusts. Income from the rental of a townhouse is an example of taxable rental real estate income.

9. A   Prize money is an example of other income reported on Form 1040.

10. A   Payment received for jury service is taxable as other income on Form 1040.

11. E   Dividend income from mutual funds that invest in tax-free government obligations is not taxable.

12. H   Qualifying medical expenses are deductible on Schedule A subject to a 7.5% of AGI floor.

13. O   Life insurance premiums are not deductible.

14. M   50% of business meals are deductible as a business expense on Schedule C.

15. K   The computer is used for business so the depreciation expense is reported on Form 4562 and is deductible on Schedule C.

16. L   Business lodging expenses while out of town are fully deductible on Schedule C.

17. L   Subscriptions to professional journals used for business are fully deductible on Schedule C.

18. G   50% of the self-employment taxes paid by an individual are deducted on Form 1040 for AGI.

19. F   Qualifying contributions to a simplified employee pension plan are fully deductible on Form 1040 to arrive at AGI.

20. K   This election is made under §179. It is reported on Form 4562 and is deductible on Schedule C.

21. F   Qualifying alimony payments are deductible on Form 1040 to arrive at AGI.

22. I   Subscriptions for investment-related publications are reported on Schedule A and are deductible subject to a 2% of AGI floor.

23. L   The money was used to finance Green's business. Therefore, the interest expense is deductible on Schedule C.

24. M   The automobile is partially used for business. Therefore, the interest expense is partially deductible on Schedule C.

25. O   The loss on the sale of a residence is a nondeductible personal loss.

SOLUTION 27-4 DEDUCTIONS FROM AGI

1. D   Employees are allowed to treat unreimbursed education expenses as a miscellaneous itemized deduction subject to the 2% of AGI limitation. The education must be to maintain or improve a skill required in the individual's employment or meets the express requirements of the employer or laws or regulations.

2. C   Contributions made that exceed the 50% limit in one year may be carried forward for five years.

3. B   Investment interest is deductible to the extent of net investment income.

4.   A   Gambling losses are first tier miscellaneous deductions (not subject to the 2% of AGI limitation) that are limited to the extent of gambling winnings. As Oate had no gambling winnings, her losses are not deductible.

5.   B   Local, state, and foreign real property taxes are deductible by the cash-basis taxpayer upon whom they are imposed in the year in which they were paid.

6.   A   Premiums for property insurance are not deductible.

7.   G   A child care credit is available up to a maximum of $2,400 for one qualifying dependent, which includes a dependent under the age of 13 for whom an exemption can be claimed.

8.   B   Interest on up to $1,000,000 of debt incurred to buy, construct, or substantially improve a first or second home is deductible as qualified residential interest.

9.   F   The amount of rental income to be included in gross income is determined on Schedule E, *Supplemental Income and Loss*, by subtracting deductible expenses from rental payments received. Real property taxes are deductible expenses.

10.   A   Gifts are tax-exempt to the recipient.

11.   E   If neither married taxpayer is an active participant in an employer-sponsored plan, both are eligible to deduct the full amount of their IRA contributions, regardless of income levels. (The candidate must make the assumption that the 2003 $3,000 contribution is for 2002.)

12.   A   Only refunds for which a taxpayer received prior tax benefits are includible in income. There is no deduction from income on a federal return for federal income taxes paid.

13.   F   Payments made to a partner for services or for the use of capital (guaranteed payments) are treated as made to one who is not a partner. These payments are deductible by the partnership and are income to the recipient.

14.   A   Life insurance proceeds paid by reason of death of the insured are excluded from gross income. If the beneficiary elects to receive the benefits in installments, the interest portion is includible in income.

15.   C   Premiums paid by the employer for up to $50,000 worth of insurance coverage is excluded

from income. $5/$1,000 x ($450,000 - $50,000) = $2,000

16.   G   Gambling winnings must be included in income. Gambling losses may be deducted from income to the extent of gambling winnings only if the taxpayer itemizes deductions.

17.   B   All interest income is included in taxable income, unless there is a specific exclusion. There is no exclusion for interest income due to a federal income tax refund.

18.   A   A single taxpayer may exclude up to $250,000 (MFJ, $500,000) of gain from the sale of a principal residence after May 6, 1997, applied once every two years without regard to pre-May 7, 1997 sales. [The old provisions may be elected past May 6, 1997, in some circumstances. If a taxpayer over the age of 55 sold his or her principal residence before August 5, 1997, then that taxpayer could elect to exclude $125,000 of any gain realized on such sale, once in a lifetime. (The original answer to this question, when the year of the sale was 1996, was J.)]

Net sales price	$ 200,000
Over 55 exclusion amount	(125,000)
Net proceeds	75,000
Basis in home	(50,000)
Recognized gain under the former provisions	$ 25,000

19.   A   Stock dividends are generally tax-free to shareholders, unless a cash option is available.

20.   O   Jacques is not an eligible dependent. Dependents must be citizens or residents of the U.S., Canada, or Mexico.

SOLUTION 27-5   TAX TREATMENT OF INDIVIDUAL ITEMS

1.   M, 4

Section 6013(a)(3) allows a spouse to file a joint return in the year of the other spouse's death, provided that the decedent did not file his or her own return before death, no executor or administrator has been appointed, and no executor or administrator is appointed before the due date of the return. If an executor or administrator is appointed after the joint return is filed, the executor or administrator may disaffirm the joint return until one year from its due date. Thus, Mrs. Vick is entitled to one personal exemption for herself and one personal exemption for the late Mr. Vick. Mrs. Vick may claim one dependency exemption each for her daughter, Joan, and for her unmarried cousin, Fran Phillips. Although Fran is not considered a relative, Fran qualifies as a dependent because she lived with the Vicks for all of the taxable year. Both Joan and Fran meet the citizenship tests and received over half of their support from the Vicks, as required. Joan's social security benefits are likely to be fully excluded from her gross income. In any case, the taxpayer's child under the age of 19 is not subject to the gross income test. Fran meets the gross income test since her gross income of zero is less than the personal exemption amount.

2.   Q, 3

For the year after Mr. Vick's death, Mrs. Vick will file as a qualifying widow with dependent child. This filing status is known in the IRC as "surviving spouse." This filing status is available for the two tax years following a spouse's death if the surviving spouse does not remarry and maintains a household for a dependent child.   Mrs. Vick is entitled to one personal exemption for herself. Mrs. Vick may claim one dependency exemption each for her daughter, Joan, and for her unmarried cousin, Fran Phillips. See the answer to question #1, above, for an explanation of Joan's and Fran's eligibility as dependents.

3.   -0-

The disability benefits are fully excluded from gross income under §104(a)(1) and Reg. §1.104-1(b). The benefits are specifically job related, so they qualify for exclusion as workers' compensation.

4. $400

The interest from a refund from an amended tax return and interest on a savings account are included in gross income under §61(a)(4). The $100 interest on the municipal bonds is excluded from gross income under §103(a).

5. $900

Because the pension plan was a qualified plan and the contributions made entirely by Mr. Vick's employer, Mr. Vick had never included these amounts in gross income. Mrs. Vick must include all $900 in gross income as income in respect of a decedent.

6.   -0-

Gifts are excluded from gross income as long as the gift is not from the taxpayer's employer.

7.   -0-

The life insurance proceeds are excluded from gross income because they were paid to Mrs. Vick on account of the death of her insured husband.

8. $200

The jury duty pay is included in gross income. Gross income includes all income unless specifically excluded. If jury duty pay is paid to the taxpayer's employer because the employer compensated the employee during the period of jury service, the taxpayer is entitled to deduct such amount from gross income in arriving at AGI under §62(a)(13).

9. $450

The gambling winnings are included in gross income under §61(a) and Regulations §1.61-14(a).

10.   A   No deduction is allowed for personal expenses under §262(a). Premiums on personal life insurance premiums are considered a personal expense under Regulation §1.262-1(b)(1).

11.   D   Penalties on early withdrawal of a certificate of deposit are deductible for AGI.

12.   F   A cash donation to the American Red Cross is deductible under §170(a). Charitable contributions are an itemized deduction that are not subject to the 2% of AGI threshold.   Under §170(b)(1)(A), there is a 50% of AGI limit on the amount of charitable contributions that an individual may deduct in any one tax year. (Candidates must assume that the examiners meant response (F) to read "ceiling" instead of "threshold.")

13.   E   State income taxes are deductible as an itemized deduction not subject to the 2% of AGI threshold in the year paid or accrued, depending upon the taxpayer's accounting method.

14.   E   Real property taxes are deductible as an itemized deduction that is not subject to the 2% of AGI threshold in the year paid or accrued, depending upon the taxpayer's accounting method.

15.   A   The loss on the sale of the family car is a loss on the sale of a personal-use asset, and therefore is not deductible. Individuals may deduct losses from a trade or business, for a transaction entered into for the production of income, and casualty and theft losses.

16.   B   A capital expenditure that is directly related to the medical care of the taxpayer may be deducted to the extent that the expenditure exceeds the increase in the value of the residence. Medical expenses are an itemized deduction, deductible to the extent that they exceed 7.5% of AGI.

17.   B   Health insurance is included in the definition of medical expenses deductible as an

itemized deduction to the extent that they exceed 7.5% of AGI.

18. C   The CPA fees to prepare a tax return are deductible in the year paid, for a cash basis taxpayer. Tax preparation fees are not listed as a deduction in arriving at AGI unless they qualify as a trade or business expense or as a deduction attributable to rents or royalties; thus, these fees are an itemized deduction. These fees are subject to the threshold of 2% of AGI.

19. E   Points paid to refinance a mortgage on a home represent prepaid interest. Interest on a home is deductible and prepaid interest is deductible in the period to which it is allocable. Points paid to refinance the taxpayer's principal residence must be capitalized and amortized over the life of the loan. Interest is deductible as an itemized deduction that is not subject to the 2% of AGI threshold.

20. D   Half of the self-employment taxes paid are deductible from gross income in arriving at AGI.

21. E   Under §165(d), gambling losses are allowed only to the extent of gains from gambling. Since Mrs. Vick had at least $100 in gains from gambling, she may deduct the $100 in gambling losses in full. Allowable gambling losses are deductible as an itemized deduction not subject to the 2% of AGI threshold.

22. C   Union dues are an employee business expense deductible as an itemized deduction, subject to the 2% of AGI threshold.

23. A   Section 275(a) disallows any deduction for federal income taxes paid.

24. F   Funeral expenses are considered a personal expense. Generally, no deduction is allowed for personal expenses. Section 641(b) provides that the taxable income of an estate is to be determined in the same manner as that of an individual, with certain noted exceptions. Thus, the funeral expenses are not deductible on the estate's income tax return. Funeral expenses may be deducted only from the gross estate in determining the taxable estate for estate tax purposes.

25. T   Section 691(c) allows a deduction for the estate tax attributable to the income in respect of a decedent included in the recipient's gross income. Such estate tax is deductible as an itemized deduction, not subject to the 2% of AGI threshold.

26. F   The loss on property used in a real estate business is a business loss, not a casualty loss. Losses on the involuntary conversion of business property are deductible in arriving at AGI.

27. F   Section 22(a) allows the credit for the elderly and the permanently and totally disabled to be taken against the tax liability. The credit is determined by multiplying a flat 15% rate by the base for the credit. However, for a married couple filing a joint return in which neither spouse has attained age 65 by the close of the tax year, the base amount is limited to the sum of the spouses' disability income. Assuming the Vicks have not attained age 65, the base amount for the credit is limited to the $1,500 in state disability benefits. There is a phaseout of this base amount for taxpayers with AGI over a specified amount, based upon filing status. Under this phaseout, the base amount is reduced by one half of the excess of AGI over the specified amount. For a married couple filing a joint return, the specified amount is $10,000. The Vicks would lose all of the credit if their AGI is $13,000 or greater: ($13,000 – $10,000) × 50% = $1,500. Clearly, the Vicks have AGI much higher than $13,000.

28. T   Section 6695(a) requires an income tax return preparer to furnish a copy of the return to the taxpayer. The $50 penalty may be waived if the preparer can prove that the failure was due to reasonable cause and not willful neglect.

29. F   The earned income credit is allowed under the provisions of §32. There is no provision under this section that makes the income limitation for the earned income credit inapplicable for the year in which the taxpayer died. The only provision concerning death in §32 is §32(e), which provides that the taxable year must be a full taxable year except in the case of the death of the taxpayer.

30. F   The accrued vacation pay at the time of Mr. Vick's death represents income in respect of a decedent to Mrs. Vick. Income in respect of a decedent is included in the gross income of the recipient in the taxable year when received. Mrs. Vick would report the accrued vacation pay when received.

31. F   Per §53 (a) and (c), the credit can only be used against the "regular" tax in future years, not the alternative minimum tax.

SOLUTION 27-6   TAX TREATMENT OF INDIVIDUAL ITEMS

1.   ($3,000)

Under §1222(4) the Moores realized a long term capital loss of $10,000 ($15,000 – $25,000) on the sale of Revco. Under §1222(1) the Moores realized a short term capital gain of $4,000 ($8,000 – $4,000) on the sale of Abbco. The Moores have a net capital loss of $6,000 ($4,000 – $10,000) under §1222(10). Section 165(f) and §1211(b)(1) limit the amount of a net capital loss that may be deducted by taxpayers other than corporations to $3,000 a year. Thus, the Moores would show a loss of $3,000 on Form 1040 and have a $3,000 long term capital loss carryforward under §1212(b)(1).

2. $0

Under §1015(a) Joan's basis for determining gain is $60,000. The donor's basis and Joan's basis, for determining loss, is $50,000, the fair market value of the property at the time of the gift. Under Regulation §1.1015-1(a)(2), if the donee sells the property for an amount in between the basis for loss and the basis for gain, there is no gain or loss. Since Joan sold the property for $56,000, she realizes no gain or loss.

3. $0

The security deposit represents a liability, not income, because the Moores must refund the deposit to the tenant when the tenant moves.

4. $55,000

The $53,000 in wages is included in gross income under §61(a)(1). The $2,000 value of the group term life insurance in excess of $50,000 is included in gross income under §79(a).

5. $1,250

The $1,250 state income tax refund is included in gross income under the tax benefit rule of §111(a). The amount included is the lesser of the $1,250 refund received or the $1,450 amount by which their itemized deductions exceeded the standard deduction in the previous tax year. The $1,250 is listed on a separate line on Form 1040, page 1.

6. $1,300

Section 85(a) provides that unemployment compensation is included in gross income. This amount is shown on a separate line on page 1 of Form 1040. The employer's payment to an unemployment insurance fund is not unemployment compensation.

7. $2,500

The $8,400 in rental receipts is included in gross income under §61(a)(5). Expenses of rental income are deductible under §162(a) as business expenses or under §212 as expenses for the production of income depending on whether the rental activity is considered a business. Sec. 62(a) defines AGI as gross income less certain specified deductions, including those attributable to rents and royalties. Thus, expenses attributable to rental income are deductible from gross income in arriving at AGI. Rental income and expenses are reported on Schedule E and the $2,500 net rental income is transferred to Form 1040, page 1.

8. $900

Section 305(a) generally excludes the value of a distribution of stock with respect to stock in the same corporation. However, §305(b)(1) states that the exclusion will not apply to distributions made in lieu of money. Dividends are included in gross income under §61(a)(7). Section 301(b)(1) states that the amount of a dividend paid in property shall be the fair market value of the property. Thus, the Moores must include $900 in gross income. This amount will be reported on Schedule B and then transferred to Form 1040, page 1. They will also have a $900 basis in the shares received under §301(d).

9. $3,500

The §101(b) death benefit exclusion for amounts paid by an employer and received by beneficiaries or the employee's estate on account of the death of the employee is inapplicable to employees who died after August 20, 1996.

10. $5,000

Interest generally is included in gross income under §61(a)(4). Section 135(a) allows an exclusion from gross income for interest realized from a redemption of any qualified U.S. Savings Bond used to pay for a dependent's higher education tuition and fees. The Moores' AGI is below the phase-out threshold. Section 135(c)(1) states to be a qualified U.S. Savings Bond, the bond must have been issued after December 31, 1989. However, as Laura is not Tom's dependent, the interest is included in gross income.

11. $8,000

Section 215(a) allows a deduction for alimony. Section 215(b) provides that alimony means any alimony that is includible in the gross income of the recipient under §71. Section 71(a) includes alimony in the gross income of the recipient. However, §71(c)(1) excludes child support from being included in the gross income of the recipient. Temporary Regulation §1.71-1T(c) states clearly that child support is not included in the gross income of the payee and not deductible by the payor. Section 62(a) defines adjusted gross income as gross income less certain specified deductions. Alimony is listed in §62(a)(10). Thus, the $8,000 in alimony, but not the $10,000 in child support, is allowed as an adjustment to gross income in arriving at AGI.

12. A   Although Tom realized a $1,200 loss, §1091(a) disallows the recognition of any loss because he acquired the same shares within 30 days of the sale of the shares that resulted in a loss. This is referred to as a wash sale.

13. B   To be deductible, personal property taxes must be based on the value of the property (ad valorem taxes) under §164(b)(1). Section 164(a) allows a deduction for such personal property taxes. Section 62(a) defines AGI as gross income less certain specified deductions. Taxes are not listed therein. Thus, taxes are deductible as an itemized deduction. Section 67(a) allows a deduction for miscellaneous itemized deductions only to the extent that they exceed 2% of AGI. Section 67(b) defines miscellaneous itemized deductions as those itemized deductions other than those listed therein. Taxes are listed in §67(b)(2). Thus, taxes are fully deductible as an itemized deduction.

14. D   Section 170 allows a deduction for contributions to qualified charitable organizations. A church is a qualified charitable organization under §170. Regulation §1.170 provides that if a contribution is made in property other than money, the amount that may be deducted is limited to the property's fair market value. Section 62(a) defines adjusted gross income (AGI) as gross income less certain specified deductions. Charitable contributions are not listed therein. Thus, charitable contributions are deductible as an itemized deduction. Section 67(a) allows a deduction for miscellaneous itemized deductions only to the extent that they exceed 2% of AGI. Section 67(b) defines miscellaneous itemized deductions as those itemized deductions other than those listed therein. Charitable contributions are listed in Section 67(b)(4). However, §170(b)(1)(A) limits an individual's deduction for charitable contributions to 50% of AGI. Thus, the used clothes are a deductible charitable contribution as an itemized deduction up to 50% of AGI.

15. A   Premiums paid for disability income insurance are considered a personal expense. Section 262(a) disallows deductions for personal expenses unless expressly allowed. There is no provision allowing a deduction for disability income insurance premiums paid by an individual.

16. F   Since Tom is an accountant, the amount he paid for subscriptions to accounting journals qualifies as a deductible business expense under §162(a). Employee business expenses are deductible as a miscellaneous itemized deduction subject to the 2% of AGI threshold.

17. B   Section 163 allows a deduction for interest on home equity indebtedness with respect to any qualified residence of the taxpayer. Section 163 defines home equity indebtedness as any indebtedness secured by a qualified residence. The amount is limited to the extent that such indebtedness does not exceed the fair market value of such residence reduced by any acquisition indebtedness with respect to such residence. Section 163 limits the amount of qualifying home equity indebtedness to $100,000. Section 163 defines a qualified residence as the taxpayer's principal residence and one other residence selected and used by the taxpayer. The interest on this loan meets the requirements for deductibility. The interest is deductible in full as an itemized deduction on Schedule A.

18. C   Section 62(a) defines AGI as gross income less certain specified deductions. Medical expenses are not listed in §62(a). Thus, medical expenses are not deductible in arriving at AGI. Payments for prescription drugs are a medical expense under §213(b). Section 213(a) allows a deduction for medical expenses to the extent that such expenses exceed 7.5% of AGI. Thus, the medical expenses are allowed as an itemized deduction subject to a threshold of 7.5% of AGI.

19. A   Funeral expenses are considered a personal expense. Section 262(a) disallows deductions for personal expense unless expressly allowed. There is no provision allowing a deduction for funeral expenses for income tax purposes.

20. E   Section 165(c) allows an individual to deduct losses from casualty or theft. The loss is deductible as an itemized deduction because §165(h)(4)(A) allows a deduction for personal casualty losses to the extent of personal casualty gains in computing AGI. Section 165(h)(1) imposes a $100 floor on each casualty or theft. Additionally, Sec. 165(h)(2) imposes a 10% of AGI floor on all casualties and thefts combined.

21. A   Section 165(c) allows an individual to deduct losses only on business property, investment property, and losses on personal use property from casualty or theft.

22. B   Section 163 defines a qualified residence as the taxpayer's principal residence and one other residence selected and used by the taxpayer. Because the loan is under $1 million, was incurred in the acquisition of the Moores' home, and is secured by their home, the interest is deductible in full as an itemized deduction on Schedule A.

23. A   A taxpayer may deduct contributions of cash, property to a qualified charity and expenses incurred on behalf of a qualified charity. However, a taxpayer may not deduct the value of labor donated to a charity under Regulation §1.170-2(a)(2) and Regulation §1.170A-1(g).

24. F   The phaseout of personal exemptions for regular tax starts when adjusted gross income for a married couple filing jointly is $193,400 for 2000.

25. T   In the calculation of alternative minimum tax (AMT), adjustments are made for several items, including standard deductions, medical expenses, and post-1986 depreciation on tangible property. For AMT, unreimbursed medical expenses have to exceed 10% of AGI to be deductible.

26. T   The personal exemption amount for regular tax is not permitted for determining alternative minimum tax (AMT). AMT exemptions are different from the personal exemptions of regular tax calculations.

27. T   In order to avoid a penalty, taxpayers must pay the lesser of either 90% of the current year's tax, or 100% of the prior year's tax, unless AGI is more than $150,000. The Moores' AGI is less than $150,000 and they paid 100% of the prior year's tax.

28. T   Generally, withdrawals from IRA's before the owners meet the age requirements are subject to regular income tax plus an early withdrawal penalty of 10%, without regard for the use of the money. There is an exception when the life expectancy of the owner is short or the money is used to pay for medical expenses in excess of 7.5% of AGI, or for medical insurance while unemployed. The Moores do not appear to meet the exceptions.

29. F   Earned income credit is figured as a percentage of earned income up to a ceiling. For married taxpayers with one qualifying child, this amount was 34% of $6,920 for 2000. The credit was completely phased-out at $27,413 in 2000. The Moores' earned income is so far above these limits that the credit is eliminated entirely.

CHANGE ALERT

Job Creation & Worker Assistance Act of 2002 (JCWAA '02) JCWAA '02 includes business economic stimulus provisions, some general retroactively effective tax breaks, and some relief provisions only for lower-Manhattan entities affected by terrorist acts on September 11, 2001. JCWAA '02 became effective on March 9, 2002. The Bisk Education editors believe details on the provisions applicable only to lower-Manhattan are beyond the scope of the exam.

STUDY TIP: MEMORIZING TAX AMOUNTS

Many tax amounts are included in the tax chapters more to forestall candidate curiosity than to provide information necessary for the upcoming exams. These amounts, particularly the inflation-adjusted ones, have been lightly tested on past exams and will likely remain so in the future. For exam purposes, it is usually not important to know the exact amount of standard deductions and phase-out ranges, for example. The examiners are more interested in testing whether candidates know that these items exist and how to apply them.

If you question this, review the questions (which are from, or modeled after, previous exams) in these chapters, and you will perceive the relative absence of needing to know specific amounts to answer most questions.

Specific tax numbers candidates may want to commit to memory from the first two tax chapters are: the personal exemption amount, the residence gain exclusion amount, and the Section 179 amount. A feel for the approximate amounts of most other numbers is more than adequate for the exam.

CHAPTER 28

FEDERAL TAXATION: PROPERTY

EXAM COVERAGE: The individual and corporate taxation portions of the ARE section of the CPA exam are designated by the examiners to be 20 percent each of the ARE section's point value. Historically exam coverage of the topics in this chapter hovers at 3 to 7 percent of the ARE section. (Because this information is applicable to several types of taxpayers this distorts any estimation we try to make of how much the exam covers the information in this and other tax chapters.) Remember the **2002** amounts are tested on the **May 2003** exam. More information about point distribution and information eligible to be tested is included in the **Practical Advice** section of this volume.

CHAPTER 28

FEDERAL TAXATION: PROPERTY

I. BASIS

A. DEFINITION

A taxpayer's basis in property acquired in a taxable transaction is generally equal to the cost or the purchase price of the property. The cost is equal to the cash or fair market value of any property paid, plus any expenses associated with the purchase and any liabilities assumed in connection with the property.

EXAMPLE 1 ♦ BASIS

> Anna purchases an automobile for use in her business for $1,000 cash plus a promissory note of $4,000. Anna takes an initial cost basis in the automobile of $5,000.
>
> The basis is **not** altered as the debt is paid off, but is altered by depreciation charges over the asset's life.

1. Where property is acquired such that the property itself is an item of gross income (e.g., a salesman receives a new car as commission), the cost basis is the amount included in gross income—the fair market value of the property received.

2. If property is acquired and written off as a current expense in the year it is acquired, its cost basis equals zero.

B. ADJUSTED BASIS

The original cost basis of property is increased by any capital expenditures made to the property and decreased by any depreciation, amortization, or depletion deductions allowed or allowable.

EXAMPLE 2 ♦ ADJUSTED BASIS

> Gerald owns a piece of real estate. Gerald's basis is $1,000, the cash price he paid several years ago. The property is now worth $10,000. Gerald arranges for a bank to lend him $2,000, using the property as collateral. Gerald has no income, and his basis in the property **remains** $1,000. If Gerald uses that $2,000 to improve the land (e.g., by clearing it), then his basis is increased by $2,000. It is not the borrowing that increases basis; it is the expenditure of funds to improve the land.

C. PROPERTY ACQUIRED BY GIFT

If the property is acquired by gift, then the basis to the donee is determined at the time of disposal.

1. **DISPOSAL** When the property is later disposed of in a taxable transaction

   a. At a loss, then the basis used to compute the loss is the lower of the property's fair market value at the date of the gift or the adjusted basis to the donor.

   b. At a gain, then the basis used to determine the gain is the property's adjusted basis in the hands of the donor.

   c. At a price between the fair market value at the date of the gift and the adjusted basis of the property in the hands of the donor, and the fair market value of the property at the date of the gift was less than the adjusted basis to the donor, then no gain or loss is recognized on the disposition.

2. **HOLDING PERIOD** When the basis in the hands of the donor is the basis of the property to the donee, then the donee's holding period includes the holding period of the donor. If, however, the fair market value at the time of the gift is the basis to the donee, then the holding period begins on the date of the gift.

D. **PROPERTY ACQUIRED FROM DECEDENT (INHERITANCE)**
The holding period for inherited property is always deemed to be long-term. Inherited property has a basis of the property's fair market value on the date of the decedent's death or the alternate valuation date, which is six months after death.

1. If the alternate valuation date is elected, and the property is distributed or otherwise disposed of before this date, the basis is the fair market value on the date of disposition.

2. The alternate valuation date may be selected only if it decreases both the value of the gross estate and the estate tax liability.

II. COST RECOVERY

A. **GENERAL**
A deduction is allowed for the exhaustion of property used in a business or held for production of income. Cost recovery deductions impact the basis of property. The original basis of the property is decreased by any depreciation, §179 deduction, amortization, or depletion.

B. **DEPRECIATION**
Depreciation is not allowed on land or inventory. Most assets placed in service after December 31, 1980, and before January 1, 1987, are depreciated using the Accelerated Cost Recovery System (ACRS). Most assets placed in service after December 31, 1986, are depreciated using the Modified Accelerated Cost Recovery System (MACRS). Alternatively, taxpayers may use the straight-line method.

1. **DEPRECIABLE PROPERTY** MACRS divides depreciable property into two broad categories. The first category, real property (§1250 property), is further divided into two sub-classifications: (1) residential rental property and (2) nonresidential real estate, such as warehouses and office buildings. The second category, personal property (§1245 property), consists of all tangible property that is not real property. Examples include office furniture, machines, and equipment.

2. **CLASS LIVES** MACRS personal property is divided into six classes based on Asset Depreciation Range (ADR) midpoint life. There are two main lives for real property.

a. **3-YEAR** Includes property with an ADR midpoint of 4 years or less except for automobiles, light trucks, and certain horses. Examples include a breeding hog, a race horse that is more than 2 years old, and tractor units for use over the road.

b. **5-YEAR** Includes property with an ADR midpoint of more than 4 years and less than 10 years. Examples include automobiles, light trucks, research and experimentation property, and certain technological equipment, such as computers.

c. **7-YEAR** Includes property with an ADR midpoint of at least 10 and less than 16 years. Also includes property that is not classified elsewhere. Examples include office furniture and office equipment.

d. **10-YEAR** Includes property with an ADR midpoint of at least 16 and less than 20 years. Examples include vessels, barges, tugs, and similar water transportation equipment.

e. **15-YEAR** Includes property with an ADR midpoint of at least 20 years and less than 25 years. Examples include municipal wastewater treatment plants and assets used in the production of cement.

f. **20-YEAR** Includes property with an ADR midpoint class life of over 25 years that is not real property. Examples include municipal sewers and farm buildings.

g. **27½-YEAR** Includes residential rental property. Examples include duplexes and apartment buildings.

h. **39-YEAR** Includes nonresidential real property placed in service after May 13, 1993. Examples include warehouses and office buildings. Property purchased before May 1993 uses a 31½-year life.

3. **RATES** Class determines MACRS rates. 3-, 5-, 7- and 10-year property is depreciated using the 200% declining-balance method, switching to the straight-line method when it results in a greater deduction. 15- and 20-year property is depreciated using the 150% declining-balance method, switching to the straight-line method when it results in a greater deduction. 27½- and 39-year real property is depreciated using the straight-line method. Salvage value is disregarded for purposes of MACRS deductions.

4. **SECTION 179 EXPENSE** An election is available to treat the cost of qualifying (business-use personal) property as an expense rather than a capital expenditure. The maximum amount that may be expensed is $24,000 in 2002 (and $25,000 thereafter). This is reduced dollar-for-dollar by the cost of qualifying property that exceeds $200,000 placed in service during the year. In addition, the expense cannot exceed taxable income derived from active conduct of a trade or business during the year; any amount disallowed under this rule may be carried forward indefinitely.

5. **CONVENTIONS** The determination of whether to use the mid-year or the mid-quarter convention for personal property is made **after** the §179 election is assigned to specific assets. Not all property is subject to the terms of these conventions, due to JCWAA '02, discussed later in this chapter.

a. **HALF-YEAR CONVENTION** The half-year convention applies to personal MACRS property. Under this convention, property is treated as placed in service in the middle of the year. Thus, regardless of when the property is placed in service, one-half of the first year's depreciation deduction is allowed in the first year. In addition, one-half a year of depreciation expense is allowed in the year of disposal.

b. **MID-QUARTER CONVENTION** The mid-quarter convention is an exception to the half-year convention. It also applies to personal property. If more than 40% of the aggregate cost of the property placed in service during the year is placed in service in the last quarter of the year, then **all** property placed in service during the year is subject to the mid-quarter convention. The MACRS deduction is computed by first determining the deduction for a full year and then multiplying it by a percentage based on what quarter the property was placed in service. These percentages are 87.5% for property placed in service in the first quarter, 62.5% for property placed in service in the second quarter, 37.5% for property placed in service in the third quarter, and 12.5% for property placed in service in the fourth quarter.

c. **MID-MONTH CONVENTION** The mid-month convention applies to real property. Under this convention, property is deemed to be placed in service in the middle of the month regardless of the day that it is actually placed in service.

Exhibit 1 ♦ Conventions and §179

In 2003, Growing Corporation placed the following assets into service. Growing formally elected not to take the additional 30% depreciation available under the Job Creation & Worker's Assistance Act of 2002.

Asset	Date	Asset Life	Cost
Furniture	March 13	7 year	$10,000
Computer	July 30	5 year	10,000
Printer	October 21	5 year	28,000
Total			$48,000

Analysis: Without a §179 deduction, Growing Corp. has more than 40% of its assets placed into service in the last quarter of the year and must, therefore, use the mid-quarter convention. However, if Growing uses the §179 deduction on the printer purchased in the fourth quarter, Growing may use the half-year convention.

Asset	Cost		Depreciable Basis	DDB Factor	Mid-Quarter Factor	Depreciation
Furniture	$10,000		$10,000	0.285	0.875	$ 2,494
Computer	10,000		10,000	0.400	0.375	1,500
Printer	28,000		28,000	0.400	0.125	1,400
Total	$48,000		$48,000			$ 5,394

Asset	Cost	§179	Depreciable Basis	DDB Factor	Half-Year Factor	Depreciation
Furniture	$10,000		$10,000	0.285	0.50	$ 1,425
Computer	10,000		10,000	0.400	0.50	2,000
Printer	28,000	$25,000	3,000	0.400	0.50	600
Total	$48,000	$25,000	$23,000			$ 4,025

Section 179 deduction	25,000
Total cost recovery deductions for the year	$29,025

6. **Automobiles** There are additional limits on "luxury" automobiles. Some large (over 6,000 pounds) SUVs do not meet this definition. These limits assume 100% business usage and election out of the additional 30% bonus depreciation available under JCWAA '02. If an automobile is used less than 50% for business, the alternative depreciation system (ADS), which is essentially straight-line with longer recovery periods, must be used. If an automobile is used less than 100% for business, these limits must be further reduced. The depreciation deduction is limited to the depreciation on a luxury threshold. In 2002, this threshold is $15,300. For a conventional auto placed in service in 2002, the first year limit is $3,060, the second year limit is $4,900, the third year limit is $2,950, and for later years the limit is $1,775. If no election out of the JCWAA '02 bonus depreciation is made, the first year limit is $4,600 higher than the amounts listed here. (The limits for "clean fuels" and electric cars are about three times higher.)

Example 3 ♦ Automobile Depreciation Deduction Limits

In 2002, Rich, Tom, and Paula each purchase an automobile in March for $43,750, $38,300, and $12,000, respectively. They all use their cars 80% for business purposes. (Note that Tom's car was purchased for an amount that results in depreciation of exactly the "luxury" threshold.)

Required: Compute the depreciation deductions for the first year.

(continued on next page)

SOLUTION: Rich's depreciation deduction is limited to $6,128. Paula's depreciation doesn't exceed the limitation, so she may take a deduction of $1,920. Tom's deduction equals the limit. (The DDB depreciation on 5-year property for the first full year is 2 times 1/5 = 40%.)

Rich			Tom			Paula		
$43,750 x .80	=	$35,000	$38,300 x .80	=	$30,640	$12,000 x .80	=	$9,600
$35,000 x .40 x .5	=	$ 7,000	$30,640 x .40 x .5	=	$ 6,128	$ 9,600 x .40 x .5	=	$1,920
$ 7,660 x .80	=	$ 6,128	$ 7,660 x .80	=	$ 6,128	$ 7,660 x .80	=	$6,128

---

7. **ENVIRONMENTAL REMEDIATION COSTS** Taxpayers may elect to treat any *qualified environmental remediation expenditure* paid or incurred as a current expense. A *qualified environmental remediation expenditure* is paid or incurred in connection with the abatement or control of hazardous substances at a *qualified contaminated site* (i.e. property held for use in a trade or business, for the production of income, or as inventory that is certified by the appropriate state environmental agency and contains a hazardous substance). Any deduction allowed under this provision is treated as a depreciation deduction in the event of sale or other disposition. (Recapture provisions apply.) This provision applies to expenditures paid, or incurred, between August 5, 1997, and January 1, 2001.

C. AMORTIZATION

Certain *acquired* intangible assets have a uniform 15-year straight-line amortization period. Taxpayers may use 15-year amortization for certain intangibles either acquired after July 25, 1991, or just for property acquired after August 10, 1993.

1. **ELIGIBLE INTANGIBLES** The following intangibles are eligible for this write off: goodwill, going-concern value, work force in place, information bases, know-how, customer-based intangibles, supplier-based intangibles, licenses, permits and other rights granted by governmental units, covenants not to compete, franchises, trademarks, and trade names.

2. **INTANGIBLES NOT ELIGIBLE** Assets that are not eligible include: self-created intangibles, interests in a corporation, partnership, trust or estate; interests in a futures (or similar) contract; any interest in land; and interests in films, sound recordings, video tapes, books and similar property if not acquired with the assets of a trade or business.

3. **COMPUTER SOFTWARE** Although off-the-shelf computer software is not eligible for 15-year amortization, it can generally be written off over 36 months. Software bought with computer hardware generally is depreciated along with the hardware.

D. BONUS DEPRECIATION

Job Creation & Worker Assistance Act of 2002 (JCWAA '02) initiates an additional 30% of bonus depreciation in the first year of service. This shouldn't be confused with Section 179 depreciation. The JCWAA '02 bonus depreciation only applies to new personal property acquired and placed in service after September 10, 2001, and before September 11, 2004.

1. **QUALIFIED PROPERTY** The bonus depreciation essentially is for new MACRS property, for which the recovery period is 20 years or less. Other qualified property includes computer software that is depreciable (not amortizable §197 property), and some qualified leasehold improvement property.

2. **NEW YORK LIBERTY ZONE (NYLZ)** Enhanced tax breaks are available within the New York Liberty Zone. Details on NYLZ provisions are beyond the exam's scope.

3. **SECTION 179** Taxpayers may take the bonus depreciation in combination with a §179 election. Generally, the §179 election is taken first.

EXAMPLE 4 ♦ JCWAA '02 BONUS DEPRECIATION & SECTION 179

On January 1, 2002, Eagle Corporation bought several laptop computers for its sales force at a total of $35,000 and a 7000-pound SUV for its repair department for $35,000. Eagle has no support that these purchases are related, directly or indirectly, to the dramatic events of September 11, 2001. None of Eagle's business is or has been conducted in the New York Liberty Zone. Eagle has 2002 taxable income of $140,000. Eagle takes the full Section 179 election.

REQUIRED: What is Eagle Corporation's basis for determining MACRS depreciation?

SOLUTION: Property primarily used in the New York Liberty Zone (NYLZ) is eligible for enhanced tax breaks, but there is no requirement that a property acquisition be related to the events of September 11, 2001, or the NYLZ to be eligible for the basic JCWAA '02 bonus depreciation.

Assets purchased and placed in service	$70,000
Section 179 expense election	24,000
Basis for JCWAA '02 bonus depreciation	$46,000
JCWAA '02 bonus depreciation ($46,000 x 30%)	13,800
Basis for MACRS depreciation	$32,200

OBSERVATIONS: Many large SUVs aren't restricted by the luxury automobile limits, because the limits only apply to vehicles with weights under 6,000 pounds. Many SUVs are over that weight limit.

4. **ALTERNATIVE DEPRECIATION SYSTEM (ADS)** Except in limited circumstances, if property must be depreciated under the ADS, then it does not qualify for the JCWAA '02 bonus depreciation. An example is used property that's not business-related property (if it's listed property or property of tax-exempt entities). This is unlikely to be tested heavily.

5. **ELECTION** If a taxpayer does not want to take the JCWAA '02 bonus depreciation, it must make a formal election, stating that it is electing not to use the JCWAA '02 bonus depreciation.

   a. **RETROACTIVE** If a taxpayer filed a 2001 return before JCWAA '02 was passed, the taxpayer should amend the 2001 return and either take or elect not to take the JCWAA '02 bonus depreciation. As the law currently is written, if a taxpayer neither amends its 2001 return nor elect out of the JCWAA '02 bonus depreciation, the taxpayer still must reduce its basis in qualified property for the untaken JCWAA '02 bonus depreciation. In other words, unless the IRS issues additional guidance, taxpayers who have already filed (and thus didn't take the JCWAA '02 bonus depreciation) must reduce the assets' bases for the JCWAA '02 bonus depreciation that they didn't take.

   b. **CLASS ELECTION** Taxpayers have to make an election for each class to elect out of the JCWAA '02 bonus depreciation. They make a formal election by attaching a statement to the Form 4562 or 2106 stating that they wish to elect out.

6. **CONVENTIONS** The JCWAA '02 bonus depreciation is regardless of the mid-quarter or mid-year convention. It doesn't apply to mid-month convention property, because real estate is ineligible for JCWAA '02 bonus depreciation.

7. **EXCHANGES & CONVERSIONS** The JCWAA '02 bonus depreciation can be claimed on the full basis of an asset acquired in a like-kind exchange or an involuntary conversion. Section 179 precludes any portion of the carryover basis from qualifying for §179, but there is no such explicit rule for the JCWAA '02 bonus depreciation. However, an argument can be made

that would preclude bonus depreciation from being claimed on the carryover basis. While this issue is in question, it is unlikely to be tested on the CPA exam.

8. **SELF-CONSTRUCTED PROPERTY** Generally, if construction started after September 10th, then self-constructed property can qualify. Generally, taxpayers may take JCWAA '02 bonus depreciation on the costs incurred between September 11, 2001, and September 10, 2004. Although the date to put a self-constructed asset into service is advanced to December 31, 2004, the qualified costs are only the costs incurred up to September 10, 2004.

9. **LISTED PROPERTY** During 2001 and 2002, JCWAA '02 increases luxury automobile limits for the first year of service by $4,600 for vehicles placed in service after September 10, 2001.

E. **DEPLETION**
Depletion is allowed for exhaustible natural resources.

1. **COST DEPLETION** Under this method, the basis of the property is divided by the number of recoverable units. The result is the cost depletion per unit. The depletion per unit is then multiplied by the number of units extracted and sold during the year. This amount is the cost depletion deduction allowed for the year.

2. **PERCENTAGE DEPLETION** Under this method, a set percentage of gross income from the property, which cannot exceed 50%, is taken as the depletion deduction. The allowable percentage depends on the type of property being extracted. After 2003, the deduction can not exceed 100% of net income.

III. PROPERTY DISPOSITIONS

A. **GENERAL**
The sale or other disposition of property generally results in the recognition of gain or loss. Depending on the type of property, the gain or loss may be ordinary or capital. Losses on property purchased for personal use usually are not recognized.

1. **TAXABLE EXCHANGE** In a taxable exchange, the gain or loss on the disposal of property is generally equal to the difference between the amount realized in the transaction and the adjusted basis of the property relinquished. The amount realized is the sum of money received, the fair value of property received, and the amount of liability relieved.

2. **NONTAXABLE EXCHANGE** In a nontaxable exchange, no gain or loss realized is recognized currently. It is usually deferred until the property is subsequently disposed of in a taxable transaction. (The gain or loss is realized but not recognized.) Some nontaxable exchanges qualify for a permanent exclusion of income recognition.

B. **CAPITAL GAIN OR LOSS**
A capital gain (or loss) can result only from the sale or exchange of a *capital* asset. Certain gains are *treated* as if they were capital gains.

1. **DEFINITION** Capital assets are all assets **except** the following:

a. Inventory and other property held primarily for sale to customers in the ordinary course of business

b. Depreciable personal property, or real property, used in business (This property is sometimes treated as if it was a capital asset.)

c. Certain copyrights, artistic compositions, letters, etc.

d. Accounts or notes receivable acquired in the ordinary course of business for services rendered or sales of inventory

e. Any U.S. Government publication received free of charge by the taxpayer

2. **HOLDING PERIOD** There are significant differences between "long-term" and "short-term" capital gains and losses for non-corporate taxpayers. Long-term is defined as **more than** 12 months. (There are special low rates for assets held more than five years, effective for sales after December 31, 2000.)

   a. Property received in a tax-free exchange, or by gift, "tacks on" the holding period of the prior transferor.

   b. Property acquired from a decedent is **automatically** considered held for more than the requisite long-term holding period.

3. **TREATMENT** A taxpayer nets capital gains and losses to arrive at either a net capital gain or a net capital loss.

   a. The net long-term capital gains of non-corporate taxpayers are taxed at a maximum rate of 28%. Reduced maximum rates apply to gains from stocks and bonds (except qualified small business stock) as well as real property for certain entities. [These reduced maximum rates do not apply to most collectibles (artwork, antiques, stamps, coins, metals, and gems).] Individuals, but **not** corporations, are among these entities.

   b. Individuals may deduct net capital losses only to the extent of the lesser of (1) $3,000 per year or (2) taxable income. Individuals cannot carry back unused capital losses; however, they can carry the losses forward indefinitely.

   c. Corporate taxpayers may deduct capital losses only to the extent of capital gains. Corporations can carry capital losses back three years and forward five years. The corporate rates for capital gains currently equal the rates for ordinary income.

   d. Even more favorable rates apply to individuals' extended-term gains. If the taxpayer is in a 15% tax bracket, capital assets sold after December 31, 2000, have a maximum rate of 8%. If the taxpayer is in a higher bracket, capital assets that are **acquired and sold** after December 31, 2000, and that are held for five years, are subject to a maximum rate of 18%.

EXHIBIT 2 ♦ MAXIMUM CAPITAL GAIN TAX RATES FOR PROPERTY (EXCEPT COLLECTIBLES) SOLD BY NON-CORPORATE TAXPAYERS

Nature of Asset	Period Held	Maximum Tax Rate	Maximum Tax Rate in 15% Bracket
Personal Property	short-term (12 months or less)	39.6	15
	long-term	20	10
Real Property*	short-term (12 months or less)	39.6	15
	long-term	20	10

* Taxpayers receive an annual tax benefit via the deduction for depreciation on depreciable real property. If the property is held *long-term* and is later sold at a gain, the taxpayer is entitled to taxation at the lower capital gains rate. However, the tax law requires the taxpayer to *recapture* the previously taken deprecation benefit. This is accomplished by taxing a *portion* of the capital gain at a higher rate. For long-term real property sold after May 6, 1997, the recapture amount is all depreciation claimed, and the recapture rate is 25%.

C. INSTALLMENT SALES

The installment method of reporting *gains* may be elected when at least one payment is received in a tax year after the year of the sale. The installment sale method may not generally be used by dealers in property. The amount of gain that is taxable each year is computed by multiplying the payments received that year by the gross profit percentage. The gross profit percentage is equal to the anticipated total gross profit to be received divided by the total contract price.

EXAMPLE 5 ♦ INSTALLMENT SALES

In year 20X1, Ed sells Steve some personal use property for $10,000 to be paid in equal installments over a 5-year period. Ed's basis in the property is $7,000. In year 20X1, Steve pays Ed $2,000. Ed must recognize gain as follows.

$$\$10,000 - \$7,000 = \$3,000 \text{ total profit}$$
$$\$3,000 / \$10,000 = 30\% \text{ gross profit percentage}$$
$$\$2,000 \times 30\% = \$600 \text{ profit recognized in year 20X1}$$

D. SECTION 1231 PROPERTY

Section 1231 property is depreciable property or land that is used in a trade or business. If gains from §1231 property exceed losses, then the net gain is treated as a **capital** gain. If however, the losses exceed the gains, then the net losses are treated as **ordinary** losses.

E. DEPRECIATION RECAPTURE

When §1231 property is disposed of and results in a §1231 gain, some of the gain may have to be recaptured as ordinary income because of depreciation deductions previously taken. Property subject to recapture includes:

1. **SECTION 1245 PROPERTY** This is primarily depreciable personalty. All depreciation claimed must be recaptured as ordinary income.

2. **SECTION 1250 PROPERTY** This is depreciable realty. For sales or exchanges prior to May 7, 1997, all depreciation taken in **excess** of straight-line depreciation must be recaptured as ordinary income. Starting May 7, 1997, all depreciation, to the extent of the gain, is recaptured at a maximum rate of 25% for non-corporate taxpayers.

F. TRANSACTIONS BETWEEN RELATED PARTIES

No loss is allowed to be recognized with respect to sales or exchanges between related parties. A related party is defined as the following:

1. **FAMILY MEMBERS**

2. **CORPORATION** An individual and a corporation owned more than 50% either directly or indirectly by that individual

    - Stock in a corporation may be indirectly owned because of the constructive ownership rules that state that an individual shall be considered to own the stock owned directly by her/his spouse, children, grandchildren, and parents.

3. **CORPORATIONS** Two corporations that are members of the same controlled group.

4. **TRUST** Most relationships between a trust and its grantor, its fiduciary trustee, or a corporation owned 50% or more by the trust grantor. TRA '97 includes most relationships between a trust and its beneficiary, effective August 6, 1997.

G. LIKE-KIND EXCHANGES

A like-kind exchange is an exchange of property of the same nature or character. (Real property must be exchanged for real property and personal property for personal property.) No gain or loss is recognized on a like-kind exchange of property held for productive use in a trade or business or for investment, if the property received is either held for productive use in a trade or business or for investment. Property held for investment may be exchanged for property to be used in a trade or business and vice versa. The like-kind exchange rules do not apply to property held for **personal** use, stocks, bonds, notes, certificates of trust, beneficial interests, or partnership interests. Trade-in allowances are covered by the like-kind exchange rules.

1. **BASIS** When no gain is recognized from the exchange, the basis of the property received is the adjusted basis of the property given up.

2. **BOOT** If boot [money or other (not like-kind) property] is received as part of the like-kind exchange, gain is recognized to the extent of the lesser of the gain realized or the boot received. Loss, however, is never recognized. The basis of property received is equal to the basis of the property given up, plus gain recognized, plus boot given, less the fair market value of boot received.

- If liabilities are assumed by one party to the exchange, they are treated as boot. If the liability was assumed by the other party, it is treated as boot received. Likewise, if the taxpayer assumes the liability, it is treated as boot given.

EXAMPLE 6 ♦ LIKE-KIND EXCHANGE

Harry's Hardware gives Sally's Shells a computer with a fair market value of $3,000 and an adjusted basis of $1,900. In return, Sally gives Harry an old computer with a fair market value of $2,000 and an adjusted basis of $600. Sally also gives Harry $900 in cash. How much gain must each recognize?

SOLUTION:

		Harry		Sally
Amount realized	($2,000 + $900 =)	$2,900		$3,000
Amount relinquished		1,900	($600 + $900 =)	1,500
Realized gain		$1,000		$1,500
Amount of boot received		$ 900		$ 0
Recognized gain (lesser of two)		$ 900		$ 0

H. SALE OF PRINCIPAL RESIDENCE

An individual taxpayer may exclude the gain from gross income in some situations. Both the once-in-a-lifetime exclusion and the rollover deferral (applicable to all eligible sales before May 7, 1997, and elected sales before August 6, 1997) could have been applied to one transaction, affecting the basis of the current residence. Sales after May 6, 1997, that are not impacted by a rollover deferral election, may be eligible for a straight exclusion.

1. **STRAIGHT EXCLUSION** An exclusion of gain ($500,000 married filing jointly or $250,000 for a single individual or HH) is available to a taxpayer who owned and occupied the home as a principal residence in two of the five years immediately preceding the sale after May 6, 1997. This exclusion may be claimed as frequently as once every two years.

EXAMPLE 7 ♦ PRO RATA EXCLUSION

Fred sold his principal residence in 20X1, after living there 1 year, due to an employment relocation. His gain on the sale of the home is $20,000. As a single taxpayer, he would be eligible for a $250,000 exclusion of gain, had he lived there 2 years. Fred may exclude $20,000 of gain, because it is less than the pro rata exclusion. ($250,000 X 50% = $125,000)

a. Taxpayers may claim a ratable portion of the exclusion, if they do not meet the two year requirement due to health problems, employment relocation, or other unforeseen circumstances.

b. A $250,000 exclusion may be used by a spouse whose residence is sold if a married couple did not share a principal residence. The marriage of a taxpayer, to someone who recently used a $250,000 exclusion, does not preclude the use of another $250,000 exclusion for that couple.

c. Taxpayers may claim the straight exclusion without regard to previous claims of the $125,000 exclusion.

2. ROLLOVER DEFERRAL A gain from the sale of a principal residence reinvested in a new residence formerly could have been deferred. The basis of the new residence is the purchase price less the deferred gain of the former home.

a. The new residence must have been purchased within a period beginning two years before and ending two years after the sale of the old residence.

b. The adjusted sale price of the old residence equals the amount **realized** on the sale, reduced by (1) any qualified expenses of fixing up the old residence so that it can be sold and (2) any once-in-a-lifetime exclusion.

3. ONCE-IN-A-LIFETIME EXCLUSION A once-in-a-lifetime exclusion of $125,000 was available to a taxpayer who attained age 55 before the sale and used the property as her/his principal residence for at least three of the five years preceding the sale. If a married couple filed a joint return, only one spouse had to be 55 to qualify for the exclusion. However, married couples were entitled to one exclusion per couple, not per person.

EXAMPLE 8 ♦ SALE OF RESIDENCE COMBINING TWO PROVISIONS

Sam sold his old home for $275,000 in March 1997 when he was 59. His basis in the old home was $100,000. Sam bought his current home for $140,000 in January 1999. Sam minimized his 1997 taxable gain with the rollover deferral and the once-in-a-lifetime exclusion.

REQUIRED: Calculate Sam's basis in his current home.

SOLUTION: Sam had a gain of $175,000, but only $10,000 was taxable in 1997.

Sales proceeds	$ 275,000
Once-in-a-lifetime exclusion	(125,000)
Net proceeds (amount to be "rolled over")	$ 150,000
Principal residence rollover (new house)	(140,000)
Maximum required taxable gain (compare to realized gain less exclusion)	$ 10,000
Realized gain ($275,000 – $100,000)	$ 175,000
Once-in-a-lifetime exclusion	(125,000)
Recognized gain (lower of $10,000 or $50,000)	(10,000)
Deferred gain from sale of old home	$ 40,000
Purchase price of current home	$ 140,000
Deferred gain from sale of old home	(40,000)
Basis in current home	$ 100,000

IV. INVOLUNTARY CONVERSIONS

A. DEFINITION

An involuntary conversion takes place when money, similar, or dissimilar property is received for property that has been damaged, stolen, or condemned.

B. GAIN OR LOSS RECOGNITION

No gain is recognized if the property is converted directly into similar-use property. (Similar-use is a stricter standard than like-kind.) In addition, the taxpayer may **elect** to not recognize gain on an involuntary conversion, if the taxpayer replaces the property with property that is similar or related in service or use to the property converted. Alternatively, the taxpayer may purchase an 80% controlling interest in a corporation owning or, within a specified time, acquiring replacement property. Gain is then recognized only to the extent that gain realized on the conversion exceeds the cost of the replacement property. The recognition or nonrecognition of **loss** is **not** affected by the involuntary conversion rules. C corporations (and certain partnerships with corporate partners) are not entitled to defer gain, if the replacement property is purchased from a related party, for involuntary conversions occurring after June 8, 1997. This denial applies to any other taxpayer (including individuals) with an aggregate realized gain over $100,000 for the taxable year.

C. REPLACEMENT PERIOD
The property must be replaced within a period beginning with the date the property was (1) damaged, stolen, condemned, etc., or (2) the earlier of the date the condemnation was first threatened or became imminent, and ending two years after the close of the first tax year in which **any** part of the gain is **realized**. This two-year period is extended to three years when **real property** is condemned or threatened to be condemned. Condemnations are held only to the standard of like-kind, not similar-use.

D. SPECIAL DISASTER RELIEF
Special relief is available for people whose qualified property is involuntarily converted as a result of a disaster for which a presidential declaration is made. The provision applies to main homes and/or contents, trade, business, and investment property. There are three special breaks.

1. **EXCLUDE** Taxpayers may exclude insurance proceeds received for unscheduled personal property.

2. **POOL** The insurance proceeds for a home or its contents are treated as a common pool of funds received for a single item of property. A taxpayer may elect not to recognize gain currently on this pool of funds to the extent it is timely reinvested in another home (or contents).

3. **PERIOD** The period of time for the replacement of property involuntarily converted due to a disaster ends 4 years after the close of the first tax year in which any part of the gain upon conversion is realized.

V. SECURITIES

A. TRANSACTIONS
The trade date is the date of sale.

1. **WASH SALES** A loss from the sale or other disposition of stock is disallowed if substantially the same stock is purchased during a time period beginning 30 days prior to the sale and ending 30 days after that date. In the case where a loss is not allowed, the basis of the disposed stock is carried over to the newly acquired stock.

2. **STOCK DIVIDENDS** Generally, when stock dividends are received, it is a nontaxable transaction and thus they are not included in gross income. The basis of the original stock is allocated proportionally between the original stock and the dividends received based on their fair market values as of the dates of distribution. If there is an option to receive cash instead of the stock dividend, the transaction is taxable, even if the stock dividend is received.

B. WORTHLESS STOCK
The basis of the stock is deductible in the year that it becomes **completely** worthless. If the stock was a capital asset to the taxpayer, then generally, the loss is a capital loss. However, there is an exception, known as §1244 stock, for investment in a small business investment company. An investor is allowed an ordinary rather than a capital loss for such stock.

C. **SMALL BUSINESS STOCK**

A noncorporate taxpayer who holds qualified small-business stock for more than 5 years to exclude 50% of any gain on the sale or exchange of the stock. The amount of gain eligible for the exclusion is limited to the greater of (1) 10 times the taxpayer's basis in the stock, or (2) a $10 million gain from the stock. The $10 million limit is applied on a shareholder-by-shareholder basis.

1. **ELIGIBLE STOCK** The stock must be acquired by the taxpayer after August 10, 1993, at the original issuance in exchange for money, other property (not including stock), or as compensation for services provided to the corporation (other than services performed as an underwriter of the stock).

2. **QUALIFIED CORPORATIONS** The small business must be a C corporation, have less than $50 million of aggregated capital as of the date of stock issuance, and at least 80%, by value, of corporate assets must be used in the active conduct of one or more trades or businesses. The corporation cannot be involved in the performance of personal services (e.g., health, law, accounting, etc.) or in the finance, banking, leasing, real estate, farming, mineral extraction, or hospitality industries.

CHAPTER 28—FEDERAL TAXATION: PROPERTY

PROBLEM 28-1 MULTIPLE CHOICE QUESTIONS (50 to 63 minutes)

1.   Fred Berk bought a plot of land with a cash payment of $40,000 and a purchase money mortgage of $50,000. In addition, Berk paid $200 for a title insurance policy. Berk's basis in this land is
a. $40,000.
b. $40,200.
c. $90,000.
d. $90,200.   (11/90, PII, #29, 1613)

2.   Which one of the following statements is correct with regard to an individual taxpayer who has elected to amortize the premium on a bond that yields taxable interest?
a.   The amortization is treated as an itemized deduction.
b.   The amortization is **not** treated as a reduction of taxable income.
c.   The bond's basis is reduced by the amortization.
d.   The bond's basis is increased by the amortization.
                                       (11/90, PII, #34, 1615)

ITEMS 3 AND 4 are based on the following:

In 20X0, Flora Ring bought a diamond necklace for her own use, at a cost of $10,000. In 20X3, when the fair market value was $12,000, Iris and her husband gave this necklace to her daughter, Ruth. No gift tax was due.

3.   Ruth's holding period for this gift
a.   Starts in 20X3.
b.   Starts in 20X0.
c.   Depends on whether the necklace is sold by Ruth at a gain or at a loss.
d.   Is irrelevant because Ruth received the necklace for no consideration of money or money's worth.
                                       (Editors, 1625)

4.   If Ruth sells this diamond necklace in 20X3 for $13,000, Ruth's recognized gain would be
a. $3,000.
b. $2,000.
c. $1,000.
d. $0.   (Editors, 1627)

ITEMS 5 AND 6 are based on the following:

On March 1, 20X5, Lois Wheat was bequeathed 1,000 shares of Lane Corp. common stock under the will of her uncle, Pat Prisy. Pat had paid $5,000 for the Lane stock in 20X0. Fair market value of the Lane stock on March 1, 20X5, the date of Pat's death, was $8,000 and had increased to $11,000 six months later. The executor of Pat's estate elected the alternate valuation date for estate tax purposes. Lois sold the Lane stock for $9,000 on May 1, 20X5, the date that the executor distributed the stock to her.

5.   How much should Lois include in her individual income tax return for the inheritance of the 1,000 shares of Lane stock which she received from Pat's estate?
a. $0
b. $ 5,000
c. $ 8,000
d. $11,000   (Editors, 1635)

6.   Lois' basis for gain or loss on sale of the 1,000 shares of Lane stock is
a. $ 5,000.
b. $ 8,000.
c. $ 9,000.
d. $11,000.   (Editors, 9263)

7.   Which of the following conditions must be satisfied for a taxpayer to expense, in the year of purchase, under Internal Revenue Code Section 179, the cost of new or used tangible depreciable personal property?

I.   The property must be purchased for use in the taxpayer's active trade or business.
II. The property must be purchased from an unrelated party.

a.   I only.
b.   II only.
c.   Both I and II.
d.   Neither I nor II.   (R/01, AR, #23, 7008)

8.   In 2002, Browne, a self-employed taxpayer, had business net income of $100,000 prior to any expense deduction for equipment purchases. Browne purchased and placed into service, for business use, office machinery costing $30,000. This was Browne's only capital expenditure during this year. Browne's business establishment was not in an economically distressed area. Browne made a proper and timely expense election to deduct the maximum amount. Browne was not a member of any pass-through entity. What is Browne's deduction under the election?
a. $ 5,000
b. $10,000
c. $24,000
d. $30,000   (5/95, AR, #2, amended, 5420)

9. On August 1, 2002, Graham purchased and placed into service an office building costing $264,000 including $30,000 for the land. What was Graham's MACRS deduction for the office building in 2002?
a. $9,600
b. $6,000
c. $3,600
d. $2,250   (5/95, AR, #5, amended, 5423)

10. Lee qualified as head of a household for tax purposes. Lee's 2002 taxable income was $100,000, exclusive of capital gains and losses. Lee had a net long-term loss of $8,000 in 2002. What amount of this capital loss can Lee offset against 2002 ordinary income?
a. $0
b. $3,000
c. $4,000
d. $8,000   (11/92, PII, #15, amended, 3349)

11. Carol sold a painting for $15,000 that she had bought for her personal use five years ago at a cost of $11,000. In her return, Carol should treat the sale of the painting as a transaction resulting in
a. Ordinary income.
b. Long-term capital gain.
c. Section 1231 gain.
d. No taxable gain.   (Editors, 1616)

12. For a cash basis taxpayer, gain or loss on a year-end sale of listed stock arises on the
a. Date of delivery of stock certificate.
b. Settlement date.
c. Date of receipt of cash proceeds.
d. Trade date.   (5/91, PII, #21, amended, 1610)

13. Capital assets include
a. A corporation's accounts receivable from the sale of its inventory.
b. Seven-year MACRS property used in a corporation's trade or business.
c. A manufacturing company's investment in U.S. Treasury bonds.
d. A corporate real estate developer's unimproved land that is to be subdivided to build homes, which will be sold to customers.
      (11/95, AR, #6, 5750)

14. Baker Corp., a calendar year C corporation, realized taxable income of $36,000 from its regular business operations for calendar year 20X1. In addition, Baker had the following capital gains and losses:

Short-term capital gain	$ 8,500
Short-term capital loss	(4,000)
Long-term capital gain	1,500
Long-term capital loss	(3,500)

Baker did not realize any other capital gains or losses since it began operations. What is Baker's total taxable income for 20X1?
a. $46,000
b. $42,000
c. $40,500
d. $38,500   (11/95, AR, #7, amended, 5751)

15. On January 2, 2000, Bates Corp. purchased and placed into service 7-year MACRS tangible property costing $100,000. On December 31, 2002, Bates sold the property for $102,000, after having taken $47,525 in MACRS depreciation deductions. What amount of the gain should Bates recapture as ordinary income?
a. $0
b. $ 2,000
c. $47,525
d. $49,525   (11/94, AR, #34, amended, 5011)

16. The following information pertains to install-ment sales of personal use property made by Carl Woode in his retail furniture store:

Year of sale	Installment sales	Gross profit	Collections in 20X3
20X1	$100,000	$ 30,000	$20,000
20X2	150,000	60,000	60,000
20X3	200,000	100,000	80,000

These sales were **not** under a revolving credit plan. Under the installment method, Woode should report a gross profit for 20X3 of
a. $ 70,000.
b. $100,000.
c. $160,000.
d. $260,000.   (Editors, 1624)

17. Among which of the following related parties are losses from sales and exchanges **not** recognized for tax purposes?
a. Father-in-law and son-in-law
b. Brother-in-law and sister-in-law
c. Grandfather and granddaughter
d. Ancestors, lineal descendants, and all in-laws
      (11/92, PII, #18, 3352)

ITEMS 18 AND 19 are based on the following:

Conner purchased 300 shares of Zinco stock for $30,000 in 20X0. On May 23, 20X2, Conner sold all the stock to his daughter Alice for $20,000, its then fair market value. Conner realized no other gain or loss during 20X2. On July 26, 20X2, Alice sold the 300 shares of Zinco for $25,000.

18. What amount of the loss from the sale of Zinco stock can Conner deduct in 20X2?
a. $0
b. $ 3,000
c. $ 5,000
d. $10,000   (5/95, AR, #3, amended, 5421)

19. What was Alice's recognized gain or loss on her sale?
a. $5,000 long-term loss
b. $5,000 long-term gain
c. $5,000 short-term loss
d. $0   (5/95, AR, #4, amended, 5422)

20. Leker exchanged a van that was used exclusively for business and had an adjusted tax basis of $20,000 for a new van. The new van had a fair market value of $10,000, and Leker also received $3,000 in cash. What was Leker's tax basis in the acquired van?
a. $20,000
b. $17,000
c. $13,000
d. $ 7,000   (5/98, AR, #1, 6638)

21. Patty Leave owned an apartment house for ten years. Depreciation was taken on a straight-line basis. When Patty's adjusted basis for this property was $300,000, she traded it for an office building having a fair market value of $700,000. The apartment house has 100 dwelling units, while the office building has 40 units rented to business enterprises. The properties are not located in the same city. What is Patty's reportable gain on this exchange?
a. $400,000 Section 1250 gain
b. $400,000 Section 1231 gain
c. $400,000 long-term capital gain
d. $0   (Editors, 1630)

22. The following information pertains to the sale of Al Bran's former principal residence:

Date of sale	April 1997
Date of purchase	May 1987
Net sales price	$260,000
Adjusted basis	$ 70,000

In May 1997, Bran (age 70) bought a smaller residence for $90,000. Bran elected to avail himself of any exclusion of realized gain available to him. He had never before used the once-in-a-lifetime exclusion. What is Bran's basis in his current residence?
a. $0
b. $45,000
c. $70,000
d. $90,000   (Editors, 1617)

23. Kelly is single with no dependents. Kelly's principal residence was sold for the net amount of $400,000 after all selling expenses. Kelly bought the house in 1970 and occupied it until sold. On the date of sale, the house had a basis of $80,000. What is the maximum exclusion of gain on sale of the residence that may be claimed in Kelly's income tax return?
a. $250,000
b. $220,000
c. $125,000
d. $0   (Editors, 3342)

24. An office building owned by Bob Elin was condemned by the state on January 2, 20X0. Bob received the condemnation award on March 1, 20X1. In order to qualify for nonrecognition of gain on this involuntary conversion, what is the last date for Bob to acquire qualified replacement property?
a. August 1, 20X2
b. January 2, 20X3
c. March 1, 20X4
d. December 31, 20X4   (Editors, 9267)

25. Smith, an individual calendar-year taxpayer, purchased 100 shares of Core Co. common stock for $15,000 on December 15, 20X1, and an additional 100 shares for $13,000 on December 30, 20X1. On January 3, 20X2, Smith sold the shares purchased on December 15, 20X1, for $13,000. What amount of loss from the sale of Core's stock is deductible on Smith's 20X1 and 20X2 income tax returns?

	20X1	20X2
a.	$0	$0
b.	$0	$2,000
c.	$1,000	$1,000
d.	$2,000	$0

(11/93, PII, #25, amended, 4454)

PROBLEM 28-2 ADDITIONAL MULTIPLE CHOICE QUESTIONS (18 to 23 minutes)

26. Hall was bequeathed 500 shares of common stock under his father's will. Hall's father had paid $2,500 for the stock ten years ago. Fair market value of the stock on February 1, 20X1, the date of his father's death, was $4,000 and had increased to $5,500 six months later. The executor of the estate elected the alternate valuation date for estate tax purposes. Hall sold the stock for $4,500 on June 1, 20X1, the date that the executor distributed the stock to him. How much income should Hall include in his individual income tax return for the inheritance of the 500 shares of stock which he received from his father's estate?
a. $5,500
b. $4,000
c. $2,500
d. $0   (5/94, AR, #32, amended, 4637)

27. On June 1, 20X1, Ben Rork sold 500 shares of Kul Corp. stock. Rork had received this stock on May 1 as a bequest from the estate of his uncle, who died on March 1, 20X1. Rork's basis was determined by reference to the stock's fair market value on March 1, 20X1. Rork's holding period for this stock was
a. Short-term.
b. Long-term.
c. Short-term if sold at a gain; long-term if sold at a loss.
d. Long-term if sold at a gain; short-term if sold at a loss.   (5/89, PII, #52, amended, 1618)

28. Data Corp., a calendar year corporation, purchased and placed into service office equipment during November, 2002. No other equipment was placed into service during the year. Data qualifies to use the general MACRS depreciation system. Data wants to take the largest deduction possible. What convention will Data use?
a. Full-year
b. Half-year
c. Mid-quarter
d. Mid-month   (11/95, AR, #5, amended, 5749)

29. Tim and Jane Rook are married and file jointly. A capital loss
a. Will be allowed only to the extent of capital gains.
b. Will be allowed to the extent of capital gains, plus up to $3,000 of ordinary income.
c. May be carried forward up to a maximum of five years.
d. Is **not** an allowable loss.   (Editors, 1619)

30. Archer Corp. sold machinery for $40,000 on December 31, 20X3. This machinery was purchased on January 2, 20X0, for $34,000, and had an adjusted basis of $20,000 at the date of sale. For 20X3, Archer should report
a. Ordinary income of $6,000 and §1231 gain of $14,000.
b. Ordinary income of $14,000 and §1231 gain of $6,000.
c. Ordinary income of $20,000.
d. §1231 gain of $20,000.   (Editors, 9264)

31. Platt owns land that is operated as a parking lot. A shed was erected on the lot for the related transactions with customers. With regard to capital assets and Section 1231 assets, how should these assets be classified?

	Land	Shed
a.	Capital	Capital
b.	Section 1231	Capital
c.	Capital	Section 1231
d.	Section 1231	Section 1231

     (11/92, PII, #17, 3351)

32. Fay sold 100 shares of Gym Co. stock to her son, Martin, for $11,000. Fay had paid $15,000 for the stock six years ago. Subsequently in the same year, Martin sold the stock to an unrelated third party for $16,000. What amount of gain from the sale of the stock to the third party should Martin report on his income tax return?
a. $0
b. $1,000
c. $4,000
d. $5,000   (11/93, PII, #29, amended, 4458)

33. Wright exchanged investment real property, with an adjusted basis of $80,000 and subject to a mortgage of $35,000, and received from Lloyd $15,000 cash and other investment real property having a fair market value of $125,000. Lloyd assumed the mortgage. What is Wright's recognized gain in the year of exchange on the exchange?
a. $15,000
b. $35,000
c. $45,000
d. $50,000   (Editors, 9266)

34. In January 1996, Derek purchased a new residence for $200,000. During that same month he sold his former residence for $80,000 and paid the realtor a $5,000 commission. The former residence, his first home, had cost $65,000 in 1986. Derek added a bathroom for $5,000 in 1995. What is the basis of Derek's current residence?
a. $205,000
b. $200,000
c. $195,000
d. $125,000   (5/94, AR, #1, amended, 4606)

SOLUTION 28-1 MULTIPLE CHOICE ANSWERS

ADJUSTED BASIS

1. (d) When mortgaged property is purchased, its basis is the cash paid, or FMV of other property given, the amount of any mortgage assumed, plus any other costs connected with the purchase.

2. (c) Amortization of the bond premium reduces the basis of that bond. The amount of the amortized premium on taxable bonds is permitted as an interest deduction and is considered a recovery of the cost or basis of the bond. For bonds purchased after December 31, 1987, the premium amortization is an offset to the interest income.

GIFT

3. (b) Since the fair market value of the gift on the date of the gift exceeds the donor's adjusted basis for the property on this date, the donor's adjusted basis will be used in all gain or loss situations. Since the donee's basis for the gift property is determined with reference to the adjusted basis of the property in the hands of the donor, the donee's holding period includes the donor's holding period [§1223(2)].

4. (a) Since the FMV of the gift on the date of the gift exceeds the donor's adjusted basis for the property on this date, the donor's adjusted basis of $10,000 will be used in all gain or loss situations. Ruth's recognized gain is determined as follows:

Cash proceeds received	$ 13,000
Less: Adjusted basis of necklace to Ruth	(10,000)
Capital gain	$ 3,000

INHERITANCE

5. (a) Section 102(a) provides that gross income does not include the value of property acquired by gift, bequest, devise, or inheritance.

6. (c) Section 1014 provides that when the alternate valuation date is elected, the basis of property inherited by the decedent is equal to the value of the property as it is determined under §2032. Under §2032, the value of property distributed from the estate after the date of death, but before the alternate valuation date, is equal to the FMV on the date of distribution [§2032]. Thus, Lois' basis in the stock is $9,000, i.e., the stock's FMV on the date of distribution.

COST RECOVERY

7. (c) In order to qualify for the Section 179 expense deduction, the property must be purchased for use in the taxpayer's active trade or business, and it must be purchased from an unrelated party.

8. (c) The equipment constitutes §179 property under §179(d)(1) and §1245(a)(3). Section 179 property is tangible, depreciable personal property that is purchased for use in a trade or business. Section 179 authorizes a deduction for §179 property placed in service during the year, but limits this deduction to $24,000 in 2002 ($25,000 in 2003). [For the 2003 exams, know the 2002 amounts. For the May 2004 exam, know the 2003 amounts.] Under §179(b)(2), this maximum is reduced by $1 for each $1 of §179 property placed in service during the year that exceeds $200,000. This reduction does not apply in this case. Section 179(b)(3) limits this deduction to the net income from the active conduct of any trade or business before the §179 deduction. Browne's deduction is not affected by this limit. [The examiners say they will test the amount in effect 6 months prior to the exam.] The JCWAA '02 30% bonus depreciation generally is taken after applicable §179 deductions.

9. (d) Only the $234,000 allocated to the cost of the building ($264,000 − $30,000) is subject to cost recovery. The office building is nonresidential

real property and is subject to a recovery period of 39 years, salvage value disregarded, under §168. For the office building, the convention that must be used in determining the cost recovery deduction is the mid-month convention. Thus, the property is deemed to have been placed in service in the middle of August, leaving 4.5 months of cost recovery for 2002. The straight-line method of cost recovery must be used for nonresidential real property, as provided by §168(b)(3)(A). Therefore, the cost recovery (MACRS) deduction for the office building for 2002 is ($234,000 / 39) × (4.5 / 12) = $2,250. (Same answer for 2003.)

SECTION 1231 & CAPITAL ASSETS

10. (b) Individuals may use up to $3,000 of capital losses per year to offset ordinary income. Any additional amounts may be carried forward for an unlimited amount of time until they are fully utilized.

11. (b) The painting is considered a capital asset because it does not fall within one of the five categories that would exclude it from being a capital asset (§1221). The painting is not ordinary income property because it was not held primarily for sale to customers in the ordinary course of the business. Nor is the painting §1231 property because it is not depreciable property used in the taxpayer's trade or business. The sale of the painting is taxable as it was sold for an amount that was greater than its basis.

12. (d) The trade date (i.e., the date the broker completes the transaction on the stock exchange) is the date of sale. The holding period for the stock sold ends with the trade date. The settlement date—the date the cash or other property is paid to the seller of the stock—is not relevant in determining the date of sale. The date of delivery of the stock certificate is also not relevant in determining the date of sale.

13. (c) Section 1221 defines capital assets as property held by the taxpayer except for a number of items listed. Section 1221(4) excludes accounts receivable from the sale of inventory from being treated as capital assets. Section 1221 excludes depreciable property used in a business and excludes inventory or property held primarily for sale to customers in the ordinary course of business from the definition of capital assets. Section 1237(a) provides that real property in the hands of a taxpayer other than a corporation shall not be treated as held primarily for sale to customers in the ordinary course of business, if certain conditions are met. The real estate developer holds the unimproved land to be subdivided to build homes to be sold to customers.

Therefore, the unimproved land does not qualify for the exception provided by §1237(a) and is not a capital asset under §1221(1). Investments in bonds or other assets are not excluded from the definition of capital assets in §1221.

14. (d) Section 1211(a) allows a corporation to deduct capital losses only against capital gains. However, corporations may offset a net long-term capital loss against a net short-term capital gain. Baker Corp. does not have a net capital loss, but rather has capital gain net income of $2,500 under §1222(9). The capital gains are included in gross income under §61(a)(3) and the capital losses are deducted from gross income under §165(f) up to the amount of capital gains under §1211(a).

Taxable Income from Regular Operations		$36,000
Short-Term Capital Gain	$ 8,500	
Short-Term Capital Loss	(4,000)	
Net Short-Term Capital Gain		$ 4,500
Long-Term Capital Gain	$ 1,500	
Long-Term Capital Loss	(3,500)	
Net Long-Term Capital Loss		$(2,000)
Net Capital Gain Income		2,500
Taxable Income		$38,500

15. (c) On a sale of depreciable personal property, ordinary income under §1245 is generally equal to the lesser of (1) the total gain realized or (2) the accumulated depreciation. Section 1231 treats any remaining gain as a §1231 gain, which is not ordinary income under §64. The §1245 gain and the remaining §1231 gain are computed as follows:

Amount realized		$102,000
Cost	$100,000	
Less: Accum. depr.	(47,525)	
Less: adjusted basis		(52,475)
Gain realized		$ 49,525
Sec. 1245 (ordinary) gain		
(lesser of $49,525 or $47,525)		$ 47,525
Sec. 1231 (capital) gain		2,000
Total gain realized		$ 49,525

INSTALLMENT SALES

16. (b) After January 1, 1988, a "dealer" in real estate or a "merchant" selling personal property can no longer use the "installment sales method" for tax purposes. Woode is a merchant selling personal property; therefore, he must report the full amount of gross profit, $100,000.

RELATED PARTY TRANSACTIONS

17. (c) In-laws are not related parties. Ancestors and lineal descendants are related parties.

18. (a) Conner realizes a $10,000 loss ($20,000 – $30,000) under §1001(a). Because the sale was to a related party, none of the loss is recognized. Section 267(a)(1) disallows the deduction of any loss on the sale or exchange of property between certain related parties, as defined in §267(b). Section 267(b)(1) includes members of a family, as defined in §267(c)(4), as related parties. Section 267(c)(4) includes brothers, sisters, spouse, ancestors and lineal descendants as family members who are related parties under §267. None of Conner's loss may be recognized, notwithstanding the fact that the sale was for the stock's fair market value.

19. (d) Alice acquired a cost basis of $20,000 in the stock under §1012. When Alice sells the stock for $25,000, she realizes a $5,000 gain ($25,000 – $20,000) under §1001(a). Usually, all of this gain would be recognized under §1001(c). However, §267(d) provides any loss not recognized under the provision of §267(a)(1) because it was a related party loss, may be used to offset gain recognized on a subsequent sale by the related party purchaser. The previously disallowed loss may not be used to create or add to a loss on a subsequent sale by the related party purchaser. Therefore, Alice may use $5,000 of the $10,000 previously disallowed loss to Conner when Alice bought the stock to completely eliminate her recognized gain. The $5,000 remainder of the previously disallowed loss is lost forever.

EXCHANGES

20. (b) The basis in the new van is the basis in the assets surrendered less the fair market value of the boot. ($20,000 – $3,000)

21. (d) Under §1031, no gain or loss is recognized on like-kind exchanges of property. To qualify as a like-kind exchange, the properties must be of "a similar nature or character"; the grade or quality of the properties is not important in this determination. Since both properties involved realty that was held for investment, the exchange would come within §1031, and Patty would report no gain.

SALE OF PRINCIPAL RESIDENCE

22. (c) If a taxpayer over the age of 55 sold her/his principal residence before August 6, 1997, then that taxpayer could elect to exclude $125,000 of any gain that is realized on such sale. A taxpayer was also able to defer the recognition of a gain on

the sale of a principal residence before August 6, 1997, if the taxpayer reinvested the proceeds from such sale into another house within 2 years (§1034).

Net sales price	$ 260,000
Over 55 exclusion amount	(125,000)
Adjusted selling price	135,000
Amount reinvested (maximum allowable deferred gain)	(90,000)
Gain recognized on the sale	$ 45,000
Adjusted selling price	$ 135,000
Basis of former home	70,000
Realized gain	$ 65,000
Cost of new residence	$ 90,000
Less: Deferred gain (65 – 45)	(20,000)
Basis of new residence	$ 70,000

23. (a) A single taxpayer may exclude up to $250,000 of gain from the sale of a principal residence after August 5, 1997. The exclusion may be applied once every two years without regard to sales under the old provisions. Generally, neither the $125,000 nor the replacement exclusion is available if the residence is sold after August 6, 1997.

INVOLUNTARY CONVERSIONS

24. (d) Section 1033(a)(2) provides that in order to qualify for nonrecognition of gain, a taxpayer, in the case of an involuntary conversion into money, has to acquire qualified replacement property within 2 years after the close of the first taxable year in which any part of the gain upon conversion is realized. Section 1033(g)(4) extends this period another year in the case of a condemnation of real property held for productive use in a trade or business or for investment. Part of the gain was first realized on March 31, 20X1. Thus, the taxpayer has until 3 years from the close of 20X1, i.e., until December 31, 20X4, to replace the condemned office building.

SECURITIES

25. (a) Smith realized a loss of $2,000 under §1001(a) on the sale of the 100 shares bought on December 15 [$13,000 – $15,000 = ($2,000)]. However, none of this loss is recognized in 20X1 because no loss was realized in 20X1. The loss is not recognized in the next year either, under the wash sale provisions of §1091. Smith bought 100 identical shares on December 30, 20X1, which is within 30 days either side of the date of sale. The loss not recognized adds to the basis of the 100 shares bought on December 30, 20X1, as provided by §1091. Thus, the basis of the 100 shares bought on December 30, 20X1 is $15,000 ($13,000 + $2,000).

SOLUTION 28-2 ADDITIONAL MULTIPLE CHOICE ANSWERS

INHERITANCE

26. **(d)** Inheritances are excluded from taxable income. For Hall to have taxable income, the stock must be sold at a gain. In general, §1014 provides that the basis of property acquired from a decedent shall be its fair market value as of the date of the decedent's death. However, §1014 provides an exception if the executor elects under §2032 to use the alternative valuation date. In such a case, §1014 provides that the basis of property acquired from a decedent shall be its value at the applicable valuation date under §2032. Section 2032 provides that if the executor elects the alternative valuation date, the basis of property distributed within 6 months of the decedent's death shall be its value as of the date of distribution. Section 2032 states that under the alternative valuation date, the value of property not distributed within 6 months of the decedent's death shall be its value as of the date 6 months after the decedent's death. In this case, Hall received the property within 6 months of the decedent's death. Thus, Hall's basis is the $4,500 value of the property as of the date of distribution. He sold the property immediately for $4,500. The amount realized of $4,500 less his basis of $4,500 results in zero recognized gain under §1001.

27. **(b)** Property acquired from a decedent is automatically considered to have been held for more than the requisite long-term holding period (§1223). Thus, Rork's holding period will be long-term.

COST RECOVERY

28. **(b)** Under §168(d)(3), if the aggregate basis of depreciable personal property placed in service during the last 3 months of the taxable year exceed 40% of the aggregate basis of such property placed in service during the taxable year, then the taxpayer must use the mid-quarter convention for all such property placed in service during the year. In this case, the taxpayer purchased and placed into service 100% of depreciable personal property in the last 3 months of the taxable year. Because this percentage is greater than 40%, Data Corp. ordinarily must use the mid-quarter convention in determining MACRS deductions with respect to the office equipment. Taxpayers who have September 11, 2001, in the third or fourth quarter of the 2001 tax year may elect not to apply the mid-quarter convention pursuant to IRS Notice 2001-70. This election is not available during tax year 2002. However, in 2002, if the property qualifies for JCWAA '02 bonus depreciation, the mid-quarter convention doesn't apply.

SECTION 1231 & CAPITAL ASSETS

29. **(b)** Under §1211(b), individuals are allowed to offset capital losses to the extent of capital gains plus up to $3,000 of ordinary income (assuming they have enough capital loss). For this purpose, married couples filing jointly are considered as one individual. Unused capital losses are carried forward indefinitely until they are absorbed.

30. **(b)** Section 1245(a)(1) provides that upon the sale of depreciable business property (other than depreciable real property), the seller must recapture as ordinary income an amount equal to the lesser of (1) the realized gain on the sale or (2) the depreciation claimed over the life of the property, *notwithstanding any other income tax provision*. Section 1231 governs the tax treatment of gains and losses from the sale or exchange of property used in a trade or business. The machinery was sold for a realized gain of $20,000 ($40,000 sales price less $20,000 adjusted basis). Up to the time of sale, $14,000 of depreciation had been claimed on the machinery. Thus, <u>$14,000</u> is recognized as ordinary income under §1245. The remaining <u>$6,000</u> of gain is treated as §1231 gain.

31. **(d)** Section 1231 assets are land or depreciable assets that are used in a trade or business. Both the parking lot and the shed qualify as §1231 assets.

RELATED PARTY TRANSACTIONS

32. **(b)** Fay realized a loss of $4,000 ($15,000 – $11,000) on the sale of the shares to her son Martin. However, none of this loss is recognized because §267 provides that no loss may be recognized on the sale of property to a related party. Section 267 states that a related party includes members of a family. Section 267 includes lineal descendants in the definition of family members. Martin has a cost basis of $11,000 in the shares under §1012. When Martin sells the shares to an unrelated party for $16,000, he realizes a gain of $5,000 ($16,000 – $11,000) under §1001(a). However, §267 provides that the gain recognized is reduced by the previously disallowed loss. Thus, Martin's recognized gain is $1,000 ($5,000 – $4,000).

EXCHANGES

33. **(d)** In a like-kind exchange under §1031, the taxpayer is required to recognize gain in an amount equal to the lesser of (1) the realized gain or (2) the amount of money and/or other property, i.e.,

boot, received in the exchange. Liabilities assumed by the other party are treated as boot received by the taxpayer. Therefore, the net reduction in the taxpayer's mortgage indebtedness is treated as money or other property received [Reg. §1.1031(d)-2]. In this problem, Wright realized a gain of $95,000 ($15,000 cash + $125,000 FMV of property received + $35,000 reduction in indebtedness − $80,000 adjusted basis of property exchanged). However, only $50,000 of gain is recognized because of the receipt of money or other property ($15,000 cash + $35,000 reduction in mortgage indebtedness).

SALE OF PRINCIPAL RESIDENCE

34. (c)   Section 1034 requires that a gain on the sale of a principal residence before August 5, 1997, be recognized only to the extent that the adjusted sales price of the old residence exceeds the cost of the new residence. Because Derek purchased a new principal residence in the same month, he meets the criteria for gain deferral under §1034. Also, the new principal residence must be purchased within 2 years on either side of the sale date of the old residence. The gain recognized is the lesser of the gain realized or the adjusted sales price of the old home less the cost of the new home. The cost of the bathroom is a capital improvement that adds to the basis of the home sold. The gain recognized is the lesser of (1) the $5,000 gain realized or (2) the excess of the adjusted sales price over the cost of the new residence. The adjusted basis in the new home is the purchase price less the deferred gain of the old home.

Contract Sales Price		$ 80,000
Less: Realtor's Commission		(5,000)
Amount Realized		$ 75,000
Original Cost	$65,000	
Cost of Added Bathroom	5,000	
Less Adjusted Basis		(70,000)
Gain Realized		$ 5,000
Amount Realized		$ 75,000
Less: Fixing-up Expenses		(0)
Adjusted Sales Price		$ 75,000
Less: Cost of New Residence		(200,000)
Gain Recognized in 1996 (Zero if negative)		$ 0
Cost of New Residence		$ 200,000
Less: Deferred Gain on New Home		(5,000)
Basis of Replacement Residence		$ 195,000

PERFORMANCE BY SUBTOPICS

Each category below parallels a subtopic covered in Chapter 28. Record the number and percentage of questions you correctly answered in each subtopic area.

Adjusted Basis

Question #	Correct √
1	
2	
# Questions	2

Correct _____
% Correct _____

Gift

Question #	Correct √
3	
4	
# Questions	2

Correct _____
% Correct _____

Inheritance

Question #	Correct √
5	
6	
# Questions	2

Correct _____
% Correct _____

Cost Recovery

Question #	Correct √
7	
8	
9	
# Questions	3

Correct _____
% Correct _____

Section 1231 & Capital Assets

Question #	Correct √
10	
11	
12	
13	
14	
15	
# Questions	6

Correct _____
% Correct _____

Installment Sales

Question #	Correct √
16	
# Questions	1

Correct _____
% Correct _____

Related Party Transactions

Question #	Correct √
17	
18	
19	
# Questions	3

Correct _____
% Correct _____

Exchanges

Question #	Correct √
20	
21	
# Questions	2

Correct _____
% Correct _____

Sale of Principal Residence

Question #	Correct √
22	
23	
# Questions	2

Correct _____
% Correct _____

Involuntary Conversions

Question #	Correct √
24	
# Questions	1

Correct _____
% Correct _____

Securities

Question #	Correct √
25	
# Questions	1

Correct _____
% Correct _____

FREQUENTLY ASKED QUESTIONS: FEDERAL TAXATION

FAQ: *Why is alimony included in gross income and then deducted from AGI?*

A: Alimony **received** is included in gross income. Alimony **paid** is deducted from gross income to arrive at adjusted gross income (AGI). Usually alimony received and alimony paid are **not** on the same return. For example, if a former husband pays alimony to a former wife, the former husband deducts the alimony on his return to calculate his AGI and the former wife includes it in her gross income.

FAQ: *What is the purpose of the alimony recapture rules?*

A: Alimony recapture rules preclude a divorced person from deducting an in-substance property settlement to a former spouse [non-deductible by the paying former spouse (PFS)] that is spread over a two year period as alimony payments (deductible by the PFS). In essence, if the alimony payments in the first and second years of a divorce exceed the alimony payments of the third year (plus a cushion of $15,000), the IRS will reclassify the excess payments as a property settlement. (The PFS will have to recapture this as income.)

FAQ: *How does the discharge of debt create taxable income?*

A: **Gross income includes all income unless there is a specific exclusion provided by law.** The receipt of loan proceeds is not income at the time of receipt. If the loan is not repaid, the taxpayer has effectively received income. There is not an exclusion for this.

FAQ: *Why is the loss on the sale of a personal-use sailboat not deductible from income?*

A: **No expenditures are tax deductible unless there is a specific provision allowing their deduction.** There are very few provisions for personal expenses or losses.

(FAQ are not necessarily heavily tested by the examiners, merely frequently asked by candidates. They are not intended to summarize, or identify highlights of, the tax chapters. For more complete discussions, see the related material in the text and explanations to questions.)

2002 TAX ACT

The Job Creation & Worker Assistance Act of 2002 (JCWAA '02) includes business economic stimulus provisions, some general retroactively effective tax breaks, and some relief provisions only for lower-Manhattan entities affected by terrorist acts on September 11, 2001. The Bisk Education editors believe details on the provisions applicable only to lower-Manhattan are beyond the scope of the exam. JCWAA '02 became effective on March 9, 2002.

Bisk Education CPA review materials are designed to help you pass the current exam. Provisions that are not yet effective are not tested; thus you unnecessarily would add time to your review by studying them. We do not discourage your interest in these provisions, but we caution you not to delude yourself that this study is exam preparation. Generally, provisions that are not effective until 2004 or later are not in this edition—which already is more than you are likely to need. Some future changes to current provisions are discussed when the additional space to do so is not significant. Future editions and updating supplements will provide information about provisions as they become eligible for testing. Study those provisions that are applicable to your exam.

CHAPTER 29

FEDERAL TAXATION: CORPORATIONS

EXAM COVERAGE: The corporate taxation portion of the ARE section of the CPA exam is designated by the examiners to be 20 percent of the section's point value. Historically exam coverage of the topics in this chapter hovers at 15 to 20 percent of the ARE section due to coverage of some parts of this topic in Chapter 28 *Federal Taxation: Property* and to a lesser extent Chapter 27 *Federal Taxation: Individuals*. More information about the point value of different topics is included in the **Practical Advice** section of this volume.

CHAPTER 29

FEDERAL TAXATION: CORPORATIONS

I. OVERVIEW

Many of the concepts that apply to individuals also apply to corporations. Therefore, we will concentrate on explaining and highlighting how the tax rules for a corporation are different from those for individuals. To help you understand the flow of corporate tax liability, we begin by outlining Form 1120, the Corporate Income Tax Return.

STEP ONE: DETERMINE INCOME

	Gross receipts
LESS:	Cost of goods sold (Schedule A)
EQUALS:	Gross profit
PLUS:	1. Dividends (Schedule C)
	2. Interest
	3. Rent
	4. Royalties
	5. Capital gains (Schedule D)
	6. Other gains and losses (Form 4797)
	7. Other income

STEP TWO: LESS DEDUCTIONS

1. Compensation of officers (Schedule E)
2. Salaries and wages
3. Repairs and maintenance
4. Bad debts
5. Rents
6. Taxes and licenses
7. Interest
8. Charitable contributions
9. Depreciation (Form 4562)
10. Depletion
11. Advertising
12. Pension, profit sharing plans
13. Employee benefit programs
14. Other deductions
15. Net operating loss
16. Dividends received deduction (Schedule C)

STEP THREE: EQUALS TAXABLE INCOME

STEP FOUR: COMPUTE TAX (Schedule J)

STEP FIVE: LESS PAYMENTS

1. Prior year overpayment applied to current year
2. Estimated payments
3. Payment with extension

STEP SIX: LESS CREDITS

    1.   Credit from regulated investment companies
    2.   Credit for federal tax on fuels

STEP SEVEN: EQUALS OVERPAYMENT OR AMOUNT DUE

A.   CHARACTERISTICS

A corporation is an entity formed by associates to conduct a business venture and divide the profits among the investors. A corporation files a charter and articles of incorporation with a state government. It also prepares bylaws, has a board of directors, and issues shares of stock.

- Treasury regulations set forth the definition of a corporation for federal tax purposes. An entity satisfying the definition is taxed as a corporation. Those same regulations also provide for the federal tax treatment of entities not meeting the corporate definition. Those entities may elect to be treated as either corporations or partnerships for federal tax purposes. Prior to January 1, 1997, corporate treatment of non-corporate entities was based on the presence of a majority of four characteristics: limited liability, free transferability of ownership interest, centralized management, and continuity of life.

B.   TRANSFERS IN EXCHANGE FOR STOCK

No gain or loss is recognized if property is transferred to a corporation solely in exchange for stock if, immediately after the transfer, the transferor(s) are in control of the corporation.

1.   Property includes everything except services.

2.   Control is defined for purposes of these rules as owning 80% of the voting power and 80% of the nonvoting stock.

3.   Receipt of boot (property other than stock) triggers gain recognition. However, no loss is recognized. *Non-qualified preferred stock* is treated as boot.

    a.   Non-qualified preferred stock has one of the following characteristics:

        (1)   The holder has the right to require the issuer (or a related person) to redeem or purchase the stock;

        (2)   The issuer is required to redeem or purchase the stock;

        (3)   The issuer has the right to redeem or purchase the stock and, as of the issue date, it is more likely than not that this right will be exercised; or

        (4)   The dividend rate on the stock varies according to interests rates, commodity price, or similar indices, in form or substance.

    b.   The following exchanges are excluded from this gain recognition;

        (1)   Certain exchanges of preferred stock for comparable preferred stock of the same or lesser value;

        (2)   Exchange of preferred stock for common stock;

        (3)   Certain exchanges of debt securities for preferred stock of the same or lesser value; and

        (4)   Exchanges of stock in certain recapitalizations of family-owned corporations.

4.   If property that is subject to a liability is transferred, gain is recognized if the liabilities exceed the basis of the property transferred.

5. The shareholder's basis in the stock is equal to the *adjusted basis* of the property transferred plus any gain recognized, less any boot received.

6. The basis of the property to the *corporation* is the transferor's adjusted basis plus any gain recognized by the transferor on the transfer.

C. FILING REQUIREMENTS

A C corporation must file Form 1120, *U.S. Corporation Income Tax Return*, with the IRS on or before the 15th day of the third month after the close of its tax year. For a calendar year corporation, the return is due March 15.

1. If the due date falls on a weekend or a legal holiday, the return is due on the next business day.

2. An automatic six month extension is available by filing Form 7004. However, this extends the time for filing the return, not for paying the tax.

D. ESTIMATED PAYMENTS

If a corporation's tax liability is $500 or more, it must make quarterly estimated tax payments. The installments are due on the 15th day of the fourth, sixth, ninth, and twelfth month of the tax year. For a calendar year corporation, the installments are due April 15, June 15, September 15, and December 15. If any of the due dates fall on a weekend or a legal holiday, the payment is due on the next business day. For 2001 and 2004, EGTRRA '01 extends the September 15 deadline until October 1. The September 15 deadline is applicable to 2002 and 2003.

E. TAX RATES

Certain personal service corporations must pay a flat rate of tax of 35%, regardless of their taxable income.

EXHIBIT 1 ♦ TAX RATES

Taxable Income	Tax Rate	Taxable Income	Tax Rate
$0 - $ 50,000	15%	$ 335,001 - $10,000,000	34%
$ 50,001 - $ 75,000	25%	$10,000,001 - $15,000,000	35%
$ 75,001 - $100,000	34%	$15,000,001 - $18,333,333	38%
$100,001 - $335,000	39%	Over $18,333,333	35%

- The 5% surtax on corporate income between $100,000 and $335,000 is imposed to phase out the benefit of the 15% and 25% bracket for high income corporations. The 3% surtax on corporate income between $15 million and $18,333,333 is also imposed to phase out the benefit of the 34% rate.

II. CORPORATE INCOME TAX

A. GROSS INCOME

All deductible corporate expenses are assumed to be incurred in the furtherance of trade or business, and are directly subtracted from gross income. The concepts of adjusted gross income, itemized deductions, the standard deduction, and personal exemptions that apply to the taxation of individuals do not apply to corporations

B. ORGANIZATIONAL EXPENSES

These are costs incurred incident to the creation of the corporation, are chargeable to a capital account, and if the corporation had a limited life, they would be amortizable over that life. Examples of organizational expenses include the costs of temporary directors, organizational meetings, and legal expenses associated with the formation of the corporation.

1. A corporation may elect to amortize its organizational expenses over a period of at least 60 months. To qualify for the election, the expenses must be incurred before the end of the first tax year in which the corporation is in business. Expenses that qualify for this election include state incorporation fees, and legal and accounting expenses incidental to the organization.

2. Costs related to the issuance of stock are **not** organizational expenses. (Stock issuance costs are netted against the proceeds in the tax year in which they are incurred.)

C.   DIVIDENDS-RECEIVED DEDUCTION

C Corporations are entitled to a special deduction for dividends received from domestic corporations. The deduction is limited to a percentage of the dividends received based on the percentage ownership of the distributing corporation by the recipient corporation.

EXHIBIT 2 ♦ DIVIDEND-RECEIVED-DEDUCTION PERCENTAGES

Percentage of ownership by corporate shareholder	Deduction percentage
Less than 20%	70%
20% or more (but less than 80%)	80%
80% or more (affiliated groups)	100%

1. Generally, the deduction is limited to 80% (70% if less than 20% ownership) of taxable income computed **without** regard to the dividends-received deduction. However, if taking the full dividends-received deduction creates a net operating loss, the taxable income limitation is **not** applicable.

EXAMPLE 1 ♦ DIVIDENDS-RECEIVED DEDUCTION

For 20X1, Tree Sap Corporation had $500,000 of income from logging operations, $550,000 in expenses, and $100,000 of dividend income from a 40% owned corporation. Based on this information, Tree Sap is able to deduct 80% of the dividends it received, resulting in a $30,000 net operating loss.

Income from logging operations	$ 500,000
Dividend income	100,000
Total income	$ 600,000
Less: Expenses	(550,000)
Tentative taxable income (computed without regard to the 80% dividends-received deduction)	50,000
Less: 80% dividends-received deduction	(80,000)
Net operating loss for 20X1	$ (30,000)*

*NOTE: Taking the 80% dividends-received deduction from tentative taxable income results in a net operating loss. Therefore, the deduction is allowed for $80,000 (the full 80% of the dividends). The 80%-of-taxable-income limitation does **not** apply whenever use of the 80% dividend-received deduction results in a net operating loss.

2. No deduction is allowed for stock that is held for short periods of time. For purposes of this rule, the holding period is measured from the dividend date to the disposition date. Generally, stock must be held for more than 45 days during a 90-day period beginning 45 days before the taxpayer becomes entitled to receive the dividend. For preferred stock, the holding period is more than 90 days during a 180-day period beginning 90 days before the taxpayers becomes entitled to receive the dividend. (This provision was aimed at preventing hedging or short sales by the taxpayer to protect itself against the risk of loss.)

D.   KEYMAN LIFE INSURANCE

Premiums on keyman life insurance policies are **not** deductible by the corporation. The proceeds from these policies are **not** included in taxable corporate income.

E.   CHARITABLE CONTRIBUTIONS

A corporation's deduction for charitable contributions is limited to 10% of taxable income without regard to (1) the deduction for charitable contributions, (2) the dividends-received deduction, (3) any net operating loss carryback to that year, and (4) any capital loss carryback to that year. The current and carried forward deduction is limited each year to 10% of taxable income. Any contributions that are not currently deductible because of the 10% rule may be carried forward for **five** years.

F.   CAPITAL GAINS & LOSSES

Corporate capital losses are deductible only against capital gains. In other words, unlike individuals, corporations are **not** allowed to deduct any net capital losses.

1.   Excess capital losses may be carried back three years and carried forward five years.

2.   Capital losses that are carried forward or back are treated as **short-term** capital losses.

G.   NET OPERATING LOSS (NOL)

When deductions exceed income, the result is a net operating loss. This loss may be carried back two years and forward **twenty**. Carrybacks and carryforwards are not included in the computation of a current year NOL. The Job Creation & Worker Assistance Act of 2002 (JCWAA '02) temporarily modifies this provision.

1.   **CHANGE** For 2001 and 2002, the carryback period is extended to **five** years, so taxpayers may carry back NOLs for five years rather than the normal two.

2.   **AMT** Additionally for 2001 and 2002, AMT may offset 100%, rather than 90% of AMTI calculated without regard to this deduction. The former law says that a AMT NOL may offset up to 90% of AMTI calculated without regard to this deduction. What this does is allows the full use or 100%, use of that AMT NOL.

3.   **DISCUSSION** JCWAA '02 extends the allowance previously only for casualty and theft type of losses to almost any business NOL. It does not apply to certain interest expense relating to equity reduction transactions and similar items beyond the scope of the exam. Generally, most businesses may take their NOLs for a five-year carryback period without adjustment.

III. ALTERNATIVE MINIMUM TAX (AMT)

A.   GENERAL

The purpose of the alternative minimum tax rules is to ensure that corporations pay a minimum amount of tax. If a corporation's tentative alternative tax exceeds its regular tax liability, the excess is paid in **addition** to the regular tax due. The starting point for computing a corporation's alternative minimum taxable income is regular taxable income.

B.   ADJUSTMENTS

Corporate adjustments for AMT are very similar to individual adjustments for AMT. Adjustments can be either positive or negative. Examples include

1.   Long-term contracts

2.   Installment sales of certain property

3.   Excess depreciation of post-1986 **real** property over straight-line. Excess depreciation of post-1986 **personal** property over 150% MACRS. TRA '97 changed the recovery **periods** for assets placed in service after December 31, 1998. (The 150% and straight-line **rates** remain the same as pre-TRA '97.) This provision is modified by JCWAA '02, as discussed in Chapter 27.

4.   Basis adjustments in determining gain or loss from the sale or exchange of property

5. Passive activities

6. Certain loss limitations

C. PREFERENCES

Corporate preferences for AMT are very similar to individual preferences for AMT. Preferences are always positive. Examples of preferences are

1. Percentage depletion

2. Tax-exempt interest from private activity bonds issued after August 7, 1986

3. Appreciated property given to charity

4. Intangible drilling costs

5. Accelerated depreciation on pre-1987 real property

D. ADJUSTED CURRENT EARNINGS (ACE)

The most distinctive difference between individual and corporate AMT calculations is the adjustment for ACE. Certain adjustments are made to alternative minimum taxable income (AMTI) to arrive at ACE. If ACE exceeds AMTI, 75% of this difference becomes a positive adjustment to AMTI. The ACE adjustment can be negative; however, any negative adjustments are limited to prior positive adjustments. These adjustments to arrive at ACE include

1. Municipal interest income

2. Dividend-received deduction (under 20% ownership)

E. EXEMPTION

Corporations are allowed a $40,000 exemption when computing the alternative minimum tax. This exemption is phased out by 25% of alternative minimum taxable income that exceeds $150,000. Therefore, the exemption is zero when corporate alternative minimum income is $310,000.

EXAMPLE 2 ♦ AMT

Max Corporation has minimum taxable income of $250,000 and a foreign tax credit of $10,000. Max is ineligible for the small business exception.

REQUIRED: Compute Max's AMT exemption and liability.

SOLUTION:

Standard Exemption		$ 40,000
Minimum Taxable Income (MTI)	$ 250,000	
Phaseout Threshold	(150,000)	
Excess MTI Over Threshold	100,000	
Reduction Percentage	.25	
Reduction		(25,000)
Max Corporation's AMT Exemption		$ 15,000
Minimum Taxable Income		$250,000
Less: AMT Exemption		(15,000)
AMT Taxable Income		235,000
AMT Rate		.20
Alternative Minimum Tax		47,000
Less: Foreign Tax Credit		(10,000)
Alternative Tax Liability		$ 37,000

F.   EXCEPTION

Corporate AMT for small business corporations is repealed. A corporation with average gross receipts of less than $5 million for the 3-year period before the current tax year is a small business corporation. A corporation that meets the $5 million gross receipts test will continue to be treated as a small business corporation exempt from the alternative minimum tax so long as its average gross receipts for the 3-year period before the current tax year do not exceed $7.5 million. A former small business corporation is subject to corporate AMT only with respect to preferences and adjustments relating to transactions entered into after losing its small business corporation status. The AMT credit allowable to a small business corporation is limited to the amount by which the corporation's regular tax liability (reduced by other credits) exceeds 25% of the excess of the corporation's regular tax (reduced by other credits) over $25,000.

G.   AMT CREDIT

To the extent AMT exceeds the regular tax liability, the corporation is entitled to a credit for the excess AMT. This credit may be carried over indefinitely, but can be used only to offset the corporation's regular tax.

EXAMPLE 3 ♦ AMT CREDIT

> In 20X0, Alpha Corporation's regular tax liability was $30,000, and its AMT liability was $45,000. Thus, Alpha was entitled to a $15,000 AMT credit. For 20X1, the regular tax is $60,000 and the AMT only $50,000. Alpha is entitled to reduce its 20X1 regular tax liability by the AMT credit carryover, but not below the 20X1 alternative tax amount. Thus, Alpha will reduce its regular tax by $10,000 (from $60,000 to $50,000) and carry over the unused $5,000 portion of the credit to 20X2 and subsequent years.

IV.   RECONCILIATION OF BOOK INCOME TO TAXABLE INCOME

A.   SCHEDULE M-1

Book income may not equal taxable income due to temporary and permanent differences. Unlike in financial accounting, it is not necessary to distinguish permanent and temporary differences for purposes of reconciling the book income to taxable income. Schedule M-1 of Form 1120 is used to reconcile book income to taxable income. The net book income is adjusted until it reconciles with the taxable income.

B.   ADDITIONS TO BOOK INCOME

1.   Federal income tax expense.

2.   The excess of capital losses over capital gains.

3.   Income items for tax purposes that are not included in book income, e.g., prepaid rents, royalties, interest, and service fees.

4.   Expenses deducted for book purposes that are not deductible for tax purposes, e.g., accrued contingent liabilities, premiums on keyman life insurance policies, business gifts to the extent that they exceed $25, charitable contributions in excess of the 10% of taxable income limitation, expenses incurred in connection with tax-exempt income, and different methods used for computing depreciation.

C.   SUBTRACTIONS FROM BOOK INCOME

1.   Income reported on the books but not for tax, e.g., interest on municipal bonds and life insurance proceeds on keyman life insurance.

2. Deductions reported on the tax return but not charged against book income, e.g., the dividends-received deduction, charitable contribution carryovers, and different methods used for computing depreciation.

V. EARNINGS & PROFITS

A. DEFINITION

It is important to understand the concept of earnings and profits (E&P) because distributions made by the corporation to its shareholders are taxable as dividends to the extent of E&P. The term "earnings and profits" is not defined explicitly in the Code. E&P is similar to, but not the same as, retained earnings. There are two types of earnings and profits: **current** and **accumulated**. Accumulated E&P is the sum of all previous years' current E&P as computed on the first day of each taxable year. Even though distributions are taxable to the extent of total E&P, it is necessary to distinguish between current E&P and accumulated E&P for the following reasons:

1. If current E&P is positive and accumulated E&P is negative, then distributions are treated as dividends to the extent of **current** E&P.

2. If current E&P is negative and accumulated E&P is positive, then the two accounts are netted at the date of the distribution. If the net result is less than or equal to zero, the distribution is a **return of capital**. If the net result is positive, the distribution is a **dividend** to the extent of net E&P.

3. Current E&P is allocated on a **pro rata** basis to the distributions made during the year. Accumulated E&P, on the other hand, is applied to the distributions in the order that they are made.

EXAMPLE 4 ♦ EARNINGS & PROFITS

X Corporation has an accumulated deficit in E&P, yet it has current E&P of $500. It makes a cash dividend distribution of $600 and has no income or loss on the distribution. The shareholders have dividend income of $500 and a tax-free return of capital of $100, that reduces their basis in the stock, but not below zero. Once the tax basis of the stock has been reduced to zero, further distributions are treated as capital gains.

B. COMPUTATION

E&P is computed in a similar manner as taxable income. Once taxable income is computed, there are several adjustments that must be made to arrive at E&P.

1. **ADDITIONS TO TAXABLE INCOME**

   a. Tax-exempt income

   b. Key-man life insurance proceeds

   c. Charitable contributions deduction carried over from a previous year

   d. Percentage depletion

   e. Accelerated depreciation greater than straight-line amount

   f. Deferred gain on an installment sale

   g. Intangible drilling costs deducted currently

   h. Mine exploration and development costs

2. **SUBTRACTIONS TO TAXABLE INCOME**

    a. Federal income taxes

    b. Loss on sale between related parties

    c. Key-man life insurance premiums

    d. Charitable contributions made in excess of the 10% taxable income limitation

C. DISTRIBUTIONS

Distributions can be made in cash, property, or stock. Generally, stock dividends are tax-free to the shareholder.

1. **EFFECT OF PROPERTY DIVIDEND TO SHAREHOLDER** When the corporation distributes property to a shareholder, the distribution is equal to the fair market value of the property on the date of the distribution. First, the distribution is treated as a dividend to the extent of E&P. Then it is treated as a tax-free return of capital to the extent of the shareholder's basis in the corporation's stock. Any remaining amount is a capital gain to the shareholder.

2. **EFFECT OF PROPERTY DIVIDEND TO CORPORATION** When the corporation distributes property, it is treated as if it sold the property to its shareholders for the property's fair market value. The corporation recognizes gain, but not loss, on the distribution of property.

3. **EFFECT OF DISTRIBUTIONS ON E&P** When the corporation makes a distribution, E&P is reduced by the amount of cash distributed and by the greater of the fair market value or adjusted basis of any property distributed, less the amount of any liability on the property. E&P is increased by the gain recognized on any property distributed.

EXAMPLE 5 ♦ PROPERTY DISTRIBUTIONS

Service Corporation distributed property with a basis of $50,000 and a fair market value of $100,000 to its two shareholders. Shareholder A is a 50% owner of Service Corporation and has a basis in her stock of $50,000. Shareholder B is also a 50% owner in Service Corporation and has a basis in his stock of $30,000. Service Corporation has a balance in its current E&P account of $20,000 and $40,000 in its accumulated E&P account, before considering the effect of the distribution. Service Corporation recognizes a gain of $50,000 on the distribution ($100,000 FMV – $50,000 adj. basis). Thus current E&P increases to $70,000. E&P is then reduced by the fair market value of the distribution, which is $100,000. Therefore, current E&P is reduced to $0, accumulated E&P is reduced to $10,000, and each shareholder receives a $50,000 taxable dividend.

VI. REDEMPTIONS & LIQUIDATIONS

A. STOCK REDEMPTION

If a corporation buys back its own stock from its shareholders, the transaction is treated like a sale for tax purposes. The shareholders will generally recognize a capital gain or loss on the redemption if one of the following five tests is met; otherwise, the redemption proceeds will be taxable as a dividend.

1. The redemption is not essentially equivalent to a dividend. This has been interpreted to mean that there has been a meaningful reduction in the shareholder's voting rights, share in the earnings, and share of the assets upon liquidation.

2. The redemption is substantially disproportionate. This is met if, after the redemption, the shareholder owns less than 50% of the total number of voting shares outstanding and less than 80% of the percentage s/he owned immediately before the redemption.

3.   All of the shareholder's stock is redeemed.

4.   The redemption is from a noncorporate shareholder in a partial liquidation.

5.   The redemption is effected to pay death taxes.

B.   COMPLETE LIQUIDATIONS
A complete liquidation is a distribution by a corporation in a single or series of transactions that redeem all of the corporation's stock.

1.   **CONSEQUENCES TO SHAREHOLDERS** Shareholders recognize gain or loss on the distribution to the extent that the money and FMV of property received (less liabilities subject to or assumed) differ from their bases in the stock.

  a.   If the stock is a capital asset in the hands of the shareholder, then the distribution equals a capital gain or loss.

  b.   The basis of the property received is its FMV at the date of distribution.

2.   **CONSEQUENCES TO LIQUIDATING CORPORATION** Generally, the corporation recognizes gain or loss on the distribution of its assets in a complete liquidation.

  a.   The gain or loss is computed as if the corporation had sold the property to the distributee at FMV.

  b.   If the distributed property is subject to a liability or the shareholder assumes a liability in excess of the basis of the distributed property, FMV is deemed to be at least the amount of the liability.

  c.   A corporation does not recognize gain or loss on a liquidating distribution to a controlling corporate shareholder that takes a carryover basis in the distributed property (e.g., a subsidiary is liquidated into its parent).

VII. PENALTY TAXES

A.   ACCUMULATED EARNINGS TAX
This tax is imposed on the accumulation of earnings beyond the reasonable needs of the business. Reasonable needs for accumulation of earnings include expansion, retirement of debt, and working capital needs. The purpose of the accumulated earnings tax is to penalize corporations that accumulate earnings to avoid the taxation of their shareholders.

1.   The number of shareholders has no effect on whether or not the tax is imposed. However, the following corporations are exempt from the tax: S Corporations, personal holding companies, foreign personal holding companies, tax-exempt organizations, and passive foreign investment companies.

2.   Corporations are allowed a credit equal to $250,000 ($150,000 for certain service corporations) plus dividends paid during the first 2½ months of the tax year, minus accumulated E&P at the close of the preceding tax year. In other words, a corporation is allowed to accumulate up to the credit amount before it has to prove that there is a reasonable need for the accumulation.

3.   The accumulated earnings tax is 39.6% of accumulated taxable income.

B.   PERSONAL HOLDING COMPANY TAX
The purpose of the personal holding company tax is to discourage the sheltering of certain types of passive income in corporations. Similar to the accumulated earnings tax, the personal holding company tax is designed to encourage the distribution of corporate earnings to the shareholders. If

a corporation passes a gross income test and a stock ownership test, it is considered a personal holding company.

1. **GROSS INCOME TEST** This test is met if 60% or more of the corporation's adjusted ordinary gross income (AOGI) consists of certain passive income (PHC income). Examples of PHC income include dividends, interest, rents, royalties, and personal service contracts.

2. **STOCK OWNERSHIP TEST** This test is met if more than 50% of the value of the outstanding stock is owned either directly or indirectly by five or fewer individuals at any time during the last half of the tax year.

3. **PENALTY TAX** A corporation that is classified as a PHC must pay a penalty tax in addition to the regular corporate income tax. The PHC tax rate is 39.6%. The PHC tax is self-assessed by filing Form PH with the 1120.

4. **CONSENT DIVIDENDS** A corporation that meets the definition of a PHC may avoid the tax if the shareholders agree to receive **consent dividends**. These are hypothetical dividends that the shareholders pay tax on, even though nothing is actually received.

VIII. CORPORATE REORGANIZATIONS

A. TYPES OF REORGANIZATIONS
There are seven types of corporate reorganizations.

1. **TYPE "A"** A statutory merger or consolidation. A merger occurs when one corporation absorbs another. A consolidation occurs when two corporations form a new corporation and the former corporations dissolve.

2. **TYPE "B"** The acquisition of at least 80% of the voting power of all classes of stock and at least 80% of the total number of shares of nonvoting stock in exchange for all or part of the acquiring company's voting stock. No boot may be exchanged.

3. **TYPE "C"** The acquisition of substantially all of the assets of a corporation in exchange for voting stock. The acquired corporation must distribute all of the consideration that it receives, as well as all of its property. "Substantially all of the assets" means at least 90% of the FMV of net assets and at least 70% of the FMV of the gross assets.

4. **TYPE "D"** A transfer by a corporation of all or part of its assets to another corporation if, immediately after the transfer, the transferor or at least one of its shareholders owns at least 80% of the voting power of all classes of stock and at least 80% of the nonvoting stock.

5. **TYPE "E"** A recapitalization where there is a major change in the character and amount of the capital structure.

6. **TYPE "F"** A mere change in identity, form, or place of organization.

7. **TYPE "G"** A bankruptcy reorganization.

B. TAX CONSEQUENCES OF REORGANIZATION
A corporate reorganization is considered a mere restructuring of the form of business and is a tax-free event except to the extent of any boot.

1. **GAIN OR LOSS RECOGNITION** In a tax-free reorganization, the acquiring corporation does not recognize gain or loss unless it transfers appreciated property to the transferor corporation. The transferor corporation does not recognize gain or loss unless it fails to distribute other property received in the exchange or it distributes appreciated property to its shareholders.

2. **BASIS** The basis of property received by the acquiring corporation from the transferor corporation is equal to the transferor's basis plus any gain recognized by the transferor on the transfer.

EXAMPLE 6 ♦ BASIS

> Transferor Corporation transfers assets with a FMV of $75,000 and a basis of $20,000 to Acquiring Corporation for $75,000 worth of stock in Acquiring Corporation. This qualifies as a type "D" reorganization. Neither corporation recognizes a gain on the exchange. The Transferor's basis in the Acquiring Corporation's stock is $20,000.

EXAMPLE 7 ♦ GAIN OR LOSS RECOGNITION

> The same facts as in Example 6 except that Acquiring Corporation transfers stock worth $50,000 and property with a FMV of $25,000 and a basis of $10,000. In this case, Acquiring will recognize a gain of $15,000. If Transferor does not distribute the property, it will have to recognize a gain equal to the lesser of the gain realized or $25,000.

IX. AFFILIATED & CONTROLLED CORPORATIONS

A. COMPARISON

A controlled group refers to both parent-subsidiary and brother-sister corporations, while an affiliated group includes only parent-subsidiary corporations.

1. A parent-subsidiary relationship exists within an affiliated group when one corporation (the parent) owns 80% of the total voting power of all classes of stock **and** 80% of the value of nonvoting stock of another corporation (the subsidiary). This relationship exists within a controlled group when one corporation (the parent) owns 80% of the total voting power of all classes of stock **or** 80% of the total value of all classes of stock.

2. A brother-sister relationship exists within a controlled group when a shareholder group of five or fewer individuals, estates, or trusts meets both a total ownership test and a common ownership test. The total ownership test is met if the shareholder group owns at least 80% of the voting power of all classes of stock **or** at least 80% of the value of all classes of stock of each corporation. The common ownership test is met if the shareholder group owns more than 50% of the total combined voting power of all classes of stock **or** more than 50% of the total value of all classes of stock of each corporation.

B. CONTROLLED GROUP CHARACTERISTICS

1. The members are treated as one corporation for purposes of the first $75,000 of taxable income being taxed at less than 34%, the accumulated earnings credit, the AMTI exemption, the Section 179 expense deduction, etc.

2. Any loss realized on an intercompany sale is disallowed. If, however, the property is subsequently sold to an unrelated third party at a gain, the gain is reduced by the amount of the loss previously disallowed.

3. Any gain recognized on an intercompany sale of depreciable property must be recognized as ordinary income.

C. AFFILIATED GROUP CHARACTERISTICS

The members may elect to file a consolidated tax return. Once the election is made, it is binding on all future returns.

1.   If a consolidated return is filed, intercompany dividends are eliminated. If separate returns are filed, dividends from affiliated corporations are eligible for the 100% dividends-received deduction.

2.   The filing of a consolidated return enables the members of the affiliated group to defer any gains on intercompany profits.

X. S CORPORATIONS

A.   S STATUS ELECTION

An S corporation has the advantage of being classified as a corporation while generally being taxed at the shareholder level instead of at the corporate level. All current shareholders, plus any shareholders who held stock during the taxable year before the date of the election, must consent to the election. The election is made on Form 2553.

1.   To be valid for the current year, the election may be made either (a) during the preceding year, or (b) on or before the 15th day of the third month of the current taxable year. A late election is considered an election for the subsequent year.

2.   If the election is ineffective at the time it is made (e.g., a shareholder failed to consent or the corporation had too many shareholders) but the situation is corrected after the election date, it is considered an election for the subsequent year.

B.   ELIGIBILITY

1.   No more than 75 shareholders. Husband and wife are treated as one shareholder, and each beneficiary of a voting trust is considered a shareholder.

2.   Only one class of stock is allowed. A corporation with shares of stock that differ solely in voting rights will not be treated as having more than one class of stock.

3.   Shareholders may be individuals, estates (testamentary and bankruptcy), and trusts including the following: (a) grantor trusts during the life of the grantor plus 60 days, or plus 2 years if the trust is includable in the grantor's gross estate, (b) testamentary trusts for 60 days after the stock is transferred to the trust, (c) stock voting trusts, (d) qualified Subchapter S trusts, or (e) electing small business trusts. Tax-exempt entities may be S corporation shareholders. Nonresident aliens, corporations, and foreign trusts may not be shareholders.

4.   Ineligible corporations generally include members of affiliated groups, some corporations owning 80% subsidiaries, financial institutions, insurance companies, companies electing the possessions tax credit, and Domestic International Sales Corporations (DISCs). Certain banks that do not use the reserve method of accounting for bad debts may elect S status. S corporations may own certain 80% subsidiaries.

C.   TAXABLE YEAR

An S corporation is generally required to adopt a December 31 year end or a fiscal year that is the same as the fiscal year used by shareholders owning more than 50% of the corporation's stock.

1.   If a valid business purpose exists, an S corporation may ask for IRS approval to adopt a different fiscal year. A valid business purpose exists if for three consecutive years at least 25% of the S corporation's gross receipts are received in the last two months of the selected fiscal year.

2.   An S corporation may elect under Section 444 to use a fiscal year as long as the fiscal year does not result in a deferral period that is greater than 3 months.

•   If an S corporation elects to use a fiscal year under Section 444, then it must make required payments to the IRS every year. In essence, this required payment is a refundable, noninterest-bearing deposit that is intended to compensate the government for the revenue lost as a result of the tax deferral. The payment is determined by a formula and is due on May 15 each year. This payment must be recomputed each year. Note that if for any year the required payment is $500 or less, the S corporation is exempted from making the payment.

D.   COMPUTATION OF TAXABLE INCOME
In general, S corporations pass items of income, loss, deductions, and credits through to their shareholders. Consequently, taxes on S corporation income generally are paid at the shareholder level instead of at the corporate level. S corporations file Form 1120S instead of Form 1120. Form 1120S is due on the 15th day of the third month following the end of the tax year. For a calendar year S corporation, the due date is March 15th. If the due date falls on a weekend or legal holiday, the return is due on the following business day. The return is an informational return that reports total corporate income and each shareholder's pro rata share of this income. Shareholders then pay tax on their pro rata share of S corporation income regardless of whether or not any income was actually distributed to them. There are two types of income that are passed through to shareholders: nonseparately stated income and separately stated income.

1.   NONSEPARATELY STATED INCOME   This type of income is netted at the corporate level and then passed through to shareholders. It consists of ordinary income such as income derived from the active conduct of business and depreciation deductions recaptured as ordinary income. This income is reported on page 1 of Form 1120S.

2.   SEPARATELY STATED INCOME   This income retains its original character as it passes through to the shareholders. Any limitations are computed at the shareholder level instead of at the corporate level.

  a.   This income is reported in total on Schedule K and each shareholder receives a Schedule K-1 which denotes her/his pro rata share of S corporation income.

  b.   Examples of separately stated income include capital gains and losses; Section 1231 gains and losses; tax-exempt interest income; foreign income, losses, and taxes; passive gains, losses, and credits; interest and dividend income; royalty income; Section 179 expense deduction; tax preferences; depletion; investment income and expenses; charitable contributions; net income or loss from real estate activity; and net income or loss from rental activity.

3.   PRO RATA SHARE   A shareholder's pro rata share of each corporate item is computed on a daily basis according to the number of shares of stock held by the shareholder on each day of the corporation's taxable year.

  a.   If stock changes hands on a particular day, it is considered owned by the transferee on that day. If the relative interests of the shareholders do not change during the year, a daily calculation is not necessary.

  b.   If a shareholder terminates her/his interest, there is an election available to allocate S corporation income as if the taxable year ended on the date the shareholder's interest was terminated.

4.   CORPORATE LEVEL TAXATION   There are some instances in which the S corporation is required to pay taxes at the corporate level. Examples include excess capital gains, passive investment income, LIFO recapture, and built-in gains (the excess of the FMV of assets over their bases at the beginning of the first year in which the S corporation is effective).

E.   DEDUCTION OF LOSSES
A shareholder may not be able to currently deduct her/his entire share of corporate losses because there are basis, at-risk, and passive loss limitations.

1. **BASIS LIMITATIONS** A shareholder is not allowed to deduct losses in excess of her/his basis in the S corporation's stock and debt. Losses first reduce a shareholder's basis in the stock of the S corporation. Once this basis is reduced to zero, any additional losses reduce the shareholder's basis in S corporation debt. Any losses that are not currently deductible are carried over until the shareholder has sufficient basis to absorb the losses. A shareholder's initial basis in the corporation's stock is increased by the shareholder's pro rata share of non-separately stated income, separately stated income, and depletion in excess of basis in the property. In addition to the shareholder's pro rata share of losses, basis in stock is reduced by separately stated deduction items, distributions not reported as income by the share-holder (AAA distributions), and nondeductible expenses of the corporation. Debt basis is restored (up to the original amount) before basis is restored in stock.

2. **AT-RISK RULES** Generally, a shareholder is considered at risk with respect to an activity to the extent of cash and the adjusted basis of other property contributed to the activity plus amounts borrowed with respect to the activity to the extent the taxpayer is personally liable for the repayment or has pledged property not used in the activity that is used as security for the borrowed amount.

3. **PASSIVE LOSS RULES** A shareholder can deduct passive losses only to the extent of passive income. Any losses that are not currently deductible are carried forward until there is suffi-cient passive income to absorb them. The basis and at-risk limitations are applied before the passive loss limitations.

F. **ACCUMULATED ADJUSTMENTS ACCOUNT (AAA)**
This account is the cumulative total of undistributed net income items for S corporation taxable years beginning after 1982. Prior to 1982, S corporations had earnings and profits similar to C corporations. The adjustments made to AAA are similar to those made to the shareholders' stock bases, except that there is no adjustment for tax-exempt income and related expenses or for federal taxes paid attributable to a C corporation tax year. Tax-exempt income and related expenses are reported in the Other Adjustments Account (OAA). Unlike a shareholder's stock basis, AAA can have a negative balance. In addition, any decreases in stock basis have no impact on AAA when AAA is negative. The AAA balance is computed at the end of the taxable year.

G. **DISTRIBUTIONS TO SHAREHOLDER**
The amount of any distribution to a shareholder is equal to the cash plus the FMV of any property received. There are two sets of rules that apply to distributions depending on whether or not the S corporation has accumulated E&P.

1. **S CORPORATION WITHOUT ACCUMULATED E&P** The distributions are tax-free to the extent of the shareholder's basis in the stock of the S corporation. Any excess distributions are treated as gain from the sale of stock.

2. **S CORPORATION WITH ACCUMULATED E&P** The tax consequences of the distributions follow a layered approach. First distributions are made out of AAA. These are tax-free to the extent of AAA (limited to the shareholder's basis in the stock). The distribution reduces both AAA and the shareholders' bases in their stock. The AAA balance is computed at the end of the tax year, not when the distribution is made. If more than one distribution is made during the year, a pro rata portion of each distribution is treated as made from AAA. After AAA is exhausted, the distribution is tax-free to the extent of any previously taxed income (PTI) from pre-1983 tax years if the distribution is made in cash. Once PTI is exhausted, the dis-tribution is a dividend to the extent of accumulated E&P. Once accumulated E&P is used up, any remaining amounts are treated as a tax-free return of capital. Any distributions in excess of the shareholder's basis in the stock are treated as gains from the sale of stock.

H. **FRINGE BENEFITS**
Fringe benefits provided to a more than 2% shareholder-employee must be included in that share-holder's gross income and are not deductible by the S corporation. However, accident and health premiums paid by the S corporation for a more than 2% shareholder are deductible by the

corporation and included in the income of the shareholder, but they are not treated as wages for FICA purposes.

I. S STATUS TERMINATION

Termination of S corporation status may be by the failure to satisfy the eligibility requirements, by the receipt of excess passive investment income while an S corporation, or by voluntary termination.

1. Revocation may be made by the consent of shareholders collectively owning a majority of the stock. The revocation may specify any prospective revocation date. If no date is specified, the revocation is retroactive to the first day of the taxable year if made on or before the 15th day of the third month of the year; otherwise, it is effective the first day of the subsequent year.

2. If S status is terminated due to failure to satisfy an eligibility requirement, the termination is effective as of the date the eligibility requirement was violated.

3. Termination will occur if the S corporation has passive investment income exceeding 25% of its gross receipts for each of three consecutive years **and**, if during these three years, the corporation was a corporation with accumulated earnings and profits attributable to prior C corporation status. The termination is effective as of the first day of the fourth taxable year. Passive investment income includes receipts from rents, royalties, dividends, interest, annuities, and the gain from sales or exchanges of stock or securities.

4. Once S status has been terminated, it cannot be re-elected for five years unless permission for an earlier re-election is granted by the IRS. If S status is terminated inadvertently, and the situation is corrected, the IRS may treat the event as if it had never occurred.

CHAPTER 29—FEDERAL TAXATION: CORPORATIONS

PROBLEM 29-1 MULTIPLE CHOICE QUESTIONS (180 to 225 minutes)

ITEMS 1 THROUGH 3 are based on the following:

Lind and Post organized Ace Corp., which issued voting common stock with a fair market value of $120,000. They each transferred property in exchange for stock as follows:

	Property	Adjusted Basis	Fair market Value	Percentage of Ace stock acquired
Lind	Building	$40,000	$82,000	60%
Post	Land	$ 5,000	$48,000	40%

The building was subject to a $10,000 mortgage that was assumed by Ace.

1. What amount of gain did Lind recognize on the exchange?
a. $0
b. $10,000
c. $42,000
d. $52,000　　　(11/96, AR, #8, amended, 6301)

2. What was Ace's basis in the building?
a. $30,000
b. $40,000
c. $72,000
d. $82,000　　　(11/96, AR, #9, amended, 6302)

3. What was Lind's basis in Ace stock?
a. $82,000
b. $40,000
c. $30,000
d. $0　　　(11/96, AR, #10, amended, 6303)

4. Adams, Beck, and Carr organized Flexo Corp. with authorized voting common stock of $100,000. Adams received 10% of the capital stock in payment for the organizational services that he rendered for the benefit of the newly formed corporation. Adams did not contribute property to Flexo and was under no obligation to be paid by Beck or Carr. Beck and Carr transferred property in exchange for stock as follows:

	Adjusted basis	Fair market value	Percentage of Flexo stock acquired
Beck	5,000	20,000	20%
Carr	60,000	70,000	70%

What amount of gain did Carr recognize from this transaction?

a. $40,000
b. $15,000
c. $10,000
d. $0　　　(11/94, AR, #52, 5028)

5. Feld, the sole stockholder of Maki Corp., paid $50,000 for Maki's stock in 20X1. In 20X2, Feld contributed a parcel of land to Maki but was not given any additional stock for this contribution. Feld's basis for the land was $10,000, and its fair market value was $18,000 on the date of the transfer of title. What is Feld's adjusted basis for the Maki stock?
a. $50,000
b. $52,000
c. $60,000
d. $68,000　　　(11/92, PII, #19, amended, 3353)

6. Jones incorporated a sole proprietorship by exchanging all the proprietorship's assets for the stock of Nu Co., a new corporation. To qualify for tax-free incorporation, Jones must be in control of Nu immediately after the exchange. What percentage of Nu's stock must Jones own to qualify as "control" for this purpose?
a. 50.00%
b. 51.00%
c. 66.67%
d. 80.00%　　　(11/93, PII, #45, 4474)

7. When computing a corporation's income tax expense for estimated income tax purposes, which of the following should be taken into account?

	Corporate tax credits	Alternative minimum tax
a.	No	No
b.	No	Yes
c.	Yes	No
d.	Yes	Yes

(11/93, PII, #43, 4472)

8. Jackson Corp., a calendar year corporation, mailed its 20X1 tax return to the Internal Revenue Service by certified mail on Friday, March 10, 20X2. The return, postmarked March 10, 20X2, was delivered to the Internal Revenue Service on March 20, 20X2. The statute of limitations on Jackson's corporate tax return begins on
a. December 31, 20X1.
b. March 10, 20X2.
c. March 16, 20X2.
d. March 20, 20X2.

(11/94, AR, #54, amended, 5030)

9. A civil fraud penalty can be imposed on a corporation that underpays tax by
a. Omitting income as a result of inadequate recordkeeping.
b. Failing to report income it erroneously considered **not** to be part of corporate profits.
c. Maintaining false records and reporting fictitious transactions to minimize corporate tax liability.
d. Filing an incomplete return with an appended statement, making clear that the return is incomplete. (11/95, AR, #16, amended, 5760)

10. Bass Corp., a calendar year C corporation, made qualifying 20X1 estimated tax deposits based on its actual 20X0 tax liability. On March 15, 20X2, Bass filed a timely automatic extension request for its 20X1 corporate income tax return. Estimated tax deposits and the extension payment totaled $7,600. This amount was 95% of the total tax shown on Bass' final 20X1 corporate income tax return. Bass paid $400 additional tax on the final 20X1 corporate income tax return filed before the extended due date. For the 20X1 calendar year, Bass was subject to pay

I. Interest on the $400 tax payment made in 20X2.
II. A tax delinquency penalty.

a. I only
b. II only
c. Both I and II
d. Neither I nor II (11/95, AR, #23, amended, 5767)

11. Edge Corp., a calendar year C corporation, had a net operating loss and zero tax liability for its 20X0 tax year. To avoid the penalty for underpayment of estimated taxes, Edge could compute its first quarter 20X1 estimated income tax payment using the

	Annualized income method	Preceding year method
a.	Yes	Yes
b.	Yes	No
c.	No	Yes
d.	No	No

(11/95, AR, #24, amended, 5768)

12. A corporation's tax year can be reopened after all statutes of limitations have expired if

I. The tax return has a 50% nonfraudulent omission from gross income.
II. The corporation prevails in a determination allowing a deduction in an open tax year that was taken erroneously in a closed tax year.

a. I only
b. II only
c. Both I and II
d. Neither I nor II (11/95, AR, #25, 5769)

13. Micro Corp., a calendar year, accrual basis corporation, purchased a 5-year, 8%, $100,000 taxable corporate bond for $108,530, on July 1, 20X1, the date the bond was issued. The bond paid interest semiannually. For Micro's tax return, the bond premium amortization for 20X1 should be

I. Computed under the constant yield to maturity method.
II. Treated as an offset to the interest income on the bond.

a. Neither I nor II
b. Both I and II
c. I only
d. II only (11/94, AR, #35, amended, 5012)

14. Axis Corp. is an accrual basis calendar year corporation. On December 13, 20X1, the Board of Directors declared a two percent of profits bonus to all employees for services rendered during 20X1 and notified them in writing. None of the employees own stock in Axis. The amount represents reasonable compensation for services rendered and was paid on March 10, 20X2. Axis' bonus expense may
a. Not be deducted on Axis' tax return because payment is a disguised dividend.
b. Be deducted on Axis' 20X1 tax return.
c. Be deducted on Axis' 20X2 tax return.
d. Not be deducted on Axis' 20X1 tax return because the per share employee amount **cannot** be determined with reasonable accuracy at the time of the declaration of the bonus.
(11/94, AR, #36, amended, 5013)

15. In 20X1, Stewart Corp. properly accrued $5,000 for an income item on the basis of a reasonable estimate. In 20X2, after filing its 20X1 federal income tax return, Stewart determined that the exact amount was $6,000. Which of the following statements is correct?
a. No further inclusion of income is required as the difference is less than 25% of the original amount reported and the estimate had been made in good faith.
b. The $1,000 difference is includible in Stewart's 20X2 income tax return.
c. Stewart is required to file an amended return to report the additional $1,000 of income.
d. Stewart is required to notify the IRS within 30 days of the determination of the exact amount of the item. (11/95, AR, #10, amended, 5754)

16. Which of the following costs is not included in inventory under the Uniform Capitalization rules for goods manufactured by the taxpayer?
a. Research
b. Warehousing costs
c. Quality control
d. Taxes excluding income taxes
(R/01, AR, #28, 7013)

17. Banks Corp., a calendar year corporation, provides meals for employees for its own convenience. The employees are present at the meals, which are neither lavish nor extravagant, and the reimbursement is not treated as wages subject to withholdings. For the current year, what percentage of the meal expense may Banks deduct?
a. 0%
b. 50%
c. 80%
d. 100% (11/94, AR, #31, 5008)

18. Rame Corp.'s operating income for the year ended December 31, 20X1, amounted to $100,000. In 20X1, a machine owned by Rame was completely destroyed in an accident. This machine's adjusted basis immediately before the casualty was $30,000. The machine was not insured and had no salvage value. In Rame's 20X1 tax return, what amount should be deducted for the casualty loss?
a. $ 5,000
b. $ 5,400
c. $29,900
d. $30,000 (Editors, 1688)

19. For the first tax year in which a corporation has qualifying research and experimental expenditures, the corporation
a. Has a choice of either deducting such expenditures as current business expenses, or capitalizing these expenditures.
b. Has to treat such expenditures in the same manner as they are accounted for in the corporation's financial statements.
c. Is required to deduct such expenditures currently as business expenses or lose the deductions.
d. Is required to capitalize such expenditures and amortize them ratably over a period of not less than 60 months. (Editors, 1689)

20. Which of the following taxpayers may use the cash method of accounting?
a. A tax shelter
b. A qualified personal service corporation
c. A C corporation with annual gross receipts of $50,000,000
d. A manufacturer (R/01, AR, #29, 7014)

21. In the case of a corporation that is **not** a financial institution, which of the following statements is correct with regard to the deduction for bad debts?
a. Either the reserve method or the direct charge-off method may be used, if the election is made in the corporation's first taxable year.
b. On approval from the IRS, a corporation may change its method from direct charge-off to reserve.
c. If the reserve method was consistently used in prior years, the corporation may take a deduction for a reasonable addition to the reserve for bad debts.
d. A corporation is required to use the direct charge-off method rather than the reserve method. (11/91, PII, #47, 2495)

22. Which of the following costs are amortizable organizational expenditures?
a. Professional fees to issue the corporate stock
b. Printing costs to issue the corporate stock
c. Legal fees for drafting the corporate charter
d. Commissions paid by the corporation to an underwriter (11/94, AR, #38, 5015)

23. Haze Corp., an accrual-basis, calendar-year C corporation, began business on January 1, and incurred the following costs:

Underwriting fees to issue corporate stock $ 2,000
Legal fees to draft the corporate charter 16,000

Haze elected to amortize its organization costs. What was the maximum amount of the costs that Haze could deduct for tax purposes on its first calendar year income tax return?
a. $0
b. $2,000
c. $3,200
d. $3,600 (11/98, AR, #10, amended, 6676)

24. Pierce Corp., an accrual-basis, calendar-year C corporation, had the following 20X1 receipts:

20X2 advance rental payments for a
  lease ending in 20X3 $250,000
Lease cancellation payment from a five-
  year lease tenant 100,000

Pierce had no restrictions on the use of the advance rental payments and renders no services in connection with the rental income. What amount of gross income should Pierce report on its 20X1 tax return?
a. $350,000
b. $250,000
c. $100,000
d. $0 (11/98, AR, #11, amended, 6677)

25. A corporation may reduce its regular income tax by taking a tax credit for
a. Dividends-received exclusion.
b. Foreign income taxes.
c. State income taxes.
d. Accelerated depreciation. (11/95, AR, #17, 5761)

26. In 20X1, Best Corp., an accrual-basis calendar year C corporation, received $100,000 in dividend income from the common stock that it held in an unrelated domestic corporation. The stock was not debt-financed, and was held for over a year. Best recorded the following information for 20X1:

Loss from Best's operations	$ (10,000)
Dividends received	100,000
Taxable income (before dividends-received deduction)	$ 90,000

Best's dividends-received deduction on its 20X1 tax return was
a. $100,000.
b. $ 80,000.
c. $ 70,000.
d. $ 63,000. (11/95, AR, #4, amended, 5748)

27. In the current year, Acorn Inc. had the following items of income and expense:

Sales	$500,000
Cost of sales	250,000
Dividends received	25,000

The dividends were received from a corporation of which Acorn owns 30%. In Acorn's corporate income tax return, what amount should be reported as income before special deductions?
a. $525,000
b. $505,000
c. $275,000
d. $250,000 (5/93, PII, #41, amended, 4147)

28. Tech Corp. files a consolidated return with its wholly owned subsidiary, Dow Corp. During 20X1, Dow paid a cash dividend of $20,000 to Tech. What amount of this dividend is taxable on the 20X1 consolidated return?
a. $20,000
b. $14,000
c. $ 6,000
d. $0 (5/94, AR, #23, amended, 4628)

29. Kisco Corp.'s taxable income before taking the dividends received deduction was $70,000. This includes $10,000 in dividends from an unrelated taxable domestic corporation. Given the following tax rates, what would Kisco's income tax be before any credits?

Partial rate table	Tax rate
Up to $50,000	15%
Over $50,000 but not over $75,000	25%

a. $10,000
b. $10,750
c. $12,500
d. $15,750 (5/94, AR, #24, amended, 4629)

30. Mell Corporation's $55,000 income before income taxes includes $10,000 of life insurance policy proceeds. The life insurance policy proceeds represent a lump-sum payment in full as a result of the death of Mell's controller. Mell was the owner and beneficiary of this policy. In its income tax return, Mell should report taxable life insurance proceeds of
a. $10,000.
b. $ 8,000.
c. $ 5,000.
d. $0. (Editors, 9271)

ITEMS 31 AND 32 are based on the following:

John Budd is the sole stockholder of Ral Corp., an accrual basis taxpayer engaged in wholesaling operations. Ral's retained earnings at January 1, 20X1, amounted to $1,000,000. For the year ended December 31, 20X1, Ral's book income, before federal income tax, was $300,000. Included in the computation of this $300,000 were the following:

Keyman insurance premiums paid on Budd's life (Ral is the beneficiary of this policy)	3,000
Group term insurance premiums paid on $10,000 life insurance policies for each of Ral's four employees (the employees' spouses are the beneficiaries)	4,000
Contribution to a recognized, qualified charity (this contribution was authorized by Ral's board of directors in December 20X1, to be paid on January 31, 20X2)	75,000

31. What amount should Ral deduct for keyman and group life insurance premiums in computing taxable income for 20X1?
a. $0
b. $3,000
c. $4,000
d. $7,000 (5/90, PII, #32, amended, 4584)

32. With regard to Ral's contribution to the recognized, qualified charity, Ral
a. Can elect to deduct in its 20X1 return any portion of the $75,000 that does **not** exceed the deduction ceiling for 20X1.
b. Can elect to carry forward indefinitely any portion of the $75,000 **not** deducted in 20X1 or 20X2.
c. Can deduct the entire $75,000 in its 20X1 return because Ral reports on the accrual basis.
d. Cannot deduct any portion of the $75,000 in 20X1 because the contribution was **not** paid in 20X1. (5/90, PII, #34, amended, 4586)

33. In 20X1, Cable Corp., a calendar year C corporation, contributed $80,000 to a qualified charitable organization. Cable's 20X1 taxable income before the deduction for charitable contributions was $820,000 after a $40,000 dividends-received deduction. Cable also had carryover contributions of $10,000 from 20X0. In 20X1, what amount can Cable deduct as charitable contributions?
a. $90,000
b. $86,000
c. $82,000
d. $80,000 (11/95, AR, #8, amended, 5752)

34. If a corporation's charitable contributions exceed the limitation for deductibility in a particular year, the excess
a. Is **not** deductible in any future or prior year.
b. May be carried back or forward for one year at the corporation's election.
c. May be carried forward to a maximum of five succeeding years.
d. May be carried back to the third preceding year. (11/95, AR, #9, 5753)

35. Tapper Corp., an accrual-basis calendar-year corporation, was organized on January 2, 20X1. During 20X1, revenue was exclusively from sales proceeds and interest income. The following information pertains to Tapper:

Taxable income before charitable
    contributions for 20X1 $500,000
Tapper's matching contribution to
    employee-designated qualified
    universities made during 20X1   10,000
Board of Directors' authorized
    contribution to a qualified charity
    (authorized December 1, 20X1,
    made February 1, 20X2)   30,000

What is the maximum allowable deduction that Tapper may take as a charitable contribution on its tax return for the year ended December 31, 20X1?
a. $0
b. $10,000
c. $30,000
d. $40,000 (11/94, AR, #37, amended, 5014)

36. In a C corporation's computation of the maximum allowable deduction for contributions, what percentage limitation should be applied to the applicable base amount?
a. 5%
b. 10%
c. 30%
d. 50% (11/91, PII, #46, 2494)

37. How are a C corporation's net capital losses used?
a. Deducted from the corporation's ordinary income only to the extent of $3,000.
b. Carried back three years and forward five years.
c. Carried forward 20 years.
d. Deductible in full from the corporation's ordinary income. (11/97, AR, #5, amended, 6533)

38. Taylor Corporation has existed since 1995. For the calendar year 2002, Taylor Corp. had a net operating loss of $200,000. Taxable income for the earlier years of corporate existence, computed without reference to the net operating loss, was as follows:

Taxable income	
1995	$40,000
1996	$50,000
1997	$ 5,000
1998	$10,000
1999	$20,000
2000	$30,000
2001	$40,000

If Taylor makes **no** special election to waive the net operating loss carryback, what amount of net operating loss will be available to Taylor for 2003?
a. $200,000
b. $130,000
c. $ 95,000
d. $ 5,000 (11/94, AR, #33, amended, 5010)

39. A corporation's capital loss carryback or carryover is
a. Not allowable under current law.
b. Limited to $3,000.
c. Always treated as a long-term capital loss.
d. Always treated as a short-term capital loss. (11/91, PII, #41, 2489)

40. John Budd is the sole stockholder of Ral Corp., an accrual basis taxpayer engaged in wholesaling operations. Ral's retained earnings at January 1, 20X1 amounted to $1,000,000. For the year ended December 31, 20X1, Ral's book income, before federal income tax, was $300,000. Included in the computation of this $300,000 was a $5,000 loss on sale of investment in stock of an unaffiliated corporation (this stock had been held for two years; Ral had no other capital gains or losses). In computing taxable income for 20X1, Ral should deduct a capital loss of
a. $0.
b. $2,500.
c. $3,000.
d. $5,000.   (5/90, PII, #30, amended, 9273)

41. If a corporation's tentative minimum tax exceeds the regular tax, the excess amount is
a. Carried back to the first preceding taxable year.
b. Carried back to the third preceding taxable year.
c. Payable in addition to the regular tax.
d. Subtracted from the regular tax.
     (5/93, PII, #57, 4162)

42. Eastern Corp., a calendar year corporation, was formed January 3, 20X0, and on that date placed five-year property in service. The property was depreciated under the general MACRS system. Eastern did not elect to use the straight-line method. In 20X0, Eastern had gross receipts of $6,000,000 and taxable income of $300,000. The following information pertains to Eastern:

Adjustment for the accelerated depreciation
  taken on 20X0 five-year property   1,000
20X0 tax-exempt interest from specified
  private activity bonds issued after
  August 7, 1986   5,000

What was Eastern's alternative minimum taxable income before the adjusted current earnings (ACE) adjustment?
a. $306,000
b. $305,000
c. $304,000
d. $301,000   (11/95, AR, #15, amended, 5759)

43. Bent Corp., a calendar-year C corporation, purchased and placed into service residential real property during February. No other property was placed into service during the year. What convention must Bent use to determine the depreciation deduction for the alternative minimum tax?
a. Full-year.
b. Half-year.
c. Mid-quarter.
d. Mid-month.   (R/00, AR, #7, amended, 6912)

44. Rona Corp.'s alternative minimum taxable income was $200,000. The exempt portion of Rona's alternative minimum taxable income was
a. $0.
b. $12,500.
c. $27,500.
d. $52,500.   (5/91, PII, #55, amended, 1647)

45. On January 2, 20X1, Shaw Corp., an accrual-basis, calendar-year C corporation, purchased all the assets of a sole proprietorship, including $300,000 in goodwill. Federal income tax expense of $110,100 and $7,500 for impairment of goodwill were deducted to arrive at Shaw's reported book income of $239,200. What should be the amount of Shaw's 20X1 taxable income, as reconciled on Shaw's Schedule M-1 of Form 1120, U.S. Corporation Income Tax Return?
a. $239,200
b. $329,300
c. $336,800
d. $349,300   (R/99, AR, #5, amended, 6794)

46. Media Corp. is an accrual-basis, calendar-year C corporation. Its reported book income included $6,000 in municipal bond interest income. Its expenses included $1,500 of interest incurred on indebtedness used to carry municipal bonds and $8,000 in advertising expense. What is Media's net M-1 adjustment on its Form 1120, U.S. Corporation Income Tax Return, to reconcile to its taxable income?
a. $(4,500)
b. $ 1,500
c. $ 3,500
d. $ 9,500   (11/98, AR, #9, amended, 6675)

47. On January 2, Tek Corp., an accrual-basis calendar-year C corporation, purchased all the assets of a sole proprietorship, including $60,000 in goodwill. Tek's reported book income before federal income taxes was $400,000, including a $1,500 deduction for impairment of goodwill. What should be the amount of Tek's taxable income, as reconciled on Tek's Schedule M-1 of Form 1120, U.S. Corporation Income Tax Return?
a. $389,500
b. $397,500
c. $400,000
d. $401,500   (11/96, AR, #7, amended, 6300)

48. In 20X1, Cape Co. reported book income of $140,000. Included in that amount was $50,000 for meals and entertainment expense and $40,000 for federal income tax expense. In Cape's Schedule M-1 of Form 1120, which reconciles book income and taxable income, what amount should be reported as 20X1 taxable income?

a. $205,000
b. $180,000
c. $165,000
d. $140,000   (11/93, PII, #42, amended, 4471)

49. The following information pertains to Dahl Corp.:

Accumulated earnings and profits at
  January 1, 20X0 $120,000
Earnings and profits for the year ended
  December 31, 20X0   160,000
Cash distributions to individual stock
  holders during 20X0   360,000

What is the total amount of distributions taxable as dividend income to Dahl's stockholders in 20X0?
a. $0
b. $160,000
c. $280,000
d. $360,000   (11/95, AR, #19, amended, 5763)

50. Lincoln Corp., a calendar-year C corporation, made a nonliquidating cash distribution of $1,500,000 to its shareholders with respect to its stock. At that time, Lincoln's current and accumulated earnings and profits totaled $825,000 and its total paid in capital for tax purposes was $10,000,000. Lincoln had no corporate shareholders. Which of the following statements is(are) correct regarding Lincoln's cash distribution?

I.   The distribution was taxable as $1,500,000 in ordinary income to its shareholders.
II. The distribution reduced its shareholders' adjusted bases in Lincoln stock by $675,000.

a. I only
b. II only
c. Both I and II
d. Neither I nor II   (11/98, AR, #15, 6681)

51. On January 1, 20X1, Locke Corp., an accrual-basis, calendar-year C corporation, had $30,000 in accumulated earnings and profits. For 20X1, Locke had current earnings and profits of $20,000, and made two $40,000 cash distributions to its shareholders, one in April and one in September. What amount of these distributions is classified as dividend income to Locke's shareholders?
a. $0
b. $20,000
c. $50,000
d. $80,000   (R/00, AR, #8, amended, 6913)

52. Dahl Corp. was organized and commenced operations in 20X0. At December 31, 20X5, Dahl had accumulated earnings and profits of $9,000 before dividend declaration and distribution. On December 31, 20X5, Dahl distributed cash of $9,000 and a vacant parcel of land to Green, Dahl's only stockholder. At the date of distribution, the land had a basis of $5,000 and a fair market value of $40,000. What was Green's taxable dividend income in 20X5 from these distributions?
a. $ 9,000
b. $14,000
c. $44,000
d. $49,000   (11/90, PII, #26, amended, 1650)

53. Kent Corp. is a calendar year, accrual basis C corporation. In 20X1, Kent made a nonliquidating distribution of property with an adjusted basis of $150,000 and a fair market value of $200,000 to Reed, its sole shareholder. The following information pertains to Kent:

Reed's basis in Kent stock at
  January 1, 20X1 $500,000
Accumulated earnings and profits at
  January 1, 20X1   125,000
Current earnings and profits for 20X1   60,000

What was taxable as dividend income to Reed for 20X1?
a. $ 60,000
b. $150,000
c. $185,000
d. $200,000   (5/95, AR, #24, amended, 5442)

54. Dart Corp., a calendar year domestic C corporation, is not a personal holding company. For purposes of the accumulated earnings tax, Dart has accumulated taxable income for 20X0. Which step(s) can Dart take to eliminate or reduce any 20X0 accumulated earnings tax?

I.   Demonstrate that the "reasonable needs" of its business require the retention of all or part of the 2000 accumulated taxable income.
II. Pay dividends by March 15, 20X1.

a. I only
b. II only
c. Both I and II
d. Neither I nor II (11/95, AR, #14, amended, 5758)

55. The accumulated earnings tax can be imposed
a. On both partnerships and corporations.
b. On companies that make distributions in excess of accumulated earnings.
c. On personal holding companies.
d. Regardless of the number of stockholders in a corporation.   (11/95, AR, #18, 5762)

56. Kari Corp., a manufacturing company, was organized on January 2, 20X0. Its 20X0 federal taxable income was $400,000 and its federal income tax was $100,000. What is the maximum amount of accumulated taxable income that may be subject to the accumulated earnings tax for 20X0 if Kari takes only the minimum accumulated earnings credit?
a. $300,000
b. $150,000
c. $ 50,000
d. $0 (5/93, PII, #55, amended, 4160)

57. Kane Corp. is a calendar year domestic personal holding company. Which deduction(s) must Kane make from 20X0 taxable income to determine undistributed personal holding company income prior to the dividend-paid deduction?

	Federal income taxes	Net long-term capital gain less related federal income taxes
a.	Yes	Yes
b.	Yes	No
c.	No	Yes
d.	No	No

(11/95, AR, #12, amended, 5756)

58. The following information pertains to Hull, Inc., a personal holding company, for the year ended December 31, 20X0:

Undistributed personal holding company income	$100,000
Dividends paid during 20X0	20,000
Consent dividends reported in the 20X0 individual income tax returns of the holders of Hull's common stock, but not paid by Hull to its stockholders	10,000

In computing its 20X0 personal holding company tax, what amount should Hull deduct for dividends paid?
a. $0
b. $10,000
c. $20,000
d. $30,000 (5/91, PII, #54, amended, 1646)

59. Edge Corp. met the stock ownership requirements of a personal holding company. What sources of income must Edge consider to determine if the income requirements for a personal holding company has been met?

I. Interest earned on tax-exempt obligations
II. Dividends received from an unrelated domestic corporation

a. I only
b. II only
c. Both I and II
d. Neither I nor II (5/95, AR, #23, 5441)

60. Zero Corp. is an investment company authorized to issue only common stock. During the last half of the current year, Edwards owned 450 of the 1,000 outstanding shares of stock in Zero. Another 350 shares of stock outstanding were owned, 10 shares each, by 35 shareholders who are neither related to each other nor to Edwards. Zero could be a personal holding company if the remaining 200 shares of common stock were owned by
a. An estate where Edwards is the beneficiary.
b. Edwards' brother-in-law.
c. A partnership where Edwards is **not** a partner.
d. Edwards' cousin.

(11/94, AR, #45, amended, 9275)

61. Keen Holding Corp. has 80 unrelated equal stockholders. For the year ended December 31, Keen's income comprised the following:

Net rental income	$1,000
Commissions earned on sales of franchises	2,000
Dividends from taxable domestic corporations	9,000

Deductible expenses for the year totaled $10,000. Keen paid no dividends for the past three years. Keen's liability for personal holding company tax will be based on
a. $12,000.
b. $11,000.
c. $ 9,000.
d. $0. (Editors, 1686)

62. Ace Corp. and Bate Corp. combine in a qualifying reorganization and form Carr Corp., the only surviving corporation. This reorganization is tax-free to the

	Shareholders	Corporation
a.	Yes	Yes
b.	Yes	No
c.	No	Yes
d.	No	No

(11/95, AR, #22, 5766)

63. Pursuant to a plan of corporate reorganization adopted in July 20X1, Gow exchanged 500 shares of Lad Corp. common stock that he had bought in January 20X1 at a cost of $5,000 for 100 shares of Rook Corp. common stock having a fair market value of $6,000. Gow's recognized gain on this exchange was

a. $1,000 long-term capital gain.
b. $1,000 short-term capital gain.
c. $1,000 ordinary income.
d. $0.   (5/91, PII, #43, amended, 1637)

64. In a type B reorganization, as defined by the Internal Revenue Code, the

I. Stock of the target corporation is acquired solely for the voting stock of either the acquiring corporation or its parent.
II. Acquiring corporation must have control of the target corporation immediately after the acquisition.

a. I only
b. II only
c. Both I and II
d. Neither I nor II   (11/94, AR, #53, 5029)

65. Jaxson Corp. has 200,000 shares of voting common stock issued and outstanding. King Corp. has decided to acquire 90 percent of Jaxson's voting common stock solely in exchange for 50 percent of its voting common stock and retain Jaxson as a subsidiary after the transaction. Which of the following statements is true?
a. King must acquire 100 percent of Jaxson stock for the transaction to be a tax-free reorganization.
b. The transaction will qualify as a tax-free reorganization.
c. King must issue at least 60 percent of its voting common stock for the transaction to qualify as a tax-free reorganization.
d. Jaxson must surrender assets for the transaction to qualify as a tax-free reorganization.
                              (5/95, AR, #25, 5443)

66. Bank Corp. owns 80% of Shore Corp.'s outstanding capital stock. Shore's capital stock consists of 50,000 shares of common stock issued and outstanding. Shore's 20X0 net income was $140,000. During 20X0, Shore declared and paid dividends of $60,000. In conformity with generally accepted accounting principles, Bank recorded the following entries in 20X0:

	Debit	Credit
Investment in Shore Corp.		
common stock	$112,000	
Equity in earnings of subsidiary		$112,000
Cash	48,000	
Investment in Shore Corp. common stock		48,000

In its 20X0 consolidated tax return, Bank should report dividend revenue of
a. $48,000.
b. $14,400.
c. $ 9,600.
d. $0.   (11/95, AR, #13, amended, 5757)

67. Potter Corp. and Sly Corp. file consolidated tax returns. In January 20X1, Potter sold land with a basis of $60,000 and a fair value of $75,000 to Sly for $100,000. Sly sold the land in December 20X2 for $125,000. In its 20X2 and 20X1 tax returns, what amount of gain should be reported for these transactions in the consolidated return?

	20X2	20X1
a.	$25,000	$40,000
b.	$50,000	$0
c.	$50,000	$25,000
d.	$65,000	$0

                              (5/93, PII, #49, amended, 4154)

68. Dane Corp. owns stock in Seaco Corp. For Dane and Seaco to qualify for the filing of consolidated returns, at least what percentage of Seaco's total voting power and total value of stock must be directly owned by Dane?

	Total voting power	Total value of stock
a.	51%	51%
b.	51%	80%
c.	80%	51%
d.	80%	80% (Editors, 1666)

69. With regard to consolidated tax returns, which of the following statements is correct?
a. Operating losses of one group member may be used to offset operating profits of the other members included in the consolidated return.
b. Only corporations that issue their audited financial statements on a consolidated basis may file consolidated returns.
c. Of all intercompany dividends paid by the subsidiaries to the parent, 70% are excludable from taxable income on the consolidated return.
d. The common parent must directly own 51% or more of the total voting power of all corporations included in the consolidated return.
                              (11/94, AR, #46, 5022)

70. In the filing of a consolidated tax return for a corporation and its wholly owned subsidiaries, intercompany dividends between the parent and subsidiary corporations are
a. Not taxable.
b. Included in taxable income to the extent of 20%.
c. Included in taxable income to the extent of 80%.
d. Fully taxable.   (11/94, AR, #47, 5023)

71. How does a noncorporate shareholder treat the gain on a redemption of stock that qualifies as a partial liquidation of the distributing corporation?
a. Entirely as capital gain
b. Entirely as a dividend
c. Partly as capital gain and partly as a dividend
d. As a tax-free transaction   (11/89, PII, #52, 1665)

72. Sky Corp. was a wholly-owned subsidiary of Jet Corp. Both corporations were domestic C corporations. Jet received a liquidating distribution of property in cancellation of its Sky stock when Jet's tax basis in Sky stock was $100,000. The distributed property had an adjusted basis of $135,000 and a fair market value of $250,000. What amount of taxable gain did Jet, the parent corporation, recognize on the receipt of the property?
a. $250,000
b. $150,000
c. $ 35,000
d. $0   (11/98, AR, #14, 6680)

73. Elm Corp. is an accrual-basis calendar-year C corporation with 100,000 shares of voting common stock issued and outstanding as of December 28, 1996. On Friday, December 29, 1996, Hall surrendered 2,000 shares of Elm stock to Elm in exchange for $33,000 cash. Hall had no direct or indirect interest in Elm after the stock surrender. Additional information follows:

Hall's adjusted basis in 2,000 shares
  of Elm on December 29, 1996
  ($8 per share) $16,000
Elm's accumulated earnings and
  profits at January 1, 1996   25,000
Elm's 1996 net operating loss   (7,000)

What amount of income did Hall recognize from the stock surrender?
a. $33,000 dividend
b. $25,000 dividend
c. $18,000 capital gain
d. $17,000 capital gain   (11/97, AR, #6, 6534)

74. Mintee Corp., an accrual-basis calendar-year C corporation, had no corporate shareholders when it liquidated in 20X0. In cancellation of all their Mintee stock, each Mintee shareholder received in 20X0, a liquidating distribution of $2,000 cash and land with a tax basis of $5,000 and a fair market value of $10,500. Before the distribution, each shareholder's tax basis in Mintee stock was $6,500. What amount of gain should each Mintee shareholder recognize on the liquidating distribution?

a. $0
b. $ 500
c. $4,000
d. $6,000   (11/97, AR, #7, amended, 6535)

75. A corporation was completely liquidated and dissolved during the current year. The filing fees, professional fees, and other expenditures incurred in connection with the liquidation and dissolution are
a. Deductible in full by the dissolved corporation.
b. Deductible by the shareholders and **not** by the corporation.
c. Treated as capital losses by the corporation.
d. Not deductible either by the corporation or shareholders. (11/93, PII, #46, amended, 4475)

76. Par Corp. acquired the assets of its wholly owned subsidiary, Sub Corp., under a plan that qualified as a tax-free complete liquidation of Sub. Which of the following of Sub's unused carryovers may be transferred to Par?

	Excess charitable contributions	Net operating loss
a.	No	Yes
b.	Yes	No
c.	No	No
d.	Yes	Yes

(11/91, PII, #45, 2493)

77. Krol Corp. distributed marketable securities in redemption of its stock in a complete liquidation. On the date of distribution, these securities had a basis of $100,000 and a fair market value of $150,000. What gain does Krol have as a result of the distribution?
a. $0
b. $50,000 capital gain
c. $50,000 Section 1231 gain
d. $50,000 ordinary gain   (5/90, PII, #28, 1652)

78. Which of the following conditions will prevent a corporation from qualifying as an S Corporation?
a. The corporation has both common and preferred stock.
b. The corporation has one class of stock with different voting rights.
c. One shareholder is an estate.
d. One shareholder is a grantor trust.
                                (5/93, PII, #51, 4156)

79. Dart Corp., a calendar-year S corporation, had 60,000 shares of voting common stock and 40,000 shares of nonvoting common stock issued and outstanding. On February 23, 20X5, Dart filed a revocation statement with the consent of shareholders holding 30,000 shares of its voting common stock and 5,000 shares of its nonvoting common stock. Dart's S corporation election
a. Did **not** terminate.
b. Terminated as of January 1, 20X5.
c. Terminated on February 24, 20X5.
d. Terminated as of January 1, 20X6.
(11/98, AR, #13, amended, 6679)

80. Bristol Corp. was formed as a C corporation on January 1, 1980, and elected S corporation status on January 1, 1986. At the time of the election, Bristol had accumulated C corporation earnings and profits which have not been distributed. Bristol has had the same 25 shareholders throughout its existence. In 2001, Bristol's S election will terminate if it
a. Increases the number of shareholders to 75.
b. Adds a decedent's estate as a shareholder to the existing shareholders.
c. Takes a charitable contribution deduction.
d. Has passive investment income exceeding 90% of gross receipts in each of the three consecutive years ending December 31, 2000.
(11/94, AR, #42, amended, 5019)

81. Village Corp., a calendar year corporation, began business in 20X1. Village made a valid S Corporation election on December 5, 20X6, with the unanimous consent of its shareholders. The eligibility requirements for S status continued to be met throughout 20X7. On what date did Village's S status become effective?
a. January 1, 20X6
b. January 1, 20X7
c. December 5, 20X6
d. December 5, 20X7
(5/95, AR, #21, amended, 5439)

82. After a corporation's status as an S corporation is revoked or terminated, how many years is the corporation required to wait before making a new S election, in the absence of IRS consent to an earlier election?
a. 1
b. 3
c. 5
d. 10
(5/91, PII, #57, 1649)

83. Zinco Corp. was a calendar year S corporation. Zinco's S status terminated on April 1, 20X1, when Case Corp. became a shareholder. During 20X1 (365-day calendar year), Zinco had non-separately computed income of $310,250. If no election was made by Zinco, what amount of the income, if any, was allocated to the S short year for 20X1?
a. $233,750
b. $155,125
c. $ 76,500
d. $0
(11/94, AR, #41, amended, 5018)

84. Bern Corp., an S corporation, had an ordinary loss of $36,500 for the year ended December 31, 20X0. At January 1, 20X0, Meyer owned 50% of Bern's stock. Meyer held the stock for 40 days in 20X0 before selling the entire 50% interest to an unrelated third party. Meyer's basis for the stock was $10,000. Meyer was a full-time employee of Bern until the stock was sold. Meyer's share of Bern's 20X0 loss was
a. $0.
b. $ 2,000.
c. $10,000.
d. $18,250.
(5/91, PII, #56, amended, 1648)

85. Graphite Corp. has been a calendar-year S corporation since its inception on January 2, 20X0. On January 1, 20X3, Smith and Tyler each owned 50% of the Graphite stock, in which their respective bases were $12,000 and $9,000. For the year ended December 31, 20X3, Graphite had $80,000 in ordinary business income and $6,000 in tax-exempt income. Graphite made a $53,000 cash distribution to each shareholder on December 31, 20X3. What total amount of income from Graphite is includible in Smith's adjusted gross income?
a. $96,000
b. $93,000
c. $43,000
d. $40,000
(11/98, AR, #12, amended, 6678)

86. Beck Corp. has been a calendar-year S corporation since its inception on January 2, 20X0. On January 1, 20X3, Lazur and Lyle each owned 50% of the Beck stock, in which their respective tax bases were $12,000 and $9,000. For the year ended December 31, 20X3, Beck had $81,000 in ordinary business income and $10,000 in tax-exempt income. Beck made a $51,000 cash distribution to each shareholder on December 31, 20X3. What was Lazur's tax basis in Beck after the distribution?
a. $ 1,500
b. $ 6,500
c. $52,500
d. $57,500
(R/99, AR, #10, 6799)

87. Lane Inc., an S corporation, pays single coverage health insurance premiums of $4,800 per year and family coverage premiums of $7,200 per year. Mill is a ten percent shareholder-employee in Lane. On Mill's behalf, Lane pays Mill's family coverage under the health insurance plan. What amount of insurance premiums is includible in Mill's gross income?

a. $0
b. $ 720
c. $4,800
d. $7,200   (R/99, AR, #4, 6793)

88. A shareholder's basis in the stock of an S corporation is increased by the shareholder's pro rata share of income from

	Tax-exempt interest	Taxable interest
a.	No	No
b.	No	Yes
c.	Yes	No
d.	Yes	Yes

(5/95, AR, #22, 5440)

89. An S corporation is **not** permitted to take a deduction for
a. Compensation of officers.
b. Charitable contributions.
c. Interest paid to individuals who are **not** stockholders of the S corporation.
d. Employee benefit programs established for individuals who are **not** stockholders of the S corporation.   (Editors, 9278)

90. With regard to S corporations and their stockholders, the "at risk" rules applicable to losses
a. Apply at the shareholder level rather than at the corporate level.
b. Are subject to the elections made by the S corporation's stockholders.
c. Take into consideration the S corporation's ratio of debt to equity.
d. Depend on the type of income reported by the S corporation.   (Editors, 1663)

PROBLEM 29-2 ADDITIONAL MULTIPLE CHOICE QUESTIONS (38 to 48 minutes)

91. A corporation's penalty for underpaying federal estimated taxes is
a. Not deductible.
b. Fully deductible in the year paid.
c. Fully deductible if reasonable cause can be established for the underpayment.
d. Partially deductible.   (11/94, AR, #48, 5024)

92. The following information pertains to treasury stock sold by Ram Corp. to an unrelated broker:

Proceeds received	$100,000
Cost	60,000
Par value	18,000

What amount of capital gain should Ram recognize on the sale of this treasury stock?

a. $0
b. $16,000
c. $40,000
d. $61,000   (Editors, 9268)

93. The rule limiting the allowability of passive activity losses and credits applies to
a. Partnerships.
b. Personal service corporations.
c. Widely held C corporations.
d. S corporations.   (5/91, PII, #44, 1638)

94. For 20X1, Kelly Corp. had net income per books of $300,000 before the provision for Federal income taxes. Included in the net income were the following items:

Dividend income from an unaffiliated
  domestic taxable corporation (taxable
  income limitation does not apply and
  there is no portfolio indebtedness) $50,000
Bad debt expense (represents the increase
  in the allowance for doubtful accounts)   80,000

Assuming no bad debt was written off, what is Kelly's taxable income for 20X1?

a. $250,000
b. $330,000
c. $345,000
d. $380,000   (11/94, AR, #32, amended, 5009)

95. The uniform capitalization method must be used by

I. Manufacturers of tangible personal property.
II. Retailers of personal property with $2 million dollars in average annual gross receipts for the 3 preceding years.

a. I only
b. II only
c. Both I and II
d. Neither I nor II   (11/95, AR, #11, 5755)

96. Which of the following taxpayers may use the cash basis as its method of accounting for tax purposes?
a. Partnership that is designated as a tax shelter
b. Retail store with a $2 million inventory
c. An international accounting firm
d. Office cleaning business with average annual income of $8 million   (R/99, AR, #9, 6798)

97. The corporate dividends-received deduction
a. Must exceed the applicable percentage of the recipient shareholder's taxable income.
b. Is affected by a requirement that the investor corporation must own the investee's stock for a specified minimum holding period.
c. Is unaffected by the percentage of the investee's stock owned by the investor corporation.
d. May be claimed by S corporations.
        (5/91, PII, #47, 1641)

98. Lyle Corp. is a distributor of pharmaceuticals and sells only to retail drug stores. Lyle received unsolicited samples of nonprescription drugs from a manufacturer. Lyle donated these drugs to a qualified exempt organization and deducted their fair market value as a charitable contribution. What should be included as gross income in Lyle's return for receipt of these samples?
a. Fair market value
b. Net discounted wholesale price
c. $25 nominal value assigned to gifts
d. $0   (11/91, PII, #42, amended, 2490)

99. When a corporation has an unused net capital loss that is carried back or carried forward to another tax year,
a. It can be used to offset ordinary income up to the amount of the carryback or carryover.
b. It is treated as a short-term capital loss whether or not it was short-term when sustained.
c. It is treated as a long-term capital loss whether or not it was long-term when sustained.
d. It retains its original identity as short-term or long-term.   (5/93, PII, #47, amended, 4153)

100. A corporation's tax preference items that must be taken into account for alternative minimum tax purposes include
a. Use of the percentage-of-completion method of accounting for long-term contracts.
b. Capital gains.
c. Accelerated depreciation on pre-1987 real property to the extent of the excess over straight-line depreciation.
d. Casualty losses.   (Editors, 9274)

101. On January 1, 20X0, Kee Corp., a C corporation, had a $50,000 deficit in earnings and profits. For 20X0, Kee had current earnings and profits of $10,000 and made a $30,000 cash distribution to its stockholders. What amount of the distribution is taxable as dividend income to Kee's stockholders?
a. $30,000
b. $20,000
c. $10,000
d. $0   (5/94, AR, #25, amended, 4630)

102. Tank Corp., which had earnings and profits of $500,000, made a nonliquidating distribution of property to its shareholders in the current year as a dividend in kind. This property, which had an adjusted basis of $20,000 and a fair market value of $30,000 at the date of distribution, did not constitute assets used in the active conduct of Tank's business. How much gain did Tank recognize on this distribution?
a. $30,000
b. $20,000
c. $10,000
d. $0   (11/94, AR, #51, amended, 5027)

103. Acme Corp. has two common stockholders. Acme derives all of its income from investments in stocks and securities, and it regularly distributes 51% of its taxable income as dividends to its stockholders. Acme is a
a. Corporation subject to tax only on income **not** distributed to stockholders.
b. Corporation subject to the accumulated earnings tax.
c. Regulated investment company.
d. Personal holding company.
        (5/93, PII, #52, 4157)

104. Portal Corp. received $100,000 in dividends from Sal Corp., its 80%-owned subsidiary. What net amount of dividend income should Portal include in its consolidated tax return?
a. $100,000
b. $ 80,000
c. $ 70,000
d. $0   (5/93, PII, #43, amended, 4149)

105. Plant Corp. and Stem Corp. file consolidated returns on a calendar-year basis. In January 20X1, Stem sold land, which it had used in its operations, to Plant for $150,000. Immediately before this sale, Stem's basis for the land was $90,000. Plant held the land primarily for sale to customers in the ordinary course of business. In July 20X2, Plant sold the land to Dubin, an unrelated individual, for $180,000. In determining the consolidated Section 1231 net gain for 20X2, how much should Stem take

into account as a result of the 20X1 sale of the land from Stem to Plant?
a. $90,000
b. $60,000
c. $45,000
d. $30,000 (Editors, 9276)

106. For the collapsible corporation provisions to be imposed, the holding period of the corporation's stock
a. Must be a minimum of six months.
b. Must be a minimum of 12 months.
c. Is irrelevant.
d. Depends on the stockholder's basis for gain or loss. (Editors, 1670)

107. An S Corporation has 30,000 shares of voting common stock and 20,000 shares of non-voting common stock issued and outstanding. The S election can be revoked voluntarily with the consent of the shareholders holding, on the day of the revocation,

	Shares of voting stock	Shares of nonvoting stock
a.	0	20,000
b.	7,500	5,000
c.	10,000	16,000
d.	20,000	0

(5/94, AR, #21, 4626)

108. If a calendar-year S corporation does **not** request an automatic six-month extension of time to file its income tax return, the return is due by
a. June 30.
b. April 15.
c. March 15.
d. January 31. (Editors, 9277)

109. On January 1, 20X0, Kane owned all 100 issued shares of Manning Corp., a calendar year S corporation. On the 41st day of 20X0, Kane sold 25 of the Manning shares to Rodgers. For the year ended December 31, 20X0 (a 366-day calendar year), Manning had $73,200 in non-separately stated income and made no distributions to its shareholders. What amount of non-separately stated income from Manning should be reported on Kane's 20X0 tax return?
a. $56,900
b. $54,900
c. $16,300
d. $0 (11/94, AR, #43, amended, 5020)

110. If an S corporation has **no** accumulated earnings and profits, the amount distributed to a shareholder
a. Must be returned to the S corporation.
b. Increases the shareholder's basis for the stock.
c. Decreases the shareholder's basis for the stock.
d. Has **no** effect on the shareholder's basis for the stock. (11/93, PII, #44, 4473)

OTHER OBJECTIVE FORMAT QUESTIONS

PROBLEM 29-3 (20 to 25 minutes)

Reliant Corp., an accrual-basis calendar year C corporation, filed its 20X3 federal income tax return on March 15, 20X4. Reliant does not meet the definition of a small corporation for AMT purposes, but is a small business for disabled access credit purposes. Reliant formally elected not to take the 30% bonus depreciation allowed by JCWAA '02.

ITEMS 1 THROUGH 6 each require two responses. Determine the amount of Reliant's 20X3 Schedule M-1 adjustment. Indicate if the adjustment (I) increases, (D) decreases, or (N) has no effect, on Reliant's taxable income.

1. Reliant's disbursements included reimbursed employees' expenses for travel of $100,000, and business meals of $30,000. The reimbursed expenses met the conditions of deductibility and were properly substantiated under an accountable plan. The reimbursement was not treated as employee compensation.

2. Reliant's books expensed $7,000 for the term life insurance premiums on the corporate officers. Reliant was the policy owner and beneficiary.

3. Reliant's books indicated an $18,000 state franchise tax expense for 20X3. Estimated state tax payments for 20X3 were $15,000.

4. Book depreciation on computers for 20X3 was $10,000. These computers, costing $50,000, were placed in service on January 2, 20X2. Tax depreciation used MACRS with the half-year convention. No election was made to expense part of the computer cost or to use a straight-line method or the alternative depreciation system.

5. Reliant's books showed a $4,000 short-term capital gain distribution from a mutual fund corporation and a $5,000 loss on the sale of Retro

stock that was purchased in 20X0. The stock was an investment in an unrelated corporation. There were no other 20X3 gains or losses and no loss carryovers from prior years.

6. Reliant's taxable income before the charitable contribution and the dividends received deductions was $500,000. Reliant's books expensed $15,000 in board-of-director authorized charitable contributions that were paid on January 5, 20X4. Charitable contributions paid and expense during 20X3 were $35,000. All charitable contributions were properly substantiated. There were no net operating losses or charitable contributions that were carried forward.

FOR ITEMS 7 THROUGH 11, indicate if the expenses are (F) fully deductible, (P) partially deductible, or (N) nondeductible for regular tax purposes on Reliant's federal income tax return.

7. Reliant purchased theater tickets for its out of town clients. The performances took place after Reliant's substantial and bona fide business negotiations with its clients.

8. Reliant accrued advertising expenses to promote a new product line. Ten percent of the new product line remained in ending inventory.

9. Reliant incurred interest expense on a loan to purchase municipal bonds.

10. Reliant paid a penalty for the underpayment of 20X2 estimated taxes.

11. On December 9, 20X3, Reliant's board of directors voted to pay a $500 bonus to each non-stockholder employee for 20X3. The bonuses were paid on February 3, 20X4.

FOR ITEMS 12 THROUGH 16, indicate if the following items are (F) fully taxable, (P) partially taxable, or (N) nontaxable for regular tax purposes on Reliant's 20X3 federal income tax return. All transactions occurred during 20X3.

ITEMS 12 THROUGH 16 are based on the following:

Reliant filed an amended federal income tax return for 20X2 and received a refund that included both the overpayment of the federal taxes and interest.

12. The portion of Reliant's refund that represented the overpayment of the 20X2 federal taxes.

13. The portion of Reliant's refund that is attributable to the interest on the overpayment of federal taxes.

14. Reliant received dividend income from a mutual fund that solely invests in municipal bonds.

15. Reliant, the lessor, benefited from the capital improvements made to its property by the lessee in 20X3. The lease agreement is for one year ending December 31, 20X3, and provides for a reduction in rental payments by the lessee in exchange for the improvements.

16. Reliant collected the proceeds on the term life insurance policy on the life of a debtor who was not a shareholder. The policy was assigned to Reliant as collateral security for the debt. The proceeds exceeded the amount of the debt.

FOR ITEMS 17 THROUGH 21, indicate if the following (I) increase, (D) decrease, or (N) have no effect on Reliant's 20X3 alternative minimum taxable income (AMTI) *prior to* the adjusted current earnings adjustment (ACE).

17. Reliant used the 70% dividends-received deduction for regular tax purposes.

18. Reliant received interest from a state's general obligation bonds.

19. Reliant used MACRS depreciation on seven-year personal property placed into service January 3, 20X3, for regular tax purposes. No expense or depreciation election was made.

20. Depreciation on nonresidential real property placed into service on January 3, 20X2, was under the general MACRS depreciation system for regular tax purposes.

21. Reliant had only cash charitable contributions for 20X3.

FOR ITEMS 22 THROUGH 28, indicate if the statement is true (T) or false (F) regarding Reliant's compliance with tax procedures, tax credits and the alternative minimum tax.

22. Reliant's exemption for alternative minimum tax is reduced by 20% of the excess of the alternative minimum taxable income over $150,000.

23. The statute of limitations on Reliant's fraudulent 20X0 federal income tax return expires six years after the filing date of the return.

24. The statute of limitations on Reliant's 20X1 federal income tax return, which omitted 30% of gross receipts, expires 2 years after the filing date of the return.

25. The targeted job tax credit may be combined with other business credits to form part of Reliant's general business credit.

26. Reliant incurred qualifying expenditures to remove existing access barriers at the place of employment in 20X3. As a small business, Reliant qualifies for the disabled access credit.

27. Reliant's tax preparer, a CPA firm, may use the 20X3 corporate tax return information to prepare corporate officers' tax returns without the consent of the corporation.

28. Reliant must file an amended return for 20X3 within 1 year of the filing date.

(5/95, AR, #3, amended, 5503-5536)

PROBLEM 29-4 (20 to 25 minutes)

Capital Corp., an accrual-basis calendar-year C corporation, began operations on January 2, 20X0. Capital timely filed its 20X1 federal income tax return on Wednesday, March 15, 20X2.

ITEMS 1 THROUGH 4 each require two responses. Determine the amount of Capital's 20X1 Schedule M-1 adjustment necessary to reconcile book income to taxable income. In addition, determine if the Schedule M-1 adjustment necessary to reconcile book income to taxable income (I) increases, (D) decreases, or (N) has no effect on Capital's 20X1 taxable income.

1. At its corporate inception in 20X0, Capital incurred and paid $40,000 in organizational costs for legal fees to draft the corporate charter. In 20X0, Capital correctly elected, for book purposes, to amortize the organizational expenditures over 40 years and for the minimum required period on its federal income tax return. For 20X1, Capital amortized $1,000 of the organizational costs on its books.

2. Capital's 20X1 disbursements included $10,000 for reimbursed employees' expenses for business and entertainment. The reimbursed expenses met the conditions of deductibility and were properly substantiated under an accountable plan. The disbursement was not treated as employee compensation.

3. Capital's 20X1 disbursements included $15,000 life insurance premium expense paid for its executives as part of their taxable compensation. Capital is neither the direct nor the indirect beneficiary of the policy, and the amount of the compensation is reasonable.

4. In 20X1, Capital increased its allowance for uncollectible accounts by $10,000. No bad debt was written off in 20X0.

Sunco Corp., an accrual-basis calendar-year C corporation, timely filed its 20X1 federal income tax return on Wednesday, March 15, 20X2.

FOR ITEMS 5 AND 6, determine if the following 20X1 items are (F) fully taxable, (P) partially taxable, or (N) nontaxable for regular income tax purposes on Sunco's 20X1 federal income tax return.

5. Sunco received dividend income from a 35%-owned domestic corporation. The dividends were not from debt-financed portfolio stock, and the taxable income limitation did not apply.

6. Sunco received a $2,800 lease cancellation payment from a three-year lease tenant.

Quest Corp., an accrual-basis calendar-year C corporation, timely filed its 2002 federal income tax return on Wednesday, March 15, 2003. Quest did not make any elections not to apply any provisions of JCWAA '02.

FOR ITEMS 7 AND 8, determine if the following 20X1 items are (F) fully deductible, (P) partially deductible, or (N) nondeductible for regular income tax purposes on Quest's 2002 federal income tax return.

7. Quest's 2002 taxable income before charitable contributions and dividends-received deduction was $200,000. Quest's Board of Directors authorized a $38,000 contribution to a qualified charity on December 1, 2002. The payment was made on February 1, 2003. All charitable contributions were properly substantiated.

8. During 2002 Quest was assessed and paid a $300 uncontested penalty for failure to pay its 2001 federal income taxes on time.

On its 20X1 federal income tax return, Gelco Corp., an accrual-basis calendar-year C corporation, reported the same amounts for regular income tax and alternative minimum tax purposes.

FOR ITEMS 9 THROUGH 11, determine if each 20X1 item, taken separately, contributes to (O) overstating, (U) understating, or (C) correctly stating Gelco's 20X1 alternative minimum taxable income (AMTI) prior to the adjusted current earnings adjustment (ACE).

9. For regular tax purposes, Gelco deducted the maximum MACRS depreciation on seven-year

personal property placed in service on January 1, 20X1. Gelco made no Internal Revenue Code Section 179 election to expense the property in 20X1.

10. For regular income tax purposes, Gelco depreciated nonresidential real property placed in service on January 1, 20X1, under the general MACRS depreciation system for a 39-year depreciable life.

11. Gelco excluded state highway construction general obligation bond interest income earned in 20X1 for regular income tax and alternative minimum tax (AMT) purposes.

(5/97, AR, #1, amended, 6340-6354)

PROBLEM 29-5 (15 to 20 minutes)

Lan Corp., an accrual-basis calendar year repair-service corporation, began business on January 1, 20X1. Lan's valid S corporation election took effect retroactively on January 1, 20X1.

FOR ITEMS 1 THROUGH 4, determine the amount, if any, using the fact pattern for each item.

1. Lan's 20X1 books recorded the following:

Gross receipts	$7,260
Interest income on investments	50
Charitable contributions	1,000
Supplies	1,120

What amount of net business income should Lan report on its 20X1 Form 1120S, U.S. Income Tax Return for an S Corporation, Schedule K?

2. As of January 1, 20X1, Taylor and Barr each owned 100 shares of the 200 issued shares of Lan stock. On January 31, 20X1, Taylor and Barr each sold 20 shares to Pike. No election was made to terminate the tax year. Lan had net business income of $14,520 for the year ended December 31, 20X1, and made no distributions

to its shareholders. (The 20X1 calendar year had 365 days.) What amount of net business income should have been reported on Pike's 20X1 Schedule K-1 from Lan? Round the answer to the nearest hundred.

3. Pike purchased 40 Lan shares on January 31, 20X1, for $4,000. Lan made no distributions to shareholders, and Pike's 20X1 Schedule K-1 from Lan reported:

Ordinary business loss	$(1,000)
Municipal bond interest income	150

What was Pike's basis in his Lan stock at December 31, 20X1?

4. On January 1, 20X1, Taylor and Barr each owned 100 shares of the 200 issued shares of Lan stock. Taylor's basis in Lan shares on that date was $10,000. Taylor sold all of his Lan shares to Pike on January 31, 20X1, and Lan made a valid election to terminate its tax year. Taylor's share of ordinary income from Lan prior to the sale was $2,000. Lan made a cash distribution of $3,000 to Taylor on January 30, 20X1. What was Taylor's basis in Lan shares for determining gain or loss from the sale to Pike?

FOR ITEMS 5 AND 6, indicate if the statement is true or false.

5. Lan issues shares of both preferred and common stock to shareholders at inception on January 1, 20X1. This will not affect Lan's S corporation eligibility.

6. Lan, an S corporation since inception, has passive investment income for 3 consecutive years following the year a valid S corporation election takes effect. Lan's S corporation election is terminated as of the first day of the fourth year.

(11/95, AR, #76-81, amended, 5819-5824)

SOLUTION 29-1 MULTIPLE CHOICE ANSWERS

FORMATION

1. (a) No gain or loss is recognized if property is transferred to a corporation solely in exchange for stock if, immediately after the transfer, the transferors are in control of the corporation.

2. (b) As no gain or loss was recognized, Ace Corporation's basis is the same as Lind's basis.

3. (c) Lind's basis in Ace's stock was the adjusted basis of the building that Lind exchanged for stock less the mortgage that Ace assumed.

4. (d) Section 351(a) provides that no gain or loss will be recognized to the transferors of property to a corporation, solely in exchange for its stock if the transferors are in control of the corporation immediately after the transfer. Control is defined in §368(c) as ownership of at least 80% of the voting

stock and at least 80% of all other classes of stock. Beck and Carr are transferors of property and own 90% of Flexo Corp. immediately after the exchange. They received solely stock in exchange for their property and thereby meet the requirements of §351(a). Neither Beck nor Carr would recognize any gain. Adams would recognize ordinary income equal to the fair market value of the stock that was received in exchange for the services rendered.

5. (c) Feld's adjusted basis in the stock is the $50,000 originally paid for it plus Feld's adjusted basis in the land contributed, which is $10,000, for a total basis of $60,000.

6. (d) Under §351(a) and 368(c), the transferors of property to a corporation for its stock must be in control of at least 80% of the stock of the corporation in order for the transfer to be tax deferred.

FILING REQUIREMENTS

7. (d) Under §6655(g), a corporation's "tax" for estimated tax purposes is the excess of: the sum of its regular corporate tax, the alternative minimum tax, the environmental tax, and the tax on gross transportation income, over the sum of its tax credits.

8. (c) Under §6072, the due date for a calendar year corporation's income tax return is March 15 following the close of the tax year. Under §7502, the return is deemed to have been filed when it is postmarked. Thus, Jackson's return is deemed to have been filed on 3/10/X2. Section 6501 states that for purposes of determining the statute of limitations, an early return is treated as if filed on its due date. Thus, for determining the statute of limitations on assessment, Jackson's return is deemed to have been filed on 3/15/X2. The statute of limitations begins to run the day after the due date, which is 3/16/X2.

9. (c) Section 6663 imposes a penalty of 75% of a tax underpayment attributable to fraud. Section 7454(a) places the burden of proof for fraud on the Secretary of the Treasury. Tax Court Rule 142(b) states that such burden is to be carried by clear and convincing evidence. Fraud implies that the taxpayer had bad faith, intentionally understated his tax liability, or had a sinister motive. To be guilty of fraud the taxpayer must have intentionally engaged in wrongful activities to avoid the payment of taxes. Maintaining false records and reporting fictitious transactions to minimize the corporate tax liability would be evidence of fraud. Omitting income as a result of inadequate recordkeeping would be indicative of negligence under §6662(b) and §6662(c), not fraud. Under Regulations §1.6662-3(b)(1) negligence includes any failure by the taxpayer to keep adequate books and records or to substantiate items properly. The penalty for negligence is 20% of the tax underpayment attributable to negligence under §6662(a). Failing to report income that the taxpayer did not consider to be included in gross income is not fraud because there is no bad faith. Whether this action constitutes negligence depends on whether the taxpayer intentionally or recklessly disregarded rules and regulations. Likewise, filing an incomplete return with adequate disclosure is not fraud because there is no evidence of bad faith.

10. (a) Section 6601(a) imposes interest as an addition to tax when the tax is not paid on or before the last date prescribed for payment. Section 6601(b)(1) states that the last date prescribed for payment is to be determined without regard to extensions of time for payment. Under §6651(a)(2) there is a penalty for failure to pay tax when due equal to 0.5% of the net tax due for each month or fraction thereof that the tax is not paid. This penalty in the aggregate may not exceed 25% of the net tax due. However, this provision states that the penalty will not apply if the taxpayer shows reasonable cause for not paying the tax on time. Regulations §301.6651-1(c)(4) provides that reasonable cause will be presumed if a corporation files a timely request for extension to file its return, pays in at least 90% of the tax due by the due date without regard to the extension, and pays the balance due on or before the extended due date. Thus, Bass Corp. must pay interest on the $400 balance due. However, Bass Corp. demonstrated reasonable cause for late payment and thereby avoids the tax delinquency penalty of §6651(a)(2).

11. (b) Section 6655(d)(1)(B) provides that a corporation may avoid the penalty for underpayment of estimated tax by making a payment equal to 100% of the tax for the preceding year. However, this rule does not apply if the corporation did not file a return for the previous tax year showing a liability for tax. Since Edge Corp. had a net operating loss and a zero tax liability for 20X0, Edge Corp. may not use the preceding year method to avoid penalty for underpayment of its 20X1 estimated tax. Section 6655(e) allows a corporation to use the annualized income method to determine its estimated tax for the first quarter of 20X1.

12. (b) Section 6501(e)(1)(A) extends the statute of limitations on assessment to 6 years from the later of the date due or the date filed for a nonfraudulent substantial omission of income. Once this period has expired, the statute of limitations cannot be reopened unless the omission was fraudulent. The statute of limitations can be reopened under the

mitigation provisions under §1311(a) if the taxpayer is able to take a deduction in an open year that the taxpayer deducted previously in a year that is now closed as provided in §1312(2).

INCOME & DEDUCTIONS

13. (b) Section 171(a) states that the amortizable bond premium on a taxable bond may be taken as a deduction. However, §171(c) provides that in the case of a bond on which the interest is not excludable from gross income, §171 shall apply only if the taxpayer so elects. Section 171 provides that the bond is to be amortized using the constant yield to maturity method and in the case of any taxable bond in lieu of any deduction, the amortization of the bond premium may be taken as an offset to the interest payment on such bond.

14. (b) Section 162(a) authorizes a deduction for all ordinary and necessary business expenses paid or accrued during the taxable year. Section 461(h) limits the deduction for accrued expenses until economic performance has occurred and provides that if services are to be performed for the taxpayer by another person, economic performance occurs as such person provides the services. Reg. §1.461-1(a)(2) provides that, for a taxpayer using the accrual method of accounting, no deduction may be taken until all events have occurred that establish the fact of the liability, and the amount of the liability can be determined with reasonable accuracy. In this case, the liability meets both the all events test and the economic performance test.

15. (b) Section 451(a) provides that any item of gross income is to be included in the year received unless the amount is properly included in a different period under the taxpayer's method of accounting. Regulations §1.451-1(a) states that under the accrual method of accounting, income is includible when all the events have occurred that fix the right to receive the income and the amount can be determined with reasonable accuracy. This regulation further provides that if an amount is properly accrued on the basis of a reasonable estimate and the exact amount is subsequently determined, the difference is to be taken into account for the taxable year in which the taxpayer makes the subsequent determination. Thus, the $1,000 difference is properly included in Stewart's 20X2 income tax return.

16. (a) Research and experimental expenditures are specifically excepted from the uniform capitalization rules. The costs of warehousing, quality control, and taxes not based on income are required to be capitalized.

17. (d) Banks Corp. may deduct the cost of the reimbursed meals as an ordinary and necessary business expense under §162(a). RRA '93 generally limits the deduction for business meals to 50% of the amount of the expense. Banks meets the requirements that the cost of the meals is not extravagant and that the taxpayer or the taxpayer's employee be present at the meals. TRA '97 allows the full deduction of meals provided to employees for the convenience of the employer.

18. (d) All activities of a corporation are considered to be business activities. Therefore, corporations may fully deduct their losses because all losses are considered business losses. Unlike individuals, corporations do not have to reduce casualty losses by either the $100 statutory floor or by 10% of AGI (the term AGI is not applicable to corporations).

19. (a) Section 174 sets forth the treatment accorded to research and experimentation (R&D) expenditures. The law permits three alternatives for the handling of research and experimentation expenditures. These expenditures may be expensed in the year paid or incurred, or they may be deferred and amortized. If neither of these two methods is elected, R&D costs must be capitalized. If the costs are capitalized, a deduction may not be available until the research project is abandoned or is deemed worthless.

20. (b) A qualified personal service corporation may use the cash method of accounting as long as it clearly reflects income. Tax shelters, C corporations, and taxpayers with inventories (e.g., manufacturers) must use the accrual method.

21. (d) For businesses other than financial institutions, bad debts *must* be deducted under the direct charge-off method rather than the reserve method.

22. (c) Corporations may elect to amortize organization costs over a period of not fewer than 60 months under §248. Section 248(b) defines organization costs as costs incident to the creation of the corporation and chargeable to a capital account. Regulation §1.248-1(b) includes costs of drafting the corporate charter as costs eligible for amortization and includes professional fees, printing costs, and commissions incurred in the issuing or selling of stock as costs that are **not** eligible for amortization as organization costs. These costs are treated as a reduction in the corporation's capital.

23. (c) Organization costs are amortized over 60 months. ($16,000 / 60 months x 12 months = $3,200) Underwriting fees to issue corporate stock are not organization costs.

24. (a) Rent is income when received, regardless of the taxpayer's basis of accounting.

25. (b) Section 27(a) allows a tax credit for foreign income taxes paid. The other answers are allowed as deductions, not credits.

DIVIDENDS RECEIVED DEDUCTION

26. (d) Section 243(a)(1) allows a corporation to deduct 70% of the dividends received from a taxable domestic corporation. Thus, the tentative dividends received deduction (DRD) is $70,000 ($100,000 x 70%). However, §246(b)(1) limits this deduction to 70% of taxable income before the DRD and certain other deductions. Hence, the DRD limit is $63,000 ($90,000 x 70%). Section 246(b)(2) waives this limitation for any year in which the taxpayer has a net operating loss. The tentative dividends received deduction does not result in a net operating loss ($90,000 – $70,000 = $20,000).

27. (c) The dividends received deduction is a special deduction. The question asks for income before special deductions, $500,000 sales + $25,000 dividends received – $250,000 cost of sales = $275,000 income before special deductions. Cost of sales needs to be subtracted because it is not a special deduction. The dividends need to be included in income in total and then the appropriate percentage is subtracted as a special deduction.

28. (d) Dow must include the $20,000 dividend in its gross income under §61(a)(7). However, under §243(a)(3) and §243(b) Dow is allowed a deduction for 100% of the dividends received from a corporation that is a member of the same affiliated group. Thus, Dow is entitled to a dividends received deduction of $20,000. The net result is this $20,000 dividend is not taxed on the consolidated return.

29. (b) Section 243(a)(1) provides for a 70% dividends received deduction for corporations that received dividends from taxable domestic corporations. This deduction is limited to 70% of taxable income determined without regard to the DRD and other specified deductions. In this case, the taxable income limitation of §246(b)(1) is greater than the tentative DRD: $70,000 x 70% = $49,000. Thus, the DRD is $7,000.

Taxable income before DRD	$70,000
Dividends received deduction ($10,000 x 70%)	(7,000)
Taxable Income [Sec. 63(a)]	$63,000
First tier ($50,000 x 15%)	$ 7,500
($63,000 – $50,000 = $13,000; $13,000 x 25%)	3,250
Income Tax (Sec. 11(b))	$10,750

KEYMAN LIFE INSURANCE

30. (d) Life insurance proceeds which are payable upon the death of an individual are generally tax-free upon receipt [§101(a)]. Therefore, Mell would not recognize any of the proceeds as taxable income.

31. (c) A corporation can deduct premiums paid for group term life insurance for its employees, as long as the death benefit does not exceed $50,000. A corporation can not deduct keyman life insurance premiums as long as it is the beneficiary.

CHARITABLE CONTRIBUTIONS

32. (a) An accrual basis corporation can elect to deduct amounts paid to a charitable organization if the board of directors authorizes a charitable contribution during the year and the payment of such contribution is made on or before the 15th day of the third month following the close of such year. Since Ral Corp.'s board of directors authorized the contribution and the payment was made before March 15, 20X2, it can deduct any amounts which do not exceed the 10% income limitation in 20X1.

33. (b) Section 170(a) allows a deduction for charitable contributions. However, §170(b)(2) limits a corporation's deduction for charitable contributions to 10% of taxable income determined without regard to the charitable contributions deduction, without regard to Part VIII except §248, net operating loss carrybacks, and capital loss carrybacks. Part VIII includes §243 that authorizes the dividends received deduction for corporations. Section 170(d)(2)(A) provides that a corporation's charitable contributions in excess of the 10% limit of §170(b)(2) shall be carried over for up to 5 years. However, charitable contributions made in the current year are to be deducted first. Cable Corp.'s tentative charitable contributions deduction for 20X1 includes the carryover of $10,000 from 20X0. The dividends received deduction must be added back to taxable income before the charitable contributions deduction to determine the limit imposed by §170(b)(2).

Charitable contributions made in 20X1	$ 80,000
Charitable contributions carryover from 20X0	10,000
Tentative charitable contributions deduction	$ 90,000
Taxable income before charitable contributions	$820,000
Add: Dividends received deduction	40,000
Taxable income for purposes of the limit	$860,000
	x 10%
Limit on Charitable Contributions Deductions	$ 86,000

34. (c) Section 170(d)(2)(A) provides that a corporation's charitable contributions in excess of the 10% limit of §170(b)(2) shall be carried over for up to 5 years.

35. (d) Section 170(a) allows a deduction for a charitable contribution made during the year and allows a corporation on the accrual basis of accounting to elect to take a deduction for a charitable contribution in the year that such contribution was authorized by its board of directors, if the corporation makes the contribution on or before the 15th day of the third month following the close of such tax year. Therefore, the corporation may deduct the $10,000 contribution and the payment authorized in 20X1, but paid in 20X2. Section 170(b)(2) limits a corporation's charitable contributions to 10% of taxable income, determined without regard to the deduction for charitable contributions. The charitable contributions are less than this limit ($500,000 x 10% = $50,000) and are thus allowed in full.

36. (b) For corporate taxpayers, the deduction for charitable contributions made to qualified donees is limited to 10% of taxable income computed without regard to the following: (1) deductions for charitable contributions, (2) deductions for dividends received, (3) net operating loss carryback, and (4) capital loss carryback. The 30% and 50% deduction limits apply to individuals.

GAINS & LOSSES

37. (b) Unlike individuals, corporations are not allowed to deduct net capital losses. Excess capital losses may be carried back three years and carried forward five years. Generally, for tax years beginning after August 5, 1997, NOLs may be carried back 2 years and forward 20 years. For 2001 and 2002, JCWAA '02 allows NOLs to be carried back 5 years and forward 20 years.

38. (c) Section 172(a) allows a deduction for net operating loss (NOL) carryovers and NOL carrybacks. Generally, NOLs arising in taxable years beginning after August 5, 1997, have 2-year carryback and 20-year carryforward periods, except for NOLs of farmers and small businesses attributable to losses incurred in presidentially declared disaster areas. For 2001 and 2002, JCWAA '02 allows NOLs to be carried back 5 years and forward 20 years. The sum of the taxable income for each of the five previous tax years is $105,000 ($5,000 + $10,000 + $20,000 + $30,000 + $40,000). A $95,000 ($200,000 − $105,000) NOL is carried forward.

39. (d) A corporation's carryback and carryforward capital losses are always treated as short-term capital losses in the year to which they are carried. Excess capital losses of a corporation can be carried back three years and forward five. The $3,000 limit for offsetting capital losses against ordinary income applies only to individuals. Corporations only use capital losses to offset capital gains.

40. (a) A corporation can deduct capital losses only against capital gains. Since Ral Corp. has no capital gains, the entire capital loss is disallowed.

ALTERNATIVE MINIMUM TAX

41. (c) The alternative minimum tax is imposed to insure that corporations pay a minimum amount of tax. The portion of the tentative minimum tax which exceeds the regular tax liability is added to the regular tax liability so that the corporation is paying the minimum tax amount.

42. (a) Section 55(b)(2) defines alternative minimum taxable income (AMTI) as the taxable income determined with regard to adjustments provided in §56 and §58 and increased by the amount of tax preference items as described in §57. Section 56(a)(1)(A)(ii) requires that the taxpayer use 150% declining balance method switching to the straight line method when the straight line method results in a larger deduction in computing AMTI. Section 168(b)(1) provides that for MACRS the taxpayer use the 200% declining balance method switching to straight line method when the straight line method results in a larger deduction. Thus, Eastern Corp. must add back the adjustment for depreciation since the depreciation under MACRS would result in a larger deduction than is allowed in computing AMTI. Section 57(a)(5)(A) states that interest on specified private activity bonds is a tax preference item. Section 57(a)(5)(C)(i) defines specified private activity bonds as any private activity bond as defined in §141 that was issued after August 7, 1986, and the interest thereon is excluded from gross income under §103. Eastern Corp. must add back the interest on the specified private activity bonds; such interest is a tax preference item.

43. (d) Both residential and nonresidential real property are depreciated using the mid-month convention for both AMT and regular tax.

44. (c) The alternative minimum tax (AMT) applicable to corporations is 20% of alternative minimum taxable income (AMTI) that exceeds the exemption amount. The exemption amount for a corporation is $40,000 reduced by 25% of the amount that AMTI exceeds $150,000. Thus, the exempt portion of Rona's AMTI is $27,500 (i.e., $40,000 – [($200,000 – $150,000) x 25%]).

SCHEDULE M-1

45. (c) For tax purposes, goodwill is amortized straight-line for 15 years. Federal income taxes are not deductible. $239,200 + $110,100 + $7,500 – ($300,000 / 15) = $336,800

46. (a) The $6,000 in municipal bond interest income must be removed from book income to reconcile to taxable income, as it is not taxable income. The $1,500 of interest incurred to carry a tax-exempt investment is not an expense deductible for taxes and thus must be included in book income to reconcile to taxable income. The advertising expense is deductible for both tax and book purposes; no adjustment need be made for it.

47. (b) OBRA '93 allows a uniform 15-year straight-line amortization period for certain intangible assets, including goodwill. [$400,000 + $1,500 – ($60,000 / 15) = $397,500]

48. (a)

Book income	$140,000
Add: Non-deductible federal income tax	40,000
Add: Non-deductible 50% portion of meals and entertainment expense	25,000
Taxable income	$205,000

DIVIDEND DISTRIBUTIONS

49. (c) Section 301(c)(1) provides that a distribution with respect to a corporation's stock is treated as a dividend as defined in §316 and included in gross income. Section 316(a) defines a dividend as a distribution of property made by a corporation to its shareholders out of accumulated earnings and profits and out of earnings and profits of the taxable year. Section 317(a) includes money in the definition of property. Thus, the taxable dividend income to Dahl Corp.'s shareholders is $280,000 ($120,000 + $160,000). The $80,000 ($360,000 – $280,000) of the distribution that is not a dividend reduces the basis of the shareholder's stock, but not below zero, under §301(c)(2). Any remaining distribution is treated as a gain on the sale of the stock under §301(c)(3).

50. (b) Distributions over the current and accumulated earnings and profits are a return of capital. A return of capital is not taxable.

51. (c) Dividends paid from earnings and profits (E&P) are income ($20,000 + $30,000 = $50,000). Dividends paid beyond E&P are a return of capital.

52. (c) Corporate distributions to shareholders on their stock are taxed as dividends to the extent of the corporation's current and/or accumulated earnings and profits. Also, the distributing corporation recognizes gain on any distribution of appreciated property as if such property were sold at its FMV. Here, the distribution of the vacant land was considered to have been sold at its FMV of $40,000, resulting in a gain of $35,000 (i.e., $40,000 – $5,000) to the corporation. This gain brought the total of accumulated earnings and profits up to $44,000 (i.e., $9,000 + $35,000), all considered to be taxable dividends. The $5,000 [($9,000 + $40,000) – $44,000] of the distribution in excess of existing accumulated earnings and profits is treated as a return of capital.

53. (c) Kent Corp. must recognize a gain of $50,000 ($200,000 – $150,000) on the distribution of the property under §311(b)(1). Section 312(b)(1) requires that the corporation's earnings and profits be increased by the amount of the gain. However, because the $60,000 current earnings and profits for 20X1 is given, the gain on the distribution has already been included in current earnings and profits. This is true because §316(a) states that current earnings and profits are determined at the close of the taxable year without any reduction for distributions made during the year. The amount of the distribution is the $200,000 fair market value of the property under §301(b)(1). Section 301(c)(1) states that the portion which is a dividend under §316 must be included in the shareholder's gross income. Section 316(a) provides that a distribution is a dividend, first, to the extent of the corporation's current earnings and profits, and second, out of the corporation's accumulated earnings and profits. Because the amount of the distribution exceeds the sum of the current earnings and profits and the accumulated earnings and profits, the distribution is a dividend in the amount of $185,000 ($60,000 + $125,000). The $15,000 remainder of the distribution reduces the shareholder's basis in the stock, and any amount in excess of the basis of the stock is treated as a gain on the deemed sale of the stock under §301(c). The shareholder has a $200,000 basis in the property under §301(d).

ACCUMULATED EARNINGS TAX

54. (c) Section 535(a) states that accumulated taxable income is taxable income adjusted by the items noted in §535(b) and less the sum of the accumulated earnings credit and the dividends paid deduction. Section 535(c)(1) states that (the general rule) accumulated earnings credit is equal to the earnings and profits for the taxable year that are retained for the reasonable needs of the business less the net capital gains adjustment. Section 561(a) allows a deduction for dividends paid during the taxable year. Section 563(a) states that a dividend paid after the taxable year and on or before the 15th day of the third month following the close of the taxable year shall be considered as paid during such taxable year.

55. (d) Section 532(c) provides that the accumulated earnings tax can be imposed on a corporation without regard to the number of shareholders of such corporations. Partnerships are not subject to the accumulated earnings tax as §531 states that the tax is imposed on the accumulated taxable income of every corporation. Section 532(b)(1) states that the accumulated earnings tax does not apply to personal holding companies. Section 535(a) states that the dividends paid deduction is allowed in computing the accumulated taxable income. Section 561(a) allows a deduction for dividends paid during the taxable year. Thus, if distributions exceed the accumulated earnings there would be no accumulated taxable income and therefore no accumulated earnings tax.

56. (c) Starting with its federal taxable income of $400,000, Kari is allowed a deduction for the federal income tax of $100,000. The minimum credit is $250,000. Therefore, the maximum amount that may be subject to the accumulated earnings tax is $400,000 − $100,000 − $250,000 = $50,000.

PERSONAL HOLDING COMPANY TAX

57. (a) Section 545(b)(1) allows a deduction for federal income taxes (FIT) in computing undistributed personal holding company (PHC) income. Section 545(b)(5) allows a deduction for net capital gains less the taxes thereon in computing personal holding company income. Section 1222(11) defines a net capital gain as the excess of a net long-term capital gain over any net short term capital loss. Thus, §545(b)(5) allows a deduction for a net long-term capital gain less the related FIT in determining undistributed PHC income.

58. (d) The tax base upon which a personal holding company (PHC) is taxed is undistributed PHC income. Basically, this amount is taxable income, subject to certain adjustments, minus the dividends-paid deduction. Dividends actually paid during the tax year ordinarily qualify for the dividends-paid deduction. However, such distributions must be pro rata. They must exhibit no preference to any shares of stock over shares of the same class or to any other class of stock over other classes outstanding. The consent dividend procedure involves a hypothetical distribution of corporate income taxed to the PHC shareholders. Since the consent dividend is taxable to the PHC shareholders, a dividends-paid deduction is allowed for the corporation. Therefore, the amount that Hull should deduct for dividends paid is $30,000, the sum of the $20,000 of dividends paid and the $10,000 of consent dividends reported in the individual income tax returns of the PHC shareholders.

59. (b) Dividends are included in personal holding company (PHC) income under §543(a)(1). Interest earned on tax-exempt obligations is not included in PHC income because §542(a)(1) states that for the income test to be met for the corporation to be a personal holding company at least 60% of the corporation's ordinary gross income must be PHC income. Section 543(b)(2) defines ordinary gross income as gross income less the sum of capital gains and §1231 gains. Section 103(a) excludes interest on state and local bonds from gross income. Thus, interest on tax exempt obligations cannot be a part of ordinary gross income and is, therefore, not PHC income.

60. (a) A corporation is a personal holding company (PHC) if two conditions are met. First, under §541(a), at least 60% of the corporation's adjusted ordinary gross income is PHC income. In general, PHC income consists of investment type income such as dividends and interest. Since Zero Corp. is an investment company, one can assume that Zero Corp. meets this income test. The second condition provided by §541(a)(2) is that at any time during the last half of the taxable year, more than 50% in value of the outstanding stock of the corporation be owned directly or indirectly by 5 or fewer individuals. There is no requirement that these 5 individuals be related. The best answer is (a) because under §544(a)(1), stock owned by an estate is deemed to be owned proportionately by its beneficiaries. Thus, Edwards, would be deemed to own the 200 shares owned by the estate, since he is **the** beneficiary of the estate. Edwards would then be deemed to own 650 shares of the 1,000 shares outstanding. **NOTE:** Answers (b) and (d) are also correct because 2 individuals would own 65% (650/1000) of the stock of Zero Corp. during the last

half of the taxable year. One cannot determine if answer (c) is correct or not. Under §544(a)(1), stock owned by a partnership is deemed to be owned proportionately by its partners. Answer (a) seems best because the question implies that it is testing the candidate's knowledge of the attribution rules of §544.

61. (d)   Kee has no personal holding company tax liability as it does not meet the two tests for a personal holding company [§542(a)]. A substantial portion (60% or more) of corporate income (adjusted ordinary gross income) must be comprised of passive types of income such as dividends, interest, rents, royalties, or certain personal service income. This test is met. However, more than 50% of the value of the outstanding stock must be owned by five or fewer individuals at any time during the last half of the taxable year. This test is not met.

REORGANIZATIONS

62. (a)   This business combination is a statutory consolidation and is a reorganization under §368(a)(1)(A). Section 354(a)(1) provides that no gain or loss shall be recognized if stock or securities in a corporation that is a party to the reorganization are exchanged, pursuant to a plan of reorganization, solely for stock or securities in such corporation or in another corporation that is a party to the reorganization. Thus, under this reorganization, neither shareholders nor any corporation recognizes gain or loss.

63. (d)   Section 354 provides for the nonrecognition of any gain or loss on property transferred to a corporation pursuant to a corporate reorganization in exchange solely for stock or securities of such corporation or in another corporation that is party to the reorganization. Because the taxpayer received only stock in the exchange, no gain or loss is recognized.

64. (c)   Section 368(a)(1)(B) provides that a reorganization, known as a type B reorganization, is the acquisition of the stock of one corporation by another corporation, solely in exchange for the acquiring corporation's voting stock or of the voting stock of a corporation that is in control of the acquiring corporation. Immediately after the acquisition, the acquiring corporation must be in control of the target corporation, as defined in §368(c).

65. (b)   Under §368(a)(1)(B) this transaction will qualify as a Type B reorganization and, therefore, will be tax free under §354(a)(1). King Corp. acquires control of Jaxson Corp. by exchanging King's voting stock for Jaxson's voting stock. King acquires 90% of Jaxson's voting stock, which means

meeting the 80% or more requirement to be in control of Jaxson.

CONSOLIDATED RETURNS

66. (d)   Section 61(a)(7) provides that dividends are included in gross income. However, §243(a)(3) allows a deduction for 100% of dividends received from a taxable domestic corporation that are qualifying dividends. Qualifying dividends are any dividends received from a member of the same affiliated group and paid out of the earnings and profits of a taxable year of the distributing corporation which ends after December 31, 1963. Section 243(b)(2) states that the term affiliated group has the same meaning as in §1504(a). Section 1504(a) provides that an affiliated group consists of corporations with a common parent if the parent owns at least 80% of the voting power and value of the stock of an affiliated corporation. Thus, on a consolidated tax return, the dividend income would be eliminated.

67. (d)   The gain on the sale from Potter to Sly is not recognized at the time of the sale because Porter and Sly file a consolidated tax return. Instead it is recognized when Sly sells the land to an unrelated third party in a fully taxable transaction.

68. (d)   Under §1504(a)(2), at least 80% of the total voting power and 80% of the total value of the stock of the subsidiary must be owned directly by the parent company to be eligible to file a consolidated return.

69. (a)   There is no requirement in the IRC that only corporations that issue audited financial statements on a consolidated basis are eligible to file a consolidated return. Under §243, 100%, not 70%, of the dividends paid by a subsidiary to a parent are deductible from gross income. Section 1501 allows an affiliated group of corporations to file a consolidated return. Under §1504(a), an affiliated group consists of corporations connected through a common parent, if the common parent owns at least 80% of the total voting power and at least 80% of the total value of the stock of at least one corporation. Also, one or more of the other corporations must directly own at least 80% of the stock of the remaining corporations. Regulation §1.1502-11(a)(1) provides that the consolidated taxable income shall take into account the separate taxable income of each member of the group.

70. (a)   Under §243, there is a 100% dividends-received deduction for dividends received from a member of an affiliated group. Thus, the dividends received are effectively not taxable, because their

inclusion in gross income under §61 is offset by the 100% dividends-received deduction.

REDEMPTIONS & LIQUIDATIONS

71. (a) Gain which is incurred by a noncorporate shareholder on the redemption of stock that qualifies as a partial liquidation of the distributing company is treated as a capital gain under §302.

72. (d) This event is a tax-free reorganization.

73. (d) Hall's gain is the sale price less the basis in the stock ($33,000 − $16,000 = $17,000). Usually amounts distributed in complete liquidation of a corporation are treated as full payment in exchange for the stock and are a capital gain or loss. Dividends are distributions from a corporation that result in the same ownership percentage by the shareholders. Hall has no ownership interest in the corporation after the transaction, so this is not a dividend. [This question is unchanged from the Nov. 1997 exam. Note that the examiners asked about tax year 1996, even though they specify that candidates should know the law in effect six months before the exam. In this case, the law is the same in 2002 and 2003 as in 1996.]

74. (d) Shareholders recognize gain or loss on a liquidating distribution to the extent that the FMV of property received is greater than their stock bases.

75. (a) These are deductible as business expenses under §162(a).

76. (d) Gain or loss is generally not recognized upon the complete liquidation of a subsidiary. Instead, the basis of the subsidiary's assets and other tax attributes, such as the net operating loss deduction and excess charitable contributions, are carried over by the parent.

77. (b) A corporation recognizes gain or loss on the distribution of property in complete liquidation as if such property had been sold to the distributee at FMV. The type of gain which is recognized depends on the type of property sold. Krol recognizes $50,000 (i.e., $150,000 − $100,000) of capital gain since it is assumed that the securities were a capital asset in the hands of Krol.

S CORPORATION STATUS

78. (a) An S corporation may only have one class of stock. The stock may have different voting rights and still be classified as one class of stock. An estate may be an S corporation shareholder. A grantor trust may be an S corporation shareholder.

79. (a) Voluntary revocation of S corporation status is made by shareholders collectively holding a majority of stock.

80. (d) Section 1362(d)(3)(A) states that the S election terminates when an S corporation has subchapter C earnings and profits and more than 25% of its gross receipts for each of 3 consecutive years are passive investment income. An S corporation may have up to 75 shareholders. An S corporation may have an estate as a shareholder. S corporations are allowed to deduct charitable contributions. The charitable contributions are passed down to the shareholders as a separately stated item.

81. (b) Section 1362(b)(3) states that if a corporation makes the S election after the first 2-1/2 months of the tax year, the election becomes effective at the beginning of the following tax year. Because the election was made in December 20X6 and Village Corp. is a calendar year corporation, the S election becomes effective on January 1, 20X7.

82. (c) After a corporation's status as an S corporation is revoked or terminated, §1362(g) enforces a five-year waiting period before a new election can be made. The Code does, however, allow the IRS to make exceptions to this rule to permit an earlier reelection by the corporation. The IRS may allow an early reelection if (1) there is a more than 50% change in ownership after the first year for which the termination is applicable or (2) the event causing the termination was not reasonably within the control of the S corporation or its majority shareholders.

S CORPORATION INCOME & BASIS

83. (c) Since no election was made to use an interim closing of the books, §1362(e)(2) requires that the non-separately computed income must be allocated on a daily basis between the short S year and the short C year. Zinco Corp.'s income allocated to the short S year is $76,500 ([90 ÷ 365] x $310,250). The days in the short S year are computed as follows: January days 31 + February days 28 + March days 31 = 90 days.

84. (b) One major advantage of an S election is the ability to pass through any net operating loss (NOL) of the corporation directly to the shareholders. The NOL is allocated on a daily basis to all shareholders. Meyer's share of Bern's loss is computed by multiplying Bern's NOL for the year by the percentage of Bern's stock owned by Meyer and the proportion of days that Meyer owned the stock (i.e., $36,500 x 50% x 40/365 = $2,000).

85. (d) S corporations are similar to partnerships, in that the distribution of income is inconsequential to its recognition and that tax-exempt income retains its character.

86. (b) Without debt transactions, a partner's adjusted basis in a partnership interest is the beginning basis plus income minus distributions. $12,000 + 50% x ($81,000 + $10,000) − $51,000 = $6,500

87. (d) Fringe benefits provided to a more than 2% shareholder-employee must be include in the shareholder's gross income.

88. (d) Section 1367(a)(1)(A) requires an increase in the shareholder's basis of stock in an S corporation for items of income separately stated in §1366(a)(1)(A). Section 1366(a)(1)(A) specifically includes tax-exempt income. Thus, the shareholder's basis in her/his stock of an S corporation is increased for her/his share of tax-exempt interest. Section 1367(a)(1)(B) also requires an increase in a shareholder's basis of stock in an S corporation for nonseparately computed income. Taxable interest would be included in non-separately computed income. Thus, the shareholder's basis in her/his stock of an S corporation is increased for her/his share of taxable interest.

89. (b) An S corporation passes through those items of income, loss, deduction, or credit which could affect the tax liability of its shareholders differently. This includes charitable contributions, dividends, and foreign taxes. Answers (a), (c), and (d) are all items that are deductible by an S corporation.

90. (a) The at-risk rules allow a shareholder of an S corporation to deduct only the losses which are passed to him from the S corporation to the extent he has amounts which are considered at-risk. Since the S corporation is not a taxpaying entity in general, and all of its income and losses are passed through to its shareholders, the at-risk rules would apply only to the shareholders.

SOLUTION 29-2 ADDITIONAL MULTIPLE CHOICE ANSWERS

FILING REQUIREMENTS

91. (a) Section 162(f) disallows any deduction for fines or penalties paid to a government for violation of any law. Therefore, the penalty is not deductible.

INCOME & DEDUCTIONS

92. (a) Under §1032, when a corporation exchanges its own stock (i.e., treasury stock) for property or money, no gain or loss is recognized on the exchange.

93. (b) The passive activity loss rules apply to (1) noncorporate taxpayers, (2) *closely* held C corporations, and (3) personal service corporations. For S corporations and partnerships, passive income or loss flows through to the owners, and the passive activity loss rules are applied at the owner level. The passive activity loss rules apply to *closely* held C corporations—not to *widely* held C corporations.

94. (c) Section 243(a) allows corporations to deduct 70% of the amount of dividends received from taxable domestic corporations. The allowance method of accounting for bad debts is not allowed for tax purposes. Section §166(a) provides that bad debts are deductible when wholly worthless or when the taxpayer can prove that a debt is recoverable only in part (the specific charge off method of accounting for bad debts). An increased allowance for doubtful accounts represents an increase in bad debts expense for book purposes.

Book income	$300,000
Less: DRD ($50,000 x 70%)	(35,000)
Add: Addition to allowance for doubtful accounts	80,000
Taxable income	$345,000

95. (a) Section 263A(b)(1) provides that the Uniform Capitalization Rules apply to tangible personal property produced by the taxpayer. Section 263A(b)(2)(A) provides that the Uniform Capitalization Rules apply to inventory acquired by the taxpayer for resale. However, §263A(b)(b)(2)(B) provides that the Uniform Capitalization Rules will not apply to inventory that the taxpayer acquires for resale if the taxpayer's average annual gross receipts for the 3 taxable years period ending with the taxable year preceding such taxable year do not exceed $10 million.

96. (c) Generally, C corporations, taxpayers with inventories, and tax shelter entities must use the accrual method. An entity that is not a tax shelter may use the cash method, if it is a qualified personal service corporation or if the entity meets the under $5 million gross receipts test.

97. (b) Section 243 indicates that no DRD is allowed if stock is held less than 46 days or if the taxpayer must make related payments on other

property. In addition, §243 states that the deduction is equal to 100% for members of an affiliated group. An 80% deduction is permitted if the recipient owns between 20% and 80%, and 70% can be claimed when holdings are less than 20%. The DRD is *limited* to a percentage of a corporation's taxable income. Per §243(a), the amount of the DRD depends upon the ownership percentage the corporate shareholder holds in the domestic corporation making the distribution (e.g., a 10% level of ownership results in a 70% deduction, while a 40% level results in an 80% deduction). Certain provisions of the Code governing the computation of taxable income applicable only to corporations, such as the DRD, do not apply to S corporations.

98. (a) A taxpayer that deducts the fair market value of unsolicited sample merchandise donated to charity must take into income the fair market value of such property upon contribution.

GAINS & LOSSES

99. (b) Capital losses that a corporation carries back or forward are deemed to be short-term regardless of whether they were short-term or long-term losses when sustained. A corporation can not use capital losses to offset ordinary income.

ALTERNATIVE MINIMUM TAX

100. (c) Tax preference items for alternative minimum tax purposes are listed under §57 and include the accelerated depreciation taken on pre-1987 real property that exceeds the depreciation that would have been allowed under the straight-line method. Using the percentage-of-completion method is an adjustment not a tax preference. The Code distinguishes between adjustments and preferences. Casualty losses are a deduction; and capital gains used to be a preference *before* the Tax Reform Act of 1986.

DIVIDEND DISTRIBUTIONS

101. (c) Section 301(c)(1) provides that when a distribution of property is from a corporation to a shareholder with respect to its stock, it will be a taxable dividend as defined in §316. Section 316(a) provides that a dividend is any distribution made to shareholders out of accumulated earnings and profits or out of current earnings and profits. Regulation §1.316-2(a) provides that consideration should be given to current earnings and profits first and then to accumulated earnings and profits. In this case, the $30,000 distribution is a dividend to the extent of the $10,000 current earnings and profits. The $50,000

deficit in accumulated earnings and profits is not netted against the current earnings and profits.

102. (c) Section 311(b)(1) provides that if a corporation distributes property to a shareholder, the corporation must recognize gain as if the property were sold for its fair market value. Section 1001(a) states that the gain on the sale of property is the amount realized less the property's adjusted basis.

PERSONAL HOLDING COMPANY

103. (d) If, at any time during the last half of the tax year, more than 50% of the value of the outstanding stock of a corporation is owned directly or indirectly by five or fewer individuals and at least 60% of the corporation's adjusted ordinary gross income is personal holding company income, then the corporation is a personal holding company.

CONSOLIDATED RETURNS

104. (d) Portal prepares a consolidated return, therefore dividends received from Sal are eliminated at the consolidated level and no dividend income is reported on the consolidated tax return.

105. (b) The transaction represents the sale of property between a parent and a subsidiary filing a consolidated tax return, and, thus, it is referred to as a deferred intercompany transaction and receives special treatment. Stem realizes a gain of $60,000 ($150,000 − $90,000) on the sale of the land to Plant. The gain realized is deferred in a suspense account until the restoration event, the sale of the land by Plant to Dubin. In 20X2, Stem recognizes the $60,000 gain realized in 20X1. Plant recognizes a gain of $30,000 ($180,000 − $150,000) as its basis in the land includes the deferred gain of Stem ($90,000 + $60,000 = $150,000).

LIQUIDATIONS

106. (c) When a corporation is liquidated or sold before three years pass after the manufacture, construction, or purchase of certain types of property is completed, and before the corporation realizes 2/3 of the income to be derived from that property, the corporation is collapsible. The stockholder's holding period is irrelevant.

S CORPORATIONS

107. (c) Under §1362(d)(1)(B) an election to be an S corporation may be revoked voluntarily only if shareholders holding more than 1/2 of the shares of stock of the corporation on the day the revocation is made consent to the revocation. Regulation

§18.1362-3 states that such shares include nonvoting shares. With 50,000 shares outstanding, shareholders holding more than 25,000 shares must consent to the revocation. The 10,000 voting shares and 16,000 nonvoting shares total 26,000 shares, which is greater than 25,000 shares.

108. (c)   Returns of corporations, made on the basis of the calendar year, are to be filed on or before the 15th day of March following the close of the calendar year [§6072(b)].

109. (a)   Section 1366(a)(1) requires that the shareholders of an S corporation must report their pro rata share of the S corporation's income.

$73,200 x (40 / 366) x (100 / 100)	$ 8,000
$73,200 x (326 / 366) x (75 / 100)	48,900
Kane's pro rata share	$56,900

110. (c)   Under §1368(b) a distribution to a shareholder in an S corporation that has no accumulated earnings and profits, in respect of the shareholder's stock in the S corporation, shall not be included in the shareholder's gross income except to the extent that the amount of the distribution exceeds the adjusted basis of the stock. Section 1367(a)(2)(A) provides that distributions by the S corporation that were not includible in income under §1368 shall decrease the basis of the shareholder's stock in the S corporation.

PERFORMANCE BY SUBTOPICS

Each category below parallels a subtopic covered in Chapter 29. Record the number and percentage of questions you correctly answered in each subtopic area.

Formation

Question #	Correct √
1	
2	
3	
4	
5	
6	
# Questions	6
# Correct	
% Correct	

Filing Requirements

Question #	Correct √
7	
8	
9	
10	
11	
12	
# Questions	6
# Correct	
% Correct	

Income & Deductions

Question #	Correct √
13	
14	
15	
16	
17	
18	
19	
20	
21	
22	
23	
24	
25	
# Questions	13
# Correct	
% Correct	

Dividends Received Deduction

Question #	Correct √
26	
27	
28	
29	
# Questions	4
# Correct	
% Correct	

Keyman Life Insurance

Question #	Correct √
30	
31	
# Questions	2
# Correct	
% Correct	

Charitable Contributions

Question #	Correct √
32	
33	
34	
35	
36	
# Questions	5
# Correct	
% Correct	

Gains & Losses

Question #	Correct √
37	
38	
39	
40	
# Questions	4
# Correct	
% Correct	

Alternative Minimum Tax

Question #	Correct √
41	
42	
43	
44	
# Questions	4
# Correct	
% Correct	

Schedule M-1

Question #	Correct √
45	
46	
47	
48	
# Questions	4
# Correct	
% Correct	

Dividend Distributions

Question #	Correct √
49	
50	
51	
52	
53	
# Questions	5
# Correct	
% Correct	

Accumulated Earnings Tax

Question #	Correct √
54	
55	
56	
# Questions	3
# Correct	
% Correct	

Personal Holding Company Tax	
Question #	Correct √
57	
58	
59	
60	
61	
# Questions	5
# Correct	_____
% Correct	_____

Consolidated Returns	
Question #	Correct √
66	
67	
68	
69	
70	
# Questions	5
# Correct	_____
% Correct	_____

S Corporation Status	
Question #	Correct √
78	
79	
80	
81	
82	
# Questions	5
# Correct	_____
% Correct	_____

S Corporation Income & Basis	
Question #	Correct √
83	
84	
85	
86	
87	
88	
89	
90	
# Questions	8
# Correct	_____
% Correct	_____

Reorganizations	
Question #	Correct √
62	
63	
64	
65	
# Questions	4
# Correct	_____
% Correct	_____

Redemptions & Liquidations	
Question #	Correct √
71	
72	
73	
74	
75	
76	
77	
# Questions	7
# Correct	_____
% Correct	_____

OTHER OBJECTIVE FORMAT QUESTION SOLUTIONS

SOLUTION 29-3 CORPORATE TAXES

1. $15,000, I

Section 162(a)(2) allows a deduction for traveling expenses, including meals, incurred in a trade or business. Section 274(n)(1) limits the deduction for business meals to 50% of the cost of such meals.

All of the travel cost and the cost of meals were deducted on Reliant's financial accounting books. Because 50% of the cost of business meals may **not** be deducted for tax purposes, such amount must be added back to the financial accounting income in arriving at taxable income ($30,000 x 50%).

2. $7,000, I

The $7,000 in life insurance premiums was deducted in arriving at financial accounting income. However, §264(a)(1) disallows any deduction for life insurance premiums paid on the life of a corporate officer when the taxpayer is the beneficiary of the policy.

3. $0, N

Under §461(a) the amount of any deduction is to be taken in the proper taxable year under the method of accounting used in computing taxable income. Because Reliant is an accrual basis taxpayer, the franchise tax expense is generally deducted in the

year accrued. However, §461(h)(4) requires that all events have occurred that fix the fact of the liability and that the amount can be determined with reasonable accuracy. Also, §461(h)(1) states that the all-events test is not deemed to be satisfied until economic performance has occurred. Under Regulation §1.461-4(g)(6) economic performance occurs for a tax liability when the tax liability is paid. However, §461(h)(3)(A) provides an exception for recurring items. For recurring items, the economic performance test is waived if (1) the all-events test is satisfied, (2) economic performance occurs within the shorter of a reasonable time after the close of the tax year or 8-1/2 months after the close of the tax year, (3) the item is recurring in nature and is consistently treated by the taxpayer, and (4) the item is not material or results in a better matching of income and deductions. The accrual of the franchise tax liability should meet the recurring item exception. Therefore, $18,000 should be deducted in arriving at Reliant's taxable income.

4. $6,000, D

Section 168(e)(3)(B)(iv) provides that any qualified technological equipment is 5-year property. Section 168(i)(2) includes computers in the definition of qualified technological equipment; thus, computers are 5-year MACRS property. Section 168(b)(1) requires the double-declining-balance method, with a switch to the straight-line method when the straight-line method provides a greater deduction.

Section 68(b)(4) states that salvage value is to be ignored. The straight-line depreciation rate would be 20% a year (100% / 5 years). Therefore, the double-declining-balance rate is 40% (20% x 2). Section 168(d) (1) requires the use of the half-year convention. Section 168(d) (4)(A) states that the half-year convention treats all property placed in service during the year as placed in service at the mid-point of the year. Therefore, the MACRS deductions for these computers for tax years 20X2 and 20X3 are determined as follows:

For tax year 20X2: $50,000 x 40% x 1/2 = $10,000
For tax year 20X3: ($50,000 – $10,000) x 40% = $16,000

The MACRS deduction for tax purposes is $6,000 ($16,000 – $10,000) more than the book depreciation.

5. $1,000, I

The $4,000 capital gain distribution was included and the $5,000 loss on the sale of the Retro stock was deducted in arriving at Reliant's financial accounting income. For tax purposes, §§165(f) and 1211(a) limit the deduction of a corporation's capital losses only to the extent of the corporation's capital gains. The $4,000 capital gain distribution is included in Reliant's gross income under §61(a). However, only $4,000 of the $5,000 capital loss is deductible in arriving at taxable income.

6. $0, N

Reliant would have deducted the $35,000 in charitable contributions made during 20X3 and the $15,000 in charitable contributions accrued in 20X3 and paid in 20X4 on its financial accounting books for 20X3. Section 170(a)(1) authorizes a deduction for charitable contributions paid during the taxable year. Also, §170(a) (2) authorizes a deduction for a corporation on the accrual basis of accounting for charitable contributions, authorized by its board of directors during the taxable year, if payment is made by the 15th day of the third month following the taxable year. Thus, Reliant has a potential deduction for charitable contributions of $50,000 ($35,000 + $15,000) for 20X3. However, §170(b)(2) limits a corporation's deduction for charitable contributions to 10% of its taxable income, determined without regard to charitable contributions, the DRD, any NOL carryback, and any net capital loss carryback. Since Reliant's taxable income before the charitable contributions and DRD was $500,000, Reliant's charitable contributions deduction is limited to $50,000 ($500,000 x 10%). The limit equals the potential deduction, and Reliant may deduct all $50,000 in charitable contributions for 20X3.

7. P   The theater tickets are deductible under §162(a) as an ordinary and necessary business expense. Reliant meets the requirement of §274(a) (1) (A) that the entertainment is associated with its business. However, §274(n) (1) (B) allows only 50% of the cost of entertainment (that is otherwise deductible) as a deduction.

8. F   Advertising expenses are fully deductible as an ordinary and necessary business expense in the year paid or incurred under §162(a). Under §461(a) the amount of any deduction is to be taken in the proper taxable year under the method of accounting used in computing taxable income. The fact that 10% of the new product line remains in inventory is irrelevant.

9. N   Section 265(a) (2) disallows any deduction for interest on indebtedness incurred to purchase or to carry tax exempt obligations. According to §103(a) interest on municipal bonds is tax exempt.

10. N   Section 162(f) disallows any deduction for business expense for any fine or similar penalty paid to a government for the violation of any law. Regulation §1.162-21(b) (1) states that such a penalty includes civil penalties that are additions to taxes.

11. F   The bonus is deductible as an ordinary and necessary business expense under §162(a). Under §461(a) the amount of any deduction is to be taken in the proper taxable year under the method of accounting used in computing taxable income. Reliant is an accrual basis taxpayer. However, §461(h)(4) requires that all events have occurred that fix the fact of the liability and that the amount can be determined with reasonable accuracy. Also, §461(h)(1) states that the all-events test is not deemed to be satisfied until economic performance has occurred. Section 461(h)(2)(A)(i) states that if the liability arises out of the performance of services by another person for the taxpayer, economic performance occurs when the other person performs such services. The all-events test is satisfied because the bonus to be paid is a legal liability of the corporation and the amount of the liability is fixed. Economic performance occurred when the employee performed the services. Thus, the bonus is fully deductible in the year accrued. Section 267(a) (2) would delay the deduction until the year paid if the recipients were related parties within the meaning of §267. In this case, the bonus is to be paid to nonstockholders only. Thus, they are not related parties within the meaning of §267 and Reliant is entitled to deduct the bonus in 20X3.

12.   N   Section 275(a)(1) disallows any deduction for federal income taxes. When Reliant receives a refund of federal income tax that Reliant previously paid, the refund is excluded from gross income because Reliant received no tax benefit from paying the federal income taxes. Although not directly applicable because Reliant's payment of the federal income taxes was not deductible, see §111 relating to the tax benefit rule. Under this rule, an amount received as a refund of an item previously deducted is included in gross income only to the extent that the deduction provided a tax benefit in a previous tax year.

13.   F   Interest income from the Internal Revenue Service is fully included in gross income under §61(a)(4).

14.   N   Section 103(a) excludes from gross income the interest on any state or local bond. The income from the mutual fund retains its character under §852(b)(5).

15.   F   In general, under §109 a lessor's gross income does not include any improvements made by the lessee on the lessor's property. However, the lessor will recognize gross income to the extent that the rental payments are reduced as a result of the improvements under Regulation §1.109-1(a), §61(a)(5), and §1.61-1(a). The lessor will also receive a basis in the improvements equal to the gross income recognized as a result of the reduction in rental payments.

16.   P   When a life insurance policy is transferred for valuable consideration, §101(a)(2) provides that the life insurance proceeds received may be excluded from gross income only to the extent of the taxpayer's basis in the consideration and subsequent premiums paid by the taxpayer. The amount of the proceeds in excess of the debt will be included in Reliant's gross income under §61(a).

17.   N   Under §56(g)(4)(C)(i) the 70% dividends received deduction is added back in computing adjusted current earnings (ACE). Therefore, it is a part of the ACE adjustment and has no effect on Reliant's alternative minimum taxable income prior to the ACE adjustment.

18.   N   Under §57(a)(5) interest on specified private activity bonds is a tax preference for purposes of the alternative minimum tax. However, interest on a state's general obligation bonds has no effect on alternative minimum taxable income.

19.   I   Under §56(a)(1)(A) taxpayers must use the alternative depreciation system (ADS) in computing alternative minimum taxable income (AMTI). In the year of acquisition, the depreciation under the ADS will be less than it is under MACRS. Thus, the adjustment will increase AMTI. This adjustment comes prior to the adjusted current earnings (ACE) adjustment. While TRA '97 results in the use of the same recovery periods for regular taxes and AMT, the AMT rules continue to require the 150%, rather than 200%, declining balance method for certain assets. (This provision is effective for assets placed in service after December 31, 1998.)

20.   I   Under §56(a)(1)(A) taxpayers must use the alternative depreciation system (ADS) in computing alternative minimum taxable income (AMTI). In the year of acquisition, the depreciation under the ADS will be less than it is under MACRS. This is true even though for MACRS the nonresidential real property must be depreciated straight-line over 39 years under §§168(b)(3)(A) and 168(c)(1). The reason is that, under §168(g)(2), the ADS uses a 40-year straight-line method. (TRA '97 changes this for assets placed in service after December 31, 1998.) Thus, the adjustment will increase AMTI. This adjustment comes prior to the adjusted current earnings (ACE) adjustment.

21.   N   There is no adjustment listed in §56 for cash charitable contributions. Cash charitable contributions are also not listed as a tax preference in §57.

22.   F   Section 55(d)(3)(A) states that the exemption for the alternative minimum tax (AMT) is reduced by 25% of the amount by which the AMT income exceeds $150,000.

23.   F   Section 6501(c)(1) states that in the case of a fraudulent return, the tax may be assessed or a proceeding in court for collection of such tax may be begun without assessment at any time. There is no statute of limitations if a fraudulent return is filed.

24.   F   Section 6501(e)(1)(A) provides that if the taxpayer omits gross income on a return greater than 25% of the gross income shown on the return, the tax may be assessed within 6 years after the return was filed. Because §6501(b)(1) states that a return filed early will, for purposes of §6501, be considered as filed on the due date, the statute of limitations in this case is 6 years from the later of the date due or the date filed.

25.   T   Section 38(b) lists the targeted jobs credit as one of a number of tax credits that must be added together to determine the current year business credit. The title of §38 is general business

credit. Section 38(a)(2) lists the current year business credit as one of three items that must be added together to arrive at the general business credit.

26. **T** Under §44, Reliant qualifies for the disabled access credit. Reliant is a small business within the meaning of §44(b). Reliant's expenditures to remove existing access barriers qualify under §44(c)(2)(A).

27. **T** Section 6713(a) imposes a civil penalty on tax return preparers for the unauthorized use or disclosure of information obtained while preparing a tax return. However, Reg. §301.7216-2(e)(2) allows a tax return preparer who is lawfully engaged in the practice of law or accountancy to take tax return information into account and act on it in the course of performing legal or accounting services for a client other than the taxpayer. The tax return information may not be disclosed to a person who is not an employee or member of the law or accounting firm unless allowed by another provision. Because a CPA firm is lawfully engaged in the practice of accounting, the CPA firm should be able to use the information obtained in preparing the corporate return to assist in preparing the corporate officers' returns without the consent of the corporation.

28. **F** Section 6511(a) states that a claim for refund must be made within 3 years from the time a return was filed or 2 years from the time the tax was paid, whichever is later. The statute of limitations on assessment is generally 3 years from the later of the date due or the date filed under §§ 6501(a) and 6501(b)(1). Under §6501(c)(7) if an amended return is filed within 60 days of the termination of the statute of limitations on assessment, the statute of limitations on assessment will not expire until 60 days after the IRS receives the amended return.

SOLUTION 29-4 SCHEDULE M-1 & AMT

1. $7,000, D

A corporation may elect to amortize organizational expenses over a period of 60 months or more. The increase of an expense decreases taxable income. $40,000 / 60 x 12 = $8,000) ($8,000 − $1,000 = $7,000)

2. $5,000, I

Only 50% of meal and entertainment expenses are deductible. The reduction of an expense increases taxable income.

3. -0-, N

Premiums on employee life insurance policies are deductible if the corporation is not the beneficiary.

4. $10,000, I

Only the direct write-off method of recognizing bad debt is allowed for tax purposes. The reduction of an expense increases taxable income.

5. **P** A dividend-received-deduction shields part of the dividend income from a 35% owned corporation.

6. **F** For tax purposes, rental income is recognized when received, regardless of the taxpayer's basis of accounting.

7. **P** A corporation's deduction for charitable contributions is limited to 10% of taxable income without regard to the deduction for charitable contributions, the DRD, any NOL carry-back to that year, and any capital loss carry-back to that year.

8. **N** Penalties are not deductible.

9. **C** As JCWAA '02 is written, property eligible for the 30% bonus depreciation—whether taken or not—is exempt from an AMT depreciation adjustment. MACRS depreciation (200%) is higher in the first year of service than the 150% that is allowed for personal property under AMT prior to JCWAA '02. Prior to JCWAA '02, because this overstates deductions, income is understated.

10. **U** Straight-line depreciation over 40, not 39, years is appropriate for AMT purposes for real property. Because the deduction is overstated, income is understated.

11. **C** Tax-exempt interest from private activity bonds issued after August 7, 1986 is a preference. However, state highway construction is not a private activity.

SOLUTION 29-5 S CORPORATIONS

1. $6,140

Section 1366(a)(1) requires that an S corporation take into account the shareholder's pro rata share of items of income, deduction, loss, or credit that could affect the liability for tax of any shareholder. Section 1566(a)(2) requires that the S corporation take into account the shareholder's pro rata share of non-separately computed income or loss. The interest income is stated separately because it is necessary in determining the deduction for investment interest expense under §163(d). Charitable contributions are separately stated because they are treated as an itemized deduction under §170 up to 50% of AGI on an individual's return. The net business income (nonseparately computed income) is determined as follows:

Gross receipts	$7,260
Less: Supplies	(1,120)
Net business income	$6,140

2. $2,700

335 days are used since Pike did not own shares for 30 days out of the 365 day year that began on January 1. Pike's share of the S corporation's income (to the nearest hundred) under §1366(a) is determined as follows:

$$\frac{40 \text{ shares}}{200 \text{ shares}} \times \frac{335 \text{ days}}{365 \text{ days}} \times \$14,520 = \$2,665$$

$$= \text{approx. } \$2,700$$

3. $3,150

Pike obtains a cost basis of $4,000 on the purchase of the shares under §1012. His basis is increased for his share of the tax-exempt municipal bond interest income under §§1367(a)(1)(A) and 1366(a)(1)(A). His basis is reduced by his share of the $1,000 ordinary business loss under and §1366(a)(1)(B) and §1367(a)(2)(C).

Cost basis for shares purchased	$ 4,000
Add: Municipal bond interest income	150
Less: Ordinary business loss	(1,000)
Pike's basis at December 31	$ 3,150

4. $9,000

Taylor's basis is increased by his share of the ordinary income under §§1367(a)(1)(B) and 1366(a)(1)(B). Taylor's basis is decreased by the distribution under §1367(a)(2)(A).

Taylor's basis on January 1	$10,000
Add: Ordinary income	2,000
Less: Distribution	(3,000)
Taylor's basis at January 31	$ 9,000

5. F   Under §1361(b)(1) an S corporation must be a small business corporation with only one class of stock. Section 1362(d)(2)(A) provides that the S election will terminate whenever the corporation ceases to be a small business corporation.

6. F   Under §1362(d)(3) the S election will terminate if the corporation has gross receipts from passive sources of 25% or more of its receipts for 3 consecutive years. An additional requirement before termination is effective is that the S corporation must have C corporation earnings and profits at the end of those 3 consecutive years. In this case, the S election is not terminated since Lan has never been a C corporation.

2002 TAX ACT

The Job Creation & Worker Assistance Act of 2002 (JCWAA '02) includes business economic stimulus provisions, some general retroactively effective tax breaks, and some relief provisions only for lower-Manhattan entities affected by terrorist acts on September 11, 2001. The Bisk Education editors believe details on the provisions applicable only to lower-Manhattan are beyond the scope of the exam. JCWAA '02 became effective on March 9, 2002.

Bisk Education CPA review materials are designed to help you pass the current exam. Provisions that are not yet effective are not tested; thus you unnecessarily would add time to your review by studying them. We do not discourage your interest in these provisions, but we caution you not to delude yourself that this study is exam preparation. Generally, provisions that are not effective until 2004 or later are not in this edition—which already is more than you are likely to need. Some future changes to current provisions are discussed when the additional space to do so is not significant. Future editions and updating supplements will provide information about provisions as they become eligible for testing. Study those provisions that are applicable to your exam.

EXAM COVERAGE: The partnership taxation portion of the ARE section of the CPA exam is designated by the examiners to be 10% of the section's point value. Estate and trust taxation exempt organizations and preparers' responsibilities together have a point value designated at 10%. Exam coverage of estate and trust taxation hovers at approximately 4 to 8% of the ARE section frequently appearing in the other objective question format. Point value hovers at 2 to 5% each for exempt organizations and preparers' responsibilities. More information about point distribution is included in the **Practical Advice** section of this volume.

CHAPTER 30

FEDERAL TAXATION: PARTNERSHIPS & OTHER TOPICS

CHAPTER 30

FEDERAL TAXATION: PARTNERSHIPS & OTHER TOPICS

I. PARTNERSHIP TAXATION

A. OVERVIEW

Generally, partnerships are not tax-paying entities. Rather, they are conduits through which several types of income, loss, deductions, and credits are passed to the partners [IRC §701].

1. **ENTITY CLASSIFICATION** Under *check-the-box* regulations, an eligible entity may elect its classification for federal tax purposes. An eligible entity is an entity that does not meet the definition of a corporation under the regulations, is not a single owner entity, is not a trust, or is not otherwise subject to special treatment under the IRC. If the entity fails to elect a classification, the regulation provides a default classification. The use is broader than the common law meaning and may include groups not commonly called partnerships.

    a. A partnership is a syndicate, group, pool, joint venture, or other unincorporated entity through which a business is carried on, and which is not a corporation, trust, or estate.

    b. Mere co-ownership of property is **not** a partnership. However, if the entity provides **services** in conjunction with the use of the property by the lessee or licensee, the entity may be characterized as a partnership.

    c. Limited partnerships are subject to the same rules as general partnerships.

    d. Limited liability entities may be classified for federal tax purposes as either corporations or as partnerships. Limited liability companies (LLC), limited liability partnerships, professional limited liability companies, etc. are frequently designed to take advantage of the pass-through tax status of partnerships and the limited legal liability of corporations, but the partnership tax status is **not** automatic. Unless a limited liability entity meets conditions that require it to be taxed as a corporation or it elects to be so treated, it is treated as a partnership for tax purposes.

2. **INFORMATION RETURN** Partnerships must file an information tax return (Form 1065) showing partnership income and deductions with each partner's share (Schedule K-1). Failure to file a return can result in a penalty being assessed against the partnership, the amount based on the number of partners. In general, partnerships with more than 100 partners must provide Form 1065 and copies of each partner's Schedule K-1 to the IRS on magnetic media. Returns are due March 15 for calendar-year partnerships.

3. **TAX YEAR** The partnership's taxable year is generally the same as that of its partners owning a majority interest in the partnership, unless a business purpose can be established for designating a different taxable year [IRC §706(b)(1)].

    a. If partners owning a majority interest do not have the same taxable year, the partnership must adopt the taxable year of its principal partners. Principal partners are partners having an interest of 5% or more in the partnership's profits or capital.

    b. If neither partners owning a majority interest nor principal partners have the same taxable year, the partnership must adopt a calendar year as its taxable year.

    c. A partnership can elect to use a fiscal year instead of a calendar year as long as the fiscal year does not result in a deferral period that is greater than 3 months [IRC §444]. Therefore, a partnership that is normally required to have a calendar year under IRC §706 can elect to have a fiscal year if the fiscal year ends on September 30, October 31, or November 30. For more information, see S Corporations.

4. PARTNER LEVEL Each partner reports her/his **distributive share** of income, loss, deduction, and credit for the partnership's taxable year that ends within or with the partner's taxable year [IRC §706(a)].

EXAMPLE 1 ♦ TIMING OF INCOME RECOGNITION

A.   Both the partnership's and the individual partners' taxable years end on December 31, 2000. The partners report their shares of 2000 partnership income, etc., on their 2000 returns.

B.   An individual partner is on a calendar-year basis, while her partnership is on a fiscal-year basis ending January 31. The partner's share of partnership income, etc., for the partnership year ending January 31, 2000, is reported on her 2000 return, i.e., the return filed in 2001.

B. DISTRIBUTIVE SHARE
Each partner must account for her/his share of partnership items. The partner is taxed on the distributive share **regardless** of actual distributions. The actual distributions are rarely taxable events, but merely a return of previous investment or previously taxed partnership income.

1. PARTNERSHIP AGREEMENT Generally, the distributive share is determined by the partnership agreement, unless the allocation in the agreement does not have substantial economic effect [IRC §704]. An allocation has substantial economic effect if it may actually affect the dollar amount of the partners' shares of the total partnership income or loss independently of tax consequences. If the allocation does not have substantial economic effect, the partnership agreement concerning the distribution is ignored, and the distribution is made according to the partners' interests in the partnership.

2. PROFITS AND LOSSES If the partnership agreement makes no provision for the distributive share, it is determined in the same manner that the partnership agreement provides for the division of the general profits and losses.

3. LIMITATIONS A partner's distributive share of partnership loss cannot exceed the partner's adjusted basis in her/his partnership interest. A partner's loss deduction is also limited by the "at-risk" and passive loss rules (see Corporations). Any unused loss is carried forward.

4. SEPARATELY REPORTED ITEMS Separately reported items, also accounted for by distributive share, include the following [IRC §702]:

a.   Long-term capital gains and losses

b.   Short-term capital gains and losses

c.   Gains and losses from sales of certain business property and certain involuntary conversions [IRC §1231(b) property]

d.   Charitable contributions

e.   Dividend income

f.   Foreign taxes paid

g.   Taxable income (or loss) other than items already separately stated

EXAMPLE 2 ♦ INCOME RECOGNITION

The partnership of Bond and Felton has a fiscal year ending March 31. John Bond files his tax return on a calendar-year basis. The partnership paid Bond what the partnership calls a guaranteed salary of $1,000 per month during calendar year 20X0 and $1,500 per month during calendar year 20X1. (The IRC calls this a guaranteed payment.) After deducting this salary, the partnership realized ordinary income of $80,000 for the year ended March 31, 20X1, and $90,000 for the year ended March 31, 20X2. Bond's share of the profits is the salary paid him plus 40% of the ordinary income after deducting this salary. For 20X1, Bond should report taxable income from the partnership of $45,500.

COMPUTATIONS:

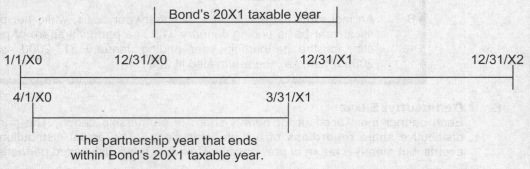

The partnership year that ends
within Bond's 20X1 taxable year.

A partner includes in his personal gross income only his pro rata share of partnership income (distributed or undistributed) for his taxable year ending with or within the taxable year of the partnership. Bond's 20X1 taxable year ends on December 31, 20X1. However, the partnership's taxable year begins on April 1, 20X0, and ends on March 31, 20X1. Therefore, Bond's share of partnership income for calendar year 20X1 is:

$1,000/month x 9 months of 20X0	$9,000	
$1,500/month x 3 months of 20X1	4,500	
Salary received from April 1, 20X0, to March 31, 20X1		$13,500
Add Bond's share of partnership income realized during		
April 1, 20X0 - March 31, 20X1 (80,000 x 40%)		32,000
Bond's 20X1 taxable income from the partnership		$45,500

The $13,500 salary that Bond received during the last nine months of 20X1 must be considered in determining his taxable income from the partnership for 20X2. The same applies to his pro rata share of the $90,000 partnership income realized during the partnership's fiscal year, beginning on April 1, 20X1, and ending on March 31, 20X2. This is because it relates to the partnership year that ends with or within Bond's 20X2 taxable year.

EXAMPLE 3 ♦ INCOME FLOW-THROUGH FROM PARTNERSHIP

X-Y Partnership Items		Trial Balance	Partnership	Partners
(A)	Sales	$100,000	$100,000	
(B)	Cost of goods sold	(50,000)	(50,000)	
(C)	Salaries	(20,000)	(20,000)	
(D)	Other operating expenses	(10,000)	(10,000)	
(E)	Guaranteed payments	(5,000)	(5,000)	
(F)	Dividends	1,000		$ 1,000
(G)	Short-term capital gains	2,000		2,000
(H)	Short-term capital losses	(4,000)		(4,000)
(I)	Long-term capital gains	10,000		$10,000
(J)	Section 1231 casualty loss	(3,000)		(3,000)
(K)	Section 1231 gain	5,000		5,000
(L)	Charitable contributions	(1,000)		(1,000)
(M)	Section 1245 gain	3,000	3,000	
Net income from operations (A, B, C, D, E, M)			$ 18,000	

(1)   Items F through L pass through the partnership's return and are not considered in arriving at the partnership's net income from operations. These items are treated individually by the two partners, X and Y, based on special allocations (if having substantial economic effect) or profit-and-loss sharing ratios, and are dealt with in the tax returns of the individual partners. Note that items F through L are items of income and expense that are generally subject to individual taxpayer limitations. Such limitations apply to each individual partner of the partnership. For example, item F, Dividends, is not considered at the partnership level but is passed through and dealt with on the returns of the partners. Thus, in the case of a corporate partner, the dividends are eligible for the 80% deduction of IRC §243.

(2)   The partnership's net income from operations, $18,000, is computed on the basis of items A, B, C, D, E, and M. This net taxable income is divided among the partners according to their profit-and-loss sharing ratios.

C.   TRANSACTIONS BETWEEN PARTNER & PARTNERSHIP

Generally, a partner can engage in a transaction with her/his partnership, and the transaction will be considered as occurring between two completely independent entities. Payments made to a partner for services or for the use of capital (**guaranteed payments**) are treated as made to one who is not a member of the partnership [IRC §707(c)]. The partnership deducts the guaranteed payments and the recipients must report such payments as income. Furthermore, certain transactions between a partner and the partnership will be recharacterized as arm's-length transactions. These transactions involve the performance of services or property transfers in exchange for direct or indirect allocations or distributions to one of the partners [IRC §707(a)(2)]. Exceptions (also applicable to sales of property between **two** commonly controlled partnerships) are:

1.   Losses from sales of property between a controlling partner (**over** 50% interest) and her/his partnership are not allowed [IRC §707(b)(1)].

2.   Gains from the sale of property between a controlling partner (**over** 50% interest) and her/his partnership are characterized as **ordinary** income [IRC §707(b)(2)].

II. PARTNERSHIP FORMATION & OPERATION

A.   CONTRIBUTIONS

No gain or loss is recognized by the partnership or any partner when property is contributed to the partnership in exchange for an interest in the partnership [IRC §721(a)].

1.   **EXCLUSIONS** Note that this provision excludes both (a) a contribution of **services** for an interest, and (b) a contribution of property for anything **other than** a partnership interest.

Where a partnership interest is received in exchange for the contribution of services, the contributing partner includes in **ordinary** income an amount equal to the excess of the FMV of the partnership interest received for the services performed over the amount paid for the partnership interest [IRC §83(a)].

- Note also that, unlike IRC §351 transfers to a corporation, there is **no** control requirement on transfers to a partnership.

2. **PARTNER'S BASIS** The basis of the partner's interest resulting from this contribution of property is the **sum** of the following [IRC §722]:

   a. Amount of money contributed

   b. Adjusted basis of property contributed

   c. Gain, if any, recognized to the partner under IRC §721(b) on the transfer

3. **HOLDING PERIOD** A partner's holding period for a partnership interest acquired through contribution of a capital asset or an asset used in the partner's trade or business includes the holding period for the contributed property. If the contributed property is not a capital asset or used in the partner's trade or business, her/his holding period in the partnership interest begins on the date that the interest is acquired.

4. **PARTNERSHIP'S BASIS IN ASSETS** The partnership's basis in the assets that are contributed to it by the partners is equal to the partners' bases, increased by the amount of gain recognized by such partners. The holding period of the contributed property includes the period during which the property was held by the contributing partner.

B. BASIS OF DISTRIBUTED PROPERTY

1. **NONLIQUIDATING** The basis of property (other than money) distributed to a partner in a nonliquidating distribution is equal to the basis of such property in the partnership's hands immediately before the distribution [IRC §732(a)(1)]. However, the basis of the property distributed may not exceed the basis of the partner's interest in the partnership (as reduced by any money distributed in the same transaction) [IRC §732(a)(2)].

   EXAMPLE 4 ♦ NONLIQUIDATING DISTRIBUTION

   > Partnership CD distributes to partner D $3,000 cash and equipment with a FMV of $10,000 and a basis of $5,000. Assuming that D's basis in his partnership interest was $7,000 immediately prior to the distribution, his basis in the equipment is $4,000, computed as follows:
   >
   > | | |
   > |---|---:|
   > | D's basis in partnership interest prior to distribution | $ 7,000 |
   > | Less cash distributed to D | (3,000) |
   > | IRC §732(a)(2) limitation on the basis of noncash assets distributed | $ 4,000 |
   > | | |
   > | Basis of equipment, i.e., lesser of (a) the asset's basis in the partnership's hands immediately before the distribution ($5,000) or (b) the IRC §732(a)(2) limitation ($4,000) | $ 4,000 |

2. **LIQUIDATING** The basis of property (other than money) distributed to a partner in a liquidating distribution is equal to the adjusted basis of the partner's interest in the partnership (as reduced by any cash received by the partner in the liquidation) [IRC §732(b)].

EXAMPLE 5 ♦ LIQUIDATING DISTRIBUTION

> Partnership XYZ distributes $12,000 cash and a computer, with a FMV of $7,000 and a basis of $3,000, to Y in liquidation of Y's interest in the partnership. If Y's basis in his partnership interest immediately before the distribution is equal to $25,000, his basis in the computer (assuming that XYZ has no liabilities) is equal to $13,000, i.e., $25,000 basis in Y's partnership interest less $12,000 cash received in the distribution.

3. **EXCESSIVE** In the case of liquidating distributions and nonliquidating distributions to which the IRC §732(a)(2) limitation applies, the basis of the partner's interest in the partnership (as reduced by cash received) is allocated **first** to any unrealized receivables and inventory items in an amount equal to the adjusted basis of such receivables and inventory.

   a. Any remaining basis adjustment, if an increase, is allocated among properties with an unrealized appreciation in proportion to their respective amounts of unrealized appreciation, to the extent of each property's appreciation, and then in proportion to their respective fair market values.

   b. Any remaining basis adjustment, if a decrease, is allocated among properties with unrealized depreciation in proportion to their respective amounts of unrealized depreciation, to the extent of each property's depreciation, and then in proportion to their respective adjusted bases, taking into account the adjustments already made. A remaining basis adjustment that is a decrease arises when the partnership's total adjusted basis in the distributed properties exceeds the amount of the basis in the distributed properties, the partner's basis in its partnership interest, and the latter amount is the basis to be allocated among the distributed properties.

C. ADJUSTED BASIS OF PARTNERSHIP INTEREST

If a partner acquires a partnership interest from another partner, the basis of the acquired interest is equal to the sum of the cash and the FMV of the other consideration paid for the interest. A partner's adjusted basis in her/his partnership interest frequently changes.

EXAMPLE 6 ♦ PARTNER'S ADJUSTED BASIS

> Assume partner X contributes property worth $20,000 with a basis to him of $14,000, subject to liabilities of $16,000, to a new partnership in exchange for a 50% interest in partnership profit, loss, and capital. Assume further that Y contributes $4,000 of cash to the partnership. The bases for X's and Y's partnership interests are computed as follows:
>
> | | |
> |---|---:|
> | X's basis in the contributed property [IRC §722] | $ 14,000 |
> | Plus X's 50% share of partnership liabilities [IRC §752(a)] | 8,000 |
> | Less liability subject to which the partnership acquires the property [IRC §752(b)] | (16,000) |
> | Initial basis of X's partnership interest | $ 6,000 |
> | | |
> | Y's basis in the contributed property [IRC §722] | $ 4,000 |
> | Plus Y's 50% share of partnership liabilities | 8,000 |
> | Initial basis of Y's partnership interest | $ 12,000 |

1. **DISTRIBUTIVE SHARE** The adjusted basis is increased by the partner's share of income and reduced by her/his share of losses (i.e., her/his distributive share) [IRC §705(a)].

2. **DISTRIBUTIONS** The adjusted basis is reduced by actual distributions to the partner. The amount of the distribution is generally the amount of money distributed and the adjusted basis to the partnership of any other property distributed [IRC §733].

3. **LIABILITIES** The partner's share of liabilities affects her/his adjusted basis.

a. An **increase** in a partner's share of liabilities of the partnership, or an increase in the partner's liabilities by reason of the partner's assumption of the partnership's liabilities, is considered a contribution of money by the partner and thus will increase her/his basis in her/his partnership interest [IRC §752(a)].

b. A **decrease** in a partner's share of liabilities of the partnership, or a decrease in the partner's liabilities by reason of the partnership's assumption of the partner's individual liabilities, is considered a distribution of money to the partner by the partnership, and thus will result in a decrease in the basis of her/his partnership interest (but not below zero) [IRC §752(b)].

D. DISTRIBUTIONS
No gain or loss is recognized by a partner on the distribution of money or other property by the partnership to the partner, **except** the following [IRC §731]:

1. EXCESSIVE Gain is recognized to the extent that money distributed **exceeds** the partner's adjusted basis in her/his partnership interest (see I., C., above).

2. LOSSES Loss is recognized **only** in liquidating distributions where the property received consists solely of money, unrealized receivables (see III., C., below), and inventory items.

3. BUILT-IN GAIN "Built-in" gain to be recognized by a **contributing** partner on the distribution of property to another partner within the five-year period after the property is contributed to the partnership. For most property contributed after June 8, 1997, the period in which a partner recognizes pre-contribution gain with respect to property contributed to a partnership is extended to **seven** years.

E. ELECTING LARGE PARTNERSHIPS
Generally, an electing large partnership (ELP) is a partnership with 100 or more partners in the preceding taxable year that elects the simplified flow-through provisions. The election applies to all subsequent years and may only be revoked with IRS consent. For tax purposes, an ELP will not terminate merely due to the sale or exchange of 50% of its interests within a 12-month period. If substantially all of the partners perform services or the partnership's principal business is commodity trading, the partnership is ineligible for the simplified flow-through provisions.

1. SIMPLIFIED FLOW-THROUGH RULES The taxable income of an ELP is computed in the same manner as that of an individual, except that certain items are separately stated and certain modifications are made. These modifications include disallowing the deduction for personal exemptions, the net operating loss deduction and certain itemized deductions.

a. All limitations and other provisions affecting the computation of taxable income or any credit (except for the at-risk, passive loss and itemized deduction limitations, and any other provision specified in regulations) are applied at the partnership (and not the partner) level.

b. The provision provides that each partner takes into account separately the partner's distributive share of the following items, which are determined at the partnership level: (1) taxable income or loss from passive loss limitation activities; (2) taxable income or loss from other activities, such as portfolio income or loss; (3) net capital gain or loss to the extent allocable to passive loss limitation activities and other activities; (4) tax-exempt interest; (5) net alternative minimum tax adjustment separately computed for passive loss limitation activities and other activities; (6) general credits; (7) low-income housing credit; (8) rehabilitation credit; (9) credit for producing fuel from a nonconventional source; (10) creditable foreign taxes and foreign source items; and (11) any other items as determined by the IRS.

2. DUE DATE FOR INFORMATION REPORTING An ELP must furnish information returns to partners by the first March 15th following the close of the partnership's taxable year.

3. **SIMPLIFIED AUDIT** ELPs and their partners continue to be subject to unified audit rules. Unlike non-electing partnerships, ELP adjustments generally flow through to the partners for the year in which the adjustment takes effect. Consequently, the current-year partners' share of current-year ELP items of income, gains, losses, deductions, or credits will be adjusted to reflect ELP adjustments that take effect in that year. The adjustments generally will not affect prior-year returns of any partners, except for changes to distributive shares.

a. Instead of flowing an adjustment through to its partners, the partnership may elect to pay an imputed underpayment. The imputed underpayment generally is calculated by netting the adjustments to the income and loss items of the partnership, multiplied by the highest individual or corporate tax rate. A partner may not file a claim for credit or refund of her/his allocable share of the payment.

b. Regardless of whether a partnership adjustment flows through to the partners, an adjustment must be offset if it requires another adjustment in a year after the adjusted year and before the year the offset adjustment takes effect. In addition, the ELP generally is liable for any interest and penalties that result from a partnership adjustment.

c. Any payment (for federal income taxes, interest, or penalties) that an ELP is required to make is not deductible. All accuracy penalty criteria and waiver criteria are determined on the basis that the ELP is a taxable individual. Accuracy and fraud penalties are assessed and accrue interest as if asserted against a taxable individual.

d. If a petition for readjustment of partnership items is filed by the ELP, the court in which the petition is filed will have jurisdiction to determine the tax treatment of all partnership items of the ELP for the partnership taxable year to which the notice of partnership adjustment relates, and the proper allocation of such items among the partners. (The court's jurisdiction is not limited to the items adjusted in the notice.)

e. Without an agreement to extend the statute of limitations, the IRS generally cannot adjust a partnership item of an ELP more than three years after the later of the filing of the ELP return or the last day for the filing of the ELP return. Special rules apply to false or fraudulent returns, a substantial omission of income, or the failure to file a return. The IRS would assess and collect any deficiency of a partner that arises from any adjustment to a partnership item subject to the limitations period on assessments and collection applicable to the year the adjustment takes effect.

4. **PARTNERS SEPARATE FROM ELP** Each ELP must designate a partner or other person to act on its behalf. Only the ELP can petition for a readjustment of partnership items. If a partnership ceases to exist before a partnership adjustment takes effect, the former partners are required to take the adjustment into account.

a. A partner is not permitted to report any partnership items inconsistently with the partnership return, even if the partner notifies the IRS of the inconsistency.

b. The IRS may challenge the reporting position of an ELP by conducting a single administrative proceeding to resolve the issue with respect to all partners. Individually, partners have no right to participate in settlement conferences or to request a refund.

c. The IRS may send notice of a partnership adjustment to the ELP and is not required to give notice to individual partners of an administrative proceeding or a final adjustment.

III. PARTNERSHIP DISSOLUTION

A. TERMINATION
If within a 12-month period, **no** part of the partnership's business is carried on **or** 50% or more of the total interests in the partnership are sold [IRC §708(b)], it terminates.

1. **MERGER** In a merger, the resulting partnership is a continuation of the merging partnership whose partners have a more than 50% interest in the resulting partnership.

2. **DIVISION** In a division, a resulting partnership is a continuation of the prior partnership if the resulting partnership's partners had a more than 50% interest in the prior partnership.

3. **ELECTING LARGE PARTNERSHIP** An *electing large partnership* does not terminate merely due to the sale or exchange of 50% of its interests within a 12-month period.

B. TAXABLE YEAR
The taxable year of a partnership generally is not affected by the entry of new partners or the death or retirement of old partners.

1. **TERMINATION** The taxable year closes upon termination of the partnership.

2. **WITH RESPECT TO A PARTNER** The taxable year of a partnership closes *with respect to a partner* whose entire interest in the partnership terminates, whether by death, liquidation, sales, exchange, or otherwise. The taxable year of a partnership does not close with respect to a partner who disposes of **less** than her/his **entire** interest in the partnership, but that partner's distributive share must reflect her/his varying interests during the year.

C. SALE OR EXCHANGE OF PARTNERSHIP INTEREST
The gains or losses from the sale or exchange of partnership interests, and gains or losses recognized on partnership distributions or liquidation, are generally characterized as **capital** gains or losses. Any gain or loss attributable to **unrealized receivables** or **inventory** items is **ordinary** in character [IRC §751(a)].

1. **CALCULATION** The amount that a partner realizes on the sale of a partnership interest includes any cash received, plus any partnership liabilities that are assumed by the buyer.

2. **DISTRIBUTIVE SHARE** Distributions must bear a pro rata share of these ordinary income items. If not, the transaction is recast as if there were such a pro rata distribution followed by a taxable exchange of properties, to achieve the result of the actual distribution [IRC §751(b)].

3. **UNREALIZED RECEIVABLES** Unrealized receivables are primarily those amounts due for property or services previously provided but not yet included in income. A typical example is the accounts receivable of a cash-basis partnership. Unrealized receivables also include any potential depreciation recapture in the partnership assets [IRC §751(c)].

4. **INVENTORY** Inventory items are those items that if sold by the partnership, would produce ordinary income. A typical example is inventory. For sales before August 6, 1997, there is a further requirement for items to be classified as inventory items: the item must be substantially appreciated (fair market value exceeds 120% of basis). [IRC §751(d)].

IV. ESTATE & TRUST INCOME TAXATION

A. OVERVIEW
Estates and trusts are separate income tax-paying entities. Beneficiaries also may be taxed, but there is no double taxation. Either the estate or trust or the beneficiaries are taxed on the income, but not both entities. In any discussion of estates and trusts, it is important to keep in mind the distinction between the assets of the estate or trust, known as the principal or the corpus, and the income earned from those assets.

1. **CONDUIT** The estate or trust is said to be a conduit. A double tax is prevented by virtue of a distribution deduction [IRC §§651 and 661]. Basically, the estate or trust reports all income earned but then gets a deduction for distributions (actual or constructive) to the beneficiaries (but only to the extent the beneficiaries must include the distribution in income).

2. **ESTATE FORMATION** An estate is created when an individual dies. On that date, all the decedent's income-producing assets begin generating income for a new taxpayer, the estate.

3. **TRUST FORMATION** A trust is an arrangement whereby a trustee takes legal title to property and manages the property for beneficiaries. A trust may be created by will (a testamentary trust) or during life (an inter vivos trust). **NOTE**: So called "short-term trusts" are not considered to be trusts subject to taxation.

4. **TRUST CLASSIFICATION** Trusts are classified as simple or complex. A simple trust is a trust that requires all income to be distributed each year, that does not allow charitable contributions to be made, and that actually does not make any distributions except out of current income. All other trusts are complex.

    a. Estates and complex trusts are subject to the same rules.

    b. A trust may be a simple trust one year and a complex trust another year.

5. **INCOME CALCULATION** The taxable income of an estate or trust is basically computed the same as that of an individual [IRC §641(b)]. The estate or trust gets a distribution deduction for income distributed to beneficiaries. Because of the "conduit" theory at work, income may be split between estate or trust and beneficiary. If this occurs, most deductions and credits must also be allocated. Estates and trusts are entitled to a personal exemption, as follows [IRC §642(b)]:

    a. Estates—$600

    b. Simple trusts—$300

    c. Complex trusts—$100

6. **TIMING** A simple trust's income is taxed to the beneficiary in the year the income is required to be distributed, whether or not it is actually distributed [IRC §652(a)]. The income is taxable to the beneficiary for her/his taxable year in which the estate or trust taxable year ends.

7. **TAXABLE YEAR** An estate has the option of choosing a fiscal or calendar year. For taxable years after 1986, most trusts must adopt a calendar year. However, a trust that qualifies as an IRC §501(a) tax-exempt organization or a charitable trust described in IRC §4947(a) can elect to use a fiscal year.

8. **FILING REQUIREMENTS** A trust or an estate must file an income tax return (Form 1041) if it has gross income of $600 or more and pay the tax by the 15th day of the fourth month after the end of its taxable year.

9. **ESTIMATED PAYMENTS** All trusts are required to make estimated quarterly tax payments. Estates are required to make estimated tax payments with regard to any taxable year ending two years after the date of the decedent's death.

B. **DISTRIBUTABLE NET INCOME**
Distributable net income (DNI) has application only in the context of the income taxation of estates and trusts. DNI determines the amount of the distribution deduction to the estate or trust and the amount of the corresponding inclusion in the beneficiary's gross income. The character of the income is preserved as it passes through to the beneficiary. For example, tax-exempt interest and long-term capital gains retain their character to the beneficiary.

1. **DESCRIPTION** The taxable income of the estate or trust, modified as follows [IRC §643(a)]:

    a. Before the distribution deduction.

> **b.** Before the personal exemption.
>
> **c.** Capital gains and losses are normally excluded, as they are usually allocated to principal rather than income.
>
> **d.** Tax-exempt interest income is included.

2. **EFFECT** Any distribution of money or property to a beneficiary is taken out of DNI for the current year and thereby requires the beneficiary to take that amount of the distribution into income to the extent that the distributed items are taxable.

C. DISTRIBUTIONS OF PROPERTY
Distributions of property are subject to several different rules.

1. **SPECIFIC BEQUESTS** Specific bequests of property found in a will or trust instrument produce no income to the beneficiary, regardless of DNI. Furthermore, no gain or loss is recognized by the estate or trust on the transfer of the property.

EXAMPLE 7 ♦ SPECIFIC BEQUEST

> A will provides that the decedent's automobile, worth $5,000, is specifically devised to Sam. Since the auto is being distributed by a specific bequest, Sam has no income. In the absence of this specific bequest, the distribution of the auto would produce $5,000 income to Sam.

2. **REPLACEMENT OF SPECIFIC BEQUEST** If a specific bequest is satisfied by other property, the distribution is a taxable transfer to the estate or trust.

EXAMPLE 8 ♦ OTHER PROPERTY

> A will specifically leaves Chris $5,000 cash. In satisfaction of this bequest, Chris accepts an auto with a value of $5,000 and an adjusted basis to the estate of $4,000. The estate has $1,000 of gross income on the distribution.

D. COMPLEX TRUSTS
Complex trusts may accumulate income, and consequently, they accrue income tax liability each year. If, on some future date, the accumulated income is distributed, a throwback rule comes into play. Generally, the accumulated income is carried back to the year it was earned, and the beneficiary is taxed as if it were received in that year. The beneficiary then gets credit for the taxes actually paid by the trust.

E. TRANSFERS OF APPRECIATED PROPERTY TO TRUST
If a settlor transfers appreciated property to a trust and the property is sold by the trust within two years, the trust is taxed on the gain based on the settlor's tax rates. This is to avoid the transfer of appreciated property by high-bracket taxpayers to lower-bracket trusts so as to tax the gain upon sale at a lower rate.

F. UNUSED LOSSES & DEDUCTIONS IN YEAR OF TRUST TERMINATION
If the trust or estate has unused loss carryovers, capital loss carryovers, or current year deductions in the year of termination, these unused items may be passed on to the beneficiaries.

G. FUNERAL TRUST
A pre-need funeral trust is an arrangement where an individual purchases funeral services or merchandise from a funeral home for the benefit of a specified person in advance of that person's death. The beneficiary may be either the purchaser or another person. Part or all of the price is held in trust during the beneficiary's lifetime and is paid to the seller upon the beneficiary's death.

1. **GENERAL RULE** Pre-need funeral trusts generally are treated as grantor trusts, and the annual income earned by those trusts is taxable income to the purchaser/grantor of the trust.

2. **ELECTION** If the proper election is made, a qualified funeral trust is not treated as a grantor trust and the amount of tax paid with respect to each purchaser's trust is determined in accordance with the income tax rate schedule generally applicable to estates and trusts, but no personal exemption deduction is allowed under IRC §642(b). The tax on the annual earnings of the trust is payable by the trustee.

    a. **QUALIFIED FUNERAL TRUST** A qualified funeral trust is any domestic trust if (1) the trust arises as a result of a contract with a business engaged in providing funeral or burial services or related property; (2) the purpose of the trust is to hold, invest, and use funds solely to make payments for funeral or burial services or property for the trust beneficiary; (3) the only trust beneficiaries are individuals who have entered into contracts to have funeral or burial services or merchandise provided upon their death; (4) the only contributions to the trust are by or for the benefit of the trust beneficiary; and (5) the trustee makes the proper election (for each purchaser's trust).

    b. **CONTRIBUTION LIMITATION** A limitation is placed on the aggregate contributions that may be made to all qualified funeral trusts for one beneficiary. For contracts entered into in 2001, the limit is $7,500.

    c. **CANCELLATION** The beneficiary doesn't recognize gain or loss for payments from the trust upon cancellation of the contract. The beneficiary takes a carryover basis in any assets received from the trust upon cancellation.

H. COVERDELL EDUCATION SAVINGS ACCOUNT (CESA)
A CESA is a trust established with an approved trustee to pay qualifying education expenses of the beneficiary. The CESA previously was named an Educational IRA (EIRA), although it has little to do with retirement, because it operates in a similar manner as a Roth IRA.

1. **QUALIFYING EXPENSES** Qualifying expenses include tuition, fees, room and board, reduced by scholarships and other nontaxable educational assistance. Room and board expenses qualify only if the student attends school at least half-time. EGTRRA '01 allows qualified elementary and secondary school expenses connected with enrollment or attendance at a public, private, or religious school. EGTRRA '01 includes special needs services in qualified expenses.

2. **CONTRIBUTIONS** Any taxpayer, subject to an income phase-out rule, can contribute up to $2,000 in cash annually to an CESA. Any number of individuals can contribute to CESAs for any number of beneficiaries, but the total annual contributions for any one beneficiary cannot exceed the ceiling. Contributions are not deductible from income. Contributions may be deemed to be made on the last day of the preceding year if made before April 15.

    a. The maximum contribution is reduced on a pro rata basis for a taxpayer with MAGI in the following ranges: single, $95,000 to $110,000; and married filing jointly, $190,000 to $220,000, exactly twice the range for single taxpayers. MAGI is AGI increased by exempt foreign income. Corporations and other entities (including tax-exempt organizations) may contribute to education IRAs, regardless of income.

    b. EGTRRA '01 repealed the excise tax, starting in 2002, on contributions to a CESA in the same year in which contributions are also made to a QTP for the same beneficiary.

3. **DISTRIBUTIONS** Distributions from the trust are nontaxable, if they do not exceed the total qualifying education expenses for the year. Funds distributed in excess of the qualifying expenses are subject to income tax and a 10% penalty tax. Starting in 2002, EGTRRA '01 allows, so long as the CESA distribution is not used for the same educational expenses for

the same student for which a credit is claimed, a taxpayer to claim a Hope or Lifetime Learning credit and exclude CESA distributions from gross income in the same year.

    a.   The penalty is waived if the distribution is due to the beneficiary's death or disability, or to the extent that the beneficiary receives nontaxable scholarships or other allowances.

    b.   Funds in the CESA not used by the beneficiary's 30th birthday are deemed distributed, subject to regular income taxes and 10% penalty taxes.

    c.   Prior to the beneficiary's 30th birthday, any unused balance may be transferred to another family member (while still remaining in the trust), including a former spouse under a divorce agreement. Starting in 2002, a cousin is deemed to be a family member for this purpose.

4.   **GIFT** A CESA contribution is considered a completed gift of a present interest and qualifies for the annual gift tax exemption, but not the additional educational gift tax exclusion of IRC §2503(e). The contribution is also exempt from the generation-skipping tax.

    a.   A transfer from one beneficiary to another is not subject to gift tax if both beneficiaries are members of the same family and generation. If these two criteria are not met, the transfer may give rise to gift tax liability if it exceeds the annual exclusion amount.

    b.   The value of an CESA is included in the estate of a beneficiary, never a contributor.

5.   **SPECIAL NEED BENEFICIARIES** Starting in 2002, EGTRRA '01 exempts CESAs for a special needs beneficiary (SNB) from certain requirements. For a SNB, contributions may continue to be made to an EIRA after the beneficiary attains age 18. No deemed distribution occurs when a SNB reaches age 30. The age 30 limit does not apply to a rollover contribution for the benefit of a SNB or a change in beneficiaries to a SNB.

I.   **QUALIFIED TUITION PROGRAMS**
Several states have qualified tuition payment programs (QTP) with tax-exempt status. Most tuition plans commonly are prepaid plans under which future tuition is locked in at current rates. Some plans are savings plan trusts that are operated like a mutual fund.

1.   **QUALIFIED PLANS** The program must be established and maintained by a state (or one of its agencies) under which a person may either purchase tuition credits, that constitute a waiver or payment of qualified higher education costs, or contribute to an account designed to meet the education costs. Starting in 2002, EGTRRA '01 allows a private institution to be treated as qualified if it has received a ruling or determination form the IRS that it satisfies applicable requirements and it holds the program assets in a trust organized in the U.S. for the exclusive benefit of plan beneficiaries, with a independent responsible party as its trustee.

    a.   Qualified higher education costs include tuition, fees, books, room and board costs, and equipment for attendance at college, university or certain vocational schools.

    b.   Contributions must be cash. A contributor is prohibiting from directly or indirectly directing the investment of any contribution.

    c.   Investment account earnings may be refunded to the contributor or beneficiary, but the program must impose a more than *de minimis* refund penalty, unless the refund is

        (1)   Used for beneficiary's qualified higher education expenses;

        (2)   Made on account of the beneficiary's death or disability; or

        (3)   Made on account of a scholarship received by the student to the extent that the refund does not exceed the scholarship amount used for qualified expenses.

2. **TRANSFERS** Contributions after 1997 to a QTP are completed gifts of a present interest and qualify for the annual gift tax exemption. The contribution is also exempt from the generation-skipping transfer tax. However, the amount does not qualify for the additional educational gift tax exclusion of IRC §2503(e).

   a. A transfer from one beneficiary to another is not subject to the gift tax if both beneficiaries are members of the same family and generation. (The original beneficiary's spouse is deemed a member of the same family.) If these two criteria are not met, the transfer may give rise to gift tax liability if it exceeds the annual exclusion amount. Starting in 2002, EGTRRA '01 includes a first cousin of the original beneficiary as a member of the family.

   b. The value of a QTP account is included in the estate of a beneficiary. (In no event is the value to be included in the estate of a contributor.)

3. **DISTRIBUTIONS** The deferred income is taxable income to the beneficiary unless it can be excluded under another provision of the tax law. If amounts are distributed to a contributor, the amount is taxed to the extent it exceeds the amounts originally contributed.

   a. Distributions are treated as pro rata shares of principal and income. The distributee, or a taxpayer claiming the distributee as a dependent, can use the distribution as a basis for claiming either the Hope or Lifetime Learning credits, assuming requirements for these credits are met.

   b. EGTRRA '01 excludes distributions from gross income, to the extent such distributions are used to pay for qualified higher education expenses. Also, EGTRRA '01 allows a taxpayer to claim a Hope or Lifetime Learning credit and exclude from gross income amounts distributed from a qualified program on behalf of the same student in the same year as long as the distribution is not used for expenses for which a credit is claimed.

   c. Starting in 2004, EGTRRA '01 extends the distribution exclusion to distributions from non-state programs.

4. **INCOMPLETE GIFT** Pre-1998 contributions to the program are incomplete gifts, deferring any potential gift tax implications until program distributions are made. Waivers (or payments) of qualified expenses are treated as qualified transfers, excluding them from gift tax. Contributions to a program (and earnings thereon) are included in the estate of a contributor if the contributor dies before the funds are distributed.

V. TRANSFER TAXES

A. ESTATE TAX
The estate tax is a transfer tax (not an income tax), imposed on the value of property "transferred" by a decedent at death. The gift tax is also a transfer tax based on the same tax rate schedule as the estate tax. However, the gift tax is imposed on inter vivos transfers of property. Thus, a transfer tax cannot be avoided simply by giving property away before death. EGTRRA '01 repeals the estate tax, but not the gift tax, effective in 2010.

EXAMPLE 9 ♦ TAXABLE ESTATE

Jennifer Bohl died on March 3, 2002. She and her husband, Mark, owned a home in joint tenancy subject to a $30,000 mortgage with annual principal payments due on December 31. She had four specific bequests. The remainder of the estate is left 1/3 to Mark and 2/3 to Susan. The executor selected the alternate valuation date. The car was given to Carol on April 3, 2002. Funeral expenses were $22,000.

Specific Bequests

Carol, a niece	car
Susan, a daughter	necklace
Mark	home
United Charities	$12,000

Asset Valuation

Assets	March 3, 2002	April 3, 2002	September 3, 2002
Home	$ 240,000	$ 240,000	$ 240,000
Car	30,000	29,500	29,000
Necklace	12,000	10,000	11,000
Investments	3,010,000	$2,990,000	$3,009,000

REQUIRED: What is the taxable estate?

SOLUTION:

Value of home	$240,000	
Less: Indebtedness on home	(30,000)	
Net value of home	$210,000	
Estate's portion of home (which goes to Mark) [$210,000 x 50%]		$ 105,000
Mark's portion of investments [$3,009,000 - $12,000)/3]		999,000
Marital deduction		$ 1,104,000
Value of car on distribution date		$ 29,500
Estate's portion of home		105,000
Value of necklace		11,000
Value of investments		3,009,000
Gross estate		$ 3,154,500
Less: Funeral expenses		(22,000)
Adjusted gross estate		$ 3,132,500
Less: Charitable deduction		(12,000)
Less: Marital deduction		(1,104,000)
Taxable estate		$ 2,016,500

NOTE: The $1 million of 2002 exclusion amount is still in the taxable estate. There is no deduction of $1 million. Instead, a tax credit shelters $1 million of the estate.

1. **GROSS ESTATE** The first step in determining the estate tax due is to obtain the value of the gross estate (see schematic, below). The value of the gross estate can be placed at the time of death or at an alternative valuation date, which is six months after the date of death. But to be able to use the alternative valuation date, the election must decrease the value of the gross estate and it must reduce any estate tax liability [IRC §2032]. The gross estate includes not only property actually owned by the decedent, but also property constructively owned by her/him. In addition, certain gifts, such as life insurance policies, made within three years of death may be includable in the gross estate.

2. **DEDUCTIONS** The gross estate is reduced by nondiscretionary deductions to arrive at the adjusted gross estate. The adjusted gross estate is further reduced by discretionary deductions to obtain the taxable estate.

3. **ADJUSTED TAXABLE GIFTS** To the taxable estate we must add post-1976 adjusted taxable gifts other than gifts that were included in the gross estate. This equals the tentative tax base, on which a tentative estate tax is determined based on the table in IRC §2001(c). The next step is to subtract from this tentative tax the amount of taxes that would have been payable (at the IRC §2001(c) rates in effect at date of death) on gifts included in the tentative tax base. The objective of this whole scheme is to increase the marginal rates at which the estate is taxed (i.e., by increasing the tax base by the amount of gifts made); however, double taxation of gifts is prevented by providing for the reduction of the tentative estate tax by the amount of gift taxes that would have been payable on the gifts themselves.

4. **FAMILY-OWNED BUSINESS DEDUCTION** An executor may elect special treatment for qualified *family-owned business interests* (FOBI), if interests passed to qualified heirs comprise more than 50% of a decedent's adjusted gross estate. As this deduction is of limited applicability, many details are omitted here. The deduction may be taken only to the extent that the deduction plus the amount effectively exempted by the unified credit does not exceed $1.3 million. This deduction is not applicable to generation-skipping or gift taxes. EGTRRA '01 repeals this deduction for the estates of decedents dying after December 31, 2003, although the recapture provisions for previous deductions remain in effect.

    a. **QUALIFIED FAMILY-OWNED BUSINESS INTERESTS** A qualified interest is any FOBI in a United States trade or business that is owned at least 50% by the decedent and members of her/his family, or 70% by two families, or 90% by three families. An interest does not qualify if the business's (or a related entity's) stock or securities were publicly traded at any time within three years of the decedent's death. Generally, an interest does not qualify if more than 35% of the business's adjusted ordinary gross income for the year of the decedent's death was personal holding company income. In the case of multiple family ownership, the decedent's family must own at least 30% of the business. For purposes of this provision, an individual's family includes the decedent's spouse; the decedent's ancestors; lineal descendants of the decedent's spouse or parents; and the spouses of any such lineal descendants.

    b. **QUALIFIED HEIRS** Qualified heirs include any individual who has been actively employed by the trade or business for at least 10 years prior to the date of the decedent's death, and members of the decedent's family.

    c. **OTHER REQUIREMENTS** To be eligible for the deduction, the decedent must have owned and materially participated in the business for at least five of the eight years preceding the decedent's death. The decedent must have been a U.S. citizen or resident at the time of death. In addition, each qualified heir (or a member of the qualified heir's family) must materially participate in the business for at least five years of any eight-year period within 10 years following the decedent's death.

    d. **RECAPTURE PROVISIONS** The benefit of this deduction is subject to recapture if, within 10 years of the decedent's death and before the qualified heir's death, the principal business place of the business is not located in the United States or the qualified heir ceases to meet the various requirements.

5. **CREDITS** The last two items in the tax computation are credits against the estate tax: the unified tax credit and other miscellaneous tax credits. These adjustments taken together produce the estate tax due. For 2002, the unified credit effective exemption amount is $1 million.

B. **GIFT TAX**
Gift tax is an excise tax imposed on the transfer of property during the life of the donor. Property, for gift tax purposes, is broadly defined to include real and personal as well as tangible and intangible property. Gifts are similarly defined to include any transfer of property, outright or in trust, to the extent it is made without full and adequate consideration.

1. **SIMILAR TO ESTATE TAX** Although the estate tax is an excise tax on transfers made at death, while the gift tax is an excise on transfers made during life, essentially the same concepts apply. The only aspect that is different is the timing of the gift. Thus, if it is made during life, it is subject to the gift tax; if at death, it is subject to the estate tax. Transfers at death and lifetime taxable gifts are taxed on a cumulative basis.

2. **COMPUTATION** The gift tax schematic illustrates the computation of the tax, beginning with the total gross amount of gifts for the calendar year. This amount includes the total amount of cash and the FMV of other property gifted. Included are gifts created by transfer to a trust by the donor (e.g., donor-grantor transfers an apartment building to a trust, with the income to himself, and the remainder fee-simple interest in the building to the donee); by creation of joint interests (the donor with the donee); by purchase of an insurance policy (the donor purchases an insurance policy and transfers all rights in the policy to the donee).

3. **TOTAL GIFTS** The statutory total amount of gifts made during the calendar year equals the total gross amount of gifts for the year made by the donor, reduced by the gift-splitting provisions of IRC §2513 and the inflation-adjusted annual per-donee exclusion of IRC §2503. For 2002, this exclusion is $11,000. Total taxable gifts for the calendar year is the residual amount remaining after the statutory total amount of gifts made during the calendar year is reduced by the unlimited marital and charitable deductions. (See below for further explanation on these exclusions and deductions.) Note that certain qualified transfers are excluded when determining total taxable gifts. Qualified transfers include the amount paid **directly** to the institution on behalf of another individual (regardless of the relationship to the donor) for tuition at an accredited educational institution or for medical care. The exclusion for tuition does not include payment for dormitory fees, supplies, or textbooks.

4. **CUMULATIVE** The gift tax is a cumulative tax, which causes the most recently made gifts to be taxed at a higher marginal transfer tax rate than gifts made in prior years. Mechanically, this is accomplished by adding all taxable gifts made in the current calendar year (Schedule A, Form 709) to all taxable gifts from prior years (Schedule B, Form 709). This total equals total taxable gifts.

5. **TENTATIVE TAX** The actual computation of the gift tax due requires a "with and without" type of calculation. Using the unified transfer tax schedule of IRC §2001(c), a tentative tax is computed on total taxable gifts. A tentative tax is computed separately on the amount of taxable gifts from prior years (Schedule B). The difference between the two tentative taxes produces the tentative tax for the current calendar year before the unified credit. This tentative tax is reduced by the amount of the unified credit remaining to the donor and is further reduced by any foreign tax credits. The tax remaining equals the gift tax due.

C. **GENERATION-SKIPPING TRANSFER TAX**
This is a separate tax that is imposed in addition to the gift tax and the estate tax. It applies to transfers to beneficiaries who are more than one generation below the transferor's generation and is taxed at a flat rate of 55%. This tax is inapplicable if the transfer is to a grandchild if the child's parent (the decedent's child) predeceases the transferor. This exception extends to other generation-skipping transfers, if the decedent has no living lineal descendants at the time of the transfer. For example, a decedent without living lineal descendants may make a transfer to a grandniece, if the grandniece's parent (the decedent's niece or nephew) is also dead, without incurring the generation-skipping tax. An exemption from the generation-skipping transfer tax is available to all taxpayers. For 2002, this inflation-adjusted exemption is $1,100,000.

D. **SCHEMATIC OF ESTATE TAX COMPUTATION**
In the following schematic, we expound upon the overview by summarizing each block in the flow chart with textual material to the right of the chart. As you read down the chart, keep in mind the main objective of the estate tax—to identify, value, and levy an appropriate tax on the transfer of all of a decedent's property. To simplify the schematic, the family-owned business exclusion is omitted.

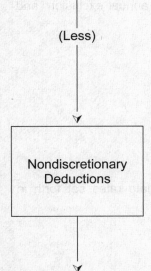

Gross Estate

The gross estate of a decedent who is a U.S. citizen or resident includes the value at the date of death (or alternate valuation date six months after date of death) of all of the decedent's worldwide property, both real and personal, tangible and intangible (IRC §2031). This all-inclusive definition of property identified to the gross estate includes the following:

- The value of all property to the extent of the decedent's beneficial interest, including income due the decedent at the time of her/his death in the form of salary, rents, royalties, dividends, insurance proceeds payable to the estate's executor as the estate's representative, and business interests (IRC §2033). This income is also included in the estate's fiduciary income tax return, since it is considered income in respect of the decedent, or IRD.

- The value of any interest in property gratuitously transferred by the decedent during life but over which the decedent retained control during her/his life. Thus, if the decedent transferred securities, real rental property, or other income-producing property but retained the right to control the property and/or its income stream, the entire value of the property is included in her/his gross estate (IRC §2036). Similarly included are gratuitous transfers conditioned on the transferee's surviving the decedent (IRC §2037).

- The value of property gratuitously transferred during life to the extent of the portion of the property over which the decedent had a right to revoke. Thus, if the decedent during life gifted securities to her/his son with income to her/his daughter and with a right to revoke the income gift, the discounted value of the income, but not the value of the security, is included (IRC §2038).

- The value of a joint and survivor annuity purchased by the decedent for her/him and another is included (IRC §2039).

- One-half the fair market value of community property, and one-half the fair market value of property held by spouses in joint tenancy or tenancy in the entirety.

The gross estate, as identified and valued above, is reduced by the following deductions:

- Funeral expenses
- Administration expenses
- Claims against the estate
- Casualty and theft losses
- Indebtedness of property included in gross estate
- Certain taxes (however, income taxes accrued after death and state estate or inheritance taxes are not deductible)

(Less)

Nondiscretionary Deductions

Observation: Ordinary and necessary administration expenses, including commissions and other selling expenses, can either be taken as a deduction in computing the Estate Tax (Form 706) or the Fiduciary Income Tax (Form 1041). In order for these administrative expenses to be deducted for income tax purposes, the executor must waive the right to take the deduction for Estate Tax purposes.

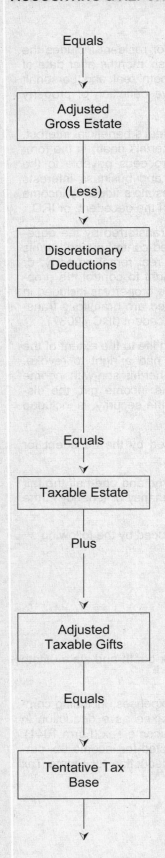

Equals

Adjusted Gross Estate

The value of the gross estate minus nondiscretionary deductions equals the adjusted gross estate.

The adjusted gross estate is diminished by the discretionary deductions. The most common discretionary deductions are the following:

(Less)

Discretionary Deductions

- Contributions to a charitable organization if the decedent's will specifically provides for the contribution and the recipient is a qualified charitable organization. The amount of the transfer is limited only by the value of the gross estate [IRC §2055].

- The marital deduction, which is generally unlimited. Thus, as with the charitable deduction, the decedent could give the entire net estate after expenses to her/his surviving spouse. The only limitation on the marital deduction is that the marital deduction interest consist of a non-terminable interest in property included in the gross estate. A terminable interest is an interest in property given to the surviving spouse that will lapse after a certain time (e.g., life estate or term of years), or upon the occurrence of an event or contingency or its failure to occur (e.g., until wife's remarriage, or only if decedent's daughter does not marry by age 30) [IRC §2056].

Equals

Taxable Estate

In 1976, the unified transfer tax system was introduced. Under this system, one transfer tax schedule [IRC §2001(c)] is used to compute gift tax as well as estate tax. The system also requires the inclusion of all lifetime gifts in the determination of the tentative tax base. The adjusted taxable gifts inclusion brings into the computation all taxable gifts (net of the annual exclusion, and net of all gifts made within three years of death).

Plus

Adjusted Taxable Gifts

Equals

Tentative Tax Base

The tentative tax base is applied against the appropriate rates set forth in IRC §2001(c).

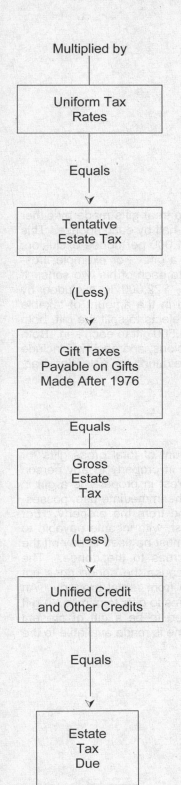

The tentative tax, as computed above, is then reduced by gift taxes payable on gifts made after 1976. Since adjusted taxable gifts (gifts not included in the gross estate by IRC §2035) were pulled into the tentative tax base for the estate tax computation using the uniform tax rates, a reduction is allowed for gift taxes payable on those gifts to avoid double taxation.

The tentative estate tax is further reduced by the unified credit against estate tax. Therefore, if an estate is valued at the threshold or less, it won't owe any federal estate tax, nor will it be required to file an estate tax return. Additionally, a limited credit is allowed the estate for certain state death taxes paid [IRC §§2010 and 2011]. In 2002, the effective exclusion amount is $1 million.

The executor or administrator of the estate is required to file the estate tax return [IRC §6018] and pay any estate tax due [IRC §2002]. If an estate tax return (Form 706) is required, then it must be filed nine months after the date of the decedent's death. Where no executor or administrator has been named in the will and/or appointed by the court, property transferees receiving property from the estate may be liable for the return and any tax due.

E.   SCHEMATIC OF GIFT TAX COMPUTATION

1.   COMPUTATION OF TOTAL TAXABLE GIFTS

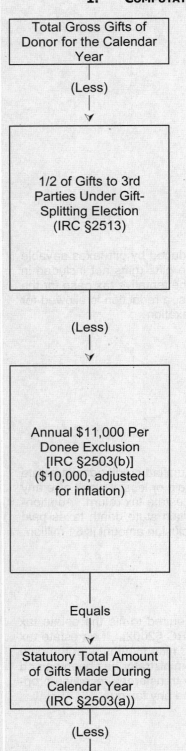

This section allows a husband and wife to elect to treat gifts made by either of them to a third party as having been made one-half by each spouse. This election has the effect of doubling the annual $11,000 per donee exclusion, because each spouse is treated as having made a gift. For example, husband wishes to give $27,000 worth of securities to each of his two sons. If wife does not elect to split the husband's gift, $22,000 is excluded by IRC §2503 (see below), and $32,000 is included in the amount of taxable gifts for the year (Schedule A). However, if wife elects to split the gift, both she and her husband are treated as making a $13,500 gift to each son. Both spouses can utilize two $11,000 per donee exclusions, and each will include $5,000 as their statutory total amount of gifts made during the calendar year.

Each donor is entitled to exclude from the amount of total gross gifts for 2002 up to $11,000 of gifts of a present interest in property to any person during a calendar year. A gift of a present interest in property is a gift in which the donee obtains an unrestricted right to the immediate use, possession, or enjoyment of the property or the income from the property. For example, donor transfers rental property to a trust, with income payable to his son. However, the rental revenue generated must be used to pay off the mortgage indebtedness before any revenue accrues to the donee. The donor is not entitled to the gift tax exclusion because the donee does not have a present interest in the gift of the income from rental property. An exception to the present interest requirement applies to gifts to minors. A gift to a person under 21 years of age is considered to be a gift of present interest, as long as all of the property and its income is made available to the donee upon obtaining age 21.

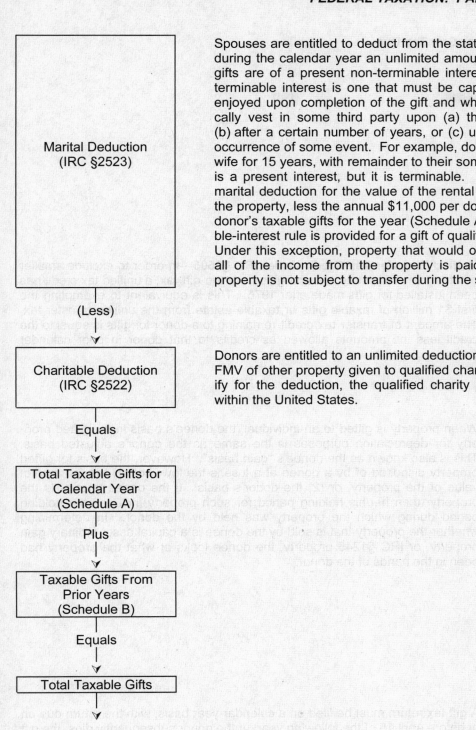

Marital Deduction
(IRC §2523)

(Less)

Charitable Deduction
(IRC §2522)

Equals

Total Taxable Gifts for
Calendar Year
(Schedule A)

Plus

Taxable Gifts From
Prior Years
(Schedule B)

Equals

Total Taxable Gifts

Spouses are entitled to deduct from the statutory total amount of gifts made during the calendar year an unlimited amount of gifts to each other if these gifts are of a present non-terminable interest in property. A present non-terminable interest is one that must be capable of instantly being used or enjoyed upon completion of the gift and which must not end and automatically vest in some third party upon (a) the death of the donee spouse, (b) after a certain number of years, or (c) upon the occurrence or failure of occurrence of some event. For example, donor gives a rental property to his wife for 15 years, with remainder to their son after the fifteenth year. The gift is a present interest, but it is terminable. Therefore, the husband has no marital deduction for the value of the rental property. The entire amount of the property, less the annual $11,000 per donee exclusion, is included in the donor's taxable gifts for the year (Schedule A). An exception to the terminable-interest rule is provided for a gift of qualified terminable interest property. Under this exception, property that would otherwise be terminable is not, if all of the income from the property is paid to the spouse-donee and the property is not subject to transfer during the spouse-donee's lifetime.

Donors are entitled to an unlimited deduction for the amount of cash plus the FMV of other property given to qualified charities. However, in order to qualify for the deduction, the qualified charity must use the donated property within the United States.

2. COMPUTATION OF GIFT TAX DUE

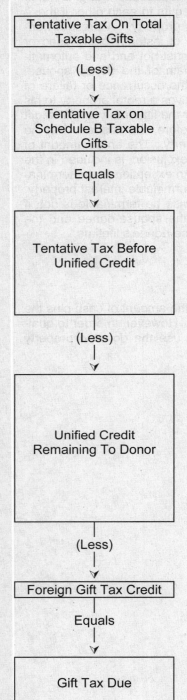

Tentative Tax On Total Taxable Gifts

(Less)

Tentative Tax on Schedule B Taxable Gifts

Equals

Tentative Tax Before Unified Credit

(Less)

Unified Credit Remaining To Donor

(Less)

Foreign Gift Tax Credit

Equals

Gift Tax Due

Unified Transfer Tax Credit Under IRC §2505—In order to exclude smaller estates from the estate tax and gifts from the gift tax, a unified tax credit has been installed for gifts made after 1976. This is equivalent to exempting the first $1 million of taxable gifts or taxable estate from the unified transfer tax. The amount of transfer tax credit remaining to a donor for gifts is equal to the credit less the amounts allowed as credits to that donor in prior calendar years.

When property is gifted to an individual, the donee's basis in the gifted property for depreciation purposes is the same as the donor's adjusted basis. This is also known as the donee's "gain basis". However, the basis for gifted property disposed of by a donee at a loss is the lower of (1) the fair market value of the property, or (2) the donor's basis. If the donee later sells the property, then her/his holding period for such property includes the holding period during which the property was held by the donor. In determining whether the property that is sold by the donee is a capital asset ordinary gain property, or IRC §1245 property, the donee looks at what the property had been in the hands of the donor.

A gift tax return must be filed on a calendar-year basis, with the return due on or before April 15 of the following year. If the donor subsequently dies, the gift tax return is due no later than the date for filing the federal estate tax return (9 months after the date of death).

VI. EXEMPT ORGANIZATIONS

A. TYPES OF ORGANIZATIONS

The Internal Revenue Code (IRC) provides for the types of organizations that are exempt from income tax [IRC §501(c)]. There is no other requirement that the entity must meet in order for it to be eligible to be exempt from income taxes. The only real criterion is that the entity be of a type specified by the IRC. The following are some of the more common types:

1. Corporations organized under an act of Congress as a U.S. instrumentality if, under the act, the corporation is exempt from federal income taxes.

2. Corporations and any community chest, fund, or foundation, organized and operated exclusively for religious, charitable, scientific, testing for public safety, literary, or educational purposes, to foster national or international amateur sports competition (so long as none of its activities involve the providing of athletic facilities or equipment), or for the prevention of cruelty to children or animals.

3. Business leagues, civic leagues, chambers of commerce, real estate boards, boards of trade, labor organizations, or professional football leagues that are not organized for profit.

4. A social or recreation club organized and operated exclusively for the pleasure and recreation of its members, supported solely by membership fees, dues, and assessments.

5. Employee's pension and profit sharing trusts.

6. Private foundations.

7. A condominium management association can qualify as a tax-exempt organization with regard to the exempt function of collecting income, such as dues, fees, and assessments. To qualify as a tax-exempt organization, a special election must be filed every year by the due date of its return.

B. REQUIREMENTS FOR EXEMPTION

An exempt organization may be either a corporation or trust. To qualify for exemption, the organization (1) must be a qualifying organization, (2) must apply to be exempt, and (3) must not engage in prohibited transactions.

1. **APPLICATION** An entity can apply for tax-exempt status by filing a form with the IRS or a written statement if no official form is provided within fifteen months after the close of the month during which the organization comes into existence. Once the tax-exempt status is granted, then the status is retroactive to the date of the organization's formation. If the form is filed after this deadline, it takes effect as of the day the notice is received. (Tax-exempt status is not retroactive.)

2. **REVOCATION** The IRS can retroactively revoke an organization's tax-exempt status.

3. **PRIVATE FOUNDATION** A private foundation is a tax-exempt organization other than a public charity. Generally, a private foundation receives less than 1/3 of its annual support from its members and the general public. To retain its tax-exempt status, a private foundation is subject to additional statutory restrictions on its activities and contributions.

4. **DISQUALIFIED** The following organizations are specifically stated as **not** being able to qualify as tax exempt organizations: (a) one that is created to influence legislation, (b) a feeder organization that is primarily conducting business for profit, even if it gives 100% of its profits to tax-exempt organizations, or (c) an organization that is created to foster national or international amateur sports competition by providing athletic facilities and equipment.

5. **RETURN** A tax-exempt organization is required to file an informational-type return every year unless it has $25,000 or less in gross receipts. Other organizations that do not have to file an annual return regardless of their income include churches and their internally supported auxiliaries, church-affiliated elementary and high schools, religious orders and mission societies, certain state institutions and exempt entities organized under an act of Congress. Regardless of their receipts, **private** foundations must file an annual return. This return is due by the 15th day of the fifth month following the close of the organization's accounting period. This annual information return must identify all substantial contributors, in addition to the amount of contributions that are received by the organization.

C. **UNRELATED BUSINESS TAXABLE INCOME (UBTI)**

Regardless of its status, a tax-exempt organization is required to pay tax on its "unrelated business taxable income" (UBTI). The tax imposed is computed under the regular rates applicable to a corporation if it is treated as a corporation under IRC §511(a) or the rates for a trust if it is treated as a trust under IRC §511(b). The tax itself must be paid at the time the return is filed or by the date an extension to file the return is filed. If a tax-exempt organization has more than $1,000 of UBI, it must file a return within two and a half months after the end of its year-end (March 15 for calendar year organizations). A tax exempt entity that generates UBI is required to make estimated tax payments each quarter under the same as the rules that govern corporate estimated tax payments.

1. **INCOME SUBJECT TO TAX** To become subject to tax under IRC §511, the tax-exempt organization must have income from a trade or business that is (a) **regularly** carried on by the organization, and (b) **not** substantially related to the purpose that serves as a basis for the organization's exemption from tax.

2. **COMPUTATION** The income from the unrelated activity is computed in the same manner as other taxable income. This means that the entity's income is generally computed the same as that of a corporation with certain modifications. Deductions directly connected to the taxable income are allocated to it. If the income is partially taxable, a proportionate part of the deductions attributable to the income is allowed in reducing UBTI. Furthermore, a specific deduction is allowed, so that the first $1,000 of UBTI is not subject to tax.

3. **EXEMPT INCOME** Activities specifically exempted from classification as unrelated trade or business income include

a. Royalties, dividends, interest, and annuities, except certain annuities and interest derived from debt-financed investments.

b. An activity where substantially all the work is performed by volunteers.

c. The sale of merchandise received by gift or contribution.

d. Income of a business conducted for the convenience of the organization's members, students, officers, or employees.

e. Income derived from conducting games of chance in a locality where such activity is legal and in a state that confines such activity to nonprofit organizations.

VII. **PREPARER RESPONSIBILITIES**

A. **PREPARERS**

A preparer is one who is paid to prepare a substantial portion of a return or claim for refund.

1. **DISCLOSURE** The IRC provides penalties for disclosures of confidential information to persons unnecessary to the preparation or filing of a taxpayer's return. Preparers may disclose information in a peer or quality review, for processing, or pursuant to an administrative order from a state agency that registers tax return preparers.

2. **UNREALISTIC POSITION** A return preparer may be liable for a $250 penalty if the return or refund claim reflects an understatement of tax liability that is based on a position that does not have a realistic chance of being sustained on its merits. This is interpreted by the Regulations to mean that a reasonable and well-informed analysis by a person knowledgeable in tax law would conclude that the position had less than a one in three chance of being sustained.

   a. The penalty will be assessed if the preparer knew or should have known that the position had a less than one in three chance of being sustained, the preparer did not disclose this, and cannot show reasonable cause for taking the position.

   b. This penalty can be avoided if a nonfrivolous position is adequately disclosed. What constitutes adequate disclosure depends on whether or not the preparer **signed** the return. For a signing preparer, disclosure is adequate only when filed with the IRS. For a nonsigning preparer, disclosure is considered adequate if the preparer advises the taxpayer or another preparer that disclosure is necessary.

3. **DUE DILIGENCE** There is a $100 penalty for a tax return preparer who does not comply with due diligence requirements of claiming the earned income credit.

4. **WILLFUL OR RECKLESS DISREGARD** The preparer may be liable for a $1,000 penalty if the understatement is willful or due to the preparer's intentional disregard of a rule or regulation. To avoid the penalty, the preparer must disclose the position to the IRS and include support indicating that the position represents a good faith challenge to the regulation's validity.

B. **"NOT FRIVOLOUS" STANDARD**
   The "not frivolous" standard is replaced with a "reasonable basis" standard for taxpayers, but not for tax preparers. The disclosure exception will no longer be relevant for purposes of the negligence penalty because a taxpayer generally will not be considered to have been negligent regarding a return position, regardless of whether it was disclosed, if the position has a reasonable basis.

What is this I've been hearing about the computerized exam?

The AICPA is in the process of converting the CPA exam into a computer-based test (CBT). Currently, candidates read questions from a printed page, darken ovals on a machine-readable sheet for the objective answers, and write essay answers on lined paper. To some extent, the exam is already computerized; the objective answers are machine-graded.

The next step in this conversion is likely to be essentially the same exam, with candidates reading questions from, and entering answers into, a personal computer. Before this happens, laws in many jurisdictions must change to allow this format, among other things.

The examination division has targeted May 2004 as the date for this next stage. There may be only pilot groups who sit for the computerized exam in May 2004. Candidates are unlikely to have much say in whether they will be part of a pilot group.

As we go to press, the AICPA has not yet decided most details; even the implementation date is subject to change (it has changed twice already). There has been some discussion regarding eliminating essay questions from the exam, in order that the entire exam may be computer-graded. When the exam becomes "computerized," Bisk Education will provide necessary details in its updating supplements, just as it provides information regarding new pronouncements, laws, and other related material.

Because the CBT details are subject to change, we don't recommend that candidates wait to take the exam in order, say, to avoid the essay questions. After waiting, candidates may find that the CBT has essay questions after all.

FYI: A further step in the conversion to a computerized exam may involve the computer selecting additional sets of questions based on a candidate's responses to a first set of questions. As opposed to current types of essay questions, candidates instead may complete research tasks (given a CD-ROM library) and express conclusions in written form.

Candidates interested in learning more about the computerized exam should contact the AICPA. As we go to press, the AICPA web-site (www.aicpa.org) has an exposure draft available for downloading. However, do not confuse time spent learning about proposals for the computerized exam with review time. Bisk Education's updating supplements will include a concise summary of need-to-know information for candidates, when it becomes relevant to passing the exam.

CHAPTER 30—FEDERAL TAXATION: PARTNERSHIPS & OTHER TOPICS

PROBLEM 30-1 MULTIPLE CHOICE QUESTIONS (150 to 188 minutes)

1. In computing the ordinary income of a partnership, a deduction is allowed for
a. Contributions to recognized charities.
b. The first $100 of dividends received from qualifying domestic corporations.
c. Short-term capital losses.
d. Guaranteed payments to partners.

(11/93, PII, #53, 4482)

2. The method used to depreciate partnership property is an election made by
a. The partnership and must be the same method used by the "principal partner."
b. The partnership and may be any method approved by the IRS.
c. The "principal partner."
d. Each individual partner. (11/93, PII, #51, 4480)

3. Basic Partnership, a cash-basis calendar year entity, began business on February 1, 20X1. Basic incurred and paid the following in 20X1.

Filing fees incident to the creation of the
partnership $ 3,600
Accounting fees to prepare the
representations in offering materials   12,000

Basic elected to amortize costs. What was the maximum amount that Basic could deduct on the 20X1 partnership return?
a. $11,000
b. $ 3,300
c. $ 2,860
d. $ 660 (5/96, AR, #3, amended, 6200)

4. At partnership inception, Black acquires a 50% interest in Decorators Partnership by contributing property with an adjusted basis of $250,000. Black recognizes a gain if

I. The fair market value of the contributed property exceeds its adjusted basis.
II. The property is encumbered by a mortgage with a balance of $100,000.

a. I only
b. II only
c. Both I and II
d. Neither I nor II (11/95, AR, #28, 5772)

5. On June 1, Kelly received a 10% interest in Rock Co., a partnership, for services contributed to the partnership. Rock's net assets at that date had a basis of $70,000 and a fair market value of $100,000. In Kelly's income tax return, what amount must Kelly include as income from transfer of partnership interest?
a. $ 7,000 ordinary income
b. $ 7,000 capital gain
c. $10,000 ordinary income
d. $10,000 capital gain

(11/93, PII, #49, amended, 4478)

6. The holding period of a partnership interest acquired in exchange for a contributed capital asset begins on the date
a. The partner is admitted to the partnership.
b. The partner transfers the asset to the partnership.
c. The partner's holding period of the capital asset began.
d. The partner is first credited with the proportionate share of partnership capital.

(11/91, PII, #60, 2508)

ITEMS 7 AND 8 are based on the following:

Jones and Curry formed Major Partnership as equal partners by contributing the assets below:

	Asset	Adjusted basis	Fair market value
Jones	Cash	$45,000	$45,000
Curry	Land	30,000	57,000

The land was held by Curry as a capital asset, subject to a $12,000 mortgage, that was assumed by Major.

7. What was Curry's initial basis in the partnership interest?
a. $45,000
b. $30,000
c. $24,000
d. $18,000 (5/96, AR #1, 6198)

8. What was Jones' initial basis in the partnership interest?
a. $51,000
b. $45,000
c. $39,000
d. $33,000 (5/96, AR #2, 6199)

9. Peters has a one-third interest in the Spano Partnership. Peters received a $16,000 guaranteed payment, which was deductible by the partnership, for services rendered to Spano. Spano reported a operating loss of $70,000 before the guaranteed payment. What is(are) the net effect(s) of the guaranteed payment?

I. The guaranteed payment increases Peters' tax basis in Spano by $16,000.
II. The guaranteed payment increases Peters' ordinary income by $16,000.

a. I only.
b. II only.
c. Both I and II.
d. Neither I nor II.   (R/99, AR, #12, amended, 6801)

10. The partnership of Marks & Sparks sustained an ordinary loss of $42,000 in 20X1. The partnership, as well as the two partners, are on a calendar-year basis. The partners share profits and losses equally. At December 31, 20X1, Marks had an adjusted basis of $18,000 for his partnership interest, before consideration of the loss. On his 20X1 individual tax return, Marks should deduct an (a)
a. Ordinary loss of $18,000.
b. Ordinary loss of $21,000.
c. Ordinary loss of $18,000 and a capital loss of $3,000.
d. Capital loss of $21,000.   (Editors, 9281)

11. Which of the following limitations will apply in determining a partner's deduction for that partner's share of partnership losses?

	At-risk	Passive loss
a.	Yes	No
b.	No	Yes
c.	Yes	Yes
d.	No	No	(11/91, PII, #55, 2503)

12. Freeman, a single individual, reported the following income in the current year:

• Guaranteed payment from services rendered to a partnership $50,000
• Ordinary income from an S corporation $20,000

What amount of Freeman's income is subject to self-employment tax?
a. $0
b. $20,000
c. $50,000
d. $70,000   (R/01, AR, #26, 7011)

ITEMS 13 AND 14 are based on the following:

Flagg and Miles are each 50% partners in Decor Partnership. Each partner had a $200,000 tax basis in the partnership on January 1. Decor's net business income before guaranteed payments was $45,000. During the year, Decor made a $7,500 guaranteed payment to Miles for deductible services rendered.

13. What total amount from Decor is includible in Flagg's tax return?
a. $15,000
b. $18,750
c. $22,500
D. $37,500   (11/98, AR, #16, amended, 6682)

14. What is Miles' tax basis in Decor on December 31?
a. $211,250
b. $215,000
c. $218,750
d. $222,500   (11/98, AR, #17, amended, 6683)

15. Dean is a 25% partner in Target Partnership. Dean's tax basis in Target on January 1, 20X1, was $20,000. At the end of 20X1, Dean received a non-liquidating cash distribution of $8,000 from Target. Target's accounts recorded municipal bond interest income of $12,000 and ordinary income of $40,000 for the year. What was Dean's tax basis in Target on December 31, 20X1?
a. $15,000
b. $23,000
c. $25,000
d. $30,000   (5/95, AR, #26, amended, 5444)

16. When a partner's share of partnership liabilities increases, that partner's basis in the partnership
a. Increases by the partner's share of the increase.
b. Decreases by the partner's share of the increase.
c. Decreases, but **not** to less than zero.
d. Is **not** affected.   (11/93, PII, #54, 4483)

17. Smith and White contributed $4,000 and $6,000 in cash, respectively, and formed the Macro General Partnership. The partnership agreement allocated profits and losses 40% to Smith and 60% to White. Macro purchased property from an unrelated seller for $10,000 cash and a $40,000 mortgage note that was the general liability of the partnership. Macro's liability
a. Increases Smith's partnership basis by $16,000.
b. Increases Smith's partnership basis by $20,000.
c. Increases Smith's partnership basis by $24,000.
d. Has **no** effect on Smith's partnership basis.
   (11/95, AR, #30, amended, 5774)

18. At January 1, 20X0, Paul owned a 25% interest in Associates partnership. During 20X0, a new partner was admitted and Paul's interest was reduced to 20%. The partnership liabilities at January 1 were $150,000, but decreased to $100,000 at December 31. Paul's and the other partners' capital accounts are in proportion to their respective interests. Disregarding any income, loss or drawings for 20X0, the basis of Paul's partnership interest at December 31, compared to the basis of his interest at January 1, was
a. Decreased by $37,500.
b. Increased by $20,000.
c. Decreased by $17,500.
d. Decreased by $5,000.
(5/94, AR, #30, amended, 4635)

19. Ryan's adjusted basis in his Lux Partnership interest was $18,000 at the time Ryan received the following nonliquidating distributions of partnership property:

Cash $10,000
Land—Adjusted basis   14,000
Land—Fair market value   20,000

What is Ryan's tax basis in the land received from the partnership?
a. $0
b. $ 8,000
c. $14,000
d. $20,000   (11/98, AR, #18, 6684)

20. Stone's basis in Ace Partnership was $70,000 at the time he received a nonliquidating distribution of partnership capital assets. These capital assets had an adjusted basis of $65,000 to Ace, and a fair market value of $83,000. Ace had no unrealized receivables, appreciated inventory, or properties which had been contributed by its partners. What was Stone's recognized gain or loss on the distribution?
a. $18,000 ordinary income
b. $13,000 capital gain
c. $ 5,000 capital loss
d. $0   (11/95, AR, #32, 5776)

ITEMS 21 AND 22 are based on the following:

The adjusted basis of Jody's partnership interest was $50,000 immediately before Jody received a current distribution of $20,000 cash and property with an adjusted basis to the partnership of $40,000 and a fair market value of $35,000.

21. What amount of taxable gain must Jody report as a result of this distribution?

a. $0
b. $ 5,000
c. $10,000
d. $20,000   (11/93, PII, #55, 4484)

22. What is Jody's basis in the distributed property?
a. $0
b. $30,000
c. $35,000
d. $40,000   (11/93, PII, #56, 4485)

23. The adjusted basis of Vance's partnership interest in Lex Associates was $180,000 immediately before receiving the following distribution in complete liquidation of Lex:

	Basis to Lex	Fair market value
Cash	$100,000	$100,000
Real estate	70,000	96,000

What is Vance's basis in the real estate?
a. $96,000
b. $83,000
c. $80,000
d. $70,000   (11/93, PII, #57, 4486)

24. A guaranteed payment by a partnership to a partner for services rendered, may include an agreement to pay

I. A salary of $5,000 monthly without regard to partnership income.
II. A 25% interest in partnership profits.

a. I only
b. II only
c. Both I and II
d. Neither I nor II   (5/95, AR, #29, 5447)

25. Don and Lisa are equal partners in the capital and profits of Sabal & Noel, but are otherwise unrelated. The following information pertains to 300 shares of Mast Corporation stock sold by Lisa to Sabal & Noel:

Year of purchase   1997
Year of sale   2000
Basis (cost) $8,000
Sales price (equal to fair market value) $3,000

The amount of long-term capital loss that Lisa realized on the sale of this stock was
a. $5,000.
b. $3,000.
c. $2,500.
d. $0.   (Editors, 1723)

26. Kaye owns an 85% interest in the capital and profits of Amor Antiques, a partnership. In 20X2, Kaye sold an oriental lamp to Amor for $6,000. Kaye bought this lamp in 20X0 for her personal use at a cost of $2,000 and had used the lamp continuously in her home until the lamp was sold to Amor. Amor purchased the lamp as inventory for sale to customers in the ordinary course of business. What is Kaye's reportable gain in 20X2 on the sale of the lamp to Amor?
a. $4,000 ordinary income
b. $4,000 capital gain
c. $3,400 ordinary income
d. $3,400 capital gain   (Editors, 9282)

27. Partnership Abel, Benz, Clark & Day is in the real estate and insurance business. Abel owns a 40% interest in the capital and profits of the partnership, while Benz, Clark, and Day each owns a 20% interest. All use a calendar year. At November 1, the real estate and insurance business is separated, and two partnerships are formed: Partnership Abel & Benz takes over the real estate business, and Partnership Clark & Day takes over the insurance business. Which one of the following statements is correct for tax purposes?
a. Partnership Abel & Benz is considered to be a continuation of Partnership Abel, Benz, Clark & Day.
b. In forming Partnership Clark & Day, partners Clark and Day are subject to a penalty surtax if they contribute their entire distributions from Partnership Abel, Benz, Clark & Day.
c. Before separating the two businesses into two distinct entities, the partners must obtain approval from the IRS.
d. Before separating the two businesses into two distinct entities, Partnership Abel, Benz, Clark & Day must file a formal dissolution with the IRS on the prescribed form.
     (5/90, PII, #21, amended, 1711)

28. Under which of the following circumstances is a partnership that is not an electing large partnership considered terminated for income tax purposes?

I. Fifty-five percent of the total interest in partnership capital and profits is sold within a 12-month period.
II. The partnership's business and financial operations are discontinued.

a. I only
b. II only
c. Both I and II
d. Neither I nor II   (11/97, AR, #8, 6536)

29. Curry's sale of her partnership interest causes a partnership termination. The partnership's business and financial operations are continued by the other members. What is(are) the effect(s) of the termination?

I. There is a deemed distribution of assets to the remaining partners and the purchaser.
II. There is a hypothetical recontribution of assets to a new partnership.

a. I only
b. II only
c. Both I and II
d. Neither I nor II   (11/95, AR, #34, 5778)

30. Which one of the following statements regarding a partnership's tax year is correct?
a. A partnership formed on July 1 is required to adopt a tax year ending on June 30.
b. A partnership may elect to have a tax year other than the generally required tax year if the deferral period for the tax year elected does **not** exceed three months.
c. A "valid business purpose" can **no** longer be claimed as a reason for adoption of a tax year other than the generally required tax year.
d. Within 30 days after a partnership has established a tax year, a form must be filed with the IRS as notification of the tax year adopted.
     (5/90, PII, #25, 1715)

31. On December 31, after receipt of his share of partnership income, Clark sold his interest in a limited partnership for $30,000 cash and relief of all liabilities. On that date, the adjusted basis of Clark's partnership interest was $40,000, consisting of his capital account of $15,000 and his share of the partnership liabilities of $25,000. The partnership has no unrealized receivables or substantially appreciated inventory. What is Clark's gain or loss on the sale of his partnership interest?
a. Ordinary loss of $10,000
b. Ordinary gain of $15,000
c. Capital loss of $10,000
d. Capital gain of $15,000
     (11/93, PII, #59, amended, 4488)

ITEMS 32 AND 33 are based on the following:

The personal service partnership of Allen, Baker & Carr had the following cash basis balance sheet at December 31, 20X1:

Assets	Adjusted basis per books	Market value
Cash	$102,000	$102,000
Unrealized accounts receivable	--	420,000
Totals	$102,000	$522,000

Liability and Capital		
Note payable	$ 60,000	$ 60,000
Allen, capital	14,000	154,000
Baker, capital	14,000	154,000
Carr, capital	14,000	154,000
Totals	$102,000	$522,000

Carr, an equal partner, sold his partnership interest to Dole, an outsider, for $154,000 cash on January 1, 20X2. In addition Dole assumed Carr's share of the partnership's liability.

32. What was the total amount realized by Carr on the sale of his partnership interest?
a. $174,000
b. $154,000
c. $140,000
d. $134,000   (5/90, PII, #22, amended, 1712)

33. What amount of ordinary income should Carr report in his 20X2 income tax return on the sale of his partnership interest?
a. $0
b. $ 20,000
c. $ 34,000
d. $140,000   (5/90, PII, #23, amended, 1713)

34. A complex trust is a trust that
a. Is exempt from payment of income tax since the tax is paid by the beneficiaries.
b. Invests only in corporate securities and is prohibited from engaging in short-term transactions.
c. Permits accumulation of current income, provides for charitable contributions, or distributes principal during the taxable year.
d. Must distribute income currently, but is prohibited from distributing principal during the taxable year.   (Editors, 1741)

35. The 2002 standard deduction for a trust or an estate in the fiduciary income tax return is
a. $0.
b. $100.
c. $300.
d. $600.   (11/91, PII, #24, amended, 2472)

36. For income tax purposes, the estate's initial taxable period for a decedent who died on October 24
a. May be either a calendar year, or a fiscal year beginning on the date of the decedent's death.
b. Must be a fiscal year beginning on the date of the decedent's death.
c. May be either a calendar year, or a fiscal year beginning on October 1 of the year of the decedent's death.
d. Must be a calendar year beginning on January 1 of the year of the decedent's death.   (R/00, AR, #9, 6914)

37. An executor of a decedent's estate that has only U.S. citizens as beneficiaries is required to file a fiduciary income tax return, if the estate's gross income for the year is at least
a. $ 400.
b. $ 500.
c. $ 600.
d. $1,000.   (5/91, PII, #37, 1697)

38. With regard to estimated income tax, estates
a. Must make quarterly estimated tax payments starting no later than the second quarter following the one in which the estate was established.
b. Are exempt from paying estimated tax during the estate's first two taxable years.
c. Are **not** required to make payments of estimated tax.
d. Must make quarterly estimated tax payments only if the estate's income is required to be distributed currently.   (Editors, 1740)

39. On January 1, 1997, Carlt created a $300,000 trust that provided his mother with a lifetime income interest starting on January 1, 1997, with the remainder interest to go to his son. Carlt expressly retained the power to revoke both the income interest and the remainder interest at any time. Who will be taxed on the trust's 1997 income?
a. Carlt's mother
b. Carlt's son
c. Carlt
d. The trust   (11/98, AR, #19, 6685)

40. A distribution to an estate's sole beneficiary for the 20X1 calendar year equaled $15,000, the amount currently required to be distributed by the will. The estate's 20X1 records were as follows:

Estate income
$40,000 Taxable interest

Estate disbursements
$34,000 Expenses attributable to taxable interest

What amount of the distribution was taxable to the beneficiary?
a. $40,000
b. $15,000
c. $ 6,000
d. $0   (11/95, AR, #35, amended, 5779)

ITEMS 41 AND 42 are based on the following:

Astor, a cash-basis taxpayer, died on February 3, 20X1. During 20X1, the estate's executor made a distribution of $12,000 from estate income to Astor's sole heir and adopted a calendar year to determine the estate's taxable income. The following additional information pertains to the estate's income and disbursements in 20X1:

Estate income:
Taxable interest $65,000
Net long-term capital gains allocable
   to corpus   5,000

Estate disbursements:
Administrative expenses attributable
   to taxable income   14,000
Charitable contributions from gross
   income to a public charity, made
   under the terms of the will   9,000

41. For the calendar year, what was the estate's distributable net income (DNI)?
a. $39,000
b. $42,000
c. $58,000
d. $65,000   (R/99, AR, #13, amended, 6802)

42. Astor's executor does not intend to file an extension request for the estate fiduciary income tax return. By what date must the executor file the Form 1041, U.S. Fiduciary Income Tax Return, for the estate's 20X1 calendar year?
a. Wednesday, March 15, 20X2
b. Monday, April 17, 20X2
c. Thursday, June 15, 20X2
d. Friday, September 15, 20X2
                    (5/95, AR, #32, amended, 5450)

43. The charitable contribution deduction on an estate's fiduciary income tax return is allowable
a. If the decedent died intestate.
b. To the extent of the same adjusted gross income limitation as that on an individual income tax return.
c. Only if the decedent's will specifically provides for the contribution.
d. Subject to the 2% threshold on miscellaneous itemized deductions.   (5/91, PII, #38, 1698)

44. Income in respect of a cash basis decedent
a. Covers income earned before the taxpayer's death but **not** collected until after death.
b. Receives a stepped-up basis in the decedent's estate.
c. Must be included in the decedent's final income tax return.
d. Cannot receive capital gain treatment.
                          (11/90, PII, #39, 1709)

45. Rose, a calendar-year, cash-basis taxpayer who died in June was entitled to receive a $10,000 fee that had not been collected before the date of death. The executor of Rose's estate collected the full $10,000 in July. This $10,000 should appear in
a. Only the decedent's final individual income tax return.
b. Only the estate's fiduciary income tax return.
c. Only the estate tax return.
d. Both the fiduciary income tax return and the estate tax return.   (Editors, 1733)

46. Which of the following credits may be offset against the gross estate tax to determine the net estate tax of a U.S. Citizen?

	Unified credit	Credit for gift taxes paid on gifts made after 1976
a.	Yes	Yes
b.	No	No
c.	No	Yes
d.	Yes	No (11/92, PII, #20, 3354)

47. What amount of a decedent's taxable estate is effectively tax-free in 2002 if the maximum unified estate and gift credit is taken?
a. $0
b. $ 11,000
c. $ 675,000
d. $1,000,000   (11/93, PII, #39, amended, 4468)

48. If the executor of a decedent's estate elects the alternate valuation date and none of the property included in the gross estate has been sold or distributed, the estate assets must be valued as of how many months after the decedent's death?

a. 12
b. 9
c. 6
d. 3   (11/94, AR, #58, 5034)

49. Under the provisions of a decedent's will, the following cash disbursements were made by the estate's executor:

I. A charitable bequest to the American Red Cross.
II. Payment of the decedent's funeral expenses.

What deduction(s) is(are) allowable in determining the decedent's taxable estate?
a. I only
b. II only
c. Both I and II
d. Neither I nor II   (11/97, AR, #9, 6537)

50. Fred and Amy Kehl, both U.S. citizens, are married. All of their real and personal property is owned by them as tenants by the entirety or as joint tenants with right of survivorship. The gross estate of the first spouse to die
a. Includes 50% of the value of all property owned by the couple, regardless of which spouse furnished the original consideration.
b. Includes only the property that had been acquired with the funds of the deceased spouse.
c. Is governed by the federal statutory provisions relating to jointly held property, rather than by the decedent's interest in community property vested by state law, if the Kehls reside in a community property state.
d. Includes one-third of the value of all real estate owned by the Kehls, as the dower right in the case of the wife or curtesy right in the case of the husband.   (5/91, PII, #35, 1695)

51. Within how many months after the date of a decedent's death is the federal estate tax return (Form 706) due if **no** extension of time for filing is granted?
a. 9
b. 6
c. 4½
d. 3½   (11/91, PII, #27, 2475)

52. Following are the fair market values of Wald's assets at the date of death:

Personal effects and jewelry	$ 150,000
Land bought by Wald with Wald's funds five years prior to death and held with Wald's sister as joint tenants with right of survivorship	1,800,000

The executor of Wald's estate did not elect the alternate valuation date. The amount includible as Wald's gross estate in the federal estate tax return is
a. $ 150,000.
b. $1,150,000.
c. $1,800,000.
d. $1,950,000.   (11/90, PII, #37, amended, 1707)

53. Proceeds of a life insurance policy payable to the estate's executor, as the estate's representative, are
a. Includible in the decedent's gross estate only if the premiums had been paid by the insured.
b. Includible in the decedent's gross estate only if the policy was taken out within three years of the insured's death under the "contemplation of death" rule.
c. Never includable in the decedent's gross estate.
d. Always includable in the decedent's gross estate.   (Editors, 9283)

54. Alan Maade, a U.S. citizen, died on March 1, leaving an adjusted gross estate with a fair market value of $1,600,000 at the date of death. Under the terms of Alan's will, $475,000 was bequeathed outright to his widow, free of all estate and inheritance taxes. The remainder of Alan's estate was left to his mother. Alan made no taxable gifts during his lifetime. In computing the taxable estate, the executor of Alan's estate should claim a marital deduction of
a. $ 250,000.
b. $ 475,000.
c. $ 600,000.
d. $1,125,000.   (Editors, 1746)

55. The generation-skipping transfer tax is imposed
a. Instead of the gift tax.
b. Instead of the estate tax.
c. As a separate tax in addition to the gift and estate taxes.
d. On transfers of future interest to beneficiaries who are more than one generation above the donor's generation.   (11/91, PII, #38, 2486)

56. Steve and Kay Briar, U.S. citizens, were married for the entire 2002 calendar year. In 2002, Steve gave a $30,000 cash gift to his sister. The Briars made no other gifts in 2002. They each signed a timely election to treat the $30,000 gift as made one-half by each spouse. Disregarding the unified credit and estate tax consequences, what amount of the gift is taxable to the Briars?
a. $30,000
b. $19,000
c. $ 8,000
d. $0   (11/95, AR, #36, amended, 5780)

57. Under the unified rate schedule,
a. Lifetime taxable gifts are taxed on a noncumulative basis.
b. Transfers at death are taxed on a noncumulative basis.
c. Lifetime taxable gifts and transfers at death are taxed on a cumulative basis.
d. The gift tax rates are 5% higher than the estate tax rates. (11/91, PII, #37, 2485)

58. During 2002, Blake transferred a corporate bond with a face amount and fair market value of $20,000 to a trust for the benefit of her 16-year old child. Annual interest on this bond is $2,000, which is to be accumulated in the trust and distributed to the child on reaching the age of 21. The bond is then to be distributed to the donor or her successor-in-interest in liquidation of the trust. Present value of the total interest to be received by the child is $8,710. The amount of the gift that is excludable from taxable gifts is
a. $20,000.
b. $11,000.
c. $ 8,710.
d. $0. (11/91, PII, #26, amended, 2474)

59. In 2002, Sayers, who is single, gave an outright gift of $50,000 to a friend, Johnson, who needed the money to pay medical expenses. In filing the gift tax return, Sayers was entitled to a maximum exclusion of
a. $0.
b. $11,000.
c. $22,000.
d. $50,000. (5/94, AR, #33, amended, 4638)

60. On July 1, 2002, Vega made a transfer by gift in an amount sufficient to require the filing of a gift tax return. Vega was still alive in 2003. If Vega did not request an extension of time for filing the 2002 gift tax return, the due date for filing was
a. March 15, 2003.
b. Monday, April 17, 2003.
c. June 15, 2003.
d. June 30, 2003. (5/91, PII, #40, amended, 1700)

61. When Jim and Nina became engaged in April 2002, Jim gave Nina a ring that had a fair market value of $50,000. After their wedding in July 2002, Jim gave Nina $75,000 in cash so that Nina could have her own bank account. Both Jim and Nina are U.S. citizens. What was the amount of Jim's 2002 marital deduction?
a. $0
b. $ 75,000
c. $115,000
d. $125,000 (11/90, PII, #36, amended, 1706)

62. The organizational test to qualify a public service charitable entity as tax exempt requires the articles of organization to

I. Limit the purpose of the entity to the charitable purpose.
II. State that an information return should be filed annually with the Internal Revenue Service.

a. I only
b. II only
c. Both I and II
d. Neither I nor II (11/95, AR, #37, 5781)

63. Which of the following exempt organizations must file annual information returns?
a. Churches
b. Internally supported auxiliaries of churches
c. Private foundations
d. Those with gross receipts of less than $5,000 in each taxable year (5/95, AR, #35, 5453)

64. The private foundation status of an exempt organization will terminate if it
a. Becomes a public charity.
b. Is a foreign corporation.
c. Does **not** distribute all of its net assets to one or more public charities.
d. Is governed by a charter that limits the organization's exempt purposes. (5/95, AR, #34, 5452)

65. To qualify as an exempt organization other than a church or an employees' qualified pension or profit-sharing trust, the applicant
a. Cannot operate under the "lodge system" under which payments are made to its members for sick benefits.
b. Need **not** be specifically identified as one of the classes on which exemption is conferred by the Internal Revenue Code, provided that the organization's purposes and activities are of a nonprofit nature.
c. Is barred from incorporating and issuing capital stock.
d. Must file a written application with the Internal Revenue Service. (5/94, AR, #34, 4639)

66. Maple Avenue Assembly, a tax-exempt religious organization, operates an outreach program for the poor in its community. A candidate for the local city council has endorsed Maple's anti-poverty program. Which of the following activities is(are) consistent with Maple's tax-exempt status?

I. Endorsing the candidate to members.
II. Collecting contributions from members for the candidate.

a. I only
b. II only
c. Both I and II
d. Neither I nor II   (11/97, AR, #10, 6538)

67.   Hope is a tax-exempt religious organization. Which of the following activities is(are) consistent with Hope's tax-exempt status?

I.   Conducting weekend retreats for business organizations.
II.   Providing traditional burial services that maintain the religious beliefs of its members.

a. I only.
b. II only.
c. Both I and II.
d. Neither I nor II.   (R/99, AR, #14, 6803)

68.   If an exempt organization is a corporation, the tax on unrelated business taxable income is
a. Computed at corporate income tax rates.
b. Computed at rates applicable to trusts.
c. Credited against the tax on recognized capital gains.
d. Abated.   (5/93, PII, #58, 4163)

69.   During the current year, Help Inc., an exempt organization, derived income of $15,000 from conducting bingo games. Conducting bingo games is legal in Help's locality and is confined to exempt organizations in Help's state. Which of the following statements is true regarding this income?
a. The entire $15,000 is subject to tax at a lower rate than the corporate income tax rate.
b. The entire $15,000 is exempt from tax on unrelated business income.
c. Only the first $5,000 is exempt from tax on unrelated business income.
d. Since Help has unrelated business income, Help automatically forfeits its exempt status for the current year.   (5/93, PII, #60, amended, 4165)

70.   An incorporated exempt organization subject to tax on its current year unrelated business income
a. Must make estimated tax payments if its tax can reasonably be expected to be $100 or more.
b. Must comply with the Code provisions regarding installment payments of estimated income tax by corporations.
c. Must pay at least 70% of the tax due as shown on the return when filed, with the balance of tax payable in the following quarter.
d. May defer payment of the tax for up to nine months following the due date of the return.
          (5/90, PII, #38, amended, 1717)

71.   Which of the following statements is correct regarding the unrelated business income of exempt organizations?
a. If an exempt organization has any unrelated business income, it may result in the loss of the organization's exempt status.
b. Unrelated business income relates to the performance of services, but **not** to the sale of goods.
c. An unrelated business does **not** include any activity where all the work is performed for the organization by unpaid volunteers.
d. Unrelated business income tax will **not** be imposed if profits from the unrelated business are used to support the exempt organization's charitable activities.   (11/93, PII, #47, 4476)

72.   Which one of the following statements is correct with regard to unrelated business income of an exempt organization?
a. An exempt organization that earns any unrelated business income in excess of $100,000 during a particular year will lose its exempt status for that particular year.
b. An exempt organization is not taxed on unrelated business income of less than $1,000.
c. The tax on unrelated business income can be imposed even if the unrelated business activity is intermittent and is carried on once a year.
d. An unrelated trade or business activity that results in a loss is excluded from the definition of unrelated business.   (11/94, AR, #60, 5036)

73.   Morgan, a sole practitioner CPA, prepares individual and corporate income tax returns. What documentation is Morgan required to retain concerning each return prepared?
a. An unrelated party compliance statement.
b. Taxpayer's name and identification number or a copy of the tax return.
c. Workpapers associated with the preparation of each tax return.
d. A power of attorney.   (11/97, AR, #11, 6539)

74.   Which of the following acts constitute(s) grounds for a tax preparer penalty?

I.   Without the taxpayer's consent, the tax preparer disclosed taxpayer income tax return information under an order from a state court.
II.   At the taxpayer's suggestion, the tax preparer deducted the expenses of the taxpayer's personal domestic help as a business expense on the taxpayer's individual tax return.

a. I only.
b. II only.
c. Both I and II.
d. Neither I nor II.   (R/00, AR, #10, 6915)

75. To avoid tax return preparer penalties for a return's understated tax liability due to an intentional disregard of the regulations, which of the following actions must a tax preparer take?

a. Audit the taxpayer's corresponding business operations
b. Review the accuracy of the taxpayer's books and records
c. Make reasonable inquiries if the taxpayer's information is incomplete
d. Examine the taxpayer's supporting documents

(11/98, AR, #20, 6686)

PROBLEM 30-2 ADDITIONAL MULTIPLE CHOICE QUESTIONS (50 to 63 minutes)

76. Barker acquired a 50% interest in Kode Partnership by contributing $20,000 cash and a building with an adjusted basis of $26,000 and a fair market value of $42,000. The building was subject to a $10,000 mortgage which was assumed by Kode. The other partners contributed cash only. The basis of Barker's interest in Kode is
a. $36,000.
b. $41,000.
c. $52,000.
d. $62,000.   (11/95, AR, #27, 5771)

77. Ola Associates is a limited partnership engaged in real estate development. Hoff, a civil engineer, billed Ola $40,000 for consulting services rendered. In full settlement of this invoice, Hoff accepted a $15,000 cash payment plus the following:

	Fair market value	Carrying amount on Ola's books
3% limited partnership interest in Ola	$10,000	N/A
Surveying equipment	7,000	$3,000

What amount should Hoff, a cash-basis taxpayer, report in his income tax return as income for the services rendered to Ola?
a. $15,000
b. $28,000
c. $32,000
d. $40,000   (11/91, PII, #56, amended, 2504)

78. Strom acquired a 25% interest in Ace Partnership by contributing land having an adjusted basis of $16,000 and a fair market value of $50,000. The land was subject to a $24,000 mortgage, which was assumed by Ace. No other liabilities existed at the time of the contribution. What was Strom's basis in Ace?
a. $0
b. $16,000
c. $26,000
d. $32,000   (5/95, AR, #27, 5445)

79. Guaranteed payments made by a partnership to partners for services rendered to the partnership, that are deductible business expenses under the Internal Revenue Code, are

I. Deductible expenses on the U.S. Partnership Return of Income, Form 1065, in order to arrive at partnership income (loss).
II. Included on schedules K-1 to be taxed as ordinary income to the partners.

a. I only
b II only
c. Both I and II
d. Neither I nor II   (5/94, AR, #29, 4634)

80. The basis to a partner of property distributed "in kind" in complete liquidation of the partner's interest is the
a. Adjusted basis of the partner's interest increased by any cash distributed to the partner in the same transaction.
b. Adjusted basis of the partner's interest reduced by any cash distributed to the partner in the same transaction.
c. Adjusted basis of the property to the partnership.
d. Fair market value of the property.

(11/91, PII, #54, 2502)

81. On January 3, the partners' percentage interest in the capital, profits, and losses of Able Partnership were:

Dean	25%
Poe	30%
Ritt	45%

On February 4, Poe sold her entire interest to an unrelated party. Dean sold his 25% interest in Able to another unrelated party on December 20. No other transactions took place during the year. For tax purposes, which of the following statements is correct with respect to Able?

a. Able terminated as of February 4.
b. Able terminated as of December 20.
c. Able terminated as of December 31.
d. Able did **not** terminate.

(11/95, AR, #33, amended, 5777)

82. Which of the following should be used in computing the basis of a partner's interest acquired from another partner?

	Cash paid by transferee to transferor	Transferee's share of partnership liabilities
a.	No	Yes
b.	Yes	No
c.	No	No
d.	Yes	Yes

(11/91, PII, #59, 2507)

83. Raff died in 2001 leaving her entire estate to her only child. Raff's will gave full discretion to the estate's executor with regard to distributions of income. For 2002, the estate's distributable net income was $15,000, of which $9,000 was paid to the beneficiary. None of the income was tax exempt. What amount can be claimed on the estate's 2002 fiduciary income tax return for the distributions deduction?

a. $0
b. $ 6,000
c. $ 9,000
d. $15,000   (5/91, PII, #39, amended, 1699)

84. Which of the following fiduciary entities are required to use the calendar year as their taxable period for income tax purposes?

	Estates	Trusts (except those that are tax exempt)
a.	Yes	Yes
b.	No	No
c.	Yes	No
d.	No	Yes

(11/91, PII, #25, 2473)

85. Ordinary and necessary administration expenses paid by the fiduciary of an estate are deductible

a. Only on the fiduciary income tax return (Form 1041) and never on the federal estate tax return (Form 706).
b. Only on the federal estate tax return and never on the fiduciary income tax return.
c. On the fiduciary income tax return only if the estate tax deduction is waived for these expenses.
d. On both the fiduciary income tax return and on the estate tax return by adding a tax computed

on the proportionate rates attributable to both returns.   (11/91, PII, #39, 2487)

86. A distribution from estate income, that was *currently* required, was made to the estate's sole beneficiary during its calendar year. The maximum amount of the distribution to be included in the beneficiary's gross income is limited to the estate's

a. Capital gain income.
b. Ordinary gross income.
c. Distributable net income.
d. Net investment income.   (5/95, AR, #33, 5451)

87. End and Law, both U.S. citizens, died in 2002. End made taxable lifetime gifts of $150,000 that are **not** included in End's gross estate. Law made no lifetime gifts. At the dates of death, End's gross estate was $600,000, and Law's gross estate was $500,000. A federal tax return must be filed for

	End	Law
a.	No	No
b.	No	Yes
c.	Yes	No
d.	Yes	Yes (Editors, 1730)

88. Which of the following requires filing a gift tax return, if the transfer exceeds the available annual gift tax exclusion?

a. Medical expenses paid directly to a physician on behalf of an individual unrelated to the donor.
b. Tuition paid directly to an accredited university on behalf of an individual unrelated to the donor.
c. Payments for college books, supplies, and dormitory fees on behalf of an individual unrelated to the donor.
d. Campaign expenses paid to a political organization.   (11/91, PII, #40, 2488)

89. Andi Corp. issued $1,000,000 face amount of bonds in 1995 and established a sinking fund to pay the debt at maturity. The bondholders appointed an independent trustee to invest the sinking fund contributions and to administer the trust. In 2001, the sinking fund earned $60,000 in interest on bank deposits and $8,000 in net long-term capital gains. All of the trust income is accumulated with Andi's periodic contributions so that the aggregate amount will be sufficient to pay the bonds when they mature. What amount of trust income was taxable to Andi in 2001?

a. $0
b. $ 8,000
c. $60,000
d. $68,000   (11/91, PII, #44, amended, 2492)

90. For federal estate taxation, the alternate valuation date
a. If elected on the first return filed for the estate, may be revoked in an amended return provided that the first return was filed on time.
b. Is required to be used if the fair market value of the estate's assets has increased since the decedent's date of death.
c. Must be used for valuation of the estate's liabilities if such date is used for valuation of the estate's assets.
d. Can be elected only if its use decreases both the value of the gross estate and the estate tax liability. (Editors, 1731)

91. Which of the following is (are) deductible from a decedent's gross estate?

I. Expenses of administering and settling the estate.
II. State inheritance or estate tax.

a. I only
b. II only
c. Both I and II
d. Neither I nor II (11/93, PII, #40, 4469)

92. Jan, an unmarried individual, gave the following outright gifts:

Donee	Amount	Use by Donee
Jones	$15,000	Down payment on house
Craig	15,000	College tuition
Kande	5,000	Vacation trip

Jan's exclusions for gift tax purposes total
a. $31,000.
b. $27,000.
c. $20,000.
d. $11,000. (11/90, PII, #35, amended, 1705)

93. Which of the following activities regularly conducted by a tax exempt organization will result in unrelated business income?

I. Selling articles made by handicapped persons as part of their rehabilitation, when the organization is involved exclusively in their rehabilitation.
II. Operating a grocery store almost fully staffed by emotionally handicapped persons as part of a therapeutic program.

a. I only
b. II only
c. Both I and II
d. Neither I nor II (11/95, AR, #38, 5782)

94. Carmen Fund, organized and operated exclusively for charitable purposes, provides insurance coverage, at amounts substantially below cost, to exempt organizations involved in the prevention of cruelty to children. Carmen's insurance activities are
a. Subject to the same tax provisions as those applicable to insurance companies.
b. Treated as unrelated business income.
c. Considered "commercial-type" as defined by the Internal Revenue Code.
d. Exempt from tax. (Editors, 9279)

95. Which one of the following statements is **not** correct with regard to exempt organizations?
a. Exempt status of an organization may be retroactively revoked.
b. Exempt organizations that are required to file annual information returns need not disclose the identity of substantial contributors.
c. An organization will not automatically forfeit its exempt status if any executive or other employee of the organization is paid compensation in excess of $150,000 per year, even if such compensation is reasonable.
d. An organization is not automatically exempt from tax merely by meeting the statutory requirements for exemption. (Editors, 1748)

96. The filing of a return covering unrelated business income
a. Is required of all exempt organizations having at least $1,000 of unrelated business taxable income for the year.
b. Relieves the organization of having to file a separate annual information return.
c. Is **not** necessary if all of the organization's income is used exclusively for charitable purposes.
d. Must be accompanied by a minimum payment of 50% of the tax due as shown on the return, with the balance of tax payable six months later. (Editors, 9280)

97. Salud Welfare Associates is an exempt organization that operates under a corporate charter granted by the state in which Salud's principal office is located. Salud's tax on unrelated business taxable income is
a. Computed at corporate income tax rates.
b. Credited against the tax on recognized capital gains.
c. Computed at rates applicable to trusts.
d. Abated. (5/91, PII, #41, amended, 1701)

98. A tax return preparer is subject to a penalty for knowingly or recklessly disclosing corporate tax return information, if the disclosure is made

a. To enable a third party to solicit business from the taxpayer.
b. To enable the tax processor to electronically compute the taxpayer's liability.
c. For peer review.
d. Under an administrative order by a state agency that registers tax return preparers.

(11/94, AR, #55, 5031)

99. Which, if any, of the following could result in penalties against an income tax return preparer?

I. Knowing or reckless disclosure or use of tax information obtained in preparing a return
II. A willful attempt to understate any client's tax liability on a return or claim for refund

a. Neither I nor II
b. I only
c. II only
d. Both I and II

(5/94, AR, #20, 4625)

100. Vee Corp. retained Water, CPA, to prepare its 20X4 income tax return. During the engagement, Water discovered that Vee had failed to file its 20X0 income tax return. What is Water's professional responsibility regarding Vee's unfiled 20X0 income tax return?

a. Prepare Vee's 20X0 income tax return and submit it to the IRS.
b. Advise Vee that the 20X0 income tax return has not been filed and recommend that Vee ignore filing its 20X0 return since the statute of limitations has passed.
c. Advise the IRS that Vee's 20X0 income tax return has not been filed.
d. Consider withdrawing from preparation of Vee's 20X4 income tax return until the error is corrected. (R/99, AR, #15, amended, 6804)

OTHER OBJECTIVE FORMAT QUESTIONS

PROBLEM 30-3 (5 to 10 minutes)

During 20X1, Adams, a general contractor, Brinks, an architect, and Carson, an interior decorator, formed the Dex Home Improvement General Partnership by contributing the assets below:

	Asset	Adjusted basis	Fair market value	% of partner share in capital, profits & losses
Adams	Cash	$40,000	$40,000	50%
Brinks	Land	$12,000	$21,000	20%
Carson	Inventory	$24,000	$24,000	30%

The land was a capital asset to Brinks, subject to a $5,000 mortgage, which was assumed by the partnership.

FOR ITEMS 1 AND 2, determine the initial basis of the partner's interest in Dex.

1. Brinks

2. Carson

During 20X1, the Dex Partnership breaks even but decides to make distributions to each partner.

FOR ITEMS 3 THROUGH 8, determine whether the statement is true (T) or false (F).

3. A nonliquidating cash distribution may reduce the recipient partner's basis in her/his partnership interest below zero.

4. A nonliquidating distribution of unappreciated inventory reduces the recipient partner's basis in her/his partnership interest.

5. In a liquidating distribution of property other than money, where the partnership's basis of the distributed property exceeds the basis of the partner's interest, the partner's basis in the distributed property is limited to her/his predistribution basis in the partnership interest.

6. Gain is recognized by the partner who receives a nonliquidating distribution of property, where the adjusted basis of the property exceeds her/his basis in the partnership interest before the distribution.

7. In a nonliquidating distribution of inventory, where the partnership has no unrealized receivables or appreciated inventory, the basis of inventory that is distributed to a partner cannot exceed the inventory's adjusted basis to the partnership.

8. The partnership's nonliquidating distribution of encumbered property to a partner who assumes the mortgage, does not affect the other partners' bases in their partnership interests.

(11/94, AR, #2, amended, 5037-5044)

PROBLEM 30-4 (5 to 10 minutes)

Before his death, Remsen, a U.S. citizen, made cash gifts of $7,000 each to his four sisters. In 20X1, Remsen also paid $2,000 in tuition directly to his grandchild's university on the grandchild's behalf. Remsen made no other lifetime transfers. Remsen died on January 9, 20X1, and was survived by his wife and only child, both of whom were U.S. citizens. The Remsens did not live in a community property state.

At his death, Remsen owned:

Cash	$650,000
Marketable securities (Fair market value)	900,000
Life insurance policy with Remsen's wife named as the beneficiary (fair market value)	500,000

Under the provisions of Remsen's will, the net cash, after payment of executor's fees and medical and funeral expenses, was bequeathed to Remsen's son. The marketable securities were bequeathed to Remsen's spouse. During 20X1, Remsen's estate paid:

Executor's fees to distribute the decedent's property (deducted on the fiduciary tax return)	$15,000
Decedent's funeral expenses	25,000

The estate's executor extended the time to file the estate tax return.

On January 3, 20X2, the estate's executor paid the decedent's outstanding $10,000 20X1 medical expense and filed the extended estate tax return.

REQUIRED:

FOR ITEMS 1 THROUGH 5, identify the federal estate tax treatment for each item. An answer may be selected once, more than once, or not at all.

Estate Tax Treatments	
F	Fully includible in Remsen's gross estate.
P	Partially includible in Remsen's gross estate.
N	Not includible in Remsen's gross estate.

1. What is the estate tax treatment of the $7,000 cash gift to each sister?

2. What is the estate tax treatment of the life insurance proceeds?

3. What is the estate tax treatment of the marketable securities?

4. What is the estate tax treatment of the $2,000 tuition payment?

5. What is the estate tax treatment of the $650,000 cash?

REQUIRED:

FOR ITEMS 6 THROUGH 10, identify the federal estate tax treatment for each item. An answer may be selected once, more than once, or not at all.

Estate Tax Treatments	
G	Deductible from Remsen's gross estate to arrive at Remsen's taxable estate.
I	Deductible on Remsen's 20X1 individual income tax return.
E	Deductible on either Remsen's estate tax return or Remsen's 20X1 individual income tax return.
N	Not deductible on either Remsen's estate tax return or Remsen's 20X1 individual income tax return.

6. What is the estate tax treatment of the executor's fees?

7. What is the estate tax treatment of the cash bequest to Remsen's son?

8. What is the estate tax treatment of the life insurance proceeds paid to Remsen's spouse?

9. What is the estate tax treatment of the funeral expenses?

10. What is the estate tax treatment of the $10,000 20X1 medical expense incurred before the decedent's death and paid by the executor on January 3, 20X2?

(5/98, AR, #2, amended, 6646-6655)

PROBLEM 30-5 (10 to 15 minutes)

Scott Lane, an unmarried U.S. citizen, made no lifetime transfers prior to the current year. During 2002, Lane made the following transfers:

- Gave a $10,000 cash gift to Kamp, a close friend.
- Made two separate $10,000 cash gifts to his only child.

- Created an **irrevocable** trust beginning in 2002 that provided his aunt with an income interest to be paid for the next five years. The remainder interest is to pass to Lane's sole cousin. The income interest is valued at $26,000 and the remainder interest is valued at $74,000.
- Paid $25,000 tuition directly to his grandchild's university on his grandchild's behalf.
- Created an **irrevocable** trust that provided his brother with a lifetime income interest beginning in two years, after which a remainder interest passes to their sister.
- Created a **revocable** trust with his niece as the sole beneficiary. During 2002, the niece received $15,000 interest income from the trust.

REQUIRED:

FOR ITEMS 1 THROUGH 7, determine whether the transactions are fully taxable, partially taxable, or not taxable to Lane in the current year for gift tax purposes after considering the gift tax annual exclusion. Ignore the unified credit when answering the items. An answer may be selected once, more than once, or not at all.

Gift Tax Treatments
F. Fully taxable to Lane in 2002 for gift tax purposes
P. Partially taxable to Lane in 2002 for gift tax purposes
N. Not taxable to Lane in 2002 for gift tax purposes

1. What is the gift tax treatment of Lane's gift to Kamp?

2. What is the gift tax treatment of Lane's cash gifts to his child?

3. What is the gift tax treatment of the trust's income interest to Lane's aunt?

4. What is the gift tax treatment of the trusts remainder interest to Lane's cousin?

5. What is the gift tax treatment of the tuition payment to Lane's grandchild's university?

6. What is the gift tax treatment of the trust's income interest to Lane's brother?

7. What is the gift tax treatment of the $11,000 interest income that Lane's niece received from the revocable trust?

(11/98, AR, #3, amended, 6691-6697)

PROBLEM 30-6 (10 to 15 minutes)

Various clients went to Rowe, CPA, for tax advice concerning possible gift tax liability on transfers they made throughout the year.

FOR ITEMS 1 THROUGH 9, indicate whether the transfer of cash, the income interest, or the remainder interest is a gift of present interest (P), a gift of a future interest (F), or not a completed gift (N).

Cobb created a $500,000 trust that provided his mother with an income interest for her life and the remainder interest to go to his sister at the death of his mother. Cobb expressly retained the power to revoke both the income interest and the remainder interest at any time.

1. The income interest at the trust's creation.
2. The remainder interest at the trust's creation.

Kane created a $100,000 trust that provided her nephew with the income interest until he reached 45 years of age. When the trust was created, Kane's nephew was 25. The income distribution is to start when Kane's nephew is 29. After Kane's nephew reaches the age of 45, the remainder interest is to go to Kane's niece.

3. The income interest.

During 2002, Hall, an unmarried taxpayer, made a $10,000 cash gift to his son in May and a further $12,000 cash gift to him in August.

4. The cash transfers.

During the current year, Yeats transferred property worth $20,000 to a trust with the income to be paid to her 22-year-old niece Jane. After Jane reaches the age of 30, the remainder interest is to be distributed to Yeats' brother. The income interest is valued at $9,700 and the remainder interest at $10,300.

5. The income interest.
6. The remainder interest.

Tom and Ann Curry, U.S. citizens, were married for the entire calendar year. Tom gave a $40,000 cash gift to his uncle, Grant. The Currys made no other gifts to Grant in the current year. Tom and Ann each signed a timely election stating that each made one half of the $40,000 gift.

7. The cash transfer.

Murry created a $1,000,000 trust that provided his brother with an income interest for ten years, after which the remainder interest passes to Murry's sister. Murry retained the power to revoke the remainder interest at any time. The income interest was valued at $600,000.

8. The income interest.
9. The remainder interest.

FOR ITEM 10, determine whether the transfer is subject to the generation skipping tax (A), the gift tax (B), or both taxes (C). Disregard the use of any exclusions and the unified credit.

10. Martin's daughter, Kim, has one child, Dale. In 2002, Martin made an outright $5,000,000 gift to Dale. (5/96, AR, #7-16, amended, 6204-6213)

PROBLEM 30-7 (5 to 10 minutes)

A CPA sole practitioner has tax preparers' responsibilities when preparing tax returns for clients.

ITEMS 1 THROUGH 9 each represent an independent factual situation in which a CPA sole practitioner has prepared and signed the taxpayer's income tax return. For each item, select from the following list the correct response regarding the tax preparer's responsibilities. A response may be selected once, more than once, or not at all.

Selections
P. The tax preparer's action constitutes an act of tax preparer misconduct subject to the Internal Revenue Code penalty.
E. The Internal Revenue Service will examine the facts and circumstances to determine whether the reasonable cause exception applies; the good faith exception applies; or both exceptions apply.
N. The tax preparer's action does not constitute an act of tax preparer misconduct.

1. The tax preparer disclosed taxpayer income tax return information under an order from a state court, without the taxpayer's consent.

2. The tax preparer relied on the advice of an advisory preparer to calculate the taxpayer's tax liability. The tax preparer believed that the advisory preparer was competent and that the advice was reasonable. Based on the advice, the taxpayer had understated income tax liability.

3. The tax preparer did not charge a separate fee for the tax return preparation and paid the taxpayer the refund shown on the tax return less a discount. The tax preparer negotiated the actual refund check for the tax preparer's own account after receiving power of attorney from the taxpayer.

4. The tax preparer relied on information provided by the taxpayer regarding deductible travel expenses. The tax preparer believed that the taxpayer's information was correct but inquired about the existence of the travel expense records. The tax preparer was satisfied by the taxpayer's representations that the taxpayer had adequate records for the deduction. Based on this information, the income tax liability was understated.

5. The taxpayer provided the tax preparer with a detailed check register to compute business expenses. The tax preparer knowingly overstated the expenses on the income tax return.

6. The tax preparer disclosed taxpayer income tax return information during a quality review conducted by CPAs. The tax preparer maintained a record of the review.

7. The tax preparer relied on incorrect instructions on an IRS tax form that were contrary to the regulations. The tax preparer was not aware of the regulations nor the IRS announcement pointing out the error. The understatement was immaterial as a result of the isolated error.

8. The tax preparer used income tax return information without the taxpayer's consent to solicit additional business.

9. The tax preparer knowingly deducted the expenses of the taxpayer's personal domestic help as wages paid in the taxpayer's business on the taxpayer's income tax return.

(11/96, AR, #2, 6308-6316)

SOLUTION 30-1 MULTIPLE CHOICE ANSWERS

PARTNERSHIP INCOME

1.   (d)   Section 707(c) provides that payments to a partner for services or the use of capital made without regard to the partnership's income shall be considered as payments made to one who is not a partner for purposes of §162(a), which allows a deduction for all ordinary and necessary business expenses. Charitable contributions and short term capital losses must be separately stated for deduction on the partner's return. There has not been any $100 exclusion for dividends in many years.

2.   (b)   Section 703(b) provides that any election affecting the taxable income of a partnership shall be made by the partnership with three noted exceptions. None of the exceptions applies to the depreciation method.

3.   (d)   Section 709(b)(1) allows a partnership to elect to amortize organization costs over a period of not less than 60 months beginning with the month the partnership begins business. Legal fees to prepare the partnership agreement are considered an organization cost eligible for amortization under Reg. §1.709-2(a). Reg. §1.709-2(b) specifically disallows accounting fees to prepare the representations in offering materials as an organization cost eligible for amortization. These costs must be capitalized and not amortized. As there are only 11 months from February 1 to the end of the calendar year, only 11 months worth of amortization is allowed. Only the filing fees are organizational costs. [(($3,600 / 60) x 11 = $660]

CONTRIBUTIONS

4.   (d)   Section 721(a) provides that no gain or loss is recognized by the partnership or by any partner on the contribution of property to the partnership in exchange for a partnership interest. The net debt relief is less than the adjusted basis of the property.

5.   (c)   Kelly has ordinary gross income from services rendered in an amount equal to the fair value of the property received as compensation under §61 and §83. Regulation §1.61-2(d)(1) states"...if services are paid for in property, the fair market value of the property taken in payment must be included in income as compensation." Thus, Kelly has $10,000 gross income ($100,000 x 10%). Although the partnership interest obtained will be a capital asset, the income for services performed to obtain such partnership interest is ordinary under §64.

6.   (c)   A partner's holding period for a partnership interest acquired through contribution of a *capital asset*, or an asset used in his trade or business, includes the holding period for the contributed property. The holding period begins on the date the partnership interest is acquired only if the contributed property is *not* a capital asset or was not used in the partner's trade or business.

7.   (c)   Curry's initial basis in the partnership interest is Curry's adjusted basis in the land less the debt assumed by the partnership plus Curry's portion of the debt assumed by the partnership. [$30,000 – $12,000 + $6,000 = $24,000]

8.   (a)   Jones' initial basis in the partnership interest is Jones' adjusted basis in the cash plus Jones' portion of the debt assumed by the partnership. [$45,000 + $6,000 = $51,000]

PARTNER'S INCOME

9.   (b)   Generally, a guaranteed payment to a partner is treated as if the partner were unrelated, and thus is a deduction from partnership income and ordinary income to the partner. As there is no indication that the payment was credited to Peters' ownership account as opposed to being paid outright, Peters' partnership basis doesn't increase.

10.   (a)   Because Marks and Sparks share profits and losses equally, Marks is allocated $21,000 of the ordinary loss (i.e., 50% of $42,000). Section 704(d) provides that a partner's distributive share of partnership loss is allowed only to the extent of the adjusted basis in that partner's partnership interest. Any loss disallowed under §704(d) will be allowed as a deduction at the end of the first succeeding taxable year to the extent that the partner's adjusted basis at the end of such year exceeds zero [Reg. §1.704-1(d)(1)]. Thus, Marks should deduct an ordinary loss of $18,000. The remaining $3,000 is carried forward and may be deducted in succeeding tax years.

11.   (c)   A partner's loss deduction generally cannot exceed the amount "at risk" in the activity at the end of the year. Once the amount of loss that is unrestricted by the basis limitation and at risk rules is determined, pass through losses may be further restricted by the passive activity rules. The partnership provides all partners with a breakdown of income, credit and deduction items from each of its passive activities, because passive activity losses can generally only offset passive activity income.

12. (c) Guaranteed payments from a partnership for services rendered are income from self-employment. Ordinary income received from an S corporation was earned by the S corp, not Freeman, and retains its character as it passes through to the taxpayer.

13. (b) ($45,000 − $7,500) x 0.50 = $18,750.

ADJUSTED BASIS

14. (c) As Miles' guaranteed payment was paid, it did not increase Miles' basis. ($45,000 − 7,500) x 0.50 + $200,000 = $218,750

15. (c) Dean's basis in her/his partnership interest is increased by her/his distributive share of the partnership's ordinary income. Her/his basis in the partnership interest is increased by her/his distributive share of the partnership's tax-exempt income. Her/his basis in the partnership interest is reduced, but not below zero, by cash distributions.

Basis, January 1 distributions	$20,000
Share of municipal bond interest income ($12,000 x 25%)	3,000
Share of ordinary income ($40,000 x 25%)	10,000
Basis before distribution	$33,000
Less: Distribution	(8,000)
Basis, December 31	$25,000

16. (a) The partner's share of an increase in partnership liabilities is treated as a contribution of money from the partner to the partnership under §752(a). The partner then gets to increase her/his basis in the partnership for this deemed contribution of money under §722.

17. (a) Smith's share of the partnership's liability is $16,000 ($40,000 x 40%). An increase in a partner's share of the partnership's liabilities is treated as a contribution of money by the partner to the partnership. This deemed contribution of money increases the partner's basis in the partnership interest under §722. Thus, Macro's liability increases Smith's basis in the partnership interest by $16,000.

18. (c) Under §752(a), a partner's share of the debts of the partnership is treated as a contribution of money to the partnership for which the partner obtains basis under §722. Under §752(b), a decrease in a partner's share of the debts of the partnership is treated as a distribution of money from the partnership to the partner. This deemed distribution reduces the partner's basis in her/his partnership interest under §733.

Paul's share of debts, Jan. 1 ($150,000 x 25%)	$ 37,500
Paul's share of debts, Dec. 31 ($100,000 x 20%)	(20,000)
Decrease in basis in Paul's partnership interest	$ 17,500

NON-LIQUIDATING DISTRIBUTION

19. (b) The basis of property distributed to a partner is generally its adjusted basis to the partnership immediately before the distribution. Section 732(a)(2) limits the adjusted basis to the adjusted basis in the partner's interest in the partnership reduced by any money distributed in the same transaction. ($18,000 − $10,000 = $8,000)

20. (d) Section 731(a)(1) provides that a partner does not recognize gain on receiving a distribution from a partnership except to the extent that any money distributed exceeds the adjusted basis of her/his partnership interest immediately before the distribution. Section 731(a)(2) provides that a partner does not recognize loss on a distribution of property from the partnership except in certain liquidating distributions. Section 731(b) also provides that the partnership does not recognize any gain or loss on a distribution to a partner. Since the distribution was a non-liquidating distribution, Stone recognizes no gain or loss.

21. (a) Section 731(a)(1) provides that no gain shall be recognized on a distribution from a partnership to a partner except to the extent that any money distributed exceeds the adjusted basis of such partner's interest in the partnership. The adjusted basis in Jody's partnership interest was $50,000. The money distributed of $20,000 is less than the adjusted basis in Jody's partnership interest.

22. (b) Section 733 provides that the adjusted basis in the partnership interest shall be reduced by the amount of money distributed. Thus, Jody's adjusted basis in the partnership interest is reduced by $20,000 to $30,000. Section 732(a)(1) provides that the adjusted basis of property distributed in a current distribution to a partner is generally equal to the adjusted basis of the property in the hands of the partnership. This would give Jody a $40,000 basis in the property. However, §732(a)(2) provides a limitation on this amount. The limit is the adjusted basis of the partnership interest. Thus, Jody's adjusted basis in the partnership of $30,000 is less than the $40,000 adjusted basis of the property in the hands of the partnership. Therefore, Jody's basis in the property is $30,000. Jody's basis in the partnership interest is reduced by this $30,000 under §733. This leaves Jody with a zero basis in the partnership interest.

LIQUIDATING DISTRIBUTION

23. (c) Section 732(b) provides that the adjusted basis of property received by a partner in complete liquidation of the partner's interest in the

partnership shall be an amount equal to the partner's adjusted basis in the partnership reduced by any money distributed in the same transaction ($180,000 – $100,000).

PARTNERS' TRANSACTION WITH PARTNERSHIP

24.   (a)   Section 707(c) states that guaranteed payments are payments to a partner for services or for the use of capital to the extent determined without regard to the income of the partnership. The $5,000 monthly salary is guaranteed because it is not determined by any reference to the income of the partnership. The payment of 25% of the partnership's profits is not a guaranteed payment because it is determined by taking into account the income of the partnership.

25.   (a)   If a partner enters into a sale of an asset with such partnership and if the partner owns *more* than 50% of the partnership, no loss is recognized. Since Lisa owns *only* 50% of the partnership, the entire loss on the sale of the stock (i.e., $8,000 – $3,000) is recognized by Lisa as a long-term capital loss.

26.   (a)   While a partner may engage in a transaction with her/his partnership in a capacity other than as a member of such partnership [§707(a)], if the partner owns, directly or indirectly, more than 50% of the capital or profits interests in such partnership, then the gain upon the sale or exchange of property between them which, in the hands of the *transferee*, is not a capital asset as defined in §1221, shall be considered as ordinary income [§707(b)]. Since Kaye owned 85% of the capital and profits interest of the partnership, her $4,000 (i.e., $6,000 – $2,000) gain is characterized as *ordinary income*.

TERMINATION

27.   (a)   Since more than 50% ownership of the prior partnership continues as the Abel & Benz Partnership, that partnership is considered to be a continuation of Partnership Abel, Benz, Clark & Day. No tax is generally imposed on a person who contributes property to a partnership. A partnership does not need IRS approval to separate a business nor does a partnership have to file its formal dissolution on a prescribed form with the IRS.

28.   (c)   Except for electing large partnerships, a partnership terminates if no part of its business is carried on within a 12-month period, or if within a 12-month period, 50% or more of the total interest in the partnership are sold [IRC §708(b)].

29.   (c)   Regulations §1.708-1(b)(1)(iv) provides that if a partnership is terminated by a sale or exchange of an interest that (1) the partnership is deemed to have distributed its properties to the purchaser and the remaining partners in proportion to their respective interests in the partnership properties and (2) immediately thereafter, the purchaser and the other remaining partners are deemed to contribute such properties to the partnership.

TAXABLE YEAR

30.   (b)   Code §444 requires a partnership to use a calendar year or a year that does not create a deferral period which exceeds three months. A partnership formed during the year must elect to have a taxable year that ends in September, October, November, or December. A partnership can elect to have a taxable year other than a required taxable year as long as the deferral period does not exceed three months. The only form which must be filed with the IRS to adopt its tax year is Form 1065, U.S. Partnership Return of Income, which is due three and a half months after the end of its tax year.

TRANSFER OF PARTNERSHIP INTEREST

31.   (d)   The amount realized by Clark is equal to the cash and the debt relief under §1001(b). The $55,000 amount realized less the $40,000 adjusted basis equals a gain realized of $15,000 under §1001(a). The sale of a partnership interest is considered the sale of a capital asset under §741 except as provided in §751 for unrealized receivables and substantially appreciated inventory ("hot assets"). There were no hot assets in this partnership.

32.   (a)   The amount which a partner realizes on the sale of a partnership interest includes any cash received, plus any partnership liabilities which are assumed by the buyer. The total amount realized by Carr on the sale of his partnership interest is $174,000 (cash plus partnership liabilities).

33.   (d)   If a partner sells her/his partnership interest and the partnership has unrealized receivables which have not been recognized as income by the partnership, then the partner has to recognize the proceeds which s/he received for the unrealized receivables as ordinary income. Since Carr's share of the partnership's unrealized receivables is $140,000 (i.e., $420,000 ÷ 3), he has to recognize this amount as ordinary income.

FIDUCIARY INCOME

34. (c)   A "simple" trust is one which provides that all of its trust accounting income is required to be distributed currently and does not provide that any amounts are to be paid, permanently set aside, or used for charitable purposes. Any nonexempt trust which is not "simple" is "complex." Only answer (c) correctly describes the statutory characteristics of a complex trust. Answers (a), (b), and (d) contain elements common to both simple and complex trusts.

35. (a)   The standard deduction is not available to estates, trusts, corporations, or partnerships. Estates and trusts may have a personal exemption.

36. (a)   Estates have the option of choosing a calendar year or a fiscal year based on the date of the decedent's death. Most trusts established after 1986 must use a calendar year.

37. (c)   An executor of a decedent's estate that has only U.S. citizens as beneficiaries is required to file a fiduciary income tax return if the estate's gross income for the year is $600 or more.

38. (b)   Estates are required to make estimated tax payments with respect to any taxable year ending two or more years after the date of the decedent's death.

39. (c)   The lifetime income interest and the remainder interest are both incomplete transfers, as Carlt retained the power to revoke them. Thus, the assets remain Carlt's, and Carlt is taxed on the income from the assets. (Same answer in 2002.)

40. (c)   Section 652(a) provides that beneficiaries of estates and trusts must include in their gross income the amount of income required to be distributed to them. However, the income to be included may not exceed the distributable net income (DNI) of the estate or trust. Section 643(a) defines DNI as the taxable income of the estate or trust computed with certain modifications. Section 643(a)(2) provides that the estate may not take an exemption deduction in computing DNI. Thus, the DNI is $6,000 ($40,000 – $34,000). Because this amount is less than the $15,000 distributed, the beneficiary must include $6,000 in gross income from the estate under §61(a)(15).

41. (b)   Capital gains and losses are normally excluded from DNI, as they are usually allocated to principal rather than income. Distribution on money or property to a beneficiary is removed from DNI for the current year.

42. (b)   Section 6072(a) states that returns required to be filed by §6012 are to be filed on or before the 15th day of April following the close of the taxable year if the taxpayer is a calendar year taxpayer. Section 7503 provides that if the last day for filing is on a Saturday, Sunday, or legal holiday, the return will be considered filed in a timely manner if it is filed by the succeeding day after the due date that is not a Saturday, Sunday, or legal holiday.

43. (c)   The charitable contribution deduction on an estate's fiduciary income tax return is allowable only if the charitable bequest is specified by a provision in the decedent's will. Generally speaking, a deduction does not materialize when an individual dies intestate (without a will). Estates are not subject to a limitation on the extent of their deductible charitable contributions for the year (e.g., to a percentage of taxable or AGI).

DECEDENT'S INCOME

44. (a)   Income in respect to a cash basis decedent is income that has been earned by the decedent up to the point of death, but is not reported on the final income tax return because it has not been received. It will be included in the estate tax return at its fair market value.

45. (d)   As a cash basis taxpayer, Rose would not recognize the $10,000 fee until she actually or constructively received it. Because this receipt occurs after Rose's death, the $10,000 is called "income in respect of the decedent" (IRD). IRD must be reported on *both* the estate's fiduciary income tax return under §691(a), and the estate tax return under §2033.

ESTATE TAX

46. (d)   The amount of gift tax paid on post-1976 gifts is subtracted to arrive at the gross estate tax. Once the amount of gross estate tax is determined, the unified credit is taken to go from the gross estate tax to the net estate tax due.

47. (d)   In 2002, the effect of the unified credit is to exempt up to $1,000,000 of a decedent's estate from estate taxation.

48. (c)   If the executor elects and the assets were not sold or distributed within 6 months after the date of the decedent's death, the assets in the decedent's gross estate are to be valued 6 months after the date of the decedent's death.

49. (c)   The gross estate is reduced by non-discretionary deductions to arrive at the adjusted gross estate, which is further reduced by

discretionary deductions to obtain the taxable estate. Funeral expenses are non-discretionary deductions. Charitable deductions are discretionary deductions.

50. (a) The decedent's fractional share of property is included in the gross estate [Reg. §20.20401(a)(1)]. In this case, two individuals are involved; therefore 50% of the value of property owned is included. The question of who furnished the original consideration is not considered.

51. (a) If an estate tax return is required, then it must be filed nine months after the date of the decedent's death. Six months after the date of the decedent's death is the time frame for the "alternate valuation date" of the gross estate.

52. (d) All property owned by the decedent at the time of death is included in the gross estate [§2033]. No distinction is made between personal effects and those belonging to a business interest. Wald's gross estate includes the personal items and jewelry as well as the jointly held land.

53. (d) Proceeds of insurance on the life of the decedent, payable to the executor as the estate's representative are always includible in the gross estate under §2042(1).

54. (b) The marital deduction is allowed for property included in the deceased spouse's gross estate that passes or has passed to the surviving spouse. The marital deduction is unlimited in amount.

GENERATION SKIPPING TAX

55. (c) The generation-skipping transfer tax is a separate tax imposed in addition to the gift tax and the estate tax. The generation-skipping transfer tax applies to transfers to beneficiaries who are more than one generation *below* the transferor's generation.

GIFT TAX

56. (c) The election to treat a gift to a third party as made equally by husband and wife is allowed by §2513. In 2002, §2503(b) allows a $11,000 exclusion from taxable gifts for each gift to each donee of a present interest in property. Steve and Kay are each considered as having made a $15,000 ($30,000 / 2) gift for which each is entitled to this $11,000 exclusion. Thus, Steve and Kay each have made a taxable gift of $4,000 ($15,000 − $11,000). Thus, their total taxable gifts are $8,000 ($4,000 + $4,000) before the unified credit.

57. (c) Under the unified transfer tax system, one transfer tax schedule is used to compute the gift tax as well as the estate tax. Transfers at death and lifetime taxable gifts are taxed on a cumulative basis.

58. (d) No part of the value of a gift of *future interest* may be excluded in determining the total amount of taxable gifts. However, no part of a transfer for the benefit of a minor will be considered a gift of future interest *if:* (1) the property *and* its income may be expended by or for the benefit of the minor before he reaches 21; and (2) any portion of the property and its income not so expended will pass to the minor upon reaching 21, or will go either to his estate or as he may appoint under the general powers of appointment. Because the property (the bond) is to be distributed to the donor or successor-in-interest instead of the minor upon his reaching the age of 21, the transfer to the trust is considered a gift of future interest. Therefore, a gift tax exclusion is not permitted.

59. (b) Section 2503(b) provides for an exclusion from taxable gifts of $11,000 per donee per year. Section 2503(e)(2)(B) provides that all of the gift is excluded from taxable gifts if the gift was made on behalf of an individual to any person who provides medical care. Sayers is not entitled to exclude all of the gift because the amount was paid directly to Johnson and not to a person who provided Johnson with medical care. Sayers could exclude $22,000 if s/he were married and Sayers and her/his spouse consented under §2513 to have the gift treated as made one half by each. However, Sayers is single and therefore is entitled to only the $11,000 annual exclusion under §2503(b) for 2002.

60. (b) Pursuant to §6075(b), when a gift tax return is due, it must be filed on or before April 15 following the year of gift, regardless of whether the taxpayer uses a calendar year or a fiscal year, unless an extension of time for filing is requested. (Also see the explanation to #42.)

61. (b) Section 2523 indicates that where a donor transfers by gift an interest in property to his spouse, a deduction will be allowed in computing taxable gifts for the calendar year equal to the amount of the gift. The ring was given prior to the marriage, thus only the $75,000 is a marital deduction.

EXEMPT ORGANIZATIONS

62. (a) Section 501(c)(3) lists a number of examples of public service charities that are exempt from tax under §501(a). Regulations §1.501(c)(3)-1(b)(1) provides that such an exempt organization must provide a paragraph in its articles of organization that limits its purposes to one or more exempt

purposes. Section 6033(a)(1) requires exempt organizations to file annual returns. Section 6033(a)(2) provides for a number of exceptions to the requirement that exempt organizations file an annual return. In any case, there is no requirement that the articles of organization include any provision stating that a return should be filed with the IRS.

63. (c) In general, §6033(a)(1) requires every exempt organization to file an annual return. However, §6033(a)(2)(A) exempts churches, integrated auxiliaries of churches, and any organization other than a private foundation that normally has gross receipts of not more than $5,000 a year.

64. (a) Under §507(b)(1) the private foundation status of an exempt organization will terminate if it becomes a public charity by distributing all of its net assets to one or more of the various public charities listed in §170(b)(1)(A). Each of these organizations must have been in existence for at least 60 calendar months immediately preceding the distribution.

65. (d) Regulation §1.501(a)-1(a)(2) requires an organization other than an employees' trust described in §401(a) to file an application form with the District Director requesting exempt status.

66. (d) To qualify for exemption from tax, an organization must not engage in prohibited transactions, which include any attempts to carry on propaganda or otherwise attempt to influence legislation.

67. (b) Conducting burial services that maintain members' beliefs is consistent with a religious organization's tax-exempt status. Conducting retreats for businesses is generally not a related activity for a religious organization.

UBTI

68. (a) Unless the exempt organization is taxable as a trust, the tax it must pay on income which is not related to its exempt purpose is computed at regular corporate tax rates.

69. (b) Generally an exempt organization is subject to the tax on unrelated business income. There is an exception, which states that the proceeds from bingo games conducted by most exempt organizations and political organizations are not unrelated business income if the games are conducted in accordance with local law and do not compete with profit-making businesses. Help meets this exception, and therefore the entire $15,000 is exempt from the tax on unrelated business income.

70. (b) If a tax-exempt organization generates unrelated business income, it must make estimated tax payments. These payments are governed by the same rules which govern corporate estimated tax payments.

71. (c) Under §513(a)(1), if an exempt organization engages in an activity and all the work is performed by unpaid volunteers, then the activity is not considered an unrelated trade or business.

72. (b) Section 511(a) imposes a tax on the unrelated business taxable income of exempt organizations. Section 512(a)(1) states that the unrelated business income is the gross income derived by an organization from any unrelated trade or business less allowable deductions directly connected with the trade or business and taking into account the modifications specified in §512(b). One of these modifications is that a specific deduction of $1,000 is allowed. Section 501(b) provides that an exempt organization may be subject to tax on its unrelated business income, but is still considered as an organization exempt from income tax. Section 512(a)(1) provides that the unrelated business must be regularly carried on by the exempt organization in order to be subject to the tax on unrelated business income. Thus, if the business activity is intermittent and carried on only once a year, no tax on unrelated business income would be imposed. Under §513(c), when an activity that has a profit motive constitutes an unrelated business, it will not lose its status as such merely because it does not result in profit.

PREPARER RESPONSIBILITIES

73. (b) The tax return preparer must keep a copy of the return or a list of taxpayer names, identification numbers, and tax years for 3 years following the close of the return period.

74. (b) A preparer properly discloses information without the taxpayer's consent under a court order, for a peer review, for processing purposes, or under an order from a state agency that registers tax return preparers. A preparer may be liable for a penalty if the return reflects an understatement of tax liability based on a position that does not have a realistic chance of being sustained on its merits.

75. (c) A preparer generally may rely in good faith without verification upon information furnished by a taxpayer. The preparer is not required to audit, examine, or review the taxpayer's records or operations. The preparer must make reasonable inquiries if the furnished information appears to be incorrect or incomplete.

SOLUTION 30-2 ADDITIONAL MULTIPLE CHOICE ANSWERS

PARTNERSHIPS

76. (b) Barker obtains an increase in basis for the contribution of the cash and building under §722. Under §752(b) the partnership's assumption of the mortgage is a reduction in Barker's debt that is treated as a distribution of money from the partnership to Barker, reducing Barker's basis under §733. As a 50% partner, Barker's share of the partnership's mortgage debt has increased by $5,000 ($10,000 x 50%). This increase in Barker's share of the partnership's debt is treated as a contribution under §752(a). This deemed contribution increases Barker's basis under §722.

Cash Contributed	$ 20,000
Adjusted Basis of Building Contributed	26,000
Increase in Share of Partnership's Debt	5,000
Less: Decrease in Personal Debt	(10,000)
Barker's Basis in Partnership Interest	$ 41,000

77. (c) Gross income can be received in different forms, such as money, property, or services. The fair market value of property or services received must be included in gross income. Thus, Hoff must include the fair market value of the surveying equipment in gross income. Additionally, where a partnership interest is received in exchange for the contribution of services, the contributing partner includes in ordinary income an amount equal to the excess of fair market value of the partnership interest received for the services performed less the amount paid for the partnership interest. Thus, the amount included in gross income for services rendered equals the cash received, the fair market value of the partnership interest, and the surveying equipment (i.e., $15,000 + $10,000 + $7,000).

78. (a) Under §§ 722 and 705(a) Strom's basis in her/his partnership interest is increased by the adjusted basis of property contributed. Under §752(a), an increase in a partner's share of the debts of the partnership is considered as a contribution of money to the partnership for which the partner receives an increase in the basis of her/his partnership interest. Strom's share of the partnership's debts increased by $6,000 ($24,000 x 25%). However, Strom was relieved of the $24,000 mortgage as a personal debt. Section 752(b) provides that a decrease in a partner's personal liabilities because the partnership assumed such liabilities is treated as a distribution of money from the partnership to the partner. Section 752(c) provides that to the extent of the property's fair market value a liability to which property is subject shall be considered as a liability of the owner. The $24,000 deemed cash distribution reduces the partner's basis in her/his partnership interest below zero. Thus, Strom's basis in her/his partnership interest is reduced to zero. The excess of the deemed cash distribution over the partner's adjusted basis in her/his partnership interest is treated as a $2,000 gain on the sale of the partnership interest under §731(a)(1). The following computation summarizes the effects on Strom's basis in her/his Ace Partnership interest:

Contribution of property	$ 16,000
Increase in share of partnership debts ($24,000 x 25%)	6,000
Basis before deemed cash distribution	$ 22,000
Reduction in personal debts (limited to $22,000)	(22,000)
Strom's basis in Ace Partnership	$ 0

79. (c) Section 707(c) provides that payments made to a partner for services or the use of capital determined without reference to the income of the partnership are to be considered as made to a person that is not a member of the partnership only for the purposes of (1) §61(a) relating to gross income and (2) §162(a) relating to the deductibility of ordinary and necessary business expenses, subject to the requirements of §263 to capitalize costs that are properly chargeable to a capital account. Thus, the guaranteed payments are includible as ordinary gross income on the recipient partners' respective income tax returns. The guaranteed payments are also deductible by the partnership as an ordinary and necessary business expense.

80. (b) The basis of property (other than money) distributed to a partner in a liquidating distribution is equal to the adjusted basis of the partner's interest in the partnership, *reduced* by any cash received by the partner in the liquidation. The partnership's adjusted basis in the property becomes the partner's basis in a *non-liquidating* distribution. It is a *shareholder* that takes the fair market value of property distributed by a *corporation* as her/his basis in the distributed property.

81. (b) Section 708(b)(1) provides that a partnership is considered as terminated if within a 12-month period there is a sale or exchange of 50% or more of the total interest in partnership capital and profits. Poe sold a 30% interest on February 4, and Dean sold his 25% interest on December 20. Thus, on December 20, 55% of the interest in the partnership's capital and profits had been sold within a 12-month period.

82. (d) If a partner acquires a partnership interest from another partner, the basis of the acquired interest is equal to the sum of the cash and the fair market value of the other consideration paid for the interest. An assumption of partnership liabilities is considered a contribution of money by the partner and increases the basis of a partner's interest. The partnership's assumption of a partner's liabilities is considered a distribution of money from the partnership resulting in a decrease in the basis of a partner's interest.

ESTATES & TRUSTS

83. (c)   As long as a distribution to a beneficiary does not exceed the distributable net income of the estate, the estate is allowed a deduction for the amount of the distribution that is subject to income tax on the beneficiary's return. Thus, the estate may claim a distribution deduction of $9,000 (i.e., $9,000 < $15,000) on its fiduciary income tax return.

84. (d)   For taxable years after 1986, most trusts must adopt a calendar year. Only a trust which qualifies as a §501(a) tax-exempt organization or a charitable trust described in §4947(a) can elect to use a fiscal year. An estate has the option of choosing a fiscal or calendar year.

85. (c)   Ordinary and necessary administration expenses, including commissions and other selling expenses, can *either* be taken as a deduction in computing the estate tax (Form 706) *or* the fiduciary income tax return (Form 1041). Administration expenses cannot be taken on *both* Form 706 and Form 1041. In order for administration expenses to be deducted for income tax purposes the executor must waive the right to take the deduction for estate tax purposes and file a statement that the amount involved has not already been allowed as a deduction for estate tax purposes.

86. (c)   Under §652(a) the income required to be distributed currently from an estate or trust is included in the gross income of the beneficiaries to whom the income is required to be distributed. However, §652(a) limits the amount to be included in the gross income of the beneficiary to the beneficiary's share of distributable net income.

87. (a)   An estate tax return is required to be filed in 2002 for any estate where the value at the date of death exceeds $1,000,000 (§6018). Since End's estate and Law's estate each are worth less than $1,000,000 (i.e., $750,000 for End and $500,000 for Law), no estate tax return is required to be filed for either of their estates. End's estate is valued at $750,000 because any taxable gifts that are made during a decedent's lifetime are added back to the estate in determining if an estate tax return has to be filed by the executor of the estate.

88. (c)   Certain qualified transfers are excluded when determining total taxable gifts. Qualified transfers include amounts paid on the behalf of another individual (regardless of their relationship to the donor) for tuition at an accredited educational institution or for medical care. The exclusion for tuition does not include payment for dormitory fees, supplies, or textbooks.

89. (d)   The money in a sinking fund or trust is an asset of the corporation, even if a trustee is authorized to invest and reinvest the trust funds. Any income (including capital gains) generated from the sinking fund assets, is included in the gross income of the corporation (Reg. §1.61-13). Therefore, both the interest income of $60,000 and the $8,000 of net long-term capital gains are taxable to the corporation.

90. (d)   The alternative valuation date can be used only to value a decedent's estate if the election will decrease the value of the estate and if it will reduce any estate tax liability (§2032). The election can be used only if the election will decrease the value of the estate. The election once made is irrevocable and cannot be changed by filing an amended return. The election applies only to the gross estate and not to the net value of the estate (i.e., after liabilities and allowable deductions).

91. (a)   The expenses of administering an estate are deductible under §2053(a)(2). The state inheritance or estate tax is not deductible from a decedent's gross estate. Rather, §2011 provides for a credit against the federal estate tax for any state inheritance or estate tax.

92. (b)   Section 2503(b) allows the first $11,000 of a gift to any person to be excluded from the total amount of gifts made during 2002. Therefore, Jan may exclude up to $11,000 on each of the gifts made to Jones and Craig, and all of the $5,000 made to Kande. To meet the tuition exclusion criteria, a donor must directly pay the institution.

EXEMPT ORGANIZATIONS

93. (d)   Regulations §1.513-1(d)(4)(ii) provides specifically that in the case of a §501(c)(3) organization engaged in a program of rehabilitation of handicapped persons, income from the sale of articles made by such handicapped persons as part of their rehabilitation is not gross income from an unrelated business. Section 513(a)(1) and Regulations §1.513-1(e)(1) provide that unrelated business income does not include income from any trade or business in which substantially all the work is performed for the organization without compensation.

The grocery store's employees are handicapped persons working as a part of their therapeutic program. Hence, they would not be compensated. Thus, the income from each activity is not unrelated business income.

94. (d) Corporations organized and operated for religious, charitable, scientific, literary, and educational purposes are exempt from tax under §501(c)(3). However, exempt corporations are taxed on their unrelated business income (UBI). To be UBI, the income must be from a continuous trade or business activity that is substantially unrelated to the exempt purpose or function of the organization. Providing low cost insurance coverage to other organizations that serve a charitable purpose is substantially related to Carmen's own charitable function, and thus, is not an activity producing UBI.

95. (b) Exempt organizations that are required to file annual information returns must disclose the total contributions during the year, and the names and addresses of all substantial contributors. The exempt status of an organization may be retroactively revoked. Reasonable compensation is allowed. To qualify for exemption, the organization must file a written application with the IRS (even when no official forms are provided) and must not engage in prohibited transactions.

96. (a) Pursuant to Regulation §1.6012-2(e), exempt organizations having at least $1,000 of unrelated business income must file an income tax return (Form 990-T). The filing of Form 990-T does *not* relieve the organization from having to file a separate annual information return (Form 990) under other code provisions.

97. (a) Under §511, unless an organization is taxable as a trust, its unrelated business taxable income is subject to the regular corporate income tax rates.

PREPARER RESPONSIBILITIES

98. (a) Section 6713 authorizes a civil penalty and §7216 authorizes a criminal penalty for the unauthorized disclosure by a tax preparer of information furnished to the preparer by a taxpayer. Regulation §301.7216-2(o) allow disclosure for the purpose of a quality or peer review. Regulation §301.7216-2(c) allows disclosure pursuant to an administrative order by a state agency that registers tax return preparers. Regulation §301.7216-2(h) allows disclosure for the purpose of processing the tax return, including electronic filing. Disclosure for the purpose of enabling a third party to solicit from the taxpayer is not an exception to the general prohibition.

99. (d) Section 7216(a) prohibits a tax preparer from disclosing or using, for a purpose unrelated to the preparation of the taxpayer's tax return, information provided to him in connection with the preparation of any such return. A preparer who is guilty of such a violation is subject to a penalty of $1,000 and/or 1 year imprisonment, plus the costs of prosecution. Section 6694(b) provides a penalty of $1,000 for any tax preparer who willfully attempts to understate any client's tax liability.

100. (d) Section 7216(a) prohibits a tax preparer from disclosing, for a purpose unrelated to the preparation of the taxpayer's tax return, information provided in connection with the preparation of such return.

PERFORMANCE BY SUBTOPICS

Each category below parallels a subtopic covered in Chapter 30. Record the number and percentage of questions you correctly answered in each subtopic area.

Partnership Income

Question #	Correct √
1	
2	
3	
# Questions	3

Correct _____
% Correct _____

Contributions

Question #	Correct √
4	
5	
6	
7	
8	
# Questions	5

Correct _____
% Correct _____

Partner's Income

Question #	Correct √
9	
10	
11	
12	
13	
# Questions	5

Correct _____
% Correct _____

Adjusted Basis

Question #	Correct √
14	
15	
16	
17	
18	
# Questions	5

Correct _____
% Correct _____

Nonliquidating Distribution

Question #	Correct √
19	
20	
21	
22	
# Questions	4

Correct _____
% Correct _____

Liquidating Distribution

Question #	Correct √
23	
# Questions	1

Correct _____
% Correct _____

Partners' Transactions With Partnership

Question #	Correct √
24	
25	
26	
# Questions	3

Correct _____
% Correct _____

Termination

Question #	Correct √
27	
28	
29	
# Questions	3

Correct _____
% Correct _____

Taxable Year

Question #	Correct √
30	
# Questions	1

Correct _____
% Correct _____

Transfer of Partnership Interest

Question #	Correct √
31	
32	
33	
# Questions	3

Correct _____
% Correct _____

Fiduciary Income

Question #	Correct √
34	
35	
36	
37	
38	
39	
40	
41	
42	
43	
# Questions	10

Correct _____
% Correct _____

Decedent's Income

Question #	Correct √
44	
45	
# Questions	2

Correct _____
% Correct _____

Estate Tax

Question #	Correct √
46	
47	
48	
49	
50	
51	
52	
53	
54	
# Questions	9

Correct _____
% Correct _____

Generation Skipping Tax

Question #	Correct √
55	
# Questions	1

Correct _____
% Correct _____

Gift Tax

Question #	Correct √
56	
57	
58	
59	
60	
61	
# Questions	6

Correct _____
% Correct _____

Exempt Organizations

Question #	Correct √
62	
63	
64	
65	
66	
67	
# Questions	6

Correct _____
% Correct _____

UBTI

Question #	Correct √
68	
69	
70	
71	
72	
# Questions	5

Correct _____
% Correct _____

Preparer Responsibilities

Question #	Correct √
73	
74	
75	
# Questions	3

Correct _____
% Correct _____

OTHER OBJECTIVE FORMAT QUESTION SOLUTIONS

SOLUTION 30-3 PARTNERSHIP TAXATION

1. $8,000

Brinks' basis in the partnership interest includes the $12,000 adjusted basis of property contributed in exchange for such interest under §722. The $5,000 mortgage assumed by the partnership on the land contributed by Brinks reduces Brinks' basis in the partnership interest by $5,000 under §733. Brinks' 20% share of the mortgage assumed by the partnership is a deemed contribution of money to the partnership by Brinks.

Adjusted basis of property transferred	$12,000
Less: Debt assumed by partnership	(5,000)
Add: Share of partnership's debt ($5,000 X 20%)	1,000
Initial basis in Dex partnership interest	$ 8,000

2. $25,500

Carson obtains a basis in the partnership interest equal to the $24,000 adjusted basis of the inventory contributed under §722. In addition, Carson is deemed to have contributed money to the partnership equal to Carson's share of the partnership's debts. Thus, Carson is deemed to have contributed $1,500 ($5,000 x 30%) in money for which Carson obtains additional basis. Therefore, Carson's initial basis in the Dex partnership interest is $25,500 ($24,000 + $1,500).

3. F   Section 733 states that a partner's basis in her/his partnership interest is to be reduced—but not below zero—by money distributed to the partner in a nonliquidating distribution.

4. T   Section 733 states that a partner's basis in her/his partnership interest is to be reduced—but not below zero—by a nonliquidating distribution of property other than money by the amount of the basis to such partner of distributed property, as determined under §732. Section 732(a)(1) provides that in the case of a nonliquidating distribution, the partner's basis in distributed property is the adjusted basis of the distributed property in the hands of the partnership. However, §732(a)(2) limits the partner's basis in the distributed property to the adjusted basis in the partnership interest.

5. T   Section 732(b) provides that in a liquidating distribution, the partner's basis in distributed property is equal to the adjusted basis in her/his partnership interest reduced by any money distributed in the same transaction.

6. F   Section 731(a)(1) provides that gain will not be recognized on a distribution to a partner, except to the extent that money distributed exceeds the adjusted basis of the partnership interest immediately before the distribution. If the adjusted basis of the property distributed exceeds the adjusted basis in the partnership interest, no gain is recognized, and the adjusted basis in the partnership interest becomes the partner's adjusted basis in the distributed property. The partner's adjusted basis in the partnership interest would then be reduced to zero.

7. T   The basis of inventory distributed to a partner in a nonliquidating distribution is the partnership's adjusted basis in the inventory, not to exceed the partner's adjusted basis in the partnership interest under §732(a). The partnership's adjusted basis in the inventory cannot exceed itself.

8. F   The other partners' basis in their respective partnership interests would be affected. The reduction in each partner's share of the partnership's liabilities would be treated as a distribution of money to them under §752(b). The deemed distribution of money would reduce their bases in their partnership interests under §733.

SOLUTION 30-4 ESTATE & GIFT TAX

1. N   Gifts made within 3 years of the donor's death usually are not included in the gross estate, unless the donor retained powers to amend or revoke the gift.

2. F   The gross estate includes the value of all property to the extent of the decedent's beneficial interest, including insurance proceeds in which the decedent retained a beneficial interest. (Note that the fact pattern states, "At his death, Remsen owned:…Life insurance policy….") The policy would not be included in the gross estate if an employer, for example, owned it without the employee having any beneficial interest.

3. F   The gross estate includes the value of all property to the extent of the decedent's beneficial interest, including marketable securities.

4. N   The annual per-donee exclusion of IRC §2503 is $11,000 for 2002. Gifts meeting this exclusion are not taxed. In addition, tuition or medical bills paid directly to an accredited institution or medical care provider is exempt from gift tax even if it exceeds the $11,000 limit.

5. F The gross estate includes the value of all property to the extent of the decedent's beneficial interest, including cash.

6. N The executor's fees to distribute property were deducted on the fiduciary tax return, so they may not be deducted on the estate tax return as well. (In order to be deducted for income tax purposes, the executor must waive the right to take the deduction for estate tax purposes.)

7. N There is no exemption or deduction for bequests to a son or daughter.

8. G There is an unlimited martial deduction for bequests to a spouse.

9. G Funeral expenses are a nondiscretionary deduction that reduces the gross estate.

10. E Medical expenses are either an itemized deduction on the decedent's income tax return or a nondiscretionary deduction that reduces the gross estate.

SOLUTION 30-5 GIFTS & TRANSFERS

1. N Section 2503(b) indicates that the first $11,000 of a gift to any person may be excluded from the total amount of gifts made during 2002.

2. P Section 2503(b) indicates that the first $11,000 of a gift to any person may be excluded from the total amount of gifts made during 2002. The gifts during the year that exceed this amount are taxable.

3. P Section 2503(b) indicates that the first $11,000 of a gift to any person may be excluded from the total amount of gifts made during the year.

4. F No part of the value of a gift of future interest may be excluded in determining the total amount of taxable gifts.

5. N Certain qualified transfers are excluded when determining total taxable gifts. Qualified transfers include amounts paid on the behalf of another individual for tuition at an accredited educational institution or for medical care. (The payment must be made directly to the institution or care provider.)

6. F No part of the value of a gift of future interest may be excluded in determining the total amount of taxable gifts.

7. P Section 2503(b) indicates that the first $11,000 of a gift to any person may be excluded from the total amount of gifts made during the year.

SOLUTION 30-6 GIFTS & TRANSFERS

1. N Because Cobb may revoke the income interest at any time, this is not a completed gift.

2. N Because Cobb may revoke the remainder interest at any time, this is not a completed gift.

3. F Because the income distribution will not start for 4 years, this is a gift of future interest.

4. P The gift cannot be revoked and is in control of the recipient.

5. P The gift cannot be revoked and is in control of the recipient.

6. F Because the income distribution will not start for 8 years, this is a gift of future interest.

7. P The gift cannot be revoked and is in control of the recipient.

8. P The gift cannot be revoked and is in control of the recipient.

9. N Because Murry may revoke the remainder interest at any time, this is not a completed gift.

10. C Transfers are subject to the generation-skipping tax if a taxpayer gives gifts to a grandchild. (For 2002, there is a $1,100,000 exemption to the generation-skipping tax.) Transfers are subject to the gift tax if a taxpayer gives a gift larger than $11,000 in 2002. Both these conditions are met.

SOLUTION 30-7 PREPARER RESPONSIBILITIES

1. N A court order is an appropriate exception to the confidentially provisions per §6103(d).

2. E A return preparer may be liable for a $250 penalty if the return reflects an understatement of tax liability based on a position that does not have a realistic change of being sustained. Other preparers are not generally considered substantial authorities. This situation would probably call for more investigation.

3. P A tax return preparer may not negotiate a client's refund check.

4. N Section 6604 imposes a penalty on any income tax return preparer who willfully attempts to understate a taxpayer's liability for tax. However, a preparer may generally rely in good faith without verification upon information furnished by the taxpayer.

5. P   Section 6604 imposes a penalty on any income tax return preparer who willfully attempts to understate a taxpayer's liability for tax.

6. N   Regulation §301.7216-20) allows disclosure for the purpose of a quality or peer review.

7. E   The preparer is responsible for preparing the return correctly, regardless of instructions on the form. The preparer may be liable for a $1,000 penalty if the understatement is willful or due to the preparer's intentional disregard of a rule or regulation.

8. P   Section 7216(a) prohibits a tax preparer from disclosing or using, for a purpose unrelated to the preparation of the taxpayer's return, information provide in connection with the preparation of a tax return.

9. P   Section 6694(b) provides a $1,000 penalty for any tax preparer who willfully attempts to understate any client's tax liability.

ARE HOT•SPOT™ VIDEO DESCRIPTIONS
(Taxation subjects only; subject to change without notice.)

CPA 3205 PROPERTY TAXATION
Robert Monette covers the adjusted basis of property (purchases, gifts, and inheritances), depreciation, depreciation recapture, amortization, capital assets, holding periods, calculation of gain or loss, like-kind exchanges, related party transactions, involuntary conversions, stock sales, wash sale losses, Section 1244, the sale of a principal residence, and personal losses.

CPA 3277 GENERAL TAXATION
Learn the federal income tax treatment of gross income inclusions and exclusions. This program illustrates computing tax liability, including the alternative minimum tax, the self-employment tax, and various business credits. The impacts of passive activity losses, statutes of limitations, and certain business expenses are explained.

CPA 3400 INDIVIDUAL TAXATION
This program covers dependents, exemptions, filing status, deductions allowed in computing adjusted gross income, standard deductions, itemized deductions, and personal tax credits. The tax benefit rule and when to itemize deductions as opposed to taking the standard deductions are examined.

CPA 3402 CORPORATE TAXATION
In this program, Robert Monette covers both C and S corporations. The tax effects of corporate formation, basis calculations, income, deductions, capital gains & losses, dividends, stock redemptions, and corporate reorganizations are clarified. Administrative items, selected tax forms, consolidated tax returns, accumulated earnings tax, and alternative minimum tax are also discussed.

CPA 3404 PARTNERSHIPS & OTHER TAX TOPICS
Learn the federal income tax treatment of partnerships, including related party transactions, contribution basis, holding periods, partnership liabilities, "pass-through" rules, non-liquidating and liquidating distributions, and calculation of capital accounts. Robert Monette highlights the differences between partnership accounting and tax treatment. The differences and similarities of simple and complex trusts are explained. The process of estate taxation is explored, including gross estate, deductions, and credits. Exempt organizations also are discussed.

Call a customer representative toll-free at 1 (800) 874-7877 for more details about videos.

APPENDIX A
PRACTICE EXAMINATION

Editor's Note: There is only one practice (or final) examination. Do not take this exam until you are ready for it. If you did not mark the answers on the diagnostic exam, it can be used as a second "final" exam.

PROBLEM 1 MULTIPLE CHOICE QUESTIONS (120 to 150 minutes)

1. For governmental fund types, which item is considered the primary measurement focus?
a. Income determination
b. Flows and balances of financial resources
c. Capital maintenance
d. Cash flows and balances

2. In which of the following fund types of a city government are revenues and expenditures recognized on the same basis of accounting as the general fund?
a. Nonexpendable trust
b. Internal service
c. Enterprise
d. Debt service

3. Kellick City has adopted GASB Statement No. 34, *Basic Financial Statements—and Management's Discussion and Analysis—for State and Local Governments*. It is inappropriate to record depreciation expense in the government-wide financial statements related to the assets in which of Kellick's funds?
a. Agency fund
b. Enterprise fund
c. General fund
d. Special revenue fund

4. Flax City has adopted GASB Statement No. 34, *Basic Financial Statements—and Management's Discussion and Analysis—for State and Local Governments*. Flax previously had reported a 20-year building rental agreement in the general fixed asset account group. Where should the lease liability be reported in Flax's financial statements?
a. General fund in the fund financial statements
b. General long-term debt account group in the fund financial statements
c. The governmental activities column of the government-wide financial statements
d. The governmental activities column of the government-wide and the general fund in the fund financial statements

5. Which of the following accounts is closed out at the end of the fiscal year?
a. Fund balance
b. Expenditures
c. Vouchers payable
d. Reserve for encumbrances

6. Fixed assets utilized in a city-owned utility are accounted for in which of the following?

	Enterprise fund	General fixed assets group of accounts
a.	No	No
b.	No	Yes
c.	Yes	No
d.	Yes	Yes

7. If a credit was made to the fund balance in the process of recording a budget for a governmental unit, it can be assumed that
a. Estimated revenues exceed appropriations.
b. Estimated expenses exceed actual revenues.
c. Actual expenses exceed estimated expenses.
d. Appropriations exceed estimated revenues.

8. Which of the following funds of a governmental unit integrates budgetary accounts into the accounting system?
a. Enterprise
b. Special revenue
c. Internal service
d. Nonexpendable trust

9. When fixed assets purchased from general fund revenues were received, the appropriate journal entry was made in the general fixed asset account group. What account, if any, should have been debited in the general fund?
a. No journal entry should have been made in the general fund.
b. Fixed assets
c. Expenditures
d. Due from general fixed asset account group

10. Property taxes levied in fiscal year 20X1 to finance the general fund budget of fiscal year 20X2 should be reported as general fund revenues in fiscal year 20X2
a. Regardless of the fiscal year in which collected.
b. For the amount collected in fiscal year 20X2 only.
c. For the amount collected before the end of fiscal year 20X2 only.
d. For the amount collected before the end of fiscal year 20X2 or shortly thereafter.

11. Pine City's year end is June 30. Pine levies property taxes in January of each year for the calendar year. One-half of the levy is due in May and one-half is due in October. Property tax revenue is budgeted for the period in which payment is due. The following information pertains to Pine's property taxes for the period from July 1, 20X1, to June 30, 20X2:

	Calendar year	
	20X1	20X2
Levy	$2,000,000	$2,400,000
Collected in:		
May	950,000	1,100,000
July	50,000	60,000
October	920,000	
December	80,000	

The $40,000 balance due for the May 2001 installments was expected to be collected in August 20X2. What amount should Pine recognize for property tax revenue for the year ended June 30, 20X2?
a. $2,160,000
b. $2,200,000
c. $2,360,000
d. $2,400,000

12. Which of the following accounts of a governmental unit is credited when supplies previously ordered are received?
a. Fund balance reserved for encumbrances
b. Encumbrances control
c. Expenditures control
d. Appropriations control

13. Japes City issued $1,000,000 general obligation bonds at 101 to build a new city hall. As part of the bond issue, the city also paid a $500 underwriter fee and $2,000 in debt issue costs. What amount should Japes City report as other financing sources?
a. $1,010,000
b. $1,008,000
c. $1,007,500
d. $1,000,000

14. The billings for transportation services provided to other governmental units are recorded by the internal service fund as
a. Interfund exchanges.
b. Intergovernmental transfers.
c. Transportation appropriations.
d. Operating revenues.

15. Gem City's internal service fund received a residual equity transfer of $50,000 cash from the general fund. This $50,000 transfer should be reported in Gem's internal service fund as a credit to
a. Revenues.
b. Other Financing Sources.
c. Accounts Payable.
d. Contributed Capital.

16. Hunt Community Development Agency (HCDA), a financially independent authority, provides loans to commercial businesses operating in Hunt County. This year, HCDA made loans totaling $500,000. How should HCDA classify the disbursements of loans on the cash flow statement?
a. Operating activities.
b. Noncapital financing activities.
c. Capital and related financing activities.
d. Investing activities.

17. Allan Rowe established a $100,000 endowment, the income from which is to be paid to Elm Hospital for general operating purposes. The present value of the income is estimated at $95,000. Elm does not control the endowment's principal. Rowe appointed West National Bank as trustee. What journal entry is required by Elm to record the establishment of the endowment?

		Debit	Credit
a.	Beneficiary Interest in Trust	$ 95,000	
	Nonexpendable Endowment:		
	Net Assets		$ 95,000
b.	Beneficiary Investment in Trust	$ 95,000	
	Permanently Restricted		
	Revenues: Contributions		$ 95,000
c.	Beneficiary Interest in Trust	$100,000	
	Permanently Restricted		
	Revenues: Contributions		$100,000
d.	Memorandum entry only	--	--

18. Midtown Church received a donation of marketable equity securities from a church member. The securities had appreciated in value after they were purchased by the donor, and they continued to appreciate through the end of Midtown's fiscal year. At what amount should Midtown report its investment in marketable equity securities in its year-end balance sheet?
a. Donor's cost
b. Market value at the date of receipt
c. Market value at the balance sheet date
d. Market value at either the date of receipt or the balance-sheet date

19. Plainfield Company manufactures Part G for use in its production cycle. The costs per unit for 10,000 units of Part G are as follows:

Direct materials	$ 3
Direct labor	15
Variable overhead	6
Fixed overhead	8
	$32

Verona Company has offered to sell Plainfield 10,000 units of Part G for $30 per unit. If Plainfield accepts Verona's offer, the released facilities could be used to save $45,000 in relevant costs in the manufacture of Part H. In addition, $5 per unit of the fixed overhead applied to Part G would be totally eliminated. What alternative is more desirable and by what amount is it more desirable?

	Alternative	Amount
a.	Manufacture	$10,000
b.	Manufacture	$15,000
c.	Buy	$35,000
d.	Buy	$65,000

20. During May, Roy Co. produced 10,000 units of Product X. Costs incurred by Roy during May were as follows:

Direct Materials	$10,000
Direct labor	20,000
Variable manufacturing overhead	5,000
Variable selling and general	3,000
Fixed manufacturing overhead	9,000
Fixed selling and general	4,000
Total	$51,000

Under absorption costing, Product X's unit cost was
a. $5.10.
b. $4.40.
c. $3.80.
d. $3.50.

21. Which of the following is (are) acceptable regarding the allocation of joint product cost to a by-product?

	Some portion allocated	None allocated
a.	Acceptable	Not acceptable
b.	Acceptable	Acceptable
c.	Not acceptable	Acceptable
d.	Not acceptable	Not acceptable

22. Baby Frames, Inc., evaluates manufacturing overhead in its factory by using variance analysis. The following information applies to the month of May:

	Actual	Budgeted
Number of frames manufactured	19,000	20,000
Variable overhead costs	$4,100	$2 per direct labor hour
Fixed overhead costs	$22,000	$20,000
Direct labor hours	2,100 hours	0.1 hour per frame

What is the fixed overhead spending variance?
a. $1,000 favorable
b. $1,000 unfavorable
c. $2,000 favorable
d. $2,000 unfavorable

23. The benefits of a just-in-time system for raw materials usually include
a. Elimination of nonvalue adding operations.
b. Increase in the number of suppliers, thereby ensuring competitive bidding.
c. Maximization of the standard delivery quantity, thereby lessening the paperwork for each delivery.
d. Decrease in the number of deliveries required to maintain production.

24. The estimates necessary to compute the economic order quantity are
a. Annual usage in units, cost per order, and annual cost of carrying one unit in stock.
b. Annual usage in units, cost per unit of inventory, and annual cost of carrying one unit in stock.
c. Annual cost of placing orders, and annual cost of carrying one unit in stock.
d. Cost per unit of inventory, annual cost of placing orders, and annual carrying cost.

25. Nell Brown's husband died in 20X0. Nell did not remarry, and continued to maintain a home for herself and her dependent infant child during 20X1, 20X2, and 20X3, providing full support for herself and her child during these three years. For 20X0, Nell properly filed a joint return. For 20X3, Nell's filing status is
a. Single.
b. Married filing joint return.
c. Head of household.
d. Qualifying widow with dependent child.

26. In the current calendar year, Alan Cox provided more than half the support for the following relatives, none of whom qualified as a member of Alan's household: a cousin, a nephew, and a foster parent. None of these relatives had any income, nor did any of these relatives file an individual or a joint return. All of these relatives are U.S. citizens. Which of these relatives could be claimed as a dependent on Alan's current year return?
a. No one
b. Nephew
c. Cousin
d. Foster parent

27. Morris Babb, CPA, reports on the cash basis. In March, Babb billed a client $1,000 for accounting services rendered in connection with the client's divorce settlement. No part of the $1,000 fee was ever paid. In July, the client went bankrupt and the $1,000 obligation became totally worthless. What loss can Babb deduct on his tax return?
a. $0
b. $1,000 short-term capital loss
c. $1,000 business bad debt
d. $1,000 nonbusiness bad debt

28. Brad Hart files a joint return with his wife. Hart's employer pays 100% of the cost of all employees' group-term life insurance under a qualified plan. Under this plan, the maximum amount of tax-free coverage that may be provided for Hart by his employer is
a. $100,000.
b. $ 50,000.
c. $ 10,000.
d. $ 5,000.

29. John Budd was 58 at the date of his death on July 1, 2002. Emma, his widow, received life insurance proceeds of $60,000 under a group policy paid for by John's employer, upon John's death. In addition, an employee death benefit of $7,500 was paid to Emma by John's employer, Toob Company. How much of the group life insurance proceeds should be excluded from taxable income?
a. $0
b. $ 5,000
c. $50,000
d. $60,000

30. Which of the following conditions must be present in a post-1984 divorce agreement for a payment to qualify as deductible alimony?

I. Payments must be in cash.
II. The payments must end at the recipient's death.

a. I only.
b. II only.
c. Both I and II.
d. Neither I nor II.

31. On January 2, 2000, the Philips paid $50,000 cash and obtained a $200,000 mortgage to purchase a home. In 2001, they borrowed $15,000 secured by their home, and used the cash to add a new room to their residence. That same year they took out a $5,000 auto loan. The following information pertains to interest paid in 2002:

Mortgage interest	$17,000
Interest on room construction loan	1,500
Auto loan interest	500

For 2002, how much interest is deductible, prior to any itemized deduction limitations?
a. $17,000
b. $17,500
c. $18,500
d. $19,000

32. Paul and Sally Lee, both age 42, are married and filed a joint return for the current year. Their adjusted gross income was $180,000, including Paul's $89,000 salary and Sally's $90,000 investment income. Neither spouse was covered by an employer-sponsored pension plan. What amount could the Lee's contribute to IRAs for the current year to take advantage of their maximum allowable IRA deduction in their current year return?
a. $0
b. $2,000
c. $3,000
d. $6,000

33. Don Mills, a single taxpayer, had $70,000 in taxable income before personal exemptions. Mills had no tax preferences. His itemized deductions were as follows:

State and local income taxes $5,000
Home mortgage interest on loan to
    acquire residence   6,000
Miscellaneous deductions that exceed
    2% of adjusted gross income   2,000

What amount did Mills report as alternative minimum taxable income before the AMT exemption?
a. $72,000
b. $75,000
c. $77,000
d. $83,000

34. Chris Baker's adjusted gross income on her 2001 tax return was $190,000. The amount covered a 12-month period. For the 2002 tax year, Baker may avoid the penalty for the underpayment of estimated tax if the timely estimated tax payments equal the required annual amount of

I. 90% of the tax on the return for the current year, paid in four equal installments.
II. 100% of prior year's tax liability, paid in four equal installments.

a. I only
b. II only
c. Both I and II
d. Neither I nor II

35. On March 1, Harry Beech received a gift of income-producing real estate having a donor's adjusted basis of $50,000 at the date of the gift. Fair market value of the property at the date of the gift was $40,000. Beech sold the property for $46,000 on August 1. How much gain or loss should Beech report for the current year?
a. No gain or loss
b. $6,000 short-term capital gain
c. $4,000 short-term capital loss
d. $4,000 ordinary loss

36. Price owned machinery which he had bought three years ago at a cost of $100,000. During the current year, the machinery was destroyed by fire. At that time it had an adjusted basis of $86,000. The insurance proceeds awarded to Price amounted to $125,000, and he immediately acquired a similar machine for $110,000. What should Price report as ordinary income resulting from the involuntary conversion for the current year?
a. $14,000
b. $15,000
c. $25,000
d. $39,000

ITEMS 37 AND 38 are based on the following:

On March 1 of the current year, Lois Rice learned that she was bequeathed 1,000 shares of Elin Corp. common stock under the will of her uncle, Pat Prevor. Pat had paid $5,000 for the Elin stock ten years ago. Fair market value of the Elin stock on March 1, the date of Pat's death, was $8,000 and had increased to $11,000 six months later. The executor of Pat's estate elected the alternate valuation date for estate tax purposes. Lois sold the Elin stock for $9,000 on May 1, the date that the executor distributed the stock to her.

37. How much should Lois include in her current year individual income tax return for the inheritance of the 1,000 shares of Elin stock which she received from Pat's estate?
a. $0
b. $ 5,000
c. $ 8,000
d. $11,000

38. Lois' basis for gain or loss on sale of the 1,000 shares of Elin stock is
a. $ 5,000.
b. $ 8,000.
c. $ 9,000.
d. $11,000.

39. Beck Corp. has been a calendar-year S corporation since its inception on January 2, 20X0. On January 1, 20X3, Lazur and Lyle each owned 50% of the Beck stock, in which their respective tax bases were $12,000 and $9,000. For the year ended December 31, 20X3, Beck had $81,000 in ordinary business income and $10,000 in tax-exempt income. Beck made a $51,000 cash distribution to each shareholder on December 31, 20X3. What was Lazur's tax basis in Beck after the distribution?
a. $ 1,500
b. $ 6,500
c. $52,500
d. $57,500

40. Pierce Corp., an accrual-basis, calendar-year C corporation, had the following 20X1 receipts:

20X2 advance rental payments for a lease ending in 20X3	$250,000
Lease cancellation payment from a five-year lease tenant	100,000

Pierce had no restrictions on the use of the advance rental payments and renders no services in connection with the rental income. What amount of gross income should Pierce report on its 20X1 tax return?
a. $350,000
b. $250,000
c. $100,000
d. $0

41. A corporation's capital loss carryback or carryover is
a. Not allowable under current law.
b. Limited to $3,000.
c. Always treated as a long-term capital loss.
d. Always treated as a short-term capital loss.

ITEMS 42 AND 43 are based on the following:

Max Finch was the sole stockholder of Burr, Inc., a company engaged principally in manufacturing operations. Total organization costs of $12,000 were incurred in January 20X0, and are being amortized over a 12-year period for financial statement purposes. Burr's retained earnings at December 31, 20X2, amounted to $1,000,000. For the year ended December 31, 20X3, Burr's book income, before income taxes, was $300,000. Included in the computation of this $300,000 were the following:

Keyman insurance premiums paid on Finch's life (Burr is beneficiary)	3,000
Group life insurance premiums paid on employees' lives (employees' dependents are beneficiaries)	9,000
Amortization of organization costs	1,000

42. In computing taxable income for 20X3, how much can Burr deduct for keyman and group life insurance premiums?
a. $0
b. $ 3,000
c. $ 9,000
d. $12,000

43. In computing taxable income for 20X3, what is the maximum deduction that Burr can claim for organization costs, assuming that the appropriate election was made on a timely basis?
a. $0
b. $ 600
c. $1,000
d. $2,400

44. Roper Corp. had operating income of $200,000, after deducting $12,000 for contributions, but not including dividends of $20,000 received from a 40%-owned domestic taxable corporation. How much is the base amount to which the percentage limitation should be applied in computing the maximum allowable deduction for contributions?
a. $212,000
b. $216,000
c. $220,000
d. $232,000

45. The following information pertains to treasury stock sold by Lee Corp. to an unrelated broker in the current year:

Proceeds received	$50,000
Cost	30,000
Par value	9,000

What amount of capital gain should Lee recognize in the current year on the sale of this treasury stock?
a. $0
b. $ 8,000
c. $20,000
d. $30,500

46. In 20X1, Acorn Inc. had the following items of income and expense:

Sales	$500,000
Cost of sales	250,000
Dividends received	25,000

The dividends were received from a corporation of which Acorn owns 30%. In Acorn's corporate income tax return, what amount should be reported as income before special deductions?
a. $525,000
b. $505,000
c. $275,000
d. $250,000

47. To qualify for tax-free incorporation, a sole proprietor must be in control of the transferee corporation immediately after the exchange of the proprietorship's assets for the corporation's stock. "Control" for this purpose means ownership of stock amounting to at least
a. 80.00%.
b. 66.67%.
c. 51.00%.
d. 50.00%.

48. Pursuant to a plan of corporate reorganization adopted in July 20X1, Gow exchanged 500 shares of Lad Corp. common stock that he had bought in January 20X1 at a cost of $5,000 for 100 shares of Rook Corp. common stock having a fair market value of $6,000. Gow's recognized gain on this exchange was
a. $1,000 long-term capital gain.
b. $1,000 short-term capital gain.
c. $1,000 ordinary income.
d. $0.

49. The partnership of Marks & Sparks sustained an ordinary loss of $42,000 in 20X1. The partnership, as well as the two partners, are on a calendar-year basis. The partners share profits and losses equally. At December 31, 20X1, Marks had an adjusted basis of $18,000 for his partnership interest, before consideration of the 20X1 loss. On his individual tax return for 20X1, Marks should deduct an (a)
a. Ordinary loss of $18,000.
b. Ordinary loss of $21,000.
c. Ordinary loss of $18,000 and a capital loss of $3,000.
d. Capital loss of $21,000.

50. On June 1, 20X1, Kelly received a 10% interest in Rock Co., a partnership, for services contributed to the partnership. Rock's net assets at that date had a basis of $70,000 and a fair market value of $100,000. In Kelly's 20X1 income tax return, what amount must Kelly include as income from transfer of partnership interest?
a. $7,000 ordinary income
b. $7,000 capital gain
c. $10,000 ordinary income
d. $10,000 capital gain

51. When a partner's share of partnership liabilities increases, that partner's basis in the partnership
a. Increases by the partner's share of the increase.
b. Decreases by the partner's share of the increase.
c. Decreases, but **not** to less than zero.
d. Is **not** affected.

52. Stone's basis in Ace Partnership was $70,000 at the time he received a nonliquidating distribution of partnership capital assets. These capital assets had an adjusted basis of $65,000 to Ace, and a fair market value of $83,000. Ace had no unrealized receivables, appreciated inventory, or properties which had been contributed by its partners. What was Stone's recognized gain or loss on the distribution?
a. $18,000 ordinary income
b. $13,000 capital gain
c. $ 5,000 capital loss
d. $0

53. Don and Lisa are equal partners in the capital and profits of Sabal & Noel, but are otherwise unrelated. The following information pertains to 300 shares of Mast Corporation stock sold by Lisa to Sabal & Noel:

Year of purchase	20X1
Year of sale	20X5
Basis (cost)	$8,000
Sales price (equal to fair market value)	$3,000

The amount of long-term capital loss that Lisa realized in 20X5 on the sale of this stock was
a. $5,000.
b. $3,000.
c. $2,500.
d. $0.

54. Under which of the following circumstances is a partnership that is not an electing large partnership considered terminated for income tax purposes?

I. Fifty-five percent of the total interest in partnership capital and profits is sold within a 12-month period.
II. The partnership's business and financial operations are discontinued.

a. I only
b. II only
c. Both I and II
d. Neither I nor II

55. Raff died in 20X0 leaving her entire estate to her only child. Raff's will gave full discretion to the estate's executor with regard to distributions of income. For 20X1, the estate's distributable net income was $15,000, of which $9,000 was paid to the beneficiary. None of the income was tax exempt. What amount can be claimed on the estate's 20X1 fiduciary income tax return for the distributions deduction?

a. $0
b. $ 6,000
c $ 9,000
d. $15,000

56. With regard to estimated income tax, estates

a. Must make quarterly estimated tax payments starting no later than the second quarter following the one in which the estate was established.
b. Are exempt from paying estimated tax during the estate's first two taxable years.
c. Are **not** required to make payments of estimated tax.
d. Must make quarterly estimated tax payments only if the estate's income is required to be distributed currently.

57. What amount of a decedent's taxable estate is effectively tax-free in 2001, if the maximum unified estate and gift credit is taken?

a. $0
b. $220,550
c. $500,000
d. $675,000

58. Within how many months after the date of a decedent's death is the federal estate tax return (Form 706) due if **no** extension of time for filing is granted?

a. 9
b. 6
c. 4½
d. 3½

59. If an exempt organization is a corporation, the tax on unrelated business taxable income is

a. Computed at corporate income tax rates.
b. Computed at rates applicable to trusts.
c. Credited against the tax on recognized capital gains.
d. Abated.

60. A tax return preparer is subject to a penalty for knowingly or recklessly disclosing corporate tax return information, if the disclosure is made

a. To enable a third party to solicit business from the taxpayer.
b. To enable the tax processor to electronically compute the taxpayer's liability.
c. For peer review.
d. Under an administrative order by a state agency that registers tax return preparers.

OTHER OBJECTIVE FORMAT QUESTIONS

PROBLEM 2 (8 to 15 minutes)

Dane City has adopted GASB Statement No. 34. The following information relates to Dane City during its fiscal year ended December 31, 20X1:

- On October 31, 20X1, to finance the construction of a city hall annex, Dane issued 8% 10-year general obligation bonds at their face value of $600,000. Construction expenditures during the period equaled $364,000.
- Dane reported $109,000 from hotel room taxes, restricted for tourist promotion, in a special revenue fund. The fund paid $81,000 for general promotions and $22,000 for a motor vehicle.

- 20X1 general fund revenues of $104,500 were transferred to a debt service fund and used to repay $100,000 of 9% 15-year term bonds, and to pay $4,500 of interest. The bonds were used to acquire a citizens' center.
- At December 31, 20X1, as a consequence of past services, city firefighters had accumulated entitlements to compensated absences valued at $86,000. General fund resources available at December 31, 20X1, are expected to be used to settle $17,000 of this amount, and $69,000 is expected to be paid out of future general fund resources.
- At December 31, 20X1, Dane was responsible for $83,000 of outstanding general fund encumbrances, including the $8,000 for supplies indicated below.

- Dane uses the purchases method to account for supplies. The following information relates to supplies:

Inventory—1/1/X1	$ 39,000
12/31/X1	42,000
Encumbrances outstanding—1/1/X1	6,000
12/31/X1	8,000
Purchase orders during 20X1	190,000
Amounts credited to vouchers payable during 20X1	$181,000

FOR ITEMS 61 THROUGH 70, determine the amounts based solely on the above information.

61. What is the amount of 20X1 general fund operating transfers out?

62. How much should be reported as 20X1 general fund liabilities from entitlements for compensated absences?

63. What is the 20X1 reserved amount of the general fund balance?

64. What is the 20X1 capital projects fund balance?

65. What is the 20X1 fund balance on the special revenue fund for tourist promotion?

66. What is the amount of 20X1 debt service fund expenditures?

67. What amount should be included in the general fund for capital assets acquired in 20X1?

68. What amount stemming from 20X1 transactions and events decreased the long-term liabilities reported in the government activities column of the government-wide statements?

69. Using the purchases method, what is the amount of 20X1 supplies expenditures?

70. What was the total amount of 20X1 supplies encumbrances?

PROBLEM 3 (32 to 40 minutes)

ITEMS 71 THROUGH 75 are based on the following:

Alex and Myra Burg, married and filing joint income tax returns, derive their entire income from the operation of their retail candy shop. Their 20X0 adjusted gross income was $50,000. The Burgs itemized their deductions on Schedule A for 20X0. The following unreimbursed cash expenditures were among those made by the Burgs during 20X0:

State income tax	1,200
Self-employment tax	7,650
Repair of glass vase accidentally broken in home by dog; vase cost $500 in 1989; fair value $600 before accident and $200 after accident	90
Fee for breaking lease on prior apartment residence located 20 miles from new residence	500
Repair and maintenance of motorized wheelchair for physically handicapped dependent child	300
Tuition, meals, and lodging at special school for physically handicapped dependent child in the institution primarily for the availability of medical care, with meals and lodging furnished as necessary incidents to that care	4,000
Four tickets to a theater party sponsored by a qualified charitable organization; not considered a business expense; similar tickets would cost $25 each at the box office	160
Security deposit placed on apartment at new location	900

71. Without regard to the adjusted gross income percentage threshold, what amount may the Burgs claim in their return as qualifying medical expenses?

72. What amount should the Burgs deduct for taxes in their itemized deductions on Schedule A?

73. What amount should the Burgs deduct for gifts to charity in their itemized deductions on Schedule A?

74. Without regard to the $100 "floor" and the adjusted gross income percentage threshold, what amount should the Burgs deduct for the casualty loss in their itemized deductions on Schedule A?

75. What amount should the Burgs deduct for moving expenses for adjusted gross income?

ITEMS 76 THROUGH 77 are based on the following:

Hall, a divorced person and custodian of her 12-year-old child, filed her 20X5 federal income tax return as head of a household.

- The divorce agreement, executed in 20X0, provides for Hall to receive $3,000 per month, of which $600 is designated as child support. After the child reaches 18, the monthly payments are to be reduced to $2,400 and are to continue until Hall's remarriage or death. However, for 20X5, Hall received a total of only $5,000 from her former husband. Hall paid an attorney $2,000 in 20X5 in a suit to collect the alimony owed.

- Hall spent a total of $1,000 for state lottery tickets. Her lottery winnings totaled $200.
- Hall paid the following expenses pertaining to the home that she owns: realty taxes, $3,400; mortgage interest, $7,000; casualty insurance, $490; assessment by city for construction of a sewer system, $910. Hall does not rent out any portion of the home.

76. What amount should be reported in Hall's return as alimony income?

77. Hall's lottery transactions should be reported as follows:

<table>
<tr><td></td><td colspan="3">Schedule A
Itemized Deductions</td></tr>
<tr><td></td><td colspan="3">Other miscellaneous deductions</td></tr>
<tr><td>Other income
on page 1</td><td>Subject to
2% AGI floor</td><td>Not subject to
2% AGI floor</td></tr>
<tr><td>A.</td><td>$0</td><td>$0</td><td>$0</td></tr>
<tr><td>B.</td><td>$200</td><td>$0</td><td>$200</td></tr>
<tr><td>C.</td><td>$200</td><td>$200</td><td>$0</td></tr>
<tr><td>D.</td><td>$200</td><td>$0</td><td>$0</td></tr>
</table>

FOR ITEMS 78 THROUGH 80, select the best answer from the following list of options:

A. A deduction in arriving at adjusted gross income.
B. An itemized deduction subject to the 2% of adjusted gross income floor.
C. An itemized deduction not subject to the 2% of adjusted gross income floor.
D. An itemized deduction with the realty taxes as an itemized deduction for taxes.
E. An itemized deduction subject to the $100 floor and the 10% of adjusted gross income floor.
F. A nondeductible personal expense.

78. The $2,000 legal fee that Hall paid to collect alimony should be treated as

79. The $910 sewer system assessment imposed by the city is

80. The casualty insurance premium of $490 is

ITEMS 81 THROUGH 84 are based on the following:

Sam and Ann Hoyt, filed a joint federal income tax return for the calendar year 20X5. Sam is 72 and has normal vision. Ann is age 67, and is legally blind. The Hoyts itemized their deductions. Their adjusted gross income was $34,000.

Among the Hoyt's cash receipts were the following:

- $4,000 net proceeds from sale of 100 shares of listed corporation stock bought in 20X0 for $9,000. The Hoyts had no other capital gains or losses in the current or prior years.
- $6,000 first installment on a $75,000 life insurance policy payable to Ann in annual installments of $6,000 each over a 15-year period, as beneficiary of the policy on her uncle, who died in 20X4.

Among the Hoyt's cash expenditures were the following:

- $2,000 transportation expenses required under the terms of Sam's employment contract were paid by Sam, an outside salesman. No reimbursement was received.
- $2,500 repairs in connection with 20X5 fire damage to the Hoyt residence. This property has a basis of $50,000. Fair market value was $60,000 before the fire and $55,000 after the fire. Insurance on the property had lapsed in 20X3 for nonpayment of premium.
- $800 appraisal fee to determine amount of fire loss.
- $3,000 real estate tax on residence; $400 state and city sales taxes; $900 state income tax.
- $100 contribution to a recognized political party.

81. What was the allowable amount of long-term capital loss that the Hoyts could offset against ordinary income on their return?

82. What portion of the $6,000 installment on the life insurance policy is excludable from 20X5 gross income in arriving at Hoyt's adjusted gross income?

83. What amount of fire loss were the Hoyts entitled to deduct as an itemized deduction on their 20X5 return?

84. What total amount was deductible as an itemized deduction for taxes on Hoyt's 20X5 return?

FOR ITEMS 85 AND 86, select the best answer from the accompanying list of options.

85. The unreimbursed employee's transportation expenses paid by Sam in 20X5 were

86. The appraisal fee to determine the amount of Hoyt's fire loss was

A. Deductible from gross income in arriving at adjusted gross income.
B. Subject to the 2% of adjusted gross income floor for miscellaneous itemized deductions.
C. Fully deductible as an itemized deduction.
D. Deductible after reducing the amount by $100.
E. Not deductible.

PROBLEM 4 (20 to 25 minutes)

Capital Corp., an accrual-basis calendar-year C corporation, began operations on January 2, 20X0. Capital timely filed its 20X1 federal income tax return on Wednesday, March 15, 20X2.

ITEMS 87 THROUGH 90 each require two responses. Determine the amount of Capital's 20X1 Schedule M-1 adjustment necessary to reconcile book income to taxable income. In addition, determine if the Schedule M-1 adjustment necessary to reconcile book income to taxable income (I) increases, (D) decreases, or (N) has no effect on Capital's 20X1 taxable income.

87. At its corporate inception in 20X0, Capital incurred and paid $40,000 in organizational costs for legal fees to draft the corporate charter. In 20X0, Capital correctly elected, for book purposes, to amortize the organizational expenditures over 40 years and for the minimum required period on its federal income tax return. For 20X1, Capital amortized $1,000 of the organizational costs on its books.

88. Capital's 20X1 disbursements included $10,000 for reimbursed employees' expenses for business and entertainment. The reimbursed expenses met the conditions of deductibility and were properly substantiated under an accountable plan. The disbursement was not treated as employee compensation.

89. Capital's 20X1 disbursements included $15,000 life insurance premium expense paid for its executives as part of their taxable compensation. Capital is neither the direct nor the indirect beneficiary of the policy, and the amount of the compensation is reasonable.

90. In 20X1, Capital increased its allowance for uncollectible accounts by $10,000. No bad debt was written off in 20X0.

Sunco Corp., an accrual-basis calendar-year C corporation, timely filed its 20X1 federal income tax return on Wednesday, March 15, 20X2.

FOR ITEMS 91 AND 92, determine if the following 20X1 items are (F) fully taxable, (P) partially taxable, or (N) nontaxable for regular income tax purposes on Sunco's 20X1 federal income tax return.

91. Sunco received dividend income from a 35%-owned domestic corporation. The dividends were not from debt-financed portfolio stock, and the taxable income limitation did not apply.

92. Sunco received a $2,800 lease cancellation payment from a three-year lease tenant.

Quest Corp., an accrual-basis calendar-year C corporation, timely filed its 20X1 federal income tax return on Wednesday, March 15, 20X2.

FOR ITEMS 93 AND 94, determine if the following 20X1 items are (F) fully deductible, (P) partially deductible, or (N) nondeductible for regular income tax purposes on Quest's 20X1 federal income tax return.

93. Quest's 20X1 taxable income before charitable contributions and dividends-received deduction was $200,000. Quest's Board of Directors authorized a $38,000 contribution to a qualified charity on December 1, 20X1. The payment was made on February 1, 20X2. All charitable contributions were properly substantiated.

94. During 20X1 Quest was assessed and paid a $300 uncontested penalty for failure to pay its 20X0 federal income taxes on time.

On its 20X1 federal income tax return, Gelco Corp., an accrual-basis calendar-year C corporation, reported the same amounts for regular income tax and alternative minimum tax purposes.

FOR ITEMS 95 THROUGH 97, determine if each 20X1 item, taken separately, contributes to (O) overstating, (U) understating, or (C) correctly stating Gelco's 20X1 alternative minimum taxable income (AMTI) prior to the adjusted current earnings adjustment (ACE).

95. For regular tax purposes, Gelco deducted the maximum MACRS depreciation on seven-year personal property placed in service on January 1, 20X1. Gelco made no Internal Revenue Code Section 179 election to expense the property in 20X1.

96. For regular income tax purposes, Gelco depreciated nonresidential real property placed in service on January 1, 20X1, under the general MACRS depreciation system for a 39-year depreciable life.

97. Gelco excluded state highway construction general obligation bond interest income earned in 20X1 for regular income tax and alternative minimum tax (AMT) purposes.

PROBLEM 5 (10 to 15 minutes)

Scott Lane, an unmarried U.S. citizen, made no lifetime transfers prior to the current year. During 20X1, Lane made the following transfers:

- Gave a $10,000 cash gift to Kamp, a close friend.
- Made two separate $10,000 cash gifts to his only child.
- Created an **irrevocable** trust beginning in the current year that provided his aunt with an income interest to be paid for the next five years. The remainder interest is to pass to Lane's sole cousin. The income interest is valued at $26,000 and the remainder interest is valued at $74,000.
- Paid $25,000 tuition directly to his grandchild's university on his grandchild's behalf.
- Created an **irrevocable** trust that provided his brother with a lifetime income interest beginning in two years, after which a remainder interest passes to their sister.
- Created a **revocable** trust with his niece as the sole beneficiary. During the current year, the niece received $11,000 interest income from the trust.

REQUIRED:

FOR ITEMS 98 THROUGH 104, determine whether the transactions are fully taxable, partially taxable, or not taxable to Lane in 20X1 for gift tax purposes after considering the gift tax annual exclusion. Ignore the unified credit when answering the items. An answer may be selected once, more than once, or not at all.

Gift Tax Treatments

F. Fully taxable to Lane in 20X1 for gift tax purposes
P. Partially taxable to Lane in 20X1 for gift tax purposes
N. Not taxable to Lane in 20X1 for gift tax purposes

98. What is the gift tax treatment of Lane's gift to Kamp?

99. What is the gift tax treatment of Lane's cash gifts to his child?

100. What is the gift tax treatment of the trust's income interest to Lane's aunt?

101. What is the gift tax treatment of the trusts remainder interest to Lane's cousin?

102. What is the gift tax treatment of the tuition payment to Lane's grandchild's university?

103. What is the gift tax treatment of the trust's income interest to Lane's brother?

104. What is the gift tax treatment of the $11,000 interest income that Lane's niece received from the revocable trust?

MULTIPLE CHOICE QUESTION SOLUTIONS

CHAPTER 21: GOVERNMENTAL OVERVIEW

1. (b) GASB §1300.102(a) states, "Governmental fund measurement focus is on determination of financial position and changes in financial position (sources, uses, and balances of financial resources), rather than on net income determination."

2. (d) Both the General Fund and the Debt Service Fund use the modified accrual basis of accounting. The modified accrual basis is the appropriate basis of accounting for governmental funds (i.e., General, Special Revenue, Capital Projects, and Debt Service), Expendable Trust Funds, and Agency Funds. Nonexpendable Trust Funds, Enterprise Funds, and Internal Service Funds all use the accrual basis of accounting.

3. (a) GASB 34 (¶73) states, "Agency funds should be used to report resources held by the reporting government in a purely custodial capacity (assets equal liabilities). Agency funds typically involve only the receipt, temporary investment, and remittance of fiduciary resources to individuals, private organizations, or other governments." Agency funds generally have neither capital assets nor expenses.

4. (c) The long-term debt incurred by a government under a capital lease should be reported in the governmental activities column of the government-wide statements, but not in any of the fund statements. The GASB 34 reporting model specifies the use of neither the general long-term debt account group nor the general fixed asset account group.

CHAPTER 22: GOVERNMENTAL FUNDS & ACCOUNT GROUPS

5. (b) There are three types of funds: governmental, proprietary, and fiduciary funds. Only governmental funds—which include the general, special revenue, capital projects, and debt service funds—integrate budgetary accounts into their accounting system. Proprietary funds are used for self supporting activities and thus are accounted for in a manner similar to commercial enterprise accounting. Fiduciary funds, such as trust and agency funds, are used to account for monies held in custody by the governmental unit for others and thus do not include budgetary accounts in their accounting system.

6. (c) A city-owned utility resembles a commercial entity in that it provides a service to users who are directly charged for this service. Therefore, like a commercial enterprise, a city utility must know the cost of providing those services, which includes depreciation on property, plant, and equipment. Thus, a city utility will account for its fixed assets in its own enterprise fund, rather than record them in the general fixed assets group of accounts.

7. (a) In recording the budget for a governmental fund, the account *Estimated Revenues* is debited while *Appropriations* is credited; any difference between the two amounts will be posted directly to *Fund Balance*. Estimated revenues (debit) must have exceeded appropriations (credit).

8. (b) In fund accounting, nominal accounts (i.e., revenues and expenditures) and budgetary accounts (i.e., estimated revenues and appropriations) are closed out to fund balance at the end of the period. *Expenditures* is a nominal account and thus is closed out. *Fund Balance* and *Reserve for Encumbrances* are both equity accounts. *Reserve for Encumbrances* is somewhat similar to appropriated retained earnings in commercial enterprises. *Vouchers Payable* is a liability account.

9. (c) Governmental funds record all outlays as "expenditures"—there is no differentiation between "expense" and "capital" outlays. The expenditure must be recorded in order to indicate that cash has been paid out or a liability (payable) incurred. Fixed assets are recorded in the fixed asset account group—not in the general fund. Answer (d) is erroneous because a "due from" account is only debited when a payment is due from another fund, which is not the case here.

10. (d) Governmental funds use the modified accrual basis of accounting, under which, revenues are recognized when they become measurable and available for use. "Available for use" means that the revenues will be collected within the current period or collected early enough in the next period to be used to pay for expenditures incurred in the current period. Therefore, the property taxes collected before the end of fiscal year 20X2 or shortly thereafter should be reported as General Fund revenues in fiscal year 20X2.

11. (b) Governmental funds use the modified accrual basis of accounting, under which revenues are recognized when they become measurable and available for use. "Available for use" means that the revenues will be collected within the current period or collected early enough in the next period (e.g., within 60 days or so) to be used to pay for expenditures incurred in the current period. Therefore, for fiscal year 20X2, Pine should recognize property tax revenue of $2,200,000. This amount is comprised of (1) $1,000,000 (i.e., $920,000 + $80,000) of property taxes levied in January 20X1 that were collected in October and December and (2) $1,200,000 (i.e., $1,100,000 + $60,000 + $40,000) of property taxes levied in January 20X2 that were collected in May, July, and August.

12. (b) When $100 of supplies are ordered, the following entry is made:

Encumbrances Control (expected cost of supplies)	100	
Reserve for Encumbrances		100

Upon receipt of the supplies for $105, the following entries are made:

Reserve for Encumbrances (reverse original entry)	100	
Encumbrances Control		100
Expenditures (actual cost)	105	
Vouchers Payable		105

13. (a) GASB 34 requires long-term debt issued ($1,000,000) to be reported as an other financing source. Premiums ($10,000) and discounts are reported as other financing sources and uses, respectively. Debt issue costs paid out of proceeds are reported as expenditures. Therefore, the city should report the entire $1,010,000 as an other financing source, not net of expenditures.

14. (d) Billings for services provided to other governmental units are recorded by the Internal Service Fund as operating revenues.

15. (d) Residual equity transfers are nonrecurring or nonroutine transfers of equity between funds. Residual equity transfers to proprietary funds are reported as additions to contributed capital of the proprietary fund.

CHAPTER 23: NONPROFIT ACCOUNTING

16. (a) Hunt Community Development Agency provides loans as its operating activity, not as financing or investing activities.

17. (b) The establishment of an endowment requires a nonprofit organization (NPO) to recognize restricted contribution revenue. The NPO includes an asset in its balance sheet. When a beneficiary has an unconditional right to specific cash flows from a trust, the beneficiary interest is measured and subsequently remeasured at fair value, using a valuation technique such as the present value of the estimated expected future cash flows. (SFAS 136, ¶15).

18. (c) Investments of nonprofit organizations are recorded initially at cost, except that donated securities are recorded at their fair market value at date of receipt. Thereafter, marketable equity and debit securities are accounted for in accordance with SFAS 124.

CHAPTER 24: DECISION MAKING

19. (c) Buying the parts will result in $35,000 savings (i.e., $290,000 – $255,000).

	Make	Buy
Variable cost		
[($3 + $15 + $6) x 10,000]	$240,000	
Fixed OH [($8 – $3) x 10,000]	50,000	
Purchase ($30 x 10,000)		$300,000
Savings, Part H		(45,000)
Total Relevant Costs	$290,000	$255,000

20. (b) Absorption costing considers fixed manufacturing overhead to be a product cost. A portion of fixed manufacturing overhead is included in the cost of a unit of product, along with direct materials, direct labor, and variable manufacturing overhead. The selling and general administrative costs ($3,000 and $4,000, respectively) are period costs and are expensed when incurred.

Direct materials	$ 10,000
Direct labor	20,000
Variable manufacturing overhead	5,000
Fixed manufacturing overhead	9,000
Total product costs incurred	$ 44,000
Units produced during period	/ 10,000
Unit cost, absorption costing, Product X	$ 4.40

CHAPTER 25: COST ACCOUNTING

21. (b) By-products result from the joint production process and have a relatively minor sales value compared to the main product. Conceptually, a portion of the joint process costs should be allocated to by-products proportionally to their relative sales value. Due to the immaterial amounts involved, however, it is acceptable to account for the sales value of by-products as a reduction of the cost of the main product.

22. (d) An unfavorable variance exists when actual cost exceeds standard cost. Since Baby Frames actually overspent the fixed overhead budget by $2,000, the spending variance is $2,000 unfavorable.

CHAPTER 26: PLANNING & CONTROL

23. (a) The benefits of a just-in-time (JIT) system usually include elimination of nonvalue added (NVA) operations—that is, operations that do not affect how customers perceive a product. Eliminating NVA added operations saves the manufacturer money and does no harm to customer relations. Holding inventory is a NVA activity. Hence, under a JIT system, inventory is regarded as an evil, and limits are imposed on all inventories, from raw materials through all stages of production. A JIT system would not seek the maximization of the standard delivery quantity of raw materials or a decrease in the number of deliveries of raw materials required to maintain production because the objective is to minimize inventory levels. A JIT system may decrease the number of suppliers and reduce competitive bidding.

24. (a) The three numbers necessary to compute the economic order quantity are the annual demand or usage, the cost of placing each order, and the annual cost of carrying one unit in inventory. The cost per unit of inventory is **not** used to compute the economic order quantity.

CHAPTER 27: FEDERAL TAXATION—INDIVIDUALS

25. (c) Since Nell's husband died more than two years ago, she cannot qualify as a surviving spouse. However, under §2(b), Nell will be a head of household because she was not married at the close of her tax year, was not a surviving spouse, and maintained her home as a household for her dependent child.

26. (b) In order to qualify as a dependent, an individual must pass five tests. The first four, gross income, support, joint return, and citizenship or residence tests are passed by all of the relatives. However, the fifth test an individual must pass is the relationship test or the member of household test. Since none of the relatives qualified as a member of Alan's household, only the ones which pass the relationship test may be claimed as a dependent. Per §152, the following pass the relationship test: child or dependent of child; stepchild; brother or sister (including half-blood); stepbrother or stepsister; father, mother, or ancestor of either; stepfather or stepmother; nephew or niece; uncle or aunt; and brother-, sister-, father-, mother-, son-, or daughter-in-law.

27. (a) A deduction is allowed for any debt which becomes totally worthless during the year. However, the deduction is only allowed with respect to debts that represent items which have been previously taken into income. A cash basis taxpayer does not take an item into income until payment is received. Since no part of the fee in question was taken into income, no deduction is allowed for the worthlessness of the debt.

28. (b) Section 79(a) provides that up to $50,000 of group-term life insurance provided by an employer is excludible from gross income for an employee. Any amounts expended by the employer for additional life insurance coverage will be included in the employee's gross income.

29. (d) Gross income does not include life insurance proceeds, if such amounts are paid by reason of the death of the insured [§101(a)(1)]. Thus, the entire $60,000 should be excluded.

30. (c) To qualify as alimony, payments must be: made pursuant to a divorce or separate maintenance agreement, made in cash, not made to someone in the same household, stopped upon the death of the payee-spouse, and not designated as anything other than alimony.

31. (c) Section 163 allows a deduction for all interest paid or accrued within the taxable year on indebtedness. However, the interest on the auto loan is not deductible because no deduction is allowed for personal interest. An auto loan is not mentioned in the exceptions to personal interest listed in §163. However, §163 excludes any qualified residence interest from the term personal interest and includes interest on acquisition indebtedness as qualified residence interest. Section 163 states that acquisition indebtedness includes any indebtedness incurred in acquiring, constructing, or substantially improving any qualified residence of the taxpayer, and is secured by such residence. Section 163 limits the aggregate amount of acquisition indebtedness to $1,000,000. Section 163 defines a qualified residence as the taxpayer's principal residence and one other residence that the taxpayer uses as a residence. The mortgage interest and the interest on the room construction loan meet the definition and are within the limit to qualify as interest on acquisition indebtedness. Thus, the mortgage interest and the interest on the room construction loan are qualified residence interest.

32. (d) Since neither Paul nor Sally was covered by an employer-sponsored pension plan, the Lees could take a total IRA deduction of $6,000, regardless of who had earned the income.

33. (c) Section 56(b)(1)(A)(i) disallows any deduction for an individual's miscellaneous itemized deductions in computing alternative minimum taxable (AMT) income. Section 56(b)(1)(A)(ii) disallows any deduction for taxes described in §164(a). Section 164(a)(3) includes state and local income taxes. Hence, state and local income taxes are not deductible in arriving at AMT income. Section 56(b)(1)(C)(i) disallows the deduction for qualified residence interest in arriving at AMT income. Instead §56(e) allows a deduction for qualified housing interest which includes interest on acquisition indebtedness but not other home equity loans, unless the taxpayer used the loan proceeds to improve the residence. Thus, the home mortgage interest on a loan to acquire a residence is deductible in arriving at AMT income and accordingly does not have to be added back to taxable income. Section 55(b)(2) defines AMT income as the taxable income of the taxpayer, determined with regard to the adjustments required by §§56 and 58 and increased by the preferences described in §57. Taxable income, as defined in §63(a), is gross income minus deductions. Section 56(b)(1)(E) disallows the standard deduction and deduction for personal exemptions in arriving at AMT income.

Taxable income before personal exemption	$70,000
Add back: Miscellaneous itemized deductions	2,000
State and local income taxes	5,000
AMT income before the AMT exemption	$77,000

34. (a) Section 6654 allows an individual to avoid the penalty for underpayment of estimated tax by paying in 90% of the tax shown on the return in timely installments. In general, §6654 provides that an individual may avoid the penalty for under-payment of estimated tax by paying 100% of the tax shown on the return for the preceding tax year. However, §6654 states that if an individual's adjusted gross income in 2001 exceeds $150,000, the individual may avoid the penalty for underpayment of estimated tax for 2002, by paying 112%, rather than 100%, of the tax shown on the return for the previous year. (Thereafter, paying 110% of the tax shown on the previous year's return would be adequate for avoiding the penalty.)

CHAPTER 28: FEDERAL TAXATION—PROPERTY

35. (a) In general, the donee's basis in gifted property is the same as the donor's basis in such property. However, if, on the date of the gift, the FMV of the property is less than the donor's basis, the donee's basis for determining loss upon a sub-sequent disposition is the FMV on the date of the gift. Harry's "gain" basis for the real estate is $50,000 (the donor's adjusted basis in the property at the time of the gift). Harry's "loss" basis is $40,000 (the FMV of the property on the date of the gift). When property is sold or otherwise disposed of for an amount between the "gain" and "loss" basis, no gain or loss results.

36. (a) Note that the question only asks for the amount of ordinary income. While there is a $15,000 recognized gain ($125,000 – $110,000), only $14,000 (accumulated depreciation) is ordinary income.

37. (a) Section 102(a) provides that gross income does not include the value of property acquired by gift, bequest, devise, or inheritance. Thus, Lois should not include any amount on her tax return for the inheritance of the stock.

38. (c) Section 1014(a)(2) provides that when the alternate valuation date is elected, the basis of property inherited by the decedent is equal to the value of the property as it is determined under §2032. Under §2032, the value of property distrib-uted from the estate after the date of death, but before the alternate valuation date, is equal to the FMV on the date of distribution [§2032(a)(1)]. Thus, Lois' basis in the stock is $9,000, i.e., the stock's FMV on the date of distribution.

CHAPTER 29: FEDERAL TAXATION—CORPORATIONS

39. (b) Without debt transactions, a partner's adjusted basis in a partnership interest is the beginning basis plus income minus distributions. $12,000 + 50% x ($81,000 + $10,000) – $51,000 = $6,500

40. (a) Rent is income when received, regard-less of the taxpayer's basis of accounting.

41. (d) A corporation's carryback and carryfor-ward capital losses are always treated as short-term capital losses in the year to which they are carried. Excess capital losses of a corporation can be carried back three years and forward five. The $3,000 limit for offsetting capital losses against ordinary income applies only to individuals. Unlike individuals, corpo-rations only use capital losses to offset capital gains (not ordinary income).

42. (c) In general, insurance premiums are a deductible business expense. However, §264(a)(1) provides that no deduction is allowed on life insur-ance premiums paid on a policy covering the life of any officer or employee if the taxpayer is the direct or indirect beneficiary under the policy. Thus, the keyman insurance premiums are not deductible, while the group life insurance premiums are deductible.

43. (d) Organizational expenditures can be deducted for tax purposes over a period of not less than 60 months [§248(a)]. These costs totaled $12,000 and they can be amortized at a maximum rate of $200 per month, i.e., $12,000 / 60 months. Thus, the maximum deduction that Burr can claim in one full year is $2,400 (i.e., $200 per month maxi-mum x 12 months).

44. (d) Section 170(b)(2) provides that total deductions for charitable contributions for the year cannot exceed 10% of the corporation's taxable income computed without regard to deductions for (1) charitable contributions, (2) dividends received, (3) NOL carrybacks, and (4) capital loss carrybacks. For purposes of computing the §170(b)(2) limitation, Roper must add to its $200,000 operating income both the $20,000 of unincluded dividends and the $12,000 of contributions already deducted.

45. (a) Under Section 1032, when a corpora-tion exchanges its own stock (i.e., treasury stock) for property or money, no gain or loss is recognized on the exchange. Thus, Lee Corp. will recognize no gain on this sale.

46. (c)   The dividends received deduction is a special deduction. The question asks for income before special deductions, $500,000 Sales + $25,000 Dividends received − $250,000 Cost of sales = $275,000 Income before special deductions. Cost of sales needs to be subtracted because it is not a special deduction. The dividends need to be included in income in total and then the appropriate percentage is subtracted as a special deduction.

47. (a)   Pursuant to §351(a) and §368(c), *control* means ownership of stock possessing at least 80% of the total combined voting power of all classes of stock entitled to vote and at least 80% of the total number of shares of all classes of stock of the corporation.

48. (d)   Section 354 provides for the nonrecognition of any gain or loss on property transferred to a corporation pursuant to a corporate reorganization in exchange solely for stock or securities of such corporation or in another corporation that is party to the reorganization. Because the taxpayer received only stock in the exchange, no gain or loss is recognized.

CHAPTER 30: FEDERAL TAXATION—PARTNERSHIPS & OTHER TOPICS

49. (a)   Because Marks and Sparks share profits and losses equally, Marks is allocated $21,000 of the ordinary loss (i.e., 50% of $42,000). Section 704(d) provides that a partner's distributive share of partnership loss is allowed only to the extent of the adjusted basis in that partner's partnership interest. Any loss disallowed under §704(d) will be allowed as a deduction at the end of the first succeeding taxable year to the extent that the partner's adjusted basis at the end of such year exceeds zero [Reg. §1.704-1(d)(1)]. Thus, Marks should deduct an ordinary loss of $18,000 in 20X1. The remaining $3,000 is carried forward and may be deducted in succeeding tax years.

50. (c)   Kelly has ordinary gross income from services rendered in an amount equal to the fair value of the property received as compensation under §61 and §83. Regulation §1.61-2(d)(1) states "...if services are paid for in property, the fair market value of the property taken in payment must be included in income as compensation." Thus, Kelly has $10,000 gross income ($100,000 x 10%). Although the partnership interest obtained will be a capital asset, the income for services performed to obtain such partnership interest is deemed ordinary under §64.

51. (a)   The partner's share of an increase in partnership liabilities is treated as a contribution of money from the partner to the partnership under §752(a). The partner then gets to increase his or her basis in the partnership for this deemed contribution of money under §722.

52. (d)   Section 731(a)(1) provides that a partner does not recognize gain on receiving a distribution from a partnership except to the extent that any money distributed exceeds the adjusted basis of his or her partnership interest immediately before the distribution. Section 731(a)(2) provides that a partner does not recognize loss on a distribution of property from the partnership except in certain liquidating distributions. Section 731(b) also provides that the partnership does not recognize any gain or loss on a distribution to a partner. Since the distribution was a non-liquidating distribution, Stone recognizes no gain or loss.

53. (a)   If a partner enters into a sale of an asset with such partnership and if the partner owns *more* than 50% of the partnership, no loss is recognized. Since Lisa owns *only* 50% of the partnership, the entire loss on the sale of the stock (i.e., $8,000 − $3,000) is realized by Lisa as a long-term capital loss.

54. (c)   Except for electing large partnerships, a partnership terminates if no part of its business is carried on within a 12-month period, or if within a 12-month period, 50% or more of the total interest in the partnership are sold [IRC §708(b)].

55. (c)   As long as a distribution to a beneficiary does not exceed the distributable net income of the estate, the estate is allowed a deduction for the amount of the distribution that is subject to income tax on the beneficiary's return. Thus, the estate may claim a distribution deduction of $9,000 (i.e., $9,000 < $15,000) on its fiduciary income tax return.

56. (b)   Estates are required to make estimated tax payments with respect to any taxable year ending two or more years after the date of the decedent's death.

57. (d)   The amount of the unified credit against the estate and gift tax in 2001 is $220,550 under §2010(a). The effect of the credit is to exempt up to $675,000 of a decedent's estate from estate taxation. [The examiners have previously asked prior year questions on the November exams].

58. (a) If an estate tax return is required, then it must be filed nine months after the date of the decedent's death. Six months after the date of the decedent's death is the time frame for the "alternate valuation date" of the gross estate.

59. (a) Unless the exempt entity is taxable as a trust, the tax it must pay on income that is not related to its exempt purpose is computed at regular corporate tax rates.

60. (a) Section 6713 authorizes a civil penalty and §7216 authorizes a criminal penalty for the unauthorized disclosure by a tax preparer of information furnished to the preparer by a taxpayer. Regulation §301.7216-2(o) allow disclosure for the purpose of a quality or peer review. Regulation §301.7216-2(c) allows disclosure pursuant to an administrative order by a state agency that registers tax return preparers. Regulation §301.7216-2(h) allows disclosure for the purpose of processing the tax return, including electronic filing. Disclosure for the purpose of enabling a third party to solicit from the taxpayer is not an exception to the general prohibition.

PERFORMANCE BY TOPICS

The final examination questions corresponding to each chapter of the Accounting & Reporting text are listed below. To assess your preparedness for the CPA exam, record the number and percentage of questions you correctly answered in each topic area. The point distribution of the multiple choice questions (not counting the other objective format questions) approximates that of the exam.

Chapter 21:
Governmental
Overview

Question #	Correct √
1	
2	
3	
4	
# Questions	4

Correct _____
% Correct _____

Chapter 22:
Governmental Funds
& Transactions

Question #	Correct √
5	
6	
7	
8	
9	
10	
11	
12	
13	
14	
15	
# Questions	11

Correct _____
% Correct _____

Chapter 23:
Nonprofit Accounting

Question #	Correct √
16	
17	
18	
# Questions	3

Correct _____
% Correct _____

Chapter 24:
Decision Making

Question #	Correct √
19	
20	
# Questions	2

Correct _____
% Correct _____

Chapter 25:
Cost Accounting

Question #	Correct √
21	
22	
# Questions	2

Correct _____
% Correct _____

Chapter 26:
Planning & Control

Question #	Correct √
23	
24	
# Questions	2

Correct _____
% Correct _____

Chapter 27:
Federal Taxation—
Individuals

Question #	Correct √
25	
26	
27	
28	
29	
30	
31	
32	
33	
34	
# Questions	10

Correct _____
% Correct _____

Chapter 28:
Federal Taxation—
Property

Question #	Correct √
35	
36	
37	
38	
# Questions	4

Correct _____
% Correct _____

Chapter 29:
Federal Taxation—
Corporations

Question #	Correct √
39	
40	
41	
42	
43	
44	
45	
46	
47	
48	
# Questions	10

Correct _____
% Correct _____

Chapter 30:
Federal Taxation—
Partnerships & Other
Topics

Question #	Correct √
49	
50	
51	
52	
53	
54	
55	
56	
57	
58	
59	
60	
# Questions	12

Correct _____
% Correct _____

OTHER OBJECTIVE FORMAT QUESTION SOLUTIONS

SOLUTION 2 GOVERNMENTAL ACCOUNTING

61. $104,500

The general fund operating transfers out (other financing uses) are composed of the $104,500 for bond principal and interest payment.

62. $17,000

Compensated absences are valued at the salary and wage rates in effect as of the balance sheet date. The liabilities in the general fund are the amounts expected to be settled with resources available at the balance sheet date. The remainder of $69,000 would appear in the government-wide statement of net assets as long-term liability but is not booked in the general fund.

63. $125,000

The reserved amount is the $83,000 for total encumbrances outstanding at December 31 and the $42,000 in ending supplies inventory. The reserve for supplies inventory indicates that a portion of fund balance is not available.

64. $236,000

The capital projects fund fund balance is $600,000 – $364,000 = $236,000.

65. $6,000

The special revenue fund fund balance is $109,000 – $81,000 – $22,000 = $6,000.

66. $104,500

The debt service fund expenditures for 20X1 are the $100,000 of principal repaid and the $4,500 of interest paid.

67. $0

The cost of capital assets acquired in 20X1 is $22,000 from the special revenue fund's purchase of a motor vehicle plus $364,000 from the capital projects fund. This appears in the government-wide financial statements in the governmental activities column, but is not booked in the general fund.

68. $100,000

The $100,000 repayment of debt decreased the reported long-term liabilities.

69. $181,000

Under the encumbrances method, the amount of 20X1 supplies expenditures is the $181,000 credited to the *Vouchers Payable* account during 20X1 less the $6,000 credited to *Vouchers Payable* account and debited to the *Fund Balance Reserved for Encumbrances* account for the encumbrances outstanding as of 1/1/X1. Under the purchases method, the fund balance is not reserved for prior year encumbrances, and thus the amount for 20X1 expenditures is the full $181,000.

70. $190,000

The $190,000 of purchase orders issued during 20X1 is the total amount of 20X1 supplies encumbrances.

SOLUTION 3 FEDERAL TAXATION—INDIVIDUALS

71. $4,300

The repair and maintenance of the motorized wheelchair qualify as a medical expense. The cost of the school qualifies as well because it provides medical care, and the meals and lodging costs are incidental to the cost of the medical care.

72. $1,200

The state income taxes paid by the Burgs are deductible on Schedule A. The self-employment tax, however, is not deductible on Schedule A. Half of the amount of self-employment tax paid is allowed as a deduction *for* AGI.

73. $60

A charitable deduction is allowed for the purchase of the theater tickets to the extent that the purchase price exceeds the fair market value of the tickets. Since the four tickets would cost a total of $100 if purchased at the box office, only the excess $60 is allowed as a charitable deduction.

74. $0

A casualty loss is a loss that is caused by a sudden, unexpected, or unusual event such as a fire, storm, or shipwreck. Although the Burgs may consider the broken vase to be a casualty, the repair costs are not deductible on their tax return.

75. $0

Moving expenses are deductible for AGI if the move is related to the commencement of work in a new location and the amount deducted is reasonable. To qualify for the moving deduction, the new work place must be at least 50 miles away from the taxpayer's old residence. The facts do not specify that the reason for the move was work related. In addition, the mileage requirement is not met.

76. $0

If the divorce or separation instrument provides for an amount to be paid for both alimony and child support, and the payment is less than the amount specified, the payment is first treated as child support to the extent provided in the instrument. Because the total payments received by Hall were less than the annual child support payment of $7,200 (i.e., $600 x 12) required in the divorce agreement, the entire amount received is classified as child support. Therefore, *no* portion of the amount received is classified as alimony income.

77.   B   Gambling winnings are included in gross income. Gambling losses are only deductible as itemized deductions (not subject to the 2% of AGI limitation) to the extent of gambling winnings.

78.   B   Legal fees attributable to the production or collection of taxable alimony are deductible by the payee under §212. Expenses of producing such income are considered miscellaneous itemized deductions subject to the 2% of AGI limitation. Legal expenses related to divorce, separation or a support decree are nondeductible personal expenses *except* for those attributable to the production or collection of alimony.

79.   F   Special assessment taxes paid for local benefits, such as streets and sewer systems are *not* deductible, except to the extent the tax assessment is made for maintenance or repair purposes.

80.   F   No deduction is allowed for personal, living, or family expenses, except as specifically provided for in the Code. No provision exists to allow a deduction for insurance premiums to cover a taxpayer's residence against casualty loss.

81. $3,000

Code Section 1211 allows an individual taxpayer to offset a certain amount of his taxable income by any net capital losses that are incurred during the year. The allowable losses are limited to the least of: (1) taxable income, (2) $3,000, or (3) the sum of net short-term losses and net long-term losses. Therefore, the Hoyts are allowed to use $3,000 in capital losses to offset their ordinary income since $3,000 is less than the Hoyts' taxable income or the total amount of their capital losses.

82. $5,000

Generally, a taxpayer is able to exclude any life insurance proceeds that are received upon the death of the insured from the taxpayer's gross income (§101). However, if the proceeds are to be paid over a period of time, then an allocation must be made between the tax-free payment of the insurance proceeds and any interest (i.e., gross income).

Cash received	$ 6,000
Portion representing cost of annuity ($75,000 ÷ 15)	(5,000)
Interest income—taxable	$ 1,000

83. $1,500

A nonbusiness casualty loss that is incurred by an individual is limited to the actual loss that is incurred reduced by 10% of the taxpayer's AGI. The loss itself is further reduced by any reimbursement (i.e., insurance proceeds received) and $100 [§165(h)]. The amount of a casualty loss is the lesser of (1) the fair market value of the property immediately before the casualty reduced by the fair market value immediately after the casualty or (2) the adjusted basis of the property. The cost of the repairs is not considered in determining the amount of the casualty loss nor are the appraisal fees considered a part of the casualty loss; rather such fees can be deducted as a miscellaneous deduction that is subject to the 2% limitation.

FMV before casualty	$ 60,000
FMV after casualty	(55,000)
Casualty loss	$ 5,000
10% of adjusted gross income ($34,000 x 10%)	(3,400)
Casualty loss floor	(100)
Deductible casualty loss	$ 1,500

84. $3,900

The Tax Reform Act of 1986 repealed the deduction for the payment of sales taxes (§164). For tax years after 1986, sales taxes are capitalized as a cost of the purchased asset. Therefore, the Hoyts can only claim a deduction for the $3,000 real estate taxes paid on their residence and the $900 in state income taxes paid. This results in a total deduction for taxes of $3,900.

85. B   An employee is allowed to treat all unreimbursed traveling expenses incurred in connection with a job as a miscellaneous itemized deduction that is subject to the 2% of AGI limitation. (Travel expenses do not include commuting expenses.)

86. B   Appraisal fees incurred in connection with a casualty loss are considered an itemized deduction that is subject to the 2% of AGI limitation.

SOLUTION 4 FEDERAL TAXATION—CORPORATIONS

87. $7,000, D

A corporation may elect to amortize organizational expenses over a period of 60 months or more. The increase of an expense decreases taxable income. $40,000 / 60 x 12 = $8,000) ($8,000 − $1,000 = $7,000)

88. $5,000, I

Only 50% of meal and entertainment expenses are deductible. The reduction of an expense increases taxable income.

89. -0-, N

Premiums on employee life insurance policies are deductible if the corporation is not the beneficiary.

90. $10,000, I

Only the direct write-off method of recognizing bad debt is allowed for tax purposes. The reduction of an expense increases taxable income.

91. P   A dividend-received-deduction shields part of the dividend income from a 35% owned corporation.

92. F   For tax purposes, rental income is recognized when received, regardless of the taxpayer's basis of accounting.

93. P   A corporation's deduction for charitable contributions is limited to 10% of taxable income

without regard to the deduction for charitable contributions, the DRD, any NOL carry-back to that year, and any capital loss carry-back to that year.

94. N   Penalties are not deductible.

95. U   MACRS depreciation (200%) is higher in the first year of service than the 150% that is allowed for personal property under AMT. Because this overstates deductions, income is understated.

96. U   Straight-line depreciation over 40, not 39, years is appropriate for AMT purposes for real property. Because the deduction is overstated, income is understated.

97. C   Tax-exempt interest from private activity bonds issued after August 7, 1986 is a preference. However, state highway construction is not a private activity.

SOLUTION 5 FEDERAL TAXATION—GIFTS & TRANSFERS

98. N   Section 2503(b) indicates that the first $10,000 of a gift to any person may be excluded from the total amount of gifts made during the year.

99. P   Section 2503(b) indicates that the first $10,000 of a gift to any person may be excluded from the total amount of gifts made during the year. The gifts during the year that exceed this amount are taxable.

100. P   Section 2503(b) indicates that the first $10,000 of a gift to any person may be excluded from the total amount of gifts made during the year.

101. F   No part of the value of a gift of future interest may be excluded in determining the total amount of taxable gifts.

102. N   Certain qualified transfers are excluded when determining total taxable gifts. Qualified transfers include amounts paid on the behalf of another individual for tuition at an accredited educational institution or for medical care. (The payment must be made directly to the institution or care provider.)

103. F   No part of the value of a gift of future interest may be excluded in determining the total amount of taxable gifts.

104. P   Section 2503(b) indicates that the first $10,000 of a gift to any person may be excluded from the total amount of gifts made during the year.

APPENDIX B
PRACTICAL ADVICE

Your first step toward an effective CPA Review program is to **study** the material in this appendix. It has been carefully developed to provide you with essential information that will help you succeed on the CPA exam. This material will assist you in organizing an efficient study plan and will demonstrate effective techniques and strategies for taking the CPA exam.

SECTION ONE: GENERAL COMMENTS ON THE CPA EXAM

The difficulty and comprehensiveness of the CPA exam is a well-known fact to all candidates. However, success on the CPA exam is a **reasonable**, **attainable** goal. You should keep this point in mind as you study this appendix and develop your study plan. A positive attitude toward the examination, combined with determination and discipline, will enhance your opportunity to pass.

PURPOSE OF THE CPA EXAM

The CPA exam is designed as a licensing requirement to measure the technical competence of CPA candidates. Although licensing occurs at the State Board level, it is a uniform exam with national acceptance. Generally, passing the CPA exam in one jurisdiction allows a candidate to obtain a reciprocal certificate or license if they meet all the requirements imposed by the jurisdiction from which reciprocity is being sought.

State Boards also rely upon other means to ensure that candidates possess the necessary technical and character attributes, including interviews, letters of reference, affidavits of employment, ethics examinations, and educational requirements. Addresses of state boards are listed in this section of the **Practical Advice** appendix or (along with applicable links) on the web site of the National Association of the State Boards of Accountancy (http://www.nasba.org).

Generally speaking, the CPA exam is essentially an academic examination that tests the breadth of material covered by good accounting curricula. It also emphasizes the body of knowledge required for the practice of public accounting. It is to your advantage to take the exam as soon as possible after completing the formal education requirements. We also recommend that you study for the entire examination the first time you take it, since there is a **synergistic** learning effect to be derived through preparing for all four parts. That is, all sections of the exam share some common subjects (particularly Financial Accounting & Reporting, Accounting & Reporting, and Auditing); so as you study for one section, you are also studying for the others.

EXAMINATION SCHEDULE AND FORMAT

The CPA exam is given twice a year, on Wednesday and Thursday of the first week of May and November. AICPA-scheduled exam dates are May 7 and 8, 2003, and November 5 and 6, 2003. As the exam is becoming further computerized, projections past November 2003 are subject to greater uncertainty than in the past.

The four sections of the exam cover the following:

1. **Business Law & Professional Responsibilities**—This section covers the legal implications of business transactions generally confronted by CPAs, and the CPA's professional responsibility to the public and the profession (formerly covered in the Auditing section). This section's name is frequently abbreviated as BLPR. (3 hours)

2. **Auditing**—This section covers the generally accepted auditing standards, procedures, and related topics. The CPA's professional responsibility is no longer tested in this area. This section's name is frequently abbreviated as AUD. (4½ hours)

3. **Accounting & Reporting-Taxation, Managerial, and Governmental and Not-for-Profit Organizations**—This section covers federal taxation, managerial accounting, and accounting for governmental and nonprofit organizations. This section consists of multiple choice and other objective format questions only. This section has no essay questions or problems. This section's name is frequently abbreviated as ARE. (3½ hours)

4. **Financial Accounting & Reporting**—This section covers generally accepted accounting principles for business enterprises. This section's name is frequently abbreviated as FARE. (4½ hours)

The examination has the following formats and times:

Section	Format Multiple Choice	Other Objective Answer Formats	Essays or Problems	Day and Time			Duration	
BLPR	50-60%	20-30%	20-30%	Wed.	9:00	-12:00	3	hours
Auditing	50-60%	20-30%	20-30%	Wed.	1:30	- 6:00	4 1/2	hours
ARE	50-60%	40-50%	---	Thur.	8:30	-12:00	3 1/2	hours
FARE	50-60%	20-30%	20-30%	Thur.	1:30	- 6:00	4 1/2	hours
							15 1/2 hours	

CONDITIONAL STATUS

You will receive four scores. A passing score for each section is 75. Individual Boards of Accountancy may grant conditional status to those candidates who receive a passing grade in some, but not all, sections. Some Boards of Accountancy grant conditional status to candidates who pass only one section, while other Boards require that at least two sections be passed before conditional status is awarded. Many Boards require a minimum grade in the sections failed to receive conditional credit for the sections passed. Candidates should check with their State Board of Accountancy concerning details on conditional status.

ATTORNEYS' WAIVER

Some Boards of Accountancy may waive the Business Law section for members of the state bar. Once again, candidates should check with their particular state Board of Accountancy concerning this matter.

WRITING SKILLS CONTENT

Answers to selected essay responses from Business Law & Professional Responsibilities, Auditing, and Financial Accounting & Reporting sections will be used to assess candidates' writing skills. Additional information regarding writing skills is included in the **Accounting for 5%** section of those volumes. Five percent of the points available on each of these sections will be allocated to writing skills. Effective writing skills include the following six characteristics:

1. Coherent organization
2. Conciseness
3. Clarity
4. Use of standard English
5. Responsiveness to the requirements of the question
6. Appropriateness for the reader

REFERENCE MATERIALS

All the material you need to review to pass the CPA exam is in your Bisk Education *CPA Comprehensive Review* texts! However, should you desire more detailed coverage in any area, you should consult the actual promulgations. Individual copies of recent pronouncements are available from the FASB or AICPA. To order materials from the **FASB** or **AICPA** contact:

FASB Order Department
P.O. Box 5116
Norwalk, CT 06856-5116
Telephone (203) 847-0700

AICPA Order Department
P.O. Box 1003
New York, NY 10108-1003
Telephone (800) 334-6961

The FASB offers a student discount that varies depending on the publication. The AICPA offers a 30% educational discount, which students may claim by submitting proof of their eligibility (e.g., copy of ID card or teacher's letter). AICPA members get a 20% discount and delivery time is speedier because members may order by phone.

THE NONDISCLOSED EXAM

The Uniform CPA Examination is nondisclosed. This means that candidates are not allowed to keep (or receive) their examination booklets after the test. Candidates are also required to sign a statement of confidentiality in which they promise not to reveal questions or answers. After the exam, only the Institute will have access to the tests themselves. (The AICPA releases a small number of questions with unofficial answers from each nondisclosed exam.) Bisk Education's editors will continue to update our diagnostic tests for your convenience, with questions based upon the representative items, items from previously disclosed tests, and the teaching expertise of our editors.

BACKGROUND

The AICPA made this change (beginning May 1996), in order to increase consistency, facilitate possible future computer administration of the test, and improve examination quality by pretesting questions. Because the examination is no longer completely changed every year, statistical equating methods will be more relevant, and the usefulness of specific questions as indicators of candidates' knowledge can be tested.

EFFECTS ON TIME MANAGEMENT

Approximately 10% of the multiple choice questions in every section of every nondisclosed exam are questions that are being pretested. These questions are not included in candidates' final grades; they are presented only so that the Board of Examiners may evaluate them for effectiveness and possible ambiguity. The Scholastic Achievement Test and the Graduate Record Exam both employ similar but not identical strategies: those tests include an extra section that is being pretested, and test-takers do not know which section is the one which will not be graded. On the Uniform CPA Examination, however, the extra questions are mixed in among the graded questions. This makes time management even more crucial. Candidates who are deciding how much time to spend on a difficult multiple choice question must keep in mind that there is a 10% chance that the answer to the question will not affect them either way. Also, candidates should not allow a question that seems particularly difficult or confusing to shake their confidence or affect their attitude towards the rest of the test; it may not even count. This experimental 10% works against candidates who are not sure whether they have answered enough questions to earn 75%. Candidates should try for a safety margin, so that they will have accumulated enough correct answers to pass, even though some of their correctly answered questions will not be scored.

POST-EXAM DIAGNOSTICS

The AICPA Board of Examiners' Advisory Grading Service provides boards of accountancy with individual diagnostic reports for all candidates along with the candidates' grades. The accountancy boards may mail the diagnostic reports to candidates along with their grades. Candidates should contact the state board in their jurisdiction to find out its policy on this issue. A sample of a diagnostic report is in Section Five of this appendix. As before, grades are mailed approximately 90 days after the examination.

DISCUSSING THE EXAM

Remember that candidates are required to sign a statement of confidentiality in which they promise not to reveal questions or answers. Due to the nondisclosure requirements, Bisk Education's editors are no longer able to address questions about specific examination questions, although we continue to supply help with similar study problems and questions in our texts.

QUESTION RE-EVALUATION

Candidates who believe that an examination question contains errors that will affect the grading should fax their complaint to the AICPA Examinations Division, at (201) 938-3443, within 4 days after taking the examination. Only this method of communication will satisfy the requirements of the AICPA. The Advisory Grading Service asks candidates to be as precise as possible about the question and their reason for believing that it should be re-evaluated, and, if possible, to supply references to support their position. Since candidates are no longer able to keep or discuss the examination questions, it is important to remember as much detail as possible about a disputed question.

AICPA
Uniform CPA Examination
Candidate Diagnostic Report

Jurisdiction _____SAMPLE_____   Candidate Number 0-00-0000   Examination Date ____May 2001____

SECTION	GRADE	CONTENT AREA AND SECTION COVERAGE		PERCENTAGE OF AREA EARNED					
				≤ 50	51-60	61-70	71-80	81-90	> 90
LPR	64	I	PROFESSIONAL AND LEGAL RESPONSIBILITIES 15%			♦			
		II	BUSINESS ORGANIZATIONS 20%				♦		
		III	CONTRACTS 10%		♦				
		IV	DEBTOR-CREDITOR RELATIONSHIPS 10%	♦					
		V	GOVERNMENT REGULATION OF BUSINESS 15%				♦		
		VI	UNIFORM COMMERCIAL CODE 20%	♦					
		VII	PROPERTY 10%						♦
			100%						
AUDIT	68	I	EVALUATE CLIENT AND PLAN ENGAGEMENT 40%				♦		
		II	OBTAIN AND DOCUMENT INFORMATION 35%			♦			
		III	REVIEW ENGAGEMENT 5%				♦		
		IV	PREPARE COMMUNICATION 20%		♦				
			100%						
ARE	78	I	FEDERAL TAXATION—INDIVIDUALS 20%			♦			
		II	FEDERAL TAXATION—CORPORATIONS 20%						♦
		III	FEDERAL TAXATION—PARTNERSHIPS 10%			♦			
		IV	FEDERAL TAXATION—OTHER 10%				♦		
		V	GOVERNMENTAL AND NOT-FOR-PROFIT ORGANIZATIONS 30%			♦			
		VI	MANAGERIAL ACCOUNTING 10%				♦		
			100%						
FARE	80	I	CONCEPTS AND STANDARDS FOR FINANCIAL STATEMENTS 20%					♦	
		II	TYPICAL ITEMS IN FINANCIAL STATEMENTS 40%			♦			
		III	SPECIFIC TRANSACTIONS AND EVENTS IN FINANCIAL STATEMENTS 40%					♦	
			100%						

AICPA NONDISCLOSED EXAMINATION COVERAGE SUMMARY

The following chart provides an analysis of the AICPA Content Specification Outline coverage for the Accounting and Reporting section of the November 1999 through November 2001 Uniform CPA Examinations, all "nondisclosed" exams. This summary, provided by the AICPA, is intended only as a study aid and should not be used to predict the content of future examinations. (There are no essay questions in the ARE section of the exam.) More detail on the content specification outline is available on pages B-21 and B-22 of the printed book.

	Multiple Choice					OOAFs				
	N01	M01	N00	M00	N99	N01	M01	N00	M00	N99
Accounting & Reporting-- Taxation, Managerial, and Governmental and Not-for-Profit Organizations	75 (60%)	75 (60%)	75 (60%)	75 (60%)	75 (60%)	38 (40%)	45 (40%)	65 40%	52 40%	40%
I. Federal Taxation-- Individuals (20%)	13* (10.4%)	25* (20%)	12* (9.6%)	12* (9.6%)	25 (20%)	10* (10%)		20* (10%)	10* (10%)	
A.					9					
B.					5					
C.					4					
D.					1					
E.					1					
F.					2					
G.					2					
H.					1					
II. Federal Taxation-- Corporations (20%)	25* (20%)	13* (10.4%)	25* (20%)	13* (10.4%)	19 (15%)		10* (10%)		12* (10%)	5%
A.										5%
B.					1					
C. (S Corporations)					6					
D.										
E.					2					
F.					2					
G.					2					
H.					6					
III. Federal Taxation-- Partnerships (10%)		6* (4.8%)		12* (9.6%)		10* (10%)	8* (5%)	10* (10%)		10%
A.										5%
B.										2%
C.										
D.										
E.										
F.										3%
G.										

*The AICPA did not provide further information about the composition of these percentages.

	Multiple Choice					OOAFs				
	N01	M01	N00	M00	N99	N01	M01	N00	M00	N99
IV. Federal Taxation--Estates and Trusts, Exempt Organizations, and Preparers' Responsibilities (10%)	6* (4.8%)		7* (5.6%)	7* (5.6%)		10* (5%)	10* (10%)	18* (5%)	8* (5%)	10%
A.										
B.										5%
C.										5%
V. Accounting for Governmental and Not-for-Profit Organizations (30%)	19* (15.2%)	19* (15.2%)	19* (15.2%)	19* (15.2%)	19 (15%)	18* (15%)	17* (15%)	17* (15%)	22* (15%)	15%
A.					11					10%
B.					8					5%
VI. Managerial Accounting (10%)	12* (9.6%)	12* (9.6%)	12* (9.6%)	12* (9.6%)	12 (10%)					
A.					1					
B.					2					
C.					1					
D.										
E.					1					
F.										
G.					1					
H.					2					
I.										
J.					1					
K.					1					
L.					2					

The percentages indicate the format and subject of questions on the November 1999 through November 2001 CPA exams. For instance, on the Accounting & Reporting section of the November 1999 exam, 60 percent of the questions were multiple choice and 40 percent of the questions were other objective format (OOAF).

The actual number of some multiple choice questions asked for each area and group of the Content Specification Outline is also provided. For example, under the *Federal Taxation—Corporations* area on the November 1999 exam, there were 19 multiple choice questions: of those, 6 dealt with the *S Corporations* group. The percentage, but not the actual number, of OOAF questions for each section is indicated. For example, under the *Federal Taxation—Corporations* area on the November 1999 exam, 5 percent of the questions were OOAF.

---

*The AICPA did not provide further information about the composition of these percentages.

STATE BOARDS OF ACCOUNTANCY

Certified Public Accountants are licensed to practice by individual State Boards of Accountancy. Application forms and requirements to sit for the CPA exam should be requested from your individual State Board. IT IS EXTREMELY IMPORTANT THAT YOU COMPLETE THE APPLICATION FORM CORRECTLY AND RETURN IT TO YOUR STATE BOARD BEFORE THE SPECIFIED DEADLINE. Errors and/or delays may result in the rejection of your application. Be extremely careful in filling out the application and be sure to enclose all required materials. In many states, applications must be received by the State Board at least ninety days before the examination date. Requirements as to education, experience, internship, and other matters vary. If you have not already done so, take a moment to call the appropriate State Board for specific and current requirements. Complete the application in a timely manner. Some states arrange for an examination administrator, such CPA Examination Services [a division of the National Association of State Boards of Accountancy (NASBA), (800) CPA-EXAM (272-3926)] or Continental Examination Services [(800) 717-1201], to handle candidate registration, examination administration, etc.

It may be possible to sit for the exam in another state as an out-of-state candidate. Candidates wishing to do so should also contact the State Board of Accountancy in the state where they plan to be certified. NASBA has links (**http://www.nasba.org**) to some state board sites.

Approximately one month before the exam, check to see that your application to sit for the exam has been processed. DON'T ASSUME THAT YOU ARE PROPERLY REGISTERED UNLESS YOU HAVE RECEIVED YOUR CANDIDATE ID NUMBER.

The AICPA publishes a booklet entitled *Information for CPA Candidates*, usually distributed by State Boards of Accountancy to candidates upon receipt or acceptance of their applications. To request a complimentary copy, write your **State Board** or the **AICPA**, Examination Division, 1211 Avenue of the Americas, New York, NY 10036.

EXAMINATION SERVICES

CPA Examination Services, a division of the National Association of State Boards of Accountancy (NASBA), administers the examination for 25 states. Contact CPA Examination Services at (800) CPA-EXAM (272-3926), (615) 880-4250, or www.nasba.org.

CO	CT	DE	GA	HI	IA	IN	KS	LA	MA	ME	MI
MO	NJ	NM	NY	OH	PA	PR	RI	SC	TN	VA	VT	WA

Continental Testing Services at (800) 717-1201 administers the examination for WI.

The following are the telephone numbers and addresses of the boards in states that administer the exam themselves.

STATE	ADDRESS	PHONE NUMBER
AK	P.O. Box 110806, Juneau 99811-0806	907/465-2580
AL	P.O. Box 300375, Montgomery 36130-0375	334/242-5700
AR	101 E. Capitol Avenue, Ste. 430, Little Rock 72201	501/682-1520
AZ	3877 North Seventh Street, Ste. 106, Phoenix 85014	602/255-3648
CA	2000 Evergreen St., Ste. 250, Sacramento 95815-3832	916/263-3680
DC	614 H Street, N.W., Room 910, P.O. Box 37200, Washington, DC 20013-7200	202/442-4461
FL	2610 N.W. 43rd St., Ste. 1A, Gainesville 32606-4599	352/333-2500
GU	P.O. Box P, Agana, GU 96910	671/477-1050
ID	P.O. Box 83720, Boise 83720-0002	208/334-2490
IL	505 E. Green, Room 216, Champaign 61820-5723	217/333-1565
KY	332 W. Broadway, Ste. 310, Louisville 40202-2115	502/595-3037
MD	501 St. Paul Place, 9th Floor, Baltimore 21202-2272	410/333-6322
MN	85 East 7th Place, Ste. 125, St. Paul 55101	651/296-7937
MS	653 North State Street, Jackson 39202-3304	601/354-7320
MT	111 N. Jackson, P.O. Box 200513, Helena 59620-0513	406/841-2388
NC	P.O. Box 12827, Raleigh 27605-2827	919/733-4222
ND	2701 S. Columbia Road, Grand Forks 58201	800/532-5904
NE	P.O. Box 94725, Lincoln 68509-4725	402/471-3595
NH	57 Regional Dr., Concord 03301	603/271-3286
NV	200 South Virginia Street, Ste. 670, Reno 89501-2408	775/786-0231
OK	4545 N. Lincoln Blvd., Ste. 165, Oklahoma City 73105-3413	405/521-2397
OR	3218 Pringle Rd. S.E., Ste. 110, Salem 97302-6307	503/378-4181
SD	301 E. 14th St., Ste. 200, Sioux Falls 57104	605/367-5770
TX	333 Guadalupe Tower III, Suite 900, Austin 78701-3900	512/305-7850
UT	P.O. Box 146741, Salt Lake City 84114-6741	801/359-4417
VI	P.O. Box Y, Christiansted, St. Croix VI, 00822	340/773-2226
WI	P.O. Box 8935, Madison 53708-8935 [Call 800/717-1201]	608/266-5511
WV	201 L&S Bldg., 812 Quarrier Street, Charleston 25301-2695	304/558-3557
WY	2020 Carey Avenue Ste. 100, Cheyenne 82002-0610	307/777-7551

These addresses and phone numbers are subject to change without notice. Bisk Education assumes no responsibility with regard to their accuracy.

TEN ATTRIBUTES OF EXAMINATION SUCCESS

1.	**Positive Mental Attitude**	6.	**Examination Grading**
2.	**Development of a Plan**	7.	**Solutions Approach™**
3.	**Adherence to the Plan**	8.	**Examination Strategies**
4.	**Time Management**	9.	**Focus on Ultimate Objective—Passing!**
5.	**Knowledge**	10.	**Examination Confidence**

We believe that successful CPA candidates possess these ten characteristics that contribute to their ability to pass the exam. Because of their importance, we will consider each attribute individually.

1. Positive Mental Attitude

Preparation for the CPA exam is a long, intense process. A positive mental attitude, above all else, can be the difference between passing and failing.

2. Development of a Plan

The significant commitment involved in preparing for the exam requires a plan. We have prepared a Study Plan in the preceding "Getting Started" section. Take time to read this plan. Whether you use our "Study Plan" or create your own, the importance of this attribute can't be overlooked.

3. Adherence to the Plan

You cannot expect to accomplish a successful and comprehensive review without adherence to your study plan.

4. Time Management

We all lead busy lives, and the ability to budget study time is a key to success. We have outlined steps to budgeting time in the **Personalized Training Plan** found in the "Getting Started" section.

5. Knowledge

There is a distinct difference between understanding the material and knowing the material. A superficial understanding of accounting, auditing, and business law is not enough. You must **know** the material likely to be tested on the exam. Your Bisk Education text is designed to help you acquire the working knowledge that is essential to exam success.

6. Examination Grading

An understanding of the CPA exam grading procedure will help you to **maximize** grading points on the exam. Remember that your objective is to score 75 points on each section. Points are assigned to individual questions by the grader who reads your exam. In essence, your job is to **satisfy the grader** by writing answers that closely conform to the grading guide. In Section Two, we explain AICPA grading procedures and show you how to **tailor your answer** to the grading guide and thus earn more points on the exam.

7. Solutions Approach™

The Solutions Approach™ is an efficient, systematic method of organizing and solving questions found on the CPA exam. This Approach will permit you to organize your thinking and your written answers in a logical manner that will maximize your exam score. Candidates who do not use a systematic answering method often neglect to show all their work on difficult problems or essays—work that could earn partial credit if it were presented to the grader in an orderly fashion. The Solutions Approach™ will help you avoid drawing "blanks" on the exam; with it, you always know where to begin.

Many candidates have never developed an effective problem-solving methodology in their undergraduate studies. The "cookbook" approach, in which students work problems by following examples, is widespread among accounting schools. Unfortunately, it is not an effective problem-solving method for the CPA exam or for problems you will encounter in your professional career. Our Solutions Approach™ teaches you to derive solutions independently, without an example to guide you.

Our **Solutions Approach™** and grader orientation skills, when properly developed, can be worth at least 10 to 15 points for most candidates. These 10 to 15 points can often make the difference between passing and failing.

The **Solutions Approach™** for objective questions, problems, and essays is outlined in Section Three. Examples are worked and explained.

8. Examination Strategies

You should be familiar with the format of the CPA exam and know exactly what you will do when you enter the examination room. In Section Four, we discuss the steps you should take from the time you receive the test booklet, until you hand in your answer sheet. Planning in advance how you will spend your examination time will save you time and confusion on exam day.

9. Focus on Ultimate Objective—Passing!

Your primary goal in preparing for the CPA exam is to attain a grade of 75 or better on all sections and, thus, **pass the examination**. Your review should be focused on this goal. Other objectives, such as learning new material or reviewing old material, are important only insofar as they assist you in passing the exam.

10. Examination Confidence

Examination confidence is actually a function of the other nine attributes. If you have acquired a good working knowledge of the material, an understanding of the grading system, a tactic for answering the problems or essays, and a plan for taking the exam, you can go into the examination room **confident** that you are in control.

SECTION TWO: EXAMINATION GRADING ORIENTATION

The CPA exam is prepared and graded by the AICPA Examinations Division. It is administered by the various State Boards of Accountancy.

An understanding of the grading procedure will help you maximize grading points on the CPA exam. Remember that your objective is to pass the exam. You cannot afford to spend time on activities that will not affect your grade, or to ignore opportunities to increase your points. The following material abstracted from the *Information for CPA Candidates* booklet summarizes the important substantive aspects of the Uniform CPA Examination itself and the grading procedures used by the AICPA.

SECURITY

The examination is prepared and administered under tight security measures. The candidates' anonymity is preserved throughout the examination and grading process. Unusual similarities in answers among candidates are reported to the appropriate State Boards.

OBJECTIVE QUESTIONS

Objective questions consist of four-option, multiple-choice questions and other objective answer formats, which include: yes-no, true-false, matching, and questions requiring a numerical response. Objective questions are machine graded. Thus, you will accomplish nothing (and only waste time) by writing explanations beside your answers—only the blackened response is considered by the optical scanner. It is also important to understand that there is **no grade reduction** for incorrect responses to objective questions—your total objective question grade is determined solely by the number of correct answers. Thus, you **should answer every question**. If you do not know the answer, make an intelligent guess.

There are two or three formats for questions on each section of the CPA exam. In the past, difficulty points were assigned to these parts as a means of curving the entire section. This no longer occurs. Instead, difficulty points are assigned to the exam as a whole, not to each individual question. The point to remember is to avoid getting "bogged down" on one answer. Move along and answer **all** the questions. This helps you avoid leaving questions unanswered or panic-answering questions due to poor budgeting of test time.

GRADING IMPLICATIONS FOR CPA CANDIDATES

To summarize this review of the AICPA's grading procedure, we can offer the following conclusions that will help you to **satisfy the grader** and maximize your score:

1. Attempt an answer on every question.

2. Do not explain answers to multiple choice questions or other objective answer formats.

3. Respond directly to the requirements of the questions.

4. Answer all requirements.

5. Develop a **Solutions Approach™** to each question type.

6. Allocate your examination time based on AICPA point value.

———————————

SECTION THREE: THE SOLUTIONS APPROACH™

The **Bisk Education Solutions Approach™** is an efficient, systematic method of organizing and solving questions found on the CPA exam. Remember that all the knowledge in the world is worthless unless you can get it down on paper. Conversely, a little knowledge can go a long way if you use a proper approach. The Solutions Approach™ was developed by our Editorial Board in 1971; all subsequently developed stereotypes trace their roots from the original "Approach" that we formulated. Our Solutions Approach™ and grader orientation skills, when properly developed, can be worth at least 10 to 15 points for most candidates. These 10 to 15 points often make the difference between passing and failing.

We will suggest a number of steps for deriving a solution that will help maximize your grade on the exam. Although you should remember the important steps in our suggested approach, don't be afraid to adapt these steps to your own taste and requirements. When you work the questions at the conclusion of each chapter, make sure you use your variation of the Solutions Approach™. It is also important for you to attempt to pattern the organization and format of your written solution to the unofficial answer reprinted after the text of the questions. However, DO NOT CONSULT THE UNOFFICIAL ANSWER UNTIL YOU FINISH THE QUESTION. The worst thing you can do is look at old questions and then turn to the answer before working the problem. This will build false confidence and provide no skills in developing a Solutions Approach™.

SOLUTIONS APPROACH™ FOR OBJECTIVE QUESTIONS

The **Solutions Approach™** is also adaptable to objective questions. We recommend the following framework:

1. Read the "Instructions to Candidates" section on your particular exam to determine if the AICPA's standard is the same. Generally, your objective portion will be determined by the number of correct answers with no penalty for incorrect answers.

2. Read the question carefully, noting exactly what the question is asking. Negative requirements are easily missed. Underline key words and note when the requirement is an exception (e.g., "except for...," or "which of the following does **not**..."). Perform any intermediate calculations necessary to the determination of the correct answer.

3. Anticipate the answer by covering the possible answers and seeing if you **know** the correct answer.

4. Read the answers given.

5. Select the best alternative. Very often, one or two possible answers will be clearly incorrect. Of the other alternatives, be sure to select the alternative that **best answers the question asked**.

6. Mark the correct answer on the examination booklet itself. After completing all of the individual questions in an overall question, transfer the answers to the machine readable answer sheet with extreme care. Before you hand in your answer sheet, **go back** and double check your answers—make sure the answer is correct and make sure the sequence is correct. The AICPA uses answer sheets with varying formats; it is extremely important to follow the correct sequence (across the sheet vs. down or vice versa). READ THE INSTRUCTIONS CAREFULLY.

7. Answer the questions in order. This is a proven, systematic approach to objective test taking. You will generally be limited to a maximum of 2 minutes per multiple choice question. Under no circumstances should you allow yourself to fall behind schedule. If a question is too difficult, too long, or is a multiple question fact situation, be sure you remain cognizant of the time you are using. If after a minute or so you feel that it is too costly to continue on with a particular question, select the letter answer you tentatively feel is the best answer and go on. Return to these questions at a later time and attempt to finally answer them when you have time for more consideration. If you cannot find a better answer when you return to the question, use your preliminary answer because your first impressions are often correct. However, as you read other question(s), if something about these subsequent questions or answers jogs your memory, return to the previous tentatively answered question(s) and make a note of the idea for later consideration (time permitting).

A particularly challenging format is a group of objective questions based on one hypothetical situation. In this case, you should skim all the related questions (but not answer possibilities) before you begin answering, since an overall view of the problem will guide you in the work you do.

Note also that many incorrect answer choices are based on the erroneous application of one or more items in the text of the question. Thus, it is extremely important to **anticipate** the answer before you read the alternatives. Otherwise, you may be easily persuaded by an answer choice that is formulated through the incorrect use of the given data.

Let's consider a multiple choice question adapted from a past examination.

EXAMPLE 1

Which basis of accounting should a voluntary health and welfare organization use?
a.   Cash basis for all funds.
b.   Modified accrual basis for all funds.
c.   Accrual basis for all funds.
d.   Accrual basis for some funds and modified accrual basis for other funds.

APPLYING THE SOLUTIONS APPROACH

Let's look at the steps you should go through to arrive at your objective question solution.

In **Step 1** , you must carefully read the instructions that precede your particular objective CPA exam portion.

In **Step 2**, you must read the question and its requirements carefully.

In **Step 3**, you must anticipate the correct answer **after** reading the question but before reading the possible answers.

In **Step 4**, you must read the answer carefully and select the alternative that best answers the question asked. Ideally, the best alternative will immediately present itself because it roughly or exactly corresponds with the answer you anticipated before looking at the other possible choices.

In **Step 5**, you select the best alternative. If there are two close possibilities, make sure you select the **best** one in light of the **facts** and **requirements** of the question.

In **Step 6**, you must make sure you accurately mark the **correct answer** in the proper sequence. If **anything** seems wrong, stop, go back and double-check your answer sheet. As a fail-safe mechanism, circle the correct letter on the exam sheet first, before you move it to the answer sheet.

In **Step 7**, you must make sure you answer the questions on the answer sheet in order, with due regard to time constraints.

Solution: The answer is (c). Voluntary health and welfare organizations use the accrual basis of accounting for all their funds.

_____

SECTION FOUR: EXAMINATION STRATEGIES

The CPA exam is more than a test of your knowledge and technical competence. It is also a test of your ability to function under psychological pressure. You could easily be thrown off balance by an unexpected turn of events during the days of the exam. Your objective is to avoid surprises and eliminate hassles and distractions that might shake your confidence. You want to be in complete control so that you can concentrate on the exam material, rather than the exam situation. By taking charge of the exam, you will be able to handle pressure in a constructive manner. The keys to control are adequate preparation and an effective examination strategy.

OVERALL PREPARATION

Advance preparation will arm you with the confidence you need to overcome the psychological pressure of the exam. As you complete your comprehensive review, you will cover most of the material that will be tested on the exam; it is unlikely that an essay, problem, or series of objective questions will deal with a topic you have not studied. But if an unfamiliar topic **is** tested, you will not be dismayed because you have learned to use the **Solutions Approach™** to derive the best possible answer from the knowledge you possess. Similarly, you will not feel pressured to write "perfect" answers, because you understand the grading process. You recognize that there is a limit to the points you can earn for each answer, no matter how much you write.

The components of your advance preparation program have previously been discussed in this appendix. Briefly summarizing, they include:

1. Comprehensive review materials such as your Bisk Education CPA Review Program.

2. A method for pre-review and ongoing self-evaluation of your level of proficiency.

3. A study plan that enables you to review each subject area methodically and thoroughly.

4. A **Solutions Approach™** for each type of examination question.

5. An understanding of the grading process and grader orientation skills.

CPA EXAM STRATEGIES

The second key to controlling the exam is to develop effective strategies for the days during which the exam is given. Your objective is to avoid surprises and frustrations so that you can focus your full concentration on the questions and your answers.

You should be familiar with the format of the CPA exam and know exactly what you will do when you enter the examination room. Remember to carefully read the instructions on the cover page of the exam booklet AND for each problem. Disregarding the instructions may mean loss of points.

On the following pages, we discuss the steps you should take from the time you receive the test booklet until the time you hand in your booklet. Planning in advance how you will spend your examination time will save you time and confusion on exam day.

INVENTORY OF THE EXAMINATION

You should spend the first few minutes of the exam surveying the exam booklet and planning your work. **Do not** plunge head-first into answering the questions without a plan of action. You do not want to risk running out of time, becoming frustrated by a difficult question, or losing the opportunity to answer a question that you could have answered well. Your inventory should take no longer than five minutes. The time you spend will help you "settle in" to the examination and develop a feel for your ability to answer the questions.

1. Carefully read the "Instructions to Candidates" on the cover page.

2. Note the number of questions/problems on the cover page.

3. Once permission is given, go through the booklet and see what topics each question covers. Jot down the topics and devise a time schedule on the front cover, forming a table of contents.

ORDER OF ANSWERING QUESTIONS

Once you have completed your inventory of the exam, the next step is to develop an order for answering the objective questions and problems/essays. We recommend that you begin with the objective questions and then proceed to the problems/essays, beginning with the problem/essay that you feel is the least difficult.

Objective questions comprise the entire point value of the ARE section. Because of their objective nature, the correct solution is listed as one of the answer choices, except when the answer is an amount. By solving these questions, not only do you gain confidence, but they often involve the same or a related topic to that covered in one of the questions where the answers are amounts.

A very effective and efficient manner of answering the objective questions is to make **two passes** through the questions. On the first pass, you should answer those questions that you find the easiest. If you come across a question that you find difficult to solve, mark it and proceed to the next one. This will allow you to avoid wasting precious time and will enable your mind to clear and start anew on your **second pass**. On the second pass, you should go back and solve those questions you left unanswered on the first pass. Some of these questions you may have skipped over without an attempt, while in others you may have been able to eliminate one or two of the answer choices. Either way, you should come up with an answer on the second pass, even if you have to guess! After completing all of the individual questions in an overall question, transfer the answers to the machine readable answer sheet with extreme care. Simply make note of those questions that gave you difficulty and then proceed to the problems or essays.

EXAMINATION TIME BUDGETING

You must **plan** how you will use your examination time and adhere faithfully to your schedule. If you budget your time carefully, you should be able to answer all parts of all questions. To demonstrate a realistic time budget, refer again to the time parameters in the examination booklet.

The time limitation on the exam is 3½ hours for the ARE section. You should subtract five minutes for your initial inventory on each section. Assuming you will use the **Solutions Approach™**, your time budget may be similar to the one below. The actual exam may differ from this scenario so be sure to adjust your time budget to accommodate the number and type of questions asked.

	Minutes			
	FAR	ARE	Auditing	BLPR
Inventory examination	5	5	5	5
Answer objective questions	120	190	180	120
Write problem solutions (45-50 min. for each)	90			
Key word outline essays (10 min. for each)	20		20	20
Write essay solutions (10-30 min. for each)	20		50	20
Review answers	15	15	15	15
	270	210	270	180

Your objective in time budgeting is to avoid running out of time to answer a question. Work quickly but efficiently (i.e., use the **Solutions Approach™**). Remember, a reasoned guess is better than no answer at all.

PSYCHOLOGY OF EXAMINATION SUCCESS

As stated previously, the CPA exam is in itself a physical and mental strain. You can minimize this strain by avoiding all unnecessary distractions and inconveniences during exam week. For example:

- **Make reservations for lodging well in advance**. It's best to reserve a room for Tuesday night so that you can check in, get a good night's sleep, and locate the exam site early the next morning.

- **Stick to your normal eating, sleeping, and exercise habits**. Eat lightly before the exam, and take small candies with you for quick energy. Watch your caffeine and alcohol intake. If you are accustomed to regular exercise, continue a regular routine during exam week.

- **Visit the examination facilities before the examination** and familiarize yourself with the surroundings.

- **Arrive early for the exam**. Allow plenty of time for unexpected delays. Nothing is more demoralizing than getting caught in a traffic jam ten minutes before the exam is scheduled to begin.

- **Avoid possible distractions**, such as friends and pre-exam conversation, immediately before the exam.

- In general, **you should not attempt to study on the nights before exam sessions**. It's better to relax—go to a movie, read a novel, or watch television. If you feel you must study, spend half an hour or so going over the chapter outlines in the text.

- **Don't discuss exam answers with other candidates**: Not only have you signed a statement of confidentiality, but someone is sure to disagree with your answer, and if you are easily influenced by his or her reasoning, you can become doubtful of your own ability. Wait and analyze the entire exam yourself after you have finished all sections.

COMPUTER-BASED TESTING

The AICPA is in the process of converting the CPA exam into a computer-based test (CBT). Currently, candidates read questions from a printed page, darken ovals on a machine-readable sheet for the objective answers, and write essay answers on lined paper. To some extent, the exam is already computerized; the objective answers are machine-graded. The next step in this conversion is likely to be essentially the same exam, with candidates reading questions from, and entering answers into, a personal computer. Before this happens, laws in many jurisdictions must change to allow this format, among other things.

The examination division tentatively has targeted 2004 as the date for this next stage. There may be only pilot groups who sit for the computerized exam in 2004. Candidates are unlikely to have much say in whether they will be part of a pilot group. As we go to press, the AICPA has not yet decided most details; even the implementation date is subject to change. When the exam becomes "computerized," Bisk Education will provide necessary details in its updating supplements, just as it provides information regarding new pronouncements, laws, and other related material. Because the details of the computerized exam are subject to change, we don't recommend that candidates wait to take the exam in order, say, to avoid the essay questions. After waiting, candidates may find that the CBT has essay questions after all.

Candidates interested in learning more about the computerized exam should contact the AICPA. As we go to press, the AICPA web-site (www.aicpa.org) has an exposure draft available for downloading. However, do not confuse time spent learning about proposals for the computerized exam with review time. Bisk Education's updating supplements will include a concise summary of need-to-know information for candidates, when it becomes relevant to passing the exam.

AICPA General Rules Governing Examination

1. Read carefully the identification card assigned to you; sign it; make note of your number for future reference; when it is requested, return the card to the examiner. Only the examination number on your card shall be used on your papers for the purpose of identification. The importance of remembering this number and recording it on your examination paper correctly cannot be over-emphasized. If a question calls for an answer involving a signature, **do not** sign your own name or initials.

2. Seating during the exam is assigned according to your ID number in most states.

3. Answers must be submitted on paper furnished by the Board and must be completed in the total time allotted for each subject stated on the printed examinations. Begin your answer to each question on a separate page.

4. Answers should be written in pencil using No. 2 lead. **Neatness and orderly presentation of work are important**. Credit cannot be given for answers that are illegible.

5. Use a soft No. 2 lead pencil to blacken the spaces on the answer sheets for the objective-type questions.

6. Supplies furnished by the Board shall remain its property and must be returned whether used or not. You must hand in your printed examination booklet before leaving the examination room or your examination will not be graded.

7. Any reference during the examination to books or other matters or the exchange of information with other persons shall be considered misconduct sufficient to bar you from further participation in the examination.

8. The only aids candidates are permitted to have in the examination room are pens, pencils, and erasers. Calculators will be provided. Handbags and purses must be placed on the floor at candidates' locations during the entire time they are taking the exam. Briefcases, files, books, and other material brought to the examination site by candidates must be placed in a designated area before the start of the examination.

9. The fixed time for each session must be observed by all candidates. Each period will start and end promptly. It is the candidate's responsibility to be present and ready at the start of the period and to stop writing when told to do so.

10. Candidates arriving late should not be permitted any extension of time, but may be allowed to take the examination with proctor approval.

11. Smoking is allowed only in designated areas away from the general examination area.

12. No telephone calls are permitted during the examination session.

13. Only two time warnings are given: (1) thirty minutes prior to the end of session, and (2) five minutes prior to the end of session. (Additional warnings are not considered necessary.)

CPA Exam Week Checklist

WHAT TO PACK FOR EXAM WEEK:

1. CPA exam registration material.

2. Hotel confirmation.

3. Cash and/or a major credit card.

4. Alarm clock—Don't rely on a hotel wake-up call.

5. Comfortable clothing that can be layered to suit varying temperatures.

6. A watch.

7. Appropriate review materials, pencils, erasers, and pencil sharpener.

8. Healthy snack foods.

EVENINGS BEFORE EXAM SECTIONS:

1. Read through your Bisk Education chapter outlines for the next day's section(s).

2. Eat lightly and monitor your intake of alcohol and caffeine. Get a good night's rest.

3. Do **not** try to cram. A brief review of your notes will help to focus your attention on important points and remind you that you are well prepared, but too much cramming can shatter your self-confidence. If you have reviewed conscientiously, you are already well-prepared for the CPA exam.

THE MORNING OF EACH EXAM SECTION:

1. Eat a satisfying breakfast. It will be several hours before your next meal. Eat enough to ward off hunger, but not so much that you feel uncomfortable.

2. Dress appropriately. Wear layers you can take off to suit varying temperatures in the room.

3. Take ample supplies.

4. Arrive at the exam center thirty minutes early. Check in as soon as you are allowed to do so.

WHAT TO BRING TO THE EXAM:

1. ID card—This is your official entrance permit to the exam.

2. Several sharpened No. 2 pencils, erasers, and a small pencil sharpener. Some states provide pencils and do not allow candidates to bring their own.

3. A watch.

4. Tissues, small candies, gum, and aspirin.

5. Do **not** take articles that will not be allowed in the exam room. Highlighters are not allowed.

DURING THE EXAM:

1. Always read all instructions and follow the directions of the exam administrator. If you don't understand any written or verbal instructions, or if something doesn't seem right, ASK QUESTIONS. Remember that an error in following directions could invalidate your **entire** exam.

2. Budget your time. Always keep track of the time and avoid getting too involved with one question.

3. **Satisfy the grader**. Remember that the grader cannot read your mind. You must explain every point. Focus on key words and concepts. Tell the grader what you know, don't **worry** about any points you don't know.

4. Answer every question, even if you must guess.

5. Use **all** the allotted time. If you finish a section early, go back and reconsider the more difficult questions.

6. Check the answer sheet frequently to see that the number of each answer corresponds to the number of the question you intended. Many examinees get out of sequence on the answer sheet.

7. Stop working **immediately** when time is called. You do not want to risk being disqualified just to get one last answer recorded.

8. Get up and stretch if you feel sluggish. Walk around if you are allowed. Breathe deeply; focus your eyes on distant objects to avoid eye strain. Do some exercises to relax muscles in the face, neck, fingers, and back.

9. Take enough time to write neatly and organize your answer. Legible, well-organized answers will impress the grader.

10. Remember that you are well-prepared for the CPA exam, and that you can **expect to pass**! A confident attitude will help you overcome examination anxiety.

SECTION FIVE: CONTENT SPECIFICATION OUTLINES AND FREQUENTLY TESTED AREAS

The AICPA Board of Examiners has developed a **Content Specification Outline** of each section of the exam to be tested. These outlines list the areas, groups, and topics to be tested and indicate the approximate percentage of the total test score devoted to each area. The content of the examination is based primarily on results of national studies of public accounting practice and the evaluation of CPA practitioners and educators.

I. **Federal Taxation--Individuals (20%)**

A. Inclusions in Gross Income

B. Exclusions and Adjustments to Arrive at Adjusted Gross Income

C. Deductions From Adjusted Gross Income

D. Filing Status and Exemptions

E. Tax Accounting Methods

F. Tax Computations, Credits, and Penalties

G. Alternative Minimum Tax

H. Tax Procedures

II. **Federal Taxation--Corporations (20%)**

A. Determination of Taxable Income or Loss

B. Tax Accounting Methods

C. S Corporations

D. Personal Holding Companies

E. Consolidated Returns

F. Tax Computations, Credits, and Penalties

G. Alternative Minimum Tax

H. Other

   1. Distributions

   2. Incorporation, Reorganization, Liquidation, and Dissolution

   3. Tax Procedures

III. **Federal Taxation--Partnerships (10%)**

A. Basis of Partner's Interest and Bases of Assets Contributed to the Partnership

B. Determination of Partner's Share of Income, Credits, and Deductions

C. Partnership and Partner Elections

D. Partner Dealing With Own Partnership

E. Treatment of Partnership Liabilities

F. Distribution of Partnership Assets

G. Termination of Partnership

IV. **Federal Taxation--Estates and Trusts, Exempt Organizations, and Preparers' Responsibilities (10%)**

A. Estates and Trusts

   1. Income Taxation

   2. Determination of Beneficiary's Share of Taxable Income

   3. Estates and Gift Taxation

B. Exempt Organizations

   1. Types of Organizations

   2. Requirements for Exemption

   3. Unrelated Business Income Tax

C. Preparers' Responsibilities

V. Accounting for Governmental and Nonprofit Organizations (30%)

A. Governmental Organizations

1. Measurement Focus and Basis of Accounting
2. Objectives of Financial Reporting
3. Uses of Fund Accounting
4. Budgetary Process
5. Financial Reporting Entity
6. Elements of Financial Statements
7. Conceptual Reporting Issues

8. Accounting and Financial Reporting for State and Local Governments

   a. Governmental-Type Funds and Account Groups
   b. Proprietary-Type Funds
   c. Fiduciary-Type Funds

9. Accounting and Financial Reporting for Governmental Not-for-profit Organizations (Including Hospitals, Colleges and Universities, Voluntary Health and Welfare Organizations and Other Governmental Not-for-profit Organizations

B. Nongovernmental Not-for-profit Organizations

1. Objectives of Financial Reporting
2. Elements of Financial Statements
3. Formats of Financial Statements

4. Accounting and Financial Reporting for Nongovernmental Not-for-profit Organizations

   a. Revenues and Contributions
   b. Restrictions on Resources
   c. Expenses, Including Depreciation

VI. Managerial Accounting (10%)

A. Cost Estimation, Cost Determination, and Cost Drivers
B. Job Costing, Process Costing, and Activity Based Costing
C. Standard Costing and Flexible Budgeting
D. Inventory Planning, Inventory Control, and Just-in-Time Purchasing
E. Budgeting and Responsibility Accounting
F. Variable and Absorption Costing
G. Cost-Volume-Profit Analysis
H. Cost Allocation and Transfer Pricing
I. Joint and By-Product Costing
J. Capital Budgeting
K. Special Analyses for Decision Making
L. Product and Service Pricing

From the AICPA's *Information for CPA Candidates*:

"Candidates are responsible for knowing accounting and auditing pronouncements, including the pronouncements in the governmental and not-for-profit organizations area, six months after a pronouncement's *effective* date, unless early application is permitted. When early application is permitted, candidates are responsible for knowing the new pronouncement six months after the *issuance* date. In this case, candidates are responsible for knowing both the old and new pronouncements until the old pronouncement is superseded. For the federal taxation area, candidates are responsible for knowing the Internal Revenue Code and federal tax regulations in effect six months before the examination date."

Although recent changes in describing content coverage make it difficult to know with certainty what the AICPA will now ask, we can use exam history to highlight those areas that have been emphasized. Based on analysis of past exams, we have identified the areas most heavily tested in the past. Keep in mind that lightly tested areas may be heavily tested on any one exam and there is the potential for **any area** to be tested.

Candidates frequently review this information and then ask, "Yes, but how do the Bisk Education chapters correspond to these specifications?" The coverage changes slightly with each exam; Bisk provides the following chart to demonstrate the variation on past exams. In order to present information in the most easily assimilated manner possible, the text is not aligned exactly with the divisions in the content specifications.

Frequently Tested Areas

Ch. 21   Governmental Overview
Ch. 22   Governmental Funds & Transactions
Ch. 23   Nonprofit Accounting
Ch. 26   Planning & Control
Ch. 27   Federal Taxation: Individuals
Ch. 29   Federal Taxation: Corporations & Exempt Organizations
Ch. 30   Federal Taxation: Partnerships & Other Topics

More precise "predictions" of what will be heavily tested on any one exam are highly speculative.

_____

Accounting & Reporting Coverage

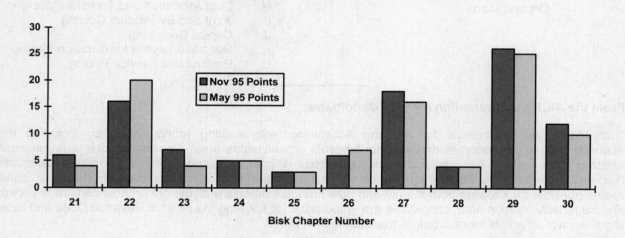

While reviewing this graph, please be aware that the content specification slightly decreased individual and corporate taxation coverage and increased partnership and other topics coverage since the November 1995 exam (the last fully disclosed exam).

_____

SECTION SIX:
AUTHORITATIVE PRONOUNCEMENTS CROSS-REFERENCE

Pronouncement	Bisk Education Chapter Number(s)	Statements of the Governmental Accounting Standards Board
GASB 18	21	Accounting for Municipal Solid Waste Landfill Closure and Postclosure Care Costs
GASB 19	21	Governmental College and University Omnibus Statement
GASB 20	22	Accounting and Financial Reporting For Proprietary Funds and Other Governmental Entities That Use Proprietary Fund Accounting
GASB 21	21	Accounting for Escheat Property
GASB 22	22	Accounting for Taxpayer-Assessed Revenues in Governmental Funds
GASB 23	22	Accounting and Financial Reporting for Refundings of Debt Reported by Proprietary Activities
GASB 24	22	Accounting and Reporting for Certain Grants and Other Financial Assistance
GASB 25	21	Financial Reporting For Defined Benefit Plans and Note Disclosures for Defined Contribution Plans
GASB 26	21	Financial Reporting for Postemployment Healthcare Plans Administered by Defined Benefit Pension Plans
GASB 27	21	Accounting For Pensions by State and Local Employers
GASB 28	21	Accounting and Financial Reporting for Securities Lending Transactions
GASB 29	22	The Use of Not-For-Profit Accounting and Financial Reporting Principles by Governmental Entities
GASB 30	21	Risk Financing Omnibus
GASB 31	21	Accounting and Financial Reporting for Certain Investments and for External Investment Pools
GASB 32	21	Accounting and Financial Reporting for Internal Revenue Code Section 457 Deferred Compensation Plans
GASB 33	21	Nonexchange Transactions
GASB 34	21, 22	Basic Financial Statements—and Management's Discussion & Analysis—for State and Local Governments
GASB 35	21, 22	Basic Financial Statements—and Management's Discussion & Analysis—for Public Colleges and Universities
GASB 36	21	Recipient Reporting for Certain Shared Nonexchange Revenues
GASB 37	21, 22	Basic Financial Statements—and Management's Discussion & Analysis—for State and Local Governments: Omnibus—an Amendment of GASB Statements No. 21 and No. 34
GASB 38	21	Certain Financial Statement Note Disclosures
GASB 39	21	Determining Whether Certain Organizations Are Component Units
		GASB Concepts Statements
1	21	Objectives of Financial Reporting

Pronouncement	Bisk Education Chapter Number(s)	Statements of Financial Accounting Standards
SFAS 93	23	Recognition of Depreciation by Not-for-profit Organizations
SFAS 95	23	Statement of Cash Flows
SFAS 116	23	Contributions Received and Contributions Made
SFAS 117	23	Financial Statements for Not-for-Profit Entities
SFAS 124	23	Accounting for Certain Investments Held by Not-for-Profit Organizations
SFAS 136	23	Transfers of Assets to a Not-for-profit Organization or Charitable Trust That Raises or Holds Contributions for Others

---

BENEFITS OF THE SOLUTIONS APPROACH™

The **Solutions Approach™** may seem cumbersome the first time you attempt it; candidates frequently have a tendency to answer a question as they read it. The Solutions Approach™ will help you arrive at a solution that meets the question requirements. It will also help you recall information under the pressure of the exam. The technique assists you in directing your thoughts toward the information required for the answer. Without a Solutions Approach™, you are apt to become distracted or confused by details that are irrelevant to the answer. Finally, the Solutions Approach™ is a **faster** way to answer exam questions. The approach may seem time-consuming at first, but as you become comfortable using it, you will see that it actually saves time and results in a better answer.

We urge you to give the **Solutions Approach™** a good try by using it throughout your CPA review (see page B-13). As you practice, you may adapt or modify it to your own preferences and requirements. The important thing is to develop a system so that you do not approach exam questions with a storehouse of knowledge that you can not put down on paper.

APPENDIX C
COMPOUND INTEREST TABLES

TABLE 1—FUTURE VALUE OF $1

$$FV = PV(1 + r)^n$$

r = interest rate; n = number of periods until valuation; PV = \$1

	1%	2%	3%	4%	5%	6%	7%	8%	10%	12%	15%	20%	25%
$n = 1$	1.010000	1.020000	1.030000	1.040000	1.050000	1.060000	1.070000	1.080000	1.100000	1.120000	1.150000	1.200000	1.250000
2	1.020100	1.040400	1.060900	1.081600	1.102500	1.123600	1.144900	1.166400	1.210000	1.254400	1.322500	1.440000	1.562500
3	1.030301	1.061208	1.092727	1.124864	1.157625	1.191016	1.225043	1.259712	1.331000	1.404928	1.520875	1.728000	1.953125
4	1.040604	1.082432	1.125509	1.169859	1.215506	1.262477	1.310796	1.360489	1.464100	1.573519	1.749006	2.073600	2.441406
5	1.051010	1.104081	1.159274	1.216653	1.276282	1.338226	1.402552	1.469328	1.610510	1.762342	2.011357	2.488320	3.051758
6	1.061520	1.126162	1.194052	1.265319	1.340096	1.418519	1.500730	1.586874	1.771561	1.973823	2.313061	2.985984	3.814697
7	1.072135	1.148686	1.229874	1.315932	1.407100	1.503630	1.605781	1.713824	1.948717	2.210681	2.660020	3.583181	4.768372
8	1.082857	1.171659	1.266770	1.368569	1.477455	1.593848	1.718186	1.850930	2.143589	2.475963	3.059023	4.299817	5.960464
9	1.093685	1.195093	1.304773	1.423312	1.551328	1.689479	1.838459	1.999005	2.357948	2.773079	3.517876	5.159781	7.450581
10	1.104622	1.218994	1.343916	1.480244	1.628895	1.790848	1.967151	2.158925	2.593743	3.105848	4.045558	6.191737	9.313226
11	1.115668	1.243374	1.384234	1.539454	1.710339	1.898299	2.104852	2.331639	2.853117	3.478550	4.652391	7.430084	11.64153
12	1.126825	1.268242	1.425761	1.601032	1.795856	2.012197	2.252192	2.518170	3.138428	3.895976	5.350250	8.916101	14.55192
13	1.138093	1.293607	1.468534	1.665074	1.885649	2.132928	2.409845	2.719624	3.452271	4.363493	6.152788	10.69932	18.18989
14	1.149474	1.319479	1.512590	1.731676	1.979932	2.260904	2.578534	2.937194	3.797498	4.887112	7.075706	12.83918	22.73737
15	1.160969	1.345868	1.557967	1.800943	2.078928	2.396558	2.759032	3.172169	4.177248	5.473566	8.137062	15.40702	28.42171
16	1.172579	1.372786	1.604706	1.872981	2.182875	2.540352	2.952164	3.425943	4.594973	6.130394	9.357621	18.48843	35.52714
17	1.184304	1.400241	1.652848	1.947900	2.292018	2.692773	3.158815	3.700018	5.054471	6.866041	10.76126	22.18611	44.40892
18	1.196147	1.428246	1.702433	2.025816	2.406619	2.854339	3.379932	3.996019	5.559917	7.689965	12.37545	26.62333	55.51115
19	1.208109	1.456811	1.753506	2.106849	2.526950	3.025599	3.616528	4.315701	6.115909	8.612761	14.23177	31.94800	69.38894
20	1.220190	1.485947	1.806111	2.191123	2.653298	3.207135	3.869684	4.660957	6.727500	9.646293	16.36654	38.33760	86.73618
22	1.244716	1.545980	1.916103	2.369919	2.925261	3.603537	4.430402	5.436540	8.140275	12.10031	21.64475	55.20615	135.5253
24	1.269735	1.608437	2.032794	2.563304	3.225100	4.048934	5.072367	6.341180	9.849733	15.17863	28.62518	79.49685	211.7582
26	1.295256	1.673418	2.156591	2.772470	3.555673	4.549383	5.807353	7.396353	11.91818	19.04007	37.85680	114.4755	330.8723
28	1.321291	1.741024	2.287928	2.998703	3.920129	5.111687	6.648839	8.627106	14.42099	23.88387	50.06562	164.8447	516.9879
30	1.347849	1.811362	2.427262	3.243397	4.321942	5.743491	7.612255	10.06266	17.44940	29.95992	66.21178	237.3763	807.7936
32	1.374941	1.884541	2.575083	3.508059	4.764942	6.453386	8.715271	11.73708	21.11378	37.58172	87.56509	341.8219	1262.177
34	1.402577	1.960676	2.731905	3.794316	5.253348	7.251025	9.978113	13.69013	25.54767	47.14251	115.8048	492.2236	1972.152
36	1.430769	2.039887	2.898278	4.103932	5.791816	8.147252	11.42394	15.96817	30.91268	59.13557	153.1519	708.8019	3081.488
38	1.459527	2.122299	3.074783	4.438813	6.385478	9.154252	13.07927	18.62527	37.40435	74.17966	202.5434	1020.675	4814.825
40	1.488864	2.208040	3.262038	4.801021	7.039989	10.28572	14.97446	21.72452	45.25926	93.05096	267.8636	1469.772	7523.164
45	1.564811	2.437854	3.781596	5.841176	8.985008	13.76461	21.00245	31.92045	72.89049	163.9876	538.7694	3657.262	22958.88
50	1.644632	2.691588	4.383906	7.106683	11.46740	18.42015	29.45703	46.90161	117.3909	289.0022	1083.658	9100.439	70064.92
100	2.704814	7.244646	19.21863	50.50494	131.5013	339.3020	867.7164	2199.761	13780.61	83522.24	117×10^4	828×10^5	491×10^7

EXAMPLE 1 ♦ FUTURE VALUE OF A SINGLE SUM

REQUIRED: Find the future value of a \$100 certificate of deposit at 8% for three years, (A) compounded annually and (B) compounded quarterly.

SOLUTION A: Let   Principal = P = \$100,   Interest Rate = r = 8%,   Period = n = 3 years
Future Value Interest Factor at r Rate for n Periods = FVIF(r, n)
Future Value = FV = P x FVIF(r, n)

FVIF(8%, 3 years) = 1.2597 (from Table 1)

FV = \$100 x 1.2597 = \$125.97

SOLUTION B: Let   Principal = P = \$100
Interest Rate = r = 8% ÷ 4 quarters = 2%,   Period = n = 12 quarters
Future Value Interest Factor at r Rate for n Periods = FVIF(r, n)
Future Value = FV = P x FVIF(r, n)

FVIF(2%, 12 quarters) = 1.2682 (from Table 1)

FV = \$100 x 1.2682 = \$126.82

TABLE 2—PRESENT VALUE OF $1

$$PV = \frac{FV}{(1 + r)^n}$$

r = discount rate; n = number of periods until payment; FV = $1

	1%	2%	3%	4%	5%	6%	7%	8%	10%	12%	15%	20%	25%
n = 1	0.990099	0.980392	0.970874	0.961538	0.952381	0.943396	0.934579	0.925926	0.909091	0.892857	0.869565	0.833333	0.800000
2	0.980296	0.961169	0.942596	0.924556	0.907029	0.889996	0.873439	0.857339	0.826446	0.797194	0.756144	0.694444	0.640000
3	0.970590	0.942322	0.915142	0.888996	0.863838	0.839619	0.816298	0.793832	0.751315	0.711780	0.657516	0.578704	0.512000
4	0.960980	0.923845	0.888487	0.854804	0.822702	0.792094	0.762895	0.735030	0.683013	0.635518	0.571753	0.482253	0.409600
5	0.951466	0.905731	0.862609	0.821927	0.783526	0.747258	0.712986	0.680583	0.620921	0.567427	0.497177	0.401878	0.327680
6	0.942045	0.887971	0.837484	0.790315	0.746215	0.704961	0.666342	0.630170	0.564474	0.506631	0.432328	0.334898	0.262144
7	0.932718	0.870560	0.813092	0.759918	0.710681	0.665057	0.622750	0.583490	0.513158	0.452349	0.375937	0.279082	0.209715
8	0.923483	0.853490	0.789409	0.730690	0.676839	0.627412	0.582009	0.540269	0.466507	0.403883	0.326902	0.232568	0.167772
9	0.914340	0.836755	0.766417	0.702587	0.644609	0.591898	0.543934	0.500249	0.424098	0.360610	0.284262	0.193807	0.134218
10	0.905287	0.820348	0.744094	0.675564	0.613913	0.558395	0.508349	0.463194	0.385543	0.321973	0.247185	0.161506	0.107374
11	0.896324	0.804263	0.722421	0.649581	0.584679	0.526788	0.475093	0.428883	0.350494	0.287476	0.214943	0.134588	0.085899
12	0.887449	0.788493	0.701380	0.624597	0.556837	0.496969	0.444012	0.397114	0.318631	0.256675	0.186907	0.112157	0.068719
13	0.878663	0.773033	0.680951	0.600574	0.530321	0.468839	0.414964	0.367698	0.289664	0.229174	0.162528	0.093464	0.054976
14	0.869963	0.757875	0.661118	0.577475	0.505068	0.442301	0.387817	0.340461	0.263331	0.204620	0.141329	0.077887	0.043980
15	0.861349	0.743015	0.641862	0.555265	0.481017	0.417265	0.362446	0.315242	0.239392	0.182696	0.122894	0.064905	0.035184
16	0.852821	0.728446	0.623167	0.533908	0.458112	0.393646	0.338735	0.291890	0.217629	0.163122	0.106865	0.054088	0.028147
17	0.844378	0.714163	0.605016	0.513373	0.436297	0.371364	0.316574	0.270269	0.197845	0.145644	0.092926	0.045073	0.022518
18	0.836017	0.700159	0.587395	0.493628	0.415521	0.350344	0.295864	0.250249	0.179859	0.130040	0.080805	0.037561	0.018014
19	0.827740	0.686431	0.570286	0.474642	0.395734	0.330513	0.276508	0.231712	0.163508	0.116107	0.070265	0.031301	0.014412
20	0.819544	0.672971	0.553676	0.456387	0.376889	0.311805	0.258419	0.214548	0.148644	0.103667	0.061100	0.026084	0.011529
22	0.803396	0.646839	0.521892	0.421955	0.341850	0.277505	0.225713	0.183941	0.122846	0.082643	0.046201	0.018114	0.007379
24	0.787566	0.621722	0.491934	0.390121	0.310068	0.246979	0.197147	0.157699	0.101526	0.065882	0.034934	0.012579	0.004722
26	0.772048	0.597579	0.463695	0.360689	0.281241	0.219810	0.172195	0.135202	0.083905	0.052521	0.026415	0.008735	0.003022
28	0.756836	0.574375	0.437077	0.333477	0.255094	0.195630	0.150402	0.115914	0.069343	0.041869	0.019974	0.006066	0.001934
30	0.741923	0.552071	0.411987	0.308319	0.231377	0.174110	0.131367	0.099377	0.057309	0.033378	0.015103	0.004213	0.001238
32	0.727304	0.530633	0.388337	0.285058	0.209866	0.154957	0.114741	0.085200	0.047362	0.026609	0.011420	0.002926	0.000792
34	0.712973	0.510028	0.366045	0.263552	0.190355	0.137912	0.100219	0.073045	0.039143	0.021212	0.008635	0.002032	0.000507
36	0.698925	0.490223	0.345032	0.243669	0.172657	0.122741	0.087535	0.062625	0.032349	0.016910	0.006529	0.001411	0.000325
38	0.685153	0.471187	0.325226	0.225285	0.156605	0.109239	0.076457	0.053690	0.026735	0.013481	0.004937	0.000980	0.000208
40	0.671653	0.452890	0.306557	0.208289	0.142046	0.097222	0.066780	0.046031	0.022095	0.010747	0.003733	0.000680	0.000133
45	0.639055	0.410197	0.264439	0.171198	0.111297	0.072650	0.047613	0.031328	0.013719	0.006098	0.001856	0.000273	0.000044
50	0.608039	0.371528	0.228107	0.140713	0.087204	0.054288	0.033948	0.021321	0.008519	0.003460	0.000923	0.000110	0.000014
100	0.369711	0.138033	0.052033	0.019800	0.007604	0.002947	0.001152	0.000455	0.000073	0.000012	0.000001	0.000000	0.000000

Note: The future value factor is equal to 1 divided by the present value factor.

EXAMPLE 2 ♦ PRESENT VALUE OF A SINGLE SUM

REQUIRED: Find the present value of $100 paid three years from now if the market rate of interest is 8% (A) compounded annually and (B) compounded quarterly.

SOLUTION A: Let   Principal = P = $100,   Interest Rate = r = 8%,   Period = n = 3 years
    Present Value Interest Factor at r Rate for n Periods = PVIF(r, n)
    Present Value = PV = P x PVIF(r, n)

    PVIF(8%, 3 years) = 0.7938 (from Table 2)

PV = $100 x 0.7938 = $79.38

SOLUTION B: Let   Principal = P = $100,   Interest Rate = r = 2%,   Period = n = 12 quarters
    Present Value Interest Factor at r Rate for n Periods = PVIF(r, n)
    Present Value = PV = P x PVIF(r, n)

    PVIF(2%, 12 quarters) = 0.7885 (from Table 2)

PV = $100 x 0.7885 = $78.85

TABLE 3—FUTURE VALUE OF ANNUITY OF $1 IN ARREARS

$$FV = \frac{(1 + r)^n - 1}{r} \qquad r = \text{interest rate; } n = \text{number of payments}$$

	1%	2%	3%	4%	5%	6%	7%	8%	10%	12%	15%	20%	25%
n = 1	1.000000	1.000000	1.000000	1.000000	1.000000	1.000000	1.000000	1.000000	1.000000	1.000000	1.000000	1.000000	1.000000
2	2.010000	2.020000	2.030000	2.040000	2.050000	2.060000	2.070000	2.080000	2.100000	2.120000	2.150000	2.200000	2.250000
3	3.030100	3.060400	3.090900	3.121600	3.152500	3.183600	3.214900	3.246400	3.310000	3.374400	3.472500	3.640000	3.812500
4	4.060401	4.121608	4.183627	4.246464	4.310125	4.374616	4.439943	4.506112	4.641000	4.779328	4.993375	5.368000	5.765625
5	5.101005	5.204040	5.309136	5.416323	5.525631	5.637093	5.750739	5.866601	6.105100	6.352847	6.742381	7.441600	8.207031
6	6.152015	6.308121	6.468410	6.632976	6.801913	6.975318	7.153291	7.335929	7.715610	8.115189	8.753738	9.929920	11.25879
7	7.213535	7.434283	7.662462	7.898294	8.142009	8.393838	8.654021	8.922803	9.487171	10.08901	11.06680	12.91590	15.07349
8	8.285670	8.582969	8.892336	9.214226	9.549109	9.897468	10.25980	10.63663	11.43589	12.29969	13.72682	16.49908	19.84186
9	9.368527	9.754628	10.15911	10.58280	11.02656	11.49132	11.97799	12.48756	13.57948	14.77566	16.78584	20.79890	25.80232
10	10.46221	10.94972	11.46388	12.00611	12.57789	13.18079	13.81645	14.48656	15.93742	17.54873	20.30372	25.95868	33.25290
11	11.56683	12.16872	12.80780	13.48635	14.20679	14.97164	15.78360	16.64549	18.53117	20.65458	24.34928	32.15042	42.56613
12	12.68250	13.41209	14.19203	15.02581	15.91713	16.86994	17.88845	18.97713	21.38428	24.13313	29.00167	39.58050	54.20766
13	13.80933	14.68033	15.61779	16.62684	17.71298	18.88214	20.14064	21.49530	24.52271	28.02911	34.35192	48.49660	68.75957
14	14.94742	15.97394	17.08632	18.29191	19.59863	21.01507	22.55049	24.21492	27.97498	32.39260	40.50471	59.19592	86.94947
15	16.09690	17.29342	18.59891	20.02359	21.57856	23.27597	25.12902	27.15211	31.77248	37.27971	47.58041	72.03511	109.6868
16	17.25786	18.63929	20.15688	21.82453	23.65749	25.67253	27.88805	30.32428	35.94973	42.75328	55.71748	87.44213	138.1086
17	18.43044	20.01207	21.76159	23.69751	25.84037	28.21288	30.84022	33.75023	40.54470	48.88367	65.07510	105.9306	173.6357
18	19.61475	21.41231	23.41443	25.64541	28.13239	30.90565	33.99903	37.45024	45.59917	55.74971	75.83636	128.1167	218.0446
19	20.81090	22.84056	25.11687	27.67123	30.53900	33.75999	37.37896	41.44626	51.15909	63.43968	88.21181	154.7400	273.5558
20	22.01900	24.29737	26.87037	29.77808	33.06596	36.78559	40.99549	45.76196	57.27500	72.05244	102.4436	186.6880	342.9447
22	24.47159	27.29898	30.53678	34.24797	38.50521	43.39229	49.00574	55.45675	71.40275	92.50258	137.6317	271.0307	538.1011
24	26.97346	30.42186	34.42647	39.08260	44.50200	50.81557	58.17667	66.76476	88.49733	118.1552	184.1679	392.4843	843.0330
26	29.52563	33.67091	38.55304	44.31174	51.11345	59.15638	68.67647	79.95441	109.1818	150.3339	245.7120	567.3773	1319.489
28	32.12910	37.05121	42.93092	49.96758	58.40258	68.52811	80.69769	95.33883	134.2099	190.6989	327.1041	819.2233	2063.951
30	34.78489	40.56808	47.57542	56.08494	66.43885	79.05818	94.46078	113.2832	164.4940	241.3327	434.7452	1181.882	3227.174
32	37.49407	44.22703	52.50276	62.70147	75.29883	90.88978	110.2182	134.2135	201.1378	304.8477	577.1005	1704.110	5044.710
34	40.25770	48.03380	57.73018	69.85791	85.06696	104.1838	128.2588	158.6267	245.4767	384.5210	765.3655	2456.118	7884.609
36	43.07688	51.99437	63.27594	77.59831	95.83633	119.1209	148.9135	187.1021	299.1268	484.4631	1014.346	3539.010	12321.95
38	45.95272	56.11494	69.15945	85.97034	107.7095	135.9042	172.5610	220.3159	364.0435	609.8305	1343.622	5098.374	19255.30
40	48.88637	60.40198	75.40126	95.02551	120.7998	154.7620	199.6351	259.0565	442.5926	767.0914	1779.091	7343.858	30088.66
45	56.48108	71.89271	92.71986	121.0294	159.7002	212.7435	285.7493	386.5056	718.9048	1358.230	3585.129	18281.31	91831.50
50	64.46318	84.57940	112.7969	152.6671	209.3480	290.3359	406.5289	573.7701	1163.909	2400.018	7217.718	45497.20	280255.7
100	170.4814	312.2323	607.2877	1237.624	2610.025	5638.368	12381.66	27484.51	137796.1	696010.5	783×10^4	414×10^6	196×10^8

Note: To convert from this table to values of an annuity in advance, determine the annuity in arrears factor above for one more period and subtract 1.

EXAMPLE 3 ♦ FUTURE VALUE OF AN ANNUITY IN ARREARS

REQUIRED: Jones plans to save $300 a year for three years. If Jones deposits money at the end of each period in a savings plan that yields 24%, how much will Jones have at the end of the three years if Jones deposits (A) $75 at the end of each quarter? (B) $25 at the end of every month?

SOLUTION A: Let Payment = P = $75, Interest Rate = r = 6%, Period = n = 12 quarters
Future Value of an Annuity Factor at r Rate for n Periods = FVAF(r, n)
Future Value of the Annuity = FVA = P x FVAF(r, n)

FVAF(6%, 12 quarters) = 16.8699 (from Table 3)

FVA = $75 x 16.8699 = $1,265.24

SOLUTION B: Let Payment = P = $25, Interest Rate = r = 2%, Period = n = 36 months
Future Value of an Annuity Factor at r Rate for n Periods = FVAF(r, n)
Future Value of the Annuity = FVA = P x FVAF(r, n)

FVAF(2%, 36 months) = 51.9944 (from Table 3)

FVA = $25 x 51.9944 = $1,299.86

TABLE 4—PRESENT VALUE OF ANNUITY OF $1 IN ARREARS

$$PV = \frac{1 - (1 + r)^{-n}}{r} \qquad r = \text{discount rate; } n = \text{number of payments}$$

	1%	2%	3%	4%	5%	6%	7%	8%	10%	12%	15%	20%	25%
n = 1	0.990099	0.980392	0.970874	0.961538	0.952381	0.943396	0.934579	0.925926	0.909091	0.892857	0.869565	0.833333	0.800000
2	1.970395	1.941561	1.913470	1.886095	1.859410	1.833393	1.808018	1.783265	1.735537	1.690051	1.625709	1.527778	1.440000
3	2.940985	2.883883	2.828611	2.775091	2.723248	2.673012	2.624316	2.577097	2.486852	2.401831	2.283225	2.106482	1.952000
4	3.901966	3.807729	3.717098	3.629895	3.545950	3.465106	3.387211	3.312127	3.169865	3.037349	2.854978	2.588735	2.361600
5	4.853431	4.713459	4.579707	4.451822	4.329477	4.212364	4.100197	3.992710	3.790787	3.604776	3.352155	2.990612	2.689280
6	5.795476	5.601431	5.417192	5.242137	5.075692	4.917325	4.766540	4.622880	4.355261	4.111407	3.784483	3.325510	2.951424
7	6.728195	6.471991	6.230283	6.002055	5.786374	5.582381	5.389289	5.206370	4.868419	4.563756	4.160419	3.604592	3.161139
8	7.651678	7.325481	7.019692	6.732745	6.463213	6.209794	5.971299	5.746639	5.334926	4.967640	4.487321	3.837160	3.328911
9	8.566017	8.162237	7.786109	7.435332	7.107821	6.801692	6.515232	6.246888	5.759024	5.328250	4.771584	4.030966	3.463129
10	9.471305	8.982585	8.530203	8.110896	7.721735	7.360087	7.023582	6.710082	6.144567	5.650223	5.018768	4.192472	3.570503
11	10.36763	9.786848	9.252625	8.760477	8.306415	7.886875	7.498674	7.138964	6.495061	5.937699	5.233712	4.327060	3.656403
12	11.25508	10.57534	9.954004	9.385074	8.863252	8.383844	7.942686	7.536078	6.813692	6.194374	5.420619	4.439217	3.725122
13	12.13374	11.34837	10.63496	9.985648	9.393573	8.852683	8.357651	7.903776	7.103356	6.423549	5.583147	4.532681	3.780098
14	13.00370	12.10625	11.29607	10.56312	9.898641	9.294984	8.745468	8.244237	7.366687	6.628168	5.724475	4.610567	3.824078
15	13.86505	12.84926	11.93793	11.11839	10.37966	9.712249	9.107914	8.559479	7.606080	6.810864	5.847370	4.675473	3.859262
16	14.71787	13.57771	12.56110	11.65230	10.83777	10.10590	9.446649	8.851369	7.823709	6.973986	5.954235	4.729560	3.887410
17	15.56225	14.29187	13.16612	12.16567	11.27407	10.47726	9.763223	9.121638	8.021553	7.119631	6.047161	4.774634	3.909928
18	16.39827	14.99203	13.75351	12.65930	11.68959	10.82760	10.05909	9.371887	8.201412	7.249670	6.127965	4.812195	3.927943
19	17.22601	15.67846	14.32380	13.13394	12.08532	11.15812	10.33560	9.603600	8.364920	7.365777	6.198231	4.843496	3.942354
20	18.04555	16.35143	14.87747	13.59033	12.46221	11.46992	10.59401	9.818148	8.513564	7.469444	6.259331	4.869580	3.953883
22	19.66038	17.65805	15.93692	14.45112	13.16300	12.04158	11.06124	10.20074	8.771541	7.644646	6.358663	4.909431	3.970485
24	21.24339	18.91393	16.93554	15.24696	13.79864	12.55036	11.46933	10.52876	8.984744	7.784316	6.433771	4.937104	3.981111
26	22.79520	20.12104	17.87684	15.98277	14.37519	13.00317	11.82578	10.80998	9.160945	7.895660	6.490564	4.956323	3.987911
28	24.31644	21.28127	18.76411	16.66306	14.89813	13.40616	12.13711	11.05108	9.306566	7.984423	6.533508	4.969668	3.992263
30	25.80771	22.39646	19.60044	17.29203	15.37245	13.76483	12.40904	11.25778	9.426914	8.055184	6.565979	4.978936	3.995048
32	27.26959	23.46833	20.38877	17.87355	15.80268	14.08404	12.64655	11.43500	9.526376	8.111594	6.590533	4.985373	3.996831
34	28.70267	24.49859	21.13184	18.41120	16.19290	14.36814	12.85401	11.58693	9.608575	8.156565	6.609098	4.989842	3.997972
36	30.10751	25.48884	21.83225	18.90828	16.54685	14.62099	13.03521	11.71719	9.676508	8.192414	6.623137	4.992946	3.998702
38	31.48466	26.44064	22.49246	19.36786	16.86789	14.84602	13.19347	11.82887	9.732652	8.220994	6.633752	4.995101	3.999169
40	32.83469	27.35548	23.11477	19.79277	17.15909	15.04630	13.33171	11.92461	9.779051	8.243777	6.641778	4.996598	3.999468
45	36.09451	29.49016	24.51871	20.72004	17.77407	15.45583	13.60552	12.10840	9.862807	8.282516	6.654293	4.998633	3.999826
50	39.19612	31.42361	25.72976	21.48219	18.25593	15.76186	13.80075	12.23349	9.914814	8.304499	6.660514	4.999451	3.999943
100	63.02888	43.09835	31.59891	24.50500	19.84791	16.61755	14.26925	12.49432	9.999274	8.333234	6.666661	5.000000	4.000000

Note: To convert from this table to values of an annuity in advance, determine the annuity in arrears factor above for one less period and add 1.

EXAMPLE 4 ♦ PRESENT VALUE OF AN ANNUITY IN ARREARS AND PRESENT VALUE OF AN ANNUITY DUE

REQUIRED: Smith can make annual mortgage payments (not including taxes, etc.) of $4,800. How much can Smith borrow at 8% interest and repay in 20 years: (A) making 20 equal payments at the end of the year? (B) making 20 equal payments at the beginning of the year?

SOLUTION A: Let Payment = P = $4,800, Interest Rate = r = 8%, Period = n = 20 years
Present Value of an Annuity Factor at r Rate for n Periods = PVAF(r, n)
Present Value of the Annuity = PVA = P x PVAF(r, n)

PVAF(8%, 20 years) = 9.8181 (from Table 4)

Loan = PVA = $4,800 x 9.8181 = $47,126.88

SOLUTION B: Let Payment = P = $4,800, Interest Rate = r = 8%, Period = n = 20 years
Present Value of an Annuity Factor at r Rate for n Periods = PVAF(r, n)
Present Value of the Annuity in Advance = PVAA = P x [PVAF(r, n – 1) + 1]

PVAF(8%, 19 years) = 9.6036 (from Table 4)

Loan = PVAA = $4,800 x (9.6036 + 1) = $50,897.28

EXAMPLE 5 ♦ CAPITAL LEASE OBLIGATION

Alpha Company has a 10 year capital lease with an implicit interest rate of 8%. The $40,000 payments are made at the beginning of each year.

REQUIRED: What is the capital lease obligation (the present value of the lease payments)?

SOLUTION: Let   Payment = P = $40,000,   Interest Rate = r = 8%,   Period = n = 10 years
Present Value of an Annuity Factor at r Rate for n Periods = PVAF(r, n)
Present Value of the Annuity in Advance = PVAA = P x [PVAF(r, n – 1) + 1]

PVAF(8%, 9 years) = 6.246888 (from Table 4)

Capital Lease Obligation = PVAA = $40,000 x (6.246888 + 1) = $289,875.52

This is the same as: Capital Lease Obligation = Initial Payment + PVA (where r = 8%, n = 9)
= Initial Payment + P x PVAF(8%, 9)
= $40,000   + $40,000 x 6.246888
= $289,875.52

EXAMPLE 6 ♦ INTERNAL RATE OF RETURN

Beta Company is considering the purchase of a machine for $12,500. Beta expects a net year-end cash inflow of $5,000 annually over the machine's 3-year life. [The IRR is that rate at which NPV = 0. For more information on internal rate of return (IRR) and net present value (NPV), see Chapter 26 in the ARE volume.]

REQUIRED: What is this project's approximate internal rate of return?

SOLUTION: This example involves a present single sum and an annuity. The present value of the single sum paid today is $12,500. In this situation, NPV is the present value of the purchase price (P) less the present value of the future annual cash inflow (PVA).

Let   Single Payment = P = $12,500   Interest Rate = r = ?
Annual Cash Inflow = A = $5,000   Period = n = 3 years
Present Value of an Annuity Factor at r Rate for n Periods = PVAF(r, n)

NPV = P – PVA   and NPV = 0   Thus,   P – PVA = 0

PVA = A x PVAF(r, n) so   P – [A x PVAF(r, n)] = 0   or
P = A x PVAF(r, n)   or
P / A = PVAF(r, n)   and substituting known values:
$12,500 / $5,000 = PVAF(r, 3 years) or
PVAF(r, 3 years) = 2.5

Looking in the 3 period row of Table 4, we find the interest rate that produces the interest factor closest to 2.5 is in the 10% column. (Examiners generally narrow the field somewhat by supplying half a dozen values instead of a whole table, but they frequently also provide values from tables that are misleading. For instance, they may supply future values of annuities or present values of single sums.)

PVAF(8%, 3 years) = 2.577097 rounds to 2.6
PVAF(10%, 3 years) = 2.486852 rounds to 2.5 Thus, r (or IRR) is about <u>10%</u>.
PVAF(12%, 3 years) = 2.401831 rounds to 2.4

INDEX

ENHANCE THE POWER OF OUR BOOKS
with
Bisk CPA REVIEW PRODUCTS

BiskCPA**Review • Discount Coupon**

$50 OFF – AUDIO or SOFTWARE

This coupon is good for $50 off the complete
Bisk Audio Tutor Lecture Series – Audio CD or Cassette or a
Bisk Multimedia CD-ROM CPA Review Package

To receive your discount, Call toll-free **1-888-CPA-BISK**,
fax your order to us at **1-800-345-8273** or visit our Web site at **www.cpaexam.com/03**
Be sure to include your source code number.

* Limit one discount coupon per purchase.
This coupon may not be used in conjunction with any other Bisk coupons, discounts, special offers or promotions.

Source Code #14B73

BiskCPA**Review • Discount Coupon**

$100 OFF – VIDEO

This coupon is good for $100 off
the purchase of 5 or more Hot•Spot™ Videos OR
a full set of Intensive Review Videos

To receive your discount, Call toll-free **1-888-CPA-BISK**,
fax your order to us at **1-800-345-8273** or visit our Web site at **www.cpaexam.com/03**
Be sure to include your source code number.

* Limit one discount coupon per purchase.
This coupon may not be used in conjunction with any other Bisk coupons, discounts, special offers or promotions.

Source Code #14B73

BiskCPA**Review • Discount Coupon**

$200 OFF – ONLINE

This coupon is good for $200 off
the complete Bisk Online CPA Review Course

To receive your discount, Call toll-free **1-888-CPA-BISK**,
fax your order to us at **1-800-345-8273** or visit our Web site at **www.cpaexam.com/03**
Be sure to include your source code number.

* Limit one discount coupon per purchase.
This coupon may not be used in conjunction with any other Bisk coupons, discounts, special offers or promotions.

Source Code #14B73

Bisk CPA Review Guarantees You Will Pass the CPA Exam Or Your Money Back!*

AMERICA'S BEST CPA REVIEW SINCE 1971!

Dear Future CPA:

Welcome to your Bisk CPA Review textbook! As you study for the nation's most difficult professional certification exam, please be aware that Bisk CPA Review is here to help. We've helped Gold Medal winners like Paul Ito and Stephanie Seiberg pass (see opposite page) and we want to see you pass as well.

In fact, purchase our **Bisk Multimedia CD-ROM CPA Review** (*$50 OFF coupon located at the back of this book*) or the **Bisk Online CPA Review** (*$200 OFF coupon at back of book*) and **we guarantee you will pass the CPA Exam the very next time you sit or your money back!***

I am confident you will find this textbook to be a valuable tool in preparing for the CPA Exam. The following pages contain:

• A special Getting Started section to assist you in developing a training plan that will ensure exam success
• Thousands of up-to-date review questions
• Bisk's exclusive Solutions Approach™ to problem solving
• And much more, *including:*

A Diagnostic Exam & A Final Practice Exam

Take the diagnostic exam now, before you start studying, to determine your strengths and weaknesses and direct your studies. Take the Final Practice Exam closer to the actual exam to test your exam preparedness.

During your studies, if an academic question arises please don't hesitate to call our toll-free help line at 1-888-272-2475. Bisk CPA Review also offers video and audio products for your learning convenience. For example, listen to our **Audio Tutor** when you are in your car or view our **Hot•Spot videos** for a specific topic section and gain valuable study time each week! To receive FREE, no-obligation demos of our Online, CD-ROM, video and audio CPA Review products, simply fill out the Request Form at the back of this book.

The award-winning Bisk CPA Review also provides the opportunity to earn up to 13 college credits through the ACE program. To meet the 150-hour rule and beyond – take undergraduate courses or earn your MBA from regionally accredited universities made available online by Bisk!

Thank you for choosing Bisk CPA Review! I look forward to welcoming you as a fellow CPA, and to fulfilling your accounting, graduate and continuing professional education needs in the years to come.

Sincerely,

Nathan M. Bisk, JD, CPA (FL)
Publisher & Editor-in-Chief

*Call for details.

It's All About Passing. Prepare with America's Best...Bisk CPA Review.

Bisk Online CPA Review Package
The Greatest e-Learning Innovation to Hit the Review Industry in 30 Years!

Better than a live classroom!
Boasts the hands-on guidance, structure and support of a live class review combined with the flexibility, convenience and 24/7 access of web-based learning.

Our Exclusive Internet Features Include:

Online Classes
- **Personalized Classes** – Class sizes are small to ensure you'll get the attention you deserve.
- **Structured Program** – Set curriculum with planned study goals and assignments keep you on track.

Online Video Lectures
- **50+ Hours of Streaming Video Lectures** – In-depth coverage on the most difficult exam concepts available to view at your convenience.
- **America's Best CPA Review Instructors** – Nationally known experts such as Bob Monette and Ivan Fox.

Communication Tools
- **Chat rooms** – Lively professor-led discussion groups, "study buddy" chats and office hour visitations with your professor.
- **Internet Bulletin Board** – Posted homework assignments keep you on track to pass the exam.
- **Email** – Private messages with professors and online classmates.
- **Support Help-line** – Technical and editorial assistance, when you need it, toll-free call or email.

Learning Tools
- **The Bisk Personal Trainer** – Match your weakest areas against the most heavily tested exam topics (according to AICPA specs). Develop a customized study plan just for you.
- **Embedded Text** – The definitions and concepts behind review questions with online links to more than 2,900 pages of comprehensive text.
- **Diagnostic Exams** – Pinpoint your test-taking strengths and weaknesses.
- **Exam Simulator** – Unlimited number of unique final exams for practice, practice, practice.
- **Automatic Grading & Statistics** – Complete statistics to track your progress. Instant grading using AICPA-style keywords and phrases.
- **Bisk's Super Search** – Powerful Internet search engine model.

★ *Included: Comprehensive 4-volume set of textbooks for your offline studying convenience!*

Get a Jump on Test Preparation!
10 <u>FREE</u> Online Lectures
Check out the high quality content and presentation of the Bisk Online CPA Review. View 10 streaming video lectures FREE.

Call today for your password

(a $150 Value)

Call Toll-Free 1-888-CPA-BISK

Achieve the Career Success You Desire with Bisk Education

Providing High-Quality, Career-Boosting e-Learning and Multimedia-based Professional Education Programs for Over 31 Years!

Everything You Need to Move Up...

Move Faster...

Or Move On to Another Level

Career Development

CPA Review

America's Best CPA Review Since 1971!

- Online courses with streaming video lectures – better than live! Plus, CD-ROM software, video and audio.
- Pass the exam guaranteed with America's best CPA Review since 1971.*
- More than 140,000 candidates, including gold medal winners, have passed the CPA Exam thanks to Bisk CPA Review.
- The only CPA Review developed exclusively for one of the "Big 4" that is now available to individuals and firms. Plus, Bisk is a provider of CPA Review materials for all of the "Big 4."
- Bisk CPA Review for College Credit allows you to earn up to 13 college credits *without going to class.*
- Has your state instituted the 150-hour education requirement to sit for the CPA Exam? If so, use Bisk CPA Review as fifth-year accounting courses to help you meet the requirement.

Our promise to you...